HUMANITIES
IN THE
Modern World

An Africana Emphasis

SECOND EDITION

Wendell Jackson
GENERAL EDITOR

Frances Alston
ASSOCIATE EDITOR

Linda M. Carter
ASSOCIATE EDITOR

Lillian Dunmars Roland
ASSOCIATE EDITOR

Cover Art:
Male head, late 15-early 16th c. Edo peoples, Benin Kingdom, Nigeria. National Museum of African Art, Smithsonian Institution, Washington, D.C. Courtesy of Aldo Tutino/Art Resource, New York.

Taj Mahal, Agra, Uttar Pradesh, India. Mausoleum built by Moghul emperor Shah Jahan in memory of his wife, 1632-43. Courtesy of Scala/Art Resource, New York.

"Sharecropper," by Elizabeth Catlett. Courtesy of National Museum of American Art, Smithsonian Institution, Washington, D.C. Copyright © Elizabeth Catlett/Licensed by VAGA, New York, NY.

"The Creation of Adam," by Michelangelo, Sistine Chapel, Vatican Palace. Courtesy of Scala/Art Resource, New York.

Copyright © 1998 by Simon & Schuster Custom Publishing.
Copyright © 2001 by Pearson Custom Publishing.
All rights reserved.

This copyright covers material written expressly for this volume by the editor/s as well as the compilation itself. It does not cover the individual selections herein that first appeared elsewhere. Permission to reprint these has been obtained by Pearson Custom Publishing for this edition only. Further reproduction by any means, electronic or mechanical, including photocopying and recording, or by any information storage or retrieval system, must be arranged with the individual copyright holders noted.

Printed in the United States of America

10 9 8 7 6 5 4 3 2 1

Please visit our web site at www.pearsoncustom.com

ISBN 0-536-62324-4

BA 992777

Pearson Custom Publishing
75 Arlington Street, Suite 300
Boston, MA 02116

Copyright Acknowledgments

Grateful acknowledgment is made to the following sources for permission to reprint material copyrighted or controlled by them:

"Stopping by Woods on a Snowy Evening," by Robert Frost, reprinted from *The Poetry of Robert Frost,* edited by Edward Connery Lathem, by permission of Henry Holt & Company, Inc. Copyright © 1923 by Robert Frost, renewed 1951. Copyright © 1969 by Henry Holt and Company, Inc. Copyright © 1997 by Edward Connery Lathem.

"The Waking," by Theodore Roethke, reprinted from *Collected Poems of Theodore Roethke,* by permission of Doubleday, a division of Bantam Doubleday Dell Publishing Group. Copyright 1953 by Theodore Roethke.

"Day of Absence," by Douglas Turner Ward, reprinted from *Happy Ending and Day of Absence,* 1966, Dramatists Play Service, William Morris Agency.

The following are reprinted from *The Selected Poems of Claude McKay,* by Claude McKay, 1953, Twayne Publishers: "Baptism," "America," "If We Must Die."

"Song of the Son," by Jean Toomer, reprinted from *Cane,* by permission of Liveright Publishing Corporation. Copyright © 1923 by Boni & Liveright, renewed 1951 by Jean Toomer.

"Strong Men," by Sterling A. Brown, reprinted from *The Collected Poems of Sterling A. Brown,* edited by Michael S. Harper, by permission of HarperCollins Publishers, Inc. Copyright © 1932 by Harcourt Brace & Company, renewed 1960 by Sterling A. Brown.

"A Black Man Talks of Reaping," by Arna Bontemps, reprinted from *Personals,* by permission of Harold Ober Associates. Copyright © 1963 by Arna Bontemps.

The following are reprinted from *Collected Poems,* by Langston Hughes, by permission of Alfred A. Knopf, Inc. Copyright © 1994 by the Estate of Langston Hughes: "Afro-American Fragment," "As I Grew Older," "Ballad of the Landlord," "The Negro Speaks of Rivers," "Harlem," "Theme for English B."

The following are reprinted by permission from *Color,* by Countee Cullen, 1925, HarperCollins Publishers: "Incident," "Yet Do I Marvel." Copyrights administrated by Thompson & Thompson, New York, NY.

The following are reprinted from *The Black Poets,* written and edited by Dudley Randall, 1971, by permission of Broadside Press: "Ballad of Birmingham," "Booker T. and W.E.B.," "The Southern Road."

"For My People," by Margaret Walker, reprinted from *This is My Century: New and Collected Poems,* 1989, by permission of University of Georgia Press.

The following are reprinted from *Blacks* by Gwendolyn Brooks, 1991, Third World Press. Copyright © 1991 by Gwendolyn Brooks: "The Mother," "We Real Cool." Reprinted by permission of the author.

"I Am a Black Woman," by Mari Evans, reprinted from *I Am a Black Woman*, 1970, William Morrow & Co. Reprinted by permission of the author.

"And Still I Rise," by Maya Angelou, reprinted from *And Still I Rise*, 1978, by permission of Random House, Inc. Copyright © 1978 by Maya Angelou.

"Nikki-Rosa," by Nikki Giovanni, reprinted from *Black Feeling, Black Talk, Black Judgement*, by permission of William Morrow & Company, Inc. Copyright © 1968, 1970 by Nikki Giovanni.

"The Ethics of Living Jim Crow: An Autobiographical Sketch," by Richard Wright, reprinted from *Uncle Tom's Children*, by permission of HarperCollins Publishers, Inc. Copyright © 1937 by Richard Wright, renewed by Ellen Wright.

"The Man Who Lived Underground," by Richard Wright, reprinted from *Eight Men*, 1944, by permission of HarperCollins Publishers, Inc. Copyright © 1944 by L. B. Fischer Publishing Corp. Copyright © 1961 by Richard Wright.

"In Darkness and Confusion," by Ann Petry, reprinted from *Cross-Section 1947*, edited by Edwin Seaver, 1947, Harper Trophy/HarperCollins Publishers, Inc.

"In One Day My Mother Grew Old," by Courtney Moyah, reprinted from *Drumbeats*, Vol. II, No. 5, April 1969, Institute of American Indian Arts, Santa Fe, NM.

"The Man From Washington," by James Welch, reprinted by permission from *South Dakota Review*, Vol. 7, No. 2, Summer 1969.

"One Chip of Human Bone," by Ray Young Bear, reprinted from *Pembroke Magazine*, 1971, Pembroke State University, NC. Copyright © 1971 by Ray Young Bear.

Excerpt from *Black Elk Speaks*, by John G. Neihardt. Copyright © 1932, 1959, 1972 by John G. Neihardt, renewed 1961 by John G. Neihardt Trust. Reprinted by permission of University of Nebraska Press.

"Ma Lucia, the Great Story Teller," by Esteban Montejo, reprinted from *The Autobiography of a Runaway Slave*, edited by Miguel Barnet, translated by Jocasta Innes, 1968, by permission of Pantheon Books, a division of Random House, Inc. Copyright © 1968 by The Bodley Head, Ltd.

"The Garden Forking Paths," by Jorge Luis Borges, reprinted from *Labyrinths*, translated by Donald A. Yates, by permission of New Directions Publishing Corporation. Copyright © 1962, 1964 by New Directions Publishing Corporation.

"Ballade," by François Villon or François de Montcorbier, reprinted from *The Poems of François Villon*, translated by Galway Kinnell, by permission of Houghton Mifflin Co. All rights reserved. Copyright © 1965, 1977 by Galway Kinnell.

"Do Not Go Gentle Into That Good Night," by Dylan Thomas, reprinted from *Poems of Dylan Thomas*, 1993, by permission of New Directions Publishing Corporation. Copyright © 1952 by Dylan Thomas.

Excerpt from *Metamorphosis,* by Franz Kafka, translated by Willa and Edwin Muir. Copyright ©1935 by Schocken Verlag, Berlin, renewed 1946, 1948 by Schocken Books, Inc. Reprinted by permission of Schocken Books, distributed by Pantheon Books, a division of Random House, Inc.

"Home-Coming Son," by Tsegaye Gabre Medhen, reprinted from *Black African Voices,* edited by James E. Miller, et. al., 1970, Scott Foresman & Company and Dr. R. Pankhurst, Director of the Institute of Ethiopia.

"Message to Mputu Antoinette, Girl of the Bush, Friend of My Childhood," by Tshakatumba, reprinted from *The African Assertion: A Critical Anthology of African Literature,* edited by Austin J. Shelton, State, 1968, *Afrique* and Odyssey Press, a division of Western Publishing Company.

"Homecoming," by Lenrie Peters, reprinted from *The African Assertion: A Critical Anthology of African Literature,* edited by Austin J. Shelton, State, 1968, Odyssey Press, a division of Western Publishing Company.

"African Heaven," by Francis E. K. Parkes, reprinted from *The African Assertion: A Critical Anthology of African Literature,* edited by Austin J. Shelton, State, 1968, Ghana Broadcasting Corporation and Odyssey Press, a division of Western Publishing Company.

"The Village," by Marina Gashe, reprinted from *Poems from Black Africa,* edited by Langston Hughes, 1969, Indiana University Press and Harold Ober Associates. Copyright © 1969 by Marina Gashe.

"Prayer of a Modern Woman," by Rebeka Njau, reprinted from *Kenya Women Heroes and Their Mystical Power*, by permission of Risk Publications. Copyright ©1984 by Rebeka Njau and Gideon Mulaki.

The following are reprinted from *Poems from Black Africa,* by Francesca Yetunde Pereira, edited by Langston Hughes, 1969, Indiana University Press and Harold Ober Associates: "Mother Dark" and "The Paradox."

The following are reprinted from *The African Assertion: A Critical Anthology of African Literature,* by Leopold Sedar Senghor, edited by Austin J. Shelton, State, 1968, Presses Universitaires de France and Odyssey Press, a division of Western Publishing Company: "Night of Sine" and "Totem."

The following are reprinted from *Poems from Black Africa* by David Diop, edited by Langston Hughes, translated by Ulli Beier, 1969, Indiana University Press and Presses Universitaires de France: "The Vultures" and "Africa."

"Seeking a Mooring," by Wang Wei, reprinted from *Women Poets of China,* edited by Kenneth Rexroth and Ling Chung, 1972, by permission of New Directions Publishing Corporation. Copyright © 1973 by Kenneth Rexroth and Ling Chung.

"Declaration," by Bei Dau, reprinted from *The Red Azalea: Chinese Poetry Since the Cultural Revolution,* edited by Edward Morin, 1990, by permission of University of Hawaii Press.

"Lemon Elegy," by Takamura Kotaro, reprinted from *Chieko and Other Poems of Takamura Kotaro,* translated by Hiroaki Sato, 1980, by permission of University of Hawaii Press.

The following are reprinted from *A Haiku Garden: The Four Seasons in Poems and Prints*, edited and translated by Stephen Addiss, with Fumiko and Akira Yamamoto, 1996, Weather Hill, Inc. Copyright © 1996 by Stephen Addiss: "Spring Passes," "Leaves Unfold," "The Piercing Voice," and "Withered by Winter."

"I Stand As Though," by Yaichu Aizu, reprinted from *Anthology of Modern Japanese Poetry*, translated by Edith Marcombe Shiffert, by permission of Charles E. Tuttle Company. Copyright © 1972 by Charles E. Tuttle Company, Inc. Rutland, Vermont and Tokyo, Japan.

"Girl Cutting Reed," by Suju Takano, reprinted from *Anthology of Modern Japanese Poetry*, translated by Edith Marcombe Shiffert, 1972, by permission of Charles E. Tuttle Company. Copyright © 1972 by Charles E. Tuttle Company, Inc. Rutland, Vermont and Tokyo, Japan.

Contributors

Frances Alston: African Background, African Narrative; Biographies of Chinua Achebe, Gwendolyn Brooks, Sterling Brown, Ralph Ellison, James Weldon Johnson, Claude McKay

Ruth McKnight Antoine: African-American Music

Gerri Bates: Biographies of Maya Angelou, Mari Evans, Nikki Giovanni, Margaret Walker, Phillis Wheatley

*****Michael Bayton:** European-American Introduction, European-American Narrative, European-American Poetry; Biographies of Kate Chopin, Emily Dickinson, Robert Frost, Edgar Allan Poe, Adrienne Rich, Theodore Roethke

Nila Bowden: Biography of Richard Wright

Linda M. Carter: American Background, African-American Narrative, Native-American Introduction; Biographies of Ray A. Young Bear, Arna Bontemps, Paul Laurence Dunbar, Olaudah Equiano, Langston Hughes, Harriet Jacobs, Dudley Randall, James Welch, William Wells Brown, August Wilson

Jewell Chambers: African-American Theater

Karl Henzy: European Narrative; Biographies of Feodor Dostoevsky, Franz Kafka

Edith Jackson: Latin-American Narrative

Wendell Jackson: Asian Background, Humanities Today, Biographies of Rabindranath Tagore, Mao Tse-Tung

Mary Jane Lupton: African-American Art; Biography of Lorraine Hansberry

*****Margaret Ann Reid:** African Poetry, African-American Poetry; Biographies of David Diop, Tsegaye Gabre-Medhen, Rebeka Njau (Marina Gashe), Francis E. K. Parkes, Francesca Yetunde Pereira, Lenrie Peters, Léopold Sédar Senghor

Lillian Dunmars Roland: European Background, European Drama; Biographies of Francesco Petrarch, William Shakespeare, Dylan Thomas

Sylvia Saunders: Biographies of Countee Cullen, Ann Petry

Ella Stevens: Biography of Jean Toomer

Minnie Washington: African-American Introduction

Judy White: Biographies of John Donne, John Keats, William Wordsworth, François Villon

Annette Williams: Biographies of Frederick Douglass, Douglas Turner Ward

---

* Special Contributor

Dedication

To Ruthe T. Sheffey, Professor of English and Language Arts,
Whose foresight in 1971 and in years following
Has made possible at Morgan State University
the basic Humanities courses as we now know them

Contents

Copyright Acknowledgments iii
Contributors vii
Dedication viii
Preface xix
Note to Instructors xxi
Acknowledgments xxiii
The Humanities Today xxv

Part I: The American Perspective 1

American Background 3

European-American Literature 9

European-American Poetry 13

Emily Dickinson (1830–1886) 14
Because I Could Not Stop for Death 15

Robert Frost (1874–1963) 16
Stopping by Woods on a Snowy Evening 17

Theodore Roethke (1908–1963) 18
The Waking 19

European-American Narrative 21

Edgar Allan Poe (1809–1849) 22
The Cask of Amontillado 24

Kate Chopin (1851–1904) 28
The Awakening 29

African-American Literature 101

African-American Theater 107

Douglas Turner Ward (1930–) 112
Day of Absence 113

African-American Poetry **133**

Phillis Wheatley (c. 1753–1784) **136**
   To S. M., a Young *African* Painter, on Seeing His Works 138

Paul Laurence Dunbar (1872–1906) **140**
   Sympathy 142
   We Wear the Mask 143

Claude McKay (1889–1948) **144**
   Baptism 146
   America 147
   If We Must Die 148

Jean Toomer (1894–1967) **149**
   Song of the Son 151

Sterling A. Brown (1901–1989) **152**
   Strong Men 154

Arna Bontemps (1902–1973) **156**
   A Black Man Talks of Reaping 158

Langston Hughes (1902–1967) **159**
   Afro-American Fragment 161
   As I Grew Older 162
   Ballad of the Landlord 163
   The Negro Speaks of Rivers 164
   Harlem 165
   Theme for English B 166

Countee Cullen (1903–1946) **168**
   Incident 169
   Yet Do I Marvel 170

Dudley Randall (1914–) **171**
   Ballad of Birmingham 172
   Booker T. and W. E. B. 173
   The Southern Road 174

Margaret Walker (1915–1998) **175**
   For My People 177

Gwendolyn Brooks (1917–) **179**
   The Mother 181
   We Real Cool 182

Mari Evans (1923–) ... 183
I Am a Black Woman ... 185

Maya Angelou (1928–) ... 186
Still I Rise ... 188

Nikki Giovanni (1943–) ... 190
Nikki-Rosa ... 192

African-American Narrative ... 193

Olaudah Equiano (c. 1745–1797) ... 194
The Interesting Narrative of the Life of Olaudah Equiano ... 195

Harriet Jacobs (c. 1813–1897) ... 217
Incidents in the Life of a Slave Girl Written by Herself ... 218

Frederick Douglass (1817–1895) ... 271
Narrative of the Life of Frederick Douglass: An American Slave ... 272

Richard Wright (1908–1960) ... 316
The Ethics of Living Jim Crow, an Autobiographical Sketch ... 318
The Man Who Lived Underground ... 325

Ann Petry (1911–1997) ... 353
In Darkness and Confusion ... 354

African-American Music ... 373

African-American Art ... 377

Native-American Literature ... 381

Navajo
The Night Chant ... 383

Courtney Moyah
In One Day My Mother Grew Old ... 385

James Welch (1940–) ... 386
The Man from Washington ... 387

Ray A. Young Bear (1950–) ... 388
One Chip of Human Bone ... 389

Black Elk (1863–1950) ... 390
from *Black Elk Speaks: Being the Life of a Holy Man of the Oglala Sioux* ... 390

Latin-American Literature **399**

Estaban Montejo (1858?–1966) and Miguel Barnet (1940–) from *The Autobiography of a Runaway Slave* 400

Jorge Luis Borges
The Garden of Forking Paths 402

Part II: The European Perspective **409**

European Background **411**

European Drama **419**

William Shakespeare (1564–1616) **422**
The Tragedy of King Lear 423
The Tragedy of Othello, The Moor of Venice 506

European Poetry

Francesco Petrarch (1304–1374) **601**
Sonnet 3
It Was the Morning of That Blessed Day 602

François Villon (1431–1463?) **603**
Ballade 604

William Shakespeare (1564–1616)
from Sonnets
Shall I Compare Thee to a Summer's Day? 606
Let Me Not to the Marriage of True Minds 607
Tis Better To Be Vile Than Vile Esteemed 607

John Donne (1572–1631) **608**
The Relic 610

William Wordsworth (1770–1850) **611**
To Toussaint L'ouverture 613
I Wandered Lonely as a Cloud 614

John Keats (1795–1821) **615**
Ode to a Nightingale 617
Ode on a Grecian Urn 620

Dylan Thomas (1914–1953) **622**
Do Not Go Gentle into That Good Night 623

European Narrative ... **625**

Feodor Mikhailovich Dostoevsky (1821–1881) ... **629**
Notes from the Underground ... 630

Franz Kafka (1883–1924) ... **686**
Metamorphosis (Die Verwandlung) ... 688

Part III: The African Perspective ... **713**

African Background ... **715**

African Poetry ... **721**

Tsegaye Gabre-Medhen (1935–) ... **724**
Home-Coming Son ... 725
Message To Mputu Antoinette, Girl Of The Bush, Friend Of My Childhood ... 726

Lenrie Peters (1932–) ... **727**
Homecoming ... 728

Francis Ernest Kobina Parkes (1932–) ... **729**
African Heaven ... 730

Rebekah Njau (1932–) ... **733**
The Village ... 734
Prayer Of A Modern Woman ... 735

Francesca Yetunde Pereira (1933–) ... **737**
Mother Dark ... 738
The Paradox ... 740

Léopold Sédar Senghor (1906–) ... **742**
Night Of Sine ... 743
The Totem ... 744

David Diop (1927–1960) ... **745**
The Vultures ... 746
Africa ... 747

African Narrative ... **749**

Contents

Part IV: The Asian Perspective 751

Asian Background 753

Poetry

Chinese 757

Wang Wei (17th Century)
Seeking a Mooring 757

Mao Zedong (1893–1976) 758
Tune: "Spring in [Princess] Ch'in's Garden" 759

Bei Dau (1949–1970)
Declaration 760

Japanese 761

Bashō (1644–1694)
Fall: "The Piercing Voice" 761
Winter: "Withered by Winter" 762

Buson (d. 1714)
Spring: "Spring Passes" 763
Summer: "Leaves Unfold" 764

Yaichi Aizu (1881–1956)
I Stand As Though 765

Takamura Kotaro (1883–1956)
Lemon Elegy 766

Suju Takano (1893–?)
The Girl Cutting Reeds 767

Narrative

Chinese 768

Ts'ao Hsüeh-Ch'in (1715?–1763?)
from "The Dream of the Red Chamber" 768

Indian 775

Sir Rabindranath Tagore (1861–1941) 775
The Editor 776

Appendices 779

Appendix A: African-American Narrative 781

Appendix B: Supplementary Biographies 787
William Wells Brown (1814–1884) 788
James Weldon Johnson (1871–1938) 790
Ralph Waldo Ellison (1914–1994) 792
Adrienne Rich (1929–) 794
Chinua Achebe (1930–) 795
Lorraine Hansberry (1930–1965) 797
August Wilson (1945–) 799

Course Syllabus 801

Black and White Illustrations

European-American Painting, Sculpture and Architecture

Robert Mills (1848–1884)
Washington Monument. Baltimore, Maryland A-1

Frank Lloyd Wright (1867–1959)
Interior and Exterior. Solomon R. Guggenheim Museum A-1

Andy Warhol (1925–1987)
100 Cans A-2

African-American Painting and Sculpture

Edmonia Lewis (1849–1890?)
Forever Free A-3

Horace Pippin (1888–1946)
The End of the War: Starting Home A-4

Jacob Lawrence (1917–)
During the World War There Was a Great Migration North by
Southern Negroes [1940–41] A-4

Faith Ringgold (1934–)
The Flag Is Bleeding A-5

European Painting, Sculpture, and Architecture

Donato Bramante (c. 1444–1514)
Damascus Court. Vatican Palace, Rome. A-6

Auguste Rodin (1840–1917)
Le Penseur (The Thinker) A-7

African Art, Sculpture, and Architecture

Baule
Mask A-8
Standing Male and Female Figures. A-9

Benin
Head of Oba (King) A-10
Head of a Queen-Mother A-11
Male Head of Early Period and Male Head of Late Period. A-12

Ife
Heads from Ita Yemoo A-13
Mask from Wunmonije and Head from Wunmonije A-14

Yoruba
Palace Door. A-15

Asian Painting and Architecture

Ming Dynasty (1368–1644)
The Great Wall with Watchtower, Hopei Province. A-16

Kitagawa Sosetsu
Summer Flowers A-17

Safawid
The Royal Square, Mosque, and Palace, Isfahan. A-18

Mughal
The Taj Mahal, Agra. A-19

Color Illustrations

European-American Painting

Jackson Pollock (1912–1956)
Autumn Rhythm A-20

African-American Painting and Sculpture

Robert S. Duncanson (1821–1871)
Blue Hole, Flood Waters, Little Miami River A-21

Edward Mitchell Bannister (1828–1901)
Approaching Storm A-22

Henry Ossawa Tanner (1859–1937)
The Banjo Lesson A-22

Aaron Douglass (1898–1979)
Building More Stately Mansions A-23

Lois Mailou Jones (1905–1998)
Jardin du Luxembourg A-23

Elizabeth Catlett (1919–)
Sharecropper A-24

James Hampton
The Throne of the Third Heaven of the Nations Millennium
General Assembly A-24

European Painting

Leonardo Da Vinci (1452–1519)
Mona Lisa. Louvre, Paris. A-25
The Last Supper. Refectory, Santa Maria Delle Grazie, Milan. A-26

Michelangelo (1475–1564)
The Creation of Man. Sistine Chapel, Vatican, Rome. A-27

Paul Gaugin (1848–1903)
Ta Matete (The Market). Kunstmuseum, Basel. A-28

Henri Matisse (1869–1954)
Poppies.. A-29

Pablo Picasso (1881–1973)
Les Demoiselles D'Avignon. A-30

African Sculpture
Baule Mask A-31

Preface

Since the early 1950s the Department of English and Language Arts at Morgan State University has conducted a humanities studies program. In those early days, the underlying aim of humanities studies was to expose students to European philosophy, literature, history, and art in order to enhance their liberal training as well as to prepare for post-graduate study those students who would take the Graduate Record Examination (G.R.E) and other graduate-level entrance tests. In the late 1960s and early 1970s, however, the humanities program expanded its canon by including in the curriculum many African-American, Native-American, African, and Asian materials. This globalization of the curriculum, which over the years has won many compliments from accrediting agencies, occurred one or two decades before the now common expansion of the literary, artistic, and philosophical canons. While building upon this tradition of intellectual diversity, this text, *Humanities in the Modern World: An Africana Emphasis,* acknowledges the fact that its primary audience will be young African-American women and men, who need to explore African-American and African intellectual traditions, so as to strengthen their understanding of themselves, of their heritage, and of their potential in the world. Through the sheer weight of readings and commentaries from this tradition, the emphasis of this text is Africana. However, all readers will derive significant benefit from the text because of its broad scope, its inclusive point of view, and the deeper and more creative fusion that it may bring about between student readers and other peoples and cultures of the world.

Note to Instructors

With a few exceptions, this text includes all materials needed for a course on humanities in the modern world, with an Africana emphasis. Certain pieces could not be included because of production difficulties. One such selection is Chinua Achebe's *Things Fall Apart,* which the student should purchase separately. Further, though Douglas Turner Ward's *Day of Absence* is part of the current text, neither Lorraine Hansberry's *A Raisin in the Sun* nor August Wilson's *Fences* is. Should the instructor feel strongly that one or the other of these be read instead of *Day of Absence,* then the student must also purchase the chosen play along with the current text. Some may wish students to purchase and read Ralph Ellison's *Invisible Man.* Biographies for all of these individuals, together with the course syllabus, may be found in the appendix.

Acknowledgments

In the early 1970s, Ruthe T. Sheffey, then chairperson of the Morgan State College Department of English, initiated an important change in the direction of the humanities studies program, from focusing primarily upon European civilization to pursuing a curriculum that was truly transcultural. The new curriculum took into account the insight, creativity, and history of African and Asian peoples. Hence, gratitude is extended to Ruthe Sheffey for her pioneering leadership and insight. The editors and contributors are likewise indebted to Burney J. Hollis, dean of the College of Arts and Sciences, for his early and defining advice, direction, and encouragement, without which the time needed to complete this project would have been doubled. Recognition also must be extended to DeLois Flemons and Jean F. Turpin and to the late Nick Aaron Ford, Harry L. Jones, and Iva G. Jones, who contributed so generously of their time, energy, and thought to the growth of the humanities program. Particular recognition must be extended to the departmental Humanities Committee, not only for preserving the program for over 40 years without pause, but also, in the last year, for taking initiative to approve the project proposal for this text, to create guidelines for its production, and to provide other helpful suggestions and frameworks. Last, the editors acknowledge gratefully the help of Ivan Johnson, and they make special recognition of the extensive and tireless assistance of Maxine Thompson in typing and preparing large portions of the manuscript.

The Humanities Today

When we consider how strange our lives are, how utterly peculiar our circumstances, we cannot be surprised that one of the continuing elements of our experience is the tendency to question, to wonder who we are, what we are, and why we are here—on what must be the strangest of the planets in an even stranger solar system. This questioning we share with all of the humanity that has come before us; and very likely, those who come after us will ask similar, if not identical, questions.

Even stranger is the fact that none of the answers we find or that we accept from others can be regarded as thorough, infallible, or permanent. All, while illumining some part of our existence, leave other parts in shadow. In the past, answers came to us from religion or philosophy or art; in the present, we have added to these sources responses from the physical and social sciences and from technology. But as the responses change from culture to culture, age to age, and individual to individual, the basic questions remain, partly because the only tool we have to explain the mysteries of our existence is our *consciousness*—our ability to observe, feel, reason, will, and act. These are poor tools often—but all we have.

It is from this duality—the outer world (or existence) and the inner world (or consciousness)—that the Humanities arise; for the Humanities are those disciplines, fields, and areas of study which attempt to interpret, explain, or clarify the human condition, usually starting the explanation from the inside out. In other words, the Humanities attempt to explore what we value or despise, what we aspire to or what limitations hold us back, as well as what we can (or should) do in relation to our environment (i.e., anything which is "the other")—an environment which includes not just our solar system, not just our planet, our cultures, communities, or families but also our own physical bodies, the vehicles by which we come to know that environment. As such, the Humanities can encompass literature, music, philosophy (including ethics), religion, painting, sculpture, architecture, or indeed any expression employing the mind, the emotions, and the innate sense of beauty, to explore the meaning, the significance behind our existence.

In coming to understand the Humanities, however, it is necessary to take as big a view as possible. We must first accept that no one of us has all (if any) of the answers. No one can claim to have a monopoly on perception. We can claim only to have part of the Truth, which must remain (at the same time) an elusive mystery. Just as we learn different lessons from different people whom we contact, so we will learn different aspects of the truth by examining the wisdom of different cultures, by attempting to experience vicariously different angles of vision, different bents, and different assumptions as to good and evil, right action and wrong action, or selfless or selfish objectives. Hence, though the bulk of the literature and art in *Humanities in the Modern World* explores African-American and African experience and concerns, we likewise set this material alongside the experiences of the European-American, the Native-American, the Latin-American, European, African, and Asian points of view. We offer, in other words, a global perspective—one which is welcome (and unavoidable), as humanity enters the 21st century.

During the modern age, the Americas were particularly influenced by the initial clashes between indigenous peoples, such as the Native American, the Aztec, and Incas, and the European peoples in search of wealth and areas in which to colonize an overflowing European population. In many instances, this contact among cultures produced amalgam civilizations and a diversity and cultural richness that benefitted all parties. In other respects, the contact was disastrous, leading to a destruction of the existing civilizations in the Americas and to the devaluation of their contributions to civilization. A similar experience awaited millions of Africans forced to endure slavery in the New World. On the one hand, the emerging civilizations became "melting pots." On the other hand, the issues of race and class arising from colonial contacts continue powerfully.

In Europe, the modern age was characterized by intense religious and socio-political conflicts stemming (between the 1400s and 1600s) from the displacing of Catholicism as the primary religious voice, in favor of rival Protestant doctrines and attitudes brought on by the Reformation. Intensifying the religious debate was a new scientism beginning with Copernicus' development of a heliocentric rather than geocentric view of the cosmos and with Harvey's discovery of the systems governing the circulation of blood in the human body. This European scientific movement, culminating today in new advances in genetic engineering or technological breakthroughs in the use of computers, seems to sweep aside questions of divinity and ultimate human purpose in favor of a study of matter itself—not the spirit or soul but the vehicle which the spirit or soul may or may not inhabit. Thus science, technology, and mercantilism, having all but smothered such questions, left European intellectuals and artists to complain (especially in the 19th and 20th centuries) of "alienation" from their own culture.

In Africa, a blend of traditional African religious views and Islamic practice dominant in thriving feudal kingdoms was often overshadowed by Christianity, a competing religion which at times proved a first step towards colonization. Colonization frequently produced among indigenous peoples in Africa a special kind of alienation. There arose a situation in which Africans, separated from their cultural roots and unable completely to assimilate European models, were left with a feeling of isolation from both. The modern African challenge seems to be, therefore, the reconstruction of a world which, while retaining useful technological concepts, values the past, seeking to blend it with the present and future.

Similar in its development to Africa was modern Asia which (country by country) faced a setting aside of traditional values because of internal or external challenges. Countries such as India, China, and Japan experienced rapid (often traumatic) modernization, with its inevitable alienation from ancient tradition—leading invariably to a later type of reconciliation or bridging between the old and new.

In all of the above areas of the world, the Humanities have played a decisive role. The exploration of ethical questions rising from the interaction between cultures, classes, and genders has never been more needed. The arts and literature have never been more relevant, if we are to understand our complex psychological and spiritual plight. An appreciation of the diversity of contributions of the many cultures of the world has never been more critical to the survival and triumph of the human spirit.

Part I: The American Perspective

American Background

American history/culture did not begin in 1492 with Christopher Columbus' voyage to the New World. Instead it originated as many as 11,000 to 35,000 years earlier when men and women walked across the Bering Strait from northeastern Asia into the area now known as Alaska. America's original ancestors, crossing from one large land mass to another as they hunted animals, eventually migrated as far south as South America.

Two major concerns have evolved over centuries: liberty and identity. Whether Native-American, European-American, African-American, Latin-American, or other ethnic Americans, and regardless of gender, age, and class status, individuals maintained a keen interest in freedom of expression and action and in identity issues such as a search for spiritual origins, assimilation, self-assertion, and self-definition. These dominant, dual motifs remain of special interest in the history, literature, music, and art of the Americas.

The Pre-Colonial period in the United States (dating to about 1584) began with the arrival of the Bering Strait pilgrims and ended with the initial English explorations to the New World. The offspring of the northeastern Asians, born in the United States and Canada, were Native-American. Hunting and farming were their preoccupations, yet they, the creators of American literature, left a vast oral legacy of tribal songs, prayers, stories, myths, and histories. The earliest forms of visual arts in the New World and the forerunners of American literature were Native-American pictorial representations (carvings and paintings) on cave walls.

America was the exclusive domain of Native Americans until European explorers arrived. Pedro Alonzo Nino (1492), Diego el Negro (1502), Peter Mexia (1512), and Estevanico (1528; 1538–39) were among the Africans (usually as slaves/servants) who were involved in the various Colonial explorations. These explorations began to gradually influence Native-American culture as Europeans and Africans imported their languages, traditions, etc. to the New World; these were reciprocal encounters because Native Americans also influenced the explorers. As early as 1526, the first African slaves were brought by Spaniards to what is now the United States. Also that year the New World witnessed the first North American slave revolt when Africans set fire to a settlement in territory that is now South Carolina and then fled to live with Native Americans. In 1565 Africans were among the settlers who founded St. Augustine in Florida.

The Colonial period in the United States (1584–1765) began with England's first colonization attempt and ended with the Stamp Act. In 1584 Sir Walter Raleigh led an English attempt to found a colony in present-day Virginia, yet habitation there was temporary. More successful were the founders of settlements, such as Jamestown (1607) and Plymouth (1620).

The colonists' literature, with few notable exceptions, was prosaic expression consisting of various modes of non-fiction (sermons, diaries, autobiographies, etc). In general, they wrote about what was most important to them—adapting to a new environment and maintaining their religious beliefs. Among the colonists' literary achievements were the establishment of America's first printing press (1639) and the consequent production of the *Bay Psalm Book* (1640), the first book printed in America; Anne Bradstreet's *The Tenth Muse Lately Sprung Up in America* (1650), the first published volume of poetry by an American woman; and Jonathan Edwards' fierce sermon, *Sinners in the Hands of an Angry God* (1741).

Religion was likewise important to Black Americans, as illustrated by Jupiter Hammon's "An Evening Thought, Salvation by Christ, with Penitential Cries" (1760). This poem was the

New World's first African-American publication, but it was not the first poem by a Black writer. In 1746, 16-year-old Lucy Terry, recalling a Native-American ambush, wrote "Bars Flight"; however, the poem was not published until 1855. Hammon and Terry were slaves who wrote during the Colonial period when 20 Black indentured servants arrived in Jamestown (1619); Virginia was the first colony to transfer a mother's status (free or slave) to her child, and African Americans fought in the French and Native-American Wars (1756–63).

During the Colonial period, as well, the oral tradition thrived among Native Americans as they added to their legacy of tribal songs, prayers, stories, myths, and histories, often ignoring the colonists who encouraged them to abandon the oral tradition in favor of writing.

The Revolutionary period (1765–1829) witnessed America's quest for independence from England; among the most significant events were the Boston Massacre (1770), the Boston Tea Party (1773), the First Continental Congress (1774), the Revolutionary War (1775–83), repeal of the Stamp Act (1766), signing of the Declaration of Independence (1776), ratification of the Constitution (1788), and the formation of the federal government (1789). While these events were the causes (and oftentimes effects) of America's separation from England, two other milestones were the Louisiana Purchase (1803) which doubled the size of the new nation and the Monroe Doctrine (1823) which demonstrated the United States' ability to stand up to European nations that interfered in South American governments.

Two European-American literary milestones occurred during the Revolutionary period. The new nation's first play authored by an American and staged in the United States was Godfrey's tragedy, *The Prince of Parthia* (1767). America's first novel was *The Power of Sympathy*, by William Hill Brown (1789). It is interesting to note that European Americans founded the Library of Congress in 1800 after they began generating their own creative literature.

For African Americans, the Revolutionary era was a time of many tribulations with few triumphs. Crispus Attucks was the first American to die in the Boston Massacre (1770); Blacks fought at Lexington and Concord, Bunker Hill as well as other battles of the Revolutionary War (1775–83); the Declaration of Independence (1776) did not include the anti-slavery statement proposed by Thomas Jefferson; the Constitution (1788) identified a slave as three-fifths of one person; Congress passed the Fugitive Slave Act (1793); and the invention of the cotton gin greatly increased the demand for slaves (1793). Among African-American highlights were artist Joshua Johnson who opened a studio in Baltimore (1796) and Alexander Twilight who was the first Black to graduate from college (1823).

African-American writers produced landmark publications during the Revolutionary period. At the time of the publication in 1773, of *Poems on Various Subjects, Religious and Moral,* Phillis Wheatley, enslaved, was the first African American to publish a book of poetry in the New World because Jupiter Hammon's 1760 publication was a single poem. Wheatley was the first Black and second female author to publish a volume of verse in the United States. Hammon's poem "An Address to Miss Phillis Wheatley" (1778) may be the first published instance of an African-American male praising an African-American female. The rich tradition of Black autobiography began with *The Interesting Narrative of the Life of Olaudah Equiano, or Gustavus Vassa, the African, Written by Himself;* Equiano's work was published in England in 1789, two years prior to its American publication debut. A free Black American who was also a mariner, entrepreneur, philanthropist, and African colonizer, published two important works in 1812: *Memoir of Captain Paul Cuffee: A Man of Colour,* and *A Brief Account of the Settlement and Present Situation of the Colony of Sierra Leone . . . as Communicated by Paul Cuffee.* Some years earlier, Cuffee and six other free African Americans successfully protested taxation without representation. Cuffee was the first African-American male granted full legal rights in Massachusetts.

Cuffee's father was Ashanti, and his mother was Wampanoag; thus he was an African-Native American. The first book published by a Native American was Samson Accom's *A Sermon Preached at the Execution of Moses Paul, an Indian* (1771). Accom, who was a member of the Mohegan tribe, authored a second book, *Collections of Hymns and Spiritual Songs* (1774).

During the First Seminole War (1816–18), escaped slaves and Native Americans united in Florida to fight the American government.

Historically, the Romantic period in the United States (1829–1860) witnessed westward expansion and increased debate over slavery. These years heralded the invention of the first steam locomotive (1829); the discovery of gold in California (1848); the popularity of the phrase, "Go West, young man" (1851); and the rail connection from New York to Chicago (1853). Although publishing companies existed in America as early as 1639, mass publishing of books did not become standard procedure until the Romantic era. Advances in bookbinding and printing, improved roads and rail systems, along with the Post Office's special book mailing rate, empowered the publishing industry to meet the demands of an increased American readership.

Although this period marked continued expansion and mechanical advancement, it was also a time of great creativity, especially in the literary arena. A number of the greatest European-American writers are associated with the Romantic period, including novelists James Fenimore Cooper, Nathaniel Hawthorne (also a short story writer), Washington Irving, and Herman Melville; poets Henry Wadsworth Longfellow, James Russell Lowell, Walt Whitman, and John Greenleaf Whittier; essayists and poets Ralph Waldo Emerson and Henry David Thoreau; and poet, short story writer, and critic Edgar Allan Poe. Among the era's highlights were Whittier's *Ballads and Anti-Slavery Poems* (1838) and *Voices of Freedom* (1844); Poe's short story, "The Cask of Amontillado" (1846) and poem, "Annabel Lee" (1849); Hawthorne's *The Scarlet Letter* (1850); Melville's *Moby Dick* (1851); and Thoreau's *Walden* (1854). Slavery and mistreatment of Native Americans are topics of concern for Thoreau in his earlier work, "Civil Disobedience" (1849).

The Romantic period witnessed great African-American activity. During this time, Nat Turner led a slave revolt (1831); coed Oberlin College adopted a nondiscriminatory admissions policy (1835); Frederick Douglass escaped from slavery (1838); the Underground Railroad was established (1838); Douglass delivered his first anti-slavery speech (1841) and spoke at a women's rights convention (1848); Harriet Tubman escaped from slavery and began her work with the Underground Railroad (1849); a "separate but equal" precedent was set almost a half-century prior to Plessy versus Ferguson (1840); Lucy Session was the first African-American woman to graduate from college (1850); Sojourner Truth delivered her "Ain't I a Woman" speech (1851); the U.S. Supreme Court ruled in the Dred Scott case that Blacks were not citizens (1857); and White abolitionist John Brown raided Harper's Ferry, Virginia (1859).

During the Romantic period, African-American authors produced a number of works that are regarded as classics. The pamphlet, *David Walker's Appeal, in Four Articles; Together with a Preamble, to the Coloured Citizens of the World, but in Particular, and Very Expressly, to Those of the United States of America* (1829), urged Blacks to become abolitionists and created extreme angst among slave owners. Another voice for freedom was Frances E. W. Harper; her *Poems on Miscellaneous Subjects* (1854) contains anti-slavery verse including "Ethiopia," "The Slave Auction," and "The Slave Mother—A Tale of Ohio." Other themes in Harper's anthology are religion, women's rights, Black history, and temperance. African-American autobiographies were written by Douglass and William Wells Brown. Two of Douglass' three autobiographies were published during this period: *The Narrative of the Life of Frederick Douglass: An American Slave, Written by Himself* (1845) and *My Bondage and My Freedom* (1855). *The Narrative of William W. Brown, a Fugitive Slave, Written by Himself* (1847) was followed by Brown's novel, *Clotel, or the President's Daughter* (1853). *Clotel,* originally published in England, is the first novel by an African American. Another early African-American novel that was also published in England was Frank Webb's *The Garies and Their Friends* (1857); Webb's novel was the first to focus on the lives of free, northern Blacks. African-American women produced significant contributions during this period. *The Narrative of Sojourner Truth: A Bondswoman of Olden Times* (1850) was the result of Truth's dictating her life story to Olive Gilbert. Nine years later, Harriet Wilson published *Our Nig or, Sketches from the Life of a Free Black,* the first novel by an African-American woman and more importantly, the first Black novel published in America.

Among works generated by Native Americans during the Romantic era were two by African-Native Americans. Considered the first Native-American autobiography is William Apes' *A Son of the Forest: The Experience of William Apes, A Native of the Forest* (1829; revised and expanded 1831). Apes, a member of the Pequot tribe, originally wrote about his Native-American identity and religious views. His revised autobiography contains more criticism of European Americans. Ann Plato's *Essays: Including Biographies and Miscellaneous Pieces of Prose and Poetry* (1841) contains verse that rejoices in the termination of slavery in the British West Indies and agonizes over her Native-American father's grief that European Americans have displaced him. The Romantic period also produced the first Native-American novel, *The Life and Adventures of Joaquin Murieta* (1854), by John Rollin Ridge, a Cherokee journalist, poet, and novelist.

The Realistic and Naturalistic period (1860–1914) witnessed America's transformation from an agrarian nation into an industrialized society. The monumental events of the era were the Civil War (1861–65) and the onset of World War I (1914), but the period is also remembered for the invention of the telephone (1876); the addition of the 14th amendment to the Constitution: rights of citizens (1868); the addition of the 15th amendment to the Constitution: right to vote (1869); the production of the first electric streetcar (1887); the introduction of motion pictures (1896); the Wright Brothers' airplane (1903); and the mass production of the model T Ford (1909).

Among the major European-American novels of this period were Henry James' *The Portrait of a Lady* (1881); Mark Twain's *Adventures of Huckleberry Finn* (1884); William Dean Howells' *The Rise of Silas Lapham* (1885); Stephan Crane's *The Red Badge of Courage* (1895); Kate Chopin's *The Awakening* (1899); Theodore Dreiser's *Sister Carrie* (1900); and Edith Wharton's *Ethan Fromme* (1911). This era marked the posthumous publication of Emily Dickinson's verse entitled *Poems* (1890), *Poems: Second Series* (1891), and *Poems: Third Series* (1896).

In addition to the 1860–1914 events cited previously, other occurrences of significance in African-American history were the Emancipation Proclamation (1863); the founding of a number of Black institutions of higher learning including Morgan State College (1867), Howard University (1867), and Tuskegee Institute (1881); the founding of the NAACP (1909); the Supreme Court's separate but equal decision in the Plessy versus Ferguson case (1896); and the beginning of masses of Blacks migrating to the North (1910).

African-American literature continued to thrive during this period. Autobiographies were well represented by Harriet Jacob's *Incidents in the Life of a Slave Girl* (1861); Douglass' third memoir, *Life and Times of Frederick Douglass* (1884); and Booker T. Washington's *Up From Slavery* (1914). *Lyrics of Lowly Life* (1896) established Paul Laurence Dunbar as an important poetic voice, and W. E. B. DuBois produced a provocative collection of essays, *The Souls of Black Folk* (1903), that remains a milestone in African-American intellectualism. The genres of short stories and novels were the domain of Charles W. Chesnutt, who was the leading Black American fiction writer of the late 1800s and early 1900s; among his publications are *The Conjure Woman and Other Tales* (1899), *The Wife of His Youth* (1899), *The House Behind the Cedars* (1900), and *The Marrow of Tradition* (1901).

For Native Americans, wars were a major concern during 1860–1914. They fought on both sides of the Civil War as the Cherokee, Choctaw, Chickasaw, Creek, and Seminole participated in the battles. Chief Opothayohola led 1,000 Native Americans and Blacks as they fought Confederates (1861). Native Americans continued to fight European Americans in many battles including Little Big Horn (1876) and Wounded Knee (1890). They endured Geronimo's captivity (1886) and mourned the murders of Crazy Horse (1877) and Sitting Bull (1890).

During this time of intense exploitation and devastation, Native Americans continued to write. One example is Sarah Winnemucca Hopkins' tribal history and memoir, *Life Among the Piutes* (1885), yet the theme that dominates is Native-American and European-American interaction. An important milestone was reached in 1891 with the publication of Sophia Alice Callahan's *Wynema: A Child of the Forest*. Although Callahan's novel is not the first published Native-American novel, it is the first published novel about Native-American life by a Native American and defends the rights of Native Americans and women.

The Modern period in American literature began in 1914. History recorded the end of World War I (1918); the 19th Constitutional Amendment: suffrage (1920); first commercial radio broadcast (1920); first "talking" movies (1928); the stock market crash leading to the onset of the Depression (1929); World War II (1939–45); atomic bomb tests (1946); President John F. Kennedy's assassination (1963); escalation of the Vietnam War (1967); Senator Robert Kennedy's assassination (1968); large scale anti-war demonstrations (1969); Neil Armstrong and Edwin Aldrin's walk on the moon (1969); four Kent State University students, protesting the Vietnam War, killed by National Guardsmen (1970); Watergate (1972); end of the Vietnam War (1973); American Bicentennial (1976); and the explosion of the space shuttle Challenger (1986).

Among the important European-American novels published during this period are Edith Wharton's *The Age of Innocence* (1911), Willa Cather's *My Antonia* (1918), Sinclair Lewis' *Main Street* (1920), Theodore Dreiser's *An American Tragedy* (1925), F. Scott Fitzgerald's *The Great Gatsby* (1925); Ernest Hemingway's *The Sun Also Rises,* Thomas Wolfe's *Look Homeward Angel* (1929), William Faulkner's *The Sound and the Fury* (1929), John Steinbeck's *Of Mice and Men* (1937), and Saul Bellow's *Herzog* (1964). The era's significant European-American poetic works include Robert Frost's *North of Boston* (1914), Carl Sandburg's *Chicago Poems* (1916), T. S. Eliot's *The Waste Land* (1922), Theodore Roethke's *The Waking Poems 1933–1953* (1953), and Adrienne Rich's *Dark Fields of the Republic: Poems 1991–1995* (1995).

Of great interest in the Modern era is the plethora of African-American, Native-American, and Latin-American writers who have emerged. In addition to the events cited above, other occurrences frame African-American literature; among them are the Harlem Renaissance (1920s); the Civil Rights Movement of the 1950s and 1960s highlighted by Rosa Parks' refusal to sit at the back of a bus (1955); the A & T college students' sit-in at Woolworth's (1960); the freedom rides; the bombing of the Birmingham church where four girls died (1963); the march on Washington (1963); Malcolm X's assassination (1965); Edward Brookes' election to the Senate (1966); Thurgood Marshall's appointment as a Supreme Court judge (1967); and Martin Luther King's assassination as well as the subsequent riots (1968). There are many important African-American novels including Zora Neale Hurston's *Their Eyes Were Watching God* (1937), Richard Wright's *Native Son* (1940), Chester Himes' *If He Hollers Let Him Go* (1945), Ann Petry's *The Street* (1946), Dorothy West's *The Living Is Easy* (1948), Ralph Ellison's *Invisible Man* (1952), James Baldwin's *Go Tell It on the Mountain* (1953), Toni Morrison's *Beloved* (1988), and Gloria Naylor's *Mama Day* (1988). The genre of autobiographies is well represented by Langston Hughes' *The Big Sea* (1940), Hurston's *Dust Tracks on a Road* (1942), Wright's *Black Boy* (1945), Malcolm X and Alex Haley's *The Autobiography of Malcolm X* (1965), W. E. B. DuBois' *The Autobiography of W. E. B. DuBois* (1968), Maya Angelou's *I Know Why the Caged Bird Sings* (1970), Himes' *The Quality of Hurt* (1972), and Sarah and A. Elizabeth Delany's *Having Our Say: The Delany Sisters' First 100 Years* (1993). Lorraine Hansberry's *A Raisin in the Sun* (1959) and August Wilson's *Fences* (1990) are two examples of African-American drama. Among the many impressive volumes of poetry are Claude McKay's *Harlem Shadows* (1922), Countee Cullen's *Color* (1925), Hughes' *The Weary Blues* (1926), Sterling Brown's *Southern Road* (1932), Margaret Walker's *For My People* (1942), Gwendolyn Brooks' *A Street in Bronzeville* (1945), Don L. Lee's (now Haki Madhubuti) *Think Black* (1967); Nikki Giovanni's *Black Feeling, Black Talk* (1968), and Mari Evans' *I Am a Black Woman* (1970).

For Native-American authors, the Modern period is a time of prolific written expression grounded in the oral tradition. Autobiographies are represented by *Black Elk Speaks: Being the Life Story of the Oglala Sioux* (1932), *Pretty Shield, Medicine Woman of the Crows* (1932), and Maria Chona's *The Autobiography of a Papaga Woman* (1936); these works were narrated by Elk, Shield, and Chona to European-American recorders. More contemporary examples of Native-American autobiography are Mary Rave Bird's *Lakota Woman* (1990) and its sequel, *Ohitka Woman* (1993). Modern Native-American novels include Dallas Eagle Chief's *Winter Count* (1967), N. Scott Momaday's Pulitzer Prize-winning *House Made of Dawn* (1969), Hyemeyohsts Storm's *Seven Arrows* (1972), and James Welch's *Winter in the Blood* (1974).

Novels by Native-American women include Leslie Marmon Silko's *Ceremony* (1977), Paula Gunn Allen's *The Woman Who Owned the Shadows* (1983), and Louise Erdrich's *Love Medicine* (1984) and *Tracks* (1988). Native-American verse continues to thrive in the 20th century, and among the many poets are Paula Gunn Allen, Courtney Moyah, Anita Endrezze Probst, Wendy Rose, Leslie Marmon Silko, James Welch, and Ray Young Bear.

Although Latin-American literature was virtually ignored by non Latin-Americans until the 1940s, Latin-American writers have been publishing for centuries. Jorge Luis Borges, Bioy Casares, and Silvina Ocampo edited *Anthology of Fantastic Literature* (1940) that ushered in a Latin-American literary renaissance; the zenith was reached during the 1960s (known as the Boom period in Latin-American literature) when writers produced a plethora of works. No longer are Latin-American writers ignored; today the world lauds the talents of such gifted authors as Borges, Lydia Cabrera, Alejandro Carpentier, Carlos Fuentes, Gabriel Garcia Marquez, Pablo Neruda, Gabriela Mistral, Victoria Ocampo, and Cesar Vallejo.

Thus an overview of American literature since its origin reveals that it is inclusive rather than exclusive. Native Americans, European Americans, African Americans, Latin Americans and others individually and collectively define manhood, womanhood, ethnic status, and citizenry as they offer rich, varied insight into the American experience as well as the importance of liberty and identity. The readers of this text assume the responsibility of discovering additional thematic similarities as well as contrasts among the works presented for perusal.

Selected Bibliography

Andrew, William L., Frances Smith Foster, and Trudier Harris, eds. *The Oxford Companion to African American Literature*. New York: Oxford University Press, 1997.
Christian, Charles M. *Black Saga: The African American Experience*. Boston: Houghton Mifflin, 1995.
Elliott, Emory et al., eds. *The Columbia Literary History of the United States*. New York: Columbia University Press, 1988.
Hart, James D. *The Oxford Companion to American Literature*. 6th ed. New York: Oxford University Press, 1995.
Kaplan, Sidney. *The Black Presence in the Era of the American Revolution*. Rev. ed. Amherst: University of Massachusetts Press, 1989.
Lincoln, Kenneth. *Native American Renaissance*. Berkeley: University of California Press, 1983.

European-American Literature

The term European-American literature usually refers to the English-settling colonies and their influence upon what later would become a distinctive "American literature." The early Protestant communities that developed first in Virginia and the New England areas brought with them the traditions of their European background, including the English language, which in this new landscape produced utilitarian materials; that is, the literature had some immediate purpose, religious, political, or economic. Settlers were familiar with the rich tradition of European literature, despite the majority of settlers having little if any literary background. But the peculiarity of this new American landscape called for something new and unique. This was a New World in which a new Eden could be established. This new Eden was foreshadowed in Shakespeare's *The Tempest,* where Prospero, on his new island, must harmonize the forces of Caliban (the rough new world) and Ariel (the older European sphere). This sense of novelty is especially true for the Puritans, who recorded their daily travails with the sense of historic destiny and mission. They were in a new landscape, a new frontier that they believed was divinely inspired, despite their difficulty in finding a place for the native peoples of America as well as the African in this "Eden." What developed in these early years was a body of literature written for European as well as new American readers.

Colonial literature (1588–1765)—diaries and autobiographies, accounts of voyages, sermons, promotion tracts and polemical treaties—is mostly devoid of imaginative material. Conditions did not permit such. The frontier landscape and Puritanism did not create a suitable environment for either drama or the novel. Some poetry was produced but almost all of it conforming to 17th and 18th century English literature. Two early standouts are Anne Bradstreet (1612–1672) and Phillis Wheatley (1753–1784). The sermon was the most sophisticated literary form, which is no surprise since these early settlers were seeking religious freedom as well as wealth. Diaries and autobiographies were instrumental in promoting an examination of one's life. Early writers in this form are William Bradford (1590–1657), John Smith (1579–1631), Samuel Sewall (1652–1730), and John Winthrop (1588–1649). Colonial literature's best representative of both sermon and autobiography, however, is Jonathan Edwards (1703–1758). Although a late Puritan, Edwards embodies better than any other the tenets of Puritanism, with its long-lasting effects on American culture. His "Sinners in the Hands of an Angry God" (1741) is still powerful, and its style and vision find echoes in the sermons of the popular TV ministers of today.

As American literature progressed into the 18th century, Puritanism loses some of its hold on the culture. The oddity is that Jonathan Edwards, as its best exemplar of the old religious fervor, wrote his most memorable work during Puritanism's waning days. A direct literary descendant of Edwards is Benjamin Franklin (1706–1790), who best represents this new period. His *Autobiography* (1784, 1788) recounts his industrious and long career as writer, scientist, diplomat, sage, and friend—a truly enlightened mind. As America's first rags-to-riches hero, Franklin also elevates making money to the level of saving souls. He takes Edwards' Puritanism and couples it with the eighteenth century's more nationalistic attitudes. It is during this period that so much political turmoil occurs—leading to the Revolutionary War, the ratification of the Constitution, the Louisiana Purchase, and the Missouri Compromise. Thus, Thomas Jefferson,

Thomas Paine, and a chorus of others (some of whom championed the equality of the slave and women) are prominent during this time.

Aside from the political writings, diaries, and autobiographies, the 18th century also produced significant developments in poetry and fiction. Distinctive voices are heard in the poetry of Philip Freneau (1753–1832) and William Cullen Bryant (1794–1878). Though meritorious poets in their own right, they provide a transition to American Romanticism, when many feel American literature had reached its height.

In fiction, the prejudice against American literature was slowly subsiding. Early novels, such as Charles Brocken Brown's Gothic tale *Wieland* (1798), were very much in the tradition of their English counterparts. The writer who gave the novel its distinctive American flavor is James Fenimore Cooper (1789–1851). His *Leather-Stocking Tales* (1823–1841), such as *The Last of the Mohicans* (1826), are one of America's earliest fictional works that use setting and characters from the American landscape. It would take barely a few years before all of American literature flowered.

American Romanticism (1829–1860), also known as the American Renaissance, begins American literature's course toward independence from its European models. The spokesman for this movement is Ralph Waldo Emerson (1803–1882), who saw in the American experience (especially in its landscape) material rich enough to stand alongside "old" European works. His "The American Scholar" (1837) called for artists, in communion with Nature, to produce works that inspire recognition of a divinity within each person, an idea found in English Romanticism. Joining Emerson in promoting this new ideal of American individualism and democracy were such writers as Henry David Thoreau, known as The Transcendentalists, a designation sometimes applied to Nathaniel Hawthorne (1804–1864), Edgar Allan Poe (1809–1849), Herman Melville (1819–1891), and Walt Whitman (1819–1892). These writers, in their inimitable styles, worked to define the essential American and his or her relation to the landscape. Emerson and Thoreau see more of the promise of the American hero in relation to environment. Poe, Hawthorne, and Melville explore a darker side of this same hero. Whitman, however, celebrates all aspects of the American hero—both the promise and failings. Fiction and poetry finally come into their own during this period. When one speaks of the "classic" novel, one cites many of the novels from this period. They include Hawthorne's *The Scarlet Letter* (1850) and *The Blithedale Romance* (1852) and Melville's *Moby Dick* (1851). This period also produced America's first great poet—Walt Whitman. In his person and works are evidenced all of the ideals of a democratic humanism. Whitman was a pioneer in creating a new verse form—free verse—capable of expressing the expansiveness of the nation itself. The more reflective, personal style of Emily Dickinson's poetry complements Whitman's bravado. Her phrasing and poetic voice make her, along with Whitman, one of America's first true poets.

The period after the Civil War up to the First World War, called Realism and Naturalism (1860–1914), sees more emphasis on "realism" in the literature. Technological advancements, developments in science, especially in biology and psychology, and the general movement away from an agricultural to an industrial world form the basis for much of the heightened awareness of the tensions in life that this literature describes. This tension is best explained by Henry Adams (1838–1918) in "The Dynamo and the Virgin," Chapter XXV in *The Education of Henry Adams* (1918). Language, setting, and choice of characters also define this period of realism. The major writers in this tradition include Samuel L. Clemens (Mark Twain) (1835–1910), William Dean Howells, and Henry James. Twain's *Adventures of Huckleberry Finn* (1884), Howells' *The Rise of Silas Lapham* (1885), and any of James' novels, especially *The Portrait of a Lady* (1881) and *The Golden Bowl* (1904) are excellent examples of works of realism. Ironically, as one of the greatest practitioners of realistic fiction, Henry James is often considered English as well as American. His novels define the artistic limits of realism in such a way that he is often placed within the English literary tradition, along with George Eliot, D. H. Lawrence, and James Joyce.

Naturalism, sometimes deemed a more "authentic" form of realism, was practiced by such writers as Stephen Crane (1871–1900), Frank Norris (1870–1902), and Theodore Dreiser (1871–1945). In such works as Crane's *Maggie, a Girl of the Streets* (1893), Norris' *The Octopus*

(1901), and Dreiser's *Sister Carrie* (1900), the lives of characters are determined by forces in nature. These are largely social forces and the chemical reactions within. Nature is indifferent to man, and events often end violently. In the naturalistic novel, characters are seldom responsible for their actions.

Modern American literature, known as the period between the First World War, the Depression, and World War II, was one in which all genres of American literature come of age. The novel had already demonstrated artistic merit. Now American poetry and drama evidenced a similar achievement. Much of this literature was critical of America. From Sinclair Lewis' popular novel, *Babbitt* (1922), to Eugene O'Neill's *The Hairy Ape* (1922), the literature during this period evidences an overwhelming pessimism.

The novel continued to command attention worldwide. Drawing upon native material as well as European trends, the American novelist created works of great power, beauty, and craft. F. Scott Fitzgerald, William Faulkner, and Ernest Hemingway are highly esteemed as the best practitioners of their craft. Fitzgerald's *The Great Gatsby* (1925), Faulkner's *The Sound and the Fury* (1929), and Hemingway's *The Sun Also Rises* (1926) reveal a matching of craft with imaginative power. As Hemingway's novel notes, this indeed was "the lost generation."

The poets of the time also commanded world attention. T.S. Eliot (1888–1965) defined the modern world in *The Waste Land* (1922). Along with his European counterparts, Eliot recreated much of the poetic landscape with sharply defined images and language. Other poets, such as Edwin Arlington Robinson (1869–1935), Carl Sandburg (1878–1967), and Robert Frost (1874–1963) also explore the complications of modern life.

For the first time, American drama was esteemed by audiences beyond its shores. Although Elmer Rice had explored realism and expressionism in *The Adding Machine* (1923) and *Street Scene* (1929), it was Eugene O'Neill's *Emperor Jones* (1921) that changed the landscape in American drama. He would go on to write works that drew heavily on European models and that assimilated them into an American setting. *Desire Under the Elms* (1925) and *Mourning Becomes Electra* (1931) make O'Neill a dominant figure in modern American drama.

European-American Poetry

The selected poets follow a clear tradition of American individualism. They also exhibit in their works a quiet intensity. Deceptively uncomplicated, their writing contains depth of meaning. Emily Dickinson's apparent simplicity is belied by her subtle phrasing and imagery. Frost's work, too, appears simple but lends itself to complex interpretations. Poetically, Roethke's selection may seem more complicated than Frost's, but both writers concern themselves with fundamental issues of life.

Emily Dickinson (1830–1886)

Emily Dickinson, the premier female poet of the nineteenth century, was born in Amherst, Massachusetts, December 10, 1830. During her lifetime only seven of her poems were published. Beginning in 1890, editions of her poems were published but not in any sequential order. The first volume of her poetry appeared posthumously in 1892. Yet Dickinson, like Walt Whitman, is responsible for giving American poetry its defining voice. Her reclusiveness did nothing to diminish her towering presence in American poetry.

There is much that is paradoxical about the life and work of Dickinson. She was reared in the tradition of stern New England Puritanism and grew increasingly withdrawn from life. Yet her voice is often humorous, passionate, playful, and daring. She grew up in a home characterized by austere dignity. Her father, once a member of Congress, was the Honorable Edward Dickinson, who was also the treasurer of Amherst College. She was educated at the Amherst Academy and Mount Holyoke; however, some event occurred within her life to make her a recluse. A sense of tragedy, a concentration on death, and stunted emotional relationships all describe her life as well as her work. With her poetic heirs including Donne, the Brownings, and Emerson, Dickinson is regarded with Whitman as being responsible for establishing modern poetry.

Dickinson was 16 when Emerson's first volume of poetry was published. She was writing poetry during the time of Longfellow, Whittier, Lowell, and Whitman. As a somewhat younger contemporary of these male writers, she and her work have risen in critical estimation, while all but Whitman's have declined. Despite her seclusion, Emily Dickinson apparently lived a full life, evidenced in her cryptic and poignant experiences. Her descriptive terms, her feminine point of view, her jestingly reverent intimacy with God, and the personal poignancy of her reflections, all explain the full wealth of Dickinson's poetry.

Selected Bibliography

Anderson, Charles Roberts. *Emily Dickinson's Poetry: Stairway of Surprise.* New York: Holt, Rinehart and Winston, 1960.

Blake, Caesar R., and Carlton F. Wells, eds. *The Recognition of Emily Dickinson: Selected Criticism Since 1890.* Ann Arbor: University of Michigan Press, 1968.

Dickinson, Emily. *Poems.* Thomas H. Johnson, ed. 3 Vols. Cambridge: Belknap Press of Harvard University Press, 1955.

Griffith, Clark. *The Long Shadow: Emily Dickinson's Tragic Poetry.* Princeton, N.J.: Princeton University Press, 1964.

Miller, Ruth. *The Poetry of Emily Dickinson.* Middletown, Conn.: Wesleyan University Press, 1968.

Because I Could Not Stop for Death

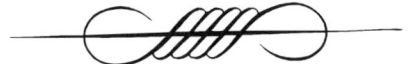

Emily Dickinson

Because I could not stop for Death—
He kindly stopped for me—
The Carriage held but just Ourselves—
And Immortality.

We slowly drove—He knew no haste   5
And I had put away
My labor and my leisure too,
For His Civility—

We passed the School, where Children strove
At Recess—in the Ring—   10
We passed the Fields of Gazing Grain—
We passed the Setting Sun—

Or rather—He passed Us—
The Dews drew quivering and chill—
For only Gossamer, my Gown—   15
My Tippet—only Tulle—

We paused before a House that seemed
A Swelling of the Ground—
The Roof was scarcely visible—
The Cornice—in the Ground—   20

Since then—'tis Centuries—and yet
Feels shorter than the Day
I first surmised the Horses Heads
Were toward Eternity—

Robert Frost (1874–1963)

Although Robert Frost was born in San Francisco, his ancestry is that of New England, where he lived most of his life. This New England influence informs many of his poems. As a poet Frost was a traditionalist in both poetic form and in the philosophical traditions of Emerson and Thoreau. His college education was intermittent; he studied at Dartmouth and Harvard but never received a degree from either institution. His early life consisted of farming, teaching, and writing poetry, each endeavor earning him little money. For a brief time, between 1912 and 1915, he and his family lived in England, where his first two volumes of poetry, *A Boy's Will* (1913) and *North of Boston* (1914), were published and received enthusiastically. Upon his return to America in 1915, Frost had gained a respectful and admiring audience for his poetry. He resumed his old activities of farming and teaching but now gave more time to his writing. The several volumes of verse that he published include *Mountain Interval* (1916), *New Hampshire* (1924), *West-Running Brook (1928), A Further Range (1936), A Witness Tree* (1942), *A Masque of Reason* (1945), *A Masque of Mercy* (1947), *Complete Poems* (1949), and *In the Clearing* (1962). The Pulitzer Award for poetry was awarded to Frost four times: 1924, 1931, 1937, and 1943.

Robert Frost had a long poetic career. His major volumes of poetry constitute a body of consistent excellence, and yet from the beginning Frost aimed at the widest possible audience. The typical Frost poem is written in consistent meters, for which he chose exact rhyme over off-rhyme, while often employing a melodic and enduring spoken American vernacular.

Although the poems are simply constructed, they contain rich meaning. Often Frost describes a scene and leaves it to the reader to search for any implied meaning. The farms, lush woodlands, old houses, and stone fences are subjects for his poems. Other subjects are the rugged folk of the New England area and their hard lives in tilling the land.

In many ways he is America's quintessential poet, embodying much of what it has celebrated within its distinctive history—the primacy of the New England region in American literature, a studied focus on individualism, and a celebration of the democratic spirit—all the while believing that the poem provides only a moment of lucidity amid confusion.

Selected Bibliography

Brower, Reuben Arthur. *The Poetry of Robert Frost: Constellations of Intention.* New York: Oxford University Press, 1963.
Cook, Reginald Lansing. *The Dimensions of Robert Frost.* New York: Barnes & Noble, 1968.
Frost, Robert. *Complete Poems of Robert Frost.* New York: Henry Holt, 1949.
Gould, Jean. *Robert Frost: The Aim Was Song.* New York: Dodd, Mead, 1964.

Stopping by Woods on a Snowy Evening

Robert Frost

Whose woods these are I think I know.
His house is in the village though;
He will not see me stopping here
To watch his woods fill up with snow.

My little horse must think it queer 5
To stop without a farmhouse near
Between the woods and frozen lake
The darkest evening of the year.

He gives his harness bells a shake
To ask if there is some mistake. 10
The only other sound's the sweep
Of easy wind and downy flake.

The woods are lovely, dark and deep,
But I have promises to keep,
And miles to go before I sleep, 15
And miles to go before I sleep.

Theodore Roethke (1908–1963)

Born in Saginaw, Michigan, in 1908, Theodore Roethke grew up greatly influenced by his father's florist business. He used the greenhouse image to counter the pervasive view of man alienated from his world. In many ways he is heir to Whitman and Emily Dickinson, for Nature is the antidote to modern living.

Roethke began his writing career somewhat late in his life. After receiving his M.A. (1936) from the University of Michigan, he taught in several colleges, Lafayette, Pennsylvania State and Bennington, during which time he was perfecting his craft. He had his first volume of poetry published in 1941 *(Open House)* when he was 32 years old. Later volumes include *The Lost Son and Other Poems* (1948), *Praise to the End* (1949), and *The Waking Poems 1933–1953* (1953), for which he received the Pulitzer Prize. His collected poems, *Words for the Wind,* won him the National Book Award in 1959. He was also the recipient of two Guggenheim Awards and the Bollingen Award for his collected poems, *Words for the Wind* (1958).

Roethke's early poems, the nature poems, are a kind of spiritual autobiography in that they explore, reveal, and celebrate the self. Later collections explore the possibilities of language, as in *The Lost Son.* His later love poems, *Words for the Wind* and *The Far Field,* offer for the reader some momentary pleasure and release. Roethke, despite his literary successes, suffered tremendously in his personal life with several mental breakdowns and bouts of alcoholism. He had a heart attack and died at the age of 55 in 1963.

Selected Bibliography

Malkoff, Karl. *Theodore Roethke: an Introduction to the Poetry.* New York: Columbia University Press, 1966.
Seager, Allan. *The Glass House: the Life of Theodore Roethke.* New York: McGraw-Hill, 1968.
Stein, Arnold Sidney, ed. *Theodore Roethke: Essays on the Poetry.* Seattle: University of Washington Press, 1965.

The Waking

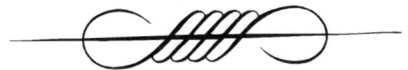

Theodore Roethke

I wake to sleep, and take my waking slow.
I feel my fate in what I cannot fear.
I learn by going where I have to go.

We think by feeling. What is there to know?
I hear my being dance from ear to ear.
I wake to sleep, and take my waking slow.

Of those so close beside me, which are you?
God bless the Ground! I shall walk softly there,
And learn by going where I have to go.

Light takes the Tree; but who can tell us how?
The lowly worm climbs up a winding stair;
I wake to sleep, and take my waking slow.

Great Nature has another thing to do
To you and me; so take the lively air,
And, lovely, learn by going where to go.
This shaking keeps me steady. I should know.
What falls away is always. And is near.
I wake to sleep, and take my waking slow.
I learn by going where I have to go.

European-American Narrative

In this section are a short story from Edgar Allan Poe and a novel by Kate Chopin. "The Cask of Amontillado" is from a rather large collection of more than 70 stories, titled *Tales of the Grotesque and Arabesque* (1840). Poe's method of composition was quite modern in his creating in his reader a specific set of emotions or responses. This psychological emphasis, evident in all his works, endears him still to a wide audience.

Kate Chopin's interest is psychological, as well. Initially her audience was not receptive to *The Awakening* (1899). For the turn of the century, Chopin's story about a married woman's growing consciousness and awareness of her sexuality was unconventional. Today, however, Chopin is celebrated for being one of this country's earliest writers to depict frankly the desires and psychology of a female protagonist.

Edgar Allan Poe (1809–1849)

Probably no other American writer has appealed to popular imagination more than Edgar Allan Poe. As Daniel Hoffman notes in his aptly titled *Poe Poe Poe Poe Poe Poe Poe,* Poe the author is not Poe the Persona. French critics recognized early his literary skill. Like the director of a movie, Poe orchestrated all toward a single effect. Unlike Hawthorne's stained Puritanism and Melville's dark symbolism that keep the reader debating meaning, Poe's stories are "arabesques" (i.e., having an element of wonder) and "grotesques" (i.e., evoking terror or horror). He wrote the first detective story, "The Murders in the Rue Morgue," and the first American science fiction stories, in "The Descent into the Maelstrom" and in "Narrative of Arthur Gordon Pym."

Poe was born in Boston, January 19, 1809, into a wandering theatrical family. Orphaned at two, after the disappearance of his father and the death of his mother, Poe became a member of the Allan family of Richmond, Virginia. Though never legally adopted, he shared in the advantages accruing from the social standing and wealth of John Allan, who eventually became a prominent tobacco merchant in Richmond. Increasingly, friction grew between Poe and his foster father, who was by turns indulgent and exacting. Poe's final break with Allan came in 1832, after withdrawing from the University of Virginia in less than one year's attendance, service in the army (1827–29), and a brief time at West Point (1830–1831). John Allan died in 1834 without making any provision for Poe.

Despite a life of struggle and poverty, Poe managed to live by his pen. Even before his break with his foster father, Poe had published three books of poetry—*Tamerlane and Other Poems* (1827), *Al Aaraaf, Tamerlane, and Minor Poems* (1829), and *Poems* (1831). Because none of these volumes was financially successful, Poe turned to writing tales. In 1833 "The MS. Found in a Bottle" won him a one-hundred dollar prize. He also soon began a career as an editor, serving on the staff of the *Southern Literary Messenger* (1835–37), *Burton's Gentleman's Magazine* (1839), *Graham's Magazine* (1841–42). Although an alert editor, Poe never had much success.

In 1831 Poe moved to Baltimore to live with a cousin of his mother, Mrs. Maria Clemm. But it was a household of poverty and sickness. In 1835 he married his 13 year old cousin, Virginia, who was always in fragile health and died at the early age of 26. Faced with his wife's poor health, financial problems, and little recognition for his literary talents, Poe would periodically go on drinking sprees, though his constitution could tolerate little alcohol. By 1845 Poe had gained some literary recognition; he had published *The Raven and Other Poems,* a collection of his verse. But the publication of a volume of his stories, *Tales of the Grotesque and Arabesque* was not a financial success. Poe died in Baltimore, October 7, 1849, helpless and insensible.

Poe was outstanding as a critic, as a fiction-writer and as a poet. As a critic, he was perceptive, independent, and articulate. His judgments, which were often brutal, have been tested by time. He defined and practiced logical concentration as a principle of art and sought to show how he reached his effects by conscious processes.

As a fiction-writer he made the short story more compressed, rid it of sentimentality common in stories of his time, and gave the form a definite structure. With a keen mind, which made him an outstanding journalistic critic, he developed a successful formula for contriving his stories. This formula was that of the single effect; that is, the writer of a tale should subordinate everything in it to the effect the writer wanted the narrative to have upon the reader. More of his tales have outlasted many of the more popular and lesser stories written during his time.

Poe's poetic narrative style and "single effect" theory are also important to his poetry. Poe regarded poetry as the rhythmical creation of beauty; goodness and truth are subordinated. All details and imagery must harmonize so as to achieve a unity of effect on the mind of the reader. Melancholy, which Poe regarded as the most powerful of the emotions, was often the intended effect. Although much of Poe's poetry may be too contrived in technique to satisfy modern taste, others such as "Romance," "To Helen," and "Israfel" confirm his poetic craftsmanship.

Selected Bibliography

Hoffman, Daniel. *Poe Poe Poe Poe Poe Poe Poe*. Garden City, N.Y.: Doubleday, 1972.

Quinn, Arthur Hobson. *Edgar Allan Poe, A Critical Biography*. New York: D. Appleton-Century, 1941.

Wagenknecht, Edward. *Edgar Allan Poe: the Man Behind the Legend*. New York: Oxford University Press, 1963.

Walker, I. M., ed. *Edgar Allan Poe: the Critical Heritage*. New York: Routledge & K. Paul, 1986.

The Cask of Amontillado

Edgar Allan Poe

The thousand injuries of Fortunato I had borne as I best could, but when he ventured upon insult I vowed revenge. You, who so well know the nature of my soul, will not suppose, however, that I gave utterance to a threat. *At length* I would be avenged; this was a point definitively settled—but the very definitiveness with which it was resolved precluded the idea of risk. I must not only punish but punish with impunity. A wrong is unredressed when retribution overtakes its redresser. It is equally unredressed when the avenger fails to make himself felt as such to him who has done the wrong.

It must be understood that neither by word nor deed had I given Fortunato cause to doubt my good will. I continued, as was my wont, to smile in his face, and he did not perceive that my smile *now* was at the thought of his immolation.

He had a weak point—this Fortunato—although in other regards he was a man to be respected and even feared. He prided himself upon his connoisseurship in wine. Few Italians have the true virtuoso spirit. For the most part their enthusiasm is adopted to suit the time and opportunity, to practice imposture upon the British and Austrian *millionaires*. In painting and gemmary, Fortunato, like his countrymen, was a quack, but in the matter of old wines he was sincere. In this respect I did not differ from him materially;—I was skilful in the Italian vintages myself, and bought largely whenever I could.

It was about dusk, one evening during the supreme madness of the carnival season, that I encountered my friend. He accosted me with excessive warmth, for he had been drinking much. The man wore motley. He had on a tight-fitting parti-striped dress, and his head was surmounted by the conical cap and bells. I was so pleased to see him that I thought I should never have done wringing his hand.

I said to him—"My dear Fortunato, you are luckily met. How remarkably well you are looking to-day. But I have received a pipe of what passes for Amontillado, and I have my doubts."

"How?" said he. "Amontillado? A pipe? Impossible! And in the middle of the carnival!"

"I have my doubts," I replied; "and I was silly enough to pay the full Amontillado price without consulting you in the matter. You were not to be found, and I was fearful of losing a bargain."

"Amontillado!"

"I have my doubts."

"Amontillado!"

"And I must satisfy them."

"Amontillado!"

"As you are engaged, I am on my way to Luchresi. If any one has a critical turn it is he. He will tell me—"

"Luchresi cannot tell Amontillado from Sherry."

"And yet some fools will have it that his taste is a match for your own."

"Come, let us go."

"Whither?"

"To your vaults."

"My friend, no; I will not impose upon your good nature. I perceive you have an engagement. Luchresi—"

"I have no engagement;—come."

"My friend, no. It is not the engagement, but the severe cold with which I perceive you are afflicted. The vaults are insufferably damp. They are encrusted with nitre."

"Let us go, nevertheless. The cold is merely nothing. Amontillado! You have been imposed upon. And as for Luchresi, he cannot distinguish Sherry from Amontillado."

Thus speaking, Fortunato possessed himself of my arm; and putting on a mask of black silk and drawing a *roquelaire* closely about my person, I suffered him to hurry me to my palazzo.

There were no attendants at home; they had absconded to make merry in honour of the time. I had told them that I should not return until the morning, and had given them explicit orders not to stir from the house. These orders were sufficient, I well knew, to insure their immediate disappearance, one and all, as soon as my back was turned.

I took from their sconces two flambeaux, and giving one to Fortunato, bowed him through several suites of rooms to the archway that led into the vaults. I passed down a long and winding staircase, requesting him to be cautious as he followed. We came at length to the foot of the descent, and stood together upon the damp ground of the catacombs of the Montresors.

The gait of my friend was unsteady, and the bells upon his cap jingled as he strode.

"The pipe," said he.

"It is farther on," said I; "but observe the white web-work which gleams from these cavern walls."

He turned towards me, and looked into my eyes with two filmy orbs that distilled the rheum of intoxication.

"Nitre?" he asked, at length.

"Nitre," I replied. "How long have you had that cough?"

"Ugh! ugh! ugh!—ugh! ugh! ugh!—ugh! ugh !ugh!—ugh! ugh! ugh!—ugh ugh! ugh!"

My poor friend found it impossible to reply for many minutes.

"It is nothing," he said, at last.

"Come," I said, with decision, "we will go back; your health is precious. You are rich, respected, admired, beloved; you are happy, as once I was. You are a man to be missed. For me it is no matter. We will go back; you will be ill, and I cannot be responsible. Besides, there is Luchresi—"

"Enough," he said; "the cough is a mere nothing; it will not kill me. I shall not die of a cough."

"True—true," I replied; "and, indeed, I had no intention of alarming you unnecessarily—but you should use all proper caution. A draught of this Medoc will defend us from the damps."

Here I knocked off the neck of a bottle which I drew from a long row of its fellows that lay upon the mould.

"Drink," I said, presenting him the wine

He raised it to his lips with a leer. He paused and nodded to me familiarly, while his bells jingled.

"I drink," he said, "to the buried that repose around us."

"And I to your long life."

He again took my arm, and we proceeded.

"These vaults," he said, "are extensive."

"The Montresors," I replied, "were a great and numerous family."

"I forget your arms."

"A huge human foot d'or, in a field azure; the foot crushes a serpent rampant whose fangs are imbedded in the heel."

"And the motto?"

"Nemo me impune lacessit."

"Good!" he said.

The wine sparkled in his eyes and the bells jingled. My own fancy grew warm with the Medoc. We had passed through long walls of piled skeletons, with casks and puncheons intermingling, into the inmost recesses of the catacombs. I paused again, and this time I made bold to seize Fortunato by an arm above the elbow.

"The nitre!" I said; "see, it increases. It hangs like moss upon the vaults. We are below the river's bed. The drops of moisture trickle among the bones. Come, we will go back ere it is too late. Your cough—"

"It is nothing," he said; "let us go on. But first, another draught of the Medoc."

I broke and reached him a flacon of De Grâve. He emptied it at a breath. His eyes flashed with a fierce light. He laughed and threw the bottle upwards with a gesticulation I did not understand.

I looked at him in surprise. He repeated the movement—a grotesque one.

"You do not comprehend?" he said.

"Not I," I replied.

"Then you are not of the brotherhood."

"How?"

"You are not of the masons."

"Yes, yes," I said; "yes, yes."

"You? Impossible! A mason?"

"A mason," I replied.

"A sign," he said, "a sign."

"It is this," I answered, producing from beneath the folds of my *roquelaire* a trowel.

"You jest," he exclaimed, recoiling a few paces. "But let us proceed to the Amontillado."

"Be it so," I said, replacing the tool beneath the cloak and again offering him my arm. He leaned upon it heavily. We continued our route in search of the Amontillado. We passed through a range of low arches, descended, passed on, and descending again, arrived at a deep crypt, in which the foulness of the air caused our flambeaux rather to glow than flame.

At the most remote end of the crypt there appeared another less spacious. Its walls had been lined with human remains, piled to the vault overhead, in the fashion of the great catacombs of Paris. Three sides of this interior crypt were still ornamented in this manner. From the fourth side the bones had been thrown down, and lay promiscuously upon the earth, forming at one point a mound of some size. Within the wall thus exposed by the displacing of the bones, we perceived a still interior crypt or recess, in depth about four feet, in width three, in height six or seven. It seemed to have been constructed for no especial use within itself, but formed merely the interval between two of the colossal supports of the roof of the catacombs, and was backed by one of their circumscribing walls of solid granite.

It was in vain that Fortunato, uplifting his dull torch, endeavoured to pry into the depth of the recess. Its termination the feeble light did not enable us to see.

"Proceed," I said; "herein is the Amontillado. As for Luchresi—"

"He is an ignoramus," interrupted my friend, as he stepped unsteadily forward, while I followed immediately at his heels. In an instant he had reached the extremity of the niche, and finding his progress arrested by the rock, stood stupidly bewildered. A moment more and I had fettered him to the granite. In its surface were two iron staples, distant from each other about two feet, horizontally. From one of these depended a short chain, from the other a padlock. Throwing the links about his waist, it was but the work of a few seconds to secure it. He was too much astounded to resist. Withdrawing the key I stepped back from the recess.

"Pass your hand," I said, "over the wall; you cannot help feeling the nitre. Indeed, it is *very* damp. Once more let me *implore* you to return. No? Then I must positively leave you. But I will first render you all the little attentions in my power."

"The Amontillado!" ejaculated my friend, not yet recovered from his astonishment.

"True," I replied; "the Amontillado."

As I said these words I busied myself among the pile of bones of which I have before spoken. Throwing them aside, I soon uncovered a quantity of building stone and mortar. With these materials and with the aid of my trowel, I began vigorously to wall up the entrance of the niche.

I had scarcely laid the first tier of the masonry when I discovered that the intoxication of Fortunato had in great measure worn off. The earliest indication I had of this was a low moaning cry from the depth of the recess. It was *not* the cry of a drunken man. There was then a long and obstinate silence. I laid the second tier, and the third, and the fourth; and then I heard the furious vibration of the chain. The noise lasted for several minutes, during which, that I might hearken to it with the more satisfaction, I ceased my labours and sat down upon the bones. When at last the clanking subsided, I resumed the trowel, and finished without interruption the fifth, the sixth, and the seventh tier. The wall was now nearly upon a level with my breast. I again paused, and holding the flambeaux over the mason-work, threw a few feeble rays upon the figure within.

A succession of loud and shrill screams, bursting suddenly from the throat of the chained form, seemed to thrust me violently back. For a brief moment I hesitated, I trembled. Unsheathing my rapier, I began to grope with it about the recess; but the thought of an instant reassured me. I placed my hand upon the solid fabric of the catacombs and felt satisfied. I reapproached the wall. I replied to the yells of him who clamoured. I re-echoed, I aided, I surpassed them in volume and in strength. I did this, and the clamourer grew still.

It was now midnight, and my task was drawing to a close. I had completed the eighth, the ninth and the tenth tier. I had finished a portion of the last and the eleventh; there remained but a single stone to be fitted and plastered in. I struggled with its weight; I placed it partially in its destined position. But now there came from out the niche a low laugh that erected the hairs upon my head. It was succeeded by a sad voice, which I had difficulty in recognizing as that of the noble Fortunato. The voice said—

"Ha! ha! ha!—he! he, he!—a very good joke, indeed—an excellent jest. We will have many a rich laugh about it at the palazzo—he! he! he!—over our wine—he! he! he!"

"The Amontillado!" I said.

"He! he! he!—he! he! he!—yes, the Amontillado. But is it not getting late? Will not they be awaiting us at the palazzo—the Lady Fortunato and the rest? Let us be gone."

"Yes," I said, "let us be gone."

"For the love of God, Montresor!"

"Yes," I said, "for the love of God!"

But to these words I hearkened in vain for a reply. I grew impatient. I called aloud—

"Fortunato!"

No answer. I called again—

"Fortunato!"

No answer still. I thrust a torch through the remaining aperture and let it fall within. There came forth in return only a jingling of the bells. My heart grew sick; it was the dampness of the catacombs that made it so. I hastened to make an end of my labour. I forced the last stone into its position; I plastered it up. Against the new masonry I re-erected the old rampart of bones. For the half of a century no mortal has disturbed them. *In pace requiescat!*

Kate Chopin (1851–1904)

Although Katherine O'Flaherty (later Chopin) was born and grew up in St. Louis, she is easily identified with New Orleans and its Bayou culture. At the age of 20 she married Oscar Chopin, who ran a prosperous cotton business. Her decade spent in New Orleans provided Kate Chopin all the material she needed for her writing. After the failure of her husband's business and his early death because of swamp fever, Chopin returned to St. Louis, where she brought up her six children. Soon after she began writing, her first story was published in 1889. *At Fault,* her first novel, appeared the following year. But Chopin was known for her fierce independence as much as for her work. Her inclusion in the literary canon parallels the history of the suffragette movement in this country.

In a relatively short time, about ten years, Kate Chopin published two novels, more than 150 stories, as well as poetry and criticism. *Bayou Folk* (1894), the work which brought her national recognition as a local color writer, was a collection of stories of Louisiana rural life. *The Awakening,* Chopin's major work, was published in 1899 and greeted with hostility from many critics. The novel aroused so much controversy because of its heroine, Edna Pontellier, who is an independent spirit and unrepentant sensualist. For this, Chopin suffered the chilly reception to her novel. Disappointed, she wrote very little after *The Awakening.*

Selected Bibliography

Martin, Wendy, ed. *New Essays on The Awakening*. New York: Cambridge University Press, 1988.

Seyersted, Per. *Kate Chopin: A Critical Biography*. Baton Rouge: Louisiana State University Press, 1969.

The Awakening

Kate Chopin

I

A green and yellow parrot, which hung in a cage outside the door, kept repeating over and over:

"*Allez vous-en! Allez vous-en! Sapristi!*[1] That's all right!"

He could speak a little Spanish, and also a language which nobody understood, unless it was the mocking bird that hung on the other side of the door, whistling his fluty notes out upon the breeze with maddening persistence.

Mr. Pontellier, unable to read his newspaper with any degree of comfort, arose with an expression and an exclamation of disgust. He walked down the gallery and across the narrow "bridges" which connected the Lebrun cottages one with the other. He had been seated before the door of the main house. The parrot and the mocking bird were the property of Madame Lebrun, and they had the right to make all the noise they wished. Mr. Pontellier had the privilege of quitting their society when they ceased to be entertaining.

He stopped before the door of his own cottage, which was the fourth one from the main building and next to the last. Seating himself in a wicker rocker which was there, he once more applied himself to the task of reading the newspaper. The day was Sunday; the paper was a day old. The Sunday papers had not yet reached Grand Isle. He was already acquainted with the market reports, and he glanced restlessly over the editorials and bits of news which he had not had time to read before quitting New Orleans the day before.

Mr. Pontellier wore eye glasses. He was a man of forty, of medium height and rather slender build; he stooped a little. His hair was brown and straight, parted on one side. His beard was neatly and closely trimmed.

Once in a while he withdrew his glance from the newspaper and looked about him. There was more noise than ever over at the house. The main building was called "the house," to distinguish it from the cottages. The chattering and whistling birds were still at it. Two young girls, the Farival twins, were playing a duet from "Zampa" upon the piano. Madame Lebrun was bustling in and out, giving orders in a high key to a yard boy whenever she got inside the house, and directions in an equally high voice to a dining room servant whenever she got outside. She was a fresh, pretty woman, clad always in white with elbow sleeves. Her starched skirts crinkled as she came and went. Farther down, before one of the cottages, a lady in black was walking demurely up and down, telling her beads. A good many persons of the *pension* had gone over to the *Chênière Caminada* in Beaudelet's lugger to hear mass. Some young people were out under the water oaks playing croquet. Mr. Pontellier's two children were there—sturdy little fellows of four and five. A quadroon nurse followed them about with a far-away, meditative air.

Mr. Pontellier finally lit a cigar and began to smoke, letting the paper drag idly from his hand. He fixed his gaze upon a white sunshade that was advancing at snail's pace from the beach. He could see it plainly between the gaunt trunks of the water oaks and across the stretch of yellow camomile. The gulf looked far away, melting hazily into the blue of the horizon. The sunshade continued to approach slowly. Beneath its pink-lined shelter were his wife, Mrs. Pontellier, and young Robert Lebrun. When they reached the cottage, the two seated themselves with some appearance of fatigue upon the upper step of the porch, facing each other, each leaning against a supporting post.

"What folly! to bathe at such an hour in such heat!" exclaimed Mr. Pontellier. He himself had taken a plunge at daylight. That was why the morning seemed long to him.

"You are burnt beyond recognition," he added, looking at his wife as one looks at a valuable piece of personal property which has suffered some damage. She held up her hands, strong, shapely hands, and surveyed them critically, drawing up her lawn sleeves above the wrists. Looking at them reminded her of her rings, which she had given to her husband before leaving for the beach. She silently reached out to him, and he, understanding, took the rings from his vest pocket and dropped them into her open palm. She slipped them upon her fingers; then clasping her knees, she looked across at Robert and began to laugh. The rings sparkled upon her fingers. He sent back an answering smile.

"What is it?" asked Pontellier, looking lazily and amused from one to the other. It was some utter nonsense; some adventure out there in the water, and they both tried to relate it at once. It did not seem half so amusing when told. They realized this, and so did Mr. Pontellier. He yawned and stretched himself. Then he got up, saying he had half a mind to go over to Klein's hotel and play a game of billiards.

"Come go along, Lebrun," he proposed to Robert. But Robert admitted quite frankly that he preferred to stay where he was and talk to Mrs. Pontellier.

"Well, send him about his business when he bores you, Edna," instructed her husband as he prepared to leave.

"Here, take the umbrella," she exclaimed, holding it out to him. He accepted the sunshade, and lifting it over his head descended the steps and walked away.

"Coming back to dinner?" his wife called after him. He halted a moment and shrugged his shoulders. He felt in his vest pocket; there was a ten-dollar bill there. He did not know; perhaps he would return for the early dinner and perhaps he would not. It all depended upon the company which he found over at Klein's and the size of "the game." He did not say this, but she understood it, and laughed, nodding good-by to him.

Both children wanted to follow their father when they saw him starting out. He kissed them and promised to bring them back bonbons and peanuts.

II

Mrs. Pontellier's eyes were quick and bright, they were a yellowish brown, about the color of her hair. She had a way of turning them swiftly upon an object and holding them there as if lost in some inward maze of contemplation or thought.

Her eyebrows were a shade darker than her hair. They were thick and almost horizontal, emphasizing the depth of her eyes. She was rather handsome than beautiful. Her face was captivating by reason of a certain frankness of expression and a contradictory subtle play of features. Her manner was engaging.

Robert rolled a cigarette. He smoked cigarettes because he could not afford cigars, he said. He had a cigar in his pocket which Mr. Pontellier had presented him with, and he was saving it for his afterdinner smoke.

This seemed quite proper and natural on his part. In coloring he was not unlike his companion. A clean-shaved face made the resemblance more pronounced than it would otherwise have been.

There rested no shadow of care upon his open countenance. His eyes gathered in and reflected the light and languor of the summer day.

Mrs. Pontellier reached over for a palm-leaf fan that lay on the porch and began to fan herself, while Robert sent between his lips light puffs from his cigarette. They chatted incessantly: about the things around them; their amusing adventure out in the water—it had again assumed its entertaining aspect; about the wind, the trees, the people who had gone to the *Chênière;* about the children playing croquet under the oaks, and the Farival twins, who were now performing the overture to "The Poet and the Peasant."

Robert talked a good deal about himself. He was very young, and did not know any better. Mrs. Pontellier talked a little about herself for the same reason. Each was interested in what the other said. Robert spoke of his intention to go to Mexico in the autumn, where fortune awaited him. He was always intending to go to Mexico, but some way never got there. Meanwhile he held on to his modest position in a mercantile house in New Orleans, where an equal familiarity with English, French and Spanish gave him no small value as a clerk and correspondent

He was spending his summer vacation, as he always did, with his mother at Grand Isle. In former times, before Robert could remember, "the house" had been a summer luxury of the Lebruns. Now, flanked by its dozen or more cottages, which were always filled with exclusive visitors from the *"Quartier Français,"* it enabled Madame Lebrun to maintain the easy and comfortable existence which appeared to be her birthright

Mrs. Pontellier talked about her father's Mississippi plantation and her girlhood home in the old Kentucky bluegrass country. She was an American woman, with a small infusion of French which seemed to have been lost in dilution. She read a letter from her sister, who was away in the East, and who had engaged herself to be married. Robert was interested, and wanted to know what manner of girls the sisters were, what the father was like, and how long the mother had been dead.

When Mrs. Pontellier folded the letter it was time for her to dress for the early dinner.

"I see Léonce isn't coming back," she said, with a glance in the direction whence her husband had disappeared. Robert supposed he was not, as there were a good many New Orleans club men over at Klein's.

When Mrs. Pontellier left him to enter her room, the young man descended the steps and strolled over toward the croquet players, where, during the half-hour before dinner, he amused himself with the little Pontellier children, who were very fond of him.

III

It was eleven o'clock that night when Mr. Pontellier returned from Klein's hotel. He was in an excellent humor, in high spirits, and very talkative. His entrance awoke his wife, who was in bed and fast asleep when he came in. He talked to her while he undressed, telling her anecdotes and bits of news and gossip that he had gathered during the day. From his trousers pockets he took a fistful of crumpled bank notes and a good deal of silver coin, which he piled on the bureau indiscriminately with keys, knife, handkerchief, and whatever else happened to be in his pockets. She was overcome with sleep, and answered him with little half utterances.

He thought it very discouraging that his wife, who was the sole object of his existence, evinced so little interest in things which concerned him, and valued so little his conversation.

Mr. Pontellier had forgotten the bonbons and peanuts for the boys. Notwithstanding he loved them very much, and went into the adjoining room where they slept to take a look at them and make sure that they were resting comfortably. The result of his investigation was far from satisfactory. He turned and shifted the youngsters about in bed. One of them began to kick and talk about a basket full of crabs.

Mr. Pontellier returned to his wife with the information that Raoul had a high fever and needed looking after. Then he lit a cigar and went and sat near the open door to smoke it.

Mrs. Pontellier was quite sure Raoul had no fever. He had gone to bed perfectly well, she said, and nothing had ailed him all day. Mr. Pontellier was too well acquainted with fever symptoms to be mistaken. He assured her the child was consuming at that moment in the next room.

He reproached his wife with her inattention, her habitual neglect of the children. If it was not a mother's place to look after children, whose on earth was it? He himself had his hands full with his brokerage business. He could not be in two places at once; making a living for his family on the street and staying at home to see that no harm befell them. He talked in a monotonous, insistent way.

Mrs. Pontellier sprang out of bed and went into the next room. She soon came back and sat on the edge of the bed, leaning her head down on the pillow. She said nothing, and refused to answer her husband when he questioned her. When his cigar was smoked out he went to bed, and in half a minute he was fast asleep.

Mrs. Pontellier was by that time thoroughly awake. She began to cry a little, and wiped her eyes on the sleeve of her *peignoir*. Blowing out the candle, which her husband had left burning, she slipped her bare feet into a pair of satin *mules* at the foot of the bed and went out on the porch, where she sat down in the wicker chair and began to rock gently to and fro.

It was then past midnight. The cottages were all dark. A single faint light gleamed out from the hallway of the house. There was no sound abroad except the hooting of an old owl in the top of a water-oak, and the everlasting voice of the sea, that was not uplifted at that soft hour. It broke like a mournful lullaby upon the night.

The tears came so fast to Mrs. Pontellier's eyes that the damp sleeve of her *peignoir* no longer served to dry them. She was holding the back of her chair with one hand; her loose sleeve had slipped almost to the shoulder of her uplifted arm. Turning, she thrust her face, steaming and wet into the bend of her arm, and she went on crying there, not caring any longer to dry her face, her eyes, her arms. She could not have told why she was crying. Such experiences as the foregoing were not uncommon in her married life. They seemed never before to have weighed much against the abundance of her husband's kindness and a uniform devotion which had come to be tacit and self-understood.

An indescribable oppression, which seemed to generate in some unfamiliar part of her consciousness, filled her whole being with a vague anguish. It was like a shadow, like a mist passing across her soul's summer day. It was strange and unfamiliar; it was a mood. She did not sit there inwardly upbraiding her husband, lamenting at Fate, which had directed her footsteps to the path which they had taken. She was just having a good cry all to herself. The mosquitoes made merry over her, biting her firm, round arms and nipping at her bare insteps.

The little stinging, buzzing imps succeeded in dispelling a mood which might have held her there in the darkness half a night longer.

The following morning Mr. Pontellier was up in good time to take the rockaway which was to convey him to the steamer at the wharf. He was returning to the city to his business, and they would not see him again at the Island till the coming Saturday. He had regained his composure, which seemed to have been somewhat impaired the night before. He was eager to be gone, as he looked forward to a lively week in Carondelet Street.

Mr. Pontellier gave his wife half of the money which he had brought away from Klein's hotel the evening before. She liked money as well as most women, and accepted it with no little satisfaction.

"It will buy a handsome wedding present for Sister Janet!" she exclaimed, smoothing out the bills as she counted them one by one.

"Oh! we'll treat Sister Janet better than that, my dear," he laughed, as he prepared to kiss her good-by.

The boys were tumbling about, clinging to his legs, imploring that numerous things be brought back to them. Mr. Pontellier was a great favorite, and ladies, men, children, even nurses, were always on hand to say good-by to him. His wife stood smiling and waving, the boys shouting, as he disappeared in the old rockaway down the sandy road.

A few days later a box arrived for Mrs. Pontellier from New Orleans. It was from her husband. It was filled with *friandises,*[2] with luscious and toothsome bits—the finest of fruits, *patés,* a rare bottle or two, delicious syrups, and bonbons in abundance.

Mrs. Pontellier was always very generous with the contents of such a box; she was quite used to receiving them when away from home. The *patés* and fruit were brought to the dining-room; the bonbons were passed around. And the ladies, selecting with dainty and discriminating fingers and a little greedily, all declared that Mr. Pontellier was the best husband in the world. Mrs. Pontellier was forced to admit that she knew of none better.

IV

It would have been a difficult matter for Mr. Pontellier to define to his own satisfaction or any one else's wherein his wife failed in her duty toward their children. It was something which he felt rather than perceived, and he never voiced the feeling without subsequent regret and ample atonement.

If one of the little Pontellier boys took a tumble whilst at play, he was not apt to rush crying to his mother's arms for comfort; he would more likely pick himself up, wipe the water out of his eyes and the sand out of his mouth, and go on playing. Tots as they were, they pulled together and stood their ground in childish battles with doubled fists and uplifted voices, which usually prevailed against the other mother-tots. The quadroon nurse was looked upon as a huge encumbrance, only good to button up waists and panties and to brush and part hair; since it seemed to be a law of society that hair must be parted and brushed.

In short, Mrs. Pontellier was not a mother-woman. The mother-women seemed to prevail that summer at Grand Isle. It was easy to know them, fluttering about with extended, protecting wings when any harm, real or imaginary, threatened their precious brood. They were women who idolized their children, worshiped their husbands, and esteemed it a holy privilege to efface themselves as individuals and grow wings as ministering angels.

Many of them were delicious in the rôle; one of them was the embodiment of every womanly grace and charm. If her husband did not adore her, he was a brute, deserving of death by slow torture. Her name was Adèle Ratignolle. There are no words to describe her save the old ones that have served so often to picture the bygone heroine of romance and the fair lady of our dreams. There was nothing subtle or hidden about her charms; her beauty was all there, flaming and apparent: the spun-gold hair that comb nor confining pin could restrain; the blue eyes that were like nothing but sapphires; two lips that pouted, that were so red one could only think of cherries or some other delicious crimson fruit in looking at them. She was growing a little stout, but it did not seem to detract an iota from the grace of every step, pose, gesture. One would not have wanted her white neck a mite less full or her beautiful arms more slender. Never were hands more exquisite than hers, and it was a joy to look at them when she threaded her needle or adjusted her gold thimble to her taper middle finger as she sewed away on the little night-drawers or fashioned a bodice or a bib.

Madame Ratignolle was very fond of Mrs. Pontellier, and often she took her sewing and went over to sit with her in the afternoons. She was sitting there the afternoon of the day the box arrived from New Orleans. She had possession of the rocker, and she was busily engaged in sewing upon a diminutive pair of night drawers.

She had brought the pattern of the drawers for Mrs. Pontellier to cut out—a marvel of construction, fashioned to enclose a baby's body so effectually that only two small eyes might look out from the garment, like an Eskimo's. They were designed for winter wear, when treacherous drafts came down chimneys and insidious currents of deadly cold found their way through keyholes.

Mrs. Pontellier's mind was quite at rest concerning the present material needs of her children, and she could not see the use of anticipating and making winter night garments the subject of her summer meditations. But she did not want to appear unamiable and uninterested, so she had brought forth newspapers, which she spread upon the floor of the gallery, and under Madame Ratignolle's directions she had cut a pattern of the impervious garment.

Robert was there, seated as he had been the Sunday before, and Mrs. Pontellier also occupied her former position on the upper step, leaning listlessly against the post. Beside her was a box of bonbons, which she held out at intervals to Madame Ratignolle.

That lady seemed at a loss to make a selection, but finally settled upon a stick of nougat, wondering if it were not too rich; whether it could possibly hurt her. Madame Ratignolle had been married seven years. About every two years she had a baby. At that time she had three babies, and was beginning to think of a fourth one. She was always talking about her "condition." Her "condition" was in no way apparent, and no one would have known a thing about it but for her persistence in making it the subject of conversation.

Robert started to reassure her, asserting that he had known a lady who had subsisted upon nougat during the entire—but seeing the color mount into Mrs. Pontellier's face he checked himself and changed the subject.

Mrs. Pontellier, though she had married a Creole, was not thoroughly at home in the society of Creoles; never before had she been thrown so intimately among them. There were only Creoles that summer at Lebrun's. They all knew each other, and felt like one large family, among whom existed the most amicable relations. A characteristic which distinguished them and which impressed Mrs. Pontellier most forcibly was their entire absence of prudery. Their freedom of expression was at first incomprehensible to her, though she had no difficulty in reconciling it with a lofty chastity which in the Creole woman seems to be inborn and unmistakable.

Never would Edna Pontellier forget the shock with which she heard Madame Ratignolle relating to old Monsieur Farival the harrowing story of one of her *accouchements,* withholding no intimate detail. She was growing accustomed to like shock, but she could not keep the mounting color back from her cheeks. Oftener than once her coming had interrupted the droll story with which Robert was entertaining some amused group of married women.

A book had gone the rounds of the *pension.* When it came her turn to read it, she did so with profound astonishment She felt moved to read the book in secret and solitude, though none of the others had done so—to hide it from view at the sound of approaching footsteps. It was openly criticised and freely discussed at table. Mrs. Pontellier gave over being astonished, and concluded that wonders would never cease.

V

They formed a congenial group sitting there that summer afternoon—Madame Ratignolle sewing away, often stopping to relate a story or incident with much expressive gesture of her perfect hands; Robert and Mrs. Pontellier sitting idle, exchanging occasional words, glances or smiles which indicated a certain advanced stage of intimacy and *camaraderie.*

He had lived in her shadow during the past month. No one thought anything of it. Many had predicted that Robert would devote himself to Mrs. Pontellier when he arrived. Since the age of fifteen, which was eleven years before, Robert each summer at Grand Isle had constituted himself the devoted attendant of some fair dame or damsel. Sometimes it was a young girl, again a widow; but as often as not it was some interesting married woman.

For two consecutive seasons he lived in the sunlight of Mademoiselle Duvigné's presence. But she died between summers; then Robert posed as an inconsolable, prostrating himself at the feet of Madame Ratignolle for whatever crumbs of sympathy and comfort she might be pleased to vouchsafe.

Mrs. Pontellier liked to sit and gaze at her fair companion as she might look upon a faultless Madonna.

"Could any one fathom the cruelty beneath that fair exterior?" murmured Robert. "She knew that I adored her once, and she let me adore her. It was 'Robert, come; go; stand up; sit down; do this; do that; see if the baby sleeps; my thimble, please, that I left God knows where. Come and read Daudet to me while I sew.'"

"*Par example!* I never had to ask. You were always there under my feet, like a troublesome cat."

"You mean like an adoring dog. And just as soon as Ratignolle appeared on the scene, then it was like a dog. *'Passez! Adieu! Allez vous-en!'*"[3]

"Perhaps I feared to make Alphonse jealous," she interjoined, with excessive naïveté. That made them all laugh. The right hand jealous of the left! The heart jealous of the soul! But for that matter, the Creole husband is never jealous; with him the gangrene passion is one which has become dwarfed by disuse.

Meanwhile Robert, addressing Mrs. Pontellier, continued to tell of his one time hopeless passion for Madame Ratignolle; of sleepless nights, of consuming flames till the very sea sizzled when he took his daily plunge. While the lady at the needle kept up a little running, contemptuous comment:

"Blagueur—farceur—gros bête, va!"[4]

He never assumed this serio-comic tone when alone with Mrs. Pontellier. She never knew precisely what to make of it; at that moment it was impossible for her to guess how much of it was jest and what proportion was earnest. It was understood that he had often spoken words of love to Madame Ratignolle, without any thought of being taken seriously. Mrs. Pontellier was glad he had not assumed a similar rôle toward herself. It would have been unacceptable and annoying.

Mrs. Pontellier had brought her sketching materials, which she sometimes dabbled with in an unprofessional way. She liked the dabbling. She felt in it satisfaction of a kind which no other employment afforded her.

She had long wished to try herself on Madame Ratignolle. Never had that lady seemed a more tempting subject than at that moment, seated there like some sensuous Madonna, with the gleam of the fading day enriching her splendid color.

Robert crossed over and seated himself upon the step below Mrs. Pontellier, that he might watch her work. She handled her brushes with a certain ease and freedom which came, not from long and close acquaintance with them, but from a natural aptitude. Robert followed her work with close attention, giving forth little ejaculatory expressions of appreciation in French, which he addressed to Madame Ratignolle.

"Mais ce n'est pas mal! Elle s'y connait, elle a de la force, oui."[5]

During his oblivious attention he once quietly rested his head against Mrs. Pontellier's arm. As gently she repulsed him. Once again he repeated the offense. She could not but believe it to be thoughtlessness on his part, yet that was no reason she should submit to it. She did not remonstrate, except again to repulse him quietly but firmly. He offered no apology.

The picture completed bore no resemblance to Madame Ratignolle. She was greatly disappointed to find that it did not look like her. But it was a fair enough piece of work, and in many respects satisfying.

Mrs. Pontellier evidently did not think so. After surveying the sketch critically she drew a broad smudge of paint across its surface, and crumpled the paper between her hands.

The youngsters came tumbling up the steps, the quadroon following at the respectful distance which they required her to observe. Mrs. Pontellier made them carry her paints and things into the house. She sought to detain them for a little talk and some pleasantry. But they were greatly in earnest. They had only come to investigate the contents of the bonbon box. They accepted without murmuring what she chose to give them, each holding out two chubby hands scoop-like, in the vain hope that they might be filled; and then away they went.

The sun was low in the west, and the breeze soft and languorous that came up from the south, charged with the seductive odor of the sea. Children, freshly befurbelowed, were gathering for their games under the oaks. Their voices were high and penetrating.

Madame Ratignolle folded her sewing, placing thimble, scissors and thread all neatly together in the roll, which she pinned securely. She complained of faintness. Mrs. Pontellier flew for the cologne water and a fan. She bathed Madame Ratignolle's face with cologne, while Robert plied the fan with unnecessary vigor.

The spell was soon over, and Mrs. Pontellier could not help wondering if there were not a little imagination responsible for its origin, for the rose tint had never faded from her friend's face.

She stood watching the fair woman walk down the long line of galleries with the grace and majesty which queens are sometimes supposed to possess. Her little ones ran to meet her. Two of them clung about her white skirts, the third she took from its nurse and with a thousand endearments bore it along in her own fond, encircling arms. Though, as everybody well knew, the doctor had forbidden her to lift so much as a pin!

"Are you going bathing?" asked Robert of Mrs. Pontellier. It was not so much a question as a reminder.

"Oh, no," she answered, with a tone of indecision. "I'm tired; I think not." Her glance wandered from his face away toward the Gulf, whose sonorous murmur reached her like a loving but imperative entreaty.

"Oh, come!" he insisted. "You mustn't miss your bath. Come on. The water must be delicious; it will not hurt you. Come."

He reached up for her big, rough straw hat that hung on a peg outside the door, and put it on her head. They descended the steps, and walked away together toward the beach. The sun was low in the west and the breeze was soft and warm.

VI

Edna Pontellier could not have told why, wishing to go to the beach with Robert, she should in the first place have declined, and in the second place have followed in obedience to one of the two contradictory impulses which impelled her.

A certain light was beginning to dawn dimly within her—the light which, showing the way, forbids it.

At that early period it served but to bewilder her. It moved her to dreams, to thoughtfulness, to the shadowy anguish which had overcome her the midnight when she had abandoned herself to tears.

In short, Mrs. Pontellier was beginning to realize her position in the universe as a human being, and to recognize her relations as an individual to the world within and about her. This may seem like a ponderous weight of wisdom to descend upon the soul of a young woman of twenty-eight—perhaps more wisdom than the Holy Ghost is usually pleased to vouchsafe to any woman.

But the beginning of things, of a world especially, is necessarily vague, tangled, chaotic, and exceedingly disturbing. How few of us ever emerge from such beginning! How many souls perish in its tumult!

The voice of the sea is seductive; never ceasing, whispering, clamoring, murmuring, inviting the soul to wander for a spell in abysses of solitude; to lose itself in mazes of inward contemplation.

The voice of the sea speaks to the soul. The touch of the sea is sensuous, enfolding the body in its soft, close embrace.

VII

Mrs. Pontellier was not a woman given to confidences, a characteristic hitherto contrary to her nature. Even as a child she had lived her own small life all within herself. At a very early period she had apprehended instinctively the dual life—that outward existence which conforms, the inward life which questions.

That summer at Grand Isle she began to loosen a little the mantle of reserve that had always enveloped her. There may have been—there must have been—influences, both subtle and apparent, working in their several ways to induce her to do this; but the most obvious was the influence of Adèle Ratignolle. The excessive physical charm of the Creole had first attracted her, for Edna had a sensuous susceptibility to beauty. Then the candor of the woman's whole existence, which every one might read, and which formed so striking a contrast to her own habitual reserve—this might have furnished a link. Who can tell what metals the gods use in forging the subtle bond which we call sympathy, which we might as well call love.

The two women went away one morning to the beach together, arm in arm, under the huge white sunshade. Edna had prevailed upon Madame Ratignolle to leave the children behind, though she could not induce her to relinquish a diminutive roll of needlework, which Adele begged to be allowed to slip into the depths of her pocket. In some unaccountable way they had escaped from Robert.

The walk to the beach was no inconsiderable one, consisting as it did of a long, sandy path, upon which a sporadic and tangled growth that bordered it on either side made frequent and unexpected inroads. There were acres of yellow camomile reaching out on either hand. Further away still, vegetable gardens abounded, with frequent small plantations of orange or lemon trees intervening. The dark green clusters glistened from afar in the sun.

The women were both of goodly height, Madame Ratignolle possessing the more feminine and matronly figure. The charm of Edna Pontellier's physique stole insensibly upon you. The lines of her body were long, clean and symmetrical; it was a body which occasionally fell into splendid poses; there was no suggestion of the trim, stereotyped fashion-plate about it. A casual and indiscriminating observer, in passing, might not cast a second glance upon the figure. But with more feeling and discernment he would have recognized the noble beauty of its modeling, and the graceful severity of poise and movement, which made Edna Pontellier different from the crowd.

She wore a cool muslin that morning—white with a waving vertical line of brown running through it; also a white linen collar and the big straw hat which she had taken from the peg outside the door. The hat rested any way on her yellow-brown hair, that waved a little, was heavy, and clung close to her head.

Madame Ratignolle, more careful of her complexion, had twined a gauze veil about her head. She wore doeskin gloves, with gauntlets that protected her wrists. She was dressed in pure white, with a fluffiness of ruffles that became her. The draperies and fluttering things which she wore suited her rich, luxuriant beauty as a greater severity of line could not have done.

There were a number of bathhouses along the beach, of rough but solid construction, built with small, protecting galleries facing the water. Each house consisted of two compartments, and each family at Lebrun's possessed a compartment for itself, fitted out with all the essential paraphernalia of the bath and whatever other conveniences the owners might desire. The two women had no intention of bathing; they had just strolled down to the beach for a walk and to be alone and near the water. The Pontellier and Ratignolle compartments adjoined one another under the same roof.

Mrs. Pontellier had brought down her key through force of habit. Unlocking the door of her bathroom she went inside, and soon emerged, bringing a rug, which she spread upon the floor of the gallery, and two huge hair pillows covered with crash, which she placed against the front of the building.

The two seated themselves there in the shade of the porch, side by side, with their backs against the pillows and their feet extended. Madame Ratignolle removed her veil, wiped her face with a rather delicate handkerchief, and fanned herself with the fan which she always carried suspended somewhere about her person by a long, narrow ribbon. Edna removed her collar and opened her dress at the throat. She took the fan from Madame Ratignolle and began to fan both herself and her companion. It was very warm, and for a while they did nothing but exchange remarks about the heat, the sun, the glare. But there was a breeze blowing, a choppy, stiff wind that whipped the water into froth. It fluttered the skirts of the two women and kept them for a while engaged in adjusting, readjusting, tucking in, securing hair-pins and hatpins. A few persons were sporting some distance away in the water. The beach was very still of human sound at that hour. The lady in black was reading her morning devotions on the porch of a neighboring bath-house. Two young lovers were exchanging their hearts' yearnings beneath the children's tent, which they had found unoccupied.

Edna Pontellier, casting her eyes about, had finally kept them at rest upon the sea. The day was clear and carried the gaze out as far as the blue sky went; there were a few white clouds suspended idly over the horizon. A lateen sail was visible in the direction of Cat Island, and others to the south seemed almost motionless in the far distance.

"Of whom—of what are you thinking?" asked Adèle of her companion, whose countenance she had been watching with a little amused attention, arrested by the absorbed expression which seemed to have seized and fixed every feature into a statuesque repose.

"Nothing," returned Mrs. Pontellier, with a start, adding at once: "How stupid! But it seems to me it is the reply we make instinctively to such a question. Let me see," she went on, throwing back her head and narrowing her fine eyes till they shone like two vivid points of light. "Let me see. I was really not conscious of thinking of anything, but perhaps I can retrace my thoughts."

"Oh! never mind!" laughed Madame Ratignolle. "I am not quite so exacting. I will let you off this time. It is really too hot to think, especially to think about thinking."

"But for the fun of it," persisted Edna. "First of all, the sight of the water stretching so far away, those motionless sails against the blue sky, made a delicious picture that I just wanted to sit and look at. The hot wind beating in my face made me think—without any connection that I can trace—of a summer day in Kentucky, of a meadow that seemed as big as the ocean to the very little girl walking through the grass, which was higher than her waist. She threw out her arms as if swimming when she walked, beating the tall grass as one strikes out in the water. Oh, I see the connection now!"

"Where were you going that day in Kentucky, walking through the grass?"

"I don't remember now. I was just walking diagonally across a big field. My sunbonnet obstructed the view. I could see only the stretch of green before me, and I felt as if I must walk on forever, without coming to the end of it. I don't remember whether I was frightened or pleased. I must have been entertained.

"Likely as not it was Sunday," she laughed; "and I was running away from prayers, from the Presbyterian service, read in a spirit of gloom by my father that chills me yet to think of."

"And have you been running away from prayers ever since, *ma chére?*" asked Madame Ratignolle, amused.

"No! oh, no!" Edna hastened to say. "I was a little unthinking child in those days, just following a misleading impulse without question. On the contrary, during one period of my life religion took a firm hold upon me; after I was twelve and until—until—why, I suppose until now, though I never thought much about it—just driven along by habit. But do you know," she broke off, turning her quick eyes upon Madame Ratignolle and leaning forward a little so as to bring her face quite close to that of her companion, "sometimes I feel this summer as if I were walking through the green meadow again, idly, aimlessly, unthinking and unguided."

Madame Ratignolle laid her hand over that of Mrs. Pontellier, which was near her. Seeing that the hand was not withdrawn, she clasped it firmly and warmly. She even stroked it a little, fondly, with the other hand, murmuring in an undertone, *"Pauvre chérie."*

The action was at first a little confusing to Edna, but she soon lent herself readily to the Creole's gentle caress. She was not accustomed to an outward and spoken expression of affection, either in herself or in others. She and her younger sister, Janet, had quarreled a good deal through force of unfortunate habit. Her older sister, Margaret, was matronly and dignified, probably from having assumed matronly and housewifely responsibilities too early in life, their mother having died when they were quite young. Margaret was not effusive; she was practical. Edna had had an occasional girl friend, but whether accidentally or not, they seemed to have been all of one type—the self-contained. She never realized that the reserve of her own character had much, perhaps everything, to do with this. Her most intimate friend at school had been one of rather exceptional intellectual gifts who wrote fine-sounding essays, which Edna admired and strove to imitate; and with her she talked and glowed over the English classics, and sometimes held religious and political controversies.

Edna often wondered at one propensity which sometimes had inwardly disturbed her without causing any outward show or manifestation on her part. At a very early age—perhaps it was when she traversed the ocean of waving grass—she remembered that she had been passionately enamored of a dignified and sad-eyed cavalry officer who visited her father in Kentucky. She could not leave his presence when he was there, nor remove her eyes from his face, which was something like Napoleon's, with a lock of black hair falling across the forehead. But the cavalry officer melted imperceptibly out of her existence.

At another time her affections were deeply engaged by a young gentleman who visited a lady on a neighboring plantation. It was after they went to Mississippi to live. The young man was engaged to be married to the young lady, and they sometimes called upon Margaret, driving over of afternoons in a buggy. Edna was a little miss, just merging into her teens; and the realization that she herself was nothing, nothing, nothing to the engaged young man was a bitter affliction to her. But he, too, went the way of dreams.

She was a grown young woman when she was overtaken by what she supposed to be the climax of her fate. It was when the face and figure of a great tragedian began to haunt her imagination and stir her senses. The persistence of the infatuation lent it an aspect of genuineness. The hopelessness of it colored it with the lofty tones of a great passion.

The picture of the tragedian stood enframed upon her desk. Any one may possess the portrait of a tragedian without exciting suspicion or comment. (This was a sinister reflection which she cherished.) In the presence of others she expressed admiration for his exalted gifts, as she handed the photograph around and dwelt upon the fidelity of the likeness. When alone she sometimes picked it up and kissed the cold glass passionately.

Her marriage to Léonce Pontellier was purely an accident, in this respect resembling many other marriages which masquerade as the decrees of Fate. It was in the midst of her secret great passion that she met him. He fell in love, as men are in the habit of doing, and pressed his suit with an earnestness and an ardor which left nothing to be desired. He pleased her; his absolute devotion flattered her. She fancied there was a sympathy of thought and taste between them, in which fancy she was mistaken. Add to this the violent opposition of her father and her sister Margaret to her marriage with a Catholic, and we need seek no further for the motives which led her to accept Monsieur Pontellier for her husband.

The acme of bliss, which would have been a marriage with the tragedian, was not for her in this world. As the devoted wife of a man who worshiped her, she felt she would take her place with a certain dignity in the world of reality, closing the portals forever behind her upon the realm of romance and dreams.

But it was not long before the tragedian had gone to join the cavalry officer and the engaged young man and a few others; and Edna found herself face to face with the realities. She grew fond of her husband, realizing with some unaccountable satisfaction that no trace of passion or excessive and fictitious warmth colored her affection, thereby threatening its dissolution.

She was fond of her children in an uneven, impulsive way. She would sometimes gather them passionately to her heart; she would sometimes forget them. The year before they had spent part of the summer with their grandmother Pontellier in Iberville. Feeling secure regarding their happiness and welfare, she did not miss them except with an occasional intense longing. Their absence was a sort of relief, though she did not admit this, even to herself. It seemed to free her of a responsibility which she had blindly assumed and for which Fate had not fitted her.

Edna did not reveal so much as all this to Madame Ratignolle that summer day when they sat with faces turned to the sea. But a good part of it escaped her. She had put her head down on Madame Ratignolle's shoulder. She was flushed and felt intoxicated with the sound of her own voice and the unaccustomed taste of candor. It muddled her like wine, or like a first breath of freedom.

There was the sound of approaching voices. It was Robert, surrounded by a troop of children, searching for them. The two little Pontelliers were with him, and he carried Madame Ratignolle's little girl in his arms. There were other children besides, and two nursemaids followed, looking disagreeable and resigned.

The women at once rose and began to shake out their draperies and relax their muscles. Mrs. Pontellier threw the cushions and rug into the bath-house. The children all scampered off to the awning, and they stood there in a line, gazing upon the intruding lovers, still exchanging their vows and sighs. The lovers got up, with only a silent protest, and walked slowly away somewhere else.

The children possessed themselves of the tent, and Mrs. Pontellier went over to join them.

Madame Ratignolle begged Robert to accompany her to the house; she complained of cramp in her limbs and stiffness of the joints. She leaned draggingly upon his arm as they walked.

VIII

"Do me a favor, Robert," spoke the pretty woman at his side, almost as soon as she and Robert had started on their slow, homeward way. She looked up in his face, leaning on his arm beneath the encircling shadow of the umbrella which he had lifted.

"Granted; as many as you like," he returned, glancing down into her eyes that were full of thoughtfulness and some speculation.

"I only ask for one; let Mrs. Pontellier alone."

"*Tiens!*" he exclaimed, with a sudden, boyish laugh. "*Voila que Madame Ratignolles est jalouse!*"[6]

"Nonsense! I'm in earnest; I mean what I say. Let Mrs. Pontellier alone."

"Why?" he asked; himself growing serious at his companion's solicitation.

"She is not one of us; she is not like us. She might make the unfortunate blunder of taking you seriously."

His face flushed with annoyance, and taking off his soft hat he began to beat it impatiently against his leg as he walked. "Why shouldn't she take me seriously?" he demanded sharply. "Am I a comedian, a clown, a jack-in-the-box? Why shouldn't she? You Creoles! I have no patience with you! Am I always to be regarded as a feature of an amusing programme? I hope Mrs. Pontellier does take me seriously. I hope she has discernment enough to find in me something besides the *blagueur*.[7] If I thought there was any doubt—"

"Oh, enough, Robert!" she broke into his heated outburst. "You are not thinking of what you are saying. You speak with about as little reflection as we might expect from one of those children down there playing in the sand. If your attentions to any married women here were ever offered with any intention of being convincing, you would not be the gentleman we all know you to be, and you would be unfit to associate with the wives and daughters of the people who trust you."

Madame Ratignolle had spoken what she believed to be the law and the gospel. The young man shrugged his shoulders impatiently.

"Oh! well! That isn't it," slamming his hat down vehemently upon his head. "You ought to feel that such things are not flattering to say to a fellow."

"Should our whole intercourse consist of an exchange of compliments? *Ma foi!*"[8]

"It isn't pleasant to have a woman tell you—" he went on, unheedingly, but breaking off suddenly: "Now if I were like Arobin—you remember Alcée Arobin and that story of the consul's wife at Biloxi?" And he related the story of Alcée Arobin and the consul's wife, and another about the tenor of the French Opera, who received letters which should never have been written, and still other stories, grave and gay, till Mrs. Pontellier and her possible propensity for taking young men seriously was apparently forgotten.

Madame Ratignolle, when they had regained her cottage, went in to take the hour's rest which she considered helpful. Before leaving her, Robert begged her pardon for the impatience—he called it rudeness—with which he had received her well-meant caution.

"You made one mistake, Adèle," he said, with a light smile; "there is no earthly possibility of Mrs. Pontellier ever taking me seriously. You should have warned me against taking myself seriously. Your advice might then have carried some weight and given me subject for some reflection. *Au revoir.* But you look tired," he added, solicitously. "Would you like a cup of bouillon? Shall I stir you a toddy? Let me mix you a toddy with a drop of Angostura."

She acceded to the suggestion of bouillon, which was grateful and acceptable. He went himself to the kitchen, which was a building apart from the cottages and lying to the rear of the house. And he himself brought her the golden-brown bouillon, in a dainty Sèvres cup, with a flaky cracker or two on the saucer.

She thrust a bare, white arm from the curtain which shielded her open door, and received the cup from his hands. She told him he was a *bon garçon,* and she meant it. Robert thanked her and turned away toward "the house."

The lovers were just entering the grounds of the *pension.* They were leaning toward each other as the water oaks bent from the sea. There was not a particle of earth beneath their feet. Their heads might have been turned upside down, so absolutely did they tread upon blue ether. The lady in black, creeping behind them, looked a trifle paler and more jaded than usual. There was no sign of Mrs. Pontellier and the children. Robert scanned the distance for any such apparition. They would doubtless remain away till the dinner hour. The young man ascended to his mother's room. It was situated at the top of the house, made up of odd angles and a queer, sloping ceiling. Two broad dormer windows looked out toward the Gulf, and as far across it as a man's eye might reach. The furnishings of the room were light, cool, and practical.

Madame Lebrun was busily engaged at the sewing machine. A little black girl sat on the floor, and with her hands worked the treadle of the machine. The Creole woman does not take any chances which may be avoided of imperiling her health.

Robert went over and seated himself on the broad sill of one of the dormer windows. He took a book from his pocket and began energetically to read it, judging by the precision and frequency with which he turned the leaves. The sewing machine made a resounding clatter in the room; it was of a ponderous, bygone make. In the lulls, Robert and his mother exchanged bits of desultory conversation.

"Where is Mrs. Pontellier?"

"Down at the beach with the children."

"I promised to lend her the Goncourt. Don't forget to take it down when you go; it's there on the bookshelf over the small table." Clatter, clatter, clatter, bang! for the next five or eight minutes.

"Where is Victor going with the rockaway?"

"The rockaway? Victor?"

"Yes, down there in front. He seems to be getting ready to drive away somewhere."

"Call him." Clatter, clatter!

Robert uttered a shrill, piercing whistle which might have been heard back at the wharf.

"He won't look up."

Madame Lebrun flew to the window. She called "Victor!" She waved a handkerchief and called again. The young fellow below got into the vehicle and started the horse off at a gallop.

Madame Lebrun went back to the machine, crimson with annoyance. Victor was the younger son and brother—a *tête montée*,[9] with a temper which invited violence and a will which no ax could break.

"Whenever you say the word I'm ready to thrash any amount of reason into him that he's able to hold."

"If your father had only lived!" Clatter, clatter, clatter, clatter, bang! It was a fixed belief with Madame Lebrun that the conduct of the universe and all things pertaining thereto would have been manifestly of a more intelligent and higher order had not Monsieur Lebrun been removed to other spheres during the early years of their married life.

"What do you hear from Montel?" Montel was a middle-aged gentleman whose vain ambition and desire for the past twenty years had been to fill the void which Monsieur Lebrun's taking off had left in the Lebrun household. Clatter, clatter, bang, clatter!

"I have a letter somewhere," looking in the machine drawer and finding the letter in the bottom of the workbasket. "He says to tell you he will be in Vera Cruz the beginning of next month"—clatter, clatter!—"and if you still have the intention of joining him"—bang! clatter, clatter, bang!

"Why didn't you tell me so before, mother? You know I wanted—" Clatter, clatter, clatter!

"Do you see Mrs. Pontellier starting back with the children? She will be in late to luncheon again. She never starts to get ready for luncheon till the last minute." Clatter, clatter! "Where are you going?"

"Where did you say the Goncourt was?"

IX

Every light in the hall was ablaze, every lamp turned as high as it could be without smoking the chimney or threatening explosion. The lamps were fixed at intervals against the wall, encircling the whole room. Some one had gathered orange and lemon branches, and with these fashioned graceful festoons between. The dark green of the branches stood out and glistened against the white muslin curtains which draped the windows, and which puffed, floated, and flapped at the capricious will of a stiff breeze that swept up from the Gulf.

It was Saturday night a few weeks after the intimate conversation held between Robert and Madame Ratignolle on their way from the beach. An unusual number of husbands, fathers, and friends had come down to stay over Sunday, and they were being suitably entertained by their families, with the material help of Madame Lebrun. The dining tables had all been removed to one end of the hall, and the chairs ranged about in rows and in clusters. Each little family group had had its say and exchanged its domestic gossip earlier in the evening. There was now an apparent disposition to relax, to widen the circle of confidences and give a more general tone to the conversation.

Many of the children had been permitted to sit up beyond their usual bedtime. A small band of them were lying on their stomachs on the floor looking at the colored sheets of the comic papers which Mr. Pontellier had brought down. The little Pontellier boys were permitting them to do so, and making their authority felt.

Music, dancing, and a recitation or two were the entertainments furnished, or rather, offered. But there was nothing systematic about the programme, no appearance of prearrangement nor even premeditation.

At an early hour in the evening the Farival twins were prevailed upon to play the piano. They were girls of fourteen, always clad in the Virgin's colors, blue and white, having been dedicated to the Blessed Virgin at their baptism. They played a duet from "Zampa," and at the earnest solicitation of everyone present followed it with the overture to "The Poet and the Peasant."

"*Allez vous-en! Sapristi!*" shrieked the parrot outside the door. He was the only being present who possessed sufficient candor to admit that he was not listening to these gracious performances for the first time that summer. Old Monsieur Farival, grandfather of the twins, grew indignant over the interruption, and insisted upon having the bird removed and consigned to regions of darkness. Victor Lebrun objected, and his decrees were as immutable as those of Fate. The parrot fortunately offered no further interruption to the entertainment, the whole venom of his nature apparently having been cherished up and hurled against the twins in that one impetuous outburst.

Later a young brother and sister gave recitations, which everyone present had heard many times at winter evening entertainments in the city.

A little girl performed a skirt dance in the center of the floor. The mother played her accompaniments and at the same time watched her daughter with greedy admiration and nervous apprehension. She need have had no apprehension. The child was mistress of the situation. She had been properly dressed for the occasion in black tulle and black silk tights. Her little neck and arms were bare, and her hair, artificially crimped, stood out like fluffy black plumes over her head. Her poses were full of grace, and her little black-shod toes twinkled as they shot out and upward with a rapidity and suddenness which were bewildering.

But there was no reason why everyone should not dance. Madame Ratignolle could not, so it was she who gaily consented to play for the others. She played very well, keeping excellent waltz time and infusing an expression into the strains which was indeed inspiring. She was keeping up her music on account of the children, she said, because she and her husband both considered it a means of brightening the home and making it attractive.

Almost everyone danced but the twins, who could not be induced to separate during the brief period when one or the other should be whirling around the room in the arms of a man. They might have danced together, but they did not think of it.

The children were sent to bed. Some went submissively; others with shrieks and protests as they were dragged away. They had been permitted to sit up till after the ice cream, which naturally marked the limit of human indulgence.

The ice cream was passed around with cake—gold and silver cake arranged on platters in alternate slices; it had been made and frozen during the afternoon back of the kitchen by two black women, under the supervision of Victor. It was pronounced a great success—excellent if it had only contained a little less vanilla or a little more sugar, if it had been frozen a degree harder, and if the salt might have been kept out of portions of it. Victor was proud of his achievement, and went about recommending it and urging everyone to partake of it to excess.

After Mrs. Pontellier had danced twice with her husband, once with Robert, and once with Monsieur Ratignolle, who was thin and tall and swayed like a reed in the wind when he danced, she went out on the gallery and seated herself on the low window sill, where she commanded a view of all that went on in the hall and could look out toward the Gulf. There was a soft effulgence in the east. The moon was coming up, and its mystic shimmer was casting a million lights across the distant, restless water.

"Would you like to hear Mademoiselle Reisz play?" asked Robert, coming out on the porch where she was. Of course Edna would like to hear Mademoiselle Reisz play; but she feared it would be useless to entreat her.

"I'll ask her," he said. "I'll tell her that you want to hear her. She likes you. She will come." He turned and hurried away to one of the far cottages, where Mademoiselle Reisz was shuffling away. She was dragging a chair in and out of her room, and at intervals objecting to the crying of a baby, which a nurse in the adjoining cottage was endeavoring to put to sleep. She was a disagreeable little woman, no longer young, who had quarreled with almost everyone, owing to a temper which was self-assertive and a disposition to trample upon the rights of others. Robert prevailed upon her without any too great difficulty.

She entered the hall with him during a lull in the dance. She made an awkward, imperious little bow as she went in. She was a homely woman, with a small weazened face and body and eyes that glowed. She had absolutely no taste in dress, and wore a batch of rusty black lace with a bunch of artificial violets pinned to the side of her hair.

"Ask Mrs. Pontellier what she would like to hear me play," she requested of Robert. She sat perfectly still before the piano, not touching the keys, while Robert carried her message to Edna at the window. A general air of surprise and genuine satisfaction fell upon everyone as they saw the pianist enter. There was a settling down, and a prevailing air of expectancy everywhere. Edna was a trifle embarrassed at being thus signaled out for the imperious little woman's favor. She would not dare to choose, and begged that Mademoiselle Reisz would please herself in her selections.

Edna was what she herself called very fond of music. Musical strains, well rendered, had a way of evoking pictures in her mind. She sometimes liked to sit in the room of mornings when Madame Ratignolle played or practiced. One piece which that lady played Edna had entitled "Solitude." It was a short, plaintive, minor strain. The name of the piece was something else, but she called it "Solitude." When she heard it there came before her imagination the figure of a man standing beside a desolate rock on the seashore. He was naked. His attitude was one of hopeless resignation as he looked toward a distant bird winging its flight away from him.

Another piece called to her mind a dainty young woman clad in an Empire gown, taking mincing dancing steps as she came down a long avenue between tall hedges. Again, another reminded her of children at play, and still another of nothing on earth but a demure lady stroking a cat.

The very first chords which Mademoiselle Reisz struck upon the piano sent a keen tremor down Mrs. Pontellier's spinal column. It was not the first time she had heard an artist at the piano. Perhaps it was the first time she was ready, perhaps the first time her being was tempered to take an impress of the abiding truth.

She waited for the material pictures which she thought would gather and blaze before her imagination. She waited in vain. She saw no pictures of solitude, of hope, of longing, or of despair. But the very passions themselves were aroused within her soul, swaying it, lashing it, as the waves daily beat upon her splendid body. She trembled, she was choking, and the tears blinded her.

Mademoiselle had finished. She arose, and bowing her stiff, lofty bow, she went away, stopping for neither thanks nor applause. As she passed along the gallery she patted Edna upon the shoulder.

"Well, how did you like my music?" she asked. The young woman was unable to answer; she pressed the hand of the pianist convulsively. Mademoiselle Reisz perceived her agitation and even her tears. She patted her again upon the shoulder as she said:

"You are the only one worth playing for. Those others? Bah!" and she went shuffling and sidling on down the gallery toward her room.

But she was mistaken about "those others." Her playing had aroused a fever of enthusiasm. "What passion!" "What an artist!" "I have always said no one could play Chopin like Mademoiselle Reisz!" "That last prelude! Bon Dieu! It shakes a man!"

It was growing late, and there was a general disposition to disband. But some one, perhaps it was Robert, thought of a bath at that mystic hour and under that mystic moon.

X

At all events Robert proposed it, and there was not a dissenting voice. There was not one but was ready to follow when he led the way. He did not lead the way, however, he directed the way; and he himself loitered behind with the lovers, who had betrayed a disposition to linger and hold themselves apart. He walked between them, whether with malicious or mischievous intent was not wholly clear, even to himself.

The Pontelliers and Ratignolles walked ahead; the women leaning upon the arms of their husbands. Edna could hear Robert's voice behind them, and could sometimes hear what he said. She wondered why he did not join them. It was unlike him not to. Of late he had sometimes held away from her for an entire day, redoubling his devotion upon the next and the next, as though to make up for hours that had been lost. She missed him the days when some pretext served to take him away from her, just as one misses the sun on a cloudy day without having thought much about the sun when it was shining.

The people walked in little groups toward the beach. They talked and laughed; some of them sang. There was a band playing down at Klein's hotel, and the strains reached them faintly, tempered by the distance. There were strange, rare odors abroad—a tangle of the sea smell and of weeds and damp, new-plowed earth, mingled with the heavy perfume of a field of white blossoms somewhere near. But the night sat lightly upon the sea and the land. There was no weight of darkness; there were no shadows. The white light of the moon had fallen upon the world like the mystery and the softness of sleep.

Most of them walked into the water as though into a native element. The sea was quiet now, and swelled lazily in broad billows that melted into one another and did not break except upon the beach in little foamy crests that coiled back like slow, white serpents.

Edna had attempted all summer to learn to swim. She had received instructions from both the men and women, in some instances from the children. Robert had pursued a system of lessons almost daily, and he was nearly at the point of discouragement in realizing the futility of his efforts. A certain ungovernable dread hung about her when in the water, unless there was a hand near by that might reach out and reassure her.

But that night she was like the little tottering, stumbling, clutching child, who of a sudden realizes its powers, and walks for the first time alone, boldly and with overconfidence. She could have shouted for joy. She did shout for joy, as with a sweeping stroke or two she lifted her body to the surface of the water.

A feeling of exultation overtook her, as if some power of significant import had been given her to control the working of her body and her soul. She grew daring and reckless, overestimating her strength. She wanted to swim far out, where no woman had swum before.

Her unlooked-for achievement was the subject of wonder, applause, and admiration. Each one congratulated himself that his special teachings had accomplished this desired end.

"How easy it is!" she thought. "It is nothing," she said aloud; "why did I not discover before that it was nothing. Think of the time I have lost splashing about like a baby!" She would not join the groups in their sports and bouts, but intoxicated with her newly conquered power, she swam out alone.

She turned her face seaward to gather in an impression of space and solitude, which the vast expanse of water, meeting and melting with the moonlit sky, conveyed to her excited fancy. As she swam she seemed to be reaching out for the unlimited in which to lose herself.

Once she turned and looked toward the shore, toward the people she had left there. She had not gone any great distance—that is, what would have been a great distance for an experienced swimmer. But to her unaccustomed vision the stretch of water behind her assumed the aspect of a barrier which her unaided strength would never be able to overcome.

A quick vision of death smote her soul, and for a second of time appalled and enfeebled her senses. But by an effort she rallied her staggering faculties and managed to regain the land.

She made no mention of her encounter with death and her flash of terror, except to say to her husband, "I thought I should have perished out there alone."

"You were not so very far, my dear; I was watching you," he told her.

Edna went at once to the bath-house, and she had put on her dry clothes and was ready to return home before the others had left the water. She started to walk away alone. They all called to her and shouted to her. She waved a dissenting hand, and went on, paying no further heed to their renewed cries which sought to detain her.

"Sometimes I am tempted to think that Mrs. Pontellier is capricious," said Madame Lebrun, who was amusing herself immensely and feared that Edna's abrupt departure might put an end to the pleasure.

"I know she is," assented Mr. Pontellier, "sometimes, not often."

Edna had not traversed a quarter of the distance on her way home before she was overtaken by Robert.

"Did you think I was afraid?" she asked him, without a shade of annoyance.

"No; I knew you weren't afraid."

"Then why did you come? Why didn't you stay out there with the others?"

"I never thought of it."

"Thought of what?"

"Of anything. What difference does it make?"

"I'm very tired," she uttered, complainingly.

"I know you are."

"You don't know anything about it. Why should you know? I never was so exhausted in my life. But it isn't unpleasant A thousand emotions have swept through me to-night. I don't comprehend half of them. Don't mind what I'm saying; I am just thinking aloud. I wonder if I shall ever be stirred again as Mademoiselle Reisz's playing moved me tonight. I wonder if any night on earth will ever again be like this one. It is like a night in a dream. The people about me are like some uncanny half-human beings. There must be spirits abroad tonight."

"There are," whispered Robert "Didn't you know this was the twenty-eighth of August?"

"The twenty-eighth of August?"

"Yes. On the twenty-eighth of August, at the hour of midnight, and if the moon is shining—the moon must be shining—a spirit that has haunted these shores for ages rises up from the Gulf. With its own penetrating vision the spirit seeks some one mortal worthy to hold him company, worthy of being exalted for a few hours into realms of the semicelestials. His search has always hitherto been fruitless, and he has sunk back, disheartened, into the sea. But tonight he found Mrs. Pontellier. Perhaps he will never wholly release her from the spell. Perhaps she will never again suffer a poor, unworthy earthling to walk in the shadow of her divine presence."

"Don't banter me," she said, wounded at what appeared to be his flippancy. He did not mind the entreaty, but the tone with its delicate note of pathos was like a reproach. He could not explain; he could not tell her that he had penetrated her mood and understood. He said nothing except to offer her his arm, for, by her own admission, she was exhausted. She had been walking alone with her arms hanging limp, letting her white skirts trail along the dewy path. She took his arm, but she did not lean upon it. She let her hand lie listlessly, as though her thoughts were elsewhere—somewhere in advance of her body, and she was striving to overtake them.

Robert assisted her into the hammock which swung from the post before her door out to the trunk of a tree.

"Will you stay out here and wait for Mr. Pontellier?" he asked.

"I'll stay out here. Goodnight"

"Shall I get you a pillow?"

"There's one here," she said, feeling about, for they were in the shadow.

"It must be soiled; the children have been tumbling it about."

"No matter." And having discovered the pillow, she adjusted it beneath her head. She extended herself in the hammock with a deep breath of relief. She was not a supercilious or an over-dainty woman. She was not much given to reclining in the hammock, and when she did so it was with no catlike suggestion of voluptuous ease, but with a beneficent repose which seemed to invade her whole body.

"Shall I stay with you till Mr. Pontellier comes?" asked Robert, seating himself on the outer edge of one of the steps and taking hold of the hammock rope which was fastened to the post

"If you wish. Don't swing the hammock. Will you get my white shawl which I left on the window sill over at the house?"

"Are you chilly?"

"No; but I shall be presently."

"Presently?" he laughed. "Do you know what time it is? How long are you going to stay out here?"

"I don't know. Will you get the shawl?"

"Of course I will," he said, rising. He went over to the house, walking along the grass. She watched his figure pass in and out of the strips of moonlight. It was past midnight. It was very quiet.

When he returned with the shawl she took it and kept it in her hand. She did not put it around her.

"Did you say I should stay till Mr. Pontellier came back?"

"I said you might if you wished to."

He seated himself again and rolled a cigarette, which he smoked in silence. Neither did Mrs. Pontellier speak. No multitude of words could have been more significant than those moments of silence, or more pregnant with the first-felt throbbings of desire.

When the voices of the bathers were heard approaching, Robert said goodnight. She did not answer him. He thought she was asleep. Again she watched his figure pass in and out of the strips of moonlight as he walked away.

XI

"What are you doing out here, Edna? I thought I should find you in bed," said her husband, when he discovered her lying there. He had walked up with Madame Lebrun and left her at the house. His wife did not reply.

"Are you asleep?" he asked, bending down close to look at her.

"No." Her eyes gleamed bright and intense, with no sleepy shadows, as they looked into his.

"Do you know it is past one o'clock? Come on," and he mounted the steps and went into their room.

"Edna!" called Mr. Pontellier from within, after a few moments had gone by.

"Don't wait for me," she answered. He thrust his head through the door.

"You will take cold out there," he said, irritably. "What folly is this? Why don't you come in?"

"It isn't cold; I have my shawl."

"The mosquitoes will devour you."

"There are no mosquitoes."

She heard him moving about the room; every sound indicating impatience and irritation. Another time she would have gone in at his request. She would, through habit, have yielded to his desire; not with any sense of submission or obedience to his compelling wishes, but unthinkingly, as we walk, move, sit, stand, go through the daily treadmill of the life which has been portioned out to us.

"Edna, dear, are you not coming in soon?" he asked again, this time fondly, with a note of entreaty.

"No; I am going to stay out here."

"This is more than folly," he blurted out. "I can't permit you to stay out there all night. You must come in the house instantly."

With a writhing motion she settled herself more securely in the hammock. She perceived that her will had blazed up, stubborn and resistant. She could not at that moment have done other than denied and resisted. She wondered if her husband had ever spoken to her like that before, and if she had submitted to his command. Of course she had; she remembered that she had. But she could not realize why or how she should have yielded, feeling as she then did.

"Léonce, go to bed," she said. "I mean to stay out here. I don't wish to go in, and I don't intend to. Don't speak to me like that again; I shall not answer you."

Mr. Pontellier had prepared for bed, but he slipped on an extra garment. He opened a bottle of wine, of which he kept a small and select supply in a buffet of his own. He drank a glass of the wine and went out on the gallery and offered a glass to his wife. She did not wish any. He drew up the rocker, hoisted his slippered feet on the rail, and proceeded to smoke a cigar. He smoked two cigars; then he went inside and drank another glass of wine. Mrs. Pontellier again declined to accept a glass when it was offered to her. Mr. Pontellier once more seated himself with elevated feet, and after a reasonable interval of time smoked some more cigars.

Edna began to feel like one who awakens gradually out of a dream, a delicious, grotesque, impossible dream, to feel again the realities pressing into her soul. The physical need for sleep began to overtake her; the exuberance which had sustained and exalted her spirit left her helpless and yielding to the conditions which crowded her in.

The stillest hour of the night had come, the hour before dawn, when the world seems to hold its breath. The moon hung low, and had turned from silver to copper in the sleeping sky. The old owl no longer hooted, and the water-oaks had ceased to moan as they bent their heads.

Edna arose, cramped from lying so long and still in the hammock. She tottered up the steps, clutching feebly at the post before passing into the house.

"Are you coming in, Léonce?" she asked, turning her face toward her husband.

"Yes, dear," he answered, with a glance following a misty puff of smoke. "Just as soon as I have finished my cigar."

XII

She slept but a few hours. They were troubled and feverish hours, disturbed with dreams that were intangible, that eluded her, leaving only an impression upon her half-awakened senses of something unattainable. She was up and dressed in the cool of the early morning. The air was invigorating and steadied somewhat her faculties. However, she was not seeking refreshment or help from any source, either external or from within. She was blindly following whatever impulse moved her, as if she had placed herself in alien hands for direction, and freed her soul of responsibility.

Most of the people at that early hour were still in bed and asleep. A few, who intended to go over to the *Chênière* for mass, were moving about. The lovers, who had laid their plans the night before, were already strolling toward the wharf. The lady in black, with her Sunday prayerbook, velvet and gold-clasped, and her Sunday silver beads, was following them at no great distance. Old Monsieur Farival was up, and was more than half inclined to do anything that suggested itself. He put on his big straw hat, and taking his umbrella from the stand in the hall, followed the lady in black, never overtaking her.

The little negro girl who worked Madame Lebrun's sewing machine was sweeping the galleries with long, absent-minded strokes of the broom. Edna sent her up into the house to awaken Robert.

"Tell him I am going to the *Chênière*. The boat is ready; tell him to hurry."

He had soon joined her. She had never sent for him before. She had never asked for him. She had never seemed to want him before. She did not appear conscious that she had done anything unusual in commanding his presence. He was apparently equally unconscious of anything extraordinary in the situation. But his face was suffused with a quiet glow when he met her.

They went together back to the kitchen to drink coffee. There was no time to wait for any nicety of service. They stood outside the window and the cook passed them their coffee and a roll, which they drank and ate from the window sill. Edna said it tasted good. She had not thought of coffee nor of anything. He told her he had often noticed that she lacked forethought.

"Wasn't it enough to think of going to the *Chênière* and waking you up" she laughed. "Do I have to think of everything?—as Léonce says when he's in a bad humor. I don't blame him; he'd never be in a bad humor if it weren't for me."

They took a short cut across the sands. At a distance they could see the curious procession moving toward the wharf—the lovers, shoulder to shoulder, creeping; the lady in black, gaining steadily upon them; old Monsieur Farival, losing ground inch by inch, and a young barefooted Spanish girl, with a red kerchief on her head and a basket on her arm, bringing up the rear.

Robert knew the girl, and he talked to her a little in the boat. No one present understood what they said. Her name was Mariequita. She had a round, sly, piquant face and pretty black eyes. Her hands were small, and she kept them folded over the handle of her basket. Her feet were broad and coarse. She did not strive to hide them. Edna looked at her feet, and noticed the sand and slime between her brown toes.

Beaudelet grumbled because Mariequita was there, taking up so much room. In reality he was annoyed at having old Monsieur Farival, who considered himself the better sailor of the two. But he would not quarrel with so old a man as Monsieur Farival, so he quarreled with Mariequita. The girl was deprecatory at one moment, appealing to Robert. She was saucy the next, moving her head up and down, making "eyes" at Robert and making "mouths" at Beaudelet.

The lovers were all alone. They saw nothing, they heard nothing. The lady in black was counting her beads for the third time. Old Monsieur Farival talked incessantly of what he knew about handling a boat, and of what Beaudelet did not know on the same subject.

Edna liked it all. She looked Mariequita up and down, from her ugly brown toes to her pretty black eyes, and back again.

"Why does she look at me like that?" inquired the girl of Robert.

"Maybe she thinks you are pretty. Shall I ask her?"

"No. Is she your sweetheart?"

"She's a married lady, and has two children."

"Oh! well! Francisco ran away with Sylvano's wife, who had four children. They took all his money and one of the children and stole his boat."

"Shut up!"

"Does she understand?"

"Oh, hush!"

"Are those two married over there—leaning on each other?"

"Of course not," laughed Robert.

"Of course not," echoed Mariequita, with a serious, confirmatory bob of the head.

The sun was high up and beginning to bite. The swift breeze seemed to Edna to bury the sting of it into the pores of her face and hands. Robert held his umbrella over her.

As they went cutting sidewise through the water, the sails bellied taut, with the wind filling and overflowing them. Old Monsieur Farival laughed sardonically at something as he looked at the sails, and Beaudelet swore at the old man under his breath.

Sailing across the bay to the *Chênière Caminada,* Edna felt as if she were being borne away from some anchorage which had held her fast, whose chains had been loosening—had snapped the night before when the mystic spirit was abroad, leaving her free to drift whithersoever she chose to set her sails. Robert spoke to her incessantly; he no longer noticed Mariequita. The girl had shrimps in her bamboo basket. They were covered with Spanish moss. She beat the moss down impatiently, and muttered to herself sullenly.

"Let us go to Grande Terre tomorrow?" said Robert in a low voice.

"What shall we do there?"

"Climb up the hill to the old fort and look at the little wriggling gold snakes, and watch the lizards sun themselves."

She gazed away toward Grande Terre and thought she would like to be alone there with Robert, in the sun, listening to the oceans roar and watching the slimy lizards writhe in and out among the ruins of the old fort.

"And the next day or the next we can sail to the Bayou Brulow," he went on.

"What shall we do there?"

"Anything—cast bait for fish."

"No; we'll go back to Grande Terre. Let the fish alone."

"We'll go wherever you like," he said. "I'll have Tonie come over and help me patch and trim my boat. We shall not need Beaudelet nor any one. Are you afraid of the pirogue?"

"Oh, no."

"Then I'll take you some night in the pirogue when the moon shines. Maybe your Gulf spirit will whisper to you in which of these islands the treasures are hidden—direct you to the very spot, perhaps."

"And in a day we should be rich!" she laughed. "I'd give it all to you, the pirate gold and every bit of treasure we could dig up. I think you would know how to spend it. Pirate gold isn't a thing to be hoarded or utilized. It is something to squander and throw to the four winds, for the fun of seeing the golden specks fly."

"We'd share it, and scatter it together," he said. His face flushed.

They all went together up to the quaint little Gothic church of Our Lady of Lourdes, gleaming all brown and yellow with paint in the sun's glare.

Only Beaudelet remained behind, tinkering at his boat, and Mariequita walked away with her basket of shrimps, casting a look of childish ill-humor and reproach at Robert from the corner of her eye.

XIII

A feeling of oppression and drowsiness overcame Edna during the service. Her head began to ache, and the lights on the altar swayed before her eyes. Another time she might have made an effort to regain her composure; but her one thought was to quit the stifling atmosphere of church and reach the open air. She arose, climbing over Robert's feet with a muttered apology. Old Monsieur Farival, flurried, curious, stood up, but upon seeing that Robert had followed Mrs. Pontellier, he sank back into his seat. He whispered an anxious inquiry of the lady in black, who did not notice him or reply, but kept her eyes fastened upon the pages of her velvet prayer-book.

"I felt giddy and almost overcome," Edna said, lifting her hands instinctively to her head and pushing her straw hat up from her forehead. "I couldn't have stayed through the service." They were outside in the shadow of the church. Robert was full of solicitude.

"It was folly to have thought of going in the first place, let alone staying. Come over to Madame Antoine's; you can rest there." He took her arm and led her away, looking anxiously and continuously down into her face.

How still it was, with only the voice of the sea whispering through the reeds that grew in the salt-water pools! The long line of little gray, weather-beaten houses nestled peacefully among the orange trees. It must always have been God's day on that low, drowsy island, Edna thought. They stopped, leaning over a jagged fence made of sea drift, to ask for water. A youth, a mild-faced Acadian, was drawing water from the cistern, which was nothing more than a rusty buoy, with an opening on one side, sunk in the ground. The water which the youth handed to them in a tin pail was not cold to taste, but it was cool to her heated face, and it greatly revived and refreshed her.

Madame Antoine's cot was at the far end of the village. She welcomed them with all the native hospitality, as she would have opened her door to let the sunlight in. She was fat, and walked heavily and clumsily across the floor. She could speak no English, but when Robert made her understand that the lady who accompanied him was ill and desired to rest, she was all eagerness to make Edna feel at home and to dispose of her comfortably.

The whole place was immaculately clean, and the big, four-posted bed, snow-white, invited one to repose. It stood in a small side room which looked out across a narrow grass plot toward the shed, where there was a disabled boat lying keel upward.

Madame Antoine had not gone to mass. Her son Tonie had, but she supposed he would soon be back, and she invited Robert to be seated and wait for him. But he went and sat outside the door and smoked. Madame Antoine busied herself in the large front room preparing dinner. She was boiling mullets over a few red coals in the huge fireplace.

Edna, left alone in the little side room, loosened her clothes, removing the greater part of them. She bathed her face, her neck and arms in the basin that stood between the windows. She took off her shoes and stockings and stretched herself in the very center of the high, white bed. How luxurious it felt to rest thus in a strange, quaint bed, with its sweet country odor of laurel lingering about the sheets and mattress! She stretched her strong limbs that ached a little. She ran her fingers through her loosened hair for a while. She looked at her round arms as she held them straight up and rubbed them one after the other, observing closely, as if it were something she saw for the first time, the fine, firm quality and texture of her flesh. She clasped her hands easily above her head, and it was thus she fell asleep.

She slept lightly at first, half awake and drowsily attentive to the things about her. She could hear Madame Antoine's heavy, scraping tread as she walked back and forth on the sanded floor. Some chickens were clucking outside the windows, scratching for bits of gravel in the grass. Later she half heard the voices of Robert and Tonie talking under the shed. She did not stir. Even her eyelids rested numb and heavily over her sleepy eyes. The voices went on—Tonie's slow, Acadian drawl, Robert's quick, soft, smooth French. She understood French imperfectly unless directly addressed, and the voices were only part of the other drowsy, muffled sounds lulling her senses.

When Edna awoke it was with the conviction that she had slept long and soundly. The voices were hushed under the shed. Madame Antoine's step was no longer to be heard in the adjoining room. Even the chickens had gone elsewhere to scratch and cluck. The mosquito bar was drawn over her; the old woman had come in while she slept and let down the bar. Edna arose quietly from the bed, and looking between the curtains of the window, she saw by the slanting rays of the sun that the afternoon was far advanced. Robert was out there under the shed, reclining in the shade against the sloping keel of the overturned boat. He was reading from a book. Tonie was no longer with him. She wondered what had become of the rest of the party. She peeped out at him two or three times as she stood washing herself in the little basin between the windows.

Madame Antoine had laid some coarse, clean towels upon a chair, and had placed a box of *poudre de riz* within easy reach. Edna dabbed the powder upon her nose and cheeks as she looked at herself closely in the little distorted mirror which hung on the wall above the basin. Her eyes were bright and wide awake and her face glowed.

When she had completed her toilet she walked into the adjoining room. She was very hungry. No one was there. But there was a cloth spread upon the table that stood against the wall, and a cover was laid for one, with a crusty brown loaf and a bottle of wine beside the plate. Edna bit a piece from the brown loaf, tearing it with her strong, white teeth. She poured some of the wine into the glass and drank it down. Then she went softly out of doors, and plucking an orange from the low-hanging bough of a tree, threw it at Robert, who did not know she was awake and up.

An illumination broke over his whole face when he saw her and joined her under the orange tree.

"How many years have I slept?" she inquired. "The whole island seems changed. A new race of beings must have sprung up, leaving only you and me as past relics. How many ages ago did Madame Antoine and Tonie die? and when did our people from Grand Isle disappear from the earth?"

He familiarly adjusted a ruffle upon her shoulder.

"You have slept precisely one hundred years. I was left here to guard your slumbers; and for one hundred years I have been out under the shed reading a book. The only evil I couldn't prevent was to keep a broiled fowl from drying up."

"If it has turned to stone, still will I eat it," said Edna, moving with him into the house. "But really, what has become of Monsieur Farival and the others?"

"Gone hours ago. When they found that you were sleeping they thought it best not to awake you. Any way, I wouldn't have let them. What was I here for?"

"I wonder if Léonce will be uneasy!" she speculated, as she seated herself at table.

"Of course not; he knows you are with me," Robert replied, as he busied himself among sundry pans and covered dishes which had been left standing on the hearth.

"Where are Madame Antoine and her son!" asked Edna.

"Gone to Vespers, and to visit some friends, I believe. I am to take you back in Tonie's boat whenever you are ready to go."

He stirred the smoldering ashes till the broiled fowl began to sizzle afresh. He served her with no mean repast, dripping the coffee anew and sharing it with her. Madame Antoine had cooked little else than the mullets, but while Edna slept Robert had foraged the island. He was childishly gratified to discover her appetite, and to see the relish with which she ate the food which he had procured for her.

"Shall we go right away!" she asked, after draining her glass and brushing together the crumbs of the crusty loaf.

"The sun isn't as low as it will be in two hours," he answered.

"The sun will be gone in two hours."

"Well, let it go; who cares!"

They waited a good while under the orange trees, till Madame Antoine came back, panting, waddling, with a thousand apologies to explain her absence. Tonie did not dare to return. He was shy, and would not willingly face any woman except his mother.

It was very pleasant to stay there under the orange trees, while the sun dipped lower and lower, turning the western sky to flaming copper and gold. The shadows lengthened and crept out like stealthy, grotesque monsters across the grass.

Edna and Robert both sat upon the ground—that is, he lay upon the ground beside her, occasionally picking at the hem of her muslin gown.

Madame Antoine seated her fat body, broad and squat, upon a bench beside the door. She had been talking all the afternoon, and had wound herself up to the story-telling pitch.

And what stories she told them! But twice in her life she had left the *Chênière Caminada,* and then for the briefest span. All her years she had squatted and waddled there upon the island, gathering legends of the Baratarians and the sea. The night came on, with the moon to lighten it Edna could hear the whispering voices of dead men and the click of muffled gold.

When she and Robert stepped into Tonie's boat, with the red lateen sail, misty spirit forms were prowling in the shadows and among the reeds, and upon the water were phantom ships, speeding to cover.

XIV

The youngest boy, Étienne, had been very naughty, Madame Ratignolle said, as she delivered him into the hands of his mother. He had been unwilling to go to bed and had made a scene; whereupon she had taken charge of him and pacified him as well as she could. Raoul had been in bed and asleep for two hours.

The youngster was in his long white nightgown, that kept tripping him up as Madame Ratignolle led him along by the hand. With the other chubby fist he rubbed his eyes, which were heavy with sleep and ill humor. Edna took him in her arms, and seating herself in the rocker, began to coddle and caress him, calling him all manner of tender names, soothing him to sleep.

It was not more than nine o'clock. No one had yet gone to bed but the children.

Léonce had been very uneasy at first, Madame Ratignolle said, and had wanted to start at once for the *Chênière*. But Monsieur Farival had assured him that his wife was only overcome with sleep and fatigue, that Tonie would bring her safely back later in the day; and he had thus been dissuaded from crossing the bay. He had gone over to Klein's, looking up some cotton broker whom he wished to see in regard to securities, exchanges, stocks, bonds or something of the sort, Madame Ratignolle did not remember what. He said he would not remain away late. She herself was suffering from heat and oppression, she said. She carried a bottle of salts and a large fan. She would not consent to remain with Edna, for Monsieur Ratignolle was alone, and he detested above all things to be left alone.

When Étienne had fallen asleep Edna bore him into the back room, and Robert went and lifted the mosquito bar that she might lay the child comfortably in his bed. The quadroon had vanished. When they emerged from the cottage Robert bade Edna good-night.

"Do you know we have been together the whole livelong day, Robert—since early this morning?" she said at parting.

"All but the hundred years when you were sleeping. Good-night."

He pressed her hand and went away in the direction of the beach. He did not join any of the others, but walked alone toward the Gulf.

Edna stayed outside, awaiting her husband's return. She had no desire to sleep or to retire; nor did she feel like going over to sit with the Ratignolles, or to join Madame Lebrun and a group whose animated voices reached her as they sat in conversation before the house. She let her mind wander back over her stay at Grand Isle, and she tried to discover wherein this summer had been different from any and every other summer of her life. She could only realize that she herself—her present self—was in some way different from the other self. That she was seeing with different eyes and making the acquaintance of new conditions in herself that colored and changed her environment, she did not yet suspect.

She wondered why Robert had gone away and left her. It did not occur to her to think he might have grown tired of being with her the livelong day. She was not tired, and she felt that he was not. She regretted that he had gone. It was so much more natural to have him stay, when he was not absolutely required to leave her.

As Edna waited for her husband she sang low a little song that Robert had sung as they crossed the bay. It began with "Ah! *Si tu savais,*" and every verse ended with *"si tu savais."*[10]

Robert's voice was not pretentious. It was musical and true. The voice, the notes, the whole refrain haunted her memory.

XV

When Edna entered the dining room one evening a little late, as was her habit, an unusually animated conversation seemed to be going on. Several persons were talking at once, and Victor's voice was predominating, even over that of his mother. Edna had returned late from her bath, had dressed in some haste, and her face was flushed. Her head, set off by her dainty white gown, suggested a rich, rare blossom. She took her seat at table between old Monsieur Farival and Madame Ratignolle.

As she seated herself and was about to begin to eat her soup, which had been served when she entered the room, several persons informed her simultaneously that Robert was going to Mexico. She laid her spoon down and looked about her bewildered. He had been with her, reading to her all the morning, and had never even mentioned such a place as Mexico. She had not seen him during the afternoon; she had heard some one say he was at the house, upstairs with his mother. This she had thought nothing of, though she was surprised when he did not join her later in the afternoon, when she went down to the beach.

She looked across at him, where he sat beside Madame Lebrun, who presided. Edna's face was a blank picture of bewilderment, which she never thought of disguising. He lifted his eyebrows with the pretext of a smile as he returned her glance. He looked embarrassed and uneasy.

"When is he going?" she asked of everybody in general, as if Robert were not there to answer for himself.

"Tonight!" "This very evening!" "Did you ever!" "What possesses him!" were some of the replies she gathered, uttered simultaneously in French and English.

"Impossible!" she exclaimed. "How can a person start off from Grand Isle to Mexico at a moment's notice, as if he were going over to Klein's or to the wharf or down to the beach?"

"I said all along I was going to Mexico; I've been saying so for years!" cried Robert, in an excited and irritable tone, with the air of a man defending himself against a swarm of stinging insects.

Madame Lebrun knocked on the table with her knife handle.

"Please let Robert explain why he is going, and why he is going tonight," she called out. "Really, this table is getting to be more and more like Bedlam every day, with everybody talking at once. Sometimes—I hope God will forgive me—but positively, sometimes I wish Victor would lose the power of speech."

Victor laughed sardonically as he thanked his mother for her holy wish, of which he failed to see the benefit to anybody, except that it might afford her a more ample opportunity and license to talk herself.

Monsieur Farival thought that Victor should have been taken out in midocean in his earliest youth and drowned. Victor thought there would be more logic in thus disposing of old people with an established claim for making themselves universally obnoxious. Madame Lebrun grew a trifle hysterical; Robert called his brother some sharp, hard names.

"There's nothing much to explain, mother," he said, though he explained, nevertheless—looking chiefly at Edna—that he could only meet the gentleman whom he intended to join at Vera Cruz by taking such and such a steamer, which left New Orleans on such a day; that Beaudelet was going out with his lugger-load of vegetables that night, which gave him an opportunity of reaching the city and making his vessel in time.

"But when did you make up your mind to all this?" demanded Monsieur Farival.

"This afternoon," returned Robert, with a shade of annoyance.

"At what time this afternoon?" persisted the old gentleman, with nagging determination, as if he were cross-questioning a criminal in a court of justice.

"At four o'clock this afternoon, Monsieur Farival," Robert replied, in a high voice and with a lofty air, which reminded Edna of some gentleman on the stage.

She had forced herself to eat most of her soup, and now she was picking the flaky bits of a *court bouillon* with her fork.

The lovers were profiting by the general conversation on Mexico to speak in whispers of matters which they rightly considered were interesting to no one but themselves. The lady in black had once received a pair of prayer-beads of curious workmanship from Mexico, with very special indulgence attached to them, but she had never been able to ascertain whether the indulgence extended outside the Mexican border. Father Fochel of the Cathedral had attempted to explain it; but he had not done so to her satisfaction. And she begged that Robert would interest himself, and discover, if possible, whether she was entitled to the indulgence accompanying the remarkably curious Mexican prayer-beads.

Madame Ratignolle hoped that Robert would exercise extreme caution in dealing with the Mexicans, who, she considered, were a treacherous people, unscrupulous and revengeful. She trusted she did them no injustice in thus condemning them as a race. She had known personally but one Mexican, who made and sold excellent tamales, and whom she would have trusted implicitly, so soft-spoken was he. One day he was arrested for stabbing his wife. She never knew whether he had been hanged or not.

Victor had grown hilarious, and was attempting to tell an anecdote about a Mexican girl who served chocolate one winter in a restaurant in Dauphine Street. No one would listen to him but old Monsieur Farival, who went into convulsions over the droll story.

Edna wondered if they had all gone mad, to be talking and clamoring at that rate. She herself could think of nothing to say about Mexico or the Mexicans.

"At what time do you leave?" she asked Robert.

"At ten," he told her. "Beaudelet wants to wait for the moon."

"Are you all ready to go?"

"Quite ready. I shall only take a handbag, and shall pack my trunk in the city."

He turned to answer some question put to him by his mother, and Edna, having finished her black coffee, left the table.

She went directly to her room. The little cottage was close and stuffy after leaving the outer air. But she did not mind; there appeared to be a hundred different things demanding her attention indoors. She began to set the toilet stand to rights, grumbling at the negligence of the quadroon, who was in the adjoining room putting the children to bed. She gathered together stray garments that were hanging on the backs of chairs, and put each where it belonged in closet or bureau drawer. She changed her gown for a more comfortable and commodious wrapper. She rearranged her hair, combing and brushing it with unusual energy. Then she went in and assisted the quadroon in getting the boys to bed.

They were very playful and inclined to talk—to do anything but lie quiet and go to sleep. Edna sent the quadroon away to her supper and told her she need not return. Then she sat and told the children a story. Instead of soothing it excited them, and added to their wakefulness. She left them in heated argument, speculating about the conclusion of the tale which their mother promised to finish the following night.

The little black girl came in to say that Madame Lebrun would like to have Mrs. Pontellier go and sit with them over at the house till Mr. Robert went away. Edna returned answer that she had already undressed, that she did not feel quite well, but perhaps she would go over to the house later. She started to dress again, and got as far advanced as to remove her *peignoir.* But changing her mind once more she resumed the *peignoir,* and went outside and sat down before her door. She was overheated and irritable, and fanned herself energetically for a while. Madame Ratignolle came down to discover what was the matter.

"All that noise and confusion at the table must have upset me," replied Edna, "and moreover, I hate shocks and surprises. The idea of Robert starting off in such a ridiculously sudden and dramatic way! As if it were a matter of life and death! Never saying a word about it all morning when he was with me."

"Yes," agreed Madame Ratignolle. "I think it was showing us all—you especially—very little consideration. It wouldn't have surprised me in any of the others; those Lebruns are all given to heroics. But I must say I should never have expected such a thing from Robert. Are you not coming down? Come on, dear; it doesn't look friendly."

"No," said Edna, a little sullenly. "I can't go to the trouble of dressing again; I don't feel like it."

"You needn't dress; you look all right; fasten a belt around your waist. Just look at me!"

"No," persisted Edna; "but you go on. Madame Lebrun might be offended if we both stayed away."

Madame Ratignolle kissed Edna goodnight and went away, being in truth rather desirous of joining in the general and animated conversation which was still in progress concerning Mexico and the Mexicans.

Somewhat later Robert came up, carrying his handbag.

"Aren't you feeling well?" he asked.

"Oh, well enough. Are you going right away?" He lit a match and looked at his watch. "In twenty minutes," he said. The sudden and brief flare of the match emphasized the darkness for a while. He sat down upon a stool which the children had left out on the porch.

"Get a chair," said Edna.

"This will do," he replied. He put on his soft hat and nervously took it off again, and wiping his face with his handkerchief, complained of the heat.

"Take the fan," said Edna, offering it to him.

"Oh, no! Thank you. It does no good; you have to stop fanning sometime, and feel all the more uncomfortable afterward."

"That's one of the ridiculous things which men always say. I have never known one to speak otherwise of fanning. How long will you be gone?"

"Forever, perhaps. I don't know. It depends upon a good many things."

"Well, in case it shouldn't be forever, how long will it be?"

"I don't know."

"This seems to me perfectly preposterous and uncalled for. I don't like it. I don't understand your motive for silence and mystery, never saying a word to me about it this morning." He remained silent, not offering to defend himself. He only said, after a moment:

"Don't part from me in an ill-humor. I never knew you to be out of patience with me before."

"I don't want to part in any ill-humor," she said. "But can't you understand? I've grown used to seeing you, to having you with me all the time, and your action seems unfriendly, even unkind.

You don't even offer an excuse for it. Why, I was planning to be together, thinking of how pleasant it would be to see you in the city next winter."

"So was I," he blurted. "Perhaps that's the—" He stood up suddenly and held out his hand. "Good-by, my dear Mrs. Pontellier; good-by. You won't—I hope you won't completely forget me." She clung to his hand, striving to detain him.

"Write to me when you get there, won't you, Robert?" she entreated.

"I will, thank you. Good-by."

How unlike Robert! The merest acquaintance would have said something more emphatic than "I will, thank you; good-by," to such a request.

He had evidently already taken leave of the people over at the house, for he descended the steps and went to join Beaudelet, who was out there with an oar across his shoulder waiting for Robert. They walked away in the darkness. She could only hear Beaudelet's voice; Robert had apparently not even spoken a word of greeting to his companion.

Edna bit her handkerchief convulsively, striving to hold back and to hide, even from herself as she would have hidden from another, the emotion which was troubling—tearing—her. Her eyes were brimming with tears.

For the first time she recognized anew the symptoms of infatuation which she had felt incipiently as a child, as a girl in her earliest teens, and later as a young woman. The recognition did not lessen the reality, the poignancy of the revelation by any suggestion or promise of instability. The past was nothing to her; offered no lesson which she was willing to heed. The future was a mystery which she never attempted to penetrate. The present alone was significant, was hers, to torture her as it was doing then with the biting which her impassioned, newly awakened being demanded.

XVI

"Do you miss your friend greatly?" asked Mademoiselle Reisz one morning as she came creeping up behind Edna, who had just left her cottage on her way to the beach. She spent much of her time in the water since she had acquired finally the art of swimming. As their stay at Grand Isle drew near its close, she felt that she could not give too much time to a diversion which afforded her the only pleasurable moments that she knew. When Mademoiselle Reisz came and touched her upon the shoulder and spoke to her, the woman seemed to echo the thought which was ever in Edna's mind, or, better, the feeling which constantly possessed her,

Robert's going had some way taken the brightness, the color, the meaning out of everything. The conditions of her life were in no way changed, but her whole existence was dulled, like a faded garment which seems to be no longer worth wearing. She sought him everywhere—in others whom she induced to talk about him. She went up in the mornings to Madame Lebrun's room, braving the clatter of the old sewing-machine. She sat there and chatted at intervals as Robert had done. She gazed around the room at the pictures and photographs hanging upon the wall, and discovered in some corner an old family album, which she examined with the keenest interest, appealing to Madame Lebrun for enlightenment concerning the many figures and faces which she discovered between its pages.

There was a picture of Madame Lebrun with Robert as a baby, seated in her lap, a round-faced infant with a fist in his mouth. The eyes alone in the baby suggested the man. And that was he also in kilts, at the age of five, wearing long curls and holding a whip in his hand. It made Edna laugh, and she laughed, too, at the portrait in his first long trousers; while another interested her, taken when he left for college, looking thin, long-faced, with eyes full of fire, ambition and great intentions. But there was no recent picture, none which suggested the Robert who had gone away five days ago, leaving a void and wilderness behind him.

"Oh, Robert stopped having his pictures taken when he had to pay for them himself! He found wiser use for his money, he says," explained Madame Lebrun. She had a letter from him, written before he left New Orleans. Edna wished to see the letter, and Madame Lebrun told her to look for it either on the table or the dresser, or perhaps it was on the mantelpiece.

The letter was on the bookshelf. It possessed the greatest interest and attraction for Edna; the envelope, its size and shape, the post-mark, the handwriting. She examined every detail of the outside before opening it. There were only a few lines, setting forth that he would leave the city that afternoon, that he had packed his trunk in good shape, that he was well, and sent her his love and begged to be affectionately remembered to all. There was no special message to Edna except a postscript saying that if Mrs. Pontellier desired to finish the book which he had been reading to her, his mother would find it in his room, among other books there on the table. Edna experienced a pang of jealously because he had written to his mother rather than to her.

Everyone seemed to take for granted that she missed him. Even her husband, when he came down the Saturday following Robert's departure, expressed regret that he had gone.

"How do you get on without him, Edna?" he asked.

"It's very dull without him," she admitted. Mr. Pontellier had seen Robert in the city, and Edna asked him a dozen questions or more. Where had they met? On Carondelet Street, in the morning. They had gone "in" and had a drink and a cigar together. What had they talked about? Chiefly about his prospects in Mexico, which Mr. Pontellier thought were promising. How did he look? How did he seem—grave, or gay, or how? Quite cheerful, and wholly taken up with the idea of his trip, which Mr. Pontellier found altogether natural in a young fellow about to seek fortune and adventure in a strange, queer country.

Edna tapped her foot impatiently, and wondered why the children persisted in playing in the sun when they might be under the trees. She went down and led them out of the sun, scolding the quadroon for not being more attentive.

It did not strike her as in the least grotesque that she should be making of Robert the object of conversation and leading her husband to speak of him. The sentiment which she entertained for Robert in no way resembled that which she felt for her husband, or had ever felt, or ever expected to feel. She had all her life long been accustomed to harbor thoughts and emotions which never voiced themselves. They had never taken the form of struggles. They belonged to her and were her own, and she entertained the conviction that she had a right to them and that they concerned no one but herself. Edna had once told Madame Ratignolle that she would never sacrifice herself for her children, or for any one. Then had followed a rather heated argument; the two women did not appear to understand each other or to be talking the same language. Edna tried to appease her friend, to explain.

"I would give up the unessential; I would give my money, I would give my life for my children, but I wouldn't give myself. I can't make it more clear; it's only something which I am beginning to comprehend, which is revealing itself to me."

"I don't know what you would call the essential, or what you mean by the unessential," said Madame Ratignolle, cheerfully, "but a woman who would give her life for her children could do no more than that—your Bible tells you so. I'm sure I couldn't do more than that."

"Oh, yes you could!" laughed Edna.

She was not surprised at Mademoiselle Reisz's question the morning that lady, following her to the beach, tapped her on the shoulder and asked if she did not greatly miss her young friend.

"Oh, good morning, Mademoiselle; is it you? Why, of course I miss Robert. Are you going down to bathe?"

"Why should I go down to bathe at the very end of the season when I haven't been in the surf all summer," replied the woman, disagreeably.

"I beg your pardon," offered Edna, in some embarrassment, for she should have remembered that Mademoiselle Reisz's avoidance of the water had furnished a theme for much pleasantry. Some among them thought it was on account of her false hair, or the dread of getting the violets wet, while others attributed it to the natural aversion for water sometimes believed to accompany the artistic temperament. Mademoiselle offered Edna some chocolates in a paper bag, which she took from her pocket, by way of showing that she bore no ill feeling. She habitually ate chocolates for their sustaining quality; they contained much nutriment in small compass, she said. They saved her from starvation, as Madame Lebrun's table was utterly impossible, and no one save so impertinent a woman as Madame Lebrun could think of offering such food to people and requiring them to pay for it.

"She must feel very lonely without her son," said Edna, desiring to change the subject "Her favorite son, too. It must have been quite hard to let him go."

Mademoiselle laughed maliciously.

"Her favorite son! Oh, dear! Who could have been imposing such a tale upon you? Aline Lebrun lives for Victor, and for Victor alone. She has spoiled him into the worthless creature he is. She worships him and the ground he walks on. Robert is very well in a way, to give up all the money he can earn to the family, and keep the barest pittance for himself. Favorite son, indeed! I miss the poor fellow myself, my dear. I liked to see him and to hear him about the place—the only Lebrun who is worth a pinch of salt. He comes to see me often in the city. I like to play to him. That Victor! hanging would be too good for him. It's a wonder Robert hasn't beaten him to death long ago."

"I thought he had great patience with his brother," offered Edna, glad to be talking about Robert, no matter what was said.

"Oh! he thrashed him well enough a year or two ago," said Mademoiselle. "It was about a Spanish girl, whom Victor considered that he had some sort of claim upon. He met Robert one day talking to the girl, or walking with her, or bathing with her, or carrying her basket—I don't remember what—and he became so insulting and abusive that Robert gave him a thrashing on the spot that has kept him comparatively in order for a good while. It's about time he was getting another."

"Was her name Mariequita?" asked Edna.

"Mariequita—yes, that was it; Mariequita. I had forgotten. Oh, she's a sly one, and a bad one, that Mariequita!"

Edna looked down at Mademoiselle Reisz and wondered how she could have listened to her venom so long. For some reason she felt depressed, almost unhappy. She had not intended to go into the water; but she donned her bathing suit, and left Mademoiselle alone, seated under the shade of the children's tent. The water was growing cooler as the season advanced. Edna plunged and swam about with an abandon that thrilled and invigorated her. She remained a long time in the water, half hoping that Mademoiselle Reisz would not wait for her.

But Mademoiselle waited. She was very amiable during the walk back, and raved much over Edna's appearance in her bathing suit. She talked about music. She hoped that Edna would go to see her in the city, and wrote her address with the stub of a pencil on a piece of card which she found in her pocket.

"When do you leave?" asked Edna.

"Next Monday; and you?"

"The following week," answered Edna, adding, "It has been a pleasant summer, hasn't it, Mademoiselle?"

"Well," agreed Mademoiselle Reisz, with a shrug, "rather pleasant, if it hadn't been for the mosquitoes and the Farival twins."

XVII

The Pontelliers possessed a very charming home on Esplanade Street in New Orleans. It was a large, double cottage, with a broad front veranda, whose round, fluted columns supported the sloping roof. The house was painted a dazzling white; the outside shutters, or jalousies, were green. In the yard, which was kept scrupulously neat, were flowers and plants of every description which flourishes in South Louisiana. Within doors the appointments were perfect after the conventional type. The softest carpets and rugs covered the floors; rich and tasteful draperies hung at doors and windows. There were paintings, selected with judgment and discrimination, upon the walls. The cut glass, the silver, the heavy damask which daily appeared upon the table were the envy of many women whose husbands were less generous than Mr. Pontellier.

Mr. Pontellier was very fond of walking about his house examining its various appointments and details, to see that nothing was amiss. He greatly valued his possessions, chiefly because they were his, and derived genuine pleasure from contemplating a painting, a statuette, a rare lace curtain—no matter what—after he had bought it and placed it among his household gods.

On Tuesday afternoons—Tuesday being Mrs. Pontellier's reception day—there was a constant stream of callers—women who came in carriages or in the streetcars, or walked when the air was soft and distance permitted. A light-colored mulatto boy, in dress coat and bearing a diminutive silver tray for the reception of cards, admitted them. A maid, in white fluted cap, offered the callers liqueur, coffee, or chocolate, as they might desire. Mrs. Pontellier, attired in a handsome reception gown, remained in the drawing room the entire afternoon receiving her visitors. Men sometimes called in the evening with their wives.

This had been the programme which Mrs. Pontellier had religiously followed since her marriage, six years before. Certain evenings during the week she and her husband attended the opera or sometimes the play.

Mr. Pontellier left his home in the mornings between nine and ten o'clock, and rarely returned before half-past six or seven in the evening—dinner being served at half-past seven.

He and his wife seated themselves at table one Tuesday evening, a few weeks after their return from Grand Isle. They were alone together. The boys were being put to bed; the patter of their bare, escaping feet could be heard occasionally, as well as the pursuing voice of the quadroon, lifted in mild protest and entreaty. Mrs. Pontellier did not wear her usual Tuesday reception gown; she was in ordinary house dress. Mr. Pontellier, who was observant about such things, noticed it, as he served the soup and handed it to the boy in waiting.

"Tired out, Edna? Whom did you have? Many callers?" he asked. He tasted his soup and began to season it with pepper, salt, vinegar, mustard—everything within reach.

"There were a good many," replied Edna, who was eating her soup with evident satisfaction. "I found their cards when I got home; I was out."

"Out!" exclaimed her husband, with something like genuine consternation in his voice as he laid down the vinegar cruet and looked at her through his glasses. "Why, what could have taken you out on Tuesday? What did you have to do?"

"Nothing. I simply felt like going out, and I went out."

"Well, I hope you left some suitable excuse," said her husband, somewhat appeased, as he added a dash of cayenne pepper to the soup.

"No, I left no excuse. I told Joe to say I was out, that was all."

"Why, my dear, I should think you'd understand by this time that people don't do such things; we've got to observe *les convenances*[11] if we ever expect to get on and keep up with the procession. If you felt that you had to leave home this afternoon, you should have left some suitable explanation for your absence.

"This soup is really impossible; it's strange that woman hasn't learned yet to make a decent soup. Any free lunch stand in town serves a better one. Was Mrs. Belthrop here?"

"Bring the tray with the cards, Joe. I don't remember who was here."

The boy retired and returned after a moment, bringing the tiny silver tray, which was covered with ladies' visiting cards. He handed it to Mrs. Pontellier.

"Give it to Mr. Pontellier," she said.

Joe offered the tray to Mr. Pontellier, and removed the soup.

Mr. Pontellier scanned the names of his wife's callers, reading some of them aloud, with comments as he read.

"'The Misses Delasidas.' I worked a big deal in futures for their father this morning; nice girls; it's time they were getting married. 'Mrs. Belthrop.' I tell you what it is, Edna; you can't afford to snub Mrs. Belthrop. Why, Belthrop could buy and sell us ten times over. His business is worth a good, round sum to me. You'd better write her a note. 'Mrs. James Highcamp.' Hugh!

the less you have to do with Mrs. Highcamp, the better. 'Madame Laforcé.' Came all the way from Carrolton, too, poor old soul. 'Miss Wiggs,' 'Mrs. Eleanor Boltons.'" He pushed the cards aside.

"Mercy!" exclaimed Edna, who had been fuming. "Why are you taking the thing so seriously and making such a fuss over it?"

"I'm not making any fuss over it. But it's just such seeming trifles that we've got to take seriously; such things count."

The fish was scorched. Mr. Pontellier would not touch it. Edna said she did not mind a little scorched taste. The roast was in some way not to his fancy, and he did not like the manner in which the vegetables were served.

"It seems to me," he said, "we spend money enough in this house to procure at least one meal a day which a man could eat and retain his self-respect."

"You used to think the cook was a treasure," returned Edna, indifferently.

"Perhaps she was when she first came; but cooks are only human. They need looking after, like any other class of persons that you employ. Suppose I didn't look after the clerks in my office, just let them run things their own way; they'd soon make a nice mess of me and my business."

"Where are you going?" asked Edna, seeing that her husband arose from table without having eaten a morsel except a taste of the highly-seasoned soup.

"I'm going to get my dinner at the club. Good night." He went into the hall, took his hat and stick from the stand, and left the house.

She was somewhat familiar with such scenes. They had often made her very unhappy. On a few previous occasions she had been completely deprived of any desire to finish her dinner. Sometimes she had gone into the kitchen to administer a tardy rebuke to the cook. Once she went to her room and studied the cookbook during an entire evening, finally writing out a menu for the week, which left her harassed with a feeling that, after all, she had accomplished no good that was worth the name.

But that evening Edna finished her dinner alone, with forced deliberation. Her face was flushed and her eyes flamed with some inward fire that lighted them. After finishing her dinner she went to her room, having instructed the boy to tell any other callers that she was indisposed.

It was a large, beautiful room, rich and picturesque in the soft, dim light which the maid had turned low. She went and stood at an open window and looked out upon the deep tangle of the garden below. All the mystery and witchery of the night seemed to have gathered there amid the perfumes and the dusky and tortuous outlines of flowers and foliage. She was seeking herself and finding herself in just such sweet, half darkness which met her moods. But the voices were not soothing that came to her from the darkness and the sky above and the stars. They jeered and sounded mournful notes without promise, devoid even of hope. She turned back into the room and began to walk to and fro down its whole length, without stopping, without resting. She carried in her hands a thin handkerchief, which she tore into ribbons, rolled into a ball, and flung from her. Once she stopped, and taking off her wedding ring, flung it upon the carpet. When she saw it lying there, she stamped her heel upon it, striving to crush it. But her small boot heel did not make an indenture, not a mark upon the little glittering circlet.

In a sweeping passion she seized a glass vase from the table and flung it upon the tiles of the hearth. She wanted to destroy something. The crash and clatter were what she wanted to hear.

A maid, alarmed at the din of breaking glass, entered the room to discover what was the matter.

"A vase fell upon the hearth," said Edna. "Never mind; leave it till morning."

"Oh! you might get some of the glass in your feet, ma'am," insisted the young woman, picking up bits of the broken vase that were scattered upon the carpet. "And here's your ring, ma'am, under the chair."

Edna held out her hand, and taking the ring, slipped it upon her finger.

XVIII

The following morning, Mr. Pontellier, upon leaving for his office, asked Edna if she would not meet him in town in order to look at some new fixtures for the library.

"I hardly think we need new fixtures, Léonce. Don't let us get anything new; you are too extravagant. I don't believe you ever think of saving or putting by."

"The way to become rich is to make money, my dear Edna, not to save it," he said. He regretted that she did not feel inclined to go with him and select new fixtures. He kissed her good-by, and told her she was not looking well and must take care of herself. She was unusually pale and very quiet.

She stood on the front veranda as he quitted the house, and absently picked a few sprays of jessamine that grew upon a trellis near by. She inhaled the odor of the blossoms and thrust them into the bosom of her white morning gown. The boys were dragging along the banquette a small "express wagon," which they had filled with blocks and sticks. The quadroon was following them with little quick steps, having assumed a fictitious animation and alacrity for the occasion. A fruit vender was crying his wares in the street.

Edna looked straight before her with a self-absorbed expression upon her face. She felt no interest in anything about her. The street, the children, the fruit vender, the flowers growing there under her eyes, were all part and parcel of an alien world which had suddenly become antagonistic.

She went back into the house. She had thought of speaking to the cook concerning her blunders of the previous night; but Mr. Pontellier had saved her that disagreeable mission, for which she was so poorly fitted. Mr. Pontellier's arguments were usually convincing with those whom he employed. He left home feeling quite sure that he and Edna would sit down that evening, and possibly a few subsequent evenings, to a dinner deserving of the name.

Edna spent an hour or two in looking over some of her old sketches. She could see their short-comings and defects, which were glaring in her eyes. She tried to work a little, but found she was not in the humor. Finally she gathered together a few of the sketches—those which she considered the least discreditable; and she carried them with her when, a little later, she dressed and left the house. She looked handsome and distinguished in her street gown. The tan of the seashore had left her face, and her forehead was smooth, white, and polished beneath her heavy, yellow-brown hair. There were a few freckles on her face, and a small, dark mole near the under lip and one on the temple, half-hidden in her hair.

As Edna walked along the street she was thinking of Robert. She was still under the spell of her infatuation. She had tried to forget him, realizing the inutility of remembering. But the thought of him was like an obsession, ever pressing itself upon her. It was not that she dwelt upon details of their acquaintance, or recalled in any special or peculiar way his personality; it was his being, his existence, which dominated her thought, fading sometimes as if it would melt into the mist of the forgotten, reviving again with an intensity which filled her with an incomprehensible longing.

Edna was on her way to Madame Ratignolle's. Their intimacy, begun at Grand Isle, had not declined, and they had seen each other with some frequency since their return to the city. The Ratignolles lived at no great distance from Edna's home, on the corner of a side street, where Monsieur Ratignolle owned and conducted a drug store which enjoyed a steady and prosperous trade. His father had been in the business before him, and Monsieur Ratignolle stood well in the community and bore an enviable reputation for integrity and clearheadedness. His family lived in commodious apartments over the store, having an entrance on the side within the *porte cochère*. There was something which Edna thought very French, very foreign, about their whole manner of living. In the large and pleasant salon which extended across the width of the house, the Ratignolles entertained their friends once a fortnight with a *soiree musicale*,[12] sometimes diversified by card-playing. There was a friend who played upon the 'cello. One brought his flute and another his violin, while there were some who sang and a number who performed upon the piano with various degrees of taste and agility. The Ratignolles' *soirees musicales* were widely known, and it was considered a privilege to be invited to them.

Edna found her friend engaged in assorting the clothes which had returned that morning from the laundry. She at once abandoned her occupation upon seeing Edna, who had been ushered without ceremony into her presence.

"Cité can do it as well as I; it is really her business," she explained to Edna, who apologized for interrupting her. And she summoned a young black woman, whom she instructed, in French, to be very careful in checking off the list which she handed her. She told her to notice particularly if a fine linen handkerchief of Monsieur Ratignolle's, which was missing last week, had been returned; and to be sure to set to one side such pieces as required mending and darning.

Then placing an arm around Edna's waist, she led her to the front of the house, to the salon, where it was cool and sweet with the odor of great roses that stood upon the hearth in jars.

Madame Ratignolle looked more beautiful than ever there at home, in a negligee which left her arm's almost wholly bare and exposed the rich, melting curves of her white throat.

"Perhaps I shall be able to paint your picture some day," said Edna with a smile when they were seated. She produced the roll of sketches and started to unfold them. "I believe I ought to work again. I feel as if I wanted to be doing something, what do you think of them? Do you think it worth while to take it up again and study some more? I might study for a while with Laidpore."

She knew that Madame Ratignolle's opinion in such a matter would be next to valueless, that she herself had not alone decided, but determined; but she sought the words of praise and encouragement that would help her to put heart into her venture.

"Your talent is immense, dear!"

"Nonsense!" protested Edna, well pleased.

"Immense, I tell you," persisted Madame Ratignolle, surveying the sketches one by one, at close range, then holding them at arm's length, narrowing her eyes, and dropping her head on one side. "Surely, this Bavarian peasant is worthy of framing; and this basket of apples! never have I seen anything more lifelike. One might almost be tempted to reach out a hand and take one."

Edna could not control a feeling which bordered upon complacency at her friend's praise, even realizing, as she did, its true worth. She retained a few of the sketches, and gave all the rest to Madame Ratignolle, who appreciated the gift far beyond its value and proudly exhibited the pictures to her husband when he came up from the store a little later for his midday dinner.

Mr. Ratignolle was one of those men who are called the salt of the earth. His cheerfulness was unbounded, and it was matched by his goodness of heart, his broad charity, and common sense. He and his wife spoke English with an accent which was only discernible through its un-English emphasis and a certain carefulness and deliberation. Edna's husband spoke English with no accent whatever. The Ratignolles understood each other perfectly. If ever the fusion of two human beings into one has been accomplished on this sphere it was surely in their union.

As Edna seated herself at table with them she thought, "Better a dinner of herbs," though it did not take her long to discover that it was no dinner of herbs, but a delicious repast, simple, choice, and in every way satisfying.

Monsieur Ratignolle was delighted to see her, though he found her looking not so well as at Grand Isle, and he advised a tonic. He talked a good deal on various topics, a little politics, some city news and neighborhood gossip. He spoke with an animation and earnestness that gave an exaggerated importance to every syllable he uttered. His wife was keenly interested in everything he said, laying down her fork the better to listen, chiming in, taking the words out of his mouth.

Edna felt depressed rather than soothed after leaving them. The little glimpse of domestic harmony which had been offered her, gave her no regret, no longing. It was not a condition of life which fitted her, and she could see in it but an appalling and hopeless ennui. She was moved by a kind of commiseration for Madame Ratignolle—a pity for that colorless existence which never uplifted its possessor beyond the region of blind contentment, in which no moment of anguish ever visited her soul, in which she would never have the taste of life's delirium. Edna vaguely wondered what she meant by "life's delirium." It had crossed her thought like some unsought, extraneous impression.

XIX

Edna could not help but think that it was very foolish, very childish, to have stamped upon her wedding ring and smashed the crystal vase upon the tiles. She was visited by no more outbursts, moving her to such futile expedients. She began to do as she liked and to feel as she liked. She completely abandoned her Tuesdays at home, and did not return the visits of those who had called upon her. She made no ineffectual efforts to conduct her household *en bonne ménagère,* going and coming as it suited her fancy, and, so far as she was able, lending herself to any passing caprice.

Mr. Pontellier had been a rather courteous husband so long as he met a certain tacit submissiveness in his wife. But her new and unexpected line of conduct completely bewildered him. It shocked him. Then her absolute disregard for her duties as a wife angered him. When Mr. Pontellier became rude, Edna grew insolent. She had resolved never to take another step backward.

"It seems to me the utmost folly for a woman at the head of a household, and the mother of children, to spend in an atelier days which would be better employed contriving for the comfort of her family."

"I feel like painting," answered Edna. "Perhaps I shan't always feel like it."

"Then in God's name paint! but don't let the family go to the devil. There's Madame Ratignolle; because she keeps up her music, she doesn't let everything else go to chaos. And she's more of a musician than you are a painter."

"She isn't a musician, and I'm not a painter. It isn't on account of painting that I let things go."

"On account of what, then?"

"Oh! I don't know. Let me alone; you bother me."

It sometimes entered Mr. Pontellier's mind to wonder if his wife were not growing a little unbalanced mentally. He could see plainly that she was not herself. That is, he could not see that she was becoming herself and daily casting aside that fictitious self which we assume like a garment with which to appear before the world.

Her husband let her alone as she requested, and went away to his office. Edna went up to her atelier—a bright room in the top of the house. She was working with great energy and interest, without accomplishing anything, however, which satisfied her even in the smallest degree. For a time she had the whole household enrolled in the service of art. The boys posed for her. They thought it amusing at first, but the occupation soon lost its attractiveness when they discovered that it was not a game arranged especially for their entertainment. The quadroon sat for hours before Edna's palette, patient as a savage, while the housemaid took charge of the children, and the drawing room went undusted. But the housemaid, too, served her term as model when Edna perceived that the young woman's back and shoulders were molded on classic lines, and that her hair, loosened from its confining cap, became an inspiration. While Edna worked she sometimes sang low the little air, *"Ah! Sit tu savais!"*

It moved her with recollections. She could hear again the ripple of the water, the flapping sail. She could see the glint of the moon upon the bay, and could feel the soft, gusty beating of the hot south wind. A subtle current of desire passed through her body, weakening her hold upon the brushes and making her eyes burn.

There were days when she was very happy without knowing why. She was happy to be alive and breathing, when her whole being seemed to be one with the sunlight, the color, the odors, the luxuriant warmth of some perfect Southern day. She liked then to wander alone into strange and unfamiliar places. She discovered many a sunny, sleepy corner, fashioned to dream in. And she found it good to dream and to be alone and unmolested.

There were days when she was unhappy, she did not know why—when it did not seem worth while to be glad or sorry, to be alive or dead, when life appeared to her like a grotesque pandemonium and humanity like worms struggling blindly toward inevitable annihilation. She could not work on such a day, nor weave fancies to stir her pulses and warm her blood.

XX

It was during such a mood that Edna hunted up Mademoiselle Reisz. She had not forgotten the rather disagreeable impression left upon her by their last interview; but she nevertheless felt a desire to see her—above all, to listen while she played upon the piano. Quite early in the afternoon she started upon her quest for the pianist Unfortunately she had mislaid or lost Mademoiselle Reisz's card, and looking up her address in the city directory, she found that the woman lived on Bienville Street, some distance away. The directory which fell into her hands was a year or more old, however, and upon reaching the number indicated, Edna discovered that the house was occupied by a respectable family of mulattoes who had *chambres garnies*[13] to let. They had been living there for six months, and knew absolutely nothing of a Mademoiselle Reisz. In fact, they knew nothing of any of their neighbors; their lodgers were all people of the highest distinction, they assured Edna. She did not linger to discuss class distinctions with Madame Pouponne, but hastened to a neighboring grocery store, feeling sure that Mademoiselle would have left her address with the proprietor.

He knew Mademoiselle Reisz a good deal better than he wanted to know her, he informed his questioner. In truth, he did not want to know her at all, or anything concerning her—the most disagreeable and unpopular woman who ever lived in Bienville Street. He thanked heaven she had left the neighborhood, and was equally thankful that he did not know where she had gone.

Edna's desire to see Mademoiselle Reisz had increased tenfold since these unlooked-for obstacles had arisen to thwart it. She was wondering who could give her the information she sought, when it suddenly occurred to her that Madame Lebrun would be the one most likely to do so. She knew it was useless to ask Madame Ratignolle, who was on the most distant terms with the musician, and preferred to know nothing concerning her. She had once been almost as emphatic in expressing herself upon the subject as the corner grocer.

Edna knew that Madame Lebrun had returned to the city, for it was the middle of November. And she also knew where the Lebruns lived, on Chartres Street.

Their home from the outside looked like a prison, with iron bars before the door and lower windows. The iron bars were a relic of the old *régime,* and no one had ever thought of dislodging them. At the side was a high fence enclosing the garden. A gate or door opening upon the street was locked. Edna rang the bell at this side garden gate, and stood upon the banquette, waiting to be admitted.

It was Victor who opened the gate for her. A black woman, wiping her hands upon her apron, was close at his heels. Before she saw them Edna could hear them in altercation, the woman—plainly an anomaly—claiming the right to be allowed to perform her duties, one of which was to answer the bell

Victor was surprised and delighted to see Mrs. Pontellier, and he made no attempt to conceal either his astonishment or his delight. He was a dark-browed, good-looking youngster of nineteen, greatly resembling his mother, but with ten times her impetuosity. He instructed the black woman to go at once and inform Madame Lebrun that Mrs. Pontellier desired to see her. The woman grumbled a refusal to do part of her duty when she had not been permitted to do it all, and started back to her interrupted task of weeding the garden. Whereupon Victor administered a rebuke in the form of a volley of abuse, which, owing to its rapidity and incoherence, was all but incomprehensible to Edna. Whatever it was, the rebuke was convincing, for the woman dropped her hoe and went mumbling into the house.

Edna did not wish to enter. It was very pleasant there on the side porch, where there were chairs, a wicker lounge, and a small table. She seated herself, for she was tired from her long tramp; and she began to rock gently and smooth out the folds of her silk parasol. Victor drew up his chair beside her. He at once explained that the black woman's offensive conduct was all due to imperfect training, as he was not there to take her in hand. He had only come up from the island the morning before, and expected to return next day. He stayed all winter at the island; he lived there, and kept the place in order and got things ready for the summer visitors.

But a man needed occasional relaxation, he informed Mrs. Pontellier, and every now and again he drummed up a pretext to bring him to the city. My! but he had had a time of it the evening before! He wouldn't want his mother to know, and he began to talk in a whisper. He was scintillant with recollections. Of course, he couldn't think of telling Mrs. Pontellier all about it, she being a woman and not comprehending such things. But it all began with a girl peeping and smiling at him through the shutters as he passed by. Oh! but she was a beauty! Certainly he smiled back, and went up and talked to her. Mrs. Pontellier did not know him if she supposed he was one to let an opportunity like that escape him. Despite herself, the youngster amused her. She must have betrayed in her look some degree of interest or entertainment The boy grew more daring, and Mrs. Pontellier might have found herself, in a little while, listening to a highly colored story but for the timely appearance of Madame Lebrun.

That lady was still clad in white, according to her custom of the summer. Her eyes beamed an effusive welcome. Would not Mrs. Pontellier go inside? Would she partake of some refreshment? Why had she not been there before? How was that dear Mr. Pontellier and how were those sweet children? Had Mrs. Pontellier ever known such a warm November?

Victor went and reclined on the wicker lounge behind his mother's chair, where he commanded a view of Edna's face. He had taken her parasol from her hands while he spoke to her, and he now lifted it and twirled it above him as he lay on his back. When Madame Lebrun complained that it was *so* dull coming back to the city; that she saw *so* few people now; that even Victor, when he came up from the island for a day or two, had *so* much to occupy him and engage his time; then it was that the youth went into contortions on the lounge and winked mischievously at Edna. She somehow felt like a confederate in crime, and tried to look severe and disapproving.

There had been but two letters from Robert, with little in them, they told her. Victor said it was really not worth while to go inside for the letters, when his mother entreated him to go in search of them. He remembered the contents, which in truth he rattled off very glibly when put to the test.

One letter was written from Vera Cruz and the other from the City of Mexico. He had met Montel, who was doing everything toward his advancement. So far, the financial situation was no improvement over the one he had left in New Orleans, but of course the prospects were vastly better. He wrote of the City of Mexico, the buildings, the people and their habits, the conditions of life which he found there. He sent his love to the family. He enclosed a check to his mother, and hoped she would affectionately remember him to all his friends. That was about the substance of the two letters. Edna felt that if there had been a message for her, she would have received it. The despondent frame of mind in which she had left home began again to overtake her, and she remembered that she wished to find Mademoiselle Reisz.

Madame Lebrun knew where Mademoiselle Reisz lived. She gave Edna the address, regretting that she would not consent to stay and spend the remainder of the afternoon, and pay a visit to Mademoiselle Reisz some other day. The afternoon was already well advanced.

Victor escorted her out upon the banquette, lifted her parasol, and held it over her while he walked to the car with her. He entreated her to bear in mind that the disclosures of the afternoon were strictly confidential. She laughed and bantered him a little, remembering too late that she should have been dignified and reserved.

"How handsome Mrs. Pontellier looked!" said Madame Lebrun to her son.

"Ravishing!" he admitted. "The city atmosphere has improved her. Some way she doesn't seem like the same woman."

XXI

Some people contended that the reason Mademoiselle Reisz always chose apartments up under the roof was to discourage the approach of beggars, peddlars and callers. There were plenty of windows in her little front room. They were for the most part dingy, but as they were nearly always open it did not make so much difference. They often admitted into the room a good deal of smoke and soot; but at the same time all the light and air that there was came through them. From her windows could be seen the crescent of the river, the masts of ships and the big chimneys of the Mississippi steamers. A magnificent piano crowded the apartment. In the next room she slept, and in the third and last she harbored a gasoline stove on which she cooked her meals when disinclined to descend to the neighboring restaurant. It was there also that she ate, keeping her belongings in a rare old buffet, dingy and battered from a hundred years of use.

When Edna knocked at Mademoiselle Reisz's front room door and entered, she discovered that person standing beside the window, engaged in mending or patching an old prunella gaiter. The little musician laughed all over when she saw Edna. Her laugh consisted of a contortion of the face and all the muscles of the body. She seemed strikingly homely, standing there in the afternoon light She still wore the shabby lace and the artificial bunch of violets on the side of her head.

"So you remembered me at last," said Mademoiselle. "I had said to myself, 'Ah, bah! she will never come.'"

"Did you want me to come?" asked Edna with a smile.

"I had not thought much about it," answered Mademoiselle. The two had seated themselves on a little bumpy sofa which stood against the wall. "I am glad, however, that you came. I have the water boiling back there, and was just about to make some coffee. You will drink a cup with me. And how is *la belle dame?* Always handsome! always healthy! always contented!" She took Edna's hand between her strong wiry fingers, holding it loosely without warmth, and executing a sort of double theme upon the back and palm.

"Yes," she went on; "I sometimes thought: 'She will never come. She promised as those women in society always do, without meaning it. She will not come.' For I really don't believe you like me, Mrs. Pontellier."

"I don't know whether I like you or not," replied Edna, gazing down at the little woman with a quizzical look.

The candor of Mrs. Pontellier's admission greatly pleased Mademoiselle Reisz. She expressed her gratification by repairing forthwith to the region of the gasoline stove and rewarding her guest with the promised cup of coffee. The coffee and the biscuit accompanying it proved very acceptable to Edna, who had declined refreshment at Madame Lebrun's and was now beginning to feel hungry. Mademoiselle set the tray which she brought in upon a small table near at hand, and seated herself once again on the lumpy sofa.

"I have had a letter from your friend," she remarked, as she poured a little cream into Edna's cup and handed it to her.

"My friend?"

"Yes, your friend Robert. He wrote to me from the City of Mexico."

"Wrote to *you?*" repeated Edna in amazement, stirring her coffee absently.

"Yes, to me. Why not? Don't stir all the warmth out of your coffee; drink it. Though the letter might as well have been sent to you; it was nothing but Mrs. Pontellier from beginning to end."

"Let me see it," requested the young woman, entreatingly.

"No; a letter concerns no one but the person who writes it and the one to whom it is written."

"Haven't you just said it concerned me from beginning to end?"

"It was written about you, not to you. 'Have you seen Mrs. Pontellier? How is she looking?' he asks. 'As Mrs. Pontellier says,' or 'as Mrs. Pontellier once said.' 'If Mrs. Pontellier should call upon you, play for her that Impromptu of Chopin's, my favorite. I heard it here a day or two ago, but not as you play it. I should like to know how it affects her,' and so on, as if he supposed we were constantly in each other's society."

"Let me see the letter."

"Oh, no."

"Have you answered it?"

"No."

"Let me see the letter."

"No, and again, no."

"Then play the Impromptu for me."

"It is growing late; what time do you have to be home?"

"Time doesn't concern me. Your question seems a little rude. Play the Impromptu."

"But you have told me nothing of yourself. What are you doing?"

"Painting!" laughed Edna. "I am becoming an artist. Think of it!"

"Ah! an artist! You have pretensions, Madame."

"Why pretensions? Do you think I could not become an artist?"

"I do not know you well enough to say. I do not know your talent or your temperament. To be an artist includes much; one must possess many gifts—absolute gifts—which have not been acquired by one's own effort. And, moreover, to succeed, the artist must possess the courageous soul."

"What do you mean by the courageous soul?"

"Courageous, *ma foi!* The brave soul. The soul that dares and defies."

"Show me the letter and play for me the Impromptu. You see that I have persistence. Does that quality count for anything in art?"

"It counts with a foolish old woman whom you have captivated," replied Mademoiselle, with her wriggling laugh.

The letter was right there at hand in the drawer of the little table upon which Edna had just placed her coffee cup. Mademoiselle opened the drawer and drew forth the letter, the topmost one. She placed it in Edna's hands, and without further comment arose and went to the piano.

Mademoiselle played a soft interlude. It was an improvisation. She sat low at the instrument, and the lines of her body settled into ungraceful curves and angles that gave it an appearance of deformity. Gradually and imperceptibly the interlude melted into the soft opening minor chords of the Chopin Impromptu.

Edna did not know when the Impromptu began or ended. She sat in the sofa corner reading Robert's letter by the fading light. Mademoiselle had glided from the Chopin into the quivering love notes of Isolde's song, and back again to the Impromptu with its soulful and poignant longing.

The shadows deepened in the little room. The music grew strange and fantastic—turbulent, insistent, plaintive and soft with entreaty. The shadows grew deeper. The music filled the room. It floated out upon the night, over the housetops, the crescent of the river, losing itself in the silence of the upper air.

Edna was sobbing, just as she had wept one midnight at Grand Isle when strange, new voices awoke in her. She arose in some agitation to take her departure. "May I come again, Mademoiselle?" she asked at the threshold.

"Come whenever you feel like it. Be careful; the stairs and landings are dark; don't stumble."

Mademoiselle reentered and lit a candle. Robert's letter was on the floor. She stooped and picked it up. It was crumpled and damp with tears. Mademoiselle smoothed the letter out, restored it to the envelope, and replaced it in the table drawer.

XXII

One morning on his way into town Mr. Pontellier stopped at the house of his old friend and family physician, Doctor Mandelet. The Doctor was a semiretired physician, resting, as the saying is, upon his laurels. He bore a reputation for wisdom rather than skill—leaving the active practice of medicine to his assistants and younger contemporaries—and was much sought for in matters of consultation. A few families, united to him by bonds of friendship, he still attended when they required the services of a physician. The Pontelliers were among these.

Mr. Pontellier found the Doctor reading at the open window of his study. His house stood rather far back from the street, in the center of a delightful garden, so that it was quiet and peaceful at the old gentleman's study window. He was a great reader. He stared up disapprovingly over his eyeglasses as Mr. Pontellier entered, wondering who had the temerity to disturb him at that hour of the morning.

"Ah, Pontellier! Not sick, I hope. Come and have a seat. What news do you bring this morning?" He was quite portly, with a profusion of gray hair, and small blue eyes which age had robbed of much of their brightness but none of their penetration.

"Oh! I'm never sick, Doctor. You know that I come of tough fiber—of that old Creole race of Pontelliers that dry up and finally blow away. I came to consult—no, not precisely to consult—to talk to you about Edna. I don't know what ails her."

"Madame Pontellier not well?" marveled the Doctor. "Why, I saw her—I think it was a week ago—walking along Canal Street, the picture of health, it seemed to me."

"Yes, yes; she seems quite well," said Mr. Pontellier, leaning forward and whirling his stick between his two hands; "but she doesn't act well. She's odd, she's not like herself. I can't make her out, and I thought perhaps you'd help me."

"How does she act?" inquired the doctor.

"Well, it isn't easy to explain," said Mr. Pontellier, throwing himself back in his chair. "She lets the housekeeping go to the dickens."

"Well, well; women are not all alike, my dear Pontellier. We've got to consider—"

"I know that; I told you I couldn't explain. Her whole attitude—toward me and everybody and everything—has changed. You know I have a quick temper, but I don't want to quarrel or be rude to a woman, especially my wife; yet I'm driven to it, and feel like ten thousand devils after I've made a fool of myself. She's making it devilishly uncomfortable for me," he went on nervously. "She's got some sort of notion in her head concerning the eternal rights of women; and—you understand—we meet in the morning at the breakfast table."

The old gentleman lifted his shaggy eyebrows, protruded his thick nether lip, and tapped the arms of his chair with his cushioned fingertips.

"What have you been doing to her, Pontellier?"

"Doing! *Parbleu!*"

"Has she," asked the Doctor, with a smile, "has she been associating of late with a circle of pseudointellectual women—superspiritual superior beings? My wife has been telling me about them."

"That's the trouble," broke in Mr. Pontellier, "she hasn't been associating with any one. She has abandoned her Tuesdays at home, has thrown over all her acquaintances, and goes tramping about by herself, moping in the street cars, getting in after dark. I tell you she's peculiar. I don't like it; I feel a little worried over it."

This was a new aspect for the Doctor. "Nothing hereditary?" he asked, seriously. "Nothing peculiar about her family antecedents, is there?"

"Oh, no, indeed! She comes of sound old Presbyterian Kentucky stock. The old gentleman, her father, I have heard, used to atone for his weekday sins with his Sunday devotions. I know for a fact, that his race horses literally ran away with the prettiest bit of Kentucky farming land I ever laid eyes upon. Margaret—you know Margaret—she has all the Presbyterianism undiluted.

And the youngest is something of a vixen. By the way, she gets married in a couple of weeks from now."

"Send your wife up to the wedding," exclaimed the Doctor, foreseeing a happy solution. "Let her stay among her own people for awhile; it will do her good."

"That's what I want her to do. She won't go to the marriage. She says a wedding is one of the most lamentable spectacles on earth. Nice thing for a woman to say to her husband!" exclaimed Mr. Pontellier, fuming anew at the recollection.

"Pontellier," said the Doctor, after a moment's reflection, "let your wife alone for a while. Don't bother her, and don't let her bother you. Woman, my dear friend, is a very peculiar and delicate organism—a sensitive and highly organized woman, such as I know Mrs. Pontellier to be, is especially peculiar. It would require an inspired psychologist to deal successfully with them. And when ordinary fellows like you and me attempt to cope with their idiosyncrasies the result is bungling. Most women are moody and whimsical. This is some passing whim of your wife, due to some cause or causes which you and I needn't try to fathom. But it will pass happily over, especially if you let her alone. Send her around to see me."

"Oh! I couldn't do that; there'd be no reason for it," objected Mr. Pontellier.

"Then I'll go around and see her," said the Doctor. "I'll drop in to dinner some evening *en bon ami.*"[14]

"Do! by all means," urged Mr. Pontellier. "What evening will you come? Say Thursday. Will you come Thursday?" he asked, rising to take his leave.

"Very well; Thursday. My wife may possibly have some engagement for me Thursday. In case she has, I shall let you know. Otherwise, you may expect me."

Mr. Pontellier turned before leaving to say:

"I am going to New York on business very soon. I have a big scheme on hand, and want to be on the field proper to pull the ropes and handle the ribbons. We'll let you in on the inside if you say so, Doctor," he laughed.

"No, I thank you, my dear sir," returned the Doctor. "I leave such ventures to you younger men with the fever of life still in your blood."

"What I wanted to say," continued Mr. Pontellier, with his hand on the knob; "I may have to be absent a good while. Would you advise me to take Edna along?"

"By all means, if she wishes to go. If not, leave her here. Don't contradict her. The mood will pass, I assure you. It may take a month, two, three months—possibly longer, but it will pass; have patience."

"Well good-by, *a jeudi,*"[15] said Mr. Pontellier, as he let himself out.

The Doctor would have liked during the course of conversation to ask, "Is there any man in the case?" but he knew his Creole too well to make such a blunder as that.

He did not resume his book immediately, but sat for a while meditatively looking out into the garden.

XXIII

Edna's father was in the city, and had been with them several days. She was not very warmly or deeply attached to him, but they had certain tastes in common, and when together they were companionable. His coming was in the nature of a welcome disturbance; it seemed to furnish a new direction for her emotions.

He had come to purchase a wedding gift for his daughter, Janet, and an outfit for himself in which he might make a creditable appearance at her marriage. Mr. Pontellier had selected the bridal gift, as everyone immediately connected with him always deferred to his taste in such matters. And his suggestions on the question of dress—which too often assumes the nature of a problem—were of inestimable value to his father-in-law. But for the past few days the old gentleman had been upon Edna's hands, and in his society she was becoming acquainted with a new set of sensations. He had been a colonel in the Confederate army, and still maintained, with the title, the military bearing which had always accompanied it. His hair and mustache were white and silky, emphasizing the rugged bronze of his face. He was tall and thin, and wore his coats padded, which gave a fictitious breadth and depth to his shoulders and chest. Edna and her father looked very distinguished together, and excited a good deal of notice during their perambulations. Upon his arrival she began by introducing him to her atelier and making a sketch of him. He took the whole matter very seriously. If her talent had been tenfold greater than it was, it would not have surprised him, convinced as he was that he had bequeathed to all of his daughters the germs of a masterful capability, which only depended upon their own efforts to be directed toward successful achievement.

Before her pencil he sat rigid and unflinching, as he had faced the cannon's mouth in days gone by. He resented the intrusion of the children, who gaped with wondering eyes at him, sitting so stiff up there in their mother's bright atelier. When they drew near he motioned them away with an expressive action of the foot, loath to disturb the fixed lines of his countenance, his arms, or his rigid shoulders.

Edna, anxious to entertain him, invited Mademoiselle Reisz to meet him, having promised him a treat in her piano playing; but Mademoiselle declined the invitation. So together they attended a *soiree musicale* at the Ratignolles'. Monsieur and Madame Ratignolle made much of the Colonel, installing him as the guest of honor and engaging him at once to dine with them the following Sunday, or any day which he might select. Madame coquetted with him in the most captivating and naive manner, with eyes, gestures, and a profusion of compliments, till the Colonel's old head felt thirty years younger on his padded shoulders. Edna marveled, not comprehending. She herself was almost devoid of coquetry.

There were one or two men whom she observed at the *soiree musicale;* but she would never have felt moved to any kittenish display to attract their notice—to any feline or feminine wiles to express herself toward them. Their personality attracted her in an agreeable way. Her fancy selected them, and she was glad when a lull in the music gave them an opportunity to meet her and talk with her. Often on the street the glance of strange eyes had lingered in her memory, and sometimes had disturbed her.

Mr. Pontellier did not attend these *soirees musicales*. He considered them *bourgeois,* and found more diversion at the club. To Madame Ratignolle he said the music dispensed at her *soirees* was too "heavy," too far beyond his untrained comprehension. His excuse flattered her. But she disapproved of Mr. Pontellier's club, and she was frank enough to tell Edna so.

"It's a pity Mr. Pontellier doesn't stay home more in the evenings. I think you would be more—well, if you don't mind my saying it—more united, if he did."

"Oh! dear no!" said Edna, with a blank look in her eyes. "What should I do if he stayed home? We wouldn't have anything to say to each other."

She had not much of anything to say to her father, for that matter; but he did not antagonize her. She discovered that he interested her, though she realized that he might not interest her long; and for the first time in her life she felt as if she were thoroughly acquainted with him. He kept her busy serving him and ministering to his wants. It amused her to do so. She would not permit a servant or one of the children to do anything for him which she might do herself. Her husband noticed, and thought it was the expression of a deep filial attachment which he had never suspected.

The Colonel drank numerous "toddies" during the course of the day, which left him, however, unperturbed. He was an expert at concocting strong drinks. He had even invented some, to which he had given fantastic names, and for whose manufacture he required diverse ingredients that it devolved upon Edna to procure for him.

When Doctor Mandelet dined with the Pontelliers on Thursday he could discern in Mrs. Pontellier no trace of that morbid condition which her husband had reported to him. She was excited and in a manner radiant. She and her father had been to the race course, and their thoughts when they seated themselves at table were still occupied with the events of the afternoon, and their talk was still of the track. The Doctor had not kept pace with turf affairs. He had certain recollections of racing in what he called "the good old times" when the Lecompte stables flourished, and he drew upon this fund of memories so that he might not be left out and seem wholly devoid of the modern spirit. But he failed to impose upon the Colonel, and was even far from impressing him with this trumped-up knowledge of bygone days. Edna had staked her father on his last venture, with the most gratifying results to both of them. Besides, they had met some very charming people, according to the Colonel's impressions. Mrs. Mortimer Merriman and Mrs. James Highcamp, who were there with Alcée Arobin, had joined them and had enlivened the hours in a fashion that warmed him to think of.

Mr. Pontellier himself had no particular leaning toward horse racing, and was even rather inclined to discourage it as a pastime, especially when he considered the fate of that bluegrass farm in Kentucky. He endeavored, in a general way, to express a particular disapproval, and only succeeded in arousing the ire and opposition of his father-in-law. A pretty dispute followed, in which Edna warmly espoused her father's cause and the Doctor remained neutral.

He observed his hostess attentively from under his shaggy brows, and noted a subtle change which had transformed her from the listless woman he had known into a being who, for the moment, seemed palpitant with the forces of life. Her speech was warm and energetic. There was no repression in her glance or gesture. She reminded him of some beautiful, sleek animal waking up in the sun.

The dinner was excellent. The claret was warm and the champagne was cold, and under their beneficent influence the threatened unpleasantness melted and vanished with the fumes of the wine.

Mr. Pontellier warmed up and grew reminiscent. He told some amusing plantation experiences, recollections of old Iberville and his youth, when he hunted 'possum in company with some friendly darky; thrashed the pecan trees, shot the grosbec, and roamed the woods and fields in mischievous idleness.

The Colonel, with little sense of humor and of the fitness of things, related a somber episode of those dark and bitter days, in which he had acted a conspicuous part and always formed a central figure. Nor was the Doctor happier in his selection, when he told the old, ever new and curious story of the waning of a woman's love, seeking strange, new channels, only to return to its legitimate source after days of fierce unrest. It was one of the many little human documents which had been unfolded to him during his long career as a physician. The story did not seem especially to impress Edna. She had one of her own to tell, of a woman who paddled away with her lover one night in a pirogue and never came back. They were lost amid the Baratarian Islands, and no one ever heard of them or found trace of them from that day to this. It was a pure invention. She said that Madame Antoine had related it to her. That, also, was an invention. Perhaps it was a dream she had had. But every glowing word seemed real to those who listened. They could feel the hot breath of the Southern night; they could hear the long sweep of the pirogue through the glistening moonlit water, the beating of birds' wings, rising startled from among the reeds in the salt-water pools; they could see the faces of the lovers, pale, close together, rapt in oblivious forgetfulness, drifting into the unknown.

The champagne was cold, and its subtle fumes played fantastic tricks with Edna's memory that night.

Outside, away from the glow of the fire and the soft lamplight, the night was chill and murky. The Doctor doubled his old-fashioned cloak across his breast as he strode home through the darkness. He knew his fellow creatures better than most men, knew that inner life which so seldom unfolds itself to unanointed eyes. He was sorry he had accepted Pontellier's invitation. He was growing old, and beginning to need rest and an unperturbed spirit. He did not want the secrets of other lives thrust upon him.

"I hope it isn't Arobin," he muttered to himself as he walked. "I hope to heaven it isn't Alcée Arobin."

XXIV

Edna and her father had a warm, and almost violent dispute upon the subject of her refusal to attend her sister's wedding. Mr. Pontellier declined to interfere, to interpose either his influence or his authority. He was following Doctor Mandelet's advice, and letting her do as she liked. The Colonel reproached his daughter for her lack of filial kindness and respect, her want of sisterly affection and womanly consideration. His arguments were labored and unconvincing. He doubted if Janet would accept any excuse—forgetting that Edna had offered none. He doubted if Janet would ever speak to her again, and he was sure Margaret would not.

Edna was glad to be rid of her father when he finally took himself off with his wedding garments and his bridal gifts, with his padded shoulders, his Bible reading, his "toddies" and ponderous oaths.

Mr. Pontellier followed him closely. He meant to stop at the wedding on his way to New York and endeavor by every means which money and love could devise to atone somewhat for Edna's incomprehensible action.

"You are too lenient, too lenient by far, Léonce," asserted the Colonel. "Authority, coercion are what is needed. Put your foot down good and hard; the only way to manage a wife. Take my word for it."

The Colonel was perhaps unaware that he had coerced his own wife into her grave. Mr. Pontellier had a vague suspicion of it which he thought it needless to mention at that late day.

Edna was not so consciously gratified at her husband's leaving home as she had been over the departure of her father. As the day approached when he was to leave her for a comparatively long stay, she grew melting and affectionate, remembering his many acts of consideration and his repeated expressions of an ardent attachment. She was solicitous about his health and his welfare. She bustled around, looking after his clothing, thinking about heavy underwear, quite as Madame Ratignolle would have done under similar circumstances. She cried when he went away, calling him her dear, good friend, and she was quite certain she would grow lonely before very long and go to join him in New York.

But after all, a radiant peace settled upon her when she at last found herself alone. Even the children were gone. Old Madame Pontellier had come herself and carried them off to Iberville with their quadroon. The old madame did not venture to say she was afraid they would be neglected during Léonce's absence; she hardly ventured to think so. She was hungry for them—even a little fierce in her attachment. She did not want them to be wholly "children of the pavement," she always said when begging to have them for a space. She wished them to know the country, with its streams, its fields, its woods, its freedom, so delicious to the young. She wished them to taste something of the life their father had lived and known and loved when he, too, was a little child.

When Edna was at last alone, she breathed a big, genuine sigh of relief. A feeling that was unfamiliar but very delicious came over her. She walked all through the house, from one room to another, as if inspecting it for the first time. She tried the various chairs and lounges, as if she had never sat and reclined upon them before. And she perambulated around the outside of the house, investigating, looking to see if windows and shutters were secure and in order. The flowers were like new acquaintances; she approached them in a familiar spirit, and made herself at home among them. The garden walks were damp, and Edna called to the maid to bring out her rubber sandals. And there she stayed, and stooped, digging around the plants, trimming, picking dead, dry leaves. The children's little dog came out, interfering, getting in her way. She scolded him, laughed at him, played with him. The garden smelled so good and looked so pretty in the afternoon sunlight Edna picked all the bright flowers she could find, and went into the house with them, she and the little dog.

Even the kitchen assumed a sudden interesting character which she had never before perceived. She went in to give directions to the cook, to say that the butcher would have to bring much less meat, that they would require only half their usual quantity of bread, of milk and groceries. She told the cook that she herself would be greatly occupied during Mr. Pontellier's absence, and she begged her to take all thought and responsibility of the larder upon her own shoulders.

That night Edna dined alone. The candelabra, with a few candles in the center of the table, gave all the light she needed. Outside the circle of light in which she sat, the large dining room looked solemn and shadowy. The cook, placed upon her mettle, served a delicious repast—a luscious tenderloin broiled à point. The wine tasted good; the marron glacé seemed to be just what she wanted. It was so pleasant, too, to dine in a comfortable peignoir.

She thought a little sentimentally about Léonce and the children, and wondered what they were doing. As she gave a dainty scrap or two to the doggie, she talked intimately to him about Étienne and Raoul. He was beside himself with astonishment and delight over these companionable advances, and showed his appreciation by his little quick, snappy barks and a lively agitation.

Then Edna sat in the library after dinner and read Emerson until she grew sleepy. She realized that she had neglected her reading, and determined to start anew upon a course of improving studies, now that her time was completely her own to do with as she liked.

After a refreshing bath, Edna went to bed. And as she snuggled comfortably beneath the eiderdown a sense of restfulness invaded her, such as she had not known before.

XXV

When the weather was dark and cloudy Edna could not work. She needed the sun to mellow and temper her mood to the sticking point. She had reached a stage when she seemed to be no longer feeling her way, working, when in the humor, with sureness and ease. And being devoid of ambition, and striving not toward accomplishment, she drew satisfaction from the work in itself.

On rainy or melancholy days Edna went out and sought the society of the friends she had made at Grand Isle. Or else she stayed indoors and nursed a mood with which she was becoming too familiar for her own comfort and peace of mind. It was not despair, but it seemed to her as if life were passing by, leaving its promise broken and unfulfilled. Yet there were other days when she listened, was led on and deceived by fresh promises which her youth held out to her.

She went again to the races, and again. Alcée Arobin and Mrs. Highcamp called for her one bright afternoon in Arobin's drag. Mrs. Highcamp was a worldly but unaffected, intelligent, slim, tall blonde woman in the forties, with an indifferent manner and blue eyes that stared. She had a daughter who served her as a pretext for cultivating the society of young men of fashion. Alcée Arobin was one of them. He was a familiar figure at the race course, the opera, the fashionable clubs. There was a perpetual smile in his eyes, which seldom failed to awaken a corresponding cheerfulness in any one who looked into them and listened to his good-humored voice. His manner was quiet, and at times a little insolent He possessed a good figure, a pleasing face, not overburdened with depth of thought or feeling; and his dress was that of the conventional man of fashion.

He admired Edna extravagantly, after meeting her at the races with her father. He had met her before on other occasions, but she had seemed to him unapproachable until that day. It was at his instigation that Mrs. Highcamp called to ask her to go with them to the Jockey Club to witness the turf event of the season.

There were possibly a few track men out there who knew the race horse as well as Edna, but there was certainly none who knew it better. She sat between her two companions as one having authority to speak. She laughed at Arobin's pretensions, and deplored Mrs. Highcamp's ignorance. The race horse was a friend and intimate associate of her childhood. The atmosphere of the stables and the breath of the bluegrass paddock revived in her memory and lingered in her nostrils. She did not perceive that she was talking like her father as the sleek geldings ambled in review before them. She played for very high stakes, and fortune favored her. The fever of the game flamed in her cheeks and eyes, and it got into her blood and into her brain like an intoxicant.

People turned their heads to look at her, and more than one lent an attentive ear to her utterances, hoping thereby to secure the elusive but ever-desired "tip." Arobin caught the contagion of excitement which drew him to Edna like a magnet. Mrs. Highcamp remained, as usual, unmoved, with her indifferent stare and uplifted eyebrows.

Edna stayed and dined with Mrs. Highcamp upon being urged to do so. Arobin also remained and sent away his drag.

The dinner was quiet and uninteresting, save for the cheerful efforts of Arobin to enliven things. Mrs. Highcamp deplored the absence of her daughter from the races, and tried to convey to her what she had missed by going to the "Dante reading" instead of joining them. The girl held a geranium leaf up to her nose and said nothing, but looked knowing and noncommittal. Mr. Highcamp was a plain, bald-headed man, who only talked under compulsion. He was unresponsive. Mrs. Highcamp was full of delicate courtesy and consideration toward her husband. She addressed most of her conversation to him at table. They sat in the library after dinner and read the evening papers together under the droplight, while the younger people went into the drawing room near by and talked. Miss Highcamp played some selections from Grieg upon the piano. She seemed to have apprehended all of the composer's coldness and none of his poetry. While Edna listened she could not help wondering if she had lost her taste for music.

When the time came for her to go home, Mr. Highcamp grunted a lame offer to escort her, looking down at his slippered feet with tactless concern. It was Arobin who took her home. The car ride was long, and it was late when they reached Esplanade Street. Arobin asked permission to enter for a second to light his cigarette—his match safe was empty. He filled his match safe, but did not light his cigarette until he left her, after she had expressed her willingness to go to the races with him again.

Edna was neither tired nor sleepy. She was hungry again, for the Highcamp dinner, though of excellent quality, had lacked abundance. She rummaged in the larder and brought forth a slice of "Gruyère" and some crackers. She opened a bottle of beer which she found in the icebox. Edna felt extremely restless and excited. She vacantly hummed a fantastic tune as she poked at the wood embers on the hearth and munched a cracker.

She wanted something to happen—something, anything; she did not know what. She regretted that she had not made Arobin stay a half hour to talk over the horses with her. She counted the money she had won. But there was nothing else to do, so she went to bed, and tossed there for hours in a sort of monotonous agitation.

In the middle of the night she remembered that she had forgotten to write her regular letter to her husband; and she decided to do so next day and tell him about her afternoon at the Jockey Club. She lay wide awake composing a letter which was nothing like the one which she wrote next day. When the maid awoke her in the morning Edna was dreaming of Mr. Highcamp playing the piano at the entrance of a music store on Canal Street, while his wife was saying to Alcée Arobin, as they boarded an Esplanade Street car:

"What a pity that so much talent has been neglected! but I must go."

When, a few days later, Alcée Arobin again called for Edna in his drag, Mrs. Highcamp was not with him. He said they would pick her up. But as that lady had not been apprised of his intention of picking her up, she was not at home. The daughter was just leaving the house to attend the meeting of a branch Folk Lore Society, and regretted that she could not accompany them. Arobin appeared nonplused, and asked Edna if there were any one else she cared to ask.

She did not deem it worth while to go in search of any of the fashionable acquaintances from whom she had withdrawn herself. She thought of Madame Ratignolle, but knew that her fair friend did not leave the house, except to take a languid walk around the block with her husband after nightfall. Mademoiselle Reisz would have laughed at such a request from Edna. Madame Lebrun might have enjoyed the outing, but for some reason Edna did not want her. So they went alone, she and Arobin.

The afternoon was intensely interesting to her. The excitement came back upon her like a remittent fever. Her talk grew familiar and confidential. It was no labor to become intimate with

Arobin. His manner invited easy confidence. The preliminary stage of becoming acquainted was one which he always endeavored to ignore when a pretty and engaging woman was concerned.

He stayed and dined with Edna. He stayed and sat beside the wood fire. They laughed and talked; and before it was time to go he was telling her how different life might have been if he had known her years before. With ingenuous frankness he spoke of what a wicked, ill-disciplined boy he had been, and impulsively drew up his cuff to exhibit upon his wrist the scar from a saber cut which he had received in a duel outside of Paris when he was nineteen. She touched his hand as she scanned the red cicatrice on the inside of his white wrist. A quick impulse that was somewhat spasmodic impelled her fingers to close in a sort of clutch upon his hand. He felt the pressure of her pointed nails in the flesh of his palm.

She arose hastily and walked toward the mantel.

"The sight of a wound or scar always agitates and sickens me," she said. "I shouldn't have looked at it."

"I beg your pardon," he entreated, following her; "it never occurred to me that it might be repulsive."

He stood close to her, and the effrontery in his eyes repelled the old, vanishing self in her, yet drew all her awakening sensuousness. He saw enough in her face to impel him to take her hand and hold it while he said his lingering good night.

"Will you go to the races again?" he asked.

"No," she said. "I've had enough of the races. I don't want to lose all the money I've won, and I've got to work when the weather is bright, instead of—"

"Yes; work; to be sure. You promised to show me your work. What morning may I come up to your atelier? Tomorrow?"

"No!"

"Day after?"

"No, no."

"Oh, please don't refuse me! I know something of such things. I might help you with a stray suggestion or two."

"No. Good night. Why don't you go after you have said good night? I don't like you," she went on in a high, excited pitch, attempting to draw away her hand. She felt that her words lacked dignity and sincerity, and she knew that he felt it.

"I'm sorry you don't like me. I'm sorry I offended you. How have I offended you? What have I done? Can't you forgive me?" And he bent and pressed his lips upon her hand as if he wished never more to withdraw them.

"Mr. Arobin," she complained, "I'm greatly upset by the excitement of the afternoon; I'm not myself. My manner must have misled you in some way. I wish you to go, please." She spoke in a monotonous, dull tone. He took his hat from the table, and stood with eyes turned from her, looking into the dying fire. For a moment or two he kept an impressive silence.

"Your manner has not misled me, Mrs. Pontellier," he said finally. "My own emotions have done that. I couldn't help it. When I'm near you, how could I help it? Don't think anything of it, don't bother, please. You see, I go when you command me. If you wish me to stay away, I shall do so. If you let me come back, I—oh! you will let me come back?"

He cast one appealing glance at her, to which she made no response. Alcée Arobin's manner was so genuine that it often deceived even himself.

Edna did not care or think whether it were genuine or not. When she was alone she looked mechanically at the back of her hand which he had kissed so warmly. Then she leaned her head down on the mantelpiece. She felt somewhat like a woman who in a moment of passion is betrayed into an act of infidelity, and realizes the significance of the act without being wholly awakened from its glamour. The thought was passing vaguely through her mind, "What would he think?"

She did not mean her husband; she was thinking of Robert Lebrun. Her husband seemed to her now like a person whom she had married without love as an excuse.

She lit a candle and went up to her room. Alcée Arobin was absolutely nothing to her. Yet his presence, his manners, the warmth of his glances, and above all the touch of his lips upon her hand had acted like a narcotic upon her.

She slept a languorous sleep, interwoven with vanishing dreams.

XXVI

Alcée Arobin wrote Edna an elaborate note of apology, palpitant with sincerity. It embarrassed her, for in a cooler, quieter moment it appeared to her absurd that she should have taken his action so seriously, so dramatically. She felt sure that the significance of the whole occurrence had lain in her own self-consciousness. If she ignored his note it would give undue importance to a trivial affair. If she replied to it in a serious spirit it would still leave in his mind the impression that she had in a susceptible moment yielded to his influence. After all, it was no great matter to have one's hand kissed. She was provoked at his having written the apology. She answered in as light and bantering a spirit as she fancied it deserved, and said she would be glad to have him look in upon her at work whenever he felt the inclination and his business gave him the opportunity.

He responded at once by presenting himself at her home with all his disarming naïveté. And then there was scarcely a day which followed that she did not see him or was not reminded of him. He was prolific in pretexts. His attitude became one of good-humored subservience and tacit adoration. He was ready at all times to submit to her moods, which were as often kind as they were cold. She grew accustomed to him. They became intimate and friendly by imperceptible degrees, and then by leaps. He sometimes talked in a way that astonished her at first and brought the crimson into her face; in a way that pleased her at last, appealing to the animalism that stirred impatiently within her.

There was nothing which so quieted the turmoil of Edna's senses as a visit to Mademoiselle Reisz. It was then, in the presence of that personality which was offensive to her, that the woman, by her divine art, seemed to reach Edna's spirit and set it free.

It was misty, with heavy, lowering atmosphere, one afternoon, when Edna climbed the stairs to the pianist's apartments under the roof. Her clothes were dripping with moisture. She felt chilled and pinched as she entered the room. Mademoiselle was poking at a rusty stove that smoked a little and warmed the room indifferently. She was endeavoring to heat a pot of chocolate on the stove. The room looked cheerless and dingy to Edna as she entered. A bust of Beethoven, covered with a hood of dust, scowled at her from the mantelpiece.

"Ah! here comes the sunlight!" exclaimed Mademoiselle, rising from her knees before the stove. "Now it will be warm and bright enough; I can let the fire alone."

She closed the stove door with a bang, and approaching, assisted in removing Edna's dripping mackintosh.

"You are cold; you look miserable. The chocolate will soon be hot. But would you rather have a taste of brandy? I have scarcely touched the bottle which you brought me for my cold." A piece of red flannel was wrapped around Mademoiselle's throat; a stiff neck compelled her to hold her head on one side.

"I will take some brandy," said Edna, shivering as she removed her gloves and overshoes. She drank the liquor from the glass as a man would have done. Then flinging herself upon the uncomfortable sofa she said, "Mademoiselle, I am going to move away from my house on Esplanade Street."

"Ah!" ejaculated the musician, neither surprised nor especially interested. Nothing ever seemed to astonish her very much. She was endeavoring to adjust the bunch of violets which had become loose from its fastening in her hair. Edna drew her down upon the sofa, and taking a pin from her own hair, secured the shabby artificial flowers in their accustomed place.

"Aren't you astonished?"

"Passably. Where are you going? to New York? to Iberville? to your father in Mississippi? where?"

"Just two steps away," laughed Edna, "in a little four-room house around the corner. It looks so cozy, so inviting and restful, whenever I pass by; and it's for rent. I'm tired looking after that big house. It never seemed like mine, anyway—like home. It's too much trouble. I have to keep too many servants. I am tired bothering with them."

"That is not your true reason, *ma belle*. There is no use in telling me lies. I don't know your reason, but you have not told me the truth." Edna did not protest or endeavor to justify herself.

"The house, the money that provides for it, are not mine. Isn't that enough reason?"

"They are your husband's," returned Mademoiselle, with a shrug and a malicious elevation of the eyebrows.

"Oh! I see there is no deceiving you. Then let me tell you: It is a caprice. I have a little money of my own from my mother's estate, which my father sends me by driblets. I won a large sum this winter on the races, and I am beginning to sell my sketches. Laidpore is more and more pleased with my work; he says it grows in force and individuality. I cannot judge of that myself, but I feel that I have gained in ease and confidence. However, as I said, I have sold a good many through Laidpore. I can live in the tiny house for little or nothing, with one servant. Old Celestine, who works occasionally for me, says she will come stay with me and do my work. I know I shall like it, like the feeling of freedom and independence."

"What does your husband say?"

"I have not told him yet. I only thought of it this morning. He will think I am demented, no doubt. Perhaps you think so."

Mademoiselle shook her head slowly. "Your reason is not yet clear to me," she said.

Neither was it quite clear to Edna herself; but it unfolded itself as she sat for a while in silence. Instinct had prompted her to put away her husband's bounty in casting off her allegiance. She did not know how it would be when he returned. There would have to be an understanding, an explanation. Conditions would some way adjust themselves, she felt; but whatever came, she had resolved never again to belong to another than herself.

"I shall give a grand dinner before I leave the old house!" Edna exclaimed. "You will have to come to it, Mademoiselle. I will give you everything that you like to eat and to drink. We shall sing and laugh and be merry for once." And she uttered a sigh that came from the very depths of her being.

If Mademoiselle happened to have received a letter from Robert during the interval of Edna's visits she would give her the letter unsolicited. And she would seat herself at the piano and play as her humor prompted her while the young woman read the letter.

The little stove was roaring; it was redhot, and the chocolate in the tin sizzled and sputtered. Edna went forward and opened the stove door, and Mademoiselle rising, took a letter from under the bust of Beethoven and handed it to Edna.

"Another! so soon!" she exclaimed, her eyes filled with delight. "Tell me, Mademoiselle, does he know that I see his letters?"

"Never in the world! He would be angry and would never write to me again if he thought so. Does he write to you? Never a line. Does he send you a message? Never a word. It is because he loves you, poor fool, and is trying to forget you, since you are not free to listen to him or to belong to him."

"Why do you show me his letters, then?"

"Haven't you begged for them? Can I refuse you anything? Oh! you cannot deceive me," and Mademoiselle approached her beloved instrument and began to play. Edna did not at once read the letter. She sat holding it in her hand, while the music penetrated her whole being like an effulgence, warming and brightening the dark places of her soul. It prepared her for joy and exultation.

"Oh!" she exclaimed, letting the letter fall to the floor. "Why did you not tell me?" She went and grasped Mademoiselle's hands up from the keys. "Oh! unkind! malicious! Why did you not tell me?"

"That he was coming back? No great news, *ma foi*. I wonder he did not come long ago."

"But when, when?" cried Edna, impatiently. "He does not say when."

"He says 'very soon.' You know as much about it as I do; it is all in the letter."

"But why? Why is he coming? Oh, if I thought—" and she snatched the letter from the floor and turned the pages this way and that way, looking for the reason, which was left untold.

"If I were young and in love with a man," said Mademoiselle, turning on the stool and pressing her wiry hands between her knees as she looked down at Edna, who sat on the floor holding the letter, "it seems to me he would have to be some *grand esprit,* a man with lofty aims and ability to reach them; one who stood high enough to attract the notice of his fellow-men. It seems to me if I were young and in love I should never deem a man of ordinary caliber worthy of my devotion."

"Now it is you who are telling lies and seeking to deceive me, Mademoiselle; or else you have never been in love, and know nothing about it. Why," went on Edna, clasping her knees and looking up into Mademoiselle's twisted face, "do you suppose a woman knows why she loves? Does she select? Does she say to herself: 'Go to! Here is a distinguished statesman with presidential possibilities; I shall proceed to fall in love with him.' Or, 'I shall set my heart upon this musician, whose fame is on every tongue?' Or, 'This financier, who controls the world's money markets?'"

"You are purposely misunderstanding me, *ma reine.* Are you in love with Robert?"

"Yes," said Edna. It was the first time she had admitted it, and a glow overspread her face, blotching it with red spots.

"Why?" asked her companion. "Why do you love him when you ought not to?"

Edna, with a motion or two, dragged herself on her knees before Mademoiselle Reisz, who took the glowing face between her two hands.

"Why? Because his hair is brown and grows away from his temples; because he opens and shuts his eyes, and his nose is a little out of drawing, because he has two lips and a square chin, and a little finger which he can't straighten from having played baseball too energetically in his youth. Because—"

"Because you do, in short," laughed Mademoiselle. "What will you do when he comes back?" she asked.

"Do? Nothing, except feel glad and happy to be alive."

She was already glad and happy to be alive at the mere thought of his return. The murky, lowering sky, which had depressed her a few hours before, seemed bracing and invigorating as she splashed through the streets on her way home.

She stopped at a confectioner's and ordered a huge box of bonbons for the children in Iberville. She slipped a card in the box, on which she scribbled a tender message and sent an abundance of kisses.

Before dinner in the evening Edna wrote a charming letter to her husband, telling him of her intention to move for a while into the little house around the block, and to give a farewell dinner before leaving, regretting that he was not there to share it, to help her out with the menu and assist her in entertaining the guests. Her letter was brilliant and brimming with cheerfulness.

XXVII

"What is the matter with you?" asked Arobin that evening. "I never found you in such a happy mood." Edna was tired by that time, and was reclining on the lounge before the fire.

"Don't you know the weather prophet has told us we shall see the sun pretty soon?"

"Well, that ought to be reason enough," he acquiesced. "You wouldn't give me another if I sat here all night imploring you." He sat close to her on a low tabouret, and as he spoke his fingers lightly touched the hair that fell a little over her forehead. She liked the touch of his fingers through her hair, and closed her eyes sensitively.

"One of these days," she said, "I'm going to pull myself together for a while and think—try to determine what character of a woman I am, for, candidly, I don't know. By all the codes which I am acquainted with, I am a devilishly wicked specimen of the sex. But some way I can't convince myself that I am. I must think about it."

"Don't. What's the use? Why should you bother thinking about it when I can tell you what manner of woman you are." His fingers strayed occasionally down to her warm, smooth cheeks and firm chin, which was growing a little full and double.

"Oh, yes! You will tell me that I am adorable, everything that is captivating. Spare yourself the effort."

"No, I shan't tell you anything of the sort, though I shouldn't be lying if I did."

"Do you know Mademoiselle Reisz?" she asked irrelevantly.

"The pianist? I know her by sight. I've heard her play."

"She says queer things sometimes in a bantering way that you don't notice at the time and you find yourself thinking about afterward."

"For instance?"

"Well, for instance, when I left her today, she put her arms around me and felt my shoulder blades, to see if my wings were strong, she said. 'The bird that would soar above the level plain of tradition and prejudice must have strong wings. It is a sad spectacle to see the weaklings bruised, exhausted, fluttering back to earth.'"

"Whither would you soar?"

"I'm not thinking of any extraordinary flights. I only half comprehend her."

"I've heard she's partially demented," said Arobin.

"She seems to me wonderfully sane," Edna replied.

"I'm told she's extremely disagreeable and unpleasant. Why have you introduced her at a moment when I desired to talk of you?"

"Oh! talk of me if you like," cried Edna, clasping her hands beneath her head; "but let me think of something else while you do."

"I'm jealous of your thoughts tonight. They're making you a little kinder than usual, but some way I feel as if they were wandering, as if they were not here with me." She only looked at him and smiled. His eyes were very near. He leaned upon the lounge with an arm extended across her, while the other hand still rested upon her hair. They continued silently to look into each other's eyes. When he leaned forward and kissed her, she clasped his head, holding his lips to hers.

It was the first kiss of her life to which her nature had really responded. It was a flaming torch that kindled desire.

XXVIII

Edna cried a little that night after Arobin left her. It was only one phase of the multitudinous emotions which had assailed her. There was with her an overwhelming feeling of irresponsibility. There was the shock of the unexpected and the unaccustomed. There was her husband's reproach looking at her from the external things around her which he had provided for her external existence. There was Robert's reproach making itself felt by a quicker, fiercer, more over-powering love, which had awakened within her toward him. Above all, there was understanding. She felt as if a mist had been lifted from her eyes, enabling her to look upon and comprehend the significance of life, that monster made up of beauty and brutality. But among the conflicting sensations which assailed her, there was neither shame nor remorse. There was a dull pang of regret because it was not the kiss of love which had inflamed her, because it was not love which had held this cup of life to her lips.

XXIX

Without even waiting for an answer from her husband regarding his opinion or wishes in the matter, Edna hastened her preparations for quitting her home on Esplanade Street and moving into the little house around the block. A feverish anxiety attended her every action in that direction. There was no moment of deliberation, no interval of repose between the thought and its fulfillment. Early upon the morning following those hours passed in Arobin's society, Edna set about securing her new abode and hurrying her arrangements for occupying it. Within the precincts of her home she felt like one who has entered and lingered within the portals of some forbidden temple in which a thousand muffled voices bade her begone.

Whatever was her own in the house, everything which she had acquired aside from her husband's bounty, she caused to be transported to the other house, supplying simple and meager deficiencies from her own resources.

Arobin found her with rolled sleeves, working in company with the house maid when he looked in during the afternoon. She was splendid and robust, and had never appeared handsomer than in the old blue gown, with a red silk handkerchief knotted at random around her head to protect her hair from the dust. She was mounted upon a high stepladder, unhooking a picture from the wall when he entered. He had found the front door open, and had followed his ring by walking in unceremoniously.

"Come down!" he said. "Do you want to kill yourself?" She greeted him with affected carelessness, and appeared absorbed in her occupation.

If he had expected to find her languishing, reproachful, or indulging in sentimental tears, he must have been greatly surprised.

He was no doubt prepared for any emergency, ready for any one of the foregoing attitudes, just as he bent himself easily and naturally to the situation which confronted him.

"Please come down," he insisted, holding the ladder and looking up at her.

"No," she answered; "Ellen is afraid to mount the ladder. Joe is working over at the 'pigeon house'—that's the name Ellen gives it, because it's so small and looks like a pigeon house—and someone has to do this."

Arobin pulled off his coat, and expressed himself ready and willing to tempt fate in her place. Ellen brought him one of her dust caps, and went into contortions of mirth, which she found it impossible to control, when she saw him put it on before the mirror as grotesquely as he could. Edna herself could not refrain from smiling when she fastened it at his request. So it was he who in turn mounted the ladder, unhooking pictures and curtains, and dislodging ornaments as Edna directed. When he had finished he took off his dust-cap and went out to wash his hands.

Edna was sitting on the tabouret, idly brushing the tips of a feather duster along the carpet when he came in again.

"Is there anything more you will let me do?" he asked.

"That is all," she answered. "Ellen can manage the rest." She kept the young woman occupied in the drawing-room, unwilling to be left alone with Arobin.

"What about the dinner?" he asked; "the grand event, the *coup d' état?*"

"It will be a day after tomorrow. Why do you call it the *'coup d' état?'* Oh! it will be very fine; all my best of everything—crystal, silver and gold, Sèvres, flowers, music, and champagne to swim in. I'll let Léonce pay the bills. I wonder what he'll say when he sees the bills."

"And you ask me why I call it a *coup d' état?*" Arobin had put on his coat, and he stood before her and asked if his cravat was plumb. She told him it was, looking no higher than the tip of his collar.

"When do you go to the 'pigeon house?'—with all due acknowledgment to Ellen."

"Day after tomorrow, after the dinner. I shall sleep there."

"Ellen, will you very kindly get me a glass of water?" asked Arobin. "The dust in the curtains, if you will pardon me for hinting such a thing, has parched my throat to a crisp."

"While Ellen gets the water," said Edna, rising, "I will say good-by and let you go. I must get rid of this grime, and I have a million things to do and think of."

"When shall I see you?" asked Arobin, seeking to detain her, the maid having left the room.

"At the dinner, of course. You are invited."

"Not before?—not tonight or tomorrow morning or tomorrow noon or night? or the day after morning or noon? Can't you see yourself, without my telling you, what an eternity it is?"

He had followed her into the hall and to the foot of the stairway, looking up at her as she mounted with her face half turned to him.

"Not an instant sooner," she said. But she laughed and looked at him with eyes that at once gave him courage to wait and made it torture to wait.

XXX

Though Edna had spoken of the dinner as a very grand affair, it was in truth a very small affair and very select, in so much as the guests invited were few and were selected with discrimination. She had counted upon an even dozen seating themselves at her round mahogany board, forgetting for the moment that Madame Ratignolle was to the last degree *souffrante*[16] and unpresentable, and not forseeing that Madame Lebrun would send a thousand regrets at the last moment. So there were only ten, after all, which made a cozy, comfortable number.

There were Mr. and Mrs. Merriman, a pretty, vivacious little woman in the thirties; her husband, a jovial fellow, something of a shallow-pate, who laughed a good deal at other people's witticisms, and had thereby made himself extremely popular. Mrs. Highcamp had accompanied them. Of course, there was Alcée Arobin, and Mademoiselle Reisz had consented to come. Edna had sent her a fresh bunch of violets with black lace trimmings for her hair. Monsieur Ratignolle brought himself and his wife's excuses. Victor Lebrun, who happened to be in the city, bent upon relaxation, had accepted with alacrity. There was a Miss Mayblunt, no longer in her teens, who looked at the world through lorgnettes and with the keenest interest. It was thought and said that she was intellectual; it was suspected of her that she wrote under a *nom de guerre*. She had come with a gentleman by the name of Gouvernail, connected with one of the daily papers, of whom nothing special could be said, except that he was observant and seemed quiet and inoffensive. Edna herself made the tenth, and at half-past eight they seated themselves at table, Arobin and Monsieur Ratignolle on either side of their hostess.

Mrs. Highcamp sat between Arobin and Victor Lebrun. Then came Mrs. Merriman, Mr. Gouvernail, Miss Mayblunt, Mr. Merriman, and Mademoiselle Reisz next to Monsieur Ratignolle.

There was something extremely gorgeous about the appearance of the table, an effect of splendor conveyed by a cover of pale yellow satin under strips of lacework There were wax candles in massive brass candelabra, burning softly under yellow silk shades; full, fragrant roses, yellow and red, abounded. There were silver and gold, as she had said there would be, and crystal which glittered like the gems which the women wore.

The ordinary stiff dining chairs had been discarded for the occasion and replaced by the most commodious and luxurious which could be collected throughout the house. Mademoiselle Reisz, being exceedingly diminutive, was elevated upon cushions, as small children are sometimes hoisted at table upon bulky volumes.

"Something new, Edna?" exclaimed Miss Mayblunt, with lorgnette directed toward a magnificent cluster of diamonds that sparkled, that almost sputtered, in Edna's hair, just over the center of her forehead.

"Quite new, 'brand' new, in fact, a present from my husband. It arrived this morning from New York. I may as well admit that this is my birthday, and that I am twenty-nine. In good time I expect you to drink my health. Meanwhile, I shall ask you to begin with this cocktail, composed—would you say 'composed?'" with an appeal to Miss Mayblunt—"composed by my father in honor of Sister Janet's wedding."

Before each guest stood a tiny glass that looked and sparkled like a garnet gem.

"Then, all things considered," spoke Arobin, "it might not be amiss to start out by drinking the Colonel's health in the cocktail which he composed, on the birthday of the most charming of women—the daughter whom he invented."

Mr. Merriman's laugh at this sally was such a genuine outburst and so contagious that it started the dinner with an agreeable swing that never slackened.

Miss Mayblunt begged to be allowed to keep her cocktail untouched before her, just to look at. The color was marvelous! She could compare it to nothing she had ever seen, and the garnet lights which it emitted were unspeakably rare. She pronounced the Colonel an artist, and stuck to it.

Monsieur Ratignolle was prepared to take things seriously: the *mets*, the *entre-mets*,[17] the service, the decorations, even the people. He looked up from his pompano and inquired of Arobin if he were related to the gentleman of that name who formed one of the firm of Laitner and Arobin, lawyers. The young man admitted that Laitner was a warm personal friend, who permitted Arobin's name to decorate the firm's letterheads and to appear upon a shingle that graced Perdido Street.

"There are so many inquisitive people and institutions abounding," said Arobin, "that one is really forced as a matter of convenience these days to assume the virtue of an occupation if he has it not."

Monsieur Ratignolle stared a little, and turned to ask Mademoiselle Reisz if she considered the symphony concerts up to the standard which had been set the previous winter. Mademoiselle Reisz answered Monsieur Ratignolle in French, which Edna thought a little rude, under the circumstances, but characteristic. Mademoiselle had only disagreeable things to say of the symphony concerts, and insulting remarks to make of all the musicians of New Orleans, singly and collectively. All her interest seemed to be centered upon the delicacies placed before her.

Mr. Merriman said that Mr. Arobin's remark about inquisitive people reminded him of a man from Waco the other day at the St. Charles Hotel—but as Mr. Merriman's stories were always lame and lacking point, his wife seldom permitted him to complete them. She interrupted him to ask if he remembered the name of the author whose book she had bought the week before to send to a friend in Geneva. She was talking "books" with Mr. Gouvernail and trying to draw from him his opinion upon current literary topics. Her husband told the story of the Waco man privately to Miss Mayblunt, who pretended to be greatly amused and to think it extremely clever.

Mrs. Highcamp hung with languid but unaffected interest upon the warm and impetuous volubility of her left-hand neighbor, Victor Lebrun. Her attention was never for a moment withdrawn from him after seating herself at table; and when he turned to Mrs. Merriman, who was prettier and more vivacious than Mrs. Highcamp, she waited with easy indifference for an opportunity to reclaim his attention. There was the occasional sound of music, of mandolins, sufficiently removed to be an agreeable accompaniment rather than an interruption to the conversation. Outside the soft, monotonous splash of a fountain could be heard; the sound penetrated into the room with the heavy odor of jessamine that came through the open windows.

The golden shimmer of Edna's satin gown spread in rich folds on either side of her. There was a soft fall of lace encircling her shoulders. It was the color of her skin, without the glow, the myriad living tints that one may sometimes discover in vibrant flesh. There was something in her attitude, in her whole appearance when she leaned her head against the high-backed chair and spread her arms, which suggested the regal woman, the one who rules, who looks on, who stands alone.

But as she sat there amid her guests, she felt the old ennui overtaking her, the hopelessness which so often assailed her, which came upon her like an obsession, like something extraneous, independent of volition. It was something which announced itself; a chill breath that seemed to issue from some vast cavern wherein discords wailed. There came over her the acute longing which always summoned into her spiritual vision the presence of the beloved one, overpowering her at once with a sense of the unattainable.

The moments glided on, while a feeling of good fellowship passed around the circle like a mystic cord, holding and binding these people together with jest and laughter. Monsieur Ratignolle was the first to break the pleasant charm. At ten o'clock he excused himself. Madame Ratignolle was waiting for him at home. She was *bien souffrante,* and she was filled with vague dread, which only her husband's presence could allay.

Mademoiselle Reisz arose with Monsieur Ratignolle, who offered to escort her to the car. She had eaten well; she had tasted the good, rich wines, and they must have turned her head, for she bowed pleasantly to all as she withdrew from table. She kissed Edna upon the shoulder, and whispered: *"Bonne nuit, ma reine; soyez sage."*[18] She had been a little bewildered upon rising, or rather, descending from her cushions, and Monsieur Ratignolle gallantly took her arm and led her away.

Mrs. Highcamp was weaving a garland of roses, yellow and red. When she had finished the garland, she laid it lightly upon Victor's black curls. He was reclining far back in the luxurious chair, holding a glass of champagne to the light.

As if a magician's wand had touched him, the garland of roses transformed him into a vision of Oriental beauty. His cheeks were the color of crushed grapes and his dusky eyes glowed with a languishing fire.

"Sapristi!" exclaimed Arobin.

But Mrs. Highcamp had one more touch to add to the picture. She took from the back of her chair a white silken scarf, with which she had covered her shoulders in the early part of the evening. She draped it across the boy in graceful folds, and in a way to conceal his black, conventional evening dress. He did not seem to mind what she did to him, only smiled, showing a faint gleam of white teeth, while he continued to gaze with narrowing eyes at the light through his glass of champagne.

"Oh! to be able to paint in color rather than in words!" exclaimed Miss Mayblunt, losing herself in a rhapsodic dream as she looked at him.

> "'There was a graven image of Desire
> Painted with red blood on a ground of gold.'"

murmured Gouvernail, under his breath.

The effect of the wine upon Victor was, to change his accustomed volubility into silence. He seemed to have abandoned himself to a reverie, and to be seeing pleasing visions in the amber bead.

"Sing," entreated Mrs. Highcamp. "Won't you sing to us?"

"Let him alone," said Arobin.

"He's posing," offered Mr. Merriman; "let him have it out."

"I believe he's paralyzed," laughed Mrs. Merriman. And leaning over the youth's chair, she took the glass from his hand and held it to his lips. He sipped the wine slowly, and when he had drained the glass she laid it upon the table and wiped his lips with her little filmy handkerchief.

"Yes, I'll sing for you," he said, turning in his chair toward Mrs. Highcamp. He clasped his hands behind his head, and looking up at the ceiling began to hum a little, trying his voice like a musician tuning an instrument. Then, looking at Edna, he began to sing:

"Ah! si tu savais!"

"Stop!" she cried, "don't sing that. I don't want you to sing it," and she laid her glass so impetuously and blindly upon the table as to shatter it against a carafe. The wine spilled over Arobin's legs and some of it trickled down upon Mrs. Highcamp's black gauze gown. Victor had lost all idea of courtesy, or else he thought his hostess was not in earnest, for he laughed and went on:

"Ah! si tu savais
Ce que tes yeux me disent"—[19]

"Oh! you mustn't! you mustn't," exclaimed Edna, and pushing back her chair she got up, and going behind him placed her hand over his mouth. He kissed the soft palm that pressed upon his lips.

"No, no, I won't, Mrs. Pontellier. I didn't know you meant it," looking up at her with caressing eyes. The touch of his lips was like a pleasing sting to her hand. She lifted the garland of roses from his head and flung it across the room.

"Come, Victor; you've posed long enough. Give Mrs. Highcamp her scarf."

Mrs. Highcamp undraped the scarf from about him with her own hands. Miss Mayblunt and Mr. Gouvernail suddenly conceived the notion that it was time to say good night. And Mr. and Mrs. Merriman wondered how it could be so late.

Before parting from Victor, Mrs. Highcamp invited him to call upon her daughter, who she knew would be charmed to meet him and talk French and sing French songs with him. Victor expressed his desire and intention to call upon Miss Highcamp at the first opportunity which presented itself. He asked if Arobin were going his way. Arobin was not.

The mandolin players had long since stolen away. A profound stillness had fallen upon the broad, beautiful street. The voices of Edna's disbanding guests jarred like a discordant note upon the quiet harmony of the night.

XXXI

"Well?" questioned Arobin, who had remained with Edna after the others had departed.

"Well," she reiterated, and stood up, stretching her arms, and feeling the need to relax her muscles after having been so long seated.

"What next?" he asked.

"The servants are all gone. They left when the musicians did. I have dismissed them. The house has to be closed and locked, and I shall trot around to the pigeon house, and shall send Celestine over in the morning to straighten things up."

He looked around, and began to turn out some of the lights.

"What about upstairs?" he inquired.

"I think it is all right; but there may be a window or two unlatched. We had better look; you might take a candle and see. And bring me my wrap and hat on the foot of the bed in the middle room."

He went up with the light, and Edna began closing doors and windows. She hated to shut in the smoke and the fumes of the wine. Arobin found her cape and hat, which he brought down and helped her to put on.

When everything was secured and the lights put out, they left through the front door, Arobin locking it and taking the key, which he carried for Edna. He helped her down the steps.

"Will you have a spray of jessamine?" he asked, breaking off a few blossoms as he passed.

"No; I don't want anything."

She seemed disheartened, and had nothing to say. She took his arm, which he offered her, holding up the weight of her satin train with the other hand. She looked down, noticing the black line of his leg moving in and out so close to her against the yellow shimmer of her gown. There was the whistle of a railway train somewhere in the distance, and the midnight bells were ringing. They met no one in their short walk.

The "pigeon-house" stood behind a locked gate, and a shallow *parterre* that had been somewhat neglected. There was a small front porch, upon which a long window and the front door opened. The door opened directly into the parlor; there was no side entry. Back in the yard was a room for servants, in which old Celestine had been ensconced.

Edna had left a lamp burning low upon the table. She had succeeded in making the room look habitable and homelike. There were some books on the table and a lounge near at hand. On the floor was a fresh matting, covered with a rug or two, and on the walls hung a few tasteful pictures. But the room was filled with flowers. These were a surprise to her. Arobin had sent them, and had had Celestine distribute them during Edna's absence. Her bedroom was adjoining, and across a small passage were the dining room and kitchen.

Edna seated herself with every appearance of discomfort.

"Are you tired?" he asked.

"Yes, and chilled, and miserable. I feel as if I had been wound up to a certain pitch—too tight—and something inside of me had snapped." She rested her head against the table upon her bare arm.

"You want to rest," he said, "and to be quiet. I'll go; I'll leave you and let you rest."

"Yes," she replied.

He stood up beside her and smoothed her hair with his soft, magnetic hand. His touch conveyed to her a certain physical comfort. She could have fallen quietly asleep there if he had continued to pass his hand over her hair. He brushed the hair upward from the nape of her neck.

"I hope you will feel better and happier in the morning," he said. "You have tried to do too much in the past few days. The dinner was the last straw; you might have dispensed with it."

"Yes," she admitted; "it was stupid."

"No, it was delightful; but it has worn you out." His hand had strayed to her beautiful shoulders, and he could feel the response of her flesh to his touch. He seated himself beside her and kissed her lightly upon the shoulder.

"I thought you were going away," she said, in an uneven voice.

"I am, after I have said good night."

"Good night," she murmured.

He did not answer, except to continue to caress her. He did not say good night until she had become supple to his gentle, seductive entreaties.

XXXII

When Mr. Pontellier learned of his wife's intention to abandon her home and take up her residence elsewhere, he immediately wrote her a letter of unqualified disapproval and remonstrance. She had given reasons which he was unwilling to acknowledge as adequate. He hoped she had not acted upon her rash impulse; and he begged her to consider first, foremost, and above all else, what people would say. He was not dreaming of scandal when he uttered this warning; that was a thing which would never have entered into his mind to consider in connection with his wife's name or his own. He was simply thinking of his financial integrity. It might get noised about that the Pontelliers had met with reverses, and were forced to conduct their *ménage* on a humbler scale than heretofore. It might do incalculable mischief to his business prospects.

But remembering Edna's whimsical turn of mind of late, and foreseeing that she had immediately acted upon her impetuous determination, he grasped the situation with his usual promptness and handled it with his well-known business tact and cleverness.

The same mail which brought to Edna his letter of disapproval carried instructions—the most minute instructions—to a well-known architect concerning the remodeling of his home, changes which he had long contemplated, and which he desired carried forward during his temporary absence.

Expert and reliable packers and movers were engaged to convey the furniture, carpets, pictures—everything movable, in short—to places of security. And in an incredibly short time the Pontellier house was turned over to the artisans. There was to be an addition—a small snuggery; there was to be frescoing, and hardwood flooring was to be put into such rooms as had not yet been subjected to this improvement

Furthermore, in one of the daily papers appeared a brief notice to the effect that Mr. and Mrs. Pontellier were contemplating a summer sojourn abroad, and that their handsome residence on Esplanade Street was undergoing sumptuous alterations, and would not be ready for occupancy until their return. Mr. Pontellier had saved appearances!

Edna admired the skill of his maneuver, and avoided any occasion to balk his intentions. When the situation as set forth by Mr. Pontellier was accepted and taken for granted, she was apparently satisfied that it should be so.

The pigeon-house pleased her. It at once assumed the intimate character of a home, while she herself invested it with a charm which it reflected like a warm glow. There was with her a feeling of having descended in the social scale, with a corresponding sense of having risen in the spiritual. Every step which she took toward relieving herself from obligations added to her strength and expansion as an individual. She began to look with her own eyes; to see and to apprehend the deeper undercurrents of life. No longer was she content to "feed upon opinion" when her own soul had invited her.

After a little while, a few days, in fact, Edna went up and spent a week with her children in Iberville. They were delicious February days, with all the summer's promise hovering in the air.

How glad she was to see the children! She wept for very pleasure when she felt their little arms clasping her; their hard, ruddy cheeks pressed against her own glowing cheeks. She looked into their faces with hungry eyes that could not be satisfied with looking. And what stories they had to tell their mother! About the pigs, the cows, the mules! About riding to the mill behind Gluglu, fishing back in the lake with their Uncle Jasper, picking pecans with Lidie's little black brood, and hauling chips in their express wagon. It was a thousand times more fun to haul real chips for old lame Susie's real fire than to drag painted blocks along the banquette on Esplanade Street!

She went with them herself to see the pigs and the cows, to look at the darkies laying the cane, *to thrash the pecan trees,* and catch fish in the back lake. She lived with them a whole week long, giving them all of herself, and gathering and filling herself with their young existence. They listened, breathless, when she told them the house in Esplanade Street was crowded with workmen, hammering, nailing, sawing, and filling the place with clatter. They wanted to know where their bed was, what had been done with their rocking horse; and where did Joe sleep, and where had Ellen gone, and the cook? But, above all, they were fired with a desire to see the little house around the block. Was there any place to play? Were there any boys next door? Raoul, with pessimistic foreboding, was convinced that there were only girls next door. Where would they sleep, and where would papa sleep? She told them the fairies would fix it all right.

The old Madame was charmed with Edna's visit, and showered all manner of delicate attentions upon her. She was delighted to know that the Esplanade Street house was in a dismantled condition. It gave her the promise and pretext to keep the children indefinitely.

It was with a wrench and a pang that Edna left her children. She carried away with her the sound of their voices and the touch of their cheeks. All along the journey homeward their presence lingered with her like the memory of a delicious song. But by the time she had regained the city the song no longer echoed in her soul. She was again alone.

XXXIII

It happened sometimes when Edna went to see Mademoiselle Reisz that the little musician was absent, giving a lesson or making some small necessary household purchase. The key was always left in a secret hiding place in the entry, which Edna knew. If Mademoiselle happened to be away, Edna would usually enter and wait for her return.

When she knocked at Mademoiselle Reisz's door one afternoon there was no response; so unlocking the door, as usual, she entered and found the apartment deserted, as she had expected.

Her day had been quite filled up, and it was for a rest, for a refuge, and to talk about Robert, that she sought out her friend.

She had worked at her canvas—a young Italian character study—all the morning, completing the work without the model, but there had been many interruptions, some incident to her modest housekeeping, and others of a social nature.

Madame Ratignolle had dragged herself over, avoiding the too public thoroughfares, she said. She complained that Edna had neglected her much of late. Besides, she was consumed with curiosity to see the little house and the manner in which it was conducted. She wanted to hear all about the dinner party; Monsieur Ratignolle had left *so* early. What had happened after he left? The champagne and grapes which Edna sent over were *too* delicious. She had so little appetite; they had refreshed and toned her stomach. Where on earth was she going to put Mr. Pontellier in that little house, and the boys? And then she made Edna promise to go to her when her hour of trial overtook her.

"At any time—any time of the day or night, dear," Edna assured her.

Before leaving Madame Ratignolle said:

"In some way you seem to me like a child, Edna. You seem to act without a certain amount of reflection which is necessary in this life. That is the reason I want to say you mustn't mind if I advise you to be a little careful while you are living here alone. Why don't you have someone come and stay with you? Wouldn't Mademoiselle Reisz come?"

"No; she wouldn't wish to come, and I shouldn't want her always with me."

"Well, the reason—you know how evil-minded the world is—someone was talking of Alcée Arobin visiting you. Of course, it wouldn't matter if Mr. Arobin had not such a dreadful reputation. Monsieur Ratignolle was telling me that his attentions alone are considered enough to ruin a woman's name."

"Does he boast of his successes?" asked Edna, indifferently, squinting at her picture.

"No, I think not. I believe he is a decent fellow as far as that goes. But his character is so well known among the men. I shan't be able to come back and see you; it was very, very imprudent today."

"Mind the step!" cried Edna.

"Don't neglect me," entreated Madame Ratignolle; "and don't mind what I said about Arobin, or having someone to stay with you."

"Of course not," Edna laughed. "You may say anything you like to me." They kissed each other good-by. Madame Ratignolle had not far to go, and Edna stood on the porch a while watching her walk down the street.

Then in the afternoon Mrs. Merriman and Mrs. Highcamp had made their "party call." Edna felt that they might have dispensed with the formality. They had also come to invite her to play *vingt-et-un* one evening at Mrs. Merriman's. She was asked to go early, to dinner, and Mr. Merriman or Mr. Arobin would take her home. Edna accepted in a half-hearted way. She sometimes felt very tired of Mrs. Highcamp and Mrs. Merriman.

Late in the afternoon she sought refuge with Mademoiselle Reisz, and stayed there alone, waiting for her, feeling a kind of repose invade her with the very atmosphere of the shabby, unpretentious little room.

Edna sat at the window, which looked out over the housetops and across the river. The window frame was filled with pots of flowers, and she sat and picked the dry leaves from a rose geranium. The day was warm, and the breeze which blew from the river was very pleasant. She removed her hat and laid it on the piano. She went on picking the leaves and digging around the plants with her hat pin. Once she thought she heard Mademoiselle Reisz approaching. But it was a young black girl, who came in, bringing a small bundle of laundry which she deposited in the adjoining room, and went away.

Edna seated herself at the piano, and softly picked out with one hand the bars of a piece of music which lay open before her. A half hour went by. There was the occasional sound of people going and coming in the lower hall. She was growing interested in her occupation of picking out the aria, when there was a second rap at the door. She vaguely wondered what these people did when they found Mademoiselle's door locked.

"Come in," she called, turning her face toward the door. And this time it was Robert Lebrun who presented himself. She attempted to rise; she could not have done so without betraying the agitation which mastered her at sight of him, so she fell back upon the stool, only exclaiming, "Why, Robert!"

He came and clasped her hand, seemingly without knowing what he was saying or doing.

"Mrs. Pontellier! How do you happen—oh! how well you look! Is Mademoiselle Reisz not here? I never expected to see you."

"When did you come back?" asked Edna in an unsteady voice, wiping her face with her handkerchief. She seemed ill at ease on the piano stool, and he begged her to take the chair by the window. She did so, mechanically, while he seated himself on the stool.

"I returned day before yesterday," he answered, while he leaned his arm on the keys, bringing forth a crash of discordant sound.

"Day before yesterday!" she repeated, aloud; and went on thinking to herself, "day before yesterday," in a sort of an uncomprehending way. She had pictured him seeking her at the very first hour, and he had lived under the same sky since day before yesterday, while only by accident had he stumbled upon her. Mademoiselle must have lied when she said, "Poor fool, he loves you."

"Day before yesterday," she repeated, breaking off a spray of Mademoiselle's geranium; "then if you had not met me here today you wouldn't—when—that is, didn't you mean to come and see me?"

"Of course, I should have gone to see you. There have been so many things—" he turned the leaves of Mademoiselle's music nervously. "I started in at once yesterday with the old firm. After all there is as much chance for me here as there was there—that is, I might find it profitable some day. The Mexicans were not very congenial."

So he had come back because the Mexicans were not congenial; because business was as profitable here as there; because of any reason, and not because he cared to be near her. She remembered the day she sat on the floor, turning the pages of his letter, seeking the reason which was left untold.

She had not noticed how he looked—only feeling his presence; but she turned deliberately and observed him. After all, he had been absent but a few months, and was not changed. His hair—the color of hers—waved back from his temples in the same way as before. His skin was not more burned than it had been at Grand Isle. She found in his eyes, when he looked at her for one silent moment, the same tender caress, with an added warmth and entreaty which had not been there before—the same glance which had penetrated to the sleeping places of her soul and awakened them.

A hundred times Edna had pictured Robert's return, and imagined their first meeting. It was usually at her home, whither he had sought her out at once. She always fancied him expressing or betraying in some way his love for her. And here, the reality was that they sat ten feet apart, she at the window, crushing geranium leaves in her hand and smelling them, he twirling around on the piano stool, saying:

"I was very much surprised to hear of Mr. Pontellier's absence; it's a wonder Mademoiselle Reisz did not tell me; and your moving—mother told me yesterday. I should think you would have gone to New York with him, or to Iberville with the children, rather than be bothered here with housekeeping. And you are going abroad, too, I hear. We shan't have you at Grand Isle next summer; it won't seem—do you see much of Mademoiselle Reisz? She often spoke of you in the few letters she wrote."

"Do you remember that you promised to write to me when you went away?" A flush overspread his whole face.

"I couldn't believe that my letters would be of any interest to you."

"That is an excuse; it isn't the truth." Edna reached for her hat on the piano. She adjusted it, sticking the hat pin through the heavy coil of hair with some deliberation.

"Are you not going to wait for Mademoiselle Reisz?" asked Robert.

"No; I have found when she is absent this long, she is liable not to come back till late." She drew on her gloves, and Robert picked up his hat.

"Won't you wait for her?" asked Edna.

"Not if you think she will not be back till late," adding, as if suddenly aware of some discourtesy in his speech, "and I should miss the pleasure of walking home with you." Edna locked the door and put the key back in its hiding place.

They went together, picking their way across muddy streets and sidewalks encumbered with the cheap display of small tradesmen. Part of the distance they rode in the car, and after disembarking, passed the Pontellier mansion, which looked broken and half torn asunder. Robert had never known the house, and looked at it with interest.

"I never knew you in your former home," he remarked.

"I am glad you did not."

"Why?" She did not answer. They went on around the corner, and it seemed as if her dreams were coming true after all, when he followed her into the little house.

"You must stay and dine with me, Robert. You see I am all alone, and it is so long since I have seen you. There is so much I want to ask you."

She took off her hat and gloves. He stood irresolute, making some excuse about his mother who expected him; he even muttered something about an engagement. She struck a match and lit the lamp on the table; it was growing dusk. When he saw her face in the lamp-light, looking pained, with all the soft lines gone out of it, he threw his hat aside and seated himself.

"Oh! you know I want to stay if you will let me!" he exclaimed. All the softness came back. She laughed, and went and put her hand on his shoulder.

"This is the first moment you have seemed like the old Robert. I'll go tell Celestine." She hurried away to tell Celestine to set an extra place. She even sent her off in search of some added delicacy which she had not thought of for herself. And she recommended great care in dripping the coffee and having the omelet done to a proper turn.

When she reentered, Robert was turning over magazines, sketches, and things that lay upon the table in great disorder. He picked up a photograph, and exclaimed:

"Alcée Arobin! What on earth is his picture doing here?"

"I tried to make a sketch of his head one day," answered Edna, "and he thought the photograph might help me. It was at the other house. I thought it had been left there. I must have packed it up with my drawing materials."

"I should think you would give it back to him if you have finished with it."

"Oh! I have a great many such photographs. I never think of returning them. They don't amount to anything." Robert kept on looking at the picture.

"It seems to me—do you think his head worth drawing? Is he a friend of Mr. Pontellier's? You never said you knew him."

"He isn't a friend of Mr. Pontellier's; he's a friend of mine. I always knew him—that is, it is only of late that I know him pretty well. But I'd rather talk about you, and know what you have been seeing and doing and feeling out there in Mexico." Robert threw aside the picture.

"I've been seeing the waves and the white beach of Grand Isle, the quiet, grassy street of the *Chênière,* the old fort at Grande Terre. I've been working like a machine, and feeling like a lost soul. There was nothing interesting."

She leaned her head upon her hand to shade her eyes from the light.

"And what have you been seeing and doing and feeling all these days?" he asked,

"I've been seeing the waves and the white beach of Grand Isle, the quiet, grassy street of the *Chênière Caminada,* the old sunny fort at Grande Terre. I've been working with a little more comprehension than a machine, and still feeling like a lost soul. There was nothing interesting."

"Mrs. Pontellier, you are cruel," he said, with feeling, closing his eyes and resting his head back in his chair. They remained in silence till old Celestine announced dinner.

XXXIV

The dining room was very small. Edna's round mahogany would have almost filled it. As it was there was but a step or two from the little table to the kitchen, to the mantel, the small buffet, and the side door that opened out on the narrow brick-paved yard.

A certain degree of ceremony settled upon them with the announcement of dinner. There was no return to personalities. Robert related incidents of his sojourn in Mexico, and Edna talked of events likely to interest him, which had occurred during his absence. The dinner was of ordinary quality, except for the few delicacies which she had sent out to purchase. Old Celestine, with a bandana *tignon* twisted about her head, hobbled in and out, taking personal interest in everything; and she lingered occasionally to talk patois with Robert, whom she had known as a boy.

He went out to a neighboring cigar stand to purchase cigarette papers, and when he came back he found that Celestine had served the black coffee in the parlor.

"Perhaps I shouldn't have come back," he said. "When you are tired of me, tell me to go."

"You never tire me. You must have forgotten the hours and hours at Grand Isle in which we grew accustomed to each other and used to being together."

"I have forgotten nothing at Grand Isle," he said, not looking at her, but rolling a cigarette. His tobacco pouch, which he laid upon the table, was a fantastic embroidered silk affair, evidently the handiwork of a woman.

"You used to carry your tobacco in a rubber pouch," said Edna, picking up the pouch and examining the needlework.

"Yes; it was lost."

"Where did you buy this one? In Mexico?"

"It was given to me by a Vera Cruz girl; they are very generous," he replied, striking a match and lighting his cigarette.

"They are very handsome, I suppose, those Mexican women; very picturesque, with their black eyes and their lace scarfs."

"Some are; others are hideous. Just as you find women everywhere."

"What was she like—the one who gave you the pouch? You must have known her very well."

"She was very ordinary. She wasn't of the slightest importance. I knew her well enough."

"Did you visit at her house? Was it interesting? I should like to know and hear about the people you met, and the impressions they made on you."

"There are some people who leave impressions not so lasting as the imprint of an oar upon the water."

"Was she such a one?"

"It would be ungenerous for me to admit that she was of that order and kind." He thrust the pouch back in his pocket, as if to put away the subject with the trifle which had brought it up.

Arobin dropped in with a message from Mrs. Merriman, to say that the card party was postponed on account of the illness of one of her children.

"How do you do, Arobin?" said Robert, rising from the obscurity.

"Oh! Lebrun. To be sure! I heard yesterday you were back. How did they treat you down in Mexique?"

"Fairly well."

"But not well enough to keep you there. Stunning girls, though, in Mexico. I thought I should never get away from Vera Cruz when I was down there a couple of years ago."

"Did they embroider slippers and tobacco pouches and hatbands and things for you?" asked Edna.

"Oh! my! no! I didn't get so deep in their regard. I fear they made more impression on me than I made on them."

"You were less fortunate than Robert, then."

"I am always less fortunate than Robert. Has he been imparting tender confidences?"

"I've been imposing myself long enough," said Robert, rising, and shaking hands with Edna. "Please convey my regards to Mr. Pontellier when you write."

He shook hands with Arobin and went away.

"Fine fellow, that Lebrun," said Arobin when Robert had gone. "I never heard you speak of him."

"I knew him last summer at Grand Isle," she replied. "Here is that photograph of yours. Don't you want it?"

"What do I want with it? Throw it away." She threw it back on the table.

"I'm not going to Mrs. Merriman's," she said. "If you see her, tell her so. But perhaps I had better write. I think I shall write now, and say that I am sorry her child is sick, and tell her not to count on me."

"It would be a good scheme," acquiesced Arobin. "I don't blame you; stupid lot!"

Edna opened the blotter, and having procured paper and pen, began to write the note. Arobin lit a cigar and read the evening paper, which he had in his pocket.

"What is the date?" she asked. He told her.

"Will you mail this for me when you go out?"

"Certainly." He read to her little bits out of the newspaper, while she straightened things on the table.

"What do you want to do?" he asked, throwing aside the paper. "Do you want to go out for a walk or a drive or anything? It would be a fine night to drive."

"No; I don't want to do anything but just be quiet. You go away and amuse yourself. Don't stay."

"I'll go away if I must; but I shan't amuse myself. You know that I only live when I am near you."

He stood up to bid her good night.

"Is that one of the things you always say to women?"

"I have said it before, but I don't think I ever came so near meaning it," he answered with a smile. There were no warm lights in her eyes; only a dreamy, absent look.

"Good night. I adore you. Sleep well," he said, and he kissed her hand and went away.

She stayed alone in a kind of reverie—a sort of stupor. Step by step she lived over every instant of the time she had been with Robert after he had entered Mademoiselle Reisz's door. She recalled his words, his looks. How few and meager they had been for her hungry heart! A vision—a transcendently seductive vision of a Mexican girl arose before her. She writhed with a jealous pang. She wondered when he would come back. He had not said he would come back. She had been with him, had heard his voice and touched his hand. But some way he had seemed nearer to her off there in Mexico.

XXXV

The morning was full of sunlight and hope. Edna could see before her no denial—only the promise of excessive joy. She lay in bed awake, with bright eyes full of speculation. "He loves you, poor fool." If she could but get that conviction firmly fixed in her mind, what mattered about the rest? She felt she had been childish and unwise the night before in giving herself over to despondency. She recapitulated the motives which no doubt explained Robert's reserve. They were not insurmountable; they would not hold if he really loved her; they could not hold against her own passion, which he must come to realize in time. She pictured him going to his business that morning. She even saw how he was dressed, how he walked down one street, and turned the corner of another, saw him bending over his desk, talking to people who entered the office, going to his lunch, and perhaps watching for her on the street. He would come to her in the afternoon or evening, sit and roll his cigarette, talk a little, and go away as he had done the night before.

But how delicious it would be to have him there with her! She would have no regrets, nor seek to penetrate his reserve if he still chose to wear it

Edna ate her breakfast only half dressed. The maid brought her a delicious printed scrawl from Raoul, expressing his love, asking her to send him some bonbons, and telling her they had found that morning ten tiny white pigs all lying in a row beside Lidie's big white pig,

A letter also came from her husband, saying he hoped to be back early in March, and then they would get ready for that journey abroad which he had promised her so long, which he felt now fully able to afford; he felt able to travel as people should, without any thought of small economies—thanks to his recent speculations in Wall Street.

Much to her surprise she received a note from Arobin, written at midnight from the club. It was to say good morning to her, to hope that she had slept well, to assure her of his devotion, which he trusted she in some faintest manner returned.

All these letters were pleasing to her. She answered the children in a cheerful frame of mind, promising them bonbons, and congratulating them upon their happy find of the little pigs.

She answered her husband with friendly evasiveness,—not with any fixed design to mislead him, only because all sense of reality had gone out of her life; she had abandoned herself to Fate, and awaited the consequences with indifference.

To Arobin's note she made no reply. She put it under Celestine's stove lid.

Edna worked several hours with much spirit. She saw no one but a picture dealer, who asked her if it were true that she was going abroad to study in Paris.

She said possibly she might, and he negotiated with her for some Parisian studies to reach him in time for the holiday trade in December.

Robert did not come that day. She was keenly disappointed. He did not come the following day, nor the next. Each morning she awoke with hope, and each night she was a prey to despondency. She was tempted to seek him out. But far from yielding to the impulse, she avoided any occasion which might throw her in his way. She did not go to Mademoiselle Reisz's nor pass by Madame Lebrun's, as she might have done if he had still been in Mexico.

When Arobin, one night, urged her to drive with him, she went—out to the lake, on the Shell Road. His horses were full of mettle, and even a little unmanageable. She liked the rapid gait at which they spun along, and the quick, sharp sound of the horses' hoofs on the hard road. They did not stop anywhere to eat or to drink. Arobin was not needlessly imprudent. But they ate and they drank when they regained Edna's little dining room—which was comparatively early in the evening.

It was late when he left her. It was getting to be more than a passing whim with Arobin to see her and be with her. He had detected the latent sensuality, which unfolded under his delicate sense of her nature's requirements like a torpid, torrid, sensitive blossom.

There was no despondency when she fell asleep that night, nor was there hope when she awoke in the morning.

XXXVI

There was a garden out in the suburbs, a small, leafy corner, with a few green tables under the orange trees. An old cat slept all day on the stone step in the sun, and an old *mulatresse* slept her idle hours away in her chair at the open window, till someone happened to knock on one of the green tables. She had milk and cream cheese to sell, and bread and butter. There was no one who could make such excellent coffee or fry a chicken so golden brown as she.

The place was too modest to attract the attention of people of fashion, and so quiet as to have escaped the notice of those in search of pleasure and dissipation. Edna had discovered it accidentally one day when the high board gate stood ajar. She caught sight of a little green table, blotched with the checkered sunlight that filtered through the quivering leaves overhead. Within she had found the slumbering *mulatresse,* the drowsy cat, and a glass of milk which reminded her of the milk she had tasted in Iberville.

She often stopped there during her perambulations; sometimes taking a book with her, and sitting an hour or two under the trees when she found the place deserted. Once or twice she took a quiet dinner there alone, having instructed Celestine beforehand to prepare no dinner at home. It was the last place in the city where she would have expected to meet any one she knew.

Still she was not astonished when, as she was partaking of a modest dinner late in the afternoon, looking into an open book, stroking the cat, which had made friends with her—she was not greatly astonished to see Robert come in at the tall garden gate.

"I am destined to see you only by accident," she said, shoving the cat off the chair beside her. He was surprised, ill at ease, almost embarrassed at meeting her thus so unexpectedly.

"Do you come here often?" he asked.

"I almost live here," she said.

"I used to drop in very often for a cup of Catiche's good coffee. This is the first time since I came back."

"She'll bring you a plate, and you will share my dinner. There's always enough for two—even three." Edna had intended to be indifferent and as reserved as he when she met him; she had reached the determination by a laborious train of reasoning, incident to one of her despondent moods. But her resolve melted when she saw him before her, seated there beside her in the little garden, as if a designing Providence had led him into her path.

"Why have you kept away from me, Robert?" she asked, closing the book that lay open upon the table.

"Why are you so personal, Mrs. Pontellier? Why do you force me to idiotic subterfuges?" he exclaimed with sudden warmth. "I suppose there's no use telling you I've been very busy, or that I've been sick, or that I've been to see you and not found you at home. Please let me off with any one of these excuses."

"You are the embodiment of selfishness," she said. "You save yourself something—I don't know what—but there is some selfish motive, and in sparing yourself you never consider for a moment what I think, or how I feel your neglect and indifference. I suppose this is what you would call unwomanly; but I have got into a habit of expressing myself. It doesn't matter to me, and you may think me unwomanly if you like."

"No; I only think you cruel, as I said the other day. Maybe not intentionally cruel; but you seem to be forcing me into disclosures which can result in nothing; as if you would have me bare a wound for the pleasure of looking at it, without the intention or power of healing it."

"I'm spoiling your dinner, Robert; never mind what I say. You haven't eaten a morsel."

"I only came in for a cup of coffee." His sensitive face was all disfigured with excitement.

"Isn't this a delightful place?" she remarked. "I am so glad it has never actually been discovered. It is so quiet, so sweet, here. Do you notice there is scarcely a sound to be heard? It's so out of the way; and a good walk from the car. However, I don't mind walking. I always feel so sorry for women who don't like to walk; they miss so much—so many rare little glimpses of life; and we women learn so little of life on the whole."

"Catiche's coffee is always hot. I don't know how she manages it, here in the open air. Celestine's coffee gets cold bringing it from the kitchen to the dining room. Three lumps! How can you drink it so sweet? Take some of the cress with your chop; it's so biting and crisp. Then there's the advantage of being able to smoke with your coffee out here. Now, in the city—aren't you going to smoke?"

"After a while," he said, laying a cigar on the table.

"Who gave it to you?" she laughed.

"I bought it. I suppose I'm getting reckless; I bought a whole box." She was determined not to be personal again and make him uncomfortable.

The cat made friends with him, and climbed into his lap when he smoked his cigar. He stroked her silky fur, and talked a little about her. He looked at Edna's book, which he had read; and he told her the end, to save her the trouble of wading through it, he said.

Again he accompanied her back to her home; and it was after dusk when they reached the little "pigeon-house." She did not ask him to remain, which he was grateful for, as it permitted him to stay without the discomfort of blundering through an excuse which he had no intention of considering. He helped her to light the lamp; then she went into her room to take off her hat and to bathe her face and hands.

When she came back Robert was not examining the pictures and magazines as before; he sat off in the shadow, leaning his head back on the chair as if in a reverie. Edna lingered a moment beside the table, arranging the books there. Then she went across the room to where he sat. She bent over the arm of his chair and called his name.

"Robert," she said, "are you asleep?"

"No," he answered, looking up at her.

She leaned over and kissed him—a soft, cool, delicate kiss, whose voluptuous sting penetrated his whole being—then she moved away from him. He followed, and took her in his arms, just holding her close to him. She put her hand up to his face and pressed his cheek against her own. The action was full of love and tenderness. He sought her lips again. Then he drew her down upon the sofa beside him and held her hand in both of his.

"Now you know," he said, "now you know what I have been fighting against since last summer at Grand Isle, what drove me away and drove me back again."

"Why have you been fighting against it?" she asked. Her face glowed with soft lights.

"Why? Because you were not free; you were Léonce Pontellier's wife. I couldn't help loving you if you were ten times his wife, but so long as I went away from you and kept away I could help telling you so." She put her free hand up to his shoulder, and then against his cheek, rubbing it softly. He kissed her again. His face was warm and flushed.

"There in Mexico I was thinking of you all the time, and longing for you."

"But not writing to me," she interrupted.

"Something put into my head that you cared for me, and I lost my senses. I forgot everything but a wild dream of your some way becoming my wife."

"Your wife!"

"Religion, loyalty, everything would give way if only you cared."

"Then you must have forgotten that I was Léonce Pontellier's wife."

"Oh! I was demented, dreaming of wild, impossible things, recalling men who had set their wives free, we have heard of such things."

"Yes, we have heard of such things."

"I came back full of vague, mad intentions. And when I got here—"

"When you got here you never came near me!" She was still caressing his cheek.

"I realized what a cur I was to dream of such a thing, even if you had been willing."

She took his face between her hands and looked into it as if she would never withdraw her eyes more. She kissed him on the forehead, the eyes, the cheeks, and the lips.

"You have been a very, very foolish boy, wasting your time dreaming of impossible things when you speak of Mr. Pontellier setting me free! I am no longer one of Mr. Pontellier's possessions to dispose of or not. I give myself where I choose. If he were to say, 'Here, Robert, take her and be happy, she is yours,' I should laugh at you both."

His face grew a little white. "What do you mean?" he asked.

There was a knock at the door. Old Celestine came in to say that Madame Ratignolle's servant had come around the back way with a message that Madame had been taken sick and begged Mrs. Pontellier to go to her immediately.

"Yes, yes," said Edna, rising; "I promised. Tell her yes—to wait for me. I'll go back with her."

"Let me walk over with you," offered Robert.

"No," she said; "I will go with the servant." She went into her room to put on her hat, and when she came in again she sat once more upon the sofa beside him. He had not stirred. She put her arms about his neck.

"Good-by, my sweet Robert. Tell me good-by." He kissed her with a degree of passion which had not before entered into his caress, and strained her to him.

"I love you," she whispered, "only you, no one but you. It was you who awoke me last summer out of a life-long stupid dream. Oh! you have made me so unhappy with your indifference. Oh! I have suffered, suffered! Now you are here we shall love each other, my Robert. We shall be everything to each other. Nothing else in the world is of any consequence. I must go to my friend; but you will wait for me? No matter how late; you will wait for me, Robert?"

"Don't go, don't go! Oh! Edna, stay with me," he pleaded. "Why should you go? Stay with me, stay with me."

"I shall come back as soon as I can; I shall find you here." She buried her face in his neck, and said good-by again. Her seductive voice, together with his great love for her, had enthralled his senses, had deprived him of every impulse but the longing to hold her and keep her.

XXXVII

Edna looked in at the drug store. Monsieur Ratignolle was putting up a mixture himself, very carefully, dropping a red liquid into a tiny glass. He was grateful to Edna for having come, her presence would be a comfort to his wife. Madame Ratignolle's sister, who had always been with her at such trying times, had not been able to come up from the plantation, and Adèle had been inconsolable until Mrs. Pontellier so kindly promised to come to her. The nurse had been with them at night for the past week, as she lived a great distance away. And Dr. Mandelet had been coming and going all the afternoon. They were then looking for him any moment.

Edna hastened upstairs by a private stairway that led from the rear of the store to the apartments above. The children were all sleeping in a back room. Madame Ratignolle was in the salon, whither she had strayed in her suffering impatience. She sat on the sofa, clad in an ample white *peignoir,* holding a handkerchief tight in her hand with a nervous clutch. Her face was drawn and pinched, her sweet blue eyes haggard and unnatural. All her beautiful hair had been drawn back and plaited. It lay in a long braid on the sofa pillow, coiled like a golden serpent. The nurse, a comfortable looking *Griffe* woman in white apron and cap, was urging her to return to her bedroom.

"There is no use, there is no use," she said at once to Edna. "We must get rid of Mandelet; he is getting too old and careless. He said he would be here at half-past seven; now it must be eight. See what time it is, Josephine."

The woman was possessed of a cheerful nature, and refused to take any situation too seriously, especially a situation with which she was so familiar. She urged Madame to have courage and patience. But Madame only set her teeth hard into her under lip, and Edna saw the sweat gather in beads on her white forehead. After a moment or two she uttered a profound sigh and wiped her face with the handkerchief rolled in a ball. She appeared exhausted. The nurse gave her a fresh handkerchief, sprinkled with cologne water.

"This is too much!" she cried. "Mandelet ought to be killed! Where is Alphonse? Is it possible I am to be abandoned like this—neglected by everyone?"

"Neglected, indeed!" exclaimed the nurse. Wasn't she there? And here was Mrs. Pontellier leaving, no doubt, a pleasant evening at home to devote to her? And wasn't Monsieur Ratignolle coming that very instant through the hall? And Josephine was quite sure she had heard Doctor Mandelet's coupé. Yes, there it was, down at the door.

Adèle consented to go back to her room. She sat on the edge of a little low couch next to her bed.

Doctor Mandelet paid no attention to Madame Ratignolle's upbraidings. He was accustomed to them at such times, and was too well convinced of her loyalty to doubt it.

He was glad to see Edna, and wanted her to go with him into the salon and entertain him. But Madame Ratignolle would not consent that Edna should leave her for an instant. Between agonizing moments, she chatted a little, and said it took her mind off her sufferings.

Edna began to feel uneasy. She was seized with a vague dread. Her own like experiences seemed far away, unreal, and only half remembered. She recalled faintly an ecstasy of pain, the heavy odor of chloroform, a stupor which had deadened sensation, and an awakening to find a little new life to which she had given being, added to the great unnumbered multitude of souls that come and go.

She began to wish she had not come; her presence was not necessary. She might have invented a pretext for staying away; she might even invent a pretext now for going. But Edna did not go. With an inward agony, with a flaming, outspoken revolt against the ways of Nature, she witnessed the scene torture.

She was still stunned and speechless with emotion when later she leaned over her friend to kiss her and softly say good-by. Adèle, pressing her cheek, whispered in an exhausted voice: "Think of the children, Edna. Oh think of the children! Remember them!"

XXXVIII

Edna still felt dazed when she got outside in the open air. The Doctor's coupé had returned for him and stood before the *porte cochère*. She did not wish to enter the coupé, and told Doctor Mandelet she would walk; she was not afraid, and would go alone. He directed his carriage to meet him at Mrs. Pontellier's, and he started to walk home with her.

Up—away up, over the narrow street between the tall houses, the stars were blazing. The air was mild and caressing, but cool with the breath of spring and the night. They walked slowly, the Doctor with a heavy, measured tread and his hands behind him; Edna, in an absent-minded way, as she had walked one night at Grand Isle, as if her thoughts had gone ahead of her and she was striving to overtake them.

"You shouldn't have been there, Mrs. Pontellier," he said. "That was no place for you. Adèle is full of whims at such times. There were a dozen women she might have had with her, unimpressionable women. I felt that it was cruel, cruel. You shouldn't have gone."

"Oh, well!" she answered, indifferently. "I don't know that it matters after all. One has to think of the children some time or other, the sooner the better."

"When is Léonce coming back?"

"Quite soon. Some time in March."

"And you are going abroad?"

"Perhaps—no, I am not going. I'm not going to be forced into doing things. I don't want to go abroad. I want to be let alone. Nobody has any right—except children, perhaps—and even then, it seems to me—or it did seem—" She felt that her speech was voicing the incoherency of her thoughts, and stopped abruptly.

"The trouble is," sighed the Doctor, grasping her meaning intuitively, "that youth is given up to illusions. It seems to be a provision of Nature, a decoy to secure mothers for the race. And Nature takes no account of moral consequences, of arbitrary conditions which we create, and which we feel obliged to maintain at any cost."

"Yes," she said. "The years that are gone seem like dreams—if one might go on sleeping and dreaming—but to wake up and find—oh! well! perhaps it is better to wake up after all, even to suffer, rather than to remain a dupe to illusions all one's life."

"It seems to me, my dear child," said the Doctor at parting, holding her hand, "you seem to me to be in trouble. I am not going to ask for your confidence. I will only say that if ever you feel moved to give it to me, perhaps I might help you. I know I would understand, and I tell you there are not many who would—not many, my dear."

"Some way I don't feel moved to speak of things that trouble me. Don't think I am ungrateful or that I don't appreciate your sympathy. There are periods of despondency and suffering which take possession of me. But I don't want anything but my own way. That is wanting a good deal, of course, when you have to trample upon the lives, the hearts, the prejudices of others—but no matter—still, I shouldn't want to trample upon the little lives. Oh! I don't know what I'm saying, Doctor. Good night. Don't blame me for anything."

"Yes, I will blame you if you don't come and see me soon. We will talk of things you never have dreamt of talking about before. It will do us both good. I don't want you to blame yourself, whatever comes. Good night, my child."

She let herself in at the gate, but instead of entering she sat upon the step of the porch. The night was quiet and soothing. All the tearing emotion of the last few hours seemed to fall away from her like a somber, uncomfortable garment, which she had but to loosen to be rid of. She went back to that hour before Adèle had sent for her; and her senses kindled afresh in thinking of Robert's words, the pressure of his arms, and the feeling of his lips upon her own. She could picture at that moment no greater bliss on earth than possession of the beloved one. His expression of love had already given him to her in part. When she thought that he was there at hand, waiting for her, she grew numb with the intoxication of expectancy. It was so late; he would be asleep perhaps. She would awaken him with a kiss. She hoped he would be asleep that she might arouse him with her caresses.

Still, she remembered Adèle's voice whispering, "Think of the children; think of them." She meant to think of them; that determination had driven into her soul like a death wound—but not tonight. Tomorrow would be time to think of everything.

Robert was not waiting for her in the little parlor. He was nowhere at hand. The house was empty. But he had scrawled on a piece of paper that lay in the lamplight:

"I love you. Good-by—because I love you."

Edna grew faint when she read the words. She went and sat on the sofa. Then she stretched herself out there, never uttering a sound. She did not sleep. She did not go to bed. The lamp sputtered and went out She was still awake in the morning, when Celestine unlocked the kitchen door and came in to light the fire.

XXXIX

Victor, with hammer and nails and scraps of scantling, was patching a corner of one of the galleries. Mariequita sat near by, dangling her legs, watching him work, and handing him nails from the tool box. The sun was beating down upon them. The girl had covered her head with her apron folded into a square pad. They had been talking for an hour or more. She was never tired of hearing Victor describe the dinner at Mrs. Pontellier's. He exaggerated every detail, making it appear a veritable Lucillean feast. The flowers were in tubs, he said. The champagne was quaffed from huge golden goblets. Venus rising from the foam could have presented no more entrancing a spectacle than Mrs. Pontellier, blazing with beauty and diamonds at the head of the board, while the other women were all of them youthful houris, possessed of incomparable charms.

She got it into her head that Victor was in love with Mrs. Pontellier, and he gave her evasive answers, framed so as to confirm her belief. She grew sullen and cried a little, threatening to go off and leave him to his fine ladies. There were a dozen men crazy about her at the *Chênière,* and since it was the fashion to be in love with married people, why, she could run away any time she liked to New Orleans with Célina's husband.

Célina's husband was a fool, a coward, and a pig, and to prove it to her, Victor intended to hammer his head into a jelly the next time he encountered him. This assurance was very consoling to Mariequita. She dried her eyes, and grew cheerful at the prospect.

They were still talking of the dinner and the allurements of city life when Mrs. Pontellier herself slipped around the corner of the house. The two youngsters stayed dumb with amazement before what they considered to be an apparition. But it was really she in flesh and blood, looking tired and a little travel-stained.

"I walked up from the wharf," she said, "and heard the hammering. I supposed it was you, mending the porch. It's a good thing. I was always tripping over those loose planks last summer. How dreary and deserted everything looks!"

It took Victor some little time to comprehend that she had come in Beaudelet's lugger, that she had come alone, and for no purpose but to rest.

"There's nothing fixed up yet, you see. I'll give you my room; it's the only place."

"Any corner will do," she assured him.

"And if you can stand Philomel's cooking," he went on, "though I might try to get her mother while you are here. Do you think she would come?" turning to Mariequita.

Mariequita thought that perhaps Philomel's mother might come for a few days, and money enough.

Beholding Mrs. Pontellier make her appearance, the girl had at once suspected a lovers' rendezvous. But Victor's astonishment was so genuine, and Mrs. Pontellier's indifference so apparent, that the disturbing notion did not lodge long in her brain. She contemplated with the greatest interest this woman who gave the most sumptuous dinners in America, and who had all the men in New Orleans at her feet.

"What time will you have dinner?" asked Edna. "I'm very hungry; but don't get anything extra."

"I'll have it ready in little or no time," he said, bustling and packing away his tools. "You may go to my room to brush up and rest yourself. Mariequita will show you."

"Thank you," said Edna. "But, do you know, I have a notion to go down to the beach and take a good wash and even a little swim, before dinner?"

"The water is too cold!" they both exclaimed. "Don't think of it."

"Well, I might go down and try—dip my toes in. Why, it seems to me the sun is hot enough to have warmed the very depths of the ocean. Could you get me a couple of towels? I'd better go right away, so as to be back in time. It would be a little too chilly if I waited till this afternoon."

Mariequita ran over to Victor's room, and returned with some towels, which she gave to Edna.

"I hope you have fish for dinner" said Edna, as she started to walk away, "but don't do anything extra if you haven't."

"Run and find Philomel's mother," Victor instructed the girl. "I'll go to the kitchen and see what I can do. By Giminy! Women have no consideration! She might have sent me word."

Edna walked on down to the beach rather mechanically, not noticing anything special except that the sun was hot. She was not dwelling upon any particular train of thought. She had done all the thinking which was necessary after Robert went away, when she lay awake upon the sofa till morning.

She had said over and over to herself: "Today it is Arobin; tomorrow it will be someone else. It makes no difference to me, it doesn't matter about Léonce Pontellier—but Raoul and Étienne!" She understood now clearly what she had meant long ago when she said to Adèle Ratignolle that she would give up the unessential, but she would never sacrifice herself for her children.

Despondency had come upon her there in the wakeful night, and had never lifted. There was no one thing in the world that she desired. There was no human being whom she wanted near her except Robert; and she even realized that the day would come when he, too, and the thought of him would melt out of her existence, leaving her alone. The children appeared before her like antagonists who had overcome her, who had overpowered and sought to drag her into the soul's slavery for the rest of her days. But she knew a way to elude them. She was not thinking of these things when she walked down to the beach.

The water of the Gulf stretched out before her, gleaming with the million lights of the sun. The voice of the sea is seductive, never ceasing, whispering, clamoring, murmuring, inviting the soul to wander in abysses of solitude. All along the white beach, up and down, there was no living thing in sight. A bird with a broken wing was beating the air above, reeling, fluttering, circling disabled down, down to the water.

Edna had found her old bathing suit still hanging, faded, upon its accustomed peg.

She put it on, leaving her clothing in the bathhouse. But when she was there beside the sea, absolutely alone, she cast the unpleasant, pricking garments from her, and for the first time in her life she stood naked in the open air, at the mercy of the sun, the breeze that beat upon her, and the waves that invited her.

How strange and awful it seemed to stand naked under the sky! how delicious! She felt like some new-born creature, opening its eyes in a familiar world that it had never known.

The foamy wavelets curled up to her white feet, and coiled like serpents about her ankles. She walked out. The water was chill, but she walked on. The water was deep, but she lifted her white body and reached out with a long, sweeping stroke. The touch of the sea is sensuous, enfolding the body in its soft, close embrace.

She went on and on. She remembered the night she swam far out, and recalled the terror that seized her at the fear of being unable to regain the shore. She did not look back now, but went on and on, thinking of the bluegrass meadow that she had traversed when a little child, believing that it had no beginning and no end.

Her arms and legs were growing tired.

She thought of Léonce and the children. They were a part of her life. But they need not have thought that they could possess her, body and soul. How Mademoiselle Reisz would have laughed, perhaps sneered, if she knew! "And you call yourself an artist! What pretensions, Madame! The artist must possess the courageous soul that dares and defies."

Exhaustion was pressing upon and overpowering her.

"Good-by—because, I love you." He did not know; he did not understand. He would never understand. Perhaps Doctor Mandelet would have understood if she had seen him—but it was too late; the shore was far behind her, and her strength was gone.

She looked into the distance, and the old terror flamed up for an instant, then sank again. Edna heard her father's voice and her sister Margaret's. She heard the barking of an old dog that was chained to the sycamore tree. The spurs of the cavalry officer clanged as he walked across the porch. There was the hum of bees, and the musky odor of pinks filled the air.

Notes

1. Get out! Get out! Damn it!
2. Delicacies
3. Get along! Good-by! Out with you!
4. Hoaxer-jokester-great beast, go!
5. But it's not bad. She knows what she's doing, she has ability, hasn't she.
6. Can it be that Madame Ratignolle is jealous?
7. Braggart; a pretentious fellow.
8. Indeed! Literally, My faith!
9. An excitable and willful fellow.
10. If you knew.
11. The conventions.
12. An evening of musical entertainment.
13. Furnished rooms.
14. Informally; as a good friend.
15. Until Thursday.
16. In pain; in labor.
17. The food, the side dishes.
18. Goodnight, my queen; be good.
19. Ah! If you knew what your eyes say to me.

African-American Literature

African-American literature traces its origins to the slave writers of the 1700s. Begun by those who modeled the Western aesthetic, this literature was nourished by slave narratives and folktales, which gave voice and identity to the Black experience in America. In spite of the dualistic legal system which sought to silence that voice during pre-slavery years, African-American literature continued to speak the truth about Blacks' burden in a racist society. The voice grew louder after the Civil War when many Southern Blacks began to migrate North. Simultaneously, educational and job opportunities increased, and Black writers began to glory in the pride of race. Most notable of the post Civil War era are the Harlem Renaissance writers who are responsible for many of the modern Black themes, technical concerns and conflicts in modern African-American literature. When the period ended (around 1929), the works of those writers were ignored (or the writings disappeared altogether). By the end of World War II, Black writers were under pressure to ignore the reality of racial problems in America and instead, were advised to portray in their writing the Western ideals of the United States. Some writers met these demands for portrayals of American ideals, but others stood their ground and continued to offer realistic images of Black life in America. This tension between the presentation of approved American images and American realism remained until the Civil Rights Movement that brought with it an overriding sense of Black pride in African Americans. This pride expressed a radical freedom. Since the civil protests of the sixties, Black writers have built on the legacy of contention, conflict, and crisis—all of which are a continuing part of their life experience in America.

African-American literature is bound together by common themes and historical conflicts that reach back (in some cases) to Africa. These common themes and historical conflicts were first noted by such poets as Lucy Terry, Jupiter Hammon, and Phillis Wheatley and by slave narrative writers like Olaudah Equiano—all of whom created a space for Black writers that would expand and command recognition from critics and readers alike. These early offerings signaled two approaches for future efforts of Black writers: (1) writers like Wheatley and Martin R. Delaney demonstrated an effort to consciously achieve the style of Western aesthetics; (2) folk material, on the other hand, ignored Western models and concerned itself with presenting the raw experience of African-American life in America. Original in diction, metaphor, and imagery, these pieces give a variety of expressions of African-American culture and identity. Wheatley and Hammon, for example, seemed to justify slavery, whereas the oral folktales depict Black experience more honestly. Animal tales, work and prison songs, folk sermons, slave tales, gospel and blues songs, spirituals, "haunt" tales, street cries, and children's songs and games are all a part of the folk literature of early African-American literature. Rich in humor and symbolism, these folk materials have contributed much to the development of Black literature. In fact, the songs, spirituals, gospel and blues contain the earliest expressions of the African-American racial consciousness. Although they expressed the disillusionment and agony of slave life, they emphasized the Black individuals' ability to transcend their pain through determination and spiritual guidance.

However, during the post-slavery years, 1860–1950, the works of African Americans, sensitive to the impact of "Jim Crow Laws," developed primarily along the lines of European aesthetic models. These "Jim Crow" laws encouraged the negative stereotypes of Blacks and made it almost impossible for Black writers to give an honest portrayal of their people. Although they were hampered and many times forced to write within the constraints of this compromise, Charles Chesnutt and Paul Laurence Dunbar made recognizable contributions. Even more than these two, W. E. B. DuBois exposed the hypocrisy of White America and pointed to the value and capabilities of Black individuals. In 1909 he helped form the NAACP and began its influential Black journal, *Crisis.* Similarly, in 1912, Johnson published his compelling novel, *The Autobiography of an Ex-Colored Man,* which depicted the moral struggles of a Black musician who passed for White. This theme of a mulatto's passing as White had long appeared in fiction of White writers, but Johnson gave this theme a different turn; his protagonist, in betraying his blackness and living as a White man, admits to a moral failure.

Shortly after the Civil War, African Americans began their immigration to the North, and by 1915, there were large numbers of Blacks living in the urban areas of the North. Simultaneously, educational opportunities for Blacks increased. Consequently, better job opportunities for Blacks were available, and African Americans began to believe that they could share in the "American Dream." America's participation in World War I opened the door for Black soldiers to defend America, and this fact heightened the sense of pride among people in the Black community. By 1920, Black cultural societies began to flourish; jazz provoked a growing White interest in Black culture and tradition; Black writing gained a wide critical audience; the influx of Black immigrants from Africa and the Caribbean developed new interests in Black origins and heritage. And Harlem emerged as one of the major cultural centers in the U.S. As Black artistry began to thrive under this new interest and freedom, new themes began to appear in Black literature: (a) a pride in "Blackness," both in the more immediate Southern past as well as in more distant African origins; (b) a consideration of the Black experience in an urban, rather than an agrarian setting; and (c) dramatization of the inner lives of African Americans.

Many of the writers of the Harlem Renaissance rejected the former stereotypes of African Americans in favor of realistic portrayals of their people. Chief among such writers were the poets Claude McKay and Countee Cullen, and the writers of fiction, Rudolph Fisher and Eric Walrond. Arguably, the two greatest writers of that era were Langston Hughes and Jean Toomer. These two were accomplished authors in several genres. Hughes' major achievement was his ability to use Black folk tradition in modern literary works; Toomer's strength was his ability to portray the sense of Black heritage and culture through psychological techniques. Many modern Black themes and technical concerns are rooted in what came to be called the Harlem Renaissance. Racial pride, concern with racial origins, emphasis on the problems of the urban African America, the sense of Black militancy—all stem, to some degree, from this period in Black literature.

The stock market crash in 1929 signaled the end of the Harlem Renaissance, and many of the Black writers and their works disappeared. They were ignored by the dominant society; thus began the growth of realism and naturalism. The Writer's Project of the WPA offered an opportunity for some Black writers. And they seized the chance to examine with realism racial prejudice, the Black struggle for racial and economic equality, the dual legal codes, and the frustrations and degradations suffered by African Americans. This period of 1930 to 1945 created a disenchantment with the capitalistic system and fostered a growing interest in socialism and communism. Black writers stressed the effects of environment and culture in determining the growth and development of the individual. Among these writers were Sterling Brown, Arna Bontemps, Zora Neale Hurston, and Langston Hughes (who continued the work he had begun during the twenties). Undoubtedly the most dominant voice of Black protest arose during the thirties, Richard Wright. He continues to be one of the major influences in Black literature. During the early forties, several new Black writers followed Wright in his brutal dramatization of Black anguish and frustration. Chester Himes was one of the writers who was greatly influenced by Wright. Focusing mostly on the plight of urban Blacks as deprived, rootless, isolated individuals, the works of that period rejected the lyricism of the Harlem Renaissance in favor of the voice of protest.

By the end of World War II, this emphasis on realism had begun to wane. America's emergence as a world leader made it essential that she bring unity to her own people. In 1946 President Truman created the Commission of Civil Rights, which, in 1947, issued a 34-point recommendation for integrating African Americans into the mainstream of American society. The NAACP grew in power, and Black Americans gained entrance into schools, housing districts, and political and business spheres which had previously been closed to them. Larger social and political issues, such as the Cold War with Communist Russia, the threat of atomic annihilation, and the loss of individuality and spiritual values in an increasingly technological decade held the attention of Black and White leaders. Simultaneously, a growing number of educated Blacks and their leaders sought more intensely their full rights in a Democratic society. The NAACP's struggle for racial integration was matched by the growing insistence on a full integration of Black literature into the mainstream of American literature. Notable Black critics, such as J. Saunders Redding, Arthur P. Davis, Hugh Gloster and Sterling Brown, began to provide credible and perceptive criticism of Black literature, applying all of the standards which were pertinent to Anglo-American work. This new movement benefitted Black writers. At the same time, these critics urged Black writers to leave the subject of racial experience and to dramatize the broader resources of American life and heritage. Frank Yerby and Willard Motley were among those writers who heeded this message and adapted their talents to the dramatization of traditional Anglo-American materials. James Baldwin's *Giovanni's Room* is another work in that same direction.

However, as America entered the fifties, Black critical thinking underwent a revision. Critics agreed that Black writers should demonstrate aesthetic and technical skills required of any writer, but they should concern themselves primarily with a portrayal of Black life and heritage, since only Black writers could understand and adequately communicate racial experience. In fact, it would be Black writers' literary skill which would gain them entrance into the mainstream of American literature; their subject, provided it was treated honestly, would not hinder recognition. Ralph Ellison, Margaret Walker, James Baldwin, Gwendolyn Brooks, and Lorraine Hansberry are among those writers of the mid-1950s who demonstrated their ability to handle Black themes with aesthetic perfection. They were among the first Blacks to gain critical recognition by White America and to be accepted into the mainstream of American literature. This period, then, was a time when Black writers perfected the tools of their trade, even while linking the Black experience to the more universal experience (a goal of the late 1940s and early 1950s)—an experience characterized by Blacks' isolation, their loss of identity, and their search for meaning and value in a world which seemed to be devoid of meaning.

Readers who extract from this historical background of African-American literature come to recognize certain common themes or trends. The literature of any new race or nation normally develops along similar thematic lines and is generally divided into three categories:

1. Initial and Early Writing, which attempts to depict the role of this group or race within the total national experience;
2. Middle Writing, which dramatizes the alienation and protest of this group against the surrounding majority or other antagonistic force; and
3. Later Writing, which concentrates on racial identity, experience, and heritage.

American literature, for example, moves from the detailing of the American experience, through the second period of alienation and protest against the British in the writings of Thomas Paine, Philip Freneau, and Thomas Jefferson; and into its third stage in the myth-creating works of Henry David Thoreau, Walt Whitman, and Mark Twain. African-American literature, although stemming from different experiences, follows a similar thematic development.

The first Black writers tried to define the concept "American," as it was reflected in the society around them. These works depict the respective inferior/superior socio-political positions of Blacks and Whites, but they also encompass the American concepts of independence, freedom, human dignity, and opportunity. In African-American folk materials, White masters might have the physical power, but they could still be outdone by their independent but clever slaves: Chesnutt's "Uncle Julius," who always outwits the White owner of the post-war plantation; Paul Laurence Dunbar's "Josh," in "The Ingrate," who demonstrates his equality by becoming a sergeant in the Yankee army; and Rudolph Fisher's "David" and "Miss Cynthie," who portray independence and intelligence in 20th century Harlem. Appearing almost simultaneously with these works are those which point out the disparity between the promise of America and the reality which Blacks came to experience. Lincoln's Emancipation Proclamation gave legal freedom to African Americans, but state and federal courts repeatedly denied their freedom and equality. Dunbar's "Mr. Cornelius Johnson, Office Seeker," portrays White politicians' use of Black leaders; Chesnutt's "The Sheriff's Children" demonstrates the stupidity of the racial conflict in America, seen from the angle of miscegenation; and Toomer's "Blood Burning Moon" depicts the White men's abuse of Black women and the powerlessness of Black men to intervene. With World War I, however, the themes in Black literature took on harsher tones. Black men fought for America; as they experienced equality and acceptance by the Europeans, they also became more educationally mobile, and they refused to allow their human rights to be ignored. The Black writers' awareness of their dissatisfaction began to be reflected in themes of deprivation, injustice, and struggle.

One of the major themes was alienation of individuals. An important example is found in Ellison's *Invisible Man*. Other examples are represented in Fisher's "City of Refuge," Toomer's "Avey," and Hughes' "One Christmas Eve." Racial discrimination and the tension, conflict, and suffering it brought also became a constant in the works of Black writers. Wright's *Native Son*, Hansberry's *A Raisin in the Sun*, Hughes' "Something in Common," Yerby's "Health Card," Dunbar's "Sympathy" and "We Wear the Mask," Petry's "Like a Winding Sheet" and "In Darkness and Confusion" all touch on the evil of racial prejudice and the problems of a racially oppressed people. Other common themes were the concern with the changing Black family, as well as struggles between parents and children concerning old values of religion, parental authority, and morality. Wright's wayward protagonist, Bigger Thomas, rejects his mother's authority in his life, and Hansberry's Walter and Beneatha present constant challenges to their Christian mother. Clearly, the generation gap found its way into the mainstream of African-American literature. Baldwin's "Rockpile" and Ellison's "King of the Bingo Game" are portrayals of deep emotion and intense suffering in the Black family.

Another theme that surfaced was the African-American struggle for identity. The question of duality had to be confronted. What does it mean to be Black and American? How do Blacks fuse the two? How do African Americans reconcile their struggle for equality as Americans with the constant reminder of their "inferiority" because they are Black? Countee Cullen's "Yet Do I Marvel" and "Incident," Toomer's "Avey," Wright's "Bright and Morning Star," Baldwin's "This Morning, This Evening, So Soon," and Ellison's "Flying Home" are just a few of the pieces that reflect this theme. Gradually, being Black and proud swept like wildfire across the nation. Writers like Eldridge Cleaver (who wrote *Soul on Ice*) began to honor Blackness and embrace their racial ancestry in a way that they never had before. Symbols of Black culture became intrusive in American society; the "Afro" or "bush" hairstyle, ethnic clothing, the raised fist as a symbol of Black power were all visible manifestations of new African Americans, who affirmed their beauty and worth in American society. This new racial expression was illustrated in two closely connected thematic strands: (a) pride in the bi-culturalism of the social group and (b) the creation of cultural and historical, mythical figures and events. The writers began to depict with sensitivity, pride, and honesty, the lives, philosophy, religion, motivation, social ties, and in-race problems of their people. They no longer made the effort to appear White or to please White audiences. For the most part, they wrote to illustrate the African-American experience, showing the good, the bad, and the ugly; the joy and pain; the admirable and the despicable; and they illustrated this experience with pride. No longer would they apologize for being Black. Hughes, Baldwin, Ellison, Ernest Gaines, Paule Marshall, Douglas Turner Ward, Arna Bontemps, and Margaret Walker are among some of the representatives of those who wrote from a racial pride that had been too long restrained. The second step in this developing pride in the bi-cultural self-awareness of African Americans is more complex. If there is to be a lasting racial pride, a pride which does not ultimately lead to complete immersion into Anglo-American society, there must be a lasting and unmistakable African-American basis for this pride. It cannot be founded solely on language, social system, or geographical affinity; for these things normally change. Rather there must be a philosophical comprehension of the inherent identity and value of the racial group.

Anglo-Americans, in separating themselves from their European ancestry, found inherent value in the image of America as the new "Eden," and Anglo-Americans themselves as the new "Adams" and "Eves." Their sense of American identity has found physical expression in the mythico-historic figures of Washington, Lincoln, Kennedy, and in the mythical literary figures provided in Anglo-American literature. In like manner, African Americans are finding their racial identity in the mythico-historic figures of the anonymous writers of spirituals, gospel, blues songs; in socio-political figures like Harriet Tubman, Booker T. Washington, W. E. B. DuBois, Martin R. Delaney, Martin Luther King, Jr., Malcolm X, Jessie Jackson, and Hank Aaron; and in such mythico-literary figures as John Henry, Aunt Dicey, and Ella Speed.

African-American Theater

Story, along with music and song, has been a part of the African-American tradition since the first Blacks came to the New World in the 1500s. Yet the overwhelming necessity of dealing with the basic elements of survival—and slavery—precluded the development of drama during the first 200 years of their presence. It was not until 1816 that William Brown, a retired seaman of means, established a theater in his home in New York's Greenwich Village. From a beginning of acts of singing, dancing, and recitation, Brown expanded his operation. In 1821 he built the African Grove Theatre at 56 Mercer Street, opening with a production of Shakespeare's *Richard III* starring Black actor James Hewitt. In 1823 Brown produced the first Black play in the United States, *The Drama of King Shotaway,* which deals with an uprising of Blacks on the West Indian island of St. Vincent in the 1790s. After a long battle to survive, for political and social reasons, his theater was closed by city sheriff Mordecai Noah, ostensibly for disturbing the peace and violating city ordinances. In the plays he produced and his resistance to external interference, Brown began the Black theater traditions of using drama to make a political statement and of not yielding to pressure from the White establishment.

Ira Aldridge (1807–1867) also performed with this company and, upon its demise, migrated to London and Europe where he became a star Shakespearean actor until his death in Lodz, Poland. He also adapted and produced a French play, *The Black Doctor* (1847). Other Black efforts in Europe included those of Victor Sejour, a New Orleans native who moved to France where he wrote and staged 21 plays, mainly full-length historical dramas in the mode of Victor Hugo and with no Black characters. In 1856 the first Black dramatist, William Wells Brown, who was also the first Black novelist, wrote *Experience, or How to Give a Northern Man a Backbone,* and in 1858 he wrote *Escape, or a Leap to Freedom.* Brown, a self-educated escaped slave, was a commanding anti-slavery speaker on the abolition of slavery. While there is no record of his plays having been performed, Brown read them to his audience.

For the remainder of the 19th century, most Blacks were concerned with abolition, economic survival, education, and securing citizenship. Most Black theatrical activity was confined to minstrel shows, which began in the 1840s and featured songs, dances, riddles, and skits in which White men, with their faces blackened with burnt cork, satirized Black speech, dress, and music. Unfortunately, minstrel shows implanted in the American consciousness the stereotypes of Blacks as passive or scheming, over-dull or over-sharp but always irresponsible. And these caricatures are alive and well in drama today, whether in theater, film, or television sitcoms.

After the Civil War African-American minstrel shows—for many years the only outlet for Black stage talent—developed, and these Black performers had to continue to play demeaning stereotypes if they wanted commercial success. The 1890s saw the rise of the coon show, a Black minstrel musical. Many were written for downtown White audiences by Bob Coles, James Weldon Johnson and his brother J. Rosamond Johnson, Will Marion Cook, and Paul Laurence Dunbar. Typical coon shows were *A Trip to Coontown* (1890), *The Octoroon* (1895), *The Shoefly Regiment,* and *Jes Lak White Folks.* Bert Williams and James Walker became performers known around the world for their work in coon shows.

Yet, beginning in 1880, Black drama began to appear. Paul Laurence Dunbar wrote several plays which were widely read, and Pauline E. Hopkins produced a historical musical. William Easton wrote two plays about the 1790 Haitian revolution: *Dessalines* (1893), the first Black play to be staged; and *Christopher* (1911), which chronicled the overthrow of Dessalines, the revolutionary general.

Historians have called the period between 1877 and 1900 the nadir of African-American life and history as rights painfully gained after the Civil War were swiftly stripped away, culminating in 1896 with the Supreme Court's decision on Plessy versus Ferguson which made segregation the law of the land. Nevertheless, a spark flickered in Black theater. In 1901 Joseph Cotter wrote *Caleb the Degenerate* which was never performed; it pointed out the backwardness of many Blacks and espoused the industrial education and work ethic put forth by Booker T. Washington, whom he admired greatly. In 1913 W. E. B. DuBois wrote a Black pageant *The Star of Ethiopia,* which considered the contributions of Africans to the Western world to counter some of the negative Black images in use by the press, literature, theater, and new film industry—even before Griffin's *Birth of a Nation* (1915). In 1916 Angelina Grimke, known for her work with the Washington NAACP, wrote and produced *Rachel,* which is believed to be the first Black non-musical play with an all-Black cast.

Aside from the works of DuBois and Grimke, no professional works appeared until 1923. Yet Black playwrights were busy writing for high schools, colleges, and little theater groups. Schoolteachers created educational materials to show the Black experience; others wrote folk plays showing aspects of Southern rural Black life or comedies of Black humor or satire. A popular subject was Black heroes and heroines who persevered in the face of intense racism. More than 100 plays were entered in writing contests in the NAACP's *Crisis* and the Urban League's *Opportunity* magazines; few were actually produced. In 1926 DuBois founded the Krigwa Players to produce African-American plays. Here many of the contest winners had their plays performed. As a totally Black undertaking, Krigwa was largely ignored by the White press.

Four Black plays appeared on Broadway during the 1920s. In 1923 Willis Richardson's one-act play *The Chip Woman's Fortune* was the first Black Broadway drama; it dealt with a Black man falsely accused of a White woman's rape. In 1925 San Francisco bellhop Garland Anderson's *Appearances* was the first full-length Black play on Broadway. Frank Wilson's *Brother Mose* (originally named *Meek Mose*) appeared briefly on Broadway in 1928, and in 1929 Wallace Thurman, collaborating with White author Jourdan Rapp, wrote *Harlem,* which supposedly gave White viewers a trip to the Black capital of the world.

It was during this time that DuBois and Alain Locke, author of *The New Negro* (1925) set forth their differences on the purpose of Black theater. DuBois saw drama reflecting the "outer life." Characters were from the mold of model humans or historical figures and pined with frustrated hopes. Themes should prick the conscience of Whites, and the language should be thought-provoking and literate. Theater had a political end; it could capture the mass imagination and thus change the racial situation in the United States, that is, an impact on the "outer life." Characters should come from the streets, joints, and dives. And while they might "cut the fool," they expressed honest and personal emotions irrespective of politics. Themes would be directed almost exclusively toward Blacks, and the language would be that of ordinary folk, dressed up with poetry, music, dance. The aim of theater was to depict Black life without White misinterpretation. In an effort to promote a positive self-respect and self-reliance, it would repudiate social dependency. These two frames of reference still form the backbone of African-American drama. As time passed, playwrights have mutated and combined the themes, yet both can still be seen, and neither school is more right or wrong, more dated or modern than the other.

During the 1930s, given the economic impact of the Depression, there was less theatrical productivity. Yet the Depression showcased the works of more Black playwrights than had the boom years of the 1920s. In 1935 more minority units were seen in the Federal Theater Project in more than 20 cities. The most active of these units were in New York, Newark, Chicago, and Seattle. Many had resident playwrights. The Newark Federal Theater produced Frank Wilson's *Walk Together Children* (1936), the Countee Cullen and Arna Bontemps adaptation of Rudolph Fisher's novel *Conjure Man Dies* (1936), and Theodore Browne's *Natural Man* (1937). In Chicago, Theodore Ward's *Big White Fog* (1938) suggested American Blacks might turn to communism as a reaction to racism, discrimination, and segregation. From the federal theater came Hughes Allison's *The Trial of Dr. Beck,* a murder mystery turning on differences in Black skin colors; Hall Johnson's *Run Little Chillun* (1933), a musical folk play; and J. Augustus Smith's *Turpentine,* a social drama written with Peter Morrell.

Without a doubt, Langston Hughes was the most productive Black playwright during the 1930s. He wrote *Mulatto* based on the theme of the tragic mulatto, which became the longest running Black Broadway play until Lorraine Hansberry's *A Raisin in the Sun* appeared nearly 25 years later. His other works include two grassroots urban comedies, *Little Ham* (1836) and *Joy to My Soul; Troubled Island* (1949), a historical tragedy; and *Front Porch,* a satire which pokes fun at the Black bourgeoisie. Hughes co-authored with Arna Bontemps *When Jack Hollers,* and in Harlem, Hughes opened the short-lived Suitcase Theater for which he wrote *Don't You Want to Be Free* (1937).

This decade also witnessed the beginning of the Black college theater movement. Randolph Edmonds founded the intercollegiate Theatre Association in 1930 and the National Association of Dramatic and Speech Arts in 1936. As early as the 1930s at Howard University and Florida A. and M. and through the mid-1950s at Black colleges as far north as Morgan State College, programs existed. Seeing material that was "safe" and would not antagonize college administrators, these educators wrote for student productions. Often the dramas were concerned with the relationship between and among Blacks, especially within the family. Representative works are Thomas Pawley's *Judgment Day* (1938), Randolph Edmond's *Gangsters Over Harlem* (1942), Owen Dobson's *The Christmas Miracle* (1955), and Arthur Lamb's *Roughshod up the Mountain* (1956).

The entrance of the United States into World War II halted much theater activity. However, in 1941 Paul Green and Richard Wright adapted *Native Son* for the stage. Abram Hill founded the American Negro Theater (ANT) with Frederick O'Neal and Austin Briggs-Hall and wrote two dramas for the group: *Striver's Row* (1940), a farce about Harlem's Black bourgeoisie; and *Walk Hard,* a look at a Black prizefighter. He also rewrote Philip Yourdan's *Anna Lucasta,* a play about a Polish prostitute, into a long-running Broadway and London play and then refashioned it into an all-Black cast for ANT. After the war, the bitter scramble for jobs and basic human dignity, especially by returning Black veterans, seemed to stifle Black writers. But Theodore Ward's *Our Lan',* about thwarted Black hopes during Reconstruction, appeared briefly on Broadway. Bontemps and Cullen wrote the Broadway musical *St. Louis Woman* based on Bontemps' unpublished novel, *Chariots in the Cloud* (1929). Hughes likewise wrote lyrics for Kurt Weill's *Street Scene.*

With the prosperity of the golden 1950s, Black dramatists achieved a measure of success and recognition in mainstream theater never anticipated by earlier playwrights. In 1950 Alice Childress wrote the one-act play *Florence* and adapted a number of Hughes' "Simple" columns into a musical, *Just a Little Simple.* In 1955 she became the first Black dramatist to win an Obie for her off-Broadway production *Of Trouble in Mind,* a full-length play about Black actors in a White playwright's production, said to be based on her experiences in *Anna Lucasta.* Other off-Broadway plays included William Branch's *In Splendid Error* (1954), which looked at Douglass' indecision about joining John Brown in the raid on Harper's Ferry; and Loften Mitchell's *A Land Beyond the River* (1957), which dealt with a Southern civil rights struggle that became a part of Brown. In 1951 William Branch opened *A Medal for Willie* in Harlem; the play raised questions about wartime service by Blacks in the armed forces, while Black soldiers and their families were openly denied equal rights at home. On Broadway Louis Peterson's *Take a Giant Step* (1953) looked at a Black teenager's coming of age in a White environment, and Hughes' musical comedy *Simply Heavenly* (1957) moved to the Great White Way. By any account, the most successful drama of the decade was Lorraine Hansberry's *A Raisin in the Sun* (1959) which starred Sidney Poitier. The first play by a Black female to reach Broadway, *A Raisin in the Sun* proved that Black playwrights did have a role in so-called mainstream theater. Hansberry became the first Black to win the New York Drama Critics Circle Award.

Racial concerns continued to dominate the 1960s theater. Ossie Davis used humor in his *Purlie Victorious* (1961) to point out prejudice in the Southern social order. William Branch found a heroine in Mary Church Terrell for his drama, *To Follow the Phoenix*. Reflecting rising African nationalism he also wrote *A Wreath for Udomo,* based on South African Peter Abraham's novel about the rise and fall of an African prime minister. Hansberry's *The Sign in Sidney Brustein's Window* (1964), a socio-political drama set in Greenwich Village with a nearly all-White cast, closed the day after she died at age 34 in 1968. Adrienne Kennedy, in 1963, won an Obie for *Funnyhouse of a Negro,* a play dealing with the problems of a bi-racial young girl.

Langston Hughes wrote three gospel musicals: *Black Nativity* (1961), *Jericho Jim Crow* (1963), and *Tambourines to Glory* (1963). Other Black 1960s musicals included *Ballad for Bimshire* (1963), a Caribbean satire by Loften Michell and Irving Burgie; *Kicks and Company*, by Oscar Brown, Jr.; and *Fly Blackbird* (1962), by the West Coast team of James Hatch and C. Bernard Jackson. James Baldwin returned to the theater writing *Blues for Mister Charlie* (1964) and *The Amen Corner* (1965).

Douglas Turner Ward, one of the founders of the Negro Ensemble Company, wrote two very popular one-act plays: *Day of Absence* (1965), a reverse minstrel show with Black actors in White faces, in which all African Americans in a Southern town disappear; and *Happy Ending* (1965), in which two domestics discover that their easy life is about to end as their employers are about to divorce. The Negro Ensemble Company also presented Errol Johns' Caribbean drama, *Moon on a Rainbow Shawl* and Thomas Pawley's *The Tumult and the Shouting,* about the lives of professors on a Black college campus, which also appeared on New York stages. In 1968 Lonnie Elder's *Ceremonies in Dark Old Men* became the first Black play nominated for a Pulitzer Prize.

As the civil rights movement transformed into the Black Power movement in the mid-1960s, the raised fist and the "in-your-face" attitude of the streets were reflected in the theater. If Brown in 1816 and DuBois 110 years later saw the desperate need for a Black theater, Amiri Baraka (then known as Leroi Jones), in 1965, now demanded a theater that was exclusively African American. Already established as a Black poet and essayist, Baraka now turned to the stage. His plays, primarily one-act pieces, used violence, allegory, myth, and foul language to acidly show the position of Blacks in the United States. In 1964 *Dutchman, The Slave,* and *The Toilet* were uncompromising in their attacks upon both White racism and Black Uncle Tomism in what they perceived to be an outright war between the races. Closely associated with Baraka as a progenitor of the Black Theater movement is Ed Bullins, one-time Minister of Culture for the Black Panthers. In 1968 his first one-act plays, *Clara's Ole Man, The Electronic Nigger,* and *A Son, Come Home* were produced off-Broadway.

The 1970s also saw a dramatic increase in the number of Black dramatists winning awards for their works. In 1970 Charles Gordone, for *No Place to be Somebody,* became the first African American to win a Pulitzer Prize for drama. Obies went to J. E. Gaines' *What If It Had Turned Up Heads?* (1971), to Paul Carter Harrison's *The Great McDaddy* (1974), to Leslie Lee's *The First Breeze of Summer* (1975), to Joseph Walker's *The River Niger* (1976), and to Ntozake Shange's *for colored girls who have considered suicide /when the rainbow is enuf* (1976). Others received Drama Desk and Dramatists Guild awards. Melvin Van Peebles' *Ain't Supposed to Die a Natural Death* (1971) and Samm-Art Williams' *Home* (1976) were nominated for Tonys and received other prestigious awards.

During the last two decades of the 20th century, August Wilson has become the dominant and most prolific Black dramatic voice with his series of plays chronicling the life of African Americans through the 20th century. His first play, *Ma Rainey's Black Bottom,* set in the 1920s, won the Drama Critics award in 1982. This was followed by *Fences,* which starred James Earl Jones and won the 1987 Pulitzer Prize. In 1990 *The Piano Lesson* won a Pulitzer and nearly every other theatrical award for which it was eligible. Other plays in his series are *Joe Turner's Come and Gone* (1984), *Two Trains Running* (1989), and *Seven Guitars* (1996). Wilson is not alone. Charles Fuller won the 1981 Pulitzer for *A Soldier's Play,* which looks at racial hostility in a segregated army camp, and George Wolfe received the 1986 Dramatists Guild award for *The Colored Museum* which satirizes Black stereotypes. Anna Denvere Smith won critical acclaim for *Fires in the Mirror,* which explores the often-incendiary relationship between Brooklyn's largely West Indian and orthodox Jewish population. African-American playwrights continue to prick White and African-American consciences as their characters run the spectrum from historical figures to imaginary beings. Like the fabrics in a quilt, the works of these playwrights are snippets of the people they represent—many classes, many problems, much humor, much sadness, and much indomitability.

Selected Bibliography

Andrews, William L. et al., eds. *The Oxford Companion to African American Literature*. New York: Oxford University Press, 1997.

Branch, William, ed. *Black Thunder: An Anthology of Contemporary African American Drama*. New York: Penguin, 1992.

Bullins, Ed, ed. *The New Lafayette Theatre Presents*. Garden City, NY: Doubleday, 1974.

Elam, Harry, and Robert Alexander. *Colored Contradictions: An Anthology of Contemporary African American Plays*. New York: Penguin, 1996.

Harrison, Paul Carter, ed. *Totem Voices: Plays from the Black World Repertory*. New York: Grove, 1989.

Hatch, James V., and Ted Shine, eds. *Black Theatre USA*. Rev. ed. 2 vols. New York: Simon and Schuster, 1996.

Hay, Samuel A. *African American Theatre: An Historical and Critical Analysis*. New York: Cambridge University Press, 1994.

King, Woodie, and Ron Milner, eds. *Black Drama Anthology*. New York: New American, 1972.

Mahone, Sydne. *Moon Marked and Touched by Sun*. New York: Theatre Communications, 1994.

Ntiri, Daphne Williams, ed. *Roots and Blossoms: African American Plays for Today*. Troy, MI: Bedford, 1991.

Patterson, Lindsay, comp. Black Theater: *A 20th Century Collection of the Work of Its Best Playwrights*. New York: New American, 1971.

Riley, Clayton. Introduction. *A Black Quartet*. New York: New American, 1970.

Wilkerson, Margaret, ed. *Nine Plays by Black Women*. New York: New American, 1986.

Douglas Turner Ward (1930–)

Douglas Turner Ward (actor, producer, director, playwright) continues to be a vital voice in African-American theater. In 1967 he, along with Robert Hooks and Gerald Krone, founded the Negro Ensemble Company, a highly touted performing and touring company.

Ward was born on May 5, 1930, in Burnside, Louisiana. He was the only child of Roosevelt and Dorothy Ward, struggling farm crop workers. Seeking economic opportunity, the elder Ward moved his family to New Orleans. It was there during his high school years that Ward realized an interest in writing. After attending Wilberforce University and the University of Michigan respectively, he migrated to New York City where he enrolled in the Paul Mann Actor's Workshop. His first acting role was in Eugene O'Neill's *The Iceman Cometh*. He also enacted the role of Walter Younger in a production of Lorraine Hansberry's *A Raisin in the Sun*.

Concerned about the void in African-American theatrical expression, Ward collaborated with Hooks and Krone to provide a vehicle for actors and playwrights to freely perfect and present their works. His production preferences ultimately reflected that sense of freedom. New York City's St. Marks Playhouse became the home base for ensemble presentations. Notably, *Happy Ending* (1965), *Day of Absence* (1965), *The Reckoning* (1969), and *The River Niger* (1972) were produced, directed, and/or acted in by Ward.

He is the recipient of The Vernon Rice Drama Award (1966), the Obie Award (1966), the Lambda Kappa Nu citation (1968), a special Tony award (1969), and a Brandeis University creative arts award (1969). All of these honors were acknowledgments of *Happy Ending* and *Day of Absence*. Additionally, *The Reckoning* was cited for a Drama Desk citation (1969) and an Obie award (1970).

Selected Bibliography

Locher, Frances Carol, ed. *Contemporary Authors*. Vols. 81–84. Detroit: Gale Research, 1979.

Moritz, Charles, ed. *Current Biography Yearbook*. New York: Wilson, 1977.

Day of Absence

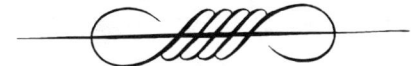

Douglas Turner Ward

SCENE: *Street.*
TIME: *Early morning.*

CLEM. *(Sitting under a sign suspended by invisible wires and bold-printed with the lettering: "STORE.")* 'Morning, Luke . . .
LUKE. *(Sitting a few paces away under an identical sign.)* 'Morning, Clem . . .
CLEM. Go'n' be a hot day.
LUKE. Looks that way . . .
CLEM. Might rain though . . .
LUKE. Might.
CLEM. Hope it does . . .
LUKE. Me, too . . .
CLEM. Farmers could use a little wet spell for a change . . . How's the Missis?
LUKE. Same.
CLEM. 'N' the kids?
LUKE. Them, too . . . How's yourns?
CLEM. Fine, thank you . . . *(They both lapse into drowsy silence, waving lethargically from time to time at imaginary passersby.)* Hi, Joe . . .
LUKE. Joe . . .
CLEM. How'd it go yesterday, Luke?
LUKE. Fair.
CLEM. Same wit' me . . . Business don't seem to git no better or no worse. Guess we in a rut, Luke, don't it 'pear that way to you?—Morning, ma'am.
LUKE. Morning . . .
CLEM. Tried display, sales, advertisement, stamps—everything, yet merchandising stumbles 'round in the same old groove. But—that's better than plunging downwards, I reckon.
LUKE. Guess it is.
CLEM. Morning, Bret. How's the family? . . . That's good.
LUKE. Bret—

113

CLEM. Morning, Sue.

LUKE. How do, Sue.

CLEM. *(Staring after her.)* . . . Fine hunk of woman.

LUKE. Sure is.

CLEM. Wonder if it's any good?

LUKE. Bet it is.

CLEM. Sure like to find out!

LUKE. So would I.

CLEM. You ever try?

LUKE. Never did . . .

CLEM. Morning, Gus . . .

LUKE. Howdy, Gus.

CLEM. Fine, thank you. *(They lapse into silence again. Clem rouses himself slowly, begins to look around quizzically.)* Luke . . . ?

LUKE. Huh?

CLEM. Do you . . . er, er—feel anything—funny . . . ?

LUKE. Like what?

CLEM. Like . . . er—something—strange?

LUKE. I dunno . . . haven't thought about it.

CLEM. I mean . . . like something's wrong—outta place, unusual?

LUKE. I don't know . . . What you got in mind?

CLEM. Nothing . . . just that—just that—like somp'ums outta kilter. I got a funny feeling somp'ums not up to snuff. Can't figger out what it is . . .

LUKE. Maybe it's in your haid?

CLEM. No, not like that . . . Like somp'ums happened—or happening—gone haywire, loony.

LUKE. Well, don't worry 'bout it, it'll pass.

CLEM. Guess you right. *(Attempts return to somnolence but doesn't succeed.)* . . . I'm sorry, Luke, but you sure you don't feel nothing peculiar . . . ?

LUKE. *(Slightly irked.)* Toss it out your mind, Clem! We got a long day ahead of us. If something's wrong, you'll know 'bout it in due time. No use worrying about it 'till it comes and if it's coming, it will. Now, relax!

CLEM. All right, you right . . . Hi, Margie . . .

LUKE. Marge.

CLEM. *(Unable to control himself.)* Luke, I don't give a damn what you say. Somp'ums topsy-turvy, I just know it!

LUKE. *(Increasingly irritated.)* Now look here, Clem—it's a bright day, it looks like it's go'n' git hotter. You say the wife and kids are fine and the business is no better or no worse? Well, what else could be wrong? . . . If somp'ums go'n' happen, it's go'n' happen anyway and there ain't a damn fool thing you kin do to stop it! So you ain't helping me, yourself or nobody else by thinking 'bout it. It's not go'n' be no better or no worse when it gits here. It'll come to you when it gits ready to come and it's go'n' be the same whether you worry about it or not. So stop letting it upset you! *(Luke settles back in his chair. Clem does likewise. Luke shuts his eyes. After a few moments, they reopen. He forces them shut again. They reopen in greater curiosity. Fi-*

nally, he rises slowly to an upright position in the chair, looks around frowningly. Turns slowly to Clem.) . . . Clem? . . . You know something? . . . Somp'um is peculiar . . .

CLEM. *(Vindicated.)* I knew it, Luke! I just knew it! Ever since we been sitting here, I been having that feeling! *(Scene is blacked out abruptly. Lights rise on another section of the stage where a young couple lie in bed under an invisible-wire-suspension-sign lettered: "HOME." Loud insistent sounds of baby yells are heard. John, the husband, turns over trying to ignore the cries, Mary, the wife, is undisturbed. John's efforts are futile, the cries continue until they cannot be denied. He bolts upright, jumps out of bed and disappears offstage. Returns quickly and tries to rouse Mary.)*

JOHN. Mary . . . *(Nudges her, pushes her, yells into her ear, but she fails to respond.)* Mary, get up . . . Get up!

MARY. Ummm . . . *(Shrugs away, still sleeping.)*

JOHN. GET UP!

MARY. UMMMMMMMMM!

JOHN. Don't you hear the baby bawling! . . . NOW GET UP!

MARY. *(Mumbling drowsily.)* . . . What baby . . . whose baby . . . ?

JOHN. Yours!

MARY. Mine? That's ridiculous . . . what'd you say . . . ? Somebody's baby bawling? . . . How could that be so? *(Hearing screams.)* Who's crying? Somebody's crying! . . . What's crying? . . . WHERE'S LULA?!

JOHN. I don't know. You better get up.

MARY. That's outrageous! . . . What time is it?

JOHN. Late 'nuff! Now rise up!

MARY. You must be joking . . . I'm sure I still have four or five hours sleep in store—even more after that head-splittin' blow-out last night . . . *(Tumbles back under covers.)*

JOHN. Nobody told you to gulp those last six bourbons—

MARY. Don't tell me how many bourbons to swallow, not after you guzzled the whole stinking bar! . . . Get up? . . . You must be cracked . . . Where's Lula? She must be here, she always is . . .

JOHN. Well, she ain't here yet, so get up and muzzle that brat before she does drive me cuckoo!

MARY. *(Springing upright, finally realizing gravity of situation.)* Whaddaya mean Lula's not here? She's always here, she must be here . . . Where else kin she be? She supposed to be . . . She just can't not be here—CALL HER! *(Blackout as John rushes offstage. Scene shifts to a trio of Telephone Operators perched on stools before imaginary switchboards. Chaos and bedlam are taking place to the sound of buzzes. PRODUCTION NOTE: Effect of following dialogue should simulate rising pandemonium.)*

FIRST OPERATOR. The line is busy—

SECOND OPERATOR. Line is busy—

THIRD OPERATOR. Is busy—

FIRST OPERATOR. Doing best we can—

SECOND OPERATOR. Having difficulty—

THIRD OPERATOR. Soon as possible—

FIRST OPERATOR. Just one moment—

SECOND OPERATOR. Would you hold on—

THIRD OPERATOR. Awful sorry, madam—

FIRST OPERATOR. Would you hold on, please—
SECOND OPERATOR. Just a second, please—
THIRD OPERATOR. Please hold on, please—
FIRST OPERATOR. The line is busy—
SECOND OPERATOR. The line is busy—
THIRD OPERATOR. The line is busy—
FIRST OPERATOR. Doing best we can—
SECOND OPERATOR. Hold on please—
THIRD OPERATOR. Can't make connections—
FIRST OPERATOR. Unable to put it in—
SECOND OPERATOR. Won't plug through—
THIRD OPERATOR. Sorry madam—
FIRST OPERATOR. If you'd wait a moment—
SECOND OPERATOR. Doing best we can—
THIRD OPERATOR. Sorry—
FIRST OPERATOR One moment—
SECOND OPERATOR. Just a second—
THIRD OPERATOR. Hold on—
FIRST OPERATOR. YES—
SECOND OPERATOR. STOP IT!—
THIRD OPERATOR. HOW DO I KNOW—
FIRST OPERATOR. YOU ANOTHER ONE!
SECOND OPERATOR. HOLD ON DAMMIT!
THIRD OPERATOR. UP YOURS, TOO!
FIRST OPERATOR. THE LINE IS BUSY—
SECOND OPERATOR. THE LINE IS BUSY—
THIRD OPERATOR. THE LINE IS BUSY—*(The switchboard clamors a cacophony of buzzes as Operators plug connections with the frenzy of a Chaplin movie. Their replies degenerate into a babble of gibberish. At the height of frenzy, the Supervisor appears.)*
SUPERVISOR. WHAT'S THE SNARL-UP???!!!
FIRST OPERATOR. Everybody calling at the same time, ma'am!
SECOND OPERATOR. Board can't handle it!
THIRD OPERATOR. Like everybody in big New York City is trying to squeeze a call through to li'l' ole us!
SUPERVISOR. God! . . . Somp'un terrible musta happened! . . . Buzz the emergency frequency hookup to the Mayor's office and find out what the hell's going on! *(Scene blacks out quickly to Clem and Luke.)*
CLEM. *(Something slowly dawning on him.)* Luke . . . ?
LUKE. Yes, Clem?
CLEM. *(Eyes roving around in puzzlement.)* Luke . . . ?
LUKE. *(Irked.)* I said what, Clem!
CLEM. Luke . . . ? Where—where is—the—the—?

LUKE. THE WHAT?!

CLEM. Nigras . . . ?

LUKE. ?????What . . . ?

CLEM. Nigras . . . Where is the Nigras, where is they, Luke . . . ? ALL THE NIGRAS! . . . I don't see no Nigras . . . ?!

LUKE. Whatcha mean . . . ?

CLEM. *(Agitatedly.)* Luke, there ain't a darky in sight . . . And if you remember, we ain't spied a nappy hair all morning . . . The Nigras, Luke! We ain't laid eyes on nary a coon this whole morning!!!

LUKE. You must be crazy or something, Clem!

CLEM. Think about it, Luke, we been sitting here for an hour or more—try and recollect if you remember seeing jist one go by?!!

LUKE. *(Confused.)* . . . I don't recall . . . But . . . but there musta been some . . . The heat musta got you, Clem! How in hell could that be so?!!!

CLEM. *(Triumphantly.)* Just think, Luke! . . . Look around ya . . . Now, every morning mosta people walkin' 'long this street is colored. They's strolling by going to work, they's waiting for the buses, they's sweeping sidewalks, cleaning stores, starting to shine shoes and wetting the mops—right?! . . . Well, look around you, Luke—where is they? *(Luke paces up and down, checking.)* I told you, Luke, they ain't nowheres to be seen.

LUKE. ???? . . . This . . . this . . . some kind of holiday for 'em—or something?

CLEM. I don't know, Luke . . . but . . . but what I do know is they ain't here 'n' we haven't seen a solitary one . . . It's scaryfying, Luke . . . !

LUKE. Well . . . maybe they's jist standing 'n' walking and shining on other streets.—Let's go look! *(Scene blacks out to John and Mary. Baby cries are as insistent as ever.)*

MARY. *(At end of patience.)* SMOTHER IT!

JOHN. *(Beyond his.)* That's a hell of a thing to say 'bout your own child! You should know what to do to hush her up!

MARY. Why don't you try?!

JOHN. You had her!

MARY. You shared in borning her?!

JOHN. Possibly not!

MARY. Why, you lousy—!

JOHN. What good is a mother who can't shut up her own daughter?!

MARY. I told you she yells louder every time I try to lay hands on her.—Where's Lula? Didn't you call her?!

JOHN. I told you I can't get the call through!

MARY. Try ag'in—

JOHN. It's no use! I tried numerous times and can't even git through to the switchboard. You've got to quiet her down yourself. *(Firmly.)* Now, go in there and clam her up 'fore I lose my patience! *(Mary exits. Soon, we hear the yells increase. She rushes back in.)*

MARY. She won't let me touch her, just screams louder!

JOHN. Probably wet 'n' soppy!

MARY. Yes! Stinks something awful! Phooooey! I can't stand that filth and odor!

JOHN. That's why she's screaming! Needs her didee changed.—Go change it!

MARY. How you 'spect me to when I don't know how?! Suppose I faint?!

JOHN. Well let her blast away. I'm getting outta here.

MARY. You can't leave me here like this!

JOHN. Just watch me! . . . See this nice split-level cottage, peachy furniture, multi-colored teevee, hi-fi set 'n' the rest? . . . Well, how you think I scraped 'em together while you curled up on your fat li'l' fanny? . . . By gitting outta here—not only on time . . . but EARLIER!—Beating a frantic crew of nice young executives to the punch—gitting there fustest with the mostest brown-nosing you ever saw! Now if I goof one day—just ONE DAY!—You reckon I'd stay ahead? NO! . . . There'd be a wolf-pack trampling over my prostrate body, racing to replace my smiling face against the boss' left rump! . . . NO, MAM! I'm zooming outta here on time, just as I always have and what's more—you go'n' fix me some breakfast, I'M HUNGRY!

MARY. But—

JOHN. No buts about it! *(Flash blackout as he gags on a mouthful of coffee.)* What you trying to do, STRANGLE ME!!! *(Jumps up and starts putting on jacket.)*

MARY. *(Sarcastically.)* What did you expect?

JOHN. *(In biting fury.)* That you could possibly boil a pot of water, toast a few slices of bread and fry a coupler eggs! . . . It was a mistaken assumption!

MARY. So they aren't as good as Lula's!

JOHN. That is an overstatement. Your efforts don't result in anything that could possibly be digested by man, mammal, or insect! . . . When I married you, I thought I was fairly acquainted with your faults and weaknesses—I chalked 'em up to human imperfection . . . But now I know I was being extremely generous, over-optimistic and phenomenally deluded!—You have no idea how useless you really are!

MARY. Then why'd you marry me?!

JOHN. Decoration!

MARY. You shoulda married Lula!

JOHN. I might've if it wasn't 'gainst the segregation law! . . . But for the sake of my home, my child and my sanity, I will even take a chance on sacrificing my slippery grip on the status pole and drive by her shanty to find out whether she or someone like her kin come over here and prevent some ultimate disaster. *(Storms toward door, stopping abruptly at exit.)* Are you sure you kin make it to the bathroom wit'out Lula backing you up?!!! *(Blackout. Scene shifts to Mayor's office where a cluttered desk stands c. amid papered debris.)*

MAYOR. *(Striding determinedly toward desk, stopping midways, bellowing.)* WOODFENCE! . . . WOODFENCE! . . . WOODFENCE! *(Receiving no reply, completes distance to desk.)* JACKSON! . . . JACKSON!

JACKSON. *(Entering worriedly.)* Yes, sir . . .

MAYOR. Where's Vice-Mayor Woodfence, that no-good brother-in-law of mine?!

JACKSON. Hasn't come in yet, sir.

MAYOR. HASN'T COME IN?!!! . . . Damn bastard! Knows we have a crucial conference. Soon as he staggers through that door, tell him to shoot in here! *(Angrily focusing on his disorderly desk and littered surroundings.)* And git Mandy here to straighten up this mess—Rufus too! You know he shoulda been waiting to knock dust off my shoes soon as I step in. Get 'em in here! . . . What's the matter wit' them lazy Nigras? . . . Already had to dress myself because of JC, fix my own coffee without MayBelle, drive myself to work 'counta Bubber, feel my old Hag's tits after Sapphi—NEVER MIND!—Git 'em in here—QUICK!

JACKSON. *(Meekly.)* They aren't . . . they aren't here, sir . . .

MAYOR. Whaddaya mean they aren't here? Find out where they at. We got important business, man! You can't run a town wit' laxity like this. Can't allow things to git snafued jist because a bunch of lazy Nigras been out gitting drunk and living it up all night! Discipline, man, discipline!

JACKSON. That's what I'm trying to tell you, sir . . . they didn't come in, can't be found . . . none of 'em.

MAYOR. Ridiculous, boy! Scare 'em up and tell 'em scoot here in a hurry befo' I git mad and fire the whole goddamn lot of 'em!

JACKSON. But we can't find 'em, sir.

MAYOR. Hogwash! Can't nobody in this office do anything right?! Do I hafta handle every piddling little matter myself?! Git me their numbers, I'll have 'em here befo' you kin shout to—*(Three men burst into room in various states of undress.)*

ONE. Henry—they vanished!

TWO. Disappeared into thin air!

THREE. Gone wit'out a trace!

TWO. Not a one on the street!

THREE. In the house!

ONE. On the job!

MAYOR. Wait a minute!! . . . Hold your water! Calm down—!

ONE. But they've gone, Henry—GONE! All of 'em!

MAYOR. What the hell you talking 'bout? Gone? Who's gone—?

ONE. The Nigras, Henry! They gone!

MAYOR. Gone? . . . Gone where?

TWO. That's what we trying to tell ya—they just disappeared! The Nigras have disappeared, swallowed up, vanished! All of 'em! Every last one!

MAYOR. Have everybody 'round here gone batty? . . . That's impossible, how could the Nigras vanish?

THREE. Beats me, but it's happened!

MAYOR. You mean a whole town of Nigras just evaporate like this—poof !—Overnight?

ONE. Right!

MAYOR. Y'all must be drunk! Why, half this town is colored. How could they just sneak out!

TWO. Don't ask me, but there ain't one in sight!

MAYOR. Simmer down 'n' put it to me easy-like.

ONE. Well . . . I first suspected somp'um smelly when Sarah Jo didn't show up this morning and I couldn't reach her—

TWO. Dorothy Jane didn't 'rive at my house—

THREE. Georgia Mae wasn't at mine neither—and SHE sleeps in!

ONE. When I reached the office, I realized I hadn't seen nary one Nigra all morning! Nobody else had either—wait a minute—Henry, have you?!

MAYOR. ???Now that you mention it . . . no, I haven't . . .

ONE. They gone, Henry . . . Not a one on the street, not a one in our homes, not a single, last living one to be found nowheres in town. What we gon' do?!

MAYOR. *(Thinking.)* Keep heads on your shoulders 'n' put clothes on your back, . . . They can't be far . . . Must be 'round somewheres . . . Probably playing hide 'n' seek, that's it! . . . JACKSON!

JACKSON. Yessir?

MAYOR. Immediately mobilize our Citizens Emergency Distress Committee!—Order a fleet of sound trucks to patrol streets urging the population to remain calm—situation's not as bad as it looks—everything's under control! Then, have another squadron of squawk buggies drive slowly through all Nigra alleys, ordering them to come out wherever they are. If that don't git 'em, organize a vigilante search-squad to flush 'em outta hiding! But most important of all, track down that lazy goldbricker, Woodfence, and tell him to git on top of the situation! By God, we'll find 'em even if we hafta dig 'em outta the ground! *(Blackout. Scene shifts back to John and Mary a few hours later. A funereal solemnity pervades their mood. John stands behind Mary who sits, in a scene duplicating the famous "American gothic" painting.)*

JOHN. . . . Walked up to the shack, knocked on door, didn't git no answer. Hollered: "LULA? LULA . . . ?—Not a thing. Went 'round the side, peeped in window—nobody stirred. Next door—nobody there. Crossed other side of street and banged on five or six other doors—not a colored person could be found! Not a man, neither woman or child—not even a little black dog could be seen, smelt or heard for blocks around . . . They've gone, Mary.

MARY. What does it all mean, John?

JOHN. I don't know, Mary . . .

MARY. I always had Lula, John. She never missed a day at my side . . . That's why I couldn't accept your wedding proposal until I was sure you'd welcome me and her together as a package. How am I gonna git through the day? My baby don't know me, I ain't acquainted wit' it. I've never lifted cover off pot, swung a mop or broom, dunked a dish or even pushed a dustrag. I'm lost wit'out Lula, I need her, John, I need her. *(Begins to weep softly. John pats her consolingly.)*

JOHN. Courage, honey . . . Everybody in town is facing the same dilemma. We mustn't crack up . . . *(Blackout. Scene shifts back to Mayor's office later in day. Atmosphere and tone resembles a wartime headquarters at the front. Mayor is poring over huge map.)*

INDUSTRIALIST. Half the day is gone already, Henry. On behalf of the factory owners of this town, you've got to bail us out! Seventy-five percent of all production is paralyzed. With the Nigra absent, men are waiting for machines to be cleaned, floors to be swept, crates lifted, equipment delivered and bathrooms to be deodorized. Why, restrooms and toilets are so filthy until they not only cannot be sat in, but it's virtually impossible to get within hailing distance because of the stench!

MAYOR. Keep your shirt on, Jeb—

BUSINESSMAN. Business is even in worse condition, Henry. The volume of goods moving 'cross counters has slowed down to a trickle—almost negligible. Customers are not only not purchasing—but the absence of handymen, porters, sweepers, stockmovers, deliverers and miscellaneous dirty-work doers is disrupting the smooth harmony of marketing!

CLUB WOMAN. Food poisoning, severe indigestitis, chronic diarrhea, advanced diaper chafings and a plethora of unsanitary household disasters dangerous to life, limb and property! . . . As a representative of the Federation of Ladies' Clubs, I must sadly report that unless the trend is reversed, a complete breakdown in family unity is imminent . . . Just as homosexuality and debauchery signalled the fall of Greece and Rome, the downgrading of Southern Bellesdom might very well prophesy the collapse of our indigenous institutions . . . Remember—it has always been pure, delicate, lily-white images of Dixie femininity which provided backbone, inspiration and ideology for our male warriors in their defense against the on-rushing black horde. If our gallant men are drained of this worship and idolatry—God knows! The cause won't be worth a Confederate nickel!

MAYOR. Stop this panicky defeatism, y'all hear me! All machinery at my disposal is being utilized. I assure you wit' great confidence the damage will soon repair itself.—Cheerful progress reports are expected any moment now.—Wait! See, here's Jackson . . . Well, Jackson?

JACKSON. *(Entering.)* As of now, sir, all efforts are fruitless. Neither hide nor hair of them has been located. We have not unearthed a single one in our shack-to-shack search. Not a single one has heeded our appeal. Scoured every crick and cranny inside their hovels, turning furniture upside down and inside out, breaking down walls and tearing through ceilings. We made determined efforts to discover where 'bouts of our faithful uncle Toms and informers—but even they have vanished without a trace . . . Searching squads are on the verge of panic and hysteria, sir, wit' hotheads among 'em campaigning for scorched earth policies. Nigras on a whole lack cellars, but there's rising sentiment favoring burning to find out whether they're underground—DUG IN!

MAYOR. Absolutely counter such foolhardy suggestions! Suppose they are tombed in? We'd only accelerate the gravity of the situation using incendiary tactics! Besides, when they're rounded up where will we put 'em if we've already burned up their shacks—IN OUR OWN BEDROOMS?!!!

JACKSON. I agree, sir, but the mood of the crowd is becoming irrational. In anger and frustration, they's forgetting their original purpose was to FIND the Nigras!

MAYOR. At all costs! Stamp out all burning proposals! Must prevent extremist notions from gaining ascendancy. Git wit' it . . . Wait—'n' for Jehovah's sake, find out where the hell is that trifling slacker, WOODFENCE!

COURIER. *(Rushing in.)* Mr. Mayor! Mr. Mayor! . . . We've found some! We've found some!

MAYOR. *(Excitedly.)* Where?!

COURIER. In the—in the—*(Can't catch breath.)*

MAYOR. *(Impatiently.)* Where, man? Where?!!!

COURIER. In the colored wing of the city hospital!

MAYOR. The hos—? The hospital! I shoulda known! How could those helpless, crippled, cut and shot Nigras disappear from a hospital! Shoulda thought of that! . . . Tell me more, man!

COURIER. I—I didn't wait, sir . . . I—I ran in to report soon as I heard—

MAYOR. WELL GIT BACK ON THE PHONE, YOU IDIOT, DON'T YOU KNOW WHAT THIS MEANS!

COURIER. Yes, sir. *(Races out.)*

MAYOR. Now we gitting somewhere! . . . Gentlemen, if one sole Nigra is among us, we're well on the road to rehabilitation! Those Nigras in the hospital must know somp'um 'bout the others where'bouts . . . Scat back to your colleagues, boost up their morale and inform 'em that things will zip back to normal in a jiffy! *(They start to file out, then pause to observe the Courier reentering dazedly.)* Well . . . ? Well, man . . . ? WHAT'S THE MATTER WIT' YOU, NINNY, TELL ME WHAT ELSE WAS SAID?!

COURIER. They all . . . they all . . . they all in a—in a—a coma, sir . . .

MAYOR. They all in a what . . . ?

COURIER. In a coma, sir

MAYOR. Talk sense, man! . . . Whaddaya mean, they all in a coma?

COURIER. Doctor says every last one of the Nigras are jist laying in bed . . . STILL . . . not moving . . . neither live or dead . . . laying up there in a coma . . . every last one of 'em . . .

MAYOR. *(Sputters, then grabs phone.)* Get me Confederate Memorial . . . Put me through to the Staff Chief . . . YES, this is the Mayor . . . Sam? . . . What's this I hear? . . . But how could they be in a coma, Sam? . . . You don't know! Well, what the hell you think the city's paying you for! . . . You've got 'nuff damn hacks and quacks there to find out! . . .—How could it be somp'um unknown? You mean Nigras know somp'um 'bout drugs your damn butchers don't?! . . . Well, what the crap good are they! . . . All right, all right, I'll be calm . . . Now, tell me . . . Uh huh, uh huh . . . Well, can't you give 'em some injections or somp'um . . . ?—You did . . . uh huh . . . DID YOU TRY A LI'L' ROUGH TREATMENT?—that too, huh . . . All right, Sam, keep trying . . . *(Puts phone down delicately, continuing absently.)* Can't wake 'em up. Just lay there. Them that's sick won't git no sicker, them that's half-well won't git no better, babies that's due won't be born and them that's come won't show no life. Nigras wit' cuts won't bleed and them which need blood won't be transfused . . . He say dying Nigras is even refusing to pass away! *(Is silently perplexed for a moment, then suddenly breaks into action.)* JACKSON?! . . . Call up the police—THE JAIL! Find out what's going on there! Them Nigras are captives! If there's one place we got darkies under control, it's there! Them sonsabitches too onery to act right either for colored or white! *(Jackson exits. The Courier follows.)* Keep your fingers crossed, citizens, them Nigras in jail are the most important Nigras we got! *(All hands are raised conspicuously aloft, fingers prominently ex-ed. Seconds tick by. Soon Jackson returns crestfallen.)*

JACKSON. Sheriff Bull says they don't know whether they still on premises or not. When they went to rouse Nigra jailbirds this morning, cell-block doors refused to swing open. Tried everything—even exploded dynamite charges—but it just wouldn't budge . . . Then they hoisted guards up to peep through barred windows, but couldn't see good 'nuff to tell whether Nigras was inside or not. Finally, gitting desperate, they power-hosed the cells wit' water but had to cease 'cause Sheriff Bull said he didn't wanta jeopardize drowning the Nigras since it might spoil his chance of shipping a record load of cotton pickers to the State Penitentiary for cotton-snatching jubilee . . . Anyway—they ain't heard a Nigra-squeak all day.

MAYOR. ???That so . . . ? WHAT 'BOUT TRAINS 'N' BUSSES PASSING THROUGH? There must be some dinges riding through?

JACKSON. We checked . . . not a one on board.

MAYOR. Did you hear whether any other towns lost their Nigras?

JACKSON. Things are status-quo everywhere else.

MAYOR. *(Angrily.)* Then what the hell they picking on us for!

COURIER. *(Rushing in.)* MR. MAYOR! Your sister jist called—HYSTERICAL! She says Vice-Mayor Woodfence went to bed wit' her last night, but when she woke up this morning he was gone! Been missing all day!

MAYOR. ???Could Nigras be holding brother-in-law Woodfence hostage?!

COURIER. No, sir. Besides him—investigations reveal that dozens or more prominent citizens—two City Council members, the chairman of the Junior Chamber of

Commerce, our City College All-Southern half-back, the chairlady of the Daughters of the Confederate Rebellion, Miss Cotton-Sack Festival of the Year and numerous other miscellaneous nobodies—are all absent wit'out leave. Dangerous evidence points to the conclusion that they have been infiltrating!

MAYOR. Infiltrating???

COURIER. Passing all along!

MAYOR ???PASSING ALL ALONG???

COURIER. Secret Nigras all the while!

MAYOR. NAW! *(Club Woman keels over in faint. Jackson, Businessman and Industrialist begin to eye each other suspiciously.)*

COURIER. Yessir!

MAYOR. PASSING???

COURIER. Yessir!

MAYOR. SECRET NIG—!???

COURIER. Yessir!

MAYOR. *(Momentarily stunned to silence.)* The dirty mongrelizers! . . . Gentlemen, this is a grave predicament indeed. It pains me to surrender priority of our states' right credo, but it is my solemn task and frightening duty to inform you that we have no other recourse but to seek outside help for deliverance. *(Blackout. Lights re-rise on Huntley-Brinkley-Murrow-Severeid-Cronkite-Reasoner-type Announcer grasping a hand-held microphone [imaginary] a few hours later. He is vigorously, excitedly mouthing his commentary, but no sound escapes his lips . . . During this dumb, wordless section of his broadcast, a bedraggled assortment of figures marching with picket signs occupy his attention. On their picket signs are inscribed various appeals and slogans. "CINDY LOU UNFAIR TO BABY JOE" . . . "CAP'N SAM MISS BIG BOY" . . . "RETURN LI'L BLUE TO MARSE JIM" . . . "INFORMATION REQUESTED 'BOUT MAMMY GAIL" . . . "BOSS NATHAN PROTEST TO FAST LEROY." Trailing behind the marchers, forcibly isolated, is a woman dressed in widow-black holding a placard which reads: "WHY DIDN'T YOU TELL US—YOUR DEFILED WIFE AND TWO ABSENT MONGRELS.")*

ANNOUNCER. *(Who has been silently mouthing his delivery during the picketing procession, is suddenly heard as if caught in the midst of commentary.)* . . . Factories standing idle from the loss of non-essential workers. Stores shuttered from the absconding of uncrucial personnel. Uncollected garbage threatening pestilence and pollution . . . Also, each second somewheres in this former utopia below the Mason and Dixon, dozens of decrepit old men and women usually tended by faithful nurses and servants are popping off like flies—abandoned by sons, daughters and grandchildren whose refusal to provide their doddering relatives with bedpans and other soothing necessities result in their hasty, nasty, messy corpus delicties . . . But most critically affected of all by this complete drought of Afro-American resources are policemen and other public safety guardians denied their daily quota of Negro arrests. One officer known affectionately as "TWO-A-DAY-PETE" because of his unblemished record of TWO Negro headwhippings per day has already been carted off to the County Insane Asylum—straight-jacketed, screaming and biting, unable to withstand the shock of having his spotless slate sullied by interruption . . . It is feared that similar attacks are soon expected among municipal judges prevented for the first time in years of distinguished benchsitting from sentencing one single Negro to a hoosegow or pokey . . . Ladies and gentlemen, as you trudge in from the joys and headaches of workday chores and dusk begins to descend on this sleepy Southern hamlet, we REPEAT—today—before early morning dew had dried upon magnolia blossoms, your comrade citizens of this lovely Dixie village awoke to the realization that some—pardon me! Not some—but ALL OF THEIR NEGROES were missing . . . Absent, vamoosed, departed, at bay, fugitive, away, gone and so-far unretrieved . . . In order to dispel your incredulity, gauge the temper of your suffering compatriots and just possibly prepare you for the likelihood of an equally nightmarish eventuality, we have gathered a cross-section of this city's most distinguished leaders for exclusive interviews . . . First, Mr. Council Clan, grand-dragoon of this area's most active civic organizations and staunch bell-wether of the political opposition . . . Mr. Clan, how do you ACCOUNT for this incredible disappearance?

CLAN. A PLOT, plain and simple, that's what it is, as plain as the corns on your feet!

ANNOUNCER. Whom would you consider responsible?

CLAN. I could go on all night.

ANNOUNCER. Cite a few?

CLAN. Too numerous.

ANNOUNCER. Just one?

CLAN. Name names when time comes.

ANNOUNCER. Could you be referring to native Negroes?

CLAN. Ever try quaranteening lepers from their spots?

ANNOUNCER. Their organizations?

CLAN. Could you slice a nose off a mouth and still keep a face?

ANNOUNCER. Commies?

CLAN. Would you lop off a titty from a chest and still have a breast?

ANNOUNCER. Your city government?

CLAN. Now you talkin'!

ANNOUNCER. State administration?

CLAN. Warming up!

ANNOUNCER. Federal?

CLAN. Kin a blind man see?!

ANNOUNCER. The Court?

CLAN. Is a pig clean?!

ANNOUNCER. Clergy?

CLAN. Do a polecat stink?!

ANNOUNCER. Well, Mr. Clan, with this massive complicity, how do you think the plot could've been prevented from succeeding?

CLAN. If I'da been in office, it never woulda happened.

ANNOUNCER. Then you're laying major blame at the doorstep of the present administration?

CLAN. Damn tooting!

ANNOUNCER. But from your oft-expressed views, Mr. Clan, shouldn't you and your followers be delighted at the turn of events? After all—isn't it one of the main policies of your society to *drive* the Negroes away? Drive 'em back where they came from?

CLAN. DRIVVVE, BOY! DRIIIIVVVE! That's right! . . . When we say so and not befo'. Ain't supposed to do nothing 'til we tell 'em. Got to stay put until we exercise our God-given right to tell 'em when to git!

ANNOUNCER. But why argue if they've merely jumped the gun? Why not rejoice at this premature purging of undesirables?

CLAN. The time ain't ripe yet, boy . . . The time ain't ripe yet.

ANNOUNCER. Thank you for being so informative, Mr. Clan—Mrs. Aide? Mrs. Aide? Over here, Mrs. Aide . . . Ladies and gentlemen, this city's Social Welfare Commissioner, Mrs. Handy Anna Aide . . . Mrs. Aide, with all your Negroes *AWOL,* haven't developments alleviated the staggering demands made upon your Welfare Department? Reduction of relief requests, elimination of case loads, removal of chronic welfare dependents, et cetera?

AIDE. Quite the contrary. Disruption of our pilot projects among Nigras saddles our white community with extreme hardship . . . You see, historically, our agencies have always been foremost contributors to the Nigra Git-A-Job movement. We pioneered in enforcing social welfare theories which oppose coddling the fakers. We strenuously believe in helping Nigras help themselves by participating in meaningful labor. "Relief is Out, Work is In," is our motto. We place them as maids, cooks, butlers, and breast-feeders, cesspool-diggers, wash-basin maintainers, shoe-shine boys, and so on—mostly on a volunteer self-work basis.

ANNOUNCER. Hired at prevailing salaried rates, of course?

AIDE. God forbid! Money is unimportant. Would only make 'em worse. Our main goal is to improve their ethical behavior. "Rehabilitation Through Positive Participation" is another motto of ours. All unwed mothers, loose-living malingering fathers, bastard children and shiftless grandparents are kept occupied through constructive muscle-therapy. This provides the Nigra with less opportunity to indulge his pleasure-loving amoral inclinations.

ANNOUNCER. They volunteer to participate in these pilot projects?

AIDE. Heavens no! They're notorious shirkers. When I said the program is voluntary, I meant white citizens in overwhelming majorities do the volunteering. Placing their homes, offices, appliances and persons at our disposal for use in "Operation Uplift." We would never dare place such a decision in the hands of the Nigra. It would never get off the ground! . . . No, they have no choice in the matter. "Work or Starve" is the slogan we use to stimulate Nigra awareness of what's good for survival.

ANNOUNCER. Thank you, Mrs. Aide, and good luck . . . Rev? . . . Rev? . . . Ladies and gentlemen, this city's foremost spiritual guidance counselor, Reverend Reb Pious . . . How does it look to you, Reb Pious?

PIOUS. *(Continuing to gaze skyward.)* It's in *His* hands, son, it's in *His* hand.

ANNOUNCER. How would you assess the disappearance, from a moral standpoint?

PIOUS. An immoral act, son, morally wrong and ethically indefensible. A perversion of Christian principles to be condemned from every pulpit of this nation.

ANNOUNCER. Can you account for its occurrence after the many decades of the Church's missionary activity among them?

PIOUS. It's basically a reversion of the Nigra to his deep-rooted primitivism . . . Now, at last, you can understand the difficulties of the Church in attempting to anchor God's kingdom among ungratefuls. It's a constant, unrelenting, no-holds-barred struggle against Satan to wrestle away souls locked in his possession for countless centuries! Despite all our aid, guidance, solace and protection, Old BeezleBub still retains tenacious grips upon the Nigras' childish loyalty—comparable to the lure of bright flames to an infant.

ANNOUNCER. But actual physical departure, Reb Pious? How do you explain that?

PIOUS. Voodoo, my son, voodoo . . . With Satan's assist, they have probably employed some heathen magic which we cultivated, sophisticated Christians know absolutely nothing about. However, before long we are confident about counteracting this evil witch-doctory and triumphing in our Holy Savior's name. At this perilous juncture, true believers of all denominations are participating in joint, 'round-the-clock observances, offering prayers for our Master's swiftest intercession. I'm optimistic about the outcome of his intervention . . . Which prompts me—if I may, sir—to offer these words of counsel to our delinquent Nigras . . . I say to you without rancor or vengeance, quoting a phrase of one of your greatest prophets, Booker T. Washington: "Return your buckets to where they lay and all will be forgiven."

ANNOUNCER. A very inspirational appeal, Reb Pious. I'm certain they will find the tug of its magnetic sincerity irresistible. Thank you, Reb Pious . . . All in all—as you have witnessed, ladies and gentlemen—this town symbolizes the face of disaster. Suffering as severe a prostration as any city wrecked, ravaged and devastated by the holocaust of war. A vital, lively, throbbing organism brought to a screeching halt by the strange enigma of the missing Negroes . . . We take you now to offices of the one man into whose hands has been thrust the final responsibility of rescuing this shuddering metropolis from the precipice of destruction . . . We give you the honorable Mayor, Henry R. E. Lee . . . Hello, Mayor Lee.

MAYOR. *(Jovially.)* Hello, Jack.

ANNOUNCER. Mayor Lee, we have just concluded interviews with some of your city's leading spokesmen. If I may say so, sir, they don't sound too encouraging about the situation.

MAYOR. Nonsense, Jack! The situation's well-in-hand as it could be under the circumstances. Couldn't be better in hand. Underneath every dark cloud, Jack, there's always a ray of sunlight, ha, ha, ha.

ANNOUNCER. Have you discovered one, sir?

MAYOR. Well, Jack, I'll tell you . . . Of course we've been faced wit' a little crisis, but look at it like this—we've faced 'em befo': Sherman marched through Georgia—ONCE! Lincoln freed the slaves—MOMENTARILY! Carpetbaggers even put Nigras in the Governor's mansion, state legislature, Congress and the Senate of the United States. But what happened?—Ole Dixie bounced right on back up . . . At this moment the Supreme Court's trying to put Nigras in our schools and the Nigra has got it in his haid to put hisself everywhere . . . But what you 'spect go'n' happen?—Ole Dixie will kangaroo back even higher. Southern courage, fortitude, chivalry and superiority always wins out . . . SHUCKS! We'll have us some Nigras befo' daylight is gone!

ANNOUNCER. Mr. Mayor, I hate to introduce this note, but in an earlier interview, one of your chief opponents, Mr. Clan, hinted at your own complicity in the affair—

MAYOR. A LOT OF POPPYCOCK! Clan is politicking! I've beaten him four times outta four and I'll beat him four more times outta four! This is no time for partisan politics! What we need now is level-headedness and across-the-board unity. This typical, rash, mealy-mouth, shooting-off-at-the-lip of Clan and his ilk proves their insincerity and voters will remember that in the next election! Won't you, voters?! *(Has risen to the height of campaign oratory.)*

ANNOUNCER. Mr. Mayor! . . . Mr. Mayor! . . . Please—

MAYOR. . . . I tell you, I promise you—

ANNOUNCER. PLEASE, MR. MAYOR!

MAYOR. Huh? . . . Oh—yes, carry on.

ANNOUNCER. Mr. Mayor, your cheerfuless and infectious good spirits lead me to conclude that startling new developments warrant fresh-found optimism. What concrete, declassified information do you have to support your claim that Negroes will reappear before nightfall?

MAYOR. Because we are presently awaiting the pay-off of a masterful five-point supra-recovery program which can't help but reap us a bonanza of Nigras 'fore sundown! . . . First: Exhaustive efforts to pinpoint the where'bouts of our own missing darkies continue to zero in on the bullseye . . . Second: The President of the United States, following an emergency cabinet meeting, has designated us the prime disaster area of the century—National Guard is already on the way . . . Third: In an unusual, but bold maneuver, we have appealed to the NAACP 'n' all other Nigra conspirators to help us git to the bottom of the vanishing act . . . Fourth: We have exercised our non-reciprocal option and requested that all fraternal southern states express their solidarity by lending us some of their Nigras temporarily on credit . . . Fifth and foremost: We have already gotten consent of the Governor to round up all stray, excess and incorrigible Nigras to be shipped to us under escort of the State Militia . . . That's why we've stifled pessimism and are brimming wit' confidence that this fullscale concerted mobilization will ring down a jackpot of jigaboos 'fore light vanishes from sky!—

ANNOUNCER. Congratulations! What happens if it fails?

MAYOR. Don't even think THAT! Absolutely no reason to suspect it will . . . *(Peers over shoulder, then whispers confidentially while placing hand over mouth by Announcer's imaginary mike.)* . . . But speculating on the dark side of your question— if we don't turn up some by nightfall, it may be all over. The harm has already been done. You see the South has always been glued together by the uninterrupted presence of its darkies. No telling how unstuck we might git if things keep on like they have.—Wait a minute, it musta paid off already! Mission accomplished 'cause here's Jackson head a time wit' the word . . . Well, Jackson, what's new?

JACKSON. Situation on the home front remains static sir—can't uncover scent or shadow. The NAACP and all other Nigra front groups 'n' plotters deny any knowledge or connection wit' the missing Nigras. Maintained this even after appearing befo' a Senate Emergency Investigating Committee which subpoenaed 'em to Washington post haste and threw 'em in jail for contempt. A handful of Nigras who agreed to make spectacular appeals for ours to come back to us, have themselves mysteriously disappeared. But, worst news of all, sir, is our sister cities and counties, inside and outside the state, have changed their minds, fallen back on their promises and refused to lend us any Nigras, claiming they don't have 'nuff for themselves.

MAYOR. What 'bout Nigras promised by the Governor?!

JACKSON. Jailbirds and vagrants escorted here from chain-gangs and other reservations either revolted and escaped enroute or else vanished mysteriously on approaching our city limits . . . Deterioration rapidly escalates, sir. Estimates predict we kin hold out only one more hour before overtaken by anarchistic turmoil . . . Some citizens seeking haven elsewheres have already fled, but on last report were being forcibly turned back by armed sentinels in other cities who wanted no parts of 'em— claiming they carried a jinx.

MAYOR. That bad, huh?

JACKSON. Worse, sir . . . we've received at least five reports of plots on your life.

MAYOR. What?!—We've gotta act quickly then!

JACKSON. Run out of ideas, sir.

MAYOR. Think harder, boy!

JACKSON. Don't have much time, sir. One measly hour, then all hell go'n' break loose.

MAYOR. Gotta think of something drastic, Jackson!

JACKSON. I'm dry, sir.

MAYOR. Jackson! Is there any planes outta here in the next hour?

JACKSON. All transportation's been knocked out, sir.

MAYOR. I thought so!

JACKSON. What were you contemplating, sir?

MAYOR. Don't ask me what I was contemplating! I'm still boss 'round here! Don't forget it!

JACKSON. Sorry, sir.

MAYOR. . . . Hold the wire! . . . Wait a minute . . . ! Waaaaait a minute—GODAMMIT! All this time crapping 'round, diddling and fotsing wit' puny li'l' solutions—all the while neglecting our ace in the hole, our trump card! Most potent weapon for digging Nigras outta the woodpile!!! All the while right befo' our eyes! . . . Ass! Why didn't you remind me?!!!

JACKSON. What is it, sir?

MAYOR. . . . ME—THAT'S WHAT! ME! A personal appeal from ME! *Directly to them!* . . . Although we wouldn't let 'em march to the polls and express their affection for me through the ballot box, we've always known I'm held highest in their esteem. A direct address from their beloved Mayor! . . . If they's anywheres close within the sound of my voice, they'll shape up! Or let us know by a sign they's ready to!

JACKSON. You sure that'll turn the trick, sir?

MAYOR. As sure as my ancestors befo' me who knew that when they puckered their lips to whistle, ole Sambo was gonna come a-lickety-splitting to answer the call! . . . That same chips-down blood courses through these Confederate gray veins of Henry R. E. Lee!!!

ANNOUNCER. I'm delighted to offer our network's facilities for such a crucial public interest address, sir. We'll arrange immediately for your appearance on an international hookup, placing you in the widest proximity to contact them wherever they may be.

MAYOR. Thank you, I'm very grateful . . . Jackson, re-grease the machinery and set wheels in motion. Inform townspeople what's being done. Tell 'em we're all in this together. The next hour is countdown. I demand absolute cooperation, city-wide silence and inactivity. I don't want the Nigras frightened if they's nearby. This is the most important hour in town's history. Tell 'em if one single Nigra shows up during hour of decision, victory is within sight. I'm gonna git 'em that one—maybe all! Hurry and crack to it! (*Announcer rushes out, followed by Jackson. Blackout. Scene reopens, with Mayor seated, eyes front, spotlight illuminating him in semi-darkness. Shadowy figures stand in the background, prepared to answer phones or aid in any other manner. Mayor waits patiently until "GO!" signal is given. Then begins, his voice combining elements of confidence, tremolo and gravity.*) Good evening . . . Despite the fact that millions of you wonderful people throughout the nation are viewing and listening to this momentous broadcast—and I thank you for your concern and sympathy in this hour of our peril—I primarily want to concentrate my attention and address these remarks solely for the benefit of our departed Nigra friends who may be listening somewhere in our far-flung land to the sound of my voice . . . If you are—it is with heart-felt emotion and fond memories of our happy association that I ask— "Where are you . . . ?" Your absence has left a void in the bosom of every single man, woman and child of our great city. I tell you—you don't know what it means for us to wake up in the morning and discover that your cheerful, grinning, happy-go-lucky faces are missing! . . . From the depths of my heart, I can only meekly, humbly suggest what it means to me personally . . . You see—the one face I will never be able to erase from my memory is the face—not of my Ma, not of Pa, neither wife or child—but the image of the first woman I came to love so well when just a wee lad— the vision of the first human I laid clear sight on at childbirth—the profile—better yet, the full face of my dear old . . . Jemimah—God rest her soul . . . Yes! My dear ole mammy, wit' her round ebony moonbeam gleaming down upon me in the crib, teeth shining, blood-red bandana standing starched, peaked and proud, gazing down upon me affectionately as she crooned me a Southern lullaby . . . OH! It's a memorable picture I will eternally cherish in permanent treasure chambers of my heart, now and forever always . . . Well, if this radiant image can remain so infinitely vivid to me all these many years after her unfortunate demise in the Po' folks home—THINK of the misery the rest of us must be suffering after being *freshly* denied your soothing presence?! We need ya. If you kin hear me, just contact this station 'n' I will welcome you back personally. Let me just tell you that since you eloped, nothing has been the same. How could it? You're part of us, you belong to us. Just give us a sign and we'll be contented that all is well . . . Now if you've skipped away on a little fun-fest, we understand, ha, ha. We know you like a good time and we don't begrudge it to ya. Hell—er, er, we like a good time ourselves—who doesn't? . . . In fact, think of all the good times we've had together, huh? We've had some real fun, you and us, yesiree! . . . Nobody knows better than you and I what fun we've had together. You singing us those old Southern coon songs and dancing those Nigra jigs and us clapping, prodding 'n' spurring you on! Lots of fun, huh?! . . . OH BOY! The times we've had together . . . If you've snucked away for a bit of fun by yourself, we'll go 'long wit' ya—long as you let us know where you at so we won't be worried about you . . . We'll go 'long wit' you long as you don't take the joke too far. I'll admit a joke is a joke and you've played a LULU! . . . I'm warning you, we can't stand much more horsing 'round from you! Business is business 'n' fun is fun! You've had your fun so now let's get down to business! Come on back, YOU HEAR ME!!! . . . If you been hoodwinked by agents of some foreign government, I've been authorized by the President of these United States to inform you that this liberty-loving Republic is prepared to rescue you from their clutches. Don't pay no 'tention to their sireeen songs and atheistic promises! You better off under our control and you know it! . . . If you been bamboozled by rabble-rousing nonsense of your own so-called leaders, we prepared to offer same protection. Just call us up! Just give us a sign! . . . Come on, give us a sign . . . give us a sign—even a teeny-weeny one . . . ??!! *(Glances around checking on possible communications. A bevy of headshakes indicate no success. Mayor returns to address with desperate fervor.)* Now look—you don't know what you doing! If you persist in this disobedience, you know all too well the consequences! We'll track you to the end of the earth, beyond the galaxy, across the stars! We'll capture you and chastise you with all the vengeance we command! 'N' you know only too well how stern we kin be when double-crossed! The city, the state and the entire nation will crucify you for this unpardonable defiance! *(Checks again.)* No call . . . ? No sign . . . ? Time is running out! Deadline slipping past! They gotta respond! They gotta! *(Resuming.)* Listen to me! I'm begging y'all, you've gotta come back . . . ! LOOK, GEORGE! *(Waves dirty rag aloft.)* I brought the rag you wax the car wit' . . . Don't this bring back memories, George, of all the days you spent shining that automobile to shimmering perfection . . . ? And you, Rufus?! . . . Here's the shoe polisher and the brush! . . . 'Member, Rufus? . . . Remember the happy mornings you spent popping this rag and whisking this brush so furiously 'till it created music that was sympho-nee to the ear . . . ? And you—MANDY? . . . Here's the waste-basket you didn't dump this morning. I saved it just for you! . . . LOOK, all y'all out there . . . ? *(Signals and a three-person procession parades one after the other before the imaginary camera.)*

DOLL WOMAN. *(Brandishing a crying baby [doll] as she strolls past and exits.)* She's been crying ever since you left, Caldonia . . .

MOP MAN. *(Flashing mop.)* It's been waiting in the same corner, Buster . . .

BRUSH MAN. *(Flagging toilet brush in one hand and toilet plunger in other.)* It's been dry ever since you left, Washington . . .

MAYOR. *(Jumping in on the heels of the last exit.)* Don't these things mean anything to y'all? By God! Are your memories so short?! Is there nothing sacred to ya? . . . Please come back, for my sake, please! All of you—even you questionable ones! I promise no harm will be done to you! Revenge is disallowed! We'll forgive everything! Just come on back and I'll git down on my knees—*(Immediately drops to knees.)* I'll be kneeling in the middle of Dixie Avenue to kiss the first shoe of the first one 'a you to show up . . . *I'll smooch any other spot you request* . . . Erase this nightmare 'n' we'll concede any demand you make, just come on back—please???!!— . . . PLEEEEEZE?!!!

VOICE. *(Shouting.)* TIME!!!

MAYOR. *(Remaining on knees, frozen in a pose of supplication. After a brief, deadly silence, he whispers almost inaudibly.)* They wouldn't answer . . . they wouldn't answer . . . *(Blackout as bedlam erupts offstage. Total blackness holds during a sufficient interval where offstage sound-effects create the illusion of complete pandemonium, followed by a diminution which trails off into an expressionistic simulation of a city coming to a strickened stand-still: industrial machinery clanks to halt, traffic blares to silence, etc. . . . The stage remains dark and silent for a long moment, then lights re-arise on the Announcer.)*

ANNOUNCER. A pitiful sight, ladies and gentlemen. Soon after his unsuccessful appeal, Mayor Lee suffered a vicious pummeling from the mob and barely escaped with his life. National Guardsmen and State Militia were impotent in quelling the fury of a town venting its frustration in an orgy of destruction—a frenzy of rioting, looting and all other aberrations of a town gone berserk . . . Then—suddenly—as if a magic wand had been waved, madness evaporated and something more frightening replaced it: Submission . . . Even whimperings ceased. The city: exhausted, benumbed.—Slowly its occupants slinked off into shadows, and by midnight, the town was occupied exclusively by zombies. The fight and life had been drained out . . . Pooped . . . Hope ebbed away as completely as the beloved, absent Negroes . . . As our crew packed gear and crept away silently, we treaded softly—as if we were stealing away from a mausoleum . . . The Face Of A Defeated City. *(Blackout. Lights rise slowly at the sound of rooster-crowing, signalling the approach of a new day, the next morning. Scene is same as opening of play. Clem and Luke are huddled over dazedly, trancelike. They remain so for a long count. Finally, a figure drifts on stage, shuffling slowly.)*

LUKE. *(Gazing in silent fascination at the approaching figure.)* . . . Clem . . . ? Do you see what I see or am I dreaming . . . ?

CLEM. It's a . . . a Nigra, ain't it, Luke . . . ?

LUKE. Sure looks like one, Clem—but we better make sure—eyes could be playing tricks on us . . . Does he still look like one to you, Clem?

CLEM. He still does, Luke—but I'm scared to believe—

LUKE. . . . Why . . . ? It looks like Rastus, Clem!

CLEM. Sure does, Luke . . . but we better not jump to no hasty conclusion . . .

LUKE. *(In timid softness.)* That you, Rastus . . . ?
RASTUS. *(Stepin Fetchit, Willie Best, Nicodemus, B. McQueen and all the rest rolled into one.)* Why . . . howdy . . . Mr. Luke . . . Mr. Clem . . .
CLEM. It is him, Luke! It is him!
LUKE. Rastus?
RASTUS. Yas . . . sah?
LUKE. Where was you yesterday?
RASTUS. *(Very, very puzzled.)* Yes . . . ter . . . day? . . . Yester . . . day . . . ? Why . . . right . . . here . . . Mr. Luke . . .
LUKE. No you warn't, Rastus, don't lie to me! Where was you yestiddy?
RASTUS. Why . . . I'm sure I was . . . Mr. Luke . . . Remember . . . I made . . . that . . . delivery for you . . .
LUKE. That was MONDAY, Rastus, yestiddy was TUESDAY.
RASTUS. Tues . . . day . . . ? You don't say . . . Well . . . well . . . well . . .
LUKE. Where was you 'n' all the other Nigras yesterday, Rastus?
RASTUS. I . . . thought . . . yestiddy . . . was . . . Monday, Mr. Luke—I coulda swore it . . . ! . . . See how . . . things . . . kin git all mixed up? . . . I coulda swore it . . .
LUKE. TODAY is WEDNESDAY, Rastus. Where was you TUESDAY?
RASTUS. Tuesday . . . huh? That's somp'um . . . I . . . don't . . . remember . . . missing . . . a day . . . Mr. Luke . . . but I guess you right . . .
LUKE. Then where was you!!!???
RASTUS. Don't rightly know, Mr. Luke. I didn't know I had skipped a day.—But that jist goes to show you how time kin fly, don't it, Mr. Luke . . . Uuh, uuh, uuh . . . *(He starts shuffling off, scratching head, a flicker of a smile playing across his lips. Clem and Luke gaze dumbfoundedly as he disappears.)*
LUKE. *(Eyes sweeping around in all directions.)* Well . . . There's the others, Clem . . . Back jist like they useta be . . . Everything's same as always . . .
CLEM. ?? . . . . Is it . . . Luke . . . ! *(Slow fade.)*

Curtain

Property Plot

First Scene:
    2 chairs, 2 "STORE" signs (optional)

Second Scene:
    Cot-bed, blanket coverlet, 1 "HOME" sign (optional)

Third Scene:
    3 high stools

Fourth Scene:
    Same as first scene (signs struck)

Fifth Scene:
    Bare stage, coffee cups and jacket (for John)

Sixth Scene:
    Mayor's table, 1 chair, phone without wires atop table, litter paper atop table

Seventh Scene:
    1 chair

Eighth Scene:
    Same as sixth scene, toy walkie-talkie and map on table added

Ninth Scene:
    Announcer's mike (head without wires), picket signs, bare stage

Tenth Scene:
    Small table, chair, waste basket (filled), mop, car rag, shoe rag, shoe polish, shoe brush, crying doll, toilet brush and toilet plunger

Eleventh Scene:
    Bare stage, announcer's mike

Twelfth Scene:
    Same as first scene (signs struck)

African-American Poetry

"Yet do I marvel at this curious thing: To make a poet black, and bid him sing!" are two lines from Countee Cullen's poem which summon the curiosity about the 200 plus years of poetry by African Americans. Coming from their native lands into a foreign, hostile, inhospitable environment with no knowledge of the language, the culture, nor the customs, these foreigners were forced to communicate by any means necessary. There were the sorrow songs, the slave ditties, the spirituals, the field songs; some of the songs happy, some plaintive. As these slaves and free people began to learn the language, they began to put their experiences, their thoughts, and feelings on paper. In their writings, African Americans maintained the rhythms, a mainstay of poetry, of their songs.

One of the first of these slaves to be recognized as a poet is Lucy Terry from Deerfield, Massachusetts. Her extant poem, written in 1746 about a Native American raid is entitled "Bars Fight." "Bars" is an archaic word meaning meadow. Jupiter Hammon, who wrote a religious poem which was published as a broadside in 1760, is considered the first African American to be published. Phillis Wheatley is recognized through her 124 page book as the first African American to publish a volume of poetry, although it was printed in London. Thus the die was cast.

As these people learned their letters through secret schoolings, reading the Bible, Greek literature, hymn books, and other books, they still drew upon their own cultural experiences and used their new language, fused with their native language to create their dialect. Because of the popularity of dialect poetry among White American writers in the late 1800s, it was no surprise that Paul Laurence Dunbar would be honorably praised and recognized as a dialect poet. Most notable of these cultural experiences were the folk literature and the secular and spiritual music which emanated from the slave plantations of the South and were drawn from the oral literature from the motherland. This richness and diversity of their heritage provided these new poets with their striking imagery and metaphorical language, and profound allusions. Of course, reason and rhythm were innate. Their imitation of the English and American poets cannot be ignored. They imitated the style, structure, language, and other modes of versification. Greek literature, Shakespeare, the 17th and 18th century poets, the Romantic poets—all were models for the developing African-American poets. They experimented with the various types of poetry, including odes, epics, sonnets, and ballads.

The African-American poets used these modes to voice their protest, subtly and blatantly, about the harsh socio-economic, political climate which pervaded America. Slavery was a reality which affected the enslaved and the free. While African Americans were not prolific writers, there was a cadre of poets who poeticized their call for the abolition of slavery. Among these many abolitionist poets, the most prolific and best known is Frances Ellen Watkins Harper who reportedly sold more than 50,000 copies of her two-volume poetry while on tours lecturing against the evils of slavery. Other notables, abolitionist poets among many, were Albery A. Whitman, George Moses Horton, James M. Whitfield, Charles Reason, and George B. Vashon. This fundamental theme of protest is the common denominator which links all poetry by African Americans. This is not to say that African Americans did not write about love and other human interest themes. One must not forget that George Moses Horton started out writing love poems for students at the University of North Carolina, Chapel Hill. This was what J. Saunders Redding called "the literature of necessity" which was spawned by the "spore of a cankerous growth" called slavery which another writer calls the bankruptcy of American democracy.

Although slavery was abolished in 1865, there was still an urgent need to rail against the conditions under which African Americans lived. Fifty-five years later during the Harlem Renaissance, poets such as Langston Hughes, Countee Cullen, Claude McKay, W. E. B. DuBois, Anne Spencer, Helene Johnson, Georgia Douglas Johnson, and James Weldon Johnson were among the many who protested the lynchings, segregation, illicit miscegenation, and other social injustices. Although African-American soldiers fought in America's war, they were not afforded equal rights on jobs or at voting polls. Poets, now more educated, used the formal styles and imagery of language to couch their protests. For instance, Claude McKay's "If We Must Die" is a tightly controlled sonnet form in which the rage of protest is rigidly restrained, yet the poem is very effective protest. On the other hand, Hughes experimented with a freer style of versification, often using the diction of the African Americans to speak out against the brutalities of the South as well as the North. Langston Hughes and Sterling Brown used the blues form, another African-American cultural phenomenon in their poetry as many others did.

The blight of urban life was one of the themes of some of the later poets, such as Gwendolyn Brooks, who poignantly describes tenement life in her *In the Mecca*. Margaret Walker's magnum opus *For My People* summarizes historically the grief-filled sojourn of her people in America. Walker and Brooks often use historical events as the backdrop for their poems. Walker's volume of verse *Prophets for a New Day* can be considered a history book on events of the turbulent 1960s, a pandemoniac period during which civil unrest was at its height. Not unlike the "Red Summer" of 1919, the 1960s can be called the Red Decade. As African Americans took to the streets, they used their pens as swords. The people and the poets were defiant, and this defiance was demonstrated in the poetry. Just like the people defied the likes of Bull Connor and his police dogs, the poets defied the classical forms, imagery, and language. Instead of traditional forms, the poets scattered words across the page, used the diction, syntax, and grammar of the man on the street, even using profanity and abbreviations, and they venerated African-American heroes, used the symbols, ideology, folklore of African-American culture. They no longer cared about Western aesthetics and refused to be judged by such standards. Not only was this a period, known as the Revolutionary 1960s; it was a period of protest but a period of affirmation. Haki Madhubuti (Don L. Lee), Nikki Giovanni, A. B. Spellman, Carolyn Rodgers, Sonia Sanchez, and Amiri Baraka (considered the Dean of the Black Arts Movement) exhorted African Americans to affirm their blackness and their self-worth and to accept that "I yam what I yam." "I am Black and proud!" "I am Somebody!" "Black is Beautiful!" These listed poets and many, many more carved on the tradition of protest poetry, which started in the 18th century but with much more vehemence.

So this "curious thing" of which Countee Cullen wrote in 1925 was no longer a curiosity, nor a curio to be ridiculed or mistreated. The African-American poets for more than two hundred years had protested their existence in an unjust society, while keeping a bloodied head unbowed. At this we all marvel.

Selected Bibliography

Andrews, William L., Frances Smith Foster, and Trudier Harris, Eds. *The Oxford Companion to African American Literature*. New York: Oxford UP, 1997.

Barksdale, Richard and Keneth Kinnamon. *Black Writers of America: A Comprehensive Anthology*. New York: Macmillan, 1972.

Davis, Arthur P. and J. Saunders Redding, eds. *Calvacade: Negro American Writing From 1760 to the Present*. New York: Houghton Mifflin, 1971.

Ford, Nick Aaron. *Black Insights: Significant Literature by Black Americans—1760 to the Present*. Waltham, MA: Xerox, 1971.

Gates, Henry Louis, Jr. and Nellie Y. McKay, eds. *Norton Anthology of African American Literature.* New York: Norton, 1997.

Henderson, Stephen. *Understanding the New Black Poetry: Black Speech and Black Music as Poetic References.* New York: William Morrow, 1973.

Hill, Patricia Liggins et al., eds. *Call and Response: The Riverside Anthology of African American Literary Tradition.* New York: Houghton Mifflin, 1998.

Hughes, Langston and Arna Bontemps, eds. *The Poetry of the Negro 1746–1970.* Garden City, New York: Anchor Press/Doubleday, 1970.

King, Woodie, Jr., ed. *The Forerunners: Black Poets in America.* Washington, D.C.: Howard, 1981.

Lee, Don L. *Dynamite Voices: Black Poets of the 60s.* Detroit: Broadside Press. 1971.

Nelson, Emmanuel S., Ed. *African American Authors, 1745–1945: A Bio-Bibliographical Critical Sourcebook.* Westport, CT: Greenwood, 2000.

Reid, Margaret. "A Rhetorical Analysis of Protest Poetry of the Harlem Renaissance and the Sixties." Diss., Ann Arbor, MI: University Microfilms, 1980.

Stetson, Erlene, ed. *Black Sister: Poetry by Black American Women, 1746–1980.* Bloomington, Indiana Press, 1981.

Wagner, Jean. *Black Poets of the United States Paul Laurence Dunbar to Langston Hughes.* Trans. Kenneth Douglas. Chicago: University of Illinois Press, 1973.

Phillis Wheatley (c. 1753–1784)

In the mid 1700s, an African girl of the Gambian Fulani tribe was kidnapped and transported aboard the slave ship, Phillis, to Boston to be sold as a slave. In July 1761, Wheatley was purchased by John Wheatley, a tailor, to attend his wife Susanna and daughter Mary. The Wheatley family instructed her religiously in the Puritan tradition. As a young learned slave in Boston, Wheatley could read fluently the most difficult parts of the Bible 16 months after arriving in the Americas. She learned grammar, history, geography, and astronomy and was astute in the Latin classics of Virgil and Ovid. Her favorite work was Alexander Pope's translation of Homer. Wheatley was such an avid student that she was not given the laborious chores of the ordinary slave, and the delicateness of her physical condition prohibited this. Instead, Wheatley wrote poetry and performed light household chores. At age 13, she wrote her first poem entitled "On Being Brought from Africa to America." Her only publication is one book of 46 poems entitled *Poems on Various Subjects, Religious and Moral by Phillis Wheatley, Negro Servant to Mr. John Wheatley, of Boston, in New England* (1773).

Wheatley conversed with some of Boston's and England's most elite citizens. Wheatley met with or received correspondence from the Earl of Dartmouth; Benjamin Franklin; John Hancock; Samuel Mather, brother of Cotton Mather; and George Washington. Wheatley underwent an oral comprehensive before several of Boston's elevated and elitist citizenry of White males to prove that her intellectual capability was authentic. They were so awestruck over Wheatley's precociousness, race, and gender that General George Washington invited her to confer with him. Several days later he opened the doors of the Continental Army to African Americans.

John Wheatley emancipated Phillis in 1773. After her emancipation she expressed her opposition to slavery in a letter addressed to Samson Occom. Thus the belief that she demonstrated race ambivalence is untrue. In 1778 Wheatley married John Peters, a pursuer of dreams who had little success in his many occupations. The two had three children who died in succession. Phillis Wheatley died on December 5, 1784.

Wheatley's poetry contains her thoughts of the day-to-day experiences of Bostonians. She adhered to the European standard, for she had no other models. Wheatley modeled her work after the neoclassical poet Alexander Pope and is considered an occasional poet, one interested in the clever crafting of verse. Her reading public was the White elite to whom she provided themes of the Christian versus the heathen. Her British poetic style is elaborate; she prefers the heroic couplet and uses hyperbole, allusion, personification, invocation, and elegiac convention for effect. One-third of her poems are elegiac. All of Wheatley's poetry is dedicated to individuals or reflects events that mattered to her.

Wheatley wrote raceless poetry. It contained little propaganda or protest and little indication that she was an African American. Some critics say that Wheatley neither excelled nor failed in poetic creativity but is an accomplished imitator. Yet she does have a place in African-American literary history. The publication of her book influenced African-American literature in general, as well as the African-American woman's literary tradition.

Selected Bibliography

Baker, Houston A., Jr. *The Journey Back: Issues in Black Literature and Criticism.* Chicago: University of Chicago Press, 1980.
Foster, Frances Smith. *Written by Herself: Literary Production by African American Women, 1746–1892.* Bloomington, IN: Indiana University Press, 1993.
Gates, Henry Louis, Jr. *Figures in Black: Words, Signs, and the "Racial" Self.* New York: Oxford University Press, 1987.
Hine, Darlene Clark, ed. *Black Women in America: An Historical Encyclopedia.* Vol. 2. Brooklyn: Carlson, 1993.
Nelson, Emmanuel S., Ed. *African American Authors, 1745–1945: A Bio-Bibliographical Critical Sourcebook.* Westport, CT: Greenwood, 2000.
Robinson, William H., ed. *Black New England Letters: The Uses of Writing in Black New England.* Boston: National Endowment for the Humanities,1977.
___, ed. *Phillis Wheatley and Her Writings.* New York: Garland, 1984.

To S. M., a Young *African* Painter, on Seeing His Works

Phillis Wheatley

To show the lab'ring bosom's deep intent,
And thought in living characters to paint,
When first thy pencil did those beauties give,
And breathing figures learnt from thee to live,
How did those prospects give my soul delight, 5
A new creation rushing on my sight?
Still, wond'rous youth! each noble path pursue,
On deathless glories fix thine ardent view:
Still may the painter's and the poet's fire
To aid thy pencil, and thy verse conspire! 10
And may the charms of each seraphic theme
Conduct thy footsteps to immortal fame!
High to the blissful wonders of the skies
Elate thy soul, and raise thy wishful eyes.
Thrice happy, when exalted to survey 15
That splendid city, crown'd with endless day,
Whose twice six gates on radiant hinges ring:
Celestial *Salem* blooms in endless spring.

Calm and serene thy moments glide along,
And may the muse inspire each future song! 20
Still, with the sweets of contemplation bless'd,
May peace with balmy wings your soul invest!
But when these shades of time are chas'd away,
And darkness ends in everlasting day,
On what seraphic pinions shall we move, 25
And view the landscapes in the realms above?
There shall thy tongue in heav'nly murmurs flow,
And there my muse with heav'nly transport glow:
No more to tell of *Damon's* tender sighs,
Or rising radiance of *Aurora's* eyes, 30

For nobler themes demand a nobler strain,
And purer language on th' ethereal plain.
Cease, gentle muse! the solemn gloom of night
Now seals the fair creation from my sight.

Paul Laurence Dunbar (1872–1906)

Paul Laurence Dunbar, poet, short story writer, novelist as well as author of articles, dramatic sketches, and song lyrics, was born on June 27, 1872, to former slaves Joshua and Matilda Dunbar. Although Dunbar was a prolific author of four volumes of short stories, four novels and other works in various genres, his greatest literary contributions were poetic.

Dunbar was a published poet as early as 1888; the *Dayton Herald* published his verse while he was in high school. In 1889 Dunbar founded a newspaper, the *Dayton Tattler,* which was printed by his classmate Orville Wright (who later made aviation history with his brother), but the paper quickly folded. During his senior year, Dunbar, who was the only African-American student at Dayton High, was editor-in-chief of the school's paper, president of the literary society, class president, and class poet. Despite his stellar high school record, Dunbar could only find employment after his 1891 graduation as a hotel elevator operator. Undaunted, Dunbar continued to write poems at work.

In 1893, the same year Frederick Douglass hired Dunbar to work as his assistant at the Chicago World Fair's Haitian Pavilion, the young, unknown poet spent his spare time selling copies of his first volume of poems, *Oak and Ivy.* His second volume, *Majors and Minors* (1895), was favorably reviewed by William Dean Howells, America's leading literary critic. Howells wrote the introduction to Dunbar's next book, *Lyrics of Lowly Life* (1896); Dunbar's talent, publicized by Howells' endorsement and a major national publishing company's printing of *Lyrics of Lowly Life,* catapulted Dunbar to national and international attention. Dunbar traveled to various sections of America as well as England to read his poetry to audiences. He published eight more volumes of poetry: *Lyrics of the Hearthside* (1899), *Poems of Cabin and Field* (1899), *Candle-Lightin' Time* (1901), *When Malindy Sings* (1903), *Lyrics of Love and Laughter* (1903), *Li'l Gal* (1904), *Lyrics of Sunshine and Shadow* (1905), and *Howdy, Honey, Howdy* (1905). To date, the most complete edition of Dunbar's poems is *The Collected Poetry of Paul Laurence Dunbar* (1994).

Although Dunbar was a prolific, critically acclaimed poet, he was frequently frustrated. White America praised his dialect poetry, while virtually ignoring his standard verse. He was not the first Black to employ dialect in poetry. During Dunbar's lifetime, America could accept an African-American poet who wrote in dialect about carefree slaves on a plantation; America could not accept a Black poet lamenting his loss of freedom as a writer and individual as Dunbar did in "Sympathy," written in standard verse. Still Dunbar, who originally wrote in dialect to attract an audience, was not swayed by the whims of America; he authored two-thirds of his poems in standard verse. Diagnosed with tuberculosis a decade before his death in 1906, Dunbar refused to allow his illness to interfere with his writing. Dunbar's writing career only lasted 13 years, yet he remains an American literary pioneer.

Selected Bibliography

Andrews, William L., Frances Smith Foster, and Trudier Harris, eds. *The Oxford Companion to African American Literature*. New York: Oxford University Press, 1997.

Nelson, Emmanuel S., Ed. *African American Authors, 1745–1945: A Bio-Bibliographical Critical Sourcebook*. Westport, CT: Greenwood, 2000.

Sympathy

Paul Laurence Dunbar

I know what the caged bird feels, alas!
When the sun is bright on the upland slopes;
When the wind stirs soft through the springing grass,
And the river flows like a stream of glass;
When the first bird sings and the first bud opes, 5
And the faint perfume from its chalice steals—
I know what the caged bird feels!

I know why the caged bird beats his wing
Till its blood is red on the cruel bars;
For he must fly back to his perch and cling 10
When he fain would be on the bough a-swing;
And a pain still throbs in the old, old scars
And they pulse again with a keener sting—
I know why he beats his wing!

I know why the caged bird sings, ah me, 15
When his wing is bruised and his bosom sore,—
When he beats his bars and he would be free;
It is not a carol of joy or glee,
But a prayer that he sends from his heart's deep core,
But a plea, that upward to Heaven he flings— 20
I know why the caged bird sings!

We Wear the Mask

Paul Laurence Dunbar

We wear the mask that grins and lies,
It hides our cheeks and shades our eyes,—
This debt we pay to human guile;
With torn and bleeding hearts we smile,
And mouth with myriad subtleties. 5

Why should the world be overwise,
In counting all our tears and sighs?
Nay, let them only see us, while
   We wear the mask.

We smile, but, O great Christ, our cries 10
To Thee from tortured souls arise.
We sing, but oh, the clay is vile
Beneath our feet, and long the mile;
But let the world dream otherwise,
   We wear the mask. 15

Claude McKay (1889–1948)

Claude McKay, the youngest of eleven children, was born in Clarendon Hills of Jamaica, British West Indies. He was initially educated by his older brother, a schoolteacher whose interest in free thought and philosophy in general affected the younger Claude. As an adolescent McKay met Edward Jekyll, an English scholar of Jamaican folklore, whose library and active instruction aided McKay in the writing of his early dialect poetry. Before McKay came to America, he was a well-known poet in his native dialect. In 1912 McKay published *Songs of Jamaica,* a volume written largely in the dialect of the island's peasants and giving a realistic picture of their lives. His second work, *Constab Ballads,* both describes the author's personal experience as an island constable and focuses on his sympathy for the people. These books were so highly respected that McKay became the first Black to receive the medal of the Jamaican Institute of Arts and Sciences, which came with a substantial cash award.

McKay, determined to use the prize to finance his education at Tuskegee Institute in Alabama, arrived in the United States in 1912. After a few months, he departed from Tuskegee in frustration at local conditions. Then McKay transferred to Kansas State College to study agricultural science for two years (1912–1914). Anxious to resume his career as a writer, McKay left for Harlem. Supporting himself as a waiter, porter, and restaurant proprietor, he familiarized himself with the New York literary scene. He was soon befriended by such important White figures as Edward Arlington Robinson and Waldo Frank, a Jewish radical novelist and cultural critic. McKay's first break came in 1917 when Frank published two of his sonnets, "The Harlem Dancer" and "Invocation," in the December issue of *The Seven Arts,* a highly respected avant-garde magazine. Short story writer Frank Harris, who published several of McKay's poems in *Pearson's*, another magazine, seems also to have made a major impression on the young poet.

In 1922 McKay published his most important collection of poetry, *Harlem Shadows,* which, in the opinion of some critics, virtually inaugurated the Harlem Renaissance. According to McKay, the book grew out of his urge to place the militant "If We Must Die," his most famous poem, "inside of a book." The racial violence that racked America in the summer of 1919 had inspired the sonnet which later was recited by Winston Churchill in 1939 to bolster British morale during the worst period of World War II. McKay, often regarded as the first major poet of the Harlem Renaissance, shaped the trends that would later define that literary movement. He introduced some of the principles which guided the authors of the Harlem Renaissance. McKay was perhaps the most radical of the young Black authors.

Not only did McKay write poetry, but he also published three novels. McKay's *Home to Harlem* (1928) was the first novel by an African American to be a bestseller. Reprinted five times in two months, it seems to have satisfied a consuming curiosity on the part of Americans for information about the nightlife and the lowlife of Harlem. *Banjo* (1929) is a sequel to *Home to Harlem.* It focuses on the experience of several Black seamen from the West Indies, Africa, and the United States, thrown together on a beach in Marseilles. Telling the story of a Jamaican peasant girl who has managed to retain her ties to her people in spite of a British education, the last novel, *Banana Bottom* (1933), is generally regarded as McKay's finest achievement in fiction. McKay also completed a collection of short stories *Gingertown* (1932), focusing primarily on Harlem and Jamaica.

In the mid 1930s, McKay decided to complete the autobiography, *A Long Way from Home*, that recounts his various travels and experiences. The autobiography does not focus on Claude McKay, the man; rather it is an account of McKay's struggle to reconcile his views of art with his concepts of self, blackness, and class. On May 22, 1948, McKay died of heart failure in a Chicago hospital. He had been at work on a collection of his poems, which appeared posthumously, with a biographical note by Max Eastman as *Selected Poems* (1953).

Selected Bibliography

Harris, Trudier, ed. *Dictionary of Literary Biography: Afro American Writers from the Harlem Renaissance to 1940*. Vol. 51. Detroit: Gale Research, 1987.

Baptism

Claude McKay

Into the furnace let me go alone;
Stay you without in terror of the heat
I will go naked in—for thus 'tis sweet—
Into the weird depths of the hottest zone.
I will not quiver in the frailest bone, 5
You will not note a flicker of defeat;
My heart shall tremble not its fate to meet,
My mouth give utterance to any moan.
The yawning oven spits forth fiery spears;
Red aspish tongues shout wordlessly my name. 10
Desire destroys, consumes my mortal fears,
Transforming me into a shape of flame,
I will come out, back to your world of tears,
A stronger soul within a finer frame.

America

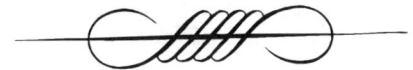

Claude McKay

Although she feeds me bread of bitterness,
And sinks into my throat her tiger's tooth,
Stealing my breath of life, I will confess
I love this cultured hell that tests my youth!
Her vigor flows like tides into my blood,
Giving me strength erect against her hate.
Her bigness sweeps my being like a flood.
Yet as a rebel fronts a king in state,
I stand within her walls with not a shred
Of terror, malice, not a word of jeer.
Darkly I gaze into the days ahead,
And see her might and granite wonders there,
Beneath the touch of Time's unerring hand,
Like priceless treasures sinking in the sand.

If We Must Die

Claude McKay

If we must die, let it not be like hogs
Hunted and penned in an inglorious spot,
While round us bark the mad and hungry dogs,
Making their mock at our accursed lot.
If we must die, O let us nobly die, 5
So that our precious blood may not be shed
In vain; then even the monsters we defy
Shall be constrained to honor us though dead!
O kinsmen! we must meet the common foe!
Though far outnumbered let us show us brave, 10
And for their thousand blows deal one deathblow!
What though before us lies the open grave?
Like men we'll face the murderous, cowardly pack,
Pressed to the wall, dying, but fighting back!

Jean Toomer (1894–1967)

Jean Toomer was born in Washington, D.C., on March 29, 1894, to Nathan and Nina Pinchback Toomer. When Nathan deserted his family less than a year later, Jean and his mother moved in with her parents, Nina and Pinckney Benton Stewart Pinchback, the former Reconstruction lieutenant governor of Louisiana and twice contested U.S. senator. Life with the Pinchbacks was not altogether easy because his grandfather fell from social and financial prominence.

Then in 1906 Nina Toomer married, and mother and son moved to New Rochelle, New York, to begin a new life with Jean's stepfather. Unfortunately, his mother passed away just three years later, and Toomer was returned to Washington, D.C., this time, as a ward of his maternal grandparents. While Toomer's relationship with his grandfather remained strained, it was his Uncle Bismarck Pinchback who planted the earliest seeds of Toomer's literary imagination. His uncle was an avid reader and a brilliant man who introduced Toomer to the world of literature. His inherited love affair with books would endure throughout Toomer's lifetime.

After graduating from Washington, D.C.'s famous M Street high school in 1914, Toomer headed for college. However, traces of his earlier restless lifestyle began to surface in his unsuccessful pursuit of a college degree. He attended six academic institutions between 1914 and 1918. The schools were as diverse as the University of Wisconsin, the Massachusetts College of Agriculture, the American College of Physical Training in Chicago, the University of Chicago, and New York University, but he did not stay long enough at any one of them to earn a degree.

A period of self-exploration followed Toomer who alternated between emotional highs and lows. He turned away briefly from his Republican, capitalist upbringing and immersed himself in socialism, soaking up Darwin, Darrow, Haeckel, and Shaw. Toomer also exhibited this restlessness of spirit by taking on a flurry of odd jobs during this period. He worked briefly in the shipyards of New Jersey and then sold cars in Chicago. His temporary positions were as diverse as grocery clerk, athletic director, and theater manager, but he proved unsuited to any of these vocations. After wandering from job to job and ideology to ideology, Toomer arrived in New York City in 1919 determined to become a writer. Now focused, Toomer became a part of the intellectual scene in Greenwich Village, where he quickly developed friendships with some of the leading writers of the day. Among the better known were Waldo Frank, Sherwood Anderson, Hart Crane, and Edwin Arlington Robinson. Ambivalent about his racial identity, Toomer moved easily between the Black and White worlds. It is not surprising, therefore, that while courting the White literati of New York, he also managed to establish close contacts with Alain Locke, Charles Johnson, Countee Cullen, and Claude McKay, all literary giants of the new Harlem Renaissance.

With the support and encouragement of his new literary contacts, Toomer began to write poems and short stories for small "avant-garde" magazines, such as *The Double Dealer, Liberator, Broom, Crisis,* and *Opportunity.* The following three years would bring Toomer closer to his Black roots than at any other period of his life.

In 1921 Toomer accepted a post as the superintendent of a small Black school in rural Sparta, Georgia. Having lived most of his life in upper middle class neighborhoods, having attended predominantly White schools while growing up, and having always appeared more White than Black physically, Toomer constantly had great difficulty identifying with Black Americans. Here was an opportunity to experience, first-hand, Black life in the heart of the South. Though the position lasted only a short while, the effects on Toomer proved deeply inspirational. The impact of this Georgia trip was greater than any other single experience on the maturation of Toomer as artist. He tirelessly devoted himself to recording artistically the pulse of Black life that he had experienced so vividly in the South.

The result of this formidable undertaking was his literary masterpiece *Cane* (1923), hailed as one of the finest examples of American modernism. *Cane* received critical acclaim from both Black and White critics, including Sherwood Anderson, Hart Crane, Countee Cullen, Allen Tate, W. E. B. DuBois, Langston Hughes, and William Stanley Braithwaite. Compared often stylistically with Anderson's *Winesburg, Ohio, Cane* is a collection of 15 poems, six prose vignettes, seven short stories, and a play unified by theme and setting. The scene shifts from rural 1920s Georgia in the first half of the book to urban Washington, D.C. and Chicago in the second section and, finally, back to the rural South in the latter part of the novel. Delving deeply in the Black psyche and breaking away from long-standing stereotypes of the African-American in literature, Toomer helped to establish a new tradition. *Cane* clearly solidified Toomer's reputation as a gifted artist and craftsman. Although it was a commercial disappointment—selling fewer than 500 copies—its critical reception was highly favorable. And today *Cane* remains one of the most celebrated texts of the Harlem Renaissance.

After *Cane,* Toomer never again returned to the subject of African-American life in his writings, nor did he ever again equal its quality in his works. What followed was another period of philosophical searching. He became obsessed with the writings of George Ivanovich Gurdjeff, a Russian psychologist and philosopher/mystic. The notion of an "ideal of man" as a spiritually and psychologically whole being consumed him. Toomer spent several summers, beginning in 1924, at Gurdjeff's Institute for the Harmonious Development of Man in France. A spiritual reformer and social critic gradually replaced the philosopher/poet of *Cane* and severely weakened Toomer's great literary talent. Other publications would follow, but none came close to the greatness of *Cane*.

Toomer's further disassociation with his Black roots widened with his first marriage in 1932 to one of his White students, Margery Latimer, who died a year later in childbirth. Then, in 1934 he married Marjorie Content, also White. Subsequently ending his long association with Gurdjeff, Toomer settled in Pennsylvania.

In 1936 he wrote "Blue Meridian," a long poem about an ideal America that replaces the old one that had been racially divided. Also published that same year was another poem "Winter on Earth." Two pamphlets followed in 1937 entitled "Living Is Developing" and "Work Ideas I." In 1939 Toomer sought a guru in India in his continual search of a higher form of consciousness. By 1940 he returned to Pennsylvania, made formal application to the Society of Friends, and became a Quaker. His writings of the 1940s were primarily religious tracts, such as "An Interpretation of Friends' Worship" published in 1947 and in 1949 "The Flavor of Man." By 1950 Toomer's health began to fail, and his final years were largely unproductive. He spent his five last days in a rest home and died on March 30, 1967.

Selected Bibliography

Benson, Brian Joseph and Mabel Mayle Dillard. *Jean Toomer*. Boston: Twayne, 1980.

Byrd, Rudolph P. *Jean Toomer's Years with Gurdjeff: Portrait of an Artist, 1923–1936*. Athens: The University of Georgia Press, 1990.

Larson, Charles R. *Invisible Darkness: Jean Toomer and Nella Larsen*. Iowa City: University of Iowa Press, 1993.

McKay, Nellie Y. *Jean Toomer, Artist: A Study of His Literary Life and Work, 1894–1936*. Chapel Hill: University of North Carolina Press, 1987.

Nelson, Emmanuel S., Ed. *African American Authors, 1745–1945: A Bio-Bibliographical Critical Sourcebook*. Westport, CT: Greenwood, 2000.

O'Daniel, Therman B., ed. *Jean Toomer: A Critical Evaluation*. Washington, D.C.: Howard University Press, 1988.

Song of the Son

Jean Toomer

Pour O pour that parting soul in song,
O pour it in the sawdust glow of night,
Into the velvet pine-smoke air to-night,
And let the valley carry it along.

And let the valley carry it along.
O land and soil, red soil and sweet-gum tree,
So scant of grass, so profligate of pines,
Now just before an epoch's sun declines
Thy son, in time, I have returned to thee,
Thy son, I have in time returned to thee.

In time, for though the sun is setting on
A song-lit race of slaves, it has not set;
Though late, O soil, it is not too late yet
To catch thy plaintive soul, leaving, soon gone,
Leaving, to catch thy plaintive soul soon gone.

O Negro slaves, dark purple ripened plums,
Squeezed, and bursting in the pine-wood air,
Passing, before they stripped the old tree bare
One plum was saved for me, one seed becomes

An everlasting song, a singing tree,
Caroling softly souls of slavery,
What they were, and what they are to me,
Caroling softly souls of slavery.

Sterling A. Brown (1901–1989)

Born on May 1, 1901, into an educated, middle-class African-American family, Sterling A. Brown was the last of six children and the only son born to Adelaide Allen Brown and the Reverend Sterling Nelson Brown. He was raised on the campus of Howard University, where his father had taught in the School of Religion since 1892. Brown grew up hearing accounts of his father's early years in Tennessee, his struggle for an education, and his friendship with noted leaders, such as Frederick Douglass and Booker T. Washington.

Brown received his entire elementary education in the public schools of Washington, D.C. He attended Dunbar High School, noted for its distinguished teachers and its tradition of graduating outstanding Black leaders and professionals. Brown entered the ivy league Williams College at the age of 17, one of few Blacks who attended on an academic scholarship. He occupied the time that was not spent with his studies serving on the debating team, waiting tables in Berkshire Hall, and playing tennis for the Common Club Tennis Team. At Williams College, Brown learned to think critically about literature. It was also at Williams College that Brown began to write poetry.

In 1922 Brown graduated Phi Beta Kappa from Williams College and entered Harvard University. As a graduate student, he studied with scholars Bliss Perry and F. O. Mathiessen. There he also discovered a book that opened new vistas in his understanding and appreciation of poetry. *Modern American Poetry* (1921), edited by Louis Untermeyer, introduced Brown to the work of the imagists, who were committed to the use of clear, crisp images, brevity, and freedom from time-worn forms. In its pages he also read Edwin Arlington Robinson and Robert Frost, both of whom greatly influenced Brown's developing literary outlook.

After earning a master's degree in 1923 from Harvard, Brown was convinced that he wanted to teach. Although he was discouraged by several friends who thought he could put his talents to better use, he was so certain of the importance of teaching that Brown influenced other William College men to go into the profession. At the suggestion of his father and of historian Carter G. Woodson, Brown went to Virginia Seminary in Lynchburg, where he taught English for the next three years. There he devoted much of his energy to writing. In 1929 Brown returned to Washington, D.C., to teach at Howard University. Seven years after coming to Howard, Brown turned his attention to the Works Progress Administration (WPA) Federal Writers' Project. From 1936 to 1940, he held the position of Editor of Negro Affairs, one of the few significant positions given to Blacks under the New Deal.

Brown's first 15 years at Howard, from 1929–1945, were his most productive years as a writer. During this period he contributed poetry, reviews, and essays to *Opportunity, New Republic, Nation, Journal of Negro Education, Phylon, Crisis,* and other publications. In a span of nine years, Brown published four books that established his reputation as an important poet and critic: *Southern Road* (1932), *The Negro in American Fiction* (1937), *Negro Poetry and Drama* (1937), and *The Negro Caravan* (1941), the classic collection of Black literature edited by Brown, Arthur P. Davis, and Ulysses Y. Lee. Perhaps more than any other single text of its day, this collection defined the range and content of Black literature. Shortly after the publication of *Southern Road,* Alain Locke hailed Sterling Brown as "The New Negro Folk Poet." Locke called Brown a folk-poet because he registered the people's sentiment in their own terms. In

1971 Howard University awarded Brown an honorary doctorate. Brown remained at Howard University until his retirement in 1969. He died in Takoma Park, Maryland, on January 13, 1989.

Although Brown produced a relatively small number of books, his achievement and influence in the field of American literature and culture are significant. He distinguished himself as a poet, folklorist, scholar, critic, and teacher.

Selected Bibliography

Gabbin, Joanne V. *Sterling A. Brown: Building the Black Aesthetic Tradition*. Charlottesville: UP of Virginia, 1985.

Harris, Trudier, ed. *Dictionary of Literary Biography: Afro-American Writers from the Harlem Renaissance to 1940*. Vol. 51. Detroit: Gale, 1987.

Henderson, Stephen. *Understanding the New Black Poetry: Black Music and Speech as Poetic References*. New York: William Morrow, 1972.

Magill, Frank N., ed. *Masterpieces of African American Literature*. New York: HarperCollins, 1992.

Nelson, Emmanuel S., Ed. *African American Authors, 1745–1945: A Bio-Bibliographical Critical Sourcebook*. Westport, CT: Greenwood, 2000.

Strong Men

Sterling A. Brown

The strong men keep coming on.
               SANDBURG.

They dragged you from homeland,
  They chained you in coffles,
  They huddled you spoon-fashion in filthy hatches,
  They sold you to give a few gentlemen ease.

They broke you in like oxen,   5
They scourged you,
They branded you,
They made your women breeders,
They swelled your numbers with bastards....
They taught you the religion they disgraced.   10

You sang:
    Keep a-inchin' along
    Lak a po' inch worm....
You sang:
    Bye and bye   15
    I'm gonna lay down dis heaby load....

You sang:
    Walk togedder, chillen,
    Dontcha git weary....
        The strong men keep a-comin' on   20
        The strong men git stronger.

They point with pride to the roads you built for them,
They ride in comfort over the rails you laid for them.
They put hammers in your hands
And said—Drive so much before sundown.   25

You sang:
  Ain't no hammah
  In dis lan',
  Strikes lak mine, bebby,
  Strikes lak mine.   30

They cooped you in their kitchens,
They penned you in their factories,
They gave you the jobs that they were too good for,
They tried to guarantee happiness to themselves
By shunting dirt and misery to you.   35

You sang:
  Me an' muh baby gonna shine, shine
  Me an' muh baby gonna shine.
      The strong men keep a-comin' on
      The strong men git stronger....   40

They bought off some of your leaders
You stumbled, as blind men will....
They coaxed you, unwontedly soft-voiced....
You followed a way.
Then laughed as usual.   45

They heard the laugh and wondered;
Uncomfortable;
Unadmitting a deeper terror....
      The strong men keep a-comin' on
      Gittin' stronger....   50

What, from the slums
Where they have hemmed you,
What, from the tiny huts
They could not keep from you—
What reaches them   55
Making them ill at ease, fearful?
Today they shout prohibition at you
"Thou shalt not this"
"Thou shalt not that"
"Reserved for whites only"   60
You laugh.

One thing they cannot prohibit—
      The strong men ... coming on
      The strong men gittin' stronger.
      Strong men....   65
      Stronger....

Arna Bontemps (1902–1973)

Arna Wendell Bontemps was born in Alexandria, Louisiana in 1902. Three years later, his family moved to California. After Bontemps' mother died, his father sent him to a predominantly White boarding school run by the Seventh-Day Adventist Church. Bontemps then enrolled in the Church's Pacific Union College and graduated in 1923. He worked in a Los Angeles post office along with his friend Wallace Thurman (before both of them became important Harlem Renaissance writers). Bontemps accepted a teaching position at the Seventh-Day Academy of Harlem; thus he lived in New York during the height of the Harlem Renaissance. Bontemps, husband and father of a growing family that eventually included six children, was forced to leave Harlem for economic reasons. For approximately the next 20 years, he lived in several locations as he pursued educational and writing careers. While serving as principal of the Shiloh Academy in Chicago, he joined the South Side Writers' Group, an organization founded by Richard Wright, in 1936, and two years later, Bontemps was appointed editorial supervisor of the Federal Writers Project of the Illinois WPA. He received a masters degree in Library Sciences from the University of Chicago in 1943. Bontemps then accepted a job as librarian at Fisk University, a position he held until his retirement in 1966.

Bontemps' initial literary efforts were poetic, and his verse received critical acclaim as early as 1924 when the *Crisis* published his poems. Bontemps extended his creativity to prose fiction as he authored four novels: the unpublished *Chariots in the Cloud* (1929), which enjoyed a brief, successful run as the Broadway musical, *St. Louis Woman* (1946); *God Sends Sunday* (1931), which focuses on race-tracks and life in the urban fast lane; *Black Thunder* (1936), which is considered Bontemps' best novel and is based on a slave revolt in Virginia; and *Drums at Dusk* (1939), which is based on a Haitian slave rebellion. Bontemps also authored short stories; including the most frequently anthologized "A Summer Tragedy" (1932). Years later 12 of his stories were collected and published as *The Old South: "A Summer Tragedy" and Other Stories of the Thirties* (1973). Poetry remained of interest to Bontemps as he compiled *Golden Slippers: An Anthology of Negro Poetry for Young Readers* (1941) and *Hold Fast to Dreams* (1969), a collection of verse by Black and White authors; Bontemps authored *Personals* (1963), another volume of verse. Turning his attention to nonfiction, Bontemps ghostwrote composer and musician W. C. Handy's autobiography, *Father of the Blues* (1941); edited *Great Slave Narratives* (1969); *The Harlem Renaissance Remembered* (1972); and collaborated with Langston Hughes on *Popo and Fifina: Children of Haiti* (1932), *The Poetry of the Negro* (1949), *The Book of Negro Folklore* (1959), and *American Negro Poetry* (1963). In addition, Bontemps wrote six children's novels as well as histories and biographies for juveniles during the 1950s and 1960s. He was writing his autobiography at the time of his death in 1973. Arna Bontemps, as poet, novelist, short story writer, editor, and writer of histories and biographies, diligently narrated the African-American experience.

Selected Bibliography

Andrews, William L., Frances Smith Foster, and Trudier Harris, eds. *The Oxford Companion to African American Literature.* New York: Oxford University Press, 1997.

Bell, Bernard W. *The Afro-American Novel and Its Tradition.* Amherst: The University of Massachusetts Press, 1987.

Nelson, Emmanuel S., Ed. *African American Authors, 1745–1945: A Bio-Bibliographical Critical Sourcebook.* Westport, CT: Greenwood, 2000.

A Black Man Talks of Reaping

Arna Bontemps

I have sown beside all waters in my day.
I planted deep, within my heart the fear
That wind or fowl would take the grain away.
I planted safe against this stark, lean year.

I scattered seed enough to plant the land   5
In rows from Canada to Mexico
But for my reaping only what the hand
Can hold at once is all that I can show.

Yet what I sowed and what the orchard yields
My brother's sons are gathering stalk and root,   10
Small wonder then my children glean in fields
They have not sown, and feed on bitter fruit.

Langston Hughes (1902–1967)

James Mercer Langston Hughes was born on February 1, 1902, in Joplin, Missouri, to James and Carrie (nee Langston) Hughes. His parents separated, and Langston lived, until the age of 12, with his maternal grandmother, Mary Langston. After her death, Langston lived with the Reed family for two years before rejoining his mother in Lincoln, Illinois. Langston, who had never written verse, was elected Class Poet by his peers. Subsequently, Langston wrote and then read a poem at his grammar school's graduation ceremony. The audience applauded, and he began to entertain thoughts of becoming a writer, much to James Hughes' dismay.

Langston visited his father, a successful businessman in Mexico, during the years immediately before and after his graduation from Cleveland's Central High School in 1920. The elder Hughes wanted Langston to be an engineer and offered to send him to college in Switzerland or Germany. Langston, inspired by his mother, who wrote poetry and took him to plays; his grandmother, who told him stories of strong individuals; and his grandfather, who had founded the Inter-State Literary Society in Kansas, told his father he wanted to become a writer. When James Hughes asserted that Black writers did not make money, Langston reminded him of Alexandre Dumas. His father, remembering the racial discrimination he experienced in the United States, countered that Dumas lived in Paris where color was unimportant. He wanted Langston to earn enough money so he could live outside the United States and away from African Americans. Yet Langston's two career goals were set: he aimed to earn a living as an author and to write about his people. Adding to his father's chagrin was Langston's keen interest in Harlem. He attended Columbia University (1921–22) merely because of its proximity to his cherished Harlem and spent the next four years traveling as a seaman to Africa and Europe before returning to the United States to study at Lincoln University in Pennsylvania. By the time he received his degree (1929), his literary career was well underway.

Langston Hughes won worldwide attention and acclaim as an author, became the most well-known Harlem Renaissance writer, enjoyed a highly successful career that spanned more than 40 years (from the Harlem Renaissance to the Black Arts Movement), became arguably the most famous African-American writer of the 20th century, and earned additional distinction as one of America's most important authors. In addition, Hughes encouraged other writers and introduced the American public to the works of African authors.

Hughes, who frequently and eloquently combined social criticism with poetry and blended jazz, blues, or bebop with traditional verse, is best known for his 17 volumes of poetry including *The Weary Blues* (1927), his first verse collection; *Fine Clothes to the Jew* (1927); *The Dream Keeper and Other Poems* (1932); *Shakespeare in Harlem* (1942); *Montage of a Dream Deferred* (1951); and the posthumous *The Panther and the Lash: Poems of Our Times* (1967). Hughes also authored two autobiographies: *The Big Sea* (1940) and *I Wonder as I Wander* (1956). He created seven collections of short stories, including five that presented Harlem's Jesse B. Semple, the fictitious character who is regarded as a Black Everyman. A prolific and versatile author, Hughes created more than 80 works including novels, plays, anthologies, children's books, essays, newspaper columns, French and Spanish translations, histories, photo essays, lyrics for dramatic musicals, song lyrics, screenplays as well as radio and television scripts. Decades have gone by since Hughes' death in 1967, yet for many people, the name Langston Hughes connotes African-American literature at its finest.

Selected Bibliography

Gates, Henry Louis, Jr. and K. A. Appiah, eds. *Langston Hughes: Critical Perspectives Past and Present*. New York: Amistad, 1993.

Nelson, Emmanuel S., Ed. *African American Authors, 1745–1945: A Bio-Bibliographical Critical Sourcebook*. Westport, CT: Greenwood, 2000.

O'Daniel, Therman B., ed. *Langston Hughes Black Genius: A Critical Evaluation*. New York: Morrow, 1971.

Rampersad, Arnold. *The Life of Langston Hughes, 1902–1967*. 2 vols. New York: Oxford University Press, 1986–88.

Afro-American Fragment

Langston Hughes

So long,
So far away
Is Africa.
Not even memories alive
Save those that history books create,
Save those that songs
Beat back into the blood—
Beat out of blood with words sad-sung
In strange un-Negro tongue—
So long,
So far away
Is Africa.

Subdued and time-lost
Are the drums—and yet
Through some vast mist of race
There comes this song
I do not understand,
This song of atavistic land,
Of bitter yearnings lost
Without a place—
So long,
So far away
Is Africa's
Dark face.

As I Grew Older

Langston Hughes

It was a long time ago.
I have almost forgotten my dream.
But it was there then,
In front of me,
Bright as a sun— 5
My dream.

And then the wall rose,
Rose slowly,
Slowly,
Between me and my dream. 10
Rose slowly, slowly,
Dimming,
Hiding,
The light of my dream.
Rose until it touched the sky— 15
The wall.

Shadow.
I am black.

I lie down in the shadow.
No longer the light of my dream before me, 20
Above me.
Only the thick wall.
Only the shadow.

My hands!
My dark hands! 25
Break through the wall!
Find my dream!
Help me to shatter this darkness,
To smash this night,
To break this shadow 30
Into a thousand lights of sun,
Into a thousand whirling dreams
Of sun!

Ballad of the Landlord

Langston Hughes

Landlord, landlord,
My roof has sprung a leak.
Don't you 'member I told you about it
Way last week?

Landlord, landlord,
These steps is broken down.
When you come up yourself
It's a wonder you don't fall down.

Ten Bucks you say I owe you?
Ten Bucks you say is due?
Well, that's Ten Bucks more'n I'll pay you
Till you fix this house up new.

What? You gonna get eviction orders?
You gonna cut off my heat?
You gonna take my furniture and
Throw it in the street?

Um-huh! You talking high and mighty.
Talk on—till you get through.
You ain't gonna be able to say a word
If I land my fist on you.

Police! Police!
Come and get this man!
And overturn the land!

Copper's whistle!
Patrol bell!
Arrest.

Precinct Station.
Iron cell.
Headlines in press:

MAN THREATENS LANDLORD

TENANT HELD NO BAIL

JUDGE GIVES NEGRO 90 DAYS IN COUNTY JAIL
1940, 1955

The Negro Speaks of Rivers

Langston Hughes

I've known rivers:
I've known rivers ancient as the world and older than the
   flow of human blood in human veins.
My soul has grown deep like the rivers.
I bathed in the Euphrates when dawns were young.
I built my hut near the Congo and it lulled me to sleep.
I looked upon the Nile and raised the pyramids above it.
I heard the singing of the Mississippi when Abe Lincoln
   went down to New Orleans, and I've seen its muddy
   bosom turn all golden in the sunset.
I've known rivers:
Ancient, dusky rivers.
My soul has grown deep like the rivers.

Harlem

Langston Hughes

What happens to a dream deferred?
    Does it dry up
    like a raisin in the sun?
    Or fester like a sore—
    And then run? 5
    Does it stink like rotten meat?
    Or crust and sugar over—
    like a syrupy sweet?

    Maybe it just sags
    like a heavy load. 10

    Or does it explode?

Theme for English B

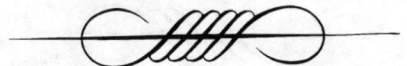

Langston Hughes

The instructor said,

> *Go home and write*
> *A page tonight.*
> *And let that page come out of you—*
> *Then, it will be true.*

I wonder if it's that simple?
I am twenty-two, colored, born in Winston-Salem.
I went to school there, then Durham, then here
to this college on the hill above Harlem.
I am the only colored student in my class.
The steps from the hill lead down into Harlem,
through a park, then I cross St. Nicholas,
Eighth Avenue, Seventh, and I come to the Y,
the Harlem Branch Y, where I take the elevator
up to my room, sit down, and write this page:

It's not easy to know what is true for you or me
at twenty-two, my age. But I guess I'm what
I feel and see and hear, Harlem, I hear you:
hear you, hear me—we two—you, me, talk on this page.
(I hear New York, too.) Me—who?
Well, I like to eat, sleep, drink, and be in love.
I like to work, read, learn, and understand life.
I like a pipe for a Christmas present,
or records—Bessie, bop, or Bach.
I guess being colored doesn't make me *not* like
the same things other folks like who are other races.
So will my page be colored that I write?
Being me, it will not be white.
But it will be
a part of you, instructor.
You are white—
yet a part of me, as I am a part of you.

That's American.
Sometimes perhaps you don't want to be a part of me.
Nor do I often want to be a part of you. 35
But we are, that's true!
As I learn from you,
I guess you learn from me—
although you're older—and white—
and somewhat more free 40

This is my page for English B.

Countee Cullen (1903–1946)

Countee Cullen, a writer of the Harlem Renaissance Period, was born Countee Porter on May 30, 1903. In 1918 he was adopted by Rev. and Mrs. Frederick Cullen. Growing up, he was influenced by Rev. Cullen's participation in the NAACP and the National Urban League. In addition to being influenced by religious and civil rights issues, Cullen's poetry is linked to the lyricism of the Romantic poets, such as Wordsworth, Shelley, and Keats.

Cullen earned his undergraduate degree at New York University and his master's degree from Harvard University. While a student, he received awards for his poetry. His first volume of poetry, *Color,* was published in 1925. Considered one of his best works, *Color* includes the poems "Incident," "Yet Do I Marvel," and "A Brown Girl Dead." Another poem, "Heritage," is considered to be one of the greatest poems of the Harlem Renaissance. "From the Dark Tower" is from Cullen's second collection, *Copper Sun,* published in 1927. The title of this poem comes from the title of the column, "The Dark Tower," that Cullen wrote for *Opportunity Magazine.* He received the Harmon Foundation Literary Award in 1927 and published *The Black Christ and Other Poems* in 1929. His only novel, *One Way to Heaven,* was published in 1932. *On These I Stand: An Anthology of the Best Poems of Countee Cullen* was published after his death in 1946.

Selected Bibliography

Lewis, David Levering. *When Harlem Was in Vogue.* New York: Oxford University Press, 1979.
Nelson, Emmanuel S., Ed. *African American Authors, 1745–1945: A Bio-Bibliographical Critical Sourcebook.* Westport, CT: Greenwood, 2000.
Shackelford, D. Dean. "The Poetry of Countee Cullen." *Masterpieces of African American Literature.* Frank N. Magill, ed. New York: HarperCollins, 1992. 382–386.

Incident

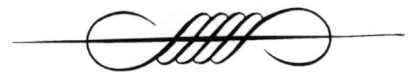

Countee Cullen

Once riding in old Baltimore,
   Heart-filled, head-filled with glee,
I saw a Baltimorean
   Keep looking straight at me.

Now I was eight and very small,
   And he was no whit bigger,
And so I smiled, but he poked out
   His tongue, and called me, "Nigger."

I saw the whole of Baltimore
   From May until December;
Of all the things that happened there
   That's all that I remember.

Yet Do I Marvel

Countee Cullen

I doubt not God is good, well-meaning, kind,
And did He stoop to quibble could tell why
The little buried mole continues blind,
why flesh that mirrors Him must some day die,
Make plain the reason tortured Tantalus   5
Is baited by the fickle fruit, declare
If merely brute caprice dooms Sisyphus
To struggle up a never-ending stair.
Inscrutable His ways are, and immune
To catechism by a mind too strewn   10
With petty cares to slightly understand
what awful brain compels His awful hand.
Yet do I marvel at this curious thing:
To make a poet black, and bid him sing!

Dudley Randall (1914–)

Dudley Randall, poet, publisher, and editor, was born on January 14, 1914, in Washington, D.C. Six years later, the Randall family moved to Detroit. Randall was a published poet at the age of 13 when his verse appeared in *The Detroit Free Press'* "Young Poets Page."

Randall worked at the Ford Motor Company in River Rouge, Michigan (1932–37) and the U.S. Postal Service in Detroit (1938–41; 1946–51). During his tenure at the post office, Randall, stationed in the South Pacific, served in the U.S. Army as a Signal Corps supply sergeant (World War II) and earned a B.A. in English from Wayne State University (1949) and a Master of Arts in Library Sciences from the University of Michigan (1951). Randall was employed as a librarian at Lincoln University in Missouri (1951–54) and Morgan State University (1954–56) before he returned to Detroit where he worked as a librarian at the Wayne County Federated Library System (1956–69), as a visiting lecturer at the University of Michigan (1969) and as librarian as well as poet-in-residence at the University of Detroit (1969–75).

Randall founded Broadside Press in 1965 in order to protect the copyrights for two of his poems that were set to music and focused on 1963 tragedies: "The Ballad of Birmingham," about the church bombing where four girls were murdered; and "Dressed in Pink," about President John F. Kennedy's assassination. While Broadside Press published established, African-American poets such as Gwendolyn Brooks, Robert Hayden, Melvin Tolson, and Margaret Walker, it provided publishing opportunities for poets who, at that time, were young and unknown including Nikki Giovanni, Etheridge Knight, Don L. Lee (now Haki Madhubuti), and Sonia Sanchez. Thus Randall, hailed as a trailblazer in African-American publishing, was instrumental in promoting the young poets who emerged in the 1960s. During the 12 years that Randall served as publisher, Broadside Press published 90 broadsides (single poems), 55 books, and a number of recordings. He sold Broadside to a Detroit church in 1977 and served as a consultant to his former company for the next 10 years.

Although Randall has promoted the works of other poets, he has gained critical acclaim for his verse. His most famous poems are "Booker T. and W. E. B.," about the contrasting viewpoints of Booker T. Washington and W. E. B. DuBois and the aforementioned "Ballad of Birmingham." Randall has authored six volumes of poetry: *Poem Counterpoem* (1966), *Cities Burning* (1968), *Love You* (1970), *More to Remember: Poems of Four Decades* (1971), *After Killing* (1973), and *A Litany of Friends* (1981). He has edited at least seven books on Black poetry: most notable is *The Black Poets* (1971). Randall, the recipient of various writing awards and academic honors, was named Detroit's poet laureate in 1981.

Selected Bibliography

Andrews, William L., Frances Smith Foster, and Trudier Harris, eds. *The Oxford Companion to African American Literature*. New York: Oxford University Press, 1997.

Barksdale, Richard and Keneth Kinnamon, eds. *Black Writers of America: A Comprehensive Anthology*. New York: Macmillan, 1972.

Bigelow, Barbara C., ed. *Contemporary Black Biography*. Vol. 8. Detroit: Gale Research, 1994.

Ballad of Birmingham

Dudley Randall

"Mother dear, may I go downtown
instead of out to play,
and march the streets of Birmingham
in a freedom march today?"

"No, baby, no, you may not go, 5
for the dogs are fierce and wild,
and clubs and hoses, guns and jails
ain't good for a little child."

"But, mother, I won't be alone.
Other children will go with me, 10
and march the streets of Birmingham
to make our country free."

"No, baby, no, you may not go,
for I fear those guns will fire.
But you may go to church instead, 15
and sing in the children's choir."

She has combed and brushed her nightdark hair,
and bathed rose petal sweet,
and drawn white gloves on her small brown hands,
and white shoes on her feet. 20

The mother smiled to know her child
was in the sacred place,
but that smile was the last smile
to come upon her face.

For when she heard the explosion, 25
her eyes grew wet and wild.
She raced through the streets of Birmingham
calling for her child.

She clawed through bits of glass and brick,
then lifted out a shoe. 30
"O, here's the shoe my baby wore,
but, baby, where are you?"

Booker T. and W. E. B.

Dudley Randall

(Booker T. Washington and W. E. B. Du Bois)

"It seems to me," said Booker T.,
"It shows a mighty lot of cheek
To study chemistry and Greek
When Mister Charlie needs a hand
To hoe the cotton on his land, 5
And when Miss Ann looks for a cook,
Why stick your nose inside a book?"

"I don't agree," said W. E. B.
"If I should have the drive to seek
Knowledge of chemistry or Greek, 10
I'll do it. Charles and Miss can look
Another place for hand or cook.
Some men rejoice in skill of hand,
And some in cultivating land,
But there are others who maintain 15
The right to cultivate the brain."

"It seems to me," said Booker T.,
"That all you folks have missed the boat
Who shout about the right to vote,
And spend vain days and sleepless nights 20
In uproar over civil rights.
Just keep your mouths shut, do not grouse,
But work, and save, and buy a house."

"I don't agree," said W. E. B., "For what can property avail
If dignity and justice fail? 25
Unless you help to make the laws,
They'll steal your house with trumped-up clause.
A rope's as tight, a fire as hot,
No matter how much cash you've got.
Speak soft, and try your little plan, 30
But as for me, I'll be a man."

"It seems to me," said Booker T.—

"I don't agree,"
Said W. E. B.

The Southern Road

Dudley Randall

There the black river, boundary to hell,
And here the iron bridge, the ancient car,
And grim conductor, who with surly yell
Forbids white soldiers where the black ones are.
And I re-live the enforced avatar
Of desperate journey to a dark abode
Made by my sires before another war;
And I set forth upon the southern road.

To a land where shadowed songs like flowers swell
And where the earth is scarlet as a scar
Friezed by the bleeding lash that fell (O fell)
Upon my fathers' flesh. O far, far, far
And deep my blood has drenched it. None can bar
My birthright to the loveliness bestowed
Upon this country haughty as a star.
And I set forth upon the southern road.
This darkness and these mountains loom a spell
Of peak-roofed town where yearning steeples soar
And the holy holy chanting of a bell
Shakes human incense on the throbbing air
Where bonfires blaze and quivering bodies char.
Whose is the hair that crisped, and fiercely glowed?
I know it; and my entrails melt like tar
And I set forth upon the southern road.

O fertile hillsides where my fathers are,
From which my griefs like troubled streams have flowed
I have to love you, though they sweep me far.
And I set forth upon the southern road.

Margaret Walker (1915–1998)

Margaret Abigail Walker was born in Birmingham, Alabama on July 7, 1915. Her father, Sigismond C. Walker, was a multilingual theologian, and her mother, Marion Dozier Walker, was a music educator. When Walker was a young girl, her parents relocated to New Orleans where they worked as professors at New Orleans University. Walker's parents provided a studious environment for their child, introducing her to the world's classics, great philosophers, and music. Communicating with each other and telling stories were natural circumstances in their home. She developed intellectually at a rapid pace and graduated from high school at 14 and college at 19. As a high school student Walker introduced herself to Langston Hughes who read his work at her school. Hughes encouraged Walker to continue her pursuits and to flee the South.

Walker entered New Orleans University but subsequently enrolled as an undergraduate at Northwestern University. Walker became a member of the Poetry Society of America, thanks to the prompting of her creative writing teacher E. B. Hungerford. She received her master's and doctoral degrees from the University of Iowa in Iowa City. To grant her financial assistance with her studies, she was awarded a Rosenwald Fellowship and a Ford Fellowship.

Walker's vocation has not only been as a writer but also as a teacher. She began her teaching career at Livingston College in Salisbury, North Carolina. She also taught at West Virginia State College and Jackson State College. In 1968 Walker became director of Jackson State's Institute for the Study of the History, Life, and Culture of Black People. In between studying and teaching, she married Firnist James Alexander on June 13, 1943, and had four children.

Walker's publications include *For My People* (1942) which was published by Yale University and became the selection of the year in the Yale University Series of Younger Poets. Her novel *Jubilee* (1966) was awarded a Houghton Mifflin Literary Fellowship and was her submission for her doctorate. This novel became significant because it told the story from the slave perspective, something that novelist Toni Morrison would later do in *Beloved* (1987). Walker also published *Ballad of the Free* (1966), *Prophets for a New Day* (1970), *How I Wrote Jubilee* (1972), *October Journey* (1973), and *For Farish Street Green* (1988).

Walker's poetry resounds with the folk tradition. She effectively combines spirituals, sermons, and preacher tales; bad women songs and blues; superstition and enchantment; and memories of slave times and free times into a skilled artistic medium. Walker is equally at ease with the sonnet tradition as she is with free verse. She emerges as the keeper of records because her poetry contains so many references to African and African-American historical past.

The proof of Margaret Walker's ability as a poet, novelist, and essayist is in her longevity. Her creative work spans three literary generations. Her signature poem "For My People," first published in *Poetry* magazine in 1937, caught the public's attention in the period of literary energy encompassing the New Negro and the Harlem Renaissance. It exhibited a race consciousness that later monopolized the Black Arts Movement. It could be said, then, that she was a forerunner to the thinking of that period. Her autobiographical collection *How I Wrote Jubilee and Other Essays on Life and Literature* (1990) remains a popular selection from The Feminist Press at City University of New York. Walker once stated that she believes in the sacredness of the individual, which is the totality of the human being. Perhaps her writing thrives because this appeal for people is evident in her creations.

Selected Bibliography

Hine, Darlene, Elsa Barkley Brown, and Rosalyn Terborg-Penn, eds. *Black Women in America: An Historical Encyclopedia.* Brooklyn: Carlson, 1993.

Collier, Eugenia. "Fields and Watered Blood: Myth and Ritual in the Poetry of Margaret Walker." *Black Women Writers 1950–1980: A Critical Evaluation.* Mari Evans, ed. Garden City, N.Y.: Anchor/Doubleday, 1984.

For My People

Margaret Walker

For my people everywhere singing their slave songs repeatedly: their dirges and their
ditties and their blues and jubilees, praying their prayers nightly to an unknown
god, bending their knees humbly to an unseen power;
For my people lending their strength to the years, to the gone years and the now years
and the maybe years, washing ironing cooking scrubbing sewing mending hoeing
plowing digging planting pruning patching dragging along never gaining never
reaping never knowing and never understanding.
For my playmates in the clay and dust and sand of Alabama backyards playing bap-
tizing and preaching and doctor and jail and soldier and school and mama and
cooking and playhouse and concert and store and hair and Miss Choomby and
company;
For the cramped bewildered years we went to school to learn to know the reasons
why and the answers to and the people who and the places where and the days
when, in memory of the bitter hours when we discovered we were black and
poor and small and different and nobody cared and nobody wondered and
nobody understood;
For the boys and girls who grew in spite of these things to be Man and Woman, to
laugh and dance and sing and play and drink their wine and religion and success,
to marry their playmates and bear children and then die of consumption and ane-
mia and lynching;
For my people thronging 47th Street in Chicago and Lenox Avenue in New York and
Rampart Street in New Orleans, lost disinherited dispossessed and happy people
filling the cabarets and taverns and other people's pockets needing bread and
shoes and milk and land and money and something—something all our own;
For my people walking blindly spreading joy, losing time being lazy, sleeping when
hungry, shouting when burdened, drinking when hopeless, tied and shackled and
tangled among ourselves by the unseen creatures who tower over us omnisciently
and laugh;
For my people blundering and groping and floundering in the dark of churches and
schools and clubs and societies, associations and councils and committees and
conventions, distressed and disturbed and deceived and devoured by money-hun-
gry glory-craving leeches, preyed on by facile force of state and fad and novelty,
by false prophet and holy believer;

For my people standing staring trying to fashion a better way from confusion, from
hypocrisy and misunderstanding, trying to fashion a world that will hold all the
people, all the faces, all the adams and eves and their countless generations;
Let a new earth rise. Let another world be born. Let a bloody peace be written in the
sky. Let a second generation full of courage issue forth; let a people loving freedom come to growth. Let a beauty full of healing and a strength of final clenching
be the pulsing in our spirits and our blood. Let the martial songs be written, let the
dirges disappear. Let a race of men now rise and take control.

1937, 1942

Gwendolyn Brooks (1917–)

Gwendolyn Brooks holds a unique position in American letters. Not only has she combined a commitment to social identity with a mastery of poetic techniques, but she also has managed to bridge the gap between the academic poets of her generation in the 1940s and the young Black militant writers of the 1960s. She generally is recognized as one of the most distinguished American poets of the 20th century. As early as 1963 she was asked to conduct a poetry workshop at Columbia College in Chicago, and she would teach there intermittently until June of 1969. During this period she taught at Elmhurst College in Elmhurst, Illinois, and at Northwestern Illinois, and at Northwestern Illinois State College, in Chicago. She was also Rennebohm Professor of English at the University of Wisconsin at Madison. Though she had resolved to quit teaching in 1969, she returned when she was invited to become the Distinguished Professor of the Arts at the City College of New York.

Brooks was born in Topeka, Kansas, in 1917. Her mother, Keziah Corrine Wims, was a schoolteacher; her father, David Anderson Brooks, was a janitor. Five weeks after her birth, the family moved to Chicago, where she spent most of her life. Brooks began writing poetry when she was seven years old; she published her first poem at 13, in *American Child* magazine. At 16 her poems were critiqued by poet and novelist James Weldon Johnson. Her poetry appeared in *Harper's Poetry, Common Ground, Yale Review, Saturday Review of Literature, Negro Story,* and other magazines.

Brooks graduated from Chicago's Englewood High School in 1934; by this time she was already a regular contributor to the weekly variety column of the *Chicago Defender.* She was making considerable progress in mastering traditional poetic form. In 1936 she graduated from Wilson Junior College and then worked briefly as a maid, an experience she found painful and inhumane and one that would serve as the basis for future poems portraying women in domestic service. She also drew upon this experience for a chapter in her novel, *Maud Martha* (1953). Her next position was worse than the domestic position. The Illinois Employment Service sent her to work as a secretary for a spiritual advisor, Dr. E. N. French, who operated in a huge slum structure known as the Mecca building and exploited the misery of the occupants and others by selling them superstitious or mystical objects. Hating to go home a failure, Brooks said that this job was the most horrible four months of her life. The misery of this job obsessed and haunted her; though she periodically tried to incorporate this experience into fiction and poetry, she was unsuccessful until her seventh volume of poems, *In the Mecca,* was published in 1968.

In 1938 Brooks had joined Chicago's NAACP Youth Council, which gave her association for the first time with young people who accepted her and valued her talents. At one of the meetings that year, she met Henry Lowington Blakely II. They were married on September 17, 1939, and have a son, born in 1940; and a daughter, born in 1951.

Brooks' major publications include *A Street in Bronzeville* (1945); *Annie Allen* (1949), which won her the Pulitzer Prize in 1950; *The Bean Eaters* (1960); *In the Mecca* (1968); and *Riot* (1969). In addition, she has published one book for children, *Bronzeville Boys and Girls* (1956); a collection of poems entitled *Selected Poems* (1963); and one short work of fiction, *Maud Martha* (1953). Brooks has been Poet Laureate of Illinois.

Selected Bibliography

Harris, Trudier, ed. *Dictionary of Literary Biography: Afro-American Writers 1940–1955.* Vol. 76. Detroit: Gale Research, 1988.
Henderson, Stephen. *Understanding the New Black Poetry: Black Speech and Black Music as Poetic References.* New York: William Morrow, 1973.
Magill, Frank N., ed. *Masterpieces of African-American Literature.* New York: HarperCollins, 1992.

The Mother

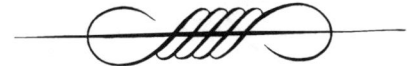

Gwendolyn Brooks

Abortions will not let you forget.
You remember the children you got that you did not get,
The damp small pulps with a little or with no hair,
The singers and workers that never handled the air.
You will never neglect or beat 5
Them, or silence or buy with a sweet.
You will never wind up the sucking-thumb
Or scuttle off ghosts that come.
You will never leave them, controlling your luscious sigh,
return for a snack of them, with gobbling mother-eye. 10

I have heard in the voices of the wind the voices of my dim
        killed children.
I have contracted. I have eased
My dim dears at the breasts they could never suck.
I have said, Sweets, if I sinned, if I seized 15
Your luck
And your lives from your unfinished reach,
If I stole your births and your names,
Your straight baby tears and your games,
Your stilted or lovely loves, your tumults, your marriages, 20
        aches, and your deaths,
If I poisoned the beginnings of your breaths,
Believe that even in my deliberateness I was not deliberate,
Though why should I whine,
Whine that the crime was other than mine?— 25
Since anyhow you are dead.
Or rather, or instead,
You were never made.
But that too, I am afraid,
Is faulty: oh, what shall I say, how is the truth to be said? 30
You were born, you had body, you died.
It is just that you never giggled or planned or cried.

Believe me, I loved you all.
Believe me, I knew you, though faintly, and I loved,
        I loved you all. 35

We Real Cool

Gwendolyn Brooks

The Pool Players.
Seven at the Golden Shovel.

We real cool. We
Left school. We

Lurk late. We
Strike straight. We

Sing sin. We
Thin gin. We

Jazz June. We
Die soon.

Mari Evans (1923–)

Mari Evans was born in Toledo, Ohio in 1923, but at age seven she had to face the world motherless as a result of her mother's premature death. Her father reared her and instilled in her a love of literature, African-American writers, and African-American consciousness. Through his influence Evans developed the fortitude and determination to pursue a writer's life.

After attending the University of Toledo, Evans sought positions where she could exercise her writing skills. Eventually, this path led her to the academic community where she held various posts in creative writing and African-American literature at institutions of higher learning, such as Indiana University at Bloomington, Northwestern University, Purdue University at Indianapolis and East Lafayette, State University of New York at Albany, Cornell University, and Washington University.

Evans' dramatic productions include *River of My Song* (1977); *Eyes* (1979), adapted from Zora Neale Hurston's *Their Eyes Were Watching God;* and *Boochie* (1979), her one-woman play about child abuse. On WTTV in Indianapolis she wrote, directed, and produced the television program *The Black Experience.*

Evans published her first book of poetry, *Where Is All the Music* (1968). She followed it with *I Am a Black Woman* (1970), *Night Star* (1981), and *A Dark and Splendid Mass* (1992). Evans' *Black Women Writers (1950–1980): A Critical Evaluation* (1984), is a valuable resource of critical essays about African-American female writers of the second half of the twentieth century. Her contribution to the field of juvenile literature includes *I Look at Me!* (1973), *Rap Stories* (1973), *Singing Black* (1976), and *Jim Flying High* (1979). Evans also published "Ethos and Creativity: The Impulse as Malleable" in David Hoppe's *Where We Live: Essays about Indiana* (1989).

A line from Evans' "I Am a Black Woman" invites the reader to look on the Black woman for renewal. As a poet she writes so eloquently of the experiences of African-American women and the African-American community and seems to be especially gifted with the grace of words to illuminate wretched conditions with beautiful, simplistic language. Indeed, reading Evans' poetry leads to feelings of being renewed.

Evans' prominence as a poet began during the period in African-American literary history known as the Black Arts Movement. It was a period of rebellion against the strictures of the previous generation, as well as White standards of poetic form, in favor of a move toward things Afrocentric. As a contributor to this literary milieu, Evans' themes were Black awareness, social revolution, African liberation, and global subjugation. Her early poetry using street vernacular and the ghetto idiom is direct but not caustic. More recently she centers on African-American male-female relationships and the plight of the African-American woman. She sends a message that to struggle is imminent but to give up is unacceptable.

Selected Bibliography

Evans, Mari. *Black Women Writers (1950–1980): a Critical Evaluation.* Garden City, N.Y.: Anchor/Doubleday, 1984.
Smith, Jessie Carney, ed. *Notable Black American Women.* Detroit: Gale Research, 1992.
Wallace, Michele. *Invisibility Blues: from Pop to Theory.* New York: Verso, 1990.

I Am a Black Woman

Mari Evans

I am a black woman
the music of my song
some sweet arpeggio of tears
is written in a minor key
and I 5
can be heard humming in the night
Can be heard
          humming
in the night.
I saw my mate leap screaming to the sea 10
and I/with these hands/cupped the lifebreath
from my issue in the canebrake
I lost Nat's swinging body in a rain of tears
and heard my son scream all the way from Anzio
for Peace he never knew. . . . I 15
learned Da Nang and Pork Chop Hill
in anguish
Now my nostrils know the gas
and these trigger tire/d fingers
seek the softness in my warrior's beard 20
I
am a black woman
tall as a cypress
strong
beyond all definition still 25
defying place
and time
and circumstance
    assailed
        impervious 30
            indestructible
Look
   on me and be
renewed

Maya Angelou (1928–)

Maya Angelou entered the world as Marguerite Annie Johnson on April 4, 1928, in St. Louis, Missouri, the younger child of Vivian and Bailey Johnson. Her older brother, Bailey, is her only sibling. After her parents divorced when she was three years old, Angelou and Bailey lived with their paternal grandmother, Annie Henderson, in Stamps, Arkansas. The ten years spent with her grandmother inspired her to assume the stance of anti-defeatism. From Annie Henderson, Angelou learned the strength-building survivalist tactics necessary to a blossoming African-American female in the South. She refused to succumb to the adversarial forces so prevalent in Stamps.

Life proved to be equally traumatic outside of the deep South. When Angelou was nearly eight years old, she visited her mother in St. Louis where she was sexually assaulted by her mother's domestic partner. Angelou had to endure the experience of her attacker's trial, his sentencing, and his subsequent murder by her uncles. Believing that she was responsible for her mother's boyfriend's death, she retreated emotionally into a world of silence, refusing to speak for five years, except on occasion to Bailey. Her mother felt compelled to return Angelou and her brother to Stamps so that Angelou could heal. During this period of muteness, another resilient southern woman, Bertha Flowers, introduced Angelou to literature and the classics. As a result of reading literature and reciting poetry, she regained her ability to speak and began to show promise as a student. By the time Angelou graduated from the eighth grade, she was at the top of her class, disproving the accusations made by the local residents that she was a moron.

After graduation Angelou and her brother joined their mother in her new home in San Francisco. She enrolled in the George Washington High School from which she graduated and took drama and dancing classes at the California Labor School. At the age of 16, Angelou gave birth to her son, Guy Johnson.

Angelou married and divorced twice, yet she retained her first husband's name. When Angelou lived in Cairo, Egypt, she edited the English language *Arab Observer*. She later moved to Ghana where she taught at the University of Ghana and worked as a journalist. Before finding her niche as a writer, Angelou held many occupations, including cook, streetcar conductor, waitress, and prostitute. She even turned to the abuse of drugs as a coping mechanism for a brief period but abandoned the practice after witnessing the devastation drugs had on her brother. Needless to say, she weathered the storms of these periods and emerged victoriously. She expresses in her writings that just because life deals defeats to people does not mean that they have to be defeated but are to use the experience to develop the power to endure.

After living a somewhat nomadic existence, she decided to devote her life to writing and took the advice of John Oliver Killens and moved to Harlem. She joined the Harlem Writers Guild whose members helped her to perfect her craft. Angelou lives a life that speaks volumes, and her autobiographical writings to date have been published in five volumes: *I Know Why the Caged Bird Sings* (1970), which was nominated for a National Book Award in 1974 and which critics believe to be the most successful of her autobiographical writings, chronicles her painful early years; *Gather Together in My Name* (1974); *Singin' and Swingin' and Gettin' Merry Like Christmas* (1976); *The Heart of a Woman* (1981); and *All God's Children Need Traveling Shoes* (1986). These volumes permit a glimpse of a very full life, but they are only the beginning of her testament.

When Angelou penned *I Know Why the Caged Bird Sings,* the literary world paid attention. This work is a masterful contribution to the African-American autobiographical tradition. It is the first of a voluminous work that presents her life in a type of chronological order. Angelou's life patterns adhere to the heroic tradition whereby she succeeds against great odds. Although her poetry receives less critical attention than her autobiographical series, she continues to produce in that genre.

Angelou's six volumes of poetry include *Just Give Me a Cool Drink of Water 'Fore I Diiie* (1971), which was nominated for a Pulitzer Prize and contains both poems of social protest and poems of love; *And Still I Rise* (1978), which includes the signature poem "Phenomenal Woman" as the celebration of womanhood, is filled with poetic rhythm; and her most recent collection is *Even the Stars Look Lonesome* (1997). At the January 21, 1993 inauguration of President William Jefferson Clinton, she delivered the poem requested by him for this occasion, "On the Pulse of Morning," establishing her as the first woman and the first African American to merit such recognition. Angelou has also written juvenile literature and screenplays for television and movies. In addition, she has acting and directing credentials.

Angelou recounts in *The Heart of a Woman* that the celebrated Billie Holiday once expressed to her that she would be famous, but her fame would have nothing to do with the night club singing that she was doing as a means of support for her and her son. Holiday's words proved to be prophetic, for Angelou has emerged as a woman of international acclaim. Though she continues to sing on occasion, it is her pen and her command of language that propel her to lofty heights.

Today Angelou holds a lifetime appointment at Wake Forest University in Winston-Salem, North Carolina, as Reynolds Professor of American Studies. Her return to the South, a place that caused so much discomfort in her early life, is perhaps a sign that strength and endurance can help a person to overcome anything.

Selected Bibliography

Elliot, Jeffrey M., ed. *Conversations with Maya Angelou.* Jackson: University of Mississippi Press, 1989

Evans, Mari, ed. *Black Women Writers (1950–1980): A Critical Evaluation.* Garden City, NY: Anchor, 1984.

McPherson, Dolly Aimee. *Order out of Chaos: The Autobiographical Works of Maya Angelou.* New York: Lang, 1990.

Tate, Claudia, ed. *Black Women Writers at Work.* New York: Continuum, 1983.

Still I Rise

Maya Angelou

You may write me down in history
With your bitter, twisted lies,
You may trod me in the very dirt
But still, like dust, I'll rise.

Does my sassiness upset you? 5
Why are you beset with gloom?
'Cause I walk like I've got oil wells
Pumping in my living room.

Just like moons and like suns,
With the certainty of tides, 10
Just like hopes springing high,
Still I'll rise.
Did you want to see me broken?
Bowed head and lowered eyes?
Shoulders falling down like teardrops, 15
Weakened by my soulful cries.

Does my haughtiness offend you?
Don't you take it awful hard
'Cause I laugh like I've got gold mines
Diggin' in my own back yard. 20

You may shoot me with your words,
You may cut me with your eyes,
You may kill me with your hatefulness,
But still, like air, I'll rise.

Does my sexiness upset you? 25
Does it come as a surprise
That I dance like I've got diamonds
At the meeting of my thighs?

Out of the huts of history's shame
I rise
from a past that's rooted in pain
I rise
I'm a black ocean, leaping and wide,
Welling and swelling I bear in the tide.
Leaving behind nights of terror and fear
I rise
Into a daybreak that's wondrously clear
I rise
Bringing the gifts that my ancestors gave,
I am the dream and the hope of the slave.
I rise
I rise
I rise.

Nikki Giovanni (1943–)

Nikki Giovanni was born in Knoxville, Tennessee, on June 7, 1943, to Gus and Yolande Giovanni. She was given her mother's name, Yolande Cornelia. Her parents and her older sister Gary relocated to Wyoming, Ohio, while Giovanni was still an infant. During her developmental years, Giovanni manifested an independent character from her maternal grandmother, Louvenia Watson, with whom she lived during her sophomore and junior years in high school.

As a freshman at Fisk University in Nashville, Tennessee, in 1960, Giovanni left campus without permission to have Thanksgiving dinner with her grandmother. Her punishment was probation, but she was unrepentant and was subsequently suspended. Giovanni returned to Fisk in 1964, a more serious and determined student. She joined the Fisk Writers Workshop under the direction of John O. Killens. He helped her to fine tune her creative skills, and he influenced her political persuasion. She was a member of the Student Nonviolent Coordinating Committee and played a significant role in getting the organization reinstated on campus. Giovanni graduated magna cum laude in February 1967 with honors in history. Later as the recipient of a Ford Foundation Grant, she pursued graduate studies at the School of Social Work at the University of Pennsylvania and the School of Fine Arts at Columbia University.

Her education and creative skills led her to seek employment on the university level, holding professorial positions at Queens College of the City University of New York, Rutgers University, Ohio State University, and the College of Mount Saint Joseph. She is currently professor of English at Virginia Polytechnic Institute and State University in Blacksburg, Virginia.

Giovanni's debut on the literary scene was as one of the New Black Poets during the era of the Black Arts Movement. Dudley Randall introduced her poetry to mainstream Black America through his Broadside Press, and her attraction within the African-American community was instantaneous. Her feistiness and spiritedness were welcome attributes during the revolutionary times of the 1960s. She evinced a commitment to race pride, Black consciousness, and social action that appealed to African-American youth. Through the language of poetic confrontation, she hoped to inspire young African Americans to dethrone those responsible for the proliferation of oppressive institutions.

Of those identified as Broadside Press poets, Giovanni was perhaps one of the most controversial. Her early poetry displayed the temperament of an aggressive revolutionary ready to become an incendiary agent for change. Giovanni's poetry professed the need for Black Americans to be openly violent and to arm themselves and rise up for the cause. She did not mince words or straddle issues. In Giovanni's early poetry she uses the language of the street, the four-letter word and other obscenities, the abbreviated word, i.e., "blk" for Black, the slashed word, the fused word, the small letter "I," the omission of capital letters, and sometimes the omission of punctuation marks. These are indicators of her revolt against the traditions of poetic form. Another innovative approach was the recording of it and the inclusion of the Negro spiritual as background music to complement her verse. The spiritualistic music somehow sanctioned the suggestions the words made. Giovanni's later poetry no longer expresses the need to end White supremacy, colonialism, and oppression through social action but centers on themes of community, life, home, heart, nature, and love.

Giovanni's collections of poetry include *Black Feeling, Black Talk* (1967), *Black Judgment* (1968), *Re-Creation* (1970), *My House* (1972), *The Women and the Men* (1975), *Shimmy Like*

My Sister Kate: Looking at the Harlem Renaissance through Poems (1995), *The Selected Poems of Nikki Giovanni* (1996), *Love Poems* (1997), and *Blues: For All the Changes: New Poems* (1999). Among her prose works are *Gemini: An Extended Autobiographical Statement on My First Twenty-Five Years of Being a Black Poet* (1971), *Dialogue: James Baldwin and Nikki Giovanni* (1973), *A Poetic Equation: Conversations between Nikki Giovanni and Margaret Walker* (1974), and *Racism 101* (1994). Giovanni's children's publications include *Spin a Soft Black Song* (1971, 1985), and *Ego-Tripping and Other Poems for Young People* (1973, 1993). Her discography titles include *Truth Is on Its Way* (1971), *Like a Ripple on a Pond* (1973), and *Cotton Candy on a Rainy Day* (1978).

Giovanni is an important figure in African-American literary history. The militancy of her early poems is an accurate reflection of the temper of the times. Her current poetry, too, is an indication of her maturity as a woman and an accurate depiction of the evolution of life in America for the African American.

Selected Bibliography

Evans, Mari, ed. *Black Women Writers (1950–1980): A Critical Evaluation*. Garden City, NY: Anchor, 1984.

Hine, Darlene Clark, ed. *Black Women in America: An Historical Encyclopedia*. Vol.1. Brooklyn: Carlson, 1993.

Tate, Claudia, ed. *Black Women Writers at Work*. New York: Continuum, 1983.

Nikki-Rosa

Nikki Giovanni

childhood remembrances are always a drag
if you're Black
you always remember things like living in Woodlawn
with no inside toilet
and if you become famous or something   5
they never talk about how happy you were to have your mother
all to yourself and
how good the water felt when you got your bath from one of those
big tubs that folk in chicago barbecue in
and somehow when you talk about home   10
it never gets across how much you
understood their feelings
as the whole family attended meetings about Hollydale
and even though you remember
your biographers never understand   15
your father's pain as he sells his stock
and another dream goes
and though you're poor it isn't poverty that
concerns you
and though they fought a lot   20
it isn't your father's drinking that makes any difference
but only that everybody is together and you
and your sister have happy birthdays and very good christmasses
and I really hope no white person ever has cause to write about me
because they never understand Black love is Black wealth and they'll   25
probably talk about my hard childhood and never understand that
all the while I was quite happy

                                    1968

African-American Narrative

The slave narratives of Olaudah Equiano, Frederick Douglass, and Harriet Jacobs are the prototypes of the African-American narrative. In the appendix are the dates, authors, and titles of key African-American narratives according to indicated periods. Naturally, the earliest narratives focus almost exclusively on slavery and freedom. Later narratives expand to include a multiplicity of themes and types.

Olaudah Equiano (c. 1745–1797)

Olaudah Equiano was born in the village of Essaka, in what is now Nigeria, around 1745; he was the youngest son of an Ibo chief. When Equiano was 11 or 12, he and his sister were captured by members of another tribe, taken to the coast, sold to British slave dealers, and subjected to the inhumanity of the Middle Passage as they sailed to the West Indies. Equiano briefly worked as a field slave before he was sent to Virginia. After he reached the American colonies, he worked as a seaman for the next ten years for various masters who also provided opportunities for him to learn English as well as shipboard and navigation skills. His first White master renamed Equiano, Gustavus Vassa in honor of a Scandinavian king because Equiano was of royal blood. When his last master sold Vassa his freedom in 1766, the newly emancipated man promptly abandoned his slave name in favor of his birth name. Equiano continued to sail to such destinations as England, Turkey, Italy, Portugal, Spain, Honduras, Nicaragua (where he lived among the Miskito Indians for six months), and the Arctic, yet he never fulfilled his dream of returning to Africa. In 1777, Equiano moved to England, and in 1792, he married Susanna Cullen, an English citizen.

Equiano was a prominent abolitionist who focused public attention on the owners of the British slave ship Zong, who filed insurance claims after 132 shackled slaves were thrown overboard. Equiano was appointed a Commissary of Provisions and Stores for the Black Poor Going to Sierra Leone, an organization to assist freed slaves in Africa. However, his greatest contribution to the anti-slavery movement was his autobiography, *The Interesting Narrative of the Life of Olaudah Equiano, or Gustavus Vassa, the African, Written by Himself* (1789 in England; 1791 in the United States). As a pioneer of the slave narrative as well as African-American autobiography, Equiano shares with his readers his firsthand knowledge of boyhood life in Africa, the trauma of captivity, the heartbreak of separation from his family and way of life, the indignities of the infamous Middle Passage, slavery in the West Indies and in the American colonies, adventures at sea, and life as a free man. Equiano died March 31, 1797 in London.

Selected Bibliography

Andrews, William L, Frances Smith Foster, and Trudier Harris, eds. *The Oxford Companion to African American Literature*. New York: Oxford University Press, 1997.

Nelson, Emmanuel S., Ed. *African American Authors, 1745–1945: A Bio-Bibliographical Critical Sourcebook*. Westport, CT: Greenwood, 2000.

The Interesting Narrative of the Life of Olaudah Equiano

Olaudah Equiano

Chapter 1

The author's account of his country, and their manners and customs—Administration of justice—Embrenche—Marriage ceremony, and public entertainments—Mode of living—Dress—Manufactures—Buildings—Commerce—Agriculture—War and religion—Superstition of the natives—Funeral ceremonies of the priests or magicians—Curious mode of discovering poison—Some hints concerning the origin of the author's countrymen, with the opinions of different writers on that subject.

I believe it is difficult for those who publish their own memoirs to escape the imputation of vanity; nor is this the only disadvantage under which they labor: it is also their misfortune that what is uncommon is rarely, if ever, believed, and what is obvious we are apt to turn from with disgust, and to charge the writer with impertinence. People generally think those memoirs only worthy to be read or remembered which abound in great or striking events, those, in short, which in a high degree excite either admiration or pity; all others they consign to contempt and oblivion. It is therefore, I confess, not a little hazardous in a private and obscure individual, and a stranger too, thus to solicit the indulgent attention of the public, especially when I own I offer here the history of neither a saint, a hero, nor a tyrant. I believe there are few events in my life which have not happened to many; it is true the incidents of it are numerous, and, did I consider myself an European, I might say my sufferings were great; but when I compare my lot with that of most of my countrymen, I regard myself as a *particular favorite of heaven,* and acknowledge the mercies of Providence in every occurrence of my life. If, then, the following narrative does not appear sufficiently interesting to engage general attention, let my motive be some excuse for its publication. I am not so foolishly vain as to expect from it either immortality or literary reputation. If it affords any satisfaction to my numerous friends, at whose request it has been written, or in the smallest degree promotes the interests of humanity, the ends for which it was undertaken will be fully attained, and every wish of my heart gratified. Let it therefore be remembered, that, in wishing to avoid censure, I do not aspire to praise.

That part of Africa, known by the name of Guinea, to which the trade for slaves is carried on, extends along the coast above 3400 miles, from Senegal to Angola, and includes a variety of kingdoms. Of these the most considerable is the kingdom of Benin, both as to extent and wealth, the richness and cultivation of the soil, the power of its king, and the number and warlike disposition of the inhabitants. It is situated nearly under the line, and extends along the coast about 170 miles, but runs back into the interior part of Africa to a distance hitherto, I believe, unexplored by any traveller, and seems only terminated at length by the empire of Abyssinia, near 1500 miles from its beginning. This kingdom is divided into many provinces or districts, in one of the most remote and fertile of which, I was born, in the year 1745, situated in a charming fruitful vale, named Essaka. The distance of this province from the capital of Benin and the sea coast must be very considerable, for I had never heard of white men or Europeans, nor of the sea; and our subjection to the king of Benin was little more than nominal, for every transaction of the government, as far as my slender observation extended, was conducted by the chief or elders of the place. The manners and government of a people who have little commerce with other countries are generally very simple, and the history of what passes in one family or village may serve as a specimen of the whole nation.

My father was one of those elders or chiefs I have spoken of, and was styled Embrenche, a term, as I remember, importing the highest distinction, and signifying in our language a *mark* of grandeur. This mark is conferred on the person entitled to it, by cutting the skin across at the top of the forehead, and drawing it down to the eyebrows; and while it is in this situation applying a warm hand, and rubbing it until it shrinks up into a thick *weal* across the lower part of the forehead. Most of the judges and senators were thus marked; my father had long borne it; I had seen it conferred on one of my brothers, and I also was *destined* to receive it by my parents. Those Embrenche, or chief men, decided disputes and punished crimes, for which purpose they always assembled together. The proceedings were generally short, and in most cases the law of retaliation prevailed.

I remember a man was brought before my father, and the other judges, for kidnapping a boy; and, although he was the son of a chief or senator, he was condemned to make recompense by a man or woman slave. Adultery, however, was sometimes punished with slavery or death, a punishment which I believe is inflicted on it throughout most of the nations of Africa, so sacred among them is the honor of the marriage bed, and so jealous are they of the fidelity of their wives. Of this I recollect an instance—a woman was convicted before the judges of adultery, and delivered over, as the custom was, to her husband, to be punished. Accordingly he determined to put her to death; but it being found, just before her execution, that she had an infant at her breast, and no woman being prevailed on to perform the part of a nurse, she was spared on account of the child. The men, however, do not preserve the same constancy to their wives which they expect from them; for they indulge in a plurality, though seldom in more than two.

Their mode of marriage is thus—both parties are usually betrothed when young by their parents (though I have known the males to betroth themselves). On this occasion a feast is prepared, and the bride and bridegroom stand up in the midst of all their friends, who are assembled for the purpose, while he declares she is henceforth to be looked upon as his wife, and that no other person is to pay any addresses to her. This is also immediately proclaimed in the vicinity, on which the bride retires from the assembly. Some time after, she is brought home to her husband, and then another feast is made, to which the relations of both parties are invited; her parents then deliver her to the bridegroom, accompanied with a number of blessings, and at the same time they tie round her waist a cotton string of the thickness of a goose-quill, which none but married women are permitted to wear; she is now considered as completely his wife; and at this time the dowry is given to the new married pair, which generally consists of portions of land, slaves, and cattle, household goods, and implements of husbandry. These are offered by the friends of both parties; besides which the parents of the bridegroom present gifts to those of the bride, whose property she is looked upon before marriage; but after it she is esteemed the sole property of her husband. The ceremony being now ended, the festival begins, which is celebrated with bonfires and loud acclamations of joy, accompanied with music and dancing.

We are almost a nation of dancers, musicians, and poets. Thus every great event, such as a triumphant return from battle or other cause of public rejoicing, is celebrated in public dances, which are accompanied with songs and music suited to the occasion. The assembly is separated into four divisions, which dance either apart or in succession, and each with a character peculiar to itself. The first division contains the married men, who in their dances frequently exhibit feats of arms and the representation of a battle. To these succeed the married women, who dance in the second division. The young men occupy the third, and the maidens the fourth. Each represents some interesting scene of real life, such as a great achievement, domestic employment, a pathetic story, or some rural sport; and as the subject is generally founded on some recent event, it is therefore ever new. This gives our dances a spirit and variety which I have scarcely seen elsewhere. We have many musical instruments, particularly drums of different kinds, a piece of music which resembles a guitar, and another much like a stickado. These last are chiefly used by betrothed virgins, who play on them on all grand festivals.

As our manners are simple, our luxuries are few. The dress of both sexes is nearly the same. It generally consists of a long piece of calico, or muslin, wrapped loosely round the body, somewhat in the form of a highland plaid. This is usually dyed blue, which is our favorite color. It is extracted from a berry, and is brighter and richer than any I have seen in Europe. Besides this, our women of distinction wear golden ornaments, which they dispose with some profusion on their arms and legs. When our women are not employed with the men in tillage, their usual occupation is spinning and weaving cotton, which they afterwards dye, and make into garments. They also manufacture earthen vessels, of which we have many kinds. Among the rest, tobacco pipes, made after the same fashion, and used in the same manner, as those in Turkey.

Our manner of living is entirely plain; for as yet the natives are unacquainted with those refinements in cookery which debauch the taste: bullocks, goats, and poultry supply the greatest part of their food. These constitute likewise the principal wealth of the country, and the chief articles of its commerce. The flesh is usually stewed in a pan; to make it savory we sometimes use pepper, and other spices, and we have salt made of wood ashes. Our vegetables are mostly plantains, eadas, yams, beans, and Indian corn. The head of the family usually eats alone; his wives and slaves have also their separate tables. Before we taste food we always wash our hands; indeed, our cleanliness on all occasions is extreme, but on this it is an indispensable ceremony. After washing, libation is made, by pouring out a small portion of the drink on the floor, and tossing a small quantity of the food in a certain place, for the spirits of departed relations, which the natives suppose to preside over their conduct and guard them from evil. They are totally unacquainted with strong or spirituous liquors; and their principal beverage is palm wine. This is got from a tree of that name, by tapping it at the top and fastening a large gourd to it; and sometimes one tree will yield three or four gallons in a night. When just drawn it is of a most delicious sweetness; but in a few days it acquires a tartish and more spirituous flavor, though I never saw anyone intoxicated by it. The same tree also produces nuts and oil. Our principal luxury is in perfumes: one sort of these is an odoriferous wood of delicious fragrance, the other a kind of earth, a small portion of which thrown into the fire diffuses a most powerful odor. We beat this wood into powder, and mix it with palm oil, with which both men and women perfume themselves.

In our buildings we study convenience rather than ornament. Each master of a family has a large square piece of ground, surrounded with a moat or fence, or enclosed with a wall made of red earth tempered, which, when dry, is as hard as brick. Within this, are his houses to accommodate his family and slaves, which, if numerous, frequently present the appearance of a village. In the middle, stands the principal building, appropriated to the sole use of the master and consisting of two apartments; in one of which he sits in the day with his family, the other is left apart for the reception of his friends. He has besides these a distinct apartment in which he sleeps, together with his male children. On each side are the apartments of his wives, who have also their separate day and night houses. The habitations of the slaves and their families are distributed throughout the rest of the enclosure. These houses never exceed one story in height; they are always built of wood, or stakes driven into the ground, crossed with wattles, and neatly plastered within and without. The roof is thatched with reeds. Our day houses are left open at the sides; but those in which we sleep are always covered, and plastered in the inside, with a composition mixed with cow-dung, to keep off the different insects which annoy us during the night. The walls and floors also of these are generally covered with mats. Our beds consist of a platform, raised three or four from the ground, on which are laid skins, and different parts of a spongy tree, called plantain. Our covering is calico or muslin, the same as our dress. The usual seats are a few logs of wood; but we have benches, which are generally perfumed to accommodate strangers: these compose the greater part of our household furniture. Houses so constructed and furnished require but little skill to erect them. Every man is a sufficient architect for the purpose. The whole neighborhood afford their unanimous assistance in building them, and in return receive and expect no other recompense than a feast.

As we live in a country where nature is prodigal of her favors, our wants are few and easily supplied; of course we have few manufactures. They consist for the most part of calicoes, earthen ware, ornaments, and instruments of war and husbandry. But these make no part of our commerce, the principal articles of which, as I have observed, are provisions. In such a state, money is of little use; however, we have some small pieces of coin, if I may call them such. They are made something like an anchor, but I do not remember either their value or denomination. We have also markets, at which I have been frequently with my mother. These are sometimes visited by stout mahogany-colored men from the south-west of us: we call the *Oye-Eboe,* which term signifies red men living at a distance. They generally bring us fire-arms, gun-powder, hats, beads, and dried fish. The last we esteemed a great rarity, as our waters were only brooks and springs. These articles they barter with us for odoriferous woods and earth, and our salt of wood ashes. They always carry slaves through our land; but the strictest account is exacted of their manner of procuring them before they are suffered to pass. Sometimes, indeed, we sold slaves to them, but they were only prisoners of war, or such among us as had been convicted of kidnapping, or adultery, and some other crimes, which we esteemed heinous. This practice of kidnapping induces me to think, that, notwithstanding all our strictness, their principal business among us was to trepan our people. I remember too, they carried great sacks along with them, which not long after, I had an opportunity of fatally seeing applied to that infamous purpose.

Our land is uncommonly rich and fruitful, and produces all kinds of vegetables in great abundance. We have plenty of Indian corn, and vast quantities of cotton and tobacco. Our pineapples grow without culture; they are about the size of the largest sugar-loaf, and finely flavored. We have also spices of different kinds, particularly pepper, and a variety of delicious fruits which I have never seen in Europe, together with gums of various kinds, and honey in abundance. All our industry is exerted to improve these blessings of nature. Agriculture is our chief employment; and everyone, even the children and women, are engaged in it. Thus we are all habituated to labor from our earliest years. Everyone contributes something to the common stock; and, as we are unacquainted with idleness, we have no beggars. The benefits of such a mode of living are obvious. The West India planters prefer the slaves of Benin or Eboe to those of any other part of Guinea, for their hardiness, intelligence, integrity, and zeal. Those benefits are felt by us in the general healthiness of the people, and in their vigor and activity; I might have added, too, in their comeliness. Deformity is indeed unknown amongst us, I mean that of shape. Numbers of the natives of Eboe now in London might be brought in support of this assertion: for, in regard to complexion, ideas of beauty are wholly relative. I remember while in Africa to have seen three Negro children who were tawny, and another quite white, who were universally regarded by myself, and the natives in general, as far as related to their complexions, as deformed. Our women, too, were, in my eye at least, uncommonly graceful, alert, and modest to a degree of bashfulness; nor do I remember to have heard of an instance of incontinence amongst them before marriage. They are also remarkably cheerful. Indeed, cheerfulness and affability are two of the leading characteristics of our nation.

Our tillage is exercised in a large plain or common, some hour's walk from our dwellings, and all the neighbors resort thither in a body. They use no beasts of husbandry; and their only instruments are hoes, axes, shovels, and beaks, or pointed iron, to dig with. Sometimes we are visited by locusts, which come in large clouds, so as to darken the air, and destroy our harvest. This, however, happens rarely, but when it does, a famine is produced by it. I remember an instance or two wherein this happened. This common is often the theatre of war; and therefore when our people go out to till their land, they not only go in a body, but generally take their arms with them for fear of a surprise; and when they apprehend an invasion, they guard the avenues to their dwellings, by driving sticks into the ground, which are so sharp at one end as to pierce the foot, and are generally dipt in poison. From what I can recollect of these battles, they appear to have been irruptions of one little state or district on the other, to obtain prisoners or booty. Perhaps they were incited to this by those traders who brought the European goods I mentioned, amongst us. Such a mode of obtaining slaves in Africa is common; and I believe more are procured this way, and by kidnapping, than any other. When a trader wants slaves, he applies to a chief for them, and tempts him with his wares. It is not extraordinary, if on this occasion he yields to the temptation with as little firmness, and accepts the price of his fellow creature's liberty, with as little reluctance as the enlightened merchant. Accordingly he falls on his neighbors, and a desperate battle ensues. If he prevails and takes prisoners, he gratifies his avarice by selling them; but, if his party be vanquished, and he falls into the hands of the enemy, he is put to death; for, as he has been known to foment their quarrels, it is thought dangerous to let him survive, and no ransom can save him, though all other prisoners may be redeemed. We have fire-arms, bows and arrows, broad two-edged swords and javelins; we have shields also which cover a man from bead to foot. All are taught the use of these weapons; even our women are warriors, and march boldly out to fight along with the men. Our whole district is a kind of militia: on a certain signal given, such as the firing of a gun at night, they all rise in arms and rush upon their enemy. It is perhaps something remarkable, that when our people march to the field a red flag or banner is borne before them.

I was once a witness to a battle in our common. We had been all at work in it one day as usual, when our people were suddenly attacked. I climbed a tree at some distance, from which I beheld the fight. There were many women as well as men on both sides; among others my mother was there, and armed with a broad sword. After fighting for a considerable time with great fury, and many had been killed, our people obtained the victory, and took their enemy's Chief a prisoner. He was carried off in great triumph, and, though he offered a large ransom for his life, he was put to death. A virgin of note among our enemies had been slain in the battle, and her arm was exposed in our marketplace, where our trophies were always exhibited. The spoils were divided according to the merit of the warriors. Those prisoners which were not sold or redeemed, we kept as slaves; but how different was their condition from that of the slaves in the West Indies! With us, they do no more work than other members of the community, even their master; their food, clothing, and lodging were nearly the same as theirs (except that they were not permitted to eat with those who were free-born); and there was scarce any other difference between them, than a superior degree of importance which the head of a family possesses in our state, and that authority which, as such, he exercises over every part of his household. Some of these slaves have even slaves under them as their own property, and for their own use.

As to religion, the natives believe that there is one Creator of all things, and that he lives in the sun, and is girted round with a belt; that he may never eat or drink, but, according to some, he smokes a pipe, which is our own favorite luxury. They believe he governs events, especially our deaths or captivity; but, as for the doctrine of eternity, I do not remember to have ever heard of it; some, however, believe in the transmigration of souls in a certain degree. Those spirits which were not transmigrated, such as their dear friends or relations, they believe always attend them, and guard them from the bad spirits or their foes. For this reason they always, before eating, as I have observed, put some small portion of the meat, and pour some of their drink, on the ground for them; and they often make oblations of the blood of beasts or fowls at their graves. I was very fond of my mother, and almost constantly with her. When she went to make these oblations at her mother's tomb, which was a kind of small solitary thatched house, I sometimes attended her. There she made her libations, and spent most of the night in cries and lamentations. I have been often extremely terrified on these occasions. The loneliness of the place, the darkness of the night, and the ceremony of libation, naturally awful and gloomy, were heightened by my mother's lamentations; and these concurring with the doleful cries of birds, by which these places were frequented, gave an inexpressible terror to the scene.

We compute the year from the day on which the sun crosses the line, and on its setting that evening, there is a general shout throughout the land; at least, I can speak from my own knowledge, throughout our vicinity. The people at the same time make a great noise with rattles, not unlike the basket rattles used by children here, though much larger, and hold up their hands to heaven for a blessing. It is then the greatest offerings are made; and those children whom our wise men foretell will be fortunate are then presented to different people. I remember many used to come to see me, and I was carried about to others for that purpose. They have many offerings, particularly at full moons; generally two, at harvest, before the fruits are taken out of the ground; and when any young animals are killed, sometimes they offer up part of them as a sacrifice. These offerings, when made by one of the heads of a family, serve for the whole. I remember we often had them at father's and my uncle's, and their families have been present. Some of our offerings are eaten with bitter herbs. We had a saying among us to anyone of a cross temper, "That if they were to be eaten, they should be eaten with bitter herbs."

We practised circumcision like the Jews, and made offerings and feasts on that occasion, in the same manner as they did. Like them also, our children were named from some event, some circumstance, or fancied foreboding, at the time of their birth. I was named *Olaudah,* which in our language signifies vicissitude, or fortunate; also, one favored, and having a loud voice and well spoken. I remember we never polluted the name of the object of our adoration; on the contrary, it was always mentioned with the greatest reverence; and we were totally unacquainted with swearing, and all those terms of abuse and reproach which find their way so readily and copiously into the language of more civilized people. The only expressions of that kind I remember were, "May you rot, or may you swell, or may a beast take you."

I have before remarked that the natives of this part of Africa are extremely cleanly. This necessary habit of decency was with us a part of religion, and therefore we had many purifications and washings; indeed almost as many, and used on the same occasions, if my recollection does not fail me, as the Jews. Those that touched the dead at any time were obliged to wash and purify themselves before they could enter a dwelling-house. Every woman, too, at certain times was forbidden to come into a dwelling-house, or touch any person, or anything we eat. I was so fond of my mother I could not keep from her, or avoid touching her at some of those periods, in consequence of which I was obliged to be kept out with her, in a little house made for that purpose, till offering was made, and then we were purified.

Though we had no places of public worship, we had priests and magicians, or wise men. I do not remember whether they had different offices, or whether they were united in the same persons, but they were held in great reverence by the people. They calculated our time, and foretold events, as their name imported, for we called them *Ah-affoe-way-cah,* which signifies calculators or yearly men, our year being called *Ah-affoe.* They wore their beards, and when they died, they were succeeded by their sons. Most of their implements and things of value were interred along with them. Pipes and tobacco were also put into the grave with the corpse, which was always perfumed and ornamented, and animals were offered in sacrifice to them. None accompanied their funerals, but those of the same profession or tribe. They buried them after sunset, and always returned from the grave by a different way from that which they went.

These magicians were also our doctors or physicians. They practised bleeding by cupping, and were very successful in healing wounds and expelling poisons. They had likewise some extraordinary method of discovering jealousy, theft, poisoning, the success of which, no doubt, they derived from the unbounded influence over the credulity and superstition of the people. I do not remember what those methods were, except that as to poisoning; I recollect an instance or two, which I hope it will not be deemed impertinent here to insert, as it may serve as a kind of specimen of the rest, as is still used by the Negroes in the West Indies. A young woman had been poisoned, but it was not known by whom; the doctors ordered the corpse to be taken up by some persons, and carried to the grave. As soon as the bearers had raised it on their shoulders, they seemed seized with some sudden impulse, and ran to and fro, unable to stop themselves. At last, after having passed through a number of thorns and prickly bushes unhurt, the corpse fell from them close to a house, and defaced it in the fall; and the owner being taken up, he immediately confessed the poisoning.

The natives are extremely cautious about poison. When they buy any eatables, the seller kisses it all round before the buyer, to shew him it is not poisoned; and the same is done when any meat or drink is presented, particularly to a stranger. We have serpents of different kinds, some of which are esteemed ominous when they appear in our houses, and these we never molest. I remember two of those ominous snakes, each of which was as thick as the calf of a man's leg, and in color resembling a dolphin in the water, crept at different times into my mother's night house, where I always lay with her, and coiled themselves into folds, and each time they crowed like a cock. I was desired by some of our wise men to touch these, that I might be interested in the good omens, which I did, for they were quite harmless, and would tamely suffer themselves to be handled; and then they were put into a large earthen pan, and set on one side of the highway. Some of our snakes, however, were poisonous; one of them crossed the road one day as I was standing on it, and passed between my feet without offering to touch me, to the great surprise of many who saw it; and these incidents were accounted by the wise men, and likewise by my mother and the rest of the people, as remarkable omens in my favor.

Such is the imperfect sketch my memory has furnished me with, of the manners and customs of a people among whom I first drew my breath. And here I cannot forbear suggesting what has long struck me very forcibly, namely, the strong analogy which even by this sketch, imperfect as it is, appears to prevail in the manners and customs of my countrymen and those of the Jews, before they reached the land of promise, and particularly the patriarchs while they were yet in that pastoral state which is described in Genesis—an analogy, which alone would induce me to think that the one people had sprung from the other. Indeed, this is the opinion of Dr. Gill, who, in his commentary on Genesis, very ably deduces the pedigree of the Africans from Afer and Afra, the descendents of Abraham by Keturah his wife and concubine (for both these titles are applied to her). It is also conformable to the sentiments of Dr. John Clarke, formerly Dean of Sarum, in his truth of the Christian religion; both these authors concur in ascribing to us this original. The reasonings of those gentlemen are still further confirmed by the scripture chronology; and if any further corroboration were required, this resemblance in so many respects, is a strong evidence in support of the opinion. Like the Israelites in their primitive state, our government was conducted by our chiefs or judges, our wise men and elders; and the head of a family with us enjoyed a similar authority over his household, with that which is ascribed to Abraham and the other patriarchs. The law of retaliation obtained almost universally with us as with them: and even their religion appeared to have shed upon us a ray of its glory, though broken and spent in its passage, or eclipsed by the cloud with which time, tradition, and ignorance might have enveloped it; for we had our circumcision (a rule, I believe, peculiar to that people), we had also our sacrifices and burnt-offerings, our washings and purifications, and on the same occasions as they did.

As to the difference of color between the Eboan Africans and the modern Jews, I shall not presume to account for it. It is a subject which has engaged the pens of men of both genius and learning, and is far above my strength. The most able and Reverend Mr. T. Clarkson, however, in his much admired *Essay on the Slavery and Commerce of the Human Species,* has ascertained the cause in a manner that at once solves every objection on that account, and, on my mind at least, has produced the fullest conviction. I shall therefore refer to that performance for the theory, contenting myself with extracting a fact as related by Dr. Mitchel. "The Spaniards, who have inhabited America, under the torrid zone, for any time, are become as dark colored as our native Indians of Virginia; of which *I myself have been a witness."* There is also another instance of a Portuguese settlement at Mitomba, a river in Sierra Leone, where the inhabitants are bred from a mixture of the first Portuguese discoverers with the natives, and are now become in their complexion, and in the woolly quality of their hair, *perfect Negroes,* retaining however a smattering of the Portuguese language.

These instances, and a great many more which might be adduced, while they show how the complexions of the same persons vary in different climates, it is hoped may tend also to remove the prejudice that some conceive against the natives of Africa on account of their color. Surely the minds of the Spaniards did not change with their complexions! Are there not causes enough to which the apparent inferiority of an African may be ascribed, without limiting the goodness of God, and supposing he forebore to stamp understanding on certainly his own image, because "carved in ebony." Might it not naturally be ascribed to their situation? When they come among Europeans, they are ignorant of their language, religion, manners, and customs. Are any pains taken to teach them these? Are they treated as men? Does not slavery itself depress the mind, and extinguish all its fire and every noble sentiment? But, above all, what advantages do not a refined people possess, over those who are rude and uncultivated? Let the polished and haughty European recollect that his ancestors were once, like the Africans, uncivilized, and even barbarous. Did Nature make *them* inferior to their sons? and should *they too* have been made slaves? Every rational mind answers, No. Let such reflections as these melt the pride of their superiority into sympathy for the wants and miseries of their sable brethren, and compel them to acknowledge that understanding is not confined to feature or color. If, when they look round the world, they feel exultation, let it be tempered with benevolence to others, and gratitude to God, "who hath made of one blood all nations of men for to dwell on all the face of the earth"; "and whose wisdom is not our wisdom, neither are our ways his ways."

Chapter 2

The author's birth and parentage—His being kidnapped with his sister—Their separation—Surprise at meeting again—Are finally separated—Account of the different places and incidents the author met with till his arrival on the coast—The effect the sight of a slave-ship had on him—He sails for the West Indies—Horrors of a slave-ship—Arrives at Barbadoes, where the cargo is sold and dispersed.

I hope the reader will not think I have trespassed on his patience in introducing myself to him with some account of the manners and customs of my country. They had been implanted in me with great care, and made an impression on my mind, which time could not erase, and which all the adversity and variety of fortune I have since experienced, served only to rivet and record: for, whether the love of one's country be real or imaginary, or a lesson of reason, or an instinct of nature, I still look back with pleasure on the first scenes of my life, though that pleasure has been for the most part mingled with sorrow.

I have already acquainted the reader with the time and place of my birth. My father, besides many slaves, had a numerous family, of which seven lived to grow up, including myself and sister, who was the only daughter. As I was the youngest of the sons, I became, of course, the greatest favorite with my mother, and was always with her; and she used to take particular pains to form my mind. I was trained up from my earliest years in the art of war: my daily exercise was shooting and throwing javelins, and my mother adorned me with emblems, after the manner of our greatest warriors. In this way I grew up till I had turned the age of eleven, when an end was put to my happiness in the following manner: Generally, when the grown people in the neighborhood were gone far in the fields to labor, the children assembled together in some of the neighboring premises to play; and commonly some of us used to get up a tree to look out for any assailant, or kidnapper, that might come upon us—for they sometimes took those opportunities of our parents' absence, to attack and carry off as many as they could seize. One day as I was watching at the top of a tree in our yard, I saw one of those people come into the yard of our next neighbor but one, to kidnap, there being many stout young people in it. Immediately on this I gave the alarm of the rogue, and he was surrounded by the stoutest of them, who entangled him with cords, so that he could not escape, till some of the grown people came and secured him. But, alas! ere long it was my fate to be thus attacked, and to be carried off, when none of the grown people were nigh.

One day, when all our people were gone out to their works as usual, and only I and my dear sister were left to mind the house, two men and a woman got over our walls, and in a moment seized us both, and, without giving us time to cry out, or make resistance, they stopped our mouths, and ran off with us into the nearest wood. Here they tied our hands, and continued to carry us as far as they could, till night came on, when we reached a small house, where the robbers halted for refreshment, and spent the night. We were then unbound, but were unable to take any food; and, being quite overpowered by fatigue and grief, our only relief was some sleep, which allayed our misfortune for a short time. The next morning we left the house, and continued travelling all the day. For a long time we had kept the woods, but at last we came into a road which I believed I knew. I had now some hopes of being delivered; for we had advanced but a little way before I discovered some people at a distance, on which I began to cry out for their assistance; but my cries had no other effect than to make them tie me faster and stop my mouth, and then they put me into a large sack. They also stopped my sister's mouth, and tied her hands; and in this manner we proceeded till we were out of sight of these people. When we went to rest the following night, they offered us victuals, but we refused it; and the only comfort we had was in being in one another's arms all that night, and bathing each other with our tears. But alas! we were soon deprived of even the small comfort of weeping together.

The next day proved a day of greater sorrow than I had yet experienced; for my sister and I were then separated, while we lay clasped in each other's arms. It was in vain that we besought them not to part us; she was torn from me, and immediately carried away, while I was left in a state of distraction not to be described. I cried and grieved continually; and for several days did not eat anything but what they forced into my mouth. At length, after many days' travelling, during which I had often changed masters, I got into the hands of a chieftain, in a very pleasant country. This man had two wives and some children, and they all used me extremely well, and did all they could do to comfort me; particularly the first wife, who was something like my mother. Although I was a great many days' journey from my father's house, yet these people spoke exactly the same language with us. This first master of mine, as I may call him, was a smith, and my principal employment was working his bellows, which were the same kind as I had seen in my vicinity. They were in some respects not unlike the stoves here in gentlemen's kitchens, and were covered over with leather; and in the middle of that leather a stick was fixed, and a person stood up, and worked it in the same manner as is done to pump water out of a cask with a hand pump. I believe it was gold he worked, for it was of a lovely bright yellow color, and was worn by the women on their wrists and ankles.

I was there I suppose about a month, and they at last used to trust me some little distance from the house. This liberty I used in embracing every opportunity to inquire the way to my own home; and I also sometimes, for the same purpose, went with the maidens, in the cool of the evenings, to bring pitchers of water from the springs for the use of the house. I had also remarked where the sun rose in the morning, and set in the evening, as I had travelled along; and I had observed that my father's house was towards the rising of the sun. I therefore determined to seize the first opportunity of making my escape, and to shape my course for that quarter; for I was quite oppressed and weighed down by grief after my mother and friends; and my love of liberty, ever great, was strengthened by the mortifying circumstance of not daring to eat with the free-born children, although I was mostly their companion.

While I was projecting my escape, one day an unlucky event happened, which quite disconcerted my plan, and put an end to my hopes. I used to be sometimes employed in assisting an elderly slave to cook and take care of the poultry; and one morning, while I was feeding some chickens, I happened to toss a small pebble at one of them, which hit it on the middle, and directly killed it. The old slave, having soon after missed the chicken, inquired after it; and on my relating the accident (for I told her the truth, for my mother would never suffer me to tell a lie), she flew into a violent passion, and threatened that I should suffer for it; and, my master being out, she immediately went and told her mistress what I had done. This alarmed me very much, and I expected an instant flogging, which to me was uncommonly dreadful, for I had seldom been beaten at home. I therefore resolved to fly; and accordingly I ran into a thicket that was hard by, and hid myself in the bushes. Soon afterwards my mistress and the slave returned, and, not seeing me, they searched all the house, but not finding me, and I not making answer when they called to me, they thought I had run away, and the whole neighborhood was raised in the pursuit of me.

In that part of the country, as in ours, the houses and villages were skirted with woods, or shrubberies, and the bushes were so thick that a man could readily conceal himself in them, so as to elude the strictest search. The neighbors continued the whole day looking for me, and several times many of them came within a few yards of the place where I lay hid. I expected every moment, when I heard a rustling among the trees, to be found out, and punished by my master; but they never discovered me, though they were often so near that I even heard their conjectures as they were looking about for me; and I now learned from them that any attempts to return home would be hopeless. Most of them supposed I had fled towards home; but the distance was so great, and the way so intricate, that they thought I could never reach it, and that I should be lost in the woods. When I heard this I was seized with a violent panic, and abandoned myself to despair. Night, too, began to approach, and aggravated all my fears. I had before entertained hopes of getting home, and had determined when it should be dark to make the attempt; but I was now convinced it was fruitless, and began to consider that, if possibly I could escape all other animals, I could not those of the human kind; and that, not knowing the way, I must perish in the woods. Thus was I like the hunted deer—

————Every leaf and every whisp'ring breath,
Convey'd a foe, and every foe a death.

I heard frequent rustlings among the leaves, and being pretty sure they were snakes, I expected every instant to be stung by them. This increased my anguish, and the horror of my situation became now quite insupportable. I at length quitted the thicket, very faint and hungry, for I had not eaten or drank anything all the day, and crept to my master's kitchen, from whence I set out at first, which was an open shed, and laid myself down in the ashes with an anxious wish for death, to relieve me from all my pains. I was scarcely awake in the morning, when the old woman slave, who was the first up, came to light the fire, and saw me in the fireplace. She was very much surprised to see me, and could scarcely believe her own eyes. She now promised to intercede for me, and went for her master, who soon after came, and, having slightly reprimanded me, ordered me to be taken care of, and not ill treated.

Soon after this, my master's only daughter, and child by his first wife, sickened and died, which affected him so much that for sometime he was almost frantic, and really would have killed himself, had he not been watched and prevented. However, in a short time afterwards he recovered, and I was again sold. I was now carried to the left of the sun's rising, through many dreary wastes and dismal woods, amidst the hideous roarings of wild beasts The people I was sold to used to carry me very often, when I was tired, either on their shoulders or on their backs. I saw many convenient well-built sheds along the road, at proper distances, to accommodate the merchants and travellers, who lay in those buildings along with their wives, who often accompany them; and they always go well armed.

From the time I left my own nation, I always found somebody that understood me till I came to the sea coast. The languages of different nations did not totally differ, nor were they so copious as those of the Europeans, particularly the English. They were therefore easily learned; and, while I was journeying thus through Africa, I acquired two or three different tongues. In this manner I had been travelling for a considerable time, when, one evening, to my great surprise, whom should I see brought to the house where I was but my dear sister! As soon as she saw me, she gave a loud shriek, and ran into my arms—I was quite overpowered; neither of us could speak, but, for a considerable time, clung to each other in mutual embraces, unable to do anything but weep. Our meeting affected all who saw us; and, indeed, I must acknowledge, in honor of those sable destroyers of human rights, that I never met with any ill treatment, or saw any offered to their slaves, except tying them, when necessary, to keep them from running away.

When these people knew we were brother and sister, they indulged us to be together; and the man, to whom I supposed we belonged, lay with us, he in the middle, while she and I held one another by the hands across his breast all night; and thus for a while we forgot our misfortunes, in the joy of being together; but even this small comfort was soon to have an end; for scarcely had the fatal morning appeared when she was again torn from me forever! I was now more miserable, if possible, than before. The small relief which her presence gave me from pain, was gone, and the wretchedness of my situation was redoubled by my anxiety after her fate, and my apprehensions lest her sufferings should be greater than mine, when I could not be with her to alleviate them. Yes, thou dear partner of all my childish sports! thou sharer of my joys and sorrows! happy should I have ever esteemed myself to encounter every misery for you and to procure your freedom by the sacrifice of my own. Though you were early forced from my arms, your image has been always riveted in my heart, from which neither time nor fortune have been able to remove it; so that, while the thoughts of your sufferings have damped my prosperity, they have mingled with adversity and increased its bitterness. To that Heaven which protects the weak from the strong, I commit the care of your innocence and virtues, if they have not already received their full reward, and if your youth and delicacy have not long since fallen victims to the violence of the African trader, the pestilential stench of a Guinea ship, the seasoning in the European colonies, or the lash and lust of a brutal and unrelenting overseer.

I did not long remain after my sister. I was again sold, and carried through a number of places, till after travelling a considerable time, I came to a town called Tinmah, in the most beautiful country I had yet seen in Africa. It was extremely rich, and there were many rivulets which flowed through it, and supplied a large pond in the centre of the town, where the people washed. Here I saw for the first time cocoanuts, which I thought superior to any nuts I had ever tasted before; and the trees, which were loaded, were also interspersed among the houses, which had commodious shades adjoining, and were in the same manner as ours, the insides being neatly plastered and whitewashed. Here I also saw and tasted for the first time, sugar-cane. Their money consisted of little white shells, the size of the finger nail. I was sold here for one hundred and seventy-two of them, by a merchant who lived and brought me there.

I had been about two or three days at his house, when a wealthy widow, a neighbor of his, came there one evening, and brought with her an only son, a young gentleman about my own age and size. Here they saw me; and, having taken a fancy to me, I was bought of the merchant, and went home with them. Her house and premises were situated close to one of those rivulets I have mentioned, and were the finest I ever saw in Africa: they were very extensive, and she had a number of slaves to attend her. The next day I was washed and perfumed, and when meal time came, I was led into the presence of my mistress, and ate and drank before her with her son. This filled me with astonishment; and I could scarce help expressing my surprise that the young gentleman should suffer me, who was bound, to eat with him who was free; and not only so, but that he would not at any time either eat or drink till I had taken first, because I was the eldest, which was agreeable to our custom. Indeed, every thing here, and all their treatment of me, made me forget that I was a slave. The language of these people resembled ours so nearly, that we understood each other perfectly. They had also the very same customs as we. There were likewise slaves daily to attend us, while my young master and I, with other boys, sported with our darts and bows and arrows, as I had been used to do at home. In this resemblance to my former happy state, I passed about two months; and I now began to think I was to be adopted into the family, and was beginning to be reconciled to my situation, and to forget by degrees my misfortunes, when all at once the delusion vanished; for, without the least previous knowledge, one morning early, while my dear master and companion was still asleep, I was awakened out of my reverie to fresh sorrow, and hurried away even amongst the uncircumcised.

Thus, at the very moment I dreamed of the greatest happiness, I found myself most miserable; and it seemed as if fortune wished to give me this taste of joy only to render the reverse more poignant. The change I now experienced was as painful as it was sudden and unexpected. It was a change indeed, from a state of bliss to a scene which is inexpressible by me, as it discovered to me an element I had never before beheld, and till then had no idea of, and wherein such instances of hardship and cruelty continually occurred, as I can never reflect on but with horror.

All the nations and people I had hitherto passed through, resembled our own in their manners, customs, and language; but I came at length to a country, the inhabitants of which differed from us in all those particulars. I was very much struck with this difference, especially when I came among a people who did not circumcise, and ate without washing their hands. They cooked also in iron pots, and had European cutlasses and cross bows, which were unknown to us, and fought with their fists among themselves. Their women were not so modest as ours, for they ate, and drank, and slept with their men. But above all, I was amazed to see no sacrifices or offerings among them. In some of those places the people ornamented themselves with scars, and likewise filed their teeth very sharp. They wanted sometimes to ornament me in the same manner, but I would not suffer them; hoping that I might some time be among a people who did not thus disfigure themselves, as I thought they did. At last I came to the banks of a large river which was covered with canoes, in which the people appeared to live with their household utensils, and provisions of all kinds. I was beyond measure astonished at this, as I had never before seen any water larger than a pond or a rivulet; and my surprise was mingled with no small fear when I was put into one of these canoes, and we began to paddle and move along the river. We continued going on thus till night, and when we came to land, and made fires on the banks, each family by themselves; some dragged their canoes on shore, others stayed and cooked in theirs, and laid in them all night. Those on the land had mats, of which they made tents, some in the shape of little houses; in these we slept; and after the morning meal, we embarked again and proceeded as before. I was often very much astonished to see some of the women, as well as the men, jump into the water, dive to the bottom, come up again, and swim about.

Thus I continued to travel, sometimes by land, sometimes by water, through different countries and various nations, till, at the end of six or seven months after I had been kidnapped, I arrived at the sea coast. It would be tedious and uninteresting to relate all the incidents which befell me during this journey, and which I have not yet forgotten; of the various hands I passed through, and the manners and customs of all the different people among whom I lived—I shall therefore only observe, that in all the places where I was, the soil was exceedingly rich; the pumpkins, eadas, plantains, yams, &c., &c., were in great abundance, and of incredible size. There were also vast quantities of different gums, though not used for any purpose, and everywhere a great deal of tobacco. The cotton even grew quite wild, and there was plenty of red-wood. I saw no mechanics whatever in all the way, except such as I have mentioned. The chief employment in all these countries was agriculture, and both the males and females, as with us, were brought up to it, and trained in the arts of war.

The first object which saluted my eyes when I arrived on the coast, was the sea, and a slave ship, which was then riding at anchor, and waiting for its cargo. These filled me with astonishment, which was soon converted into terror, when I was carried on board. I was immediately handled, and tossed up to see if I were sound, by some of the crew; and I was now persuaded that I had gotten into a world of bad spirits, and that they were going to kill me. Their complexions, too, differing so much from ours, their long hair, and the language they spoke (which was very different from any I had ever heard), united to confirm me in this belief. Indeed, such were the horrors of my views and fears at the moment, that, if ten thousand worlds had been my own, I would have freely parted with them all to have exchanged my condition with that of the meanest slave in my own country. When I looked round the ship too, and saw a large furnance of copper boiling, and a multitude of black people of every description chained together, every one of their countenances expressing dejection and sorrow, I no longer doubted of my fate; and, quite overpowered with horror and anguish, I fell motionless on the deck and fainted. When I recovered a little, I found some black people about me, who I believed were some of those who had brought me on board, and had been receiving their pay; they talked to me in order to cheer me, but all in vain. I asked them if we were not to be eaten by those white men with horrible looks, red faces, and long hair. They told me I was not, and one of the crew brought me a small portion of spirituous liquor in a wine glass; but being afraid of him, I would not take it out of his hand. One of the blacks therefore took it from him and gave it to me, and I took a little down my palate, which, instead of reviving me, as they thought it would, threw me into the greatest consternation at the strange feeling it produced, having never tasted any such liquor before. Soon after this, the blacks who brought me on board went off, and left me abandoned to despair.

I now saw myself deprived of all chance of returning to my native country, or even the least glimpse of hope of gaining the shore, which I now considered as friendly; and I even wished for my former slavery in preference to my present situation, which was filled with horrors of every kind, still heightened by my ignorance of what I was to undergo. I was not long suffered to indulge my grief; I was soon put down under the decks, and there I received such a salutation in my nostrils as I had never experienced in my life: so that, with the loathsomeness of the stench, and crying together, I became so sick and low that I was not able to eat, nor had I the least desire to taste anything. I now wished for the last friend, death, to relieve me; but soon, to my grief, two of the white men offered me eatables; and, on my refusing to eat, one of them held me fast by the hands, and laid me across, I think, the windlass, and tied my feet, while the other flogged me severely. I had never experienced anything of this kind before, and, although not being used to the water, I naturally feared that element the first time I saw it, yet, nevertheless, could I have got over the nettings, I would have jumped over the side, but I could not; and besides, the crew used to watch us very closely who were not chained down to the decks, lest we should leap into the water; and I have seen some of these poor African prisoners most severely cut, for attempting to do so, and hourly whipped for not eating. This indeed was often the case with myself.

In a little time after, amongst the poor chained men, I found some of my own nation, which in a small degree gave ease to my mind. I inquired of these what was to be done with us? They gave me to understand, we were to be carried to these white people's country to work for them. I then was a little revived, and thought, if it were no worse than working, my situation was not so desperate; but still I feared I should be put to death, the white people looked and acted, as I thought, in so savage a manner; for I had never seen among any people such instances of brutal cruelty; and this not only shown towards us blacks, but also to some of the whites themselves. One white man in particular I saw, when we were permitted to be on deck, flogged so unmercifully with a large rope near the foremast, that he died in consequence of it; and they tossed him over the side as they would have done a brute. This made me fear these people the more; and I expected nothing less than to be treated in the same manner. I could not help expressing my fears and apprehensions to some of my countrymen; I asked them if these people had no country, but lived in this hollow place (the ship)? They told me they did not, but came from a distant one. "Then," said I, "how comes it in all our country we never heard of them?" They told me because they lived so very far off. I then asked where were their women? had they any like themselves? I was told they had. "And why," said I, "do we not see them?" They answered, because they were left behind. I asked how the vessel could go? They told me they could not tell; but that there was cloth put upon the masts by the help of the ropes I saw, and then the vessel went on; and the white men had some spell or magic they put in the water when they liked, in order to stop the vessel. I was exceedingly amazed at this account, and really thought they were spirits. I therefore wished much to be from amongst them, for I expected they would sacrifice me; but my wishes were vain—for we were so quartered that it was impossible for any of us to make our escape.

While we stayed on the coast I was mostly on deck; and one day, to my great astonishment, I saw one of these vessels coming in with the sails up. As soon as the whites saw it, they gave a great shout, at which we were amazed; and the more so, as the vessel appeared larger by approaching nearer. At last, she came to an anchor in my sight, and when the anchor was let go, I and my countrymen who saw it, were lost in astonishment to observe the vessel stop—and were now convinced it was done by magic. Soon after this the other ship got her boats out, and they came on board of us, and the people of both ships seemed very glad to see each other. Several of the strangers also shook hands with us black people, and made motions with their hands, signifying I suppose, we were to go to their country, but we did not understand them.

At last, when the ship we were in, had got in all her cargo, they made ready with many fearful noises, and we were all put under deck, so that we could not see how they managed the vessel. But this disappointment was the least of my sorrow. The stench of the hold while we were on the coast was so intolerably loathsome, that it was dangerous to remain there for any time, and some of us bad been permitted to stay on the deck for the fresh air; but now that the whole ship's cargo were confined together, it became absolutely pestilential. The closeness of the place, and the heat of the climate, added to the number in the ship, which was so crowded that each had scarcely room to turn himself, almost suffocated us. This produced copious perspirations, so that the air soon became unfit for respiration, from a variety of loathsome smells, and brought on a sickness among the slaves, of which many died—thus falling victims to the improvident avarice, as I may call it, of their purchasers. This wretched situation was again aggravated by the galling of the chains, now became insupportable, and the filth of the necessary tubs, into which the children often fell, and were almost suffocated. The shrieks of the women, and the groans of the dying, rendered the whole a scene of horror almost inconceivable. Happily perhaps, for myself, I was soon reduced so low here that it was thought necessary to keep me almost always on deck; and from my extreme youth I was not put in fetters. In this situation I expected every hour to share the fate of my companions, some of whom were almost daily brought upon deck at the point of death, which I began to hope would soon put an end to my miseries. Often did I think many of the inhabitants of the deep much more happy than myself. I envied them the freedom they enjoyed, and as often wished I could change my condition for theirs. Every circumstance I met with, served only to render my state more painful, and heightened my apprehensions, and my opinion of the cruelty of the whites.

One day they had taken a number of fishes; and when they had killed and satisfied themselves with as many as they thought fit, to our astonishment who were on deck, rather than give any of them to us to eat, as we expected, they tossed the remaining fish into the sea again, although we begged and prayed for some as well as we could, but in vain; and some of my countrymen, being pressed by hunger, took an opportunity, when they thought no one saw them, of trying to get a little privately; but they were discovered, and the attempt procured them some very severe floggings.

One day, when we had a smooth sea and moderate wind, two of my wearied countrymen who were chained together (I was near them at the time), preferring death to such a life of misery, somehow made through the nettings and jumped into the sea; immediately, another quite dejected fellow, who, on account of his illness, was suffered to be out of irons, also followed their example; and I believe many more would very soon have done the same, if they had not been prevented by the ship's crew, who were instantly alarmed. Those of us that were the most active, were in a moment put down under the deck; and there was such a noise and confusion amongst the people of the ship as I never heard before, to stop her, and get the boat out to go after the slaves. However, two of the wretches were drowned, but they got the other, and afterwards flogged him unmercifully, for thus attempting to prefer death to slavery. In this manner we continued to undergo more hardships than I can now relate, hardships which are inseparable from this accursed trade. Many a time we were near suffocation from the want of fresh air, which we were often without for whole days together. This, and the stench of the necessary tubs, carried off many.

During our passage, I first saw flying fishes, which surprised me very much; they used frequently to fly across the ship, and many of them fell on the deck. I also now first saw the use of the quadrant; I had often with astonishment seen the mariners make observations with it, and I could not think what it meant. They at last took notice of my surprise; and one of them, willing to increase it, as well as to gratify my curiosity, made me one day look through it. The clouds appeared to me to be land, which disappeared as they passed along. This heightened my wonder; and I was now more persuaded than ever, that I was in another world, and that every thing about me was magic.

At last we came in sight of the island of Barbadoes, at which the whites on board gave a great shout, and made many signs of joy to us. We did not know what to think of this; but as the vessel drew nearer, we plainly saw the harbor, and other ships of different kinds and sizes, and we soon anchored amongst them, off Bridgetown. Many merchants and planters now came on board, though it was in the evening. They put us in separate parcels, and examined us attentively. They also made us jump, and pointed to the land, signifying we were to go there. We thought by this, we should be eaten by these ugly men, as they appeared to us; and, when soon after we were all put down under the deck again, there was much dread and trembling among us, and nothing but bitter cries to be heard all the night from these apprehensions, insomuch, that at last the white people got some old slaves from the land to pacify us. They told us we were not to be eaten, but to work, and were soon to go on land, where we should see many of our country people. This report eased us much. And sure enough, soon after we were landed, there came to us Africans of all languages.

We were conducted immediately to the merchant's yard, where we were all pent up together, like so many sheep in a fold, without regard to sex or age. As every object was new to me, everything I saw filled me with surprise. What struck me first, was, that the houses were built with bricks and stories, and in every other respect different from those I had seen in Africa; but I was still more astonished on seeing people on horseback. I did not know what this could mean; and, indeed, I thought these people were full of nothing but magical arts. While I was in this astonishment, one of my fellow prisoners spoke to a countryman of his, about the horses, who said they were the same kind they had in their country. I understood them, though they were from a distant part of Africa; and I thought it odd I had not seen any horses there; but afterwards, when I came to converse with different Africans, I found they had many horses amongst them, and much larger than those I then saw.

We were not many days in the merchant's custody, before we were sold after their usual manner, which is this: On a signal given (as the beat of a drum), the buyers rush at once into the yard where the slaves are confined, and make choice of that parcel they like best. The noise and clamor with which this is attended, and the eagerness visible in the countenances of the buyers, serve not a little to increase the apprehension of terrified Africans, who may well be supposed to consider them as the ministers of that destruction to which they think themselves devoted. In this manner, without scruple, are relations and friends separated, most of them never to see each other again.

I remember, in the vessel in which I was brought over, in the men's apartment, there were several brothers, who, in the sale, were sold in different lots; and it was very moving on this occasion, to see and hear their cries at parting. O, ye nominal Christians! might not an African ask you—Learned you this from your God, who says unto you, Do unto all men as you would men should do unto you? Is it not enough that we are torn from our country and friends, to toil for your luxury and lust of gain? Must every tender feeling be likewise sacrificed to your avarice? Are the dearest friends and relations, now rendered more dear by their separation from their kindred, still to be parted from each other, and thus prevented from cheering the gloom of slavery, with the small comfort of being together, and mingling their sufferings and sorrows? Why are parents to lose their children, brothers their sisters, or husbands their wives? Surely, this is a new refinement in cruelty, which, while it has no advantage to atone for it, thus aggravates distress, and adds fresh horrors even to the wretchedness of slavery.

Chapter 3

The author is carried to Virginia—His distress—Surprise at seeing a picture and a watch—Is bought by Captain Pascal, and sets out for England—His terror during the voyage—Arrives in England—His wonder at a fall of snow—Is sent to Guernsey, and in some time goes on board a ship of war with his master—Some account of the expedition against Louisburg under the command of Admiral Boscawen, in 1758.

I now totally lost the small remains of comfort I had enjoyed in conversing with my countrymen; the women too, who used to wash and take care of me were all gone different ways, and I never saw one of them afterwards.

I stayed in this island for a few days, I believe it could not be above a fortnight, when I, and some few more slaves that were not saleable amongst the rest, from very much fretting, were shipped off in a sloop for North America. On the passage we were better treated than when we were coming from Africa, and we had plenty of rice and fat pork. We were landed up a river a good way from the sea, about Virginia county, where we saw few or none of our native Africans, and not one soul who could talk to me. I was a few weeks weeding grass and gathering stones in a plantation; and at last all my companions were distributed different ways, and only myself was left. I was now exceedingly miserable, and thought myself worse off than any of the rest of my companions, for they could talk to each other, but I had no person to speak to that I could understand. In this state, I was constantly grieving and pining, and wishing for death rather than anything else.

While I was in this plantation, the gentleman, to whom I suppose the estate belonged, being unwell, I was one day sent for to his dwelling-house to fan him; when I came into the room where he was I was very much affrighted at some things I saw, and the more so as I had seen a black woman slave as I came through the house, who was cooking the dinner, and the poor creature was cruelly loaded with various kinds of iron machines; she had one particularly on her head, which locked her mouth so fast that she could scarcely speak; and could not eat nor drink. I was much astonished and shocked at this contrivance, which I afterwards learned was called the iron muzzle. Soon after I had a fan put in my hand, to fan the gentleman while he slept; and so I did indeed with great fear. While he was fast asleep I indulged myself a great deal in looking about the room, which to me appeared very fine and curious.

The first object that engaged my attention was a watch which hung on the chimney, and was going. I was quite surprised at the noise it made, and was afraid it would tell the gentleman anything I might do amiss; and when I immediately after observed a picture hanging in the room, which appeared constantly to look at me, I was still more affrighted, having never seen such things as these before. At one time I thought it was something relative to magic; and not seeing it move, I thought it might be some way the whites had to keep their great men when they died, and offer them libations as we used to do our friendly spirits. In this state of anxiety I remained till my master awoke, when I was dismissed out of the room, to my no small satisfaction and relief; for I thought that these people were all made up of wonders.

In this place I was called Jacob; but on board the *African Snow,* I was called Michael. I had been some time in this miserable, forlorn, and much dejected state, without having anyone to talk to, which made my life a burden, when the kind and unknown hand of the Creator (who in every deed leads the blind in a way they know not) now began to appear, to my comfort; for one day the captain of a merchant ship, called the *Industrious Bee,* came on some business to my master's house. This gentleman, whose name was Michael Henry Pascal, was a lieutenant in the Royal Navy, but now commanded this trading ship, which was somewhere in the confines of the county many miles off. While he was at my master's house, it happened that he saw me, and liked me so well that he made a purchase of me. I think I have often heard him say he gave thirty or forty pounds sterling for me; but I do not remember which. However, he meant me for a present to some of his friends in England: and as I was sent accordingly from the house of my then master (one Mr. Campbell) to the place where the ship lay; I was conducted on horseback by an elderly black man (a mode of travelling which appeared very odd to me). When I arrived I was carried on board a fine large ship, loaded with tobacco, &c., and just ready to sail for England.

I now thought my condition much mended; I had sails to lie on, and plenty of good victuals to eat; and everybody on board used me very kindly, quite contrary to what I had seen of any white people before; I therefore began to think that they were not all of the same disposition. A few days after I was on board we sailed for England. I was still at a loss to conjecture my destiny. By this time, however, I could smatter a little imperfect English; and I wanted to know as well as I could where we were going. Some of the people of the ship used to tell me they were going to carry me back to my own country, and this made me very happy. I was quite rejoiced at the idea of going back, and thought if I could get home what wonders I should have to tell. But I was reserved for another fate, and was soon undeceived when we came within sight of the English coast.

While I was on board this ship, my captain and master named me *Gustavus Vassa*. I at that time began to understand him a little, and refused to be called so, and told him as well as I could that I would be called Jacob; but he said I should not, and still called me Gustavus: and when I refused to answer to my new name, which I at first did, it gained me many a cuff; so at length I submitted, and by which I have been known ever since.

The ship had a very long passage; and on that account we had very short allowance of provisions. Towards the last, we had only one pound and a half of bread per week, and about the same quantity of meat, and one quart of water a day. We spoke with only one vessel the whole time we were at sea, and but once we caught a few fishes. In our extremities the captain and people told me in jest they would kill and eat me; but I thought them in earnest, and was depressed beyond measure, expecting every moment to be my last. While I was in this situation, one evening they caught, with a good deal of trouble, a large shark, and got it on board. This gladdened my poor heart exceedingly, as I thought it would serve the people to eat instead of their eating me; but very soon, to my astonishment, they cut off a small part of the tail, and tossed the rest over the side. This renewed my consternation; and I did not know what to think of these white people, though I very much feared they would kill and eat me.

There was on board the ship a young lad who had never been at sea before, about four or five years older than myself: his name was Richard Baker. He was a native of America, had received an excellent education, and was of a most amiable temper. Soon after I went on board, he showed me a great deal of partiality and attention, and in return I grew extremely fond of him. We at length became inseparable; and, for the space of two years, he was of very great use to me, and was my constant companion and instructor. Although this dear youth had many slaves of his own, yet he and I have gone through many sufferings together on shipboard; and we have many nights lain in each other's bosoms when we were in great distress. Thus such a friendship was cemented between us as we cherished till his death, which, to my very great sorrow, happened in the year 1759, when he was up the Archipelago, on board his Majesty's ship the *Preston:* an event which I have never ceased to regret, as I lost at once a kind interpreter, an agreeable companion, and a faithful friend; who, at the age of fifteen, discovered a mind superior to prejudice; and who was not ashamed to notice, to associate with, and to be the friend and instructor of one who was ignorant, a stranger, of a different complexion, and a slave!

My master had lodged in his mother's house in America; he respected him very much, and made him always eat with him in the cabin. He used often to tell him jocularly that he would kill and eat me. Sometimes he would say to me—the black people were not good to eat, and would ask me if we did not eat people in my country. I said, No; then he said he would kill Dick (as he always called him) first, and afterwards me. Though this hearing relieved my mind a little as to myself, I was alarmed for Dick, and whenever he was called I used to be very much afraid he was to be killed; and I would peep and watch to see if they were going to kill him; nor was I free from this consternation till we made the land.

One night we lost a man overboard; and the cries and noise were so great and confused, in stopping the ship, that I, who did not know what was the matter, began, as usual, to be very much afraid, and to think they were going to make an offering with me, and perform some magic; which I still believed they dealt in. As the waves were very high, I thought the Ruler of the seas was angry, and I expected to be offered up to appease him. This filled my mind with agony, and I could not any more, that night, close my eyes again to rest. However, when daylight appeared, I was a little eased in my mind; but still, every time I was called, I used to think it was to be killed. Some time after this, we saw some very large fish, which I afterwards found were called grampusses. They looked to me exceedingly terrible, and made their appearance just at dusk, and were so near as to blow the water on the ship's deck. I believed them to be the rulers of the sea; and as the white people did not make any offerings at any time, I thought they were angry with them; and, at last, what confirmed my belief was, the wind just then died away, and a calm ensued, and in consequence of it the ship stopped going. I supposed that the fish had performed this, and I hid myself in the fore part of the ship, through fear of being offered up to appease them, every minute peeping and quaking; but my good friend Dick came shortly towards me, and I took an opportunity to ask him, as well as I could, what these fish were. Not being able to talk much English, I could but just make him understand my question; and not at all, when I asked him if any offerings were to be made to them; however, he told me these fish would swallow anybody which sufficiently alarmed me. Here he was called away by the captain, who was leaning over the quarter-deck railing, and looking at the fish; and most of the people were busied in getting a barrel of pitch to light for them to play with. The captain now called me to him, having learned some of my apprehensions from Dick; and having diverted himself and others for some time with my fears, which appeared ludicrous enough in my crying and trembling, he dismissed me. The barrel of pitch was now lighted and put over the side into the water. By this time it was just dark, and the fish went after it; and, to my great joy, I saw them no more.

However, all my alarms began to subside when we got sight of land; and at last the ship arrived at Falmouth, after a passage of thirteen weeks. Every heart on board seemed gladdened on our reaching the shore, and none more than mine. The captain immediately went on shore, and sent on board some fresh provisions, which we wanted very much. We made good use of them, and our famine was soon turned into feasting, almost without ending. It was about the beginning of the spring 1757, when I arrived in England, and I was near twelve years of age at that time. I was very much struck with the buildings and the pavement of the streets in Falmouth; and, indeed, every object I saw, filled me with new surprise.

One morning, when I got upon deck, I saw it covered all over with the snow that fell over night. As I had never seen anything of the kind before, I thought it was salt: so I immediately ran down to the mate, and desired him, as well as I could, to come and see how somebody in the night had thrown salt all over the deck. He, knowing what it was, desired me to bring some of it down to him. Accordingly I took up a handful of it, which I found very cold indeed; and when I brought it to him he desired me to taste it. I did so, and I was surprised beyond measure. I then asked him what it was; he told me it was snow, but I could not in anywise understand him. He asked me, if we had no such thing in my country; I told him, No. I then asked him the use of it, and who made it; he told me a great man in the heavens, called God. But here again I was to all intents and purposes at a loss to understand him; and the more so, when a little after I saw the air filled with it, in a heavy shower, which fell down on the same day.

After this I went to church; and having never been at such a place before, I was again amazed at seeing and hearing the service. I asked all I could about it, and they gave me to understand it was worshipping God, who made us and all things. I was still at a great loss, and soon got into an endless field of inquiries, as well as I was able to speak and ask about things. However, my little friend Dick used to be my best interpreter; for I could make free with him, and he always instructed me with pleasure. And from what I could understand by him of this God, and in seeing these white people did not sell one another as we did, I was much pleased; and in this I thought they were much happier than we Africans. I was astonished at the wisdom of the white people in all things I saw; but was amazed at their not sacrificing, or making any offerings, and eating with unwashed hands, and touching the dead. I likewise could not help remarking the particular slenderness of their women, which I did not at first like; and I thought they were not so modest and shame-faced as the African women.

I had often seen my master and Dick employed in reading; and I had a great curiosity to talk to the books as I thought they did, and so to learn how all things had a beginning. For that purpose I have often taken up a book, and have talked to it, and then put my ears to it, when alone, in hopes it would answer me; and I have been very much concerned when I found it remained silent.

My master lodged at the house of a gentleman in Falmouth, who had a fine little daughter about six or seven years of age, and she grew prodigiously fond of me, insomuch that we used to eat together, and had servants to wait on us. I was so much caressed by this family that it often reminded me of the treatment I had received from my little noble African master. After I had been here a few days, I was sent on board of the ship; but the child cried so much after me that nothing could pacify her till I was sent for again. It is ludicrous enough, that I began to fear I should be betrothed to this young lady; and when my master asked me if I would stay there with her behind him, as he was going away with the ship, which had taken in the tobacco again, I cried immediately, and said I would not leave him. At last, by stealth, one night I was sent on board the ship again; and in a little time we sailed for Guernsey, where she was in part owned by a merchant, one Nicholas Doberry.

As I was now amongst a people who had not their faces scarred, like some of the African nation where I had been, I was very glad I did not let them ornament me in that manner when I was with them. When we arrived at Guernsey, my master placed me to board and lodge with one of his mates, who had a wife and family there; and some months afterwards he went to England, and left me in care of this mate, together with my friend Dick. This mate had a little daughter, aged about five or six years, with whom I used to be much delighted. I had often observed that when her mother washed her face it looked very rosy, but when she washed mine it did not look so. I therefore tried oftentimes myself if I could not by washing make my face of the same color as my little play-mate, Mary, but it was all in vain; and I now began to be mortified at the difference in our complexions. This woman behaved to me with great kindness and attention, and taught me everything in the same manner as she did her own child, and, indeed, in every respect, treated me as such. I remained here till the summer of the year 1757, when my master, being appointed first lieutenant of his Majesty's ship the *Roebuck,* sent for Dick and me, and his old mate. On this we all left Guernsey, and set out for England in a sloop, bound for London.

As we were coming up towards the Nore, where the *Roebuck* lay, a man-of-war's boat came along side to press our people, on which each man run to hide himself. I was very much frightened at this, though I did not know what it meant, or what to think or do. However I went and hid myself also under a hencoop. Immediately afterwards, the press-gang came on board with their swords drawn, and searched all about, pulled the people out by force, and put them into the boat. At last I was found out also; the man that found me held me up by the heels while they all made their sport of me, I roaring and crying out all the time most lustily; but at last the mate, who was my conductor, seeing this, came to my assistance, and did all he could to pacify me; but all to very little purpose, till I had seen the boat go off. Soon afterwards we came to the Nore, where the *Roebuck* lay; and, to our great joy, my master came on board to us, and brought us to the ship.

When I went on board this large ship, I was amazed indeed to see the quantity of men and the guns. However, my surprise began to diminish as my knowledge increased; and I ceased to feel those apprehensions and alarms which had taken such strong possession of me when I first came among the Europeans, and for some time after. I began now to pass to an opposite extreme; I was so far from being afraid of anything new which I saw, that after I had been some time in this ship, I even began to long for an engagement. My griefs, too, which in young minds are not perpetual, were now wearing away; and I soon enjoyed myself pretty well, and felt tolerably easy in my present situation. There was a number of boys on board, which still made it more agreeable; for we were always together, and a great part of our time was spent in play.

I remained in this ship a considerable time, during which we made several cruises, and visited a variety of places; among others we were twice in Holland, and brought over several persons of distinction from it, whose names I do not now remember. On the passage, one day, for the diversion of those gentlemen, all the boys were called on the quarter-deck, and were paired proportionably, and then made to fight; after which the gentlemen gave the combatants from five to nine shillings each. This was the first time I ever fought with a white boy; and I never knew what it was to have a bloody nose before. This made me fight most desperately, I suppose considerably more than an hour; and at last, both of us being weary, we were parted. I had a great deal of this kind of sport afterwards, in which the captain and the ship's company used very much to encourage me.

Sometime afterwards, the ship went to Leith in Scotland, and from thence to the Orkneys, where I was surprised in seeing scarcely any night; and from thence we sailed with a great fleet, full of soldiers, for England. All this time we had never come to an engagement, though we were frequently cruising off the coast of France; during which we chased many vessels, and took in all seventeen prizes. I had been learning many of the maneuvres of the ship during our cruise; and I was several times made to fire the guns. One evening, off Havre de Grace, just as it was growing dark, we were standing off shore, and met with a fine large French built frigate. We got all things immediately ready for fighting; and I now expected I should be gratified in seeing an engagement, which I had so long wished for in vain. But the very moment the word of command was given to fire, we heard those on board the other ship cry, "Haul down the jib"; and in that instant she hoisted English colors. There was instantly with us an amazing cry of—"Avast!" or stop firing; and I think one or two guns had been let off, but happily they did no mischief. We had hailed them several times, but they not hearing, we received no answer, which was the cause of our firing. The boat was then sent on board of her, and she proved to be the *Ambuscade,* man-of-war, to my no small disappointment.

We returned to Portsmouth, without having been in any action, just at the trial of Admiral Byng (whom I saw several times during it); and my master having left the ship, and gone to London for promotion, Dick and I were put on board the *Savage,* sloop-of-war, and we went in her to assist in bringing off the *St. George,* man-of-war, that had run ashore somewhere on the coast. After staying a few weeks on board the *Savage,* Dick and I were sent on shore at Deal, where we remained some short time, till my master sent for us to London, the place I had long desired exceedingly to see. We therefore both with great pleasure got into a wagon, and came to London, where we were received by a Mr. Guerin, a relation of my master. This gentleman had two sisters, very amiable ladies, who took much notice and great care of me.

Though I had desired so much to see London, when I arrived in it I was unfortunately unable to gratify my curiosity; for I had at this time the chilblains to such a degree that I could not stand for several months, and I was obliged to be sent to St. George's hospital. There I grew so ill that the doctors wanted to cut my leg off, at different times, apprehending a mortification; but I always said I would rather die than suffer it, and happily (I thank God) I recovered without the operation. After being there several weeks, and just as I had recovered, the smallpox broke out on me, so that I was again confined; and I thought myself now particularly unfortunate. However, I soon recovered again; and by this time, my master having been promoted to be first lieutenant of the *Preston,* man-of-war, of fifty guns, then new at Deptford, Dick and I were sent on board her, and soon after, we went to Holland to bring over the late Duke of Cumberland to England.

While I was in the ship an incident happened, which, though trifling, I beg leave to relate, as I could not help taking particular notice of it, and considered it then as a judgment of God. One morning a young man was looking up to the foretop, and in a wicked tone, common on shipboard, d——d his eyes about something. Just at the moment some small particles of dirt fell into his left eye, and by the evening it was very much inflamed. The next day it grew worse, and within six or seven days he lost it.

From this ship my master was appointed a lieutenant on board the *Royal George.* When he was going he wished me to stay on board the *Preston,* to learn the French horn; but the ship being ordered for Turkey, I could not think of leaving my master, to whom I was very warmly attached;

and I told him if he left me behind, it would break my heart. This prevailed on him to take me with him; but he left Dick on board the *Preston,* whom I embraced at parting for the last time. The *Royal George* was the largest ship I had ever seen, so that when I came on board of her I was surprised at the number of people, men, women, and children, of every denomination; and the largeness of the guns, many of them also of brass, which I had never seen before. Here were also shops or stalls of every kind of goods, and people crying their different commodities about the ship as in a town.

To me it appeared a little world, into which I was again cast without a friend, for I had no longer my dear companion Dick. We did not stay long here. My master was not many weeks on board before he got an appointment to the sixth lieutenant of the *Namur,* which was then at Spithead, fitting up for Vice-admiral Boscawen, who was going with a large fleet on an expedition against Louisburg.

The crew of the *Royal George* were turned over to her, and the flag of that gallant admiral was hoisted on board, the blue at the maintop gallant mast head. There was a very great fleet of men-of-war of every description assembled together for this expedition, and I was in hopes soon to have an opportunity of being gratified with a sea-fight. All things being now in readiness, this mighty fleet (for there was also Admiral Cornish's fleet in company, destined for the East Indies) at last weighed anchor, and sailed. The two fleets continued in company for several days, and then parted; Admiral Cornish, in the *Lenox,* having first saluted our Admiral in the *Namur,* which he returned. We then steered for America; but, by contrary winds, we were driven to Tenerife, where I was struck with its noted peak. Its prodigious height, and its form, resembling a sugar loaf, filled me with wonder. We remained in sight of this island some days, and then proceeded for America, which we soon made, and got into a very commodious harbor called St. George, in Halifax, where we had fish in great plenty, and all other fresh provisions. We were here joined by different men-of-war and transport ships with soldiers; after which, our fleet being increased to a prodigious number of ships of all kinds, we sailed for Cape Breton in Nova Scotia. We had the good and gallant General Wolfe on board our ship, whose affability made him highly esteemed and beloved by all the men. He often honored me, as well as other boys, with marks of his notice, and saved me once a flogging for fighting with a young gentleman.

We arrived at Cape Breton in the summer of 1758; and here the soldiers were to be landed, in order to make an attack upon Louisburg. My master had some part in superintending the landing; and here I was in a small measure gratified in seeing an encounter between our men and the enemy. The French were posted on the shore to receive us, and disputed our landing for a long time; but at last they were driven from their trenches, and a complete landing was effected. Our troops pursued them as far as the town of Louisburg. In this action many were killed on both sides.

One thing remarkable I saw this day. A lieutenant of the *Princess Amelia,* who, as well as my master, superintended the landing, was giving the word of command, and while his mouth was open, a musket ball went through it, and passed out at his cheek. I had that day, in my hand, the scalp of an Indian king, who was killed in the engagement; the scalp had been taken off by an Highlander. I saw the king's ornaments too, which were very curious, and made of feathers.

Our land forces laid siege to the town of Louisburg, while the French men-of-war were blocked up in the harbor by the fleet, the batteries at the same time playing upon them from the land. This they did with such effect, that one day I saw some of the ships set on fire by the shells from the batteries, and I believe two or three of them were quite burnt. At another time, about fifty boats belonging to the English men-of-war, commanded by Captain George Belfour, of the *Etna,* fire ship, and Mr. Laforey, another junior Captain, attacked and boarded the only two remaining French men-of-war in the harbor. They also set fire to a seventy-gun ship, but a sixty-four, called the *Bienfaisant,* they brought off. During my stay here, I had often an opportunity of being near Captain Belfour, who was pleased to notice me, and liked me so much that he often asked my master to let him have me, but he would not part with me; and no consideration could have induced me to leave him.

At last, Louisburg was taken, and the English men-of-war came into the harbor before it, to my very great joy; for I had now more liberty of indulging myself, and I went often on shore.

When the ships were in the harbor, we had the most beautiful procession on the water I ever saw All the Admirals and Captains of the men-of-war, full dressed, and in their barges, well ornamented with pendants, came alongside of the *Namur.* The Vice-admiral then went on shore in his barge, followed by the other officers in order of seniority, to take possession, as I suppose, of the town and fort. Some time after this, the French governor and his lady, and other persons of note, came on board our ship to dine. On this occasion our ships were dressed with colors of all kinds, from the top-gallant mast head to the deck; and this, with the firing of guns, formed a most grand and magnificent spectacle.

    As soon as everything here was settled, Admiral Boscawen sailed with part of the fleet for England, leaving some ships behind with Rear-admirals Sir Charles Hardy and Durell. It was now winter; and one evening, during our passage home, about dusk, when we were in the channel, or near soundings, and were beginning to look for land, we descried seven sail of large men-of-war, which stood off shore. Several people on board of our ship said, as the two fleets were (in forty minutes from the first sight) within hail of each other, that they were English men-of-war; and some of our people even began to name some of the ships. By this time both fleets began to mingle, and our Admiral ordered his flag to be hoisted. At that instant, the other fleet, which were French, hoisted their ensigns, and gave us a broadside as they passed by. Nothing could create greater surprise and confusion among us than this. The wind was high, the sea rough, and we had our lower and middle deck guns housed in, so that not a single gun on board was ready to be fired at any of the French ships. However, the *Royal William* and the *Somerset,* being our sternmost ships, became a little prepared, and each gave the French ships a broadside as they passed by.

    I afterwards heard this was a French squadron, commanded by Monsieur Corflans; and certainly, had the Frenchmen known our condition, and had a mind to fight us, they might have done us great mischief. But we were not long before we were prepared for an engagement. Immediately many things were tossed overboard, the ships were made ready for fighting as soon as possible, and about ten at night we had bent a new main-sail, the old one being split. Being now in readiness for fighting, we wore ship, and stood after the French fleet, who were one or two ships in number more than we. However we gave them chase, and continued pursuing them all night; and at daylight we saw six of them, all large ships of the line, and an English East Indiaman, a prize they had taken. We chased them all day till between three and four o'clock in the evening, when we came up with, and passed within a musket shot of one seventy-four-gun ship, and the Indiaman also, who now hoisted her colors, but immediately hauled them down again. On this we made a signal for the other ships to take possession of her; and, supposing the man-of-war would likewise strike, we cheered, but she did not; though if we had fired into her, from being so near we must have taken her. To my utter surprise, the *Somerset,* who was the next ship astern of the *Namur,* made way likewise; and, thinking they were sure of this French ship, they cheered in the same manner, but still continued to follow us.

    The French Commodore was about a gun-shot ahead of all, running from us with all speed; and about four o'clock he carried his foretopmast overboard. This caused another loud cheer with us; and a little after the topmast came close by us; but, to our great surprise, instead of coming up with her, we found she went as fast as ever, if not faster. The sea grew now much smoother; and the wind lulling, the seventy-four-gun ship we had passed, came again by us in the very same direction, and so near that we heard her people talk as she went by, yet not a shot was fired on either side; and about five or six o'clock, just as it grew dark, she joined her Commodore. We chased all night; but the next day we were out of sight, so that we saw no more of them; and we only had the old Indiaman (called *Carnarvon,* I think) for our trouble.

    After this we stood in for the channel, and soon made the land; and, about the close of the year 1758–9, we got safe to St. Helen's. Here the *Namur* ran aground, and also another large ship astern of us; but, by starting our water, and tossing many things overboard to lighten her, we got the ships off without any damage. We stayed for a short time at Spithead, and then went into Portsmouth harbor to refit. From whence the Admiral went to London; and my master and I soon followed, with a press-gang, as we wanted some hands to complete our complement.

Harriet Jacobs (c. 1813–1897)

Born into slavery in Edenton, North Carolina, around 1813, Harriet Jacobs' happy childhood ended shortly before her 12th birthday with the death of the kind mistress who had taught her to read, spell, and sew. Jacobs was bequeathed to her mistress' five-year-old niece, whose father, James Norcom (identified as Dr. Flint in the autobiography), began sexually harassing Jacobs when she was 15 years old. Until her escape to freedom in 1842, Jacobs endured 14 years of misery, including seven years of hiding in a crawlspace in efforts to avoid the lecherous Norcom.

After her escape to New York, Jacobs worked as a nursemaid, became active in the anti-slavery movement, and moved to Massachusetts. In 1853 Jacobs' employer purchased freedom for her and her two children, Joseph and Louisa (identified as Benny and Ellen in the autobiography). During the Civil War, Jacobs and Louisa went to Alexandria, Virginia, where they worked as nurses in the relief effort and founded the Jacobs Free School for children of the refugees. In 1866 mother and daughter moved to Savannah, Georgia, where they also offered medical and educational assistance to former slaves. Two years later, Jacobs and Louisa embarked on a fund-raising trip to England; their objectives were to establish an orphanage and senior citizens home in Savannah, but the Ku Klux Klan forced them to abandon both projects. Jacobs and Louisa returned to Massachusetts where Jacobs served briefly as a clerk of the New England Women's Club and ran a boarding house for Harvard University students. Jacobs and her daughter then moved to Washington, D.C., where Jacobs continued to assist African Americans until her death on March 7, 1897.

Jacobs, adopting the pseudonym Linda Brent, published her autobiography, *Incidents in the Life of a Slave Girl*, in 1861; yet until its 1987 Harvard University edition, its authorship and autobiographical status were questioned; some people assumed that Jacobs' book had been written by a White female abolitionist. Literary and historical scholars now recognize *Incidents* as the first extended slave narrative by a Black woman. Considered the most important feminine slave narrative, *Incidents in the Life of a Slave Girl*, along with the well-known autobiographies by Olaudah Equiano, Frederick Douglass, and William Wells Brown, bears eloquent, comprehensive witness.

Selected Bibliography

Hine, Darlene Clark, ed. *Black Women in America: An Historical Encyclopedia*. Vol 1. Brooklyn: Carlson, 1993.

Nelson, Emmanuel S., Ed. *African American Authors, 1745–1945: A Bio-Bibliographical Critical Sourcebook*. Westport, CT: Greenwood, 2000.

Smith, Jessie Carney, ed. *Notable Black American Women*. Detroit: Gale Research, 1992.

Incidents in the Life of a Slave Girl Written by Herself

Harriet A. Jacobs

I

Childhood

I was born a slave; but I never knew it till six years of happy childhood had passed away. My father was a carpenter, and considered so intelligent and skilful in his trade, that, when buildings out of the common line were to be erected, he was sent for from long distances, to be head workman. On condition of paying his mistress two hundred dollars a year, and supporting himself, he was allowed to work at his trade, and manage his own affairs. His strongest wish was to purchase his children; but, though he several times offered his hard earnings for that purpose, he never succeeded. In complexion my parents were a light shade of brownish yellow, and were termed mulattoes. They lived together in a comfortable home; and, though we were all slaves, I was so fondly shielded that I never dreamed I was a piece of merchandise, trusted to them for safe keeping, and liable to be demanded of them at any moment. I had one brother, William, who was two years younger than myself—a bright, affectionate child. I had also a great treasure in my maternal grandmother, who was a remarkable woman in many respects. She was the daughter of a planter in South Carolina, who, at his death, left her mother and his three children free, with money to go to St. Augustine, where they had relatives. It was during the Revolutionary War; and they were captured on their passage, carried back, and sold to different purchasers. Such was the story my grandmother used to tell me; but I do not remember all the particulars. She was a little girl when she was captured and sold to the keeper of a large hotel. I have often heard her tell how hard she fared during childhood. But as she grew older she evinced so much intelligence, and was so faithful, that her master and mistress could not help seeing it was for their interest to take care of such a valuable piece of property. She became an indispensable personage in the household, officiating in all capacities, from cook and wet nurse to seamstress. She was much praised for her cooking; and her nice crackers became so famous in the neighborhood that many people were desirous of obtaining them. In consequence of numerous requests of this kind, she asked permission of her mistress to bake crackers at night, after all the household work was done; and she obtained leave to do it, provided she would clothe herself and her children from the profits. Upon these terms, after working hard all day for her mistress, she began her midnight bakings, assisted by her two oldest children. The business proved profitable; and each year she laid by a little, which was saved for a fund to purchase her children. Her master died, and the property was divided among his heirs. The widow had her dower in the hotel, which she continued to keep open. My grandmother remained in her service as a slave; but her children were divided among her master's children. As she had five, Benjamin, the youngest one, was sold, in order that each heir might have an equal portion of dollars and cents. There was so little difference in our ages that he seemed more like my brother than my uncle. He was a bright, handsome lad, nearly white; for he inherited the complexion my grandmother had derived from Anglo-Saxon ancestors. Though only ten years old, seven hundred and twenty dollars were paid for him. His sale was a terrible blow to my grandmother; but she was naturally hopeful, and she went to work with renewed energy, trusting in time to be able to purchase some of her children. She had laid up three hundred dollars, which her mistress one day begged as a loan, promising to pay her soon. The reader probably knows that no promise or writing given to a slave is legally binding; for, according to Southern laws, a slave, *being* property, can *hold* no property. When my grandmother lent her hard earnings to her mistress, she trusted solely to her honor. The honor of a slaveholder to a slave!

To this good grandmother I was indebted for many comforts. My brother Willie and I often received portions of the crackers, cakes, and preserves, she made to sell; and after we ceased to be children we were indebted to her for many more important services.

Such were the unusually fortunate circumstances of my early childhood. When I was six years old, my mother died; and then, for the first time, I learned, by the talk around me, that I was a slave. My mother's mistress was the daughter of my grandmother's mistress. She was the foster sister of my mother; they were both nourished at my grandmother's breast. In fact, my mother had been weaned at three months old, that the babe of the mistress might obtain sufficient food. They played together as children; and, when they became women, my mother was a most faithful servant to her whiter foster sister. On her death-bed her mistress promised that her children should never suffer for any thing; and during her lifetime she kept her word. They all spoke kindly of my dead mother, who had been a slave merely in name, but in nature was noble and womanly. I grieved for her, and my young mind was troubled with the thought who would now take care of me and my little brother. I was told that my home was now to be with her mistress; and I found it a happy one. No toilsome or disagreeable duties were imposed upon me. My mistress was so kind to me that I was always glad to do her bidding, and proud to labor for her as much as my young years would permit. I would sit by her side for hours, sewing diligently, with a heart as free from care as that of any free-born white child. When she thought I was tired, she would send me out to run and jump; and away I bounded, to gather berries or flowers to decorate her room. Those were happy days—too happy to last. The slave child had no thought for the morrow; but there came that blight, which too surely waits on every human being born to be a chattel.

When I was nearly twelve years old, my kind mistress sickened and died. As I saw the cheek grow paler, and the eye more glassy, how earnestly I prayed in my heart that she might live! I loved her; for she had been almost like a mother to me. My prayers were not answered. She died, and they buried her in the little churchyard, where, day after day, my tears fell upon her grave.

I was sent to spend a week with my grandmother. I was now old enough to begin to think of the future; and again and again I asked myself what they would do with me. I felt sure I should never find another mistress so kind as the one who was gone. She had promised my dying mother that her children should never suffer for any thing; and when I remembered that, and recalled her many proofs of attachment to me, I could not help having some hopes that she had left me free. My friends were almost certain it would be so. They thought she would be sure to do it, on account of my mother's love and faithful service. But, alas! we all know that the memory of a faithful slave does not avail much to save her children from the auction block.

After a brief period of suspense, the will of my mistress was read, and we learned that she had bequeathed me to her sister's daughter, a child of five years old. So vanished our hopes. My mistress had taught me the precepts of God's Word: "Thou shalt love thy neighbor as thyself." "Whatsoever ye would that men should do unto you, do ye even so unto them." But I was her slave, and I suppose she did not recognize me as her neighbor. I would give much to blot out from my memory that one great wrong. As a child, I loved my mistress; and, looking back on the happy days I spent with her, I try to think with less bitterness of this act of injustice. While I was with her, she taught me to read and spell; and for this privilege, which so rarely falls to the lot of a slave, I bless her memory.

She possessed but few slaves; and at her death those were all distributed among her relatives. Five of them were my grandmother's children, and had shared the same milk that nourished her mother's children. Notwithstanding my grandmother's long and faithful service to her owners, not one of her children escaped the auction block. These God-breathing machines are no more, in the sight of their masters, than the cotton they plant, or the horses they tend.

II

The New Master and Mistress

Dr. Flint, a physician in the neighborhood, had married the sister of my mistress, and I was now the property of their little daughter. It was not without murmuring that I prepared for my new home; and what added to my unhappiness, was the fact that my brother William was purchased by the same family. My father, by his nature, as well as by the habit of transacting business as a skilful mechanic, had more of the feelings of a freeman than is common among slaves. My brother was a spirited boy; and being brought up under such influences, he early detested the name of master and mistress. One day, when his father and his mistress had happened to call him at the same time, he hesitated between the two; being perplexed to know which had the strongest claim upon his obedience. He finally concluded to go to his mistress. When my father reproved him for it, he said, "You both called me, and I didn't know which I ought to go to first."

"You are *my* child," replied our father, "and when I call you, you should come immediately, if you have to pass through fire and water."

Poor Willie! He was now to learn his first lesson of obedience to a master. Grandmother tried to cheer us with hopeful words, and they found an echo in the credulous hearts of youth.

When we entered our new home we encountered cold looks, cold words, and cold treatment. We were glad when the night came. On my narrow bed I moaned and wept, I felt so desolate and alone.

I had been there nearly a year, when a dear little friend of mine was buried. I heard her mother sob, as the clods fell on the coffin of her only child, and I turned away from the grave, feeling thankful that I still had something left to love. I met my grandmother, who said, "Come with me, Linda;" and from her tone I knew that something sad had happened. She led me apart from the people, and then said, "My child, your father is dead." Dead! How could I believe it? He had died so suddenly I had not even heard that he was sick. I went home with my grandmother. My heart rebelled against God, who had taken from me mother, father, mistress, and friend. The good grandmother tried to comfort me. "Who knows the ways of God?" said she. "Perhaps they have been kindly taken from the evil days to come." Years afterwards I often thought of this. She promised to be a mother to her grandchildren, so far as she might be permitted to do so; and strengthened by her love, I returned to my master's. I thought I should be allowed to go to my father's house the next morning; but I was ordered to go for flowers, that my mistress's house might be decorated for an evening party. I spent the day gathering flowers and weaving them into festoons, while the dead body of my father was lying within a mile of me. What cared my owners for that? he was merely a piece of property. Moreover, they thought he had spoiled his children, by teaching them to feel that they were human beings. This was blasphemous doctrine for a slave to teach; presumptuous in him, and dangerous to the masters.

The next day I followed his remains to a humble grave beside that of my dear mother. There were those who knew my father's worth, and respected his memory.

My home now seemed more dreary than ever. The laugh of the little slave-children sounded harsh and cruel. It was selfish to feel so about the joy of others. My brother moved about with a very grave face. I tried to comfort him, by saying, "Take courage, Willie; brighter days will come by and by."

"You don't know any thing about it, Linda," he replied. "We shall have to stay here all our days; we shall never be free."

I argued that we were growing older and stronger, and that perhaps we might, before long, be allowed to hire our own time, and then we could earn money to buy our freedom. William declared this was much easier to say than to do; moreover, he did not intend to *buy* his freedom. We held daily controversies upon this subject.

Little attention was paid to the slaves' meals in Dr. Flint's house. If they could catch a bit of food while it was going, well and good. I gave myself no trouble on that score, for on my various errands I passed my grandmother's house, where there was always something to spare for me. I was frequently threatened with punishment if I stopped there; and my grandmother, to avoid detaining me, often stood at the gate with something for my breakfast or dinner. I was indebted to *her* for all my comforts, spiritual or temporal. It was *her* labor that supplied my scanty wardrobe. I have a vivid recollection of the linsey-woolsey dress given me every winter by Mrs. Flint. How I hated it! It was one of the badges of slavery.

While my grandmother was thus helping to support me from her hard earnings, the three hundred dollars she had lent her mistress were never repaid. When her mistress died, her son-in-law, Dr. Flint, was appointed executor. When grandmother applied to him for payment, he said the estate was insolvent, and the law prohibited payment. It did not, however, prohibit him from retaining the silver candelabra, which had been purchased with that money. I presume they will be handed down in the family, from generation to generation.

My grandmother's mistress had always promised her that, at her death, she should be free; and it was said that in her will she made good the promise. But when the estate was settled, Dr. Flint told the faithful old servant that, under existing circumstances, it was necessary she should be sold.

On the appointed day, the customary advertisement was posted up, proclaiming that there would be a "public sale of negroes, horses, &c." Dr. Flint called to tell my grandmother that he was unwilling to wound her feelings by putting her up at auction, and that he would prefer to dispose of her at private sale. My grandmother saw through his hypocrisy; she understood very well that he was ashamed of the job. She was a very spirited woman, and if he was base enough to sell her, when her mistress intended she should be free, she was determined the public should know it. She had for a long time supplied many families with crackers and preserves; consequently, "Aunt Marthy," as she was called, was generally known, and every body who knew her respected her intelligence and good character. Her long and faithful service in the family was also well known, and the intention of her mistress to leave her free. When the day of sale came, she took her place among the chattels, and at the first call she sprang upon the auction-block. Many voices called out, "Shame! Shame! Who is going to sell *you*, aunt Marthy? Don't stand there! That is no place for *you*." Without saying a word, she quietly awaited her fate. No one bid for her. At last, a feeble voice said, "Fifty dollars." It came from a maiden lady, seventy years old, the sister of my grandmother's deceased mistress. She had lived forty years under the same roof with my grandmother; she knew how faithfully she had served her owners, and how cruelly she had been defrauded of her rights; and she resolved to protect her. The auctioneer waited for a higher bid; but her wishes were respected; no one bid above her. She could neither read nor write; and when the bill of sale was made out, she signed it with a cross. But what consequence was that, when she had a big heart overflowing with human kindness? She gave the old servant her freedom.

At that time, my grandmother was just fifty years old. Laborious years had passed since then; and now my brother and I were slaves to the man who had defrauded her of her money, and tried to defraud her of her freedom. One of my mother's sisters, called Aunt Nancy, was also a slave in his family. She was a kind, good aunt to me; and supplied the place of both housekeeper and waiting maid to her mistress. She was, in fact, at the beginning and end of every thing.

Mrs. Flint, like many southern women, was totally deficient in energy. She had not strength to superintend her household affairs; but her nerves were so strong, that she could sit in her easy chair and see a woman whipped, till the blood trickled from every stroke of the lash. She was a member of the church; but partaking of the Lord's supper did not seem to put her in a Christian frame of mind. If dinner was not served at the exact time on that particular Sunday, she would station herself in the kitchen, and wait till it was dished, and then spit in all the kettles and pans that had been used for cooking. She did this to prevent the cook and her children from eking out their meagre fare with the remains of the gravy and other scrapings. The slaves could get nothing to eat except what she chose to give them. Provisions were weighed out by the pound and ounce, three times a day. I can assure you she gave them no chance to eat wheat bread from her flour barrel. She knew how many biscuits a quart of flour would make, and exactly what size they ought to be.

Dr. Flint was an epicure. The cook never sent a dinner to his table without fear and trembling; for if there happened to be a dish not to his liking, he would either order her to be whipped, or compel her to eat every mouthful of it in his presence. The poor, hungry creature might not have objected to eating it; but she did object to having her master cram it down her throat till she choked.

They had a pet dog, that was a nuisance in the house. The cook was ordered to make some Indian mush for him. He refused to eat, and when his head was held over it, the froth flowed from his mouth into the basin. He died a few minutes after. When Dr. Flint came in, he said the mush had not been well cooked, and that was the reason the animal would not eat it. He sent for the cook, and compelled her to eat it. He thought that the woman's stomach was stronger than the dog's; but her sufferings afterwards proved that he was mistaken. This poor woman endured many cruelties from her master and mistress; sometimes she was locked up, away from her nursing baby, for a whole day and night.

When I had been in the family a few weeks, one of the plantation slaves was brought to town, by order of his master. It was near night when he arrived, and Dr. Flint ordered him to be taken to the work house, and tied up to the joist, so that his feet would just escape the ground. In that situation he was to wait till the doctor had taken his tea. I shall never forget that night. Never before, in my life, had I heard hundreds of blows fall, in succession, on a human being. His piteous groans, and his "O, pray don't, massa," rang in my ear for months afterwards. There were many conjectures as to the cause of this terrible punishment. Some said master accused him of stealing corn; others said the slave had quarrelled with his wife, in presence of the overseer, and had accused his master of being the father of her child. They were both black, and the child was very fair.

I went into the work house next morning, and saw the cowhide still wet with blood, and the boards all covered with gore. The poor man lived, and continued to quarrel with his wife. A few months afterwards Dr. Flint handed them both over to a slavetrader. The guilty man put their value into his pocket, and had the satisfaction of knowing that they were out of sight and hearing. When the mother was delivered into the trader's hands, she said, "You *promised* to treat me well." To which he replied, "You have let your tongue run too far; damn you!" She had forgotten that it was a crime for a slave to tell who was the father of her child.

From others than the master persecution also comes in such cases. I once saw a young slave girl dying soon after the birth of a child nearly white. In her agony she cried out, "O Lord, come and take me!" Her mistress stood by, and mocked at her like an incarnate fiend. "You suffer, do you?" she exclaimed. "I am glad of it. You deserve it all, and more too."

The girl's mother said, "The baby is dead, thank God; and I hope my poor child will soon be in heaven, too."

"Heaven!" retorted the mistress. "There is no such place for the like of her and her bastard."

The poor mother turned away, sobbing. Her dying daughter called her, feebly, and as she bent over her, I heard her say, "Don't grieve so, mother; God knows all about it; and HE will have mercy upon me."

Her sufferings, afterwards, became so intense, that her mistress felt unable to stay; but when she left the room, the scornful smile was still on her lips. Seven children called her mother. The poor black woman had but the one child, whose eyes she saw closing in death, while she thanked God for taking her away from the greater bitterness of life.

III

The Slaves' New Year's Day

Dr. Flint owned a fine residence in town, several farms, and about fifty slaves, besides hiring a number by the year.

Hiring-day at the south takes place on the 1st of January. On the 2d, the slaves are expected to go to their new masters. On a farm, they work until the corn and cotton are laid. They then have two holidays. Some masters give them a good dinner under the trees. This over, they work until Christmas eve. If no heavy charges are meantime brought against them, they are given four or five holidays, whichever the master or overseer may think proper. Then comes New Year's eve; and they gather together their little alls, or more properly speaking, their little nothings, and wait anxiously for the dawning of day. At the appointed hour the grounds are thronged with men, women, and children, waiting, like criminals, to hear their doom pronounced. The slave is sure to know who is the most humane, or cruel master, within forty miles of him.

It is easy to find out, on that day, who clothes and feeds his slaves well; for he is surrounded by a crowd, begging, "Please, massa, hire me this year. I will work *very* hard, massa."

If a slave is unwilling to go with his new master, he is whipped, or locked up in jail, until he consents to go, and promises not to run away during the year. Should he chance to change his mind, thinking it justifiable to violate an extorted promise, woe unto him if he is caught! The whip is used till the blood flows at his feet; and his stiffened limbs are put in chains, to be dragged in the field for days and days!

If he lives until the next year, perhaps the same man will hire him again, without even giving him an opportunity of going to the hiring-ground. After those for hire are disposed of, those for sale are called up.

O, you happy free women, contrast *your* New Year's day with that of the poor bond-woman! With you it is a pleasant season, and the light of the day is blessed. Friendly wishes meet you every where, and gifts are showered upon you. Even hearts that have been estranged from you soften at this season, and lips that have been silent echo back, "I wish you a happy New Year." Children bring their little offerings, and raise their rosy lips for a caress. They are your own, and no hand but that of death can take them from you.

But to the slave mother New Year's day comes laden with peculiar sorrows. She sits on her cold cabin floor, watching the children who may all be torn from her the next morning; and often does she wish that she and they might die before the day dawns. She may be an ignorant creature, degraded by the system that has brutalized her from childhood; but she has a mother's instincts, and is capable of feeling a mother's agonies.

On one of these sale days, I saw a mother lead seven children to the auction-block. She knew that *some* of them would be taken from her; but they took *all*. The children were sold to a slave-trader, and their mother was bought by a man in her own town. Before night her children were all far away. She begged the trader to tell her where he intended to take them; this he refused to do. How *could* he, when he knew he would sell them, one by one, wherever he could command the highest price? I met that mother in the street, and her wild, haggard face lives to-day in my mind. She wrung her hands in anguish, and exclaimed, "Gone! All gone! Why *don't* God kill me?" I had no words wherewith to comfort her. Instances of this kind are of daily, yea, of hourly occurrence.

Slaveholders have a method, peculiar to their institution, of getting rid of *old* slaves, whose lives have been worn out in their service. I knew an old woman, who for seventy years faithfully served her master. She had become almost helpless, from hard labor and disease. Her owners moved to Alabama, and the old black woman was left to be sold to any body who would give twenty dollars for her.

IV

The Slave Who Dared to Feel like a Man

Two years had passed since I entered Dr. Flint's family, and those years had brought much of the knowledge that comes from experience, though they had afforded little opportunity for any other kinds of knowledge.

My grandmother had, as much as possible, been a mother to her orphan grandchildren. By perseverance and unwearied industry, she was now mistress of a snug little home, surrounded with the necessaries of life. She would have been happy could her children have shared them with her. There remained but three children and two grandchildren, all slaves. Most earnestly did she strive to make us feel that it was the will of God: that He had seen fit to place us under such circumstances; and though it seemed hard, we ought to pray for contentment.

It was a beautiful faith, coming from a mother who could not call her children her own. But I, and Benjamin, her youngest boy, condemned it. We reasoned that it was much more the will of God that we should be situated as she was. We longed for a home like hers. There we always found sweet balsam for our troubles. She was so loving, so sympathizing! She always met us with a smile, and listened with patience to all our sorrows. She spoke so hopefully, that unconsciously the clouds gave place to sunshine. There was a grand big oven there, too, that baked bread and nice things for the town, and we knew there was always a choice bit in store for us.

But, alas! even the charms of the old oven failed to reconcile us to our hard lot. Benjamin was now a tall, handsome lad, strongly and gracefully made, and with a spirit too bold and daring for a slave. My brother William, now twelve years old, had the same aversion to the word master that he had when he was an urchin of seven years. I was his confidant. He came to me with all his troubles. I remember one instance in particular. It was on a lovely spring morning, and when I marked the sunlight dancing here and there, its beauty seemed to mock my sadness. For my master, whose restless, craving, vicious nature roved about day and night, seeking whom to devour, had just left me, with stinging, scorching words; words that scathed ear and brain like fire. O, how I despised him! I thought how glad I should be, if some day when he walked the earth, it would open and swallow him up, and disencumber the world of a plague.

When he told me that I was made for his use, made to obey his command in *every* thing; that I was nothing but a slave, whose will must and should surrender to his, never before had my puny arm felt half so strong.

So deeply was I absorbed in painful reflections afterwards, that I neither saw nor heard the entrance of any one, till the voice of William sounded close beside me. "Linda," he said, "what makes you look so sad? I love you. O, Linda, isn't this a bad world? Every body seems so cross and unhappy. I wish I had died when poor father did."

I told him that every body was *not* cross, or unhappy; that those who had pleasant homes, and kind friends, and who were not afraid to love them, were happy. But we, who were slave-children, without father or mother, could not expect to be happy. We must be good; perhaps that would bring us contentment.

"Yes," he said, "I try to be good; but what's the use? They are all the time troubling me." Then he proceeded to relate his afternoon's difficulty with young master Nicholas. It seemed that the brother of master Nicholas had pleased himself with making up stories about William. Master Nicholas said he should be flogged, and he would do it. Whereupon he went to work; but William fought bravely, and the young master, finding he was getting the better of him, undertook to tie his hands behind him. He failed in that likewise. By dint of kicking and fisting, William came out of the skirmish none the worse for a few scratches.

He continued to discourse on his young master's *meanness*; how he whipped the *little* boys, but was a perfect coward when a tussle ensued between him and white boys of his own size. On such occasions he always took to his legs. William had other charges to make against him. One was his rubbing up pennies with quicksilver, and passing them off for quarters of a dollar on an old man who kept a fruit stall. William was often sent to buy fruit, and he earnestly inquired of me what he ought to do under such circumstances. I told him it was certainly wrong to deceive the old man, and that it was his duty to tell him of the impositions practised by his young master. I assured him the old man would not be slow to comprehend the whole, and there the matter would end. William thought it might with the old man, but not with *him*. He said he did not mind the smart of the whip, but he did not like the *idea* of being whipped.

While I advised him to be good and forgiving I was not unconscious of the beam in my own eye. It was the very knowledge of my own shortcomings that urged me to retain, if possible, some sparks of my brother's God-given nature. I had not lived fourteen years in slavery for nothing. I had felt, seen, and heard enough, to read the characters, and question the motives, of those around me. The war of my life had begun; and though one of God's most powerless creatures, I resolved never to be conquered. Alas, for me!

If there was one pure, sunny spot for me, I believed it to be in Benjamin's heart, and in another's, whom I loved with all the ardor of a girl's first love. My owner knew of it, and sought in every way to render me miserable. He did not resort to corporal punishment, but to all the petty, tyrannical ways that human ingenuity could devise.

I remember the first time I was punished. It was in the month of February. My grandmother had taken my old shoes, and replaced them with a new pair. I needed them; for several inches of snow had fallen, and it still continued to fall. When I walked through Mrs. Flint's room, their creaking grated harshly on her refined nerves. She called me to her, and asked what I had about me that made such a horrid noise. I told her it was my new shoes. "Take them off," said she; "and if you put them on again, I'll throw them into the fire."

I took them off, and my stockings also. She then sent me a long distance, on an errand. As I went through the snow, my bare feet tingled. That night I was very hoarse; and I went to bed thinking the next day would find me sick, perhaps dead. What was my grief on waking to find myself quite well!

I had imagined if I died, or was laid up for some time, that my mistress would feel a twinge of remorse that she had so hated "the little imp," as she styled me. It was my ignorance of that mistress that gave rise to such extravagant imaginings.

Dr. Flint occasionally had high prices offered for me; but he always said, "She don't belong to me. She is my daughter's property, and I have no right to sell her." Good, honest man! My young mistress was still a child, and I could look for no protection from her. I loved her, and she returned my affection. I once heard her father allude to her attachment to me; and his wife promptly replied that it proceeded from fear. This put unpleasant doubts into my mind. Did the child feign what she did not feel? or was her mother jealous of the mite of love she bestowed on me? I concluded it must be the latter. I said to myself, "Surely, little children are true."

One afternoon I sat at my sewing, feeling unusual depression of spirits. My mistress had been accusing me of an offence, of which I assured her I was perfectly innocent; but I saw, by the contemptuous curl of her lip, that she believed I was telling a lie.

I wondered for what wise purpose God was leading me through such thorny paths, and whether still darker days were in store for me. As I sat musing thus, the door opened softly, and William came in. "Well, brother," said I, "what is the matter this time?"

"O Linda, Ben and his master have had a dreadful time!" said he.

My first thought was that Benjamin was killed. "Don't be frightened, Linda," said William; "I will tell you all about it."

It appeared that Benjamin's master had sent for him, and he did not immediately obey the summons. When he did, his master was angry, and began to whip him. He resisted. Master and slave fought, and finally the master was thrown. Benjamin had cause to tremble; for he had thrown to the ground his master—one of the richest men in town. I anxiously awaited the result.

That night I stole to my grandmother's house; and Benjamin also stole thither from his master's. My grandmother had gone to spend a day or two with an old friend living in the country.

"I have come," said Benjamin, "to tell you good by. I am going away."

I inquired where.

"To the north," he replied.

I looked at him to see whether he was in earnest. I saw it all in his firm, set mouth. I implored him not to go, but he paid no heed to my words. He said he was no longer a boy, and every day made his yoke more galling. He had raised his hand against his master, and was to be publicly whipped for the offence. I reminded him of the poverty and hardships he must encounter among strangers. I told him he might be caught and brought back; and that was terrible to think of.

He grew vexed, and asked if poverty and hardships with freedom, were not preferable to our treatment in slavery. "Linda," he continued, "we are dogs here; foot-balls, cattle, every thing that's mean. No, I will not stay. Let them bring me back. We don't die but once."

He was right; but it was hard to give him up. "Go," said I, "and break your mother's heart."

I repented of my words ere they were out.

"Linda," said he, speaking as I had not heard him speak that evening, "how *could* you say that? Poor mother! be kind to her, Linda; and you, too, cousin Fanny."

Cousin Fanny was a friend who had lived some years with us.

Farewells were exchanged, and the bright, kind boy, endeared to us by so many acts of love, vanished from our sight.

It is not necessary to state how he made his escape. Suffice it to say, he was on his way to New York when a violent storm overtook the vessel. The captain said he must put into the nearest port. This alarmed Benjamin, who was aware that he would be advertised in every port near his own town. His embarrassment was noticed by the captain. To port they went. There the advertisement met the captain's eye. Benjamin so exactly answered its description, that the captain laid hold on him, and bound him in chains. The storm passed, and they proceeded to New York. Before reaching that port Benjamin managed to get off his chains and throw them overboard. He escaped from the vessel, but was pursued, captured, and carried back to his master.

When my grandmother returned home and found her youngest child had fled, great was her sorrow; but, with characteristic piety, she said, "God's will be done." Each morning, she inquired if any news had been heard from her boy. Yes, news *was* heard. The master was rejoicing over a letter, announcing the capture of his human chattel.

That day seems but as yesterday, so well do I remember it. I saw him led through the streets in chains, to jail. His face was ghastly pale, yet full of determination. He had begged one of the sailors to go to his mother's house and ask her not to meet him. He said the sight of her distress would take from him all self-control. She yearned to see him, and she went; but she screened herself in the crowd, that it might be as her child had said.

We were not allowed to visit him; but we had known the jailer for years, and he was a kind-hearted man. At midnight he opened the jail door for my grandmother and myself to enter, in disguise. When we entered the cell not a sound broke the stillness. "Benjamin, Benjamin!"

whispered my grandmother. No answer. "Benjamin!" she again faltered. There was a jingle of chains. The moon had just risen, and cast an uncertain light through the bars of the window. We knelt down and took Benjamin's cold hands in ours. We did not speak. Sobs were heard, and Benjamin's lips were unsealed; for his mother was weeping on his neck. How vividly does memory bring back that sad night! Mother and son talked together. He asked her pardon for the suffering he had caused her. She said she had nothing to forgive; she could not blame his desire for freedom. He told her that when he was captured, he broke away, and was about casting himself into the river, when thoughts of *her* came over him, and he desisted. She asked if he did not also think of God. I fancied I saw his face grow fierce in the moonlight. He answered, "No, I did not think of him. When a man is hunted like a wild beast he forgets there is a God, a heaven. He forgets every thing in his struggle to get beyond the reach of the bloodhounds."

"Don't talk so, Benjamin," said she. "Put your trust in God. Be humble, my child, and your master will forgive you."

"Forgive me for *what*, mother? For not letting him treat me like a dog? No! I will never humble myself to him. I have worked for him for nothing all my life, and I am repaid with stripes and imprisonment. Here I will stay till I die, or till he sells me."

The poor mother shuddered at his words. I think he felt it; for when he next spoke, his voice was calmer. "Don't fret about me, mother. I ain't worth it," said he. "I wish I had some of your goodness. You bear every thing patiently, just as though you thought it was all right. I wish I could."

She told him she had not always been so; once, she was like him; but when sore troubles came upon her, and she had no arm to lean upon, she learned to call on God, and he lightened her burdens. She besought him to do likewise.

We overstaid our time, and were obliged to hurry from the jail.

Benjamin had been imprisoned three weeks, when my grandmother went to intercede for him with his master. He was immovable. He said Benjamin should serve as an example to the rest of his slaves; he should be kept in jail till he was subdued, or be sold if he got but one dollar for him. However, he afterwards relented in some degree. The chains were taken off, and we were allowed to visit him.

As his food was of the coarsest kind, we carried him as often as possible a warm supper, accompanied with some little luxury for the jailer.

Three months elapsed, and there was no prospect of release or of a purchaser. One day he was heard to sing and laugh. This piece of indecorum was told to his master, and the overseer was ordered to re-chain him. He was now confined in an apartment with other prisoners, who were covered with filthy rags. Benjamin was chained near them, and was soon covered with vermin. He worked at his chains till he succeeded in getting out of them. He passed them through the bars of the window, with a request that they should be taken to his master, and he should be informed that he was covered with vermin.

This audacity was punished with heavier chains, and prohibition of our visits.

My grandmother continued to send him fresh changes of clothes. The old ones were burned up. The last night we saw him in jail his mother still begged him to send for his master, and beg his pardon. Neither persuasion nor argument could turn him from his purpose. He calmly answered, "I am waiting his time."

Those chains were mournful to hear.

Another three months passed, and Benjamin left his prison walls. We that loved him waited to bid him a long and last farewell. A slave trader had bought him. You remember, I told you what price he brought when ten years of age. Now he was more than twenty years old, and sold for three hundred dollars. The master had been blind to his own interest. Long confinement had made his face too pale, his form too thin; moreover, the trader had heard something of his character, and it did not strike him as suitable for a slave. He said he would give any price if the handsome lad was a girl. We thanked God that he was not.

Could you have seen that mother clinging to her child, when they fastened the irons upon his wrists; could you have heard her heartrending groans, and seen her bloodshot eyes wander wildly from face to face, vainly pleading for mercy; could you have witnessed that scene as I saw it, you would exclaim, *Slavery is damnable!*

Benjamin, her youngest, her pet, was forever gone! She could not realize it. She had had an interview with the trader for the purpose of ascertaining if Benjamin could be purchased. She was told it was impossible, as he had given bonds not to sell him till he was out of the state. He promised that he would not sell him till he reached New Orleans.

With a strong arm and unvaried trust, my grandmother began her work of love. Benjamin must be free. If she succeeded, she knew they would still be separated; but the sacrifice was not too great. Day and night she labored. The trader's price would treble that he gave; but she was not discouraged.

She employed a lawyer to write to a gentleman, whom she knew, in New Orleans. She begged him to interest himself for Benjamin, and he willingly favored her request. When he saw Benjamin, and stated his business, he thanked him; but said he preferred to wait a while before making the trader an offer. He knew he had tried to obtain a high price for him, and had invariably failed. This encouraged him to make another effort for freedom. So one morning, long before day, Benjamin was missing. He was riding over the blue billows, bound for Baltimore.

For once his white face did him a kindly service. They had no suspicion that it belonged to a slave; otherwise, the law would have been followed out to the letter, and the *thing* rendered back to slavery. The brightest skies are often overshadowed by the darkest clouds. Benjamin was taken sick, and compelled to remain in Baltimore three weeks. His strength was slow in returning; and his desire to continue his journey seemed to retard his recovery. How could he get strength without air and exercise? He resolved to venture on a short walk. A by-street was selected, where he thought himself secure of not being met by any one that knew him; but a voice called out, "Halloo, Ben, my boy! what are you doing *here*?"

His first impulse was to run; but his legs trembled so that he could not stir. He turned to confront his antagonist, and behold, there stood his old master's next door neighbor! He thought it was all over with him now; but it proved otherwise. That man was a miracle. He possessed a goodly number of slaves, and yet was not quite deaf to that mystic clock, whose ticking is rarely heard in the slaveholder's breast.

"Ben, you are sick," said he. "Why, you look like a ghost. I guess I gave you something of a start. Never mind, Ben, I am not going to touch you. You had a pretty tough time of it, and you may go on your way rejoicing for all me. But I would advise you to get out of this place plaguy quick, for there are several gentlemen here from our town." He described the nearest and safest route to New York, and added, "I shall be glad to tell your mother I have seen you. Good by, Ben."

Benjamin turned away, filled with gratitude, and surprised that the town he hated contained such a gem—a gem worthy of a purer setting.

This gentleman was a Northerner by birth, and had married a southern lady. On his return, he told my grandmother that he had seen her son, and of the service he had rendered him.

Benjamin reached New York safely, and concluded to stop there until he had gained strength enough to proceed further. It happened that my grandmother's only remaining son had sailed for the same city on business for his mistress. Through God's providence, the brothers met. You may be sure it was a happy meeting. "O Phil," exclaimed Benjamin, "I am here at last." Then he told him how near he came to dying, almost in sight of free land, and how he prayed that he might live to get one breath of free air. He said life was worth something now, and it would be hard to die. In the old jail he had not valued it; once, he was tempted to destroy it; but something, he did not know what, had prevented him; perhaps it was fear. He had heard those who profess to be religious declare there was no heaven for self-murderers; and as his life had been pretty hot here, he did not desire a continuation of the same in another world. "If I die now," he exclaimed, "thank God, I shall die a freeman!"

He begged my uncle Phillip not to return south; but stay and work with him, till they earned enough to buy those at home. His brother told him it would kill their mother if he deserted her in her trouble. She had pledged her house, and with difficulty had raised money to buy him. Would he be bought?

"No, never!" he replied. "Do you suppose, Phil, when I have got so far out of their clutches, I will give them one red cent? No! And do you suppose I would turn mother out of her home in her old age? That I would let her pay all those hard-earned dollars for me, and never to see me? For you know she will stay south as long as her other children are slaves. What a good mother! Tell her to buy *you,* Phil. You have been a comfort to her, and I have been a trouble. And Linda, poor Linda; what'll become of her? Phil, you don't know what a life they lead her. She has told me something about it, and I wish old Flint was dead, or a better man. When I was in jail, he asked her if she didn't want *him* to ask my master to forgive me, and take me home again. She told him, No; that I didn't want to go back. He got mad, and said we were all alike. I never despised my own master half as much as I do that man. There is many a worse slaveholder than my master; but for all that I would not be his slave."

While Benjamin was sick, he had parted with nearly all his clothes to pay necessary expenses. But he did not part with a little pin I fastened in his bosom when we parted. It was the most valuable thing I owned, and I thought none more worthy to wear it. He had it still.

His brother furnished him with clothes, and gave him what money he had.

They parted with moistened eyes; and as Benjamin turned away, he said, "Phil, I part with all my kindred." And so it proved. We never heard from him again.

Uncle Phillip came home; and the first words he uttered when he entered the house were, "Mother, Ben is free! I have seen him in New York." She stood looking at him with a bewildered air. "Mother, don't you believe it?" he said, laying his hand softly upon her shoulder. She raised her hands, and exclaimed, "God be praised! Let us thank him." She dropped on her knees, and poured forth her heart in prayer. Then Phillip must sit down and repeat to her every word Benjamin had said. He told her all; only he forbore to mention how sick and pale her darling looked. Why should he distress her when she could do him no good?

The brave old woman still toiled on, hoping to rescue some of her other children. After a while she succeeded in buying Phillip. She paid eight hundred dollars, and came home with the precious document that secured his freedom. The happy mother and son sat together by the old hearthstone that night, telling how proud they were of each other, and how they would prove to the world that they could take care of themselves, as they had long taken care of others. We all concluded by saying, "He that is *willing* to be a slave, let him be a slave."

V

The Trials of Girlhood

During the first years of my service in Dr. Flint's family, I was accustomed to share some indulgences with the children of my mistress. Though this seemed to me no more than right, I was grateful for it, and tried to merit the kindness by the faithful discharge of my duties. But I now entered on my fifteenth year—a sad epoch in the life of a slave girl. My master began to whisper foul words in my ear. Young as I was, I could not remain ignorant of their import. I tried to treat them with indifference or contempt. The master's age, my extreme youth, and the fear that his conduct would be reported to my grandmother, made him bear this treatment for many months. He was a crafty man, and resorted to many means to accomplish his purposes. Sometimes he had stormy, terrific ways, that made his victims tremble; sometimes he assumed a gentleness that he thought must surely subdue. Of the two, I preferred his stormy moods, although they left me trembling. He tried his utmost to corrupt the pure principles my grandmother had instilled.

He peopled my young mind with unclean images, such as only a vile monster could think of. I turned from him with disgust and hatred. But he was my master. I was compelled to live under the same roof with him—where I saw a man forty years my senior daily violating the most sacred commandments of nature. He told me I was his property; that I must be subject to his will in all things. My soul revolted against the mean tyranny. But where could I turn for protection? No matter whether the slave girl be as black as ebony or as fair as her mistress. In either case, there is no shadow of law to protect her from insult, from violence, or even from death; all these are inflicted by fiends who bear the shape of men. The mistress, who ought to protect the helpless victim, has no other feelings towards her but those of jealousy and rage. The degradation, the wrongs, the vices, that grow out of slavery, are more than I can describe. They are greater than you would willingly believe. Surely, if you credited one half the truths that are told you concerning the helpless millions suffering in this cruel bondage, you at the north would not help to tighten the yoke. You surely would refuse to do for the master, on your own soil, the mean and cruel work which trained bloodhounds and the lowest class of whites do for him at the south.

Every where the years bring to all enough of sin and sorrow; but in slavery the very dawn of life is darkened by these shadows. Even the little child, who is accustomed to wait on her mistress and her children, will learn, before she is twelve years old, why it is that her mistress hates such and such a one among the slaves. Perhaps the child's own mother is among those hated ones. She listens to violent outbreaks of jealous passion, and cannot help understanding what is the cause. She will become prematurely knowing in evil things. Soon she will learn to tremble when she hears her master's footfall. She will be compelled to realize that she is no longer a child. If God has bestowed beauty upon her, it will prove her greatest curse. That which commands admiration in the white woman only hastens the degradation of the female slave. I know that some are too much brutalized by slavery to feel the humiliation of their position; but many slaves feel it most acutely, and shrink from the memory of it. I cannot tell how much I suffered in the presence of these wrongs, nor how I am still pained by the retrospect. My master met me at every turn, reminding me that I belonged to him, and swearing by heaven and earth that he would compel me to submit to him. If I went out for a breath of fresh air, after a day of unwearied toil, his footsteps dogged me. If I knelt by my mother's grave, his dark shadow fell on me even there. The light heart which nature had given me became heavy with sad forebodings. The other slaves in my master's house noticed the change. Many of them pitied me; but none dared to ask the cause. They had no need to inquire. They knew too well the guilty practices under that roof; and they were aware that to speak of them was an offence that never went unpunished.

I longed for some one to confide in. I would have given the world to have laid my head on my grandmother's faithful bosom, and told her all my troubles. But Dr. Flint swore he would kill me, if I was not as silent as the grave. Then, although my grandmother was all in all to me, I feared her as well as loved her. I had been accustomed to look up to her with a respect bordering upon awe. I was very young, and felt shamefaced about telling her such impure things, especially as I knew her to be very strict on such subjects. Moreover, she was a woman of a high spirit. She was usually very quiet in her demeanor; but if her indignation was once roused, it was not very easily quelled. I had been told that she once chased a white gentleman with a loaded pistol, because he insulted one of her daughters. I dreaded the consequences of a violent outbreak; and both pride and fear kept me silent. But though I did not confide in my grandmother, and even evaded her vigilant watchfulness and inquiry, her presence in the neighborhood was some protection to me. Though she had been a slave, Dr. Flint was afraid of her. He dreaded her scorching rebukes. Moreover, she was known and patronized by many people; and he did not wish to have his villainy made public. It was lucky for me that I did not live on a distant plantation, but in a town not so large that the inhabitants were ignorant of each other's affairs. Bad as are the laws and customs in a slaveholding community, the doctor, as a professional man, deemed it prudent to keep up some outward show of decency.

O, what days and nights of fear and sorrow that man caused me! Reader, it is not to awaken sympathy for myself that I am telling you truthfully what I suffered in slavery. I do it to kindle a flame of compassion in your hearts for my sisters who are still in bondage, suffering as I once suffered.

I once saw two beautiful children playing together. One was a fair white child; the other was her slave, and also her sister. When I saw them embracing each other, and heard their joyous laughter, I turned sadly away from the lovely sight. I foresaw the inevitable blight that would fall on the little slave's heart. I knew how soon her laughter would be changed to sighs. The fair child grew up to be a still fairer woman. From childhood to womanhood her pathway was blooming with flowers, and overarched by a sunny sky. Scarcely one day of her life had been clouded when the sun rose on her happy bridal morning.

How had those years dealt with her slave sister, the little playmate of her childhood? She, also, was very beautiful; but the flowers and sunshine of love were not for her. She drank the cup of sin, and shame, and misery, whereof her persecuted race are compelled to drink.

In view of these things, why are ye silent, ye free men and women of the north? Why do your tongues falter in maintenance of the right? Would that I had more ability! But my heart is so full, and my pen is so weak! There are noble men and women who plead for us, striving to help those who cannot help themselves. God bless them! God give them strength and courage to go on! God bless those, every where, who are laboring to advance the cause of humanity!

VI

The Jealous Mistress

I would ten thousand times rather that my children should be the half-starved paupers of Ireland than to be the most pampered among the slaves of America. I would rather drudge out my life on a cotton plantation, till the grave opened to give me rest, than to live with an unprincipled master and a jealous mistress. The felon's home in a penitentiary is preferable. He may repent, and turn from the error of his ways, and so find peace; but it is not so with a favorite slave. She is not allowed to have any pride of character. It is deemed a crime in her to wish to be virtuous.

Mrs. Flint possessed the key to her husband's character before I was born. She might have used this knowledge to counsel and to screen the young and the innocent among her slaves; but for them she had no sympathy. They were the objects of her constant suspicion and malevolence. She watched her husband with unceasing vigilance; but he was well practised in means to evade it. What he could not find opportunity to say in words he manifested in signs. He invented more than were ever thought of in a deaf and dumb asylum. I let them pass, as if I did not understand what he meant; and many were the curses and threats bestowed on me for my stupidity. One day he caught me teaching myself to write. He frowned, as if he was not well pleased; but I suppose he came to the conclusion that such an accomplishment might help to advance his favorite scheme. Before long, notes were often slipped into my hand. I would return them, saying, "I can't read them, sir." "Can't you?" he replied; "then I must read them to you." He always finished the reading by asking, "Do you understand?" Sometimes he would complain of the heat of the tea room, and order his supper to be placed on a small table in the piazza. He would seat himself there with a well-satisfied smile, and tell me to stand by and brush away the flies. He would eat very slowly, pausing between the mouthfuls. These intervals were employed in describing the happiness I was so foolishly throwing away, and in threatening me with the penalty that finally awaited my stubborn disobedience. He boasted much of the forbearance he had exercised towards me, and reminded me that there was a limit to his patience. When I succeeded in avoiding opportunities for him to talk to me at home, I was ordered to come to his office, to do some errand. When there, I was obliged to stand and listen to such language as he saw fit to address to me. Sometimes I so openly expressed my contempt for him that he would become violently enraged, and I wondered why he did not strike me. Circumstanced as he was, he probably thought it was better policy to be forbearing. But the state of things grew worse and worse daily. In desperation I told him that I must and would apply to my grandmother for protection. He threatened me with death, and worse than death, if I made any complaint to her. Strange to say, I did not despair. I was naturally of a buoyant disposition, and always I had a hope of somehow getting out of his clutches. Like many a poor, simple slave before me, I trusted that some threads of joy would yet be woven into my dark destiny.

I had entered my sixteenth year, and every day it became more apparent that my presence was intolerable to Mrs. Flint. Angry words frequently passed between her and her husband. He had never punished me himself, and he would not allow any body else to punish me. In that respect, she was never satisfied; but, in her angry moods, no terms were too vile for her to bestow upon me. Yet I, whom she detested so bitterly, had far more pity for her than he had, whose duty it was to make her life happy. I never wronged her, or wished to wrong her; and one word of kindness from her would have brought me to her feet.

After repeated quarrels between the doctor and his wife, he announced his intention to take his youngest daughter, then four years old, to sleep in his apartment. It was necessary that a servant should sleep in the same room, to be on hand if the child stirred. I was selected for that office, and informed for what purpose that arrangement had been made. By managing to keep within sight of people, as much as possible, during the day time, I had hitherto succeeded in eluding my master, though a razor was often held to my throat to force me to change this line of policy. At night I slept by the side of my great aunt, where I felt safe. He was too prudent to come into her room. She was an old woman, and had been in the family many years. Moreover, as a married man, and a professional man, he deemed it necessary to save appearances in some degree. But he resolved to remove the obstacle in the way of his scheme; and he thought he had planned it so that he should evade suspicion. He was well aware how much I prized my refuge by the side of my old aunt, and he determined to dispossess me of it. The first night the doctor had the little child in his room alone. The next morning, I was ordered to take my station as nurse the following night. A kind Providence interposed in my favor. During the day Mrs. Flint heard of this new arrangement, and a storm followed. I rejoiced to hear it rage.

After a while my mistress sent for me to come to her room. Her first question was, "Did you know you were to sleep in the doctor's room?"

"Yes, ma am."

"Who told you?"

"My master."

"Will you answer truly all the questions I ask?"

"Yes, ma am."

"Tell me, then, as you hope to be forgiven, are you innocent of what I have accused you?"

"I am."

She handed me a Bible, and said, "Lay your hand on your heart, kiss this holy book, and swear before God that you tell me the truth."

I took the oath she required, and I did it with a clear conscience.

"You have taken God's holy word to testify your innocence," said she. "If you have deceived me, beware! Now take this stool, sit down, look me directly in the face, and tell me all that has passed between your master and you."

I did as she ordered. As I went on with my account her color changed frequently, she wept, and sometimes groaned. She spoke in tones so sad, that I was touched by her grief. The tears came to my eyes; but I was soon convinced that her emotions arose from anger and wounded pride. She felt that her marriage vows were desecrated, her dignity insulted; but she had no compassion for the poor victim of her husband's perfidy. She pitied herself as a martyr; but she was incapable of feeling for the condition of shame and misery in which her unfortunate, helpless slave was placed.

Yet perhaps she had some touch of feeling for me; for when the conference was ended, she spoke kindly, and promised to protect me. I should have been much comforted by this assurance if I could have had confidence in it; but my experiences in slavery had filled me with distrust. She was not a very refined woman, and had not much control over her passions. I was an object of her jealousy, and, consequently, of her hatred; and I knew I could not expect kindness or confidence from her under the circumstances in which I was placed. I could not blame her. Slaveholders' wives feel as other women would under similar circumstances. The fire of her temper kindled from small sparks, and now the flame became so intense that the doctor was obliged to give up his intended arrangement.

I knew I had ignited the torch, and I expected to suffer for it afterwards; but I felt too thankful to my mistress for the timely aid she rendered me to care much about that. She now took me to sleep in a room adjoining her own. There I was an object of her especial care, though not of her especial comfort, for she spent many a sleepless night to watch over me. Sometimes I woke up, and found her bending over me. At other times she whispered in my ear, as though it was her husband who was speaking to me, and listened to hear what I would answer. If she startled me, on such occasions, she would glide stealthily away; and the next morning she would tell me I had been talking in my sleep, and ask who I was talking to. At last, I began to be fearful for my life. It had been often threatened; and you can imagine, better than I can describe, what an unpleasant sensation it must produce to wake up in the dead of night and find a jealous woman bending over you. Terrible as this experience was, I had fears that it would give place to one more terrible.

My mistress grew weary of her vigils; they did not prove satisfactory. She changed her tactics. She now tried the trick of accusing my master of crime, in my presence, and gave my name as the author of the accusation. To my utter astonishment, he replied, "I don't believe it: but if she did acknowledge it, you tortured her into exposing me." Tortured into exposing him! Truly, Satan had no difficulty in distinguishing the color of his soul! I understood his object in making this false representation. It was to show me that I gained nothing by seeking the protection of my mistress; that the power was still all in his own hands. I pitied Mrs. Flint. She was a second wife, many years the junior of her husband; and the hoary-headed miscreant was enough to try the patience of a wiser and better woman. She was completely foiled, and knew not how to proceed. She would gladly have had me flogged for my supposed false oath; but, as I have already stated, the doctor never allowed any one to whip me. The old sinner was politic. The application of the lash might have led to remarks that would have exposed him in the eyes of his children and grandchildren. How often did I rejoice that I lived in a town where all the inhabitants knew each other! If I had been on a remote plantation, or lost among the multitude of a crowded city, I should not be a living woman at this day.

The secrets of slavery are concealed like those of the Inquisition. My master was, to my knowledge, the father of eleven slaves. But did the mothers dare to tell who was the father of their children? Did the other slaves dare to allude to it, except in whispers among themselves? No, indeed! They knew too well the terrible consequences.

My grandmother could not avoid seeing things which excited her suspicions. She was uneasy about me, and tried various ways to buy me; but the neverchanging answer was always repeated: "Linda does not belong to *me*. She is my daughter's property, and I have no legal right to sell her." The conscientious man! He was too scrupulous to *sell* me; but he had no scruples whatever about committing a much greater wrong against the helpless young girl placed under his guardianship, as his daughter's property. Sometimes my persecutor would ask me whether I would like to be sold. I told him I would rather be sold to any body than to lead such a life as I did. On such occasions he would assume the air of a very injured individual, and reproach me for my ingratitude. "Did I not take you into the house, and make you the companion of my own children?" he would say. "Have I ever treated you like a negro? I have never allowed you to be punished, not even to please your mistress. And this is the recompense I get, you ungrateful girl!" I answered that he had reasons of his own for screening me from punishment, and that the course he pursued made my mistress hate me and persecute me. If I wept, he would say, "Poor child!

Don't cry! don't cry! I will make peace for you with your mistress. Only let me arrange matters in my own way. Poor, foolish girl! you don't know what is for your own good. I would cherish you. I would make a lady of you. Now go, and think of all I have promised you."

I did think of it.

Reader, I draw no imaginary pictures of southern homes. I am telling you the plain truth. Yet when victims make their escape from this wild beast of Slavery, northerners consent to act the part of bloodhounds, and hunt the poor fugitive back into his den, "full of dead men's bones, and all uncleanness." Nay, more, they are not only willing, but proud, to give their daughters in marriage to slaveholders. The poor girls have romantic notions of a sunny clime, and of the flowering vines that all the year round shade a happy home. To what disappointments are they destined! The young wife soon learns that the husband in whose hands she has placed her happiness pays no regard to his marriage vows. Children of every shade of complexion play with her own fair babies, and too well she knows that they are born unto him of his own household. Jealousy and hatred enter the flowery home, and it is ravaged of its loveliness.

Southern women often marry a man knowing that he is the father of many little slaves. They do not trouble themselves about it. They regard such children as property, as marketable as the pigs on the plantation; and it is seldom that they do not make them aware of this by passing them into the slavetrader's hands as soon as possible, and thus getting them out of their sight. I am glad to say there are some honorable exceptions.

I have myself known two southern wives who exhorted their husbands to free those slaves towards whom they stood in a "parental relation"; and their request was granted. These husbands blushed before the superior nobleness of their wives' natures. Though they had only counselled them to do that which it was their duty to do, it commanded their respect, and rendered their conduct more exemplary. Concealment was at an end, and confidence took the place of distrust.

Though this bad institution deadens the moral sense, even in white women, to a fearful extent, it is not altogether extinct. I have heard southern ladies say of Mr. Such a one, "He not only thinks it no disgrace to be the father of those little niggers, but he is not ashamed to call himself their master. I declare, such things ought not to be tolerated in any decent society!"

VII

The Lover

Why does the slave ever love? Why allow the tendrils of the heart to twine around objects which may at any moment be wrenched away by the hand of violence? When separations come by the hand of death, the pious soul can bow in resignation, and say, "Not my will, but thine be done, O Lord!" But when the ruthless hand of man strikes the blow, regardless of the misery he causes, it is hard to be submissive. I did not reason thus when I was a young girl. Youth will be youth. I loved, and I indulged the hope that the dark clouds around me would turn out a bright lining. I forgot that in the land of my birth the shadows are too dense for light to penetrate. A land

> "Where laughter is not mirth; nor thought the mind;
> Nor words a language; nor e'en men mankind.
> Where cries reply to curses, shrieks to blows,
> And each is tortured in his separate hell."

There was in the neighborhood a young colored carpenter; a free born man. We had been well acquainted in childhood, and frequently met together afterwards. We became mutually attached, and he proposed to marry me. I loved him with all the ardor of a young girl's first love. But when I reflected that I was a slave, and that the laws gave no sanction to the marriage of such, my heart sank within me. My lover wanted to buy me; but I knew that Dr. Flint was too wilful and arbitrary a man to consent to that arrangement. From him, I was sure of experiencing all sorts of opposition, and I had nothing to hope from my mistress. She would have been delighted to have got rid of me, but not in that way. It would have relieved her mind of a burden if she could have seen me sold to some distant state, but if I was married near home I should be just as much in her husband's power as I had previously been,—for the husband of a slave has no power to protect her. Moreover, my mistress, like many others, seemed to think that slaves had no right to any family ties of their own; that they were created merely to wait upon the family of the mistress. I once heard her abuse a young slave girl, who told her that a colored man wanted to make her his wife. "I will have you peeled and pickled, my lady," said she, "if I ever hear you mention that subject again. Do you suppose that I will have you tending *my* children with the children of that nigger?" The girl to whom she said this had a mulatto child, of course not acknowledged by its father. The poor black man who loved her would have been proud to acknowledge his helpless offspring.

Many and anxious were the thoughts I revolved in my mind. I was at a loss what to do. Above all things, I was desirous to spare my lover the insults that had cut so deeply into my own soul. I talked with my grandmother about it, and partly told her my fears. I did not dare to tell her the worst. She had long suspected all was not right, and if I confirmed her suspicions I knew a storm would rise that would prove the overthrow of all my hopes.

This love-dream had been my support through many trials; and I could not bear to run the risk of having it suddenly dissipated. There was a lady in the neighborhood, a particular friend of Dr. Flint's, who often visited the house. I had a great respect for her, and she had always manifested a friendly interest in me. Grandmother thought she would have great influence with the doctor. I went to this lady, and told her my story. I told her I was aware that my lover's being a free-born man would prove a great objection; but he wanted to buy me; and if Dr. Flint would consent to that arrangement, I felt sure he would be willing to pay any reasonable price. She knew that Mrs. Flint disliked me; therefore, I ventured to suggest that perhaps my mistress would approve of my being sold, as that would rid her of me. The lady listened with kindly sympathy, and promised to do her utmost to promote my wishes. She had an interview with the doctor, and I believe she pleaded my cause earnestly; but it was all to no purpose.

How I dreaded my master now! Every minute I expected to be summoned to his presence; but the day passed, and I heard nothing from him. The next morning, a message was brought to me: "Master wants you in his study." I found the door ajar, and I stood a moment gazing at the hateful man who claimed a right to rule me, body and soul. I entered, and tried to appear calm. I did not want him to know how my heart was bleeding. He looked fixedly at me, with an expression which seemed to say, "I have half a mind to kill you on the spot." At last he broke the silence, and that was a relief to both of us.

"So you want to be married, do you?" said he, "and to a free nigger."

"Yes, sir."

"Well, I'll soon convince you whether I am your master, or the nigger fellow you honor so highly. If you *must* have a husband, you may take up with one of my slaves."

What a situation I should be in, as the wife of one of his slaves, even if my heart had been interested!

I replied, "Don't you suppose, sir, that a slave can have some preference about marrying? Do you suppose that all men are alike to her?"

"Do you love this nigger?" said he, abruptly.

"Yes, sir."

"How dare you tell me so!" he exclaimed, in great wrath. After a slight pause, he added, "I supposed you thought more of yourself, that you felt above the insults of such puppies."

I replied, "If he is a puppy, I am a puppy, for we are both of the negro race. It is right and honorable for us to love each other. The man you call a puppy never insulted me, sir; and he would not love me if he did not believe me to be a virtuous woman."

He sprang upon me like a tiger, and gave me a stunning blow. It was the first time he had ever struck me; and fear did not enable me to control my anger. When I had recovered a little from the effects, I exclaimed, "You have struck me for answering you honestly. How I despise you!"

There was silence for some minutes. Perhaps he was deciding what should be my punishment; or, perhaps, he wanted to give me time to reflect on what I had said, and to whom I had said it. Finally, he asked, "Do you know what you have said?"

"Yes, sir; but your treatment drove me to it."

"Do you know that I have a right to do as I like with you,—that I can kill you, if I please?"

"You have tried to kill me, and I wish you had; but you have no right to do as you like with me."

"Silence!" he exclaimed, in a thundering voice. "By heavens, girl, you forget yourself too far! Are you mad? If you are, I will soon bring you to your senses. Do you think any other master would bear what I have borne from you this morning? Many masters would have killed you on the spot. How would you like to be sent to jail for your insolence?"

"I know I have been disrespectful, sir," I replied; "but you drove me to it; I couldn't help it. As for the jail, there would be more peace for me there than there is here."

"You deserve to go there," said he, "and to be under such treatment, that you would forget the meaning of the word *peace*. It would do you good. It would take some of your high notions out of you. But I am not ready to send you there yet, notwithstanding your ingratitude for all my kindness and forbearance. You have been the plague of my life. I have wanted to make you happy, and I have been repaid with the basest ingratitude; but though you have proved yourself incapable of appreciating my kindness, I will be lenient towards you, Linda. I will give you one more chance to redeem your character. If you behave yourself and do as I require, I will forgive you and treat you as I always have done; but if you disobey me, I will punish you as I would the meanest slave on my plantation. Never let me hear that fellow's name mentioned again. If I ever know of your speaking to him, I will cowhide you both; and if I catch him lurking about my premises, I will shoot him as soon as I would a dog. Do you hear what I say? I'll teach you a lesson about marriage and free niggers! Now go, and let this be the last time I have occasion to speak to you on this subject."

Reader, did you ever hate? I hope not. I never did but once; and I trust I never shall again. Somebody has called it "the atmosphere of hell"; and I believe it is so.

For a fortnight the doctor did not speak to me. He thought to mortify me; to make me feel that I had disgraced myself by receiving the honorable addresses of a respectable colored man, in preference to the base proposals of a white man. But though his lips disdained to address me, his eyes were very loquacious. No animal ever watched its prey more narrowly than he watched me. He knew that I could write, though he had failed to make me read his letters; and he was now troubled lest I should exchange letters with another man. After a while he became weary of silence; and I was sorry for it. One morning, as he passed through the hall, to leave the house, he contrived to thrust a note into my hand. I thought I had better read it, and spare myself the vexation of having him read it to me. It expressed regret for the blow he had given me, and reminded me that I myself was wholly to blame for it. He hoped I had become convinced of the injury I was doing myself by incurring his displeasure. He wrote that he had made up his mind to go to Louisiana; that he should take several slaves with him, and intended I should be one of the number. My mistress would remain where she was; therefore I should have nothing to fear from that quarter. If I merited kindness from him, he assured me that it would be lavishly bestowed. He begged me to think over the matter, and answer the following day.

The next morning I was called to carry a pair of scissors to his room. I laid them on the table, with the letter beside them. He thought it was my answer, and did not call me back. I went as usual to attend my young mistress to and from school. He met me in the street, and ordered me to stop at his office on my way back. When I entered, he showed me his letter, and asked me why I had not answered it. I replied, "I am your daughter's property, and it is in your power to send me, or take me, wherever you please." He said he was very glad to find me so willing to go, and that we should start early in the autumn. He had a large practice in the town, and I rather thought he had made up the story merely to frighten me. However that might be, I was determined that I would never go to Louisiana with him.

Summer passed away, and early in the autumn Dr. Flint's eldest son was sent to Louisiana to examine the country, with a view to emigrating. That news did not disturb me. I knew very well that I should not be sent with *him*. That I had not been taken to the plantation before this time, was owing to the fact that his son was there. He was jealous of his son; and jealousy of the overseer had kept him from punishing me by sending me into the fields to work. Is it strange that I was not proud of these protectors? As for the overseer, he was a man for whom I had less respect than I had for a bloodhound.

Young Mr. Flint did not bring back a favorable report of Louisiana, and I heard no more of that scheme. Soon after this, my lover met me at the corner of the street, and I stopped to speak to him. Looking up, I saw my master watching us from his window. I hurried home, trembling with fear. I was sent for, immediately, to go to his room. He met me with a blow. "When is mistress to be married?" said he, in a sneering tone. A shower of oaths and imprecations followed. How thankful I was that my lover was a free man! that my tyrant had no power to flog him for speaking to me in the street!

Again and again I revolved in my mind how all this would end. There was no hope that the doctor would consent to sell me on any terms. He had an iron will, and was determined to keep me, and to conquer me. My lover was an intelligent and religious man. Even if he could have obtained permission to marry me while I was a slave, the marriage would give him no power to protect me from my master. It would have made him miserable to witness the insults I should have been subjected to. And then, if we had children, I knew they must "follow the condition of the mother." What a terrible blight that would be on the heart of a free, intelligent father! For *his* sake, I felt that I ought not to link his fate with my own unhappy destiny. He was going to Savannah to see about a little property left him by an uncle; and hard as it was to bring my feelings to it, I earnestly entreated him not to come back. I advised him to go to the Free States, where his tongue would not be tied, and where his intelligence would be of more avail to him. He left me, still hoping the day would come when I could be bought. With me the lamp of hope had gone out. The dream of my girlhood was over. I felt lonely and desolate.

Still I was not stripped of all. I still had my good grandmother, and my affectionate brother. When he put his arms round my neck, and looked into my eyes, as if to read there the troubles I dared not tell, I felt that I still had something to love. But even that pleasant emotion was chilled by the reflection that he might be torn from me at any moment, by some sudden freak of my master. If he had known how we love each other, I think he would have exulted in separating us. We often planned together how we could get to the north. But, as William remarked, such things are easier said than done. My movements were very closely watched, and we had no means of getting any money to defray our expenses. As for grandmother, she was strongly opposed to her children's undertaking any such project. She had not forgotten poor Benjamin's sufferings, and she was afraid that if another child tried to escape, he would have a similar or a worse fate. To me, nothing seemed more dreadful than my present life. I said to myself, "William *must* be free. He shall go to the north, and I will follow him." Many a slave sister has formed the same plans.

X

A Perilous Passage in the Slave Girl's Life

After my lover went away, Dr. Flint contrived a new plan. He seemed to have an idea that my fear of my mistress was his greatest obstacle. In the blandest tones, he told me that he was going to build a small house for me, in a secluded place, four miles away from the town. I shuddered; but I was constrained to listen, while he talked of his intention to give me a home of my own, and to make a lady of me. Hitherto, I had escaped my dreaded fate, by being in the midst of people. My grandmother had already had high words with my master about me. She had told him pretty plainly what she thought of his character, and there was considerable gossip in the neighborhood about our affairs, to which the open-mouthed jealousy of Mrs. Flint contributed not a little. When my master said he was going to build a house for me, and that he could do it with little trouble and expense, I was in hopes something would happen to frustrate his scheme; but I soon heard that the house was actually begun. I vowed before my Maker that I would never enter it. I had rather toil on the plantation from dawn till dark; I had rather live and die in jail, than drag on, from day to day, through such a living death. I was determined that the master, whom I so hated and loathed, who had blighted the prospects of my youth, and made my life a desert, should not, after my long struggle with him, succeed at last in trampling his victim under his feet. I would do any thing, every thing, for the sake of defeating him. What *could* I do? I thought and thought, till I became desperate, and made a plunge into the abyss.

And now, reader, I come to a period in my unhappy life, which I would gladly forget if I could. The remembrance fills me with sorrow and shame. It pains me to tell you of it; but I have promised to tell you the truth, and I will do it honestly, let it cost me what it may. I will not try to screen myself behind the plea of compulsion from a master; for it was not so. Neither can I plead ignorance or thoughtlessness. For years, my master had done his utmost to pollute my mind with foul images, and to destroy the pure principles inculcated by my grandmother, and the good mistress of my childhood. The influences of slavery had had the same effect on me that they had on other young girls; they had made me prematurely knowing, concerning the evil ways of the world. I knew what I did, and I did it with deliberate calculation.

But, O, ye happy women, whose purity has been sheltered from childhood, who have been free to choose the objects of your affection, whose homes are protected by law, do not judge the poor desolate slave girl too severely! If slavery had been abolished, I, also, could have married the man of my choice; I could have had a home shielded by the laws; and I should have been spared the painful task of confessing what I am now about to relate; but all my prospects had been blighted by slavery. I wanted to keep myself pure; and, under the most adverse circumstances, I tried hard to preserve my self-respect; but I was struggling alone in the powerful grasp of the demon Slavery; and the monster proved too strong for me. I felt as if I was forsaken by God and man; as if all my efforts must be frustrated; and I became reckless in my despair.

I have told you that Dr. Flint's persecutions and his wife's jealousy had given rise to some gossip in the neighborhood. Among others, it chanced that a white unmarried gentleman had obtained some knowledge of the circumstances in which I was placed. He knew my grandmother, and often spoke to me in the street. He became interested for me, and asked questions about my master, which I answered in part. He expressed a great deal of sympathy, and a wish to aid me. He constantly sought opportunities to see me, and wrote to me frequently. I was a poor slave girl, only fifteen years old.

So much attention from a superior person was, of course, flattering; for human nature is the same in all. I also felt grateful for his sympathy, and encouraged by his kind words. It seemed to me a great thing to have such a friend. By degrees, a more tender feeling crept into my heart. He was an educated and eloquent gentleman; too eloquent, alas, for the poor slave girl who trusted in him. Of course I saw whither all this was tending. I knew the impassable gulf between us; but to be an object of interest to a man who is not married, and who is not her master, is agreeable to the pride and feelings of a slave, if her miserable situation has left her any pride or sentiment. It seems less degrading to give one's self, than to submit to compulsion. There is something akin to freedom in having a lover who has no control over you, except that which he gains by kindness and attachment. A master may treat you as rudely as he pleases, and you dare not speak; moreover, the wrong does not seem so great with an unmarried man, as with one who has a wife to be made unhappy. There may be sophistry in all this; but the condition of a slave confuses all principles of morality, and, in fact, renders the practice of them impossible.

When I found that my master had actually begun to build the lonely cottage, other feelings mixed with those I have described. Revenge, and calculations of interest, were added to flattered vanity and sincere gratitude for kindness. I knew nothing would enrage Dr. Flint so much as to know that I favored another; and it was something to triumph over my tyrant even in that small way. I thought he would revenge himself by selling me, and I was sure my friend, Mr. Sands, would buy me. He was a man of more generosity and feeling than my master, and I thought my freedom could be easily obtained from him. The crisis of my fate now came so near that I was desperate. I shuddered to think of being the mother of children that should be owned by my old tyrant. I knew that as soon as a new fancy took him, his victims were sold far off to get rid of them; especially if they had children. I had seen several women sold, with his babies at the breast. He never allowed his offspring by slaves to remain long in sight of himself and his wife. Of a man who was not my master I could ask to have my children well supported; and in this case, I felt confident I should obtain the boon. I also felt quite sure that they would be made free. With all these thoughts revolving in my mind, and seeing no other way of escaping the doom I so much dreaded, I made a headlong plunge. Pity me, and pardon me, O virtuous reader! You never knew what it is to be a slave; to be entirely unprotected by law or custom; to have the laws reduce you to the condition of a chattel, entirely subject to the will of another. You never exhausted your ingenuity in avoiding the snares, and eluding the power of a hated tyrant; you never shuddered at the sound of his footsteps, and trembled within hearing of his voice. I know I did wrong. No one can feel it more sensibly than I do. The painful and humiliating memory will haunt me to my dying day. Still, in looking back, calmly, on the events of my life, I feel that the slave woman ought not to be judged by the same standard as others.

The months passed on. I had many unhappy hours. I secretly mourned over the sorrow I was bringing on my grandmother, who had so tried to shield me from harm. I knew that I was the greatest comfort of her old age, and that it was a source of pride to her that I had not degraded myself, like most of the slaves. I wanted to confess to her that I was no longer worthy of her love; but I could not utter the dreaded words.

As for Dr. Flint, I had a feeling of satisfaction and triumph in the thought of telling *him*. From time to time he told me of his intended arrangements, and I was silent. At last, he came and told me the cottage was completed, and ordered me to go to it. I told him I would never enter it. He said, "I have heard enough of such talk as that. You shall go, if you are carried by force; and you shall remain there."

I replied, "I will never go there. In a few months I shall be a mother."

He stood and looked at me in dumb amazement, and left the house without a word. I thought I should be happy in my triumph over him. But now that the truth was out, and my relatives would hear of it, I felt wretched. Humble as were their circumstances, they had pride in my good character. Now, how could I look them in the face? My self-respect was gone! I had resolved that I would be virtuous, though I was a slave. I had said, "Let the storm beat! I will brave it till I die." And now, how humiliated I felt!

I went to my grandmother. My lips moved to make confession, but the words stuck in my throat. I sat down in the shade of a tree at her door and began to sew. I think she saw something unusual was the matter with me. The mother of slaves is very watchful. She knows there is no security for her children. After they have entered their teens she lives in daily expectation of trouble. This leads to many questions. If the girl is of a sensitive nature, timidity keeps her from answering truthfully, and this well-meant course has a tendency to drive her from maternal counsels. Presently, in came my mistress, like a mad woman, and accused me concerning her husband. My grandmother, whose suspicions had been previously awakened, believed what she said. She exclaimed, "O Linda! has it come to this? I had rather see you dead than to see you as you now are. You are a disgrace to your dead mother." She tore from my fingers my mother's wedding ring and her silver thimble. "Go away!" she exclaimed, "and never come to my house, again." Her reproaches fell so hot and heavy, that they left me no chance to answer. Bitter tears, such as the eyes never shed but once, were my only answer. I rose from my seat, but fell back again, sobbing. She did not speak to me; but the tears were running down her furrowed cheeks, and they scorched me like fire. She had always been so kind to me! *So* kind! How I longed to throw myself at her feet, and tell her all the truth! But she had ordered me to go, and never to come there again. After a few minutes, I mustered strength, and started to obey her. With what feelings did I now close that little gate, which I used to open with such an eager hand in my childhood! It closed upon me with a sound I never heard before.

Where could I go? I was afraid to return to my master's. I walked on recklessly, not caring where I went, or what would become of me. When I had gone four or five miles, fatigue compelled me to stop. I sat down on the stump of an old tree. The stars were shining through the boughs above me. How they mocked me, with their bright, calm light! The hours passed by, and as I sat there alone a chilliness and deadly sickness came over me. I sank on the ground. My mind was full of horrid thoughts. I prayed to die; but the prayer was not answered. At last, with great effort I roused myself, and walked some distance further, to the house of a woman who had been a friend of my mother. When I told her why I was there, she spoke soothingly to me; but I could not be comforted. I thought I could bear my shame if I could only be reconciled to my grandmother. I longed to open my heart to her. I thought if she could know the real state of the case, and all I had been bearing for years, she would perhaps judge me less harshly. My friend advised me to send for her. I did so; but days of agonizing suspense passed before she came. Had she utterly forsaken me? No. She came at last. I knelt before her, and told her the things that had poisoned my life; how long I had been persecuted; that I saw no way of escape; and in an hour of extremity I had become desperate. She listened in silence. I told her I would bear any thing and do any thing, if in time I had hopes of obtaining her forgiveness. I begged of her to pity me, for my dead mother's sake. And she did pity me. She did not say, "I forgive you;" but she looked at me lovingly, with her eyes full of tears. She laid her old hand gently on my head, and murmured, "Poor child! Poor child!"

XI

The New Tie to Life

I returned to my good grandmother's house. She had an interview with Mr. Sands. When she asked him why he could not have left her one ewe lamb,—whether there were not plenty of slaves who did not care about character,—he made no answer; but he spoke kind and encouraging words. He promised to care for my child, and to buy me, be the conditions what they might.

I had not seen Dr. Flint for five days. I had never seen him since I made the avowal to him. He talked of the disgrace I had brought on myself; how I had sinned against my master, and mortified my old grandmother. He intimated that if I had accepted his proposals, he, as a physician, could have saved me from exposure. He even condescended to pity me. Could he have offered wormwood more bitter? He, whose persecutions had been the cause of my sin!

"Linda," said he, "though you have been criminal towards me, I feel for you, and I can pardon you if you obey my wishes. Tell me whether the fellow you wanted to marry is the father of your child. If you deceive me, you shall feel the fires of hell."

I did not feel as proud as I had done. My strongest weapon with him was gone. I was lowered in my own estimation, and had resolved to bear his abuse in silence. But when he spoke contemptuously of the lover who had always treated me honorably; when I remembered that but for *him* I might have been a virtuous, free, and happy wife, I lost my patience. "I have sinned against God and myself," I replied; "but not against you."

He clinched his teeth, and muttered, "Curse you!" He came towards me, with ill-suppressed rage, and exclaimed, "You obstinate girl! I could grind your bones to powder! You have thrown yourself away on some worthless rascal. You are weak-minded, and have been easily persuaded by those who don't care a straw for you. The future will settle accounts between us. You are blinded now; but hereafter you will be convinced that your master was your best friend. My lenity towards you is a proof of it. I might have punished you in many ways. I might have had you whipped till you fell dead under the lash. But I wanted you to live; I would have bettered your condition. Others cannot do it. You are my slave. Your mistress, disgusted by your conduct, forbids you to return to the house; therefore I leave you here for the present; but I shall see you often. I will call tomorrow."

He came with frowning brows, that showed a dissatisfied state of mind. After asking about my health, he inquired whether my board was paid, and who visited me. He then went on to say that he had neglected his duty; that as a physician there were certain things that he ought to have explained to me. Then followed talk such as would have made the most shameless blush. He ordered me to stand up before him. I obeyed. "I command you," said he, "to tell me whether the father of your child is white or black." I hesitated. "Answer me this instant!" he exclaimed. I did answer. He sprang upon me like a wolf, and grabbed my arm as if he would have broken it. "Do you love him?" said he, in a hissing tone.

"I am thankful that I do not despise him," I replied.

He raised his hand to strike me; but it fell again. I don't know what arrested the blow. He sat down, with lips tightly compressed. At last he spoke. "I came here," said he, "to make you a friendly proposition; but your ingratitude chafes me beyond endurance. You turn aside all my good intentions towards you. I don't know what it is that keeps me from killing you." Again he rose, as if he had a mind to strike me.

But he resumed. "On one condition I will forgive your insolence and crime. You must henceforth have no communication of any kind with the father of your child. You must not ask any thing from him, or receive any thing from him. I will take care of you and your child. You had better promise this at once, and not wait till you are deserted by him. This is the last act of mercy I shall show towards you."

I said something about being unwilling to have my child supported by a man who had cursed it and me also. He rejoined, that a woman who had sunk to my level had no right to expect any thing else. He asked, for the last time, would I accept his kindness? I answered that I would not.

"Very well," said he; "then take the consequences of your wayward course. Never look to me for help. You are my slave, and shall always be my slave. I will never sell you, that you may depend upon."

Hope died away in my heart as he closed the door after him. I had calculated that in his rage he would sell me to a slave-trader; and I knew the father of my child was on the watch to buy me.

About this time my uncle Phillip was expected to return from a voyage. The day before his departure I had officiated as bridesmaid to a young friend. My heart was then ill at ease, but my smiling countenance did not betray it. Only a year had passed; but what fearful changes it had wrought! My heart had grown gray in misery. Lives that flash in sunshine, and lives that are born in tears, receive their hue from circumstances. None of us know what a year may bring forth.

I felt no joy when they told me my uncle had come. He wanted to see me, though he knew what had happened. I shrank from him at first; but at last consented that he should come to my room. He received me as he always had done. O, how my heart smote me when I felt his tears on my burning cheeks! The words of my grandmother came to my mind,—"Perhaps your mother and father are taken from the evil days to come." My disappointed heart could now praise God that it was so. But why, thought I, did my relatives ever cherish hopes for me? What was there to save me from the usual fate of slave girls? Many more beautiful and more intelligent than I had experienced a similar fate, or a far worse one. How could they hope that I should escape?

My uncle's stay was short, and I was not sorry for it. I was too ill in mind and body to enjoy my friends as I had done. For some weeks I was unable to leave my bed. I could not have any doctor but my master, and I would not have him sent for. At last, alarmed by my increasing illness, they sent for him. I was very weak and nervous; and as soon as he entered the room, I began to scream. They told him my state was very critical. He had no wish to hasten me out of the world, and he withdrew.

When my babe was born, they said it was premature. It weighed only four pounds; but God let it live. I heard the doctor say I could not survive till morning. I had often prayed for death; but now I did not want to die, unless my child could die too. Many weeks passed before I was able to leave my bed. I was a mere wreck of my former self. For a year there was scarcely a day when I was free from chills and fever. My babe also was sickly. His little limbs were often racked with pain. Dr. Flint continued his visits, to look after my health; and he did not fail to remind me that my child was an addition to his stock of slaves.

I felt too feeble to dispute with him, and listened to his remarks in silence. His visits were less frequent; but his busy spirit could not remain quiet. He employed my brother in his office, and he was made the medium of frequent notes and messages to me. William was a bright lad, and of much use to the doctor. He had learned to put up medicines, to leech, cup, and bleed. He had taught himself to read and spell. I was proud of my brother; and the old doctor suspected as much. One day, when I had not seen him for several weeks, I heard his steps approaching the door. I dreaded the encounter, and hid myself. He inquired for me, of course; but I was nowhere to be found. He went to his office, and despatched William with a note. The color mounted to my brother's face when he gave it to me; and he said, "Don't you hate me, Linda, for bringing you these things?" I told him I could not blame him; he was a slave, and obliged to obey his master's will. The note ordered me to come to his office. I went. He demanded to know where I was when he called. I told him I was at home. He flew into a passion, and said he knew better. Then he launched out upon his usual themes,—my crimes against him, and my ingratitude for his forbearance. The laws were laid down to me anew, and I was dismissed. I felt humiliated that my brother should stand by, and listen to such language as would be addressed only to a slave. Poor boy! He was powerless to defend me; but I saw the tears, which he vainly strove to keep back. This manifestation of feeling irritated the doctor. William could do nothing to please him. One morning he did not arrive at the office so early as usual; and that circumstance afforded his master an opportunity to vent his spleen. He was put in jail. The next day my brother sent a trader to the doctor, with a request to be sold. His master was greatly incensed at what he called his insolence. He said he had put him there to reflect upon his bad conduct, and he certainly was not giving any evidence of repentance. For two days he harassed himself to find somebody to do his office work; but every thing went wrong without William. He was released, and ordered to take his old stand, with many threats, if he was not careful about his future behavior.

As the months passed on, my boy improved in health. When he was a year old, they called him beautiful. The little vine was taking deep root in my existence, though its clinging fondness excited a mixture of love and pain. When I was most sorely oppressed I found a solace in his smiles. I loved to watch his infant slumbers; but always there was a dark cloud over my enjoyment. I could never forget that he was a slave. Sometimes I wished that he might die in infancy. God tried me. My darling became very ill. The bright eyes grew dull, and the little feet and hands were so icy cold that I thought death had already touched them. I had prayed for his death, but never so earnestly as I now prayed for his life; and my prayer was heard. Alas, what mockery it is for a slave mother to try to pray back her dying child to life! Death is better than slavery. It was a sad thought that I had no name to give my child. His father caressed him and treated him kindly, whenever he had a chance to see him. He was not unwilling that he should bear his name; but he had no legal claim to it; and if I had bestowed it upon him, my master would have regarded it as a new crime, a new piece of insolence, and would, perhaps, revenge it on the boy. O, the serpent of Slavery has many and poisonous fangs!

XIV

Another Link to Life

I had not returned to my master's house since the birth of my child. The old man raved to have me thus removed from his immediate power; but his wife vowed, by all that was good and great, she would kill me if I came back; and he did not doubt her word. Sometimes he would stay away for a season. Then he would come and renew the old threadbare discourse about his forbearance and my ingratitude. He labored, most unnecessarily, to convince me that I had lowered myself. The venomous old reprobate had no need of descanting on that theme. I felt humiliated enough. My unconscious babe was the ever-present witness of my shame. I listened with silent contempt when he talked about my having forfeited *his* good opinion; but I shed bitter tears that I was no longer worthy of being respected by the good and pure. Alas! slavery still held me in its poisonous grasp. There was no chance for me to be respectable. There was no prospect of being able to lead a better life.

Sometimes, when my master found that I still refused to accept what he called his kind offers, he would threaten to sell my child. "Perhaps that will humble you," said he.

Humble *me!* Was I not already in the dust? But his threat lacerated my heart. I knew the law gave him power to fulfil it; for slaveholders have been cunning enough to enact that "the child shall follow the condition of the *mother*" not of the *father*; thus taking care that licentiousness shall not interfere with avarice. This reflection made me clasp my innocent babe all the more firmly to my heart. Horrid visions passed through my mind when I thought of his liability to fall into the slave trader's hands. I wept over him, and said, "O my child! perhaps they will leave you in some cold cabin to die, and then throw you into a hole, as if you were a dog."

When Dr. Flint learned that I was again to be a mother, he was exasperated beyond measure. He rushed from the house, and returned with a pair of shears. I had a fine head of hair; and he often railed about my pride of arranging it nicely. He cut every hair close to my head, storming and swearing all the time. I replied to some of his abuse, and he struck me. Some months before, he had pitched me down stairs in a fit of passion; and the injury I received was so serious that I was unable to turn myself in bed for many days. He then said, "Linda, I swear by God I will never raise my hand against you again"; but I knew that he would forget his promise.

After he discovered my situation, he was like a restless spirit from the pit. He came every day; and I was subjected to such insults as no pen can describe. I would not describe them if I could; they were too low, too revolting. I tried to keep them from my grandmother's knowledge as much as I could. I knew she had enough to sadden her life, without having my troubles to bear. When she saw the doctor treat me with violence, and heard him utter oaths terrible enough to palsy a man's tongue, she could not always hold her peace. It was natural and motherlike that she should try to defend me; but it only made matters worse.

When they told me my new-born babe was a girl, my heart was heavier than it had ever been before. Slavery is terrible for men; but it is far more terrible for women. Superadded to the burden common to all, *they* have wrongs, and sufferings, and mortifications peculiarly their own.

Dr. Flint had sworn that he would make me suffer, to my last day, for this new crime against *him*, as he called it; and as long as he had me in his power he kept his word. On the fourth day after the birth of my babe, he entered my room suddenly, and commanded me to rise and bring my baby to him. The nurse who took care of me had gone out of the room to prepare some nourishment, and I was alone. There was no alternative. I rose, took up my babe, and crossed the room to where he sat. "Now stand there," said he, "till I tell you to go back!" My child bore a strong resemblance to her father, and to the deceased Mrs. Sands, her grandmother. He noticed this; and while I stood before him, trembling with weakness, he heaped upon me and my little one every vile epithet he could think of. Even the grandmother in her grave did not escape his curses. In the midst of his vituperations I fainted at his feet. This recalled him to his senses. He took the baby from my arms, laid it on the bed, dashed cold water in my face, took me up, and shook me violently, to restore my consciousness before any one entered the room. Just then my grandmother came in, and he hurried out of the house. I suffered in consequence of this treatment; but I begged my friends to let me die, rather than send for the doctor. There was nothing I dreaded so much as his presence. My life was spared; and I was glad for the sake of my little ones. Had it not been for these ties to life, I should have been glad to be released by death, though I had lived only nineteen years.

Always it gave me a pang that my children had no lawful claim to a name. Their father offered his; but, if I had wished to accept the offer, I dared not while my master lived. Moreover, I knew it would not be accepted at their baptism. A Christian name they were at least entitled to; and we resolved to call my boy for our dear good Benjamin, who had gone far away from us.

My grandmother belonged to the church; and she was very desirous of having the children christened. I knew Dr. Flint would forbid it, and I did not venture to attempt it. But chance favored me. He was called to visit a patient out of town, and was obliged to be absent during Sunday. "Now is the time," said my grandmother; "we will take the children to church, and have them christened."

When I entered the church, recollections of my mother came over me, and I felt subdued in spirit. There she had presented me for baptism, without any reason to feel ashamed. She had been married, and had such legal rights as slavery allows to a slave. The vows had at least been sacred to *her*, and she had never violated them. I was glad she was not alive, to know under what different circumstances her grandchildren were presented for baptism. Why had my lot been so different from my mother's? *Her* master had died when she was a child; and she remained with her mistress till she married. She was never in the power of any master; and thus she escaped one class of the evils that generally fall upon slaves.

When my baby was about to be christened, the former mistress of my father stepped up to me, and proposed to give it her Christian name. To this I added the surname of my father, who had himself no legal right to it; for my grandfather on the paternal side was a white gentleman. What tangled skeins are the genealogies of slavery! I loved my father; but it mortified me to be obliged to bestow his name on my children.

When we left the church, my father's old mistress invited me to go home with her. She clasped a gold chain around my baby's neck. I thanked her for this kindness; but I did not like the emblem. I wanted no chain to be fastened on my daughter, not even if its links were of gold. How earnestly I prayed that she might never feel the weight of slavery's chain, whose iron entereth into the soul!

XV

Continued Persecutions

My children grew finely; and Dr. Flint would often say to me, with an exulting smile, "These brats will bring me a handsome sum of money one of these days."

I thought to myself that, God being my helper, they should never pass into his hands. It seemed to me I would rather see them killed than have them given up to his power. The money for the freedom of myself and my children could be obtained; but I derived no advantage from that circumstance. Dr. Flint loved money, but he loved power more. After much discussion, my friends resolved on making another trial. There was a slaveholder about to leave for Texas, and he was commissioned to buy me. He was to begin with nine hundred dollars, and go up to twelve. My master refused his offers. "Sir," said he, "she don't belong to me. She is my daughter's property, and I have no right to sell her. I mistrust that you come from her paramour. If so, you may tell him that he cannot buy her for any money; neither can he buy her children."

The doctor came to see me the next day, and my heart beat quicker as he entered. I never had seen the old man tread with so majestic a step. He seated himself and looked at me with withering scorn. My children had learned to be afraid of him. The little one would shut her eyes and hide her face on my shoulder whenever she saw him; and Benny, who was now nearly five years old, often inquired, "What makes that bad man come here so many times? Does he want to hurt us?" I would clasp the dear boy in my arms, trusting that he would be free before he was old enough to solve the problem. And now, as the doctor sat there so grim and silent, the child left his play and came and nestled up by me. At last my tormentor spoke. "So you are left in disgust, are you?" said he. "It is no more than I expected. You remember I told you years ago that you would be treated so. So he is tired of you? Ha! ha! ha! The virtuous madam don't like to hear about it, does she? Ha! ha! ha!" There was a sting in his calling me virtuous madam. I no longer had the power of answering him as I had formerly done. He continued: "So it seems you are trying to get up another intrigue. Your new paramour came to me, and offered to buy you; but you may be assured you will not succeed. You are mine; and you shall be mine for life. There lives no human being that can take you out of slavery. I would have done it; but you rejected my kind offer."

I told him I did not wish to get up any intrigue; that I had never seen the man who offered to buy me.

"Do you tell me I lie?" exclaimed he, dragging me from my chair. "Will you say again that you never saw that man?"

I answered, "I do say so."

He clinched my arm with a volley of oaths. Ben began to scream, and I told him to go to his grandmother.

"Don't you stir a step, you little wretch!" said he. The child drew nearer to me, and put his arms round me, as if he wanted to protect me. This was too much for my enraged master. He caught him up and hurled him across the room. I thought he was dead, and rushed towards him to take him up.

"Not yet!" exclaimed the doctor. "Let him lie there till he comes to."

"Let me go! Let me go!" I screamed, "or I will raise the whole house." I struggled and got away; but he clinched me again. Somebody opened the door, and he released me. I picked up my insensible child, and when I turned my tormentor was gone. Anxiously I bent over the little form, so pale and still; and when the brown eyes at last opened, I don't know whether I was very happy.

All the doctor's former persecutions were renewed. He came morning, noon, and night. No jealous lover ever watched a rival more closely than he watched me and the unknown slaveholder, with whom he accused me of wishing to get up an intrigue. When my grandmother was out of the way he searched every room to find him.

In one of his visits, he happened to find a young girl, whom he had sold to a trader a few days previous. His statement was, that he sold her because she had been too familiar with the overseer. She had had a bitter life with him, and was glad to be sold. She had no mother, and no near ties. She had been torn from all her family years before. A few friends had entered into bonds for her safety, if the trader would allow her to spend with them the time that intervened between her sale and the gathering up of his human stock. Such a favor was rarely granted. It saved the trader the expense of board and jail fees, and though the amount was small, it was a weighty consideration in a slave-trader's mind.

Dr. Flint always had an aversion to meeting slaves after he had sold them. He ordered Rose out of the house; but he was no longer her master, and she took no notice of him. For once the crushed Rose was the conqueror. His gray eyes flashed angrily upon her; but that was the extent of his power. "How came this girl here?" he exclaimed. "What right had you to allow it, when you knew I had sold her?"

I answered "This is my grandmother's house, and Rose came to see her. I have no right to turn any body out of doors, that comes here for honest purposes."

He gave me the blow that would have fallen upon Rose if she had still been his slave. My grandmother's attention had been attracted by loud voices, and she entered in time to see a second blow dealt. She was not a woman to let such an outrage, in her own house, go unrebuked. The doctor undertook to explain that I had been insolent. Her indignant feelings rose higher and higher, and finally boiled over in words. "Get out of my house!" she exclaimed. "Go home, and take care of your wife and children, and you will have enough to do, without watching my family."

He threw the birth of my children in her face, and accused her of sanctioning the life I was leading. She told him I was living with her by compulsion of his wife; that he needn't accuse her, for he was the one to blame; he was the one who had caused all the trouble. She grew more and more excited as she went on. "I tell you what, Dr. Flint," said she, "you ain't got many more years to live, and you'd better be saying your prayers. It will take 'em all, and more too, to wash the dirt off your soul."

"Do you know whom you are talking to?" he exclaimed.

She replied, "Yes, I know very well who I am talking to."

He left the house in a great rage. I looked at my grandmother. Our eyes met. Their angry expression had passed away, but she looked sorrowful and weary—weary of incessant strife. I wondered that it did not lessen her love for me; but if it did she never showed it. She was always kind, always ready to sympathize with my troubles. There might have been peace and contentment in that humble home if it had not been for the demon Slavery.

The winter passed undisturbed by the doctor. The beautiful spring came; and when Nature resumes her loveliness, the human soul is apt to revive also. My drooping hopes came to life again with the flowers. I was dreaming of freedom again; more for my children's sake than my own. I planned and I planned. Obstacles hit against plans. There seemed no way of overcoming them; and yet I hoped.

Back came the wily doctor. I was not at home when he called. A friend had invited me to a small party, and to gratify her I went. To my great consternation, a messenger came in haste to say that Dr. Flint was at my grandmother's, and insisted on seeing me. They did not tell him where I was, or he would have come and raised a disturbance in my friend's house. They sent me a dark wrapper; I threw it on and hurried home. My speed did not save me; the doctor had gone away in anger. I dreaded the morning, but I could not delay it; it came, warm and bright. At an early hour the doctor came and asked me where I had been last night. I told him. He did not believe me, and sent to my friend's house to ascertain the facts. He came in the afternoon to assure me he was satisfied that I had spoken the truth. He seemed to be in a facetious mood, and I expected some jeers were coming. "I suppose you need some recreation," said he, "but I am surprised at your being there, among those negroes. It was not the place for *you*. Are you *allowed* to visit such people?"

I understood this covert fling at the white gentleman who was my friend; but I merely replied, "I went to visit my friends, and any company they keep is good enough for me."

He went on to say, "I have seen very little of you of late, but my interest in you is unchanged. When I said I would have no more mercy on you I was rash. I recall my words. Linda, you desire freedom for yourself and your children, and you can obtain it only through me. If you agree to what I am about to propose, you and they shall be free. There must be no communication of any kind between you and their father. I will procure a cottage, where you and the children can live together. Your labor shall be light, such as sewing for my family. Think what is offered you, Linda—a home and freedom! Let the past be forgotten. If I have been harsh with you at times, your wilfulness drove me to it. You know I exact obedience from my own children, and I consider you as yet a child."

He paused for an answer, but I remained silent.

"Why don't you speak?" said he. "What more do you wait for?"

"Nothing, sir."

"Then you accept my offer?"

"No, sir."

His anger was ready to break loose; but he succeeded in curbing it, and replied, "You have answered without thought. But I must let you know there are two sides to my proposition; if you reject the bright side, you will be obliged to take the dark one. You must either accept my offer, or you and your children shall be sent to your young master's plantation, there to remain till your young mistress is married; and your children shall fare like the rest of the negro children. I give you a week to consider of it."

He was shrewd; but I knew he was not to be trusted. I told him I was ready to give my answer now.

"I will not receive it now," he replied. "You act too much from impulse. Remember that you and your children can be free a week from today if you choose."

On what a monstrous chance hung the destiny of my children! I knew that my master's offer was a snare, and that if I entered it escape would be impossible. As for his promise, I knew him so well that I was sure if he gave me free papers, they would be so managed as to have no legal value. The alternative was inevitable. I resolved to go to the plantation. But then I thought how completely I should be in his power, and the prospect was appalling. Even if I should kneel before him, and implore him to spare me, for the sake of my children, I knew he would spurn me with his foot, and my weakness would be his triumph.

Before the week expired, I heard that young Mr. Flint was about to be married to a lady of his own stamp. I foresaw the position I should occupy in his establishment. I had once been sent to the plantation for punishment, and fear of the son had induced the father to recall me very soon. My mind was made up; I was resolved that I would foil my master and save my children, or I would perish in the attempt. I kept my plans to myself; I knew that friends would try to dissuade me from them, and I would not wound their feelings by rejecting their advice.

On the decisive day the doctor came, and said he hoped I had made a wise choice.

"I am ready to go to the plantation, sir," I replied.

"Have you thought how important your decision is to your children?" said he.

I told him I had.

"Very well. Go to the plantation, and my curse go with you," he replied. "Your boy shall be put to work, and he shall soon be sold; and your girl shall be raised for the purpose of selling well. Go your own ways!" He left the room with curses, not to be repeated.

As I stood rooted to the spot, my grandmother came and said, "Linda, child, what did you tell him?"

I answered that I was going to the plantation.

"*Must* you go?" said she. "Can't something be done to stop it?"

I told her it was useless to try; but she begged me not to give up. She said she would go to the doctor, and remind him how long and how faithfully she had served in the family, and how she had taken her own baby from her breast to nourish his wife. She would tell him I had been out of the family so long they would not miss me; that she would pay them for my time, and the money would procure a woman who had more strength for the situation than I had. I begged her not to go; but she persisted in saying, "He will listen to *me,* Linda." She went, and was treated as I expected. He coolly listened to what she said, but denied her request. He told her that what he did was for my good, that my feelings were entirely above my situation, and that on the plantation I would receive treatment that was suitable to my behavior.

My grandmother was much cast down. I had my secret hopes; but I must fight my battle alone. I had a woman's pride, and a mother's love for my children; and I resolved that out of the darkness of this hour a brighter dawn should rise for them. My master had power and law on his side; I had a determined will. There is might in each.

XVI

Scenes at the Plantation

Early the next morning I left my grandmother's with my youngest child. My boy was ill, and I left him behind. I had many sad thoughts as the old wagon jolted on. Hitherto, I had suffered alone; now, my little one was to be treated as a slave. As we drew near the great house, I thought of the time when I was formerly sent there out of revenge. I wondered for what purpose I was now sent. I could not tell. I resolved to obey orders so far as duty required; but within myself, I determined to make my stay as short as possible. Mr. Flint was waiting to receive us, and told me to follow him up stairs to receive orders for the day. My little Ellen was left below in the kitchen. It was a change for her, who had always been so carefully tended. My young master said she might amuse herself in the yard. This was kind of him, since the child was hateful to his sight. My task was to fit up the house for the reception of the bride. In the midst of sheets, tablecloths, towels, drapery, and carpeting, my head was as busy planning, as were my fingers with the needle. At noon I was allowed to go to Ellen. She had sobbed herself to sleep. I heard Mr. Flint say to a neighbor, "I've got her down here, and I'll soon take the town notions out of her head. My father is partly to blame for her nonsense. He ought to have broke her in long ago." The remark was made within my hearing, and it would have been quite as manly to have made it to my face. He *had* said things to my face which might, or might not, have surprised his neighbor if he had known of them. He was "a chip of the old block."

I resolved to give him no cause to accuse me of being too much of a lady, so far as work was concerned. I worked day and night, with wretchedness before me. When I lay down beside my child, I felt how much easier it would be to see her die than to see her master beat her about, as I daily saw him beat other little ones. The spirit of the mothers was so crushed by the lash, that they stood by, without courage to remonstrate. How much more must I suffer, before I should be "broke in" to that degree?

I wished to appear as contented as possible. Sometimes I had an opportunity to send a few lines home; and this brought up recollections that made it difficult, for a time, to seem calm and indifferent to my lot. Notwithstanding my efforts, I saw that Mr. Flint regarded me with a suspicious eye. Ellen broke down under the trials of her new life. Separated from me, with no one to look after her, she wandered about, and in a few days cried herself sick. One day, she sat under the window where I was at work, crying that weary cry which makes a mother's heart bleed. I was obliged to steel myself to bear it. After a while it ceased. I looked out, and she was gone. As it was near noon, I ventured to go down in search of her. The great house was raised two feet above the ground. I looked under it, and saw her about midway, fast asleep. I crept under and drew her out. As I held her in my arms, I thought how well it would be for her if she never waked up; and I uttered my thought aloud. I was startled to hear some one say, "Did you speak to me?" I looked up, and saw Mr. Flint standing beside me. He said nothing further, but turned, frowning, away. That night he sent Ellen a biscuit and a cup of sweetened milk. This generosity surprised me. I learned afterwards, that in the afternoon he had killed a large snake, which crept from under the house; and I supposed that incident had prompted his unusual kindness.

The next morning the old cart was loaded with shingles for town. I put Ellen into it, and sent her to her grandmother. Mr. Flint said I ought to have asked his permission. I told him the child was sick, and required attention which I had no time to give. He let it pass; for he was aware that I had accomplished much work in a little time.

I had been three weeks on the plantation, when I planned a visit home. It must be at night, after every body was in bed. I was six miles from town, and the road was very dreary. I was to go with a young man, who, I knew, often stole to town to see his mother. One night, when all was quiet, we started. Fear gave speed to our steps, and we were not long in performing the journey. I arrived at my grandmother's. Her bed room was on the first floor, and the window was open, the weather being warm. I spoke to her and she awoke. She let me in and closed the window, lest some late passerby should see me. A light was brought, and the whole household gathered round me, some smiling and some crying. I went to look at my children, and thanked God for their happy sleep. The tears fell as I leaned over them. As I moved to leave, Benny stirred. I turned back, and whispered, "Mother is here." After digging at his eyes with his little fist, they opened, and he sat up in bed, looking at me curiously. Having satisfied himself that it was I, he exclaimed, "O mother! you ain't dead, are you? They didn't cut off your head at the plantation, did they?"

My time was up too soon, and my guide was waiting for me. I laid Benny back in his bed, and dried his tears by a promise to come again soon. Rapidly we retraced our steps back to the plantation. About half way we were met by a company of four patrols. Luckily we heard their horses' hoofs before they came in sight, and we had time to hide behind a large tree. They passed, hallooing and shouting in a manner that indicated a recent carousal. How thankful we were that they had not their dogs with them! We hastened our footsteps, and when we arrived on the plantation we heard the sound of the hand-mill. The slaves were grinding their corn. We were safely in the house before the horn summoned them to their labor. I divided my little parcel of food with my guide, knowing that he had lost the chance of grinding his corn, and must toil all day in the field.

Mr. Flint often took an inspection of the house, to see that no one was idle. The entire management of the work was trusted to me, because he knew nothing about it; and rather than hire a superintendent he contented himself with my arrangements. He had often urged upon his father the necessity of having me at the plantation to take charge of his affairs, and make clothes for the slaves; but the old man knew him too well to consent to that arrangement.

When I had been working a month at the plantation, the great aunt of Mr. Flint came to make him a visit. This was the good old lady who paid fifty dollars for my grandmother, for the purpose of making her free, when she stood on the auction block. My grandmother loved this old lady, whom we all called Miss Fanny. She often came to take tea with us. On such occasions the table was spread with a snow-white cloth, and the china cups and silver spoons were taken from the old-fashioned buffet. There were hot muffins, tea rusks, and delicious sweetmeats. My grandmother kept two cows, and the fresh cream was Miss Fanny's delight. She invariably declared that it was the best in town. The old ladies had cosey times together. They would work and chat, and sometimes, while talking over old times, their spectacles would get dim with tears, and would have to be taken off and wiped. When Miss Fanny bade us good by, her bag was filled with grandmother's best cakes, and she was urged to come again soon.

There had been a time when Dr. Flint's wife came to take tea with us, and when her children were also sent to have a feast of "Aunt Marthy's" nice cooking. But after I became an object of her jealousy and spite, she was angry with grandmother for giving a shelter to me and my children. She would not even speak to her in the street. This wounded my grandmother's feelings, for she could not retain ill will against the woman whom she had nourished with her milk when a babe.

The doctor's wife would gladly have prevented our intercourse with Miss Fanny if she could have done it, but fortunately she was not dependent on the bounty of the Flints. She had enough to be independent; and that is more than can ever be gained from charity, however lavish it may be.

Miss Fanny was endeared to me by many recollections, and I was rejoiced to see her at the plantation. The warmth of her large, loyal heart made the house seem pleasanter while she was in it. She staid a week, and I had many talks with her. She said her principal object in coming was to see how I was treated, and whether any thing could be done for me. She inquired whether she could help me in any way. I told her I believed not. She condoled with me in her own peculiar way; saying she wished that I and all my grandmother's family were at rest in our graves, for not until then should she feel any peace about us. The good old soul did not dream that I was planning to bestow peace upon her, with regard to myself and my children; not by death, but by securing our freedom.

Again and again I had traversed those dreary twelve miles, to and from the town; and all the way, I was meditating upon some means of escape for myself and my children. My friends had made every effort that ingenuity could devise to effect our purchase, but all their plans had proved abortive. Dr. Flint was suspicious, and determined not to loosen his grasp upon us. I could have made my escape alone; but it was more for my helpless children than for myself that I longed for freedom. Though the boon would have been precious to me, above all price, I would not have taken it at the expense of leaving them in slavery. Every trial I endured, every sacrifice I made for their sakes, drew them closer to my heart, and gave me fresh courage to beat back the dark waves that rolled and rolled over me in a seemingly endless night of storms.

The six weeks were nearly completed, when Mr. Flint's bride was expected to take possession of her new home. The arrangements were all completed, and Mr. Flint said I had done well. He expected to leave home on Saturday, and return with his bride the following Wednesday. After receiving various orders from him, I ventured to ask permission to spend Sunday in town. It was granted; for which favor I was thankful. It was the first I had ever asked of him, and I intended it should be the last. It needed more than one night to accomplish the project I had in view; but the whole of Sunday would give me an opportunity. I spent the Sabbath with my grandmother. A calmer, more beautiful day never came down out of heaven. To me it was a day of conflicting emotions. Perhaps it was the last day I should ever spend under that dear, old sheltering roof! Perhaps these were the last talks I should ever have with the faithful old friend of my whole life! Perhaps it was the last time I and my children should be together! Well, better so, I thought, than that they should be slaves. I knew the doom that awaited my fair baby in slavery, and I determined to save her from it, or perish in the attempt. I went to make this vow at the graves of my poor parents, in the burying-ground of the slaves. "There the wicked cease from troubling, and there the weary be at rest. There the prisoners rest together; they hear not the voice of the oppressor; the servant is free from his master." I knelt by the graves of my parents, and thanked God, as I had often done before, that they had not lived to witness my trials, or to mourn over my sins. I had received my mother's blessing when she died; and in many an hour of tribulation I had seemed to hear her voice, sometimes chiding me, sometimes whispering loving words into my wounded heart. I have shed many and bitter tears, to think that when I am gone from my children they cannot remember me with such entire satisfaction as I remembered my mother.

The graveyard was in the woods, and twilight was coming on. Nothing broke the deathlike stillness except the occasional twitter of a bird. My spirit was overawed by the solemnity of the scene. For more than ten years I had frequented this spot, but never had it seemed to me so sacred as now. A black stump, at the head of my mother's grave, was all that remained of a tree my father had planted. His grave was marked by a small wooden board, bearing his name, the letters of which were nearly obliterated. I knelt down and kissed them, and poured forth a prayer to God for guidance and support in the perilous step I was about to take. As I passed the wreck of the old meeting house, where, before Nat Turner's time, the slaves had been allowed to meet for worship, I seemed to hear my father's voice come from it, bidding me not to tarry till I reached freedom or the grave. I rushed on with renovated hopes. My trust in God had been strengthened by that prayer among the graves.

My plan was to conceal myself at the house of a friend, and remain there a few weeks till the search was over. My hope was that the doctor would get discouraged, and, for fear of losing my value, and also of subsequently finding my children among the missing, he would consent to sell us; and I knew somebody would buy us. I had done all in my power to make my children comfortable during the time I expected to be separated from them. I was packing my things, when grandmother came into the room, and asked what I was doing. "I am putting my things in order," I replied. I tried to took and speak cheerfully; but her watchful eye detected something beneath the surface. She drew me towards her, and asked me to sit down. She looked earnestly at me, and said, "Linda, do you want to kill your old grandmother? Do you mean to leave your little, helpless children? I am old now, and cannot do for your babies as I once did for you."

I replied, that if I went away, perhaps their father would be able to secure their freedom.

"Ah, my child," said she, "don't trust too much to him. Stand by your own children, and suffer with them till death. Nobody respects a mother who forsakes her children; and if you leave them, you will never have a happy moment. If you go, you will make me miserable the short time I have to live. You would be taken and brought back, and your sufferings would be dreadful. Remember poor Benjamin. Do give it up, Linda. Try to bear a little longer. Things may turn out better than we expect."

My courage failed me, in view of the sorrow I should bring on that faithful, loving old heart. I promised that I would try longer, and that I would take nothing out of her house without her knowledge.

Whenever the children climbed on my knee, or laid their heads on my lap, she would say, "Poor little souls! what would you do without a mother? She don't love you as I do." And she would hug them to her own bosom, as if to reproach me for my want of affection; but she knew all the while that I loved them better than my life. I slept with her that night, and it was the last time. The memory of it haunted me for many a year.

On Monday I returned to the plantation, and busied myself with preparations for the important day. Wednesday came. It was a beautiful day, and the faces of the slaves were as bright as the sunshine. The poor creatures were merry. They were expecting little presents from the bride, and hoping for better times under her administration. I had no such hopes for them. I knew that the young wives of slaveholders often thought their authority and importance would be best established and maintained by cruelty; and what I had heard of young Mrs. Flint gave me no reason to expect that her rule over them would be less severe than that of the master and overseer. Truly, the colored race are the most cheerful and forgiving people on the face of the earth. That their masters sleep in safety is owing to their superabundance of heart; and yet they look upon their sufferings with less pity than they would bestow on those of a horse or a dog.

I stood at the door with others to receive the bridegroom and bride. She was a handsome, delicate-looking girl, and her face flushed with emotion at sight of her new home. I thought it likely that visions of a happy future were rising before her. It made me sad; for I knew how soon clouds would come over her sunshine. She examined every part of the house, and told me she was delighted with the arrangements I had made. I was afraid old Mrs. Flint had tried to prejudice her against me, and I did my best to please her.

All passed off smoothly for me until dinner time arrived. I did not mind the embarrassment of waiting on a dinner party, for the first time in my life, half so much as I did the meeting with Dr. Flint and his wife, who would be among the guests. It was a mystery to me why Mrs. Flint had not made her appearance at the plantation during all the time I was putting the house in order. I had not met her, face to face, for five years, and I had no wish to see her now. She was a praying woman, and, doubtless, considered my present position a special answer to her prayers. Nothing could please her better than to see me humbled and trampled upon. I was just where she would have me—in the power of a hard, unprincipled master. She did not speak to me when she took her seat at table; but her satisfied, triumphant smile, when I handed her plate, was more eloquent than words. The old doctor was not so quiet in his demonstrations. He ordered me here and there, and spoke with peculiar emphasis when he said "your *mistress*." I was drilled like a disgraced soldier. When all was over, and the last key turned, I sought my pillow, thankful that God had appointed a season of rest for the weary.

The next day my new mistress began her housekeeping. I was not exactly appointed maid of all work; but I was to do whatever I was told. Monday evening came. It was always a busy time. On that night the slaves received their weekly allowance of food. Three pounds of meat, a peck of corn, and perhaps a dozen herring were allowed to each man. Women received a pound and a half of meat, a peck of corn, and the same number of herring. Children over twelve years old had half the allowance of the women. The meat was cut and weighed by the foreman of the field hands, and piled on planks before the meat house. Then the second foreman went behind the building, and when the first foreman called out, "Who takes this piece of meat?" he answered by calling somebody's name. This method was resorted to as means of preventing partiality in distributing the meat. The young mistress came out to see how things were done on her plantation, and she soon gave a specimen of her character. Among those in waiting for their allowance was a very old slave, who had faithfully served the Flint family through three generations. When he hobbled up to get his bit of meat, the mistress said he was too old to have any allowance; that when niggers were too old to work, they ought to be fed on grass. Poor old man! He suffered much before he found rest in the grave.

My mistress and I got along very well together. At the end of a week, old Mrs. Flint made us another visit, and was closeted a long time with her daughter-in-law. I had my suspicions what was the subject of the conference. The old doctor's wife had been informed that I could leave the plantation on one condition, and she was very desirous to keep me there. If she had trusted me, as I deserved to be trusted by her, she would have had no fears of my accepting that condition. When she entered her carriage to return home, she said to young Mrs. Flint, "Don't neglect to send for them as quick as possible." My heart was on the watch all the time, and I at once concluded that she spoke of my children. The doctor came the next day, and as I entered the room to spread the tea table, I heard him say, "Don't wait any longer. Send for them to-morrow." I saw through the plan. They thought my children's being there would fetter me to the spot, and that it was a good place to break us all in to abject submission to our lot as slaves. After the doctor left, a gentleman called, who had always manifested friendly feelings towards my grandmother and her family. Mr. Flint carried him over the plantation to show him the results of labor performed by men and women who were unpaid, miserably clothed, and half famished. The cotton crop was all they thought of. It was duly admired, and the gentleman returned with specimens to show his friends. I was ordered to carry water to wash his hands. As I did so, he said, "Linda, how do you like your new home?" I told him I liked it as well as I expected. He replied, "They don't think you are contented, and to-morrow they are going to bring your children to be with you. I am sorry for you, Linda. I hope they will treat you kindly." I hurried from the room, unable to thank him. My suspicions were correct. My children were to be brought to the plantation to be "broke in."

To this day I feel grateful to the gentleman who gave me this timely information. It nerved me to immediate action.

XVII

The Flight

Mr. Flint was hard pushed for house servants, and rather than lose me he had restrained his malice. I did my work faithfully, though not, of course, with a willing mind. They were evidently afraid I should leave them. Mr. Flint wished that I should sleep in the great house instead of the servants' quarters. His wife agreed to the proposition, but said I mustn't bring my bed into the house, because it would scatter feathers on her carpet. I knew when I went there that they would never think of such a thing as furnishing a bed of any kind for me and my little one. I therefore carried my own bed, and now I was forbidden to use it. I did as I was ordered. But now that I was certain my children were to be put in their power, in order to give them a stronger hold on me, I resolved to leave them that night. I remembered the grief this step would bring upon my dear old grandmother; and nothing less than the freedom of my children would have induced me to disregard her advice. I went about my evening work with trembling steps. Mr. Flint twice called from his chamber door to inquire why the house was not locked up. I replied that I had not done my work. "You have had time enough to do it," said he. "Take care how you answer me!"

I shut all the windows, locked all the doors, and went up to the third story, to wait till midnight. How long those hours seemed, and how fervently I prayed that God would not forsake me in this hour of utmost need! I was about to risk every thing on the throw of a die; and if I failed, O what would become of me and my poor children? They would be made to suffer for my fault.

At half past twelve I stole softly down stairs. I stopped on the second floor, thinking I heard a noise. I felt my way down into the parlor, and looked out of the window. The night was so intensely dark that I could see nothing. I raised the window very softly and jumped out. Large drops of rain were falling, and the darkness bewildered me. I dropped on my knees, and breathed a short prayer to God for guidance and protection. I groped my way to the road, and rushed towards the town with almost lightning speed. I arrived at my grandmother's house, but dared not see her. She would say, "Linda, you are killing me"; and I knew that would unnerve me. I tapped softly at the window of a room, occupied by a woman, who had lived in the house several years. I knew she was a faithful friend, and could be trusted with my secret. I tapped several times before she heard me. At last she raised the window, and I whispered, "Sally, I have run away. Let me in, quick." She opened the door softly, and said in low tones, "For God's sake, don't. Your grandmother is trying to buy you and de chillern. Mr. Sands was here last week. He tole her he was going away on business, but he wanted her to go ahead about buying you and de chillern, and he would help her all he could. Don't run away, Linda. Your grandmother is all bowed down wid trouble now."

I replied, "Sally, they are going to carry my children to the plantation to-morrow; and they will never sell them to any body so long as they have me in their power. Now, would you advise me to go back?"

"No, chile, no," answered she. "When dey finds you is gone, dey won't want de plague ob de chillern; but where is you going to hide? Dey knows ebery inch ob dis house."

I told her I had a hiding-place, and that was all it was best for her to know. I asked her to go into my room as soon as it was light, and take all my clothes out of my trunk, and pack them in hers; for I knew Mr. Flint and the constable would be there early to search my room. I feared the sight of my children would be too much for my full heart; but I could not go out into the uncertain future without one last look. I bent over the bed where lay my little Benny and baby Ellen. Poor little ones! fatherless and motherless! Memories of their father came over me. He wanted to be kind to them; but they were not all to him, as they were to my womanly heart. I knelt and prayed for the innocent little sleepers. I kissed them lightly, and turned away.

As I was about to open the street door, Sally laid her hand on my shoulder, and said, "Linda, is you gwine all alone? Let me call your uncle."

"No, Sally," I replied, "I want no one to be brought into trouble on my account."

I went forth into the darkness and rain. I ran on till I came to the house of the friend who was to conceal me.

Early the next morning Mr. Flint was at my grandmother's inquiring for me. She told him she had not seen me, and supposed I was at the plantation. He watched her face narrowly, and said, "Don't you know any thing about her running off?" She assured him that she did not. He went on to say, "Last night she ran off without the least provocation. We had treated her very kindly. My wife liked her. She will soon be found and brought back. Are her children with you?" When told that they were, he said, "I am very glad to hear that. If they are here, she cannot be far off. If I find out that any of my niggers have had any thing to do with this damned business, I'll give 'em five hundred lashes." As he started to go to his father's, he turned round and added, persuasively, "Let her be brought back, and she shall have her children to live with her."

The tidings made the old doctor rave and storm at a furious rate. It was a busy day for them. My grandmother's house was searched from top to bottom. As my trunk was empty, they concluded I had taken my clothes with me. Before ten o'clock every vessel northward bound was thoroughly examined, and the law against harboring fugitives was read to all on board. At night a watch was set over the town. Knowing how distressed my grandmother would be, I wanted to send her a message; but it could not be done. Every one who went in or out of her house was closely watched. The doctor said he would take my children, unless she became responsible for them; which of course she willingly did. The next day was spent in searching. Before night, the following advertisement was posted at every corner, and in every public place for miles round:—

> "$300 REWARD! Ran away from the subscriber, an intelligent, bright, mulatto girl, named Linda, 21 years of age. Five feet four inches high. Dark eyes, and black hair inclined to curl, but it can be made straight. Has a decayed spot on a front tooth. She can read and write, and in all probability will try to get to the Free States. All persons are forbidden, under penalty of the law, to harbor or employ said slave. $150 will be given to whoever takes her in the state, and $300 if taken out of the state and delivered to me, or lodged in jail.
>
> Dr. Flint."

XVIII

Months of Peril

The search for me was kept up with more perseverance than I had anticipated. I began to think that escape was impossible. I was in great anxiety lest I should implicate the friend who harbored me. I knew the consequences would be frightful; and much as I dreaded being caught, even that seemed better than causing an innocent person to suffer for kindness to me. A week had passed in terrible suspense, when my pursuers came into such close vicinity that I concluded they had tracked me to my hiding-place. I flew out of the house, and concealed myself in a thicket of bushes. There I remained in an agony of fear for two hours. Suddenly, a reptile of some kind seized my leg. In my fright, I struck a blow which loosened its hold, but I could not tell whether I had killed it; it was so dark, I could not see what it was; I only knew it was something cold and slimy. The pain I felt soon indicated that the bite was poisonous. I was compelled to leave my place of concealment, and I groped my way back into the house. The pain had become intense, and my friend was startled by my look of anguish. I asked her to prepare a poultice of warm ashes and vinegar, and I applied it to my leg, which was already much swollen. The application gave me some relief, but the swelling did not abate. The dread of being disabled was greater than the physical pain I endured. My friend asked an old woman, who doctored among the slaves, what was good for the bite of a snake or a lizard. She told her to steep a dozen coppers in vinegar, over night, and apply the cankered vinegar to the inflamed part.

I had succeeded in cautiously conveying some messages to my relatives. They were harshly threatened, and despairing of my having a chance to escape, they advised me to return to my master, ask his forgiveness, and let him make an example of me. But such counsel had no influence with me. When I started upon this hazardous undertaking, I had resolved that, come what would, there should be no turning back. "Give me liberty, or give me death," was my motto. When my friend contrived to make known to my relatives the painful situation I had been in for twenty-four hours, they said no more about my going back to my master. Something must be done, and that speedily; but where to turn for help, they knew not. God in his mercy raised up "a friend in need."

Among the ladies who were acquainted with my grandmother, was one who had known her from childhood, and always been very friendly to her. She had also known my mother and her children, and felt interested for them. At this crisis of affairs she called to see my grandmother, as she not unfrequently did. She observed the sad and troubled expression of her face, and asked if she knew where Linda was, and whether she was safe. My grandmother shook her head, without answering. "Come, Aunt Martha," said the kind lady, "tell me all about it. Perhaps I can do something to help you." The husband of this lady held many slaves, and bought and sold slaves. She also held a number in her own name; but she treated them kindly, and would never allow any of them to be sold. She was unlike the majority of slaveholders' wives. My grandmother looked earnestly at her. Something in the expression of her face said "Trust me!" and she did trust her. She listened attentively to the details of my story, and sat thinking for a while. At last she said, "Aunt Martha, I pity you both. If you think there is any chance of Linda's getting to the Free States, I will conceal her for a time. But first you must solemnly promise that my name shall never be mentioned. If such a thing should become known, it would ruin me and my family. No one in my house must know of it, except the cook. She is so faithful that I would trust my own life with her; and I know she likes Linda. It is a great risk; but I trust no harm will come of it. Get word to Linda to be ready as soon as it is dark, before the patrols are out. I will send the housemaids on errands, and Betty shall go to meet Linda." The place where we were to meet was designated and agreed upon. My grandmother was unable to thank the lady for this noble deed; overcome by her emotions, she sank on her knees and sobbed like a child.

I received a message to leave my friend's house at such an hour, and go to a certain place where a friend would be waiting for me. As a matter of prudence no names were mentioned. I had no means of conjecturing who I was to meet, or where I was going. I did not like to move thus blindfolded, but I had no choice. It would not do for me to remain where I was. I disguised myself, summoned up courage to meet the worst, and went to the appointed place. My friend Betty was there; she was the last person I expected to see. We hurried along in silence. The pain in my leg was so intense that it seemed as if I should drop; but fear gave me strength. We reached the house and entered unobserved. Her first words were: "Honey, now you is safe. Dem devils ain't coming to search *dis* house. When I get you into missis' safe place, I will bring some nice hot supper. I specs you need it after all dis skeering." Betty's vocation led her to think eating the most important thing in life. She did not realize that my heart was too full for me to care much about supper.

The mistress came to meet us, and led me up stairs to a small room over her own sleeping apartment. "You will be safe here, Linda," said she; "I keep this room to store away things that are out of use. The girls are not accustomed to be sent to it, and they will not suspect any thing unless they hear some noise, I always keep it locked, and Betty shall take care of the key. But you must be very careful, for my sake as well as your own; and you must never tell my secret;

for it would ruin me and my family. I will keep the girls busy in the morning, that Betty may have a chance to bring your breakfast; but it will not do for her to come to you again till night. I will come to see you sometimes. Keep up your courage. I hope this state of things will not last long." Betty came with the "nice hot supper," and the mistress hastened down stairs to keep things straight till she returned. How my heart overflowed with gratitude! Words choked in my throat; but I could have kissed the feet of my benefactress. For that deed of Christian womanhood, may God forever bless her!

I went to sleep that night with the feeling that I was for the present the most fortunate slave in town. Morning came and filled my little cell with light. I thanked the heavenly Father for this safe retreat. Opposite my window was a pile of feather beds. On the top of these I could lie perfectly concealed, and command a view of the street through which Dr. Flint passed to his office. Anxious as I was, I felt a gleam of satisfaction when I saw him. Thus far I had outwitted him, and I triumphed over it. Who can blame slaves for being cunning? They are constantly compelled to resort to it. It is the only weapon of the weak and oppressed against the strength of their tyrants.

I was daily hoping to hear that my master had sold my children; for I knew who was on the watch to buy them. But Dr. Flint cared even more for revenge than he did for money. My brother William, and the good aunt who had served in his family twenty years, and my little Benny, and Ellen, who was a little over two years old, were thrust into jail, as a means of compelling my relatives to give some information about me. He swore my grandmother should never see one of them again till I was brought back. They kept these facts from me for several days. When I heard that my little ones were in a loathsome jail, my first impulse was to go to them. I was encountering dangers for the sake of freeing them, and must I be the cause of their death? The thought was agonizing. My benefactress tried to soothe me by telling me that my aunt would take good care of the children while they remained in jail. But it added to my pain to think that the good old aunt, who had always been so kind to her sister's orphan children, should be shut up in prison for no other crime than loving them. I suppose my friends feared a reckless movement on my part, knowing, as they did, that my life was bound up in my children. I received a note from my brother William. It was scarcely legible, and ran thus: "Wherever you are, dear sister, I beg of you not to come here. We are all much better off than you are. If you come, you will ruin us all. They would force you to tell where you had been, or they would kill you. Take the advice of your friends; if not for the sake of me and your children, at least for the sake of those you would ruin."

Poor William! He also must suffer for being my brother. I took his advice and kept quiet. My aunt was taken out of jail at the end of a month, because Mrs. Flint could not spare her any longer. She was tired of being her own housekeeper. It was quite too fatiguing to order her dinner and eat it too. My children remained in jail, where brother William did all he could for their comfort. Betty went to see them sometimes, and brought me tidings. She was not permitted to enter the jail; but William would hold them up to the grated window while she chatted with them. When she repeated their prattle, and told me how they wanted to see their ma, my tears would flow. Old Betty would exclaim, "Lors, chile! what's you crying 'bout? Dem young uns vil kill you dead. Don't be so chick'n hearted! If you does, you vil nebber git thro' dis world."

Good old soul! She had gone through the world childless. She had never had little ones to clasp their arms round her neck; she had never seen their soft eyes looking into hers; no sweet little voices had called her mother; she had never pressed her own infants to her heart, with the feeling that even in fetters there was something to live for. How could she realize my feelings? Betty's husband loved children dearly, and wondered why God had denied them to him. He expressed great sorrow when he came to Betty with the tidings that Ellen had been taken out of jail and carried to Dr. Flint's. She had the measles a short time before they carried her to jail, and the disease had left her eyes affected. The doctor had taken her home to attend to them. My children had always been afraid of the doctor and his wife. They had never been inside of their house. Poor little Ellen cried all day to be carried back to prison. The instincts of childhood are true. She knew she was loved in the jail. Her screams and sobs annoyed Mrs. Flint. Before night she called one of the slaves, and said, "Here, Bill, carry this brat back to the jail. I can't stand her noise. If she would be quiet I should like to keep the little minx. She would make a handy waiting-maid for my daughter by and by. But if she staid here, with her white face, I suppose I should either kill her or spoil her. I hope the doctor will sell them as far as wind and water can carry them. As for their mother, her ladyship will find out yet what she gets by running away. She hasn't so much feeling for her children as a cow has for its calf. If she had, she would have come back long ago, to get them out of jail, and save all this expense and trouble. The good-for-nothing hussy! When she is caught, she shall stay in jail, in irons, for one six months, and then be sold to a sugar plantation. I shall see her broke in yet. What do you stand there for, Bill? Why don't you go off with the brat? Mind, now, that you don't let any of the niggers speak to her in the street!"

When these remarks were reported to me, I smiled at Mrs. Flint's saying that she should either kill my child or spoil her. I thought to myself there was very little danger of the latter. I have always considered it as one of God's special providences that Ellen screamed till she was carried back to jail.

That same night Dr. Flint was called to a patient, and did not return till near morning. Passing my grandmother's, he saw a light in the house, and thought to himself, "Perhaps this has something to do with Linda." He knocked, and the door was opened. "What calls you up so early?" said he. "I saw your light, and I thought I would just stop and tell you that I have found out where Linda is. I know where to put my hands on her, and I shall have her before twelve o'clock." When he had turned away, my grandmother and my uncle looked anxiously at each other. They did not know whether or not it was merely one of the doctor's tricks to frighten them. In their uncertainty, they thought it was best to have a message conveyed to my friend Betty. Unwilling to alarm her mistress, Betty resolved to dispose of me herself. She came to me, and told me to rise and dress quickly. We hurried down stairs, and across the yard, into the kitchen. She locked the door, and lifted up a plank in the floor. A buffalo skin and a bit of carpet were spread for me to lie on, and a quilt thrown over me. "Stay dar," said she, "till I sees if dey know 'bout you. Dey say dey vil put thar hans on you afore twelve o'clock. If dey *did* know whar you are, dey won't know *now*. Dey'll be disapinted dis time. Dat's all I got to say. If dey comes rummagin 'mong *my* tings, dey'll get one bressed sarssin from dis 'ere nigger." In my shallow bed I had but just room enough to bring my hands to my face to keep the dust out of my eyes; for Betty walked over me twenty times in an hour, passing from the dresser to the fireplace. When she was alone, I could hear her pronouncing anathemas over Dr. Flint and all his tribe, every now and then saying, with a chuckling laugh, "Dis nigger's too cute for 'em dis time." When the house-maids were about, she had sly ways of drawing them out, that I might hear what they would say. She would repeat stories she had heard about my being in this, or that, or the other place. To which they would answer, that I was not fool enough to be staying round there; that I was in Philadelphia or New York before this time. When all were abed and asleep, Betty raised the plank, and said, "Come out, chile; come out. Dey don't know nottin 'bout you. 'Twas only white folks' lies, to skeer de niggers."

Some days after this adventure I had a much worse fright. As I sat very still in my retreat above stairs, cheerful visions floated through my mind. I thought Dr. Flint would soon get discouraged, and would be willing to sell my children, when he lost all hopes of making them the means of my discovery. I knew who was ready to buy them. Suddenly I heard a voice that chilled my blood. The sound was too familiar to me, it had been too dreadful, for me not to recognize at once my old master. He was in the house, and I at once concluded he had come to seize me. I looked round in terror. There was no way of escape. The voice receded. I supposed the constable was with him, and they were searching the house. In my alarm I did not forget the trouble I was bringing on my generous benefactress. It seemed as if I were born to bring sorrow on all who befriended me, and that was the bitterest drop in the bitter cup of my life. After a while I heard approaching footsteps; the key was turned in my door. I braced myself against the wall to keep from falling. I ventured to look up, and there stood my kind benefactress alone. I was too much overcome to speak, and sunk down upon the floor.

"I thought you would hear your master's voice," she said; "and knowing you would be terrified, I came to tell you there is nothing to fear. You may even indulge in a laugh at the old gentleman's expense. He is so sure you are in New York, that he came to borrow five hundred dollars to go in pursuit of you. My sister had some money to loan on interest. He has obtained it, and proposes to start for New York tonight. So, for the present, you see you are safe. The doctor will merely lighten his pocket hunting after the bird he has left behind."

XIX

The Children Sold

The doctor came back from New York, of course without accomplishing his purpose. He had expended considerable money, and was rather disheartened. My brother and the children had now been in jail two months, and that also was some expense. My friends thought it was a favorable time to work on his discouraged feelings. Mr. Sands sent a speculator to offer him nine hundred dollars for my brother William, and eight hundred for the two children. These were high prices, as slaves were then selling; but the offer was rejected. If it had been merely a question of money, the doctor would have sold any boy of Benny's age for two hundred dollars; but he could not bear to give up the power of revenge. But he was hard pressed for money, and he revolved the matter in his mind. He knew that if he could keep Ellen till she was fifteen, he could sell her for a high price; but I presume he reflected that she might die, or might be stolen away. At all events, he came to the conclusion that he had better accept the slave-trader's offer. Meeting him in the street, he inquired when he would leave town. "To-day, at ten o'clock," he replied. "Ah, do you go so soon?" said the doctor; "I have been reflecting upon your proposition, and I have concluded to let you have the three negroes if you will say nineteen hundred dollars." After some parley, the trader agreed to his terms. He wanted the bill of sale drawn up and signed immediately, as he had a great deal to attend to during the short time he remained in town. The doctor went to the jail and told William he would take him back into his service if he would promise to behave himself; but he replied that he would rather be sold. "And you *shall* be sold, you ungrateful rascal!" exclaimed the doctor. In less than an hour the money was paid, the papers were signed, sealed, and delivered, and my brother and children were in the hands of the trader.

It was a hurried transaction; and after it was over, the doctor's characteristic caution returned. He went back to the speculator, and said, "Sir, I have come to lay you under obligations of a thousand dollars not to sell any of those negroes in this state." "You come too late," replied the trader; "our bargain is closed." He had, in fact, already sold them to Mr. Sands, but he did not mention it. The doctor required him to put irons on "that rascal, Bill," and to pass through the back streets when he took his gang out of town. The trader was privately instructed to concede to his wishes. My good old aunt went to the jail to bid the children good by, supposing them to be the speculator's property, and that she should never see them again. As she held Benny in her lap, he said, "Aunt Nancy, I want to show you something." He led her to the door and showed her a long row of marks, saying, "Uncle Will taught me to count. I have made a mark for every day I have been here, and it is sixty days. It is a long time; and the speculator is going to take me and Ellen away. He's a bad man. It's wrong for him to take grandmother's children. I want to go to my mother."

My grandmother was told that the children would be restored to her, but she was requested to act as if they were really to be sent away. Accordingly, she made up a bundle of clothes and went to the jail. When she arrived, she found William handcuffed among the gang, and the children in the trader's cart. The scene seemed too much like reality. She was afraid there might have been some deception or mistake. She fainted, and was carried home.

When the wagon stopped at the hotel, several gentlemen came out and proposed to purchase William, but the trader refused their offers, without stating that he was already sold. And now came the trying hour for that drove of human beings, driven away like cattle, to be sold they knew not where. Husbands were torn from wives, parents from children, never to look upon each other again this side the grave. There was wringing of hands and cries of despair.

Dr. Flint had the supreme satisfaction of seeing the wagon leave town, and Mrs. Flint had the gratification of supposing that my children were going "as far as wind and water would carry them." According to agreement, my uncle followed the wagon some miles, until they came to an old farm house. There the trader took the irons from William, and as he did so, he said, "You are a damned clever fellow. I should like to own you myself. Them gentlemen that wanted to buy you said you was a bright, honest chap, and I must git you a good home. I guess your old master will swear to-morrow, and call himself an old fool for selling the children. I reckon he'll never git their mammy back agin. I expect she's made tracks for the north. Good by, old boy. Remember, I have done you a good turn. You must thank me by coaxing all the pretty gals to go with me next fall. That's going to be my last trip. This trading in niggers is a bad business for a fellow that's got any heart. Move on, you fellows!" And the gang went on, God alone knows where.

Much as I despise and detest the class of slave-traders, whom I regard as the vilest wretches on earth, I must do this man the justice to say that he seemed to have some feeling. He took a fancy to William in the jail, and wanted to buy him. When he heard the story of my children, he was willing to aid them in getting out of Dr. Flint's power, even without charging the customary fee.

My uncle procured a wagon and carried William and the children back to town. Great was the joy in my grandmother's house! The curtains were closed, and the candles lighted. The happy grandmother cuddled the little ones to her bosom. They hugged her, and kissed her, and clapped their hands, and shouted. She knelt down and poured forth one of her heartfelt prayers of thanksgiving to God. The father was present for a while; and though such a "parental relation" as existed between him and my children takes slight hold of the hearts or consciences of slaveholders, it must be that he experienced some moments of pure joy in witnessing the happiness he had imparted.

I had no share in the rejoicings of that evening. The events of the day had not come to my knowledge. And now I will tell you something that happened to me; though you will, perhaps, think it illustrates the superstition of slaves. I sat in my usual place on the floor near the window, where I could hear much that was said in the street without being seen. The family had retired for the night, and all was still. I sat there thinking of my children, when I heard a low strain of music. A band of serenaders were under the window, playing "Home, sweet home." I listened till the sounds did not seem like music, but like the moaning of children. It seemed as if my heart would burst. I rose from my sitting posture, and knelt. A streak of moonlight was on the floor before me, and in the midst of it appeared the forms of my two children. They vanished; but I had seen them distinctly. Some will call it a dream, others a vision. I know not how to account for it, but it made a strong impression on my mind, and I felt certain something had happened to my little ones.

I had not seen Betty since morning. Now I heard her softly turning the key. As soon as she entered, I clung to her, and begged her to let me know whether my children were dead, or whether they were sold; for I had seen their spirits in my room, and I was sure something had happened to them. "Lor, chile," said she, putting her arms round me, "you's got de highsterics. I'll sleep wid you to-night, cause you'll make a noise, and ruin missis. Something has stirred you up mightily. When you is done cryin, I'll talk wid you. De chillern is well, and mighty happy. I seed 'em myself. Does dat satisfy you? Dar, chile, be still! Somebody vill hear you." I tried to obey her. She lay down, and was soon sound asleep; but no sleep would come to my eyelids.

At dawn, Betty was up and off to the kitchen. The hours passed on, and the vision of the night kept constantly recurring to my thoughts. After a while I heard the voices of two women in the entry. In one of them I recognized the housemaid. The other said to her, "Did you know Linda Brent's children was sold to the speculator yesterday. They say ole massa Flint was mighty glad to see 'em drove out of town; but they say they've come back agin. I spect it's all their daddy's doings. They say he's bought William too. Lor! how it will take hold of ole massa Flint! I'm going roun' to aunt Marthy's to see 'bout it."

I bit my lips till the blood came to keep from crying out. Were my children with their grandmother, or had the speculator carried them off? The suspense was dreadful. Would Betty *never* come, and tell me the truth about it? At last she came, and I eagerly repeated what I had overheard. Her face was one broad, bright smile. "Lor, you foolish ting!" said she. "I'se gwine to tell you all 'bout it. De gals is eating thar breakfast, and missus tole me to let her tell you; but, poor creeter! t'aint right to keep you waitin', and I'se gwine to tell you. Brudder, chillern, all is bought by de daddy! I'se laugh more dan nuft, tinking 'bout ole massa Flint. Lor, how he *vill* swar! He's got ketched dis time, any how; but I must be getting out o' dis, or dem gals vill come and ketch *me*."

Betty went off laughing; and I said to myself "Can it be true that my children are free? I have not suffered for them in vain. Thank God!"

Great surprise was expressed when it was known that my children had returned to their grandmother's. The news spread through the town, and many a kind word was bestowed on the little ones.

Dr. Flint went to my grandmother's to ascertain who was the owner of my children, and she informed him. "I expected as much," said he. "I am glad to hear it. I have had news from Linda lately, and I shall soon have her. You need never expect to see *her* free. She shall be my slave as long as I live, and when I am dead she shall be the slave of my children. If I ever find out that you or Phillip had any thing to do with her running off I'll kill him. And if I meet William in the street, and he presumes to look at me, I'll flog him within an inch of his life. Keep those brats out of my sight!"

As he turned to leave, my grandmother said something to remind him of his own doings. He looked back upon her, as if he would have been glad to strike her to the ground.

I had my season of joy and thanksgiving. It was the first time since my childhood that I had experienced any real happiness. I heard of the old doctor's threats, but they no longer had the same power to trouble me. The darkest cloud that hung over my life had rolled away. Whatever slavery might do to me, it could not shackle my children. If I fell a sacrifice, my little ones were saved. It was well for me that my simple heart believed all that had been promised for their welfare. It is always better to trust than to doubt.

XXI

The Loophole of Retreat

A small shed had been added to my grandmother's house years ago. Some boards were laid across the joists at the top, and between these boards and the roof was a very small garret, never occupied by any thing but rats and mice. It was a pent roof, covered with nothing but shingles, according to the southern custom for such buildings. The garret was only nine feet long and seven wide. The highest part was three feet high, and sloped down abruptly to the loose board floor. There was no admission for either light or air. My uncle Phillip, who was a carpenter, had very skilfully made a concealed trap-door, which communicated with the storeroom. He had been doing this while I was waiting in the swamp. The storeroom opened upon a piazza. To this hole I was conveyed as soon as I entered the house. The air was stifling; the darkness total. A bed had been spread on the floor. I could sleep quite comfortably on one side; but the slope was so sudden that I could not turn on the other without hitting the roof. The rats and mice ran over my bed; but I was weary, and I slept such sleep as the wretched may, when a tempest has passed over them. Morning came. I knew it only by the noises I heard; for in my small den day and night were all the same. I suffered for air even more than for light. But I was not comfortless. I heard the voices of my children. There was joy and there was sadness in the sound. It made my tears flow. How I longed to speak to them! I was eager to look on their faces; but there was no hole, no crack, through which I could peep. This continued darkness was oppressive. It seemed horrible to sit or lie in a cramped position day after day, without one gleam of light. Yet I would have chosen this, rather than my lot as a slave, though white people considered it an easy one; and it was so compared with the fate of others. I was never cruelly over-worked; I was never lacerated with the whip from head to foot; I was never so beaten and bruised that I could not turn from one side to the other; I never had my heel-strings cut to prevent my running away; I was never chained to a log and forced to drag it about, while I toiled in the fields from morning till night; I was never branded with hot iron, or torn by bloodhounds. On the contrary, I had always been kindly treated, and tenderly cared for, until I came into the hands of Dr. Flint. I had never wished for freedom till then. But though my life in slavery was comparatively devoid of hardships, God pity the woman who is compelled to lead such a life!

My food was passed up to me through the trap-door my uncle had contrived; and my grandmother, my uncle Phillip, and aunt Nancy would seize such opportunities as they could, to mount up there and chat with me at the opening. But of course this was not safe in the daytime. It must all be done in darkness. It was impossible for me to move in an erect position, but I crawled about my den for exercise. One day I hit my head against something, and found it was a gimlet. My uncle had left it sticking there when he made the trap-door. I was as rejoiced as Robinson Crusoe could have been at finding such a treasure. It put a lucky thought into my head. I said to myself, "Now I will have some light. Now I will see my children." I did not dare to begin my work during the daytime, for fear of attracting attention. But I groped round; and having found the side next the street, where I could frequently see my children, I stuck the gimlet in and waited for evening. I bored three rows of holes, one above another; then I bored out the interstices between. I thus succeeded in making one hole about an inch long and an inch broad. I sat by it till late into the night, to enjoy the little whiff of air that floated in. In the morning I watched for my children. The first person I saw in the street was Dr. Flint. I had a shuddering, superstitious feeling that it was a bad omen. Several familiar faces passed by. At last I heard the merry laugh of children, and presently two sweet little faces were looking up at me, as though they knew I was there, and were conscious of the joy they imparted. How I longed to *tell* them I was there!

My condition was now a little improved. But for weeks I was tormented by hundreds of little red insects, fine as a needle's point, that pierced through my skin, and produced an intolerable burning. The good grandmother gave me herb teas and cooling medicines, and finally I got rid of them. The heat of my den was intense, for nothing but thin shingles protected me from the scorching summer's sun. But I had my consolations. Through my peeping-hole I could watch the children, and when they were near enough, I could hear their talk. Aunt Nancy brought me all the news she could hear at Dr. Flint's. From her I learned that the doctor had written to New York to a colored woman, who had been born and raised in our neighborhood, and had breathed his contaminating atmosphere. He offered her a reward if she could find out any thing about me. I know not what was the nature of her reply; but he soon after started for New York in haste, saying to his family that he had business of importance to transact. I peeped at him as he passed on his way to the steamboat. It was a satisfaction to have miles of land and water between us, even for a little while; and it was a still greater satisfaction to know that he believed me to be in the Free States. My little den seemed less dreary than it had done. He returned, as he did from his former journey to New York, without obtaining any satisfactory information. When he passed our house next morning, Benny was standing at the gate. He had heard them say that he had gone to find me, and he called out, "Dr. Flint, did you bring my mother home? I want to see her." The doctor stamped his foot at him in a rage, and exclaimed, "Get out of the way, you little damned rascal! If you don't, I'll cut off your head."

Benny ran terrified into the house, saying, "You can't put me in jail again. I don't belong to you now." It was well that the wind carried the words away from the doctor's ear. I told my grandmother of it, when we had our next conference at the trap-door; and begged of her not to allow the children to be impertinent to the irascible old man.

Autumn came, with a pleasant abatement of heat. My eyes had become accustomed to the dim light, and by holding my book or work in a certain position near the aperture I contrived to read and sew. That was a great relief to the tedious monotony of my life. But when winter came, the cold penetrated through the thin shingle roof, and I was dreadfully chilled. The winters there are not so long, or so severe, as in northern latitudes; but the houses are not built to shelter from cold, and my little den was peculiarly comfortless. The kind grandmother brought me bed-clothes and warm drinks. Often I was obliged to lie in bed all day to keep comfortable; but with all my precautions, my shoulders and feet were frostbitten. O, those long, gloomy days, with no object for my eye to rest upon, and no thoughts to occupy my mind, except the dreary past and the uncertain future! I was thankful when there came a day sufficiently mild for me to wrap myself up and sit at the loophole to watch the passers by. Southerners have the habit of stopping and talking in the streets, and I heard many conversations not intended to meet my ears. I heard slave-hunters planning how to catch some poor fugitive. Several times I heard allusions to Dr. Flint, myself, and the history of my children, who, perhaps, were playing near the gate. One would say, "I wouldn't move my little finger to catch her, as old Flint's property." Another would say, "I'll catch *any* nigger for the reward. A man ought to have what belongs to him, if he *is* a damned brute." The opinion was often expressed that I was in the Free States. Very rarely did any one suggest that I might be in the vicinity. Had the least suspicion rested on my grandmother's house, it would have been burned to the ground. But it was the last place they thought of. Yet there was no place, where slavery existed, that could have afforded me so good a place of concealment.

Dr. Flint and his family repeatedly tried to coax and bribe my children to tell something they had heard said about me. One day the doctor took them into a shop, and offered them some bright little silver pieces and gay handkerchiefs if they would tell where their mother was. Ellen shrank away from him, and would not speak; but Benny spoke up, and said, "Dr. Flint, I don't know where my mother is. I guess she's in New York; and when you go there again, I wish you'd ask her to come home, for I want to see her; but if you put her in jail, or tell her you'll cut her head off, I'll tell her to go right back."

XXIII

Still in Prison

When spring returned, and I took in the little patch of green the aperture commanded, I asked myself how many more summers and winters I must be condemned to spend thus. I longed to draw in a plentiful draught of fresh air, to stretch my cramped limbs, to have room to stand erect, to feel the earth under my feet again. My relatives were constantly on the lookout for a chance of escape; but none offered that seemed practicable, and even tolerably safe. The hot summer came again, and made the turpentine drop from the thin roof over my head.

During the long nights I was restless for want of air, and I had no room to toss and turn. There was but one compensation; the atmosphere was so stifled that even mosquitos would not condescend to buzz in it. With all my detestation of Dr. Flint, I could hardly wish him a worse punishment, either in this world or that which is to come, than to suffer what I suffered in one single summer. Yet the laws allowed *him* to be out in the free air, while I, guiltless of crime, was pent up here, as the only means of avoiding the cruelties the laws allowed him to inflict upon me! I don't know what kept life within me. Again and again, I thought I should die before long; but I saw the leaves of another autumn whirl through the air, and felt the touch of another winter. In summer the most terrible thunder storms were acceptable, for the rain came through the roof, and I rolled up my bed that it might cool the hot boards under it. Later in the season, storms sometimes wet my clothes through and through, and that was not comfortable when the air grew chilly. Moderate storms I could keep out by filling the chinks with oakum.

But uncomfortable as my situation was, I had glimpses of things out of doors, which made me thankful for my wretched hiding-place. One day I saw a slave pass our gate, muttering, "It's his own, and he can kill it if he will." My grandmother told me that woman's history. Her mistress had that day seen her baby for the first time, and in the lineaments of its fair face she saw a likeness to her husband. She turned the bondwoman and her child out of doors, and forbade her ever to return. The slave went to her master, and told him what had happened. He promised to talk with her mistress, and make it all right. The next day she and her baby were sold to a Georgia trader.

Another time I saw a woman rush wildly by, pursued by two men. She was a slave, the wet nurse of her mistress's children. For some trifling offence her mistress ordered her to be stripped and whipped. To escape the degradation and the torture, she rushed to the river, jumped in, and ended her wrongs in death.

Senator Brown, of Mississippi, could not be ignorant of many such facts as these, for they are of frequent occurrence in every Southern State. Yet he stood up in the Congress of the United States, and declared that slavery was "a great moral, social, and political blessing; a blessing to the master, and a blessing to the slave!"

I suffered much more during the second winter than I did during the first. My limbs were benumbed by inaction, and the cold filled them with cramp. I had a very painful sensation of coldness in my head; even my face and tongue stiffened, and I lost the power of speech. Of course it was impossible, under the circumstances, to summon any physician. My brother William came and did all he could for me. Uncle Phillip also watched tenderly over me; and poor grandmother crept up and down to inquire whether there were any signs of returning life. I was restored to consciousness by the dashing of cold water in my face, and found myself leaning against my brother's arm, while he bent over me with streaming eyes. He afterwards told me he thought I was dying, for I had been in an unconscious state sixteen hours. I next became delirious, and was in great danger of betraying myself and my friends. To prevent this, they stupefied me with drugs. I remained in bed six weeks, weary in body and sick at heart. How to get medical advice was the question. William finally went to a Thompsonian doctor, and described himself as having all my pains and aches. He returned with herbs, roots, and ointment. He was especially charged to rub on the ointment by a fire; but how could a fire be made in my little den? Charcoal in a furnace was tried, but there was no outlet for the gas, and it nearly cost me my life. Afterwards coals, already kindled, were brought up in an iron pan, and placed on bricks. I was so weak, and it was so long since I had enjoyed the warmth of a fire, that those few coals actually made me weep. I think the medicines did me some good; but my recovery was very slow. Dark thoughts passed through my mind as I lay there day after day. I tried to be thankful for my little cell, dismal as it was, and even to love it, as part of the price I had paid for the redemption of my children. Sometimes I thought God was a compassionate Father, who would forgive my sins for the sake of my sufferings. At other times, it seemed to me there was no justice or mercy in the divine government. I asked why the curse of slavery was permitted to exist, and why I had been so persecuted and wronged from youth upward. These things took the shape of mystery, which is to this day not so clear to my soul as I trust it will be hereafter.

In the midst of my illness, grandmother broke down under the weight of anxiety and toil. The idea of losing her, who had always been my best friend and a mother to my children, was the sorest trial I had yet had. O, how earnestly I prayed that she might recover! How hard it seemed, that I could not tend upon her, who had so long and so tenderly watched over me!

One day the screams of a child nerved me with strength to crawl to my peeping-hole, and I saw my son covered with blood. A fierce dog, usually kept chained, had seized and bitten him. A doctor was sent for, and I heard the groans and screams of my child while the wounds were being sewed up. O, what torture to a mother's heart, to listen to this and be unable to go to him!

But childhood is like a day in spring, alternately shower and sunshine. Before night Benny was bright and lively, threatening the destruction of the dog; and great was his delight when the doctor told him the next day that the dog had bitten another boy and been shot. Benny recovered from his wounds; but it was long before he could walk.

When my grandmother's illness became known, many ladies, who were her customers, called to bring her some little comforts, and to inquire whether she had every thing she wanted. Aunt Nancy one night asked permission to watch with her sick mother, and Mrs. Flint replied, "I don't see any need of your going. I can't spare you." But when she found other ladies in the neighborhood were so attentive, not wishing to be outdone in Christian charity, she also sallied forth, in magnificent condescension, and stood by the bedside of her who had loved her in her infancy, and who had been repaid by such grievous wrongs. She seemed surprised to find her so ill, and scolded uncle Phillip for not sending for Dr. Flint. She herself sent for him immediately, and he came. Secure as I was in my retreat, I should have been terrified if I had known he was so near me. He pronounced my grandmother in a very critical situation, and said if her attending physician wished it, he would visit her. Nobody wished to have him coming to the house at all hours, and we were not disposed to give him a chance to make out a long bill.

As Mrs. Flint went out, Sally told her the reason Benny was lame was, that a dog had bitten him. "I'm glad of it," replied she. "I wish he had killed him. It would be good news to send to his mother. *Her* day will come. The dogs will grab *her* yet." With these Christian words she and her husband departed, and, to my great satisfaction, returned no more.

I heard from uncle Phillip, with feelings of unspeakable joy and gratitude, that the crisis was passed and grandmother would live. I could now say from my heart, "God is merciful. He has spared me the anguish of feeling that I caused her death."

XXIX

Preparations for Escape

I hardly expect that the reader will credit me, when I affirm that I lived in that little dismal hole, almost deprived of light and air, and with no space to move my limbs, for nearly seven years. But it is a fact; and to me a sad one, even now; for my body still suffers from the effects of that long imprisonment, to say nothing of my soul. Members of my family, now living in New York and Boston, can testify to the truth of what I say.

Countless were the nights that I sat late at the little loophole scarcely large enough to give me a glimpse of one twinkling star. There, I heard the patrols and slave-hunters conferring together about the capture of runaways, well knowing how rejoiced they would be to catch me.

Season after season, year after year, I peeped at my children's faces, and heard their sweet voices, with a heart yearning all the while to say, "Your mother is here." Sometimes it appeared to me as if ages had rolled away since I entered upon that gloomy, monotonous existence. At times, I was stupefied and listless; at other times I became very impatient to know when these dark years would end, and I should again be allowed to feel the sunshine, and breathe the pure air.

After Ellen left us, this feeling increased. Mr. Sands had agreed that Benny might go to the north whenever his uncle Phillip could go with him; and I was anxious to be there also, to watch over my children, and protect them so far as I was able. Moreover, I was likely to be drowned out of my den, if I remained much longer; for the slight roof was getting badly out of repair, and uncle Phillip was afraid to remove the shingles, lest some one should get a glimpse of me. When storms occurred in the night, they spread mats and bits of carpet, which in the morning appeared to have been laid out to dry; but to cover the roof in the daytime might have attracted attention. Consequently, my clothes and bedding were often drenched; a process by which the pains and aches in my cramped and stiffened limbs were greatly increased. I revolved various plans of escape in my mind, which I sometimes imparted to my grandmother, when she came to whisper with me at the trap-door. The kind-hearted old woman had an intense sympathy for runaways. She had known too much of the cruelties inflicted on those who were captured. Her memory always flew back at once to the sufferings of her bright and handsome son, Benjamin, the youngest and dearest of her flock. So, whenever I alluded to the subject, she would groan out, "O, don't think of it, child. You'll break my heart." I had no good old aunt Nancy now to encourage me; but my brother William and my children were continually beckoning me to the north.

And now I must go back a few months in my story. I have stated that the first of January was the time for selling slaves, or leasing them out to new masters. If time were counted by heart-throbs, the poor slaves might reckon years of suffering during that festival so joyous to the free. On the New Year's day preceding my aunt's death, one of my friends, named Fanny, was to be sold at auction, to pay her master's debts. My thoughts were with her during all the day, and at night I anxiously inquired what had been her fate. I was told that she had been sold to one master, and her four little girls to another master, far distant; that she had escaped from her purchaser, and was not to be found. Her mother was the old Aggie I have spoken of. She lived in a small tenement belonging to my grandmother, and built on the same lot with her own house. Her dwelling was searched and watched, and that brought the patrols so near me that I was obliged to keep very close in my den. The hunters were somehow eluded; and not long afterwards Benny accidentally caught sight of Fanny in her mother's hut. He told his grandmother, who charged him never to speak of it, explaining to him the frightful consequences; and he never betrayed the trust. Aggie little dreamed that my grandmother knew where her daughter was concealed, and that the stooping form of her old neighbor was bending under a similar burden of anxiety and fear; but these dangerous secrets deepened the sympathy between the two old persecuted mothers.

My friend Fanny and I remained many weeks hidden within call of each other; but she was unconscious of the fact. I longed to have her share my den, which seemed a more secure retreat than her own; but had brought so much trouble on my grandmother, that it seemed wrong to ask her to incur greater risks. My restlessness increased. I had lived too long in bodily pain and anguish of spirit. Always I was in dread that by some accident, or some contrivance, slavery would succeed in snatching my children from me. This thought drove me nearly frantic, and I determined to steer for the North Star at all hazards. At this crisis, Providence opened an unexpected way for me to escape. My friend Peter came one evening, and asked to speak with me. "Your day has come, Linda," said he. "I have found a chance for you to go to the Free States. You have a fortnight to decide." The news seemed too good to be true; but Peter explained his arrangements, and told me all that was necessary was for me to say I would go. I was going to answer him with a joyful yes, when the thought of Benny came to my mind. I told him the temptation was exceedingly strong, but I was terribly afraid of Dr. Flint's alleged power over my child, and that I could not go and leave him behind. Peter remonstrated earnestly. He said such a good chance might never occur again; that Benny was free, and could be sent to me; and that for the sake of my children's welfare I ought not to hesitate a moment. I told him I would consult with uncle Phillip. My uncle rejoiced in the plan, and bade me go by all means. He promised, if his life was spared, that he would either bring or send my son to me as soon as I reached a place of safety. I resolved to go, but thought nothing had better be said to my grandmother till very near the time of departure. But my uncle thought she would feel it more keenly if I left her so suddenly. "I will reason with her," said he, "and convince her how necessary it is, not only for your sake, but for hers also. You cannot be blind to the fact that she is sinking under her burdens." I was not blind to it. I knew that my concealment was an ever-present source of anxiety, and that the older she grew the more nervously fearful she was of discovery. My uncle talked with her, and finally succeeded in persuading her that it was absolutely necessary for me to seize the chance so unexpectedly offered.

The anticipation of being a free woman proved almost too much for my weak frame. The excitement stimulated me, and at the same time bewildered me. I made busy preparations for my journey, and for my son to follow me. I resolved to have an interview with him before I went, that I might give him cautions and advice, and tell him how anxiously I should be waiting for him at the north. Grandmother stole up to me as often as possible to whisper words of counsel. She insisted upon my writing to Dr. Flint, as soon as I arrived in the Free States, and asking him to sell me to her. She said she would sacrifice her house, and all she had in the world, for the sake of having me safe with my children in any part of the world. If she could only live to know *that* she could die in peace. I promised the dear old faithful friend that I would write to her as soon as I arrived, and put the letter in a safe way to reach her; but in my own mind I resolved that not another cent of her hard earnings should be spent to pay rapacious slaveholders for what they called their property. And even if I had not been unwilling to buy what I had already a right to possess, common humanity would have prevented me from accepting the generous offer, at the expense of turning my aged relative out of house and home, when she was trembling on the brink of the grave.

I was to escape in a vessel; but I forbear to mention any further particulars. I was in readiness, but the vessel was unexpectedly detained several days. Meantime, news came to town of a most horrible murder committed on a fugitive slave, named James. Charity, the mother of this unfortunate young man, had been an old acquaintance of ours. I have told the shocking particulars of his death, in my description of some of the neighboring slaveholders. My grandmother, always nervously sensitive about runaways, was terribly frightened. She felt sure that a similar fate awaited me, if I did not desist from my enterprise. She sobbed, and groaned, and entreated me not to go. Her excessive fear was somewhat contagious, and my heart was not proof against her extreme agony. I was grievously disappointed, but I promised to relinquish my project.

When my friend Peter was apprised of this, he was both disappointed and vexed. He said, that judging from our past experience, it would be a long time before I had such another chance to throw away. I told him it need not be thrown away; that I had a friend concealed near by, who would be glad enough to take the place that had been provided for me. I told him about poor Fanny, and the kind-hearted, noble fellow, who never turned his back upon any body in distress, white or black, expressed his readiness to help her. Aggie was much surprised when she found that we knew her secret. She was rejoiced to hear of such a chance for Fanny, and arrangements were made for her to go on board the vessel the next night. They both supposed that I had long been at the north, therefore my name was not mentioned in the transaction. Fanny was carried on board at the appointed time, and stowed away in a very small cabin. This accommodation had been purchased at a price that would pay for a voyage to England. But when one proposes to go to fine old England, they stop to calculate whether they can afford the cost of the pleasure; while in making a bargain to escape from slavery, the trembling victim is ready to say, "Take all I have, only don't betray me!"

The next morning I peeped through my loophole, and saw that it was dark and cloudy. At night I received news that the wind was ahead, and the vessel had not sailed. I was exceedingly anxious about Fanny, and Peter too, who was running a tremendous risk at my instigation. Next day the wind and weather remained the same. Poor Fanny had been half dead with fright when they carried her on board, and I could readily imagine how she must be suffering now. Grandmother came often to my den, to say how thankful she was I did not go. On the third morning she rapped for me to come down to the storeroom. The poor old sufferer was breaking down under her weight of trouble. She was easily flurried now. I found her in a nervous, excited state, but I was not aware that she had forgotten to lock the door behind her, as usual. She was exceedingly worried about the detention of the vessel. She was afraid all would be discovered, and then Fanny, and Peter, and I, would all be tortured to death, and Phillip would be utterly ruined, and her house would be torn down. Poor Peter! If he should die such a horrible death as the poor slave James had lately done, and all for his kindness in trying to help me, how dreadful it would be for us all! Alas, the thought was familiar to me, and had sent many a sharp pang through my heart. I tried to suppress my own anxiety, and speak soothingly to her. She brought in some allusion to aunt Nancy, the dear daughter she had recently buried, and then she lost all control of herself. As she stood there, trembling and sobbing, a voice from the piazza called out, "Whar is you, aunt Marthy?" Grandmother was startled, and in her agitation opened the door, without thinking of me. In stepped Jenny, the mischievous housemaid, who had tried to enter my room, when I was concealed in the house of my white benefactress. "I's bin huntin ebery whar for you, aunt Marthy," said she. "My missis wants you to send her some crackers." I had slunk down behind a barrel, which entirely screened me, but I imagined that Jenny was looking directly at the spot, and my heart beat violently. My grandmother immediately thought what she had done, and went out quickly with Jenny to count the crackers locking the door after her. She returned to me, in a few minutes, the perfect picture of despair. "Poor child!" she exclaimed, "my carelessness has ruined you. The boat ain't gone yet. Get ready immediately, and go with Fanny. I ain't got another word to say against it now; for there's no telling what may happen this day."

Uncle Phillip was sent for, and he agreed with his mother in thinking that Jenny would inform Dr. Flint in less than twenty-four hours. He advised getting me on board the boat, if possible; if not, I had better keep very still in my den, where they could not find me without tearing the house down. He said it would not do for him to move in the matter, because suspicion would be immediately excited; but he promised to communicate with Peter. I felt reluctant to apply to him again, having implicated him too much already; but there seemed to be no alternative. Vexed as Peter had been by my indecision, he was true to his generous nature, and said at once that he would do his best to help me, trusting I should show myself a stronger woman this time.

He immediately proceeded to the wharf, and found that the wind had shifted, and the vessel was slowly beating down stream. On some pretext of urgent necessity, he offered two boatmen a dollar apiece to catch up with her. He was of lighter complexion than the boatmen he hired, and when the captain saw them coming so rapidly, he thought officers were pursuing his vessel in search of the runaway slave he had on board. They hoisted sails, but the boat gained upon them, and the indefatigable Peter sprang on board.

The captain at once recognized him. Peter asked him to go below, to speak about a bad bill he had given him. When he told his errand, the captain replied, "Why, the woman's here already; and I've put her where you or the devil would have a tough job to find her."

"But it is another woman I want to bring," said Peter. "*She* is in great distress, too, and you shall be paid any thing within reason, if you'll stop and take her."

"What's her name?" inquired the captain.

"Linda," he replied.

"That's the name of the woman already here," rejoined the captain. "By George! I believe you mean to betray me."

"O!" exclaimed Peter, "God knows I wouldn't harm a hair of your head. I am too grateful to you. But there really *is* another woman in great danger. Do have the humanity to stop and take her!"

After a while they came to an understanding. Fanny, not dreaming I was any where about in that region, had assumed my name, though she had called herself Johnson. "Linda is a common name," said Peter, "and the woman I want to bring is Linda Brent."

The captain agreed to wait at a certain place till evening, being handsomely paid for his detention.

Of course, the day was an anxious one for us all. But we concluded that if Jenny had seen me, she would be too wise to let her mistress know of it; and that she probably would not get a chance to see Dr. Flint's family till evening, for I knew very well what were the rules in that household. I afterwards believed that she did not see me; for nothing ever came of it, and she was one of those base characters that would have jumped to betray a suffering fellow being for the sake of thirty pieces of silver.

I made all my arrangements to go on board as soon as it was dusk. The intervening time I resolved to spend with my son. I had not spoken to him for seven years, though I had been under the same roof, and seen him every day, when I was well enough to sit at the loophole. I did not dare to venture beyond the storeroom; so they brought him there, and locked us up together, in a place concealed from the piazza door. It was an agitating interview for both of us. After we had talked and wept together for a little while, he said, "Mother, I'm glad you're going away. I wish I could go with you. I knew you was here; and I have been so afraid they would come and catch you!"

I was greatly surprised, and asked him how he had found it out.

He replied, "I was standing under the eaves, one day, before Ellen went away, and I heard somebody cough up over the wood shed. I don't know what made me think it was you, but I did think so. I missed Ellen, the night before she went away; and grandmother brought her back into the room in the night; and I thought maybe she'd been to see *you*, before she went, for I heard grandmother whisper to her, 'Now go to sleep; and remember never to tell.'"

I asked him if he ever mentioned his suspicions to his sister. He said he never did; but after he heard the cough, if he saw her playing with other children on that side of the house, he always tried to coax her round to the other side, for fear they would hear me cough, too. He said he had kept a close lookout for Dr. Flint, and if he saw him speak to a constable, or a patrol, he always told grandmother. I now recollected that I had seen him manifest uneasiness, when people were on that side of the house, and I had at the time been puzzled to conjecture a motive for his actions. Such prudence may seem extraordinary in a boy of twelve years, but slaves, being surrounded by mysteries, deceptions, and dangers, early learn to be suspicious and watchful, and prematurely cautious and cunning. He had never asked a question of grandmother, or uncle Phillip, and I had often heard him chime in with other children, when they spoke of my being at the north.

I told him I was now really going to the Free States, and if he was a good, honest boy, and a loving child to his dear old grandmother, the Lord would bless him, and bring him to me, and we and Ellen would live together. He began to tell me that grandmother had not eaten any thing all day. While he was speaking, the door was unlocked, and she came in with a small bag of money, which she wanted me to take. I begged her to keep a part of it, at least, to pay for Benny's being sent to the north; but she insisted, while her tears were falling fast, that I should take the whole. "You may be sick among strangers," she said, "and they would send you to the poorhouse to die." Ah, that good grandmother!

For the last time I went up to my nook. Its desolate appearance no longer chilled me, for the light of hope had risen in my soul. Yet, even with the blessed prospect of freedom before me, I felt very sad at leaving forever that old homestead, where I had been sheltered so long by the dear old grandmother; where I had dreamed my first young dream of love; and where, after that had faded away, my children came to twine themselves so closely round my desolate heart. As the hour approached for me to leave, I again descended to the storeroom. My grandmother and Benny were there. She took me by the hand, and said, "Linda, let us pray." We knelt down together, with my child pressed to my heart, and my other arm round the faithful, loving old friend I was about to leave forever. On no other occasion has it ever been my lot to listen to so fervent a supplication for mercy and protection. It thrilled through my heart, and inspired me with trust in God.

Peter was waiting for me in the street. I was soon by his side, faint in body, but strong of purpose. I did not look back upon the old place, though I felt that I should never see it again.

XXX

Northward Bound

I never could tell how we reached the wharf. My brain was all of a whirl, and my limbs tottered under me. At an appointed place we met my uncle Phillip, who had started before us on a different route, that he might reach the wharf first, and give us timely warning if there was any danger. A row-boat was in readiness. As I was about to step in, I felt something pull me gently, and turning round I saw Benny, looking pale and anxious. He whispered in my ear, "I've been peeping into the doctor's window, and he's at home. Good by, mother. Don't cry; I'll come." He hastened away. I clasped the hand of my good uncle, to whom I owed so much, and of Peter, the brave, generous friend who had volunteered to run such terrible risks to secure my safety. To this day I remember how his bright face beamed with joy, when he told me he had discovered a safe method for me to escape. Yet that intelligent, enterprising, noble-hearted man was a chattel! liable, by the laws of a country that calls itself civilized, to be sold with horses and pigs! We parted in silence. Our hearts were all too full for words!

Swiftly the boat glided over the water. After a while, one of the sailors said, "Don't be down-hearted, madam. We will take you safely to your husband, in ——." At first I could not imagine what he meant; but I had presence of mind to think that it probably referred to something the captain had told him; so I thanked him, and said I hoped we should have pleasant weather.

When I entered the vessel the captain came forward to meet me. He was an elderly man, with a pleasant countenance. He showed me to a little box of a cabin, where sat my friend Fanny. She started as if she had seen a spectre. She gazed on me in utter astonishment, and exclaimed, "Linda, can this be *you*? or is it your ghost?" When we were locked in each other's arms, my overwrought feelings could no longer be restrained. My sobs reached the ears of the captain, who came and very kindly reminded us, that for his safety, as well as our own, it would be prudent for us not to attract any attention. He said that when there was a sail in sight he wished us to keep below; but at other times, he had no objection to our being on deck. He assured us that he would keep a good lookout, and if we acted prudently, he thought we should be in no danger. He had represented us as women going to meet our husbands in ——. We thanked him, and promised to observe carefully all the directions he gave us.

Fanny and I now talked by ourselves, low and quietly, in our little cabin. She told me of the sufferings she had gone through in making her escape, and of her terrors while she was concealed in her mother's house. Above all, she dwelt on the agony of separation from all her children on that dreadful auction day. She could scarcely credit me, when I told her of the place where I had passed nearly seven years. "We have the same sorrows," said I. "No," replied she, "you are going to see your children soon, and there is no hope that I shall ever even hear from mine."

The vessel was soon under way, but we made slow progress. The wind was against us. I should not have cared for this, if we had been out of sight of the town; but until there were miles of water between us and our enemies, we were filled with constant apprehensions that the constables would come on board. Neither could I feel quite at ease with the captain and his men. I was an entire stranger to that class of people, and I had heard that sailors were rough, and sometimes cruel. We were so completely in their power, that if they were bad men, our situation would be dreadful. Now that the captain was paid for our passage, might he not be tempted to make more money by giving us up to those who claimed us as property? I was naturally of a confiding disposition, but slavery had made me suspicious of every body. Fanny did not share my distrust of the captain or his men. She said she was afraid at first, but she had been on board three days while the vessel lay in the dock, and nobody had betrayed her, or treated her otherwise than kindly.

The captain soon came to advise us to go on deck for fresh air. His friendly and respectful manner, combined with Fanny's testimony, reassured me, and we went with him. He placed us in a comfortable seat, and occasionally entered into conversation. He told us he was a Southerner by birth, and had spent the greater part of his life in the Slave States, and that he had recently lost a brother who traded in slaves. "But," said he, "it is a pitiable and degrading business, and I always felt ashamed to acknowledge my brother in connection with it." As we passed Snaky Swamp, he pointed to it, and said, "There is a slave territory that defies all the laws." I thought of the terrible days I had spent there, and though it was not called Dismal Swamp, it made me feel very dismal as I looked at it.

I shall never forget that night. The balmy air of spring was so refreshing! And how shall I describe my sensations when we were fairly sailing on Chesapeake Bay? O, the beautiful sunshine! the exhilarating breeze! and I could enjoy them without fear or restraint. I had never realized what grand things air and sunlight are till I had been deprived of them.

Ten days after we left land we were approaching Philadelphia. The captain said we should arrive there in the night, but he thought we had better wait till morning, and go on shore in broad daylight, as the best way to avoid suspicion.

I replied, "You know best. But will you stay on board and protect us?"

He saw that I was suspicious, and he said he was sorry, now that he had brought us to the end of our voyage, to find I had so little confidence in him. Ah, if he had ever been a slave he would have known how difficult it was to trust a white man. He assured us that we might sleep through the night without fear; that he would take care we were not left unprotected. Be it said to the honor of this captain, Southerner as he was, that if Fanny and I had been white ladies, and our passage lawfully engaged, he could not have treated us more respectfully. My intelligent friend, Peter, had rightly estimated the character of the man to whose honor he had intrusted us.

The next morning I was on deck as soon as the day dawned. I called Fanny to see the sun rise, for the first time in our lives, on free soil; for such I *then* believed it to be. We watched the reddening sky, and saw the great orb come up slowly out of the water, as it seemed. Soon the waves began to sparkle, and every thing caught the beautiful glow. Before us lay the city of strangers. We looked at each other, and the eyes of both were moistened with tears. We had escaped from slavery, and we supposed ourselves to be safe from the hunters. But we were alone in the world, and we had left dear ties behind us; ties cruelly sundered by the demon Slavery.

Frederick Douglass (1817–1895)

Frederick Douglass, an esteemed orator, abolitionist, author, and politician, had humble beginnings. Born a slave in Talbot County, Maryland in 1817, he had faint and fragile memories of his mother. Later, he presumed that a slave master was indeed his biological father. This limited familial knowledge coupled with denied access to formal schooling provoked in him a great respect for learning. Eventually, Douglass was successful in coercing the children of slave masters to teach him to read.

After a particularly brutal beating at the hands of a slave master, Douglass dared to challenge his abuser. This confrontation aroused an intense desire for freedom. After escaping from slavery in 1836, he focused on helping other slaves to escape. He forged documents, verified passes, and provided lodging for fugitive slaves. His printing shop in Rochester, New York, was an Underground Railroad station. Armed now with knowledge of the written word and a gift of oratory skill, Douglass became an advocate for the enslaved African American. He spoke with intelligence and experience, having been a slave himself. His anti-slavery campaign was extended to the *North Star,* the publication which he founded and edited. There he formed a relationship with some northern abolitionists, led by William Lloyd Garrison.

Douglass authored innumerable articles protesting the institution of slavery and advocating human rights. His most noted work, the *Narrative of the Life of Frederick Douglass, an American Slave,* was published in 1845. It is particularly important because it negates the stereotype of the intellectually inferior African American, and it presents a disquieting part of history from the perception of the slave. The first African-American short story was written by Douglass in 1841. "The Heroic Slave" depicted a ship mutiny initiated by a slave. Douglass wrote two additional autobiographies: *My Bondage and My Freedom* (1855) and *The Life and Times of Frederick Douglass* (1881).

His public/political career was highlighted by service as the United States Marshall for the District of Columbia in 1876 and the Recorder of Deeds in 1882, and in 1889 Douglass was appointed United States Minister to Haiti. Douglass died in 1895. Nearly a century after his appointment as U.S. Marshall, the United States Postal Service, in 1967, posthumously honored Douglass with the creation of a stamp in his likeness on February 14, the supposed day of his birth. Likewise, his home in the Anacostia section of Washington, D.C. has become an historic African-American landmark.

Selected Bibliography

Foner, Philip S. *The Life and Writings of Frederick Douglass.* 4 vols. New York: International, 1975.
Nelson, Emmanuel S., Ed. *African American Authors, 1745–1945: A Bio-Bibliographical Critical Sourcebook.* Westport, CT: Greenwood, 2000.

Narrative of the Life of Frederick Douglass
An American Slave

Frederick Douglass

Chapter I

I was born in Tuckahoe, near Hillsborough, and about twelve miles from Easton, in Talbot county, Maryland. I have no accurate knowledge of my age, never having seen any authentic record containing it. By far the larger part of the slaves know as little of their ages as horses know of theirs, and it is the wish of most masters within my knowledge to keep their slaves thus ignorant. I do not remember to have ever met a slave who could tell of his birthday. They seldom come nearer to it than planting-time, harvest-time, cherry-time, spring-time, or fall-time. A want of information concerning my own was a source of unhappiness to me even during childhood. The white children could tell their ages. I could not tell why I ought to be deprived of the same privilege. I was not allowed to make any inquiries of my master concerning it. He deemed all such inquiries on the part of a slave improper and impertinent, and evidence of a restless spirit. The nearest estimate I can give makes me now between twenty-seven and twenty-eight years of age. I come to this, from hearing my master say, some time during 1835, I was about seventeen years old.

My mother was named Harriet Bailey. She was the daughter of Isaac and Betsey Bailey, both colored, and quite dark. My mother was of a darker complexion than either my grandmother or grandfather.

My father was a white man. He was admitted to be such by all I ever heard speak of my parentage. The opinion was also whispered that my master was my father; but of the correctness of this opinion, I know nothing; the means of knowing was withheld from me. My mother and I were separated when I was but an infant—before I knew her as my mother. It is a common custom, in the part of Maryland from which I ran away, to part children from their mothers at a very early age. Frequently, before the child has reached its twelfth month, its mother is taken from it, and hired out on some farm a considerable distance off, and the child is placed under the care of an old woman, too old for field labor. For what this separation is done, I do not know, unless it be to hinder the development of the child's affection toward its mother, and to blunt and destroy the natural affection of the mother for the child. This is the inevitable result.

I never saw my mother, to know her as such, more than four or five times in my life; and each of these times was very short in duration, and at night. She was hired by a Mr. Stewart, who lived about twelve miles from my home. She made her journeys to see me in the night, travelling the whole distance on foot, after the performance of her day's work. She was a field hand, and a whipping is the penalty of not being in the field at sunrise, unless a slave has special permission from his or her master to the contrary—a permission which they seldom get, and one that gives to him that gives it the proud name of being a kind master. I do not recollect of ever seeing my mother by the light of day. She was with me in the night. She would lie down with me, and get me to sleep, but long before I waked she was gone. Very little communication ever took place between us. Death soon ended what little we could have while she lived, and with it her hardships and suffering. She died when I was about seven years old, on one of my master's farms, near Lee's Mill. I was not allowed to be present during her illness, at her death, or burial. She was gone long before I knew any thing about it. Never having enjoyed, to any considerable extent, her soothing presence, her tender and watchful care, I received the tidings of her death with much the same emotions I should have probably felt at the death of a stranger.

Called thus suddenly away, she left me without the slightest intimation of who my father was. The whisper that my master was my father, may or may not be true; and, true or false, it is of but little consequence to my purpose whilst the face remains, in all its glaring odiousness, that slaveholders have ordained, and by law established, that the children of slave women shall in all cases follow the condition of their mothers; and this is done too obviously to administer to their own lusts, and make gratification of their wicked desires profitable as well as pleasurable; for by this cunning arrangement, the slaveholder, in cases not a few, sustains to his slaves the double relation of master and father.

I know of such cases; and it is worthy of remark that such slaves invariably suffer greater hardships, and have more to contend with, than others. They are, in the first place, a constant offence to their mistress. She is ever disposed to find fault with them; they can seldom do any thing to please her; she is never better pleased than when she sees them under the lash, especially when she suspects her husband of showing to his mulatto children favors which he withholds from his black slaves. The master is frequently compelled to sell this class of his slaves, out of deference to the feelings of his white wife; and, cruel as the deed may strike any one to be, for a man to sell his own children to human flesh-mongers, it is often the dictate of humanity for him to do so; for, unless he does this, he must not only whip them himself, but must stand by and see one white son tie up his brother, of but few shades darker complexion than himself, and ply the gory lash to his naked back; and if he lisp one word of disapproval, it is set down to his parental partiality, and only makes a bad matter worse, both for himself and the slave whom he would protect and defend.

Every year brings with it multitudes of this class of slaves. It was doubtless in consequence of a knowledge of this fact, that one great statesman of the south predicted the downfall of slavery by the inevitable laws of population. Whether this prophecy is ever fulfilled or not, it is nevertheless plain that a very different-looking class of people are springing up at the south, and are now held in slavery, from those originally brought to this country from Africa; and if their increase will do no other good, it will do away the force of the argument, that God cursed Ham, and therefore American slavery is right. If the lineal descendants of Ham are alone to be scripturally enslaved, it is certain that slavery at the south must soon become unscriptural; for thousands are ushered into the world, annually, who, like myself, owe their existence to white fathers, and those fathers most frequently their own masters.

I have had two masters. My first master's name was Anthony. I do not remember his first name. He was generally called Captain Anthony—a title which, I presume, he acquired by sailing a craft on the Chesapeake Bay. He was not considered a rich slaveholder. He owned two or three farms, and about thirty slaves. His farms and slaves were under the care of an overseer. The overseer's name was Plummer. Mr. Plummer was a miserable drunkard, a profane swearer, and a savage monster. He always went armed with a cowskin and a heavy cudgel. I have known him to cut and slash the women's heads so horribly, that even master would be enraged at his cruelty, and would threaten to whip him if he did not mind himself. Master, however, was not a humane slaveholder. It required extraordinary barbarity on the part of an overseer to affect him. He was a cruel man, hardened by a long life of slaveholding. He would at times seem to take great pleasure in whipping a slave. I have often been awakened at the dawn of day by the most heart-rending shrieks of an own aunt of mine, whom he used to tie up to a joist, and whip upon her naked back till she was literally covered with blood. No words, no tears, no prayers, from his gory victim, seemed to move his iron heart from its bloody purpose. The louder she screamed, the harder he whipped; and where the blood ran fastest, there he whipped longest. He would whip her to make her scream, and whip her to make her hush; and not until overcome by fatigue, would he cease to swing the blood-clotted cowskin. I remember the first time I ever witnessed this horrible exhibition. I was quite a child, but I well remember it. I never shall forget it whilst I remember any thing. It was the first of a long series of such outrages, of which I was doomed to be a witness and a participant. It struck me with awful force. It was the blood-stained gate, the entrance to the hell of slavery, through which I was about to pass. It was a most terrible spectacle. I wish I could commit to paper the feelings with which I beheld it.

This occurrence took place very soon after I went to live with my old master, and under the following circumstances. Aunt Hester went out one night,—where or for what I do not know,—and happened to be absent when my master desired her presence. He had ordered her not to go out evenings, and warned her that she must never let him catch her in company with a young man, who was paying attention to her, belonging to Colonel Lloyd. The young man's name was Ned Roberts, generally called Lloyd's Ned. Why master was so careful of her, may be safely left to conjecture. She was a woman of noble form, and of graceful proportions, having very few equals, and fewer superiors, in personal appearance, among the colored or white women of our neighborhood.

Aunt Hester had not only disobeyed his orders in going out, but had been found in company with Lloyd's Ned; which circumstance, I found, from what he said while whipping her, was the chief offence. Had he been a man of pure morals himself, he might have been thought interested in protecting the innocence of my aunt; but those who knew him will not suspect him of any such virtue. Before he commenced whipping Aunt Hester, he took her into the kitchen, and stripped her from neck to waist, leaving her neck, shoulders, and back, entirely naked. He then told her to cross her hands, calling her at the same time a d——d b——h. After crossing her hands, he tied them with a strong rope, and led her to a stool under a large hook in the joist, put in for the purpose. He made her get upon the stool, and tied her hands to the hook. She now stood fair for his infernal purpose. Her arms were stretched up at their full length, so that she stood upon the ends of her toes. He then said to her, "Now, you d——d b——h, I'll learn you how to disobey my orders!" and after rolling up his sleeves, he commenced to lay on the heavy cowskin, and soon the warm, red blood (amid heart-rending shrieks from her, and horrid oaths from him) came dripping to the floor. I was so terrified and horror-stricken at the sight, that I hid myself in a closet, and dared not venture out till long after the bloody transaction was over. I expected it would be my turn next. It was all new to me. I had never seen any thing like it before. I had always lived with my grandmother on the outskirts of the plantation, where she was put to raise the children of the younger women. I had therefore been, until now, out of the way of the bloody scenes that often occurred on the plantation.

Chapter II

My master's family consisted of two sons, Andrew and Richard; one daughter, Lucretia, and her husband, Captain Thomas Auld. They lived in one house, upon the home plantation of Colonel Edward Lloyd. My master was Colonel Lloyd's clerk and superintendent. He was what might be called the overseers of the overseers. I spent two years of childhood on this plantation in my old master's family. It was here that I witnessed the bloody transaction recorded in the first chapter; and as I received my first impressions of slavery on this plantation, I will give some description of it, and of slavery as it there existed. The plantation is about twelve miles north of Easton, in Talbot county, and is situated on the border of Miles River. The principal products raised upon it were tobacco, corn, and wheat. These were raised in great abundance; so that, with the products of this and the other farms belonging to him, he was able to keep in almost constant employment a large sloop, in carrying them to market at Baltimore. This sloop was named Sally Lloyd, in honor of one of the colonel's daughters. My master's son-in-law, Captain Auld, was master of the vessel; she was otherwise manned by the colonel's own slaves. Their names were Peter, Isaac, Rich, and Jake. These were esteemed very highly by the other slaves, and looked upon as the privileged ones of the plantation; for it was no small affair, in the eyes of the slaves, to be allowed to see Baltimore.

Colonel Lloyd kept from three to four hundred slaves on his home plantation, and owned a large number more on the neighboring farms belonging to him. The names of the farms nearest to the home plantation were Wye Town and New Design. "Wye Town" was under the overseership of a man named Noah Willis. New Design was under the overseership of a Mr. Townsend. The overseers of these, and all the rest of the farms, numbering over twenty, received advice and direction from the managers of the home plantation. This was the great business place. It was the seat of government for the whole twenty farms. All disputes among the overseers were settled here. If a slave was convicted of any high misdemeanor, became unmanageable, or evinced a determination to run away, he was brought immediately here, severely whipped, put on board the sloop, carried to Baltimore, and sold to Austin Woolfolk or some other slave-trader, as a warning to the slaves remaining.

Here, too, the slaves of all the other farms received their monthly allowance of food, and their yearly clothing. The men and women slaves received, as their monthly allowance of food, eight pounds of pork, or its equivalent in fish, and one bushel of corn meal. Their yearly clothing consisted of two coarse linen shirts, one pair of linen trousers, like the shirts, one jacket, one pair of trousers for winter, made of coarse negro cloth, one pair of stockings, and one pair of shoes; the whole of which could not have cost more than seven dollars. The allowance of the slave children was given to their mothers, or the old women having the care of them. The children unable to work in the field had neither shoes, stockings, jackets, nor trousers, given to them; their clothing consisted of two coarse linen shirts per year. When these failed them, they went naked until the next allowance-day. Children from seven to ten years old, of both sexes, almost naked, might be seen at all seasons of the year.

There were no beds given the slaves, unless one coarse blanket be considered such, and none but the men and women had these. This, however, is not considered a very great privation. They find less difficulty from the want of beds, than from the want of time to sleep; for when their day's work in the field is done, the most of them having their washing, mending, and cooking to do, and having few or none of the ordinary facilities for doing either of these, very many of their sleeping hours are consumed in preparing for the field the coming day; and when this is done, old and young, male and female, married and single, drop down side by side, on one common bed,—the cold, damp floor,—each covering himself or herself with their miserable blankets; and here they sleep till they are summoned to the field by the driver's horn. At the sound of this, all must rise, and be off to the field. There must be no halting; every one must be at his or her post; and woe betides them who hear not this morning summons to the field; for if they are not awakened by the sense of hearing, they are by the sense of feeling; no age nor sex finds any favor. Mr. Severe, the overseer, used to stand by the door of the quarter, armed with a large hickory stick and heavy cowskin, ready to whip any one who was so unfortunate as not to hear, or, from any other cause, was prevented from being ready to start for the field at the sound of the horn.

Mr. Severe was rightly named: he was a cruel man. I have seen him whip a woman, causing the blood to run half an hour at the time; and this, too, in the midst of her crying children, pleading for their mother's release. He seemed to take pleasure in manifesting his fiendish barbarity. Added to his cruelty, he was a profane swearer. It was enough to chill the blood and stiffen the hair of an ordinary man to hear him talk. Scarce a sentence escaped him but that was commenced or concluded by some horrid oath. The field was the place to witness his cruelty and profanity. His presence made it both the field of blood and of blasphemy. From the rising till the going down of the sun, he was cursing, raving, cutting, and slashing among the slaves of the field, in the most frightful manner. His career was short. He died very soon after I went to Colonel Lloyd's; and he died as he lived, uttering, with his dying groans, bitter curses and horrid oaths. His death was regarded by the slaves as the result of a merciful providence.

Mr. Severe's place was filled by a Mr. Hopkins. He was a very different man. He was less cruel, less profane, and made less noise, than Mr. Severe. His course was characterized by no extraordinary demonstrations of cruelty. He whipped, but seemed to take no pleasure in it. He was called by the slaves a good overseer.

The home plantation of Colonel Lloyd wore the appearance of a country village. All the mechanical operations for all the farms were performed here. The shoemaking and mending, the blacksmithing, cartwrighting, coopering, weaving, and grain-grinding, were all performed by the slaves on the home plantation. The whole place wore a business-like aspect very unlike the neighboring farms. The number of houses, too, conspired to give it advantage over the neighboring farms. It was called by the slaves the *Great House Farm*. Few privileges were esteemed higher, by the slaves of the out-farms, than that of being selected to do errands at the Great House Farm. It was associated in their minds with greatness. A representative could not be prouder of his election to a seat in the American Congress, than a slave on one of the out-farms would be of his election to do errands at the Great House Farm. They regarded it as evidence of great confidence reposed in them by their overseers; and it was on this account, as well as a constant desire to be out of the field from under the driver's lash, that they esteemed it a high privilege, one worth careful living for. He was called the smartest and most trusty fellow, who had this honor conferred upon him the most frequently. The competitors for this office sought as diligently to please their overseers, as the office-seekers in the political parties seek to please and deceive the people. The same traits of character might be seen in Colonel Lloyd's slaves, as are seen in the slaves of the political parties.

The slaves selected to go to the Great House Farm, for the monthly allowance for themselves and their fellow-slaves, were peculiarly enthusiastic. While on their way, they would make the dense old woods, for miles around, reverberate with their wild songs, revealing at once the highest joy and the deepest sadness. They would compose and sing as they went along, consulting neither time nor tune. The thought that came up, came out—if not in the word, in the sound;—and as frequently in the one as in the other. They would sometimes sing the most pathetic sentiment in the most rapturous tone, and the most rapturous sentiment in the most pathetic tone. Into all of their songs they would manage to weave something of the Great House Farm. Especially would they do this, when leaving home. They would then sing most exultingly the following words:—

"I am going away to the Great House Farm!
O, yea! O, yea! O!"

This they would sing, as a chorus, to words which to many would seem unmeaning jargon, but which, nevertheless, were full of meaning to themselves. I have sometimes thought that the mere hearing of those songs would do more to impress some minds with the horrible character of slavery, than the reading of whole volumes of philosophy on the subject could do.

I did not, when a slave, understand the deep meaning of those rude and apparently incoherent songs. I was myself within the circle; so that I neither saw nor heard as those without might see and hear. They told a tale of woe which was then altogether beyond my feeble comprehension; they were tones loud, long, and deep; they breathed the prayer and complaint of souls boiling over with the bitterest anguish. Every tone was a testimony against slavery, and a prayer to God for deliverance from chains. The hearing of those wild notes always depressed my spirit, and filled me with ineffable sadness. I have frequently found myself in tears while hearing them. The mere recurrence to those songs, even now, afflicts me; and while I am writing these lines, an expression of feeling has already found its way down my cheek. To those songs I trace my first glimmering conception of the dehumanizing character of slavery. I can never get rid of that conception. Those songs still follow me, to deepen my hatred of slavery, and quicken my sympathies for my brethren in bonds. If any one wishes to be impressed with the soul-killing effects of slavery, let him go to Colonel Lloyd's plantation, and, on allowance-day, place himself in the deep pine woods, and there let him, in silence, analyze the sounds that shall pass through the chambers of his soul,—and if he is not thus impressed, it will only be because "there is no flesh in his obdurate heart."

I have often been utterly astonished, since I came to the north, to find persons who could speak of the singing, among slaves, as evidence of their contentment and happiness. It is impossible to conceive of a greater mistake. Slaves sing most when they are most unhappy. The songs of the slave represent the sorrows of his heart; and he is relieved by them, only as an aching heart is relieved by its tears. At least, such is my experience. I have often sung to drown my sorrow, but seldom to express my happiness. Crying for joy, and singing for joy, were alike uncommon to me while in the jaws of slavery. The singing of a man cast away upon a desolate island might be as appropriately considered as evidence of contentment and happiness, as the singing of a slave; the songs of the one and of the other are prompted by the same emotion.

Chapter III

Colonel Lloyd kept a large and finely cultivated garden, which afforded almost constant employment for four men, besides the chief gardener, (Mr. M'Durmond.) This garden was probably the greatest attraction of the place. During the summer months, people came from far and near—from Baltimore, Easton, and Annapolis—to see it. It abounded in fruits of almost every description, from the hardy apple of the north to the delicate orange of the south. This garden was not the least source of trouble on the plantation. Its excellent fruit was quite a temptation to the hungry swarms of boys, as well as the older slaves, belonging to the colonel, few of whom had the virtue or the vice to resist it. Scarcely a day passed, during the summer, but that some slave had to take the lash for stealing fruit. The colonel had to resort to all kinds of stratagems to keep his slaves out of the garden. The last and most successful one was that of tarring his fence all around; after which, if a slave was caught with any tar upon his person, it was deemed sufficient proof that he had either been into the garden, or had tried to get in. In either case, he was severely whipped by the chief gardener. This plan worked well; the slaves became as fearful of tar as of the lash. They seemed to realize the impossibility of touching tar without being defiled.

The colonel also kept a splendid riding equipage. His stable and carriage-house presented the appearance of some of our large city livery establishments. His horses were of the finest form and noblest blood. His carriage-house contained three splendid coaches, three or four gigs, besides dearborns and barouches of the most fashionable style.

This establishment was under the care of two slaves—old Barney and young Barney—father and son. To attend to this establishment was their sole work. But it was by no means an easy employment; for in nothing was Colonel Lloyd more particular than in the management of his horses. The slightest inattention to these was unpardonable, and was visited upon those, under whose care they were placed, with the severest punishment; no excuse could shield them, if the colonel only suspected any want of attention to his horse—a supposition which he frequently indulged, and one which, of course, made the office of old and young Barney a very trying one. They never knew when they were safe from punishment. They were frequently whipped when least deserving, and escaped whipping when most deserving it. Every thing depended upon the looks of the horses, and the state of Colonel Lloyd's own mind when his horses were brought to him for use. If a horse did not move fast enough, or hold his head high enough, it was owing to some fault of his keepers. It was painful to stand near the stable-door, and hear the various complaints against the keepers when a horse was taken out for use. "This horse has not had proper attention. He has not been sufficiently rubbed and curried, or he has not been properly fed; his food was too wet or too dry; he got it too soon or too late; he was too hot or too cold; he had too much hay, and not enough of grain; or he had too much grain, and not enough of hay; instead of old Barney's attending to the horse, he had very improperly left it to his son." To all these complaints, no matter how unjust, the slave must answer never a word. Colonel Lloyd could not brook any contradiction from a slave. When he spoke, a slave must stand, listen, and tremble; and such was literally the case. I have seen Colonel Lloyd make old Barney, a man between fifty and sixty years of age, uncover his bald head, kneel down upon the cold, damp ground, and receive upon his naked and toil-worn shoulders more than thirty lashes at the time. Colonel Lloyd had three son—Edward, Murray, and Daniel, and three sons-in-law, Mr. Winder, Mr. Nicholson, and Mr. Lowndes. All of these lived at the Great House Farm, and enjoyed the luxury of whipping the servants when they pleased, from old Barney down to William Wilkes, the coach-driver. I have seen Winder make one of the house-servants stand off from him a suitable distance to be touched with the end of his whip, and at every stroke raise great ridges upon his back.

To describe the wealth of Colonel Lloyd would be almost equal to describing the riches of Job. He kept from ten to fifteen house-servants. He was said to own a thousand slaves, and I think this estimate quite within the truth. Colonel Lloyd owned so many that he did not know them when he saw them; nor did all the slaves of the out-farms know him. It is reported of him, that, while riding along the road one day, he met a colored man, and addressed him in the usual manner of speaking to colored people on the public highways of the south: "Well, boy, whom do you belong to?" "To Colonel Lloyd," replied the slave. "Well, does the colonel treat you well?" "No, sir," was the ready reply. "What, does he work you too hard?" "Yes, sir." "Well, don't he give you enough to eat?" "Yes, sir, he gives me enough, such as it is."

The colonel, after ascertaining where the slave belonged, rode on; the man also went on about his business, not dreaming that he had been conversing with his master. He thought, said, and heard nothing more of the matter, until two or three weeks afterwards. The poor man was then informed by his overseer that, for having found fault with his master, he was now to be sold to a Georgia trader. He was immediately chained and handcuffed; and thus, without a moment's warning, he was snatched away, and forever sundered, from his family and friends, by a hand more unrelenting than death. This is the penalty of telling the truth, of telling the simple truth, in answer to a series of plain questions.

It is partly in consequence of such facts, that slaves when inquired of as to their condition and the character of their masters, almost universally say they are contented, and that their masters are kind. The slaveholders have been known to send in spies among their slaves, to ascertain their views and feelings in regard to their condition. The frequency of this has had the effect to establish among the slaves the maxim, that a still tongue makes a wise head. They suppress the truth rather than take the consequences of telling it, and in so doing prove themselves a part of the human family. If they have any thing to say of their masters, it is generally in their masters' favor, especially when speaking to an untried man. I have been frequently asked, when a slave, if I had a kind master, and do not remember ever to have given a negative answer; nor did I, in pursuing this course, consider myself as uttering what was absolutely false; for I always measured the kindness of my master by the standard of kindness set up among slaveholders around us. Moreover, slaves are like other people, and imbibe prejudices quite common to others. They think their own better than that of others. Many, under the influence of this prejudice, think their own masters are better than the masters of other slaves; and this, too, in some cases, when the very reverse is true. Indeed, it is not uncommon for slaves even to fall out and quarrel among themselves about the relative goodness of their masters, each contending for the superior goodness of his own over that of the others. At the very same time, they mutually execrate their masters when viewed separately. It was so on our plantation. When Colonel Lloyd's slaves met the slaves of Jacob Jepson, they seldom parted without a quarrel about their masters; Colonel Lloyd's slaves contending that he was the richest, and Mr. Jepson's slaves that he was the smartest, and most of a man. Colonel Lloyd's slaves would boast his ability to buy and sell Jacob Jepson. Mr. Jepson's slaves would boast his ability to whip Colonel Lloyd. These quarrels would almost always end in a fight between the parties, and those that whipped were supposed to have gained the point at issue. They seemed to think that the greatness of their masters was transferable to themselves. It was considered as being bad enough to be a slave; but to be a poor man's slave was deemed a disgrace indeed!

Chapter IV

Mr. Hopkins remained but a short time in the office of overseer. Why his career was so short, I do not know, but suppose he lacked the necessary severity to suit Colonel Lloyd. Mr. Hopkins was succeeded by Mr. Austin Gore, a man possessing, in an eminent degree, all those traits of character indispensable to what is called a first-rate overseer. Mr. Gore had served Colonel Lloyd, in the capacity of overseer, upon one of the out-farms, and had shown himself worthy of the high station of overseer upon the home or Great House Farm.

Mr. Gore was proud, ambitious, and persevering. He was artful, cruel, and obdurate. He was just the man for such a place, and it was just the place for such a man. It afforded scope for the full exercise of all his powers, and he seemed to be perfectly at home in it. He was one of those who could torture the slightest look, word, or gesture, on the part of the slave, into impudence, and would treat it accordingly There must be no answering back to him; no explanation was allowed a slave, showing himself to have been wrongfully accused. Mr. Gore acted fully up to the maxim laid down by slaveholders,—"It is better that a dozen slaves suffer under the lash, than that the overseer should be convicted, in the presence of the slaves, of having been at fault." No matter how innocent a slave might be—it availed him nothing, when accused by Mr. Gore of any misdemeanor. To be accused was to be convicted, and to be convicted was to be punished; the one always following the other with immutable certainty. To escape punishment was to escape accusation; and few slaves had the fortune to do either, under the overseership of Mr. Gore. He was just proud enough to demand the most debasing homage of the slave, and quite servile enough to crouch, himself, at the feet of the master. He was ambitious enough to be contented with nothing short of the highest rank of overseers, and persevering enough to reach the height of his ambition. He was cruel enough to inflict the severest punishment, artful enough to descend to the lowest trickery, and obdurate enough to be insensible to the voice of a reproving conscience. He was, of all the overseers, the most dreaded by the slaves. His presence was painful; his eye flashed confusion; and seldom was his sharp, shrill voice heard, without producing horror and trembling in their ranks.

Mr. Gore was a grave man, and, though a young man, he indulged in no jokes, said no funny words, seldom smiled. His words were in perfect keeping with his looks, and his looks were in perfect keeping with his words. Overseers will sometimes indulge in a witty word, even with the slaves; not so with Mr. Gore. He spoke but to command, and commanded but to be obeyed; he dealt sparingly with his words, and bountifully with his whip, never using the former where the latter would answer as well. When he whipped, he seemed to do so from a sense of duty, and feared no consequences. He did nothing reluctantly, no matter how disagreeable; always at his post, never inconsistent. He never promised but to fulfil. He was, in a word, a man of the most inflexible firmness and stone-like coolness.

His savage barbarity was equalled only by the consummate coolness with which he committed the grossest and most savage deeds upon the slaves under his charge. Mr. Gore once undertook to whip one of Colonel Lloyd's slaves, by the name of Demby. He had given Demby but few stripes, when, to get rid of the scourging, he ran and plunged himself into a creek, and stood there at the depth of his shoulders, refusing to come out. Mr. Gore told him that he would give him three calls, and that, if he did not come out at the third call, he would shoot him. The first call was given. Demby made no response, but stood his ground. The second and third calls were given with the same result. Mr. Gore then, without consultation or deliberation with any one, not even giving Demby an additional call, raised his musket to his face, taking deadly aim at his standing victim, and in an instant poor Demby was no more. His mangled body sank out of sight, and blood and brains marked the water where he had stood.

A thrill of horror flashed through every soul upon the plantation, excepting Mr. Gore. He alone seemed cool and collected. He was asked by Colonel Lloyd and my old master, why he resorted to this extraordinary expedient. His reply was, (as well as I can remember,) that Demby had become unmanageable. He was setting a dangerous example to the other slaves,—one which, if suffered to pass without some such demonstration on his part, would finally lead to the total subversion of all rule and order upon the plantation. He argued that if one slave refused to be corrected, and escaped with his life, the other slaves would soon copy the example; the result of which would be, the freedom of the slaves, and the enslavement of the whites. Mr. Gore's defence was satisfactory. He was continued in his station as overseer upon the home plantation. His fame as an overseer went abroad. His horrid crime was not even submitted to judicial investigation. It was committed in the presence of slaves, and they of course could neither institute a suit, nor testify against him; and thus the guilty perpetrator of one of the bloodiest and most foul murders goes unwhipped of justice, and uncensured by the community in which he lives. Mr. Gore lived in St. Michael's, Talbot country, Maryland, when I left there; and if he is still alive, he very probably lives there now; and if so, he is now, as he was then, as highly esteemed and as much respected as though his guilty soul had not been stained with his brother's blood.

I speak advisedly when I say this,—that killing a slave, or any colored person, in Talbot country, Maryland, is not treated as a crime, either by the courts or the community. Mr. Thomas Lanman, of St. Michael's, killed two slaves, one of whom he killed with a hatchet, by knocking his brains out. He used to boast of the commission of the awful and bloody deed. I have heard him do so laughingly, saying, among other things, that he was the only benefactor of his country in the company, and that when others would do as much as he had done, we should be relieved of "the d——d niggers."

The wife of Mr. Giles Hick, living but a short distance from where I used to live, murdered my wife's cousin, a young girl between fifteen and sixteen years of age, mangling her person in the most horrible manner, breaking her nose and breastbone with a stick, so that the poor girl expired in a few hours afterward. She was immediately buried, but had not been in her untimely grave but a few hours before she was taken up and examined by the coroner, who decided that she had come to her death by severe beating. The offence for which this girl was thus murdered was this:—She had been set that night to mind Mrs. Hick's baby, and during the night she fell asleep, and the baby cried. She, having lost her rest for several nights previous, did not hear the crying. They were both in the room with Mrs. Hicks. Mrs. Hicks, finding the girl slow to move, jumped from her bed, seized an oak stick of wood by the fireplace, and with it broke the girl's nose and breastbone, and thus ended her life. I will not say that this most horrid murder produced no sensation in the community. It did produce sensation, but not enough to bring the murderess to punishment. There was a warrant issued for her arrest, but it was never served. Thus she escaped not only punishment, but even the pain of being arraigned before a court for her horrid crime.

Whilst I am detailing bloody deeds which took place during my stay on Colonel Lloyd's plantation, I will briefly narrate another, which occurred about the same time as the murder of Demby by Mr. Gore.

Colonel Lloyd's slaves were in the habit of spending a part of their nights and Sundays in fishing for oysters, and in this way made up the deficiency of their scanty allowance. An old man belonging to Colonel Lloyd, while thus engaged, happened to get beyond the limits of Colonel Lloyd's, and on the premises of Mr. Beal Bondly. At this trespass, Mr. Bondly took offence, and with his musket came down to the shore, and blew its deadly contents into the poor old man.

Mr. Bondly came over to see Colonel Lloyd the next day, whether to pay him for his property, or to justify himself in what he had done, I know not. At any rate, this whole fiendish transaction was soon hushed up. There was very little said about it at all, and nothing done. It was a common saying, even among little white boys, that it was worth a half-cent to kill a "nigger," and a half-cent to bury one.

Chapter V

As to my own treatment while I lived on Colonel Lloyd's plantation, it was very similar to that of the other slave children. I was not old enough to work in the field, and there being little else than field work to do, I had a great deal of leisure time. The most I had to do was to drive up the cows at evening, keep the fowls out of the garden, keep the front yard clean, and run of errands for my old master's daughter, Mrs. Lucretia Auld. The most of my leisure time I spent in helping Master Daniel Lloyd in finding his birds, after he had shot them. My connection with Master Daniel was of some advantage to me. He became quite attached to me, and was a sort of protector of me. He would not allow the older boys to impose upon me, and would divide his cakes with me.

I was seldom whipped by my old master, and suffered little from any thing else than hunger and cold. In hottest summer and coldest winter, I was kept almost naked—no shoes, no stockings, no jacket, no trousers, nothing on but a coarse tow linen shirt, reaching only to my knees. I had no bed. I must have perished with cold, but that, the coldest nights, I used to steal a bag which was used for carrying corn to the mill. I would crawl into this bag, and there sleep on the cold, damp clay floor, with my head in and feet out. My feet have been so cracked with the frost, that the pen with which I am writing might be laid in the gashes.

We were not regularly allowanced. Our food was coarse corn meal boiled. This was called *mush*. It was put into a large wooden tray or trough, and set down upon the ground. The children were then called, like so many pigs, and like so many pigs they would come and devour the mush; some with oyster-shells, others with pieces of shingle, some with naked hands, and none with spoons. He that ate fastest got most; he that was strongest secured the best place; and few left the trough satisfied.

I was probably between seven and eight years old when I left Colonel Lloyd's plantation. I left it with joy. I shall never forget the ecstasy with which I received the intelligence that my old master (Anthony) had determined to let me go to Baltimore, to live with Mr. Hugh Auld, brother to my old master's son-in-law, Captain Thomas Auld. I received this information about three days before my departure. They were three of the happiest days I ever enjoyed. I spent the most part of all these three days in the creek, washing off the plantation scurf, and preparing myself for my departure.

The pride of appearance which this would indicate was not my own. I spent the time in washing, not so much because I wished to, but because Mrs. Lucretia had told me I must get all the dead skin off my feet and knees before I could go to Baltimore; for the people in Baltimore were very cleanly, and would laugh at me if I looked dirty. Besides, she was going to give me a pair of trousers, which I should not put on unless I got all the dirt off me. The thought of owning a pair of trousers was great indeed! It was almost a sufficient motive, not only to make me take off what would be called by pig-drovers the mange, but the skin itself. I went at it in good earnest, working for the first time with the hope of reward.

The ties that ordinarily bind children to their homes were all suspended in my case. I found no severe trial in my departure. My home was charmless; it was not home to me; on parting from it, I could not feel that I was leaving any thing which I could have enjoyed by staying. My mother was dead, my grandmother lived far off, so that I seldom saw her. I had two sisters and one brother, that lived in the same house with me; but the early separation of us from our mother had well nigh blotted the fact of our relationship from our memories. I looked for home elsewhere, and was confident of finding none which I should relish less than the one which I was leaving. If, however, I found in my new home hardship, hunger, whipping, and nakedness, I had the consolation that I should not have escaped any one of them by staying. Having already had more than a taste of them in the house of my old master, and having endured them there, I very naturally inferred my ability to endure them elsewhere, and especially at Baltimore; for I had something of the feeling about Baltimore that is expressed in the proverb, that "being hanged in England is preferable to dying a natural death in Ireland." I had the strongest desire to see Baltimore. Cousin

Tom, though not fluent in speech, had inspired me with that desire by his eloquent description of the place. I could never point out any thing at the Great House, no matter how beautiful or powerful, but that he had seen something at Baltimore far exceeding, both in beauty and strength, the object which I pointed out to him. Even the Great House itself, with all its pictures, was far inferior to many buildings in Baltimore. So strong was my desire, that I thought a gratification of it would fully compensate for whatever loss of comforts I should sustain by the exchange. I left without a regret, and with the highest hopes of future happiness.

We sailed out of Miles River for Baltimore on a Saturday morning. I remember only the day of the week, for at that time I had no knowledge of the days of the month, nor the months of the year. On setting sail, I walked aft, and gave to Colonel Lloyd's plantation what I hoped would be the last look. I then placed myself in the bows of the sloop, and there spent the remainder of the day in looking ahead, interesting myself in what was in the distance rather than in things near by or behind.

In the afternoon of that day, we reached Annapolis, the capital of the State. We stopped but a few moments, so that I had no time to go on shore. It was the first large town that I had ever seen, and though it would look small compared with some of our New England factory villages, I thought it a wonderful place for its size—more imposing even than the Great House Farm!

We arrived at Baltimore early on Sunday morning, landing at Smith's Wharf, not far from Bowley's Wharf. We had on board the sloop a large flock of sheep; and after aiding in driving them to the slaughter-house of Mr. Curtis on Louden Slater's Hill, I was conducted by Rich, one of the hands belonging on board of the sloop, to my new home in Alliciana Street, near Mr. Gardner's ship-yard, on Fells Point.

Mr. and Mrs. Auld were both at home, and met me at the door with their little son Thomas, to take care of whom I had been given. And here I saw what I had never seen before; it was a white face beaming with the most kindly emotions; it was the face of my new mistress, Sophia Auld. I wish I could describe the rapture that flashed through my soul as I beheld it. It was a new and strange sight to me, brightening up my pathway with the light of happiness. Little Thomas was told, there was his Freddy, and I was told to take care of little Thomas; and thus I entered upon the duties of my new home with the most cheering prospect ahead.

I look upon my departure from Colonel Lloyd's plantation as one of the most interesting events of my life. It is possible, and even quite probable, that but for the mere circumstance of being removed from that plantation to Baltimore, I should have to-day, instead of being here seated by my own table, in the enjoyment of freedom and the happiness of home, writing this Narrative, been confined in the galling chains of slavery. Going to live at Baltimore laid the foundation, and opened the gateway, to all my subsequent prosperity. I have ever regarded it as the first plain manifestation of that kind providence which has ever since attended me, and marked my life with so many favors. I regarded the selection of myself as being somewhat remarkable. There were a number of slave children that might have been sent from the plantation to Baltimore. There were those younger, those older, and those of the same age. I was chosen from among them all, and was the first, last, and only choice.

I may be deemed superstitious, and even egotistical, in regarding this event as a special interposition of divine Providence in my favor. But I should be false to the earliest sentiments of my soul, if I suppressed the opinion. I prefer to be true to myself, even at the hazard of incurring the ridicule of others, rather than to be false, and incur my own abhorrence. From my earliest recollection, I date the entertainment of a deep conviction that slavery would not always be able to hold me within its foul embrace; and in the darkest hours of my career in slavery, this living word of faith and spirit of hope departed not from me, but remained like ministering angels to cheer me through the gloom. This good spirit was from God, and to him I offer thanksgiving and praise.

Chapter VI

My new mistress proved to be all she appeared when I first met her at the door,—a woman of the kindest heart and finest feelings. She had never had a slave under her control previously to myself, and prior to her marriage she had been dependent upon her own industry for a living. She was by trade a weaver; and by constant application to her business, she had been in a good degree preserved from the blighting and dehumanizing effects of slavery. I was utterly astonished at her goodness. I scarcely knew how to behave towards her. She was entirely unlike any other white woman I had ever seen. I could not approach her as I was accustomed to approach other white ladies. My early instruction was all out of place. The crouching servility, usually so acceptable a quality in a slave, did not answer when manifested toward her. Her favor was not gained by it; she seemed to be disturbed by it. She did not deem it impudent or unmannerly for a slave to look her in the face. The meanest slave was put fully at ease in her presence, and none left without feeling better for having seen her. Her face was made of heavenly smiles, and her voice of tranquil music.

But, alas! this kind heart had but a short time to remain such. The fatal poison of irresponsible power was already in her hands, and soon commenced its infernal work. That cheerful eye, under the influence of slavery, soon became red with rage; that voice, made all of sweet accord, changed to one of harsh and horrid discord; and that angelic face gave place to that of a demon.

Very soon after I went to live with Mr. and Mrs. Auld, she very kindly commenced to teach me the A, B, C. After I had learned this, she assisted me in learning to spell words of three or four letters. Just at this point of my progress, Mr. Auld found out what was going on, and at once forbade Mrs. Auld to instruct me further, telling her, among other things, that it was unlawful, as well as unsafe, to teach a slave to read. To use his own words, further, he said, "If you give a nigger an inch, he will take an ell. A nigger should know nothing but to obey his master—to do as he is told to do. Learning would *spoil* the best nigger in the world. Now," said he, "if you teach that nigger (speaking of myself) how to read, there would be no keeping him. It would forever unfit him to be a slave. He would at once become unmanageable, and of no value to his master. As to himself, it could do him no good, but a great deal of harm. It would make him discontented and unhappy." These words sank deep into my heart, stirred up sentiments within that lay slumbering, and called into existence an entirely new train of thought. It was a new and special revelation, explaining dark and mysterious things, with which my youthful understanding had struggled, but struggled in vain. I now understood what had been to me a most perplexing difficulty—to wit, the white man's power to enslave the black man. It was a grand achievement, and I prized it highly. From that moment, I understood the pathway from slavery to freedom. It was just what I wanted, and I got it at a time when I the least expected it. Whilst I was saddened by the thought of losing the aid of my kind mistress, I was gladdened by the invaluable instruction which, by the merest accident, I had gained from my master. Though conscious of the difficulty of learning without a teacher, I set out with high hope, and a fixed purpose, at whatever cost of trouble, to learn how to read. The very decided manner with which he spoke, and strove to impress his wife with the evil consequences of giving me instruction, served to convince me that he was deeply sensible of the truths he was uttering. It gave me the best assurance that I might rely with the utmost confidence on the results which, he said, would flow from teaching me to read. What he most dreaded, that I most desired. What he most loved, that I most hated. That which to him was a great evil, to be carefully shunned, was to me a great good, to be diligently sought; and the argument which he so warmly urged, against my learning to read, only served to inspire me with a desire and determination to learn. In learning to read, I owe almost as much to the bitter opposition of my master, as to the kindly aid of my mistress. I acknowledge the benefit of both.

I had resided but a short time in Baltimore before I observed a marked difference, in the treatment of slaves, from that which I had witnessed in the country. A city slave is almost a freeman, compared with a slave on the plantation. He is much better fed and clothed, and enjoys privileges altogether unknown to the slave on the plantation. There is a vestige of decency, a sense of shame, that does much to curb and check those outbreaks of atrocious cruelty so commonly enacted upon the plantation. He is a desperate slaveholder, who will shock the humanity of his non-slaveholding neighbors with the cries of his lacerated slave. Few are willing to incur the odium attaching to the reputation of being a cruel master; and above all things, they would not be known as not giving a slave enough to eat. Every city slaveholder is anxious to have it known of him, that he feeds his slaves well, and it is due to them to say, that most of them do give their slaves enough to eat. There are, however, some painful exceptions to this rule. Directly opposite to us, on Philpot Street, lived Mr. Thomas Hamilton. He owned two slaves. Their names were Henrietta and Mary. Henrietta was about twenty-two years of age, Mary was about fourteen; and of all the mangled and emaciated creatures I ever looked upon, these two were the most so. His heart must be harder than stone, that could look upon these unmoved. The head, neck, and shoulders of Mary were literally cut to pieces. I have frequently felt her head, and found it nearly covered with festering sores, caused by the lash of her cruel mistress. I do not know that her master ever whipped her, but I have been an eye-witness to the cruelty of Mrs. Hamilton. I used to be in Mr. Hamilton's house nearly every day. Mrs. Hamilton used to sit in a large chair in the middle of the room, with a heavy cowskin always by her side, and scarce an hour passed during the day but was marked by the blood of one of these slaves. The girls seldom passed her without her saying, "Move faster, you *black gip!*" at the same time giving them a blow with the cowskin over the head or shoulders, often drawing the blood. She would then say, "Take that, you *black gip!*"—continuing, "If you don't move faster, I'll move you!" Added to the cruel lashings to which these slaves were subjected, they were kept nearly half-starved. They seldom knew what it was to eat a full meal. I have seen Mary contending with the pigs for the offal thrown into the street. So much was Mary kicked and cut to pieces, that she was oftener called *"pecked"* than by her name.

Chapter VII

I lived in Master Hugh's family about seven years. During this time, I succeeded in learning to read and write. In accomplishing this, I was compelled to resort to various stratagems. I had no regular teacher. My mistress, who had kindly commenced to instruct me, had, in compliance with the advice and direction of her husband, not only ceased to instruct, but had set her face against my being instructed by any one else. It is due, however, to my mistress to say of her, that she did not adopt this course of treatment immediately. She at first lacked the depravity indispensable to shutting me up in mental darkness. It was at least necessary for her to have some training in the exercise of irresponsible power, to make her equal to the task of treating me as though I were a brute.

My mistress was, as I have said, a kind and tender-hearted woman; and in the simplicity of her soul she commenced, when I first went to live with her, to treat me as she supposed one human being ought to treat another. In entering upon the duties of a slaveholder, she did not seem to perceive that I sustained to her the relation of a mere chattel, and that for her to treat me as a human being was not only wrong, but dangerously so. Slavery proved as injurious to her as it did to me. When I went there, she was a pious, warm, and tender-hearted woman. There was no sorrow or suffering for which she had not a tear. She had bread for the hungry, clothes for the naked, and comfort for every mourner that came within her reach. Slavery soon proved its ability to divest her of these heavenly qualities. Under its influence, the tender heart became stone, and the lamblike disposition gave way to one of tiger-like fierceness. The first step in her downward course was in her ceasing to instruct me. She now commenced to practise her husband's precepts. She finally became even more violent in her opposition than her husband himself. She was not satisfied with simply doing as well as he had commanded; she seemed anxious to do better. Nothing seemed to make her more angry than to see me with a newspaper. She seemed to think that here lay the danger. I have had her rush at me with a face made all up of fury, and snatch from me a newspaper, in a manner that fully revealed her apprehension. She was an apt woman; and a little experience soon demonstrated, to her satisfaction, that education and slavery were incompatible with each other.

From this time I was most narrowly watched. If I was in a separate room any considerable length of time, I was sure to be suspected of having a book, and was at once called to give an account of myself. All this, however, was too late. The first step had been taken. Mistress, in teaching me the alphabet, had given me the *inch,* and no precaution could prevent me from taking the *ell.*

The plan which I adopted, and the one by which I was most successful, was that of making friends of all the little white boys whom I met in the street. As many of these as I could, I converted into teachers. With their kindly aid, obtained at different times and in different places, I finally succeeded in learning to read. When I was sent of errands, I always took my book with me, and by going one part of my errand quickly, I found time to get a lesson before my return. I used also to carry bread with me, enough of which was always in the house, and to which I was always welcome; for I was much better off in this regard than many of the poor white children in our neighborhood. this bread I used to bestow upon the hungry little urchins, who, in return, would give me that more valuable bread of knowledge. I am strongly tempted to give the names of two or three of those little boys, as a testimonial of the gratitude and affection I bear them; but prudence forbids;—not that it would injure me, but it might embarrass them; for it is almost an unpardonable offence to teach slaves to read in this Christian country. It is enough to say of the dear little fellows, that they lived on Philpot Street, very near Durgin and Bailey's shipyard. I used to talk this matter of slavery over with them. I would sometimes say to them, I wished I could be as free as they would be when they got to be men. "You will be free as soon as you are twenty-one, *but I am a slave for life!* Have not I as good a right to be free as you have?" These words used to trouble them; they would express for me the liveliest sympathy, and console me with the hope that something would occur by which I might be free.

I was now about twelve years old, and the thought of being *a slave for life* began to bear heavily upon my heart. Just about this time, I got hold of a book entitled "The Columbian orator." Every opportunity I got, I used to read this book. Among much of other interesting matter, I found in it a dialogue between a master and his slave. The slave was represented as having run away from his master three times. The dialogue represented the conversation which took place between them, when the slave was retaken the third time. In this dialogue, the whole argument in behalf of slavery was brought forward by the master, all of which was disposed of by the slave. The slave was made to say some very smart as well as impressive things in reply to his master—things which had the desired though unexpected effect; for the conversation resulted in the voluntary emancipation of the slave on the part of the master.

In the same book, I met with one of Sheridan's mighty speeches on and in behalf of Catholic emancipation. These were choice documents to me. I read them over and over again with unabated interest. They gave tongue to interesting thoughts of my own soul, which had frequently flashed through my mind, and died away for want of utterance. The moral which I gained from the dialogue was the power of truth over the conscience of even a slaveholder. What I got from Sheridan was a bold denunciation of slavery, and a powerful vindication of human rights. The reading of these documents enabled me to utter my thoughts, and to meet the arguments brought forward to sustain slavery; but while they relieved me of one difficulty, they brought on another even more painful than the one of which I was relieved. The more I read, the more I was led to abhor and detest my enslavers. I could regard them in no other light than a band of successful robbers, who had left their homes, and gone to Africa, and stolen us from our homes, and in a strange land reduced us to slavery. I loathed them as being the meanest as well as the most wicked of men. As I read and contemplated the subject, behold! that very discontentment which Master Hugh had predicted would follow my learning to read had already come, to torment and sting my soul to unutterable anguish. As I writhed under it, I would at times feel that learning to read had been a curse rather than a blessing. It had given me a view of my wretched condition, without the remedy. I opened my eyes to the horrible pit, but to no ladder upon which to get out. In moments of agony, I envied my fellow-slaves for their stupidity. I have often wished myself a beast. I preferred the condition of the meanest reptile to my own. Any thing, no matter what, to get rid of thinking! It was this everlasting thinking of my condition that tormented me. There was no getting rid of it. It was pressed upon me by every object within sight or hearing, animate or inanimate. The silver trump of freedom had roused my soul to eternal wakefulness. Freedom now appeared, to disappear no more forever. It was heard in every sound, and seen in every thing. It was ever present to torment me with a sense of my wretched condition. I saw nothing without seeing it, I heard nothing without hearing it, and felt nothing without feeling it. It looked from every star, it smiled in every calm, breathed in every wind, and moved in every storm.

I often found myself regretting my own existence, and wishing myself dead; and but for the hope of being free, I have no doubt but that I should have killed myself, or done something for which I should have been killed. While in this state of mind, I was eager to hear any one speak of slavery. I was a ready listener. Every little while, I could hear something about the abolitionists. It was some time before I found what the word meant. It was always used in such connections as to make it an interesting word to me. If a slave ran away and succeeded in getting clear, or if a slave killed his master, set fire to a barn, or did any thing very wrong in the mind of a slaveholder, it was spoken of as the fruit of *abolition*. Hearing the word in this connection very often, I set about learning what it meant. The dictionary afforded me little or no help. I found it was "the act of abolishing;" but then I did not know what was to be abolished. Here I was perplexed. I did not dare to ask any one about its meaning, for I was satisfied that it was something they wanted me to know very little about. After a patient waiting, I got one of our city papers, containing an account of the number of petitions from the north, praying for the abolition of slavery in the District of Columbia, and of the slave trade between the States. From this time I understood the words *abolition* and *abolitionist*, and always drew near when that word was spoken, expecting to hear something of importance to myself and fellow-slaves. The light broke in upon me by degrees. I went one day down on the wharf of Mr. Waters; and seeing two Irishmen unloading a scow of stone, I went, unasked, and helped them. When we had finished, one of them came to me and asked me if I were a slave. I told him I was. He asked, "Are ye a slave for life?" I told him that I was. The good Irishman seemed to be deeply affected by the statement. He said to the other that it was a pity so fine a little fellow as myself should be a slave for life. He said it was a shame to hold me. They both advised me to run away to the north; that I should find friends there, and that I should be free. I pretended not to be interested in what they said, and treated them as if I did not understand them; for I feared they might be treacherous. White men have been known to encourage slaves to escape, and then, to get the reward, catch them and return them to their masters. I was afraid that these seemingly good men might use me so; but I nevertheless remembered their advice, and from that time I resolved to run away. I looked forward to a time at which it would be safe for me to escape. I was too young to think of doing so immediately; besides, I wished to learn how to write, as I might have occasion to write my own pass. I consoled myself with the hope that I should one day find a good chance. Meanwhile, I would learn to write.

The idea as to how I might learn to write was suggested to me by being in Durgin and Bailey's ship-yard, and frequently seeing the ship carpenters, after hewing, and getting a piece of timber ready for use, write on the timber the name of that part of the ship for which it was intended. When a piece of timber was intended for the larboard side, it would be marked thus—"L." When a piece was for the larboard side, it would be marked thus—"S." A piece for the larboard side forward, would be marked thus—"L. F." When a piece was for starboard side forward, it would be marked thus—"S. F." For starboard aft, it would be marked thus—"L. A." For starboard aft, it would be marked thus—"S. A." I soon learned the names of these letters, and for what they were intended when placed upon a piece of timber in the shipyard. I immediately commenced copying them, and in a short time was able to make the four letters named. After that, when I met with any boy who I knew could write, I would tell him I could write as well as he. The next word would be, "I don't believe you. Let me see you try it." I would then make the letters which I had been so fortunate as to learn, and ask him to beat that. In this way I got a good many lessons in writing, which it is quite possible I should never have gotten in any other way. During this time, my copy-book was the board fence, brick wall, and pavement; my pen and ink was a lump of chalk. With these, I learned mainly how to write. I then commenced and continued copying the Italics in Webster's Spelling Book, until I could make them all without looking at the book. By this time, my little Master Thomas had gone to school, and learned how to write, and had written over a number of copy-books. These had been brought home, and shown to some of our near neighbors, and then laid aside. My mistress used to go to class meeting at the Wilk Street meeting-house every Monday afternoon, and leave me to take care of the house. When left thus, I used to spend the time in writing in the spaces left in Master Thomas's copy-book, copying what he had written. I continued to do this until I could write a hand very similar to that of Master Thomas. Thus, after a long, tedious effort for years, I finally succeeded in learning how to write.

Chapter VIII

In a very short time after I went to live at Baltimore, my old master's youngest son Richard died; and in about three years and six months after his death, my old master, Captain Anthony, died, leaving only his son, Andrew, and daughter, Lucretia, to share his estate. He died while on a visit to see his daughter at Hillsborough. Cut off thus unexpectedly, he left no will as to the disposal of his property. It was therefore necessary to have a valuation of the property, that it might be equally divided between Mrs. Lucretia and Master Andrew. I was immediately sent for, to be valued with the other property. Here again my feelings rose up in detestation of slavery. I had now a new conception of my degraded condition. Prior to this, I had become, if not insensible to my lot, at least partly so. I left Baltimore with a young heart overborne with sadness, and a soul full of apprehension. I took passage with Captain Rowe, in the schooner Wild Cat, and, after a sail of about twenty-four hours, I found myself near the place of my birth. I had now been absent from it almost, if not quite, five years. I, however, remembered the place very well. I was only about five years old when I left it, to go and live with my old master on Colonel Lloyd's plantation; so that I was now between ten and eleven years old.

We were all ranked together at the valuation. Men and women, old and young, married and single, were ranked with horses, sheep, and swine. There were horses and men, cattle and women, pigs and children, all holding the same rank in the scale of being, and were all subjected to the same narrow examination. Silvery-headed age and sprightly youth, maids and matrons, had to undergo the same indelicate inspection. At this moment, I saw more clearly than ever the brutalizing effects of slavery upon both slave and slaveholder.

After the valuation, then came the division. I have no language to express the high excitement and deep anxiety which were felt among us poor slaves during this time. Our fate for life was now to be decided. We had no more voice in that decision than the brutes among whom we were ranked. A single word from the white men was enough—against all our wishes, prayers, and entreaties—to sunder forever the dearest friends, dearest kindred, and strongest ties known to human beings. In addition to the pain of separation, there was the horrid dread of falling into the hands of Master Andrew. He was known to us all as being a most cruel wretch,—a common drunkard, who had, by his reckless mismanagement and profligate dissipation, already wasted a large portion of his father's property. We all felt that we might as well be sold at once to the Georgia traders, as to pass into his hands; for we knew that that would be our inevitable condition,—a condition held by us all in the utmost horror and dread.

I suffered more anxiety than most of my fellow-slaves. I had known what it was to be kindly treated; they had known nothing of the kind. They had seen little or nothing of the world. They were in very deed men and women of sorrow, and acquainted with grief. Their backs had been made familiar with the bloody lash, so that they had become callous; mine was yet tender; for while at Baltimore I got few whippings, and few slaves could boast of a kinder master and mistress than myself; and the thought of passing out of their hands into those of Master

Andrew—a man who, but a few days before, to give me a sample of his bloody disposition, took my little brother by the throat, threw him on the ground, and with the heel of his boot stamped upon his head till the blood gushed from his nose and ears—was well calculated to make me anxious as to my fate. After he had committed this savage outrage upon my brother, he turned to me, and said that was the way he meant to serve me one of these days,—meaning, I suppose, when I came into his possession.

Thanks to a kind Providence, I fell to the portion of Mrs. Lucretia, and was sent immediately back to Baltimore, to live again in the family of Master Hugh. Their joy at my return equalled their sorrow at my departure. It was a glad day to me. I had escaped a [fate] worse than lion's jaws. I was absent from Baltimore, for the purpose of valuation and division, just about one month, and it seemed to have been six.

Very soon after my return to Baltimore, my mistress, Lucretia, died, leaving her husband and one child, Amanda; and in a very short time after her death, Master Andrew died. Now all the property of my old master, slaves included, was in the hands of strangers,—strangers who had had nothing to do with accumulating it. Not a slave was left free. All remained slaves, from the youngest to the oldest. If any one thing in my experience, more than another, served to deepen my conviction of the infernal character of slavery, and to fill me with unutterable loathing of slaveholders, it was their base ingratitude to my poor old grandmother. She had served my old master faithfully from youth to old age. She had been the source of all his wealth; she had peopled his plantation with slaves; she had become a great grandmother in his service. She had rocked him in infancy, attended him in childhood, served him through life, and at his death wiped from his icy brow the cold death-sweat, and closed his eyes forever. She was nevertheless left a slave—a slave for life—a slave in the hands of strangers; and in their hands she saw her children, her grandchildren, and her great-grandchildren, divided, like so many sheep, without being gratified with the small privilege of a single word, as to their or her own destiny. And, to cap the climax of their base ingratitude and fiendish barbarity, my grandmother, who was now very old, having outlived my old master and all his children, having seen the beginning and end of all of them, and her present owners finding she was of but little value, her frame already racked with the pains of old age, and complete helplessness fast stealing over her once active limbs, they took her to the woods, built her a little hut, put up a little mud-chimney, and then made her welcome to the privilege of supporting herself there in perfect loneliness; thus virtually turning her out to die! If my poor old grandmother now lives, she lives to suffer in utter loneliness; she lives to remember and mourn over the loss of children, the loss of grandchildren, and the loss of great-grandchildren. They are, in the language of the slave's poet, Whittier,—

> "Gone, gone, sold and gone
> To the rice swamp dank and lone,
> Where the slave-whip ceaseless swings,
> Where the noisome insect stings,
> Where the fever-demon strews
> Poison with the falling dews,
> Where the sickly sunbeams glare
> Through the hot and misty air:—
>   Gone, gone, sold and gone
>   To the rice swamp dank and lone,
>   From Virginia hills and waters—
>   Woe is me, my stolen daughters!"

The hearth is desolate. The children, the unconscious children, who once sang and danced in her presence, are gone. She gropes her way, in the darkness of age, for a drink of water. Instead of the voices of her children, she hears by day the moans of the dove, and by night the screams of the hideous owl. All is gloom. The grave is at the door. And now, when weighed down by the pains and aches of old age, when the head inclines to the feet, when the beginning and ending of human existence meet, and helpless infancy and painful old age combine together—at this time, this most needful time, the time for the exercise of that tenderness and affection which children only can exercise towards a declining parent—my poor old grandmother, the devoted mother of twelve children, is left all alone, in yonder little hut, before a few dim embers. She stands—she sits—she staggers—she falls—she groans—she dies—and there are none of her children or grandchildren present, to wipe from her wrinkled brow the cold sweat of death, or to place beneath the sod her fallen remains. Will not a righteous God visit for these things?

In about two years after the death of Mrs. Lucretia, Master Thomas married his second wife. Her name was Rowena Hamilton. She was the eldest daughter of Mr. William Hamilton. Master now lived in St. Michael's. Not long after his marriage, a misunderstanding took place between himself and Master Hugh; and as a means of punishing his brother, he took me from him to live with himself at St. Michael's. Here I underwent another most painful separation. It, however, was not so severe as the one I dreaded at the division of property; for, during this interval, a great change had taken place in Master Hugh and his once kind and affectionate wife. The influence of brandy upon him, and of slavery upon her, had effected a disastrous change in the characters of both; so that, as far as they were concerned, I thought I had little to lose by the change. But it was not to them that I was attached. It was to those little Baltimore boys that I felt the strongest attachment. I had received many good lessons from them, and was still receiving them, and the thought of leaving them was painful indeed. I was leaving, too, without the hope of ever being allowed to return. Master Thomas had said he would never let me return again. The barrier betwixt himself and brother he considered impassable.

I then had to regret that I did not at least make the attempt to carry out my resolution to run away; for the chances of success are tenfold greater from the city than from the country.

I sailed from Baltimore for St. Michael's in the sloop Amanda, Captain Edward Dodson. On my passage, I paid particular attention to the direction which the steamboats took to go to Philadelphia. I found, instead of going down, on reaching North Point they went up the bay, in a north-easterly direction. I deemed this knowledge of the utmost importance. My determination to run away was again revived. I resolved to wait only so long as the offering of a favorable opportunity. When that came, I was determined to be off.

Chapter IX

I have now reached a period of my life when I can give dates. I left Baltimore, and went to live with Master Thomas Auld, at St. Michael's, in March, 1832. It was now more than seven years since I lived with him in the family of my old master, on Colonel Lloyd's plantation. We of course were now almost entire strangers to each other. He was to me a new master, and I to him a new slave. I was ignorant of his temper and disposition; he was equally so of mine. A very short time, however, brought us into full acquaintance with each other. I was made acquainted with his wife not less than with himself. They were well matched, being equally mean and cruel. I was now, for the first time during a space of more than seven years, made to feel the painful gnawings of hunger—a something which I had not experienced before since I left Colonel Lloyd's plantation. It went hard enough with me then, when I could look back to no period at which I had enjoyed a sufficiency. It was tenfold harder after living in Master Hugh's family, where I had always had enough to eat, and of that which was good. I have said Master Thomas was a mean man. He was so. Not to give a slave enough to eat, is regarded as the most aggravated development of meanness even among slaveholders. The rule is, no matter how coarse the food, only let there be enough of it. This is the theory; and in the part of Maryland from which I came, it is the general practice, though there are many exceptions. Master Thomas gave us enough of neither coarse nor fine food. There were four slaves of us in the kitchen—my sister Eliza, my aunt Priscilla, Henny, and myself; and we were allowed less than a half bushel of corn-meal per week, and very little else, either in the shape of meat or vegetables. It was not enough for us to subsist upon. We were therefore reduced to the wretched necessity of living at the expense of our neighbors. This we did by begging and stealing, whichever came handy in the time of need, the one being considered as legitimate as the other. A great many times have we poor creatures been nearly perishing with hunger, when food in abundance lay mouldering in the safe and smoke-house, and our pious mistress was aware of the fact; and yet that mistress and her husband would kneel every morning, and pray that God would bless them in basket and store!

Bad as all slaveholders are, we seldom meet one destitute of every element of character commanding respect. My master was one of this rare sort. I do not know of one single noble act ever performed by him. The leading trait in his character was meanness; and if there were any other element in his nature, it was made subject to this. He was mean; and, like most other mean men, he lacked the ability to conceal his meanness. Captain Auld was not born a slaveholder. He had been a poor man, master only of a Bay craft. He came into possession of all his slaves by marriage; and of all men, adopted slaveholders are the worse. He was cruel, but cowardly. He commanded without firmness. In the enforcement of his rules, he was at times rigid, and at times lax. At times, he spoke to his slaves with the firmness of Napoleon and the fury of a demon; at other times, he might well be mistaken for an inquirer who had lost his way. He did nothing of himself. He might have passed for a lion, but for his ears. In all things noble which he attempted, his own meanness shone most conspicuous. His airs, words, and actions, were the airs, words, and actions of born slaveholders, and, being assumed, were awkward enough. He was not even a good imitator. He possessed all the disposition to deceive, but wanted the power. Having no resources within himself, he was compelled to be the copyist of many, and being such, he was forever the victim of inconsistency; and of consequence he was an object of contempt, and was held as such even by his slaves. The luxury of having slaves of his own to wait upon him was something new and unprepared for. He was a slaveholder without the ability to hold slaves. He found himself incapable of managing his slaves either by force, fear, or fraud. We seldom called him "master," we generally called him "Captain Auld," and were hardly disposed to title him at all. I doubt not that our conduct had much to do with making him appear awkward, and of consequence fretful. Our want of reverence for him must have perplexed him greatly. He wished to have us call him master, but lacked the firmness necessary to command us to do so. His wife used to insist upon our calling him so, but to no purpose. In August, 1832, my master attended a Methodist camp-meeting held in the Bay-side, Talbot county, and there experienced religion. I indulged a faint hope that his conversion would lead him to emancipate his slaves, and that, if he did not do this, it would, at any rate, make him more kind and humane. I was disappointed in both these respects. It neither made him to be humane to his slaves, nor to emancipate them. If it had any effect on his character, it made him more cruel and hateful in all his ways; for I believe him to have been a much worse man after his conversion than before. Prior to his conversion, he relied upon his own depravity to shield and sustain him in his savage barbarity; but after his conversion, he found religious sanction and support for his slave-holding cruelty. He made the greatest pretensions to piety. His house was the house of prayer. He prayed morning, noon, and night. He very soon distinguished himself among his brethren, and was soon made a class-leader and exhorter. His activity in revivals was great, and he proved himself an instrument in the hands of the church in converting many souls. His house was the preachers' home. They used to take great pleasure in coming there to put up; for while he starved us, he stuffed them. We have had three or four preachers there at a time. The names of those who used to come most frequently while I lived there, were Mr. Storks, Mr. Ewery, Mr. Humphry, and Mr. Hickey. I have also seen Mr. George Cookman at our house. We slaves loved Mr. Cookman. We believed him to be a good man. We thought him instrumental in getting Mr. Samuel Harrison, a very rich slaveholder, to emancipate his slaves; and by some means got the impression that he was laboring to effect the emancipation of all the slaves. When he was at our house, we were sure to be called in to prayers. When the other were there, we were sometimes called in and sometimes not. Mr. Cookman took more notice of us than either of the other ministers. He could not come among us without betraying his sympathy for us, and, stupid as we were, we had the sagacity to see it.

While I lived with my master in St. Michael's, there was a white young man, a Mr. Wilson, who proposed to keep a Sabbath school for the instruction of such slaves as might be disposed to learn to read the New Testament. We met but three times, when Mr. West and Mr. Fairbanks, both class-leaders, with many others, came upon us with sticks and other missiles, drove us off, and forbade us to meet again. Thus ended our little Sabbath school in the pious town of St. Michael's.

I have said my master found religious sanction for his cruelty. As an example, I will state one of the many facts going to prove the charge. I have seen him tie up a lame young woman, and whip her with a heavy cowskin upon her naked shoulders, causing the warm red blood to drip; and, in justification of the bloody deed, he would quote this passage of Scripture—"He that knoweth his master's will, and doeth it not, shall be beaten with many stripes."

Master would keep this lacerated young woman tied up in this horrid situation four or five hours at a time. I have known him to tie her up early in the morning, and whip her before breakfast; leave her, go to his store, return at dinner, and whip her again, cutting her in the places already made raw with his cruel lash. The secret of master's cruelty toward "Henny" is found in the act of her being almost helpless. When quite a child, she fell into the fire, and burned herself horribly. Her hands were so burnt that she never got the use of them. She could do very little but bear heavy burdens. She was to master a bill of expense; and as he was a mean man, she was a constant offence to him. He seemed desirous of getting the poor girl out of existence. He gave her away once to his sister; but, being a poor gift, she was not disposed to keep her. Finally, my benevolent master, to use his own words, "set her adrift to take care of herself." Here was a recently-converted man, holding on upon the mother, and at the same time turning out her helpless child, to starve and die! Master Thomas was one of the many pious slaveholders who hold slaves for the very charitable purpose of taking care of them.

My master and myself had quite a number of differences. He found me unsuitable to his purpose. My city life, he said, had had a very pernicious effect upon me. It had almost ruined me for every good purpose, and fitted me for every thing which was bad. One of my greatest faults was that of letting his horse run away, and go down to his father-in-law's farm, which was about five miles from St. Michael's. I would then have to go after it. My reason for this kind of carelessness, or carefulness, was, that I could always get something to eat when I went there. Master William Hamilton, my master's father-in-law, always gave his slaves enough to eat. I never left there hungry, no matter how great the need of my speedy return. Master Thomas at length said he would stand it no longer. I had lived with him nine months, during which time he had given me a number of severe whippings, all to no good purpose. He resolved to put me out, as he said, to be broken; and, for this purpose, he let me for one year to a man named Edward Covey. Mr. Covey was a poor man, a farm-renter. He rented the place upon which he lived, as also the hands with which he tilled it. Mr. Covey had acquired a very high reputation for breaking young slaves, and this reputation was of immense value to him. It enabled him to get his farm tilled with much less expense to himself than he could have had it done without such a reputation. Some slaveholders thought it not much loss to allow Mr. Covey to have their slaves one year, for the sake of the training to which they were subjected, without any other compensation. He could hire young help with great ease, in consequence of this reputation. Added to the natural good qualities of Mr. Covey, he was a professor of religion—a pious soul—a member and class-leader in the Methodist church. All of this added weight to his reputation as a "nigger-breaker." I was aware of all the facts, having been made acquainted with them by a young man who had lived there. I nevertheless made the change gladly; for I was sure of getting enough to eat, which is not the smallest consideration to a hungry man.

Chapter X

I left Master Thomas's house, and went to live with Mr. Covey, on the 1st of January, 1833. I was now, for the first time in my life, a field hand. In my new employment, I found myself even more awkward than a country boy appeared to be in a large city. I had been at my new home but one week before Mr. Covey gave me a very severe whipping, cutting my back, causing the blood to run, and raising ridges on my flesh as large as my little finger. The details of this affair are as follows: Mr. Covey sent me, very early in the morning of one of our coldest days in the month of January, to the woods, to get a load of wood. He gave me a team of unbroken oxen. He told me which was the in-hand ox, and which the off-hand one. He then tied the end of a large rope around the horns of the in-hand ox, and gave me the other end of it, and told me, if the oxen started to run, that I must hold on upon the rope. I had never driven oxen before, and of course I was very awkward. I, however, succeeded in getting to the edge of the woods with little difficulty; but I had got a very few rods into the woods, when the oxen took fright, and started full tilt, carrying the cart against trees, and over stumps, in the most frightful manner. I expected every moment that my brains would be dashed out against the trees. After running thus for a considerable distance, they finally upset the cart, dashing it with great force against a tree, and threw themselves into a dense thicket. How I escaped death, I do not know. There I was, entirely alone, in a thick wood, in a place new to me. My cart was upset and shattered, my oxen were entangled among the young trees, and there was none to help me. After a long spell of effort, I succeeded in getting my cart righted, my oxen disentangled, and again yoked to the cart. I now proceeded with my team to the place where I had, the day before, been chopping wood, and loaded my cart pretty heavily, thinking in this way to tame my oxen. I then proceeded on my way home. I had now consumed one half of the day. I got out of the woods safely, and now felt out of danger. I stopped my oxen to open the woods gate; and just as I did so, before I could get hold of my ox-rope, the oxen again started, rushed through the gate, catching it between the wheel and the body of the cart, tearing it to pieces, and coming within a few inches of crushing me against the gate-post. Thus twice, in one short day, I escaped death by the merest chance. On my return, I told Mr. Covey what had happened, and how it happened. He ordered me to return to the woods again immediately. I did so, and he followed on after me. Just as I got into the woods, he came up and told me to stop my cart, and that he would teach me how to trifle away my time, and break gates. He then went to a large gum-tree, and with his axe cut three large switches, and, after trimming them up neatly with his pocket-knife, he ordered me to take off my clothes. I made him no answer, but stood with my clothes on. He repeated his order. I still made him no answer, nor did I move to strip myself. Upon this he rushed at me with the fierceness of a tiger, tore off my clothes, and lashed me till he had worn out his switches, cutting me so savagely as to leave the marks visible for a long time after. This whipping was the first of a number just like it, and for similar offences.

I lived with Mr. Covey one year. During the first six months, of that year, scarce a week passed without his whipping me. I was seldom free from a sore back. My awkwardness was almost always his excuse for whipping me. We were worked fully up to the point of endurance. Long before day we were up, our horses fed, and by the first approach of day we were off to the field with our hoes and ploughing teams. Mr. Covey gave us enough to eat, but scarce time to eat it. We were often less than five minutes taking our meals. We were often in the field from the first approach of day till its last lingering ray had left us; and at saving-fodder time, midnight often caught us in the field binding blades.

Covey would be out with us. The way he used to stand it, was this. He would spend the most of his afternoons in bed. He would then come out fresh in the evening, ready to urge us on with his words, example, and frequently with the whip. Mr. Covey was one of the few slaveholders who could and did work with his hands. He was a hard-working man. He knew by himself just what a man or a boy could do. There was no deceiving him. His work went on in his absence almost as well as in his presence; and he had the faculty of making us feel that he was ever present with us. This he did by surprising us. He seldom approached the spot where we were at work openly, if he could do it secretly. He always aimed at taking us by surprise. Such was his cunning, that we used to call him, among ourselves, "the snake." When we were at work in the cornfield, he would sometimes crawl on his hands and knees to avoid detection, and all at once he would rise nearly in our midst, and scream out, "Ha, ha! Come, come! Dash on, dash on!" This being his mode of attack, it was never safe to stop a single minute. His comings were like a thief in the night. He appeared to us as being ever at hand. He was under every tree, behind every stump, in every bush, and at every window, on the plantation. He would sometimes mount his horse, as if bound to St. Michael's, a distance of seven miles, and in half an hour afterwards you would see him coiled up in the corner of the wood-fence, watching every motion of the slaves. He would, for this purpose, leave his horse tied up in the woods. Again, he would sometimes walk up to us, and give us orders as though he was upon the point of starting on a long journey, turn his back upon us, and make as though he was going to the house to get ready; and, before he would get half way thither, he would turn short and crawl into a fence-corner, or behind some tree, and there watch us till the going down of the sun.

Mr. Covey's *forte* consisted in his power to deceive. His life was devoted to planning and perpetrating the grossest deceptions. Every thing he possessed in the shape of learning or religion, he made conform to his disposition to deceive. He seemed to think himself equal to deceiving the Almighty. He would make a short prayer in the morning, and a long prayer at night; and, strange as it may seem, few men would at times appear more devotional than he. The exercises of his family devotions were always commenced with singing; and, as he was a very poor singer himself, the duty of raising the hymn generally came upon me. He would read his hymn, and nod at me to commence. I would at times do so; at others, I would not. My non-compliance would almost always produce much confusion. To show himself independent of me, he would start and stagger through with his hymn in the most discordant manner. In this state of mind, he prayed with more than ordinary spirit. Poor man! such was his disposition, and success at deceiving, I do verily believe that he sometimes deceived himself into the solemn belief, that he was a sincere worshipper of the most high God; and this, too, at a time when he may be said to have been guilty of compelling his woman slave to commit the sin of adultery. The facts in the case are these: Mr. Covey was a poor man; he was just commencing in life; he was only able to buy one slave; and, shocking as is the fact, he bought her, as he said, for *a breeder*. This woman was named Caroline. Mr. Covey bought her from Mr. Thomas Lowe, about six miles from St. Michael's. She was a large, able-bodied woman, about twenty years old. She had already given birth to one child, which proved her to be just what he wanted. After buying her, he hired a married man of Mr. Samuel Harrison, to live with him one year; and him he used to fasten up with her every night! The result was, that, at the end of the year, the miserable woman gave birth to twins. At this result Mr. Covey seemed to be highly pleased, both with the man and the wretched woman. Such was his joy, and that of his wife, that nothing they could do for Caroline during her confinement was too good, or too hard, to be done. The children were regarded as being quite an addition to his wealth.

If at any one time of my life more than another, I was made to drink the bitterest dregs of slavery, that time was during the first six months of my stay with Mr. Covey. We were worked in all weathers. It was never too hot or too cold; it could never rain, blow, hail, or snow, too hard for us to work in the field. Work, work, work, was scarcely more the order of the day than of the night. The longest days were too short for him, and the shortest nights too long for him. I was somewhat unmanageable when I first went there, but a few months of this discipline tamed me. Mr. Covey succeeded in breaking me. I was broken in body, soul, and spirit. My natural elasticity was crushed, my intellect languished, the disposition to read departed, the cheerful spark that lingered about my eye died; the dark night of slavery closed in upon me; and behold a man transformed into a brute!

Sunday was my only leisure time. I spent this in a sort of beast-like stupor, between sleep and wake, under some large tree. At times I would rise up, a flash of energetic freedom would dart through my soul, accompanied with a faint beam of hope, that flickered for a moment, and then vanished. I sank down again, mourning over my wretched condition. I was sometimes prompted to take my life, and that of Covey, but was prevented by a combination of hope and fear. My sufferings on this plantation seem now like a dream rather than a stern reality.

Our house stood within a few rods of the Chesapeake Bay, whose broad bosom was ever white with sails from every quarter of the habitable globe. Those beautiful vessels, robed in purest white, so delightful to the eye of freemen, were to me so many shrouded ghosts, to terrify and torment me with thoughts of my wretched condition. I have often, in the deep stillness of a summer's Sabbath, stood all alone upon the lofty banks of that noble bay, and traced, with saddened heart and tearful eye, the countless number of sails moving off to the mighty ocean. The sight of these always affected me powerfully. My thoughts would compel utterance; and there, with no audience but the Almighty, I would pour our my soul's complaint, in my rude way, with an apostrophe to the moving multitude of ships:—

"You are loosed from your moorings, and are free; I am fast in my chains, and am a slave! You move merrily before the gentle gale, and I sadly before the bloody whip! You are freedom's swift-winged angels, that fly round the world; I am confined in bands of iron! O that I were free! O, that I were on one of your gallant decks, and under your protecting wing! Alas! betwixt me and you, the turbid waters roll. Go on, go on. O, that I could also go! Could I but swim! If I could fly! O, why was I born a man, of whom to make a brute! The glad ship is gone; she hides in the dim distance. I am left in the hottest hell of unending slavery. O God, save me! God, deliver me! Let me be free! Is there any God! Why am I a slave? I will run away. I will not stand it. Get caught, or get clear, I'll try it. I had as well die with ague as the fever. I have only one life to lose. I had as well be killed running as die standing. Only think of it; one hundred miles straight north, and I am free! Try it? Yes! God helping me, I will. It cannot be that I shall live and die a slave. I will take to the water. This very bay shall yet bear me into freedom. The steamboats steered in a north-east course from North Point. I will do the same; and when I get to the head of the bay, I will turn my canoe adrift, and walk straight through Delaware into Pennsylvania. When I get there, I shall not be required to have a pass; I can travel without being disturbed. Let but the first opportunity offer, and, come what will, I am off. Meanwhile, I will try to bear up under the yoke. I am not the only slave in the world. Why should I fret? I can bear as much as any of them. Besides, I am but a boy, and all boys are bound to some one. It may be that my misery in slavery will only increase my happiness when I get free. There is a better day coming."

Thus I used to think, and thus I used to speak to myself; goaded almost to madness at one moment, and at the next reconciling myself to my wretched lot.

I have already intimated that my condition was much worse, during the first six months of my stay at Mr. Covey's, than in the last six. The circumstances leading to the change in Mr. Covey's course toward me form an epoch in my humble history. You have seen how a man was made a slave; you shall see how a slave was made a man. On one of the hottest days of the month of August, 1833, Bill Smith, William Hughes, a slave named Eli, and myself, were engaged in fanning wheat. Hughes was clearing the fanned wheat from before the fan, Eli was turning, Smith was feeding, and I was carrying wheat to the fan. The work was simple, requiring strength rather than intellect; yet, to one entirely unused to such work, it came very hard. About three o'clock of that day, I broke down; my strength failed me; I was seized with a violent aching of the head, attended with extreme dizziness; I trembled in every limb. Finding what was coming, I nerved myself up, feeling it would never do to stop work. I stood as long as I could stagger to the hopper with grain. When I could stand no longer, I fell, and felt as if held down by an immense weight. The fan of course stopped; every one had his own work to do; and no one could do the work of the other, and have his own go on at the same time.

Mr. Covey was at the house, about one hundred yards from the treading-yard where we were fanning. On hearing the fan stop, he left immediately, and came to the spot where we were. He hastily inquired what the matter was. Bill answered that I was sick, and there was no one to bring wheat to the fan. I had by this time crawled away under the side of the post and rail-fence by which the yard was enclosed, hoping to find relief by getting out of the sun. He then asked where I was. He was told by one of the hands. He came to the spot, and, after looking at me awhile, asked me what was the matter. I told him as well as I could, for I scarce had strength to speak. He then gave me a savage kick in the side, and told me to get up. I tried to do so, but fell back in the attempt. He gave me another kick, and again told me to rise. I again tried, and succeeded in gaining my feet; but, stooping to get the tub with which I was feeding the fan, I again staggered and fell. While down in this situation, Mr. Covey took up the hickory slat with which Hughes had been striking off the half-bushel measure, and with it gave me a heavy blow upon the head, making a large wound, and the blood ran freely; and with this again told me to get up. I made no effort to comply, having now made up my mind to let him do his worst. In a short time after receiving this blow, my head grew better. Mr. Covey had now left me to my fate. At this moment I resolved, for the first time, to go to my master, enter a complaint, and ask his protection. In order to [do] this, I must that afternoon walk seven miles; and this, under the circumstances, was truly a severe undertaking. I was exceedingly feeble; made so as much by the kicks and blows which I received, as by the severe fit of sickness to which I had been subjected. I, however, watched my chance, while Covey was looking in an opposite direction, and started for St. Michael's. I succeeded in getting a considerable distance on my way to the woods, when Covey discovered me, and called after me to come back, threatening what he would do if I did not come. I disregarded both his calls and his threats, and made my way to the woods as fast as my feeble state would allow; and thinking I might be overhauled by him if I kept the road, I walked through the woods, keeping far enough from the road to avoid detection, and near enough to prevent losing my way. I had not gone far before my little strength again failed me. I could go no farther. I fell down, and lay for a considerable time. The blood was yet oozing from the wound on my head. For a time I thought I should bleed to death; and think now that I should have done so, but that the blood so matted my hair as to stop the wound. After lying there about three quarters of an hour, I nerved myself up again, and started on my way, through bogs and briers, barefooted and bareheaded, tearing my feet sometimes at nearly every step; and after a journey of about seven miles, occupying some five hours to perform it, I arrived at master's store. I then presented an appearance enough to affect any but a heart of iron. From the crown of my head to my feet, I was covered with blood. My hair was all clotted with dust and blood; my shirt was stiff with blood. My legs and feet were torn in sundry places with briers and thorns, and were also covered with blood. I suppose I looked like a man who had escaped a den of wild beasts, and barely escaped them. In this state I appeared before my master, humbly entreating him to interpose his authority for my protection. I told him all the circumstances as well as I could, and it seemed, as I spoke, at times to affect him. He would then walk the floor, and seek to justify Covey by saying he expected I deserved it. He asked me what I wanted. I told him, to let me get a new home; that as sure as I lived with Mr. Covey again, I should live with but to die with him; that Covey would surely kill me; he was in a fair way for it. Master Thomas ridiculed the idea that there was any danger of Mr. Covey's killing me, and said that he knew Mr. Covey; that he was a good man, and that he could not think of taking me from him; that, should he do so, he would lose the whole year's wages; that I belonged to Mr. Covey for one year, and that I must go back to him, come what might; and that I must not trouble him with any more stories, or that he would himself *get hold of me*. After threatening me thus, he gave me a very large dose of salts, telling me that I might remain in St. Michael's that night, (it being quite late,) but that I must be off back to Mr. Covey's early in the morning; and that if I did not, he would *get hold of me,* which meant that he would whip me. I remained all night, and, according to his orders, I started off to Covey's in the morning, (Saturday morning,) wearied in body and broken in spirit. I got no supper that night, or breakfast that morning. I reached Covey's about nine o'clock; and just as I was getting over the fence that divided Mrs. Kemp's fields from ours, out ran Covey with his cowskin, to give me another whipping. Before he could reach me, I succeeded in getting to the cornfield; and as the corn was very high, it afforded me the means of hiding. He seemed very angry, and searched for me a long time. My behavior was altogether unaccountable. He finally gave up the chase, thinking, I suppose, that I must come home for something to eat; he would give himself no further trouble in looking for me. I spent that day mostly in the woods, having the alternative before me,—to go home and be whipped to death, or stay in the woods and be starved to death.

That night, I fell in with Sandy Jenkins, a slave with whom I was somewhat acquainted. Sandy had a free wife, who lived about four miles from Mr. Covey's; and it being Saturday, he was on his way to see her. I told him my circumstances, and he very kindly invited me to go home with him. I went home with him, and talked this whole matter over, and got his advice as to what course it was best for me to pursue. I found Sandy an old adviser. He told me, with great solemnity, I must go back to Covey; but that before I went, I must go with him into another part of the woods, where there was a certain *root*, which, if I would take some of it with me, carrying it *always on my right side*, would render it impossible for Mr. Covey, or any other white man, to whip me. He said he had carried it for years; and since he had done so, he had never received a blow, and never expected to while he carried it. I at first rejected the idea, that the simple carrying of a root in my pocket would have any such effect as he had said, and was not disposed to take it; but Sandy impressed the necessity with much earnestness, telling me it could do no harm, if it did no good. To please him, I at length took the root, and, according to his direction, carried it upon my right side. This was Sunday morning. I immediately started for home; and upon entering the yard gate, out came Mr. Covey on his way to meeting. He spoke to me very kindly, bade me drive the pigs from a lot near by, and passed on towards the church. Now, this singular conduct of Mr. Covey really made me begin to think that there was something in the *root* which Sandy had given me; and had it been on any other day than Sunday, I could have attributed the conduct to no other cause than the influence of that root; and as it was, I was half inclined to think the *root* to be something more than I at first had taken it to be. All went well till Monday morning. On this morning, the virtue of the *root* was fully tested. Long before daylight, I was called to go and rub, curry, and feed, the horses. I obeyed, and was glad to obey. But whilst thus engaged, whilst in the act of throwing down some blades from the loft, Mr. Covey entered the stable with a long rope; and just as I was half out of the loft, he caught hold of my legs, and was about tying me. As soon as I found what he was up to, I gave a sudden spring, and as I did so, he holding to my legs, I was brought sprawling on the stable floor. Mr. Covey seemed now to think he had me, and could do what he pleased; but at this moment—from whence came the spirit I don't know—I resolved to fight; and, suiting my action to the resolution, I seized Covey hard by the throat; and as I did so, I rose. He held on to me, and I to him. My resistance was so entirely unexpected, that Covey seemed taken all aback. He trembled like a leaf. This gave me assurance, and I held him uneasy, causing the blood to run where I touched him with the ends of my fingers. Mr. Covey soon called out to Hughes for help. Hughes came, and, while Covey held me, attempted to tie my right hand. While he was in the act of doing so, I watched my chance, and gave him a heavy kick close under the ribs. This kick fairly sickened Hughes, so that he left me in the hands of Mr. Covey. This kick had the effect of not only weakening Hughes, but Covey also. When he saw Hughes bending over with pain, his courage quailed. He asked me if I meant to persist in my resistance. I told him I did, come what might; that he had used me like a brute for six months, and that I was determined to be used so no longer. With that, he strove to drag me to a stick that was lying just out of the stable door. He meant to knock me down. But just as he was leaning over to get the stick, I seized him with both hands by his collar, and brought him by a sudden snatch to the ground. By this time, Bill came. Covey called upon him for assistance. Bill wanted to know what he could do. Covey said, "Take hold of him, take hold of him!" Bill said his master hired him out to work, and not to help to whip me; so he left Covey and myself to fight out own battle out. We were at it for nearly two hours. Covey at length let me go, puffing and blowing at a great rate, saying that if I had not resisted, he would not have whipped me half so much. The truth was, that he had not whipped me at all. I considered him as getting entirely the worst end of the bargain; for he had drawn no blood from me, but I had from him. The whole six months afterwards, that I spent with Mr. Covey, he never laid the weight of his finger upon me in anger. He would occasionally say, he didn't want to get hold of me again. "No," thought I, "you need not; for you will come off worse than you did before."

    This battle with Mr. Covey was the turning-point in my career as a slave. It rekindled the few expiring embers of freedom, and revived within me a sense of my own manhood. It recalled the departed self-confidence, and inspired me again with a determination to be free. The gratification afforded by the triumph was a full compensation for whatever else might follow, even death itself. He only can understand the deep satisfaction which I experience, who has himself repelled by force the bloody arm of slavery. I felt as I never felt before. It was a glorious resurrection, for the tomb of slavery, to the heaven of freedom. My long-crushed spirit rose, cowardice departed, bold defiance took its place; and I now resolved that, however long I might remain a slave in form, the day has passed forever when I could be a slave in fact. I did not hesitate to let it be known of me, that the white man who expected to succeed in whipping, must also succeed in killing me.

From this time I was never again what might be called fairly whipped, though I remained a slave four years afterwards. I had several fights, but was never whipped.

It was for a long time a matter of surprise to me why Mr. Covey did not immediately have me taken by the constable to the whipping-post, and there regularly whipped for the crime of raising my hand against a white man in defence of myself. And the only explanation I can now think of does not entirely satisfy me; but such as it is, I will give it. Mr. Covey enjoyed the most unbounded reputation for being a first-rate overseer and negro-breaker. It was of considerable importance to him. That reputation was at stake; and had he sent me—a boy about sixteen years old—to the public whipping-post, his reputation would have been lost; so, to save his reputation, he suffered me to go unpunished.

My term of actual service to Mr. Edward Covey ended on Christmas day, 1833. The days between Christmas and New Year's day are allowed as holidays; and, accordingly, we were not required to perform any labor, more than to feed and take care of the stock. This time we regarded as our own, by the grace of our masters; and we therefore used or abused it nearly as we pleased. Those of us who had families at a distance, were generally allowed to spend the whole six days in their society. This time, however, was spent in various ways. The staid, sober, thinking and industrious ones of our number would employ themselves in making corn-brooms, mats, horse-collars, and baskets; and another class of us would spend the time in hunting opossums, hares, and coons. But by far the larger part engaged in such sports and merriments as playing ball, wrestling, running foot-races, fiddling, dancing, and drinking whiskey; and this latter mode of spending the time was by far the most agreeable to the feelings of our masters. A slave who would work during the holidays was considered by our masters as scarcely deserving them. He was regarded as one who rejected the favor of his master. It was deemed a disgrace not to get drunk at Christmas; and he was regarded as lazy indeed, who had not provided himself with the necessary means, during the year, to get whisky enough to last him through Christmas.

From what I know of the effect of these holidays upon the slave, I believe them to be among the most effective means in the hands of the slaveholder in keeping down the spirit of insurrection. Were the slaveholders at once to abandon this practice, I have not the slightest doubt it would lead to an immediate insurrection among the slaves. These holidays serve as conductors, or safety-valves, to carry off the rebellious spirit of enslaved humanity. But for these, the slave would be forced up to the wildest desperation; and woe betide the slaveholder, the day he ventures to remove or hinder the operation of those conductors! I warn him that, in such an event, a spirit will go forth in their midst, more to be dreaded than the most appalling earthquake.

The holidays are part and parcel of the gross fraud, wrong, and inhumanity of slavery. They are professedly a custom established by the benevolence of the slaveholders; but I undertake to say, it is the result of selfishness, and one of the grossest frauds committed upon the down-trodden slave. They do not give the slaves this time because they would not like to have their work during its continuance, but because they know it would be unsafe to deprive them of it. This will be seen by the fact, that the slaveholders like to have their slaves spend those days just in such a manner as to make them as glad of their ending as of their beginning. Their object seems to be, to disgust their slaves with freedom, by plunging them into the lowest depths of dissipation, For instance, the slaveholders not only like to see the slave drink of his own accord, but will adopt various plans to make him drunk. One plan is, to make bets on their slaves, as to who can drink the most whiskey without getting drunk; and in this way they succeed in getting whole multitudes to drink to excess. Thus, when the slave asks for virtuous freedom, the cunning slaveholder, knowing his ignorance, cheats him with a dose of vicious dissipation, artfully labelled with the name of liberty. The most of us used to drink it down, and the result was just what might be supposed: many of us were led to think that there was little to choose between liberty and slavery. We felt, and very properly too, that we had almost as well be slaves to man as to rum. So, when the holidays ended, we staggered up from the filth of our wallowing, took a long breath, and marched to the field,—feeling, upon the whole, rather glad to go, from what our master had deceived us into a belief was freedom, back to the arms of slavery.

I have said that this mode of treatment is a part of the whole system of fraud and inhumanity of slavery. It is so. The mode here adopted to disgust the slave with freedom, by allowing him to see only the abuse of it, is carried out in other things. For instance, a slave loves molasses; he steals some. His master, in many cases, goes off to town, and buys a large quantity; he returns, takes his whip, and commands the slave to eat the molasses, until the poor fellow is made sick at the very mention of it. The same mode is sometimes adopted to make the slaves refrain from asking for more food than their regular allowance. A slave runs through his allowance, and applies for more. His master is enraged at him; but, not willing to send him off without food, gives him more than is necessary, and compels him to eat it within a given time. Then, if he complains that he cannot eat it, he is said to be satisfied neither full nor fasting, and is whipped for being hard to please! I have an abundance of such illustrations of the same principle, drawn from my own observation, but think the cases I have cited sufficient. The practice is a very common one.

On the first of January, 1834, I left Mr. Covey, and went to live with Mr. William Freeland, who lived about three miles from St. Michael's. I soon found Mr. Freeland a very different man from Mr. Covey. Though not rich, he was what would be called an educated southern gentleman. Mr. Covey, as I have shown, was a well-trained negro-breaker and slave-driver. The former (slaveholder though he was) seemed to possess some regard for honor, some reverence for justice, and some respect for humanity. The latter seemed totally insensible to all such sentiments. Mr. Freeland had many of the faults peculiar to slaveholders, such as being very passionate and fretful; but I must do him the justice to say, that he was exceedingly free from those degrading vices to which Mr. Covey was constantly addicted. The one was open and frank, and we always knew where to find him. The other was a most artful deceiver, and could be understood only by such as were skilful enough to detect his cunningly-devised frauds. Another advantage I gained in my new master was, he made no pretensions to, or profession of, religion; and this, in my opinion, was truly a great advantage. I assert most unhesitatingly, that the religion of the south is a mere covering for the most horrid crimes,—a justifier of the most appalling barbarity,—a sanctifier of the most hateful frauds,—and a dark shelter under, which the darkest, foulest, grossest, and most infernal deeds of slaveholders find the strongest protection. Were I to be again reduced to the chains of slavery, next to that enslavement, I should regard being the slave of a religious master the greatest calamity that could befall me. For of all slaveholders with whom I have ever met, religious slaveholders are the worst. I have ever found them the meanest and basest, and most cruel and cowardly, of all others. It was my unhappy lot not only to belong to a religious slaveholder, but to live in a community of such religionists. Very near Mr. Freeland lived the Rev. Daniel Weeden, and in the same neighborhood lived the Rev. Rigby Hopkins. These were members and ministers in the Reformed Methodist Church. Mr. Weeden owned, among others, a woman slave, whose name I have forgotten. This woman's back, for weeks, was kept literally raw, made so by the lash of this merciless, *religious* wretch. He used to hire hands. His maxim was, Behave well or behave ill, it is the duty of a master occasionally to whip a slave, to remind him of his master's authority. Such was his theory, and such his practice.

Mr. Hopkins was even worse than Mr. Weeden. His chief boast was his ability to manage slaves. The peculiar feature of his government was that of whipping slaves in advance of deserving it. He always managed to have one or more of his slaves to whip every Monday morning. He did this to alarm their fears, and strike terror into those who escaped. His plan was to whip for the smallest offences, to prevent the commission of large ones. Mr. Hopkins could always find some excuse for whipping a slave. It would astonish one, unaccustomed to a slaveholding life, to see with what wonderful ease a slaveholder can find things, of which to make occasion to whip a slave. A mere look, word, or motion,—mistake, accident, or want of power, are all matters for which a slave may be whipped at any time. Does a slave look dissatisfied? It is said, he has the devil in him, and it must be whipped out. Does he speak loudly when spoken to by his master? Then he is getting high-minded, and should be taken down a buttonhole lower. Does he forget to pull off his hat at the approach of a white person? Then he is wanting in reverence, and should be whipped for it. Does he ever venture to vindicate his conduct, when censured for it? Then he is guilty of impudence,—one of the greatest crimes of which a slave can be guilty. Does he ever venture to suggest a different mode of doing things from that pointed out by his master? He is indeed presumptuous, and getting above himself; and nothing less than a flogging will do for him. Does he, while ploughing, break a plough,—or, while hoeing, break a hoe? It is owning to his carelessness, and for it a slave must always be whipped. Mr. Hopkins could always find something of this sort to justify the use of the lash, and he seldom failed to embrace such opportunities. There was not a man in the whole county, with whom the slaves who had the getting their own home, would not prefer to live, rather than with this Rev. Mr. Hopkins. And yet there was not a man any where round, who made higher professions of religion, or was more active in revivals,—more attentive to the class, love-feast, prayer and preaching meetings, or more devotional in his family,—that prayed earlier, later, louder, and longer,—than this same reverend slave-driver, Rigby Hopkins.

But to return to Mr. Freeland, and to my experience while in his employment. He, like Mr. Covey, gave us enough to eat; but, unlike Mr. Covey, he also gave us sufficient time to take our meals. He worked us hard, but always between sunrise and sunset. He required a good deal of work to be done, but gave us good tools with which to work. His farm was large, but he employed hands enough to work it, and with ease, compared with many of his neighbors. My treatment, while in his employment, was heavenly, compared with what I experienced at the hands of Mr. Edward Covey.

Mr. Freeland was himself the owner of but two slaves. Their names were Henry Harris and John Harris. The rest of his hands he hired. These consisted of myself, Sandy Jenkins, and Handy Caldwell. Henry and John were quite intelligent, and in a very little while after I went there, I succeeded in creating in them a strong desire to learn how to read. This desire soon sprang up in the others also. They very soon mustered up some old spelling-books, and nothing would do but that I must keep a Sabbath school. I agreed to do so, and accordingly devoted my Sundays to teaching these my loved fellow-slaves how to read. Neither of them knew his letters when I went there. Some of the slaves of the neighboring farms found what was going on, and also availed themselves of this little opportunity to learn to read. It was understood, among all who came, that there must be as little display about it as possible. It was necessary to keep our religious masters at St. Michael's unacquainted with the fact, that, instead of spending the Sabbath in wrestling, boxing, and drinking whisky, we were trying to learn how to read the will of God; for they had much rather see us engaged in those degrading sports, than to see us behaving like intellectual, moral, and accountable beings. My blood boils as I think of the bloody manner in which Messrs. Wright Fairbanks and Garrison West, both class-leaders, in connection with many others, rushed in upon us with sticks and stones, and broke up our virtuous little Sabbath school, at St. Michael's—all calling themselves Christians! humble followers of the Lord Jesus Christ! But I am again digressing.

I held my Sabbath school at the house of a free colored man, whose name I deem it imprudent to mention; for should it be known, it might embarrass him greatly, though the crime of holding the school was committed ten years ago. I had at one time over forty scholars, and those of the right sort, ardently desiring to learn. They were of all ages, though mostly men and women. I look back to those Sundays with an amount of pleasure not to be expressed. They were great days to my soul. The work of instructing my dear fellow-slaves was the sweetest engagement with which I was ever blessed. We loved each other, and to leave them at the close of the Sabbath was a severe cross indeed. When I think that these precious souls are to-day shut up in the prisonhouse of slavery, my feelings overcome me, and I am almost ready to ask, "Does a righteous God govern the universe? and for what does he hold the thunders in his right hand, if not to smite the oppressor, and deliver the spoiled out of the hand of the spoiler?" These dear souls came not to Sabbath school because it was popular to do so, nor did I teach them because it was reputable to be thus engaged. Every moment they spent in that school, they were liable to be taken up, and given thirty-nine lashes. They came because they wished to learn. Their minds had been starved by their cruel masters. They had been shut up in mental darkness. I taught them, because it was the delight of my soul to be doing something that looked like bettering the condition of my race. I kept up my school nearly the whole year I lived with Mr. Freeland; and, beside my Sabbath school, I devoted three evenings in the week, during the winter, to teaching the slaves at home. And I have the happiness to know, that several of those who came to Sabbath school learned how to read; and that one, at least, is now free through my agency.

The year passed off smoothly. It seemed only about half as long as the year which preceded it. I went through it without receiving a single blow. I will give Mr. Freeland the credit of being the best master I ever had, *till I became my own master*. For the ease with which I passed the year, I was, however, somewhat indebted to the society of my fellow-slaves. They were noble souls; they not only possessed loving hearts, but brave ones. We were linked and interlinked with each other. I loved them with a love stronger than any thing I have experienced since. It is sometimes said that we slaves do not love and confide in each other. In answer to this assertion, I can say, I never loved any or confided in any people more than my fellow-slaves, and especially those with whom I lived at Mr. Freeland's. I believe we would have died for each other. We never undertook to do any thing, of any importance, without a mutual consultation. We never moved separately. We were one; and as much so by our tempers and dispositions, as by the mutual hardships to which we were necessarily subjected by our condition as slaves.

At the close of the year 1834, Mr. Freeland again hired me of my master, for the year 1835. But, by this time, I began to want to live *upon free land* as well as *with Freeland;* and I was no longer content, therefore, to live with him or any other slaveholder. I began, with the commencement of the year, to prepare myself for a final struggle, which should decide my fate one way or the other. My tendency was upward. I was fast approaching manhood, and year after year had passed, and I was still a slave. These thoughts roused me—I must do something. I therefore resolved that 1835 should not pass without witnessing an attempt, on my part, to secure my liberty. But I was not willing to cherish this determination alone. My fellow-slaves were dear to me. I was anxious to have them participate with me in this, my life-giving determination. I therefore, though with great prudence, commenced early to ascertain their views and feelings in regard to their condition, and to imbue their minds with thoughts of freedom. I bent myself to devising ways and means for our escape, and meanwhile strove, on all fitting occasions, to impress them with the gross fraud and inhumanity of slavery. I went first to Henry, next to John, then to the others. I found, in them all, warm hearts and noble spirits. They were ready to hear, and ready to act when a feasible plan should be proposed. This was what I wanted. I talked to them of our want of manhood, if we submitted to our enslavement without at least one noble effort to be free. We met often, and consulted frequently, and told our hopes and fears, recounted the difficulties, real and imagined, which we should be called on to meet. At times we were almost disposed to give up, and try to content ourselves with our wretched lot; at others, we were firm and unbending in our determination to go. Whenever we suggested any plan, there was shrinking—the odds were fearful. Our path was beset with the greatest obstacles; and if we succeeded in gaining the end of it, our right to be free was yet questionable—we were yet liable to be returned to bondage. We could see no spot, this side of the ocean, where we could be free. We knew nothing about Canada. Our knowledge of the north did not extend farther than New York; and to go there, and be forever harassed with the frightful liability of being returned to slavery—with the certainty of being treated tenfold worse than before—the thought was truly a horrible one, and one which it was not easy to overcome. The case sometimes stood thus: At every gate through which we were to pass, we saw a watchman—at every ferry a guard—on every bridge a sentinel—and in every wood a patrol. We were hemmed in upon every side. Here were the difficulties, real or imagined—the good to be sought, and the evil to be shunned. On the one hand, there stood slavery, a stern reality, glaring frightfully upon us,—its robes already crimsoned with the blood of millions, and even now feasting itself greedily upon our own flesh. On the other hand, away back in the dim distance, under the flickering light of the north star, behind some craggy hill or snow-covered mountain, stood a doubtful freedom—half frozen—beckoning us to come and share its hospitality. This in itself was sometimes enough to stagger us; but when we permitted ourselves to survey the road, we were frequently appalled. Upon either side we saw grim death, assuming the most horrid shapes. Now it was starvation, causing us to eat our own flesh;—now we were contending with the waves, and were drowned;—now we were overtaken, and torn to pieces by the fangs of the terrible bloodhound. We were stung by scorpions, chased by wild beasts, bitten by snakes, and finally, after having nearly reached the desired spot,—after swimming rivers, encountering wild beasts, sleeping in the woods, suffering hunger and nakedness,—we were overtaken by our pursuers, and, in our resistance, we were shot dead upon the spot! I say, this picture sometimes appalled us, and made us

> "rather bear those ills we had,
> Than fly to others, that we knew not of."

In coming to a fixed determination to run away, we did more than Patrick Henry, when he resolved upon liberty or death. With us it was a doubtful liberty at most, and almost certain death if we failed. For my part, I should prefer death to hopeless bondage.

Sandy, one of our number, gave up the notion, but still encouraged us. Our company then consisted of Henry Harris, John Harris, Henry Bailey, Charles Roberts, and myself. Henry Bailey was my uncle, and belonged to my master. Charles married my aunt; he belonged to my master's father-in-law, Mr. William Hamilton.

The plan we finally concluded upon was, to get a large canoe belonging to Mr. Hamilton, and upon the Saturday night previous to Easter holidays, paddle directly up the Chesapeake Bay. On our arrival at the head of the bay, a distance of seventy or eighty miles from where we lived, it was our purpose to turn our canoe adrift, and follow the guidance of the north star till we got beyond the limits of Maryland. Our reason for taking the water route was, that we were less liable to be suspected as runaways; we hoped to be regarded as fishermen; whereas, if we should take the land route, we should be subjected to interruptions of almost every kind. Any one having a white face, and being so disposed, could stop us, and subject us to examination.

The week before our intended start, I wrote several protections, one for each of us. As well as I can remember, they were in the following words, to wit:—

> "This is to certify that I, the undersigned, have given the bearer, my servant, full liberty to go to Baltimore, and spend the Easter holidays. Written with mine own hand, &c., 1835
> "WILLIAM HAMILTON,
> "Near St. Michael's, in Talbot county, Maryland."

We were not going to Baltimore; but, in going up the bay, we went toward Baltimore, and these protections were only intended to protect us while on the bay.

As the time drew near for our departure, our anxiety became more and more intense. It was truly a matter of life and death with us. The strength of our determination was about to be fully tested. At this time, I was very active in explaining every difficulty, removing every doubt, dispelling every fear, and inspiring all with the firmness indispensable to success in our undertaking; assuring them that half was gained the instant we made the move; we had talked long enough; we were now ready to move; if not now, we never should be; and if we did not intend to move now, we had as well fold our arms, sit down, and acknowledge ourselves fit only to be slaves. This, none of us were prepared to acknowledge. Every man stood firm; and at our last meeting, we pledged ourselves afresh, in the most solemn manner, that, at the time appointed, we would certainly start in pursuit of freedom. This was in the middle of the week, at the end of which we were to be off. We went, as usual, to our several fields of labor, but with bosoms highly agitated with thoughts of our truly hazardous undertaking. We tried to conceal our feelings as much as possible; and I think we succeeded very well.

After a painful waiting, the Saturday morning, whose night was to witness our departure, came. I hailed it with joy, bring what of sadness it might. Friday night was a sleepless one for me. I probably felt more anxious than the rest, because I was, by common consent, at the head of the whole affair. The responsibility of success or failure lay heavily upon me. The glory of the one, and the confusion of the other, were alike mine. The first two hours of that morning were such as I never experienced before, and hope never to again. Early in the morning; we went, as usual, to the field. We were spreading manure; and all at once, while thus engaged, I was overwhelmed with an indescribable feeling, in the fulness of which I turned to Sandy, who was near by, and said, "We are betrayed!" "Well," said he, "that thought has this moment struck me." We said no more. I was never more certain of any thing.

The horn was blown as usual, and we went up from the field to the house for breakfast. I went for the form, more than for want of any thing to eat that morning. Just as I got to the house, in looking out at the lane gate, I saw four white men, with two colored men. The white men were on horseback, and the colored ones were walking behind, as if tied. I watched them a few moments till they got up to our lane gate. Here they halted, and tied the colored men to the gatepost. I was not yet certain as to what the matter was. In a few moments, in rode Mr. Hamilton, with a speed betokening great excitement. He came to the door, and inquired if Master William was in. He was told he was at the barn. Mr. Hamilton, without dismounting, rode up to the barn with extraordinary speed. In a few moments, he and Mr. Freeland returned to the house. By this time, the three constables rode up, and in great haste dismounted, tied their horses, and met Master William and Mr. Hamilton returning from the barn; and after talking awhile, they all walked up to the kitchen door. There was no one in the kitchen but myself and John. Henry and Sandy were up at the barn. Mr. Freeland put his head in at the door, and called me by name, saying, there were some gentlemen at the door who wished to see me. I stepped to the door, and inquired what they wanted. They at once seized me, and, without giving me any satisfaction, tied me—lashing my hands closely together. I insisted upon knowing what the matter was. They at length said, that they had learned I had been in a "scrape," and that I was to be examined before my master; and if their information proved false, I should not be hurt.

In a few moments, they succeeded in tying John. They then turned to Henry, who had by this time returned, and commanded him to cross his hands. "I won't!" said Henry, in a firm tone, indicating his readiness to meet the consequences of his refusal. "Won't you?" said Tom Graham, the constable. "No, I won't!" said Henry, in a still stronger tone. With this, two of the constables pulled out their shining pistols, and swore, by their Creator, that they would make him cross his hands or kill him. Each cocked his pistol, and, with fingers on the trigger, walked up to Henry, saying, at the same time, if he did not cross his hands, they would blow his damned heart out. "Shoot me, shoot me!" said Henry; "you can't kill me but once. Shoot, shoot,—and be damned! *I won't be tied!*" This he said in a tone of loud defiance; and at the same time, with a motion as quick as lightning, he with one single stroke dashed the pistols from the hand of each constable. As he did this, all hands fell upon him, and, after beating him some time, they finally overpowered him, and got him tied.

During the scuffle, I managed, I know not how, to get my pass out, and, without being discovered, put it into the fire. We were all now tied; and just as we were to leave for Easton jail, Betsy Freeland, mother of William Freeland, came to the door with her hands full of biscuits, and divided them between Henry and John. She then delivered herself of a speech, to the following effect:—addressing herself to me, she said, *"You devil! You yellow devil!* it was you that put it into the heads of Henry and John to run away. But for you, you long-legged mulatto devil! Henry nor John would never have thought of such a thing." I made no reply, and was immediately hurried off towards St. Michael's. Just a moment previous to the scuffle with Henry, Mr. Hamilton suggested the propriety of making a search for the protections which he had understood Frederick had written for himself and the rest. But, just at the moment he was about carrying his proposal into effect, his aid was needed in helping to tie Henry; and the excitement attending the scuffle caused them either to forget, or to deem it unsafe, under the circumstances, to search. So we were not yet convicted of the intention to run away.

When we got about half way to St. Michael's, while the constables having us in charge were looking ahead, Henry inquired of me what he should do with his pass. I told him to eat it with his biscuit, and own nothing; and we passed the word around, *"Own nothing;"* and *"Own nothing!"* said we all. Our confidence in each other was unshaken. We were resolved to succeed or fail together, after the calamity had befallen us as much as before. We were now prepared for any thing. We were to be dragged that morning fifteen miles behind horses, and then to be placed in the Easton jail. When we reached St. Michael's, we underwent a sort of examination. We all denied that we ever intended to run away. We did this more to bring out the evidence against us, than from any hope of getting clear of being sold; for, as I have said, we were ready for that. The fact was, we cared but little where we went, so we went together. Our greatest concern was about separation. We dreaded that more than any thing this side of death. We found the evidence against us to be the testimony of one person; our master would not tell who it was; but we came to a unanimous decision among ourselves as to who their informant was. We were sent off to the jail at Easton. When we got there, we were delivered up to the sheriff, Mr. Joseph Graham, and by him placed in jail. Henry, John, and myself, were placed in one room together—Charles, and Henry Bailey, in another. Their object in separating us was to hinder concert.

We had been in jail scarcely twenty minutes, when a swarm of slave traders, and agents for slave traders, flocked into jail to look at us, and to ascertain if we were for sale. Such a set of beings I never saw before! I felt myself surrounded by so many fiends from perdition. A band of pirates never looked more like their father, the devil. They laughed and grinned over us, saying, "Ah, my boys! we have got you, haven't we?" And after taunting us in various ways, they one by one went into an examination of us, with intent to ascertain our value. They would impudently ask us if we would not like to have them for our masters. We would make them no answer, and leave them to find out as best they could. Then they would curse and swear at us, telling us that they could take the devil out of us in a very little while, if we were only in their hands.

While in jail, we found ourselves in much more comfortable quarters than we expected when we went there. We did not get much to eat, nor that which was very good; but we had a good clean room, from the windows of which we could see what was going on in the street, which was very much better than though we had been placed in one of the dark, damp cells. Upon the whole, we got along very well, so far as the jail and its keeper were concerned. Immediately after the holidays were over, contrary to all our expectations, Mr. Hamilton and Mr. Freeland came up to Easton, and took Charles, the two Henrys, and John, out of jail, and carried them home, leaving me alone. I regarded this separation as a final one. It caused me more pain than any thing else in the whole transaction. I was ready for any thing rather than separation. I supposed that they had consulted together, and had decided that, as I was the whole cause of the intention of the others to run away, it was hard to make the innocent suffer with the guilty; and that they had, therefore, concluded to take the others home, and sell me, as a warning to the others that remained. It is due to the noble Henry to say, he seemed almost as reluctant at leaving the prison as at leaving home to come to the prison. But we knew we should, in all probability, be separated, if we were sold; and since he was in their hands, he concluded to go peaceably home.

I was now left to my fate. I was all alone, and within the walls of a stone prison. But a few days before, and I was full of hope. I expected to have been safe in a land of freedom; but now I was covered with gloom, sunk down to the utmost despair. I thought the possibility of freedom was gone. I was kept in this way about one week, at the end of which, Captain Auld, my master, to my surprise and utter astonishment, came up, and took me out, with the intention of sending me, with a gentleman of his acquaintance, into Alabama. But, from some cause or other, he did not send me to Alabama, but concluded to send me back to Baltimore, to live again with his brother Hugh, and to learn a trade.

Thus, after an absence of three years and one month, I was once more permitted to return to my old home at Baltimore. My master sent me away, because there existed against me a very great prejudice in the community, and he feared I might be killed.

In a few weeks after I went to Baltimore, Master Hugh hired me to Mr. William Gardner, an extensive ship-builder, on Fell's Point. I was put there to learn how to calk. It, however, proved a very unfavorable place for the accomplishment of this object. Mr. Gardner was engaged that spring in building two large man-of-war brigs, professedly for the Mexican government. The vessels were to be launched in the July of that year, and in failure thereof, Mr. Gardner was to lose a considerable sum; so that when I entered, all was hurry. There was no time to learn any thing. Every man had to do that which he knew how to do. In entering the ship-yard, my orders from Mr. Gardner were, to do whatever the carpenters commanded me to do. This was placing me at the beck and call of about seventy-five men. I was to regard all these as masters. Their word was to be my law. My situation was a most trying one. At times I needed a dozen pair of hands. I was called a dozen ways in the space of a single minute. Three or four voices would strike my ear at the same moment. It was—"Fred., come help me to cant this timber here."—"Fred., come carry this timber yonder."—"Fred., bring that roller here."—"Fred., go get a fresh can of water."—"Fred., come help saw off the end of this timber."—"Fred., go quick, and get the crowbar."—"Fred., hold on the end of this fall."—"Fred, go to the blacksmith's shop, and get a new punch."—"Hurra, Fred.! run and bring me a cold chisel."—"I say, Fred., bear a hand, and get up a fire as quick as lightning under that steam-box."—"Hallo, nigger! come, turn this grindstone."—"Come, come! move, move! and *bowse* this timber forward."—"I say, darky, blast your eyes, why don't you heat up some pitch?"—"Halloo! halloo! halloo!" (Three voices at the same time.) "Come here!—Go there!—Hold on where you are! Damn you, if you move, I'll knock your brains out!"

This was my school for eight months; and I might have remained there longer, but for a most horrid fight I had with four of the white apprentices, in which my left eye was nearly knocked out, and I was horribly mangled in other respects. The facts in the case were these: Until a very little while after I went there, white and black ship-carpenters worked side by side, and no one seemed to see any impropriety in it. All hands seemed to be very well satisfied. Many of the black carpenters were freemen. Things seemed to be going on very well. All at once, the white carpenters knocked off, and said they would not work with free colored workmen. Their reason for this, as alleged, was, that if free colored carpenters were encouraged, they would soon take the trade into their own hands, and poor white men would be thrown out of employment. They therefore felt called upon at once to put a stop to it. And, taking advantage of Mr. Gardner's necessities, they broke off, swearing they would work no longer, unless he would discharge his black carpenters. Now, though this did not extend to me in form, it did reach me in fact. My fellow-apprentices very soon began to feel it degrading to them to work with me. They began to put on airs, and talk about the "niggers" taking the country, saying we all ought to be killed; and, being encouraged by the journeymen, they commenced making my condition as hard as they could, by hectoring me around, and sometimes striking me. I, of course, kept the vow I made after the fight with Mr. Covey, and struck back again, regardless of consequences; and while I kept them from combining, I succeeded very well; for I could whip the whole of them, taking them separately. They, however, at length combined, and came upon me, armed with sticks, stones, and heavy handspikes. One came in front with a half brick. There was one at each side of me, and one behind me. While I was attending to those in front, and on either side, the one behind ran up with the handspike, and struck me a heavy blow upon the head. It stunned me. I fell, and with this they all ran upon me, and fell to beating me with their fists. I let them lay on for a while, gathering strength. In an instant, I gave a sudden surge, and rose to my hands and knees. Just as I did that, one of their number gave me, with his heavy boot, a powerful kick in the left eye. My eyeball seemed to have burst. When they saw my eye closed, and badly swollen, they left me. With this I seized the handspike, and for a time pursued them. But here the carpenters interfered, and I thought I might as well give it up. It was impossible to stand my hand against so many. All this took place in sight of not less than fifty white ship-carpenters, and not one interposed a friendly word; but some cried, "Kill the damned nigger! Kill him! kill him! He struck a white person." I found my only chance for life was in flight. I succeeded in getting away without an additional blow, and barely so; for to strike a white man is death by Lynch law,—and that was the law in Mr. Gardner's ship-yard; nor is there much of any other out of Mr. Gardner's ship yard.

I went directly home, and told the story of my wrongs to Master Hugh; and I am happy to say of him, irreligious as he was, his conduct was heavenly, compared with that of his brother Thomas under similar circumstances. He listened attentively to my narration of the circumstances leading to the savage outrage, and gave many proofs of his strong indignation at it. The heart of my once overkind mistress was again melted into pity. My puffed-out eye and blood-covered face moved her to tears. She took a chair by me, washed the blood from my face, and, with a mother's tenderness, bound up my head, covering the wounded eye with a lean piece of fresh beef. It was almost compensation for my suffering to witness, once more, a manifestation of kindness from this, my once affectionate old mistress. Master Hugh was very much enraged. He gave expression to his feelings by pouring out curses upon the heads of those who did the deed. As soon as I got a little the better of my bruises, he took me with him to Esquire Watson's, on Bond Street, to see what could be done about the matter. Mr. Watson inquired who saw the assault committed. Master Hugh told him it was done in Mr. Gardner's ship-yard, at mid-day, where there were a large company of men at work. "As to that," he said, "the deed was done, and there was no question as to who did it." His answer was, he could do nothing in the case, unless some white man would come forward and testify. He could issue no warrant on my word. If I had been killed in the presence of a thousand colored people, their testimony combined would have been insufficient to have arrested one of the murderers. Master Hugh, for once, was compelled to say this state of things was too bad. Of course, it was impossible to get any white man to volunteer his testimony in my behalf, and against the white young men. Even those who may have sympathized with me were not prepared to do this. It required a degree of courage unknown to them to do so; for just at that time, the slightest manifestation of humanity toward a colored person was denounced as abolitionism, and that name subjected its bearer to frightful liabilities. The watchwords of the bloody-minded in that region, and in those days, were, "Damn the abolitionists!" and "Damn the niggers!" There was nothing done, and probably nothing would have been done if I had been killed. Such was, and such remains, the state of things in the Christian city of Baltimore.

Master Hugh, finding he could get no redress, refused to let me go back again to Mr. Gardner. He kept me himself, and his wife dressed my wound till I was again restored to health. He then took me into the ship-yard of which he was foreman, in the employment of Mr. Walter Price. There I was immediately set to calking, and very soon learned the art of using my mallet and irons. In the course of one year from the time I left Mr. Gardner's, I was able to command the highest wages given to the most experienced calkers. I was now of some importance to my master. I was bringing him from six to seven dollars per week. I sometimes brought him nine dollars per week: my wages were a dollar and a half a day. After learning how to calk, I sought my own employment, made my own contracts, and collected the money which I earned. My pathway became much more smooth than before; my condition was now much more comfortable. When I could get no calking to do, I did nothing. During these leisure times, those old notions about freedom would steal over me again. When in Mr. Gardner's employment, I was kept in such a perpetual whirl of excitement, I could think of nothing, scarcely, but my life; and in thinking of my life, I almost forgot my liberty. I have observed this in my experience of slavery,—that whenever my condition was improved, instead of its increasing my contentment, it only increased my desire to be free, and set me to thinking of plans to gain my freedom. I have found that, to make a contented slave, it is necessary to make a thoughtless one. It is necessary to darken his moral and mental vision, and, as far as possible, to annihilate the power of reason. He must be able to detect no inconsistencies in slavery; he must be made to feel that slavery is right; and he can be brought to that only when he ceases to be a man.

I was now getting, as I have said, one dollar and fifty cents per day. I contracted for it; I earned it; it was paid to me; it was rightfully my own; yet, upon each returning Saturday night, I was compelled to deliver every cent of that money to Master Hugh. And why? Not because he earned it,—not because he had any hand in earning it,—not because I owed it to him,—nor because he possessed the slightest shadow of a right to it; but solely because he had the power to compel me to give it up. The right of the grim-visaged pirate upon the high seas is exactly the same.

Chapter XI

I now come to that part of my life during which I planned, and finally succeeded in making, my escape from slavery. But before narrating any of the peculiar circumstances, I deem it proper to make known my intention not to state all the facts connected with the transaction. My reasons for pursuing this course may be understood from the following: First, were I to give a minute statement of all the facts, it is not only possible, but quite probable, that others would thereby be involved in the most embarrassing difficulties. Secondly, such a statement would most undoubtedly induce greater vigilance on the part of slaveholders than has existed heretofore among them; which would, of course, be the means of guarding a door whereby some dear brother bondman might escape his galling chains. I deeply regret the necessity that impels me to suppress any thing of importance connected with my experience in slavery. It would afford me great pleasure indeed, as well as materially add to the interest of my narrative, were I at liberty to gratify a curiosity, which I know exists in the minds of many, by an accurate statement of all the facts pertaining to my most fortunate escape. But I must deprive myself of this pleasure, and the curious of the gratification which such a statement would afford. I would allow myself to suffer under the greatest imputations which evil-minded men might suggest, rather than exculpate myself, and thereby run the hazard of closing the slightest avenue by which a brother slave might clear himself of the chains and fetters of slavery.

I have never approved of the very public manner in which some of our western friends have conducted what they call the *underground railroad*, but which, I think, by their open declarations, has been made most emphatically the *upperground railroad*. I honor those good men and women for their noble daring, and applaud them for willingly subjecting themselves to bloody persecution, by openly avowing their participation in the escape of slaves. I, however, can see very little good resulting from such a course, either to themselves or the slaves escaping; while, upon the other hand, I see and feel assured that those open declarations are a positive evil to the slaves remaining, who are seeking to escape. They do nothing towards enlightening the slave, whilst they do much towards enlightening the master. They stimulate him to greater watchfulness, and enhance his power to capture his slave. We owe something to the slaves south of the line as well as to those north of it; and in aiding the latter on their way to freedom, we should be careful to do nothing which would be likely to hinder the former from escaping from slavery. I would keep the merciless slaveholder profoundly ignorant of the means of flight adopted by the slave. I would leave him to imagine himself surrounded by myriads of invisible tormentors, ever ready to snatch from his infernal grasp his trembling prey. Let him be left to feel his way in the dark; let darkness commensurate with his crime hover over him; and let him feel that at every step he takes, in pursuit of the flying bondman, he is running the frightful risk of having his hot brains dashed out by an invisible agency. Let us render the tyrant no aid; let us not hold the light by which he can trace the footprints of our flying brother. But enough of this. I will now proceed to the statement of those facts, connected with my escape, for which I am alone responsible, and for which no one can be made to suffer by myself.

In the early part of the year 1838, I became quite restless. I could see no reason why I should, at the end of each week, pour the reward of my toil into the purse of my master. When I carried to him my weekly wages, he would, after counting the money, look me in the face with a robber-like fierceness, and ask, "Is this all?" He was satisfied with nothing less than the last cent. He would, however, when I made him six dollars, sometimes give me six cents, to encourage me. It had the opposite effect. I regarded it as a sort of admission of my right to the whole. The fact that he gave me any part of my wages was proof, to my mind, that he believed me entitled to the whole of them. I always felt worse for having received any thing; for I feared that the giving me a few cents would ease his conscience, and make him feel himself to be a pretty honorable sort of robber. My discontent grew upon me. I was ever on the look-out for means of escape; and, finding no direct means, I determined to try to hire my time, with a view of getting money with which to make my escape. In the spring of 1838, when Master Thomas came to Baltimore to purchase his spring goods, I got an opportunity, and applied to him to allow me to hire my time. He unhesitatingly refused my request, and told me this was another stratagem by which to escape. He told me I could go nowhere but that he could get me; and that, in the event of my running away, he should spare no pains in his efforts to catch me. He exhorted me to content myself, and be obedient. He told me, if I would be happy, I must lay out no plans for the future. He said, if I behaved myself properly, he would take care of me. Indeed, he advised me to complete thoughtlessness of the future, and taught me to depend solely upon him for happiness. He seemed to see fully the pressing necessity of setting aside my intellectual nature, in order to contentment in slavery. But in spite of him, and even in spite of myself, I continued to think, and to think about the injustice of my enslavement, and the means of escape.

About two months after this, I applied to Master Hugh for the privilege of hiring my time. He was not acquainted with the fact that I had applied to Master Thomas, and had been refused. He too, at first, seemed disposed to refuse; but, after some reflection, he granted me the privilege, and proposed the following terms: I was to be allowed all my time, make all contracts with those for whom I worked, and find my own employment; and, in return for this liberty, I was to pay him three dollars at the end of each week; find myself in calking tools, and in board and clothing. My board was two dollars and a half per week. This, with the wear and tear of clothing and calking tools, made my regular expenses about six dollars per week. This amount I was compelled to make up, or relinquish the privilege of hiring my time. Rain or shine, work or no work, at the end of each week the money must be forthcoming, or I must give up my privilege. This arrangement, it will be perceived, was decidedly in my master's favor. It relieved him of all need of looking after me. His money was sure. He received all the benefits of slaveholding without its evils; while I endured all the evils of a slave, and suffered all the care and anxiety of a freeman. I found it a hard bargain. But, hard as it was, I thought it better than the old mode of getting along. It was a step towards freedom to be allowed to bear the responsibilities of a freeman, and I was determined to hold on upon it. I bent myself to the work of making money. I was ready to work at night as well as day, and by the most untiring perseverance and industry, I made enough to meet my expenses, and lay up a little money every week. I went on thus from May till August. Master Hugh then refused to allow me to hire my time longer. The ground for his refusal was a failure on my part, one Saturday night, to pay him for my week's time. This failure was occasioned by my attending a camp meeting about ten miles from Baltimore. During the week, I had entered into an engagement with a number of young friends to start from Baltimore to the camp ground early Saturday evening; and being detained by my employer, I was unable to get down to Master Hugh's without disappointing the company. I knew that Master Hugh was in no special need of the money that night. I therefore decided to go to camp meeting, and upon my return pay him the three dollars. I staid at the camp meeting one day longer than I intended when I left. But as soon as I returned, I called upon him to pay him what he considered his due. I found him very angry; he could scarce restrain his wrath. He said he had a great mind to give me a severe whipping. He wished to know how I dared go out of the city without asking his permission. I told him I hired my time, and while I paid him the price which he asked for it, I did not know that I was bound to ask him when and where I should go. This reply troubled him; and, after reflecting a few moments, he turned to me, and said I should hire my time no longer; that the next thing he should know of, I would be running away. Upon the same plea, he told me to bring my tools and clothing home forthwith. I did so; but instead of seeking work, as I had been accustomed to do previously to hiring my time, I spent the whole week without the performance of a single stroke of work. I did this in retaliation. Saturday night, he called upon me as usual for my week's wages. I told him I had no wages; I had done no work that week. Here we were upon the point of coming to blows. He raved, and swore his determination to get hold of me. I did not allow myself a single word; but was resolved, if he laid the weight of his hand upon me, it should be blow for blow. He did not strike me, but told me that he would find me in constant employment in future. I thought the matter over during the next day, Sunday, and finally resolved upon the third day of September, as the day upon which I would make a second attempt to secure my freedom. I now had three weeks during which to prepare for my journey. Early on Monday morning, before Master Hugh had time to make any engagement for me, I went out and got employment of Mr. Butler, at his shipyard near the drawbridge, upon what is called the City Block, thus making it unnecessary for him to seek employment for me. At the end of the week, I brought him between eight and nine dollars. He seemed very well pleased, and asked me why I did not do the same the week before. He little knew what my plans were. My object in working steadily was to remove any suspicion he might entertain of my intent to run away; and in this I succeeded admirably. I suppose he thought I was never better satisfied with my condition than at the very time during which I was planning my escape. The second week passed, and again I carried him my full wages; and so well pleased was he, that he gave me twenty-five cents, (quite a large sum for a slaveholder to give a slave,) and bade me to make a good use of it. I told him I would.

Things went on without very smoothly indeed, but within there was trouble. It is impossible for me to describe my feelings as the time of my contemplated start drew near. I had a number of warm-hearted friends in Baltimore,—friends that I loved almost as I did my life,—and the thought of being separated from them forever was painful beyond expression. It is my opinion that thousands would escape from slavery, who now remain, but for the strong cords of affection that bind them to their friends. The thought of leaving my friends was decidedly the most painful thought with which I had to contend. The love of them was my tender point, and shook my decision more than all things else. Besides the pain of separation, the dread and apprehension of a failure exceeded what I had experienced at my first attempt. The appalling defeat I then sustained returned to torment me. I felt assured that, if I failed in this attempt, my case would be a hopeless one—it would seal my fate as a slave forever. I could not hope to get off with any thing less than the severest punishment, and being placed beyond the means of escape. It required no very vivid imagination to depict the most frightful scenes through which I should have to pass, in case I failed. The wretchedness of slavery, and the blessedness of freedom, were perpetually before me. It was life and death with me. But I remained firm, and, according to my resolution, on the third day of September, 1838, I left my chains, and succeeded in reaching New York without the slightest interruption of any kind. How I did so,—what means I adopted,—what direction I travelled, and by what mode of conveyance,—I must leave unexplained, for the reasons before mentioned.

I have been frequently asked how I felt when I found myself in a free State. I have never been able to answer the question with any satisfaction to myself. It was a moment of the highest excitement I ever experienced. I suppose I felt as one may imagine the unarmed mariner to feel when he is rescued by a friendly man-of-war from the pursuit of a pirate. In writing to a dear friend, immediately after my arrival at New York, I said I felt like one who had escaped a den of hungry lions. This state of mind, however, very soon subsided; and I was again seized with a feeling of great insecurity and loneliness. I was yet liable to be taken back, and subjected to all the tortures of slavery. This in itself was enough to damp the ardor of my enthusiasm. But the loneliness overcame me. There I was in the midst of thousands, and yet a perfect stranger; without home and without friends, in the midst of thousands of my own brethren—children of a common Father, and yet I dared not to unfold to any one of them my sad condition. I was afraid to speak to any one for fear of speaking to the wrong one, and thereby falling into the hands of money-loving kidnappers, whose business it was to lie in wait for the panting fugitive, as the ferocious beasts of the forest lie in wait for their prey. The motto which I adopted when I started from slavery was this—"Trust no man!" I saw in every white man an enemy, and in almost every colored man cause for distrust. It was a most painful situation; and, to understand it, one must needs experience it, or imagine himself in similar circumstances. Let him be a fugitive slave in a strange land—a land given up to be the hunting-ground for slaveholder—whose inhabitants are legalized kidnappers—where he is every moment subjected to the terrible liability of being seized upon by his fellow-men, as the hideous crocodile seizes upon his prey!—I say, let him place himself in my situation—without home or friends—without money or credit—wanting shelter, and no one to give it—wanting bread, and no money to buy it,—and at the same time let him feel that he is pursued by merciless men-hunters, and in total darkness as to what to do, where to go, or where to stay,—perfectly helpless both as to the means of defence and means of escape,—in the midst of plenty, yet suffering the terrible gnawings of hunger,—in the midst of houses, yet having no home,—among fellow-men, yet feeling as if in the midst of wild beasts, whose greediness to swallow up the trembling and half-famished fugitive is only equalled by that with which the monsters of the deep swallow up the helpless fish upon which they subsist,—I say, let him be placed in this most trying situation,—the situation in which I was placed,—then, and not till then, will he fully appreciate the hardships of, and know how to sympathize with, the toil-worn and whip-scarred fugitive slave.

Thank Heaven, I remained but a short time in this distressed situation. I was relieved from it by the humane hand of Mr. DAVID RUGGLES, whose vigilance, kindness, and perseverance, I shall never forget. I am glad of an opportunity to express, as far as words can, the love and gratitude I bear him. Mr. Ruggles is now afflicted with blindness, and is himself in need of the same kind offices which he was once so forward in the performance of toward others. I had been in New York but a few days, when Mr. Ruggles sought me out, and very kindly took me to his boarding-house at the corner of Church and Lespenard Streets. Mr. Ruggles was then very deeply engaged in the memorable *Darg* case, as well as attending to a number of other fugitive slaves, devising ways and means for their successful escape; and, though watched and hemmed in on almost every side, he seemed to be more than a match for his enemies.

Very soon after I went to Mr. Ruggles, he wished to know of me where I wanted to go; as he deemed it unsafe for me to remain in New York. I told him I was a calker, and should like to go where I could get work. I thought of going to Canada; but he decided against it, and in favor of my going to New Bedford, thinking I should be able to get work there at my trade. At this time, Anna, my intended wife, came on; for I wrote to her immediately after my arrival at New York, (notwithstanding my homeless, houseless, and helpless condition,) informing her of my successful flight, and wishing her to come on forthwith. In a few days after her arrival, Mr. Ruggles called in the Rev. J. W. C. Pennington, who, in the presence of Mr. Ruggles, Mrs. Michaels, and two or three others, performed the marriage ceremony, and gave us a certificate, of which the following is an exact copy:—

"THIS may certify, that I joined together in holy matrimony Frederick Johnson and Anna Murray, as man and wife, in the presence of Mr. David Ruggles and Mrs. Michaels.
"JAMES W. C. PENNINGTON.
"NEW YORK, SEPT. 15, 1838."

Upon receiving this certificate, and a five-dollar bill from Mr. Ruggles, I shouldered one part of our baggage, and Anna took up the other, and we set out forthwith to take passage on board of the steamboat John W. Richmond for Newport, on our way to New Bedford. Mr. Ruggles gave me a letter to a Mr. Shaw in Newport, and told me, in case my money did not serve me to New Bedford, to stop in Newport and obtain further assistance; but upon our arrival at Newport, we were so anxious to get to a place of safety, that, notwithstanding we lacked the necessary money to pay our fare, we decided to take seats in the stage, and promise to pay when we got to New Bedford. We were encouraged to do this by two excellent gentlemen, residents of New Bedford, whose names I afterward ascertained to be Joseph Ricketson and William C. Taber. They seemed at once to understand our circumstances, and gave us such assurance of their friendliness as put us fully at ease in their presence. It was good indeed to meet with such friends, at such a time. Upon reaching New Bedford, we were directed to the house of Mr. Nathan Johnson, by whom we were kindly received, and hospitably provided for. Both Mr. and Mrs. Johnson took a deep and lively interest in our welfare. They proved themselves quite worthy of the name of abolitionists. When the stage-driver found us unable to pay our fare, he held on upon our baggage as security for the debt. I had but to mention the fact to Mr. Johnson, and he forthwith advanced the money.

We now began to feel a degree of safety, and to prepare ourselves for the duties and responsibilities of a life of freedom. On the morning after our arrival at New Bedford, while at the breakfast-table, the question arose as to what name I should be called by. The name given me by my mother was, "Frederick Augustus Washington Bailey." I, however, had dispensed with the two middle names long before I left Maryland, so that I was generally known by the name of "Frederick Bailey." I started from Baltimore bearing the name of "Stanley." When I got to New York, I again changed my name to "Frederick Johnson," and thought that would be the last change. But when I got to New Bedford, I found it necessary again to change my name. The reason of this necessity was, that there were so many Johnsons in New Bedford, it was already quite difficult to distinguish between them. I gave Mr. Johnson the privilege of choosing me a name, but told him he must not take from me the name of "Frederick." I must hold on to that, to preserve a sense of my identity. Mr. Johnson had just been reading the "Lady of the Lake," and at once suggested that my name be "Douglass." From that time until now I have been called "Frederick Douglass;" and as I am more widely known by that name than by either of the others, I shall continue to use it as my own.

I was quite disappointed at the general appearance of things in New Bedford. The impression which I had received respecting the character and condition of the people of the north, I found to be singularly erroneous. I had very strangely supposed, while in slavery, that few of the comforts, and scarcely any of the luxuries, of life were enjoyed at the north, compared with what were enjoyed by the slaveholders of the south. I probably came to this conclusion from the fact that northern people owned no slaves. I supposed that they were about upon a level with the non-slaveholding population of the south. I knew *they* were exceedingly poor, and I had been accustomed to regard their poverty as the necessary consequence of their being non-slaveholders. I had somehow imbibed the opinion that, in the absence of slaves, there could be no wealth, and very little refinement. And upon coming to the north, I expected to meet with a rough, hard-handed, and uncultivated population, living in the most Spartan-like simplicity, knowing nothing of the ease, luxury, pomp, and grandeur of southern slaveholders. Such being my conjectures, any one acquainted with the appearance of New Bedford may very readily infer how palpably I must have seen my mistake.

In the afternoon of the day when I reached New Bedford, I visited the wharves, to take a view of the shipping. Here I found myself surrounded with the strongest proofs of wealth. Lying at the wharves, and riding in the stream, I saw many ships of the finest models, in the best order, and of the largest size. Upon the right and left, I was walled in by granite warehouses of the widest dimensions, stowed to their utmost capacity with the necessaries and comforts of life. Added to this, almost every body seemed to be at work, but noiselessly so, compared with what I had been accustomed to in Baltimore. There were no loud songs heard from those engaged in loading and unloading ships. I heard no deep oaths or horrid curses on the laborer. I saw no whipping of men; but all seemed to go smoothly on. Every man appeared to understand his work, and went at it with a sober, yet cheerful earnestness, which betokened the deep interest which he felt in what he was doing, as well as a sense of his own dignity as a man. To me this looked exceedingly strange. From the wharves I strolled around and over the town, gazing with wonder and admiration at the splendid churches, beautiful dwellings, and finely-cultivated gardens; evincing an amount of wealth, comfort, taste, and refinement, such as I had never seen in any part of slaveholding Maryland.

Every thing looked clean, new, and beautiful. I saw few or no dilapidated houses, with poverty-stricken inmates; no half-naked children and barefooted women, such as I had been accustomed to see in Hillsborough, Easton, St. Michael's, and Baltimore. The people looked more able, stronger, healthier, and happier, than those of Maryland. I was for once made glad by a view of extreme wealth, without being saddened by seeing extreme poverty. But the most astonishing as well as the most interesting thing to me was the condition of the colored people, a great many of whom, like myself, had escaped thither as a refuge from the hunters of men. I found many, who had not been seven years out of their chains, living in finer houses, and evidently enjoying more of the comforts of life, than the average of slaveholders in Maryland. I will venture to assert that my friend Mr. Nathan Johnson (of whom I can say with a grateful heart, "I was hungry, and he gave me meat; I was thirsty, and he gave me drink; I was a stranger, and he took me in") lived in a neater house; dined at a better table; took, paid for, and read, more newspapers; better understood the moral, religious, and political character of the nation,—than nine tenths of the slaveholders in Talbot county, Maryland. Yet Mr. Johnson was a working man. His hands were hardened by toil, and not his alone, but those also of Mrs. Johnson. I found the colored people much more spirited than I had supposed they would be. I found among them a determination to protect each other from the blood-thirsty kidnapper, at all hazards. Soon after my arrival, I was told of a circumstance which illustrated their spirit. A colored man and a fugitive slave were on unfriendly terms. The former was heard to threaten the latter with informing his master of his whereabouts. Straightway a meeting was called among the colored people, under the stereotyped notice, "Business of importance!" The betrayer was invited to attend. The people came at the appointed hour, and organized the meeting by appointing a very religious old gentleman as president, who, I believe, made a prayer, after which he addressed the meeting as follows: *"Friends, we have got him here, and I would recommend that you young men just take him outside the door, and kill him!"* With this, a number of them bolted at him; but they were intercepted by some more timid than themselves, and the betrayer escaped their vengeance, and has not been seen in New Bedford since. I believe there have been no more such threats, and should there be hereafter, I doubt not that death would be the consequence.

I found employment, the third day after my arrival, in stowing a sloop with a load of oil. It was new, dirty, and hard work for me; but I went at it with a glad heart and a willing hand. I was now my own master. It was a happy moment, the rapture of which can be understood only by those who have been slaves. It was the first work, the reward of which was to be entirely my own. There was no Master Hugh standing ready, the moment I earned the money, to rob me of it. I worked that day with a pleasure I had never before experienced. I was at work for myself and newly-married wife. It was to me the starting-point of a new existence. When I got through with that job, I went in pursuit of a job of calking; but such was the strength of prejudice against color, among the white calkers, that they refused to work with me, and of course I could get no employment. Finding my trade of no immediate benefit, I threw off my calking habiliments, and prepared myself to do any kind of work I could get to do. Mr. Johnson kindly let me have his wood-horse and saw, and I very soon found myself a plenty of work. There was no work too hard—none too dirty. I was ready to saw wood, shovel coal, carry the hod, sweep the chimney, or roll oil casks,—all of which I did for nearly three years in New Bedford, before I became known to the anti-slavery world.

In about four months after I went to New Bedford, there came a young man to me, and inquired if I did not wish to take the "Liberator." I told him I did; but, just having made my escape from slavery, I remarked that I was unable to pay for it then. I, however, finally became a subscriber to it. The paper came, and I read it from week to week with such feelings as it would be quite idle for me to attempt to describe. The paper became my meat and my drink. My soul was set all on fire. Its sympathy for my brethren in bond—its scathing denunciations of slaveholders—its faithful exposures of slavery—and its powerful attacks upon the upholders of the institution—sent a thrill of joy through my soul, such as I had never felt before!

I had not long been a reader of the "Liberator," before I got a pretty correct idea of the principles, measures and spirit of the anti-slavery reform. I took right hold of the cause. I could do but little; but what I could, I did with a joyful heart, and never felt happier than when in an anti-slavery meeting. I seldom had much to say at the meetings, because what I wanted to say was said so much better by others. But, while attending an anti-slavery convention at Nantucket, on the 11th of August, 1841, I felt strongly moved to speak, and was at the same time much urged to do so by Mr. William C. Coffin, a gentleman who had heard me speak in the colored people's meeting at New Bedford. It was a severe cross, and I took it up reluctantly. The truth was, I felt myself a slave, and the idea of speaking to white people weighed me down. I spoke but a few moments, when I felt a degree of freedom, and said what I desired with considerable ease. From that time until now, I have been engaged in pleading the cause of my brethren—with what success, and with what devotion, I leave those acquainted with my labors to decide.

Appendix

I find, since reading over the foregoing Narrative, that I have, in several instances, spoken in such a tone and manner, respecting religion, as may possibly lead those unacquainted with my religious views to suppose me an opponent of all religion. To remove the liability of such misapprehension, I deem it proper to append the following brief explanation. What I have said respecting and against religion, I mean strictly to apply to the *slaveholding religion* of this land, and with no possible reference to Christianity proper; for, between the Christianity of this land, and the Christianity of Christ, I recognize the widest possible difference—so wide, that to receive the one as good, pure, and holy, is of necessity to reject the other as bad, corrupt, and wicked. To be the friend of the one, is of necessity to be the enemy of the other. I love the pure, peaceable, and impartial Christianity of Christ: I therefore hate the corrupt, slaveholding, women-whipping, cradle-plundering, partial and hypocritical Christianity of this land. Indeed, I can see no reason, but the most deceitful one, for calling the religion of this land Christianity. I look upon it as the climax of all misnomers, the boldest of all frauds, and the grossest of all libels. Never was there a clearer case of "stealing the livery of the court of heaven to serve the devil in." I am filled with unutterable loathing when I contemplate the religious pomp and show, together with the horrible inconsistencies, which every where surround me. We have men-stealers for ministers, women-whippers for missionaries, and cradle-plunderers for church members. The man who wields the blood-clotted cowskin during the week fills the pulpit on Sunday, and claims to be a minister of the meek and lowly Jesus. The man who robs me of my earnings at the end of each week meets me as a class-leader on Sunday morning, to show me the way of life, and the path of salvation. He who sells my sister, for purposes of prostitution, stands forth as the pious advocate of purity. He who proclaims it a religious duty to read the Bible denies me the right of learning to read the name of the God who made me. He who is the religious advocate of marriage robs whole millions of its sacred influence, and leaves them to the ravages of wholesale pollution. The warm defender of the sacredness of the family relation is the same that scatters whole families,—sundering husbands and wives, parents and children, sisters and brothers,—leaving the hut vacant, and the hearth desolate. We see the thief preaching against theft, and the adulterer against adultery. We have men sold to build churches, women sold to support the gospel, and babes sold to purchase Bibles for the *poor heathen! all for the glory of God and the good of soul!* The slave auctioneer's bell and the church-going bell chime in with each other, and the bitter cries of the heart-broken slave are drowned in the religious shouts of his pious master. Revivals of religion and revivals in the slave-trade go hand in hand together. The slave prison and the church stand near each other. The clanking of fetters and the rattling of chains in the prison, and the pious psalm and solemn prayer in the church, may be heard at the same time. The dealers in the bodies and souls of men erect their stand in the presence of the pulpit, and they mutually help each other. The dealer gives his blood-stained gold to support the pulpit, and the pulpit, in return, covers his infernal business with the garb of Christianity. Here we have religion and robbery the allies of each other—devils dressed in angels' robes, and hell presenting the semblance of paradise.

"Just God! and these are they,
    Who minister at thine altar, God of right!
Men who their hands, with prayer and blessing, lay
    On Israel's ark of light.
"What! preach, and kidnap men?
    Give thanks, and rob thy own afflicted poor?
Talk of thy glorious liberty, and then
    Bolt hard the captive's door?
"What! servants of thy own
    Merciful Son, who came to seek and save
The homeless and the outcast, fettering down
    The tasked and plundered slave!
"Pilate and Herod friends!
    Chief priests and rulers, as of old, combine!
Just God and holy! is that church which lends
    Strength to the spoiler thine?"

    The Christianity of America is a Christianity, of whose votaries it may be as truly said, as it was of the ancient scribes and Pharisees, "They bind heavy burdens, and grievous to be borne, and lay them on men's shoulders, but they themselves will not move them with one of their fingers. All their works they do for to be seen of men.——They love the uppermost rooms at feasts, and the chief seats in the synagogues, . . . and to be called of men, Rabbi, Rabbi.——But woe unto you, scribes and Pharisees, hypocrites! for ye shut up the kingdom of heaven against men; for ye neither go in yourselves, neither suffer ye them that are entering to go in. Ye devour widows' houses, and for a pretence make long prayers; therefore ye shall receive the greater damnation. Ye compass sea and land to make one proselyte, and when he is made, ye make him twofold more the child of hell than yourselves.——Woe unto you, scribes and Pharisees, hypocrites! for ye pay tithe of mint, and anise, and cumin, and have omitted the weightier matters of the law, judgment, mercy, and faith; these ought ye to have done, and not to leave the other undone. Ye blind guides! which strain at a gnat, and swallow a camel. Woe unto you, scribes and Pharisees, hypocrites! for ye make clean the outside of the cup and of the platter; but within, they are full of extortion and excess.——Woe unto you, scribes and Pharisees, hypocrites! for ye are like unto whited sepulchres, which indeed appear beautiful outward, but are within full of dead men's bones, and of all uncleanness. Even so ye also outwardly appear righteous unto men, but within ye are full of hypocrisy and iniquity."

    Dark and terrible as is this picture, I hold it to be strictly true of the overwhelming mass of professed Christians in America. They strain at a gnat, and swallow a camel. Could any thing be more true of our churches? They would be shocked at the proposition of fellowshipping a *sheep*-stealer; and at the same time they hug to their communion a *man*-stealer, and brand me with being an infidel, if I find fault with them for it. They attend with Pharisaical strictness to the outward forms of religion, and at the same time neglect the weightier matters of the law, judgment, mercy, and faith. They are always ready to sacrifice, but seldom to show mercy. They are they who are represented as professing to love God whom they have not seen, whilst they hate their brother whom they have seen. They love the heathen on the other side of the globe. They can pray for him, pay money to have the Bible put into his hand, and missionaries to instruct him; while they despise and totally neglect the heathen at their own doors.

    Such is, very briefly, my view of the religion of this land; and to avoid any misunderstanding, growing out of the use of general terms, I mean, by the religion of this land, that which is revealed in the words, deeds, and actions, of those bodies, north and south, calling themselves Christian churches, and yet in union with slaveholders. It is against religion, as presented by these bodies, that I have felt it my duty to testify.

    I conclude these remarks by copying the following portrait of the religion of the south, (which is, by communion and fellowship, the religion of the north,) which I soberly affirm is "true to the life," and without caricature or the slightest exaggeration. It is said to have been drawn, several years before the present anti-slavery agitation began, by a northern Methodist preacher, who, while residing at the south, had an opportunity to see slaveholding morals, manners, and piety, with his own eyes. "Shall I not visit for these things? saith the Lord. Shall not my soul be avenged on such a nation as this?"

A Parody

"Come, saints and sinners, hear me tell
How pious priests whip Jack and Nell,
And women buy and children sell,
And preach all sinners down to hell,
    And sing of heavenly union.

"They'll beat and baa, dona like goats,
Gorge down black sheep, and strain at motes,
Array their backs in fine black coats,
Then seize their negroes by their throats,
    And choke, for heavenly union.

"They'll church you if you sip a dram,
And damn you if you steal a lamb;
Yet rob old Tony, Doll, and Sam,
Of human rights, and bread and ham;
    Kidnapper's heavenly union.

"They'll loudly talk of Christ's reward,
And bind his image with a cord,
And scold, and wing the lash abhorred,
And sell their brother in the Lord
    To handcuffed heavenly union.

"They'll read and sing a sacred song,
And make a prayer both loud and long,
And teach the right and do the wrong,
Hailing the brother, sister throng,
    With words of heavenly union.

"We wonder how such saints can sing,
Or praise the Lord upon the wing,
Who roar, and scold, and whip, and sting,
And to their slaves and mammon cling,
    In guilty conscience union.

"They'll raise tobacco, corn, and rye,
And drive, and thieve, and cheat, and lie,
And lay up treasures in the sky,
By making switch and cowskin fly,
    In hope of heavenly union.

"They'll crack old Tony on the skull,
And preach and roar like Bashan bull,
Or braying ass, of mischief full,
Then seize old Jacob by the wool,
    And pull for heavenly union.

"A roaring, ranting, sleek man-thief,
Who lived on mutton, veal, and beef,
Yet never would afford relief
To needy, sable sons of grief,
    Was big with heavenly union.

"'Love not the world,' the preacher said,
And winked his eye, and shook his head;
He seized on Tom, and Dick, and Ned,
Cut short their meat, and clothes, and bread,
    Yet still loved heavenly union.

"Another preacher whining spoke
Of One whose heart for sinners broke:
He tied old Nanny to an oak,
And drew the blood at every stroke,
    And prayed for heavenly union.

"Two others oped their iron jaws,
And waved their children-stealing paws;
There sat their children in gewgaws;
By stinting negroes' backs and maws,
    They kept up heavenly union.

"All good from Jack another takes,
And entertains their flirts and rakes,
Who dress as sleek as glossy snakes,
And cram their mouths with sweetened cakes;
    And this goes down for union."

    Sincerely and earnestly hoping that this little book may do something toward throwing light on the American slave system, and hastening the glad day of deliverance to the millions of my brethren in bonds—faithfully relying upon the power of truth, love, and justice, for success in my humble efforts—and solemnly pledging myself anew to the sacred cause,—I subscribe myself,

FREDERICK DOUGLASS.

LYNN, *Mass., April* 28, 1845.

Richard Wright (1908–1960)

As novelist, autobiographer, writer of short stories, poet, and essayist, Richard Nathaniel Wright played a major role in the development of African-American literature. His literary talent established him as one of America's most powerful writers. He was born on September 4, 1908 on Rucker's Plantation near Natchez, Mississippi, the first son of Nathan Wright, an illiterate sharecropper, and Ella (Wilson) Wright, a rural schoolteacher.

When Wright was a child, his family moved from Natchez to Memphis, Tennessee, where his father deserted them, causing Wright to experience hunger, anger, and pain. Wright's mother, who suffered several strokes, tried to raise Wright and his brother, but her paralysis and lack of financial resources caused her to seek the assistance of relatives. The boys lived in the homes of various relatives and even in an orphanage for a brief period. Since Wright moved often, his formal education lacked continuity. By 1920 he was attending a Seventh-Day Adventist school, while living with his grandmother in Jackson, Mississippi. About a year later, he enrolled in the public school system.

After Wright graduated as valedictorian of the ninth grade from a Jackson public school, he concluded his formal education in 1925. Following his graduation, Wright traveled to Memphis and worked a series of unskilled jobs. Subsequently, he got a job in an optical company. While there, he devised a method which permitted him to borrow books from the public library built for "Whites only." Wright read extensively and was influenced by the writings of H. L. Mencken, especially his *Book of Prefaces,* as well as the writings of other naturalists, including Theodore Dreiser, Stephen Crane, and Sinclair Lewis.

As a result of the Depression, many Blacks, including Wright, migrated to the North anticipating a better life and hoping to leave behind some of the barriers of the South: poverty, racism, segregation, and oppression. When Wright moved to Chicago in 1927, he worked a number of odd jobs, before securing a job as a postal clerk. While working in the Chicago Post Office, Wright continued to broaden his knowledge, meeting different types of people and becoming friends with both Blacks and Whites. A few of Wright's friends, along with his interest in the social genesis of racial oppression, influenced him to join the Communist Party in 1932, but he renounced the Party in 1944 because of ideological conflicts. During this period, Wright became affiliated with the John Reed Club, and in 1935, he joined the Works Progress Administration Federal Writers' Project (WPA).

Wright spent ten years in Chicago, where he concentrated his energies on developing his artistic talent. He began by publishing two poems, "Rest for the Weary" and "A Red Love Note," in an issue of *Left Front* magazine, 1934. Then in 1935, he wrote his first novel, and it was published posthumously as *Lawd Today* (1963), a naturalistic novel concerning a Black postal worker. The four novellas (long short stories) which he began writing were published at a later date as *Uncle Tom's Children,* his first book. At this time, he started the groundwork for *Native Son.*

Since Wright wanted to enhance his career, he moved to New York in 1937. Again, he joined the Writers' Project. In *American Stuff: WPA Anthology,* Wright published "The Ethics of Living Jim Crow" (1937), an autobiographical essay about some of his work experiences in the South, especially Jackson, Mississippi. Later, he completed and published *Native Son* (1940), a novel in which Bigger Thomas, the young Black protagonist, unintentionally kills his employer's daughter and subsequently murders his girlfriend. Focusing his attention on nonfiction, Wright published *Twelve Million Voices* (1941), a picture-essay book about Black American folk history. In 1944 Wright also published in its complete form his distinctive novella entitled *The Man Who Lived Underground,* a story about Fred Daniels, a Black fugitive who hides in a sewer to protect himself from the police. Wright's idea of the underground man can be traced to Dostoevsky's *Notes from the Underground* and is said to have influenced Ralph Ellison. The following year, he published *Black Boy* (1945), his autobiography about his early years in the South. It is considered one of Wright's best works.

Wright's creative genius earned him several honors. In 1938 he won first prize for *Uncle Tom's Children* from *Story* magazine, and the following year, he received a Guggenheim Fellowship. During the early 1940s, *Native Son* gained him national recognition when it was selected by the Book-of-the-Month Club and ranked as a bestseller. It also earned him the Spingarn Medal, and in 1941, *Native Son* was later produced on Broadway and made into film.

In 1939 Wright married Rose Dhimah Meadman, whom he later divorced. About two years later, he married Ellen Poplar, and they had a daughter, Julia. In 1947 Wright and his family immigrated to Paris, where their second daughter, Rachel, was born and where Wright lived as an expatriate until his death.

While in exile, Wright traveled widely and continued his literary activities, which resulted in numerous publications, fiction and nonfiction. Some of these works include three novels: *The Outsider* (1953), *Savage Holiday* (1954), and *The Long Dream* (1958). Among his nonfiction are *Black Power* (1954), *The Color Curtain* (1957), and *White Man, Listen* (1957). Aside from *Lawd Today,* three other works were published posthumously: *Eight Men* (1961), a collection of short stories; *American Hunger* (1977), the sequel to *Black Boy* which centers on Wright's years in Chicago; *Rite of Passage* (1994), a novella about a Harlem youth; and *Haiku: This Other World* (1998), a volume of 809 Haiku slelected from the more than 4,000 he wrote. Leaving several unpublished works, Wright died, apparently of a heart attack, on November 28, 1960, in Paris, France. At the time of his death, Wright had achieved international acclaim.

Selected Bibliography

Bigelow, Barbara C., ed. *Contemporary Black Biography*. 13 vols. Washington, D.C.: Gale Research, 1994. Vol 5.

Felgar, Robert. *Richard Wright*. Boston: Twayne, 1980.

Logan, Rayford W. and Michael R. Winston, eds. *Dictionary of American Negro Biography*. New York: Norton, 1982.

Metzger, Linda et al., eds. *Black Writers*. Detroit: Gale Research, 1989.

Nasso, Christine et al., eds. *Contemporary Authors*. 152 vols. Detroit: Gale Research, 1983. Vol. 108.

Nelson, Emmanuel S., Ed. *African American Authors, 1745–1945: A Bio-Bibliographical Critical Sourcebook*. Westport, CT: Greenwood, 2000.

Valade III, Roger M., ed. with Denise Kasinec. *The Schomburg Center Guide to Black Literature*. New York: Gale Research, 1996.

Walker, Margaret. *Richard Wright, Daemonic Genius*. New York: Warner, 1988.

The Ethics of Living Jim Crow, an Autobiographical Sketch

Richard Wright

I

My first lesson in how to live as a Negro came when I was quite small. We were living in Arkansas. Our house stood behind the railroad tracks. Its skimpy yard was paved with black cinders. Nothing green ever grew in that yard. The only touch of green we could see was far away, beyond the tracks, over where the white folks lived. But cinders were good enough for me and I never missed the green growing things. Arid anyhow, cinders were fine weapons. You could always have a nice hot war with huge black cinders. All you had to do was crouch behind the brick pillars of a house with your hands full of gritty ammunition. And the first woolly black head you saw pop out from behind another row of pillars was your target. You tried your very best to knock it off. It was great fun.

I never fully realized the appalling disadvantages of a cinder environment till one day the gang to which I belonged found itself engaged in a war with the white boys who lived beyond the tracks. As usual we laid down our cinder barrage, thinking that this would wipe the white boys out. But they replied with a steady bombardment of broken bottles. We doubled our cinder barrage, but they hid behind trees, hedges, and the sloping embankments of their lawns. Having no such fortifications, we retreated to the brick pillars of our homes. During the retreat a broken milk bottle caught me behind the ear, opening a deep gash which bled profusely. The sight of blood pouring over my face completely demoralized our ranks. My fellow-combatants left me standing paralyzed in the center of the yard, and scurried for their homes. A kind neighbor saw me and rushed me to a doctor, who took three stitches in my neck.

I sat brooding on my front steps, nursing my wound and waiting for my mother to come from work. I felt that a grave injustice had been done me. It was all right to throw cinders. The greatest harm a cinder could do was leave a bruise. But broken bottles were dangerous; they left you cut, bleeding and helpless.

When night fell, my mother came from the white folks' kitchen. I raced down the street to meet her. I could just feel in my bones that she would understand. I knew she would tell me exactly what to do next time. I grabbed her hand and babbled out the whole story. She examined my wound, then slapped me.

"How come yuh didn't hide?" she asked me. "How come yuh awways fightin'?"

I was outraged, and bawled. Between sobs I told her that I didn't have any trees or hedges to hide behind. There wasn't a thing I could have used as a trench. And you couldn't throw very far when you were hiding behind the brick pillars of a house. She grabbed a barrel stave, dragged me home, stripped me naked, and beat me till I had a fever of one hundred and two. She would smack my rump with the stave, and, while the skin was still smarting, impart to me gems of Jim Crow wisdom. I was never to throw cinders any more. I was never to fight any more wars. I was never, never, under any conditions, to fight *white* folks again. And they were absolutely right in clouting me with the broken milk bottle. Didn't I know she was working hard every day in the hot kitchens of the white folks to make money to take care of me? When was I ever going to learn to be a good boy? She couldn't be bothered with my fights. She finished by telling me that I ought to be thankful to God as long as I lived that they didn't kill me.

All that night I was delirious and could not sleep. Each time I closed my eyes I saw monstrous white faces suspended from the ceiling, leering at me.

From that time on, the charm of my cinder yard was gone. The green trees, the trimmed hedges, the cropped lawns grew very meaningful, became a symbol. Even today when I think of white folks, the hard, sharp outlines of white houses surrounded by trees, lawns, and hedges are present somewhere in the background of my mind. Through the years they grew into an overreaching symbol of fear.

It was a long time before I came in close contact with white folks again. We moved from Arkansas to Mississippi. Here we had the good fortune not to live behind the railroad tracks, or close to white neighborhoods. We lived in the very heart of the local Black Belt. There were black churches and black preachers; there were black schools and black teachers; black groceries and black clerks. In fact, everything was so solidly black that for a long time I did not even think of white folks, save in remote and vague terms. But this could not last forever. As one grows older one eats more. One's clothing costs more. When I finished grammar school I had to go to work. My mother could no longer feed and clothe me on her cooking job.

There is but one place where a black boy who knows no trade can get a job, and that's where the houses and faces are white, where the trees, lawns, and hedges are green. My first job was with an optical company in Jackson, Mississippi. The morning I applied I stood straight and neat before the boss, answering all his questions with sharp yessirs and nosirs. I was very careful to pronounce my *sirs* distinctly, in order that he might know that I was polite, that I knew where I was, and that I knew he was a *white* man. I wanted that job badly.

He looked me over as though he were examining a prize poodle. He questioned me closely about my schooling, being particularly insistent about how much mathematics I had had. He seemed very pleased when I told him I had had two years of algebra.

"Boy, how would you like to try to learn something around here?" he asked me.

"I'd like it fine, sir," I said, happy. I had visions of "working my way up." Even Negroes have those visions.

"All right," he said. "Come on."

I followed him to the small factory.

"Pease," he said to a white man of about thirty-five, "this is Richard. He's going to work for us."

Pease looked at me and nodded.

I was then taken to a white boy of about seventeen.

"Morrie, this is Richard, who's going to work for us."

"Whut yuh sayin' there, boy!" Morrie boomed at me.

"Fine!" I answered.

The boss instructed these two to help me, teach me, give me jobs to do, and let me learn what I could in my spare time.

My wages were five dollars a week.

I worked hard, trying to please. For the first month I got along O.K. Both Pease and Morrie seemed to like me. But one thing was missing. And I kept thinking about it. I was not learning anything and nobody was volunteering to help me. Thinking they had forgotten that I was to learn something about the mechanics of grinding lenses, I asked Morrie one day to tell me about the work. He grew red.

"Whut yuh tryin' t' do, nigger, git smart?" he asked.

"Naw; I ain' tryin' t' git smart," I said.

"Well, don't, if yuh know whut's good for yuh!"

I was puzzled. Maybe he just doesn't want to help me, I thought. I went to Pease.

"Say, are you crazy, you black bastard?" Pease asked me, his gray eyes growing hard.

I spoke out, reminding him that the boss had said I was to be given a chance to learn something.

"Nigger, you think you're *white,* don't you?"

"Naw, sir!"

"Well, you're acting mighty like it!"

"But, Mr. Pease, the boss said . . ."

Pease shook his fist in my face.

"This is a *white* man's work around here, and you better watch yourself!"

From then on they changed toward me. They said good-morning no more. When I was just a bit slow in performing some duty, I was called a lazy black son-of-a-bitch.

Once I thought of reporting all this to the boss. But the mere idea of what would happen to me if Pease and Morrie should learn that I had "snitched" stopped me. And after all, the boss was a white man, too. What was the use?

The climax came at noon one summer day. Pease called me to his workbench. To get to him I had to go between two narrow benches and stand with my back against a wall.

"Yes, sir," I said.

"Richard, I want to ask you something," Pease began pleasantly, not looking up from his work.

"Yes, sir," I said again.

Morrie came over, blocking the narrow passage between the benches. He folded his arms, staring at me solemnly.

I looked from one to the other, sensing that something was coming.

"Yes, sir," I said for the third time.

Pease looked up and spoke very slowly.

"Richard, Mr. Morrie here tells me you called me *Pease.*"

I stiffened. A void seemed to open up in me. I knew this was the showdown.

He meant that I had failed to call him Mr. Pease. I looked at Morrie. He was gripping a steel bar in his hands. I opened my mouth to speak, to protest, to assure Pease that I had never called him simply *Pease,* and that I had never had any intentions of doing so, when Morrie grabbed me by the collar, ramming my head against the wall.

"Now, be careful, nigger!" snarled Morrie, baring his teeth. "I heard yuh call 'im *Pease!* 'N' if yuh say yuh didn't, yuh're callin' me a *lie,* see?" He waved the steel bar threateningly.

If I had said: No, sir, Mr. Pease, I never called you *Pease,* I would have been automatically calling Morrie a liar. And if I had said: Yes, sir, Mr. Pease, I called you *Pease*, I would have been pleading guilty to having uttered the worst insult that a Negro can utter to a southern white man. I stood hesitating, trying to frame a neutral reply.

"Richard, I asked you a question!" said Pease. Anger was creeping into his voice.

"I don't remember calling you *Pease,* Mr. Pease," I said cautiously. "And if I did, I sure didn't mean . . ."

"You black son-of-a-bitch! You called me *Pease*, then!" he spat, slapping me till I bent sideways over a bench. Morrie was on top of me, demanding:

"Didn't yuh call 'im *Pease?* If yuh say yuh didn't, I'll rip yo' gut string loose with this bar, yuh black granny dodger! Yuh can't call a white man a lie 'n' git erway with it, you black son-of-a-bitch!"

I wilted. I begged them not to bother me. I knew what they wanted. They wanted me to leave.

"I'll leave," I promised. "I'll leave right *now.*"

They gave me a minute to get out of the factory. I was warned not to show up again, or tell the boss.

I went.

When I told the folks at home what had happened, they called me a fool. They told me that I must never again attempt to exceed my boundaries. When you are working for white folks, they said, you got to "stay in you place" if you want to keep working.

II

My Jim Crow education continued on my next job, which was portering in a clothing store. One morning, while polishing brass out front, the boss and his twenty-year old son got out of their car and half-dragged and half kicked a Negro woman into the store. A policeman standing at the corner looked on, twirling his nightstick. I watched out of the corner of my eye, never slackening the strokes of my chamois upon the brass. After a few minutes, I heard shrill screams coming from the rear of the store. Later the woman stumbled out, bleeding, crying, and holding her stomach. When she reached the end of the block, the policeman grabbed her and accused her of being drunk. Silently, I watched him throw her into a patrol wagon.

When I went to the rear of the store, the boss and his son were washing their hands at the sink. They were chuckling. The floor was bloody and strewn with wisps of hair and clothing. No doubt I must have appeared pretty shocked, for the boss slapped me reassuringly on the back.

"Boy, that's what we do to niggers when they don't want to pay their bills," he said, laughing.

His son looked at me and grinned.

"Here, hava cigarette," he said.

Not knowing what to do, I took it. He lit his and held the match for me This was a gesture of kindness, indicating that even if they had beaten the poor old woman, they would not beat me if I knew enough to keep my mouth shut.

"Yes, sir," I said, and asked no questions.

After they had gone, I sat on the edge of a packing box and stared at the bloody floor till the cigarette went out.

That day at noon, while eating in a hamburger joint, I told my fellow Negro porters what had happened. No one seemed surprised. One fellow after swallowing a huge bite, turned to me and asked:

"Huh! Is tha' all they did t' her?"

"Yeah. Wasn't tha' enough?" I asked.

"Shucks! Man, she's a lucky bitch!" he said, burying his lips deep into a juicy hamburger. "Hell, it's a wonder they didn't lay her when they got through."

III

I was learning fast, but not quite fast enough. One day, while I was delivering packages in the suburbs, my bicycle tire was punctured. I walked along the hot, dusty road, sweating and leading my bicycle by the handlebars.

A car slowed at my side.

"What's the matter, boy?" a white man called.

I told him my bicycle was broken and I was walking back to town.

"That's too bad," he said. "Hop on the running board."

He stopped the car. I clutched hard at my bicycle with one hand and clung to the side of the car with the other.

"All set?"

"Yes, sir," I answered. The car started.

It was full of young white men. They were drinking. I watched the flask pass from mouth to mouth.

"Wanna drink, boy?" one asked.

I laughed as the wind whipped my face. Instinctively obeying the freshly planted precepts of my mother, I said:

"Oh, no!"

The words were hardly out of my mouth before I felt something hard and cold smash me between the eyes. It was an empty whisky bottle. I saw stars, and fell backwards from the speeding car into the dust of the road, my feet becoming entangled in the steel spokes of my bicycle. The white men piled out and stood over me.

"Nigger, ain' yuh learned no better sense'n tha' yet?" asked the man who hit me. "Ain' yuh learned t' say *sir* t' a white man yet?"

Dazed, I pulled to my feet. My elbows and legs were bleeding. Fists doubled, the white man advanced, kicking my bicycle out of the way.

"Aw, leave the bastard alone. He's got enough," said one.

They stood looking at me. I rubbed my shins, trying to stop the flow of blood. No doubt they felt a sort of contemptuous pity, for one asked:

"Yuh wanna ride t' town now, nigger? Yuh reckon yuh know enough t' ride now?"

"I wanna walk," I said, simply.

Maybe it sounded funny. They laughed.

"Well, walk, yuh black son-of-a-bitch!"

When they left they comforted me with:

"Nigger, yuh sho better be damn glad it wuz us yuh talked t' tha' way. Yuh're a lucky bastard, cause if yuh'd said tha' t' somebody else, yuh might've been a dead nigger now."

IV

Negroes who have lived South know the dread of being caught alone upon the streets in white neighborhoods after the sun has set. In such a simple situation as this the plight of the Negro in America is graphically symbolized. While white strangers may be in these neighborhoods trying to get home, they can pass unmolested But the color of a Negro's skin makes him easily recognizable, makes him suspect, converts him into a defenseless target.

Late one Saturday night I made some deliveries in a white neighborhood. I was pedaling my bicycle back to the store as fast as I could, when a police car, swerving toward me, jammed me into the curbing.

"Get down and put up your hands!" the policemen ordered.

I did. They climbed out of the car, guns drawn, faces set, and advanced slowly.

"Keep still!" they ordered.

I reached my hands higher. They searched my pockets and packages. They seemed dissatisfied when they could find nothing incriminating. Finally, one of them said:

"Boy, tell your boss not to send you out in white neighborhoods after sundown."

As usual, I said:

"Yes, sir."

V

My next job was as hall-boy in a hotel. Here my Jim Crow education broadened and deepened. When the bellboys were busy, I was often called to assist them. As many of the rooms in the hotel were occupied by prostitutes, I was constantly called to carry them liquor and cigarettes. These women were nude most of the time. They did not bother about clothing, even for bellboys. When you went into their rooms, you were supposed to take their nakedness for granted, as though it startled you no more than a blue vase or a red rug. Your presence awoke in them no sense of shame, for you were not regarded as human. If they were alone, you could steal sidelong glimpses at them. But if they were receiving men, not a flicker of your eyelids could show. I remember one incident vividly. A new woman, a huge, snowy-skinned blonde, took a room on my floor. I was sent to wait upon her. She was in bed with a thick-set man; both were nude and uncovered. She said she wanted some liquor and slid out of bed and waddled across the floor to get her money from a dresser drawer. I watched her.

"Nigger, what in hell you looking at?" the white man asked me, raising himself upon his elbows.

"Nothing," I answered, looking miles deep into the blank wall of the room.

"Keep your eyes where they belong, if you want to be healthy!" he said.

"Yes, sir."

VI

One of the bellboys I knew in this hotel was keeping steady company with one of the Negro maids. Out of a clear sky the police descended upon his home and arrested him, accusing him of bastardy. The poor boy swore he had had no intimate relations with the girl. Nevertheless, they forced him to marry her. When the child arrived, it was found to be much lighter in complexion than either of the two supposedly legal parents. The white men around the hotel made a great joke of it. They spread the rumor that some white cow must have scared the poor girl while she was carrying the baby. If you were in their presence when this explanation was offered, you were supposed to laugh.

VII

One of the bellboys was caught in bed with a white prostitute. He was castrated and run out of town. Immediately after this all the bellboys and hall-boys were called together and warned. We were given to understand that the boy who had been castrated was a "mighty, mighty lucky bastard." We were impressed with the fact that next time the management of the hotel would not be responsible for the lives of "trouble-makin' niggers." We were silent.

VIII

One night, just as I was about to go home, I met one of the Negro maids. She lived in my direction, and we fell in to walk part of the way home together. As we passed the white night-watchman, he slapped the maid on her buttock. I turned around, amazed. The watchman looked at me with a long, hard, fixed-under stare. Suddenly he pulled his gun and asked:

"Nigger, don't yuh like it?"

I hesitated.

"I asked yuh don't yuh like it?" he asked again, stepping forward.

"Yes, sir," I mumbled.

"Talk like it, then!"

"Oh, yes, sir!" I said with as much heartiness as l could muster.

Outside, I walked ahead of the girl, ashamed to face her. She caught up with me and said:

"Don't be a fool! Yuh couldn't help it!"

This watchman boasted of having killed two Negroes in self-defense.

Yet, in spite of all this, the life of the hotel ran with an amazing smoothness. It would have been impossible for a stranger to detect anything. The maids, the hall-boys, and the bellboys were all smiles. They had to be.

IX

I had learned my Jim Crow lessons so thoroughly that I kept the hotel job till I left Jackson for Memphis. It so happened that while in Memphis I applied for a job at a branch of the optical company. I was hired. And for some reason, as long as I worked there, they never brought my past against me.

Here my Jim Crow education assumed quite a different form. It was no longer brutally cruel, but subtly cruel. Here I learned to lie, to steal, to dissemble. I learned to play that dual role which every Negro must play if he wants to eat and live.

For example, it was almost impossible to get a book to read. It was assumed that after a Negro had imbibed what scanty schooling the state furnished he had no further need for books. I was always borrowing books from men on the job. One day I mustered enough courage to ask one of the men to let me get books from the library in his name. Surprisingly, he consented. I cannot help but think that he consented because he was a Roman Catholic and felt a vague sympathy for Negroes, being himself an object of hatred. Armed with a library card, I obtained books in the following manner: I would write a note to the librarian, saying: "Please let this nigger boy have the following books." I would then sign it with the white man's name.

When I went to the library, I would stand at the desk, hat in hand, looking as unbookish as possible. When I received the books desired I would take them home. If the books listed in the note happened to be out, I would sneak into the lobby and forge a new one. I never took any chances guessing with the white librarian about what the fictitious white man would want to read. No doubt if any of the white patrons had suspected that some of the volumes they enjoyed had been in the home of a Negro, they would not have tolerated it for an instant.

The factory force of the optical company in Memphis was much larger than that in Jackson, and more urbanized. At least they liked to talk, and would engage the Negro help in conversation whenever possible. By this means I found that many subjects were taboo from the white man's point of view. Among the topics they did not like to discuss with Negroes were the following: American white women; the Ku Klux Klan; France, and how Negro soldiers fared while there; French women; Jack Johnson; the entire northern part of the United States; the Civil War; Abraham Lincoln; U.S. Grant; General Sherman; Catholics; the Pope; Jews; the Republican Party; slavery; social equality; Communism; Socialism; the 13th and 14th Amendments to the Constitution; or any topic calling for positive knowledge or manly self-assertion on the part of the Negro. The most accepted topics were sex and religion.

There were many times when I had to exercise a great deal of ingenuity to keep out of trouble. It is a southern custom that all men must take off their hats when they enter an elevator. And especially did this apply to us blacks with rigid force. One day I stepped into an elevator with my arms full of packages. I was forced to ride with my hat on. Two white men stared at me coldly. Then one of them very kindly lifted my hat and placed it upon my armful of packages. Now the most accepted response for a Negro to make under such circumstances is to look at the white man out of the corner of his eye and grin. To have said: "Thank you!" would have made the white man *think* that you *thought* you were receiving from him a personal service. For such an act I have seen Negroes take a blow in the mouth. Finding the first alternative distasteful, and the second dangerous, I hit upon an acceptable course of action which fell safely between these two poles. I immediately—no sooner than my hat was lifted—pretended that my packages were about to spill, and appeared deeply distressed with keeping them in my arms. In this fashion I evaded having to acknowledge his service, and, in spite of adverse circumstances, salvaged a slender shred of personal pride.

How do Negroes feel about the way they have to live? How do they discuss it when alone among themselves? I think this question can be answered in a single sentence. A friend of mine who ran an elevator once told me:

"Lawd, man! Ef it wuzn't fer them polices 'n' them ol' lynch-mobs, there wouldn't be nothin' but uproar down here!"

The Man Who Lived Underground

Richard Wright

I've got to hide, he told himself. His chest heaved as he waited, crouching in a dark corner of the vestibule. He was tired of running and dodging. Either he had to find a place to hide, or he had to surrender. A police car swished by through the rain, its siren rising sharply. They're looking for me all over . . . He crept to the door and squinted through the fogged plate glass. He stiffened as the siren rose and died in the distance. Yes, he had to hide, but where? He gritted his teeth. Then a sudden movement in the street caught his attention. A throng of tiny columns of water snaked into the air from the perforations of a manhole cover. The columns stopped abruptly, as though the perforations had become clogged; a gray spout of sewer water jutted up from underground and lifted the circular metal cover, juggled it for a moment, then let it fall with a clang.

He hatched a tentative plan: he would wait until the siren sounded far off, then he would go out. He smoked and waited, tense. At last the siren gave him his signal; it wailed, dying, going away from him. He stepped to the sidewalk, then paused and looked curiously at the open manhole, half expecting the cover to leap up again. He went to the center of the street and stooped and peered into the hole, but could see nothing. Water rustled in the black depths.

He started with terror; the siren sounded so near that he had the idea that he had been dreaming and had awakened to find the car upon him. He dropped instinctively to his knees and his hands grasped the rim of the manhole. The siren seemed to hoot directly above him and with a wild gasp of exertion he snatched the cover far enough off to admit his body. He swung his legs over the opening and lowered himself into watery darkness. He hung for an eternal moment to the rim by his fingertips, then he felt rough metal prongs and at once he knew that sewer workmen used these ridges to lower themselves into manholes. Fist over fist, he let his body sink until he could feel no more prongs. He swayed in dank space; the siren seemed to howl at the very rim of the man-hole. He dropped and was washed violently into an ocean of warm, leaping water. His head was battered against a wall and he wondered if this were death. Frenziedly his fingers clawed and sank into a crevice. He steadied himself and measured the strength of the current with his own muscular tension. He stood slowly in water that dashed past his knees with fearful velocity.

He heard a prolonged scream of brakes and the siren broke off. Oh, God! They had found him! Looming above his head in the rain a white face hovered over the hole. "How did this damn thing get off?" he heard a policeman ask. He saw the steel cover move slowly until the hole looked like a quarter moon turned black. "Give me a hand here," someone called. The cover clanged into place, muffling the sights and sounds of the upper world. Knee-deep in the pulsing current, he breathed with aching chest, filling his lungs with the hot stench of yeasty rot.

From the perforations of the manhole cover, delicate lances of hazy violet sifted down and wove a mottled pattern upon the surface of the streaking current. His lips parted as a car swept past along the wet pavement overhead, its heavy rumble soon dying out, like the hum of a plane speeding through a dense cloud. He had never thought that cars could sound like that; everything seemed strange and unreal under here. He stood in darkness for a long time, knee-deep in rustling water, musing.

The odor of rot had become so general that he no longer smelled it. He got his cigarettes, but discovered that his matches were wet. He searched and found a dry folder in the pocket of his shirt and managed to strike one; it flared weirdly in the wet gloom, glowing greenishly, turning red, orange, then yellow. He lit a crumpled cigarette; then, by the flickering light of the match, he looked for support so that he would not have to keep his muscles flexed against the pouring water. His pupils narrowed and he saw to either side of him two steaming walls that rose and curved inward some six feet above his head to form a dripping, mouse-colored dome. The bottom of the sewer was a sloping V-trough. To the left, the sewer vanished in ashen fog. To the right was a steep down-curve into which water plunged.

He saw now that had he not regained his feet in time, he would have been swept to death, or had he entered any other manhole he would have probably drowned. Above the rush of the current he heard sharper juttings of water; tiny streams were spewing into the sewer from smaller conduits. The match died; he struck another and saw a mass of debris sweep past him and clog the throat of the down-curve. At once the water began rising rapidly. Could he climb out before he drowned? A long hiss sounded and the debris was sucked from sight; the current lowered. He understood now what had made the water toss the manhole cover; the down-curve had become temporarily obstructed and the perforations had become clogged.

He was in danger; he might slide into a down-curve; he might wander with a lighted match into a pocket of gas and blow himself up; or he might contract some horrible disease . . . Though he wanted to leave, an irrational impulse held him rooted. To the left, the convex ceiling swooped to a height of less than five feet With cigarette slanting from pursed lips, he waded with taut muscles, his feet sloshing over the slimy bottom, his shoes sinking into spongy slop, the slate-colored water cracking in creamy foam against his knees. Pressing his flat left palm against the lowered ceiling, he struck another match and saw a metal pole nestling in a niche of the wall. Yes, some sewer workman had left it. He reached for it, then jerked his head away as a whisper of scurrying life whisked past and was still. He held the match close and saw a huge rat, wet with slime, blinking beady eyes and baring tiny fangs. The light blinded the rat and the frizzled head moved aimlessly. He grabbed the pole and let it fly against the rat's soft body; there was shrill piping and the grizzly body splashed into the dun-colored water and was snatched out of sight, spinning in the scuttling stream.

He swallowed and pushed on, following the curve of the misty cavern, sounding the water with the pole. By the faint light of another manhole cover he saw, amid loose wet brick, a hole with walls of damp earth leading into blackness. Gingerly he poked the pole into it; it was hollow and went beyond the length of the pole. He shoved the pole before him, hoisted himself upward, got to his hands and knees, and crawled. After a few yards he paused, struck to wonderment by the silence; it seemed that he had traveled a million miles away from the world. As he inched forward again he could sense the bottom of the dirt tunnel becoming dry and lowering slightly. Slowly he rose and to his astonishment he stood erect. He could not hear the rustling of the water now and he felt confoundingly alone, yet lured by the darkness and silence.

He crept a long way, then stopped, curious, afraid. He put his right foot forward and it dangled in space; he drew back in fear. He thrust the pole outward and it swung in emptiness. He trembled, imagining the earth crumbling and burying him alive. He scratched a match and saw that the dirt floor sheered away steeply and widened into a sort of cave some five feet below him. An old sewer, he muttered. He cocked his head, hearing a feathery cadence which he could not identify. The match ceased to burn.

Using the pole as a kind of ladder, he slid down and stood in darkness. The air was a little fresher and he could still hear vague noises. Where was he? He felt suddenly that someone was standing near him and he turned sharply, but there was only darkness. He poked cautiously and felt a brick wall; he followed it and the strange sounds grew louder. He ought to get out of here. This was crazy. He could not remain here for any length of time; there was no food and no place to sleep. But the faint sounds tantalized him; they were strange but familiar. Was it a motor? A baby crying? Music? A siren? He groped on, and the sounds came so clearly that he could feel the pitch and timbre of human voices. Yes, singing! That was it! He listened with open mouth. It was a church service. Enchanted, he groped toward the waves of melody.

> *Jesus, take me to your home above*
> *And fold me in the bosom of Thy love . . .*

The singing was on the other side of a brick wall. Excited, he wanted to watch the service without being seen. Whose church was it? He knew most of the churches in this area above ground, but the singing sounded too strange and detached for him to guess. He looked to the left, to the right, down to the black dirt, then upward and was startled to see a bright sliver of light slicing the darkness like the blade of a razor. He struck one of his two remaining matches and saw rusty pipes running along an old concrete ceiling. Photographically he located the exact position of the pipes in his mind. The match flame sank and he sprang upward; his hands clutched a pipe. He swung his legs and tossed his body onto the bed of pipes and they creaked, swaying up and down; he thought that the tier was about to crash, but nothing happened. He edged to the crevice and saw a segment of black men and women, dressed in white robes, singing, holding tattered songbooks in their black palms. His first impulse was to laugh, but he checked himself.

What was he doing? He was crushed with a sense of guilt. Would God strike him dead for that? The singing swept on and he shook his head, disagreeing in spite of himself. They oughtn't to do that, he thought. But he could think of no reason *why* they should not do it. Just singing with the air of the sewer blowing in on them . . . He felt that he was gazing upon something abysmally obscene, yet he could not bring himself to leave.

After a long time he grew numb and dropped to the dirt. Pain throbbed in his legs and a deeper pain, induced by the sight of those black people groveling and begging for something they could never get, churned in him. A vague conviction made him feel that those people should stand unrepentant and yield no quarter in singing and praying, yet *he* had run away from the police, had pleaded with them to believe in *his* innocence. He shook his head, bewildered.

How long had he been down here? He did not know. This was a new kind of living for him; the intensity of feelings he had experienced when looking at the church people sing made him certain that he had been down here a long time, but his mind told him that the time must have been short. In this darkness the only notion he had of time was when a match flared and measured time by its fleeting light He groped back through the hole toward the sewer and the waves of song subsided and finally he could not hear them at all. He came to where the earth hole ended and he heard the noise of the current and time lived again for him, measuring the moments by the wash of water.

The rain must have slackened, for the flow of water had lessened and came only to his ankles. Ought he to go up into the streets and take his chances on hiding somewhere else? But they would surely catch him. The mere thought of dodging and running again from the police made him tense. No, he would stay and plot how to elude them. But what could he do down here? He walked forward into the sewer and came to another manhole cover; he stood beneath it, debating. Fine pencils of gold spilled suddenly from the little circles in the manhole cover and trembled on the surface of the current. Yes, street lamps . . . It must be night . . .

He went forward for about a quarter of an hour, wading aimlessly, poking the pole carefully before him. Then he stopped, his eyes fixed and intent. What's that? A strangely familiar image attracted and repelled him. Lit by the yellow sterns from another manhole cover was a tiny nude body of a baby snagged by debris and half-submerged in water. Thinking that the baby was alive, he moved impulsively to save it, but his roused feelings told him that it was dead, cold, nothing, the same nothingness he had felt while watching the men and women singing in the church. Water blossomed about the tiny legs, the tiny arms, the tiny head, and rushed onward. The eyes were closed, as though in sleep; the fists were clenched, as though in protest; and the mouth gaped black in a soundless cry.

He straightened and drew in his breath, feeling that he had been staring for all eternity at the ripples of veined water skimming impersonally over the shriveled limbs. He felt as condemned as when the policemen had accused him. Involuntarily he lifted his hand to brush the vision away, but his arm fell listlessly to his side. Then he acted; he closed his eyes and reached forward slowly with the soggy shoe of his right foot and shoved the dead baby from where it had been lodged. He kept his eyes closed, seeing the little body twisting in the current as it floated from sight. He opened his eyes, shivered, placed his knuckles in the sockets, hearing the water speed in the somber shadows.

He tramped on, sensing at times a sudden quickening in the current as he passed some conduit whose waters were swelling the stream that slid by his feet. A few minutes later he was standing under another manhole cover, listening to the faint rumble of noises above ground. Streetcars and trucks, he mused. He looked down and saw a stagnant pool of gray-green sludge; at intervals a balloon pocket rose from the scum, glistening a bluish-purple, and burst. Then another. He turned, shook his head, and tramped back to the dirt cave by the church, his lips quivering.

Back in the cave, he sat and leaned his back against a dirt wall. His body was trembling slightly. Finally his senses quieted and he slept. When he awakened he felt stiff and cold. He had to leave this foul place, but leaving meant facing those policemen who had wrongly accused him. No, he could not go back aboveground. He remembered the beating they had given him and how he had signed his name to a confession, a confession which he had not even read. He had been too tired when they had shouted at him, demanding that he sign his name; he had signed it to end his pain.

He stood and groped about in the darkness. The church singing had stopped. How long had he slept? He did not know. But he felt refreshed and hungry. He doubled his fist nervously, realizing that he could not make a decision. As he walked about he stumbled over an old rusty iron pipe. He picked it up and felt a jagged edge. Yes, there was a brick wall and he could dig into it. What would he find? Smiling, he groped to the brick wall, sat, and began digging idly into damp cement. I can't make any noise, he cautioned himself. As time passed he grew thirsty, but there was no water. He had to kill time or go aboveground. The cement came out of the wall easily; he extracted four bricks and felt a soft draft blowing into his face. He stopped, afraid. What was beyond? He waited a long time and nothing happened; then he began digging again, soundlessly, slowly; he enlarged the hole and crawled through into a dark room and collided with another wall. He felt his way to the right; the wall ended and his fingers toyed in space, like the antennae of an insect.

He fumbled on and his feet struck something hollow, like wood. What's this? He felt with his fingers. Steps . . . He Stooped and pulled off his shoes and mounted the stairs and saw a yellow chink of light shining and heard a low voice speaking. He placed his eye to a keyhole and saw the nude waxen figure of a man stretched out upon a white table. The voice, low-pitched and vibrant, mumbled indistinguishable words, neither rising nor falling. He craned his neck and squinted to see the man who was talking, but he could not locate him. Above the naked figure was suspended a huge glass container filled with a blood-red liquid from which a white rubber tube dangled. He crouched closer to the door and saw the tip end of a black object lined with pink satin. A coffin, he breathed. This is an undertaker's establishment . . . A fine-spun lace of ice covered his body and he shuddered. A throaty chuckle sounded in the depths of the yellow room.

He turned to leave. Three steps down it occurred to him that a light switch should be nearby; he felt along the wall, found an electric button, pressed it, and a blinding glare smote his pupils so hard that he was sightless, defenseless. His pupils contracted and he wrinkled his nostrils at a peculiar odor. At once he knew that he had been dimly aware of this odor in the darkness, but the light had brought it sharply to his attention. Some kind of stuff they use to embalm, he thought. He went down the steps and saw piles of lumber, coffins, and a long workbench. In one corner was a tool chest. Yes, he could use tools, could tunnel through walls with them. He lifted the lid of the chest and saw nails, a hammer, a crowbar, a screwdriver, a light bulb, a long length of electric wire. Good! He would lug these back to his cave.

He was about to hoist the chest to his shoulders when he discovered a door behind the furnace. Where did it lead? He tried to open it and found it securely bolted. Using the crow-bar so as to make no sound, he pried the door open; it swung on creaking hinges, outward. Fresh air came to his face and he caught the faint roar of faraway sound. Easy now, he told himself. He widened the door and a lump of coal rattled toward him. A coalbin... Evidently the door led into another basement. The roaring noise was louder now, but he could not identify it, Where was he? He groped slowly over the coal pile, then ranged in darkness over a gritty floor. The roaring noise seemed to come from above him, then below, his fingers followed a wall until he touched a wooden ridge. A door, he breathed.

The noise died to a low pitch; he felt his skin prickle. It seemed that he was playing a game with an unseen person whose intelligence outstripped his. He put his ear to the flat surface of the door. Yes, voices... Was this a prize fight stadium? The sound of the voices came near and sharp, but he could not tell if they were joyous or despairing. He twisted the knob until he heard a soft click and felt the springy weight of the door swinging toward him. He was afraid to open it, yet captured by curiosity and wonder. He jerked the door wide and saw on the far side of the basement a furnace glowing red. Ten feet away was still another door, half ajar. He crossed and peered through the door into an empty, high-ceilinged corridor that terminated in a dark complex of shadow. The belling voices rolled about him and his eagerness mounted. He stepped into the corridor and the voices swelled louder. He crept on and came to a narrow stairway leading circularly upward; there was no question but what he was going to ascend those stairs.

Mounting the spiraled staircase, he heard the voices roll in a steady wave, then leap to crescendo, only to die away, but always remaining audible. Ahead of him glowed red letters: E-X-I-T. At the top of the steps he paused in front of a black curtain that fluttered uncertainly. He parted the folds and looked into a convex depth that gleamed with clusters of shimmering lights. Sprawling below him was a stretch of human faces, tilted upward, chanting, whistling, screaming, laughing. Dangling before the faces, high upon a screen of silver, were jerking shadows. A movie, he said with slow laughter breaking from his lips.

He stood in a box in the reserved section of a movie house and the impulse he had had to tell the people in the church to stop their singing seized him. These people were laughing at their lives, he thought with amazement. They were shouting and yelling at the animated shadows of themselves. His compassion fired his imagination and he stepped out of the box, walked out upon thin air, walked on down to the audience; and, hovering in the air just above them, he stretched out his hand to touch them... His tension snapped and he found himself back in the box, looking down into the sea of faces. No; it could not be done; he could not awaken them. He sighed. Yes, these people were children, sleeping in their living, awake in their dying.

He turned away, parted the black curtain, and looked out. He saw no one. He started down the white stone steps and when he reached the bottom he saw a man in trim blue uniform coming toward him. So used had he become to being underground that he thought that he could walk past the man, as though he were a ghost. But the man stopped. And he stopped.

"Looking for the men's room, sir?" the man asked, and, without waiting for an answer, he turned and pointed. "This way, sir. The first door to your right."

He watched the man turn and walk up the steps and go out of sight. Then he laughed. What a funny fellow! He went back to the basement and stood in the red darkness, watching the glowing embers in the furnace. He went to the sink and turned the faucet and the water flowed in a smooth silent stream that looked like a spout of blood. He brushed the mad image from his mind and began to wash his hands leisurely, looking about for the usual bar of soap. He found one and rubbed it in his palms until a rich lather bloomed in his cupped fingers, like a scarlet sponge. He scrubbed and rinsed his hands meticulously, then hunted for a towel; there was none. He shut off the water, pulled off his shirt, dried his hands on it; when he put it on again he was grateful for the cool dampness that came to his skin.

Yes, he was thirsty; he turned on the faucet again, bowled his fingers and when the water bubbled over the brim of his cupped palms, he drank in long, slow swallows. His bladder grew tight; he shut off the water, faced the wall, bent his head, and watched a red stream strike the floor. His nostrils wrinkled against acrid wisps of vapor; though he had tramped in the waters of the sewer, he stepped back from the wall so that his shoes, wet with sewer slime, would not touch his urine.

He heard footsteps and crawled quickly into the coalbin. Lumps rattled noisily. The footsteps came into the basement and stopped. Who was it? Had someone heard him and come down to investigate? He waited, crouching, sweating. For a long time there was silence, then he heard the clang of metal and a brighter glow lit the room. Somebody's tending the furnace, he thought. Footsteps came closer and he stiffened. Looming before him was a white face lined with coal dust, the face of an old man with watery blue eyes. Highlights spotted his gaunt cheekbones, and he held a huge shovel. There was a screechy scrape of metal against stone, and the old man lifted a shovelful of coal and went from sight.

The room dimmed momentarily, then a yellow glare came as coal flared at the furnace door. Six times the old man came to the bin and went to the furnace with shovels of coal, but not once did he lift his eyes. Finally he dropped the shovel, mopped his face with a dirty handkerchief, and sighed: "Wheeew!" He turned slowly and trudged out of the basement, his footsteps dying away.

He stood, and lumps of coal clattered down the pile. He stepped from the bin and was startled to see the shadowy outline of an electric bulb hanging above his head. Why had not the old man turned it on? Oh, yes . . . He understood. The old man had worked here for so long that he had no need for light; he had learned a way of seeing in his dark world, like those sightless worms that inch along underground by a sense of touch.

His eyes fell upon a lunch pail and he was afraid to hope that it was full. He picked it up; it was heavy. He opened it. *Sandwiches!* He looked guiltily around; he was alone. He searched farther and found a folder of matches and a half-empty tin of tobacco; he put them eagerly into his pocket and clicked off the light. With the lunch pail under his arm, he went through the door, groped over the pile of coal, and stood again in the lighted basement of the undertaking establishment. I've got to get those tools, he told himself. And turn off that light. He tiptoed back up the steps and switched off the light; the invisible voice still droned on behind the door. He crept down and, seeing with his fingers, opened the lunch pail and tore off a piece of paper bag and brought out the tin and spilled grains of tobacco into the makeshift concave. He rolled it and wet it with spittle, then inserted one end into his mouth and lit it: he sucked smoke that bit his lungs. The nicotine reached his brain, went out along his arms to his fingertips, down to his stomach, and over all the tired nerves of his body.

He carted the tools to the hole he had made in the wall. Would the noise of the falling chest betray him? But he would have to take a chance; he had to have those tools. He lifted the chest and shoved it; it hit the dirt on the other side of the wall with a loud clatter. He waited, listening; nothing happened. Head first, he slithered through and stood in the cave. He grinned, filled with a cunning idea. Yes, he would now go back into the basement of the undertaking establishment and crouch behind the coal pile and dig another hole. Sure! Fumbling, he opened the tool chest and extracted a crowbar, a screwdriver, and a hammer; he fastened them securely about his person.

With another lumpish cigarette in his flexed lips, he crawled back through the hole and over the coal pile and sat, facing the brick wall. He jabbed with the crowbar and the cement sheered away; quicker than he thought, a brick came loose. He worked an hour; the other bricks did not come easily. He sighed, weak from effort. I ought to rest a little, he thought I'm hungry. He felt his way back to the cave and stumbled along the wall till he came to the tool chest. He sat upon it, opened the lunch pail, and took out two thick sandwiches. He smelled them. Pork chops . . . His mouth watered. He closed his eyes and devoured a sandwich, savoring the smooth rye bread and juicy meat. He ate rapidly, gulping down lumpy mouthfuls that made him long for water. He ate the other sandwich and found an apple and gobbled that up too, sucking the core till the last trace of flavor was drained from it. Then, like a dog, he ground the meat bones with his teeth, enjoying the salty, tangy marrow. He finished and stretched out full length on the ground and went to sleep . . .

. . . His body was washed by cold water that gradually turned warm and he was buoyed upon a stream and swept out to sea where waves rolled gently and suddenly he found himself walking upon the water how strange and delightful to walk upon the water and he came upon a nude woman holding a nude baby in her arms and the woman was sinking into the water holding the baby above her head and screaming *help* and he ran over the water to the woman and he reached her just before she went down and he took the baby from her hands and stood watching the breaking bubbles where the woman sank and he called *lady* and still no answer yes dive down there and rescue that woman but he could not take this baby with him and he stooped and laid the baby tenderly upon the surface of the water expecting it to sink but it floated and he leaped into the water and held his breath and strained his eyes to see through the gloomy volume of water but there was no woman and he opened his mouth and called *lady* and the water bubbled and his chest ached and his arms were tired but he could not see the woman and he called again *lady lady* and his feet touched sand at the bottom of the sea and his chest felt as though it would burst and he bent his knees and propelled himself upward and water rushed past him and his head bobbed out and he breathed deeply and looked around where was the baby the baby was gone and he rushed over the water looking for the baby calling *where is it* and the empty sky and sea threw back his voice *where is it* and he began to doubt that he could stand upon the water and then he was sinking and as he struggled the water rushed him downward spinning dizzily and he opened his mouth to call for help and water surged into his lungs and he choked . . .

He groaned and leaped erect in the dark, his eyes wide. The images of terror that thronged his brain would not let him sleep. He rose, made sure that the tools were hitched to his belt, and groped his way to the coal pile and found the rectangular gap from which he had taken the bricks. He took out the crowbar and hacked. Then dread paralyzed him. How long had he slept? Was it day or night now? He had to be careful. Someone might hear him if it were day. He hewed softly for hours at the cement, working silently. Faintly quivering in the air above him was the dim sound of yelling voices. Crazy people, he muttered. They're still there in that movie . . .

Having rested, he found the digging much easier. He soon had a dozen bricks out. His spirits rose. He took out another brick and his fingers fluttered in space. Good! What lay ahead of him? Another basement? He made the hole larger, climbed through, walked over an uneven floor and felt a metal surface. He lighted a match and saw that he was standing behind a furnace in a basement; before him, on the far side of the room, was a door. He crossed and opened it; it was full of odds and ends. Daylight spilled from a window above his head.

Then he was aware of a soft, continuous tapping. What was it? A clock? No, it was louder than a clock and more irregular. He placed an old empty box beneath the window, stood upon it, and looked into an areaway. He eased the window up and crawled through; the sound of the tapping came clearly now. He glanced about; he was alone. Then he looked upward at a series of window ledges. The tapping identified itself. That's a typewriter, he said to himself. It seemed to be coming from just above. He grasped the ridges of a rain pipe and lifted himself upward; through a half-inch opening of window he saw a doorknob about three feet away. No, it was not a doorknob; it was a small circular disk made of stainless steel with many fine markings upon it. He held his breath: an eerie white hand, seemingly detached from its arm, touched the metal knob and whirled it, first to the left, then to the right. It's a safe! . . . Suddenly he could see the dial no more; a huge metal door swung slowly toward him and he was looking into a safe filled with green wads of paper money, rows of coins wrapped in brown paper, and glass jars and boxes of various sizes. His heart quickened. Good lord! The white hand went in and out of the safe, taking wads of bills and cylinders of coins. The hand vanished and he heard the muffled click of the big door as it closed. Only the steel dial was visible now. The typewriter still tapped in his ears, but he could not see it. He blinked, wondering if what he had seen was real. There was more money in that safe than he had seen in all his life.

As he clung to the rain pipe, a daring idea came to him and he pulled the screwdriver from his belt. If the white hand twirled that dial again, he would be able to see how far to the left and right it spun and he would have the combination! His blood tingled. I can scratch the numbers right here, he thought. Holding the pipe with one hand, he made the sharp edge of the screwdriver bite into the brick wall. Yes, he could do it. Now, he was set. Now, he had a reason for staying here in the underground. He waited for a long time, but the white hand did not return. Goddamn! Had he been more alert, he would have counted the twirls and he would have had the combination. He got down and stood in the areaway, sunk in reflection.

How could he get into that room? He climbed back into the basement and saw wooden steps leading upward. Was that the room where the safe stood? Fearing that the dial was now being twirled, he clambered through the window, hoisted himself up the rain pipe, and peered; he saw only the naked gleam of the steel dial. He got down and doubled his fists. Well, he would explore the basement. He returned to the basement room and mounted the steps to the door and squinted through the keyhole; all was dark, but the tapping was still somewhere near, still faint and directionless. He pushed the door in; along one wall of a room was a table piled with radios and electrical equipment. A radio shop, he muttered.

Well, he could rig up a radio in his cave. He found a sack, slid the radio into it, and slung it across his back. Closing the door, he went down the steps and stood again in the basement, disappointed. He had not solved the problem of the steel dial and he was irked. He set the radio on the floor and again hoisted himself through the window and up the rain pipe and squinted; the metal door was swinging shut. Goddamn! He's worked the combination again. If I had been patient, I'd have had it! How could he get into that room? He *had* to get into it. He could jimmy the window, but it would be much better if he could get in without any traces. To the right of him, he calculated, should be the basement of the building that held the safe; therefore, if he dug a hole right *here,* he ought to reach his goal.

He began a quiet scraping; it was hard work, for the bricks were not damp. He eventually got one out and lowered it softly to the floor. He had to be careful; perhaps people were beyond this wall. He extracted a second layer of brick and found still another. He gritted his teeth, ready to quit. I'll dig one more, he resolved. When the next brick came out he felt air blowing into his face. He waited to be challenged, but nothing happened.

He enlarged the hole and pulled himself through and stood in quiet darkness. He scratched a match to flame and saw steps; he mounted and peered through a keyhole: Darkness . . . He strained to hear the typewriter, but there was only silence. Maybe the office had closed? He twisted the knob and swung the door in; a frigid blast made him shiver. In the shadows before him were halves and quarters of hogs and lambs and steers hanging from metal hooks on the low ceiling, red meat encased in folds of cold white fat. Fronting him was frost-coated glass from behind which came indistinguishable sounds. The odor of fresh raw meat sickened him and he backed away. A meat market, he whispered.

He ducked his head, suddenly blinded by light. He narrowed his eyes; the red-white rows of meat were drenched in yellow glare. A man wearing a crimson-spotted jacket came in and took down a bloody meat clever. He eased the door to, holding it ajar just enough to watch the man, hoping that the darkness in which he stood would keep him from being seen. The man took down a hunk of steer and placed it upon a bloody wooden block and bent forward and whacked with the cleaver. The man's face was hard, square, grim; a jet of mustache smudged his upper lip and a glistening cowlick of hair fell over his left eye. Each time he lifted the cleaver and brought it down upon the meat, he let out a short, deep-chested grunt. After he had cut the meat, he wiped blood off the wooden block with a sticky wad of gunnysack and hung the cleaver upon a hook. His face was proud as he placed the chunk of meat in the crook of his elbow and left.

The door slammed and the light went off; once more he stood in shadow. His tension ebbed. From behind the frosted glass he heard the man's voice: "Forty-eight cents a pound, ma am." He shuddered, feeling that there was something he had to do. But what? He stared fixedly at the cleaver, then he sneezed and was terrified for fear that the man had heard him. But the door did not open. He took down the cleaver and examined the sharp edge smeared with cold blood. Behind the ice-coated glass a cash register rang with a vibrating, musical tinkle.

Absent-mindedly holding the meat cleaver, he rubbed the glass with his thumb and cleared a spot that enabled him to see into the front of the store. The shop was empty, save for the man who was now putting on his hat and coat Beyond the front window a wan sun shone in the streets;

people passed and now and then a fragment of laughter or the whir of a speeding auto came to him. He peered closer and saw on the right counter of the shop a mosquito netting covering pears, grapes, lemons, oranges, bananas, peaches, and plums. His stomach contracted.

The man clicked out the light and he gritted his teeth, muttering, Don't lock the icebox door ... The man went through the door of the shop and locked it from the outside. Thank God! Now, he would eat some more! He waited, trembling. The sun died and its rays lingered on in the sky, turning the streets to dusk. He opened the door and stepped inside the shop. In reverse letters across the front window was: NICK'S FRUITS AND MEATS. He laughed, picked up a soft ripe yellow pear and bit into it; juice squirted; his mouth ached as his saliva glands reacted to the acid of the fruit. He ate three pears, gobbled six bananas, and made away with several oranges, taking a bite out of their tops and holding them to his lips and squeezing them as he hungrily sucked the juice.

He found a faucet, turned it on, laid the cleaver aside, pursed his lips under the stream until his stomach felt about to burst. He straightened and belched, feeling satisfied for the first time since he had been underground. He sat upon the floor, rolled and lit a cigarette, his bloodshot eyes squinting against the film of drifting smoke. He watched a patch of sky turn red, then purple; night fell and he lit another cigarette, brooding. Some part of him was trying to remember the world he had left, and another part of him did not want to remember it. Sprawling before him in his mind was his wife, Mrs. Wooten for whom he worked, the three policemen who had picked him up ... He possessed them now more completely than he had ever possessed them when he had lived aboveground. How this had come about he could not say, but he had no desire to go back to them. He laughed, crushed the cigarette, and stood up.

He went to the front door and gazed out. Emotionally he hovered between the world aboveground and the world underground. He longed to go out, but sober judgment urged him to remain here. Then impulsively he pried the lock loose with one swift twist of the crowbar; the door swung outward. Through the twilight he saw a white man and a white woman coming toward him. He held himself tense, waiting for them to pass; but they came directly to the door and confronted him.

"I want to buy a pound of grapes," the woman said.

Terrified, he stepped back into the store. The white man stood to one side and the woman entered.

"Give me a pound of dark ones," the woman said.

The white man came slowly forward, blinking his eyes.

"Where's Nick?" the man asked.

"Were you just closing?" the woman asked.

"Yes, ma'am," he mumbled. For a second he did not breathe, then he mumbled again: "Yes. ma'am."

"I'm sorry," the woman said.

The street lamps came on, lighting the store somewhat. Ought he run? But that would raise an alarm. He moved slowly, dreamily, to a counter and lifted up a bunch of grapes and showed them to the woman.

"Fine," the woman said. "But isn't that more than a pound?"

He did not answer. The man was staring at him intently.

"Put them in a bag for me," the woman said, fumbling with her purse.

"Yes, ma'am."

He saw a pile of paper bags under a narrow ledge; he opened one and put the grapes in.

"Thanks," the woman said, taking the bag and placing a dime in his dark palm.

"Where's Nick?" the man asked again. "At supper?"

"Sir? Yes, sir," he breathed.

They left the store and he stood trembling in the doorway. When they were out of sight, he burst out laughing and crying. A trolley car rolled noisily past and he controlled himself quickly. He flung the dime to the pavement with a gesture of contempt and stepped into the warm night air. A few shy stars trembled above him. The look of things was beautiful, yet he felt a lurking threat. He went to an unattended newsstand and looked at a stack of papers. He saw a headline: HUNT NEGRO FOR MURDER.

He felt that someone had slipped up on him from behind and was stripping off his clothes; he looked about wildly, went quickly back into the store, picked up the meat cleaver where he had left it near the sink, then made his way through the icebox to the basement. He stood for a long time, breathing heavily. They know I didn't do anything, he muttered. But how could he prove it? He had signed a confession. Though innocent, he felt guilty, condemned. He struck a match and held it near the steel blade, fascinated and repelled by the dried blotches of blood. Then his fingers gripped the handle of the cleaver; with all the strength of his body, he wanted to fling the cleaver from him, but he could not. The match flame wavered and fled; he struggled through the hole and put the cleaver in the sack with the radio. He was determined to keep it, for what purpose he did not know.

He was about to leave when he remembered the safe. Where was it? He wanted to give up, but felt that he ought to make one more try. Opposite the last hole he had dug, he tunneled again, plying the crowbar. Once he was so exhausted that he lay on the concrete floor and panted. Finally he made another hole. He wriggled through and his nostrils filled with the fresh smell of coal. He struck a match; yes, the usual steps led upward. He tiptoed to a door and eased it open, A fair-haired white girl stood in front of a steel cabinet, her blue eyes wide upon him. She turned chalky and gave a high-pitched scream. He bounded down the steps and raced to his hole and clambered through, replacing the bricks with nervous haste. He paused, hearing loud voices.

"What's the matter, Alice?"

"A man . . ."

"What man? Where?"

"A man was at that door . . ."

"Oh nonsense!"

"He was looking at me through the door!"

"Aw, you're dreaming."

"I *did* see a man!"

The girl was crying now.

"There's nobody here."

Another man's voice sounded.

"What is it, Bob?"

"Alice says she saw a man in here, in that door!"

"Let's take a look."

He waited, poised for flight. Footsteps descended the stairs.

"There's nobody down here."

"The window's locked."

"And there's no door."

"You ought to fire that dame."

"Oh, I don't know. Women are that way."

"She's too hysterical."

The men laughed. Footsteps sounded again on the stairs. A door slammed. He sighed, relieved that he had escaped. But he had not done what he had set out to do; his glimpse of the room had been too brief to determine if the safe was there. He had to know. Boldly he groped through the hole once more; he reached the steps and pulled off his shoes and tiptoed up and peered through the keyhole. His head accidentally touched .the door and it swung silently in a fraction of an inch; he saw the girl bent over the cabinet, her back to him. Beyond her was the safe. He crept back down the steps, thinking exultingly; I found it!

Now he had to get the combination. Even if the window in the areaway was locked. and bolted, he could gain entrance when the office closed. He scoured through the hole he had dug and stood again in the basement where he had left the radio and the clever. Again he crawled out of the window and lifted himself. up the rain pipe and peered. The steel dial showed lonely and bright, reflecting the yellow glow of an unseen light. Resigned to a long wait, he sat and leaned against a wall. From far off came the faint sounds of life aboveground; once he looked with a baffled expression at the dark sky. Frequently he rose and climbed the pipe to see the white hand spin the dial, but nothing happened. He bit his lip with impatience. It was not the money that was luring him, but the mere fact that he could get it with impunity. Was the hand now twirling the dial? He rose and looked, but the white hand was not in sight.

Perhaps it would be better to watch continuously? Yes; he clung to the pipe and watched the dial until his eyes thickened with tears. Exhausted, he stood again in the areaway. He heard a door being shut and he clawed up the pipe and looked. He jerked tense as a vague figure passed in front of him. He stared unblinkingly, hugging the pipe with one band and holding the screwdriver with the other, ready to etch the combination upon the wall. His ears caught: *Dong . . . Dong . . . Dong . . . Dong . . . Dong . . . Dong . . .* Seven o'clock, he whispered Maybe they were closing now? What kind of a store would be open as late as this? he wondered. Did anyone live in the rear? Was there a night watchman? Perhaps the safe was *already* locked for the night! Goddamn! While he had been eating in that shop, they had locked up everything . . . Then, just as he was about to give up, the white hand touched the dial and turned it once to the right and stopped at six. With quivering fingers, he etched 1—R—6 upon the brick wall with the tip of the screwdriver. The hand twirled the dial twice to the left and stopped at two, and he engraved 2—L—R upon the wall. The dial was spun four times to the right and stopped at six again; he wrote 4—R—6. The dial rotated three times to the left and was centered straight up and down; he wrote 3—L—0 . The door swung open and again he saw the piles of green money and the rows of wrapped coins. I got it, he said grimly.

Then he was stone still, astonished. There were two hands now. A right hand lifted a wad of green bills and deftly slipped it up the sleeve of a left arm. The hands trembled; again the right hand slipped a packet of bills up the left sleeve. He's stealing, he said to himself. He grew indignant, as if the money belonged to him. Though *he* had planned to steal the money, he despised and pitied the man. He felt that his stealing the money and the man's stealing were two entirely different things. He wanted to steal the money merely for the sensation involved in getting it, and he had no intention whatever of spending a penny of it; but he knew that the man who was now stealing it was going to spend it, perhaps for pleasure. The huge steel door closed with a soft click.

Though angry, he was somewhat satisfied. The office would close soon. I'll clean the place out, he mused. He imagined the entire office staff cringing with fear; the police would question everyone for a crime they had not committed, just as they had questioned him. And they would have no idea of how the money had been stolen until they discovered the holes, he had tunneled in the walls of the basements. He lowered himself and laughed mischievously, with the abandoned glee of an adolescent.

He flattened himself against the wall as the window above him closed with rasping sound. He looked; somebody was bolting the window securely with a metal screen. That won't help you, he snickered to himself. He clung to the rain pipe until the yellow light in the office went out. He went back into the basement, picked up the sack containing the radio and cleaver, and crawled through the two holes he had dug and groped his way into the basement of the building that held the safe. He moved in slow motion, breathing softly. Be careful now, he told himself. There might be a night watchman . . . In his memory was the combination written in bold white characters as upon a blackboard. Eel-like he squeezed through the last hole and crept up the steps and put his hand on the knob and pushed the door in about three inches. Then his courage ebbed; his imagination wove dangers for him.

Perhaps the night watchman was waiting in there, ready to shoot. He dangled his cap on a forefinger and poked it past the jamb of the door. If anyone fired, they would hit his cap; but nothing happened. He widened the door, holding the crowbar high above his head, ready to beat off an assailant. He stood like that for five minutes; the rumble of a streetcar brought him to himself. He entered the room. Moonlight floated in from a wide window. He confronted the safe, then checked himself. Better take a look around first . . . He stepped about and found a closed door. Was the night watchman in there? He opened it and saw a washbowl, a faucet, and a commode. To the left was still another door that opened into a huge dark room that seemed empty; on the far side of that room he made out the shadow of still another door. Nobody's here, he told himself.

He turned back to the safe and fingered the dial; it spun with ease. He laughed and twirled it just for fun. Get to work, he told himself. He turned the dial to the figures he saw on the blackboard of his memory; it was so easy that he felt that the safe had not been locked at all. The heavy door eased loose and he caught hold of the handle and pulled hard, but the door swung open with a slow momentum of its own. Breathless, he gaped at wads of green bills, rows of wrapped coins, curious glass jars full of white pellets, and many oblong green metal boxes. He glanced guiltily over his shoulder; it seemed impossible that someone should not call to him to stop.

They'll be surprised in the morning, he thought. He opened the top of the sack and lifted a wad of compactly tied bills; the money was crisp and new. He admired the smooth, clean-cut edges. The fellows in Washington sure know how to make this stuff, he mused. He rubbed the money with his fingers, as though expecting it to reveal hidden qualities. He lifted the wad to his nose and smelled the fresh odor of ink. Just like any other paper, he mumbled. He dropped the wad into the sack and picked up another. Holding the bag, he thought and laughed.

There was in him no sense of possessiveness; he was intrigued with the form and color of the money, with the manifold reactions which he knew that men aboveground held toward it. The sack was one-third full when it occurred to him to examine the denominations of the bills; without realizing it, he had put many wads of one-dollar bills into the sack. Aw, nuts, he said in disgust. Take the big ones . . . He dumped the one-dollar bills onto the floor and swept all the hundred-dollar bills he could find into the sack, then he raked in rolls of coins with crooked fingers.

He walked to a desk upon which sat a typewriter, the same machine which the blond girl had used. He was fascinated by it; never in his life had he used one of them. It was a queer instrument of business, something beyond the rim of his life. Whenever he had been in an office where a girl was typing, he had almost always spoken in whispers. Remembering vaguely what he had seen others do, he inserted a sheet of paper into the machine; it went in lopsided and he did not know how to straighten it. Spelling in a soft diffident voice, he pecked out his name on the keys: *freddaniels*. He looked at it and laughed. He would learn to type correctly one of these days.

Yes, he would take the typewriter too. He lifted the machine and placed it atop the bulk of money in the sack, He did not feel that he was stealing, for the cleaver, the radio, the money, and the typewriter were all on the same level of value, all meant the same thing to him. They were the serious toys of the men who lived in the dead world of sunshine and rain he had left, the world that had condemned him, branded him guilty.

But what kind of a place is this? He wondered. What was in that dark room to his rear? He felt for his matches and found that he had only one left. He leaned the sack against the safe and groped forward into the room, encountering smooth, metallic objects that felt like machines. Baffled, he touched a wall and tried vainly to locate an electric switch. Well, he *had* to strike his last match. He knelt and struck it, cupping the flame near the floor with his palms. The place seemed to be a factory, with benches and tables. There were bulbs with green shades spaced about the tables; he turned on a light and twisted it low so that the glare was limited. There were stools at the benches and he concluded that men worked here at some trade. He wandered and found a few half-used folders of matches. If only he could find more cigarettes! But there were none.

But what kind of a place was this? On a bench he saw a pad of paper captioned: PEER'S—MANUFACTURING JEWELERS. His lips formed an "O," then he snapped off the light and ran back to the safe and lifted one of the glass jars and stared at the tiny white pellets. Gingerly he picked up one and found that it was wrapped in tissue paper. He peeled the paper and saw a glittering stone that looked like glass, glinting white and blue sparks. Diamonds, he breathed.

Roughly he tore the paper from the pellets and soon his palm quivered with precious fire. Trembling, he took all four glass jars from the safe and put them into the sack. He grabbed one of the metal boxes, shook it, and heard a tinny rattle. He pried off the lid with the screwdriver. Rings! Hundreds of them. . . . Were they worth anything? He scooped up a handful and jets of fire shot fitfully from the stones. These are diamonds too, he said. He pried open another box. Watches! A chorus of soft, metallic ticking filled his ears. For a moment he could not move, then he dumped all the boxes into the sack.

He shut the safe door, then stood looking around, anxious not to overlook anything. Oh! He had seen a door in the room where the machines were. What was in there? More valuables? He reentered the room, crossed the floor, and stood undecided before the door. He finally caught hold of the knob and pushed the door in; the room beyond was dark. He advanced cautiously inside and ran his fingers along the wall for the usual switch, then he was stark still. *Something had moved in the room!* What was it? Ought he to creep out, taking the rings and diamonds and money? Why risk what he already had? He waited and the ensuing silence gave him confidence to explore further. Dare he strike a match? Would not a match flame make him a good target? He tensed again as he heard a faint sigh; he was now convinced that there was something alive near him, something that lived and breathed. On tiptoe he felt slowly along the wall, hoping that he would not collide with anything. Luck was with him; he found the light switch.

No; don't turn the light on . . . Then suddenly he realized that he did not know in what direction the door was. Goddamn! He had to turn the light on or strike a match. He fingered the switch for a long time, then thought of an idea. He knelt upon the floor, reached his arm up to the switch and flicked the button, hoping that if anyone shot, the bullet would go above his head. The moment the light came on he narrowed his eyes to see quickly. He sucked in his breath and his body gave a violent twitch and was still. In front of him, so close that it made him want to bound up and scream, was a human face.

He was afraid to move lest he touch the man. If the man had opened his eyes at that moment, there was no telling what he might have done. The man—long and rawboned—was stretched out on his back upon a little cot, sleeping in his clothes, his head cushioned by a dirty pillow; his face, clouded by a dark stubble of beard, looked straight up to the ceiling. The man sighed, and he grew tense to defend himself; the man mumbled and turned his face away from the light. I've got to turn off that light, he thought. Just as he was about to rise, he saw a gun and cartridge belt on the floor at the man's aide. Yes, he would take the gun and cartridge belt, not to use them, but just to keep them, as one takes a memento from a country fair. He picked them up and was about to click off the light when his eyes fell upon a photograph perched upon a chair near the man's head; it was the picture of a woman, smiling, shown against a background of open fields; at the woman's side were two young children, a boy and a girl. He smiled indulgently; he could send a bullet into that man's brain and time would be over for him . . .

He clicked off the light and crept silently back into the room where the safe stood; he fastened the cartridge belt about him and adjusted the holster at his right hip. He strutted about the room on tiptoe, lolling his head nonchalantly, then paused abruptly, pulled the gun, and pointed it with grim face toward an imaginary foe. "Boom!" he whispered fiercely. Then he bent forward with silent laughter. That's just like they do it in the movies, he said.

He contemplated his loot for a long time, then got a towel from the washroom and tied the sack securely. When he looked up he was momentarily frightened by his shadow looming on the wall before him. He lifted the sack, dragged it down the basement steps, lugged it across the basement, gasping for breath. After he had struggled through the hole, he clumsily replaced the bricks, then tussled with the sack until he got it to the cave. He stood in the dark, wet with sweat, brooding about the diamonds, the rings, the watches, the money; he remembered the singing in the church, the people yelling in the movie, the dead baby, the nude man stretched out upon the white table . . . He saw these items hovering before his eyes and felt that some dim meaning linked them together, that some magical relationship made them kin. He stared with vacant eyes, convinced that all of these images, with their tongueless reality, were striving to tell him something . . .

Later, seeing with his fingers, he untied the sack and set each item neatly upon the dirt floor. Exploring, he took the bulb, the socket, and the wire out of the tool chest; he was elated to find a double socket at one end of the wire. He crammed the stuff into his pockets and hoisted himself upon the rusty pipes and squinted into the church; it was dim and empty. Somewhere in this wail were live electric wires; but where? He lowered himself, groped and tapped the wall with the butt of the screwdriver, listening vainly for hollow sounds. I'll just take a chance and dig, he said.

For an hour he tried to dislodge a brick, and when he struck a match, he found that he had dug a depth of only an inch! No use in digging here, he sighed. By the flickering light of a match, he looked upward, then lowered his eyes, only to glance up again, startled. Directly above his head, beyond the pipes, was a wealth of electric wiring. I'll be damned, he snickered.

He got an old dull knife from the chest and, seeing again with his fingers, separated the two strands of wire and cut away the insulation. Twice he received a slight shock. He scraped the wiring clean and managed to join the two twin ends, then screwed in the bulb. The sudden illumination blinded him and he shut his lids to kill the pain in his eyeballs. I've got that much done, he thought jubilantly.

He placed the bulb on the dirt floor and the light cast a blatant glare on the bleak clay walls. Next he plugged one end of the wire that dangled from the radio into the light socket and bent down and switched on the button; almost at once there was the harsh sound of static, but no words or music. Why won't it work? he wondered. Had he damaged the mechanism in any way? Maybe it needed grounding? Yes . . . He rummaged in the tool chest and found another length of wire, fastened it to the ground of the radio, and then tied the opposite end to a pipe. Rising and growing distinct, a slow strain of music entranced him with its measured sound. He sat upon the chest, deliriously happy.

Later he searched again in the chest and found a half-gallon can of glue; he opened it and smelled a sharp odor. Then he recalled that he had not even looked at the money. He took a wad of green bills and weighed it in his palm, then broke the seal and held one of the bills up to the light and studied it closely. *The United States of America will pay to the bearer on demand one hundred dollars,* he read in slow speech; then: *This note is legal tender for all debts, public and private* . . . He broke into a musing laugh, feeling that he was reading of the doings of people who lived on some far-off planet. He turned the bill over and saw on the other side of it a delicately beautiful building gleaming with paint and set amidst green grass. He had no desire whatever to count the money; it was what it stood for—the various currents of life swirling aboveground—that captivated him. Next he opened the rolls of coins and let them slide from their paper wrappings to the ground; the bright, new gleaming pennies and nickels and dimes piled high at his feet, a glowing mound of shimmering copper and silver. He sifted them through his fingers, listening to their tinkle as they struck the conical heap.

Oh, yes! He had forgotten. He would now write his name on the typewriter. He inserted a piece of paper and poised his fingers to write. But what was his name? He stared, trying to remember. He stood and glared about the dirt cave, his name on the tip of his lips. But it would not come to him. Why was he here? Yes, he had been running away from the police. But why? His mind was blank. He bit his lips and sat again, feeling a vague terror. But why worry? He laughed, then pecked slowly: *itwasalonghotday.* He was determined to type the sentence without making any mistakes. How did one make capital letters? He experimented and luckily discovered how to lock the machine for capital letters and then shift it back to lower case. Next he discovered how to make spaces, then he wrote neatly and correctly: *It was a long hot day.* Just why he selected that sentence he did not know; it was merely the ritual of performing the thing that appealed to him. He took the sheet out of the machine and looked around with stiff neck and hard eyes and spoke to an imaginary person:

"Yes, I'll have the contracts ready tomorrow."

He laughed. That's just the way they talk, he said. He grew weary of the game and pushed the machine aside. His eyes fell upon the can of glue, and a mischievous idea bloomed in him, filling him with nervous eagerness. He leaped up and opened the can of glue, then broke the seals on all the wads of money. I'm going to have some wallpaper, he said with a luxurious, physical laugh that made him bend at the knees. He took the towel with which he had tied the sack and balled it into a swab and dipped it into the can of glue and dabbed glue onto the wall; then he pasted one green bill by the side of another. He stepped back and cocked his head. Jesus! That's funny . . . He slapped his thighs and guffawed. He had triumphed over the world aboveground! He was free! If only people could see this! He wanted to run from this cave and yell his discovery to the world.

He swabbed all the dirt walls of the cave and pasted them with green bills; when he had finished the walls blazed with a yellow-green fire. Yes, this room would be his hideout; between him and the world that had branded him guilty would stand this mocking symbol. He had not stolen the money; he had simply picked it up, just as a man would pick up firewood in a forest. And that was how the world aboveground now seemed to him, a wild forest filled with death.

The walls of money finally palled on him and he looked about for new interests to feed his emotions. The cleaver! He drove a nail into the wall and hung the bloody cleaver upon it. Still another idea welled up. He pried open the metal boxes and lined them side by side on the dirt floor. He grinned at the gold and fire. From one box he lifted up a fistful of ticking gold watches and dangled them by their gleaming chains. He stared with an idle smile, then began to wind them up; he did not attempt to set them at any given hour, for there was no time for him now. He took a fistful of nails and drove them into the papered walls and hung the watches upon them, letting them swing down by their glittering chains, trembling and ticking busily against the backdrop of green with the lemon sheen of the electric light shining upon the metal watch casings, converting the golden disks into blobs of liquid yellow. Hardly had he hung up the last watch than the idea extended itself; he took more nails from the chest and drove them into the green paper and took the boxes of rings and went from nail to nail and hung up the golden bands. The blue and white sparks from the stones filled the cave with brittle laughter, as though enjoying his hilarious secret. People certainly can do some funny things, he said to himself.

He sat upon the tool chest, alternately laughing and shaking his head soberly. Hours later he became conscious of the gun sagging at his hip and he pulled it from the holster. He had seen men fire guns in movies, but somehow his life had never led him into contact with firearms. A desire to feel the sensation others felt in firing came over him. But someone might hear . . . Well, what if they did? They would not know where the shot had come from. Not in their wildest notions would they think that it had come from under the streets! He tightened his finger on the trigger; there was a deafening report and it seemed that the entire underground had caved in upon his eardrums; and in the same instant there flashed an orange-blue spurt of flame that died quickly but lingered on as a vivid after-image. He smelled the acrid stench of burnt powder filling his lungs and he dropped the gun abruptly.

The intensity of his feelings died and he hung the gun and cartridge belt upon the wall. Next he lifted the jars of diamonds and turned them bottom upward, dumping the white pellets upon the ground. One by one he picked them up and peeled the tissue paper from them and piled them in a neat heap. He wiped his sweaty hands on his trousers, lit a cigarette, and commenced playing another game. He imagined that he was a rich man who lived aboveground in the obscene sunshine and he was strolling through a park of a summer morning, smiling, nodding to his neighbors, sucking an after-breakfast cigar. Many times he crossed the floor of the cave, avoiding the diamonds with his feet, yet subtly gauging his footsteps so that his shoes, wet with sewer slime, would strike the diamonds at some undetermined moment. After twenty minutes of sauntering, his right foot smashed into the heap and diamonds lay scattered in all directions, glinting with a million tiny chuckles of icy laughter. Oh, shucks, he mumbled in mock regret, intrigued by the damage he had wrought. He continued walking, ignoring the brittle fire. He felt that he had a glorious victory locked in his heart.

He stooped and flung the diamonds more evenly over the floor and they showered rich sparks, collaborating with him. He went over the floor and trampled the stones just deep enough for them to be faintly visible, as though they were set delicately in the prongs of a thousand rings. A ghostly light bathed the cave. He sat on the chest and frowned. Maybe anything's right, he mumbled. Yes, if the world as men had made it was right, then anything else was right, any act a man took to satisfy himself, murder, theft, torture.

He straightened with a start. What was happening to him? He was drawn to these crazy thoughts, yet they made him feel vaguely guilty. He would stretch out upon the ground, then get up; he would want to crawl again through the holes he had dug, but would restrain himself; he would think of going again up into the streets, but fear would hold him still. He stood in the middle of the cave, surrounded by green walls and a laughing floor, trembling. He was going to do something, but what? Yes, he was afraid of himself, afraid of doing some nameless thing.

To control himself, he turned on the radio. A melancholy piece of music rose. Brooding over the diamonds on the floor was like looking up into a sky full of restless stars; then the illusion turned into its opposite: he was high up in the air looking down at the twinkling lights of a sprawling city. The music ended and a man recited news events. In the same attitude in which he had contemplated the city, so now, as he heard the cultivated tone, he looked down upon land and sea as men fought, as cities were razed, as planes scattered death upon open towns, as long lines of trenches wavered and broke. He heard the names of generals and the names of mountains and the names of countries and the names and numbers of divisions that were in action on different battle fronts. He saw black smoke billowing from the stacks of war-ships as they neared each other over wastes of water and he heard their huge guns thunder as red-hot shells screamed across the surface of night seas. He saw hundreds of planes wheeling and droning in the sky and heard the clatter of machine guns as they fought each other and he saw planes falling in plumes of smoke and blaze of fire. He saw steel tanks rumbling across fields of ripe wheat to meet other tanks and there was a loud clang of steel as numberless tanks collided. He saw troops with fixed bayonets charging in waves against other troops who held fixed bayonets and men groaned as steel ripped into their bodies and they went down to die . . . The voice of the radio faded and he was staring at the diamonds on the floor at his feet.

He shut off the radio, fighting an irrational compulsion to act. He walked aimlessly about the cave, touching the walls with his fingertips. Suddenly he stood still. *What was the matter with him?* Yes, he knew . . . It was these walls; these crazy walls were filling him with a wild urge to climb out into the dark sunshine aboveground. Quickly he doused the light to banish the shouting walls, then sat again upon the tool chest. Yes, he was trapped. His muscles were flexed taut and sweat ran down his face. He knew now that he could not stay here and he could not go out. He lit a cigarette with shaking fingers; the match flame revealed the green-papered walls with militant distinctness; the purple on the gun barrel glinted like a threat; the meat cleaver brooded with its eloquent splotches of blood; the mound of silver and copper smoldered angrily; the diamonds winked at him from the floor; and the gold watches ticked and trembled, crowning time the king of consciousness, defining the limits of living . . . The match blaze died and he bolted from where he stood and collided brutally with the nails upon the walls. The spell was broken. He shuddered, feeling that, in spite of his fear, sooner or later he would go up into that dead sunshine and somehow say something to somebody about all this.

He sat again upon the tool chest. Fatigue weighed upon his forehead and eyes. Minutes passed and he relaxed. He dozed, but his imagination was alert. He saw himself rising, wading again in the sweeping water of the sewer; he came to a manhole and climbed out and was amazed to discover that he had hoisted himself into a room filled with armed policemen who were watching him intently. He jumped awake in the dark; he had not moved. He sighed, closed his eyes, and slept again; this time his imagination designed a scheme of protection for him. His dreaming made him feel that he was standing in a room watching over his own nude body lying stiff and cold upon a white table. At the far end of the room he saw a crowd of people huddled in a corner, afraid of his body. Though lying dead upon the table, he was standing in some mysterious way at his side, warding off the people, guarding his body, and laughing to himself as he observed the situation. They're scared of me, he thought.

He awakened with a start, leaped to his feet, and stood in the center of the black cave. It was a full minute before he moved again. He hovered between sleeping and waking, unprotected, a prey of wild fears. He could neither see nor hear. One part of him was asleep; his blood coursed slowly and his flesh was numb. On the other hand he was roused to a strange, high pitch of tension. He lifted his fingers to his face, as though about to weep. Gradually his hands lowered and he struck a match, looking about, expecting to see a door through which he could walk to safety: but there was no door, only the green walls and the moving floor. The match flame died and it was dark again.

Five minutes later he was still standing when the thought came to him that he had been asleep. Yes . . . But he was not yet fully awake; he was still queerly blind and deaf. How long had he slept? Where was he? Then suddenly he recalled the green-papered walls of the cave and in the same instant he heard loud singing coming from the church beyond the wall. Yes, they woke me up, he muttered. He hoisted himself and lay atop the bed of pipes and brought his face to the narrow slit. Men and women stood here and there between pews. A song ended and a young black girl tossed back her head and closed her eyes and broke plaintively into another hymn:

*Glad, glad, glad, oh, so glad
I got Jesus in my soul . . .*

Those few words were all she sang, but what her words did not say, her emotions said as she repeated the lines, varying the mood and tempo, making her tone express meanings which her conscious mind did not know. Another woman melted her voice with the girl's, and then an old man's voice merged with that of the two women. Soon the entire congregation was singing:

*Glad, glad, glad, oh, so glad
I got Jesus in my soul . . .*

They're wrong, he whispered in the lyric darkness. He felt that their search for a happiness they could never find made them feel that they had committed some dreadful offense which they could not remember or understand. He was now in possession of the feeling that had gripped him when he had first come into the underground. It came to him in a series of questions: Why was this sense of guilt so seemingly innate, so easy to come by, to think, to feel, so verily physical? It seemed that when one felt this guilt one was retracing in one's feelings a faint pattern designed long before; it seemed that one was always trying to remember a gigantic shock that had left a haunting impression upon one's body which one could not forget or shake off, but which had been forgotten by the conscious mind, creating in one's life a state of eternal anxiety.

He had to tear himself away from this; he got down from the pipes. His nerves were so taut that he seemed to feel his brain pushing through his skull. He felt that he had to do something, but he could not figure out what it was. Yet he knew that if he stood here until he made up his mind, he would never move. He crawled through the hole he had made in the brick wall and the exertion afforded him respite from tension. When he entered the basement of the radio store, he stopped in fear, hearing loud voices.

"Come on, boy! Tell us what you did with the radio!"

"Mister, I didn't steal the radio! I swear!"

He heard a dull thumping sound and he imagined a boy being struck violently.

"Please, mister!"

"Did you take it to a pawn shop?"

"No, sir! I didn't steal the radio! I got a radio at home," the boy's voice pleaded hysterically. "Go to my home and look!"

There came to his ears the sound of another blow. It was so funny that he had to clap his hand over his mouth to keep from laughing out loud. They're beating some poor boy, he whispered to himself, shaking his head. He felt a sort of distant pity for the boy and wondered if he ought to bring back the radio and leave it in the basement. No. Perhaps it was a good thing that they were beating the boy; perhaps the beating would bring to the boy's attention, for the first time in his life, the secret of his existence, the guilt that he could never get rid of.

Smiling, he scampered over a coal pile and stood again in the basement of the building where he had stolen the money and jewelry. He lifted himself into the areaway, climbed the rain pipe, and squinted through a two-inch opening of window. The guilty familiarity of what he saw made his muscles tighten. Framed before him in a bright tableau of daylight was the night watchman sitting upon the edge of a chair, stripped to the waist, his head sagging forward, his eyes red and puffy. The watchman's face and shoulders were stippled with red and black welts. Back of the watchman stood the safe, the steel door wide open showing the empty vault. Yes, they think he did it, he mused.

Footsteps sounded in the room and a man in a blue suit passed in front of him, then another, then still another. Policemen, he breathed. Yes, they were trying to make the watchman confess, just as they had once made him confess to a crime he had not done. He stared into the room, trying to recall something. Oh . . . Those were the same policemen who had beaten him, had made him sign that paper when he had been too tired and sick to care. Now, they were doing the same thing to the watchman. His heart pounded as he saw one of the policemen shake a finger into the watchman's face.

"Why don't you admit it's an inside job, Thompson?" the policeman said.

"I've told you all I know," the watchman mumbled through swollen lips.

"But nobody was here but you!" the policeman shouted.

"I was sleeping," the watchman said. "It was wrong, but I was sleeping all that night!"

"Stop telling us that lie!"

"It's the truth!"

"When did you get the combination?"

"I don't know how to open the safe," the watchman said.

He clung to the rain pipe, tense; he wanted to laugh, but he controlled himself. He felt a great sense of power; yes, he could go back to the cave, rip the money off the walls, pick up the diamonds and rings, and bring them here and write a note, telling them where to look for their foolish toys. No . . . What good would that do? It was not worth the effort. The watchman was guilty; although he was not guilty of the crime of which he had been accused, he was guilty, had always been guilty. The only thing that worried him was that the man who had been really stealing was not being accused. But he consoled himself: they'll catch him sometime during his life.

He saw one of the policemen slap the watchman across the mouth.

"Come clean, you bastard!"

"I've told you all I know," the watchman mumbled like a child.

One of the police went to the rear of the watchman's chair and jerked it from under him; the watchman pitched forward upon his face.

"Get up!" a policeman said.

Trembling, the watchman pulled himself up and sat limply again in the chair.

"Now, are you going to talk?"

"I've told you all I know," the watchman gasped.

"Where did you hide the stuff?"

"I didn't take it!"

"Thompson, your brains are in your feet," one of the policemen said. "We're going to string you up and get them back into your skull."

He watched the policemen clamp handcuffs on the watchman's wrists and ankles; then they lifted the watchman and swung him upside-down and hoisted his feet to the edge of a door. The watchman hung, head down, his eyes bulging. They're crazy, he whispered to himself as he clung to the ridges of the pipe.

"You going to talk?" a policeman shouted into the watchman's ear.

He heard the watchman groan

"We'll let you hang there till you talk, see?"

He saw the watchman close his eyes.

"Let's take 'im down. He passed out," a policeman said.

He grinned as he watched them take the body down and dump it carelessly upon the floor. The policeman took off the handcuffs.

"Let 'im come to. Let's get a smoke," a policeman said.

The three policemen left the scope of his vision. A door slammed. He had an impulse to yell to the watchman that he could escape through the hole in the basement and live with him in the cave. But he wouldn't understand, he told himself. After a moment he saw the watchman rise and stand swaying from weakness. He stumbled across the room to a desk, opened a drawer, and took out a gun. He's going to kill himself, he thought, intent, eager, detached, yearning to see the end of the man's actions. As the watchman stared vaguely about he lifted the gun to his temple; he stood like that for some minutes, biting his lips until a line of blood etched its way down a corner of his chin. No, he oughtn't do that, he said to himself in a mood of pity.

"Don't!" he half whispered and half-yelled.

The watchman looked wildly about; he had heard him. But it did not help; there was a loud report and the watchman's head jerked violently and he fell like a log and lay prone, the gun clattering over the floor.

The three policemen came running into the room with drawn guns. One of the policemen knelt and rolled the watchman's body over and stared at a ragged, scarlet hole in the temple.

"Our hunch was right," the kneeling policeman said. "He was guilty, all right."

"Well, this ends the case," another policeman said

"He knew he was licked," the third one said with grim satisfaction.

He eased down the rain pipe, crawled back through the holes he had made, and went back into his cave. A fever burned in his bones. He had to act, yet he was afraid. His eyes stared in the darkness as though propped open by invisible hands, as though they had become lidless. His muscles were rigid and he stood for what seemed to him a thousand years.

When he moved again his actions were informed with precision, his muscular system reinforced from a reservoir of energy. He crawled through the hole of earth, dropped into the gray sewer current, and sloshed ahead. When his right foot went forward at a street intersection, he fell backward and shot down into water. In a spasm of terror his right hand grabbed the concrete ledge of a down-curve and he felt the streaking water tugging violently at his body. The current reached his neck and for a moment he was still. He knew that if he moved clumsily he would he sucked under. He held onto the ledge with both hands and slowly pulled himself up. He sighed, standing once more in the sweeping water, thankful that he had missed death.

He waded on through sludge, moving with care, until he came to a web of light sifting down from a manhole cover. He saw steel hooks running up the side of the sewer wall; he caught hold and lifted himself and put his shoulder to the cover and moved it an inch. A crash of sound came to him as he looked into a hot glare of sunshine through which blurred shapes moved. Fear scalded him and he dropped back into the pallid current and stood paralyzed in the shadows. A heavy car rumbled past overhead, jarring the pavement, warning him to stay in his world of dark light, knocking the cover back into place with an imperious clang.

He did not know how much fear he felt, for fear claimed him completely; yet it was not a fear of the police or of people, but a cold dread at the thought of the actions he knew he would perform if he went out into that cruel sunshine. His mind said no; his body said yes; and his mind could not understand his feelings. A low whine broke from him and he was in the act of uncoiling. He climbed upward and heard the faint honking of auto horns. Like a frantic cat clutching a rag, he clung to the steel prongs and heaved his shoulder against the cover and pushed it off halfway. For a split second his eyes were drowned in the terror of yellow light and he was in a deeper darkness than he had ever known in the underground.

Partly out of the hole, he blinked, regaining enough sight to make out meaningful forms. An odd thing was happening: No one was rushing forward to challenge him. He had imagined the moment of his emergence as a desperate tussle with men who wanted to cart him off to be killed; instead, life froze about him as the traffic stopped. He pushed the cover aside, stood, swaying in a world so fragile that he expected it to collapse and drop him into some deep void. But nobody seemed to pay him heed. The cars were now swerving to shun him and the gaping hole.

"Why in hell don't you put up a red light, dummy?" a raucous voice yelled.

He understood; they thought that he was a sewer workman. He walked toward the sidewalk, weaving unsteadily through the moving traffic.

"Look where you're going, nigger!"

"That's right! Stay there and get killed!"

"You blind, you bastard?"

"Go home and sleep your drunk off!"

A policeman stood at the curb, looking in the opposite direction. When he passed the policeman, he feared that he would he grabbed, but nothing happened. Where was he? Was this real? He wanted to look about to get his bearings, but felt that something awful would happen to him if he did. He wandered into a spacious doorway of a store that sold men's clothing and saw his reflection in a long mirror: his cheekbones protruded from a hairy black face; his greasy cap was perched askew upon his head and his eyes were red and glassy. His shirt and trousers were caked with mud and hung loosely. His hands were gummed with a black stickiness. He threw back his head and laughed so loudly that passersby stopped and stared.

He ambled on down the sidewalk, not having the merest notion of where he was going. Yet, sleeping within him, was the drive to go somewhere and say something to somebody. Half an hour later his ears caught the sound of spirited singing.

> *The Lamb, the Lamb, the Lamb*
>   *I hear thy voice a-calling*
> *The Lamb, the Lamb, the Lamb*
>   *I feel thy grace a-falling*

A church! he exclaimed. He broke into a run and came to brick steps leading downward to a subbasement, This is it! The church into which he had peered. Yes, he was going in and tell them. What? He did not know; but, once face to face with them, he would think of what to say. Must be Sunday, he mused. He ran down the steps and jerked the door open; the church was crowded and a deluge of song swept over him.

> *The Lamb, the Lamb, the Lamb*
>   *Tell me again your story*
> *The Lamb, the Lamb, the Lomb*
>   *Flood my, soul with your glory*

He stared at the singing faces with a trembling smile.

"Say!" he shouted.

Many turned to look at him, but the song rolled on. His arm was jerked violently.

"I'm sorry, Brother, but you can't do that in here," a man said.

"But, mister!"

"You can't act rowdy in God's house," the man said.

"He's filthy," another man said.

"But I want to tell 'em," he said loudly.

"He stinks," someone muttered.

The song had stopped, but at once another one began.

> *Oh, wondrous sight upon the cross*
>   *Vision sweet and divine*
> *Oh, wondrous sight upon the cross*
>   *Full of such love sublime*

He attempted to twist away, but other hands grabbed him and rushed him into the doorway.

"Let me alone!" he screamed, struggling.

"Get out!"

"He's drunk," somebody said. "He ought to be ashamed!"

"He acts crazy!"

He felt that he was failing and he grew frantic.

"But, mister, let me tell—"

"Get away from this door, or I'll call the police!"

He stared, his trembling smile fading in a sense of wonderment.

"The police," he repeated vacantly.

"Now, get!"

He was pushed toward the brick steps and the door banged shut. The waves of song came.

> *Oh, wondrous sight, wondrous sight*
>   *Lift my heavy heart above*
> *Oh, wondrous sight, wondrous sight*
>   *Fill my weary soul with love*

He was smiling again now. Yes, the police . . . That was it! Why had he not thought of it before? The idea had been deep down in him, and only now did it assume supreme importance. He looked up and saw a street sign: COURT STREET—HARTSDALE AVENUE. He turned and walked northward, his mind filled with the image of the police station. Yes, that was where they had beaten him, accused him, and had made him sign a confession of his guilt. He would go there and clear up everything, make a statement, What statement? He did not know. He was the statement, and since it was all so clear to him, surely he would be able to make it clear to others.

He came to the corner of Hartsdale Avenue and turned westward. Yeah, there's the station . . . A policeman came down the steps and walked past him without a glance. He mounted the stone steps and went through the door, paused; he was in a hallway where several policemen were standing, talking, smoking. One turned to him.

"What do you want, boy?"

He looked at the policeman and laughed.

"What in hell are you laughing about?" the policeman asked.

He stopped laughing and stared. His whole being was full of what he wanted to say to them, but he could not say it.

"Are you looking for the Desk Sergeant?"

"Yes, sir," he said quickly; then: "Oh, no, sir."

"Well, make up your mind, now."

Four policemen grouped themselves around him.

"I'm looking for the men," he said.

"What men?"

Peculiarly, at that moment he could not remember the names of the policemen; he recalled their beating him, the confession he had signed, and how he had run away from them. He saw the cave next to the church, the money on the walls, the guns, the rings, the cleaver, the watches, and the diamonds on the floor.

"They brought me here," he began.

"When?"

His mind flew back over the blur of the time lived in the underground blackness. He had no idea of how much time had elapsed, but the intensity of what had happened to him told him that it could not have transpired in a short space of time, yet his mind told him that time must have been brief.

"It was a long time ago." He spoke like a child relating a dimly remembered dream. "It was a long time," he repeated, following the promptings of his emotions. "They beat me . . . I was scared . . . I ran away."

A policeman raised a finger to his temple and made a derisive circle.

"Nuts," the policeman said.

"Do you know what place this is, boy?"

"Yes, sir. The police station," he answered sturdily, almost proudly.

"Well, who do you want to see?"

"The men," he said again, feeling that surely they knew the men. "You know the men," he said in a hurt tone.

"What's your name?"

He opened his lips to answer and no words came. He had forgotten. But what did it matter if he had? It was not important.

"Where do you live?"

Where did he live? It had been so long ago since he had lived up here in this strange world that he felt it was foolish even to try to remember. Then for a moment the old mood that had dominated him in the underground surged back. He leaned forward and spoke eagerly.

"They said I killed the woman."

"What woman?" a policeman asked.

"And I signed a paper that said I was guilty," he went on, ignoring their questions. "Then I ran off . . ."

"Did you run off from an institution?"

"No, sir," he said, blinking and shaking his head. "I came from under the ground. I pushed off the manhole cover and climbed out . . ."

"All right, now," a policeman said, placing an arm about his shoulder. "We'll send you to the psycho and you'll be taken care of."

"Maybe he's a Fifth Columnist!" a policeman shouted.

There was laughter and, despite his anxiety, he joined in. But the laughter lasted so long that it irked him.

"I got to find those men," he protested mildly.

"Say, boy, what have you been drinking?"

"Water," he said. "I got some water in a basement."

"Were the men you ran away from dressed in white, boy?"

"No, sir," he said brightly. "They were men like you."

An elderly policeman caught hold of his arm.

"Try and think hard. Where did they pick you up?"

He knitted his brows in an effort to remember, but he was blank inside. The policeman stood before him demanding logical answers and he could no longer think with his mind; he thought with his feelings and no words came.

"I was guilty," he said. "Oh, no, sir. I wasn't then, I mean, mister!"

"Aw, talk sense. Now, where did they pick you up?"

He felt challenged and his mind began reconstructing events in reverse; his feelings ranged back over the long hours and he saw the cave, the sewer, the bloody room where it was said that a woman had been killed.

"Oh, yes, sir," he said, smiling. "I was coming from Mrs. Wooten's."

"Who is she?"

"I work for her."

"Where does she live?"

"Next door to Mrs. Peabody, the woman who was killed."

The policemen were very quiet now, looking at him intently.

"What do you know about Mrs. Peabody's death, boy?"

"Nothing, sir. But they said I killed her. But it doesn't make any difference. I'm guilty!"

"What are you talking about, boy?"

His smile faded and he was possessed with memories of the underground; he saw the cave next to the church and his lips moved to speak. But how could he say it? The distance between what he felt and what these men meant was vast. Something told him, as he stood there looking into their faces, that he would never be able to tell them, that they would never believe him even if he told them.

"All the people I saw was guilty," he began slowly.

"Aw, nuts," a policemen muttered.

"Say," another policeman said, "that Peabody woman was killed over on Winewood. That's Number Ten's beat"

"Where's Number Ten?" a policeman asked.

"Upstairs in the swing room," someone answered.

"Take this boy up, Sam," a policeman ordered.

"O.K. Come along, boy."

An elderly policeman caught hold of his arm and led him up a flight of wooden stairs, down a long hall, and to a door.

"Squad Ten!" the policeman called through the door.

"What?" a gruff voice answered.

"Someone to see you!"

"About what?"

The old policeman pushed the door in and then shoved him into the room.

He stared, his lips open, his heart barely beating. Before him were the three policemen who had picked him up and had beaten him to extract the confession. They were seated about a small table, playing cards. The air was blue with smoke and sunshine poured through a high window, lighting up fantastic smoke shapes. He saw one of the policemen look up; the policeman's face was tired and a cigarette dropped limply from one corner of his mouth and both of his fat, puffy eyes were squinting and his hands gripped his cards.

"Lawson!" the man exclaimed.

The moment the man's name sounded he remembered the names of all of them: Lawson, Murphy, and Johnson. How simple it was. He waited, smiling, wondering how they would react when they knew that he had come back.

"Looking for me?" the man who had been called Lawson mumbled, sorting his cards. "For what?"

So far only Murphy, the red-headed one, had recognized him.

"Don't you-all remember me?" he blurted, running to the table.

All three of the policemen were looking at him now. Lawson, who seemed the leader, jumped to his feet.

"Where in hell have you been?"

"Do you know 'im, Lawson?" the old policeman asked.

"Huh?" Lawson frowned. "Oh, yes. I'll handle 'im." The old policeman left the room and Lawson crossed to the door and turned the key in the lock. "Come here, boy," he ordered in a cold tone.

He did not move; he looked from face to face. Yes, he would tell them about his cave.

"He looks batty to me," Johnson said, the one who had not spoken before.

"Why in hell did you come back here?" Lawson said.

"I—I just didn't want to run away no more," he said. "I'm all right, now." He paused; the men's attitude puzzled him.

"You've been hiding, huh?" Lawson asked in a tone that denoted that he had not heard his previous words. "You told us you were sick, and when we left you in the room, you jumped out of the window and ran away."

Panic filled him. Yes, they were indifferent to what he would say! They were waiting for him to speak and they would laugh at him. He had to rescue himself from this bog; he had to force the reality of himself upon them.

"Mister, I took a sackful of money and pasted it on the walls . . ." he began.

"I'll be damned," Lawson said.

"Listen," said Murphy, "let me tell you something for your own good. We don't want you, see? You're free, free as air. Now go home and forget it. It was all a mistake. We caught the guy who did the Peabody job. He wasn't colored at all. He was an Eyetalian."

"Shut up!" Lawson yelled. "Have you no sense!"

"But I want to tell 'im," Murphy said.

"We can't let this crazy fool go," Lawson exploded. "He acts nuts, but this may be a stunt..."

"I was down in the basement," he began in a childlike tone as though repeating a lesson learned by heart; "and I went into a movie..." His voice failed. He was getting ahead of his story. First, he ought to tell them about the singing in the church, but what words could he use? He looked at them appealingly. "I went into a shop and took a sackful of money and diamonds and watches and rings... I didn't steal 'em; I'll give 'em all back. I just took 'em to play with..." He paused, stunned by their disbelieving eyes.

Lawson lit a cigarette and looked at him coldly.

"What did you do with the money?" he asked in a quiet, waiting voice.

"I pasted the hundred-dollar bills on the walls."

"What walls?" Lawson asked.

"The walls of the dirt room," he said, smiling, "the room next to the church. I hung up the rings and the watches and I stamped the diamonds into the dirt..." He saw that they were not understanding what he was saying. He grew frantic to make them believe, his voice tumbled on eagerly. "I saw a dead baby and a dead man..."

"Aw, you're nuts," Lawson snarled, shoving him into a chair.

"But, mister..."

"Johnson, where's the paper he signed?" Lawson asked.

"What paper?"

"The confession, fool!"

Johnson pulled out his billfold and extracted a crumpled piece of paper.

"Yes, sir, mister," he said, stretching forth his hand. "That's the paper I signed..."

Lawson slapped him and he would have toppled had his chair not struck a wall behind him. Lawson scratched a match and held the paper over the flame; the confession burned down to Lawson's fingertips.

He stared, thunderstruck; the sun of the underground was fleeing and the terrible darkness of the day stood before him. They did not believe him, but he *had* to make them believe him!

"But, mister..."

"It's going to be all right, boy," Lawson said with a quiet, soothing laugh. "I've burned your confession, see? You didn't sign anything." Lawson came close to him with the black ashes cupped in his palm. "You don't remember a thing about this, do you?"

"Don't you-all be scared of me," he pleaded, sensing their uneasiness. "I'll sign another paper, if you want me to. I'll show you the cave."

"What's your game, boy?" Lawson asked suddenly.

"What are you trying to find out?" Johnson asked.

"Who sent you here?" Murphy demanded.

"Nobody sent me, mister," he said. "I just want to show you the room..."

"Aw, he's plumb bats," Murphy said. "let's ship 'im to the psycho."

"No," Lawson said. "He's playing a game and I wish to God I knew what it was."

There flashed through his mind a definite way to make them believe him; he rose from the chair with nervous excitement.

"Mister, I saw the night watchman blow his brains out because you accused him of stealing," he told them. "But he didn't steal the money and diamonds. I took 'em."

Tigerishly Lawson grabbed his collar and lifted him bodily.

"Who told you about that?"

"Don't get excited, Lawson," Johnson said. "He read about it in the papers."

Lawson flung him away.

"He couldn't have," Lawson said, pulling papers from his pocket. "I haven't turned in the reports yet."

"Then how *did* he find out?" Murphy asked.

"Let's get out of here," Lawson said with quick resolution. "Listen, boy, we're going to take you to a nice, quiet place, see?"

"Yes, sir," he said. "And I'll show you the underground."

"Goddamn," Lawson muttered, fastening the gun at his hip. He narrowed his eyes at Johnson and Murphy. "Listen," he spoke just above a whisper, "say nothing about this, you hear?"

"O.K.," Johnson said.

"Sure," Murphy said.

Lawson unlocked the door and Johnson and Murphy led him down the stairs. The hallway was crowded with policemen.

"What have you got there, Lawson?"

"What did he do, Lawson?"

"He's psycho, ain't he, Lawson?"

Lawson did not answer; Johnson and Murphy led him to the car parked at the curb, pushed him into the back seat. Lawson got behind the steering wheel and the car rolled forward.

"What's up, Lawson," Murphy asked.

"Listen," Lawson began slowly, "we tell the papers that he spilled about the Peabody job, then he escapes. The Wop is caught and we tell the papers that we steered them wrong to trap the real guy, see? Now this dope shows up and acts nuts. If we let him go, he'll squeal that we framed him, see?"

"I'm all right, mister," he said, feeling Murphy's and Johnson's arms locked rigidly into his. "I'm guilty . . . I'll show you everything in the underground. I laughed and laughed . . ."

"Shut that fool up!" Lawson ordered.

Johnson tapped him across the head with a blackjack and he fell back against the seat cushion, dazed.

"Yes, sir," he mumbled. "I'm all right."

The car sped along Hartsdale Avenue, then swung onto Pine Street and rolled to State Street, then turned south. It slowed to a stop, turned in the middle of a block, and headed north again.

"You're going around in circles, Lawson," Murphy said.

Lawson did not answer; he was hunched over the steering wheel. Finally he pulled the car to a stop at the curb.

"Say, boy, tell us the truth," Lawson asked quietly. "Where did you hide?"

"I didn't hide, mister."

The three policemen were staring at him now; he felt that for the first time they were willing to understand him.

"Then what happened?"

"Mister, when I looked through all of those holes and saw how people were living, I loved 'em . . ."

"Cut out that crazy talk!" Lawson snapped. "Who sent you back here?"

"Nobody, mister."

"Maybe he's talking straight," Johnson ventured.

"All right," Lawson said. "Nobody hid you. Now, tell us *where* you hid."

"I went underground . . ."

"What goddamn underground do you keep talking about?"

"I just went . . ." He paused and looked into the street, then pointed to a manhole cover. "I went down in there and stayed."

"In the *sewer?*"

"Yes, sir."

The policemen burst into a sudden laugh and ended quickly. Lawson swung the car around and drove to Woodside Avenue; he brought the car to a stop in front of a tall apartment building.

"What're we going to do, Lawson," Murphy asked.

"I'm taking him up to my place," Lawson said. "We've got to wait until night. There's nothing we can do now."

They took him out of the car and led him into a vestibule.

"Take the steps," Lawson muttered.

They led him up four flights of stairs and into the living room of a small apartment. Johnson and Murphy let go of his arms and he stood uncertainly in the middle of the room.

"Now, listen, boy," Lawson began, "forget those wild lies you've been telling us. Where did you hide?"

"I just went underground, like I told you."

The room rocked with laughter. Lawson went to a cabinet and got a bottle of whisky; he placed glasses for Johnson and Murphy. The three of them drank.

He felt that he could not explain himself to them. He tried to muster all the sprawling images that floated in him; the images stood out sharply in his mind, but he could not make them have the meaning for others that they had for him. He felt so helpless that he began to cry.

"He's nuts, all right," Johnson said. "All nuts cry like that."

Murphy crossed the room and slapped him.

"Stop that raving!"

A sense of excitement flooded him; he ran to Murphy and grabbed his arm.

"Let me show you the cave," he said. "Come on, and you'll see!"

Before he knew it a sharp blow had clipped him on the chin; darkness covered his eyes. He dimly felt himself being lifted and laid out on the sofa. He heard low voices and struggled to rise, but hard hands held him down. His brain was clearing now. He pulled to a sitting posture and stared with glazed eyes. It had grown dark. How long had he been out?

"Say, boy," Lawson said soothingly, "will you show us the underground?"

His eyes shone and his heart swelled with gratitude. Lawson believed him! He rose, glad; he grabbed Lawson's arm, making the policeman spill whisky from the glass to his shirt.

"Take it easy, goddammit," Lawson said.

"Yes, sir."

"O.K. We'll take you down. But you'd better be telling us the truth, you hear?"

He clapped his hands in wild joy.

"I'll show you everything!"

He had triumphed at last! He would now do what he had felt was compelling him all along. At last he would be free of his burden.

"Take 'im down," Lawson ordered.

They led him down to the vestibule; when he reached the sidewalk he saw that it was night and a fine rain was falling.

"It's just like when I went down," he told them.

"What?" Lawson asked.

"The rain," he said, sweeping his arm in a wide arc. "It was raining when I went down. The rain made the water rise and lift the cover off."

"Cut it out," Lawson snapped.

They did not believe him now, but they would. A mood of high selflessness throbbed in him. He could barely contain his rising spirits. They would see what he had seen; they would feel what he had felt. He would lead them through all the holes he had dug and . . . He wanted to make a hymn, prance about in physical ecstasy, throw his arms about the policemen in fellowship.

"Get into the car," Lawson ordered.

He climbed in and Johnson and Murphy sat at either side of him; Lawson slid behind the steering wheel and started the motor.

"Now, tell us where to go," Lawson said.

"It's right around the corner from where the lady was killed," he said.

The car rolled slowly and he closed his eyes, remembering the song he had heard in the church, the song that had wrought him to such a high pitch of terror and pity. He sang softly, lolling his head:

> *Glad, glad, glad, oh, so glad*
> *I got Jesus in my soul . . .*

"Mister," he said, stopping his song, "you ought to see how funny the rings look on the wall." He giggled. "I fired a pistol, too. Just once, to see how it felt."

"What do you suppose he's suffering from?" Johnson asked.

"Delusions of grandeur, maybe," Murphy said.

"Maybe it's because he lives in a white man's world," Lawson said.

"Say, boy, what did you eat down there?" Murphy asked, prodding Johnson anticipatorily with his elbow

"Pears, oranges, bananas, and pork chops," he said.

The car filled with laughter.

"You didn't eat any watermelon?" Lawson asked, smiling.

"No, sir," he answered calmly. "I didn't see any."

The three policemen roared harder and louder.

"Boy, you're sure some case," Murphy said, shaking his head in wonder.

The car pulled to a curb.

"All right, boy," Lawson said. "Tell us where to go."

He peered through the rain and saw where he had gone down. The streets, save for a few dim lamps glowing softly through the rain, were dark and empty.

"Right there, mister," he said, pointing.

"Come on; let's take a look," Lawson said.

"Well, suppose he did hide down there," Johnson said, "what is that supposed to prove?"

"I don't believe he hid down there," Murphy said.

"It won't hurt to look," Lawson said. "Leave things to me."

Lawson got out of the car and looked up and down the street.

He was eager to show them the cave now. If he could show them what he had seen, then they would feel what he had felt and they in turn would show it to others and those others would feel as they had felt, and soon everybody would be governed by the same impulse of pity.

"Take 'im out," Lawson ordered.

Johnson and Murphy opened the door and pushed him out; he stood trembling in the rain, smiling. Again Lawson looked up and down the street; no one was in sight. The rain came down hard, slanting like black wires across the windswept air.

"All right," Lawson said. "Show us."

He walked to the center of the street, stopped and inserted a finger in one of the tiny holes of the cover and tugged, but he was too weak to budge it.

"Did you really go down in there, boy?" Lawson asked; there was a doubt in his voice.

"Yes, sir. Just a minute. I'll show you."

"Help 'im get that damn thing off," Lawson said.

Johnson stepped forward and lifted the cover; it clanged against the wet pavement. The hole gaped round and black.

"I went down in there," he announced with pride.

Lawson gazed at him for a long time without speaking, then he reached his right hand to his holster and drew his gun.

"Mister, I got a gun just like that down there," he said, laughing and looking into Lawson's face. "I fired it once then hung it on the wall. I'll show you."

"Show us how you went down," Lawson said quietly.

"I'll go down first, mister, and then you-all can come after me, hear?" He spoke like a little boy playing a game.

"Sure, sure," Lawson said soothingly. "Go ahead. We'll come."

He looked brightly at the policemen; he was bursting with happiness. He bent down and placed his hands on the rim of the hole and sat on the edge, his feet dangling into watery darkness. He heard the familiar drone of the gray current. He lowered his body and hung for a moment by his fingers, then he went downward on the steel prongs, hand over hand, until he reached the last rung. He dropped and his feet hit the water and he felt the stiff current trying to suck him away. He balanced himself quickly and looked back upward at the policemen.

"Come on, you-all!" he yelled, casting his voice above the rustling at his feet.

The vague forms that towered above him in the rain did not move. He laughed, feeling that they doubted him. But, once they saw the things he had done, they would never doubt again.

"Come On! The cave isn't far!" he yelled. "But be careful when your feet hit the water, because the current's pretty rough down here!"

Lawson still held the gun. Murphy and Johnson looked at Lawson quizzically.

"What are we going to do, Lawson?" Murphy asked.

"We are not going to follow that crazy nigger down into that sewer, are we?" Johnson asked.

"Come on, you-all" he begged in a shout.

He saw Lawson raise the gun and point it directly at him. Lawson's face twitched, as though he were hesitating.

Then there was a thunderous report and a streak of fire ripped through his chest. He was hurled into the water, flat on his back. He looked in amazement at the blurred white faces looming above him. They shot me, he said to himself. The water flowed past him, blossoming in foam about his arms, his legs, and his head. His jaw sagged and his mouth gaped soundless. A vast pain gripped his head and gradually squeezed out consciousness. As from a great distance he heard hollow voices.

"What did you shoot him for, Lawson?"

"I had to."

"Why?"

"You've got to shoot his kind. They'd wreck things."

As though in a deep dream, he heard a metallic clank; they had replaced the manhole cover, shutting out forever the sound of wind and rain. From overhead came the muffled roar of a powerful motor and the swish of a speeding car. He felt the strong tide pushing him slowly into the middle of the sewer, turning him about. For a split second there hovered before his eyes the glittering cave, the shouting walls, and the laughing floor . . . Then his mouth was full of thick, bitter water. The current spun him around. He sighed and closed his eyes, a whirling object rushing alone in the darkness, veering, tossing, lost in the heart of the earth.

Ann Petry (1911–1997)

Ann Lane Petry was born on October 12, 1911, in Old Saybrook, Connecticut. She grew up in a middle-class family in Old Saybrook, where her father was a pharmacist. In fact, Petry graduated from the College of Pharmacy at the University of Connecticut. She became interested in writing while she was a student.

She married George Petry in 1938 and moved with him to Harlem, where she worked as a journalist for *The Amsterdam News* and *The People's Voice.* Later, they returned to Old Saybrook. She received a $2,500 literary award from Houghton Mifflin Publishing Company, which published her first novel, *The Street,* in 1946. This novel became a best seller. In 1992 the publishing company reissued *The Street.*

The heroine of the novel, Lutie Johnson, is a young, Black single parent, who is raising a son, Bub, in Harlem. Lutie encounters manipulators and preyers. For example, there is Junto, the slum lord and club owner. Another character, Boots Smith, is the band leader whom Lutie murders, when he makes sexual advances toward her and refuses to pay her after she had worked in his club as a singer. Mrs. Hedges, who is employed as Junto's madame, has an ulterior motive in befriending Lutie. Jones, the superintendent of Lutie's building, desires her; he has a negative effect on Bub when he encourages the boy to steal.

Although this novel was first published over 50 years ago, it has contemporary issues. As a single Black parent, Lutie seeks a better life for herself and Bub. She works as a maid at first; then she is offered a better-paying job working as a singer in a nightclub. This classic novel shows Lutie as she balances her schedules at work, her time with Bub, and her social life. At the end of the novel, Bub is arrested for stealing, an act which Jones instigates. In order to hire a lawyer for Bub, Lutie attempts to get her back wages from Boots Smith. After she resists Boots' sexual advances, Lutie kills Boots in self-defense. In panic, she leaves Harlem, without knowing Bub's fate.

In addition to *The Street,* Petry published two other novels, *Country Place* (1947) and *The Narrows* (1953), as well as a collection of short stories, *Miss Muriel and Other Stories* (1971), four children's books, and numerous essays. Petry died on April 28, 1997.

Selected Bibliography

Barrett, Lindon. "Analysis of *The Street.*" *Masterpieces of African American Literature.* Frank N. Magill, ed. New York: HarperCollins, 1992. 546–549.

Ervin, Hazel A. *Ann Petry: A Bio-Bibliography.* New York: G. K. Hall, 1993.

Thomas, Robert McG., Jr. "Ann Petry, 88, First to Write a Literary Portrait of Harlem." *New York Times* (April 30, 1997): A2.

In Darkness and Confusion

Ann Petry

William Jones took a sip of coffee and then put his cup down on the kitchen table. It didn't taste right and be was annoyed because he always looked forward to eating breakfast. He usually got out of bed as soon as he woke up and hurried into the kitchen. Then he would take a long time heating the corn bread left over from dinner the night before, letting the coffee brew until it was strong and c]ear, frying bacon and scrambling eggs. He would eat very slowly—savoring the early-morning quiet and the just-rightness of the food he fixed part of the day, he thought. But this Saturday morning in July it was too hot in the apartment. There were too many nagging worries that kept drifting through his mind. In the heat he couldn't think clearly—so that all of them pressed in against him, weighed him down.

He pushed his plate away from him. The eggs had cooked too long; much as he liked corn bread it tasted like sand this morning—grainy and coarse inside his throat. He couldn't help wondering if it scratched the inside of his stomach in the same way.

Pink was moving around in the bedroom. He cocked his head on one side, listening to her. He could tell exactly what she was doing, as though he were in there with her. The soft heavy sound of her stockinged feet as she walked over to the dresser. The dresser drawer being pulled out. That meant she was getting a clean slip. Then the thud of her two hundred pounds landing in the rocker by the window. She was sitting down to comb her hair. Untwisting the small braids she'd made the night before. She would unwind them one by one, putting the hairpins in her mouth as she went along. Now she was brushing it, for he could hear the creak of the rocker; she was rocking back and forth, humming under her breath as she brushed.

He decided that as soon as she came into the kitchen he would go back to the bedroom, get dressed, and go to work. For his mind was already on the mailbox. He didn't feel like talking to Pink. There simply had to be a letter from Sam today. There had to be.

He was thinking about it so hard that he didn't hear Pink walk toward the kitchen.

When he looked up she was standing in the doorway. She was a short, enormously fat woman. The only garment she had on was a bright pink slip that magnified the size of her body. The skin on her arms and shoulders and chest was startlingly black against the pink material. In spite of the brisk brushing she had given her hair, it stood up stiffly all over her head in short wiry lengths, as though she wore a turban of some rough dark-gray material.

He got up from the table quickly when he saw her. "Hot, ain't it?" he said, and patted her arm as he went past her toward the bedroom.

She looked at the food on his plate. "You didn't want no breakfast?" she asked.

"Too hot," he said over his shoulder.

He closed the bedroom door behind him gently. If she saw the door was shut, she'd know that he was kind of low in his mind this morning and that he didn't feel like talking. At first he moved about with energy—getting a clean work shirt, giving his shoes a hasty brushing, hunting for a pair of clean socks. Then he stood still in the middle of the room, holding his dark work pants in his hand while he listened to the rush and roar of water running in the bathtub.

Annie May was up and taking a bath. And he wondered if that meant she was going to work. Days when she went to work she used a hot comb on her hair before she ate her breakfast, so that before he left the house in the morning it was filled with the smell of hot irons sizzling against hair grease.

He frowned. Something had to be done about Annie May. Here she was only eighteen years old and staying out practically all night long. He hadn't said anything to Pink about it, but Annie May crept into the house at three and four and five in the morning. He would hear her key go in the latch and then the telltale click as the lock drew back. She would shut the door very softly and turn the bolt. She'd stand there awhile, waiting to see if they woke up. Then she'd take her shoes off and pad down the hall in her stockinged feet.

When she turned the light on in the bathroom, he could see the clock on the dresser. This morning it was four-thirty when she came in. Pink, lying beside him, went on peacefully snoring. He was glad that she didn't wake up easy. It would only worry her to know that Annie May was carrying on like that.

Annie May put her hands on her hips and threw her head back and laughed whenever he tried to tell her she had to come home earlier. The smoky smell of the hot irons started seeping into the bedroom and he finished dressing quickly.

He stopped in the kitchen on his way out. "Got to get to the store early today," he explained. He was sure Pink knew he was hurrying downstairs to look in the mailbox. But she nodded and held her face up for his kiss. When he brushed his lips against her forehead he saw that her face was wet with perspiration. He thought with all that weight she must feel the heat something awful.

Annie May nodded at him without speaking. She was hastily swallowing a cup of coffee. Her dark thin hands made a pattern against the thick white cup she was holding. She had pulled her hair out so straight with the hot combs that he thought it was like a shiny skullcap fitted tight to her head. He was surprised to see that her lips were heavily coated with lipstick. When she was going to work she didn't use any, and he wondered why she was up so early if she wasn't working. He could see the red outline of her mouth on the cup.

He hadn't intended to say anything. It was the sight of the lipstick on the cup that forced the words out. "You ain't workin' today?"

"No," she said lazily. "Think I'll go shopping." She winked at Pink, and it infuriated him.

"How you expect to keep a job when you don't show up half the time?" he asked.

"I can always get another one." She lifted the coffee cup to her mouth with both hands and her eyes laughed at him over the rim of the cup.

"What time did you come home last night?" he asked abruptly.

She stared out of the window at the blank brick wall that faced the kitchen. "I dunno," she said finally. "It wasn't late."

He didn't know what to say. Probably she was out dancing somewhere. Or maybe she wasn't. He was fairly certain that she wasn't. Yet he couldn't let Pink know what he was thinking. He shifted his feet uneasily and watched Annie May swallow the coffee. She was drinking it fast.

"You know you ain't too big to get your butt whipped," he said finally.

She looked at him out of the corner of her eyes. And he saw a deep smoldering sullenness in her face that startled him. He was conscious that Pink was watching both of them with a growing apprehension.

Then Annie May giggled. "You and who else?" she said lightly. Pink roared with laughter. And Annie May laughed with her.

He banged the kitchen door hard as he went out. Striding down the outside hall, he could still hear them laughing. And even though he knew Pink's laughter was due to relief because nothing unpleasant had happened, he was angry. Lately every time Annie May looked at him there was open, jeering laughter in her eyes, as though she dared him to say anything to her. Almost as though she thought he was a fool for working so hard.

She had been a nice little girl when she first came to live with them six years ago. He groped in his mind for words to describe what he thought Annie May had become. A Jezebel, he decided grimly. That was it.

And he didn't want Pink to know what Annie May was really like. Because Annie May's mother, Lottie, had been Pink's sister. And when Lottie died, Pink took Annie May. Right away she started finding excuses for anything she did that was wrong. If he scolded Annie May he had to listen to a sharp lecture from Pink. It always started off the same way: "Don't care what she done, William. You ain't goin' to lay a finger on her. She ain't got no father and mother except us . . ."

The quick spurt of anger and irritation at Annie May had sent him hurrying down the first flight of stairs. But he slowed his pace on the next flight because the hallways were so dark that he knew if he wasn't careful he'd walk over a step. As he trudged down the long flights of stairs he began to think about Pink. And the hot irritation in him disappeared as it usually did when he thought about her. She was so fat she couldn't keep on climbing all these steep stairs. They would have to find another place to live—on a first floor where it would be easier for her. They'd lived on this top floor for years, and all the time Pink kept getting heavier and heavier. Every time she went to the clinic the doctor said the stairs were bad for her. So they'd start looking for another apartment and then because the top floors cost less, why, they stayed where they were. And—

Then he stopped thinking about Pink because he had reached the first floor. He walked over to the mailboxes and took a deep breath. Today there'd be a letter. He knew it. There had to be. It had been too long a time since they had had a letter from Sam. The last ones that came he'd said the same thing. Over and over. Like a refrain. "Ma, I can't stand this much longer." And then the letters just stopped.

As he stood there, looking at the mailbox, half afraid to open it for fear there would be no letter, he thought back to the night Sam graduated from high school. It was a warm June night. He and Pink got all dressed up in their best clothes. And he kept thinking me and Pink have got as far as we can go. But Sam—he made up his mind Sam wasn't going to earn his living with a mop and a broom. He was going to earn it wearing a starched white collar, and a shine on his shoes and a crease in his pants.

After he finished high school Sam got a job redcapping at Grand Central. He started saving his money because be was going to go to Lincoln—a college in Pennsylvania. It looked like it was no time at all before he was twenty-one. And in the army. Pink cried when he left. Her huge body shook with her sobbing. He remembered that he had only felt queer and lost. There was this war and all the young men were being drafted. But why Sam—why did he have to go?

It was always in the back of his mind. Next thing Sam was in a camp in Georgia. He and Pink never talked about his being in Georgia. The closest they ever came to it was one night when she said, "I hope he gets used to it quick down there. Bein' born right here in New York there's lots he won't understand."

Then Sam's letters stopped coming. He'd come home from work and say to Pink casually, "Sam write today?" She'd shake her head without saying anything.

The days crawled past. And finally she burst out. "What you keep askin' for? You think I wouldn't tell you?" And she started crying.

He put his arm around her and patted her shoulder. She leaned hard against him. "Oh, Lord," she said. "He's my baby. What they done to him?"

Her crying like that tore him in little pieces. His mind kept going around in circles. Around and around. He couldn't think what to do. Finally one night after work he sat down at the kitchen table and wrote Sam a letter. He had written very few letters in his life because Pink had always done it for him. And now standing in front of the mailbox he could even remember the feel of the pencil in his hand; how the paper looked—blank and challenging—lying there in front of him; that the kitchen clock was ticking and it kept getting louder and louder. It was hot that night, too, and he held the pencil so tight that the inside of his hand was covered with sweat

He had sat and thought a long time. Then he wrote: "Is you all right? Your Pa." It was the best he could do. He licked the envelope and addressed it with the feeling that Sam would understand.

He fumbled for his key ring, found the mailbox key, and opened the box quickly. It was empty. Even though he could see it was empty he felt around inside it. Then he closed the box and walked toward the street door.

The brilliant sunlight outside made him blink after the darkness of the hall. Even now, so early in the morning, it was hot in the street. And he thought it was going to be a hard day to get through, what with the heat and its being Saturday and all. Lately he couldn't seem to think about anything but Sam. Even at the drugstore where he worked as a porter, he would catch himself leaning on the broom or pausing in his mopping to wonder what had happened to him.

The man who owned the store would say to him sharply, "Boy, what the hell's the matter with you? Can't you keep your mind on what you're doing?" And he would go on washing windows, or mopping the floor, or sweeping the sidewalk. But his thoughts, somehow, no matter what he was doing, drifted back to Sam.

As he walked toward the drugstore he looked at the houses on both sides of the street. He knew this street as he knew the creases in the old felt hat he wore the year round. No matter how you looked at it, it wasn't a good street to live on. It was a long cross-town street. Almost half of it on one side consisted of the backs of the three theaters on One Hundred Twenty-fifth Street—a long blank wall of gray brick. There were few trees on the street. Even these were a source of danger, for at night shadowy, vague shapes emerged from the street's darkness, lurking near the trees, dodging behind them. He had never been accosted by any of those disembodied figures, but the very stealth of their movements revealed a dishonest intent that frightened him. So when he came home at night he walked an extra block or more in order to go through One Hundred Twenty-fifth Street and enter the street from Eighth Avenue.

Early in the morning like this, the street slept. Window shades were drawn down tight against the morning sun. The few people he passed were walking briskly on their way to work. But in those houses where the people still slept the window shades would go up about noon, and radios would blast music all up and down the street. The bold-eyed women who lived in these houses would lounge in the open windows and call to each other back and forth across the street.

Sometimes when he was on his way home to lunch they would call out to him as he went past, "Come on in, Poppa!" And he would stare straight ahead and start walking faster.

When Sam turned sixteen it seemed to him the street was unbearable. After lunch he and Sam went through this block together—Sam to school and he on his way back to the drugstore. He'd seen Sam stare at the lounging women in the windows. His face was expressionless, but his eyes were curious.

"I catch you goin' near one of them women and I'll beat you up and down the block," he'd said grimly.

Sam didn't answer him. Instead he looked down at him with a strangely adult look, for even at sixteen Sam had been a good five inches taller than he. After that when they passed through the block, Sam looked straight ahead. And William got the uncomfortable feeling that he had already explored the possibilities that the block offered. Yet he couldn't be sure. And he couldn't bring himself to ask him. Instead he walked along beside him, thinking desperately, we gotta move. I'll talk to Pink. We gotta move this time for sure.

That Sunday after Pink came home from church they looked for a new place. They went in and out of apartment houses along Seventh Avenue and Eighth Avenue, One Hundred Thirty-fifth Street, One Hundred Forty-fifth Street. Most of the apartments they didn't even look at. They just asked the super how much the rents were.

It was late when they headed for home. He had irritably agreed with Pink that they'd better stay where they were. Twenty-two dollars a month was all they could afford.

"It ain't a fit place to live, though," he said. They were walking down Seventh Avenue. The street looked wide to him, and he thought with distaste of their apartment. The rooms weren't big enough for a man to move around in without bumping into something. Sometimes he thought that was why Annie May spent so much time away from home. Even at thirteen she couldn't stand being cooped up like that in such a small amount of space.

And Pink said, "You want to live on Park Avenue? With a doorman bowin' you in and out. 'Good mornin', Mr. William Jones. Does the weather suit you this mornin'?'" Her voice was sharp, like the crack of a whip.

That was five years ago. And now again they ought to move on account of Pink not being able to stand the stairs any more. He decided that Monday night after work he'd start looking for a place.

It was even hotter in the drugstore than it was in the street. He forced himself to go inside and put on a limp work coat. Then broom in hand he went to stand in the doorway. He waved to the superintendent of the building on the corner. And watched him as he lugged garbage cans out of the areaway and rolled them to the curb. Now, that's the kind of work he didn't want Sam to have to do. He tried to decide why that was. It wasn't just because Sam was his boy and it was hard work. He searched his mind for the reason. It didn't pay enough for a man to live on decently. That was it. He wanted Sam to have a job where he could make enough to have good clothes and a nice home.

Sam's being in the army wasn't so bad, he thought. It was his being in Georgia that was bad. They didn't treat colored people right down there. Everybody knew that. If he could figure out some way to get him farther north Pink wouldn't have to worry about him so much.

The very sound of the word "Georgia" did something to him inside. His mother had been born there. She had talked about it a lot and painted such vivid pictures of it that he felt he knew the place—the heat, the smell of the earth, how cotton looked. And something more. The way her mouth had folded together whenever she had said, "They hate niggers down there. Don't you never none of you children go down there."

That was years ago, yet even now, standing here on Fifth Avenue, remembering the way she said it turned his skin clammy cold in spite of the heat. And of all the places in the world, Sam had to go to Georgia. Sam, who was born right here in New York, who had finished high school here—they had to put him in the army and send him to Georgia.

He tightened his grip on the broom and started sweeping the sidewalk in long, even strokes. Gradually the rhythm of the motion stilled the agitation in him. The regular back-and-forth motion was so pleasant that he kept on sweeping long after the sidewalk was clean. When Mr. Yudkin, who owned the store, arrived at eight-thirty he was still outside with the broom. Even now he didn't feel much like talking, so he only nodded in response to the druggist's brisk, "Good morning! Hot today!"

William followed him into the store and began polishing the big mirror in back of the soda fountain. He watched the man out of the corner of his eye as he washed his hands in the back room and exchanged his suit coat for a crisp white laboratory coat. And he thought maybe when the war is over Sam ought to study to be a druggist instead of a doctor or a lawyer.

As the morning wore along, customers came in in a steady stream. They got Bromo-Seltzers, cigarettes, aspirin, cough medicine, baby bottles. He delivered two prescriptions that cost five dollars. And the cash register rang so often it almost played a tune. Listening to it he said to himself, yes, Sam ought to be a druggist. It's clean work and it pays good.

A little after eleven o'clock three young girls came in. "Cokes," they said, and climbed up on the stools in front of the fountain. William was placing new stock on the shelves and he studied them from the top of the stepladder. As far as he could see, they looked exactly alike. All three of them. And like Annie May. Too thin. Too much lipstick. Their dresses were too short and too tight. Their hair was piled on top of their heads in slicked set curls.

"Aw, I quit that job," one of them said. "I wouldn't get up that early in the morning for nothing in the world."

That was like Annie May, too. She was always changing jobs. Because she could never get to work on time. If she was due at a place at nine she got there at ten. If at ten, then she arrived about eleven. He knew, too, that she didn't earn enough money to pay for all the cheap, bright-colored dresses she was forever buying.

Her girl friends looked just like her and just like these girls. He'd seen her coming out of the movie houses on One Hundred Twenty-fifth Street with two or three of them. They were all chewing gum and they nudged each other and talked too loud and laughed too loud. They stared hard at every man who went past them.

Mr. Yudkin looked up at him sharply, and he shifted his glance away from the girls and began putting big bottles of Father John's medicine neatly on the shelf in front of him. As he stacked the bottles up he wondered if Annie May would have been different if she'd stayed in high school. She had stopped going when she was sixteen. He had spoken to Pink about it. "She oughtn't to stop school. She's too young," he'd said.

And because Annie May was Pink's sister's child all Pink had done had been to shake her head comfortably. "She's tired of going to school. Poor little thing. Leave her alone."

So he hadn't said anything more. Pink always took up for her. And he and Pink didn't fuss at each other like some folks do. He didn't say anything to Pink about it, but he took the afternoon off from work to go to see the principal of the school. He had to wait two hours to see her. And he studied the pictures on the walls in the outer office, and looked down at his shoes while he tried to put into words what he'd say—and how he wanted to say it.

The principal was a large-bosomed white woman. She listened to him long enough to learn that he was Annie May's uncle. "Ah, yes, Mr. Jones," she said. "Now in my opinion—"

And he was buried under a flow of words, a mountain of words, that went on and on. Her voice was high-pitched and loud, and she kept talking until he lost all sense of what she was saying. There was one phrase she kept using that sort of jumped at him out of the mass of words—"a slow learner."

He left her office feeling confused and embarrassed. If he could only have found the words he could have explained that Annie May was bright as a dollar. She wasn't any "slow learner." Before he knew it he was out in the street, conscious only that he'd lost a whole afternoon's pay and he never had got to say what he'd come for. And he was boiling mad with himself. All he'd wanted was to ask the principal to help him persuade Annie May to finish school. But he'd never got the words together.

When he hung up his soiled work coat in the broom closet at eight o'clock that night he felt as though he'd been sweeping floors, dusting fixtures, cleaning fountains, and running errands since the beginning of time itself. He looked at himself in the cracked mirror that hung on the door of the closet. There was no question about it; he'd grown older-looking since Sam went in the army. His hair was turning a frizzled gray at the temples His jawbones showed up sharper. There was a stoop in his shoulders.

"Guess I'll get a haircut," he said softly. He didn't really need one. But on a Saturday night the barbershop would be crowded. He'd have to wait a long time before Al got around to him. It would be good to listen to the talk that went on—the arguments that would get started and never really end. For a while all the nagging worry about Sam would be pushed so far back in his mind, he wouldn't be aware of it.

The instant he entered the barbershop he could feel himself begin to relax inside. All the chairs were full. There were a lot of customers waiting. He waved a greeting to the barbers. "Hot, ain't it?" he said and mopped his forehead.

He stood there a minute, listening to the hum of conversation, before he picked out a place to sit. Some of the talk, he knew, would be violent, and he always avoided those discussions because he didn't like violence—even when it was only talk. Scraps of talk drifted past him.

"White folks got us by the balls—"

"Well, I dunno. It ain't just white folks. There's poor white folks gettin' their guts squeezed out, too—"

"Sure. But they're white. They can stand it better."

"Sadie had two dollars on 546 yesterday and it came out and—"

"You're wrong man. Ain't no two ways about it. This country's set up so that—"

"Only thing to do, if you ask me, is to shoot all them crackers and start out new—"

He finally settled himself in one of the chairs in the corner—not too far from the window and right in the middle of a group of regular customers who were arguing hotly about the war. It was a good seat. By looking in the long mirror in front of the barbers he could see the length of the shop.

Almost immediately he joined in the conversation. "Them Japs ain't got a chance—" he started. And he was feeling good. He'd come in at just the right time. He took a deep breath before he went on. Most every time he started talking about the Japs the others listened with deep respect. Because he knew more about them than the other customers. Pink worked for some Navy people and she told him what they said.

He looked along the line of waiting customers, watching their reaction to his words. Pretty soon they'd all be listening to him. And then he stopped talking abruptly, A soldier was sitting in the far corner of the shop, staring down at his shoes. Why, that's Scummy, he thought. He's at the same camp where Sam is. He forgot what he was about to say. He got up and walked over to Scummy. He swallowed all the questions about Sam that trembled on his lips.

"Hiya, son," he said. "Sure is good to see you."

As he shook hands with the boy he looked him over carefully. He's changed, he thought. He was older. There was something about his eyes that was different than before. He didn't seem to want to talk. After that first quick look at William he kept his eyes down, staring at his shoes.

Finally William couldn't hold the question back any longer. It came out fast. "How's Sam?"

Scummy picked up a newspaper from the chair beside him. "He's all right," he mumbled. There was a long silence. Then he raised his head and looked directly at William. "Was the las' time I seen him." He put a curious emphasis on the word "las'."

William was conscious of a trembling that started in his stomach. It went all through his body. He was aware that conversation in the barbershop had stopped. There was a cone of silence in which he could hear the scraping noise of the razors—a harsh sound, loud in the silence. Al was putting thick oil on a customer's hair and he turned and looked with the hair-oil bottle still in his hand, tilted up over the customer's head. The men sitting in the tilted-back barber's chairs twisted their necks around—awkwardly, slowly—so they could look at Scummy.

"What you mean—the las' tune?" William asked sharply. The words beat against his ears. He wished the men in the barbershop would start talking again, for he kept hearing his own words. "What you mean—the las' time?" Just as though he were saying them over and over again. Something had gone wrong with his breathing, too. He couldn't seem to get enough air in through his nose.

Scummy got up. There was something about him that William couldn't give a name to. It made the trembling in his stomach worse.

"The las' time I seen him he was O.K." Scummy's voice made a snarling noise in the barbershop.

One part of William's mind said, yes, that's it. It's hate that makes him look different. It's hate in his eyes. You can see it. It's in his voice, and you can hear it. He's filled with it.

"Since I seen him las'," he went on slowly, "he got shot by a white MP. Because he wouldn't go to the nigger end of a bus. He had a bullet put through his guts. He took the MP's gun away from him and shot the bastard in the shoulder." He put the newspaper down and started toward the door; when he reached it he turned around. "They court-martialed him," he said softly. "He got twenty years at hard labor. The notice was posted in the camp the day I left." Then he walked out of the shop. He didn't look back.

There was no sound in the barbershop as William watched him go down the street. Even the razors had stopped. Al was still holding the hair-oil bottle over the head of his customer. The heavy oil was falling on the face of the man sitting in the chair. It was coming down slowly—one drop at a time.

The men in the shop looked at William and then looked away. He thought, I mustn't tell Pink. She mustn't ever get to know. I can go down to the mailbox early in the morning and I can get somebody else to look in it in the afternoon, so if a notice comes I can tear it up

The barbers started cutting hair again. There was the murmur of conversation in the shop. Customers got up out of the tilted-back chairs. Someone said to him, "You can take my place."

He nodded and walked over to the empty chair. His legs were weak and shaky. He couldn't seem to think at all. His mind kept dodging away from the thought of Sam in prison. Instead the familiar details of Sam's growing up kept creeping into his thoughts. All the time the boy was in grammar school he made good marks. Time went so fast it seemed like it was just overnight and he was in long pants. And then in high school.

He made the basketball team in high school. The whole school was proud of him, for his picture had been in one of the white papers. They got two papers that day. Pink cut the pictures out and stuck one in the mirror of the dresser in their bedroom. She gave him one to carry in his wallet.

While Al cut his hair he stared at himself in the mirror until he felt as though his eyes were crossed. First he thought, maybe it isn't true. Maybe Scummy was joking. But a man who was joking didn't look like Scummy looked. He wondered if Scummy was AWOL. That would be bad. He told himself sternly that he mustn't think about Sam here in the barbershop—wait until he got home.

He was suddenly angry with Annie May. She was just plain no good. Why couldn't something have happened to her? Why did it have to be Sam? Then he was ashamed. He tried to find an excuse for having wanted harm to come to her. It looked like all his life he'd wanted a little something for himself and Pink and then when Sam came along he forgot about those things. He wanted Sam to have all the things that he and Pink couldn't get. It got to be too late for them to have them. But Sam—again he told himself not to think about him. To wait until he got home and in bed.

Al took the cloth from around his neck, and he got up out of the chair. Then be was out on the street, heading toward home. The heat that came from the pavement seeped through the soles of his shoes. He had forgotten how hot it was. He forced himself to wonder what it would be like to live in the country. Sometimes on hot nights like this, after he got home from work, he went to sit in the park. It was always cooler there. It would probably be cool in the country. But then it might be cold in winter—even colder than the city.

The instant he got in the house he took off his shoes and his shirt. The heat in the apartment was like a blanket—it made his skin itch and crawl in a thousand places. He went into the living room, where he leaned out of the window, trying to cool off. Not yet, he told himself. He mustn't think about it yet.

He leaned farther out of the window, to get away from the innumerable odors that came from the boxlike rooms in back of him. They cut off his breath, and he focused his mind on them. There was the greasy smell of cabbage and collard greens, smell of old wood and soapsuds and disinfectant, a lingering smell of gas from the kitchen stove, and over it all Annie May's perfume.

Then he turned his attention to the street. Up and down as far as he could see, folks were sitting on the stoops. Not talking. Just sitting. Somewhere up the street a baby wailed. A woman's voice rose sharply as she told it to shut up.

Pink wouldn't be home until late. The white folks she worked for were having a dinner party tonight. And no matter how late she got home on Saturday night she always stopped on Eighth Avenue to shop for her Sunday dinner. She never trusted him to do it. It's a good thing, he thought. If she ever took a look at me tonight she'd know there was something wrong.

A key clicked in the lock, and he drew back from the window. He was sitting on the couch when Annie May came in the room.

"You're home early, ain't you?" he asked.

"Oh, I'm going out again," she said.

"You shouldn't stay out so late like you did last night," he said mildly, He hadn't really meant to say it. But what with Sam—

"What you think I'm going to do? Sit here every night and make small talk with you?" Her voice was defiant. Loud.

"No," he said, and then added, "but nice girls ain't runnin' around the streets at four o'clock in the mornin'." Now that he'd started he couldn't seem to stop. "Oh, I know what time you come home. And it ain't right. If you don't stop it you can get some other place to stay."

"It's O.K. With me," she said lightly. She chewed the gum in her mouth so it made a cracking noise. "I don't know what Auntie Pink married a little runt like you for, anyhow. It wouldn't bother me a bit if I never saw you again." She walked toward the hall. "I'm going away for the week end," she added over her shoulder. "And I'll move out on Monday."

"What you mean for the week end?" he asked sharply. "Where you goin'?"

"None of your damn business," she said, and slammed the bathroom door hard.

The sharp sound of the door closing hurt his ears so that he winced, wondering why he had grown so sensitive to sounds in the last few hours. What'd she have to say that for, anyway, he asked himself. Five feet five wasn't so short for a man. He was taller than Pink, anyhow. Yet compared to Sam, he supposed he was a runt, for Sam had just kept on growing until he was six feet tall. At the thought he got up from the chair quickly, undressed, and got in bed. He lay there trying to still the trembling in his stomach; trying even now not to think about Sam, because it would be best to wait until Pink was in bed and sound asleep so that no expression on his face, no least little motion, would betray his agitation

When he heard Pink come up the stairs just before midnight he closed his eyes. All of him was listening to her. He could hear her panting outside on the landing. There was a long pause before she put her key in the door. It took her all that time to get her breath back. She's getting old, he thought. I mustn't let her know about Sam.

She came into the bedroom, and he pretended to be asleep. He made himself breathe slowly. Evenly. Thinking, I can get through tomorrow all right. I won't get up much before she goes to church. She'll be so busy getting dressed she won't notice me.

She went out of the room and he heard the soft murmur of her voice talking to Annie May. "Don't you pay no attention, honey. He don't mean a word of it. I know menfolks. They's always tired and out of sorts by the time Saturdays come around."

"But I'm not going to stay here any more."

"Yes, you is. You think I'm goin' to let my sister's child be turned out? You goin' to be right here."

They lowered their voices. There was laughter. Pink's deep and rich and slow. Annie May's high-pitched and nervous. Pink said, "You looks lovely, honey. Now, have a good time."

The front door closed. This time Annie May didn't slam it. He turned over on his back, making the springs creak. Instantly Pink came into the bedroom to look at him. He lay still, with his eyes closed, holding his breath for fear she would want to talk to him about what he'd said to Annie May and would wake him up. After she moved away from the door he opened his eyes.

There must be some meaning in back of what had happened to Sam. Maybe it was some kind of judgment from the Lord, he thought. Perhaps he shouldn't have stopped going to church. His only concession to Sunday was to put on his best suit. He wore it just that one day, and Pink pressed the pants late on Saturday night. But in the last few years it got so that every time he went to church he wanted to stand up and yell, "You Goddamn fools! How much more you goin' to take?"

He'd get to thinking about the street they lived on, and the sight of the minister with his clean white collar turned hind side to and the sound of his buttery voice were too much. One Sunday he'd actually gotten on his feet, for the minister was talking about the streets of gold up in heaven; the words were right on the tip of his tongue when Pink reached out and pinched his behind sharply. He yelped and sat down. Someone in back of him giggled. In spite of himself a slow smile had spread over his face. He stayed quiet through the rest of the service, but after that he didn't go to church at all.

This street where he and Pink lived was like the one where his mother had lived. It looked like he and Pink ought to have gotten further than his mother had. She had scrubbed floors, washed, and ironed in the white folks' kitchens. They were doing practically the same thing.

That was another reason he stopped going to church. He couldn't figure out why these things had to stay the same, and if the Lord didn't intend it like that, why didn't He change it?

He began thinking about Sam again, so he shifted his attention to the sounds Pink was making in the kitchen. She was getting the rolls ready for tomorrow. Scrubbing the sweet potatoes. Washing the greens. Cutting up the chicken. Then the thump of the iron. Hot as it was, she was pressing his pants. He resisted the impulse to get up and tell her not to do it.

A little later, when she turned the light on in the bathroom, he knew she was getting ready for bed. And he held his eyes tightly shut, made his body rigidly still. As long as he could make her think he was sound asleep she wouldn't take a real good look at him. One real good look and she'd know there was something wrong. The bed sagged under her weight as she knelt down to say her prayers. Then she was lying down beside him. She sighed under her breath as her head hit the pillow.

He must have slept part of the time, but in the morning it seemed to him that he had looked up at the ceiling most of the night. He couldn't remember actually going to sleep.

When he finally got up, Pink was dressed and ready for church. He sat down in a chair in the living room away from the window, so the light wouldn't shine on his face. As he looked at her he wished that he could find relief from the confusion of his thoughts by taking part in the singing and the shouting that would go on in church. But he couldn't. And Pink never said anything about his not going to church. Only sometimes like today, when she was ready to go, she looked at him a little wistfully.

She had on her Sunday dress. It was made of a printed material—big red and black poppies splashed on a cream-colored background. He wouldn't let himself look right into her eyes, and in order that she wouldn't notice the evasiveness of his glance he stared at the dress. It fit snugly over her best corset, and the corset in turn constricted her thighs and tightly encased the rolls of flesh around her waist. She didn't move away, and he couldn't keep on inspecting the dress, so he shifted his gaze up to the wide cream-colored straw hat she was wearing far back on her head. Next he noticed that she was easing her feet by standing on the outer edges of the high-heeled patent-leather pumps she wore.

He reached out and patted her arm. "You look nice," he said, picking up the comic section of the paper.

She stood there looking at him while she pulled a pair of white cotton gloves over her roughened hands. "Is you, all right, honey?" she asked.

"Course," he said, holding the paper up in front of his face.

"You shouldn't talk so mean to Annie May," she said gently.

"Yeah, I know," he said, and hoped she understood that he was apologizing He didn't dare lower the paper while she was standing there looking at him so intently. Why doesn't she go, he thought.

"There's grits and eggs for breakfast."

"O.K." He tried to make his voice sound as though he were so absorbed in what he was reading that he couldn't give her all of his attention. She walked toward the door, and he lowered the paper to watch her, thinking that her legs looked too small for her body under the vastness of the printed dress, that womenfolks sure were funny—she's got that great big pocketbook swinging on her arm and hardly anything in it. Sam used to love to tease her about the size of the handbags she carried.

When she closed the outside door and started down the stairs, the heat in the little room struck him in the face. He almost called her back so that he wouldn't be there by himself—left alone to brood over Sam. He decided that when she came home from church he would make love to her. Even in the heat the softness of her body, the smoothness of her skin, would comfort him.

He pulled his chair up close to the open window. Now he could let himself go. He could begin to figure out something to do about Sam. There's gotta be something, he thought. But his mind wouldn't stay put. It kept going back to the time Sam graduated from high school. Nineteen seventy-five his dark-blue suit had cost. He and Pink had figured and figured and finally they'd managed it. Sam had looked good in the suit; he was so tall and his shoulders were so broad it looked like a tailor-made suit on him. When he got his diploma everybody went wild—he'd played center on the basketball team, and a lot of folks recognized him.

The trembling in his stomach got worse as he thought about Sam. He was aware that it had never stopped since Scummy had said those words "the las' time." It had gone on all last night until now there was a tautness and a tension in him that left him feeling as though his eardrums were strained wide open, listening for sounds. They must be a foot wide open, he thought. Open and pulsing with the strain of being open. Even his nostrils were stretched open like that. He could feel them. And a weight behind his eyes.

He went to sleep sitting there in the chair. When he woke up his whole body was wet with sweat. It musta got hotter while I slept, he thought. He was conscious of an ache in his jawbones. It's from holding 'em shut so tight. Even his tongue—he'd been holding it so still in his mouth it felt like it was glued there.

Attracted by the sound of voices, he looked out of the window. Across the way a man and a woman were arguing. Their voices rose and fell on the hot, still air. He could look directly into the room where they were standing, and he saw that they were half undressed.

The woman slapped the man across the face. The sound was like a pistol shot, and for an instant William felt his jaw relax. It seemed to him that the whole block grew quiet and waited. He waited with it. The man grabbed his belt and lashed out at the woman. He watched the belt rise and fall against her brown skin. The woman screamed with the regularity of clockwork. The street came alive again. There was the sound of voices, the rattle of dishes. A baby whined. The woman's voice became a murmur of pain in the background.

"I gotta get me some beer," he said aloud. It would cool him off. It would help him to think. He dressed quickly, telling himself that Pink wouldn't be home for hours yet and by that time the beer smell would be gone from his breath.

The street outside was full of kids playing tag. They were all dressed up in their Sunday clothes. Red socks, blue socks, danced in front of him all the way to the corner. The sight of them piled up the quivering in his stomach. Sam used to play in this block on Sunday afternoons. As he walked along, women thrust their heads out of the opened windows, calling to the children. It seemed to him that all the voices were Pink's voice saying, "You, Sammie, stop that runnin' in your good cloes!"

He was so glad to get away from the sight of the children that he ignored the heat inside the barroom of the hotel on the corner and determinedly edged his way past girls in sheer summer dresses and men in loud plaid jackets and tight-legged cream-colored pants until he finally reached the long bar.

There was such a sense of hot excitement in the place that he turned to look around him. Men with slicked, straightened hair were staring through half-closed eyes at the girls lined up at the bar. One man sitting at a table close by kept running his hand up and down the bare arm of the girl leaning against him. Up and down. Down and up. William winced and looked away. The jukebox was going full blast, filling the room with high, raw music that beat about his ears in a queer mixture of violence and love and hate and terror. He stared at the brilliantly colored moving lights on the front of the jukebox as he listened to it, wishing that he had stayed at home, for the music made the room hotter.

"Make it a beer," he, said to the bartender.

The beer glass was cold. He held it in his hand, savoring the, chill of it, before he raised it to his lips. He drank it down fast. Immediately he felt the air grow cooler. The smell of beer and whisky that hung in the room lifted.

"Fill it up again," he said. He still had that awful trembling in his stomach, but he felt as though he were really beginning to think. Really think. He found he was arguing with himself.

"Sam mighta been like this. Spendin' Sunday afternoons whorin'."

"But he was part of me and part of Pink. He had a chance—"

"Yeah. A chance to live in one of them hell-hole flats. A chance to get himself a woman to beat."

"He would a finished college and got a good job. Mebbe been a druggist or a doctor or a lawyer—"

"Yeah. Or mebbe got himself a stable of women to rent out on the block—"

He licked the suds from his lips. The man at the table nearby had stopped stroking the girl's arm. He was kissing her—forcing her closer and closer to him

"Yeah," William jeered at himself. "That coulda been Sam on a hot Sunday afternoon—"

As he stood there arguing with himself he thought it was getting warmer in the bar. The lights were dimmer. I better go home, he thought. I gotta live with this thing some time. Drinking beer in this place ain't going to help any. He looked out toward the lobby of the hotel, attracted by the sound of voices. A white cop was arguing with a frowzy-looking girl who had obviously had too much to drink.

"I got a right in here. I'm mindin' my own business," she said with one eye on the bar.

"Aw, go chase yourself." The cop gave her a push toward the door. She stumbled against a chair.

William watched her in amusement. "Better than a movie," he told himself.

She straightened up and tugged at her girdle. "You white son of a bitch," she said.

The cop's face turned a furious red. He walked toward the woman, waving his nightstick. It was then that William saw the soldier. Tall. Straight. Creases in his khaki pants. An overseas cap cocked over one eye. Looks like Sam looked that one time he was home on furlough, he thought.

The soldier grabbed the cop's arm and twisted the nightstick out of his hand. He threw it half the length of the small lobby. It rattled along the floor and came to a dead stop under a chair.

"Now what'd he want to do that for?" William said softly. He knew that night after night the cop had to come back to this hotel. He's the law, he thought, and he can't let—Then he stopped thinking about him, for the cop raised his arm. The soldier aimed a blow at the cop's chin. The cop ducked and reached for his gun. The soldier turned to run.

It's happening too fast, William thought. It's like one of those horse-race reels they run over fast at the movies. Then he froze inside. The quivering in his stomach got worse. The soldier was heading toward the door. Running. His foot was on the threshold when the cop fired. The soldier dropped. He folded up as neatly as the brown-paper bags Pink brought home from the store, emptied, and then carefully put in the kitchen cupboard.

The noise of the shot stayed in his eardrums. He couldn't get it out. "Jesus Christ!" he said. Then again, "Jesus Christ!" The beer glass was warm. He put it down on the bar with such violence some of the beer slopped over on his shirt He stared at the wet place, thinking Pink would be mad as hell. Him out drinking in a bar on Sunday. There was a stillness in which he was conscious of the stink of the beer, the heat in the room, and he could still hear the sound of the shot. Somebody dropped a glass, and the tinkle of it hurt his ears.

Then everybody was moving toward the lobby. The doors between the bar and the lobby slammed shut. High, excited talk broke out.

The tall, thin black man standing next to him said, "That ties it. It ain't even safe here where we live. Not no more. I'm goin' to get me a white bastard of a cop and nail his hide to a street sign."

"Is the soldier dead?" someone asked.

"He wasn't movin' none," came the answer.

They pushed hard against the doors leading to the lobby. The doors stayed shut.

He stood still, watching them. The anger that went through him was so great that he had to hold on to the bar to keep from falling. He felt as though he were going to burst wide open. It was like having seen Sam killed before his eyes. Then he heard the whine of an ambulance siren. His eardrums seemed to be waiting to pick it up.

"Come on, what you waitin' for?" he snarled the words at the people milling around the lobby doors. "Come on!" he repeated, running toward the street.

The crowd followed him to the One Hundred Twenty-sixth Street entrance of the hotel. He got there in time to see a stretcher bearing a limp khaki-clad figure disappear inside the ambulance in front of the door. The ambulance pulled away fast, and he stared after it stupidly.

He hadn't known what he was going to do, but he felt cheated. Let down. He noticed that it was beginning to get dark. More and more people were coming into the street. He wondered where they'd come from and how they'd heard about the shooting so quickly. Every time he looked around there were more of them. Curious, eager voices kept asking, "What happened? What happened?" The answer was always the same. Hard. Angry. "A white cop shot a soldier."

Someone said, "Come on to the hospital. Find out what happened to him."

In front of the hotel he had been in the front of the crowd, Now there were so many people in back of him and in front of him that when they started toward the hospital, he moved along with them. He hadn't decided to go—the forward movement picked him up and moved him along without any intention on his part. He got the feeling that he had lost his identity as a person with a free will of his own. It frightened him at first. Then he began to feel powerful. He was surrounded by hundreds of people like himself. They were all together. They could do anything.

As the crowd moved slowly down Eighth Avenue, he saw that there were cops lined up on both sides of the street. Mounted cops kept coming out of the side streets, shouting "Break it up! Keep moving. Keep moving."

The cops were scared of them. He could tell. Their faces were dead white in the semidarkness. He started saying the words over separately to himself. Dead. White. He laughed. White cops. White MP's. They got us coming and going, he thought. He laughed again. Dead. White. The words were funny said separately like that. He stopped laughing suddenly because a part of his mind repeated: twenty years, twenty years.

He licked his lips. It was hot as all hell tonight. He imagined what it would he like to be drinking swallow after swallow of ice-cold beer. His throat worked and he swallowed audibly.

The big black man walking beside him turned and looked down at him. "You all right, brother?" he asked curiously.

"Yeah," he nodded. "It's them sons of bitches of cops. They're scared of us." He shuddered. The heat was terrible. The tide of hate quivering in his stomach made him hotter. "Wish I had some beer," he said.

The man seemed to understand not only what he had said, but all the things he had left unsaid, For he nodded and smiled. And William thought this was an extraordinary night. It was as though, standing so close together, so many of them like this—as though they knew each other's thoughts. It was a wonderful thing.

The crowd carried him along. Smoothly. Easily. He wasn't really walking. Just gliding. He was aware that the shuffling feet of the crowd made a muffled rhythm on the concrete sidewalk. It was slow, inevitable. An ominous sound, like a funeral march. With the regularity of a drumbeat. No. It's more like a pulse beat, he thought. It isn't a loud noise. It just keeps repeating over and over. But not that regular, because it builds up to something. It keeps building up.

The mounted cops rode their horses into the crowd. Trying to break it up into smaller groups. Then the rhythm was broken. Seconds later it started again. Each time the tempo was a little faster. He found he was breathing the same way. Faster and faster. As though he were running. There were more and more cops. All of them white. They had moved the colored cops out.

"They done that before," he muttered.

"What?" said the man next to him.

"They moved the colored cops out," he said.

He heard the man repeat it to someone standing beside him. It became part of the slow shuffling rhythm on the sidewalk. "They moved the colored cops." He heard it go back and back through the crowd until it was only a whisper of hate on the still, hot air. "They moved the colored cops."

As the crowd Shuffled back and forth in front of the hospital, he caught snatches of conversation. "The soldier was dead when they put him in the ambulance." "Always tryin' to fool us." "Christ! Just let me get my hands on one of them cops."

He was thinking about the hospital and he didn't take part in any of the conversations. Even now across the long span of years he could remember the helpless, awful rage that had sent him hurrying home from this same hospital. Not saying anything. Getting home by some kind of instinct.

Pink had come to this hospital when she had had her last child. He could hear again the cold contempt in the voice of the nurse as she listened to Pink's loud grieving. "You people have too many children anyway," she said.

It left him speechless. He had his hat in his hand and he remembered how he wished afterward that he'd put it on in front of her to show her what he thought of her. As it was, all the bitter answer that finally surged into his throat seemed to choke him. No words would come out. So he stared at her lean, spare body. He let his eyes stay a long time on her flat breasts. White uniform. White shoes. White stockings. White skin.

Then he mumbled, "It's too bad your eyes ain't white, too." And turned on his heel and walked out

It wasn't any kind of answer. She probably didn't even know what he was talking about. The baby dead, and all he could think of was to tell her her eyes ought to be white. White shoes, white stockings, white uniform, white skin, and blue eyes.

Staring at the hospital, he saw with satisfaction that frightened faces were appearing at the windows. Some of the lights went out. He began to feel that this night was the first time he'd ever really been alive. Tonight everything was going to be changed. There was a growing, swelling sense of power in him. He felt the same thing in the people around him.

The cops were aware of it, too, he thought. They were out in full force. Mounties, patrolmen, emergency squads. Radio cars that looked like oversize bugs crawled through the side streets. Waited near the curbs. Their white tops stood out in the darkness. "White folks riding in white cars." He wasn't aware that he had said it aloud until he heard the words go through the crowd. "White folks in white cars." The laughter that followed the words had a rough, raw rhythm. It repeated the pattern of the shuffling feet.

Someone said, "They got him at the station house. He ain't here." And the crowd started moving toward One Hundred Twenty-third Street.

Great God in the morning, William thought everybody's out here. There were girls in thin summer dresses, boys in long coats and tight-legged pants, old women dragging kids along by the hand. A man on crutches jerked himself past to the rhythm of the shuffling feet. A blind man tapped his way, through the center of the crowd, and it divided into two separate streams as it swept by him. At every street corner William noticed someone stopped to help the blind man up over the curb.

The street in front of the police station was so packed with people that he couldn't get near it. As far as he could see they weren't doing anything. They were simply standing there. Waiting for something to happen. He recognized a few of them: the woman with the loose, rolling eyes who sold shopping bags on One Hundred Twenty-fifth Street; the lucky-number peddler—the man with the white parrot on his shoulder; three sisters of the Heavenly Rest for All movement—barefooted women in loose white robes.

Then, for no reason that he could discover, everybody moved toward One Hundred Twenty-fifth Street. The motion of the crowd was slower now because it kept increasing in size as people coming from late church services were drawn into it. It was easy to identify them, he thought. The women wore white gloves. The kids were all slicked up. Despite the more gradual movement he was still being carried along effortlessly, easily. When someone in front of him barred his way, he pushed against the person irritably, frowning in annoyance because the smooth forward flow of his progress had been stopped.

It was Pink who stood in front of him. He stopped frowning when he recognized her. She had a brown-paper bag tucked under her arm, and he knew she had stopped at the corner store to get the big bottle of cream soda she always brought home on Sundays. The sight of it made him envious, for it meant that this Sunday had been going along in an orderly, normal fashion for her while he—She was staring at him so hard he was suddenly horribly conscious of the smell of the beer that had spilled on his shirt. He knew she had smelled it, too, by the tighter grip she took on her pocketbook.

"What you doing out here in this mob? A Sunday evening and you drinking beer," she said grimly.

For a moment he couldn't answer her. All he could think of was Sam. He almost said, "I Saw Sam shot this afternoon," and he swallowed hard.

"This afternoon I saw a white cop kill a colored soldier," he said. "In the bar where I was drinking beer. I saw it. That's why I'm here. The glass of beer I was drinking went on my clothes. The cop shot him in the back. That's why I'm here."

He paused for a moment, took a deep breath. This was how it ought to be, he decided. She had to know sometime and this was the right place to tell her. In this semidarkness, in this confusion of noises, with the low, harsh rhythm of the footsteps sounding against the noise of the horses' hoofs.

His voice thickened. "I saw Scummy yesterday," he went on. "He told me Sam's doing time at hard labor. That's why we ain't heard from him. A white MP shot him when he wouldn't go to the nigger end of a bus. Sam shot the MP. They gave him twenty years at hard labor."

He knew he hadn't made it clear how to him the soldier in the bar was Sam; that it was like seeing his own son shot before his very eyes. I don't even know whether the soldier was dead, he thought. What made me tell her about Sam out here in the street like this, anyway? He realized with a sense of shock that he really didn't care that he had told her. He felt strong, powerful, aloof. All the time he'd been talking he wouldn't look right at her. Now, suddenly, he was looking at her as though she were a total stranger. He was coldly wondering what she'd do. He was prepared for anything.

But he wasn't prepared for the wail that came from her throat. The sound hung in the hot air. It made the awful quivering in his stomach worse. It echoed and re-echoed the length of the street. Somewhere in the distance a horse whinnied. A woman standing way back in the crowd groaned as though the sorrow and the anguish in that cry were more than she could bear.

Pink stood there for a moment. Silent. Brooding. Then she lifted the big bottle of soda high in the air. She threw it with all her might. It made a wide arc and landed in the exact center of the plate-glass window of a furniture store. The glass crashed in with a sound like a gunshot.

A sigh went up from the crowd. They surged toward the broken window. Pink followed close behind. When she reached the window, all the glass had been broken in. Reaching far inside, she grabbed a small footstool and then turned to hurl it through the window of the dress shop next door. He kept close behind her, watching her as she seized a new missile from each store window that she broke.

Plate-glass windows were being smashed all up and down One Hundred Twenty-fifth Street—on both sides of the street. The violent, explosive sound fed the sense of power in him. Pink had started this. He was proud of her, for she had shown herself to be a fit mate for a man of his type. He stayed as close to her as he could. So in spite of the crashing, splintering sounds and the swarming, violent activity around him, he knew the exact moment when she lost her big straw hat; when she took off the high-heeled patent-leather shoes and flung them away, striding swiftly along in her stockinged feet. That her dress was hanging crooked on her.

He was right in back of her when she stopped in front of a hat store. She carefully appraised all the hats inside the broken window. Finally she reached out, selected a small hat covered with purple violets, and fastened it securely on her head.

"Woman's got good sense," a man said.

"Man, oh, man! Let me get in there," said a rawboned woman who thrust her way forward through the jam of people to seize two hats from the window.

A roar of approval went up from the crowd. From then on when a window was smashed it was bare of merchandise when the people streamed past it. White folks owned these stores. They'd lose and lose and lose, he thought with satisfaction. The words "twenty years" re-echoed in his mind. I'll be an old man, he thought. Then: I may be dead before Sam gets out of prison.

The feeling of great power and strength left him. He was so confused by its loss that he decided this thing happening in the street wasn't real. It was so dark, there were so many people shouting and running about, that he almost convinced himself he was having a nightmare. He was aware that his hearing had now grown so acute he could pick up the tiniest sounds: the quickened breathing and the soft, gloating laughter of the crowd; even the sound of his own heart beating. He could hear these things under the noise of the breaking glass, under the shouts that were coming from both sides of the street. They forced him to face the fact that this was no dream but a reality from which he couldn't escape. The quivering in his stomach kept increasing as he walked along.

Pink was striding through the crowd just ahead of him. He studied her to see if she, too, was feeling as he did. But the outrage that ran through her had made her younger. She was tireless. Most of the time she was leading the crowd. It was all he could do to keep up with her, and finally he gave up the attempt—it made him too tired.

He stopped to watch a girl who was standing in a store window, clutching a clothes model tightly around the waist "What's she want that for?" he said aloud. For the model had been stripped of clothing by the passing crowd, and he thought its pinkish torso was faintly obscene in its resemblance to a female figure.

The girl was young and thin. Her back was turned toward him, and there was something so ferocious about the way her dark hands gripped the naked model that he resisted the onward movement of the crowd to stare in fascination. The girl turned around. Her nervous hands were tight around the dummy's waist. It was Annie May.

"Ah, no!" he said, and let his breath come out with a sigh.

Her hands crept around the throat of the model and she sent it hurtling through the air above the heads of the crowd. It landed short of a window across the street. The legs shattered. The head rolled toward the curb. The waist snapped neatly in two. Only the torso remained whole and in one piece.

Annie May stood in the empty window and laughed with the crowd when someone kicked the torso into the street. He stood there, staring at her. He felt that now for the first time he understood her. She had never had anything but badly paying jobs—working for young white women who probably despised her. She was like Sam on that bus in Georgia. She didn't want just the nigger end of things, and here in Harlem there wasn't anything else for her. All along she'd been trying the only way she knew how to squeeze out of life a little something for herself.

He tried to get closer to the window where she was standing. He had to tell her that he understood. And the crowd, tired of the obstruction that he had made by standing still, swept him up and carried him past. He stopped thinking and let himself be carried along on a vast wave of feeling. There was so much plate glass on the sidewalk that it made a grind in noise under the feet of the hurrying crowd. It was a dull, harsh sound that set his teeth on edge and quickened the trembling of his stomach.

Now all the store windows that he passed were broken. The people hurrying by him carried tables, lamps, shoeboxes, clothing. A woman next to him held a wedding cake in her hands—it went up in tiers of white frosting with a small bride and groom mounted at the top. Her hands were bleeding, and he began to look closely at the people nearest him. Most of them, too, had cuts on their hands and legs. Then he saw there was blood on the sidewalk in front of the windows; blood dripping down the jagged edges of the broken windows. And he wanted desperately to go home.

He was conscious that the rhythm of the crowd had changed. It was faster, and it had taken on an ugly note. The cops were using their nightsticks. Police wagons drew up to the curbs. When they pulled away, they were full of men and women who carried loot from the stores in their hands.

The police cars slipping through the streets were joined by other cars with loudspeakers on top. The voices coming through the loudspeakers were harsh. They added to the noise and the confusion. He tried to listen to what the voices were saying. But the words had no meaning for him. He caught one phrase over and over: "Good people of Harlem." It made him feel sick.

He repeated the words "of Harlem." We don't belong anywhere, he thought. There ain't no room for us anywhere. There wasn't no room for Sam in a bus in Georgia. There ain't no room for us here in New York. There ain't no place but top floors. The top-floor black people. And he laughed, and the sound stuck in his throat.

After that he snatched a suit from the window of a men's clothing store. It was a summer suit. The material felt crisp and cool. He walked away with it under his arm. He'd never owned a suit like that. He simply sweated out the summer in the same dark pants he wore in winter. Even while he stroked the material, a part of his mind sneered—you got summer pants; Sam's got twenty years.

He was surprised to find that he was almost at Lenox Avenue, for he hadn't remembered crossing Seventh. At the corner the cops were shoving a group of young boys and girls into a police wagon. He paused to watch. Annie May was in the middle of the group. She had a yellow-fox jacket dangling from one hand.

"Annie May!" he shouted. "Annie May!" The crowd pushed him along faster and faster. She hadn't seen him. He let himself be carried forward by the movement of the crowd. He had to find Pink and tell her that the cops had taken Annie May.

He peered into the dimness of the street ahead of him, looking for her; then he elbowed his way toward the curb so that he could see the other side of the street. He forgot about finding Pink, for directly opposite him was the music store that he passed every night coming home from work. Young boys and girls were always lounging on the sidewalk in front of it. They danced a few steps while they listened to the records being played inside the shop. All the records sounded the same—a terribly magnified woman's voice bleating out a blues song in a voice that sounded to him like that of an animal in heat—an old animal, tired and beaten, but with an insinuating know-how left in her. The white men who went past the store smiled as their eyes lingered on the young girls swaying to the music.

"White folks got us comin' and goin'. Backwards and forwards," he muttered. He fought his way out of the crowd and walked toward a no-parking sign that stood in front of the store. He rolled it up over the curb. It was heavy, and the effort made him pant. It took all his strength to send it crashing through the glass on the door.

Almost immediately an old woman and a young man slipped inside the narrow shop. He followed them. He watched them smash the records that lined the shelves. He hadn't thought of actually breaking the records, but once he started he found the crisp, snapping noise pleasant. The feeling of power began to return. He didn't like these records, so they had to be destroyed.

When they left the music store there wasn't a whole record left. The old woman came out of the store last. As he hurried off up the street he could have sworn he smelled the sharp, acrid smell of smoke. He turned and looked back. He was right. A thin wisp of smoke was coming through the store door. The old woman had long since disappeared in the crowd.

Farther up the street he looked back again. The fire in the record shop was burning merrily. It was making a glow that lit up that part of the street. There was a new rhythm now. It was faster and faster. Even the voices coming from the loud-speakers had taken on the urgency of speed.

Fire trucks roared up the street. He threw his head back and laughed when he saw them. That's right, he thought. Burn the whole damn place down. It was wonderful. Then he frowned. "Twenty years at hard labor." The words came back to him. He was a fool. Fire wouldn't wipe that out. There wasn't anything that would wipe it out.

He remembered then that he had to find Pink. To tell her about Annie May. He overtook her in the next block. She's got more stuff, he thought. She had a table lamp in one hand, a large enamel kettle in the other. The lightweight summer coat drapped across her shoulders was so small it barely covered her enormous arms. She was watching a group of boys assault the steel gates in front of a liquor store. She frowned at them so ferociously he wondered what she was going to do. Hating liquor the way she did, he half expected her to cuff the boys and send them on their way up the street.

She turned and looked at the crowd in back of her. When she saw him she beckoned to him. "Hold these," she said. He took the lamp, the kettle, and the coat she held out to him, and he saw that her face was wet with perspiration. The print dress was darkly stained with it.

She fastened the hat with the purple flowers securely on her head. Then she walked over to the gate. "Git out the way," she said to the boys. Bracing herself in front of the gate, she started tugging at it. The gate resisted. She pulled at it with a sudden access of such furious strength that he was frightened. Watching her, he got the feeling that the resistance of the gate had transformed it in her mind. It was no longer a gate—it had become the world that had taken her son, and she was wreaking vengeance on it.

The gate began to bend and sway under her assault. Then it was down She stood there for a moment, staring at her hands—big drops of blood oozed slowly over the palms. Then she turned to the crowd that had stopped to watch.

"Come on, you niggers," she said. Her eyes were little and evil and triumphant. "Come on and drink up the white man's liquor." As she strode off up the street, the beflowered, hat dangled precariously from the back of her head.

When he caught up with her she was moaning, talking to herself in husky whispers, She stopped when she saw him and put her hand on his arm.

"It's hot, ain't it?" she said, panting.

In the midst of all this violence, the sheer commonplaceness of her question startled him. He looked at her closely. The rage that had been in her was gone, leaving her completely exhausted. She was breathing too fast in uneven gasps that shook her body. Rivulets of sweat streamed down her face. It was as though her triumph over the metal gate had finished her. The gate won anyway, he thought.

"Let's go home, Pink," he said, He had to shout to make his voice carry over the roar of the crowd, the sound of breaking glass.

He realized she didn't have the strength to speak, for she only nodded in reply to his suggestion, Once we get home she'll be all right, he thought. It was suddenly urgent that they get home, where it was quiet, where he could think, where he could take something to still the tremors in his stomach. He tried to get her to walk a little faster, but she kept slowing down until, when they entered their own street, it seemed to him they were barely moving.

In the middle of the block she stood still. "I can't make it," she said. "I'm too tired."

Even as he put his arm around her she started going down. He tried to hold her up, but her great weight was too much for him. She went down slowly, inevitably, like a great ship capsizing. Until all of her huge body was crumpled on the sidewalk.

"Pink," he said, "Pink. You gotta get up," he said it over and over again.

She didn't answer. He leaned over and touched her gently. Almost immediately afterward he straightened up. All his life, moments of despair and frustration had left him speechless—strangled by the words that rose in his throat. This time the words poured out.

He sent his voice raging into the darkness and the awful confusion of noises. "The sons of bitches," he shouted, "The sons of bitches."

African-American Music

A line from "How I Got Over," a gospel song written by Clara Ward and popularized by Mahalia Jackson, exclaims, "My soul looks back and wonders how I made it over." This line undoubtedly articulates a common sentiment of Blacks during their early experiences in America, first as slaves and then as freedmen. Their music was a large part of how they "got over." As in Africa, music for Africans in America continued to be an integral part of daily life. From field hollers, to work songs, to spirituals, gospels, blues, jazz and beyond, African-American music speaks to the world of the trials, triumphs, fears, and hopes of African-Americans.

A survey of African-American music reveals at least three things: (1) that the music has retained certain Africanisms (African survivals), (2) that the music is a history of how African Americans attempted to cope with an alien and hostile culture, and (3) that the music represents a combination of the old and the new, resulting in a style that is uniquely African American.

First of all, certain characteristics of African-American music can be identified as African. Among these are strong rhythm, syncopation, polyphony, repetition, improvisation, and collective participation. African-American music, like African music, tends to be driven by the beat, a beat designed to stimulate body movement, as there is a close link between music and dance, whether sacred or secular. Syncopation is the stressing of weak or customarily unstressed beats. It is that aspect of the music that makes listeners snap their fingers or tap their feet, thus also stimulating body movement. Polyphony means many sounds; several melodies and counter melodies might be heard in one musical piece. Repetition, improvisation, and collective participation all affect the length of the performance of a piece. Performers may repeat certain parts of the music or add additional words and phrases or create their own variations of the melody, all of which can be affected by the participation of the audience. The more feedback the performers receive from the audience, the more the performers tend to repeat and improvise, thereby extending the length of the piece. African-American performers thrive on audience feedback. The above characteristics can typically be found in Negro spirituals, in the blues, in gospel songs, and in jazz.

Originating during slavery, Negro spirituals are folk songs, for they sprang up among the people and did not have specific authors. Originally sung a cappella, these songs express strong religious sentiments ("Ev'ry Time I Feel the Spirit," "Lord, I Want to Be a Christian"); alienation ("Sometimes I Feel Like a Motherless Child," "I'm a-Rolling Through an Unfriendly World"); anticipation of freedom ("Oh, Freedom," "Free at Last"); and many other themes reflective of slave life. Spirituals draw heavily upon Old Testament stories: the plight of the Hebrew children, Joshua and the battle of Jericho, Daniel in the lion's den, and so on. Some spirituals are reworkings of Anglo-Saxon hymns, such as "Amazing Grace," "Jesus, Keep Me Near the Cross," and "Leaning on the Everlasting Arms." Spirituals were also used as a kind of code language whereby the slaves could communicate with each other about the Underground Railroad. Songs such as "Wade in the Water" and "Swing Low, Sweet Chariot" might convey a message for fugitive slaves to use a water route to keep the bloodhounds off their trail or to watch for someone who would be coming to carry them to freedom—Harriet Tubman, for example. The Fisk Jubilee Singers are credited with bringing world-wide attention to the spirituals; in 1871 they embarked on a tour to raise money for a financially struggling Fisk University.

The blues, like spirituals, also came from the folk tradition. Exactly when blues came into existence is open to conjecture, but Eileen Southern in The Music of Black Americans mentions the year 1902, the year Gertrude "Ma" Rainey claimed to have first heard a girl sing a plaintive song about a broken love relationship. Rainey, in turn, learned and performed the song and others like it in her own act, and because she was frequently asked what kind of songs these were, she simply said they were blues. Southern hastens to add that other musicians contended that the blues had no beginning; they "always been." At any rate, the blues, like spirituals, also addressed the problems of African-Americans; only they reflected a different set of problems, problems centered around the movement from slavery to freedom. Many blues focus on natural disasters that affected African-American livelihood ("Backwater Blues," "Boll Weevil Blues"); about movement, often in search of jobs or to escape a bad relationship ("Freight Train Blues," "Cholly Blues"); or about infidelity ("My Man Don't Love Me," "Hey Lady, Your Husband is Cheatin' on Us"). In this way blues can be a catharsis. Composing a song and/or singing about a problem brings an emotional release for the musicians. Blues are not always sad but rather often display irony and a sense of humor. The song "Hey Lady, Your Husband is Cheatin' on Us" is a good example of both. The wife and the lover are both being cheated on, and the lover ironically complains to the wife.

Musical accompaniment for the early blues was simple. The banjo, the guitar, homemade instruments or kazoos (toy instruments) were typically used. As the blues developed from country blues to city blues to urban or contemporary blues, more instruments were added. City blues singers, for example, were sometimes accompanied by an entire orchestra.

William Christopher (W. C.) Handy (1873–1958) was a performer, writer, and publisher of blues. He published his first piece, "Memphis Blues," in 1912. Handy's most famous blues is "Saint Louis Blues," known the world over. His publications helped to popularize the blues, earning him the title Father of the Blues.

Gospel songs, like spirituals, express the African-American religious beliefs; however, whereas the spirituals tended to focus on stories from the Old Testament, gospel songs focus more on stories of the New Testament. The term "gospel" means good news, hence the emphasis on stories from the four gospels—Matthew, Mark, Luke, and John—which detail the teachings and miracles of Jesus. Gospel songs express the belief that Jesus is still working miracles and can be counted on to solve whatever problems believers may be experiencing. The development of gospel songs coincided with the migration of Africans from the rural South to urban centers like New York and Chicago. First associated with the storefront churches of the Holiness and Pentecostal sects, gospel was not readily accepted by churches of other denominations, which claimed it was too loud and too rhythmic. According to Eileen Southern, the history of gospel music began when it was publicly endorsed at the 1930 Jubilee Meeting of the National Baptist Convention (472).

Much of the credit for the development of gospel music goes to Thomas A. Dorsey (1899–1993). Dorsey had previously been a blues singer, but after a serious illness, he began to work solely with gospel. He had migrated from Villa Rica, Georgia, to Chicago and joined the Pilgrim Baptist Church there in 1921. Dorsey's songs are classic examples of the fact that, like spirituals and blues, gospel grew out of the immediacy of the experiences of African-Americans. Dorsey's first hit, "If You See My Savior, Tell Him That You Saw Me" (1926), was written upon the death of a neighbor who had died after being ill for only 24 hours. At the time, Dorsey himself had been ill for several months; and seeing this young man die so abruptly had a profound effect on him. "Precious Lord," Dorsey's most famous song, was written in 1932, shortly after his first wife and baby died in childbirth. The words were formed out of the depth of Dorsey's despair, but the tune is that of an old Anglo Saxon hymn, "Must Jesus Bear the Cross Alone"—a combination of the old and the new.

Dorsey had a far-reaching effect on the development of African-American religious music, not only because he was a prolific writer of gospel songs but also because he started a number of trends in gospel music, such as the first organized gospel choir, the use of piano as accompaniment, and the gospel music convention. He fused the blues quality with the sanctified beat of the Holiness and Pentecostal churches and created a musical style that revived a church that had become staid and cold. Another very significant contribution of Dorsey's to gospel music was his association with Mahalia Jackson, known as the world's greatest gospel singer. He wrote many of her hits and was her accompanist for many years. In his 1974 Black World interview of Dorsey, Alfred Duckett calls Dorsey the "father" of the gospel music.

The secular counterpart of gospel music is jazz. The origin of the term "jazz" is not certain; but according to Eileen Southern, the term was being commonly used by 1918. Jazz, originally jass, developed in major towns along the Mississippi. One of these towns was New Orleans. Some have gone so far as to say that jazz started in New Orleans. It is generally agreed that New Orleans did much for the development of jazz because of the presence of large numbers of marching bands and the opportunity for African-Americans to be employed as musicians in the saloons and dance halls of the infamous Storyville. Here Creoles who were formally trained in music played alongside their Black brothers, who had no formal musical training, resulting again in a music that is uniquely African-American.

The classic New Orleans jazz band consisted of a cornet, a clarinet, and a rhythm section of drums, banjos, guitars, and basses. New Orleans was the birthplace of many famous jazz musicians, including Buddy Bolden, Jelly Roll Morton, and the legendary Louis Armstrong.

Jazz combines elements from the blues, ragtime, brass band and syncopated dance music. It is a way of playing music, employing the Africanisms discussed earlier. It is folk music, for like spirituals and blues, it was neither composed by a known individual nor written down. And even when musicians began to score jazz, much of what jazz musicians did could not be represented on paper. Consequently, the best way to learn to play jazz is to hear it, for the performers also become the composers. Early jazz utilized blues, spirituals, stomps, rags, and worksongs. Some examples are "The Beale Street Blues," "When the Saints Go Marching In," "Didn't He Ramble" and "John Henry."

Finally, African-American music is rich and varied. And while the music continues to evolve, there are those who are attempting to keep alive the old traditions. For example, one can hear the Negro spirituals performed by the Moses Hogan Chorale; the Hallelujah Singers of Beaufort, South Carolina; or the famed Morgan State University choir and choirs of other historically Black colleges and universities. Preservation Hall in New Orleans carries on the tradition of early jazz, and one need only listen to the radio to know that there is a revival of traditional blues and gospels. The story of a creative people who survived the horrors of slavery, and the obstacles of discrimination and segregation after slavery, continues to be told through their music.

Selected Bibliography

Blassingame, John W. *The Slave Community: Plantation Life in the Antebellem South.* New York: Oxford University Press, 1972.

Boeckman, Charles. *Cool, Hot and Blue: A History of Jazz for Young People.* Washington, D.C.: Luce, 1968.

Boyer, Horace C. "An Analysis of His Contributions: Thomas A. Dorsey, 'Father of Gospel Music.'" *Black World.* July 1974: 20–28.

Cleveland, J. Jefferson and William B. McClain. "A Historical Account of the Negro Spiritual." *Songs of Zion: Supplemental Worship Resources 12.* Nashville: Abingdon, 1981: 73.

Cohn, Lawrence. *Nothing But the Blues: The Music and the Musicians.* New York: Abbeville, 1993.

Collier, James Lincoln. *The Making of Jazz: a Comprehensive History.* New York: Dell, 1978.

Dahl, Linda. *Stormy Weather: The Music and Lives of a Century of Black Women.* New York: Pantheon, 1984.

DuBois, William Edward Burghart. *Souls of Black Folk.* New York: Bantam, 1989.

Duckett, Alfred. "An Interview with Thomas A. Dorsey." *Black World.* July 1974: 4–18.

Haskins, James. *Black Music in America: a History Through Its People.* New York: HarperCollins, 1987.
Heilbut, Tony. *The Gospel Sound: Good News and Bad Times.* New York: Simon & Shuster, 1971.
Levine, Lawrence W. *Afro-American Folk Thought from Slavery to Freedom.* New York: Oxford University Press, 1977.
Roberts, Storm. *Black Music of Two Worlds.* New York: Praeger, 1972.
Shaw, Arnold. *The Jazz Age: Popular Music in the 1920s.* New York: Oxford University Press, 1987.
Southern, Eileen. *The Music of Black Americans: A History.* 2nd ed. New York: Norton, 1983.

African-American Art

Like African-American literature, African-American art has its roots in West African countries such as Nigeria, Ghana, and the Ivory Coast, where people for centuries have carved and decorated objects like masks and cups for religious and domestic purposes. Separated from their African traditions through the odious intervention of the slave trade, early Black Americans expressed their creativity through making pottery, quilts, and other slave-crafted objects that recalled their homelands but were at the same time innovative.

After the Civil War, many skilled artists, wanting to perfect their crafts, followed the techniques and styles of the Old Masters. Henry Ossawa Tanner (1859–1937), while he most surely engaged in portraying Black life and culture in oil paintings such as Banjo Lesson, is best remembered for his religious paintings, especially *The Two Disciples at the Tomb* and *Flight into Egypt*. A number of African Americans, for example, Nelson A. Primus (1842–1916) and Grafton Tyler Brown (1841–1918), distinguished themselves in landscape painting or portraiture, neither of which was ethnic in orientation.

But the folk tradition, begun in slavery and concerned less with artistic elegance than with strong images of Blacks, continued to inform African-American art. With its primitive shapes and bright colors, Black folk art became a leading inspiration of the Harlem Renaissance, as is evidenced in the paintings of Romare Bearden (1911–88) and William Henry Johnson (1901–70).

Johnson, who studied in France and whose early landscapes resemble the work of French impressionist painter Paul Cezanne (1839–1906), was eventually to return to the simplicity of Black folk art in depicting Bible stories, street culture, and rural Southern scenes. One famous work is a silkscreen called *Going to Church*, which shows a silhouetted Black family in a cart drawn by a mule. They are going to church, but implied in the imagery is the African-American journey to freedom. The background of this deceptively childlike drawing shows a church and a school as opposing entities, while the brightly colored horizontal and vertical shapes in the foreground suggest a road, fields, and fences.

Romare Bearden, who also studied in Paris but who lived in Harlem during much of his life, was familiar with both folk art and the art and theories of the Harlem Renaissance. One of the most admired of all African-American artists, Bearden worked in a variety of artistic media, from watercolor to photography to collage. In his watercolor *Golgotha*, Bearden washes tints of pale pink and purple and red across the central image of Christ hanging from the cross, his bent, geometrical head suggesting an African mask. *Projections* is a collage, collage being a kind of art in which objects are applied to canvas or another suitable material, thus giving the art work a three-dimensional effect. In *Projections* Bearden takes a collection of photographs of African Americans and pastes them into protruding patterns. In another collage, *Family*, done shortly before his death, he depicts a prosperous and dignified Black couple holding a baby; several friends or attendants are with them in what appears to be a Christening. The collage, which expresses the elegance and centrality of the Black family, resembles a studio portrait, even though the figures themselves have an unrealistic, almost cartoon-like quality.

The painter Jacob Lawrence (born 1917) also projects a primitive, cartoon-like style in his paintings, many of them done in ordered narratives that depict Black history and Black heroes: the Haitian revolutionary Toussaint L'Ouverture; the American slaves, Frederick Douglass and Harriet Tubman. His most applauded work is *The Migration of the Negro,* a set of 60 small canvasses that tells the story of the Black exodus from the rural South to the urban North from 1916 to 1940. Using bold colors (oranges, black, yellows) and decisive forms, Lawrence delineates such themes as hunger, loneliness, violence, and prejudice, accompanying each 12″ × 18″ painting with a short and potent script that serves as its title.

The coming to power of African-Americans several decades later, during the Civil Rights Movement of the 1960s, coincided with a similar but more radical form of Black artistic expression. Many Black painters and sculptors spoke out in protest against racism in America, either aggressively or unobtrusively. Thus Elizabeth Catlett (b. 1919) created a number of sensitive prints on noted African Americans, including Malcolm X. The prints were versions of a basic process called lithography, in which a drawing is made on a stone or other hard surface that is treated, inked, and printed. Using her lithographic skills, Catlett, in the mid 1960s, created *Sharecropper*, a portrait similar in size to Leonardo da Vinci's *Mona Lisa*. It portrays an old Black woman, wrinkled from the sun and anguished from her life of servitude.

Another Black artist, Yvonne Catchings, used the collage medium to represent violence and protest in her painting *Detroit Riot*. In an energetic application of materials, Catchings paints a blood-red background, then glues onto its surface shards of glass, rubber, and other debris to show her despair at a city in collapse.

But there seems to be no 1960s protest painting quite as disturbing as *Castration*, a large oil by William Henderson (born 1943). The painting envisions the castration of a Black man by six Southern law enforcers whose pale, cruel faces reveal that they are "pigs," clansmen, devils, and other vile characters. All participate in the destruction of an African-American male. On the table a red, white and blue hatchet ironically implicates the American government. In its dramatic rendering, *Castration* does for art what Richard Wright's poem, "Between the World and Me," does for literature; it shows the inhumanity of the White race in its mistreatment of Black Americans.

Since the Civil Rights movement, more Black artists have been accepted by the academy, as teachers, curators, and artists in residence. One very prominent painter, Sam Gilliam (born 1933), has assured his place in the history of American art by proving that, race aside, he is one of the most accomplished of contemporary abstract expressionists. A member of the Washington (D. C.) Color School, Gilliam has been innovative in his use of poured paint and of folded or unsupported canvases. His non-representational acrylic entitled *April 4, 1969* is one of many paintings which combine his vivid use of color with spontaneous emotion.

One modern African-American sculptor, though, fits no category, having until recently stood outside of the history of African-American art. James Hampton was a Washington, D. C. janitor who lived in anonymity, driven only by his compulsion to erect a monumental altar made of junk. Hampton's spectacular sculpture has a title that mirrors its enormity: *The Throne of the Third Heaven of the Nations' Millennium General Assembly*. Constructed between 1950 and 1964, *The Throne* was created from discarded pieces of furniture and other scraps of wood that Hampton covered with silver and gold foil. It consists of 180 pieces, intricately patterned and symmetrically arranged; it measures 27 feet in length. The piece, with its grand design and intense spirituality, can be compared to Michelangelo's early sixteenth century fresco painted on the ceiling of the Sistine Chapel in Rome. But Michelangelo's painting of the Creation was a project for the most part supported by the Church and intended for public viewing, whereas Hampton's Throne is the private work of a janitor who created his masterpiece at night in a garage. Fortunately, the massive sculpture was saved after Hampton's death and donated to the National Museum of American Art.

The above account of African-American artists covers only a few of the many figures who have contributed to the Humanities. One of the best sources for further study is Samella S. Lewis's book, *African-American Art and Artists*, published in 1978 and reissued in 1990. Unfortunately, though, James Hampton is not listed there. One wonders how many other Black artists, still unknown and still unrecognized, are waiting to be discovered—perhaps a TV repair person or a kindergarten teacher or someone who has no job and spends time carving small wooden birds. Such individuals, recognized or not, would be part of a tradition of artists who, from slavery and before, have sought to express their creativity through exploring the visual.

Selected Bibliography

Bearden, Romare and Harry Henderson. *Six Black Masters of American Art.* New York: Doubleday, 1972.
Campbell, Mary et al. *Harlem Renaissance: Art of Black America.* New York: Harry N. Abrams, 1987.
Davis, Lenwood G. and Janet L. Sims. *Black Artists in the United States: An Annotated Bibliography of Books, Articles, and Dissertations on Black Artists.* Westport, CT: Greenwood, 1980.
Fax, Elton. *17 Black Artists.* New York: Dodd, Mead, 1971.
Hughes, Robert. *American Visions. Time:* Special Issue. Spring 1997.
Lawrence, Jacob. *The Migration Series.* Exhibition Catalog. New York: Museum of Modern Art, 1995.
Lewis, Samella S. *African-American Art and Artists.* Berkeley: University of California Press, 1990.
___, and Ruth G. Waddy. *Black Artists on Art, II.* Los Angeles: Contemporary Crafts, 1976.
Livingston, Jane and John Beardsley. *Black Folk Art in America, 1930–80.* Jackson: University Press of Mississippi, 1989.
Neal, Larry. "Any Day Now: Black Art and Black Liberation." *Ebony.* August 1970: 54–58, 62.
"Romare Bearden, 1911–1988." A Memorial Exhibition. New York City: ACA Galleries, May 11–June 10, 1989.
Thomison, Dennis, compiler. *The Black Artist in America: An Index to Reproductions.* Lanham, MD: Scarecrow, 1991.
Willett, Frank. *African Art.* New York: Praeger, 1971.

Native-American Literature

For many centuries, Native Americans created a vast number of myths, stories, and histories via the oral tradition. In the 19th century, Native Americans began publishing their narratives; the first Native-American autobiography was William Apes' *A Son of the Forest* (1829) while the first Native-American novel with a Native-American theme was Sophia Alice Callahan's *Wynema: A Child of the Forest* (1891). Another early narrative is Simon Pokagon's 1899 novel, *O-gi-maw-kwe-Mit-I-qua-ki (Queen of the Woods);* it contrasts traditional Potawatomi life before European-American invasion and laments changes in Native-American lifestyles. The 20th century marked the publication of contemporary Native-American narratives such as N. Scott Momaday's Pulitzer Prize-winning *House Made of Dawn* (1969), James Welch's *Winter in the Blood* (1974), and Leslie Marmon Silko's *Ceremony* (1977). However *Black Elk Speaks: Being the Life Story of a Holy Man of the Oglala Sioux* (1932), as told through John G. Neihardt, remains the most widely known narrative of Native-American life.

Black Elk was born in 1863 during the period in American history referred to as the Indian Wars (1860–1890), when Native Americans unsuccessfully fought to maintain their cultural identity and independence from federal encroachment. A member of the Oglala Sioux tribe, he inherited Black Elk after his father's, grandfather's, and great grandfather's name. His father and several of his uncles were medicine men. Black Elk would grow up to be a medicine man and wichasha wakon (holy man); consequently, his tribe considered his knowledge sacred, and the Sioux believed that Black Elk had supernormal powers.

A wasichu (White person) who believed Black Elk had supernormal powers was John Neihardt, author of "Song of the Indian Wars." The poem's hero is Crazy Horse, and coincidently Neihardt, while working on another poem, was referred to Black Elk, Crazy Horse's second cousin, after Neihardt sought an interview with someone who had firsthand knowledge of the Messianic dreams that various Native Americans experienced during the Indian Wars.

Flying Hawk, the interpreter, introduced the wichasha wakon and the wasichu to each other in August 1930 when Black Elk was 66 and almost blind. Before Neihardt could ask for information, Black Elk announced he would teach him about Native-American life and told him to return in the Spring. The following May, Neihardt returned to the Sioux reservation. Black Elk only spoke Sioux, so his son Ben served as interpreter, and Neihardt's daughter Enid was the stenographer. As a result of the collaboration between Native American and wasichu and between holy man and poet (whom Black Elk named Flaming Rainbow), *Black Elk Speaks* was published 18 years before Black Elk's death.

There are 25 chapters in the narrative. In the first chapter, "The Offering of the Pipe," Black Elk agrees to tell his life story, not because an individual life is important, but because his story is universally meaningful. He is not concerned with his days as a hunter, warrior, or traveler; his story is of the great vision given to him. Even though Black Elk has stated his objective, he still does not begin the history. He makes an offering of a sacred pipe to the Great Spirit for guidance during his narration. Black Elk explains the pipe's symbolism and history. He then acknowledges the Great Spirit's omnipotence and omniscience, prays for strength, perception, and understanding, while hoping that his weak yet earnest voice would be heard. He then ends his prayer before he and Neihardt smoke the pipe. In the remaining chapters, Black Elk contrasts Native-American life before and after the arrival of the wasichus and stresses the happy life of his people in their own land, harming no one, and only desiring to be left alone. His nostalgic story offers additional insight into a Native-American culture filled with bravery and shared responsibility. The land, ancestors, traditions, and spirits are revered. Young people are cherished, encouraged, made to feel needed, and other individuals are valued for their characters rather than their possessions. What Native Americans do not value is gold, which is one of the reasons wasichus drove them from their land. The arrival of the wasichus brought broken promises, wars, and lifestyle changes. Should the tribe follow Chief Red Cloud's example and accept the wasichus? Should they heed Crazy Horse's advice and remain a separate nation? Ultimately more and more Native Americans left their tepees for the gray boxes (housing provided by the wasichus).

Assimilation is the major concern of Native-American writers and poets. From the earliest published Native-American narrative to the most recent, the struggle to survive in a hostile world while maintaining cultural identity is presented. Native-American poets such as Courtney Moyah, James Welch, and Ray Young Bear eloquently lament the loss of a way of life. The Navajo ceremonial verse "Night Chant: Concluding Rite, First Day—The Sacred Mountain" provides a glimpse into the past, a proud, and noble heritage that today's young writers cherish.

The Night Chant

Navajo

Concluding Rite, First Day

The Sacred Mountains

In a holy place with a god I walk,
In a holy place with a god I walk,
On Tsisnadzhini with a god I walk,
On a chief of mountains with a god I walk,
In old age wandering with a god I walk, 5
On a hail of beauty with a god I walk.

From the base of the east.
From the base of Tsisnadzhini.
From the house made of mirage,
From the story made of mirage, 10
From the doorway of rainbow,
The path out of which is the rainbow,
The rainbow passed out with me.
The rainbow raised up with me
Through the middle of broad fields, 15
The rainbow returned with me.
To where my house is visible,
The rainbow returned with me.
To the roof of my house,
The rainbow returned with me. 20
To the entrance of my house,
The rainbow returned with me.
To just within my house,
The rainbow returned with me.
To my fireside, 25
The rainbow returned with me.
To the center of my house,
The rainbow returned with me.
At the fore part of my house with the dawn,

The Talking God sits with me. 30
The House God sits with me.
Pollen Boy sits with me.
Grasshopper Girl sits with me.
In beauty Estsánatlehi, my mother, for her I return.
Beautifully my fire to me is restored. 35
Beautifully my possessions are to me restored.
Beautifully my soft goods to me are restored.
Beautifully my hard goods to me are restored.
Beautifully my horses to me are restored.
Beautifully my sheep to me are restored. 40
Beautifully my old men to me are restored.
Beautifully my old women to me are restored.
Beautifully my young men to me are restored.
Beautifully my young women to me are restored.
Beautifully my children to me are restored. 45
Beautifully my wife to me is restored.
Beautifully my chiefs to me are restored.
Beautifully my country to me is restored.
Beautifully my fields to me are restored.
Beautifully my house to me is restored. 50
Talking God sits with me.
House God sits with me.
Pollen Boy sits with me.
Grasshopper Girl sits with me.
Beautifully white corn to me is restored. 55
Beautifully yellow corn to me is restored.
Beautifully blue corn to me is restored.
Beautifully corn of all kinds to me is restored.
In beauty may I walk.
All day long may I walk. 60
Through the returning seasons may I walk.
[line untranslated]
Beautifully . . . will I possess again.
[line untranslated]
Beautifully birds 65
Beautifully joyful birds . . .
On the trail marked with pollen may I walk.
With grasshoppers about my feet may I walk.
With dew about my feet may I walk.
With beauty may I walk. 70
With beauty before me, may I walk.
With beauty behind me, may I walk.
With beauty above me, may I walk.
With beauty below me, may I walk.
With beauty all around me, may I walk. 75
In old age wandering on a trail of beauty, lively, may I walk.
In old age wandering on a trail of beauty, living again, may I walk.
It is finished in beauty.
It is finished in beauty.

In One Day My Mother Grew Old

Courtney Moyah

In one day my mother grew old
I walked the trail, looking down
onto the ground. In one day
my mother grew old.

I came to the end of the trail near
the river. I stopped to listen to
the flowing water. In one day
my mother grew old.

I looked at the river. I heard
waves from a river beyond sight.
The waves wanted to say something,
but went away. In one day
my mother grew old.

I walked and looked at my mother's face.
She was quiet. She was life. She
waved as I came closer and held me in
her arms until water from the river
came to my eyes.

James Welch (1940–)

James Welch, son of a Blackfoot father and a Gros Vendre mother, was born on a Blackfoot reservation in Browning, Montana, on November 18, 1940. He was enrolled in schools on Blackfoot as well as Fort Belknap reservations and in Minneapolis, Minnesota. Welch studied at the University of Minnesota and Northern Montana College prior to receiving a B.A. from the University of Montana. He worked as a laborer, forest service employee, firefighter, and counselor at the University of Montana's Upward Bound Program before deciding to write full-time. Welch was appointed to the Literature Panel of the National Endowment of the Arts and the Montana State Board of Pardons.

Welch's first book, *Riding the Earthboy 40* (1971), is a collection of poems. His poetry has been published in various anthologies and many periodicals including *New American Review, The New Yorker, Poetry, Poetry Northwest,* and *South Dakota Review.* Welch's first novel, *Winter in the Blood* (1974), focuses on a young man's search for his identity and has been hailed as a stellar example of contemporary Native-American literature. His subsequent novels, *The Death of Jim Loney* (1979), *Fools Crow* (1987), and *The Indian Lawyer* (1990) have also won critical acclaim. Welch's poems, novels, and his first nonfiction work, *Killing Custer: The Battle of the Little Bighorn and the Fate of the Plains Indians* (1994) illustrate his belief that Native-American literature must be written by Native Americans.

Selected Bibliography

Bruchac, Joseph, ed. *Songs from This Earth on Turtle's Back: Contemporary American Indian Poetry.* New York: Greenfield Review Press, 1983.

Dodge, Robert K. and Joseph B. McCullough, eds. *Voices from Wah' Kon-Tah: Contemporary Poetry of Native Americans.* New York: International, 1974.

Lincoln, Kenneth. *Native American Renaissance.* Berkeley: University of California Press, 1983.

Niatum, Duane, ed. *Carriers of the Dream Wheel: Contemporary Native American Poetry.* New York: Harper Row, 1973.

The Man from Washington

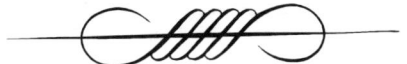

James Welch

The end came easy for most of us.
Packed away in our crude beginnings
in some far corner of a flat world,
we didn't expect much more
than firewood and buffalo robes   5
to keep us warm. The man came down,
a slouching dwarf with rainwater eyes,
and spoke to us. He promised
that life would go on as usual,
that treaties would be signed, and everyone—   10
man, woman and child—would he inoculated
against a world in which we had no part,
a world of wealth, promise and fabulous disease.

Ray A. Young Bear (1950–)

Ray A. Young Bear, a member of the Mesquaki (formerly Sauk and Fox) tribe, was born on November 12, 1950, in Tama, Iowa. He studied art at Grinnell College and the University of Northern Iowa at Cedar Falls. Young Bear, who has been writing poetry since 1966, acknowledges that he creates a poem in his native Mesquaki tongue before translating his thoughts into English. His poetry appears in many anthologies and has been published in various periodicals, such as *American Poetry Review, Northwest Review,* and *Pembroke Magazine.* Young Bear's first published collection of verse is *Winter of the Salamander* (1980), and among his more recent works are *The Invisible Musician! Poems* (1990), *Black Eagle Child: The Facepaint Narratives* (1992), and *Remnants of the First Earth* (1997). Young Bear is recognized as a leading contemporary American poet.

Selected Bibliography

Bruchac, Joseph, ed. *Songs from This Earth on Turtle's Back: Contemporary American Indian Poetry.* New York: Greenfield Review Press, 1983.

Dodge, Robert K. and Joseph B. McCullough, eds. *Voices from Wah'Kon-Tah: Contemporary Poetry of Native Americans.* New York: International, 1974.

Lourie, Dick, ed. *Come to Power: Eleven Contemporary American Indian Poets.* Trumansburg, N.Y.: Crossing Press, 1974.

Niatum, Duane, ed. *Carriers of the Dream Wheel: Contemporary Native American Poetry.* New York: Harper Row, 1973.

Rosen, Kenneth, ed. *Voices of the Rainbow: Contemporary Poetry by American Indians.* New York: Viking, 1975.

One Chip of Human Bone

Ray A. Young Bear

one chip of human bone

it is almost fitting
to die on railroad tracks.

i can easily understand
how they felt on their
staggered walks back.

there is something about
trains, drinking, and being
an indian with nothing to lose.

from *Black Elk Speaks: Being the Life of a Holy Man of the Oglala Sioux*

As Told Through John G. Neihardt (Flaming Rainbow)

Chapter III

The Great Vision

What happened after that until the summer I was nine years old is not a story. There were winters and summers, and they were good; for the Wasichus had made their iron road along the Platte and traveled there. This had cut the bison herd in two, but those that stayed in our country with us were more than could be counted, and we wandered without trouble in our land.

Now and then the voices would come back when I was out alone, like someone calling me, but what they wanted me to do I did not know. This did not happen very often, and when it did not happen, I forgot about it; for I was growing taller and was riding horses now and could shoot prairie chickens and rabbits with my bow. The boys of my people began very young to learn the ways of men, and no one taught us; we just learned by doing what we saw, and we were warriors at a time when boys now are like girls.

It was the summer when I was nine years old, and our people were moving slowly towards the Rocky Mountains. We camped one evening in a valley beside a little creek just before it ran into the Greasy Grass, and there was a man by the name of Man Hip who liked me and asked me to eat with him in his tepee.

While I was eating, a voice came and said: "It is time; now they are calling you." The voice was so loud and clear that I believed it, and I thought I would just go where it wanted me to go. So I got right up and started. As I came out of the tepee, both my thighs began to hurt me, and suddenly it was like waking from a dream, and there wasn't any voice. So I went back into the tepee, but I didn't want to eat. Man Hip looked at me in a strange way and asked me what was wrong. I told him that my legs were hurting me.

The next morning the camp moved again, and I was riding with some boys. We stopped to get a drink from a creek, and when I got off my horse, my legs crumpled under me and I could not walk. So the boys helped me up and put me on my horse; and when we camped again that evening, I was sick. The next day the camp moved on to where the different bands of our people were coming together, and I rode in a pony drag, for I was very sick. Both my legs and both my arms were swollen badly and my face was all puffed up.

When we had camped again, I was lying in our tepee and my mother and father were sitting beside me. I could see out through the opening, and there two men were coming from the clouds, headfirst like arrows slanting down, and I knew they were the same that I had seen before. Each now carried a long spear, and from the points of these a jagged lightning flashed. They came clear down to the ground this time and stood a little way off and looked at me and said: "Hurry! Come! Your Grandfathers are calling you!"

Then they turned and left the ground like arrows slanting upward from the bow. When I got up to follow, my legs did not hurt me any more and I was very light. I went outside the tepee, and yonder where the men with flaming spears were going, a little cloud was coming very fast. It came and stooped and took me and turned back to where it came from, flying fast. And when I looked down I could see my mother and my father yonder, and I felt sorry to be leaving them.

Then there was nothing but the air and the swiftness of the little cloud that bore me and those two men still leading up to where white clouds were piled like mountains on a wide blue plain, and in them thunder beings lived and leaped and flashed.

Now suddenly there was nothing but a world of cloud, and we three were there alone in the middle of a great white plain with snowy hills and mountains staring at us; and it was very still; but there were whispers.

Then the two men spoke together and they said: "Behold him, the being with four legs!"

I looked and saw a bay horse standing there, and he began to speak: "Behold me!" he said, "My life-history you shall see." Then he wheeled about to where the sun goes down, and said: "Behold them! Their history you shall know."

I looked, and there were twelve black horses yonder all abreast with necklaces of bison hoofs, and they were beautiful, but I was frightened, because their manes were lightning and there was thunder in their nostrils.

Then the bay horse wheeled to where the great white giant lives (the north) and said: "Behold!" And yonder there were twelve white horses all abreast. Their manes were flowing like a blizzard wind and from their noses came a roaring, and all about them white geese soared and circled.

Then the bay wheeled round to where the sun shines continually (the east) and bade me look; and there twelve sorrel horses, with necklaces of elk's teeth, stood abreast with eyes that glimmered like the day-break star and manes of morning light.

Then the bay wheeled once again to look upon the place where you are always facing (the south), and yonder stood twelve buckskins all abreast with horns upon their heads and manes that lived and grew like trees and grasses.

And when I had seen all these, the bay horse said: "Your Grandfathers are having a council. These shall take you; so have courage."

Then all the horses went into formation, four abreast—the blacks, the whites, the sorrels, and the buckskins—and stood behind the bay, who turned now to the west and neighed; and yonder suddenly the sky was terrible with a storm of plunging horses in all colors that shook the world with thunder, neighing back.

Now turning to the north the bay horse whinnied, and yonder all the sky roared with a mighty wind of running horses in all colors, neighing back.

And when he whinnied to the east, there too the sky was filled with glowing clouds of manes and tails of horses in all colors singing back. Then to the south he called, and it was crowded with many colored, happy horses, nickering.

Then the bay horse spoke to me again and said: "See how your horses all come dancing!" I looked, and there were horses, horses everywhere—a whole skyful of horses dancing round me.

"Make haste!" the bay horse said; and we walked together side by side, while the blacks, the whites, the sorrels, and the buckskins followed, marching four by four.

I looked about me once again, and suddenly the dancing horses without number changed into animals of every kind and into all the fowls that are, and these fled back to the four quarters of the world from whence the horses came, and vanished.

Then as we walked, there was a heaped up cloud ahead that changed into a tepee, and a rainbow was the open door of it; and through the door I saw six old men sitting in a row.

The two men with the spears now stood beside me, one on either hand, and the horses took their places in their quarters, looking inward, four by four. And the oldest of the Grandfathers spoke with a kind voice and said: "Come right in and do not fear." And as he spoke, all the horses of the four quarters neighed to cheer me. So I went in and stood before the six, and they looked older than men can ever be—old like hills, like stars.

The oldest spoke again: "Your Grandfathers all over the world are having a council, and they have called you here to teach you." His voice was very kind, but I shook all over with fear now, for I knew that these were not old men, but the Powers of the World. And the first was the Power of the West; the second, of the North; the third, of the East; the fourth, of the South; the fifth, of the Sky; the sixth, of the Earth. I knew this, and was afraid, until the first Grandfather spoke again: "Behold them yonder where the sun goes down, the thunder beings! You shall see, and have from them my power; and they shall take you to the high and lonely center of the earth that you may see; even to the place where the sun continually shines, they shall take you there to understand."

And as he spoke of understanding, I looked up and saw the rainbow leap with flames of many colors over me.

Now there was a wooden cup in his hand and it was full of water and in the water was the sky.

"Take this," he said. "It is the power to make live, and it is yours."

Now he had a bow in his hands. "Take this," he said. "It is the power to destroy, and it is yours."

Then he pointed to himself and said: "Look close at him who is your spirit now, for you are his body and his name is Eagle Wing Stretches."

And saying this, he got up very tall and started running toward where the sun goes down; and suddenly he was a black horse that stopped and turned and looked at me, and the horse was very poor and sick; his ribs stood out.

Then the second Grandfather, he of the North, arose with a herb of power in his hand, and said: "Take this and hurry." I took and held it toward the black horse yonder. He fattened and was happy and came prancing to his place again and was the first Grandfather sitting there.

The second Grandfather, he of the North, spoke again: "Take courage, younger brother," he said; "on earth a nation you shall make live, for yours shall be the power of the white giant's wing, the cleansing wind." Then he got up very tall and started running toward the north; and when he turned toward me, it was a white goose wheeling. I looked about me now, and the horses in the west were thunders and the horses of the north were geese. And the second Grandfather sang two songs that were like this:

> "They are appearing, may you behold!
> They are appearing, may you behold!
> The thunder nation is appearing, behold!
> They are appearing, may you behold!
> They are appearing, may you behold!
> The white geese nation is appearing, behold!"

And now it was the third Grandfather who spoke, he of where the sun shines continually. "Take courage, younger brother," he said, "for across the earth they shall take you!" Then he pointed to where the daybreak star was shining, and beneath the star two men were flying. "From them you shall have power," he said, "from them who have awakened all the beings of the earth with roots and legs and wings." And as he said this, he held in his hand a peace pipe which had a spotted eagle outstretched upon the stem; and this eagle seemed alive, for it was poised there, fluttering, and its eyes were looking at me. "With this pipe," the Grandfather said, "you shall walk upon the earth, and whatever sickens there you shall make well." Then he pointed to a man who was bright red all over, the color of good and of plenty, and as he pointed, the red man lay down and rolled and changed into a bison that got up and galloped toward the sorrel horses of the east, and they too turned to bison, fat and many.

And now the fourth Grandfather spoke, he of the place where you are always facing (the south), whence comes the power to grow. "Younger brother," he said, "with the powers of the four quarters you shall walk, a relative. Behold, the living center of a nation I shall give you, and with it many you shall save." And I saw that he was holding in his hand a bright red stick that was alive, and as I looked it sprouted at the top and sent forth branches, and on the branches many leaves came out and murmured and in the leaves the birds began to sing. And then for just a little while I thought I saw beneath it in the shade the circled villages of people and every living thing with roots or legs or wings, and all were happy. "It shall stand in the center of the nation's circle," said the Grandfather, "a cane to walk with and a people's heart; and by your powers you shall make it blossom."

Then when he had been still a little while to hear the birds sing, he spoke again: "Behold the earth!" So I looked down and saw it lying yonder like a hoop of peoples, and in the center bloomed the holy stick that was a tree, and where it stood there crossed two roads, a red one and a black. "From where the giant lives (the north) to where you always face (the south) the red road goes, the road of good," the Grandfather said, "and on it shall your nation walk. The black road goes from where the thunder beings live (the west) to where the sun continually shines (the east), a fearful road, a road of troubles and of war. On this also you shall walk, and from it you shall have the power to destroy a people's foes. In four ascents you shall walk the earth with power."

I think he meant that I should see four generations, counting me, and now I am seeing the third.

Then he rose very tall and started running toward the south, and was an elk; and as he stood among the buckskins yonder, they too were elks.

Now the fifth Grandfather spoke, the oldest of them all, the Spirit of the Sky. "My boy," he said, "I have sent for you and you have come. My power you shall see!" He stretched his arms and turned into a spotted eagle hovering. "Behold," he said, "all the wings of the air shall come to you, and they and the winds and the stars shall be like relatives. You shall go across the earth with my power." Then the eagle soared above my head and fluttered there; and suddenly the sky was full of friendly wings all coming toward me.

Now I knew the sixth Grandfather was about to speak, he who was the Spirit of the Earth, and I saw that he was very old, but more as men are old. his hair was long and white, his face was all in wrinkles and his eyes were deep and dim. I stared at him, for it seemed I knew him somehow; and as I stared, he slowly changed, for he was growing backwards into youth, and when he had become a boy, I knew that he was myself with all the years that would be mine at last. When he was old again, he said: "My boy, have courage, for my power shall be yours, and you shall need it, for your nation on the earth will have great troubles. Come."

He rose and tottered out through the rainbow door, and as I followed I was riding on the bay horse who had talked to me at first and led me to that place.

Then the bay horse stopped and faced the black horses of the west, and a voice said: "They have given you the cup of water to make live the greening day, and also the bow and arrow to destroy." The bay neighed, and the twelve black horses came and stood behind me, four abreast.

The bay faced the sorrels of the east, and I saw that they had morning stars upon their foreheads and they were very bright. And the voice said: "They have given you the sacred pipe and the power that is peace, and the good red day." The bay neighed, and the twelve sorrels stood behind me, four abreast.

My horse now faced the buckskins of the south, and a voice said: "They have given you the sacred stick and your nation s hoop, and the yellow day; and in the center of the hoop you shall set the stick and make it grow into a shielding tree, and bloom." The bay neighed, and the twelve buckskins came and stood behind me, four abreast.

Then I knew that there were riders on all the horses there behind me, and a voice said: "Now you shall walk the black road with these; and as you walk, all the nations that have roots or legs or wings shall fear you."

So I started, riding toward the east down the fearful road, and behind me came the horsebacks four abreast—the blacks, the whites, the sorrels, and the buckskins—and far away above the fearful road the daybreak star was rising very dim.

I looked below me where the earth was silent in a sick green light, and saw the hills look up afraid and the grasses on the hills and all the animals; and everywhere about me were the cries of frightened birds and sounds of fleeing wings. I was the chief of all the heavens riding there, and when I looked behind me, all the twelve black horses reared and plunged and thundered and their manes and tails were whirling hail and their nostrils snorted lightning. And when I looked below again, I saw the slant hail falling and the long, sharp rain, and where we passed, the trees bowed low and all the hills were dim.

Now the earth was bright again as we rode. I could see the hills and valleys and the creeks and rivers passing under. We came above a place where three streams made a big one—a source of mighty waters—and something terrible was there. Flames were rising from the waters and in the flames a blue man lived. The dust was floating all about him in the air, the grass was short and withered, the trees were wilting, two-legged and four-legged beings lay there thin and panting, and wings too weak to fly.

Then the black horse riders shouted "Hoka hey!" and charged down upon the blue man, but were driven back. And the white troop shouted, charging, and was beaten; then the red troop and the yellow.

And when each had failed, they all cried together: "Eagle Wing Stretches, hurry!" And all the world was filled with voices of all kinds that cheered me, so I charged. I had the cup of water in one hand and in the other was the bow that turned into a spear as the bay and I swooped down, and the spear's head was sharp lightning. It stabbed the blue man's heart, and as it struck I could hear the thunder rolling and many voices that cried "Un-hee!," meaning I had killed. The flames died. The trees and grasses were not withered any more and murmured happily together, and every living being cried in gladness with whatever voice it had. Then the four troops of horsemen charged down and struck the dead body of the blue man, counting coup; and suddenly it was only a harmless turtle.

You see, I had been riding with the storm clouds, and had come to earth as rain, and it was drouth that I had killed with the power that the Six Grandfathers gave me. So we were riding on the earth now down along the river flowing full from the source of waters, and soon I saw ahead the circled village of a people in the valley. And a Voice said: "Behold a nation; it is yours. Make haste, Eagle Wing Stretches!"

I entered the village, riding, with the four horse troops behind me—the blacks, the whites, the sorrels, and the buckskins; and the place was filled with moaning and with mourning for the dead. The wind was blowing from the south like fever, and when I looked around I saw that in nearly every tepee the women and the children and the men lay dying with the dead.

So I rode around the circle of the village, looking in upon the sick and dead, and I felt like crying as I rode. But when I looked behind me, all the women and the children and the men were getting up and coming forth with happy faces.

And a Voice said: "Behold, they have given you the center of the nation's hoop to make it live."

So I rode to the center of the village, with the horse troops in their quarters round about me, and there the people gathered. And the Voice said: "Give them now the flowering stick that they may flourish, and the sacred pipe that they may know the power that is peace, and the wing of the white giant that they may have endurance and face all winds with courage."

So I took the bright red stick and at the center of the nation's hoop I thrust it in the earth. As it touched the earth it leaped mightily in my hand and was a waga chun, the rustling tree, very tall and full of leafy branches and of all birds singing. And beneath it all the animals were mingling with the people like relatives and making happy cries. The women raised their tremolo of joy, and the men shouted all together: "Here we shall raise our children and be as little chickens under the mother sheo's wing."

Then I heard the white wind blowing gently through the tree and singing there, and from the east the sacred pipe came flying on its eagle wings, and stopped before me there beneath the tree, spreading deep peace around it.

Then the daybreak star was rising, and a Voice said: "It shall be a relative to them; and who shall see it, shall see much more, for thence comes wisdom; and those who do not see it shall be dark." And all the people raised their faces to the east, and the star's light fell upon them, and all the dogs barked loudly and the horses whinnied.

Then when the many little voices ceased, the great Voice said: "Behold the circle of the nation's hoop, for it is holy, being endless, and thus all powers shall be one power in the people without end. Now they shall break camp and go forth upon the red road, and your Grandfathers shall walk with them." So the people broke camp and took the good road with the white wing on their faces, and the order of their going was like this:

First, the black horse riders with the cup of water; and the white horse riders with the white wing and the sacred herb; and the sorrel riders with the holy pipe; and the buckskins with the flowering stick. And after these the little children and the youths and maidens followed in a band.

Second, came the tribe's four chieftains, and their band was all young men and women.

Third, the nation's four advisers leading men and women neither young nor old.

Fourth, the old men hobbling with their canes and looking to the earth.

Fifth, old women hobbling with their canes and looking to the earth.

Sixth, myself all alone upon the bay with the bow and arrows that the First Grandfather gave me. But I was not the last; for when I looked behind me there were ghosts of people like a trailing fog as far as I could see—grandfathers of grandfathers and grandmothers of grandmothers without number. And over these a great Voice—the Voice that was the South—lived, and I could feel it silent.

And as we went the Voice behind me said: "Behold a good nation walking in a sacred manner in a good land!"

Then I looked up and saw that there were four ascents ahead, and these were generations I should know. Now we were on the first ascent, and all the land was green. And as the long line climbed, all the old men and women raised their hands, palms forward, to the far sky yonder and began to croon a song together, and the sky ahead was filled with clouds of baby faces.

When we came to the end of the first ascent we camped in the sacred circle as before, and in the center stood the holy tree, and still the land about us was all green.

Then we started on the second ascent, marching as before, and still the land was green, but it was getting steeper. And as I looked ahead, the people changed into elks and bison and all four-footed beings and even into fowls, all walking in a sacred manner on the good red road together. And I myself was a spotted eagle soaring over them. But just before we stopped to camp at the end of that ascent, all the marching animals grew restless and afraid that they were not what they had been, and began sending forth voices of trouble, calling to their chiefs. And when they camped at the end of that ascent, I looked down and saw that leaves were falling from the holy tree.

And the Voice said: "Behold your nation, and remember what your Six Grandfathers gave you, for thenceforth your people walk in difficulties."

Then the people broke camp again, and saw the black road before them towards where the sun goes down, and black clouds coming yonder; and they did not want to go but could not stay. And as they walked the third ascent, all the animals and fowls that were the people ran here and there, for each one seemed to have his own little vision that he followed and his own rules; and all over the universe I could hear the winds at war like wild beasts fighting.

And when we reached the summit of the third ascent and camped, the nation s hoop was broken like a ring of smoke that spreads and scatters and the holy tree seemed dying and all its birds were gone. And when I looked ahead I saw that the fourth ascent would be terrible.

Then when the people were getting ready to begin the fourth ascent, the Voice spoke like some one weeping, and it said: "Look there upon your nation." And when I looked down, the people were all changed back to human, and they were thin, their faces sharp, for they were starving. Their ponies were only hide and bones, and the holy tree was gone.

And as I looked and wept, I saw that there stood on the north side of the starving camp a sacred man who was painted red all over his body, and he held a spear as he walked into the center of the people, and there he lay down and rolled. And when he got up, it was a fat bison standing there, and where the bison stood a sacred herb sprang up right where the tree had been in the center of the nation's hoop. The herb grew and bore four blossoms on a single stem while I was looking—a blue, a white, a scarlet, and a yellow—and the bright rays of these flashed to the heavens.

I know now what this meant, that the bison were the gift of a good spirit and were our strength, but we should lose them, and from the same good spirit we must find another strength. For the people all seemed better when the herb had grown and bloomed, and the horses raised their tails and neighed and pranced around, and I could see a light breeze going from the north among the people like a ghost; and suddenly the flowering tree was there again at the center of the nation's hoop where the four-rayed herb had blossomed.

I was still the spotted eagle floating, and I could see that I was already in the fourth ascent and the people were camping yonder at the top of the third long rise. It was dark and terrible about me, for all the winds of the world were fighting. It was like rapid gun-fire and like whirling smoke, and like women and children wailing and like horses screaming all over the world.

I could see my people yonder running about, setting the smoke-flap poles and fastening down their tepees against the wind, for the storm cloud was coming on them very fast and black, and there were frightened swallows without number fleeing before the cloud.

Then a song of power came to me and I sang it there in the midst of that terrible place where I was. It went like this:

> A good nation I will make live.
> This the nation above has said.
> They have given me the power to make over.

And when I had sung this, a Voice said: "To the four quarters you shall run for help, and nothing shall be strong before you. Behold him!"

Now I was on my bay horse again, because the horse is of the earth, and it was there my power would be used. And as I obeyed the Voice and looked, there was a horse all skin and bones yonder in the west, a faded brownish black. And a Voice there said: "Take this and make him over; and it was the four-rayed herb that I was holding in my hand. So I rode above the poor horse in a circle, and as I did this I could hear the people yonder calling for spirit power, "A-hey! a-hey! a-hey! a-hey!" Then the poor horse neighed and rolled and got up, and he was a big, shiny, black stallion with dapples all over him and his mane about him like a cloud. He was the chief of all the horses; and when he snorted, it was a flash of lightning and his eyes were like the sunset star. He dashed to the west and neighed, and the west was filled with a dust of hoofs, and horses without number, shiny black, came plunging from the dust. Then he dashed toward the north and neighed, and to the east and to the south, and the dust clouds answered, giving forth their plunging horses without number—whites and sorrels and buckskins, fat, shiny, rejoicing in their fleetness and their strength. It was beautiful, but it was also terrible.

Then they all stopped short, rearing, and were standing in a great hoop about their black chief at the center, and were still. And as they stood, four virgins, more beautiful than women of the earth can be, came through the circle, dressed in scarlet, one from each of the four quarters, and stood about the great black stallion in their places; and one held the wooden cup of water, and one the white wing, and one the pipe, and one the nation's hoop. All the universe was silent, listening; and then the great black stallion raised his voice and sang. The song he sang was this:

"My horses, prancing they are coming.
My horses, neighing they are coming;
Prancing, they are coming.
All over the universe they come.
They will dance; may you behold them."

(4 times)

A horse nation, they will dance. May you behold them.

(4 times)

His voice was not loud, but it went all over the universe and filled it. There was nothing that did not hear, and it was more beautiful than anything can be. It was so beautiful that nothing anywhere could keep from dancing. The virgins danced, and all the circled horses. The leaves on the trees, the grasses on the hills and in the valleys, the waters in the creeks and in the rivers and the lakes, the four-legged and the two-legged and the wings of the air—all danced together to the music of the stallion's song.

And when I looked down upon my people yonder, the cloud passed over, blessing them with friendly rain, and stood in the east with a flaming rainbow over it.

Then all the horses went singing back to their places beyond the summit of the fourth ascent, and all things sang along with them as they walked.

And a Voice said: "All over the universe they have finished a day of happiness." And looking down I saw that the whole wide circle of the day was beautiful and green, with all fruits growing and all things kind and happy.

Then a Voice said: "Behold this day, for it is yours to make. Now you shall stand upon the center of the earth to see, for there they are taking you."

I was still on my bay horse, and once more I felt the riders of the west, the north, the east, the south, behind me in formation, as before, and we were going east. I looked ahead and saw the mountains there with rocks and forests on them, and from the mountains flashed all colors upward to the heavens. Then I was standing on the highest mountain of them all, and round about beneath me was the whole hoop of the world. And while I stood there I saw more than I can tell and I understood more than I saw; for I was seeing in a sacred manner the shapes of all things in the spirit, and the shape of all shapes as they must live together like one being. And I saw that the sacred hoop of my people was one of many hoops that made one circle, wide as daylight and as starlight, and in the center grew one mighty flowering tree to shelter all the children of one mother and one father. And I saw that it was holy.

Then as I stood there, two men were coming from the east, head first like arrows flying, and between them rose the daybreak star. They came and gave a herb to me and said: "With this on earth you shall undertake anything and do it." It was the day-break-star herb, the herb of understanding, and they told me to drop it on the earth. I saw it falling far, and when it struck the earth it rooted and grew and flowered, four blossoms on one stem, a blue, a white, a scarlet, and a yellow; and the rays from these streamed upward to the heavens so that all creatures saw it and in no place was there darkness.

Then the Voice said: "Your Six Grandfathers—now you shall go back to them."

I had not noticed how I was dressed until now, and I saw that I was painted red all over, and my joints were painted black, with white stripes between the joints. My bay had lightning stripes all over him, and his mane was cloud. And when I breathed, my breath was lightning.

Now two men were leading me, head first like arrows slanting upward—the two that brought me from the earth. And as I followed on the bay, they turned into four flocks of geese that flew in circles, one above each quarter, sending forth a sacred voice as they flew: Br-r-r-p, br-r-r-p, br-r-r-p, br-r-r-p!

Then I saw ahead the rainbow flaming above the tepee of the Six Grandfathers, built and roofed with cloud and sewed with thongs of lightning; and underneath it were all the wings of the air and under them the animals and men. All these were rejoicing, and thunder was like happy laughter.

As I rode in through the rainbow door, there were cheering voices from all over the universe, and I saw the Six Grandfathers sitting in a row, with their arms held toward me and their hands, palms out; and behind them in the cloud were faces thronging, without number, of the people yet to be.

"He has triumphed!" cried the six together, making thunder. And as I passed before them there, each gave again the gift that he had given me before—the cup of water and the bow and arrows, the power to make live and to destroy; the white wing of cleansing and the healing herb; the sacred pipe; the flowering stick. And each one spoke in turn from west to south, explaining what he gave as he had done before, and as each one spoke he melted down into the earth and rose again; and as each did this, I felt nearer to the earth.

Then the oldest of them all said: "Grandson, all over the universe you have seen. Now you shall go back with power to the place from whence you came, and it shall happen yonder that hundreds shall be sacred, hundreds shall be flames! Behold!"

I looked below and saw my people there, and all were well and happy except one, and he was lying like the dead—and that one was myself. Then the oldest Grandfather sang, and his song was like this:

> "There is someone lying on earth in a sacred manner.
> There is someone—on earth he lies.
> In a sacred manner I have made him to walk."

Now the tepee, built and roofed with cloud, began to sway back and forth as in a wind, and the flaming rainbow door was growing dimmer. I could hear voices of all kinds crying from outside: "Eagle Wing Stretches is coming forth! Behold him!"

When I went through the door, the face of the day of earth was appearing with the daybreak star upon its forehead; and the sun leaped up and looked upon me, and I was going forth alone.

And as I walked alone, I heard the sun singing as it arose, and it sang like this:

> "With visible face I am appearing.
> In a sacred manner I appear.
> For the greening earth a pleasantness I make.
> The center of the nation's hoop I have made pleasant.
> With visible face, behold me!
> The four-leggeds and two-leggeds, I have made them to walk;
> The wings of the air, I have made them to fly.
> With visible face I appear.
> My day, I have made it holy."

When the singing stopped, I was feeling lost and very lonely. Then a Voice above me said: "Look back!" It was a spotted eagle that was hovering over me and spoke. I looked, and where the flaming rainbow tepee, built and roofed with cloud, had been, I saw only the tall rock mountain at the center of the world.

I was all alone on a broad plain now with my feet upon the earth, alone but for the spotted eagle guarding me. I could see my people's village far ahead, and I walked very fast, for I was homesick now. Then I saw my own tepee, and inside I saw my mother and my father bending over a sick boy that was myself. And as I entered the tepee, some one was saying: "The boy is coming to; you had better give him some water."

Then I was sitting up; and I was sad because my mother and my father didn't seem to know I had been so far away.

Latin-American Literature

Latin-American literature grows from richly diverse cultural traditions which were in contact in the New World. As early as the 14th century, Aztecs wrote in Nahuatl; Mayans narrated myths and legends in their language that are still used today. Yet what is known as Latin-American literature is the discourse that dates from the 15th century Spanish conquest. The product of the blend of the art of Africans, Asians, and Europeans who populate Central and South America, the Latin-American literary tradition has begun to gain world recognition. "The Boom," a literary movement of the 1960s, was named to mark the universal acclaim of these contemporary narratives. Among its authors, the Colombian, Gabriel Garcia Marquez, stands out as the creator of *One Hundred Years of Solitude,* for which he received the Nobel Prize (1984). Macondo, the novel's fictive world, functions as a metaphor for the social and political relations throughout Latin America, and it is a synthesis of magical realism or mythic epiphanies and historical realities.

Most typically, however, Latin-American letters tend to follow a double trajectory. Some works give priority to aesthetics (art for art's sake), while others are valued principally for reflecting the political or social commitments of their authors and times. Jorge Luis Borges (1899–1986), an Argentine aesthete, was a key contributor to the development of contemporary Latin-American narratives. His innovations in narrative techniques and his inclusion of the philosophical ideas of Schoepenhauer, Kafka, and Chesterton as transformed thematic raw material for his stories created his distinctive style. Educated in Geneva (1914–1918), Borges taught English literature at the University of Buenos Aires and lectured publicly on Anglo-Saxon languages. As the director of the Biblioteca Nacional of Buenos Aires, he had at hand the literature of the world, with which he enriched his narratives. In his stories, Borges uses the library to symbolize the universe and the labyrinth to depict enigmas and human suffering from unsolvable metaphysical questions. "The Garden of the Forking Paths" demonstrates the author's preoccupation with time, with paths that divide in simultaneous and infinite directions.

"Ma Lucia: The Great Story Teller" represents the other pole of Latin-American literary production and stands for a renewed interest in history and documentary narratives. Estaban Montejo (1858–1966), a freedman or ex-slave, dictated the narrative to Miguel Barnet, a Cuban scholar, who published the Spanish version in 1965. This excerpt is from the translation *The Autobiography of a Runaway Slave* (1993). Along with a description of Ma Lucia, Montejo mentions santeria and other practices of African inspiration, along with images of daily life among slaves on plantations in 19th century Cuba. It is one of the only two known Cuban slave testimonies to date and thus differs from the more abundant slave narratives of North America that have created their own space in the American literary tradition. Montejo's testimony moves from the margins to the center, along with voices of feminist authors, such as Rigoberta Menchu, the Nobel laureate (1994), who dictated Guatemala's strife.

from *The Autobiography of a Runaway Slave*

Estaban Montejo (1858?–1966)
and Miguel Barnet (1940–)

[Ma Lucia, the great storyteller]

What the old men enjoyed most was telling jokes and stories. They told stories all the time, morning, noon and night, they were at it constantly. There were so many stories that it was often difficult to keep track of them, you go so muddled up. I always pretended to be listening, but to be honest, by the end it was all whirling round in my head. There were three or four African elders at Ariosa. There was a difference between the Africans and the Creoles. The various Africans understood each other, but the Creoles hardly ever understood the Africans. They used to listen to them singing, but they didn't understand them. I got on all right with them because I spent my whole life listening to them. They were fond of me, too.

I still remember Ma Lucia. I first met her outside Ariosa, I don't recall whether it was at Remedios or Zulueta, but in any case I met her again long afterwards at Santa Clara, when I went there to a fiesta. I got on well with Ma Lucia. She was a black-skinned Negress, rather tall, a Lucumi by birth. After I got to know her she devoted most of her time to *santeria*. She had a big collection of godchildren, being so well-known. Ma Lucia was a great story-teller. She spent hours ironing her clothes, her white costume and cambric blouse, out of vanity, and she wore her hair in a piled-up style which you never see nowadays. She said it was African. She made sweets and *amalá* which she sold in the streets and in the plantation town when she did the rounds, and she made a lot of money.

She finally bought herself a house in Santa Clara after the war, which she left to a daughter. One day she called me and said, "You're a good, quiet man, I'm going to tell you something," and she began telling me all sorts of African stories. Unfortunately, almost all the stories and things I hear get muddled in my memory, and I don't know whether I'm talking about an elephant or a mouse. Old age does this to you. There are some things I remember clearly, but old age is old age, and it isn't given you for pleasure.

The point is, Ma Lucia started telling me about African customs which I never saw here, and nor did she either, which is why they were in her memory. She told me that in her country all the men ever did was fell trees, while the women had to clear the ground and bring in the food, and then cook meals for the family, which was very big. She said her own family was bigger than a slave settlement. I suppose this is because in Africa women give birth every year. I once saw a photograph of Africa, and all the women had swollen bellies and bare tits. I don't recall seeing such a spectacle in Cuba. Certainly it was quite different in the barracoon—the women there wore layers of clothes and covered their breasts. Well, not to wander too far from Ma Lucia, what she said about the elephants was very strange; whenever she saw one of those circuses which went from village to village, with elephants and monkeys, she would say, "Look, Creole, you don't know what an elephant is! Those aren't elephants you see in the circus, elephants in my country are much higher, high as a palm-tree heart."I was struck dumb. It really did seem a bit much to me, especially when she went on to say that in her country elephants weighed five or six hundred pounds. We boys couldn't help laughing at that, though we didn't let on to her. A lot of her stories were lies, but some might have been true. Well, let's say I thought they were lies, though the others thought they were the truth. Heaven help anyone who tried to tell one of those old women she was wrong!

I remember the story of the tortoise and the toad; she must have told it to me a hundred times. The tortoise and the toad had this big feud going for years, and the toad used to deceive the tortoise because he was frightened of her and thought she was stronger than him. One day the toad got hold of a big bowl of food and presented it to the tortoise, setting it down right under her nose, almost in her mouth. When the tortoise saw the bowl she took a fancy to it and gobbled it so fast she choked. It never even crossed her mind that the toad had put it there for a reason. She was very simple-minded, and so it was easy to trick her. After that, feeling full and satisfied, she started wandering through the forest in search of the toad, who had hidden himself in a cave. When the toad saw her in the distance, he called out "Here I am, tortoise, look." She looked but couldn't see him, and after a while she got tired and went away till she came across a heap of dry' straw and lay down to sleep. The toad seized her while she was asleep and poisoned her by peeing over her, and she didn't even wake up because she had eaten so heavily. The moral of this story is that people shouldn't be greedy, and you should trust no one. An enemy might offer you a meal merely to trick you.

Ma Lucia went on telling me about the toad. She was afraid of toads because, she said, they had a fatal poison in their veins instead of blood. The proof of this is that when you harm one by hitting it with a stick or a stone, it will follow you and poison you through the mouth or the nose, usually the mouth, because nearly everyone sleeps with their mouth open.

She told me that tigers were treacherous animals who climbed trees so as to be able to spring down on to men's backs and kill them. But they would seize women by their parts and force them to do dirty things with them, like the orang-outangs. But the orang-outangs were worse. According to Ma Lucia an orang-outang could tell a woman by her smell and capture her quite easily, so she couldn't even move. All monkeys are like that, like men with tails, but dumb.

Monkeys often fall in love with women. There have been cases like this in Cuba. I heard of two women of rich families who slept with monkeys, two sisters. One of them came from Santa Clara: I don't remember much about the other one, but she must have had children, because I saw monkeys lording it about in her house. I had to go along there one day, I can't remember why, and there was this monkey sitting in a chair in the doorway. That's why I think that the elders were sometimes speaking the truth—it was just that we had not seen these things for ourselves, so we either disbelieved them or laughed at them. Today, after so many years, I find myself thinking about all this again, and to tell the truth, I am coming to the conclusion that the African was a wise man in all matters. Some people say they were no better than monkeys off the trees—there's always some bloody white going round saying things like that—but having known them, I think differently. They weren't the least bit like animals. They taught me many things without being able to read or write—customs, which are more important than knowledge: to be polite, not to meddle in other peoples affairs, to speak softly, to be respectful and religious, to work hard. They used to say, "Water falls on the arum plant but it never gets wet," which was a warning to me not to get involved in arguments. They advised me to listen and take note so as to be able to stick up for myself, but not to talk too much. A person who talks too much ties himself in knots. Lots of people put their foot in it simply because they let their tongues run away with them.

The Garden of Forking Paths

Jorge Luis Borges

On page 22 of Liddell Hart's *History of World War I* you will read that an attack against the Serre-Montauban line by thirteen British divisions (supported by 1,400 artillery pieces), planned for the 24th of July, 1916, had to be postponed until the morning of the 29th. The torrential rains, Captain Liddell Hart comments, caused this delay, an insignificant one, to be sure.

The following statement, dictated, reread and signed by Dr. Yu Tsun, former professor of English at the *Hochschule* at Tsingtao, throws an unsuspected light over the whole affair. The first two pages of the document are missing.

". . . and I hung up the receiver. Immediately afterwards, I recognized the voice that had answered in German. It was that of Captain Richard Madden. Madden's presence in Viktor Runeberg's apartment meant the end of our anxieties and—but this seemed, *or should have seemed,* very, secondary to me—also the end of our lives. It meant that Runeberg had been arrested or murdered. Before the sun set on that day, I would encounter the same fate. Madden was implacable. Or rather, he was obliged to be so. An Irishman at the service of England, a man accused of laxity and perhaps of treason, how could he fail to seize and be thankful for such a miraculous opportunity: the discovery, capture, maybe even the death of two agents of the German Reich? I went up to my room; absurdly I locked the door and threw myself on my back on the narrow iron cot. Through the window I saw the familiar roofs and the cloud-shaded six o'clock sun. It seemed incredible to me that that day without premonitions or symbols should be the one of my inexorable death. In spite of my dead father, in spite of having been a child in a symmetrical garden of Hai Feng, was I—now—going to die? Then I reflected that everything happens to a man precisely, precisely *now*. Centuries of centuries and only in the present do things happen; countless men in the air, on the face of the earth and the sea, and all that really is happening is happening to me . . . The almost intolerable recollection of Madden's horselike face banished these wanderings. In the midst of my hatred and terror (it means nothing to me now to speak of terror, now that I have mocked Richard Madden, now that my throat yearns for the noose) it occurred to me that that tumultuous and doubtless happy warrior did not suspect that I possessed the Secret. The name of the exact location of the new British artillery park on the River Ancre. A bird streaked across the gray sky and blindly I translated it into an airplane and that airplane into many (against the French sky) annihilating the artillery station with vertical bombs. If only my mouth, before a bullet shattered it, could cry out that secret name so it could be heard in German . . . My human voice was very weak. How might I make it carry to the ear of the Chief? To the ear of that sick and hateful man who knew nothing of Runeberg and me save that we were in Staffordshire and who was waiting in vain for our report in his arid office in Berlin, endlessly examining newspapers . . . I said out loud: *I must flee*. I sat up noiselessly, in a useless perfection of silence, as if Madden were already lying in wait for me. Something—perhaps the mere vain ostentation of proving my resources were nil—made me look through my pockets. I found what I knew I would find. The American watch, the nickel chain and the square coin, the key ring with the incriminating useless keys to Runeberg's apartment, the notebook, a letter which I resolved to destroy immediately (and which I did not destroy), a crown, two shillings and a few pence, the red and blue pencil, the handkerchief, the revolver with one bullet. Absurdly, I took it in my hand and weighed it in order to inspire courage within myself. Vaguely I thought that a pistol report can be heard at a great distance. In ten minutes my plan was perfected. The telephone book listed the name of the only person capable of transmitting the message; he lived in a suburb of Fenton, less than a half hour's train ride away.

I am a cowardly man, I say it now, now that I have carried to its end, a plan who perilous nature no one can deny. I know its execution was terrible. I didn't do it for Germany, no. I care nothing for a barbarous country which imposed upon me the abjection of being a spy. Besides, I know of a man from England—a modest man—who for me is no less than Goethe. I talked with him for scarcely an hour, but during that hour he was Goethe . . . I did it because I sensed that the Chief somehow feared people of my race—for the innumerable ancestors who merge within me. I wanted to prove to him that a yellow man could save his armies. Besides, I had to flee from Captain Madden. His hands and his voice could call at my door at any moment. I dressed silently, bade farewell to myself in the mirror, went downstairs, scrutinized the peaceful street and went out. The station was not far from my home, but I judged it wise to take a cab. I argued that in this way I ran less risk of being recognized; the fact is that in the deserted street I felt myself visible and vulnerable, infinitely so. I remember that I told the cab drive to stop a short distance before the main entrance. I got out with voluntary, almost painful slowness; I was going to the village of Ashgrove but I bought a ticket for a more distant station. The train left within a very few minutes, at eight-fifty. I hurried; the next one would leave at nine-thirty. There was hardly a soul on the platform. I want through the coaches; I remember a few farmers, a woman dressed in mourning, a young boy who was reading with fervor the *Annals* of Tacitus, a wounded and happy soldier. The coaches jerked forward at last. A man whom I recognized ran in vain to the end of the platform. It was Captain Richard Madden. Shattered, trembling, I shrank into the far corner of the seat, away from the dreaded window.

From this broken state I passed into an almost abject felicity. I told myself that the duel had already begun and that I had won the first encounter by frustrating, even if for forty minutes, even if by a stroke of fate, the attack of my adversary. I argued that this slightest of victories foreshadowed a total victory. I argued (no less fallaciously) that my cowardly felicity proved that I was a man capable of carrying out the adventure successfully. From this weakness I took strength that did not abandon me. I foresee that man will resign himself each day to more atrocious undertakings; soon there will be no one but warriors and brigands; I give them this counsel: *The author of an atrocious undertaking ought to imagine that he has already accomplished it, ought to impose upon himself a future as irrevocable as the past.* Thus I proceeded as my eyes of a man already dead registered the elapsing of that day, which was perhaps the last, and the diffusion of the night. The train ran gently along, amid ash trees. It stopped, almost in the middle of the fields. No one announced the name of the station. "Ashgrove?" I asked a few lads on the platform. "Ashgrove," they replied. I got off.

A lamp enlightened the platform but the faces of the boys were in shadow. One questioned me, "Are you going to Dr. Stephen Albert's house?" Without waiting for my answer, another said, "The house is a long way from here, but you won't get lost if you take this road to the left and at every crossroads turn again to your left." I tossed them a coin (my last), descended a few stone steps and started down the solitary road. It went downhill, slowly. It was of elemental earth; overhead the branches were tangled; the low, full moon seemed to accompany me.

For an instant, I thought that Richard Madden in some way had penetrated my desperate plan. Very quickly, I understood that that was impossible. The instructions to turn always to the left reminded me that such was the common procedure for discovering the central point of certain labyrinths. I have some understanding of labyrinths: not for nothing am I the great grandson of the Ts'ui Pên who was governor of Yunnan and who renounced worldly power in order to write a novel that might be even more populous than the *Hung Lu Meng* and to construct a labyrinth in which all men would become lost. Thirteen years he dedicated to these heterogeneous tasks, but the hand of a stranger murdered him—and his novel was incoherent and no one found the labyrinth. Beneath English trees I meditated on that lost maze: I imagined it inviolate and perfect at the secret crest of a mountain; I imagined it erased by rice fields or beneath the water; I imagined it infinite, no longer composed of octagonal kiosks and returning paths, but of rivers and provinces and kingdoms . . . I thought of a labyrinth of labyrinths, of one sinuous spreading labyrinth that would encompass the past and the future and in some way involve the stars. Absorbed in these illusory images, I forgot my destiny of one pursued. I felt myself to be, for an unknown period of time, an abstract perceiver of the world. The vague, living countryside, the moon, the remains of the day worked on me, as well as the slope of the road which eliminated any possibility of weariness. The afternoon was intimate, infinite. The road descended and forked among the now confused meadows. A high-pitched, almost syllabic music approached and receded in the shifting of the wind, dimmed by leaves and distance. I thought that a man can be an enemy of other men, of the moments of other men, but not of a country; not of fireflies, words, gardens, streams of water, sunsets. Thus I arrived before a tall, rusty gate. Between the iron bars I made out a poplar grove and a pavilion. I understood suddenly two things, the first trivial, the second almost unbelievable: the music came from the pavilion, and the music was Chinese. For precisely that reason I had openly accepted it without paying it any heed. I do not remember whether there was a bell or whether I knocked with my hand. The sparkling of the music continued.

From the rear of the house within a lantern approached: a lantern that the trees sometimes striped and sometimes eclipsed, a paper lantern that had the form of a drum and the color of the moon. A tall man bore it. I didn't see his face for the light blinded me. He opened the door and said slowly, in my own language: "I see that the pious Hsi Pêng persists in correcting my solitude. You no doubt wish to see the garden?"

I recognized the name of one of our consuls and I replied, disconcerted, "The garden?"

"The garden of forking paths."

Something stirred in my memory and I uttered with incomprehensible certainty, "The garden of my ancestor Ts'ui Pên."

"Your ancestor? Your illustrious ancestor? Come in."

The damp path zigzagged like those of my childhood. We came to a library of Eastern and Western books. I recognized bound in yellow silk several volumes of the Lost Encyclopedia, edited by the Third Emperor of the Luminous Dynasty but never printed. The record on the phonograph revolved next to a bronze phoenix. I also recall a *famille rose* vase and another, many centuries older, of that shade of blue which our craftsmen copied from the potters of Persia . . .

Stephen Albert observed me with a smile. He was, as I have said, very tall, sharp-featured, with gray eyes and a gray beard. He told me that he had been a missionary in Tientsin "before aspiring to become a Sinologist."

We sat down—I on a long, low divan, he with his back to the window and a tall circular clock. I calculated that my pursuer, Richard Madden, could not arrive for at least an hour. My irrevocable determination could wait.

"An astounding fate, that of Ts'ui Pên," Stephen Albert said. "Governor of his native province, learned in astronomy, in astrology and in the tireless interpretation of the canonical books, chess player, famous poet and calligrapher—he abandoned all this in order to compose a book and a maze. He renounced the pleasures of both tyranny and justice, of his populous couch, of his banquets and even of erudition—all to close himself up for thirteen years in the Pavilion of the Limpid Solitude. When he died, his heirs found nothing save chaotic manuscripts. His family, as you may be aware, wished to condemn them to the fire; but his executor—a Taoist or Buddhist monk—insisted on their publication."

"We descendants of Ts'ui Pên," I replied, "continue to curse that monk. Their publication was senseless. The book is an indeterminate heap of contradictory drafts. I examined it once: in the third chapter the hero dies, in the fourth he is alive. As for the other undertaking of Ts'ui Pên, his labyrinth . . ."

"Here is Ts'ui Pên's labyrinth," he said, indicating a tall lacquered desk.

"An ivory labyrinth!" I exclaimed. "A minimum labyrinth."

"A labyrinth of symbols," he corrected. "An invisible labyrinth of time. To me, a barbarous Englishman, has been entrusted the revelation of this diaphanous mystery. After more than a hundred years, the details are irretrievable; but it is not hard to conjecture what happened. Ts'ui Pên must have said once: *I am withdrawing to write a book.* And another time: *I am withdrawing to construct a labyrinth.* Every one imagined two works; to no one did it occur that the book and the maze were one and the same thing. The Pavilion of the Limpid Solitude stood in the center of a garden that was perhaps intricate; that circumstance could have suggested to the heirs a physical labyrinth. Ts'ui Pên died; no one in the vast territories that were his came upon the labyrinth; the confusion of the novel suggested to me that *it* was the maze. Two circumstances gave me the correct solution of the problem. One: the curious legend that Ts'ui Pên had planned to create a labyrinth which would be strictly infinite. The other: a fragment of a letter I discovered."

Albert rose. He turned his back on me for a moment; he opened a drawer of the black and gold desk. He faced me and in his hands he held a sheet of paper that had once been crimson, but was now pink and tenuous and cross-sectioned. The fame of Ts'ui Pên as a calligrapher had been justly won. I read, uncomprehendingly and with fervor, these words written with a minute brush by a man of my blood: *I leave to the various futures (not to all) my garden of forking paths.* Wordlessly, I returned the sheet. Albert continued:

"Before unearthing this letter, I had questioned myself about the ways in which a book can be infinite. I could think of nothing other than a cyclic volume, a circular one. A book whose last page was identical with the first, a book which had the possibility of continuing indefinitely. I remembered too that night which is at the middle of the Thousand and One Nights when Scheherazade (through a magical oversight of the copyist) begins to relate word for word the story of the Thousand and One Nights, establishing the risk of coming once again to the night when she must repeat it, and thus on to infinity. I imagined as well a Platonic, hereditary work, transmitted from father to son, in which each new individual adds a chapter or corrects with pious care the pages of his elders. These conjectures diverted me; but none seemed to correspond, not even remotely, to the contradictory chapters of Ts'ui Pên. In the midst of this perplexity, I received from Oxford the manuscript you have examined. I lingered, naturally, on the sentence: *I leave to the various futures (not to all) my garden of forking paths.* Almost instantly, I understood: 'The garden of forking paths' was the chaotic novel; the phrase 'the various futures (not to all)' suggested to me the forking in time, not in space. A broad rereading of the work confirmed the theory. In all fictional works, each time a man is confronted with several alternatives, he chooses one and eliminates the others; in the fiction of Ts'ui Pên, he chooses—simultaneously—all of them. He *creates,* in this way, diverse futures, diverse times which themselves also proliferate and fork. Here, then, is the explanation of novel's contradictions. Fang, let us say, has a secret; a stranger calls at his door; Fang resolves to kill him. Naturally, there are several possible outcomes: Fang can kill the intruder, the intruder can kill Fang, they both can escape, they both can die, and so forth. In the work of Ts'ui Pên, all possible outcomes occur; each one is the point of departure for other forkings. Sometime, the paths of this labyrinth converge: for example, you arrive at this house, but in one of the possible pasts you are my enemy, in another, my friend. If you will resign yourself to my incurable pronunciation, we shall read a few pages."

His face, within the vivid circle of the lamplight, was unquestionably that of an old man but with something unalterable about it, even immortal. He read with slow precision two versions of the same epic chapter. In the first, an army marches to a battle across a lonely mountain; the horror of the rocks and shadows makes the men undervalue their lives and they gain an easy victory. In the second, the same army traverses a palace where a great festival is taking place; the resplendent battle seems to them a continuation of the celebration, and they win the victory. I listened with proper veneration to these ancient narratives, perhaps less admirable in themselves than the fact that they had been created by my blood and were being restored to me by a man of a remote empire, in the course of a desperate adventure, on a Western isle. I remember the last words, repeated in each version like a secret commandment: *Thus fought the heroes, tranquil their admirable hearts, violent their swords, resigned to kill and to die.*

From that moment on, I felt about me and within my dark body an invisible, intangible swarming. Not the swarming of the divergent, parallel and finally coalescent armies, but a more inaccessible, more intimate agitation that they in some manner prefigured. Stephen Albert continued:

"I don't believe that your illustrious ancestor played idly with these variations. I don't consider it credible that he would sacrifice thirteen years to the infinite execution of a rhetorical experiment. In your country, the novel is a subsidiary from of literature; in Ts'ui Pên's time it was a despicable form. Ts'ui Pên was a brilliant novelist, but he was also a man of letters who doubtless did not consider himself a mere novelist. The testimony of his contemporaries proclaims—and his life fully confirms—his metaphysical and mystical interests. Philosophic controversy usurps a good part of the novel. I know that of all problems, none disturbed him so greatly nor worked upon him so much as the abysmal problem of time. Now then, the latter is the only problem that does not figure in the pages of the *Garden*. He does not even use the word that signifies *time*. How do you explain this voluntary omission?"

I proposed several solutions—all unsatisfactory. We discussed them. Finally Stephen Albert said to me:

"In a riddle whose answer is chess, what is the only prohibited word?"

I thought a moment and replied, "The word *chess*."

"Precisely," said Albert. *The Garden of Forking Paths* is an enormous riddle or parable whose theme is time: this recondite cause prohibits its mention. To omit a word always, to resort to inept metaphors and obvious periphrases, is perhaps the most emphatic way of stressing it. That is the tortuous method preferred, in each of the meanderings of his indefatigable novel, by the oblique Ts'ui Pên. I have compared hundreds of manuscripts, I have corrected the errors that the negligence of the copyists has introduced, I have guessed the plan of this chaos, I have re-established—believe I have re-established—the primordial organization, I have translated the entire work: it is clear to me that not once does he employ the word 'time.' The explanation is obvious: *The Garden of Forking Paths* is an incomplete, but not false, image of the universe as Ts'ui Pên conceives it. In contrast to Newton and Schopenhauer, your ancestor did not believe in a uniform, absolute time. He believed in an infinite series of times, in a growing, dizzying net of divergent, convergent and parallel times. This network of times which approached one another, forked, broke off, or were unaware of one another for centuries, embraces *all* possibilities of time. We do not exist in the majority of these; in some you exist, and not I; in others I, and not you; in others, both of us. In the present one, which a favorable fate has granted me, you have arrived at my house; in another, while crossing the garden, you found me dead; in still another, I utter these same words, but I am a mistake, a ghost."

"In every one," I pronounced, not without a tremble to my voice. "I am grateful to you and revere you for your re-creation of the garden of Ts'ui Pên."

"Not in all," he murmured with a smile. "Time forks perpetually toward innumerable futures. In one of them I am your enemy."

Once again I felt the swarming sensation of which I have spoken. It seemed to me that the humid garden that surrounded the house was infinitely saturated with invisible persons. Those persons were Albert and my secret, busy and multiform in other dimensions of time. I raised my eyes and the tenuous nightmare dissolved. In the yellow and black garden there was only one man; but this man was as strong as a statue . . . this man was approaching along the path and he was Captain Richard Madden.

"The future already exists," I replied, "but I am your friend. Could I see the letter again?"

Albert rose. Standing tall, he opened the drawer of the tall desk; for the moment his back was to me. I had readied the revolver. I fired with extreme caution. Albert fell uncomplainingly, immediately. I swear his death was instantaneous—a lightning stroke.

The rest is unreal, insignificant. Madden broke in, arrested me. I have been condemned to the gallows. I have won out abominably; I have communicated to Berlin the secret name of the city they must attack. They bombed it yesterday; I read it in the same papers that offered to England the mystery of the learned Sinologist Stephen Albert who was murdered by a stranger, one Yu Tsun. The Chief had deciphered this mystery. He knew my problem was to indicate (through the uproar of the war) the city called Albert, and that I had found no other means to do so than to kill a man of that name. He does not know (no one can know) my innumerable contrition and weariness.

For Victoria Ocampo

Part II: The European Perspective

European Background

Modern European history and literature (from the Renaissance and Neoclassical, to the Romantic, to the Realistic and Modern eras) unfolded in exhilarating and exceedingly productive times when an abundance of creative spirits lived and wrote. Each temporal block has its distinct set of characteristics, events, beliefs, and figures. Though each historical period and movement cohabit the same space at the beginning or end of each movement, no period completely eclipses either a preceding or a succeeding epoch.

Each period's origin can be traced to a rebel seed or voice that grows out of a prior period. As this different seed matures, its dominant traits proliferate, and its key literary forms, movements, and figures become more solidly defined. Gradually, each embryonic period usurps the position held by the preceding period, then dissipates in a sequential chain whose ascent, climax, and descent link each period to the next in succession, from the earliest to the most contemporary. The more vociferous and tangible each dissenting voice becomes, the more readers are able to discern this proliferation in the architecture of the texts. Indeed, the closer readers get to the late modern period, the more narrative form and content seem to disintegrate fixed patterns and progress to a formlessness that borders on textual madness.

Just as dissenting voices can be heard in any historical era, in each literary movement, readers discern whispered voices progressing into rumblings of a freer and different chronological segment, as rebel writers deviate from the stringent "boxed-in" requirements of the preceding period. Eventually, this temporal span swells to an apogee, then loses its strength as its lines of demarcation become blurred through superimposition. Like these voices, Renaissance origins, which can be traced to the 12th and 13th centuries, overlap the decline of the Medieval period; and in the 16th century, the Renaissance divides the Dark Ages from the early modern period in Western Europe.[1] During the Renaissance, quantum cultural, economic, intellectual, and scientific leaps were made that would forever separate Western Europe from the ancient world and set the standard of contemporary thought. The word "Renaissance" conjures up in some readers' minds not just a respect for antiquity but a span of time in the distant past that has little in common with the modern world and its literatures. The term, taken from a French noun *naissance* (birth), comes primarily from the verb, *Naître,* which means "to be born." Thus, the term "Renaissance" refers to the cultural, economic, intellectual, and scientific re-awakening that flourished in Italy from the 14th to the 16th centuries and then spread, during the 17th century, to other parts of Europe.

One has to acknowledge the respect which Renaissance writers had for classical texts. For more than two millennia, pre-Christian writers of Greece, such as Homer, Aeschylus, Sophocles, and Euripides[2] and those from Rome, like Cicero, Ovid, Virgil, and Horace, developed, for its own sake and to promote human virtue, a literary style with specific requirements and conventions on which future writers relied.

First, to return to Classical conventions meant for writers to objectively record the often sensational feats of mythical, noble heroes (usually of divine or semi-divine origin), to fill their formal diction with rich epic similes and stereotyped epithets, to write dignified but simple language to avoid detracting from the story's action, to have their plots unfold in set structural patterns and stages, to make their central action more important than the details used, and to have the text's structure limit the writers' expression. Second, because Greek, Roman, and later

European civilizations valued learning and refinement and because aristocrats in these cultures revered literature and scholarship, writers had to control, not suppress, their subjectivity to make their literature appeal more to the audience's intellect than to emotions. Third, the subject matter had to address universal rather than particular themes if the works were to appeal to large populations. Fourth, since nature and its processes signified order and the universal, writers were obligated to depict the very best in nature, not reproduce good, ugly, and base copies. Last, their works had to be moral in tone in order to improve society.

The Renaissance was the seat of socio-economic, political, and military changes that led, to some extent, to democracy and to discoveries in maritime exploration, astronomy, nationalism, and literary nationalism. Craftsmen discovered or invented methods, machines, and materials, and scientists revealed new structures of the universe. For example, the old method of bookmaking, which required scribes to copy texts laboriously, was so expensive that only aristocrats could afford books. When the printing press was invented, writers were able to produce inexpensive texts more quickly and efficiently. After they had first located these texts, they then learned Greek or Latin in order to translate them. Reduced prices made books more publicly accessible, and the printing press, along with the discovery of gunpowder, made class distinctions less noticeable and raised warfare to a new, more deadly level. More sophisticated weaponry and firearms not only rendered traditional training and the wearing of body armor obsolete but leveled the playing field between commoner and aristocrat since a gun-carrying peasant could more easily wound an opponent fatally before the latter could retaliate.

Moreover, ancient writers envisioned the world as a complete, chain-linked, comprehensible whole that was planned and operated with meticulous precision by a supreme deity who was omnipotent, omniscient, and omnipresent and who maintained ties with humans. When their readers absorbed stories of faraway places recounted in ancient, recovered texts, their curiosity was piqued, and they were motivated to explore foreign lands and cultures. Columbus sought India and found America, and other explorers traveled and colonized Asia and Africa.

Renaissance people were also able to travel from one level of understanding to higher ones and, with new tools, to journey to regions impossible to navigate before. Because of Copernicus' heliocentric theory of the cosmos, people rejected Ptolemy's concept of an absolutely fixed universe, and they adopted a sun-centered one in constant flux. Two inventions dominated this period: the microscope, which enabled viewers to navigate the closer, inner life of objects from an unheard range and viewpoint; and the telescope, which permitted viewers to tour far-flung regions of space never glimpsed before.

Historical and religious changes also occurred. Charles V abdicated the Spanish throne (1556), a massacre occurred at St. Bartholomew (1572), the Spanish Armada sailed (1588), and the Edict of Nantes was written (1598). During this same period, the Protestant Reformation, manifesting in France as evangelism, was spread by two great reformers: Luther, who led the Protestant Reformation, and Calvin, who advocated a more subversive type of Protestantism. Each claimed that his way was the right way to God.[3]

These changes and accomplishments resulted in the growth of nationalism. Humanists called themselves internationalists, and local writers or patriots expressed nationalistic feelings in national languages. These Renaissance writers sought not only to understand their experiences but to use them to guide their literary creations. They believed that study of the Classics would dignify human existence, fulfill human aspirations, and, through reason, exalt the human soul.

Some of these writers were Rabelais, Ronsard, Montaigne, and the writers forming La Pleiade[4] from France; Rojas, Cervantes, and Oriosto from Spain; Machiavelli and Versalius from Italy; and More, Spencer, Sidney, Shakespeare, Donne, and Milton from England. Their works explored psychological complexities (that mimicked real emotions) appearing in characters' behaviors. Like their Classical predecessors, Renaissance writers exalted form and believed that detail, language, or other decoration should be subordinate to the story idea or action. They thought that using the three unities (of time, place, and action) would help writers to exercise self-control and moderate their emotions.[5] Their diction was formal, ordered, intellectual, reasonable, balanced, edifying, dignified, and austere, and never low or base.

On the one hand, Medieval people, who were obsessed with death, were convinced that human beings were wretched and insignificant, that they were born into sin, and that their role was, while in the flesh, to prepare for a better, spiritual existence. On the other hand, motivated by humanism and taking their cue from Greek and Roman texts, Renaissance people rejoiced in the body, stressed human greatness, and placed humans at the center of life. For them, living was praiseworthy, pleasurable, and significant. They, therefore, rejected asceticism[6] and sought to reform corruption in church and state by educating people, using moral philosophy to replace formal logic, and directing study of the Bible to replace Medieval theology. Though they believed that human creation was the climax of divine creative endeavor, they also thought that these imperfect beings could be motivated, if stimulated adequately with ancient writings, to pursue a higher, moral life.

However, like an imperfect world, neither the humanistic movement nor its human advocates were unblemished. Renaissance discoveries and inventions resulted in economic expansion which, in turn, led ultimately to colonialism, slavery, and European labeling of anything different as inferior. Though humanists pushed for human dignity, they also believed that some people were less human than others. Humanistic growth, as a necessary panacea, would change flaws in human thought and character and bring inferior others up to par. However, this philosophy, though lofty on its face, exposed humanists as members of an elite class that was guilty of class stratification, oppression, and racism. So preoccupied were the uneducated masses with staying alive each day that they had no time, money, or leisure to profit from these texts and had, therefore, no chance of evolving in humanistic terms.

Following the Renaissance was the Baroque, a term used initially to label an architectural style that was later applied to literature. The term is a French borrowing of the Portuguese word *barroco,* which means "imperfect pearl." Flourishing from the late 16th to the early 18th century, Baroque artists revolted against the imaginative, emotional exuberance and disordered technique of writers like Montaigne. Instead of an idealistic, formal, and logically ordered style, the Baroque represents itself as a realistic, arbitrary, sensational, wild, bizarre, and decadent style that was also opulent, grandiose, and full of movement and energy.

Historically, a new Baroque ruler who wanted absolute power emerged. Under the rule of Elizabeth I, literature flourished in England, but this monarchy, after the Stuart Accession, gradually changed during the next 50 years to a Republic and then reverted, after two more decades of civil war, to a limited monarchy which recognized the rights of Parliament and of ordinary citizens. During the 17th century, Louis XIV, the Sun King, not only encouraged a number of brilliant writers whose works reflected Neoclassical ideals but also assured his own immortality when he built the palace of Versailles.

In literature, the term refers to a serious, discordant style that dominated the 17th century and served as a semi-transition between the Renaissance and more modern modes of expression. Its purpose was to startle or shock readers; its mode of expression was often unusual, unexpected, obscure, grotesque, or contorted. Preciosity, a distinction in thought, speech, and behavior that reacted against the coarseness and brutality of manners wrought by the chaos of civil wars, eventually regressed into absurdity. Malherbe, a Baroque rebel writer, believed that language was either noble or low. Other distinguished writers of the period were Bacon, Donne, Jonson, Milton, and Shakespeare from England; Calderon and Cervantes from Spain; and Corneille, La Fontaine, La Rochefoucauld, Molière, Madame de Sévigné, Madame de la Fayette, and Racine from France.

The Rococo period, which followed the Baroque but preceded the Neoclassical, takes its name from the French word *rocaille,* which means "shell work." It was first applied to an architectural style characterized by elaborate ornamentation imitating foliage, scrolls, and shell work. Perceived by some as a decadent phase of the Baroque, the Rococo Style preferred decorative detail suggesting grace, intimacy, and playfulness to that evoking grandeur, gravity, and logic. It also suggests a reckless or tasteless style.

Formed as a reaction to the Baroque, the Neoclassical period, also called the Age of Reason and the Enlightenment, extended from the late 17th to the mid-18th century. This period advocated a renewed interest in the principles of classical rhetoric, that is, how to manipulate language in order to hone persuasive skills. The term "Neoclassical" was "new" in the sense that certain ideas were taken, not directly from the Greeks but from current French attitudes and from Horace, a Roman. However, after the religious and political upheavals of the 17th century, many tired of the irregular, the fantastic, and the unexpected. Like Classical writers, they yearned for tranquility and moderation, a return to order, logic, and restrained emotion. In order to maintain order, higher mental faculties were required. Neoclassical writers' recovery of Classical texts and their dependence upon scientific investigation and logic led to the Scientific Revolution, to an accompanying language and cosmological model, and to the human promotion of evolution by means of "Reason."

Vital energy was also released in other human endeavors, specifically architecture. This period of philosophical questioning on the nature, purpose, and positioning of human beings in the cosmos found voice in such thinkers and writers as Blake, Burns, Defoe, Pope, and Swift from England; and Goethe, Kant, and Schiller from Germany. Alongside these, a new group of French writers (who called themselves *les philosophes*) and a new *esprit philosophique* dominated the period as the literary nucleus around which Neoclassical writers revolved. Many French writers flourished during this time, among them giants like Diderot, Montesquieu, Rousseau, and Voltaire.

Though cultural, religious, and historical rebellions occurred from period to period, it was the early Romantic era which symbolized revolution. Romanticism can be narrowly defined as a late 18th and early 19th century movement and literary theory promoted by a group of writers from 1820 to 1850. More broadly, it is a state of mind that values emotion over reason, tenderness over tough-mindedness, and desire for and expectation of change over stasis. This state recognizes a dynamic creative imagination and diversity, with a mental focus on imperfection and the subconscious.

During the early Romantic period, revolutionary change was occurring on historical, economic, social, industrial, political, and intellectual levels. Historically, key events reached world attention, and figures became renowned for their faults or virtues. Napoleon became Emperor of France (1804), and Russia was invaded (1812). After Napoleon died (1821), the French colonized Algeria (1830–48), and revolts spread to other European countries (1848).

From more subversive, conceptual frames of reference, reason was the guide to truth, the human soul contained the potential for construction and destruction, God and human institutions provided controls to save humans from anarchy, and human beings were tested in the public arena, where meaningful experiences resulted in growth. Though Romantics accepted a social, hierarchical chain with the aristocracy at its head, when the nobility's power waned and the merchant class rose to prominence, wealth was substituted for rank. Middle-class money earned via agriculture and manufacturing bought power, educated a few underprivileged, purchased blue-veined spouses, and helped to blur class distinctions. Socially, the Industrial Revolution, through which inexpensive newspapers and cheap home lighting could be mass-produced, made life easier for many. A new class emerged, the industrial proletariat, whose abject poverty precluded their humanistic improvement. Politically, people revolted against the status quo by requiring kings to ratify constitutions guaranteeing the rights of males to suffrage and the eradication of censorship.

Romantics, who preferred liberty, equality, and fraternity to inherited hierarchical systems, relied more on individual self-control and on science than on God or institutions. Because of this leveling factor, women, children, and "savages" or "primitives" were taken seriously and were thought to be closer to nature, thus nobler, purer, and more righteous than "contaminated" civilians. Science played a revolutionary role for Romantics, by making the human playing field more equal when Darwin wrote his *Origin of the Species* (1859), which exploded public notions of the hierarchical positioning of humans in an ordered universe. Darwin's great statement on the origin, differentiation, and evolution of the species, called biological determinism, partly severed the link between human beings and their metaphysical origins. Humans were no longer special creations but chance, immoral, unjust beings placed in a world in which survival belonged to the strong, the ruthless, and the biologically fit. Emerging simultaneously was Karl Marx, whose economic determinism in *Das Kapital* (1867), contends that people band together not for righteous reasons but by economic necessity.

In literature, inspiration justified violations of social or literary traditions. Romantics, who placed no limits on subject matter, moved often from humankind or "man" to nation or ethnic group, from communal stability to individual fulfillment, from the reasonable to the emotional, and from the corrupt and civilized to the innocent or "primitive." Writers, uninhibited by genre, verse form, formal diction, or language, relied on inspiration to determine whether or not they would use a "low" or "high" style.

Propitious were the historical circumstances that bred Realism. Romantic passion had become exaggerated, grotesque, and absurd. Though superficially, business thrived, and the controlling bourgeoisie imposed Classical rules, order, respectability, and conformity on society, underneath, the rumblings of discontented workers presaged class struggle. People's reliance on science and facts and their dismissal of metaphysical concepts, like dreams, mysticism, and God, set the stage for Realism. In their realistic portrayals, writers strove to use common sense and objectivity rather than figurative language. They searched for the *"mot juste,"* the "right word," in order to render the most concise and accurate "slice of life" possible.

Concurrently, history was being made, that is, the *coup d'etat* of Louis Napoleon (1851), the Crimean War (1845–56), and the Dreyfus case (1894–1906). In literary history, such distinguished writers as Arnold, Conrad, Hardy, Kipling, Swinburne, Tennyson, Wilde, and Yeats from England; Crane, Melville, Thoreau, and Whitman from the U.S.A.; Ibsen from Norway; Baudelaire, Flaubert, Gide, Hugo, Mallarme, Rimbeau, and Verlaine from France; Dostoevsky and Tolstoy from Russia; and Marx and Nietzsche from Germany, made extraordinary contributions to literature and philosophy.

Many of the writers who created some of the world's greatest masterpieces and who owe their existence to Realism were governed, implicitly or explicitly, by other literary theories like Naturalism and Symbolism. Naturalism is often defined as Realism taken to its scientific extreme. These writers used science, yet another cure-all for human ills, to structure their works and to indicate their precise, objective study of the human species, particularly the lower classes, who were, like the primitives, more instinctive, like animals, than were the upper classes. The Naturalists, whose texts often reflected repulsive, crude, or offensive facets of human character, presented a deterministic view of life and had, as their purpose, social reform. One well-known naturalist was Zola, whose Rougon-Macquart series of novels presents, for example, case studies of alcoholism (*L'Assomoir,* 1877), labor (*Germinal,* 1885), and sex (*Nana,* 1880). Another was Gorky, from Russia, whose works depict generous peasants who lead degraded lives.

Symbolism, a literary movement which began in France as a reaction to Realism, requires writers to use symbols to describe their feelings. Often, these symbols show no logical connection but form a pattern of sensory suggestion. Mallarmè's phrase, "white bouquet of roses snowing down," for example, though illogical, freely associates words to connote ideal purity and sensual delight. Other symbolist writers are Dreiser, Emerson, and Thoreau from the U.S.A.; Joyce from England; Mann from Germany; and, of course, Mallarmè, Verlaine, and Baudelaire from France.

The early 20th century witnessed the rise of Stream-of-Consciousness, Dadaism, Surrealism, and Existentialism. Stream-of-Consciousness fiction is a rich, achronological assortment of freely-associated thoughts, sensations, and memories that emerge from obscure regions of the subconscious where past, present, and future blend, without pause, like the disorganized flow of thought. Originating with Sterne's *Tristram Shandy* (1759–67), other famous Stream-of-Consciousness writers are Garcia Lorca from Spain; Proust from France; James and Woolf from England; and Hemingway and Faulkner from the U.S.A.

Both Dada and Surrealism show the influence of Stream-of-Consciousness, both arose as revolts against Realism, and both became popular because both reflected the climate of unrest during the first half of the 20th century. Industrialization was destroying ancient ways and lifestyles. World Wars I and II (1914–18 and 1942–45) brought to much of Europe a heavy loss of human life, the Russian Revolution erupted (1917), Mussolini became dictator in Italy, the

Depression hit (1929), and the Atomic Bomb was dropped on Hiroshima (1945). These instances of a tradition overturned created in many people a distrust of government and orthodoxy and feelings of fear and insecurity. Like the people, the literature of this period was not just socially conscious but disrespectful of tradition, difficult to understand, unsure of itself, and defiant.

Dadaism, a forerunner of the anti-realistic novel and of the Theater of the Absurd,[7] was founded in Zurich, Switzerland, in 1916 by Tristan Tzara, who, shortly thereafter, moved to Paris, France. The movement began as a protest against World War I, blossomed into a revolt against all things orthodox, and attempted to destroy logical relationships between idea and statement, replacing such relationships with illogical ones. Primarily a French movement, Dada's doctrine was shaped and influenced largely by poets like Baudelaire and Rimbaud, who echoed Freud's theory of the conscious mind as a surface aspect of a larger subconscious or higher and truer human self. Dada's adherents also believed that memory and activity of the conscious mind had to be repressed and then replaced by subliminal chaos.

Dada, which argued for the writer's absolute freedom, eventually evolved into "surrealism," a term coined by Apollinaire in 1917 and later adopted by André Breton, who formulated in his *Manifeste du Surrèalisme* both the Surrealist doctrine and its school. Unlike Dada, the Surrealist movement, which rejected everything conventional, had a purpose (to change the world), a subject matter (the dream and the subconscious), and a method (use of free association and the imagination).

In the mid 20th century, the calamitous period in the history of Europe was followed by recovery and stability. People became accustomed to the Atomic Bomb, the Communist threat diminished, nationalism declined, and European unity was suggested in the creation of the Common Market (1958). However, literature, in competition with other disciplines, that is, science, social studies, politics, and big business, became progressively unstable. This social climate produced a philosophical system called Existentialism, which originated in Germany before it was popularized by Jean-Paul Sartre in the 1930s, in France.

Existentialists believe that the external world is real and absurd; since it has no meaning except that with which humans endow it, it should be regarded with nausea. The apparent stability of things is an illusion. Neither God, nor the mind, soul, or spirit exists apart from the body, which is, in itself, disgusting. Human beings first exist (as *tabula rasas*), with others, and from their existence, they create their essence through their choices and acts, which cause them to experience despair and then to become liberated. Humans are involved in absurd relationships with other people who are mirrors through which people are able to confirm their existence, but this reflected self-image is revolting. For this reason, Sartre says, in his play *Huis Clos* (*Closed Exit,* 1944), that hell is other people.

Two other "isms" found expression during this period: Impressionism and Expressionism. Impressionistic writing moves from the external world inward, to record, not how the incident, scene, or character objectively and externally appears but the artist's impressions of the incident, scene, or character. This approach uses a different logic than that employed by writers of traditional literature, for it substitutes an external, objective relationship with a momentary, subjective one that is created in the writer's mind. Readers are shown the scene, incident, or character after it has been filtered through and altered by the writer's mind, mood, and attitude. Such writing, like Impressionistic painting, appears hazy or vague in outline and often violates cause-and-effect relationships in order to build a central impression. Impressionistic writers believe that writers should not imitate nature but interpret it (the external world). Details are selected, and colors are used to suggest the writer's emotions and attitude, which are more important than the plot or its unity and coherence. Some Impressionistic writers are James from England; Balzac, Flaubert, and Claudel from France; Mansfield from New Zealand; and Conrad from Poland.

Unlike Impressionism, Expressionism, which is fourth-dimensional, mystical, and symbolic, accepts mental distortions as objective reality. An Impressionistic scene, incident, or character *is an actual person, event, or thing* that has undergone mental filtering, processing, and alteration. An expressionistic scene, incident, or character, such as Kafka's beetle (who is his character,

Gregor, after he turns into a bug in the story's opening sentence), *does not exist* as objective reality. Rather, the writer records these mental images as real ones. Thus, scenes, incidents, and characters created by such expressionistic writers as Joyce from Ireland; Kafka from Czechoslovakia; and O'Neill and Elliot, from the U.S.A., escape reality by perceiving instead unreal, usually distorted worlds.

Thus, as readers of Renaissance life and literature draw closer to the modern world and its literatures, they note changes in writers' views that also move from certainty to doubt, from wholeness to fragmentation, from belonging to isolation, from poetic censorship to poetic license, from fixed boundaries to none at all, from normalcy to abnormality, from lucid sight to hazy perspective, and from a self-regulating freedom to a no-holds-barred way of thinking, being, and acting in the world.

Notes

1. The Dark Ages was so named because of the failure of the Crusades; because of rivalry within the Medieval papacy (between supporters of the Pope and those of the Holy Roman Emperor); because of the Black Death plague, which weakened feudal society; because of the French Jacquerie Revolution in 1358; and because of the English Peasant's Revolt of 1381. However, the Middle Ages was not a period which lacked creativity. In fact, such giants as Dante and Chaucer produced literary masterpieces. In addition, there were epic poems from various nations such as *Beowulf* from England; the *Song of Roland* from France; *El Cid* from Spain; the *Elda Edda* from the Norse; and the *Nibelungenlied* from Germany. Romances, allegories (beast fables, folk tales, and anecdotes), lyrics, drama (the mystery, miracle, and morality plays), and secular works like farces and interludes were also abundant during the period.
2. This period of high achievement in Greece, known as the Periclean Age, was from 429–400 B.C.
3. Luther is known also for his *Ninety-Five Theses* and Calvin for his *Institutes*.
4. A group of Renaissance poets whose leader was Joachim du Bellay.
5. The unity of time states that the action must occur within one day or 24 hours. The unity of place requires the action to happen in one place. The unity of action requires one major plot.
6. The term "asceticism" refers to the practice of strict self-denial as a means of achieving personal and spiritual discipline in preparation for a supernatural life.
7. The Theater of the Absurd is a name given to avant-garde drama that reflects the influence of both Dada and Surrealist movements. It rejects logical devices and realistic form, and it substitutes for these a belief in the absurdity of the human condition.

Selected Bibliography

Guches, Richard C. *Sequel: A Handbook for the Critical Analysis of Literature.* Palo Alto: Peek Press, 1979.
Kafka, Franz. *The Metamorphosis.* Stanley Corngold trans. and ed., New York: Bantam, 1972.
Kershner, R.B. *The Twentieth Century Novel: An Introduction.* Boston: Bedford, 1997.

European Drama

European drama consists of comedy, tragedy, and a "peripheral" type incorporating three subtypes: the festival drama, the masque, and the history play. Renaissance writers from other European countries developed different literary genres. For example, poetry was developed by the Pleiade group of French writers, and Rabelais and Montaigne developed stories and essays. However, the beginnings of European Renaissance drama can be traced to English morality plays or interludes which servants wrote for lords or for the entertainment of religious figures. Two such short plays written for Cardinal Morton by Henry Medwall survive: *Nature* and *Fulgens and Lucrece*. Renaissance playwrights returned to Classical models in their attempts to construct sophisticated art forms.

Comedy, which was considered a much lower genre than tragedy, frequently mixed prose with poetry, and playwrights often used middle to lower class characters. To develop comedy, writers turned to two Roman dramatists, Terence and Plautus, as models. This fact means that their intricate plots had to adhere to certain standards: comedies had to contain stock characters, and they had to be divided into acts and scenes. Nicolas Udall's *Ralph Roister Doister* uses one such type of character, the braggart soldier, upon whom Shakespeare's Sir John Falstaff is patterned. Several varieties of comedy existed during the Renaissance. Romantic comedy contains noble characters involved in a love plot; domestic comedy presents a domestic situation; city comedy contains bourgeois characters; humor comedy develops type characters; and classical intrigue comedy has Classical types of characters and contains witty dialogue and complex, rapidly unfolding plots.

Like comedy, tragedy relies on both Classical and Medieval models and is based on the tragic view of the Roman goddess, Fortuna, whose turning wheel symbolizes the downfall of those in the high echelons of society. Renaissance tragedy also had to adhere to certain standards established in Aristotle's *Poetics*. European dramatists believed, like Aristotle, that the tragic hero is a person of high estate, that he does at some point recognize his plight, undergoes a reversal of fortune, then falls from grace because of his error or moral weakness. They also believed that the drama should evoke pity and fear in its viewers and thus bring about an emotional catharsis or purgation.

During the Elizabethan period, revenge tragedy had a wronged character seek revenge, villain tragedy contained an antagonist, and heroic tragedy featured a larger-than-life "tragic" hero. Festival drama was also presented by a lord's servants during a festival, as well as the masque (which was a type of court entertainment containing dialogues, songs, and dancing), and the English history play. European Renaissance drama, now thought by some to be nearly synonymous with Shakespearean drama since he exerted such an influence on drama, has been a source of pleasure and delight to readers from the time that Shakespeare's works first appeared in print. Since both Classical and Shakespearean dramas were written centuries ago, most contemporary readers may think of both as antiquated parts of the same ancient tradition. In some respects, Classical and Elizabethan dramas share common characteristics in the roles and functions of actors, in the structure of the theater, and in class structure and occupation. However, clear and distinct differences between European drama and that of its Classical predecessors are present and can be identified through a meticulous study of representative Shakespearean works. Just as Oedipus set the Classical standard, Shakespeare's works established the pattern for

Elizabethan drama. First, Shakespeare's tragic heroes exhibit many of the characteristics of their Classical counterparts, that is, their isolation from their community, their sense of their own uniqueness and virtue, their courageous leadership, and their choices and actions affecting large groups of people rather than a few. Like Grecian tragic heroes, Shakespearean tragic heroes also exhibit, in varying degrees, *hamartia, hubris, anagnorisis,* and *perepeteia*.[1]

Second, both Classical and Elizabethan dramatists framed their dramas' content within historical, cultural, and spiritual contexts. Both Greek and later Roman dramatists used public theaters that allowed their respective audiences to watch from the front and sides; both used men to play the roles of both men and women, since actresses did not perform on stage; both relied on wealthy patrons to sponsor their dramas; and both dramatic types included divine forces as prominent players who intervened in human affairs.

However, the social context for Shakespeare's works is far different from that of Classical drama. For instance, Shakespeare included current mythology in his dramas. Ghosts and goblins are in *Hamlet, Julius Caesar, Macbeth,* and *Richard III;* witches are in *Macbeth,* and a practitioner of magic is in *The Tempest.* Moreover, the depth and range of Shakespeare's learning can be traced to his exposure to a varied London culture made up of commercial and banking centers, the royal court, as well as artists, teachers, musicians, students, and writers from foreign cultures who were drawn like magnets to England because of its advanced urban cultural life.

Historically, the English optimism of the late 1500s changed to pessimism during the early 1600s and this change was mirrored in Shakespeare's works. In 1588 the English Navy's victory over the Spanish Armada created optimism and patriotism in the citizenry. The death of Queen Elizabeth I in 1603, along with England's ensuing social and economic problems, created a climate of uncertainty which bred the negativity reflected in such tragedies as *King Lear* and in comedies like *Measure for Measure* and *All's Well That Ends Well.* Furthermore, because several European countries were embroiled in war, at different times, Europeans in general had a strange fascination with violence and death. It was not unusual for them to flock to hangings of criminals or to patronize to-the-death sports like bullbaiting or bearbaiting. The constant threat of plagues increased their morbid fascination with death. Not surprisingly, Shakespeare's dramas contain themes of foreboding, bitterness, confusion, and death.

Shakespearean drama also differs from Classical tragedy in six other significant ways. One, unlike the linear progression of Classical plots, Shakespearean main and subplots are more varied and more intricate than one-plot Classical dramas. Two, Shakespearean plots, distinctly Christian, monotheistic ones, are framed by forces of light and darkness symbolizing God and the Devil. Conversely, Greek and Roman dramas depicted a mythological and polytheistic cosmos consisting of Titans and the retinue of 12 great Olympians, headed by Zeus. Three, the Greek and Roman gods and goddesses were fallible. Four, the Christian God in the European Renaissance universe was an omniscient, omnipotent, and omnipresent, perfect deity who maintained distance from his earthly subjects. However, though the gods of Classical drama had special powers, often they behaved no better than their subjects, which made mortals feel closer to and more comfortable with them. Five, though both Classical and Elizabethan tragic heroes fall from grace, in Classical drama the reversal of fortune is caused by human weaknesses or character flaws (as in the case of Sophocles' *Oedipus*), by a major character's courageous attempt to substitute his will for divine will, or by the intervention of the gods in human affairs. Six, though characters in both Classical and Shakespearean drama undergo spiritual or actual deaths, the Classical hero's life after death is not based on whether or not he is aligned with good or evil spiritual forces. Rather, regardless of the actions that a tragic hero took in physical life, the place for the dead was still Hades, which was not a place of hell and brimstone but a shadowy abode. For Shakespeare's characters, however, the fall from grace symbolizes human alignment with the second most powerful force: the devil. Thus, "to fall," in Christian terms, means to distance oneself from the good, the ordered, and the perfect and deliberately align oneself with Satan and his host of demons, an act that guarantees, for the human soul, eternal damnation.

But what precise contributions did Shakespeare make to drama? First, he conveys through his poetry and drama details about the English countryside and his boyhood environment. He also vividly evokes individuals, fairies, and animals, all of which help to define his great talent. Second, Shakespeare incorporates conceits[2] and puns[3] in his works. Third, Shakespeare, who is skilled in the employment of rhetoric, often creates elaborate linguistic structures, as in *Richard III* and in *Romeo and Juliet*. He also satirizes language in *Love's Labor Lost* and uses a variety of rhetorical devices in his early poetry. Last, Shakespeare is quite fond of using image clusters to suggest emotions or to make symbolic statements. For example, candy, dogs, ice, poison, and stones have been successfully linked to flattery, and certain other images like birds, animals, light, and darkness symbolize supernatural forces.

Clearly, then, William Shakespeare is a key figure in the traditional literary canon, one who will continue to be recognized and appreciated, worldwide, in years to come.

Notes

1. *Hamartia* is the error or flaw in the tragic hero's character; *hubris* is his abuse of power, overweening pride, or bullying nature; *anagnorisis* is the tragic hero's moment of recognition; and *perepeteia* is his reversal of fortune or change in lifestyle brought on by his actions.
2. A conceit is an idea, usually expressed through an analogy, which points to a telling parallel between two things that are essentially different.
3. A pun is a fanciful or witty expression or play on words based on similar sounds between words with different meanings. It may appear as a metaphor within a poem, for example, or the poem itself may be a huge metaphor or conceit.

Selected Bibliography

Charney, Maurice. *All of Shakespeare*. New York: Columbia University Press, 1993.
Kay, Dennis. *William Shakespeare: His Life and Times*. New York: Twayne, 1995.
Levi, Peter. *The Life and Times of William Shakespeare*. New York: Henry Holt, 1988.
Miller, Jordan Y. *The Heath Introduction to Drama*. 4th ed. Lexington: D. C. Heath, 1992.
Vena, Gary, and Andrea Nouryeh. *Drama and Performance: An Anthology*. New York: Harper-Collins, 1996.
Well, Stanley, ed. *The Cambridge Companion to Shakespeare Studies*. Cambridge: Cambridge University Press, 1993.

William Shakespeare (1564–1616)

The childhood of the great playwright, William Shakespeare, is, for the most part, shrouded in mystery. He was born around April 23, 1564, at Stratford-on-Avon and probably attended the Stratford grammar school, where he may have learned Latin. However, there is no record of his having pursued a high education at either Oxford or Cambridge. In 1582, when he was 18 years old, he married Anne Hathaway, who subsequently gave birth to a daughter a year later and then to twin boys two years thereafter. By 1592, he acted in London and became known as a playwright. Shakespeare then joined an acting company called the Lord Chamberlain's Men, which later attached itself to James I, after which the troupe became known as the King's Men.

During his early years, Shakespeare was not only England's foremost playwright but was also a lyrical poet much in demand. He published, in 1593, a mythological love poem entitled "Venus and Adonis." He dedicated this poem and another, "The Rape of Lucrece" written the next year, to the Earl of Southhampton. Shakespeare was also recognized for his sonnets which idealized a young man who was devoted to a dark, promiscuous mistress. Unlike Petrarchan sonnets, which contain an octave and a sextet, the Shakespearean sonnet consists of three quatrains (four-line stanzas) and a couplet (a rhymed two-line stanza). Structurally, the three quatrains prepare the reader for the couplet which ends the sonnet. These quatrains present a situation; ask a question; deliver a meditation on beauty, change, or time; or identify a problem. The result of the meditation, the resolution of the conflict contained in the situation, the answer to the question, or the problem's solution is given in the ending couplet.

By the turn of the century, Shakespeare had written his great Romantic comedies *As You Like It, Twelfth Night,* and *Much Ado About Nothing.* By 1597 he had become wealthy enough to invest in real estate and bought a beautiful house in Stratford. During the next decade, he produced these great tragedies: *Hamlet, Macbeth, Othello, King Lear,* and *Antony and Cleopatra,* after which time he retired to his Stratford home, where he wrote *The Tempest, Cymbeline,* and *The Winter's Tale.*

England's foremost dramatist also wrote love songs, elegies, ballads, and aubades (morning songs), most of which accompany his plays. Though Shakespeare died in 1616, his expertise in both poetic and dramatic media will endure as striking testaments to his talent and skill, his gift for humor, and his ability to deliver, with great sensory appeal, the sounds and sights of Renaissance English life.

The Tragedy of King Lear

Shakespeare

[Dramatis Personae

Lear, King of Britain
King of France
Duke of Burgundy
Duke of Cornwall, husband to Regan
Duke of Albany, husband to Goneril
Earl of Kent
Earl of Gloucester
Edgar, son to Gloucester
Edmund, bastard son to Gloucester
Curan, a courtier
Oswald, steward to Goneril
Old Man, tenant to Gloucester
Doctor
Lear's Fool
A Captain, subordinate to Edmund
Gentleman, attending on Cordelia
A Herald
Servants to Cornwall
Goneril, daughter to Lear
Regan, daughter to Lear
Cordelia, daughter to Lear
Knights attending on Lear, Officers, Messengers, Soldiers, Attendants

SCENE: Britain.]

ACT I

Scene I. *[King Lear's palace.]*

Enter Kent, Gloucester, and Edmund.

KENT. I thought the king had more affected the Duke of Albany than Cornwall.

GLOUCESTER. It did always seem so to us: but now, in the division of the kingdom, it appears not which of the dukes he values most; for equalities are so weighed, that curiosity in neither can make choice of either's moiety.

KENT. Is not this your son, my lord?

GLOUCESTER. His breeding, sir, hath been at my charge. I have so often blushed to acknowledge him, that now I am brazed to't.

KENT. I cannot conceive you.

GLOUCESTER. Sir, this young fellow's mother could; whereupon she grew round-wombed, and had, indeed, sir, a son for her cradle ere she had a husband for her bed. Do you smell a fault?

KENT. I cannot wish the fault undone, the issue of it being so proper.

GLOUCESTER. But I have, sir, a son by order of law, some year elder than this, who yet is no dearer in my account: though this knave came something saucily into the world before he was sent for, yet was his mother fair; there was good sport at his making, and the whoreson must be acknowledged. Do you know this noble gentleman, Edmund?

EDMUND. No, my lord.

GLOUCESTER. My lord of Kent. Remember him hereafter as my honourable friend.

EDMUND. My services to your lordship.

KENT. I must love you, and sue to know you better.

EDMUND. Sir, I shall study deserving.

GLOUCESTER. He hath been out nine years, and away he shall again. The king is coming.

Sound a sennet. Enter one bearing a coronet, then King Lear, then the Dukes of Cornwall and Albany, next Goneril, Regan, Cordelia, and Attendants.

LEAR. Attend the lords of France and Burgundy, Gloucester.

GLOUCESTER. I shall, my lord. *Exit [with Edmund].*

LEAR. Meantime we shall express our darker purpose.
Give me the map there. Know that we have divided
In three our kingdom; and 'tis our fast intent
To shake all cares and business from our age;

    Conferring them on younger strengths, while we 35
    Unburthened crawl toward death. Our son of Cornwall,
    And you our no less loving son of Albany,
    We have this hour a constant will to publish
    Our daughters' several dowers, that future strife
    May be prevented now. The princes, France and Burgundy, 40
    Great rivals in our youngest daughter's love,
    Long in our court have made their amorous sojourn,
    And here are to be answered. Tell me, my daughters
    (Since now we will divest us both of rule,
    Interest of territory, cares of state), 45
    Which of you shall we say doth love us most?
    That we our largest bounty may extend
    Where nature doth with merit challenge. Goneril,
    Our eldest-born, speak first.

GONERIL. Sir, I love you more than words can wield the matter; 50
    Dearer than eye-sight, space, and liberty;
    Beyond what can be valued, rich or rare;
    No less than life, with grace, health, beauty, honour;
    As much as child e'er loved, or father found;
    A love that makes breath poor, and speech unable: 55
    Beyond all manner of so much I love you.

CORDELIA. *[Aside]* What shall Cordelia do? Love, and be silent.

LEAR. Of all these bounds, even from this line to this,
    With shadowy forests and with champains riched,
    With plenteous rivers and wide-skirted meads, 60
    We make thee lady. To thine and Albany's issue
    Be this perpetual. What says our second daughter,
    Our dearest Regan, wife to Cornwall? Speak.

REGAN. Sir, I am made of the self mettle as my sister,
    And prize me at her worth. In my true heart 65
    I find she names my very deed of love;
    Only she comes too short, that I profess
    Myself an enemy to all other joys,
    Which the most precious square of sense possesses,
    And find I am alone felicitate 70
    In your dear Highness' love.

CORDELIA.   *[Aside]* Then poor Cordelia!
    And yet not so, since I am sure my love's
    More ponderous than my tongue.

LEAR. To thee and thine hereditary ever 75
    Remain this ample third of our fair kingdom,
    No less in space, validity, and pleasure,
    Than that conferred on Goneril. Now, our joy,
    Although the last and least; to whose young love
    The vines of France and milk of Burgundy 80
    Strive to be interest; what can you say to draw
    A third more opulent than your sisters? Speak.

CORDELIA. Nothing, my lord.

LEAR. Nothing!

CORDELIA. Nothing. 85

LEAR. Nothing will come of nothing. Speak again.

CORDELIA. Unhappy that I am, I cannot heave
   My heart into my mouth. I love your majesty
   According to my bond, nor more nor less.

LEAR. How, how, Cordelia? Mend your speech a little, 90
   Lest it may mar your fortunes.

CORDELIA.   Good my lord,
   You have begot me, bred me, loved me. I
   Return those duties back as are right fit,
   Obey you, love you, and most honour you. 95
   Why have my sisters husbands, if they say
   They loved you all? Haply, when I shall wed,
   That lord whose hand must take my plight shall carry
   Half my love with him, half my care and duty.
   Sure I shall never marry like my sisters, 100
   To love my father all.

LEAR. But goes thy heart with this?

CORDELIA.   Ay, good my lord.

LEAR. So young, and so untender?

CORDELIA. So young, my lord, and true. 105

LEAR. Let it be so; thy truth, then, be thy dower!
   For, by the sacred radiance of the sun,
   The mysteries of Hecate, and the night,
   By all the operation of the orbs
   From whom we do exist, and cease to be, 110
   Here I disclaim all my paternal care,
   Propinquity and property of blood,
   And as a stranger to my heart and me
   Hold thee, from this, for ever. The barbarous Scythian,
   Or he that makes his generation messes 115
   To gorge his appetite, shall to my bosom
   Be as well neighboured, pitied, and relieved,
   As thou my sometime daughter.

KENT.   Good my liege—

LEAR. Peace, Kent! 120
   Come not between the dragon and his wrath.
   I loved her most, and thought to set my rest
   On her kind nursery. Hence, and avoid my sight!
   So be my grave my peace, as here I give
   Her father's heart from her! Call France. Who stirs? 125
   Call Burgundy. Cornwall and Albany,
   With my two daughters' dowers digest this third;
   Let pride, which she calls plainness, marry her.
   I do invest you jointly with my power,
   Pre-eminence, and all the large effects 130

That troop with majesty. Ourself, by monthly course,
With reservation of an hundred knights,
By you to be sustained, shall our abode
Make with you by due turns. Only we shall retain
The name, and all th' additions to a king. The sway, 135
Revenue, execution of the rest,
Beloved sons, be yours; which to confirm,
This coronet part between you.

KENT.   Royal Lear,
    Whom I have ever honoured as my king, 140
    Loved as my father, as my master followed,
    As my great patron thought on in my prayers—

LEAR. The bow is bent and drawn, make from the shaft.

KENT. Let it fall rather, though the fork invade
    The region of my heart. Be Kent unmannerly, 145
    When Lear is mad. What wilt thou do, old man?
    Think'st thou that duty shall have dread to speak,
    When power to flattery bows? To plainness honour's bound
    When majesty stoops to folly. Reverse thy state,
    And, in thy best consideration, check 150
    This hideous rashness. Answer my life my judgment,
    Thy youngest daughter does not love thee least;
    Nor are those empty-hearted whose low sounds
    Reverbs no hollowness.

LEAR.   Kent, on thy life, no more. 155

KENT. My life I never held but as a pawn
    To wage against thy enemies; nor fear to lose it,
    Thy safety being motive.

LEAR.   Out of my sight!

KENT. See better, Lear; and let me still remain 160
    The true blank of thine eye.

LEAR. Now, by Apollo—

KENT.   Now, by Apollo, King,
    Thou swear'st thy gods in vain.

LEAR.   O, vassal! Miscreant! 165
              [Laying his hand on his sword.]

ALBANY, CORNWALL. Dear sir, forbear!

KENT. Kill thy physician, and the fee bestow
    Upon thy foul disease. Revoke thy gift,
    Or, whilst I can vent clamour from my throat,
    I'll tell thee thou dost evil. 170

LEAR.   Hear me, recreant!
    On thine allegiance, hear me!
    That thou hast sought to make us break our vows,
    Which we durst never yet, and with strained pride
    To come betwixt our sentence and our power, 180

Which nor our nature nor our place can bear,
Our potency made good, take thy reward.
Five days we do allot thee, for provision
To shield thee from diseases of the world,
And on the sixth to turn thy hated back 185
Upon our kingdom. If, on the tenth day following,
Thy banished trunk be found in our dominions,
The moment is thy death. Away! by Jupiter,
This shall not be revoked.

KENT. Fare thee well, King. Sith thus thou wilt appear, 190
Freedom lives hence, and banishment is here.
[To Cordelia] The gods to their dear shelter take thee, maid,
That justly think'st, and hast most rightly said!
[To Regan and Goneril] And your large speeches may your deeds approve, 195
That good effects may spring from words of love.
Thus Kent, O Princes, bids you all adieu;
He'll shape his old course in a country new. *Exit.*

Flourish. Enter Gloucester, with France and Burgundy; Attendants.

GLOUCESTER. Here's France and Burgundy, my noble lord.

LEAR. My Lord of Burgundy. 200
We first address towards you, who with this king
Hath rivaled for our daughter. What in the least
Will you require in present dower with her,
Or cease your quest of love?

BURGUNDY. Most royal Majesty, 205
I crave no more than hath your highness offered,
Nor will you tender less.

LEAR. Right noble Burgundy,
When she was dear to us, we did hold her so;
But now her price is fallen. Sir, there she stands. 210
If aught within that little seeming substance,
Or all of it, with our displeasure pieced,
And nothing more, may fitly like your Grace,
She's there, and she is yours.

BURGUNDY. I know no answer. 215

LEAR. Will you, with those infirmities she owes,
Unfriended, new-adopted to our hate,
Dow'red with our curse, and strangered with our oath,
Take her, or leave her?

BURGUNDY. Pardon me, royal sir; 220
Election makes not up on such conditions.

LEAR. Then leave her, sir; for, by the power that made me,
I tell you all her wealth. *[To France.]* For you, great King,
I would not from your love make such a stray
To match you where I hate; therefore beseech you 225
T' avert your liking a more worthier way
Than on a wretch whom nature is ashamed

    Almost t' acknowledge hers.

FRANCE.   This is most strange,
    That she whom even but now was your best object,   230
    The argument of your praise, balm of your age,
    The best, the dearest, should in this trice of time
    Commit a thing so monstrous, to dismantle
    So many folds of favour. Sure, her offence
    Must be of such unnatural degree   235
    That monsters it, or your fore-vouched affection
    Fall into taint; which to believe of her
    Must be a faith that reason without miracle
    Could never plant in me.

CORDELIA.   I yet beseech your Majesty,   240
    If for I want that glib and oily art
    To speak and purpose not, since what I well intend
    I'll do't before I speak, that you make known
    It is no vicious blot, murder, or foulness,
    No unchaste action, or dishonoured step,   245
    That hath deprived me of your grace and favour;
    But even for want of that for which I am richer,
    A still-soliciting eye, and such a tongue
    As I am glad I have not, though not to have it
    Hath lost me in your liking.   250

LEAR.   Better thou
    Hadst not been born than not to have pleased me better.

FRANCE. Is it but this? A tardiness in nature
    Which often leaves the history unspoke
    That it intends to do. My lord of Burgundy,   255
    What say you to the lady? Love's not love
    When it is mingled with regards that stand
    Aloof from th' entire point. Will you have her?
    She is herself a dowry.

BURGUNDY.   Royal King,   260
    Give but this portion which yourself proposed,
    And here I take Cordelia by the hand,
    Duchess of Burgundy.

LEAR. Nothing. I have sworn. I am firm.

BURGUNDY. I am sorry then you have so lost a father   265
    That you must lose a husband.

CORDELIA.   Peace be with Burgundy.
    Since that respects of fortune are his love,
    I shall not be his wife.

FRANCE. Fairest Cordelia, that art most rich being poor,   270
    Most choice, forsaken; and most loved despised,
    Thee and thy virtues here I seize upon.
    Be it lawful I take up what's cast away.
    Gods, gods! 'Tis strange that from their cold'st neglect
    My love should kindle to inflamed respect.   275

Thy dowerless daughter, king, thrown to my chance,
Is Queen of us, of ours, and our fair France.
Not all the dukes of wat'rish Burgundy
Can buy this unprized precious maid of me.
Bid them farewell, Cordelia, though unkind. 280
Thou losest here, a better where to find.

LEAR. Thou hast her, France; let her be thine; for we
Have no such daughter, nor shall ever see
That face of hers again. Therefore be gone,
Without our grace, our love, our benison. 285
Come, noble Burgundy.

[Flourish. Exeunt [Lear, Burgundy, Cornwall, Albany, Gloucester,
and Attendants].

FRANCE. Bid farewell to your sisters.

CORDELIA. The jewels of our father, with washed eyes
Cordelia leaves you. I know you what you are,
And like a sister, am most loath to call 290
Your faults as they are named. Love well our father.
To your professed bosoms I commit him
But yet, alas, stood I within his grace,
I would prefer him to a better place.
So, farewell to you both. 295

REGAN. Prescribe not us our duties.

GONERIL. Let your study
Be to content your lord, who hath received you
At Fortune's alms. You have obedience scanted,
And well are worth the want that you have wanted. 300

CORDELIA. Time shall unfold what plighted cunning hides,
Who cover faults, at last shame them derides.
Well may you prosper.

FRANCE. Come, my fair Cordelia.
Exit France and Cordelia.

GONERIL. Sister, it is not a little I have to say of what most nearly 305
appertains to us both. I think our father will hence tonight.

REGAN. That's most certain, and with you; next month with us.

GONERIL. You see how full of changes his age is. The observation
we have made of it hath not been little. He always loved our sister
most; and with what poor judgment he hath now cast her off 310
appears too grossly.

REGAN. 'Tis the infirmity of his age; yet he hath ever but slenderly
known himself.

GONERIL. The best and soundest of his time hath been but rash; then
must we look from his age to receive not alone the imperfections 315
of long-ingraffed condition, but therewithal the unruly wayward-
ness that infirm and choleric years bring with them.

REGAN. Such unconstant starts are we like to have from him as this of Kent's banishment.

GONERIL. There is further compliment of leave-taking between France and him. Pray you, let's hit together; if our father carry authority with such dispositions as he bears, this last surrender of his will but offend us.

REGAN. We shall further think of it.

GONERIL. We must do something, and i' the heat.

Exeunt.

Scene II. *[The Earl of Gloucester's castle.]*

Enter Edmund [with a letter].

EDMUND. Thou, Nature, art my goddess; to thy law
My services are bound. Wherefore should I
Stand in the plague of custom, and permit
The curiosity of nations to deprive me,
For that I am some twelve or fourteen moonshines
Lag of a brother? Why bastard? wherefore base?
When my dimensions are as well compact,
My mind as generous, and my shape as true,
As honest madam's issue? Why brand they us
With base? With baseness? Bastardy? Base, Base?
Who, in the lusty stealth of nature, take
More composition and fierce quality
Than doth, within a dull, stale, tired bed,
Go to th' creating a whole tribe of fops
Got 'tween asleep and wake? Well then,
Legitimate Edgar, I must have your land.
Our father's love is to the bastard Edmund
As to th' legitimate. Fine word, "legitimate."
Well, my legitimate, if this letter speed,
And my invention thrive, Edmund the base
Shall top th' legitimate. I grow; I prosper.
Now, gods, stand up for bastards.

Enter Gloucester.

GLOUCESTER. Kent banished thus? and France in choler parted?
And the king gone tonight! prescribed his pow'r?
Confined to exhibition? All this done
Upon the gad? Edmund, how now? What news?

EDMUND. So please your lordship, none.

GLOUCESTER. Why so earnestly seek you to put up that letter?

EDMUND. I know no news, my lord.

GLOUCESTER. What paper were you reading?

EDMUND. Nothing, my lord.

GLOUCESTER. No? What needed, then, that terrible dispatch of it into your pocket? The quality of nothing hath not such need to hide itself. Let's see. Come, if it be nothing, I shall not need spectacles.

EDMUND. I beseech you, sir, pardon me. It is a letter from my brother, that I have not all o'er-read; and for so much as I have perused, I find it not fit for your o'er-looking.

GLOUCESTER. Give me the letter, sir.

EDMUND. I shall offend, either to detain or give it. The contents, as in part I understand them, are to blame.

GLOUCESTER. Let's see, let's see.

EDMUND. I hope, for my brother's justification, he wrote this but as an essay or taste of my virtue.

GLOUCESTER. *(Reads)* "This policy and reverence of age makes the world bitter to the best of our times; keeps our fortunes from us till our oldness cannot relish them. I begin to find an idle and fond bondage in the oppression of aged tyranny, who sways, not as it hath power, but as it is suffered. Come to me, that of this I may speak more. If our father would sleep till I waked him, you should enjoy half his revenue for ever, and live the beloved of your brother,   EDGAR."
Hum! Conspiracy? "Sleep till I waked him, you should enjoy half his revenue." My son Edgar! Had he a hand to write this? A heart and brain to breed it in? When came this to you? Who brought it?

EDMUND. It was not brought me, my lord; there's the cunning of it; I found it thrown in at the casement of my closet.

GLOUCESTER. You know the character to be your brother's?

EDMUND. If the matter were good, my lord, I durst swear it were his; but, in respect of that, I would fain think it were not.

GLOUCESTER. It is his.

EDMUND. It is his hand, my lord; but I hope his heart is not in the contents.

GLOUCESTER. Hath he never heretofore sounded you in this business?

EDMUND. Never, my lord. But I have heard him oft maintain it to be fit, that, sons at perfect age, and fathers declined, the father should be as ward to the son, and the son manage his revenue.

GLOUCESTER. O villain, villain! His very opinion in the letter! Abhorred villain, unnatural, detested, brutish villain; worse than brutish! Go, sirrah, seek him. I'll apprehend him. Abominable villain! Where is he?

EDMUND. I do not well know, my lord. If it shall please you to suspend your indignation against my brother till you can derive from him better testimony of his intent, you shall run a certain course; where, if you violently proceed against him, mistaking his purpose, it would make a great gap in your own honor, and shake in pieces the heart of his obedience. I dare pawn down my life for him that he hath writ this to feel my affection to your honor, and to no other pretence of danger.

GLOUCESTER. Think you so?

EDMUND. If your honor judge it meet, I will place you where you shall hear us confer of this, and by an auricular assurance have your satisfaction; and that without any further delay than this very evening.

GLOUCESTER. He cannot be such a monster.

EDMUND. Nor is not, sure.

GLOUCESTER. To his father, that so tenderly and entirely loves him. Heaven and earth! Edmund, seek him out; wind me into him, I pray you; frame the business after your own wisdom. I would unstate myself, to be in a due resolution.

EDMUND. I will seek him, sir, presently; convey the business as I shall find means and acquaint you withal.

GLOUCESTER. These late eclipses in the sun and moon portend no good to us. Though the wisdom of Nature can reason it thus and thus, yet Nature finds itself scourged by the sequent effects. Love cools, friendship falls off, brothers divide. In cities, mutinies; in countries, discord; in palaces, treason; and the bond cracked 'twixt son and father. This villain of mine comes under the prediction; there's son against father; the King falls from bias of nature, there's father against child. We have seen the best of our time. Machinations, hollowness, treachery, and all ruinous disorders, follow us disquietly to our graves. Find out this villain, Edmund; it shall lose thee nothing. Do it carefully. And the noble and true-hearted Kent banished; his offence, honesty! 'Tis strange.

Exit.

EDMUND. This is the excellent foppery of the world, that, when we are sick in fortune, often the surfeits of our own behavior, we make guilty of our disasters the sun, the moon, and the stars; as if we were villains on necessity; fools by heavenly compulsion; knaves, thieves, and treachers by spherical predominance; drunkards, liars, and adulterers, by an enforced obedience of planetary influence; and all that we are evil in, by a divine thrusting on. An admirable evasion of whoremaster man, to lay his goatish disposition on the charge of a star. My father compounded with my mother under the Dragon's Tail; and my nativity was under Ursa Major, so that it follows, I am rough and lecherous. Fut! I should have been that I am, had the maidenliest star in the firmament twinkled on my bastardizing. Edgar—

Enter Edgar.

and pat he comes like the catastrophe of the old comedy. My cue is villanous melancholy, with a sigh like Tom o' Bedlam.—O, these eclipses do portend these divisions! Fa, sol, la, mi.

EDGAR. How now, brother Edmund! what serious contemplation are you in?

EDMUND. I am thinking, brother, of a prediction I read this other day, what should follow these eclipses. 125

EDGAR. Do you busy yourself about that?

EDMUND. I promise you, the effects he writes of succeed unhappily: as of unnaturalness between the child and the parent; death, dearth, dissolutions of ancient amities; divisions in state, menaces and maledictions against King and nobles, needless diffidences, 130 banishment of friends, dissipation of cohorts, nuptial breaches, and I know not what.

EDGAR. How long have you been a sectary astronomical?

EDMUND. Come, come; when saw you my father last?

EDGAR. Why, the night gone by. 135

EDMUND. Spake you with him?

EDGAR. Ay, two hours together.

EDMUND. Parted you in good terms? Found you no displeasure in him by word or countenance?

EDGAR. None at all. 140

EDMUND. Bethink yourself wherein you may have offended him; and at my entreaty forbear his presence till some little time hath qualified the heat of his displeasure, which at this instant so rageth in him, that with the mischief of your person it would scarcely allay. 145

EDGAR. Some villain hath done me wrong.

EDMUND. That's my fear, brother I pray you have a continent forbearance till the speed of his rage goes slower; and, as I say, retire with me to my lodging, from whence I will fitly bring you to hear my lord speak. Pray ye, go; there's my key. If you do stir abroad, 150 go armed.

EDGAR. Armed, brother?

EDMUND. Brother, I advise you to the best. Go armed. I am no honest man if there be any good meaning towards you. I have told you what I have seen and heard; but faintly, nothing like the 155 image and horror of it. Pray you, away.

EDGAR. Shall I hear from you anon?

EDMUND. I do serve you in this business.

Exit Edgar.

A credulous father! and a brother noble,
Whose nature is so far from doing harms 160
That he suspects none; on whose foolish honesty
My practices ride easy. I see the business.
Let me, if not by birth, have lands by wit.
All with me's meet that I can fashion fit. *Exit.*

Scene III. *[The Duke of Albany's palace.]*

Enter Goneril, and [Oswald, her] Steward.

GONERIL. Did my father strike my gentleman for chiding of his
   Fool?

OSWALD. Ay, madam.

GONERIL. By day and night he wrongs me. Every hour
   He flashes into one gross crime or other
   That sets us all at odds. I'll not endure it.
   His knights grow riotous, and himself upbraids us
   On every trifle. When he returns from hunting,
   I will not speak with him. Say I am sick.
   If you come slack of former services,
   You shall do well; the fault of it I'll answer.

[Horns within.]

OSWALD. He's coming, madam; I hear him.

GONERIL. Put on what weary negligence you please,
   You and your fellows. I'd have it come to question.
   If he distaste it, let him to our sister,
   Whose mind and mine I know in that are one,
   Not to be overruled. Idle old man,
   That still would manage those authorities
   That he hath given away. Now, by my life,
   Old fools are babes again; and must be used
   With checks as flatteries, when they are seen abused.
   Remember what I have said.

OSWALD.   Well, madam.

GONERIL. And let his knights have colder looks among you;
   What grows of it, no matter; advise your fellows so.
   I would breed from hence occasions, and I shall,
   That I may speak. I'll write straight to my sister
   To hold my very course. Go, prepare for dinner.

Exeunt.

Scene IV. *[A hall in the same.]*

Enter Kent, [disguised].

KENT. If but as well I other accents borrow
   That can my speech defuse, my good intent
   May carry through itself to that full issue
   For which I razed my likeness. Now, banished Kent,
   If thou canst serve where thou dost stand condemned,
   So may it come, thy master, whom thou lov'st,
   Shall find thee full of labors.

Horns within. Enter Lear, [Knights] and Attendants.

LEAR. Let me not stay a jot for dinner; go get it ready. *[Exit an Attendant.]* How now! what art thou?

KENT. A man, sir.

LEAR. What dost thou profess? What wouldst thou with us?

KENT. I do profess to be no less than I seem, to serve him truly that will put me in trust, to love him that is honest, to converse with him that is wise, and says little, to fear judgment, to fight when I cannot choose, and to eat no fish.

LEAR. What art thou?

KENT. A very honest-hearted fellow, and as poor as the King.

LEAR. If thou be'st as poor for a subject as he's for a king, thou art poor enough. What wouldst thou?

KENT. Service.

LEAR. Who wouldst thou serve?

KENT. You.

LEAR. Dost thou know me, fellow?

KENT. No, sir; but you have that in your countenance which I would fain call master.

LEAR. What's that?

KENT. Authority.

LEAR. What services canst thou do?

KENT. I can keep honest counsel, ride, run, mar a curious tale in telling it, and deliver a plain message bluntly. That which ordinary men are fit for, I am qualified in, and the best of me is diligence.

LEAR. How old art thou?

KENT. Not so young, sir, to love a woman for singing, nor so old to dote on her for anything. I have years on my back forty-eight.

LEAR. Follow me; thou shalt serve me. If I like thee no worse after dinner, I will not part from thee yet. Dinner, ho, dinner! Where's my knave? my Fool? Go you, and call my fool hither.

[Exit an Attendant.]

Enter Oswald.

You, you, sirrah, where's my daughter?

OSWALD. So please you—— *Exit.*

LEAR. What says the fellow there? Call the clotpoll back. *[Exit a Knight.]* Where's my Fool, ho? I think the world's asleep.

[Re-enter Knight.]

How now! Where's that mongrel?

KNIGHT. He says, my lord, your daughter is not well.

LEAR. Why came not the slave back to me when I called him?

KNIGHT. Sir, he answered me in the roundest manner, he would not. 45

LEAR. He would not?

KNIGHT. My lord, I know not what the matter is; but, to my judgment, your Highness is not entertained with that ceremonious affection as you were wont. There's a great abatement of kindness appears as well in the general dependants as in the Duke himself also and your daughter. 50

LEAR. Ha? Sayest thou so?

KNIGHT. I beseech you, pardon me, my lord, if I be mistaken; for my duty cannot be silent when I think your Highness wronged.

LEAR. Thou but rememb'rest me of mine own conception. I have perceived a most faint neglect of late, which I have rather blamed as mine own jealous curiosity than as a very pretence and purpose of unkindness. I will look further into't. But where's my Fool? I have not seen him this two days. 55

KNIGHT. Since my young lady's going into France, sir, the Fool hath much pined away. 60

LEAR. No more of that; I have noted it well. Go you, and tell my daughter I would speak with her. Go you, call hither my Fool.
                                                           [*Exit an Attendant.*]

Enter Oswald.

O, you, sir, you! Come you hither, sir. Who am I, sir?

OSWALD. My lady's father. 65

LEAR. "My lady's father"? My lord's knave, you whoreson dog! you slave! you cur!

OSWALD. I am none of these, my lord; I beseech your pardon.

LEAR. Do you bandy looks with me, you rascal?
                                                           [*Striking him.*]

OSWALD. I'll not be strucken, my lord. 70

KENT. Nor tripped neither, you base football player.
                                                           [*Tripping up his heels.*]

LEAR. I thank thee, fellow. Thou serv'st me, and I'll love thee.

KENT. Come, sir, arise, away. I'll teach you differences. Away, away! if you will measure your lubber's length again, tarry; but away. Go to! Have you wisdom? So.   [*Pushes Oswald out.*] 75

LEAR. Now, my friendly knave, I thank thee. There's earnest of thy service.   [*Giving Kent money.*]

Enter Fool.

FOOL. Let me hire him too. Here's my coxcomb.
                                                           [*Offering Kent his cap.*]

LEAR. How now, my pretty knave? How dost thou?

FOOL. Sirrah, you were best take my coxcomb.

KENT. Why, Fool?

FOOL. Why, for taking one's part that's out of favor. Nay, an thou canst not smile as the wind sits, thou'lt catch cold shortly. There, take my coxcomb. Why, this fellow has banished two on 's daughters, and did the third a blessing against his will; if thou follow him, thou must needs wear my coxcomb.—How now, Nuncle! Would I had two coxcombs and two daughters!

LEAR. Why, my boy?

FOOL. If I gave them all my living, I'd keep my coxcombs myself. There's mine; beg another of thy daughters.

LEAR. Take heed, sirrah—the whip.

FOOL. Truth's a dog must to kennel; he must be whipped out, when Lady the Brach may stand by th' fire and stink.

LEAR. A pestilent gall to me.

FOOL. Sirrah, I'll teach thee a speech.

LEAR. Do.

FOOL. Mark it, Nuncle.
> Have more than thou showest,
> Speak less than thou knowest,
> Lend less than thou owest,
> Ride more than thou goest,
> Learn more than thou trowest,
> Set less than thou throwest,
> Leave thy drink and thy whore,
> And keep in-a-door,
> And thou shalt have more
> Than two tens to a score.

KENT. This is nothing, Fool.

FOOL. Then 'tis like the breath of an unfeed lawyer—you gave me nothing for't. Can you make no use of nothing, Nuncle?

LEAR. Why, no, boy; nothing can be made out of nothing.

FOOL. *[To Kent]* Prithee, tell him, so much the rent of his land comes to; he will not believe a Fool.

LEAR. A bitter Fool.

FOOL. Dost thou know the difference, my boy, between a bitter Fool and a sweet one?

LEAR. No, lad; teach me.

FOOL.
> That lord that counseled thee
> To give away thy land,
> Come place him here by me,

>   Do thou for him stand.
>   The sweet and bitter fool
>   Will presently appear;
>   The one in motley here,
>   The other found out there. 125

LEAR. Dost thou call me fool, boy?

FOOL. All thy other titles thou hast given away; that thou wast born with.

KENT. This is not altogether fool, my lord.

FOOL. No, faith, lords and great men will not let me. If I had a monopoly out, they would have part on't. And ladies too, they will not let me have all fool to myself; they'll be snatching. Nuncle, give me an egg, and I'll give thee two crowns. 130

LEAR. What two crowns shall they be?

FOOL. Why, after I have cut the egg i' th, middle, and eat up the meat, the two crowns of the egg. When thou clovest thy crown i' th' middle, and gav'st away both parts, thou borest thy ass on thy back o'er the dirt. Thou hadst little wit in thy bald crown, when thou gav'st thy golden one away. If I speak like myself in this, let him be whipped that first finds it so. 135
>   *[Singing.]* Fools had ne'er less wit in a year, 140
>   For wise men are grown foppish,
>   And know not how their wits to wear,
>   Their manners are so apish.

LEAR. When were you wont to be so full of songs, sirrah?

FOOL. I have used it, Nuncle, ever since thou mad'st thy daughters thy mothers; for when thou gav'st them the rod, and put'st down thine own breeches, 145
>   *[Singing.]* Then they for sudden joy did weep,
>   And I for sorrow sung,
>   That such a king should play bo-peep 150
>   And go the fools among.

   Prithee, Nuncle, keep a schoolmaster that can teach thy Fool to lie. I would fain learn to lie.

LEAR. And you lie, sirrah, we'll have you whipped.

FOOL. I marvel what kin thou and thy daughters are. They'll have me whipped for speaking true; thou'lt have me whipped for lying; and sometimes I am whipped for holding my peace. I had rather be any kind o' thing than a Fool, and yet I would not be thee, Nuncle; thou hast pared thy wit o' both sides, and left nothing i' th' middle. Here comes one o' the parings. 155

160

Enter Goneril.

LEAR. How now, daughter! What makes that frontlet on? Methinks you are too much of late i' th' frown.

FOOL. Thou wast a pretty fellow when thou hadst no need to care for her frowning. Now thou art an O without a figure. I am better than thou art now. I am a fool, thou art nothing. *[To Goneril.]* Yes, 165

    forsooth, I will hold my tongue. So your face bids me, though you
    say nothing. Mum, mum,
        He that keeps nor crust nor crum,
        Weary of all, shall want some.
    [Pointing to Lear] That's a shealed peascod.   170

GONERIL. Not only, sir, this your all-licensed Fool,
    But other of your insolent retinue
    Do hourly carp and quarrel, breaking forth
    In rank and not-to-be endured riots. Sir,
    I had thought, by making this well known unto you   175
    To have found a safe redress, but now grow fearful,
    By what yourself too late have spoke and done,
    That you protect this course, and put it on
    By your allowance; which if you should, the fault
    Would not 'scape censure, nor the redresses sleep,   180
    Which, in the tender of a wholesome weal,
    Might in their working do you that offense,
    Which else were shame, that then necessity
    Will call discreet proceeding.

FOOL. For, you know, Nuncle,   185
        The hedge-sparrow fed the cuckoo so long,
        That its had it head bit off by it young.
    So, out went the candle, and we were left darkling.

LEAR. Are you our daughter?

GONERIL. Come, sir,   190
    I would you would make use of that good wisdom
    Whereof I know you are fraught; and put away
    These dispositions, that of late transform you
    From what you rightly are.

FOOL. May not an ass know when the cart draws the horse? Whoop,   195
    Jug, I love thee!

LEAR. Does any here know me? This is not Lear.
    Does Lear walk thus? Speak thus? Where are his eyes?
    Either his notion weakens, or his discernings
    Are lethargied—Ha! Waking? 'Tis not so.   200
    Who is it that can tell me who I am?

FOOL. Lear's shadow.

LEAR. I would learn that; for, by the marks of sovereignty, knowl-
    edge, and reason, I should be false persuaded I had daughters.

FOOL. Which they will make an obedient father.   205

LEAR. Your name, fair gentlewoman?

GONERIL. This admiration, sir, is much o' th' savor
    Of other your new pranks. I do beseech you
    To understand my purposes aright.
    As you are old and reverend, you should be wise.   210
    Here do you keep a hundred knights and squires,
    Men so disordered, so deboshed and bold,

> That this our court, infected with their manners,
> Shows like a riotous inn. Epicurism and lust
> Make it more like a tavern or a brothel 215
> Than a graced palace. The shame itself doth speak
> For instant remedy. Be then desired
> By her, that else will take the thing she begs,
> A little to disquantity your train,
> And the remainders that shall still depend, 220
> To be such men as may besort your age,
> Which know themselves, and you.

LEAR.   Darkness and devils!
> Saddle my horses; call my train together.
> Degenerate bastard! I'll not trouble thee: 225
> Yet have I left a daughter.

GONERIL. You strike my people; and your disordered rabble
> Make servants of their betters.

Enter Albany.

LEAR. Woe, that too late repents. O, sir, are you come?
> Is it your will? Speak, sir. Prepare my horses. 230
> Ingratitude! Thou marble-hearted fiend,
> More hideous when thou show'st thee in a child
> Than the sea-monster!

ALBANY.   Pray, sir, be patient.

LEAR. Detested kite, thou liest. 235
> My train are men of choice and rarest parts,
> That all particulars of duty know,
> And in the most exact regard, support
> The worships of their name. O most small fault,
> How ugly didst thou in Cordelia show! 240
> That, like an engine, wrenched my frame of nature
> From the fixed place; drew from my heart all love,
> And added to the gall. O Lear, Lear, Lear!
> Beat at this gate, that let thy folly in *[Striking his head.]*
> And thy dear judgment out. Go, go, my people. 245

ALBANY. My lord, I am guiltless, as I am ignorant
> Of what hath moved you.

LEAR.   It may be so, my lord.
> Hear, Nature, hear; dear Goddess, hear:
> Suspend thy purpose, if thou didst intend 250
> To make this creature fruitful.
> Into her womb convey sterility.
> Dry up in her the organs of increase,
> And from her derogate body never spring
> A babe to honour her. If she must teem, 255
> Create her child of spleen, that it may live
> And be a thwart disnatured torment to her.
> Let it stamp wrinkles in her brow of youth;
> With cadent tears fret channels in her cheeks,
> Turn all her mother's pains and benefits 260

      To laughter and contempt, that she may feel
      How sharper than a serpent's tooth it is
      To have a thankless child. Away, away! *Exit.*

ALBANY. Now, gods that we adore, whereof comes this?

GONERIL. Never afflict yourself to know the cause,   265
      But let his disposition have that scope
      As dotage gives it.

                  Enter Lear.

LEAR. What, fifty of my followers at a clap?
      Within a fortnight?

ALBANY.   What's the matter, sir?   270

LEAR. I'll tell thee. *[To Goneril.]* Life and death! I am ashamed
      That thou hast power to shake my manhood thus!
      That these hot tears, which break from me perforce,
      Should make thee worth them. Blasts and fogs upon thee!
      Th' untented woundings of a father's curse   275
      Pierce every sense about thee! Old fond eyes,
      Beweep this cause again, I'll pluck ye out
      And cast you, with the waters that you loose,
      To temper clay. Yea, it is come to this?
      Ha! Let it be so. I have another daughter,   280
      Who I am sure is kind and comfortable.
      When she shall hear this of thee, with her nails
      She'll flay thy wolvish visage. Thou shalt find
      That I'll resume the shape which thou dost think
      I have cast off for ever.   285

          Exit [Lear with Kent and Attendants].

GONERIL.   Do you mark that?

ALBANY. I cannot be so partial, Goneril,
      To the great love I bear you—

GONERIL. Pray you, content. What, Oswald, ho!
      [To the Fool.] You, sir, more knave than fool, after your master!   290

FOOL. Nuncle Lear, Nuncle Lear, tarry and take the Fool with thee.
            A fox, when one has caught her,
            And such a daughter,
            Should sure to the slaughter,
            If my cap would buy a halter.   295
            So the Fool follows after.   *Exit.*

GONERIL. This man hath had good counsel. A hundred knights!
      'Tis politic and safe to let him keep
      At point a hundred knights: yes, that, on every dream,
      Each buzz, each fancy, each complaint, dislike,   300
      He may enguard his dotage with their pow'rs,
      And hold our lives in mercy. Oswald, I say!

ALBANY. Well, you may fear too far.

GONERIL.   Safer than trust too far.

GONERIL.
　　Let me still take away the harms I fear, 305
　　Not fear still to be taken. I know his heart.
　　What he hath uttered I have writ my sister.
　　If she sustain him and his hundred knights,
　　When I have showed th' unfitness—

Enter Oswald.

　　　　　　　　　　　　How now, Oswald? 310
　　What, have you writ that letter to my sister?

OSWALD. Ay, madam.

GONERIL. Take you some company, and away to horse.
　　Inform her full of my particular fear,
　　And thereto add such reasons of your own 315
　　As may compact it more. Get you gone,
　　And hasten your return. *[Exit Oswald.]* No, no, my lord,
　　This milky gentleness and course of yours,
　　Though I condemn not, yet, under pardon,
　　You are much more attasked for want of wisdom 320
　　Than praised for harmful mildness.

ALBANY. How far your eyes may pierce I cannot tell;
　　Striving to better, oft we mar what's well.

GONERIL. Nay, then——

ALBANY. Well, well; th' event. *Exeunt.* 325

Scene V. [*Court before the same.*]

Enter Lear, Kent, and Fool.

LEAR. Go you before to Gloucester with these letters. Acquaint my daughter no further with anything you know than comes from her demand out of the letter. If your diligence be not speedy, I shall be there afore you.

KENT. I will not sleep, my lord, till I have delivered your letter. 5
　　Exit.

FOOL. If a man's brains were in's heels, were't not in danger of kibes?

LEAR. Ay, boy.

FOOL. Then I prithee be merry. Thy wit shall not go slipshod.

LEAR. Ha, ha, ha. 10

FOOL. Shalt see thy other daughter will use thee kindly; for though she's as like this as a crab's like an apple, yet I can tell what I can tell.

LEAR. Why, what canst thou tell, my boy?

FOOL. She will taste as like this as a crab does to a crab. Thou canst 15
tell why one's nose stands i' th' middle on's face?

LEAR. No.

FOOL. Why, to keep one's eyes of either side's nose, that what a man cannot smell out, he may spy into.

LEAR. I did her wrong.

FOOL. Canst tell how an oyster makes his shell?

LEAR. No.

FOOL. Nor I neither; but I can tell why a snail has a house.

LEAR. Why?

FOOL. Why, to put's head in; not to give it away to his daughters, and leave his horns without a case.

LEAR. I will forget my nature. So kind a father! Be my horses ready?

FOOL. Thy asses are gone about 'em. The reason why the seven stars are no moe than seven is a pretty reason.

LEAR. Because they are not eight?

FOOL. Yes, indeed. Thou wouldst make a good Fool.

LEAR. To take't again perforce! Monster ingratitude!

FOOL. If thou wert my Fool, Nuncle, I'd have thee beaten for being old before thy time.

LEAR. How's that?

FOOL. Thou shouldst not have been old till thou hadst been wise.

LEAR. O, let me not be mad, not mad, sweet heaven!
Keep me in temper; I would not be mad!

[Enter Gentleman.]

How now, are the horses ready?

GENTLEMAN. Ready, my lord.

LEAR. Come, boy.

FOOL. She that's a maid now, and laughs at my departure,
Shall not be a maid long, unless things be cut shorter.   *Exeunt.*

ACT II

Scene I. [*The Earl of Gloucester's castle.*]

Enter Edmund and Curan, severally.

EDMUND. Save thee, Curan.

CURAN. And you, sir. I have been with your father, and given him notice that the Duke of Cornwall and Regan his duchess will be here with him this night.

EDMUND. How comes that?

CURAN. Nay, I know not. You have heard of the news abroad; I mean the whispered ones, for they are yet but ear-kissing arguments?

EDMUND. Not I. Pray you, what are they?

CURAN. Have you heard of no likely wars toward, 'twixt the Dukes of Cornwall and Albany?

EDMUND. Not a word.

CURAN. You may do, then, in time. Fare you well, sir.
Exit.

EDMUND. The duke be here tonight? The better! best!
This weaves itself perforce into my business.
My father hath set guard to take my brother;
And I have one thing of a queasy question
Which I must act. Briefness and Fortune, work!
Brother, a word; descend. Brother, I say!

Enter Edgar.

My father watches. O sir, fly this place.
Intelligence is given where you are hid.
You have now the good advantage of the night.
Have you not spoken 'gainst the Duke of Cornwall?
He's coming hither; now, i' th' night, i' th' haste,
And Regan with him. Have you nothing said
Upon his party 'gainst the Duke of Albany?
Advise yourself.

EDGAR.   I am sure on't, not a word.

EDMUND. I hear my father coming. Pardon me:
In cunning I must draw my sword upon you.
Draw; seem to defend yourself; now quit you well.
Yield! Come before my father! Light, ho, here!
Fly, brother. Torches, torches!—So, farewell.
Exit Edgar.
Some blood drawn on me would beget opinion
[*Wounds his arm.*]
Of my more fierce endeavour. I have seen drunkards
Do more than this in sport. Father, father!

Stop, stop! No help?

Enter Gloucester, and Servants with torches.

GLOUCESTER. Now, Edmund, where's the villain?

EDMUND. Here stood he in the dark, his sharp sword out,
    Mumbling of wicked charms, conjuring the moon 40
    To stand auspicious mistress.

GLOUCESTER.   But where is he?

EDMUND. Look, sir, I bleed.

GLOUCESTER.   Where is the villain, Edmund?

EDMUND. Fled this way, sir. When by no means he could— 45

GLOUCESTER. Pursue him, ho! Go after.
                              [Exeunt some Servants.]
    By no means what?

EDMUND. Persuade me to the murder of your lordship;
    But that I told him the revenging gods
    'Gainst parricides did all the thunder bend; 50
    Spoke with how manifold and strong a bond
    The child was bound to th' father. Sir, in fine,
    Seeing how loathly opposite I stood
    To his unnatural purpose, in fell motion
    With his preparèd sword he charges home 55
    My unprovided body, latched mine arm;
    But when he saw my best alarumed spirits
    Bold in the quarrel's right, roused to th' encounter,
    Or whether gasted by the noise I made,
    Full suddenly he fled. 60

GLOUCESTER.   Let him fly far.
    Not in this land shall he remain uncaught;
    And found—dispatch. The noble Duke my master,
    My worthy arch and patron, comes tonight.
    By his authority I will proclaim it, 65
    That he which finds him shall deserve our thanks,
    Bringing the murderous coward to the stake.
    He that conceals him, death.

EDMUND. When I dissuaded him from his intent,
    And found him pight to do it, with curst speech 70
    I threatened to discover him. He replied,
    "Thou unpossessing bastard, dost thou think,
    If I would stand against thee, would the reposal
    Of any trust, virtue, or worth in thee
    Make thy words faithed? No. What I should deny— 75
    As this I would, ay, though thou didst produce
    My very character—I'd turn it all
    To thy suggestion, plot, and damnèd practice.
    And thou must make a dullard of the world,
    If they not thought the profits of my death 80
    Were very pregnant and potential spirits

To make thee seek it."

GLOUCESTER. O strange and fastened villain!
Would he deny his letter, said he? I never got him.

Tucket within.

Hark, the Duke's trumpets. I know not why he comes. 85
All ports I'll bar; the villain shall not 'scape;
The duke must grant me that. Besides, his picture
I will send far and near, that all the kingdom
May have the due note of him; and of my land,
Loyal and natural boy, I'll work the means 90
To make thee capable.

Enter Cornwall, Regan, and Attendants.

CORNWALL. How now, my noble friend! Since I came hither,
Which I can call but now, I have heard strange news.

REGAN. If it be true, all vengeance comes too short
Which can pursue th' offender. How dost, my lord? 95

GLOUCESTER. O madam, my old heart is cracked, it's cracked!

REGAN. What, did my father's godson seek your life?
He whom my father named? your Edgar?

GLOUCESTER. O, lady, lady, shame would have it hid.

REGAN. Was he not companion with the riotous knights 100
That tend upon my father?

GLOUCESTER. I know not, madam. 'Tis too bad, too bad.

EDMUND. Yes, madam, he was of that consort.

REGAN. No marvel then, though he were ill affected.
'Tis they have put him on the old man's death, 105
To have th' expense and waste of his revenues.
I have this present evening from my sister
Been well informed of them; and with such cautions,
That if they come to sojourn at my house,
I'll not be there. 110

CORNWALL. Nor I, assure thee, Regan.
Edmund, I hear that you have shown your father
A childlike office.

EDMUND. It was my duty, sir.

GLOUCESTER. He did bewray his practice, and received 115
This hurt you see, striving to apprehend him.

CORNWALL. Is he pursued?

GLOUCESTER. Ay, my good lord.

CORNWALL. If he be taken, he shall never more
Be fear'd of doing harm. Make your own purpose, 120
How in my strength you please. For you, Edmund,
Whose virtue and obedience doth this instant
So much commend itself, you shall be ours.

    Natures of such deep trust we shall much need;
    You we first seize on. 125

EDMUND.   I shall serve you, sir,
    Truly, however else.

GLOUCESTER.   For him I thank your Grace.

CORNWALL. You know not why we came to visit you?

REGAN. Thus out of season, threading dark-eyed night. 130
    Occasions, noble Gloucester, of some prize,
    Wherein we must have use of your advice.
    Our father he hath writ, so hath our sister,
    Of differences, which I least thought it fit
    To answer from our home; the several messengers 135
    From hence attend dispatch. Our good old friend,
    Lay comforts to your bosom; and bestow
    Your needful counsel to our businesses,
    Which craves the instant use.

GLOUCESTER.   I serve you, madam. 140
    Your Graces are right welcome.

                                            Exeunt. Flourish.

Scene II. *[Before Gloucester's castle.]*

Enter Kent and Oswald, severally.

OSWALD. Good dawning to thee, friend. Art of this house?

KENT. Ay.

OSWALD. Where may we set our horses?

KENT. I' th' mire.

OSWALD. Prithee, if thou lov'st me, tell me. 5

KENT. I love thee not.

OSWALD. Why, then, I care not for thee.

KENT. If I had thee in Lipsbury Pinfold, I would make thee care for me.

OSWALD. Why dost thou use me thus? I know thee not.

KENT. Fellow, I know thee. 10

OSWALD. What dost thou know me for?

KENT. A knave, a rascal, an eater of broken meats; a base, proud, shallow, beggarly, three-suited, hundred-pound, filthy, worsted-stocking knave; a lily-livered, action-taking whoreson, glass-gazing, superserviceable, finical rogue; one-trunk-inheriting slave; 15 one that wouldst be a bawd, in way of good service, and art nothing but the composition of a knave, beggar, coward, pander, and the son and heir of a mongrel bitch; one whom I will beat into clamorous whining, if thou deniest the least syllable of thy addition. 20

OSWALD. Why, what a monstrous fellow art thou, thus to rail on one that is neither known of thee nor knows thee!

KENT. What a brazen-faced varlet art thou, to deny thou knowest me! Is it two days ago since I tripped up thy heels, and beat thee before the King? *[Drawing his sword]* Draw, you rogue, for though it be night, yet the moon shines. I'll make a sop o' th' moonshine of you. You whoreson cullionly barbermonger, draw! 25

OSWALD. Away, I have nothing to do with thee.

KENT. Draw, you rascal. You come with letters against the King, and take Vanity the puppet's part against the royalty of her father. Draw, you rogue, or I'll so carbonado your shanks. Draw, you rascal. Come your ways! 30

OSWALD. Help, ho! Murder! Help!

KENT. Strike, you slave! Stand, rogue! Stand, you neat slave! Strike! *[Beating him.]*

OSWALD. Help, ho! Murder! Murder! 35

Enter Edmund, with his rapier drawn, Cornwall, Regan, Gloucester, Servants.

EDMUND. How now? What's the matter? Part!

KENT. With you, goodman boy, an you please! Come, I'll flesh ye, come on, young master.

GLOUCESTER. Weapons? Arms? What's the matter here?

CORNWALL. Keep peace, upon your lives. 40
He dies that strikes again. What is the matter?

REGAN. The messengers from our sister and the King.

CORNWALL. What is your difference? Speak.

OSWALD. I am scarce in breath, my lord.

KENT. No marvel, you have so bestirred your valor. You cowardly rascal, nature disclaims in thee. A tailor made thee. 45

CORNWALL. Thou art a strange fellow. A tailor make a man?

KENT. A tailor, sir. A stonecutter or painter could not have made him so ill, though he had been but two years o' th' trade.

CORNWALL. Speak yet, how grew your quarrel? 50

OSWALD. This ancient ruffian, sir, whose life I have spared at suit of his gray beard—

KENT. Thou whoreson zed, thou unnecessary letter! My lord, if you will give me leave, I will tread this unbolted villain into mortar, and daub the wall of a jakes with him. Spare my gray beard, you wagtail! 55

CORNWALL. Peace, sirrah!

You beastly knave, know you no reverence?

KENT. Yes, sir; but anger hath a privilege.

CORNWALL. Why art thou angry? 60

KENT. That such a slave as this should wear a sword,
Who wears no honesty. Such smiling rogues as these,
Like rats, oft bite the holy cords atwain
Which are too intrince t' unloose; smooth every passion
That in the natures of their lords rebel, 65
Bring oil to fire, snow to their colder moods;
Renege, affirm, and turn their halcyon beaks
With every gale and vary of their masters,
Knowing naught, like dogs, but following.
A plague upon your epileptic visage! 70
Smile you my speeches, as I were a fool?
Goose, if I had you upon Sarum Plain,
I'd drive ye cackling home to Camelot.

CORNWALL. Why, art thou mad, old fellow?

GLOUCESTER. How fell you out? Say that. 75

KENT. No contraries hold more antipathy
Than I and such a knave.

CORNWALL. Why dost thou call him a knave? What's his fault?

KENT. His countenance likes me not.

CORNWALL. No more perchance does mine, nor his, nor hers. 80

KENT. Sir, 'tis my occupation to be plain:
I have seen better faces in my time
Than stands on any shoulder that I see
Before me at this instant.

CORNWALL. This is some fellow, 85
Who, having been praised for bluntness, doth affect
A saucy roughness, and constrains the garb
Quite from his nature. He cannot flatter, he;
An honest mind and plain, he must speak truth.
And they will take it, so; if not, he's plain. 90
These kind of knaves I know, which in this plainness
Harbor more craft and more corrupter ends
Than twenty silly-ducking observants
That stretch their duties nicely.

KENT. Sir, in good faith, in sincere verity, 95
Under th' allowance of your great aspect,
Whose influence, like the wreath of radiant fire
On flick'ring Phoebus' front—

CORNWALL. What mean'st by this?

KENT. To go out of my dialect, which you discommend so much. I 100
know, sir, I am no flatterer. He that beguiled you in a plain accent
was a plain knave; which for my part, I will not be, though I
should win your displeasure to entreat me to't.

CORNWALL. What was th' offence you gave him?

OSWALD. I never gave him any. 105
   It pleased the King his master very late
   To strike at me, upon his misconstruction;
   When he, compact, and flattering his displeasure,
   Tripped me behind; being down, insulted, railed,
   And put upon him such a deal of man 110
   That worthied him, got praises of the King
   For him attempting who was self-subdued;
   And, in the fleshment of this dread exploit,
   Drew on me here again.

KENT.   None of these rogues and cowards 115
   But Ajax is their fool.

CORNWALL.   Fetch forth the stocks!
   You stubborn ancient knave, you reverend braggart,
   We'll teach you.

KENT.   Sir, I am too old to learn. 120
   Call not your stocks for me, I serve the King,
   On whose employment I was sent to you.
   You shall do small respect, show too bold malice
   Against the grace and person of my master,
   Stocking his messenger. 125

CORNWALL. Fetch forth the stocks! As I have life and honor,
   There shall he sit till noon.

REGAN. Till noon? Till night, my lord; and all night too.

KENT. Why, madam, if I were your father's dog,
   You should not use me so. 130

REGAN.   Sir, being his knave, I will.

CORNWALL. This is a fellow of the selfsame color
   Our sister speaks of. Come, bring away the stocks!

                        Stocks brought out.

GLOUCESTER. Let me beseech your Grace not to do so.
   His fault is much, and the good King his master 135
   Will check him for 't. Your purposed low correction
   Is such as basest and contemned'st wretches
   For pilf'rings and most common trespasses
   Are punished with.
   The King his master needs must take it ill 140
   That he, so slightly valued in his messenger,
   Should have him thus restrained.

CORNWALL.   I'll answer that.

REGAN. My sister may receive it much more worse,
   To have her gentleman abused, assaulted, 145
   For following her affairs. Put in his legs.
                  [Kent is put in the stocks.]
   Come, my good lord, away!
               [Exeunt all but Gloucester and Kent.]

GLOUCESTER. I am sorry for thee, friend. 'Tis the duke's pleasure,
    Whose disposition, all the world well knows
    Will not be rubbed nor stopped. I'll entreat for thee. 150

KENT. Pray do not, sir. I have watched and traveled hard.
    Some time I shall sleep out, the rest I'll whistle.
    A good man's fortune may grow out at heels.
    Give you good morrow.

GLOUCESTER. The Duke's to blame in this. 'Twill be ill taken. *Exit.* 155

KENT. Good king, that must approve the common saw,
    Thou out of Heaven's benediction com'st
    To the warm sun.
    Approach, thou beacon to this under globe,
    That by thy comfortable beams I may 160
    Peruse this letter. Nothing almost sees miracles
    But misery. I know 'tis from Cordelia,
    Who hath most fortunately been informed
    Of my obscurèd course. And shall find time
    From this enormous state, seeking to give 165
    Losses their remedies. All weary and o'erwatched,
    Take vantage, heavy eyes, not to behold
    This shameful lodging. Fortune, good night;
    Smile once more, turn thy wheel.
                              Sleeps.

[Scene III. *A wood.*]

Enter Edgar.

EDGAR. I heard myself proclaimed,
    And by the happy hollow of a tree
    Escaped the hunt. No port is free, no place,
    That guard and most unusual vigilance
    Does not attend my taking. Whiles I may 'scape, 5
    I will preserve myself; and am bethought
    To take the basest and most poorest shape
    That ever penury, in contempt of man,
    Brought near to beast; my face I'll grime with filth,
    Blanket my loins, elf all my hairs in knots, 10
    And with presented nakedness outface
    The winds and persecutions of the sky.
    The country gives me proof and precedent
    Of Bedlam beggars, who, with roaring voices,
    Strike in their numbed and mortified bare arms 15
    Pins, wooden pricks, nails, sprigs of rosemary;
    And with this horrible object, from low farms,
    Poor pelting villages, sheepcotes, and mills,
    Sometime with lunatic bans, sometime with prayers,
    Enforce their charity. Poor Turlygod, Poor Tom, 20
    That's something yet: Edgar I nothing am. *Exit.*

[Scene IV. *Before Gloucester's castle. Kent in the stocks.*]

Enter Lear, Fool, and Gentleman.

LEAR. 'Tis strange that they should so depart from home,
   And not send back my messenger.

GENTLEMAN.   As I learned,
   The night before there was no purpose in them
   Of this remove.

KENT.   Hail to thee, noble master!

LEAR. Ha!
   Mak'st thou this shame thy pastime?

KENT.   No, my lord.

FOOL. Ha, ha, he wears cruel garters. Horses are tied by the heads,
   dogs and bears by the neck, monkeys by th' loins, and men by the
   legs. When a man's over-lusty at legs, then he wears wooden neth-
   erstocks.

LEAR. What's he that hath so much thy place mistook
   To set thee here?

KENT.   It is both he and she;
   Your son and daughter.

LEAR. No.

KENT. Yes.

LEAR. No, I say.

KENT. I say yea.

LEAR. No, no, they would not.

KENT. Yes, they have.

LEAR. By Jupiter, I swear no!

KENT. By Juno, I swear ay!

LEAR.   They durst not do't;
   They could not, would not do't. 'Tis worse than murder
   To do upon respect such violent outrage.
   Resolve me, with all modest haste which way
   Thou might'st deserve or they impose this usage,
   Coming from us.

KENT.   My lord, when at their home
   I did commend your Highness' letters to them,
   Ere I was risen from the place that showed
   My duty kneeling, came there a reeking post,
   Stewed in his haste, half breathless, panting forth
   From Goneril his mistress salutations,
   Delivered letters, spite of intermission,
   Which presently they read; on whose contents
   They summoned up their meiny, straight took horse,

>   Commanded me to follow and attend
>   The leisure of their answer, gave me cold looks,
>   And meeting here the other messenger,
>   Whose welcome I perceived had poisoned mine,
>   Being the very fellow which of late   45
>   Displayed so saucily against your Highness,
>   Having more man than wit about me, drew;
>   He raised the house, with loud and coward cries.
>   Your son and daughter found this trespass worth
>   The shame which here it suffers.   50

FOOL. Winter's not gone yet, if the wild geese fly that way.
>   Fathers that wear rags
>   Do make their children blind;
>   But fathers that bear bags
>   Shall see their children kind.   55
>   Fortune, that arrant whore,
>   Ne'er turns the key to the poor.
>   But, for all this, thou shalt have as many dolors for
>   thy daughters as thou canst tell in a year.

LEAR. O, how this mother swells up toward my heart!   60
>   Hysterica passio, down, thou climbing sorrow,
>   Thy element's below. Where is this daughter?

KENT. With the earl, sir, here within.

LEAR.   Follow me not;
>   Stay here.   *Exit.*   65

GENTLEMAN. Made you no more offence but what you speak of?

KENT. None.
>   How chance the King comes with so small a number?

FOOL. And thou hadst been set i' th' stocks for that question, thou
>   hadst well deserved it.   70

KENT. Why, Fool?

FOOL. We'll set thee to school to an ant, to teach thee there's no la-
>   boring i' th' winter. All that follow their noses are led by their
>   eyes but blind men, and there's not a nose among twenty but can
>   smell him that's stinking. Let go thy hold when a great wheel runs 75
>   down a hill, lest it break thy neck with following. But the great
>   one that goes up the hill, let him draw thee after. When a wise
>   man gives thee better counsel, give me mine again. I would have
>   none but knaves follow it, since a Fool gives it.
>   That sir, which serves and seeks for gain,   80
>   And follows but for form,
>   Will pack, when it begins to rain,
>   And leave thee in the storm,
>   But I will tarry; the Fool will stay,
>   And let the wise man fly.   85
>   The knave turns Fool that runs away,
>   The Fool no knave, perdy.

KENT. Where learned you this, Fool?

FOOL. Not i' the stocks, fool.

Enter Lear and Gloucester.

LEAR. Deny to speak with me? They are sick, they are weary, 90
   They have traveled all the night? Mere fetches,
   The images of revolt and flying off!
   Fetch me a better answer.

GLOUCESTER.   My dear lord,
   You know the fiery quality of the Duke, 95
   How unremoveable and fixed he is
   In his own course.

LEAR.   Vengeance, plague, death, confusion! Fiery?
   What quality? Why, Gloucester, Gloucester, I'll speak with the
   Duke of Cornwall and his wife. 100

GLOUCESTER. Well, my good lord, I have informed them so.

LEAR. Informed them? Dost thou understand me, man?

GLOUCESTER. Ay, my good lord.

LEAR. The King would speak with Cornwall. The dear father
   Would with his daughter speak, commands—tends—service. 105
   Are they informed of this? My breath and blood!
   Fiery? The fiery Duke, tell the hot Duke that—
   No, but not yet. May be he is not well.
   Infirmity doth still neglect all office
   Whereto our health is bound. We are not ourselves 110
   When nature, being oppress'd, commands the mind
   To suffer with the body. I'll forbear;
   And am fallen out with my more headier will
   To take the indisposed and sickly fit
   For the sound man. *[Looking on Kent]* Death on my state! 115
   Wherefore
   Should he sit here? This act persuades me
   That this remotion of the Duke and her
   Is practice only. Give me my servant forth.
   Go tell the Duke and's wife I'd speak with them! 120
   Now, presently! Bid them come forth and hear me,
   Or at their chamber door I'll beat the drum
   Till it cry sleep to death.

GLOUCESTER. I would have all well betwixt you.
                                               Exit.

LEAR. O me, my heart, my rising heart! But down! 125

FOOL. Cry to it, Nuncle, as the cockney did to the eels when she put
   'em i' th' paste alive. She knapped 'em o' th' coxcombs with a
   stick, and cried "Down, wantons, down!" 'Twas her brother that,
   in pure kindness to his horse, buttered his hay.

Enter Cornwall, Regan, Gloucester, Servants.

LEAR. Good morrow to you both. 130

CORNWALL.   Hail to your grace!

Kent here set at liberty.

REGAN. I am glad to see your Highness.

LEAR. Regan, I think you are. I know what reason
I have to think so. If thou shouldst not be glad,
I would divorce me from thy mother's tomb, 135
Sepulchring an adultress. *[To Kent]* O, are you free?
Some other time for that. Beloved Regan,
Thy sister's naught. O Regan, she hath tied
Sharp-tooth'd unkindness, like a vulture, here.
[Points to his heart.]
I can scarce speak to thee. Thou'lt not believe 140
With how depraved a quality—O Regan!

REGAN. I pray you, sir, take patience. I have hope.
You less know how to value her desert
Than she to scant her duty.

LEAR. Say, how is that? 145

REGAN. I cannot think my sister in the least
Would fail her obligation. If, sir, perchance
She have restrained the riots of your followers,
'Tis on such ground, and to such wholesome end,
As clears her from all blame. 150

LEAR. My curses on her!

REGAN. O, sir, you are old.
Nature in you stands on the very verge
Of her confine. You should be ruled, and led
By some discretion that discerns your state 155
Better than you yourself. Therefore I pray you
That to our sister you do make return,
Say you have wrong'd her.

LEAR. Ask her forgiveness?
Do you but mark how this becomes the house: 160
"Dear daughter, I confess that I am old.
[Kneeling.]
Age is unnecessary. On my knees I beg
That you'll vouchsafe me raiment, bed, and food."

REGAN. Good sir, no more. These are unsightly tricks.
Return you to my sister. 165

LEAR. *[Rising]* Never, Regan.
She hath abated me of half my train;
Looked black upon me; struck me with her tongue,
Most serpentlike, upon the very heart.
All the stored vengeances of heaven fall 170
On her ingrateful top! Strike her young bones,
You taking airs, with lameness.

CORNWALL. Fie, sir, fie!

LEAR. You nimble lightnings, dart your blinding flames
Into her scornful eyes! Infect her beauty, 175

    You fen-suck'd fogs, drawn by the pow'rful sun,
    To fall and blast her pride.

REGAN.   O the blest gods!
    So will you wish on me when the rash mood is on.

LEAR. No, Regan, thou shalt never have my curse.   180
    Thy tender-hefted nature shall not give
    Thee o'er to harshness. Her eyes are fierce, but thine
    Do comfort and not burn. 'Tis not in thee
    To grudge my pleasures, to cut off my train,
    To bandy hasty words, to scant my sizes,   185
    And, in conclusion, to oppose the bolt
    Against my coming in. Thou better know'st
    The offices of nature, bond of childhood,
    Effects of courtesy, dues of gratitude.
    Thy half o' the kingdom hast thou not forgot,   190
    Wherein I thee endow'd.

REGAN.   Good sir, to th' purpose.

                              Tucket within.

LEAR. Who put my man i' th' stocks?

CORNWALL.   What trumpet's that?

REGAN. I know't—my sister's. This approves her letter,   195
    That she would soon be here.

                        Enter Oswald.

                      Is your lady come?

LEAR. This is a slave, whose easy borrowed pride
    Dwells in the fickle grace of her he follows.
    Out, varlet, from my sight!   200

CORNWALL.   What means your Grace?

LEAR. Who stocked my servant? Regan, I have good hope
    Thou didst not know on't.

                        Enter Goneril.

                    Who comes here? O heavens!
    If you do love old men, if your sweet sway   205
    Allow obedience, if yourselves are old,
    Make it your cause. Send down, and take my part.
    [To Goneril] Art not ashamed to look upon this beard?
    O Regan, wilt thou take her by the hand?

GONERIL. Why not by th' hand, sir? How have I offended?   210
    All's not offence that indiscretion finds
    And dotage terms so.

LEAR.   O sides, you are too tough!
    Will you yet hold? How came my man i' th' stocks?

CORNWALL. I set him there, sir; but his own disorders   215
    Deserved much less advancement.

LEAR.   You? Did you?

REGAN. I pray you, father, being weak, seem so.
    If till the expiration of your month
    You will return and sojourn with my sister, 220
    Dismissing half your train, come then to me.
    I am now from home, and out of that provision
    Which shall be needful for your entertainment.

LEAR. Return to her, and fifty men dismissed?
    No, rather I abjure all roofs, and choose 225
    To wage against the enmity o' th' air,
    To be a comrade with the wolf and owl,
    Necessity's sharp pinch. Return with her?
    Why, the hot-blooded France, that dowerless took
    Our youngest born, I could as well be brought 230
    To knee his throne, and, squirelike, pension beg
    To keep base life afoot. Return with her?
    Persuade me rather to be slave and sumpter
    To this detested groom. *[Pointing at Oswald.]*

GONERIL.   At your choice, sir. 235

LEAR. I prithee, daughter, do not make me mad.
    I will not trouble thee, my child; farewell.
    We'll no more meet, no more see one another.
    But yet thou art my flesh, my blood, my daughter;
    Or rather a disease that's in my flesh, 240
    Which I must needs call mine. Thou art a boil,
    A plague-sore, or embossèd carbuncle
    In my corrupted blood. But I'll not chide thee.
    Let shame come when it will, I do not call it.
    I do not bid the Thunder-bearer shoot, 245
    Nor tell tales of thee to high-judging Jove.
    Mend when thou canst; be better at thy leisure,
    I can be patient, I can stay with Regan,
    I and my hundred knights.

REGAN.   Not altogether so. 250
    I looked not for you yet, nor am provided
    For your fit welcome. Give ear, sir, to my sister,
    For those that mingle reason with your passion
    Must be content to think you old, and so—
    But she knows what she does. 255

LEAR.   Is this well spoken?

REGAN. I dare avouch it, sir. What, fifty followers?
    Is it not well? What should you need of more?
    Yea, or so many, sith that both charge and danger
    Speak 'gainst so great a number? How in one house 260
    Should many people, under two commands,
    Hold amity? 'Tis hard; almost impossible.

GONERIL. Why might not you, my lord, receive attendance
    From those that she calls servants or from mine?

REGAN. Why not, my lord? If then they chanced to slack ye, 265
    We could control them. If you will come to me
    (For now I spy a danger), I entreat you
    To bring but five and twenty. To no more
    Will I give place or notice.

LEAR. I gave you all. 270

REGAN.   And in good time you gave it.

LEAR. Made you my guardians, my depositaries,
    But kept a reservation to be followed
    With such a number. What, must I come to you
    With five-and-twenty? Regan, said you so? 275

REGAN. And speak't again, my lord. No more with me.

LEAR. Those wicked creatures yet do look well-favored,
    When others are more wicked; not being the worst
    Stands in some rank of praise. *[To Goneril]* I'll go with thee.
    Thy fifty yet doth double five-and-twenty, 280
    And thou art twice her love.

GONERIL.   Hear me, my lord;
    What need you five-and-twenty? ten? or five?
    To follow in a house where twice so many
    Have a command to tend you? 285

REGAN.   What need one?

LEAR. O reason not the need! Our basest beggars
    Are in the poorest thing superfluous.
    Allow not nature more than nature needs,
    Man's life's as cheap as beast's. Thou art a lady: 290
    If only to go warm were gorgeous,
    Why, nature needs not what thou gorgeous wear'st,
    Which scarcely keeps thee warm. But, for true need—
    You heavens, give me that patience, patience I need.
    You see me here, you gods, a poor old man, 295
    As full of grief as age; wretched in both.
    If it be you that stir these daughters' hearts
    Against their father, fool me not so much
    To bear it tamely; touch me with noble anger,
    And let not women's weapons, water drops, 300
    Stain my man's cheeks. No, you unnatural hags!
    I will have such revenges on you both
    That all the world shall—I will do such things—
    What they are, yet I know not; but they shall be
    The terrors of the earth. You think I'll weep. 305
    No, I'll not weep.
                        Storm and tempest.
    I have full cause of weeping, but this heart
    Shall break into a hundred thousand flaws
    Or ere I'll weep. O Fool, I shall go mad!
              [Exeunt Lear, Gloucester, Kent, and Fool.]

CORNWALL. Let us withdraw; 'twill be a storm. 310

REGAN. This house is little; the old man and's people
    Cannot be well bestowed.

GONERIL. 'Tis his own blame; hath put himself from rest
    And must needs taste his folly.

REGAN. For his particular, I'll receive him gladly, 315
    But not one follower.

GONERIL.   So am I purposed.
    Where is my lord of Gloucester?

CORNWALL. Followed the old man forth.

Enter Gloucester.

                                      He is returned. 320

GLOUCESTER. The King is in high rage.

CORNWALL.   Whither is he going?

GLOUCESTER. He calls to horse; but will I know not whither.

CORNWALL. 'Tis best to give him way; he leads himself.

GONERIL. My lord, entreat him by no means to stay. 325

GLOUCESTER. Alack, the night comes on, and the high winds
    Do sorely ruffle. For many miles about
    There's scarce a bush.

REGAN.   O, sir, to willful men
    The injuries that they themselves procure 330
    Must be their schoolmasters. Shut up your doors.
    He is attended with a desperate train,
    And what they may incense him to, being apt
    To have his ear abused, wisdom bids fear.

CORNWALL. Shut up your doors, my lord; 'tis a wild night. 335
    My Regan counsels well. Come out o' th' storm.

Exeunt.

ACT III

Scene I. [*A heath.*]

Storm still. Enter Kent and a Gentleman severally.

KENT. Who's there, besides foul weather?

GENTLEMAN. One minded like the weather most unquietly.

KENT. I know you. Where's the King?

GENTLEMAN. Contending with the fretful elements;
   Bids the winds blow the earth into the sea, 5
   Or swell the curlèd waters 'bove the main,
   That things might change or cease; tears his white hair,
   Which the impetuous blasts, with eyeless rage,
   Catch in their fury, and make nothing of;
   Strives in his little world of man to outscorn 10
   The to-and-fro-conflicting wind and rain.
   This night, wherein the cub-drawn bear would couch,
   The lion, and the belly-pinchèd wolf
   Keep their fur dry, unbonneted he runs,
   And bids what will take all. 15

KENT.   But who is with him?

GENTLEMAN. None but the Fool, who labors to outjest
   His heart-struck injuries.

KENT.   Sir, I do know you,
   And dare upon the warrant of my note 20
   Commend a dear thing to you. There is division,
   Although as yet the face of it be covered
   With mutual cunning, 'twixt Albany and Cornwall;
   Who have—as who have not, that their great stars
   Throned and set high?—servants, who seem no less, 25
   Which are to France the spies and speculations
   Intelligent of our state. What hath been seen,
   Either in snuffs and packings of the Dukes,
   Or the hard rein which both of them have borne
   Against the old kind King, or something deeper, 30
   Whereof, perchance, these are but furnishings—
   But, true it is, from France there comes a power
   Into this scattered kingdom, who already,
   Wise in our negligence, have secret feet
   In some of our best ports, and are at point 35
   To show their open banner. Now to you:
   If on my credit you dare build so far
   To make your speed to Dover, you shall find
   Some that will thank you, making just report
   Of how unnatural and bemadding sorrow 40
   The King hath cause to plain.
   I am a gentleman of blood and breeding,
   And from some knowledge and assurance offer

>   This office to you.
>
> GENTLEMAN. I will talk further with you.   45
>
> KENT.   No, do not.
>   For confirmation that I am much more
>   Than my out-wall, open this purse and take
>   What it contains. If you shall see Cordelia,
>   As fear not but you shall, show her this ring,   50
>   And she will tell you who your fellow is
>   That yet you do not know. Fie on this storm!
>   I will go seek the king.
>
> GENTLEMAN. Give me your hand. Have you no more to say?
>
> KENT. Few words, but, to effect, more than all yet: 55
>   That, when we have found the King—in which your pain
>   That way, I'll this—he that first lights on him,
>   Holla the other.   *Exeunt [severally].*

Scene II. [*Another part of the heath.*]

Storm still.

Enter Lear and Fool.

> LEAR. Blow, winds, and crack your cheeks. Rage, blow!
>   You cataracts and hurricanes, spout
>   Till you have drenched our steeples, drowned the cocks!
>   You sulph'rous and thought-executing fires,
>   Vaunt-couriers of oak-cleaving thunderbolts,   5
>   Singe my white head. And thou, all-shaking thunder,
>   Smite flat the thick rotundity o' th' world,
>   Crack Nature's molds, all germains spill at once,
>   That make ingrateful man.
>
> FOOL. O Nuncle, court holy-water in a dry house is better than this   10
>   rain water out o' door. Good Nuncle, in; and ask thy daughters'
>   blessing. Here's a night pities neither wise man nor fools.
>
> LEAR. Rumble thy bellyful. Spit, fire. Spout, rain!
>   Nor rain, wind, thunder, fire, are my daughters.
>   I tax not you, you elements, with unkindness.   15
>   I never gave you kingdom, called you children,
>   You owe me no subscription. Then let fall
>   Your horrible pleasure. Here I stand, your slave,
>   A poor, infirm, weak, and despised old man.
>   But yet I call you servile ministers,   20
>   That will with two pernicious daughters join
>   Your high-engender'd battles 'gainst a head
>   So old and white as this. O, ho! 'tis foul.
>
> FOOL. He that has a house to put 's head in has a good headpiece.
>   The codpiece that will house   25
>   Before the head has any,

    The head and he shall louse;
     So beggars marry many.
    The man that makes his toe
     What he his heart should make
    Shall of a corn cry woe,
     And turn his sleep to wake.
 For there was never yet fair woman but she made mouths in a glass.

       Enter Kent.

LEAR. No, I will be the pattern of all patience,
 I will say nothing.

KENT. Who's there?

FOOL. Marry, here's grace and a cod-piece; that's a wise man and a
 fool.

KENT. Alas, sir, are you here? Things that love night
 Love not such nights as these. The wrathful skies
 Gallow the very wanderers of the dark
 And make them keep their caves. Since I was man
 Such sheets of fire, such bursts of horrid thunder,
 Such groans of roaring wind and rain, I never
 Remember to have heard. Man's nature cannot carry
 The affliction nor the fear.

LEAR.   Let the great gods,
 That keep this dreadful pother o'er our heads,
 Find out their enemies now. Tremble, thou wretch,
 That hast within thee undivulged crimes
 Unwhipped of justice. Hide thee, thou bloody hand,
 Thou perjured, and thou simular of virtue
 That art incestuous. Caitiff, to pieces shake,
 That under covert and convenient seeming
 Hast practiced on man's life. Close pent-up guilts,
 Rive your concealing continents, and cry
 These dreadful summoners grace. I am a man
 More sinned against than sinning.

KENT.   Alack, bareheaded?
 Gracious my lord, hard by here is a hovel;
 Some friendship will it lend you 'gainst the tempest.
 Repose you there, while I to this hard house
 (More harder than the stones whereof 'tis raised,
 Which even but now, demanding after you,
 Denied me to come in) return, and force
 Their scanted courtesy.

LEAR.   My wits begin to turn.
 Come on, my boy. How dost, my boy? Art cold?
 I am cold myself. Where is this straw, my fellow?
 The art of our necessities is strange,
 That can make vile things precious. Come, your hovel.
 Poor fool and knave, I have one part in my heart
 That's sorry yet for thee.

FOOL. [*Singing*]
        He that has and a little tiny wit,
          With heigh-ho, the wind and the rain,
        Must make content with his fortunes fit,
          For the rain it raineth every day.

LEAR. True, my good boy. Come, bring us to this hovel.
                                        Exit [with Kent].

FOOL. This is a brave night to cool a courtesan. I'll speak a prophecy
   ere I go:
   When priests are more in word than matter;
   When brewers mar their malt with water;
   When nobles are their tailors' tutors,
   No heretics burned, but wenches' suitors;
   When every case in law is right,
   No squire in debt, nor no poor knight;
   When slanders do not live in tongues;
   Nor cutpurses come not to throngs;
   When usurers tell their gold i' th' field,
   And bawds and whores do churches build,
   Then shall the realm of Albion
   Come to great confusion.
   Then comes the time, who lives to see't,
   That going shall be used with feet.
   This prophecy Merlin shall make; for I live before his time.   *Exit.*

Scene III. [*Gloucester's castle.*]

Enter Gloucester and Edmund.

GLOUCESTER. Alack, alack, Edmund, I like not this unnatural dealing. When I desire their leave that I might pity him, they took from me the use of mine own house; charged me, on pain of their perpetual displeasure, neither to speak of him, entreat for him, or any way sustain him.

EDMUND. Most savage and unnatural!

GLOUCESTER. Go to; say you nothing. There is division betwixt the Dukes; and a worse matter than that. I have received a letter this night—'tis dangerous to be spoken—I have locked the letter in my closet. These injuries the King now bears will be revenged home; there's part of a power already footed; we must incline to the King. I will look him, and privily relieve him. Go you and maintain talk with the Duke, that my charity be not of him perceived. If he ask for me, I am ill, and gone to bed. If I die for it, as no less is threatened me, the King my old master must be relieved. There is some strange thing toward, Edmund; pray you, be careful.   *Exit.*

EDMUND. This courtesy forbid thee shall the Duke
   Instantly know; and of that letter too.
   This seems a fair deserving, and must draw me

That which my father loses—no less than all.
The younger rises when the old doth fall.

Exit.

Scene IV. [*The heath. Before a hovel.*]

Enter Lear, Kent, and Fool.

KENT. Here is the place, my lord. Good my lord, enter.
    The tyranny of the open night's too rough
    For nature to endure.

Storm still.

LEAR.   Let me alone.

KENT. Good my lord, enter here.   5

LEAR.   Wilt break my heart?

KENT. I had rather break mine own. Good my lord, enter.

LEAR. Thou think'st 'tis much that this contentious storm
    Invades us to the skin: so 'tis to thee;
    But where the greater malady is fixed,   10
    The lesser is scarce felt. Thou'ldst shun a bear;
    But if thy flight lay toward the roaring sea,
    Thou'ldst meet the bear i' th' mouth. When the mind's free,
    The body's delicate. The tempest in my mind
    Doth from my senses take all feeling else,   15
    Save what beats there. Filial ingratitude,
    Is it not as this mouth should tear this hand
    For lifting food to't? But I will punish home.
    No, I will weep no more. In such a night
    To shut me out! Pour on; I will endure.   20
    In such a night as this! O Regan, Goneril,
    Your old kind father, whose frank heart gave all—
    O, that way madness lies; let me shun that.
    No more of that.

KENT.   Good my lord, enter here.   25

LEAR. Prithee, go in thyself; seek thine own ease.
    This tempest will not give me leave to ponder
    On things would hurt me more, but I'll go in.
    [To the Fool] In, boy; go first. You houseless poverty—
    Nay, get thee in. I'll pray, and then I'll sleep.   30

Exit [Fool].

    Poor naked wretches, whereso'er you are,
    That bide the pelting of this pitiless storm,
    How shall your houseless heads and unfed sides,
    Your looped and windowed raggedness, defend you
    From seasons such as these? O, I have ta'en   35
    Too little care of this! Take physic, pomp;
    Expose thyself to feel what wretches feel,
    That thou mayst shake the superflux to them,

And show the heavens more just.

EDGAR. [*Within*] Fathom and half, fathom and half! Poor Tom! 40

Enter Fool.

FOOL. Come not in here, Nuncle, here's a spirit. Help me, help me!

KENT. Give me thy hand. Who's there?

FOOL. A spirit, a spirit. He says his name's Poor Tom.

KENT. What art thou that dost grumble there i' th' straw? 45
Come forth.

Enter Edgar [disguised as a madman].

EDGAR. Away! the foul fiend follows me. Through the sharp hawthorn blows the cold wind. Humh! Go to thy cold bed, and warm thee.

LEAR. Didst thou give all to thy two daughters? And art thou come to 50
this?

EDGAR. Who gives anything to Poor Tom? Whom the foul fiend hath led through fire and through flame, and through ford and whirlpool o'er bog and quagmire; that hath laid knives under his pillow, and halters in his pew; set ratsbane by his porridge; made 55
him proud of heart, to ride on a bay trotting horse over four-inched bridges, to course his own shadow for a traitor. Bless thy five wits, Tom's a-cold. O, do, de, do, de, do, de. Bless thee from whirlwinds, star-blasting, and taking. Do Poor Tom some charity, whom the foul fiend vexes. There could I have him now—and 60
there—and there again—and there.

Storm still.

LEAR. What, have his daughters brought him to this pass? Couldst thou save nothing? Wouldst thou give 'em all?

FOOL. Nay, he reserved a blanket, else we had been all shamed.

LEAR. Now, all the plagues that in the pendulous air 65
Hang fated o'er men's faults light on thy daughters!

KENT. He hath no daughters, sir.

LEAR. Death, traitor! nothing could have subdued nature
To such a lowness but his unkind daughters.
Is it the fashion, that discarded fathers 70
Should have thus little mercy on their flesh?
Judicious punishment—'twas this flesh begot
Those pelican daughters.

EDGAR. Pillicock sat on Pillicock Hill. Alow, alow, loo, loo!

FOOL. This cold night will turn us all to fools and madmen. 75

EDGAR. Take heed o' th' foul fiend; obey thy parents; keep thy word's justice; swear not; commit not with man's sworn spouse; set not thy sweet heart on proud array. Tom's a-cold.

LEAR. What hast thou been?

EDGAR. A serving-man, proud in heart and mind; that curled my
hair; wore gloves in my cap; served the lust of my mistress' heart,
and did the act of darkness with her; swore as many oaths as I
spake words, and broke them in the sweet face of heaven. One
that slept in the contriving of lust, and waked to do it. Wine loved
I deeply, dice dearly; and in woman out-paramoured the Turk.
False of heart, light of ear, bloody of hand; hog in sloth, fox in
stealth, wolf in greediness, dog in madness, lion in prey. Let not
the creaking of shoes nor the rustling of silks betray thy poor
heart to woman. Keep thy foot out of brothels, thy hand out of
plackets, thy pen from lenders' books, and defy the foul fiend.
Still through the hawthorn blows the cold wind; says suum, mun,
nonny. Dolphin my boy, boy, sessa! let him trot by.

Storm still.

LEAR. Thou wert better in thy grave than to answer with thy uncovered body this extremity of the skies. Is man no more than this?
Consider him well. Thou ow'st the worm no silk, the beast no
hide, the sheep no wool, the cat no perfume. Ha! here's three on's
are sophisticated! Thou art the thing itself; unaccommodated man
is no more but such a poor, bare, forked animal as thou art. Off,
off, you lendings! Come unbutton here.

[Tearing off his clothes.]

FOOL. Prithee, Nuncle, be contented; 'tis a naughty night to swim in.
Now a little fire in a wild field were like an old lecher's heart—a
small spark, all the rest on's body, cold. Look, here comes a walking
fire.

Enter Gloucester, with a torch.

EDGAR. This is the foul fiend Flibbertigibbet. He begins at curfew,
and walks till the first cock. He gives the web and the pin, squints
the eye, and makes the harelip; mildews the white wheat, and
hurts the poor creature of earth.
    Swithold footed thrice the old;
    He met the nightmare, and her nine fold;
     Bid her alight,
     And her troth plight,
    And, aroint thee, witch, aroint thee!

KENT. How fares your Grace?

LEAR. What's he?

KENT. Who's there? What is't you seek?

GLOUCESTER. What are you there? Your names?

EDGAR. Poor Tom; that eats the swimming frog, the toad, the tadpole, the wall-newt and the water; that in the fury of his heart,
when the foul fiend rages, eats cow-dung for sallets; swallows the
old rat and the ditch-dog; drinks the green mantle of the standing
pool; who is whipped from tithing to tithing, and stock-punished,
and imprisoned; who hath had three suits to his back, six shirts to
his body,

        Horse to ride, and weapon to wear,
        But mice and rats, and such small deer,
        Have been Tom's food for seven long year.
  Beware my follower! Peace, Smulkin; peace, thou fiend!   125

GLOUCESTER. What, hath your grace no better company?

EDGAR. The prince of darkness is a gentleman.
  Modo he's called, and Mahu.   130

GLOUCESTER. Our flesh and blood, my Lord, is grown so vile
  That it doth hate what gets it.

EDGAR. Poor Tom's a-cold.

GLOUCESTER. Go in with me. My duty cannot suffer
  T' obey in all your daughters' hard commands.   135
  Though their injunction be to bar my doors
  And let this tyrannous night take hold upon you,
  Yet have I ventured to come seek you out
  And bring you where both fire and food is ready.

LEAR. First let me talk with this philosopher.   140
  What is the cause of thunder?

KENT. Good my lord, take his offer; go into th' house.

LEAR. I'll talk a word with this same learned Theban.
  What is your study?

EDGAR. How to prevent the fiend, and to kill vermin.   145

LEAR. Let me ask you one word in private.

KENT. Importune him once more to go, my lord.
  His wits begin to unsettle.

GLOUCESTER.   Canst thou blame him?

Storm still.

  His daughters seek his death. Ah, that good Kent,   150
  He said it would be thus, poor banished man!
  Thou say'st the King grows mad—I'll tell thee, friend,
  I am almost mad myself. I had a son,
  Now outlawed from my blood; he sought my life
  But lately, very late. I loved him, friend,   155
  No father his son dearer. True to tell thee,
  The grief hath crazed my wits. What a night's this!
  I do beseech your Grace—

LEAR.   O, cry you mercy, sir.
  Noble philosopher, your company.   160

EDGAR. Tom's a-cold.

GLOUCESTER. In, fellow, there, into th' hovel; keep thee warm.

LEAR. Come let's in all.

KENT.   This way, my lord.

LEAR.   With him!   165
  I will keep still with my philosopher.

KENT. Good my lord, soothe him; let him take the fellow.

GLOUCESTER. Take him you on.

KENT. Sirrah, come on; go along with us.

LEAR. Come, good Athenian.

GLOUCESTER. No words, no words! Hush.

EDGAR. Child Rowland to the dark tower came;
His word was still, "Fie, foh, and fum,
I smell the blood of a British man."

Exeunt.

Scene V. *[Gloucester's castle.]*

Enter Cornwall and Edmund.

CORNWALL. I will have my revenge ere I depart his house.

EDMUND. How, my lord, I may be censured, that nature thus gives way to loyalty, something fears me to think of.

CORNWALL. I now perceive, it was not altogether your brother's evil disposition made him seek his death; but a provoking merit, set a-work by a reprovable badness in himself.

EDMUND. How malicious is my fortune, that I must repent to be just! This is the letter he spoke of, which approves him an intelligent party to the advantages of France. O heavens, that his treason were not, or not I the detector!

CORNWALL. Go with me to the Duchess.

EDMUND. If the matter of this paper be certain, you have mighty business in hand.

CORNWALL. True or false, it hath made thee Earl of Gloucester. Seek out where thy father is, that he may be ready for our apprehension.

EDMUND. [*Aside*] If I find him comforting the King, it will stuff his suspicion more fully.—I will persevere in my course of loyalty, though the conflict be sore between that and my blood.

CORNWALL. I will lay trust upon thee; and thou shalt find a dearer father in my love. *Exeunt.*

Scene VI. [*A chamber in a farmhouse adjoining the castle.*]

Enter Kent and Gloucester.

GLOUCESTER. Here is better than the open air; take it thankfully. I will piece out the comfort with what addition I can. I will not be long from you.

KENT. All the power of his wits have given way to his impatience.
    The gods reward your kindness.
                      Exit [Gloucester].

            Enter Lear, Edgar, and Fool.

EDGAR. Frateretto calls me, and tells me Nero is an angler in the
    lake of darkness. Pray, innocent, and beware the foul fiend.

FOOL. Prithee, Nuncle, tell me whether a madman be a gentleman or
    a yeoman.

LEAR. A king, a king!

FOOL. No, he's a yeoman that has a gentleman to his son; for he's a
    mad yeoman that sees his son a gentleman before him.

LEAR. To have a thousand with red burning spits
    Come hissing in upon 'em—

EDGAR. The foul fiend bites my back.

FOOL. He's mad that trusts in the tameness of a wolf, a horse's
    health, a boy's love, or a whore's oath.

LEAR. It shall be done; I will arraign them straight.
    [*To Edgar*] Come, sit thou here, most learned justice.
    [*To the Fool*] Thou, sapient sir, sit here. Now, you she-foxes—

EDGAR. Look, where he stands and glares! Want'st thou eyes at trial,
    madam?
    Come o'er the bourn, Bessy, to me.

FOOL. Her boat hath a leak,
        And she must not speak
    Why she dares not come over to thee.

EDGAR. The foul fiend haunts Poor Tom in the voice of a nightin-
    gale. Hoppedance cries in Tom's belly for two white herring.
    Croak not, black angel; I have no food for thee.

KENT. How do you, sir? Stand you not so amazed. Will you lie down
    and rest upon the cushions?

LEAR. I'll see their trial first. Bring in the evidence.
    [*To Edgar* Thou robèd man of justice, take thy place.
    [*To the Fool*] And thou, his yokefellow of equity,
    Bench by his side. [*To Kent*] You are o' th' commission;
    Sit you too.

EDGAR. Let us deal justly.
        Sleepest or wakest thou, jolly shepherd?
           Thy sheep be in the corn;
           And for one blast of thy minikin mouth
        Thy sheep shall take no harm.
    Purr, the cat is gray.

LEAR. Arraign her first. 'Tis Goneril, I here take my oath before this
    honorable assembly, she kicked the poor King her father.

FOOL. Come hither, mistress. Is your name Goneril?

LEAR. She cannot deny it.

FOOL. Cry you mercy, I took you for a joint stool.

LEAR. And here's another, whose warp'd looks proclaim
    What store her heart is made on. Stop her there!
    Arms, arms, sword, fire! Corruption in the place!   50
    False justicer, why hast thou let her 'scape?

EDGAR. Bless thy five wits!

KENT. O pity! Sir, where is the patience now
    That thou so oft have boasted to retain?

EDGAR. [*Aside*] My tears begin to take his part so much,   55
    They'll mar my counterfeiting.

LEAR. The little dogs and all,
    Tray, Blanch, and Sweetheart—see, they bark at me.

EDGAR. Tom will throw his head at them. Avaunt, you curs!
        Be thy mouth or black or white,   60
        Tooth that poisons if it bite;
        Mastiff, greyhound, mongrel grim,
        Hound or spaniel, brach or lym,
        Or bobtail tike or trundle-tail—
        Tom will make them weep and wail;   65
        For, with throwing thus my head,
        Dogs leap the hatch, and all are fled.

  Do, de, de, de. Sessa! Come, march to wakes and fairs and market towns. Poor Tom, thy horn is dry.

LEAR. Then let them anatomize Regan; see what breeds about her   70
    heart. Is there any cause in nature that makes these hard hearts?
    [*To Edgar*] You, sir, I entertain for one of my hundred; only I do
    not like the fashion of your garments. You will say they are Per-
    sian; but let them be changed.

KENT. Now, good my lord, lie here and rest awhile.   75

LEAR. Make no noise, make no noise; draw the curtains.
    So, so. We'll go to supper i' th' morning.

FOOL. And I'll go to bed at noon.

                Enter Gloucester.

GLOUCESTER. Come hither, friend. Where is the King my master?

KENT. Here, sir; but trouble him not, his wits are gone.   80

GLOUCESTER. Good friend, I prithee, take him in thy arms.
    I have o'erheard a plot of death upon him.
    There is a litter ready; lay him in't,
    And drive towards Dover, friend, where thou shalt meet
    Both welcome and protection. Take up thy master.   85
    If thou shouldst dally half an hour, his life,
    With thine and all that offer to defend him,
    Stand in assured loss. Take up, take up;
    And follow me, that will to some provision.

    Give thee quick conduct.

KENT.   Oppressèd nature sleeps.
 This rest might yet have balmed thy broken sinews,
 Which, if convenience will not allow,
 Stand in hard cure. [*To the Fool*] Come, help to bear thy master.
 Thou must not stay behind.

GLOUCESTER.   Come, come, away.
          Exeunt [all but Edgar].

EDGAR. When we our betters see bearing our woes,
 We scarcely think our miseries our foes.
 Who alone suffers suffers most i' th' mind,
 Leaving free things and happy shows behind;
 But then the mind much sufferance doth o'erskip
 When grief hath mates, and bearing fellowship.
 How light and portable my pain seems now,
 When that which makes me bend makes the King bow.
 He childed as I fathered. Tom, away.
 Mark the high noises, and thyself bewray
 When false opinion, whose wrong thought defiles thee,
 In thy just proof repeals and reconciles thee.
 What will hap more tonight, safe 'scape the King!
 Lurk, lurk.   *[Exit.]*

    Scene VII. [*Gloucester's castle.*]

  Enter Cornwall, Regan, Goneril, Edmund, and Servants.

CORNWALL. [*To Goneril*] Post speedily to my Lord your husband;
 show him this letter. The army of France is landed. [*To Servants*]
 Seek out the traitor Gloucester. [*Exeunt some of the Servants.*]

REGAN. Hang him instantly.

GONERIL. Pluck out his eyes.

CORNWALL. Leave him to my displeasure. Edmund, keep you our
 sister company. The revenges we are bound to take upon your trai-
 torous father are not fit for your beholding. Advise the Duke,
 where you are going, to a most festinate preparation. We are
 bound to the like. Our posts shall be swift and intelligent betwixt
 us. Farewell, dear sister; farewell, my Lord of Gloucester.

    Enter Oswald.

 How now? Where's the King?

OSWALD. My lord of Gloucester hath conveyed him hence.
 Some five or six and thirty of his knights,
 Hot questrists after him, met him at gate;
 Who, with some other of the lord's dependants,
 Are gone with him towards Dover; where they boast
 To have well-armed friends.

CORNWALL.   Get horses for your mistress.
                                                                      [*Exit Oswald.*]

GONERIL. Farewell, sweet lord, and sister.   20

CORNWALL. Edmund, farewell.
                                [*Exeunt Goneril and Edmund.*]
                           Go seek the traitor Gloucester,
   Pinion him like a thief, bring him before us.
                            [*Exeunt other Servants.*]
   Though well we may not pass upon his life
   Without the form of justice, yet our power   25
   Shall do a court'sy to our wrath, which men
   May blame, but not control.

         Enter Gloucester, brought in by two or three.

                       Who's there? the traitor?

REGAN. Ingrateful fox, 'tis he.

CORNWALL. Bind fast his corky arms.   30

GLOUCESTER. What mean your Graces? Good my friends, consider
   You are my guests. Do me no foul play, friends.

CORNWALL. Bind him, I say.
                                    [*Servants bind him.*]

REGAN.   Hard, hard! O filthy traitor.

GLOUCESTER. Unmerciful lady as you are, I'm none.   35

CORNWALL. To this chair bind him. Villain, thou shalt find—
                                 [*Regan plucks his beard.*]

GLOUCESTER. By the kind gods, 'tis most ignobly done
   To pluck me by the beard.

REGAN. So white, and such a traitor?

GLOUCESTER.   Naughty lady,   40
   These hairs, which thou dost ravish from my chin
   Will quicken, and accuse thee. I am your host.
   With robber's hands my hospitable favours
   You should not ruffle thus. What will you do?

CORNWALL. Come, sir, what letters had you late from France?   45

REGAN. Be simple-answererd, for we know the truth.

CORNWALL. And what confederacy have you with the traitors
   Late footed in the kingdom?

REGAN. To whose hands have you sent the lunatic King:
   Speak.   50

GLOUCESTER. I have a letter guessingly set down,
   Which came from one that's of a neutral heart,
   And not from one opposed.

CORNWALL.   Cunning.

REGAN.   And false.

CORNWALL. Where hast thou sent the King?

GLOUCESTER. To Dover.

REGAN. Wherefore to Dover? Wast thou not charged at peril—

CORNWALL. Wherefore to Dover? Let him first answer that.

GLOUCESTER. I am tied to the stake, and I must stand the course.

REGAN. Wherefore to Dover?

GLOUCESTER. Because I would not see thy cruel nails
    Pluck out his poor old eyes; nor thy fierce sister
    In his anointed flesh rash boarish fangs.
    The sea, with such a storm as his bare head
    In hell-black night endured, would have buoyed up,
    And quenched the stellèd fires.
    Yet, poor old heart, he holp the heavens to rain.
    If wolves had at thy gate howled that dearn time,
    Thou shouldst have said "Good porter, turn the key."
    All cruels else subscribed. But I shall see
    The winged vengeance overtake such children.

CORNWALL. See't shalt thou never. Fellows, hold the chair.
    Upon these eyes of thine I'll set my foot.

GLOUCESTER. He that will think to live till he be old,
    Give me some help.—O cruel! O you gods!

REGAN. One side will mock another. Th' other too.

CORNWALL. If you see vengeance——

FIRST SERVANT.   Hold your hand, my lord!
    I have served you ever since I was a child;
    But better service have I never done you
    Than now to bid you hold.

REGAN.   How now, you dog!

FIRST SERVANT. If you did wear a beard upon your chin,
    I'd shake it on this quarrel. What do you mean?

CORNWALL. My villain!

                                             Draw and fight.

FIRST SERVANT. Nay, then, come on, and take the chance of anger.

REGAN. Give me thy sword. A peasant stand up thus!

    She takes a sword and runs at him behind, kills him.

FIRST SERVANT. O, I am slain! My lord, you have one eye left
    To see some mischief on him. O!

CORNWALL. Lest it see more, prevent it. Out, vile jelly.
    Where is thy luster now?

GLOUCESTER. All dark and comfortless. Where's my son Edmund?
    Edmund, enkindle all the sparks of nature

  To quit this horrid act. 95

REGAN.   Out, treacherous villain,
 Thou call'st on him that hates thee. It was he
 That made the overture of thy treasons to us;
 Who is too good to pity thee.

GLOUCESTER. O my follies! Then Edgar was abused. 100
 Kind gods, forgive me that, and prosper him.

REGAN. Go thrust him out at gates, and let him smell
 His way to Dover.   *Exit [one] with Gloucester.*
    How is't, my lord? How look you?

CORNWALL. I have received a hurt. Follow me, lady. 105
 Turn out that eyeless villain. Throw this slave
 Upon the dunghill. Regan, I bleed apace.
 Untimely comes this hurt. Give me your arm.
              Exeunt.

SECOND SERVANT. I'll never care what wickedness I do,
 If this man come to good. 110

THIRD SERVANT.   If she live long,
 And in the end meet the old course of death,
 Women will all turn monsters.

SECOND SERVANT. Let's follow the old Earl, and get the Bedlam
 To lead him where he would. His roguish madness 115
 Allows itself to anything.

THIRD SERVANT. Go thou. I'll fetch some flax and whites of eggs
 To apply to his bleeding face. Now, heaven help him!
            [*Exeunt severally.*]

ACT IV

Scene I. [*The heath*.]

Enter Edgar.

EDGAR. Yet better thus, and known to be contemned,
Than still contemned and flattered. To be worst,
The lowest and most dejected thing of fortune,
Stands still in esperance, lives not in fear:
The lamentable change is from the best, 5
The worst returns to laughter. Welcome, then,
Thou unsubstantial air that I embrace!
The wretch that thou hast blown unto the worst
Owes nothing to thy blasts.

Enter Gloucester, led by an Old Man.

    But who comes here? 10
My father, poorly led? World, world, O world!
But that thy strange mutations make us hate thee,
Life would not yield to age.

OLD MAN. O, my good lord, I have been your tenant, and your father's tenant, these fourscore years. 15

GLOUCESTER. Away, get thee away; good friend, be gone:
Thy comforts can do me no good at all;
Thee they may hurt.

OLD MAN.   Alack, sir, you cannot see your way.

GLOUCESTER. I have no way, and therefore want no eyes; 20
I stumbled when I saw. Full oft 'tis seen,
Our means secure us, and our mere defects
Prove our commodities. O dear son Edgar,
The food of thy abused father's wrath!
Might I but live to see thee in my touch, 25
I'd say I had eyes again!

OLD MAN.   How now! Who's there?

EDGAR. [*Aside*] O gods! Who is 't can say "I am at the worst"?
I am worse than e'er I was.

OLD MAN.   'Tis poor mad Tom. 30

EDGAR. [*Aside*] And worse I may be yet: the worst is not
So long as we can say "This is the worst."

OLD MAN. Fellow, where goest?

GLOUCESTER.   Is it a beggar-man?

OLD MAN. Madman and beggar too. 35

GLOUCESTER. He has some reason, else he could not beg.
I' th' last night's storm I such a fellow saw,
Which made me think a man a worm. My son

>   Came then into my mind, and yet my mind
>   Was then scarce friends with him. I have heard more since. 40
>   As flies to wanton boys, are we to th' gods.
>   They kill us for their sport.
>
> EDGAR. [*Aside*] How should this be?
> >   Bad is the trade that must play fool to sorrow,
> >   Angering itself and others. Bless thee, master! 45
>
> GLOUCESTER. Is that the naked fellow?
>
> OLD MAN. Ay, my lord.
>
> GLOUCESTER. Then, prithee, get thee gone: if, for my sake
> >   Thou wilt o'ertake us, hence a mile or twain
> >   I' th' way toward Dover, do it for ancient love; 50
> >   And bring some covering for this naked soul,
> >   Who I'll entreat to lead me.
>
> OLD MAN. Alack, sir, he is mad.
>
> GLOUCESTER. 'Tis the times' plague, when madmen lead the blind.
> >   Do as I bid thee, or rather do thy pleasure; 55
> >   Above the rest, be gone.
>
> OLD MAN. I'll bring him the best 'parel that I have,
> >   Come on 't what will.   *Exit.*
>
> GLOUCESTER. Sirrah, naked fellow—
>
> EDGAR. Poor Tom's a-cold. [*Aside*] I cannot daub it further. 60
>
> GLOUCESTER. Come hither, fellow.
>
> EDGAR. [*Aside*] And yet I must.—Bless thy sweet eyes, they bleed.
>
> GLOUCESTER. Know'st thou the way to Dover?
>
> EDGAR. Both stile and gate, horse-way and footpath. Poor Tom hath
> > been scared out of his good wits. Bless thee, good man's son, 65
> > from the foul fiend! Five fiends have been in poor Tom at once; of
> > lust, as Obidicut; Hobbididance, prince of dumbness; Mahu, of
> > stealing; Modo, of murder; Flibbertigibbet, of mopping and mow-
> > ing, who since possesses chambermaids and waiting-women. So,
> > bless thee, master! 70
>
> GLOUCESTER. Here, take this purse, thou whom the heavens' plagues
> >   Have humbled to all strokes: that I am wretched
> >   Makes thee the happier. Heavens, deal so still!
> >   Let the superfluous and lust-dieted man, 75
> >   That slaves your ordinance, that will not see
> >   Because he doth not feel, feel your pow'r quickly;
> >   So distribution should undo excess,
> >   And each man have enough. Dost thou know Dover?
>
> EDGAR. Ay, master. 80
>
> GLOUCESTER. There is a cliff, whose high and bending head
> >   Looks fearfully in the confined deep:
> >   Bring me but to the very brim of it,

        And I'll repair the misery thou dost bear
        With something rich about me: from that place   85
        I shall no leading need.

EDGAR.   Give me thy arm:
        Poor Tom shall lead thee.   *Exeunt.*

Scene II. [*Before the Duke of Albany's palace.*]

Enter Goneril and Edmund.

GONERIL. Welcome, my lord: I marvel our mild husband
        Not met us on the way.

Enter Oswald.

        Now, where's your master?

OSWALD. Madam, within; but never man so changed.
        I told him of the army that was landed: 5
        He smiled at it. I told him you were coming;
        His answer was, "The worse." Of Gloucester's treachery,
        And of the loyal service of his son
        When I informed him, then he called me sot,
        And told me I had turned the wrong side out: 10
        What most he should dislike seems pleasant to him;
        What like, offensive.

GONERIL. [*To Edmund*] Then shall you go no further.
        It is the cowish terror of his spirit,
        That dares not undertake: he'll not feel wrongs   15
        Which tie him to an answer. Our wishes on the way
        May prove effects. Back, Edmund, to my brother;
        Hasten his musters and conduct his pow'rs.
        I must change names at home and give the distaff
        Into my husband's hands. This trusty servant   20
        Shall pass between us: ere long you are like to hear,
        If you dare venture in your own behalf,
        A mistress's command. Wear this; spare speech;

                          [*Giving a favor*]

        Decline your head. This kiss, if it durst speak,
        Would stretch thy spirits up into the air: 25
        Conceive, and fare thee well.

EDMUND. Yours in the ranks of death.

GONERIL.   My most dear Gloucester!
                          Exit [*Edmund*].
        O, the difference of man and man!
        To thee a woman's services are due: 30
        My fool usurps my body.

OSWALD.   Madam, here comes my lord.
                                      Exit.

Enter Albany.

GONERIL. I have been worth the whistle.

ALBANY.   O Goneril!
   You are not worth the dust which the rude wind
   Blows in your face. I fear your disposition:
   That nature which contemns its origin
   Cannot be bordered certain in itself;
   She that herself will sliver and disbranch
   From her material sap, perforce must wither
   And come to deadly use.

GONERIL. No more; the text is foolish.

ALBANY. Wisdom and goodness to the vile seem vile:
   Filths savour but themselves. What have you done?
   Tigers, not daughters, what have you performed?
   A father, and a gracious agèd man,
   Whose reverence even the head-lugged bear would lick,
   Most barbarous, most degenerate, have you madded.
   Could my good brother suffer you to do it?
   A man, a prince, by him so benefited!
   If that the heavens do not their visible spirits
   Send quickly down to tame these vile offenses,
   It will come,
   Humanity must perforce prey on itself,
   Like monsters of the deep.

GONERIL.   Milk-livered man!
   That bear'st a cheek for blows, a head for wrongs;
   Who hast not in thy brows an eye discerning
   Thine honor from thy suffering; that not know'st
   Fools do those villains pity who are punished
   Ere they have done their mischief. Where's thy drum?
   France spreads his banners in our noiseless land;
   With plumèd helm thy state begins to threat,
   Whilst thou, a moral fool, sits still, and cries
   "Alack, why does he so?"

ALBANY.   See thyself, devil!
   Proper deformity seems not in the fiend
   So horrid as in woman.

GONERIL.   O vain fool!

ALBANY. Thou changèd and self-covered thing, for shame,
   Be-monster not thy feature. Were 't my fitness
   To let these hands obey my blood,
   They are apt enough to dislocate and tear
   Thy flesh and bones: howe'er thou art a fiend,
   A woman's shape doth shield thee.

GONERIL. Marry, your manhood mew—

Enter a Messenger.

ALBANY. What news?

MESSENGER. O, my good lord, the Duke of Cornwall's dead,

  Slain by his servant, going to put out
  The other eye of Gloucester.   80

ALBANY.   Gloucester's eye!

MESSENGER. A servant that he bred, thrilled with remorse,
  Opposed against the act, bending his sword
  To his great master, who thereat enraged
  Flew on him, and amongst them felled him dead;   85
  But not without that harmful stroke, which since
  Hath plucked him after.

ALBANY.   This shows you are above,
  You justicers, that these our nether crimes
  So speedily can venge. But, O poor Gloucester!   90
  Lost he his other eye?

MESSENGER.   Both, both, my lord.
  This letter, madam, craves a speedy answer;
  'Tis from your sister.

GONERIL.   [*Aside*] One way I like this well;   95
  But being widow, and my Gloucester with her,
  May all the building in my fancy pluck
  Upon my hateful life. Another way,
  The news is not so tart.—I'll read, and answer.
                 Exit.

ALBANY. Where was his son when they did take his eyes?   100

MESSENGER. Come with my lady hither.

ALBANY.   He is not here.

MESSENGER. No, my good lord; I met him back again.

ALBANY. Knows he the wickedness?

MESSENGER. Ay, my good lord; 'twas he inform'd against him,   105
  And quit the house on purpose, that their punishment
  Might have the freer course.

ALBANY.   Gloucester, I live
  To thank thee for the love thou show'dst the King,
  And to revenge thine eyes. Come hither, friend: 110
  Tell me what more thou know'st.   *Exeunt.*

    [Scene III. *The French camp near Dover.*]

      Enter Kent and a Gentleman.

KENT. Why the King of France is so suddenly gone back know you
  the reason?

GENTLEMAN. Something he left imperfect in the state, which since
  his coming forth is thought of; which imports to the kingdom so
  much fear and danger, that his personal return was most required   5
  and necessary.

KENT. Who hath he left behind him general?

GENTLEMAN. The Marshal of France, Monsieur La Far.

KENT. Did your letters pierce the queen to any demonstration of grief? 10

GENTLEMAN. Ay, sir; she took them, read them in my presence,
And now and then an ample tear trilled down
Her delicate cheek: it seemed she was a queen
Over her passion; who, most rebel-like
Sought to be king o'er her. 15

KENT. O, then it moved her.

GENTLEMAN. Not to a rage: patience and sorrow strove
Who should express her goodliest. You have seen
Sunshine and rain at once: her smiles and tears
Were like a better way: those happy smilets 20
That played on her ripe lip, seemed not to know
What guests were in her eyes; which parted thence
As pearls from diamonds dropped. In brief,
Sorrow would be a rarity most beloved,
If all could so become it. 25

KENT. Made she no verbal question?

GENTLEMAN. Faith, once or twice she heaved the name of "father"
Pantingly forth, as if it pressed her heart;
Cried "Sisters! Sisters! Shame of ladies! Sisters!
Kent! Father! Sisters! What, i' th' storm? i' th' night? 30
Let pity not be believed!" There she shook
The holy water from her heavenly eyes,
And clamour moistened: then away she started
To deal with grief alone.

KENT. It is the stars, 35
The stars above us, govern our conditions;
Else one self mate and mate could not beget
Such different issues. You spoke not with her since?

GENTLEMAN. No.

KENT. Was this before the King returned? 40

GENTLEMAN. No, since.

KENT. Well, sir, the poor distressed Lear's i' th' town;
Who sometime, in his better tune remembers
What we are come about, and by no means
Will yield to see his daughter. 45

GENTLEMAN. Why, good sir?

KENT. A sovereign shame so elbows him: his own unkindness
That stripped her from his benediction, turned her
To foreign casualties, gave her dear rights
To his dog-hearted daughters: these things sting 50
His mind so venomously that burning shame
Detains him from Cordelia.

GENTLEMAN. Alack, poor gentleman!

KENT. Of Albany's and Cornwall's powers you heard not?

GENTLEMAN. 'Tis so, they are afoot. 55

KENT. Well, sir, I'll bring you to our master Lear,
    And leave you to attend him: some dear cause
    Will in concealment wrap me up awhile;
    When I am known aright, you shall not grieve
    Lending me this acquaintance. I pray you, go 60
    Along with me.   [*Exeunt.*]

[Scene IV. *The same. A tent.*]

Enter, with drum and colors, Cordelia, Doctor, and Soldiers.

CORDELIA. Alack, 'tis he: why, he was met even now
    As mad as the vexed sea; singing aloud;
    Crowned with rank fumiter and furrow-weeds,
    With hardocks, hemlock, nettles, cuckoo-flow'rs,
    Darnel, and all the idle weeds that grow 5
    In our sustaining corn. A century send forth;
    Search every acre in the high-grown field,
    And bring him to our eye. [*Exit an Officer.*] What can man's wisdom
    In the restoring his bereavèd sense?
    He that helps him take all my outward worth. 10

DOCTOR. There is means, madam:
    Our foster-nurse of nature is repose,
    The which he lacks: that to provoke in him,
    Are many simples operative, whose power
    Will close the eye of anguish. 15

CORDELIA.   All blest secrets,
    All you unpublish'd virtues of the earth,
    Spring with my tears! be aidant and remediate
    In the good man's distress! Seek, seek for him,
    Lest his ungovern'd rage dissolve the life 20
    That wants the means to lead it.

Enter Messenger.

MESSENGER. News, madam;
    The British pow'rs are marching hitherward.

CORDELIA. 'Tis known before; our preparation stands
    In expectation of them. O dear father, 25
    It is thy business that I go about;
    Therefore great France
    My mourning and importuned tears hath pitied.
    No blown ambition doth our arms incite,
    But love, dear love, and our aged father's right: 30
    Soon may I hear and see him!   *Exeunt.*

[Scene V. *Gloucester's castle.*]

Enter Regan and Oswald.

REGAN. But are my brother's pow'rs set forth?

OSWALD.   Ay, madam.

REGAN. Himself in person there?

OSWALD.   Madam, with much ado:
Your sister is the better soldier.   5

REGAN. Lord Edmund spake not with your lord at home?

OSWALD. No, madam.

REGAN. What might import my sister's letter to him?

OSWALD. I know not, lady.

REGAN. Faith, he is posted hence on serious matter.   10
It was great ignorance, Gloucester's eyes being out,
To let him live. Where he arrives he moves
All hearts against us: Edmund, I think, is gone,
In pity of his misery, to dispatch
His nighted life; moreover, to descry   15
The strength o' th' enemy.

OSWALD. I must needs after him, madam, with my letter.

REGAN. Our troops set forth tomorrow: stay with us;
The ways are dangerous.

OSWALD.   I may not, madam: 20
My lady charged my duty in this business.

REGAN. Why should she write to Edmund? Might not you
Transport her purposes by word? Belike,
Somethings I know not what. I'll love thee much,
Let me unseal the letter.   25

OSWALD.   Madam, I had rather—

REGAN. I know your lady does not love her husband;
I am sure of that: and at her late being here
She gave strange eliads and most speaking looks
To noble Edmund. I know you are of her bosom.   30

OSWALD. I, madam?

REGAN. I speak in understanding: y'are; I know't:
Therefore I do advise you, take this note:
My lord is dead; Edmund and I have talked;
And more convenient is he for my hand   35
Than for your lady's: you may gather more.
If you do find him, pray you, give him this;
And when your mistress hears thus much from you,
I pray, desire her call her wisdom to her.
So, fare you well.   40

If you do chance to hear of that blind traitor,
Preferment falls on him that cuts him off.

OSWALD. Would I could meet him, madam! I should show
What party I do follow.

REGAN.   Fare thee well.   45

Exeunt.

[Scene VI. *Fields near Dover.*]

Enter Gloucester and Edgar.

GLOUCESTER. When shall we come to th' top of that same hill?

EDGAR. You do climb up it now. Look, how we labor.

GLOUCESTER. Methinks the ground is even.

EDGAR.   Horrible steep.
Hark, do you hear the sea?   5

GLOUCESTER.   No, truly.

EDGAR. Why, then, your other senses grow imperfect
By your eyes' anguish.

GLOUCESTER.   So may it be, indeed.
Methinks thy voice is altered, and thou speak'st   10
In better phrase and matter than thou didst.

EDGAR. Y'are much deceived: in nothing am I changed
But in my garments.

GLOUCESTER.   Methinks y'are better spoken.

EDGAR. Come on, sir; here's the place: stand still. How fearful   15
And dizzy 'tis, to cast one's eyes so low!
The crows and choughs that wing the midway air
Show scarce so gross as beetles. Half way down
Hangs one that gathers samphire, dreadful trade!
Methinks he seems no bigger than his head.   20
The fishermen that walk upon the beach
Appear like mice; and yond tall anchoring bark
Diminished to her cock; her cock, a buoy
Almost too small for sight. The murmuring surge
That on th' unnumber'd idle pebbles chafes   25
Cannot be heard so high. I'll look no more,
Lest my brain turn and the deficient sight
Topple down headlong.

GLOUCESTER.   Set me where you stand.

EDGAR. Give me your hand: you are now within a foot   30
Of the extreme verge: for all beneath the moon
Would I not leap upright.

GLOUCESTER.   Let go my hand.

Here, friend, 's another purse; in it a jewel
Well worth a poor man's taking. Fairies and gods 35
Prosper it with thee! Go thou farther off;
Bid me farewell, and let me hear thee going.

EDGAR. Now fare you well, good sir.

GLOUCESTER.   With all my heart.

EDGAR. [*Aside*] Why I do trifle thus with his despair 40
Is done to cure it.

GLOUCESTER.   O you mighty gods!

He kneels

This world I do renounce, and in your sights
Shake patiently my great affliction off:
If I could bear it longer, and not fall 45
To quarrel with your great opposeless wills,
My snuff and loathed part of nature should
Burn itself out. If Edgar live, O, bless him!
Now, fellow, fare thee well.

He falls.

EDGAR.   Gone, sir, farewell. 50
And yet I know not how conceit may rob
The treasury of life, when life itself
Yields to the theft. Had he been where he thought,
By this, had thought been past. Alive or dead?
Ho, you sir! friend! Hear you, sir! speak! 55
Thus might he pass indeed: yet he revives.
What are you, sir?

GLOUCESTER.   Away, and let me die.

EDGAR. Hadst thou been aught but gossamer, feathers, air,
So many fathom down precipitating, 60
Thou'dst shiver'd like an egg: but thou dost breathe;
Hast heavy substance; bleed'st not; speak'st; art sound.
Ten masts at each make not the altitude
Which thou hast perpendicularly fell:
Thy life's a miracle. Speak yet again. 65

GLOUCESTER. But have I fall'n, or no?

EDGAR. From the dread summit of this chalky bourn.
Look up a-height; the shrill-gorged lark so far
Cannot be seen or heard: do but look up.

GLOUCESTER. Alack, I have no eyes. 70
Is wretchedness deprived that benefit,
To end itself by death? 'Twas yet some comfort,
When misery could beguile the tyrant's rage
And frustrate his proud will.

EDGAR.   Give me your arm. 75
Up, so. How is 't? Feel you your legs? You stand.

GLOUCESTER. Too well, too well.

EDGAR. This is above all strangeness.
    Upon the crown o' th' cliff, what thing was that
    Which parted from you? 80

GLOUCESTER. A poor unfortunate beggar.

EDGAR. As I stood here below, methought his eyes
    Were two full moons; he had a thousand noses,
    Horns whelked and waved like the enridged sea:
    It was some fiend; therefore, thou happy father, 85
    Think that the clearest gods, who make them honors
    Of men's impossibilities, have preserved thee.

GLOUCESTER. I do remember now: henceforth I'll bear
    Affliction till it do cry out itself
    "Enough, enough," and die. That thing you speak of, 90
    I took it for a man; often 'twould say
    "The fiend, the fiend"—he led me to that place.

EDGAR. Bear free and patient thoughts.

Enter Lear [fantastically dressed with wild flowers].

                    But who comes here?
    The safer sense will ne'er accommodate 95
    His master thus.

LEAR. No, they cannot touch me for coining; I am the King himself.

EDGAR. O thou side-piercing sight!

LEAR. Nature's above art in that respect. There's your press-money.
    That fellow handles his bow like a crow-keeper; draw me a 100
    clothier's yard. Look, look, a mouse! Peace, peace; this piece of
    toasted cheese will do't. There's my gauntlet; I'll prove it on a gi-
    ant. Bring up the brown bills. O, well flown, bird! i' th' clout, i'
    th' clout: hewgh! Give the word.

EDGAR. Sweet marjoram. 105

LEAR. Pass.

GLOUCESTER. I know that voice.

LEAR. Ha! Goneril, with a white beard! They flattered me like a dog;
    and told me I had white hairs in my beard ere the black ones were
    there. To say "ay" and "no" to everything that I said! "Ay" and 110
    "no" too was no good divinity. When the rain came to wet me
    once, and the wind to make me chatter; when the thunder would
    not peace at my bidding; there I found 'em, there I smelt 'em out.
    Go to, they are not men o' their words: they told me I was every-
    thing; 'tis a lie, I am not ague-proof. 115

GLOUCESTER. The trick of that voice I do well remember: Is't not
    the king?

LEAR. Ay, every inch a king.
    When I do stare, see how the subject quakes.
    I pardon that man's life. What was thy cause? 120
    Adultery?

> Thou shalt not die: die for adultery! No:
> The wren goes to 't, and the small gilded fly
> Does lecher in my sight.
> Let copulation thrive; for Gloucester's bastard son 125
> Was kinder to his father than my daughters
> Got 'tween the lawful sheets.
> To 't, luxury, pell-mell! for I lack soldiers.
> Behold yond simp'ring dame,
> Whose face between her forks presages snow; 130
> That minces virtue, and does shake the head
> To hear of pleasure's name.
> The fitchew, nor the soilèd horse, goes to 't
> With a more riotous appetite.
> Down from the waist they are Centaurs, 135
> Though women all above:
> But to the girdle do the gods inherit,
> Beneath is all the fiend's.
> There's hell, there's darkness, there is the sulphurous pit,
> Burning, scalding, stench, consumption; fie, fie, fie! pah, pah! 140

Give me an ounce of civet; good apothecary, sweeten my imagination: there's money for thee.

GLOUCESTER. O, let me kiss that hand!

LEAR. Let me wipe it first; it smells of mortality.

GLOUCESTER. O ruined piece of nature! This great world 145
  Shall so wear out to nought. Dost thou know me?

LEAR. I remember thine eyes well enough. Dost thou squiny at me?
  No, do thy worst, blind Cupid; I'll not love. Read thou this challenge; mark but the penning of it.

GLOUCESTER. Were all the letters suns, I could not see. 150

EDGAR. I would not take this from report: it is,
  And my heart breaks at it.

LEAR. Read.

GLOUCESTER. What, with the case of eyes?

LEAR. O, ho, are you there with me? No eyes in your head, nor no 155
  money in your purse? Your eyes are in a heavy case, your purse in
  a light; yet you see how this world goes.

GLOUCESTER. I see it feelingly.

LEAR. What, art mad? A man may see how this world goes with no
  eyes. Look with thine ears: see how yond justice rails upon yond 160
  simple thief. Hark, in thine ear: change places; and, handy-dandy,
  which is the justice, which is the thief? Thou hast seen a farmer's
  dog bark at a beggar?

GLOUCESTER. Ay, sir.

LEAR. And the creature run from the cur? There thou mightst behold 165
  the great image of authority: a dog's obeyed in office.
  Thou rascal beadle, hold thy bloody hand!

Why dost thou lash that whore? Strip thine own back;
Thou hotly lust to use her in that kind
For which thou whip'st her. The usurer hangs the cozener. 170
Through tattered clothes small vices do appear;
Robes and furr'd gowns hide all. Plate sin with gold,
And the strong lance of justice hurtless breaks;
Arm it in rags, a pigmy's straw does pierce it.
None does offend, none, I say, none; I'll able 'em: 175
Take that of me, my friend, who have the power
To seal the accuser's lips. Get thee glass eyes,
And like a scurvy politician, seem
To see the things thou dost not. Now, now, now, now.
Pull off my boots: harder, harder: so. 180

EDGAR. O, matter and impertinency mixed!
Reason in madness!

LEAR. If thou wilt weep my fortunes, take my eyes.
I know thee well enough; thy name is Gloucester:
Thou must be patient; we came crying hither: 185
Thou know'st the first time that we smell the air
We wawl and cry. I will preach to thee: mark.

GLOUCESTER. Alack, alack the day!

LEAR. When we are born, we cry that we are come
To this great stage of fools. This' a good block. 190
It were a delicate stratagem, to shoe
A troop of horse with felt: I'll put't in proof;
And when I have stol'n upon these sons-in-law,
Then, kill, kill, kill, kill, kill, kill!

Enter a Gentleman [with Attendants].

GENTLEMAN. O, here he is: lay hand upon him. Sir, 195
Your most dear daughter—

LEAR. No rescue? What, a prisoner? I am even
The natural fool of fortune. Use me well;
You shall have ransom. Let me have surgeons;
I am cut to th' brains. 200

GENTLEMAN.   You shall have any thing.

LEAR. No seconds? all myself?
Why, this would make a man a man of salt,
To use his eyes for garden water-pots,
Ay, and laying autumn's dust. 205

GENTLEMAN. Good sir—

LEAR. I will die bravely, like a bridegroom. What!
I will be jovial: come, come; I am a king,
Masters, know you that?

GENTLEMAN. You are a royal one, and we obey you. 210

LEAR. Then there's life in 't. Come, if you get it, you shall get it with
running. Sa, sa, sa, sa.

Exit [running; Attendants follow].

GENTLEMAN. A sight most pitiful in the meanest wretch,
    Past speaking of in a king! Thou hast one daughter,
    Who redeems nature from the general curse 215
    Which twain have brought her to.

EDGAR. Hail, gentle sir.

GENTLEMAN.   Sir, speed you: what's your will?

EDGAR. Do you hear aught, sir, of a battle toward?

GENTLEMAN. Most sure and vulgar: every one hears that, 220
    Which can distinguish sound.

EDGAR.   But, by your favor,
    How near's the other army?

GENTLEMAN. Near and on speedy foot; the main descry
    Stands on the hourly thought. 225

EDGAR.   I thank you, sir: that's all.

GENTLEMAN. Though that the Queen on special cause is here,
    Her army is moved on.

EDGAR.   I thank you, sir.
                              Exit [Gentleman].

GLOUCESTER. You ever-gentle gods, take my breath from me; 230
    Let not my worser spirit tempt me again
    To die before you please.

EDGAR.   Well pray you, father.

GLOUCESTER. Now, good sir, what are you?

EDGAR. A most poor man, made tame to fortune's blows; 235
    Who, by the art of known and feeling sorrows,
    Am pregnant to good pity. Give me your hand,
    I'll lead you to some biding.

GLOUCESTER.   Hearty thanks;
    The bounty and the benison of heaven 240
    To boot, and boot.

              Enter Oswald.

OSWALD.   A proclaimed prize! Most happy!
    That eyeless head of thine was first framed flesh
    To raise my fortunes. Thou old unhappy traitor,
    Briefly thyself remember: the sword is out 245
    That must destroy thee.

GLOUCESTER.   Now let thy friendly hand
    Put strength enough to 't.
                         [Edgar interposes.]

OSWALD.   Wherefore, bold peasant,
    Darest thou support a published traitor? Hence! 250
    Lest that th' infection of his fortune take
    Like hold on thee. Let go his arm.

EDGAR. Chill not let go, zir, without vurther 'casion.

OSWALD. Let go, slave, or thou diest!

EDGAR. Good gentleman, go your gait, and let poor volk pass. An 255
chud ha' bin zwaggered out of my life, 'twould not ha' bin zo
long as 'tis by a vortnight. Nay, come not near th' old man; keep
out, che vor' ye, or I'se try whether your costard or my ballow be
the harder: chill be plain with you.

OSWALD. Out, dunghill! 260
They fight.

EDGAR. Chill pick your teeth, zir: come; no matter vor your foins.
[*Oswald falls.*]

OSWALD. Slave, thou hast slain me. Villain, take my purse:
If ever thou wilt thrive, bury my body;
And give the letters which thou find'st about me
To Edmund earl of Gloucester; seek him out 265
Upon the British party. O, untimely death!
Death!
He dies.

EDGAR. I know thee well. A serviceable villain,
As duteous to the vices of thy mistress
As badness would desire. 270

GLOUCESTER.   What, is he dead?

EDGAR. Sit you down, father; rest you.
Let's see these pockets: the letters that he speaks of
May be my friends. He's dead; I am only sorry
He had no other deathsman. Let us see: 275
Leave, gentle wax; and, manners, blame us not:
To know our enemies' minds, we'd rip their hearts;
Their papers is more lawful.

Reads the letter.

"Let our reciprocal vows be remembered. You have many opportunities to cut him off: if your will want not, time and place will be 280
fruitfully offered. There is nothing done, if he return the conqueror:
then am I the prisoner, and his bed my jail; from the loathed warmth
whereof deliver me, and supply the place for your labor.
"Your—wife, so I would say—affectionate servant, and for you
her own for venture, 285
          'Goneril.'"
O indistinguished space of woman's will!
A plot upon her virtuous husband's life;
And the exchange my brother! Here, in the sands,
Thee I'll rake up, the post unsanctified 290
Of murderous lechers; and in the mature time,
With this ungracious paper strike the sight
Of the death practiced Duke: for him 'tis well
That of thy death and business I can tell.

GLOUCESTER. The king is mad: how stiff is my vile sense, 295

That I stand up, and have ingenious feeling
Of my huge sorrows! Better I were distract:
So should my thoughts be severed from my griefs,
And woes by wrong imaginations lose
The knowledge of themselves. 300

Drum afar off.

EDGAR. Give me your hand:
Far off, methinks, I hear the beaten drum.
Come, father, I'll bestow you with a friend.

Exeunt.

Scene VII. [*A tent in the French camp.*]

Enter Cordelia, Kent, Doctor, and Gentleman.

CORDELIA. O thou good Kent, how shall I live and work,
To match thy goodness? My life will be too short,
And every measure fail me.

KENT. To be acknowledged, madam, is o'erpaid. 5
All my reports go with the modest truth,
Nor more nor clipped, but so.

CORDELIA. Be better suited:
These weeds are memories of those worser hours:
I prithee, put them off.

KENT. Pardon me, dear madam; 10
Yet to be known shortens my made intent:
My boon I make it, that you know me not
Till time and I think meet.

CORDELIA. Then be 't so, my good lord. [*To the Doctor.*] How does
the King? 15

DOCTOR. Madam, sleeps still.

CORDELIA. O you kind gods!
Cure this great breach in his abused nature!
The untuned and jarring senses, O, wind up
Of this child-changèd father. 20

DOCTOR. So please your Majesty
That we may wake the King: he hath slept long.

CORDELIA. Be governed by your knowledge, and proceed
I' th' sway of your own will. Is he arrayed?

Enter Lear in a chair carried by Servants.

GENTLEMAN. Ay, madam; in the heaviness of his sleep 25
We put fresh garments on him.

DOCTOR. Be by, good madam, when we do awake him;
I doubt not of his temperance.

CORDELIA. Very well.

DOCTOR. Please you, draw near. Louder the music there!

CORDELIA. O my dear father! Restoration hang
    Thy medicine on my lips; and let this kiss
    Repair those violent harms that my two sisters
    Have in thy reverence made.

KENT.   Kind and dear Princess.

CORDELIA. Had you not been their father, these white flakes
    Did challenge pity of them. Was this a face
    To be opposed against the warring winds?
    To stand against the deep dread-bolted thunder?
    In the most terrible and nimble stroke
    Of quick, cross lightning? to watch—poor perdu!—
    With this thin helm? Mine enemy's dog,
    Though he had bit me, should have stood that night
    Against my fire; and wast thou fain, poor father,
    To hovel thee with swine and rogues forlorn,
    In short and musty straw? Alack, alack!
    'Tis wonder that thy life and wits at once
    Had not concluded all. He wakes; speak to him.

DOCTOR. Madam, do you; 'tis fittest.

CORDELIA. How does my royal lord? How fares your Majesty?

LEAR. You do me wrong to take me out o' the grave:
    Thou art a soul in bliss; but I am bound
    Upon a wheel of fire, that mine own tears
    Do scald like molten lead.

CORDELIA.   Sir, do you know me?

LEAR. You are a spirit, I know. Where did you die?

CORDELIA. Still, still, far wide.

DOCTOR. He's scarce awake: let him alone awhile.

LEAR. Where have I been? Where am I? Fair daylight?
    I am mightily abused. I should ev'n die with pity,
    To see another thus. I know not what to say.
    I will not swear these are my hands: let's see;
    I feel this pin prick. Would I were assured
    Of my condition!

CORDELIA.   O, look upon me, sir,
    And hold your hands in benediction o'er me.
    No, sir, you must not kneel.

LEAR.   Pray, do not mock me:
    I am a very foolish fond old man,
    Fourscore and upward, not an hour more nor less;
    And, to deal plainly,
    I fear I am not in my perfect mind.
    Methinks I should know you, and know this man,
    Yet I am doubtful for I am mainly ignorant
    What place this is; and all the skill I have

> Remembers not these garments; nor I know not
> Where I did lodge last night. Do not laugh at me,
> For, as I am a man, I think this lady
> To be my child Cordelia.

CORDELIA.　　　　　And so I am, I am. 80

LEAR. Be your tears wet? Yes, faith. I pray, weep not.
> If you have poison for me, I will drink it.
> I know you do not love me; for your sisters
> Have, as I do remember, done me wrong.
> You have some cause, they have not. 85

CORDELIA.　　　　　　　　No cause, no cause.

LEAR. Am I in France?

KENT.　　　　　In your own kingdom, sir.

LEAR. Do not abuse me.

DOCTOR. Be comforted, good madam: the great rage, 90
> You see, is killed in him: and yet it is danger
> To make him even o'er the time he has lost.
> Desire him to go in; trouble him no more
> Till further settling.

CORDELIA. Will 't please your Highness walk? 95

LEAR. You must bear with me. Pray you now, forget and forgive. I am old and foolish.
>　　　　　　　　*Exeunt. Mane[n]t Kent and Gentleman.*

GENTLEMAN. Holds it true, sir, that the Duke of Cornwall was so slain?

KENT. Most certain, sir. 100

GENTLEMAN. Who is conductor of his people?

KENT. As 'tis said, the bastard son of Gloucester.

GENTLEMAN. They say Edgar, his banished son, is with the Earl of Kent in Germany.

KENT. Report is changeable. 'Tis time to look about; the powers of 105
> the kingdom approach apace.

GENTLEMAN. The arbitrement is like to be bloody. Fare you well, sir.
>　　　　　　　　　　　　　*[Exit.]*

KENT. My point and period will be throughly wrought,
> Or well or ill, as this day's battle's fought. 110
>　　　　　　　　　　　　　*Exit.*

ACT V

Scene I. [*The British camp, near Dover.*]

Enter, with drum and colors, Edmund, Regan, Gentlemen, and Soldiers.

EDMUND. Know of the Duke if his last purpose hold,
 Or whether since he is advised by aught
 To change the course: he's full of alteration
 And self-reproving: bring his constant pleasure.
  [*To a Gentleman, who goes out.*]

REGAN. Our sister's man is certainly miscarried.

EDMUND. 'Tis to be doubted, madam.

REGAN.   Now, sweet lord,
 You know the goodness I intend upon you:
 Tell me, but truly, but then speak the truth,
 Do you not love my sister?

EDMUND.   In honored love.

REGAN. But have you never found my brother's way
 To the forfended place?

EDMUND.   That thought abuses you.

REGAN. I am doubtful that you have been conjunct
 And bosom'd with her, as far as we call hers.

EDMUND. No, by mine honor, madam.

REGAN. I never shall endure her: dear my lord,
 Be not familiar with her.

EDMUND.   Fear me not.—
 She and the Duke her husband!

Enter, with drum and colors, Albany, Goneril [and] Soldiers.

GONERIL. [*Aside*] I had rather lose the battle than that sister
 Should loosen him and me.

ALBANY. Our very loving sister, well be-met.
 Sir, this I hear; the King is come to his daughter,
 With others whom the rigour of our state
 Forced to cry out. Where I could not be honest,
 I never yet was valiant: for this business,
 It toucheth us, as France invades our land,
 Not bolds the king, with others, whom I fear,
 Most just and heavy causes make oppose.

EDMUND. Sir, you speak nobly.

REGAN.   Why is this reasoned?

GONERIL. Combine together 'gainst the enemy;
 For these domestic and particular broils

Are not the question here.

ALBANY. Let's then determine
With the ancient of war on our proceedings.

EDMUND. I shall attend you presently at your tent.

REGAN. Sister, you'll go with us?

GONERIL. No.

REGAN. 'Tis most convenient; pray you, go with us.

GONERIL. [*Aside*] O, ho, I know the riddle.—I will go.

Exeunt both the Armies. Enter Edgar [disguised].

EDGAR. If e'er your grace had speech with man so poor,
Hear me one word.

ALBANY. [*To those going out*] I'll overtake you. [*To Edgar*] Speak.
Exeunt [all but Albany and Edgar].

EDGAR. Before you fight the battle, ope this letter.
If you have victory, let the trumpet sound
For him that brought it: wretched though I seem,
I can produce a champion that will prove
What is avouched there. If you miscarry,
Your business of the world hath so an end,
And machination ceases. Fortune love you.

ALBANY. Stay till I have read the letter.

EDGAR. I was forbid it.
When time shall serve, let but the herald cry,
And I'll appear again.

ALBANY. Why, fare thee well: I will o'erlook thy paper.
Exit [Edgar].

Enter Edmund.

EDMUND. The enemy's in view: draw up your powers.
Here is the guess of their true strength and forces
By diligent discovery; but your haste
Is now urged on you.

ALBANY. We will greet the time. *Exit.*

EDMUND. To both these sisters have I sworn my love;
Each jealous of the other, as the stung
Are of the adder. Which of them shall I take?
Both? One? Or neither? Neither can be enjoyed,
If both remain alive: to take the widow
Exasperates, makes mad her sister Goneril;
And hardly shall I carry out my side,
Her husband being alive. Now then we'll use
His countenance for the battle; which being done,
Let her who would be rid of him devise
His speedy taking off. As for the mercy
Which he intends to Lear and to Cordelia,

The battle done, and they within our power,
Shall never see his pardon; for my state
Stands on me to defend, not to debate.   *Exit.*

Scene II. [*A field between the two camps.*]

*Alarum within. Enter, with drum and colors, Lear, Cordelia, and
Soldiers, over the stage; and exeunt.*
Enter Edgar and Gloucester.

EDGAR. Here, father, take the shadow of this tree
For your good host; pray that the right may thrive.
If ever I return to you again,
I'll bring you comfort.

GLOUCESTER.   Grace go with you, sir.   5
                                             Exit [Edgar].

Alarum and retreat within. [Re-]enter Edgar.

EDGAR. Away, old man; give me thy hand; away!
King Lear hath lost, he and his daughter ta'en:
Give me thy hand; come on.

GLOUCESTER. No further, sir; a man may rot even here.

EDGAR. What, in ill thoughts again? Men must endure   10
Their going hence, even as their coming hither:
Ripeness is all. Come on.

GLOUCESTER.   And that's true too.
                                                  Exeunt.

Scene III. [*The British camp near Dover.*]

*Enter, in conquest, with drum and colors, Edmund; Lear and
Cordelia, as prisoners; Soldiers, Captain.*

EDMUND. Some officers take them away: good guard,
Until their greater pleasure first be known
That are to censure them.

CORDELIA.   We are not the first
Who, with best meaning, have incurr'd the worst   5
For thee, oppressed King, I am cast down;
Myself could else out-frown false fortune's frown.
Shall we not see these daughters and these sisters?

LEAR. No, no, no, no! Come, let's away to prison:
We two alone will sing like birds i' th' cage: 10
When thou dost ask me blessing, I'll kneel down
And ask of thee forgiveness: so we'll live,
And pray, and sing, and tell old tales, and laugh

      At gilded butterflies, and hear poor rogues
      Talk of court news; and we'll talk with them too,   15
      Who loses and who wins; who's in, who's out;
      And take upon's the mystery of things,
      As if we were God's spies: and we'll wear out,
      In a walled prison, packs and sects of great ones
      That ebb and flow by the moon.   20

EDMUND.   Take them away.

LEAR. Upon such sacrifices, my Cordelia,
      The gods themselves throw incense. Have I caught thee?
      He that parts us shall bring a brand from heaven,
      And fire us hence like foxes. Wipe thine eyes;   25
      The good years shall devour them, flesh and fell,
      Ere they shall make us weep. We'll see 'em starve first.
      Come.   [*Exeunt Lear and Cordelia, guarded.*]

EDMUND. Come hither, captain; hark.
      Take thou this note: go follow them to prison: 30
      One step I have advanced thee; if thou dost
      As this instructs thee, thou dost make thy way
      To noble fortunes: know thou this, that men
      Are as the time is: to be tender-minded
      Does not become a sword: thy great employment   35
      Will not bear question; either say thou'lt do 't,
      Or thrive by other means.

CAPTAIN.   I'll do 't, my lord.

EDMUND. About it; and write happy when th' hast done.
      Mark; I say, instantly; and carry it so   40
      As I have set it down.

CAPTAIN. I cannot draw a cart, nor eat dried oats;
      If it be man's work, I'll do 't.   *Exit Captain.*

    Flourish. Enter Albany, Goneril, Regan, [another Captain, and]
                      Soldiers.

ALBANY. Sir, you have shown to-day your valiant strain,
      And fortune led you well: you have the captives   45
      That were the opposites of this day's strife:
      We do require them of you, so to use them
      As we shall find their merits and our safety
      May equally determine.

EDMUND.   Sir, I thought it fit   50
      To send the old and miserable King
      To some retention and appointed guard;
      Whose age has charms in it, whose title more,
      To pluck the common bosom on his side,
      An turn our impressed lances in our eyes   55
      Which do command them. With him I sent the Queen:
      My reason all the same; and they are ready
      Tomorrow, or at further space, t' appear
      Where you shall hold your session. At this time

    We sweat and bleed: the friend hath lost his friend; 60
    And the best quarrels, in the heat, are cursed
    By those that feel their sharpness.
    The question of Cordelia and her father
    Requires a fitter place.

ALBANY.   Sir, by your patience, 65
    I hold you but a subject of this war,
    Not as a brother.

REGAN.   That's as we list to grace him.
    Methinks our pleasure might have been demanded,
    Ere you had spoke so far. He led our powers; 70
    Bore the commission of my place and person;
    The which immediacy may well stand up
    And call itself your brother.

GONERIL.   Not so hot:
    In his own grace he doth exalt himself 75
    More than in your addition.

REGAN.   In my rights,
    By me invested, he compeers the best.

GONERIL. That were the most, if he should husband you.

REGAN. Jesters do oft prove prophets. 80

GONERIL.   Holla, holla!
    That eye that told you so looked but a-squint.

REGAN. Lady, I am not well; else I should answer
    From a full-flowing stomach. General,
    Take thou my soldiers, prisoners, patrimony; 85
    Dispose of them, of me; the walls are thine:
    Witness the world, that I create thee here
    My lord and master.

GONERIL.   Mean you to enjoy him?

ALBANY. The let-alone lies not in your good will. 90

EDMUND. Nor in thine, lord.

ALBANY.   Half-blooded fellow, yes.

REGAN. [*To Edmund*] Let the drum strike, and prove my title thine.

ALBANY. Stay yet; hear reason. Edmund, I arrest thee
    On capital treason; and, in thine attaint, 95
    This gilded serpent [*pointing to Goneril*] For your claim, fair sister,
    I bar it in the interest of my wife.
    'Tis she is sub-contracted to this lord,
    And I, her husband, contradict your banes.
    If you will marry, make your loves to me; 100
    My lady is bespoke.

GONERIL.   An interlude!

ALBANY. Thou art armed, Gloucester: let the trumpet sound:
    If none appear to prove upon thy person

Thy heinous, manifest, and many treasons, 105
There is my pledge [*throwing down a glove*]:
   I'll prove it on thy heart,
Ere I taste bread, thou art in nothing less
Than I have here proclaimed thee.

REGAN.   Sick, O, sick! 110

GONERIL. [*Aside*] If not, I'll ne'er trust medicine.

EDMUND. [*Throwing down a glove*] There's my exchange: what in
   the world he is
That names me traitor, villain-like he lies:
Call by thy trumpet: he that dares approach, 115
On him, on you—who not?—I will maintain
My truth and honor firmly.

ALBANY. A herald, ho!

EDMUND.   A herald, ho, a herald!

ALBANY. Trust to thy single virtue; for thy soldiers, 120
   All levied in my name, have in my name
   Took their discharge.

REGAN.   My sickness grows upon me.

ALBANY. She is not well; convey her to my tent.
                                       [*Exit Regan, led.*]

                  Enter a Herald.

Come hither, herald. Let the trumpet sound— 125
   And read out this

CAPTAIN. Sound, trumpet!

                  A trumpet sounds.

HERALD. (*Reads*) "If any man of quality or degree within the lists of
   the army will maintain upon Edmund, supposed Earl of
   Gloucester, that he is a manifold traitor, let him appear by the 130
   third sound of the trumpet: he is bold in his defence.

EDMUND. Sound!

                  First trumpet.

HERALD. Again!

                  Second trumpet.

HERALD. Again!

                  Third trumpet.

Trumpet answers within. Enter Edgar, at the third sound, armed, with
                  a trumpet before him.

ALBANY. Ask him his purposes, why he appears 135
   Upon this call o' the trumpet.

HERALD.   What are you?
   Your name, your quality? and why you answer

        This present summons?

EDGAR.   Know, my name is lost;   140
   By treason's tooth bare-gnawn and canker-bit:
   Yet am I noble as the adversary
   I come to cope.

ALBANY.   Which is that adversary?

EDGAR. What's he that speaks for Edmund Earl of Gloucester?   145

EDMUND. Himself: what say'st thou to him?

EDGAR.   Draw thy sword,
   That, if my speech offend a noble heart,
   Thy arm may do thee justice: here is mine.
   Behold, it is the privilege,   150
   The privilege of mine honors,
   My oath, and my profession. I protest,
   Maugre thy strength, youth, place, and eminence,
   Despite thy victor sword and fire-new fortune,
   Thy valour and thy heart, thou art a traitor,   155
   False to thy gods, thy brother, and thy father;
   Conspirant 'gainst this high-illustrious prince;
   And, from th' extremest upward of thy head
   To the descent and dust below thy foot,
   A most toad-spotted traitor. Say thou "No,"   160
   This sword, this arm, and my best spirits, are bent
   To prove upon thy heart, whereto I speak,
   Thou liest.

EDMUND.   In wisdom I should ask thy name,
   But, since thy outside looks so fair and warlike,   165
   And that thy tongue some say of breeding breathes,
   What safe and nicely I might well delay
   By rule of knighthood, I disdain and spurn
   Back do I toss these treasons to thy head;
   With the hell-hated lie o'erwhelm thy heart;   170
   Which, for they yet glance by and scarcely bruise,
   This sword of mine shall give them instant way,
   Where they shall rest for ever. Trumpets, speak!

        Alarums. [They] fight. [Edmund falls.]

ALBANY. Save him, save him!

GONERIL.   This is practice, Gloucester: 175
   By th' law of arms thou wast not bound to answer
   An unknown opposite; thou art not vanquished,
   But cozen'd and beguiled.

ALBANY.   Shut your mouth, dame,
   Or with this paper shall I stop it. Hold, sir;   180
   Thou worse than any name, read thine own evil.
   No tearing, lady; I perceive you know it.

GONERIL. Say, if I do, the laws are mine, not thine:
   Who can arraign me for 't?

ALBANY.   Most monstrous! O!   185
    Know'st thou this paper?

GONERIL.   Ask me not what I know.
                                                          Exit.

ALBANY. Go after her; she's desperate; govern her.

EDMUND. What you have charged me with, that have I done;
    And more, much more; the time will bring it out.   190
    'Tis past, and so am I. But what art thou
    That hast this fortune on me? If thou'rt noble,
    I do forgive thee.

EDGAR.   Let's exchange charity.
    I am no less in blood than thou art, Edmund;   195
    If more, the more thou hast wronged me.
    My name is Edgar, and thy father's son.
    The gods are just, and of our pleasant vices
    Make instruments to plague us:
    The dark and vicious place where thee he got   200
    Cost him his eyes.

EDMUND.   Th' hast spoken right, 'tis true;
    The wheel is come full circle; I am here.

ALBANY. Methought thy very gait did prophesy
    A royal nobleness: I must embrace thee: 205
    Let sorrow split my heart, if ever I
    Did hate thee or thy father!

EDGAR.   Worthy prince, I know 't.

ALBANY. Where have you hid yourself?
    How have you known the miseries of your father?   210

EDGAR. By nursing them, my lord. List a brief tale;
    And when 'tis told, O, that my heart would burst!
    The bloody proclamation to escape
    That followed me so near—O, our lives' sweetness,
    That we the pain of death would hourly die   215
    Rather than die at once!—taught me to shift
    Into a madman's rags; t' assume a semblance
    That very dogs disdained: and in this habit
    Met I my father with his bleeding rings,
    Their precious stones new lost; became his guide,   220
    Led him, begged for him, saved him from despair;
    Never—O fault!—reveal'd myself unto him,
    Until some half-hour past, when I was armed,
    Not sure, though hoping, of this good success,
    I asked his blessing, and from first to last   225
    Told him my pilgrimage. But his flawed heart—
    Alack, too weak the conflict to support—
    'Twixt two extremes of passion, joy and grief,
    Burst smilingly.

EDMUND.   This speech of yours hath moved me,   230
    And shall perchance do good: but speak you on;

You look as you had something more to say.

ALBANY. If there be more, more woeful, hold it in;
   For I am almost ready to dissolve,
   Hearing of this. 235

EDGAR.   This would have seemed a period
   To such as love not sorrow; but another,
   To amplify too much, would make much more,
   And top extremity.
   Whilst I was big in clamor, came there in a man, 240
   Who, having seen me in my worst estate,
   Shunned my abhorred society; but then, finding
   Who 'twas that so endured, with his strong arms
   He fastened on my neck, and bellowed out
   As he'd burst heaven; threw him on my father; 245
   Told the most piteous tale of Lear and him
   That ever ear received: which in recounting
   His grief grew puissant, and the strings of life
   Began to crack: twice then the trumpets sounded,
   And there I left him tranced. 250

ALBANY.   But who was this?

EDGAR. Kent, sir, the banish'd Kent; who in disguise
   Followed his enemy king, and did him service
   Improper for a slave.

Enter a Gentleman, with a bloody knife.

GENTLEMAN. Help, help, O, help! 255

EDGAR.   What kind of help?

 ALBANY.   Speak, man.

EDGAR. What means that bloody knife?

GENTLEMAN.   'Tis hot, it smokes;
   It came even from the heart of—O, she's dead! 260

ALBANY. Who dead? Speak, man.

GENTLEMAN. Your lady, sir, your lady: and her sister
   By her is poisoned; she confesses it.

EDMUND. I was contracted to them both: all three
   Now marry in an instant. 265

EDGAR.   Here comes Kent.

ALBANY. Produce their bodies, be they alive or dead.
                          [*Exit Gentleman.*]
   This judgment of the heavens, that makes us tremble,
   Touches us not with pity.

Enter Kent.

            O, is this he? 270
   The time will not allow the compliment
   Which very manners urges.

KENT.   I am come
  To bid my king and master aye good night:
  Is he not here?   275

ALBANY.   Great thing of us forgot!
  Speak, Edmund, where's the King? and where's Cordelia?
  See'st thou this object, Kent?

  The bodies of Goneril and Regan are brought in.

KENT. Alack, why thus?

EDMUND.   Yet Edmund was beloved: 280
  The one the other poisoned for my sake,
  And after slew herself.

ALBANY. Even so. Cover their faces.

EDMUND. I pant for life: some good I mean to do,
  Despite of mine own nature. Quickly send,   285
  Be brief in it, to the castle; for my writ
  Is on the life of Lear and on Cordelia:
  Nay, send in time.

ALBANY.   Run, run, O, run!

EDGAR. To who, my lord? Who hath the office? Send   290
  Thy token of reprieve.

EDMUND. Well thought on: take my sword,
  Give it the captain.

EDGAR.   Haste thee, for thy life.
                              [*Exit Messenger.*]

EDMUND. He hath commission from thy wife and me   295
  To hang Cordelia in the prison, and
  To lay the blame upon her own despair,
  That she fordid herself.

ALBANY. The gods defend her! Bear him hence awhile.
                              [*Edmund is borne off.*]

  *Enter Lear, with Cordelia in his arms [Gentleman, and others
                        following].*

LEAR. Howl, howl, howl, howl! O, you are men of stones: 300
  Had I your tongues and eyes, I'd use them so
  That heaven's vault should crack. She's gone for ever!
  I know when one is dead, and when one lives;
  She's dead as earth. Lend me a looking-glass;
  If that her breath will mist or stain the stone,   305
  Why, then she lives.

KENT.   Is this the promised end?

EDGAR. Or image of that horror?

ALBANY.   Fall, and cease!

LEAR. This feather stirs; she lives. If it be so,   310
  It is a chance which does redeem all sorrows

That ever I have felt.

KENT. O my good master!

LEAR. Prithee, away.

EDGAR. 'Tis noble Kent, your friend. 315

LEAR. A plague upon you, murderers, traitors all!
   I might have saved her; now she's gone for ever.
   Cordelia, Cordelia! stay a little. Ha,
   What is 't thou say'st? Her voice was ever soft,
   Gentle, and low, an excellent thing in woman. 320
   I killed the slave that was a-hanging thee.

GENTLEMAN. 'Tis true, my lords, he did.

LEAR. Did I not, fellow?
   I have seen the day, with my good biting falchion
   I would have made them skip: I am old now, 325
   And these same crosses spoil me. Who are you?
   Mine eyes are not o' the best: I'll tell you straight.

KENT. If fortune brag of two she loved and hated,
   One of them we behold.

LEAR. This is a dull sight. Are you not Kent? 330

KENT. The same,
   Your servant Kent. Where is your servant Caius?

LEAR. He's a good fellow, I can tell you that;
   He'll strike, and quickly too: he's dead and rotten.

KENT. No, my good lord; I am the very man. 335

LEAR. I'll see that straight.

KENT. That from your first of difference and decay,
   Have followed your sad steps.

LEAR. You are welcome hither.

KENT. Nor no man else: all's cheerless, dark, and deadly. 340
   Your eldest daughters have fordone themselves,
   And desperately are dead.

LEAR. Ay, so I think.

ALBANY. He knows not what he says, and vain is it
   That we present us to him. 345

EDGAR. Very bootless.

Enter a Messenger.

MESSENGER. Edmund is dead, my lord.

ALBANY. That's but a trifle here.
   You lords and noble friends, know our intent.
   What comfort to this great decay may come 350
   Shall be applied. For us we will resign,
   During the life of this old majesty,

>   To him our absolute power: [*To Edgar and Kent*] you, to your rights;
>   With boot, and such addition as your honors
>   Have more than merited. All friends shall taste   355
>   The wages of their virtue, and all foes
>   The cup of their deservings. O, see, see!

LEAR. And my poor fool is hanged: no, no, no life!
    Why should a dog, a horse, a rat, have life,
    And thou no breath at all? Thou'lt come no more,   360
    Never, never, never, never, never.
    Pray you, undo this button. Thank you, sir.
    Do you see this? Look on her, look, her lips,
    Look there, look there!
                                       He dies.

EDGAR.   He faints! My lord, my lord!   370

KENT. Break, heart; I prithee, break!

EDGAR.   Look up, my lord.

KENT. Vex not his ghost: O, let him pass! He hates him
    That would upon the rack of this tough world
    Stretch him out longer.   375

EDGAR.   He is gone, indeed.

KENT. The wonder is, he hath endured so long:
    He but usurped his life.

ALBANY. Bear them from hence. Our present business
    Is general woe. [*To Kent and Edgar.*] Friends of my soul, you twain,   380
    Rule in this realm, and the gored state sustain.

KENT. I have a journey, sir, shortly to go;
    My master calls me, I must not say no.

ALBANY. The weight of this sad time we must obey,
    Speak what we feel, not what we ought to say.   385
    The oldest hath borne most: we that are young
    Shall never see so much, nor live so long.
                           Exeunt, with a dead march.

FINIS

The Tragedy of Othello, The Moor of Venice

Characters in the Play

OTHELLO, a Moorish general in the Venetian army
DESDEMONA, a Venetian lady
BRABANTIO, a Venetian senator, father to Desdemona

IAGO, Othello's standard-bearer, or "ancient"
EMILIA, Iago's wife and Desdemona's attendant

CASSIO, Othello's second-in-command, or lieutentant
RODERIGO, a Venetian gentleman

Duke of Venice
LODOVICO, Venetian gentleman, kinsman to Brabantio
GRATIANO, Venetian gentleman, kinsman to Brabantio
Venetian senators

MONTANO, an official in Cyprus
BIANCA, a woman in Cyprus in love with Cassio
Clown, a comic servant to Othello and Desdemona
Gentlemen of Cyprus
Sailors

Servants, Attendants, Officers, Messengers, Herald, Musicians, Torchbearers

Act 1

Scene 1

Enter Roderigo and Iago.

RODERIGO
    Tush, never tell me! I take it much unkindly
    That thou, Iago, who hast had my purse
    As if the strings were thine, shouldst know of this.

IAGO 'Sblood, but you will not hear me!
    If ever I did dream of such a matter, 5
    Abhor me.

RODERIGO
    Thou told'st me thou didst hold him in thy hate.

IAGO Despise me
    If I do not. Three great ones of the city,
    In personal suit to make me his lieutenant, 10
    Off-capped to him; and, by the faith of man,
    I know my price, I am worth no worse a place.
    But he, as loving his own pride and purposes,
    Evades them, with a bombast circumstance,
    Horribly stuffed with epithets of war, 15
    And in conclusion,
    Nonsuits my mediators. For "Certes," says he,
    "I have already chose my officer."
    And what was he?
    Forsooth, a great arithmetician, 20
    One Michael Cassio, a Florentine,
    A fellow almost damned in a fair wife,
    That never set a squadron in the field,
    Nor the division of a battle knows
    More than a spinster—unless the bookish theoric, 25
    Wherein the togèd consuls can propose
    As masterly as he. Mere prattle without practice
    Is all his soldiership. But he, sir, had th' election;
    And I, of whom his eyes had seen the proof
    At Rhodes, at Cyprus, and on other grounds 30
    Christened and heathen, must be beleed and calmed
    By debitor and creditor. This countercaster,
    He, in good time, must his lieutenant be,
    And I, God bless the mark, his Moorship's ancient.

RODERIGO
    By heaven, I rather would have been his hangman. 35

IAGO
    Why, there's no remedy. 'Tis the curse of service.
    Preferment goes by letter and affection,
    And not by old gradation, where each second
    Stood heir to th' first. Now, sir, be judge yourself
    Whether I in any just term am affined 40
    To love the Moor.

RODERIGO
   I would not follow him, then.

IAGO   O, sir, content you.
   I follow him to serve my turn upon him.
   We cannot all be masters, nor all masters   45
   Cannot be truly followed. You shall mark
   Many a duteous and knee-crooking knave
   That, doting on his own obsequious bondage,
   Wears out his time, much like his master's ass,
   For nought but provender, and when he's old, cashiered.   50
   Whip me such honest knaves! Others there are
   Who, trimmed in forms and visages of duty,
   Keep yet their hearts attending on themselves,
   And, throwing but shows of service on their lords,
   Do well thrive by them; and when they have lined their coats 55
   Do themselves homage. These fellows have some soul,
   And such a one do I profess myself. For, sir,
   It is as sure as you are Roderigo,
   Were I the Moor, I would not be Iago.
   In following him, I follow but myself.   60
   Heaven is my judge, not I for love and duty,
   But seeming so, for my peculiar end.
   For when my outward action doth demonstrate
   The native act and figure of my heart
   In compliment extern, 'tis not long after   65
   But I will wear my heart upon my sleeve
   For daws to peck at. I am not what I am.

RODERIGO
   What a full fortune does the thick-lips owe
   If he can carry 't thus!

IAGO   Call up her father.   70
   Rouse him. Make after him, poison his delight,
   Proclaim him in the streets; incense her kinsmen,
   And, though he in a fertile climate dwell,
   Plague him with flies. Though that his joy be joy,
   Yet throw such changes of vexation on 't   75
   As it may lose some color.

RODERIGO
   Here is her father's house. I'll call aloud.

IAGO
   Do, with like timorous accent and dire yell
   As when, by night and negligence, the fire
   Is spied in populous cities.   80

RODERIGO
   What, ho, Brabantio! Signior Brabantio, ho!

IAGO
   Awake! what, ho, Brabantio! Thieves! thieves!
   Look to your house, your daughter and your bags!
   Thieves! thieves!

Enter Brabantio, above.

BRABANTIO
    What is the reason of this terrible summons? 85
    What is the matter there?

RODERIGO
    Signior, is all your family within?

IAGO
    Are your doors locked?

BRABANTIO   Why, wherefore ask you this?

IAGO
    Zounds, sir, you're robbed. For shame, put on your gown! 90
    Your heart is burst. You have lost half your soul.
    Even now, now, very now, an old black ram
    Is tupping your white ewe. Arise, arise!
    Awake the snorting citizens with the bell,
    Or else the devil will make a grandsire of you. 95
    Arise, I say!

BRABANTIO   What, have you lost your wits?

RODERIGO
    Most reverend signior, do you know my voice?

BRABANTIO Not I. What are you?

RODERIGO
    My name is Roderigo. 100

BRABANTIO   The worser welcome.
    I have charged thee not to haunt about my doors.
    In honest plainness thou hast heard me say
    My daughter is not for thee. And now, in madness,
    Being full of supper and distemp'ring draughts, 105
    Upon malicious bravery dost thou come
    To start my quiet.

RODERIGO   Sir, sir, sir—

BRABANTIO But thou must needs be sure
    My spirit and my place have in them power 110
    To make this bitter to thee.

RODERIGO
    Patience, good sir.

BRABANTIO   What tell'st thou me of robbing?
    This is Venice. My house is not a grange.

RODERIGO Most grave Brabantio, 115
    In simple and pure soul I come to you—

IAGO Zounds, sir, you are one of those that will not serve God, if the
    devil bid you. Because we come to do you service and you think
    we are ruffians, you'll have your daughter covered with a Barbary
    horse, you'll have your nephews neigh to you, you'll have 120
    coursers for cousins and jennets for germans.

BRABANTIO What profane wretch art thou?

IAGO I am one, sir, that comes to tell you your daughter and the
Moor are now making the beast with two backs.

BRABANTIO Thou art a villain. 125

IAGO You are a senator.

BRABANTIO
This thou shalt answer. I know thee, Roderigo.

RODERIGO
Sir, I will answer any thing. But, I beseech you,
[If't be your pleasure and most wise consent—
As partly I find it is—that your fair daughter, 130
At this odd-even and dull watch o' th' night,
Transported, with no worse nor better guard
But with a knave of common hire, a gondolier,
To the gross clasps of a lascivious Moor:
If this be known to you and your allowance, 135
We then have done you bold and saucy wrongs.
But if you know not this, my manners tell me
We have your wrong rebuke. Do not believe
That, from the sense of all civility
I thus would play and trifle with your Reverence. 140
Your daughter, if you have not given her leave,
I say again, hath made a gross revolt,
Tying her duty, beauty, wit and fortunes
In an extravagant and wheeling stranger
Of here and everywhere. Straight satisfy yourself.] 145
If she be in her chamber or your house,
Let loose on me the justice of the state
For thus deluding you.

BRABANTIO Strike on the tinder, ho!
Give me a taper! Call up all my people. 150
This accident is not unlike my dream.
Belief of it oppresses me already.
Light, I say! light! *He exits.*

IAGO [*To Roderigo*] Farewell; for I must leave you.
It seems not meet, nor wholesome to my place 155
To be producted, as if I stay I shall,
Against the Moor. For I do know the state,
However this may gall him with some check,
Cannot with safety cast him, for he's embarked
With such loud reason to the Cyprus wars, 160
Which even now stand in act, that, for their souls,
Another of his fathom they have none
To lead their business. In which regard,
Though I do hate him as I do hell pains,
Yet, for necessity of present life, 165
I must show out a flag and sign of love—
Which is indeed but sign. That you shall surely find him,
Lead to the Sagittary the raisèd search,

And there will I be with him. So, farewell.　　　　　*He exits.*

Enter Brabantio (in his nightgown,) with Servants and Torches.

BRABANTIO
It is too true an evil. Gone she is; 170
And what's to come of my despisèd time
Is nought but bitterness.—Now, Roderigo,
Where didst thou see her?—O unhappy girl!—
With the Moor, say'st thou?—Who would be a father?—
How didst thou know 'twas she?—O she deceives me 175
Past thought!—What said she to you?—Get more tapers.
Raise all my kindred.—Are they married, think you?

RODERIGO Truly, I think they are.

BRABANTIO
O heaven! How got she out? O treason of the blood!
Fathers, from hence trust not your daughters' minds 180
By what you see them act.—Is there not charms
By which the property of youth and maidhood
May be abused? Have you not read, Roderigo,
Of some such thing?

RODERIGO　　　　　Yes, sir, I have indeed. 185

BRABANTIO
Call up my brother.—O, would you had had her!—
Some one way, some another.—Do you know
Where we may apprehend her and the Moor?

RODERIGO
I think I can discover him, if you please,
To get good guard and go along with me. 190

BRABANTIO
Pray you, lead on. At every house I'll call.
I may command at most.—Get weapons, ho!
And raise some special officers of night.—
On, good Roderigo: I'll deserve your pains.
　　　　　　　　　　　　　　　　　　　They exit.

Scene 2

Enter Othello, Iago, Attendants with Torches.

IAGO
Though in the trade of war I have slain men,
Yet do I hold it very stuff o' th' conscience
To do no contrived murder. I lack iniquity
Sometimes to do me service. Nine or ten times
I had thought t' have yerked him here under the ribs. 5

OTHELLO
'Tis better as it is.

IAGO　　　　　Nay, but he prated
And spoke such scurvy and provoking terms

    Against your Honor,
    That, with the little godliness I have 10
    I did full hard forbear him. But, I pray you, sir,
    Are you fast married? Be assured of this,
    That the magnifico is much beloved,
    And hath in his effect a voice potential
    As double as the Duke's. He will divorce you 15
    Or put upon you what restraint and grievance
    The law (with all his might to enforce it on)
    Will give him cable.

OTHELLO   Let him do his spite:
    My services which I have done the signiory 20
    Shall out-tongue his complaints. 'Tis yet to know
    (Which, when I know that boasting is an honor,
    I shall promulgate) I fetch my life and being
    From men of royal siege, and my demerits
    May speak unbonneted to as proud a fortune 25
    As this that I have reached. For know, Iago,
    But that I love the gentle Desdemona,
    I would not my unhousèd free condition
    Put into circumscription and confine
    For the sea's worth. But, look! what lights come yond? 30

IAGO
    Those are the raisèd father and his friends:
    You were best go in.

OTHELLO Not I. I must be found.
    My parts, my title, and my perfect soul
    Shall manifest me rightly. Is it they? 35

IAGO By Janus, I think no.

Enter Cassio, with Officers, and Torches

OTHELLO
    The servants of the Duke and my lieutenant!
    The goodness of the night upon you, friends.
    What is the news?

CASSIO   The Duke does greet you, general, 40
    And he requires your haste-post-haste appearance,
    Even on the instant.

OTHELLO   What is the matter, think you?

CASSIO
    Something from Cyprus, as I may divine.
    It is a business of some heat. The galleys 45
    Have sent a dozen sequent messengers
    This very night at one another's heels,
    And many of the Consuls, raised and met,
    Are at the Duke's already. You have been hotly called for.
    When, being not at your lodging to be found, 50
    The Senate hath sent about three several quests
    To search you out.

OTHELLO 'Tis well I am found by you.
　I will but spend a word here in the house
　And go with you.　　　　　　　　　　　　　　*He* 55
exits.

CASSIO　　　　　Ancient, what makes he here?

IAGO
　Faith, he tonight hath boarded a land carrack.
　If it prove lawful prize, he's made forever.

CASSIO I do not understand.

IAGO　　　　　　　　He's married. 60

CASSIO　　　　　　　　　　To who?

IAGO Marry, to—

　　　　　Reenter Othello.

　　Come, captain, will you go?

OTHELLO Have with you.

CASSIO
　Here comes another troop to seek for you. 65

　　Enter Brabantio, Roderigo, with Officers, and Torches.

IAGO
　It is Brabantio. General, be advised,
　He comes to bad intent.

OTHELLO　　　　　Holla! stand there!

RODERIGO Signior, it is the Moor.

BRABANTIO　　　　　Down with him, thief! 70
　　　　　　They draw their swords.

IAGO
　You, Roderigo! Come, sir, I am for you.

OTHELLO
　Keep up your bright swords, for the dew will rust them.
　Good signior, you shall more command with years
　Than with your weapons.

BRABANTIO
　O thou foul thief, where hast thou stowed my daughter? 75
　Damned as thou art, thou hast enchanted her!
　For I'll refer me to all things of sense,
　[If she in chains of magic were not bound,]
　Whether a maid so tender, fair and happy,
　So opposite to marriage that she shunned 80
　The wealthy curlèd darlings of our nation,
　Would ever have, t' incur a general mock,
　Run from her guardage to the sooty bosom
　Of such a thing as thou—to fear, not to delight!
　[Judge me the world, if 'tis not gross in sense 85
　That thou hast practiced on her with foul charms,

Abused her delicate youth with drugs or minerals
That weaken motion. I'll have't disputed on.
'Tis probable and palpable to thinking.
I therefore apprehend and do attach thee]
For an abuser of the world, a practicer
Of arts inhibited and out of warrant.—
Lay hold upon him: if he do resist,
Subdue him at his peril!

OTHELLO   Hold your hands,
Both you of my inclining, and the rest.
Were it my cue to fight, I should have known it
Without a prompter.—Whither will you that I go
To answer this your charge?

BRABANTIO To prison, till fit time
Of law and course of direct session
Call thee to answer.

OTHELLO   What if I do obey?
How may the Duke be therewith satisfied,
Whose messengers are here about my side,
Upon some present business of the state,
To bring me to him?

OFFICER   'Tis true, most worthy signior.
The Duke's in council and your noble self
I am sure is sent for.

BRABANTIO   How? The Duke in council?
In this time of the night? Bring him away;
Mine's not an idle cause. The Duke himself,
Or any of my brothers of the state,
Cannot but feel this wrong as 'twere their own.
For if such actions may have passage free,
Bondslaves and pagans shall our statesmen be.

They exit.

Scene 3

Enter Duke, Senators, and Officers

DUKE, *reading a paper*
There is no composition in these news
That gives them credit.

FIRST SENATOR, *reading a paper*
Indeed, they are disproportioned.
My letters say a hundred and seven galleys.

DUKE
And mine, a hundred and forty.

SECOND SENATOR, *reading a paper*
                    And mine, two hundred.
But though they jump not on a just account

    (As in these cases, where the aim reports
    'Tis oft with difference), yet do they all confirm
    A Turkish fleet, and bearing up to Cyprus.

DUKE
    Nay, it is possible enough to judgment.
    I do not so secure me in the error,
    But the main article I do approve
    In fearful sense.

SAILOR, *within*   What, ho! what, ho! what, ho!

Enter Sailor.

OFFICER A messenger from the galleys.

DUKE Now, what's the business?

SAILOR
    The Turkish preparation makes for Rhodes.
    So was I bid report here to the state
    By Signior Angelo.

DUKE
    How say you by this change?

FIRST SENATOR   This cannot be,
    By no assay of reason. 'Tis a pageant
    To keep us in false gaze. When we consider
    Th' importancy of Cyprus to the Turk,
    And let ourselves again but understand
    That as it more concerns the Turk than Rhodes,
    So may he with more facile question bear it,
    [For that it stands not in such warlike brace,
    But altogether lacks th' abilities
    That Rhodes is dressed in—if we make thought of this,
    We must not think the Turk is so unskillful
    To leave that latest which concerns him first,
    Neglecting an attempt of ease and gain
    To wake and wage a danger profitless.]

DUKE
    Nay, in all confidence, he's not for Rhodes.

OFFICER Here is more news.

Enter a Messenger.

MESSENGER
    The Ottomites, Reverend and Gracious,
    Steering with due course towards the isle of Rhodes,
    Have there injointed them with an after fleet.

[FIRST SENATOR
    Ay, so I thought. How many, as you guess?]

MESSENGER
    Of thirty sail; and now they do restem
    Their backward course, bearing with frank appearance
    Their purposes toward Cyprus. Signior Montano,

> Your trusty and most valiant servitor,
> With his free duty recommends you thus,
> And prays you to believe him.

DUKE 'Tis certain, then, for Cyprus.
> Marcus Luccicos, is not he in town?

FIRST SENATOR
> He's now in Florence.

DUKE   Write from us to him.
> Post-post-haste. Dispatch.

FIRST SENATOR
> Here comes Brabantio and the valiant Moor.

Enter Brabantio, Othello, Cassio, Iago, Roderigo, and Officers

DUKE
> Valiant Othello, we must straight employ you
> Against the general enemy Ottoman.
> [*To Brabantio.*] I did not see you. Welcome, gentle signior;
> We lacked your counsel and your help tonight.

BRABANTIO
> So did I yours. Good your grace, pardon me.
> Neither my place nor aught I heard of business
> Hath raised me from my bed, nor doth the general care
> Take hold on me, for my particular grief
> Is of so floodgate and o'erbearing nature
> That it engluts and swallows other sorrows
> And it is still itself.

DUKE   Why, what's the matter?

BRABANTIO My daughter! O, my daughter!

FIRST SENATOR Dead?

BRABANTIO Ay, to me;
> She is abused, stol'n from me, and corrupted
> By spells and medicines bought of mountebanks;
> For nature so prepost'rously to err—
> Being not deficient, blind, or lame of sense—
> Sans witchcraft could not.

DUKE
> Whoe'er he be that in this foul proceeding
> Hath thus beguiled your daughter of herself
> And you of her, the bloody book of law
> You shall yourself read in the bitter letter
> After your own sense, yea, though our proper son
> Stood in your action.

BRABANTIO   Humbly I thank your grace.
> Here is the man—this Moor, whom now, it seems,
> Your special mandate for the state affairs
> Hath hither brought.

ALL   We are very sorry for 't.

DUKE, [*to Othello*]
    What, in your own part, can you say to this? 85

BRABANTIO Nothing, but this is so.

OTHELLO
    Most potent, grave, and reverend signiors,
    My very noble and approved good masters,
    That I have ta'en away this old man's daughter,
    It is most true; true I have married her: 90
    The very head and front of my offending
    Hath this extent, no more. Rude am I in my speech,
    And little blessed with the soft phrase of peace;
    For since these arms of mine had seven years' pith,
    Till now some nine moons wasted, they have used 95
    Their dearest action in the tented field,
    And little of this great world can I speak
    More than pertains to feats of broil and battle.
    And therefore little shall I grace my cause
    In speaking for myself. Yet, by your gracious patience, 100
    I will a round unvarnished tale deliver
    Of my whole course of love—what drugs, what charms,
    What conjuration and what mighty magic
    (For such proceeding I am charged withal)
    I won his daughter. 105

BRABANTIO   A maiden never bold,
    Of spirit so still and quiet that her motion
    Blushed at herself. And she, in spite of nature,
    Of years, of country, credit, everything,
    To fall in love with what she feared to look on! 110
    It is a judgment maimed and most imperfect
    That will confess perfection so could err
    Against all rules of nature, and must be driven
    To find out practices of cunning hell
    Why this should be. I therefore vouch again 115
    That with some mixtures powerful o'er the blood,
    Or with some dram conjured to this effect,
    He wrought upon her.

DUKE   To vouch this is no proof
    Without more wider and more overt test 120
    Than these thin habits and poor likelihoods
    Of modern seeming do prefer against him.

FIRST SENATOR But, Othello, speak:
    Did you by indirect and forced courses
    Subdue and poison this young maid's affections? 125
    Or came it by request and such fair question
    As soul to soul affordeth?

OTHELLO   I do beseech you,
    Send for the lady to the Sagittary,
    And let her speak of me before her father. 130
    If you do find me foul in her report,
    [The trust, the office I do hold of you,]

Not only take away, but let your sentence
Even fall upon my life.

DUKE Fetch Desdemona hither. 135

OTHELLO
Ancient, conduct them. You best know the place.
Iago and Attendants exit.
And till she come, as truly as to heaven
[I do confess the vices of my blood,]
So justly to your grave ears I'll present
How I did thrive in this fair lady's love, 140
And she in mine.

DUKE Say it, Othello.

OTHELLO
Her father loved me, oft invited me,
Still questioned me the story of my life
From year to year—the battles, sieges, fortunes 145
That I have passed.
I ran it through, even from my boyish days
To the very moment that he bade me tell it,
Wherein I spoke of most disastrous chances:
Of moving accidents by flood and field, 150
Of hairbreadth 'scapes i' th' imminent deadly breach,
Of being taken by the insolent foe
And sold to slavery, of my redemption thence,
And portance in my traveler's history,
Wherein of antres vast and deserts idle, 155
Rough quarries, rocks, and hills whose heads touch heaven,
It was my hint to speak—such was the process—
And of the Cannibals that each other eat,
The Anthropophagi, and men whose heads
Do grow beneath their shoulders. These things to hear 160
Would Desdemona seriously incline.
But still the house affairs would draw her thence,
Which ever as she could with haste dispatch
She'd come again, and with a greedy ear
Devour up my discourse. Which I, observing, 165
Took once a pliant hour, and found good means
To draw from her a prayer of earnest heart
That I would all my pilgrimage dilate,
Whereof by parcels she had something heard,
But not intentively. I did consent, 170
And often did beguile her of her tears
When I did speak of some distressful stroke
That my youth suffered. My story being done,
She gave me for my pains a world of sighs.
She swore, in faith, 'twas strange, 'twas passing strange, 175
'Twas pitiful, 'twas wondrous pitiful.
She wished she had not heard it, yet she wished
That heaven had made her such a man. She thanked me,
And bade me, if I had a friend that loved her,
I should but teach him how to tell my story, 180

And that would woo her. Upon this hint I spake.
   She loved me for the dangers I had passed,
   And I loved her that she did pity them.
   This only is the witchcraft I have used.
   Here comes the lady. Let her witness it. 185

   Enter Desdemona, Iago, Attendants

DUKE
   I think this tale would win my daughter too.
   Good Brabantio,
   Take up this mangled matter at the best.
   Men do their broken weapons rather use
   Than their bare hands. 190

BRABANTIO   I pray you hear her speak.
   If she confess that she was half the wooer,
   Destruction on my head if my bad blame
   Light on the man.—Come hither, gentle mistress.
   Do you perceive in all this noble company 200
   Where most you owe obedience?

DESDEMONA   My noble father,
   I do perceive here a divided duty.
   To you I am bound for life and education.
   My life and education both do learn me 205
   How to respect you; you are the lord of duty.
   I am hitherto your daughter. But here's my husband.
   And so much duty as my mother showed
   To you, preferring you before her father,
   So much I challenge that I may profess 210
   Due to the Moor my lord.

BRABANTIO God be with you! I have done.
   Please it your Grace, on to the state affairs.
   I had rather to adopt a child than get it.—
   Come hither, Moor: 215
   I here do give thee that with all my heart
   [Which, but thou hast already, with all my heart]
   I would keep from thee.—For your sake, jewel,
   I am glad at soul I have no other child,
   For thy escape would teach me tyranny, 220
   To hang clogs on them.—I have done, my lord.

DUKE
   Let me speak like yourself, and lay a sentence,
   Which, as a grise or step, may help these lovers
   Into your favor.
   When remedies are past, the griefs are ended 225
   By seeing the worst, which late on hopes depended.
   To mourn a mischief that is past and gone
   Is the next way to draw new mischief on.
   What cannot be preserved when fortune takes,
   Patience her injury a mock'ry makes. 230
   The robbed that smiles steals something from the thief;
   He robs himself that spends a bootless grief.

BRABANTIO
   So let the Turk of Cyprus us beguile,
   We lose it not so long as we can smile.
   He bears the sentence well that nothing bears   235
   But the free comfort which from thence he hears;
   But he bears both the sentence and the sorrow
   That, to pay grief, must of poor patience borrow.
   These sentences, to sugar, or to gall,
   Being strong on both sides, are equivocal.   240
   But words are words. I never yet did hear
   That the bruised heart was pierced through the ear.
   I humbly beseech you, proceed to th' affairs of state.

DUKE The Turk with a most mighty preparation makes for Cyprus.
   Othello, the fortitude of the place is best known to you; and   245
   though we have there a substitute of most allowed sufficiency, yet
   opinion, a sovereign mistress of effects, throws a more safer voice
   on you: you must therefore be content to slubber the gloss of your
   new fortunes with this more stubborn and boisterous expedition.

OTHELLO
   The tyrant custom, most grave senators,   250
   Hath made the flinty and steel couch of war
   My thrice-driven bed of down: I do agnize
   A natural and prompt alacrity
   I find in hardness, and do undertake
   These present wars against the Ottomites.   255
   Most humbly, therefore, bending to your state,
   I crave fit disposition for my wife,
   Due reference of place and exhibition,
   With such accommodation and besort
   As levels with her breeding.   260

DUKE
   Why, at her father's.

BRABANTIO   I'll will not have it so.

OTHELLO Nor I.

DESDEMONA Nor would I there reside
   To put my father in impatient thoughts   265
   By being in his eye. Most gracious duke,
   To my unfolding lend your prosperous ear
   And let me find a charter in your voice
   T' assist my simpleness.

DUKE What would you, Desdemona?   270

DESDEMONA
   That I did love the Moor to live with him
   My downright violence and storm of fortunes
   May trumpet to the world. My heart's subdued
   Even to the very quality of my lord.
   I saw Othello's visage in his mind,   275
   And to his honors and his valiant parts
   Did I my soul and fortunes consecrate.

So that, dear lords, if I be left behind,
A moth of peace, and he go to the war,
The rites for which I love him are bereft me
And I a heavy interim shall support
By his dear absence. Let me go with him.

OTHELLO Let her have your voices.
Vouch with me, heaven, I therefore beg it not,
To please the palate of my appetite,
Nor to comply with heat (the young affects
In me defunct) and proper satisfaction,
But to be free and bounteous to her mind.
And heaven defend your good souls that you think
I will your serious and great business scant
For she is with me. No, when light-winged toys
Of feathered Cupid seel with wanton dullness
My speculative and officed instruments,
That my disports corrupt and taint my business,
Let housewives make a skillet of my helm,
And all indign and base adversities
Make head against my estimation.

DUKE
Be it as you shall privately determine,
Either for her stay or going. Th' affair cries haste,
And speed must answer it.

FIRST SENATOR You must away tonight.

OTHELLO   With all my heart.

DUKE
At nine i' th' morning here we'll meet again.
Othello, leave some officer behind
And he shall our commission bring to you;
With such things else of quality and respect
As doth import you.

OTHELLO   So please your Grace, my ancient.
A man he is of honesty and trust.
To his conveyance I assign my wife,
With what else needful your good Grace shall think
To be sent after me.

DUKE   Let it be so.
Good night to every one. [*To Brabantio.*] And, noble signior,
If virtue no delighted beauty lack,
Your son-in-law is far more fair than black.

FIRST SENATOR
Adieu, brave Moor, use Desdemona well.

BRABANTIO
Look to her, Moor, if thou hast eyes to see.
She has deceived her father, and may thee.   *He exits.*

OTHELLO
My life upon her faith!

The Duke, the Senators, Cassio, and Officers exit.

                    Honest Iago,
My Desdemona must I leave to thee.
I prithee, let thy wife attend on her,
And bring them after in the best advantage.
Come, Desdemona: I have but an hour 325
Of love, of worldly matters, and direction
To spend with thee: we must obey the time.

                             Othello and Desdemona exit.

RODERIGO Iago—

IAGO What sayst thou, noble heart?

RODERIGO What will I do, think'st thou? 330

IAGO Why, go to bed and sleep.

RODERIGO I will incontinently drown myself.

IAGO If thou dost, I shall never love thee after. Why, thou silly gentleman!

RODERIGO It is silliness to live, when to live is torment, and then 335 have we a prescription to die when death is our physician.

IAGO O villainous! I have looked upon the world for four times seven years; and since I could distinguish betwixt a benefit and an injury, I never found man that knew how to love himself. Ere I would say, I would drown myself for the love of a guinea hen, I 340 would change my humanity with a baboon.

RODERIGO What should I do? I confess it is my shame to be so fond; but it is not in my virtue to amend it.

IAGO Virtue! A fig! 'Tis in ourselves that we are thus or thus. Our bodies are our gardens, to the which our wills are gardeners. So 345 that if we will plant nettles, or sow lettuce, set hyssop and weed up thyme, supply it with one gender of herbs, or distract it with many, either to have it sterile with idleness, or manured with industry, why, the power and corrigible authority of this lies in our wills. If the balance of our lives had not one scale of reason to 350 poise another of sensuality, the blood and baseness of our natures would conduct us to most preposterous conclusions: but we have reason to cool our raging motions, our carnal stings, our unbitted lusts—whereof I take this that you call love to be a sect or scion.

RODERIGO It cannot be. 355

IAGO It is merely a lust of the blood and a permission of the will. Come, be a man. Drown thyself? Drown cats and blind puppies. I have professed me thy friend and I confess me knit to thy deserving with cables of perdurable toughness. I could never better stead thee than now. Put money in thy purse. Follow thou the wars; 360 defeat thy favor with an usurped beard; I say, put money in thy purse. It cannot be that Desdemona should long continue her love to the Moor—put money in thy purse—nor he his to her. It was a violent commencement, and thou shalt see an answerable sequestration—put but money in thy purse. These Moors are changeable in their wills. Fill thy purse with money. The food that to him now is as luscious as locusts shall be to him shortly as bitter as coloquintida. She must change for youth. When she is sated with his body, she will find the error of her choice. Therefore, put money in thy purse. If thou wilt needs damn thyself, do it a more delicate way than drowning. Make all the money thou canst. If sanctimony and a frail vow betwixt an erring barbarian and a supersubtle Venetian be not too hard for my wits and all the tribe of hell, thou shalt enjoy her. Therefore make money. A pox of drowning thyself! It is clean out of the way. Seek thou rather to be hanged in compassing thy joy than to be drowned and go without her.

RODERIGO Wilt thou be fast to my hopes, if I depend on the issue?

IAGO Thou art sure of me. Go, make money. I have told thee often, and I retell thee again and again, I hate the Moor. My cause is hearted; thine hath no less reason. Let us be conjunctive in our revenge against him. If thou canst cuckold him, thou dost thyself a pleasure, me a sport. There are many events in the womb of time which will be delivered. Traverse, go, provide thy money. We will have more of this tomorrow. Adieu.

RODERIGO Where shall we meet i' th' morning?

IAGO At my lodging.

RODERIGO I'll be with thee betimes.

IAGO Go to, farewell. Do you hear, Roderigo?

RODERIGO What say you?

IAGO No more of drowning, do you hear?

RODERIGO I am changed.

IAGO Go to, farewell. Put money enough in your purse.

[RODERIGO I'll sell all my land.] *He exits.*

IAGO
    Thus do I ever make my fool my purse.
    For I mine own gained knowledge should profane,
    If I would time expend with such a snipe.
    But for my sport and profit. I hate the Moor,
    And it is thought abroad, that 'twixt my sheets
    'Has done my office. I know not if 't be true,
    But I, for mere suspicion in that kind,
    Will do as if for surety. He holds me well;
    The better shall my purpose work on him.
    Cassio's a proper man: let me see now:
    To get his place and to plume up my will
    In double knavery—How, how?—Let's see.
    After some time, to abuse Othello's ear
    That he is too familiar with his wife.
    He hath a person and a smooth dispose
    To be suspected, framed to make women false.
    The Moor is of a free and open nature

That thinks men honest that but seem to be so,
And will as tenderly be led by th' nose
As asses are.
　I have 't. It is engendered. Hell and night
Must bring this monstrous birth to the world's light. 415
He exits.

Act 2

Scene 1

Enter Montano and two Gentlemen.

MONTANO
    What from the cape can you discern at sea?

FIRST GENTLEMAN
    Nothing at all: it is a high-wrought flood.
    I cannot, 'twixt the heaven and the main
    Descry a sail.

MONTANO
    Methinks the wind hath spoke aloud at land. 5
    A fuller blast ne'er shook our battlements.
    If it hath ruffianed so upon the sea,
    What ribs of oak, when mountains melt on them,
    Can hold the mortise? What shall we hear of this?

SECOND GENTLEMAN
    A segregation of the Turkish fleet: 10
    For do but stand upon the foaming shore,
    The chidden billow seems to pelt the clouds,
    The wind-shaked surge, with high and monstrous mane,
    Seems to cast water on the burning Bear
    And quench the guards of th' ever-fixed pole. 15
    I never did like molestation view
    On the enchafèd flood.

MONTANO If that the Turkish fleet
    Be not ensheltered and embayed, they are drowned.
    It is impossible they bear it out. 20

Enter a third Gentleman.

THIRD GENTLEMAN News, lads! Our wars are done.
    The desperate tempest hath so banged the Turks
    That their designment halts. A noble ship of Venice
    Hath seen a grievous wreck and sufferance
    On most part of their fleet. 25

MONTANO
    How! Is this true?

THIRD GENTLEMAN The ship is here put in,
    A Veronesa. Michael Cassio,
    Lieutenant to the warlike Moor Othello,
    Is come on shore; the Moor himself at sea, 30
    And is in full commission here for Cyprus.

MONTANO
    I am glad on 't. 'Tis a worthy governor.

THIRD GENTLEMAN
    But this same Cassio, though he speak of comfort
    Touching the Turkish loss, yet he looks sadly,

  And prays the Moor be safe, for they were parted 35
  With foul and violent tempest.

MONTANO   Pray heaven he be;
  For I have served him, and the man commands
  Like a full soldier. Let's to the seaside, ho!
  As well to see the vessel that's come in 40
  As to throw out our eyes for brave Othello,
  [Even till we make the main and th' aerial blue
  An indistinct regard.]

THIRD GENTLEMAN Come, let's do so;
  For every minute is expectancy 45
  Of more arrivance.

      Enter Cassio.

CASSIO
  Thanks, you the valiant of this warlike isle,
  That so approve the Moor! O, let the heavens
  Give him defense against the elements,
  For I have lost him on a dangerous sea. 50

MONTANO Is he well shipped?

CASSIO
  His bark is stoutly timbered, and his pilot
  Of very expert and approved allowance;
  Therefore my hopes, not surfeited to death,
  Stand in bold cure. 55

     Voices cry within. "A sail, a sail, a sail!"

      Enter a Messenger.

CASSIO What noise?

MESSENGER
  The town is empty; on the brow o' th' sea
  Stand ranks of people, and they cry "A sail!"

CASSIO
  My hopes do shape him for the Governor.

            A Shot.

SECOND GENTLEMEN
  They do discharge their shot of courtesy. 60
  Our friends, at least.

CASSIO   I pray you, sir, go forth,
  And give us truth who 'tis that is arrived.

SECOND GENTLEMAN I shall.   *He exits.*

MONTANO
  But, good lieutenant, is your general wived? 65

CASSIO
  Most fortunately. He hath achieved a maid
  That paragons description and wild fame,
  One that excels the quirks of blazoning pens,

                    And in the essential vesture of creation
                    Does tire the ingener.   70

      Enter Second Gentleman.

      How now! Who has put in?

SECOND GENTLEMAN
 'Tis one Iago, ancient to the General.

CASSIO
 'Has had most favourable and happy speed!
 Tempests themselves, high seas, and howling winds,
 The guttered rocks and congregated sands   75
 (Traitors ensteeped to clog the guiltless keel),
 As having sense of beauty, do omit
 Their mortal natures, letting go safely by
 The divine Desdemona.

MONTANO   What is she?   80

CASSIO
 She that I spake of, our great captain's captain,
 Left in the conduct of the bold Iago,
 Whose footing here anticipates our thoughts
 A sennight's speed. Great Jove, Othello guard,
 And swell his sail with thine own powerful breath,   85
 That he may bless this bay with his tall ship,
 Make love's quick pants in Desdemona's arms,
 Give renewed fire to our extincted spirits,
 And bring all Cyprus comfort!

    Enter Desdemona, Iago, Roderigo, and Emilia

      O, behold,   90
 The riches of the ship is come on shore!
 Ye men of Cyprus, let her have your knees.
           He kneels.
 Hail to thee, lady, and the grace of heaven,
 Before, behind thee, and on every hand,
 Enwheel thee round.   *He*   95
rises.

DESDEMONA I thank you, valiant Cassio.
 What tidings can you tell me of my lord?

CASSIO
 He is not yet arrived: nor know I aught
 But that he's well and will be shortly here.

DESDEMONA
 O, but I fear—How lost you company?   100

CASSIO
 The great contention of the sea and skies
 Parted our fellowship.
      Within "A sail, a sail!" A shot.
    But hark, a sail!

SECOND GENTLEMAN
   They give their greeting to the citadel.
   This likewise is a friend.   105

CASSIO   See for the news.
                              Second Gentleman exits.
   Good ancient, you are welcome. Welcome, mistress.
                                  He kisses Emilia.
   Let it not gall your patience, good Iago,
   That I extend my manners. 'Tis my breeding
   That gives me this bold show of courtesy.   110

IAGO
   Sir, would she give you so much of her lips
   As of her tongue she oft bestows on me,
   You'll have enough.

DESDEMONA
   Alas, she has no speech!

IAGO   In faith, too much.   115
   I find it still when I have list to sleep.
   Marry, before your ladyship, I grant,
   She puts her tongue a little in her heart
   And chides with thinking.

EMILIA You have little cause to say so.   120

IAGO Come on, come on! You are pictures out of door, bells in your
   parlors, wildcats in your kitchens, saints in your injuries, devils
   being offended, players in your huswifery, and huswives in your
   beds.

DESDEMONA Oh, fie upon thee, slanderer!   125

IAGO
   Nay, it is true, or else I am a Turk:
   You rise to play and go to bed to work.

EMILIA You shall not write my praise.

IAGO   No, let me not.

DESDEMONA
   What wouldst thou write of me if thou shouldst praise me?   130

IAGO
   O, gentle lady, do not put me to 't,
   For I am nothing if not critical.

DESDEMONA
   Come on assay.—There's one gone to the harbor?

IAGO Ay, madam.

DESDEMONA, [*aside*]
   I am not merry; but I do beguile   135
   The thing I am, by seeming otherwise.—
   Come, how wouldst thou praise me?

IAGO I am about it; but indeed my invention comes from my pate as birdlime does from frieze: it plucks out brains and all. But my muse labors, and thus she is delivered:
If she be fair and wise, fairness and wit,
The one's for use, the other useth it.

DESDEMONA
Well praised! How if she be black and witty?

IAGO
If she be black, and thereto have a wit,
She'll find a white that shall her blackness hit.

DESDEMONA
Worse and worse.

EMILIA How if fair and foolish?

IAGO
She never yet was foolish that was fair,
For even her folly helped her to an heir.

DESDEMONA These are old fond paradoxes to make fools laugh i' th' alehouse. What miserable praise hast thou for her that's foul and foolish?

IAGO
There's none so foul and foolish thereunto,
But does foul pranks which fair and wise ones do.

DESDEMONA O heavy ignorance! Thou praisest the worst best. But what praise couldst thou bestow on a deserving woman indeed, one that, in the authority of her merit, did justly put on the vouch of very malice itself?

IAGO
She that was ever fair and never proud,
Had tongue at will and yet was never loud,
Never lacked gold and yet went never gay,
Fled from her wish and yet said "Now I may,"
She that being angered, her revenge being nigh,
Bade her wrong stay and her displeasure fly,
She that in wisdom never was so frail
To change the cod's head for the salmon's tail,
She that could think and ne'er disclose her mind,
[See suitors following and not look behind,]
She was a wight, if ever such wight were—

DESDEMONA To do what?

IAGO
To suckle fools and chronicle small beer.

DESDEMONA O most lame and impotent conclusion!—Do not learn of him, Emilia, though he be thy husband.—How say you, Cassio? is he not a most profane and liberal counselor?

CASSIO He speaks home, madam: You may relish him more in the soldier than in the scholar.

Cassio takes Desdemona's hand.

IAGO [*Aside*] He takes her by the palm. Ay, well said, whisper: with as little a web as this will I ensnare as great a fly as Cassio. Ay, smile upon her, do; I will gyve thee in thine own courtship. You say true, 'tis so indeed. If such tricks as these strip you out of your lieutenantry, it had been better you had not kissed your three fingers so oft, which now again you are most apt to play the sir in. Very good; well kissed; an excellent courtesy! 'Tis so, indeed. Yet again your fingers to your lips? Would they were clyster pipes for your sake! [*Trumpets within.*] The Moor. I know his trumpet.

CASSIO 'Tis truly so.

DESDEMONA Let's meet him and receive him.

CASSIO Lo, where he comes!

Enter Othello and Attendants.

OTHELLO
O my fair warrior!

DESDEMONA My dear Othello!

OTHELLO
It gives me wonder great as my content
To see you here before me. O my soul's joy!
If after every tempest come such calms,
May the winds blow till they have wakened death!
And let the labouring bark climb hills of seas
Olympus high and duck again as low
As hell's from heaven! If it were now to die,
'Twere now to be most happy; for, I fear,
My soul hath her content so absolute
That not another comfort like to this
Succeeds in unknown fate.

DESDEMONA The heavens forbid
But that our loves and comforts should increase
Even as our days do grow!

OTHELLO Amen to that, sweet powers!
I cannot speak enough of this content.
It stops me here; it is too much of joy. [*They kiss.*]
And this, and this, the greatest discords be
That e'er our hearts shall make!

IAGO [*Aside*] O, you are well tuned now,
But I'll set down the pegs that make this music,
As honest as I am.

OTHELLO Come, let us to the castle.—
News, friends; our wars are done, the Turks are drowned.
How does my old acquaintance of this isle?—
Honey, you shall be well desired in Cyprus.
I have found great love amongst them. O my sweet,
I prattle out of fashion, and I dote

In mine own comforts.—I prithee, good Iago,
Go to the bay and disembark my coffers.
Bring thou the master to the citadel.
He is a good one, and his worthiness
Does challenge much respect.—Come, Desdemona,
Once more, well met at Cyprus.

All but Iago and Roderigo exit.

IAGO, [*to a departing Attendant*] Do thou meet me presently at the harbor. [*To Roderigo.*] Come hither. If thou be'st valiant—as they say, base men being in love have then a nobility in their natures more than is native to them—list me. The Lieutenant tonight watches on the court of guard. First, I must tell thee this: Desdemona is directly in love with him.

RODERIGO With him! Why, 'tis not possible.

IAGO Lay thy finger thus, and let thy soul be instructed. Mark me with what violence she first loved the Moor but for bragging and telling her fantastical lies. And will she love him still for prating? Let not thy discreet heart think it. Her eye must be fed. And what delight shall she have to look on the devil? When the blood is made dull with the act of sport, there should be, again to inflame it and to give satiety a fresh appetite, loveliness in favor, sympathy in years, manners and beauties, all which the Moor is defective in. Now, for want of these required conveniences, her delicate tenderness will find itself abused, begin to heave the gorge, disrelish and abhor the Moor. Very nature will instruct her in it and compel her to some second choice. Now, sir, this granted—as it is a most pregnant and unforced position—who stands so eminent in the degree of this fortune as Cassio does? A knave very voluble; no further conscionable than in putting on the mere form of civil and humane seeming, for the better compassing of his salt and most hidden loose affection. Why, none, why, none! A slipper and subtle knave, a finder-out of occasions, that has an eye can stamp and counterfeit advantages, though true advantage never present itself; a devilish knave. Besides, the knave is handsome, young, and hath all those requisites in him that folly and green minds look after. A pestilent complete knave; and the woman hath found him already.

RODERIGO I cannot believe that in her. She's full of most blessed condition.

IAGO Blessed fig's end! The wine she drinks is made of grapes. If she had been blessed, she would never have loved the Moor. Blessed pudding! Didst thou not see her paddle with the palm of his hand? Didst not mark that?

RODERIGO Yes, that I did; but that was but courtesy.

IAGO Lechery, by this hand! An index and obscure prologue to the history of lust and foul thoughts. They met so near with their lips that their breaths embraced together. Villanous thoughts, Roderigo! When these mutualities so marshal the way, hard at hand comes the master and main exercise, th' incorporate conclu-

sion. Pish! But, sir, be you ruled by me. I have brought you from
Venice. Watch you tonight. For the command, I'll lay't upon you.
Cassio knows you not. I'll not be far from you. Do you find some 270
occasion to anger Cassio, either by speaking too loud, or tainting
his discipline, or from what other course you please, which the
time shall more favourably minister.

RODERIGO Well.

IAGO Sir, he is rash and very sudden in choler, and haply may strike 275
at you. Provoke him, that he may; for even out of that will I cause
these of Cyprus to mutiny; whose qualification shall come into no
true taste again but by the displanting of Cassio. So shall you have
a shorter journey to your desires by the means I shall then have to
prefer them, and the impediment most profitably removed, 280
without the which there were no expectation of our prosperity.

RODERIGO I will do this, if I can bring it to any opportunity.

IAGO I warrant thee. Meet me by and by at the citadel. I must fetch
his necessaries ashore. Farewell.

RODERIGO Adieu. *He exits* 285

IAGO
    That Cassio loves her, I do well believe 't.
    That she loves him, 'tis apt and of great credit.
    The Moor, howbeit that I endure him not,
    Is of a constant, loving, noble nature,
    And I dare think he'll prove to Desdemona 290
    A most dear husband. Now, I do love her too.
    Not out of absolute lust (though peradventure
    I stand accountant for as great a sin)
    But partly led to diet my revenge
    For that I do suspect the lusty Moor 295
    Hath leaped into my seat—the thought whereof
    Doth, like a poisonous mineral, gnaw my inwards,
    And nothing can or shall content my soul
    Till I am evened with him, wife for wife,
    Or, failing so, yet that I put the Moor 300
    At least into a jealousy so strong
    That judgment cannot cure. Which thing to do,
    If this poor trash of Venice, whom I trace
    For his quick hunting, stand the putting on,
    I'll have our Michael Cassio on the hip, 305
    Abuse him to the Moor in the rank garb
    (For I fear Cassio with my nightcap too),
    Make the Moor thank me, love me and reward me
    For making him egregiously an ass
    And practicing upon his peace and quiet 310
    Even to madness. 'Tis here, but yet confused.
    Knavery's plain face is never seen till used.
    He exits.

Scene 2

Enter Othello's Herald with a proclamation.

HERALD It is Othello's pleasure, our noble and valiant general, that upon certain tidings now arrived, importing the mere perdition of the Turkish fleet, every man put himself into triumph: some to dance, some to make bonfires, each man to what sport and revels his addiction leads him. For besides these beneficial news, it is the celebration of his nuptial. So much was his pleasure should be proclaimed. All offices are open, and there is full liberty of feasting from this present hour of five till the bell have told eleven. Heaven bless the isle of Cyprus and our noble general, Othello!

He exits.

Scene 3

Enter Othello, Desdemona, Cassio, and Attendants.

OTHELLO
Good Michael, look you to the guard tonight.
Let's teach ourselves that honorable stop
Not to outsport discretion.

CASSIO
Iago hath direction what to do,
But, notwithstanding, with my personal eye
Will I look to 't.

OTHELLO   Iago is most honest.
Michael, good night. Tomorrow with your earliest
Let me have speech with you. [*To Desdemona.*] Come, my dear love,
The purchase made, the fruits are to ensue;
That profit's yet to come 'tween me and you.—
Good night.   *Othello and Desdemona exit, with Attendants*

Enter Iago.

CASSIO
Welcome, Iago. We must to the watch.

IAGO Not this hour, lieutenant. 'Tis not yet ten o' th' clock. Our general cast us thus early for the love of his Desdemona—who let us not therefore blame; he hath not yet made wanton the night with her; and she is sport for Jove.

CASSIO She's a most exquisite lady.

IAGO And, I'll warrant her, fun of game.

CASSIO Indeed, she's a most fresh and delicate creature.

IAGO What an eye she has! Methinks it sounds a parley to provocation.

CASSIO An inviting eye, and yet methinks right modest.

IAGO And when she speaks, is it not an alarum to love?

CASSIO She is indeed perfection.

IAGO Well, happiness to their sheets! Come, lieutenant, I have a stoup of wine; and here without are a brace of Cyprus gallants that would fain have a measure to the health of black Othello.

CASSIO Not tonight, good Iago. I have very poor and unhappy brains for drinking. I could well wish courtesy would invent some other custom of entertainment.

IAGO O, they are our friends! But one cup; I'll drink for you.

CASSIO I have drunk but one cup to-night, and that was craftily qualified too, and, behold, what innovation it makes here. I am unfortunate in the infirmity and dare not task my weakness with any more.

IAGO What, man! 'Tis a night of revels. The gallants desire it.

CASSIO Where are they?

IAGO Here at the door. I pray you, call them in.

CASSIO I'll do 't, but it dislikes me.   *He exits.*

IAGO
If I can fasten but one cup upon him
With that which he hath drunk tonight already,
He'll be as full of quarrel and offense
As my young mistress' dog. Now, my sick fool Roderigo,
Whom love hath turn'd almost the wrong side out,
To Desdemona hath tonight caroused
Potations pottle-deep; and he's to watch.
Three lads of Cyprus, noble swelling spirits
That hold their honors in a wary distance,
The very elements of this warlike isle,
Have I tonight flustered with flowing cups;
And they watch too. Now, 'mongst this flock of drunkards
Am I to put our Cassio in some action
That may offend the isle. But here they come.
If consequence do but approve my dream,
My boat sails freely, both with wind and stream.

Enter Cassio, Montano, Gentlemen, followed by Servants with wine.

CASSIO 'Fore God, they have given me a rouse already.

MONTANO Good faith, a little one; not past a pint, as I am a soldier.

IAGO Some wine, ho! [*Sings.*] *And let me the canakin clink, clink,*
   And let me the canakin clink
      A soldier's a man,
      O, man's life's but a span,
      Why, then, let a soldier drink.
Some wine, boys!

CASSIO 'Fore God, an excellent song.

IAGO I learned it in England, where, indeed, they are most potent in
potting. Your Dane, your German, and your swag-bellied Hollander—drink, ho!—are nothing to your English.

CASSIO Is your Englishman so expert in his drinking?

IAGO Why, he drinks you, with facility, your Dane dead drunk; he
sweats not to overthrow your Almain. He gives your Hollander a
vomit, ere the next pottle can be filled.

CASSIO To the health of our general!

MONTANO I am for it, lieutenant; and I'll do you justice.

IAGO O sweet England!
[Sings.]   King Stephen was and-a worthy peer,
              His breeches cost him but a crown;
           He held them sixpence all too dear;
              With that he called the tailor lown.
           He was a wight of high renown,
              And thou art but of low degree;
           'Tis pride that pulls the country down,
              Then take thy auld cloak about thee.
Some wine, ho!

CASSIO 'Fore God, this is a more exquisite song than the other!

IAGO Will you hear 't again?

CASSIO No, for I hold him to be unworthy of his place that does
those things. Well, God's above all; and there be souls must be
saved, [and there be souls must not be saved.]

IAGO It's true, good lieutenant.

CASSIO For mine own part—no offense to the General, nor any man
of quality—I hope to be saved.

IAGO And so do I too, lieutenant.

CASSIO Ay, but, by your leave, not before me. The Lieutenant is to
be saved before the ancient. Let's have no more of this. Let's to
our affairs. God forgive us our sins! Gentlemen, let's look to our
business. Do not think, gentlemen, I am drunk. This is my ancient;
this is my right hand, and this is my left. I am not drunk now. I
can stand well enough, and I speak well enough.

GENTLEMEN Excellent well.

CASSIO Why, very well then; you must not think then that I am
drunk.   *He exits.*

MONTANO
   To th' platform, masters. Come, let's set the watch.
                                              [*Gentlemen exit.*]

IAGO, [*to Montano*]
   You see this fellow that is gone before?
   He is a soldier fit to stand by Caesar
   And give direction; and do but see his vice.
   'Tis to his virtue a just equinox,

The one as long as th' other. 'Tis pity of him.
I fear the trust Othello puts him in, 110
On some odd time of his infirmity,
Will shake this island.

MONTANO   But is he often thus?

IAGO
'Tis evermore the prologue to his sleep.
He'll watch the horologe a double set 115
If drink rock not his cradle.

MONTANO   It were well
The General were put in mind of it.
Perhaps he sees it not; or his good nature
Prizes the virtue that appears in Cassio 120
And looks not on his evils. Is not this true?

Enter Roderigo.

IAGO, [*aside to Roderigo*] How now, Roderigo?
I pray you, after the Lieutenant, go.

Roderigo exits.

MONTANO
And 'tis great pity that the noble Moor
Should hazard such a place as his own second 125
With one of an ingraft infirmity.
It were an honest action to say
To the Moor.

IAGO   Not I, for this fair island.
I do love Cassio well and would do much 130
To cure him of this evil—   [*"Help, help!" within.*]
But, hark! What noise?

Enter Cassio, pursuing Roderigo.

CASSIO Zounds, you rogue, you rascal!

MONTANO What's the matter, lieutenant?

CASSIO A knave teach me my duty! I'll beat the knave into a 135
twiggen bottle.

RODERIGO Beat me?

CASSIO Dost thou prate, rogue?   [*He hits Roderigo.*]

MONTANO Nay, good lieutenant. I pray you, sir, hold your hand.

CASSIO Let me go, sir, or I'll knock you o'er the mazard. 140

MONTANO Come, come, you're drunk.

CASSIO Drunk?
     [*They fight.*]

IAGO, [*aside to Roderigo*]
Away, I say! Go out and cry a mutiny.
     [*Roderigo exits.*]
Nay, good lieutenant.—God's will, gentlemen!—

Help, ho! Lieutenant—sir—Montano—sir— 145
Help, masters!—Here's a goodly watch indeed!

[*A bell is rung.*]

Who's that which rings the bell? Diablo, ho!
The town will rise. God's will, lieutenant, hold!
You will be shamed forever.

Enter Othello and Attendants

OTHELLO What is the matter here? 150

MONTANO   Zounds, I bleed still.
I am hurt to th' death. He dies!   [*He attacks Cassio.*]

OTHELLO   Hold, for your lives!

IAGO
Hold, ho! Lieutenant—sir—Montano—gentlemen—
Have you forgot all sense of place and duty? 155
Hold! The General speaks to you. Hold, for shame!

OTHELLO
Why, how now, ho! from whence ariseth this?
Are we turned Turks, and to ourselves do that
Which heaven hath forbid the Ottomites?
For Christian shame, put by this barbarous brawl! 160
He that stirs next to carve for his own rage
Holds his soul light; he dies upon his motion.
Silence that dreadful bell. It frights the isle
From her propriety. What is the matter, masters?
Honest Iago, that look'st dead with grieving, 165
Speak, Who began this? On thy love, I charge thee.

IAGO
I do not know. Friends all but now, even now,
In quarter, and in terms like bride and groom
Divesting them for bed; and then but now,
As if some planet had unwitted men, 170
Swords out, and tilting one at other's breast,
In opposition bloody. I cannot speak
Any beginning to this peevish odds,
And would in action glorious I had lost
Those legs that brought me to a part of it! 175

OTHELLO
How comes it, Michael, you are thus forgot?

CASSIO
I pray you, pardon me; I cannot speak.

OTHELLO
Worthy Montano, you were wont be civil.
The gravity and stillness of your youth
The world hath noted. And your name is great 180
In mouths of wisest censure. What's the matter
That you unlace your reputation thus,
And spend your rich opinion for the name
Of a night-brawler? Give me answer to it.

MONTANO
>Worthy Othello, I am hurt to danger.
>Your officer Iago can inform you,
>While I spare speech, which something now offends me,
>Of all that I do know; nor know I aught
>By me that's said or done amiss this night,
>Unless self-charity be sometimes a vice,
>And to defend ourselves it be a sin
>When violence assails us.

OTHELLO   Now, by heaven,
>My blood begins my safer guides to rule,
>And passion, having my best judgment collied,
>Assays to lead the way. Zounds, if I stir,
>Or do but lift this arm, the best of you
>Shall sink in my rebuke. Give me to know
>How this foul rout began, who set it on;
>And he that is approved in this offense,
>Though he had twinned with me, both at a birth,
>Shall lose me. What, in a town of war
>Yet wild, the people's hearts brimful of fear,
>To manage private and domestic quarrel,
>In night, and on the court and guard of safety?
>'Tis monstrous. Iago, who began 't?

MONTANO
>If partially affined, or leagued in office,
>Thou dost deliver more or less than truth,
>Thou art no soldier.

IAGO   Touch me not so near.
>I had rather have this tongue cut from my mouth
>Than it should do offence to Michael Cassio.
>Yet, I persuade myself, to speak the truth
>Shall nothing wrong him. Thus it is, general:
>Montano and myself being in speech,
>There comes a fellow crying out for help,
>And Cassio following him with determined sword
>To execute upon him. Sir, this gentleman
>   [*Pointing to Montano.*]
>Steps in to Cassio, and entreats his pause.
>Myself the crying fellow did pursue,
>Lest by his clamour—as it so fell out—
>The town might fall in fright. He, swift of foot,
>Outran my purpose; and I returned the rather
>For that I heard the clink and fall of swords
>And Cassio high in oath, which till tonight
>I ne'er might say before. When I came back—
>For this was brief—I found them close together
>At blow and thrust, even as again they were
>When you yourself did part them.
>More of this matter cannot I report.
>But men are men; the best sometimes forget.
>Though Cassio did some little wrong to him,

    As men in rage strike those that wish them best,
    Yet surely Cassio, I believe, received
    From him that fled some strange indignity 235
    Which patience could not pass.

OTHELLO   I know, Iago,
    Thy honesty and love doth mince this matter,
    Making it light to Cassio. Cassio, I love thee,
    But never more be officer of mine. 240

              Enter Desdemona attended.

    Look, if my gentle love be not raised up!
    I'll make thee an example.

DESDEMONA What's the matter, dear?

OTHELLO   All's well now, sweeting.
    Come away to bed. [*To Montano.*] Sir, for your hurts, 245
    Myself will be your surgeon.—Lead him off.
                        [*Montano is led off.*]
    Iago, look with care about the town
    And silence those whom this vile brawl distracted.—
    Come, Desdemona. 'Tis the soldiers' life
    To have their balmy slumbers waked with strife. 250
               [*All but Iago and Cassio exit.*]

IAGO What, are you hurt, lieutenant?

CASSIO Ay, past all surgery.

IAGO Marry, God forbid!

CASSIO Reputation, reputation, reputation! O, I have lost my reputation! I have lost the immortal part of myself, and what remains is 255
    bestial. My reputation, Iago, my reputation!

IAGO As I am an honest man, I thought you had received some bodily wound. There is more sense in that than in reputation. Reputation is an idle and most false imposition, oft got without merit, and lost without deserving. You have lost no reputation at all, 260
    unless you repute yourself such a loser. What, man, there are ways to recover the general again! You are but now cast in his mood—a punishment more in policy than in malice, even so as one would beat his offenceless dog to affright an imperious lion. Sue to him again, and he's yours. 265

CASSIO I will rather sue to be despised than to deceive so good a commander with so slight, so drunken, and so indiscreet an officer. [Drunk? And speak parrot? And squabble? Swagger? Swear? And discourse fustian with one's own shadow?] O thou invisible spirit of wine, if thou hast no name to be known by, let us call 270
    thee devil!

IAGO What was he that you followed with your sword? What had he done to you?

CASSIO I know not.

IAGO Is 't possible? 275

CASSIO I remember a mass of things, but nothing distinctly; a quarrel, but nothing wherefore. O God, that men should put an enemy in their mouths to steal away their brains! That we should, with joy, pleasance, revel and applause transform ourselves into beasts!

IAGO Why, but you are now well enough. How came you thus recovered?

CASSIO It hath pleased the devil drunkenness to give place to the devil wrath. One unperfectness shows me another, to make me frankly despise myself.

IAGO Come, you are too severe a moraler. As the time, the place, and the condition of this country stands, I could heartily wish this had not befallen. But, since it is as it is, mend it for your own good.

CASSIO I will ask him for my place again; he shall tell me I am a drunkard! Had I as many mouths as Hydra, such an answer would stop them all. To be now a sensible man, by and by a fool, and presently a beast! O strange! Every inordinate cup is unblessed and the ingredient is a devil.

IAGO Come, come, good wine is a good familiar creature, if it be well used. Exclaim no more against it. And, good lieutenant, I think you think I love you.

CASSIO I have well approved it, sir.—I drunk!

IAGO You or any man living may be drunk. at a time, man. I'll tell you what you shall do. Our general's wife is now the general: I may say so in this respect, for that he hath devoted and given up himself to the contemplation, mark, and denotement of her parts and graces. Confess yourself freely to her. Importune her help to put you in your place again. She is of so free, so kind, so apt, so blessed a disposition, she holds it a vice in her goodness not to do more than she is requested. This broken joint between you and her husband entreat her to splinter; and, my fortunes against any lay worth naming, this crack of your love shall grow stronger than it was before.

CASSIO You advise me well.

IAGO I protest, in the sincerity of love and honest kindness.

CASSIO I think it freely; and betimes in the morning I will beseech the virtuous Desdemona to undertake for me. I am desperate of my fortunes if they check me here.

IAGO You are in the right. Good night, lieutenant. I must to the watch.

CASSIO Good night, honest Iago. *Cassio exits*

IAGO
And what's he, then, that says I play the villain,
When this advice is free I give and honest,
Probal to thinking, and indeed the course
To win the Moor again? For 'tis most easy
Th' inclining Desdemona to subdue
In any honest suit. She's framed as fruitful

As the free elements. And then for her
To win the Moor—were 't to renounce his baptism,
All seals and symbols of redeemed sin—
His soul is so enfettered to her love
That she may make, unmake, do what she list, 325
Even as her appetite shall play the god
With his weak function. How am I then a villain
To counsel Cassio to this parallel course
Directly to his good? Divinity of hell!
When devils will the blackest sins put on, 330
They do suggest at first with heavenly shows,
As I do now. For whiles this honest fool
Plies Desdemona to repair his fortunes
And she for him pleads strongly to the Moor,
I'll pour this pestilence into his ear: 335
That she repeals him for her body's lust;
And by how much she strives to do him good,
She shall undo her credit with the Moor.
So will I turn her virtue into pitch,
And out of her own goodness make the net 340
That shall enmesh them all.

Enter Roderigo.

How now, Roderigo!

RODERIGO I do follow here in the chase, not like a hound that hunts, but one that fills up the cry. My money is almost spent; I have been tonight exceedingly well cudgeled, and I think the issue will 345 be I shall have so much experience for my pains, and so, with no money at all and a little more wit, return again to Venice.

IAGO
How poor are they that have not patience!
What wound did ever heal but by degrees?
Thou know'st we work by wit, and not by witchcraft, 350
And wit depends on dilatory time.
Does't not go well? Cassio hath beaten thee,
And thou, by that small hurt, hast cashiered Cassio.
Though other things grow fair against the sun,
Yet fruits that blossom first will first be ripe. 355
Content thyself awhile. By th' Mass, 'tis morning!
Pleasure and action make the hours seem short.
Retire thee; go where thou art billeted.
Away, I say; thou shalt know more hereafter.
Nay, get thee gone. *Roderigo exits.* 360

Two things are to be done:
My wife must move for Cassio to her mistress.
I'll set her on.
Myself the while to draw the Moor apart
And bring him jump when he may Cassio find 365
Soliciting his wife. Ay, that's the way.
Dull not device by coldness and delay.

He exits.

Act 3

Scene 1

Enter Cassio with Musicians.

CASSIO
 Masters, play here (I will content your pains)
 Something that's brief; and bid "Good morrow, general."
 [*They play.*]

Enter the Clown

CLOWN Why masters, have your instruments been in Naples, that they speak i' th' nose thus?

MUSICIAN How, sir, how?

CLOWN Are these, I pray you, wind instruments?

MUSICIAN Ay, marry, are they, sir.

CLOWN O, thereby hangs a tail.

MUSICIAN Whereby hangs a tale, sir?

CLOWN Marry, sir, by many a wind instrument that I know. But, masters, here's money for you; and the General so likes your music, that he desires you, for love's sake, to make no more noise with it.

MUSICIAN Well, sir, we will not.

CLOWN If you have any music that may not be heard, to 't again. But, as they say to hear music the General does not greatly care.

MUSICIAN We have none such, sir.

CLOWN Then put up your pipes in your bag, for I'll away. Go, vanish into air, away!
 Musicians exit.

CASSIO Dost thou hear, mine honest friend?

CLOWN No, I hear not your honest friend. I hear you.

CASSIO Prithee, keep up thy quillets. [*Giving money.*] There's a poor piece of gold for thee. If the gentlewoman that attends the General's wife be stirring, tell her there's one Cassio entreats her a little favor of speech. Wilt thou do this?

CLOWN She is stirring, sir. If she will stir hither, I shall seem to notify unto her.

CASSIO
 Do, good my friend. *Clown exits.*

Enter Iago.

 In happy time, Iago.

IAGO You have not been abed, then?

CASSIO Why, no. The day had broke
 Before we parted. I have made bold, Iago,
 To send in to your wife. My suit to her
 Is, that she will to virtuous Desdemona
 Procure me some access. 35

IAGO I'll send her to you presently,
 And I'll devise a mean to draw the Moor
 Out of the way, that your converse and business
 May be more free.

CASSIO
 I humbly thank you for 't. [*Iago exits.*] I never knew 40
 A Florentine more kind and honest.

 Enter Emilia.

EMILIA
 Good morrow, good lieutenant. I am sorry
 For your displeasure, but all will sure be well.
 The General and his wife are talking of it,
 And she speaks for you stoutly. The Moor replies 45
 That he you hurt is of great fame in Cyprus
 And great affinity, and that in wholesome wisdom
 He might not but refuse you. But he protests he loves you
 And needs no other suitor but his likings
 To take the safest occasion by the front 50
 To bring you in again.

CASSIO   Yet, I beseech you,
 If you think fit, or that it may be done,
 Give me advantage of some brief discourse
 With Desdemona alone. 55

EMILIA   Pray you, come in.
 I will bestow you where you shall have time
 To speak your bosom freely.

[CASSIO I am much bound to you.]
                                        They exit.

Scene 2

Enter Othello, Iago, and Gentlemen.

OTHELLO
 These letters give, Iago, to the pilot
 And by him do my duties to the Senate.
                    [*He gives Iago some papers.*]
 That done, I will be walking on the works.
 Repair there to me.

IAGO   Well, my good lord, I'll do 't. 5

OTHELLO
 This fortification, gentlemen, shall we see 't?

GENTLEMEN
We'll wait upon your Lordship.

They exit.

Scene 3

Enter Desdemona, Cassio, and Emilia

DESDEMONA
Be thou assured, good Cassio, I will do
All my abilities in thy behalf.

EMILIA
Good madam, do. I warrant it grieves my husband
As if the cause were his.

DESDEMONA
O, that's an honest fellow! Do not doubt, Cassio, 5
But I will have my lord and you again
As friendly as you were.

CASSIO Bounteous madam,
Whatever shall become of Michael Cassio,
He's never anything but your true servant. 10

DESDEMONA
I know 't. I thank you. You do love my lord;
You have known him long; and be you well assured
He shall in strangeness stand no farther off
Than in a politic distance.

CASSIO Ay, but, lady, 15
That policy may either last so long,
Or feed upon such nice and waterish diet,
Or breed itself so out of circumstance,
That, I being absent and my place supplied,
My general will forget my love and service. 20

DESDEMONA
Do not doubt that. Before Emilia here,
I give thee warrant of thy place. Assure thee,
If I do vow a friendship, I'll perform it
To the last article. My lord shall never rest:
I'll watch him tame and talk him out of patience; 25
His bed shall seem a school, his board a shrift;
I'll intermingle every thing he does
With Cassio's suit. Therefore be merry, Cassio;
For thy solicitor shall rather die
Than give thy cause away. 30

Enter Othello and Iago.

EMILIA Madam, here comes my lord.

CASSIO Madam, I'll take my leave.

DESDEMONA Why, stay, and hear me speak.

CASSIO
Madam, not now: I am very ill at ease,

Unfit for mine own purposes.   35

DESDEMONA Well, do your discretion.   *Cassio exits.*

IAGO
Ha! I like not that.

OTHELLO   What dost thou say?

IAGO
Nothing, my lord; or if—I know not what.

OTHELLO
Was not that Cassio parted from my wife?   40

IAGO
Cassio, my lord? No, sure, I cannot think it
That he would steal away so guiltylike,
Seeing you coming.

OTHELLO I do believe 'twas he.

DESDEMONA How now, my lord?   45
I have been talking with a suitor here,
A man that languishes in your displeasure.

OTHELLO Who is 't you mean?

DESDEMONA
Why, your lieutenant, Cassio. Good my lord,
If I have any grace or power to move you,   50
His present reconciliation take;
For if he be not one that truly loves you,
That errs in ignorance and not in cunning,
I have no judgment in an honest face.
I prithee, call him back.   55

OTHELLO   Went he hence now?

DESDEMONA Yes, faith, so humbled
That he hath left part of his grief with me
To suffer with him. Good love, call him back.

OTHELLO
Not now, sweet Desdemona. Some other time.   60

DESDEMONA
But shall 't be shortly?

OTHELLO   The sooner, sweet, for you.

DESDEMONA
Shall 't be tonight at supper?

OTHELLO   No, not tonight.

DESDEMONA Tomorrow dinner, then?   65

OTHELLO I shall not dine at home;
I meet the captains at the citadel.

DESDEMONA
Why, then, tomorrow night; or Tuesday morn,

    On Tuesday noon, or night; on Wednesday morn.
    I prithee, name the time, but let it not
    Exceed three days: in faith, he's penitent;
    And yet his trespass, in our common reason—
    Save that, they say, the wars must make example
    Out of their best—is not almost a fault
    T' incur a private check. When shall he come?
    Tell me, Othello. I wonder in my soul
    What you would ask me that I should deny,
    Or stand so mamm'ring on? What! Michael Cassio,
    That came a-wooing with you, and so many a time,
    When I have spoke of you dispraisingly,
    Hath ta'en your part—to have so much to do
    To bring him in! By'r Lady, I could do much—

OTHELLO
    Prithee, no more. Let him come when he will;
    I will deny thee nothing.

DESDEMONA Why, this is not a boon!
    'Tis as I should entreat you wear your gloves,
    Or feed on nourishing dishes, or keep you warm,
    Or sue to you to do a peculiar profit
    To your own person. Nay, when I have a suit
    Wherein I mean to touch your love indeed,
    It shall be full of poise and difficult weight,
    And fearful to be granted.

OTHELLO I will deny thee nothing!
    Whereon, I do beseech thee, grant me this,
    To leave me but a little to myself.

DESDEMONA
    Shall I deny you? No. Farewell, my lord.

OTHELLO
    Farewell, my Desdemona. I'll come to thee straight.

DESDEMONA
    Emilia, come.—Be as your fancies teach you.
    Whate'er you be, I am obedient.
                             Desdemona and Emilia exit

OTHELLO
    Excellent wretch! Perdition catch my soul
    But I do love thee! And when I love thee not,
    Chaos is come again.

IAGO   My noble lord—

OTHELLO
    What dost thou say, Iago?

IAGO   Did Michael Cassio,
    When you wooed my lady, know of your love?

OTHELLO
    He did, from first to last. Why dost thou ask?

IAGO
   But for a satisfaction of my thought;
   No further harm.
OTHELLO   Why of thy thought, Iago?   110
IAGO
   I did not think he had been acquainted with her.
OTHELLO
   O, yes, and went between us very oft.
IAGO Indeed?
OTHELLO
   Indeed? Ay, indeed! Discern'st thou aught in that?
   Is he not honest?   115
IAGO Honest, my lord?
OTHELLO Honest—ay, honest.
IAGO
   My lord, for aught I know.
OTHELLO   What dost thou think?
IAGO Think, my lord?   120
OTHELLO
   "Think, my lord!" By heaven, he echo'st me
   As if there were some monster in thy thought
   Too hideous to be shown. Thou dost mean something.
   I heard thee say even now, thou lik'st not that,
   When Cassio left my wife. What didst not like?   125
   And when I told thee he was of my counsel
   In my whole course of wooing, thou cried'st "Indeed?"
   And didst contract and purse thy brow together,
   As if thou then hadst shut up in thy brain
   Some horrible conceit. If thou dost love me,   130
   Show me thy thought.
IAGO My lord, you know I love you.
OTHELLO I think thou dost;
   And for I know thou 'rt full of love and honesty
   And weigh'st thy words before thou giv'st them breath,   135
   Therefore these stops of thine fright me the more.
   For such things in a false disloyal knave
   Are tricks of custom; but in a man that's just,
   They are close dilations working from the heart
   That passion cannot rule.   140
IAGO   For Michael Cassio,
   I dare be sworn I think that he is honest.
OTHELLO
   I think so too.
IAGO   Men should be what they seem;
   Or those that be not, would they might seem none!   145

OTHELLO Certain, men should be what they seem.

IAGO
  Why then, I think Cassio's an honest man.

OTHELLO Nay, yet there's more in this.
  I prithee speak to me as to thy thinkings,
  As thou dost ruminate, and give thy worst of thoughts 150
  The worst of words.

IAGO   Good my lord, pardon me.
  Though I am bound to every act of duty,
  I am not bound to that all slaves are free to.
  Utter my thoughts? Why, say they are vile and false— 155
  As where's that palace whereinto foul things
  Sometimes intrude not? Who has a breast so pure
  But some uncleanly apprehensions
  Keep leets and law days and in sessions sit
  With meditations lawful? 160

OTHELLO
  Thou dost conspire against thy friend, Iago,
  If thou but think'st him wrong'd and mak'st his ear
  A stranger to thy thoughts.

IAGO   I do beseech you,
  Though I perchance am vicious in my guess— 165
  As, I confess, it is my nature's plague
  To spy into abuses, and oft my jealousy
  Shapes faults that are not—that your wisdom
  From one that so imperfectly conceits,
  Would take no notice, nor build yourself a trouble 170
  Out of his scattering and unsure observance.
  It were not for your quiet nor your good,
  Nor for my manhood, honesty, and wisdom,
  To let you know my thoughts.

OTHELLO   What dost thou mean? 175

IAGO
  Good name in man and woman, dear my lord,
  Is the immediate jewel of their souls.
  Who steals my purse steals trash. 'Tis something, nothing;
  'Twas mine, 'tis his, and has been slave to thousands.
  But he that filches from me my good name 180
  Robs me of that which not enriches him
  And makes me poor indeed.

OTHELLO By heaven, I'll know thy thoughts.

IAGO
  You cannot, if my heart were in your hand,
  Nor shall not, whilst 'tis in my custody. 185

OTHELLO
  Ha?

IAGO O, beware, my lord, of jealousy!

It is the green-eyed monster which doth mock
The meat it feeds on. That cuckold lives in bliss
Who, certain of his fate, loves not his wronger;
But, O, what damned minutes tells he o'er
Who dotes, yet doubts; suspects, yet strongly loves!

OTHELLO O misery!

IAGO
Poor and content is rich and rich enough;
But riches fineless is as poor as winter
To him that ever fears he shall be poor.
Good God, the souls of all my tribe defend
From jealousy!

OTHELLO Why, why is this?
Think'st thou I'd make a lie of jealousy,
To follow still the changes of the moon
With fresh suspicions? No. To be once in doubt
Is once to be resolved. Exchange me for a goat
When I shall turn the business of my soul
To such exsufflicate and blown surmises,
Matching thy inference. 'Tis not to make me jealous
To say my wife is fair, feeds well, loves company,
Is free of speech, sings, plays, and dances well.
Where virtue is, these are more virtuous.
Nor from mine own weak merits will I draw
The smallest fear or doubt of her revolt,
For she had eyes, and chose me. No, Iago,
I'll see before I doubt; when I doubt, prove;
And on the proof, there is no more but this:
Away at once with love or jealousy.

IAGO
I am glad of this, for now I shall have reason
To show the love and duty that I bear you
With franker spirit. Therefore, as I am bound,
Receive it from me. I speak not yet of proof.
Look to your wife; observe her well with Cassio;
Wear your eye thus, not jealous nor secure.
I would not have your free and noble nature,
Out of self-bounty, be abused. Look to 't.
I know our country disposition well.
In Venice they do let God see the pranks
They dare not show their husbands. Their best conscience
Is not to leave 't undone, but keep 't unknown.

OTHELLO Dost thou say so?

IAGO
She did deceive her father, marrying you,
And when she seemed to shake and fear your looks,
She loved them most.

OTHELLO And so she did.

IAGO Why, go to then!

>   She that, so young, could give out such a seeming,
>   To seal her father's eyes up close as oak,   235
>   He thought 'twas witchcraft! But I am much to blame.
>   I humbly do beseech you of your pardon
>   For too much loving you.

OTHELLO I am bound to thee for ever.

IAGO
> I see this hath a little dashed your spirits.   240

OTHELLO
> Not a jot, not a jot.

IAGO   I' faith, I fear it has.
> I hope you will consider what is spoke
> Comes from my love. But I do see you're moved.
> I am to pray you not to strain my speech   245
> To grosser issues nor to larger reach
> Than to suspicion.

OTHELLO I will not.

IAGO Should you do so, my lord,
> My speech should fall into such vile success   250
> As my thoughts aim not at. Cassio's my worthy friend.
> My lord, I see you're moved.

OTHELLO   No, not much moved.
> I do not think but Desdemona's honest.

IAGO
> Long live she so! And long live you to think so!   255

OTHELLO
> And yet, how nature erring from itself—

IAGO
> Ay, there's the point. As, to be bold with you,
> Not to affect many proposèd matches
> Of her own clime, complexion, and degree,
> Whereto we see in all things nature tends—   260
> Foh! one may smell in such a will most rank,
> Foul disproportion, thoughts unnatural—
> But pardon me—I do not in position
> Distinctly speak of her, though I may fear
> Her will, recoiling to her better judgment,   265
> May fall to match you with her country forms
> And happily repent.

OTHELLO   Farewell, farewell:
> If more thou dost perceive, let me know more.
> Set on thy wife to observe. Leave me, Iago.   270

IAGO, [*beginning to exit*] My lord, I take my leave.

OTHELLO
> Why did I marry? This honest creature doubtless
> Sees and knows more, much more, than he unfolds.

IAGO, [*returning*]
    My lord, I would I might entreat your Honor
    To scan this thing no farther. Leave it to time. 275
    Although 'tis fit that Cassio have his place—
    For sure, he fills it up with great ability—
    Yet, if you please to hold him off awhile,
    You shall by that perceive him and his means.
    Note if your lady strain his entertainment 280
    With any strong or vehement importunity.
    Much will be seen in that. In the meantime,
    Let me be thought too busy in my fears—
    As worthy cause I have to fear I am—
    And hold her free, I do beseech your Honor. 285

OTHELLO Fear not my government.

IAGO I once more take my leave. *He exits.*

OTHELLO
    This fellow's of exceeding honesty,
    And knows all qualities, with a learned spirit
    Of human dealings. If I do prove her haggard, 290
    Though that her jesses were my dear heartstrings,
    I'd whistle her off and let her down the wind
    To pray at fortune. Haply, for I am black
    And have not those soft parts of conversation
    That chamberers have, or for I am declined 295
    Into the vale of years—yet that's not much—
    She's gone, I am abused, and my relief
    Must be to loathe her. O curse of marriage,
    That we can call these delicate creatures ours
    And not their appetites! I had rather be a toad 300
    And live upon the vapor of a dungeon
    Than keep a corner in the thing I love
    For others' uses. Yet 'tis the plague of great ones;
    Prerogatived are they less than the base.
    'Tis destiny unshunnable, like death. 305
    Even then this forked plague is fated to us
    When we do quicken. Look where she comes.

Enter Desdemona and Emilia

    If she be false, heaven mocks itself!
    I'll not believe 't.

DESDEMONA   How now, my dear Othello! 310
    Your dinner, and the generous islanders
    By you invited, do attend your presence.

OTHELLO I am to blame.

DESDEMONA
    Why do you speak so faintly? Are you not well?

OTHELLO
    I have a pain upon my forehead, here. 315

DESDEMONA
    'Faith, that's with watching. 'Twill away again.
    Let me but bind it hard; within this hour
    It will be well.

OTHELLO   Your napkin is too little:
    Let it alone.   [*The handkerchief falls, unnoticed.*]   320
        Come, I'll go in with you.

DESDEMONA
    I am very sorry that you are not well.

                            Othello and Desdemona exit.

EMILIA, [*picking up the handkerchief*]
    I am glad I have found this napkin.
    This was her first remembrance from the Moor:
    My wayward husband hath a hundred times   325
    Wooed me to steal it. But she so loves the token
    (For he conjured her she should ever keep it)
    That she reserves it evermore about her
    To kiss and talk to. I'll have the work ta'en out
    And give 't Iago. What he will do with it   330
    Heaven knows, not I.
    I nothing but to please his fantasy.

                      Enter Iago.

IAGO How now? What do you here alone?

EMILIA
    Do not you chide. I have a thing for you.

IAGO
    A thing for me? It is a common thing—   335

EMILIA Ha?

IAGO To have a foolish wife.

EMILIA
    O, is that all? What will you give me now
    For the same handkerchief?

IAGO   What handkerchief?   340

EMILIA What handkerchief?
    Why, that the Moor first gave to Desdemona,
    That which so often you did bid me steal.

IAGO Hast stol'n it from her?

EMILIA
    No, faith, she let it drop by negligence.   345
    And, to the advantage, I, being here, took 't up.
    Look, here it is.

IAGO   A good wench! Give it me.

EMILIA
    What will you do with 't, that you have been so earnest
    To have me filch it?   350

IAGO, [*snatching it*]   Why, what is that to you?

EMILIA
If it be not for some purpose of import,
Give 't me again. Poor lady, she'll run mad
When she shall lack it.

IAGO   Be not acknown on 't.   355
I have use for it. Go, leave me.   *Emilia exits.*
I will in Cassio's lodging lose this napkin,
And let him find it. Trifles light as air
Are to the jealous confirmations strong
As proofs of holy writ. This may do something.   360
[The Moor already changes with my poison;]
Dangerous conceits are, in their natures, poisons,
Which at the first are scarce found to distaste,
But with a little act upon the blood
Burn like the mines of sulphur.   365

Enter Othello.

                    I did say so.
Look where he comes. Not poppy, nor mandragora
Nor all the drowsy syrups of the world
Shall ever medicine thee to that sweet sleep
Which thou owedst yesterday.   370

OTHELLO Ha, ha, false to me?

IAGO
Why, how now, general? No more of that!

OTHELLO
Avaunt! Begone! Thou hast set me on the rack
I swear 'tis better to be much abused
Than but to know 't a little.   375

IAGO   How now, my lord?

OTHELLO
What sense had I of her stol'n hours of lust?
I saw 't not, thought it not, it harmed not me.
I slept the next night well, was free and merry.
I found not Cassio's kisses on her lips.   380
He that is robbed, not wanting what is stol'n,
Let him not know 't, and he's not robbed at all.

IAGO I am sorry to hear this.

OTHELLO
I had been happy if the general camp,
Pioners and all, had tasted her sweet body,   385
So I had nothing known. O, now, forever
Farewell the tranquil mind! Farewell content!
Farewell the plumèd troop, and the big wars,
That make ambition virtue! O, farewell!
Farewell the neighing steed, and the shrill trump,   390
The spirit-stirring drum, th' ear-piercing fife,

The royal banner, and all quality,
Pride, pomp, and circumstance of glorious war!
And O you mortal engines, whose rude throats
Th' immortal Jove's dread clamors counterfeit, 395
Farewell! Othello's occupation's gone!

IAGO Is 't possible, my lord?

OTHELLO
Villain, be sure thou prove my love a whore!
Be sure of it. Give me the ocular proof,
Or by the worth of man's eternal soul, 400
Thou hadst been better have been born a dog
Than answer my waked wrath.

IAGO   Is 't come to this?

OTHELLO
Make me to see 't, or at the least so prove it
That the probation bear no hinge nor loop 405
To hang a doubt on, or woe upon thy life!

IAGO My noble lord—

OTHELLO
If thou dost slander her and torture me,
Never pray more. Abandon all remorse;
On horror's head horrors accumulate; 410
Do deeds to make heaven weep, all earth amazed;
For nothing canst thou to damnation add
Greater than that.

IAGO   O grace! O heaven forgive me!
Are you a man? Have you a soul or sense? 415
God b' wi' you. Take mine office.—O wretched fool,
That liv'st to make thine honesty a vice!—
O monstrous world! Take note, take note, O world:
To be direct and honest is not safe.—
I thank you for this profit; and from hence 420
I'll love no friend, sith love breeds such offense.

OTHELLO Nay, stay. Thou shouldst be honest.

IAGO
I should be wise; for honesty's a fool
And loses that it works for.

[OTHELLO   By the world, 425
I think my wife be honest and think she is not.
I think that thou art just and think thou art not.
I'll have some proof. Her name, that was as fresh
As Dian's visage, is now begrimed and black
As mine own face. If there be cords, or knives, 430
Poison, or fire, or suffocating streams,
I'll not endure it. Would I were satisfied!]

IAGO
I see, you are eaten up with passion.

I do repent me that I put it to you.
You would be satisfied? 435

OTHELLO Would? Nay, and I will.

IAGO
And may; but, how? How satisfied, my lord?
Would you, the supervisor, grossly gape on,
Behold her topped?

OTHELLO   Death and damnation! O! 440

IAGO
It were a tedious difficulty, I think,
To bring them to that prospect. Damn them then
If ever mortal eyes do see them bolster
More than their own! What then? How then?
What shall I say? Where's satisfaction? 445
It is impossible you should see this,
Were they as prime as goats, as hot as monkeys,
As salt as wolves in pride, and fools as gross
As ignorance made drunk. But yet I say,
If imputation and strong circumstances 450
Which lead directly to the door of truth
Will give you satisfaction, you may have 't.

OTHELLO
Give me a living reason she's disloyal.

IAGO I do not like the office,
But sith I am entered in this cause so far, 455
Pricked to 't by foolish honesty and love,
I will go on. I lay with Cassio lately,
And, being troubled with a raging tooth,
I could not sleep. There are a kind of men
So loose of soul that in their sleeps will mutter 460
Their affairs. One of this kind is Cassio.
In sleep I heard him say "Sweet Desdemona,
Let us be wary, let us hide our loves."
And then, sir, would he gripe and wring my hand,
Cry "O sweet creature!" and then kiss me hard, 465
As if he plucked up kisses by the roots
That grew upon my lips: then laid his leg
Over my thigh, and sighed, and kissed; and then
Cried "Cursed fate that gave thee to the Moor!"

OTHELLO
O monstrous! Monstrous! 470

IAGO   Nay, this was but his dream.

OTHELLO
But this denoted a foregone conclusion.
'Tis a shrewd doubt, though it be but a dream.

IAGO
And this may help to thicken other proofs
That do demonstrate thinly. 475

OTHELLO I'll tear her all to pieces.

IAGO
   Nay, but be wise. Yet we see nothing done.
   She may be honest yet. Tell me but this:
   Have you not sometimes seen a handkerchief
   Spotted with strawberries in your wife's hand?   480

OTHELLO
   I gave her such a one. 'Twas my first gift.

IAGO
   I know not that; but such a handkerchief—
   I am sure it was your wife's—did I today
   See Cassio wipe his beard with.

OTHELLO   If it be that—   485

IAGO
   If it be that, or any that was hers,
   It speaks against her with the other proofs.

OTHELLO
   O, that the slave had forty thousand lives!
   One is too poor, too weak for my revenge.
   Now do I see 'tis true. Look here, Iago,   490
   All my fond love thus do I blow to heaven.
   'Tis gone.
   Arise, black vengeance, from thy hollow hell!
   Yield up, O love, thy crown and hearted throne
   To tyrannous hate! Swell, bosom, with thy fraught,   495
   For 'tis of aspics' tongues!

IAGO Yet be content.

OTHELLO O, blood, blood, blood!

IAGO
   Patience, I say. Your mind perhaps may change.

OTHELLO
   Never, [Iago. Like to the Pontic Sea,   500
   Whose icy current and compulsive course
   Ne'er feels retiring ebb, but keeps due on
   To the Propontic and the Hellespont,
   Even so my bloody thoughts, with violent pace
   Shall ne'er look back, ne'er ebb to humble love,   505
   Till that a capable and wide revenge
   Swallow them up. [*He kneels.*] Now by yond marble heaven,]
   In the due reverence of a sacred vow
   I here engage my words.

IAGO   Do not rise yet. [*Iago kneels.*]   510
   Witness, you ever-burning lights above,
   You elements that clip us round about,
   Witness that here Iago doth give up
   The execution of his wit, hands, heart
   To wronged Othello's service! Let him command,   515

And to obey shall be in me remorse,
What bloody business ever. [*They rise.*]

OTHELLO   I greet thy love
Not with vain thanks, but with acceptance bounteous,
And will upon the instant put thee to 't.
Within these three days let me hear thee say
That Cassio's not alive.

IAGO   My friend is dead.
'Tis done at your request. But let her live.

OTHELLO Damn her, lewd minx! O, damn her, damn her!
Come, go with me apart. I will withdraw
To furnish me with some swift means of death
For the fair devil. Now art thou my lieutenant.

IAGO I am your own forever.
They exit.

Scene 4

Enter Desdemona, Emilia, and Clown

DESDEMONA Do you know, sirrah, where Lieutenant Cassio lies?

CLOWN I dare not say he lies anywhere.

DESDEMONA Why, man?

CLOWN He's a soldier, and for one to say a soldier lies, 'tis stabbing.

DESDEMONA Go to! where lodges he?

[CLOWN To tell you where he lodges is to tell you where I lie.

DESDEMONA Can anything be made of this?]

CLOWN I know not where he lodges, and for me to devise a lodging and say he lies here or he lies there, were to lie in mine own throat.

DESDEMONA Can you inquire him out, and be edified by report?

CLOWN I will catechise the world for him—that is, make questions, and by them answer.

DESDEMONA Seek him, bid him come hither. Tell him I have moved my lord on his behalf, and hope all will be well.

CLOWN To do this is within the compass of man's wit, and therefore I will attempt the doing it.
Clown exits.

DESDEMONA
Where should I lose that handkerchief, Emilia?

EMILIA I know not, madam.

DESDEMONA
Believe me, I had rather have lost my purse
Full of crusadoes. And, but my noble Moor
Is true of mind and made of no such baseness

As jealous creatures are, it were enough
To put him to ill thinking.

EMILIA   Is he not jealous?

DESDEMONA
Who, he? I think the sun where he was born   25
Drew all such humors from him.

EMILIA   Look, where he comes.

Enter Othello.

DESDEMONA
I will not leave him now till Cassio
Be called to him.—How is 't with you, my lord?

OTHELLO
Well, my good lady. [*Aside.*] O, hardness to dissemble!—   30
How do you, Desdemona?

DESDEMONA   Well, my good lord.

OTHELLO
Give me your hand. [*He takes her hand.*] This hand is moist, my
lady.

DESDEMONA
It yet has felt no age nor known no sorrow.   35

OTHELLO
This argues fruitfulness and liberal heart:
Hot, hot, and moist. This hand of yours requires
A sequester from liberty, fasting and prayer,
Much castigation, exercise devout;
For here's a young and sweating devil here   40
That commonly rebels. 'Tis a good hand,
A frank one.

DESDEMONA You may, indeed, say so,
For 'twas that hand that gave away my heart.

OTHELLO
A liberal hand! The hearts of old gave hands,   45
But our new heraldry is hands, not hearts.

DESDEMONA
I cannot speak of this. Come now, your promise.

OTHELLO What promise, chuck?

DESDEMONA
I have sent to bid Cassio come speak with you.

OTHELLO
I have a salt and sorry rheum offends me.   50
Lend me thy handkerchief.

DESDEMONA   Here, my lord.

OTHELLO
That which I gave you.

DESDEMONA   I have it not about me.

OTHELLO Not?   55

DESDEMONA No, faith, my lord.

OTHELLO That'is a fault. That handkerchief
  Did an Egyptian to my mother give.
  She was a charmer, and could almost read
  The thoughts of people. She told her, while she kept it,   60
  'Twould make her amiable and subdue my father
  Entirely to her love. But if she lost it,
  Or made gift of it, my father's eye
  Should hold her loathed, and his spirits should hunt
  After new fancies. She, dying, gave it me,   65
  And bid me, when my fate would have me wived,
  To give it her. I did so; and take heed on 't,
  Make it a darling like your precious eye.
  To lose 't or give 't away were such perdition
  As nothing else could match.   70

DESDEMONA   Is 't possible?

OTHELLO
  'Tis true. There's magic in the web of it.
  A sibyl that had numbered in the world
  The sun to course two hundred compasses,
  In her prophetic fury sewed the work.   75
  The worms were hallowed that did breed the silk,
  And it was dyed in mummy, which the skillful
  Conserved of maidens' hearts.

DESDEMONA   I' faith, is 't true?

OTHELLO
  Most veritable. Therefore look to 't well.   80

DESDEMONA
  Then would to God that I had never seen 't!

OTHELLO Ha! Wherefore?

DESDEMONA
  Why do you speak so startingly and rash?

OTHELLO
  Is 't lost? Is 't gone? Speak, is 't out o' th' way?

DESDEMONA Heaven bless us!   85

OTHELLO Say you?

DESDEMONA
  It is not lost; but what an if it were?

OTHELLO How?

DESDEMONA I say it is not lost.

OTHELLO Fetch 't. Let me see 't.   90

DESDEMONA
  Why, so I can. But I will not now.
  This is a trick to put me from my suit.
  Pray you, let Cassio be received again.

OTHELLO
  Fetch me the handkerchief! [*Aside*] My mind misgives.

DESDEMONA Come, come; 95
  You'll never meet a more sufficient man.

OTHELLO
  The handkerchief!

DESDEMONA   I pray, talk me of Cassio.

OTHELLO The handkerchief!

DESDEMONA   A man that all his time 100
  Hath founded his good fortunes on your love;
  Shared dangers with you—

OTHELLO
  The handkerchief!

DESDEMONA   I' faith, you are to blame.

OTHELLO Zounds!   *Othello exits.* 105

EMILIA Is not this man jealous?

DESDEMONA I ne'er saw this before.
  Sure, there's some wonder in this handkerchief!
  I am most unhappy in the loss of it.

EMILIA
  'Tis not a year or two shows us a man. 110
  They are all but stomachs, and we all but food;
  They eat us hungerly, and when they are full,
  They belch us.

            Enter Iago and Cassio.

            Look you—Cassio and my husband!

IAGO, *to Cassio*
  There is no other way; 'tis she must do 't, 115
  And, lo, the happiness! Go, and importune her.

DESDEMONA
  How now, good Cassio, what's the news with you?

CASSIO
  Madam, my former suit. I do beseech you
  That by your virtuous means I may again
  Exist, and be a member of his love 120
  Whom I with all the office of my heart
  Entirely honor. I would not be delayed.
  If my offense be of such mortal kind
  That nor my service past nor present sorrows
  Nor purposed merit in futurity 125

Can ransom me into his love again,
But to know so must be my benefit.
So shall I clothe me in a forced content,
And shut myself up in some other course
To fortune's alms. 130

DESDEMONA   Alas, thrice-gentle Cassio,
My advocation is not now in tune.
My lord is not my lord; nor should I know him
Were he in favor as in humor altered.
So help me every spirit sanctified 135
As I have spoken for you all my best,
And stood within the blank of his displeasure
For my free speech! You must awhile be patient.
What I can do I will; and more I will
Than for myself I dare. Let that suffice you. 140

IAGO
Is my lord angry?

EMILIA   He went hence but now,
And certainly in strange unquietness.

IAGO
Can he be angry? I have seen the cannon
When it hath blown his ranks into the air 145
And, like the devil, from his very arm
Puffed his own brother—and can he be angry?
Something of moment then. I will go meet him.
There's matter in 't indeed, if he be angry.

DESDEMONA
I prithee, do so. *He exits.* 150
    Something, sure, of state,
Either from Venice, or some unhatched practice
Made demonstrable here in Cyprus to him,
Hath puddled his clear spirit; and in such cases
Men's natures wrangle with inferior things, 155
Though great ones are their object. 'Tis even so.
For let our finger ache, and it endues
Our other healthful members even to that sense
Of pain. Nay, we must think men are not gods,
Nor of them look for such observancy 160
As fits the bridal. Beshrew me much, Emilia,
I was—unhandsome warrior as I am!—
Arraigning his unkindness with my soul.
But now I find I had suborned the witness,
And he's indicted falsely. 165

EMILIA   Pray heaven it be
State matters, as you think, and no conception
Nor no jealous toy concerning you.

DESDEMONA
Alas the day! I never gave him cause.

EMILIA
>But jealous souls will not be answered so. 170
>They are not ever jealous for the cause,
>But jealous for they are jealous. It is a monster
>Begot upon itself, born on itself.

DESDEMONA
>Heaven keep that monster from Othello's mind!

EMILIA Lady, amen. 175

DESDEMONA
>I will go seek him—Cassio, walk hereabout.
>If I do find him fit, I'll move your suit
>And seek to effect it to my uttermost.

CASSIO I humbly thank your Ladyship.

Desdemona and Emilia exit.

Enter Bianca.

BIANCA
>'Save you, friend Cassio! 180

CASSIO   What make you from home?
>How is 't with you, my most fair Bianca?
>I' faith, sweet love, I was coming to your house.

BIANCA
>And I was going to your lodging, Cassio.
>What, keep a week away? Seven days and nights? 185
>Eight score eight hours, and lovers' absent hours
>More tedious than the dial eightscore times?
>O weary reck'ning!

CASSIO   Pardon me, Bianca.
>I have this while with leaden thoughts been pressed, 190
>But I shall, in a more continuate time
>Strike off this score of absence. Sweet Bianca,
>   [*Giving her Desdemona's handkerchief.*]
>Take me this work out.

BIANCA   O Cassio, whence came this?
>This is some token from a newer friend. 195
>To the felt absence now I feel a cause.
>Is 't come to this? Well, well.

CASSIO   Go to, woman!
>Throw your vile guesses in the devil's teeth,
>From whence you have them. You are jealous now 200
>That this is from some mistress, some remembrance.
>No, by my faith, Bianca.

BIANCA   Why, whose is it?

CASSIO
>I know not, neither. I found it in my chamber.
>I like the work well. Ere it be demanded, 205

    As like enough it will, I would have it copied.
    Take it, and do 't, and leave me for this time.

BIANCA Leave you! Wherefore?

CASSIO
    I do attend here on the General,
    And think it no addition, nor my wish,   210
    To have him see me womaned.

[BIANCA Why, I pray you?

CASSIO Not that I love you not.]

BIANCA But that you do not love me.
    I pray you, bring me on the way a little,   215
    And say if I shall see you soon at night.

CASSIO
    'Tis but a little way that I can bring you,
    For I attend here. But I'll see you soon.

BIANCA
    'Tis very good. I must be circumstanced.

                                            They exit.

Act 4

Scene 1

Enter Othello and Iago.

IAGO Will you think so?

OTHELLO Think so, Iago?

IAGO What, to kiss in private?

OTHELLO An unauthorized kiss!

IAGO
   Or to be naked with her friend in bed
   An hour or more, not meaning any harm?

OTHELLO
   Naked in bed, Iago, and not mean harm?
   It is hypocrisy against the devil!
   They that mean virtuously, and yet do so,
   The devil their virtue tempts, and they tempt heaven.

IAGO
   So they do nothing, 'tis a venial slip.
   But if I give my wife a handkerchief—

OTHELLO What then?

IAGO
   Why, then, 'tis hers, my lord; and, being hers,
   She may, I think, bestow't on any man.

OTHELLO
   She is protectress of her honor, too.
   May she give that?

IAGO
   Her honor is an essence that's not seen;
   They have it very oft that have it not.
   But, for the handkerchief—

OTHELLO
   By heaven, I would most gladly have forgot it.
   Thou saidst—O, it comes o'er my memory
   As doth the raven o'er the infectious house,
   Boding to all—he had my handkerchief.

IAGO Ay, what of that?

OTHELLO That's not so good now.

IAGO
   What if I had said I had seen him do you wrong?
   Or heard him say (as knaves be such abroad,
   Who having, by their own importunate suit
   Or voluntary dotage of some mistress,
   Convinced or supplied them, cannot choose
   But they must blab)—

OTHELLO Hath he said any thing?

IAGO
   He hath, my lord; but be you well assured,
   No more than he'll unswear.　　　　　　　　　　　　　　　　35

OTHELLO　　　　　　　　　What hath he said?

IAGO
   Faith, that he did—I know not what he did.

OTHELLO What? What?

IAGO
   Lie—

OTHELLO With her?　　　　　　　　　　　　　　　　　　　　　　40

IAGO　　　　　　　　With her—on her—what you will.

OTHELLO Lie with her? Lie on her? We say "lie on her" when they
   belie her. Lie with her—Zounds, that's fulsome! Handkerchief—
   confessions—handkerchief. [To confess and be hanged for his labor. First to be hanged and then to confess—I tremble at it. Nature　　45
   would not invest herself in such shadowing passion without some
   instruction. It is not words that shake me thus. Pish! Noses, ears,
   and lips—is't possible? Confess—handkerchief—O devil!]
                                            He falls in a trance

IAGO Work on,
   My medicine, work! Thus credulous fools are caught;　　　　　50
   And many worthy and chaste dames even thus,
   All guiltless, meet reproach.—What ho! My lord!
   My lord, I say! Othello!

Enter Cassio.

                How now, Cassio?

CASSIO What's the matter?　　　　　　　　　　　　　　　　　55

IAGO
   My lord is fall'n into an epilepsy.
   This is his second fit. He had one yesterday.

CASSIO
   Rub him about the temples.

IAGO　　　　　　　　　　No, forbear.
   The lethargy must have his quiet course.　　　　　　　　　　　60
   If not, he foams at mouth, and by and by
   Breaks out to savage madness. Look he stirs.
   Do you withdraw yourself a little while.
   He will recover straight. When he is gone,
   I would on great occasion speak with you.　　[*Cassio exits.*]　　65
   How is it, general? Have you not hurt your head?

OTHELLO
   Dost thou mock me?

IAGO　　　　　　　　　I mock you not, by heaven!

Would you would bear your fortune like a man!

OTHELLO
    A hornèd man's a monster and a beast.

IAGO
    There's many a beast, then, in a populous city,
    And many a civil monster.

OTHELLO
    Did he confess it?

IAGO   Good sir, be a man!
    Think every bearded fellow that's but yoked
    May draw with you. There's millions now alive
    That nightly lie in those unproper beds
    Which they dare swear peculiar. Your case is better.
    O, 'tis the spite of hell, the fiend's arch-mock,
    To lip a wanton in a secure couch
    And to suppose her chaste! No, let me know,
    And knowing what I am, I know what she shall be.

OTHELLO O, thou art wise, 'tis certain.

IAGO Stand you awhile apart.
    Confine yourself but in a patient list.
    Whilst you were here o'erwhelmèd with your grief—
    A passion most unsuiting such a man—
    Cassio came hither. I shifted him away
    And laid good 'scuses upon your ecstasy,
    Bade him anon return and here speak with me,
    The which he promised. Do but encave yourself,
    And mark the fleers, the gibes, and notable scorns
    That dwell in every region of his face.
    For I will make him tell the tale anew—
    Where, how, how oft, how long ago, and when
    He hath, and is again to cope your wife.
    I say but mark his gesture. Marry, patience,
    Or I shall say you're all in all in spleen,
    And nothing of a man.

OTHELLO Dost thou hear, Iago?
    I will be found most cunning in my patience,
    But (dost thou hear?) most bloody.

IAGO   That's not amiss.
    But yet keep time in all. Will you withdraw?
                             [*Othello withdraws.*]
    Now will I question Cassio of Bianca,
    A huswife that by selling her desires
    Buys herself bread and clothes. It is a creature
    That dotes on Cassio—as 'tis the strumpet's plague
    To beguile many and be beguiled by one.
    He, when he hears of her, cannot restrain
    From the excess of laughter. Here he comes.

                Enter Cassio.

As he shall smile, Othello shall go mad,
And his unbookish jealousy must construe
Poor Cassio's smiles, gestures, and light behaviors
Quite in the wrong.—How do you, lieutenant? 115

CASSIO
The worser that you give me the addition
Whose want even kills me.

IAGO
Ply Desdemona well, and you are sure on 't.
Now, if this suit lay in Bianco's power,
How quickly should you speed! 120

CASSIO, [*laughing*]   Alas, poor caitiff!

OTHELLO Look, how he laughs already!

IAGO I never knew woman love man so.

CASSIO
Alas, poor rogue! I think, i' faith, she loves me.

OTHELLO
Now he denies it faintly, and laughs it out. 125

IAGO
Do you hear, Cassio?

OTHELLO   Now he importunes him
To tell it o'er. Go to, well said, well said.

IAGO
She gives it out that you shall marry her.
Do you intend it? 130

CASSIO   Ha, ha, ha!

OTHELLO
Do you triumph, Roman? Do you triumph?

CASSIO I marry her? What, a customer? Prithee, bear some charity to
my wit! Do not think it so unwholesome. Ha, ha, ha!

OTHELLO So, so, so, so. They laugh that wins. 135

IAGO
Faith, the cry goes that you shall marry her.

CASSIO Prithee say true.

IAGO I am a very villain else.

OTHELLO Have you scored me? Well.

CASSIO This is the monkey's own giving out. She is persuaded I will 140
marry her, out of her own love and flattery, not out of my promise.

OTHELLO
Iago beckons me. Now he begins the story.

CASSIO She was here even now. She haunts me in every place. I was
the other day talking on the sea-bank with certain Venetians, and

thither comes the bauble. By this hand, she falls thus about my neck!

OTHELLO Crying "O dear Cassio," as it were; his gesture imports it.

CASSIO So hangs, and lolls, and weeps upon me; so shakes, and pulls me. Ha, ha, ha!

OTHELLO Now he tells how she plucked him to my chamber.—O, I see that nose of yours, but not that dog I shall throw it to.

CASSIO Well, I must leave her company.

IAGO Before me, look, where she comes.

Enter Bianca.

CASSIO 'Tis such another fitchew—marry a perfumed one!—What do you mean by this haunting of me?

BIANCA Let the devil and his dam haunt you! What did you mean by that same handkerchief you gave me even now? I was a fine fool to take it. I must take out the work? A likely piece of work, that you should find it in your chamber, and not know who left it there! This is some minx's token, and I must take out the work? There, give it your hobbyhorse. Wheresoever you had it, I'll take out no work on 't.

CASSIO
How now, my sweet Bianca! How now? How now?

OTHELLO
By heaven, that should be my handkerchief!

BIANCA If you'll come to supper tonight, you may. If you will not, come when you are next prepared for. *She exits.*

IAGO After her, after her!

CASSIO Faith, I must. She'll rail in the street else.

IAGO Will you sup there?

CASSIO Faith, I intend so.

IAGO Well, I may chance to see you, for I would very fain speak with you.

CASSIO Prithee, come. Will you?

IAGO Go to; say no more. *Cassio exits.*

OTHELLO, [*coming forward*] How shall I murder him, Iago?

IAGO Did you perceive how he laughed at his vice?

OTHELLO O Iago!

IAGO And did you see the handkerchief?

OTHELLO Was that mine?

[IAGO Yours by this hand! And to see how he prizes the foolish woman your wife! She gave it him, and he hath given it his whore.]

OTHELLO I would have him nine years a-killing! A fine woman, a fair woman, a sweet woman!

IAGO Nay, you must forget that.

OTHELLO Ay, let her rot and perish and be damned tonight, for she shall not live. No, my heart is turned to stone. I strike it, and it hurts my hand. O, the world hath not a sweeter creature! She might lie by an emperor's side and command him tasks.

IAGO Nay, that's not your way.

OTHELLO Hang her, I do but say what she is! So delicate with her needle, an admirable musician—O, she will sing the savageness out of a bear! Of so high and plenteous wit and invention!

IAGO She's the worse for all this.

OTHELLO O, a thousand thousand times!—And then, of so gentle a condition!

IAGO Ay, too gentle.

OTHELLO Nay, that's certain. But yet the pity of it, Iago! O Iago, the pity of it, Iago!

IAGO If you are so fond over her iniquity, give her patent to offend, for if it touch not you, it comes near nobody.

OTHELLO I will chop her into messes! Cuckold me?

IAGO O, 'tis foul in her.

OTHELLO With mine officer!

IAGO That's fouler.

OTHELLO Get me some poison, Iago; this night. I'll not expostulate with her, lest her body and beauty unprovide my mind again. This night, Iago.

IAGO Do it not with poison. Strangle her in her bed, even the bed she hath contaminated.

OTHELLO Good, good. The justice of it pleases. Very good.

IAGO And for Cassio, let me be his undertaker. You shall hear more by midnight.

OTHELLO
Excellent good. *[A trumpet sounds.]*
What trumpet is that same?

IAGO I warrant something from Venice.

Enter Lodovico, Desdemona, and Attendants.

'Tis Lodovico. This comes from the Duke.
See, your wife is with him.

LODOVICO God save you, worthy general.

OTHELLO With all my heart, sir.

LODOVICO
　The Duke and Senators of Venice greet you.
　　　　　　　　　　　　[*He hands Othello a paper.*]

OTHELLO
　I kiss the instrument of their pleasures.

DESDEMONA
　And what's the news, good cousin Lodovico?

IAGO
　I am very glad to see you, signior
　Welcome to Cyprus.　　　　　　　　　　　　　　　　225

LODOVICO
　I thank you. How does Lieutenant Cassio?

IAGO Lives, sir.

DESDEMONA
　Cousin, there's fall'n between him and my lord
　An unkind breach, but you shall make all well.

OTHELLO Are you sure of that?　　　　　　　　　　　230

DESDEMONA My lord?

OTHELLO, [*reading*] "This fail you not to do, as you will"—

LODOVICO
　He did not call; he's busy in the paper.
　Is there division 'twixt my lord and Cassio?

DESDEMONA
　A most unhappy one. I would do much　　　　　　235
　To atone them, for the love I bear to Cassio.

OTHELLO Fire and brimstone!

DESDEMONA My lord?

OTHELLO Are you wise?

DESDEMONA What, is he angry?　　　　　　　　　　240

LODOVICO　　　　　　　　　May be the letter moved him.
　For, as I think, they do command him home,
　Deputing Cassio in his government.

DESDEMONA By my troth, I am glad on 't.

OTHELLO Indeed?　　　　　　　　　　　　　　　245

DESDEMONA My lord?

OTHELLO I am glad to see you mad.

DESDEMONA Why, sweet Othello!

OTHELLO, [*striking her*] Devil!

DESDEMONA I have not deserved this.　　　　　　　250

LODOVICO
　My lord, this would not be believed in Venice,

>   Though I should swear I saw 't. 'Tis very much.
>   Make her amends. She weeps.
>
> OTHELLO   O devil, devil!
>   If that the earth could teem with woman's tears,
>   Each drop she falls would prove a crocodile.
>   Out of my sight!
>
> DESDEMONA   I will not stay to offend you.
>   [*She begins to leave.*]
>
> LODOVICO Truly, an obedient lady.
>   I do beseech your Lordship call her back.
>
> OTHELLO Mistress!
>
> DESDEMONA, [*turning back*] My lord?
>
> OTHELLO What would you with her, sir?
>
> LODOVICO Who, I, my lord?
>
> OTHELLO
>   Ay, you did wish that I would make her turn.
>   Sir, she can turn, and turn, and yet go on,
>   And turn again. And she can weep, sir, weep.
>   And she's obedient, as you say, obedient.
>   Very obedient.—Proceed you in your tears.—
>   Concerning this, sir—O well-painted passion!—
>   I am commanded home.—Get you away.
>   I'll send for you anon.—Sir, I obey the mandate
>   And will return to Venice.—Hence, avaunt!
>   [*Desdemona exits.*]
>   Cassio shall have my place. And, sir, tonight
>   I do entreat that we may sup together.
>   You are welcome, sir, to Cyprus. Goats and monkeys!   *He exits.*
>
> LODOVICO
>   Is this the noble Moor whom our full senate
>   Call all in all sufficient? Is this the nature
>   Whom passion could not shake, whose solid virtue
>   The shot of accident, nor dart of chance
>   Could neither graze nor pierce?
>
> IAGO   He is much changed.
>
> LODOVICO
>   Are his wits safe? Is he not light of brain?
>
> IAGO
>   He's that he is. I may not breathe my censure
>   What he might be. If what he might he is not,
>   I would to heaven he were.
>
> LODOVICO   What? strike his wife?
>
> IAGO
>   'Faith, that was not so well. Yet would I knew
>   That stroke would prove the worst.

255

260

265

270

275

280

285

LODOVICO Is it his use? 290
  Or did the letters work upon his blood
  And new-create this fault?

IAGO Alas, alas!
  It is not honesty in me to speak
  What I have seen and known. You shall observe him, 295
  And his own courses will denote him so
  That I may save my speech. Do but go after
  And mark how he continues.

LODOVICO
  I am sorry that I am deceived in him.

They exit.

Scene 2

Enter Othello and Emilia.

OTHELLO You have seen nothing then?

EMILIA
  Nor ever heard, nor ever did suspect.

OTHELLO
  Yes, you have seen Cassio and she together.

EMILIA
  But then I saw no harm, and then I heard
  Each syllable that breath made up between them. 5

OTHELLO
  What, did they never whisper?

EMILIA Never, my lord.

OTHELLO Nor send you out o' th' way?

EMILIA Never.

OTHELLO
  To fetch her fan, her gloves, her mask, nor nothing? 10

EMILIA Never, my lord.

OTHELLO That's strange.

EMILIA
  I durst, my lord, to wager she is honest,
  Lay down my soul at stake. If you think other,
  Remove your thought. It doth abuse your bosom. 15
  If any wretch have put this in your head,
  Let heaven requite it with the serpent's curse,
  For, if she be not honest, chaste, and true,
  There's no man happy. The purest of their wives
  Is foul as slander. 20

OTHELLO Bid her come hither. Go.

Emilia exits.

She says enough. Yet she's a simple bawd
That cannot say as much. This is a subtle whore,
A closet lock and key of villanous secrets.
And yet she'll kneel and pray. I have seen her do 't. 25

Enter Desdemona with Emilia.

DESDEMONA My lord, what is your will?

OTHELLO
Pray you, chuck, come hither.

DESDEMONA   What is your pleasure?

OTHELLO
Let me see your eyes. Look in my face.

DESDEMONA What horrible fancy's this? 30

OTHELLO, [*to Emilia*] Some of your function, mistress.
Leave procreants alone, and shut the door.
Cough, or cry "hem," if anybody come.
Your mystery, your mystery! Nay, dispatch.

Emilia exits.

DESDEMONA, [*kneeling*]
Upon my knees, what doth your speech import? 35
I understand a fury in your words,
But not the words.

OTHELLO Why, what art thou?

DESDEMONA
Your wife, my lord; your true and loyal wife.

OTHELLO Come, swear it. Damn thyself, 40
Lest, being like one of heaven, the devils themselves
Should fear to seize thee. Therefore be double damned.
Swear thou art honest.

DESDEMONA   Heaven doth truly know it.

OTHELLO
Heaven truly knows that thou art false as hell. 45

DESDEMONA, [*standing*]
To whom, my lord? With whom? How am I false?

OTHELLO
O Desdemona, away, away, away!

DESDEMONA
Alas the heavy day, why do you weep?
Am I the motive of these tears, my lord?
If haply you my father do suspect 50
An instrument of this your calling back,
Lay not your blame on me. If you have lost him,
Why, I have lost him too.

OTHELLO   Had it pleased heaven
To try me with affliction, had they rained 55

All kinds of sores and shames on my bare head.
　　Steeped me in poverty to the very lips,
　　Given to captivity me and my utmost hopes,
　　I should have found in some place of my soul
　　A drop of patience. But, alas, to make me 60
　　A fixed figure for the time of scorn
　　To point his slow unmoving finger at—
　　Yet could I bear that too, well, very well.
　　But there, where I have garnered up my heart,
　　Where either I must live, or bear no life, 65
　　The fountain from the which my current runs
　　Or else dries up—to be discarded thence,
　　Or keep it as a cistern for foul toads
　　To knot and gender in—turn thy complexion there,
　　Patience, thou young and rose-lipped cherubin, 70
　　Ay, there look grim as hell.

DESDEMONA
　　I hope my noble lord esteems me honest.

OTHELLO
　　O, ay; as summer flies are in the shambles,
　　That quicken even with blowing! O thou weed,
　　Who art so lovely fair, and smell'st so sweet 75
　　That the sense aches at thee, would thou hadst ne'er been born!

DESDEMONA
　　Alas, what ignorant sin have I committed?

OTHELLO
　　Was this fair paper, this most goodly book,
　　Made to write "whore" upon? What committed?
　　[Committed? O thou public commoner, 80
　　I should make very forges of my cheeks
　　That would to cinders burn up modesty,
　　Did I but speak thy deeds. What committed?]
　　Heaven stops the nose at it and the moon winks;
　　The bawdy wind that kisses all it meets 85
　　Is hushed within the hollow mine of earth
　　And will not hear 't. What committed?
　　Impudent strumpet!

DESDEMONA By heaven, you do me wrong.

OTHELLO Are you not a strumpet? 90

DESDEMONA No, as I am a Christian!
　　If to preserve this vessel for my lord
　　From any other foul unlawful touch
　　Be not to be a strumpet, I am none.

OTHELLO What, not a whore? 95

DESDEMONA No, as I shall be saved.

OTHELLO Is 't possible?

DESDEMONA
　O, heaven forgive us!

OTHELLO　　　　　　　I cry you mercy, then.
　I took you for that cunning whore of Venice
　That married with Othello.—You, mistress,

Enter Emilia.

　That have the office opposite to Saint Peter
　And keep the gate of hell—you, you, ay, you!
　We have done our course. There's money for your pains.
　　　　　　　　　　　　　[*He gives her money.*]
　I pray you, turn the key and keep our counsel.
　　　　　　　　　　　　　　　He exits.

EMILIA
　Alas, what does this gentleman conceive?
　How do you, madam? How do you, my good lady?

DESDEMONA Faith, half asleep.

EMILIA
　Good madam, what's the matter with my lord?

DESDEMONA With who?

EMILIA Why, with my lord, madam.

[**DESDEMONA** Who is thy lord?

EMILIA He that is yours, sweet lady.]

DESDEMONA
　I have none. Do not talk to me, Emilia.
　I cannot weep, nor answers have I none
　But what should go by water. Prithee, tonight
　Lay on my bed my wedding sheets. Remember.
　And call thy husband hither.

EMILIA Here's a change indeed!　　　*She exits.*

DESDEMONA
　'Tis meet I should be used so, very meet.
　How have I been behaved that he might stick
　The small'st opinion on my least misuse?

Enter Iago and Emilia.

IAGO
　What is your pleasure, madam? How is 't with you?

DESDEMONA
　I cannot tell. Those that do teach young babes
　Do it with gentle means and easy tasks.
　He might have chid me so, for, in good faith,
　I am a child to chiding.

IAGO What's the matter, lady?

EMILIA
　Alas, Iago, my lord hath so bewhored her,

    Thrown such despite and heavy terms upon her 130
    As true hearts cannot bear.

DESDEMONA Am I that name, Iago?

IAGO   What name, fair lady?

DESDEMONA
    Such as she says my lord did say I was.

EMILIA
    He called her "whore." A beggar in his drink 135
    Could not have laid such terms upon his callet.

IAGO Why did he so?

DESDEMONA
    I do not know. I am sure I am none such.

IAGO
    Do not weep, do not weep! Alas the day!

EMILIA
    Hath she forsook so many noble matches, 140
    Her father and her country and her friends,
    To be called "whore"? Would it not make one weep?

DESDEMONA It is my wretched fortune.

IAGO
    Beshrew him for 't! How comes this trick upon him?

DESDEMONA Nay, heaven doth know. 145

EMILIA
    I will be hanged if some eternal villain,
    Some busy and insinuating rogue,
    Some cogging, cozening slave, to get some office,
    Have not devised this slander. I'll be hanged else.

IAGO
    Fie, there is no such man. It is impossible. 150

DESDEMONA
    If any such there be, heaven pardon him.

EMILIA
    A halter pardon him, and hell gnaw his bones!
    Why should he call her "whore"? Who keeps her company?
    What place? What time? What form? What likelihood?
    The Moor's abused by some most villanous knave, 155
    Some base notorious knave, some scurvy fellow.
    O heaven, that such companions thou'dst unfold,
    And put in every honest hand a whip
    To lash the rascals naked through the world,
    Even from the east to th' west! 160

IAGO   Speak within door.

EMILIA
    O, fie upon them! Some such squire he was

That turned your wit the seamy side without
And made you to suspect me with the Moor.

IAGO
You are a fool. Go to.

DESDEMONA   Alas, Iago,
What shall I do to win my lord again?
Good friend, go to him. For, by this light of heaven,
I know not how I lost him. [*She kneels.*] [Here I kneel.
If e'er my will did trespass 'gainst his love,
Either in discourse of thought or actual deed,
Or that mine eyes, mine ears, or any sense,
Delighted them in any other form,
Or that I do not yet, and ever did,
And ever will—though he do shake me off
To beggarly divorcement—love him dearly,
Comfort forswear me! [*She stands.*] Unkindness may do much,
And his unkindness may defeat my life,
But never taint my love. I cannot say "whore"—
It does abhor me now I speak the word.
To do the act that might the addition earn,
Not the world's mass of vanity could make me.]

IAGO
I pray you, be content. 'Tis but his humor.
The business of the state does him offense,
And he does chide with you.

DESDEMONA
If 'twere no other—

IAGO   'Tis but so, I warrant.

Trumpets sound.

Hark, how these instruments summon to supper.
The messengers of Venice stay the meat.
Go in and weep not. All things shall be well.

Desdemona and Emilia exit.

Enter Roderigo.

How now, Roderigo?

RODERIGO   I do not find
That thou deal'st justly with me.

IAGO What in the contrary?

RODERIGO Every day thou daff'st me with some device, Iago, and rather, as it seems to me now, keep'st from me all conveniency than suppliest me with the least advantage of hope. I will indeed no longer endure it. Nor am I yet persuaded to put up in peace what already I have foolishly suffered.

IAGO Will you hear me, Roderigo?

RODERIGO Faith, I have heard too much, for your words and performances are no kin together.

IAGO You charge me most unjustly.

RODERIGO With naught but truth. I have wasted myself out of my means. The jewels you have had from me to deliver to Desdemona would half have corrupted a votaress. You have told me she hath received them, and returned me expectations and comforts of sudden respect and acquaintance, but I find none.

IAGO Well, go to! Very well.

RODERIGO "Very well." "Go to!" I cannot go to, man, nor 'tis not very well! By this hand, I say 'tis very scurvy, and begin to find myself fopped in it.

IAGO Very well.

RODERIGO I tell you 'tis not very well! I will make myself known to Desdemona. If she will return me my jewels, I will give over my suit and repent my unlawful solicitation. If not, assure yourself I will seek satisfaction of you.

IAGO You have said now.

RODERIGO Ay, and said nothing but what I protest intendment of doing.

IAGO Why, now I see there's mettle in thee, and even from this instant to build on thee a better opinion than ever before. Give me thy hand, Roderigo. Thou hast taken against me a most just exception, but yet, I protest, I have dealt most directly in thy affair.

RODERIGO It hath not appeared.

IAGO I grant indeed it hath not appeared, and your suspicion is not without wit and judgment. But, Roderigo, if thou hast that in thee indeed, which I have greater reason to believe now than ever—I mean purpose, courage, and valour—this night show it. If thou the next night following enjoy not Desdemona, take me from this world with treachery and devise engines for my life.

RODERIGO Well, what is it? Is it within reason and compass?

IAGO Sir, there is especial commission come from Venice to depute Cassio in Othello's place.

RODERIGO Is that true? Why, then Othello and Desdemona return again to Venice.

IAGO O, no. He goes into Mauritania and takes away with him the fair Desdemona, unless his abode be lingered here by some accident—wherein none can be so determinate as the removing of Cassio.

RODERIGO How do you mean, removing of him?

IAGO Why, by making him uncapable of Othello's place: knocking out his brains.

RODERIGO And that you would have me to do?

IAGO Ay, if you dare do yourself a profit and a right. He sups tonight with a harlotry, and thither will I go to him. He knows not yet of his honorable fortune. If you will watch his going thence (which I will fashion to fall out between twelve and one), you may take him at your pleasure. I will be near to second your attempt, and he shall fall between us. Come, stand not amazed at it, but go along with me. I will show you such a necessity in his death that you shall think yourself bound to put it on him. It is now high suppertime, and the night grows to waste. About it!

RODERIGO I will hear further reason for this.

IAGO And you shall be satisfied. *They exit.*

Scene 3

Enter Othello, Lodovico, Desdemona, Emilia, and Attendants.

LODOVICO
I do beseech you, sir, trouble yourself no further.

OTHELLO
O, pardon me, 'twill do me good to walk.

LODOVICO
Madam, good night. I humbly thank your Ladyship.

DESDEMONA Your Honor is most welcome.

OTHELLO
Will you walk, sir?—O, Desdemona—

DESDEMONA   My lord?

OTHELLO Get you to bed on th' instant. I will be returned forthwith.
Dismiss your attendant there. Look 't be done.

DESDEMONA I will, my lord.   *All but Desdemona and Emilia exit.*

EMILIA
How goes it now? He looks gentler than he did.

DESDEMONA
He says he will return incontinent,
He hath commanded me to go to bed,
And bade me to dismiss you.

EMILIA   Dismiss me?

DESDEMONA
It was his bidding. Therefore, good Emilia,
Give me my nightly wearing, and adieu.
We must not now displease him.

EMILIA I would you had never seen him.

DESDEMONA
So would not I. My love doth so approve him
That even his stubbornness, his checks, his frowns—
Prithee, unpin me—have grace and favor in them.

EMILIA
I have laid those sheets you bade me on the bed.

DESDEMONA
All's one. Good faith, how foolish are our minds!
If I do die before thee, prithee, shroud me
In one of those same sheets. 25

EMILIA Come, come you talk!

DESDEMONA
My mother had a maid called Barbary.
She was in love, and he she loved proved mad
And did forsake her. She had a song of willow,
An old thing 'twas, but it expressed her fortune, 30
And she died singing it. That song tonight
Will not go from my mind. [I have much to do,
But to go hang my head all at one side
And sing it like poor Barbary. Prithee, dispatch.

EMILIA Shall I go fetch your nightgown? 35

DESDEMONA No, unpin me here.
This Lodovico is a proper man.

EMILIA A very handsome man.

DESDEMONA He speaks well.

EMILIA I know a lady in Venice would have walked barefoot to 40
Palestine for a touch of his nether lip.

DESDEMONA, [*singing*]
The poor soul sat sighing by a sycamore tree,
 Sing all a green willow.
Her hand on her bosom, her head on her knee,
 Sing willow, willow, willow. 45
The fresh streams ran by her, and murmured her moans,
 Sing willow, willow, willow;
Her salt tears fell from her, and softened the stones—
Lay by these.
 Sing willow, willow, willow. 50
Prithee hie thee! He'll come anon.
 Sing all a green willow must be my garland.
 Let nobody blame him, his scorn I approve.
Nay, that's not next.] Hark, who is 't that knocks?

EMILIA It's the wind. 55

DESDEMONA
[*I called my love false love, but what said he then?*
 Sing willow, willow, willow.
If I court more women, you'll couch with more men.]—
So, get thee gone. Good night. Mine eyes do itch;
Doth that bode weeping? 60

EMILIA 'Tis neither here nor there.

[DESDEMONA
	I have heard it said so. O, these men, these men!
	Dost thou in conscience think—tell me, Emilia—
	That there be women do abuse their husbands
	In such gross kind? 65

EMILIA   There be some such, no question.]

DESDEMONA
	Wouldst thou do such a deed for all the world?

EMILIA
	Why, would not you?

DESDEMONA   No, by this heavenly light!

EMILIA
	Nor I neither by this heavenly light. 70
	I might do't as well i' th' dark.

DESDEMONA
	Wouldst thou do such a deed for all the world?

EMILIA The world's a huge thing. It is a great price for a small vice.

DESDEMONA In troth, I think thou wouldst not.

EMILIA In troth, I think I should, and undo 't when I had done it. 75
	Marry, I would not do such a thing for a joint ring, nor for measures of lawn, nor for gowns, petticoats, nor caps, nor any petty exhibition. But for the whole world—'Uds pity! Who would not make her husband a cuckold to make him a monarch? I should venture purgatory for 't. 80

DESDEMONA Beshrew me, if I would do such a wrong for the whole world!

EMILIA Why the wrong is but a wrong i' th' world; and, having the world for your labor, tis a wrong in your own world, and you might quickly make it right. 85

DESDEMONA I do not think there is any such woman.

EMILIA Yes, a dozen; and as many to th' vantage as would store the world they played for.
	[But I do think it is their husbands' faults
	If wives do fall. Say that they slack their duties, 90
	And pour our treasures into foreign laps;
	Or else break out in peevish jealousies,
	Throwing restraint upon us. Or say they strike us,
	Or scant our former having in despite.
	Why, we have galls, and though we have some grace, 95
	Yet have we some revenge. Let husbands know
	Their wives have sense like them. They see, and smell,
	And have their palates both for sweet and sour,
	As husbands have. What is it that they do
	When they change us for others? Is it sport? 100
	I think it is. And doth affection breed it?
	I think it doth. Is 't frailty that thus errs?

It is so too. And have not we affections,
Desires for sport, and frailty, as men have?
Then let them use us well. Else let them know, 105
The ills we do, their ills instruct us so.]

DESDEMONA
Good night, good night. God me such uses send,
Not to pick bad from bad, but by bad mend. *They exit.*

Act 5

Scene 1

Enter Iago and Roderigo

IAGO
Here, stand behind this bulk. Straight will he come.
Wear thy good rapier bare, and put it home.
Quick, quick! Fear nothing. I'll be at thy elbow.
It makes us, or it mars us—think on that,
And fix most firm thy resolution. 5

RODERIGO
Be near at hand. I may miscarry in 't.

IAGO
Here, at thy hand. Be bold, and take thy stand.
[*He moves aside.*]

RODERIGO
I have no great devotion to the deed,
And yet he hath given me satisfying reasons.
'Tis but a man gone. Forth, my sword! He dies. 10
[*He draws his sword.*]

IAGO, [*aside*]
I have rubbed this young quat almost to the sense,
And he grows angry. Now, whether he kill Cassio,
Or Cassio him, or each do kill the other,
Every way makes my gain. Live Roderigo,
He calls me to a restitution large 15
Of gold and jewels that I bobbed from him
As gifts to Desdemona.
It must not be. If Cassio do remain,
He hath a daily beauty in his life
That makes me ugly. And, besides, the Moor 20
May unfold me to him. There stand I in much peril.
No, he must die. Be 't so. I hear him coming.

Enter Cassio.

RODERIGO
I know his gait. 'Tis he!—Villain, thou diest!
He thrusts at Cassio.

CASSIO
That thrust had been mine enemy indeed
But that my coat is better than thou know'st. 25
I will make proof of thine.
[*He draws, and stabs Roderigo.*]

RODERIGO   O, I am slain!
[*Roderigo falls.*]
Iago stabs Cassio in the leg, and exits.

CASSIO
I am maimed forever. Help, ho! Murder! murder!

Enter Othello.

OTHELLO
The voice of Cassio! Iago keeps his word.

RODERIGO O, villain that I am! 30

OTHELLO, [*aside*] It is even so.

CASSIO O, help ho! Light! A surgeon!

OTHELLO, [*aside*]
'Tis he! O brave Iago, honest and just,
That hast such noble sense of thy friend's wrong!
Thou teachest me.—Minion, your dear lies dead, 35
And your unblest fate hies. Strumpet, I come.
Forth of my heart those charms, thine eyes, are blotted.
Thy bed, lust-stained, shall with lust's blood be spotted.
Othello exits.

Enter Lodovico and Gratiano.

CASSIO
What, ho! No watch? No passage? Murder, murder!

GRATIANO
'Tis some mischance. The voice is very direful. 40

CASSIO O, help!

LODOVICO Hark!

RODERIGO O wretched villain!

LODOVICO
Two or three groan. 'Tis a heavy night.
These may be counterfeits. Let's think 't unsafe 45
To come in to the cry without more help.

RODERIGO
Nobody come? Then shall I bleed to death.

Enter Iago with a light.

LODOVICO Hark!

GRATIANO
Here's one comes in his shirt, with light and weapons.

IAGO
Who's there? Whose noise is this that cries on murder? 50

LODOVICO
We do not know.

IAGO Did not you hear a cry?

CASSIO Here, here! For heaven's sake, help me!

IAGO What's the matter?

GRATIANO, [*to Lodovico*]
This is Othello's ancient, as I take it. 55

LODOVICO
  The same indeed; a very valiant fellow.
IAGO, [*to Cassio*]
  What are you here that cry so grievously?
CASSIO
  Iago? O, I am spoiled, undone by villains.
  Give me some help!
IAGO
  O me, lieutenant! What villains have done this? 60
CASSIO
  I think that one of them is hereabout
  And cannot make away.
IAGO   O treacherous villains!
  [*To Lodovico and Gratiano*] What are you there?
  Come in, and give some help. 65
RODERIGO O, help me here!
CASSIO
  That's one of them.
IAGO, [*to Roderigo*] O murd'rous slave! O villain!
                              He stabs Roderigo.
RODERIGO
  O damned Iago! O inhuman dog!
IAGO
  Kill men i' th' dark!—Where be these bloody thieves?— 70
  How silent is this town! Ho, murder, murder!—
  What may you be? Are you of good or evil?
LODOVICO
  As you shall prove us, praise us.
IAGO   Signior Lodovico?
LODOVICO He, sir. 75
IAGO
  I cry you mercy. Here's Cassio hurt by villains.
GRATIANO Cassio?
IAGO
  How is 't, brother?
CASSIO   My leg is cut in two.
IAGO Marry, heaven forbid! 80
  Light, gentlemen. I'll bind it with my shirt.
                              Enter Bianca.
BIANCA
  What is the matter, ho? Who is 't that cried?

IAGO
Who is 't that cried?

BIANCA   O, my dear Cassio,
My sweet Cassio! O, Cassio, Cassio, Cassio!   85

IAGO
O notable strumpet! Cassio, may you suspect
Who they should be that have thus many led you?

CASSIO No.

GRATIANO
I am to find you thus; I have been to seek you.

[IAGO
Lend me a garter. So.—O, for a chair   90
To bear him easily hence!]

BIANCA
Alas, he faints! O Cassio, Cassio, Cassio!

IAGO
Gentlemen all, I do suspect this trash
To be a party in this injury.—
Patience awhile, good Cassio.—Come, come;   95
Lend me a light. [*Peering at Roderigo.*] Know we this face or no?
Alas my friend and my dear countryman
Roderigo? No! Yes, sure. O heaven, Roderigo!

GRATIANO What, of Venice?

IAGO Even he, sir. Did you know him?   100

GRATIANO Know him? Ay.

IAGO
Signior Gratiano? I cry your gentle pardon.
These bloody accidents must excuse my manners
That so neglected you.

GRATIANO   I am glad to see you.   105

IAGO
How do you, Cassio?—O, a chair, a chair!

GRATIANO Roderigo?

IAGO
He, he 'tis he! [*A chair is brought in.*] O, that's well said; the chair.—
Some good man bear him carefully from hence.   110
I'll fetch the General's surgeon.—For you, mistress,
Save you your labor.—He that lies slain here, Cassio,
Was my dear friend. What malice was between you?

CASSIO
None in the world; nor do I know the man.

IAGO, [*to Bianca*]
What, look you pale?—O, bear him out o' the air.   115

[*Cassio, in the chair, and Roderigo are carried off.*]
[*To Gratiano and Lodovico.*] Stay you, good gentlemen.—Look
you pale, mistress?—
 Do you perceive the gastness of her eye?—
 Nay, if you stare, we shall hear more anon.—
 Behold her well. I pray you, look upon her.
 Do you see, gentlemen? Nay, guiltiness will speak
 Though tongues were out of use.

Enter Emilia.

EMILIA
 Alas, what's the matter? What's the matter, husband?

IAGO
 Cassio hath here been set on in the dark
 By Roderigo and fellows that are scaped.
 He's almost slain, and Roderigo dead.

EMILIA
 Alas, good gentleman! Alas, good Cassio!

IAGO
 This is the fruit of whoring. Prithee, Emilia,
 Go know of Cassio where he supped tonight.
 [*To Bianca.*] What, do you shake at that?

BIANCA
 He supped at my house; but I therefore shake not.

IAGO
 O, did he so? I charge you, go with me.

EMILIA O fie upon thee, strumpet!

BIANCA
 I am no strumpet; but of life as honest
 As you that thus abuse me.

EMILIA As I? Faugh! Fie upon thee!

IAGO
 Kind gentlemen, let's go see poor Cassio dressed.—
 Come, mistress, you must tell's another tale.—
 Emilia run you to the citadel
 And tell my lord and lady what hath happed.—
 Will you go on afore? [*Aside.*] This is the night
 That either makes me or fordoes me quite.
  They exit in different directions.

Scene 2

Enter Othello with a light, and Desdemona in her bed.

OTHELLO
 It is the cause, it is the cause, my soul,
 Let me not name it to you, you chaste stars.
 It is the cause. Yet I'll not shed her blood,

Nor scar that whiter skin of hers than snow,
And smooth as monumental alabaster. 5
Yet she must die, else she'll betray more men.
Put out the light, and then put out the light.
If I quench thee, thou flaming minister,
I can again thy former light restore
Should I repent me. But once put out thy light, 10
Thou cunning'st pattern of excelling nature,
I know not where is that Promethean heat
That can thy light relume. When I have plucked the rose,
I cannot give it vital growth again.
It must needs wither. I'll smell it on the tree 15
O balmy breath, that dost almost persuade
Justice to break her sword! [*He kisses her.*] One more, one more.
Be thus when thou art dead, and I will kill thee
And love thee after. One more, and this the last.

[*He kisses her.*]

So sweet was ne'er so fatal. I must weep, 20
But they are cruel tears. This sorrow's heavenly:
It strikes where it doth love. She wakes.

DESDEMONA
Who's there? Othello?

OTHELLO   Ay. Desdemona.

DESDEMONA Will you come to bed, my lord? 25

OTHELLO
Have you prayed tonight, Desdemona?

DESDEMONA Ay, my lord.

OTHELLO
If you bethink yourself of any crime
Unreconciled as yet to heaven and grace,
Solicit for it straight. 30

DESDEMONA   Alack, my lord,
What do you mean by that?

OTHELLO
Well, do it, and be brief; I will walk by.
I would not kill thy unprepared spirit.
No, heaven forfend! I would not kill thy soul. 35

DESDEMONA Talk you of killing?

OTHELLO
Ay, I do.

DESDEMONA Then heaven have mercy on me.

OTHELLO Amen, with all my heart!

DESDEMONA
If you say so, I hope you will not kill me. 40

OTHELLO Humh.

DESDEMONA
    And yet I fear you, for you're fatal then
    When your eyes roll so. Why I should fear I know not,
    Since guiltiness I know not; but yet I feel I fear.

OTHELLO
    Think on thy sins.   45

DESDEMONA   They are loves I bear to you.

OTHELLO Ay, and for that thou diest.

DESDEMONA
    That death's unnatural that kills for loving.
    Alas, why gnaw you so your nether lip?
    Some bloody passion shakes your very frame.   50
    These are portents, but yet I hope, I hope,
    They do not point on me.

OTHELLO   Peace, and be still.

DESDEMONA
    I will so. What's the matter?

OTHELLO   That handkerchief   55
    Which I so loved and gave thee, thou gav'st to Cassio.

DESDEMONA
    No, by my life and soul! Send for the man
    And ask him.

OTHELLO
    Sweet soul, take heed, take heed of perjury.
    Thou art on thy deathbed.   60

DESDEMONA
    Ay, but not yet to die.

OTHELLO   Yes, presently.
    Therefore confess thee freely of thy sin.
    For to deny each article with oath
    Cannot remove nor choke the strong conception   65
    That I do groan withal. Thou art to die.

DESDEMONA
    Then Lord have mercy on me!

OTHELLO   I say "Amen."

DESDEMONA
    And have you mercy too. I never did
    Offend you in my life, never loved Cassio   70
    But with such general warranty of heaven
    As I might love. I never gave him token.

OTHELLO
    By heaven, I saw my handkerchief in 's hand!
    O perjured woman, thou dost stone my heart
    And mak'st me call what I intend to do   75
    A murder, which I thought a sacrifice!

I saw the handkerchief!

DESDEMONA   He found it, then.
I never gave it him. Send for him hither.
Let him confess a truth.   80

OTHELLO   He hath confessed.

DESDEMONA What, my lord?

OTHELLO
That he hath used thee.

DESDEMONA   How? Unlawfully?

OTHELLO Ay.   85

DESDEMONA
He will not say so.

OTHELLO   No. His mouth is stopped.
Honest Iago hath ta'en order for 't.

DESDEMONA
O! my fear interprets. What, is he dead?

OTHELLO
Had all his hairs been lives, my great revenge   90
Had stomach for them all.

DESDEMONA
Alas, he is betrayed and I undone.   [*She weeps.*]

OTHELLO
Out, strumpet! Weep'st thou for him to my face?

DESDEMONA
O banish me, my lord, but kill me not!

OTHELLO Down, strumpet!   95

DESDEMONA
Kill me tomorrow, let me live tonight.

OTHELLO Nay, if you strive—

DESDEMONA
But half an hour!

[OTHELLO   Being done, there is no pause.]

DESDEMONA
But while I say one prayer!   100

OTHELLO   It is too late.
                                    He smothers her.

EMILIA, [*within*]
My lord, my lord? What, ho! My lord, my lord!

OTHELLO
What noise is this?—Not dead? Not yet quite dead?
I that am cruel am yet merciful.
I would not have thee linger in thy pain.   105

So, so.

EMILIA, [within] What, ho! My lord, my lord!

OTHELLO Who's there?

EMILIA, [within]
  O, good my lord, I would speak a word with you.

OTHELLO
  Yes. 'Tis Emilia.—By and by.—She's dead.
  'Tis like she comes to speak of Cassio's death.
  The noise was here. Ha, no more moving?
  Still as the grave. Shall she come in? Were 't good?
  I think she stirs again. No. What's best to do?
  If she come in, she'll sure speak to my wife.
  My wife, my wife! What wife? I have no wife.
  O insupportable! O heavy hour!
  Methinks it should be now a huge eclipse
  Of sun and moon, and that th' affrighted globe
  Should yawn at alteration.

EMILIA, [within] I do beseech you
  That I may speak with you. O, good my lord—

OTHELLO
  I had forgot thee. O, come in, Emilia.—
  Soft, by and by, let me the curtains draw.—
  Where art thou?

  Enter Emilia.

  What's the matter with thee now?

EMILIA
  O, my good lord, yonder's foul murders done!

OTHELLO What? Now?

EMILIA But now, my lord.

OTHELLO
  It is the very error of the moon.
  She comes more nearer earth than she was wont
  And makes men mad.

EMILIA Cassio, my lord, hath killed
  A young Venetian called Roderigo.

OTHELLO
  Roderigo killed? And Cassio killed?

EMILIA No, Cassio is not killed.

OTHELLO
  Not Cassio killed? Then murder's out of tune,
  And sweet revenge grows harsh.

DESDEMONA O, falsely, falsely murdered!

EMILIA
  O Lord, what cry is that? 140

OTHELLO   That? What?

EMILIA
  Out, and alas, that was my lady's voice!
  Help! Help ho! Help! O lady, speak again!
  Sweet Desdemona, O sweet mistress, speak!

DESDEMONA A guiltless death I die. 145

EMILIA O, who hath done this deed?

DESDEMONA Nobody. I myself. Farewell.
  Commend me to my kind lord. O, farewell.

                              [*She dies.*]

OTHELLO
  Why, how should she be murdered?

EMILIA   Alas, who knows? 150

OTHELLO
  You heard her say herself, it was not I.

EMILIA
  She said so. I must needs report the truth.

OTHELLO
  She's like a liar, gone to burning hell!
  'Twas I that killed her.

EMILIA
  O, the more angel she, and you the blacker devil! 155

OTHELLO
  She turned to folly, and she was a whore.

EMILIA
  Thou dost belie her, and thou art a devil.

OTHELLO She was false as water.

EMILIA Thou art rash as fire to say
  That she was false. O, she was heavenly true! 160

OTHELLO
  Cassio did top her. Ask thy husband else.
  O, I were damned beneath all depth in hell
  But that I did proceed upon just grounds
  To this extremity. Thy husband knew it all.

EMILIA My husband? 165

OTHELLO Thy husband.

EMILIA That she was false to wedlock?

OTHELLO
  Ay, with Cassio. Had she been true,
  If heaven would make me such another world
  Of one entire and perfect chrysolite, 170

I'd not have sold her for it.

EMILIA My husband?

OTHELLO
Ay, 'twas he that told me on her first.
An honest man he is, and hates the slime
That sticks on filthy deeds.

EMILIA My husband?

OTHELLO
What needs this iteration, woman? I say, thy husband.

[EMILIA
O mistress, villany hath made mocks with love!—
My husband say she was false?

OTHELLO   He, woman.
I say thy husband. Dost understand the word?
My friend, thy husband; honest, honest Iago.]

EMILIA
If he say so, may his pernicious soul
Rot half a grain a day! He lies to th' heart!
She was too fond of her most filthy bargain.

[*He draws his sword.*]

OTHELLO Hah?

EMILIA Do thy worst!
This deed of thine is no more worthy heaven
Than thou wast worthy her.

OTHELLO   Peace, you were best!

EMILIA
Thou hast not half that power to do me harm
As I have to be hurt. O gull! O dolt,
As ignorant as dirt! Thou hast done a deed—
I care not for thy sword. I'll make thee known,
Though I lost twenty lives. Help! Help, ho! Help!
The Moor hath killed my mistress! Murder! murder!

Enter Montano, Gratiano, and Iago.

MONTANO
What is the matter? How now, general?

EMILIA
O, are you come, Iago? you have done well,
That men must lay their murders on your neck.

GRATIANO What is the matter?

EMILIA, [*to Iago*]
Disprove this villain, if thou be'st a man.
He says thou told'st him that his wife was false.
I know thou didst not. Thou'rt not such a villain.
Speak, for my heart is full.

IAGO
    I told him what I thought, and told no more 205
    Than what he found himself was apt and true.

EMILIA
    But did you ever tell him she was false?

IAGO I did.

EMILIA
    You told a lie, an odious, damned lie!
    Upon my soul, a lie, a wicked lie! 210
    She false with Cassio? Did you say with Cassio?

IAGO
    With Cassio, mistress. Go to! Charm your tongue.

EMILIA
    I will not charm my tongue. I am bound to speak.
    [My mistress here lies murder'd in her bed.

ALL O heavens forfend! 215

EMILIA, [to Iago]
    And your reports have set the murder on!

OTHELLO
    Nay, stare not, masters; it is true, indeed.

GRATIANO 'Tis a strange truth.

MONTANO
    O monstrous act!

EMILIA   Villainy, villainy, villainy! 220
    I think upon 't. I think! I smell 't! O villainy!
    I thought so then. I'll kill myself for grief!
    O villainy! Villainy!]

IAGO
    What, are you mad? I charge you, get you home.

EMILIA
    Good gentlemen, let me have leave to speak. 225
    'Tis proper I obey him, but not now.
    Perchance, Iago, I will ne'er go home.

OTHELLO O, O, O!   *Othello falls on the bed.*

EMILIA Nay, lay thee down and roar!
    For thou hast killed the sweetest innocent 230
    That e'er did lift up eye.

OTHELLO, [standing]   O, she was foul!—
    I scarce did know you, uncle. There lies your niece,
    Whose breath, indeed, these hands have newly stopped.
    I know this act shows horrible and grim. 235

GRATIANO
    Poor Desdemona, I am glad thy father's dead.
    Thy match was mortal to him, and pure grief

>   Shore his old thread in twain. Did he live now,
>   This sight would make him do a desperate turn,
>   Yea, curse his better angel from his side,
>   And fall to reprobation.

240

OTHELLO
>   'Tis pitiful. But yet Iago knows
>   That she with Cassio hath the act of shame
>   A thousand times committed. Cassio confessed it,
>   And she did gratify his amorous works
>   With that recognizance and pledge of love
>   Which I first gave her. I saw it in his hand.
>   It was a handkerchief, an antique token
>   My father gave my mother.

245

EMILIA O God! O heavenly God!

250

IAGO Zounds, hold your peace.

EMILIA 'Twill out, 'twill out. I peace?
>   No, I will speak as liberal as the north.
>   Let heaven and men and devils, let them all,
>   All, all, cry shame against me, yet I'll speak.

255

IAGO Be wise, and get you home.

[He draws his sword.]

EMILIA
>   I will not.

GRATIANO   Fie, your sword upon a woman!

EMILIA
>   O thou dull Moor! that handkerchief thou speak'st of
>   I found by fortune and did give my husband—
>   For often, with a solemn earnestness
>   (More than indeed belonged to such a trifle),
>   He begged of me to steal 't.

260

IAGO   Villainous whore!

EMILIA
>   She give it Cassio? No, alas! I found it,
>   And I did give 't my husband.

265

IAGO   Filth, thou liest!

EMILIA
>   By heaven, I do not, I do not, gentlemen!
>   *[To Othello.]* O murd'rous coxcomb, what should such a fool
>   Do with so good a wife?

270

OTHELLO Are there no stones in heaven
>   But what serve for the thunder?—Precious villain!

The Moor runs at Iago but is disarmed. Iago kills his wife.

GRATIANO
>   The woman falls! Sure he hath killed his wife.

EMILIA
    Ay, ay! O, lay me by my mistress' side.   *Iago exits.*

GRATIANO He's gone, but his wife's killed.   275

MONTANO
    'Tis a notorious villain. Take you this weapon
    Which I have here recovered from the Moor.
    Come, guard the door without. Let him not pass,
    But kill him rather. I'll after that same villain,
    For 'tis a damned slave.   280
                Montano and Gratiano exit.

OTHELLO   I am not valiant neither,
    But ever puny whipster gets my sword.
    But why should honour outlive honesty?
    Let it go all.

[EMILIA   What did thy song bode, lady?   285
    Hark, canst thou hear me? I will play the swan.
    And die in music.
    [*She sings.*] *Willow, willow, willow.*]
    Moor, she was chaste. She loved thee, cruel Moor.
    So come my soul to bliss, as I speak true.   290
    So speaking as I think, alas, I die.   *She dies.*

OTHELLO
    I have another weapon in this chamber.
    It is a sword of Spain, the ice-brook's temper.
    O, here it is.—Uncle, I must come forth.

GRATIANO, [*within*]
    If thou attempt it, it will cost thee dear;   295
    Thou hast no weapon, and perforce must suffer.

OTHELLO
    Look in upon me then and speak with me,
    Or naked as I am, I will assault thee.

                Enter Gratiano.

GRATIANO
    What is the matter?

OTHELLO   Behold, I have a weapon.   300
    A better never did itself sustain
    Upon a soldier's thigh. I have seen the day
    That with this little arm and this good sword,
    I have made my way through more impediments
    Than twenty times your stop. But—O vain boast!—   305
    Who can control his fate? 'Tis not so now.
    [Be not afraid, though you do see me weaponed.
    Here is my journey's end, here is my butt
    And very sea-mark of my utmost sail.
    Do you go back dismayed? 'Tis a lost fear.   310
    Man but a rush against Othello's breast,
    And he retires. Where should Othello go?
                [*He looks toward the bed.*]

Now, how dost thou look now? O ill-starred wench,]
Pale as thy smock, when we shall meet at compt,
This look of thine will hurl my soul from heaven, 315
And fiends will snatch at it. Cold, cold, my girl?
Even like thy chastity.—O cursèd, cursèd slave!—
Whip me, you devils,
From the possession of this heavenly sight!
Blow me about in winds, roast me in sulfur, 320
Wash me in steep-down gulfs of liquid fire!
O Desdemona! Dead, Desdemon! Dead! O, O!

Enter Lodovico, Cassio in a chair, Montano, and Iago, with Officers.

LODOVICO
　Where is this rash and most unfortunate man?

OTHELLO
　That's he that was Othello. Here I am.

LODOVICO
　Where is that viper? Bring the villain forth. 325
　　　　　　　　　　　　[Iago is brought forward.]

OTHELLO
　I look down towards his feet; but that's a fable.—
　If that thou be'st a devil, I cannot kill thee.
　　　　　　　　　　　　　　[He stabs Iago.]

LODOVICO　Wrench his sword from him.
　　　　　　　　　　　　　[Othello is disarmed.]

IAGO　I bleed, sir, but not killed.

OTHELLO
　I am not sorry neither: I'd have thee live, 330
　For, in my sense, 'tis happiness to die.

LODOVICO
　O thou Othello, thou wert once so good,
　Fall'n in the practice of a damnèd slave,
　What shall be said to thee?

OTHELLO　　　　　　　　　Why, anything. 335
　An honorable murderer, if you will,
　For naught I did in hate, but all in honor.

LODOVICO
　This wretch hath part confessed his villainy.
　Did you and he consent in Cassio's death?

OTHELLO　Ay. 340

CASSIO
　Dear general, I never gave you cause.

OTHELLO
　I do believe it, and I ask your pardon.
　Will you, I pray, demand that demi-devil
　Why he hath thus ensnared my soul and body?

IAGO
    Demand me nothing. What you know, you know. 345
    From this time forth I never will speak word.

LODOVICO What? Not to pray?

GRATIANO Torments will ope your lips.

OTHELLO Well, thou dost best.

LODOVICO Sir,
    You shall understand what hath befall'n, 350
    Which, as I think, you know not. Here is a letter
    Found in the pocket of the slain Roderigo,
    And here another. [*He shows papers.*] The one of them imports
    The death of Cassio, to be undertook
    By Roderigo. 355

OTHELLO O villain!

CASSIO Most heathenish and most gross.

LODOVICO
    Now here's another discontented paper
    Found in his pocket, too; and this, it seems
    Roderigo meant to have sent this damnèd villain, 360
    But that, belike, Iago in the interim
    Came in and satisfied him.

OTHELLO O, thou pernicious caitiff!—
    How came you, Cassio, by that handkerchief
    That was my wife's? 365

CASSIO   I found it in my chamber.
    And he himself confessed but even now,
    That there he dropped it for a special purpose
    Which wrought to his desire.

OTHELLO   O fool, fool, fool! 370

CASSIO
    There is besides in Roderigo's letter,
    How he upbraids Iago, that he made him
    Brave me upon the watch, whereon it came
    That I was cast. And even but now he spake,
    After long seeming dead, Iago hurt him, 375
    Iago set him on.

LODOVICO, [*to Othello*]
    You must forsake this room, and go with us.
    Your power and your command is taken off,
    And Cassio rules in Cyprus. For this slave,
    If there be any cunning cruelty 380
    That can torment him much and hold him long,
    It shall be his. You shall close prisoner rest,
    Till that the nature of your fault be known
    To the Venetian state.—Come, bring away.

OTHELLO
Soft you. A word or two before you go. 385
I have done the state some service, and they know 't.
No more of that. I pray you, in your letters,
When you shall these unlucky deeds relate,
Speak of me as I am. Nothing extenuate,
Nor set down aught in malice. Then must you speak 390
Of one that loved not wisely, but too well;
Of one not easily jealous, but being wrought,
Perplexed in the extreme; of one whose hand,
Like the base Judean, threw a pearl away
Richer than all his tribe; of one whose subdued eyes, 395
Albeit unused to the melting mood,
Drop tears as fast as the Arabian trees
Their medicinal gum. Set you down this,
And say besides, that in Aleppo once,
Where a malignant and a turbanned Turk 400
Beat a Venetian and traduced the state,
I took by th' throat the circumcised dog,
And smote him, thus. *He stabs himself.*

LODOVICO O bloody period!

GRATIANO All that's spoke is marred. 405

OTHELLO, [*to Desdemona*]
I kissed thee ere I killed thee. No way but this
Killing myself, to die upon a kiss. *He dies.*

CASSIO
This did I fear, but thought he had no weapon,
For he was great of heart.

LODOVICO, [*to Iago*]   O Spartan dog, 410
More fell than anguish, hunger, or the sea,
Look on the tragic loading of this bed.
This is thy work.—The object poisons sight.
Let it be hid.—Gratiano, keep the house,
And seize upon the fortunes of the Moor, 415
For they succeed on you. [*To Cassio.*] To you, lord governor,
Remains the censure of this hellish villain.
The time, the place, the torture, O, enforce it.
Myself will straight aboard, and to the state
This heavy act with heavy heart relate. 420
They exit.

European Poetry

Francesco Petrarch (1304–1374)

Francesco Petrarch, one of Italy's greatest lyric poets, was born on July 20, 1304, in Arezzo, Italy, where his father was exiled because of political problems. Seven months later, he and his mother moved to Ancisa, his father's hometown. When a second child, Gerardo, was born in 1307, the family moved again to Avignon, France. After receiving private instruction for several years, Petrarch began law studies first at Montpellier and then in Bologna. In April, 1326, at the time of his father's death, Petrarch developed an interest in literary study. Petrarch had to support himself financially, so he decided to become a priest. In 1330 he served as chaplain to Cardinal Giovanni Colonna, after which time he received the first of several canonries. Though Petrarch was involved in other literary works, at this time, he began writing his *Africa,* an epic poem about Scipio Africanus, who conquered Hannibal; and *Deviris Illustribus,* containing the biographies of men in antiquity. Neither work was completed. His fame spreading by 1340, Petrarch was crowned poet laureate by the Roman Senate on April 8, 1341.

Petrarch fell in love with a young woman named Laura, who did not return his love. However, his unrequited love was the inspiration for lyrics after which love poetry was patterned for many centuries. In 1398 Laura was struck down by the Black Death.

Petrarch did not believe that his ambitions and aspirations would prevent him from receiving Christian salvation. He saw his achievements and knowledge with new eyes when he situated his accomplishments within the context of Christianity, for they revealed both the person's potential to sink to great depths or to rise to great heights. Petrarch began to travel more to Parma, Milan, Padua, and Venice to fulfill writing engagements and religious duties and to try to outrun the Black Death plague. On one trip, he stopped in Florence where he met Giovanni Boccaccio, and the two became lifelong friends. He finally settled in Arqua in 1370. Four years later, on July 19, 1374, he died.

Sonnet

Francesco Petrarch

Sonnet 3

It Was the Morning of That Blessed Day

It was the morning of that blessèd day
Whereon the Sun in pity veiled his glare
For the Lord's agony, that, unaware,
I fell a captive, Lady, to the sway

Of your swift eyes: that seemed no time to stay　　　5
The strokes of Love: I stepped into the snare
Secure, with no suspicion: then, and there
I found my cue in man's most tragic play.
Love caught me naked to his shaft, his sheaf,
The entrance for his ambush and surprise　　　10
Against the head wide open through the eyes,

The constant gate and fountain of my grief:
How craven so to strike me stricken so,
Yet from you fully armed conceal his bow!

François Villon (1431–1463?)

François Villon was the greatest lyric poet of French Medieval literature. He led a rogue's life, the story of which has grown into myth over the centuries, yet he wrote some of the most original poetry of his time. In his two greatest works, *Le petit testament* and *Le grand testament,* Villon writes with a candor not seen before in Medieval French poetry. Like Chaucer, he praises or skewers other people or professions as he sees fit and thus gives us a discerning look at his world and times. However, Villon did not spare himself from self-criticism; some of the most painfully honest introspection ever seen in European literature appears in *Le grand testament.* At the same time, though, the imagery he uses in his flights of contemplation sometimes possesses an uncanny beauty. From Villon's works, we get a portrait of a highly intelligent and sensitive man who nonetheless failed to resist the call of the streets.

Villon was born in 1431, either in Paris or a nearby village. His real name is thought to be François de Moncorbier. Little is known about his childhood except that he lost his father at an early age. Fortunately, however, Guillaume de Villon, a chaplain, took an interest in his welfare and became his mentor; the poet took his name in tribute to his generosity. Villon matriculated at the Sorbonne, where he earned both the bachelor of arts (1449) and the master of arts (1452) degrees, despite his reputation for boisterous behavior. Within three years of his graduation, however, he got into serious trouble by killing a priest in a street fight and then, a year later, participating in the theft of 500 crowns from a chapel in Paris. There is no record of his punishment for the murder, but for the theft he was banished from the city.

Villon was arrested again in Orleans three years later and imprisoned, although he was pardoned by Louis XI; again, back in Paris in 1462, he was arrested in another street brawl and condemned to death. Though his sentence was commuted, he was banished from Paris a second time.

Le petit testament and *Le grand testament* are written in the form of burlesque wills. His greatest technical achievements can be seen in the rondeaux and ballades he included in *Le grand testament.* The rondeau was originally a lyric form, the words of which were meant to be sung. Villon reworked the song form into a purely literary form which became the standard; his revision consisted of 13 lines divided into three stanzas, with an unrhymed refrain. He also experimented with the ballade form.

Ballade

François Villon

Brother humans who live on after us
Don't let your hearts harden against us
For if you have pity on wretches like us
More likely God will show mercy to you
You see us five, six, hanging here 5

As for the flesh we loved too well
A while ago it was eaten and has rotted away
And we the bones turn to ashes and dust
Let no one make us the butt of jokes
But pray God that he absolve us all. 10

Don't be insulted that we call you
Brothers, even if it was by Justice
We were put to death, for you understand
Not every person has the same good sense
Speak up for us, since we can't ourselves 15

Before the son of the virgin Mary
That his mercy toward us shall keep flowing
Which is what keeps us from hellfire
We are dead, may no one taunt us
But pray God that he absolve us all. 20

The rain has rinsed and washed us
The sun dried us and turned us black
Magpies and ravens have pecked out our eyes
And plucked our beards and eyebrows
Never ever can we stand still 25

Now here, now there, as the wind shifts
At its whim it keeps swinging us
Pocked by birds worse than a sewing thimble
Therefore don't join in our brotherhood
But pray God that he absolve us all. 30

Prince Jesus, master over all
Don't let us fall into hell's dominion
We've nothing to do or settle down there
Men, there's nothing here to laugh at
But pray God that he absolve us all. 35

from Sonnets

William Shakespeare (1564–1616)

Sonnet No. 18

Shall I Compare Thee to a Summer's Day?

Shall I compare thee to a summer's day?
Thou art more lovely and more temperate:
Rough winds do shake the darling buds of May,
And summer's lease hath all too short a date:
Sometime too hot the eye of heaven shines, 5
And often is his gold complexion dimm'd;
And every fair from fair sometime declines,
By chance, or nature's changing course untrimm'd:
But thy eternal summer shall not fade,
Nor lose possession of that fair thou ow'st; 10
Nor shall Death brag thou wand'rest in his shade,
When in eternal lines to time thou grow'st:
   So long as men can breathe or eyes can see,
   So long lives this, and this gives life to thee.

Sonnet No. 116

Let Me Not to the Marriage of True Minds

Let me not to the marriage of true minds
Admit impediments. Love is not love
Which alters when it alteration finds,
Or bends with the remover to remove.
O, no! it is an ever-fixed mark   5
That looks on tempests and is never shaken;
It is the star to every wand'ring bark,
Whose worth's unknown, although his height be taken.
Love's not Time's fool, though rosy lips and cheeks
Within his bending sickle's compass come;   10
Love alters not with his brief hours and weeks,
But bears it out even to the edge of doom.
    If this be error and upon me proved,
    I never writ, nor no man ever loved.

Sonnet No. 121

Tis Better To Be Vile Than Vile Esteemed

'Tis better to be vile than vile esteemed,
When not to be, receives reproach of being,
And the just pleasure lost, which is so deemed,
Not by our feeling, but by others' seeing.
For why should others' false adulterate eyes   5
Give salutation to my sportive blood?
Or on my frailties why are frailer spies,
Which in their wills count bad what I think good?
No, I am that I am, and they that level
At my abuses, reckon up their own: 10
I may be straight though they themselves be bevel;
By their rank thoughts my deeds must not be shown;
    Unless this general evil they maintain,
    All men are bad, and in their badness reign.

John Donne (1572–1631)

John Donne was the founder and leader of the school of metaphysical poetry. His poetical works are best known for their complex and arresting imagery and elaborate, often unique metrical patterns. However, they can hardly be considered apart from the man who composed them. By turns sensual and spiritual, earthy and erudite, Donne's poems give voice to his attempts to strike a healthy balance among the contrasting strains of his personality. Donne was also known for his religious works (his public sermons and tracts, in which he expressed his own faith and dissected the beliefs of others) and profoundly personal meditations and sonnets.

Born in London to a middle-class Roman Catholic family, Donne matriculated at both Oxford and Cambridge before settling into legal studies at Lincoln's Inn. It was during this time that he composed his first book of poems, *Satires*. Both Satires and his second effort, a volume of love poems titled *Songs and Sonnets,* were privately circulated in manuscript form long before they were published. It was also during this time, or shortly after, that he renounced his affiliation with the Roman Catholic church.

After satisfying his thirst for adventure by joining a naval expedition to the port of Cadiz, Spain, Donne returned to London and took the position of personal secretary to Sir Thomas Egerton, a man he hoped would become a mentor and patron. Donne took the opportunity to sit in Elizabeth's last parliament and cultivate the patronage of various members of the peerage; it was the only way a man of his class, with merely a small inheritance, could mold his own future. But Donne soon fell in love with Egerton's niece, Anne More, and in December 1601, the couple secretly married. Donne could not have made a more disastrous career move; Egerton dismissed him from his secretarial post at the urging of Anne's father, Sir George More, and even had Donne thrown in prison for a brief time. The courts declared the marriage valid. John and Anne Donne were said to be truly in love, but that reality did not temper the fact that Donne had no money and no position and now had a wife to support.

In practical terms, the ill-advised marriage had a lifelong influence on the fortunes of the couple: without funds, they had to take the lodging that was offered by a cousin, accommodations which were well outside London and kept them away from family, friends, and, just as importantly, the bustling social and political life of the city. Nor was the episode forgotten in royal circles; James I, installed as monarch upon the death of the Queen, turned away Donne's application for a position at court, citing his aversion to Donne's improprieties and adding that he would only consider the poet for a position within the Anglican church.

For the next decade or so, Donne took makeshift assignments to help support his growing family. Ann was to give birth to 12 children in a little over 15 years, and there is no doubt that financial concerns were a major worry throughout their marriage. Yet, by most accounts, they were a happy couple. In fact, Anne was not just an inspiration to Donne but a catalyst, for she provided the means by which he could examine the complex double nature of his attraction to her—the sacred and the profane, the spiritual and the erotic. In fact, Donne's most famous poems, such as "The Flea" and "The Ecstasy," celebrate their twin marriage—the union of flesh and soul.

As Donne approached middle age, his prose writing reflected a deep and abiding melancholy. His thoughts turned to the reconsideration of the tenets of Catholicism and of Christianity in general. He wrote an essay (*Biathantos*) in which he argued that the act of suicide is not inherently sinful; in association with Thomas Morton, Dean of Gloucester, but more importantly Chaplain to the Earl of Rutland and defender of the Church of England, he composed two anti-Catholic tracts, *Pseudo-Martyr* (1610) and *Ignatius His Conclave* (1611). Thus, his renunciation of the Roman Catholic church was made complete, and the stage was set for Donne to become active in the Anglican church.

Donne had once refused to take Anglican orders; however, his vast intellectual capacity and rhetorical talents had come to the notice of James I, who had been the first to urge him to become an Anglican minister. In 1615 Donne was ordained. He was eventually appointed Reader of Divinity at Lincoln's Inn, and it was here that he won a stellar reputation as a preacher who combined intellectual rigor with passion and drama.

Just as John Donne found his wings amidst his flock of lawyers at the Inn, he suffered the greatest tragedy of all: Anne Donne died in 1617, a week after giving birth to their twelfth child. The grief he suffered upon her death pushed him to an even more profound depth of contemplation about the nature of the soul and the meaning of love beyond the time-bound world. Contemporary accounts also suggest that he became obsessed with death at this time. In an eerie coincidence, Donne preached what many considered to be his own funeral oration, *Death's Duell* (1631), a few weeks before he died, and draped himself up in his own funeral shroud for what turned out to be his final portrait.

In his most renowned poems, Donne characteristically uses the *conceit*, an elaborately constructed metaphor which brings together dissimilar elements, both natural and man-made, to produce an image that is often disturbing. For the metaphysical poets, the conceit was often the means by which they exercised their intellectual muscle and established the beginnings of an uneasy union between science and faith. Donne was also creative in his metrical schemes. His poetry is notable because he rarely, if ever, repeated a metrical pattern, but it is also noteworthy because he was the first to break with an established, artificial poetic style and reproduce recognizable speech patterns in poetic form.

Selected Bibliography

Carey, John. *John Donne: Life, Mind, and Art.* New York: Oxford University Press, 1981.
Parfitt, George. *John Donne: A Literary Life.* New York: St. Martin's Press, 1989.
Parker, Derek. *John Donne and His World.* London: Thames and Hudson, 1975.

The Relic

John Donne

    When my grave is broke up again
    Some second guest to entertain,
    (For graves have learn'd that woman-head
    To be to more than one a bed)
        And he that digs it, spies 5
A bracelet of bright hair about the bone,
        Will he not let' us alone,
And think that there a loving couple lies,
Who thought that this device might be some way
To make their souls, at the last busy day, 10
Meet at this grave, and make a little stay?

    If this fall in a time, or land,
    Where mis-devotion doth command,
    Then, he that digs us up, will bring
    Us, to the Bishop, and the King, 15
        To make us relics; then
Thou shalt be a Mary Magdalen, and I
        A something else thereby;
All women shall adore us, and some men;
And since at such time, miracles are sought, 20
I would have that age by this paper taught
What miracles we harmless lovers wrought.

    First, we lov'd well and faithfully,
    Yet knew not what we lov'd, nor why,
    Difference of sex no more we knew, 25
    Than our guardian angels do;
        Coming and going, we
Perchance might kiss, but not between those meals;
        Our hands ne'er touch'd the seals,
Which nature, injur'd by late law, sets free: 30
These miracles we did; but now alas,
All measure, and all language, I should pass,
Should I tell what a miracle she was.

William Wordsworth (1770–1850)

William Wordsworth was one of the Lake Poets and a founder of the English Romantic literary movement. With his friend Samuel Taylor Coleridge, he published *Lyrical Ballads,* a slim volume which reflected a revolutionary way of thinking about poetry. For Wordsworth, the farmer, the shepherd, and even the idiot in his "Idiot Boy" were subjects as worthy of celebration as the heroes exalted in the popular poetry of the day. He also used the language of common folk to tell their stories. To these, Wordsworth added an even more disturbing notion: that poetry should not be self-consciously artificial and modeled on Classical forms but should be based on "emotion recollected in tranquillity." When *Lyrical Ballads* was born, poetry was transformed into a means of intimate interaction between a writer and his audience, rather than an ostentatious display of wit and style.

Wordsworth was born in the Lake District of northern England on April 7, 1770, to a well-respected, middle-class family. His was a happy childhood. From an early age, he was allowed to roam the fields and wetlands of the area, and it was there that he developed his early fascination with the beauty of nature. These experiences left an indelible imprint; years later, Wordsworth would describe his childhood with much affection in his autobiographical masterwork, *The Prelude*.

Wordsworth attended St. John's College at Cambridge; at the end of his third year, he took a walking tour through Switzerland and France, where he first became enthralled with the ideals set forth in the French Revolution: liberty, equality, fraternity. He returned in 1791, months after he had obtained his Bachelor of Arts degree and stayed long enough to witness the blood of royalists staining the streets of Paris. He also fell in love with a French woman, Annette Vallon, who bore him a daughter in December 1792. Although he may have intended to marry her, the lack of financial resources and growing anti-British sentiment forced him to return to London. He did return to France on several occasions and kept in touch with Annette, though he eventually married Mary Hutchinson, a friend from childhood.

With the benefit of a considerable bequest, Wordsworth eventually settled down in Dorsetshire, first with his sister Dorothy and later with the rest of his family. However, they soon made a move which would change both their lives forever. In 1797 they relocated to Alfoxden, Somersetshire, to be close to Samuel Taylor Coleridge and his family. The friendship between the two families, which only ended with Coleridge's death in 1834, was thus sealed. Within another year, Wordsworth and Coleridge had embarked on a literary collaboration, which resulted in the publication of *Lyrical Ballads* in 1798.

Wordsworth, stung by the curt dismissal of the Ballads by critics and the poor sales of the volume, composed a defense of his literary theories and published them in a preface to the second edition of *Lyrical Ballads*. While "the Preface" is now considered a landmark in literary history, its original publication only served to alienate more of the reading public. Fortunately, the charming quality of the poems themselves eventually won over many of Wordsworth's readers and became quite popular, especially with young people.

The years 1800–1805 were Wordsworth's most productive years. The result was the publication of *Poems in Two Volumes,* a collection of 113 poems of varying lengths and moods, in 1807. "Ode on the Intimations of Immortality," long considered to be the poet's greatest ode, closed the second volume. Unable to make a satisfactory living writing poetry, Wordsworth took a position as a civil servant in 1813. Later, two of his children, Catherine and Thomas, died within six months of each other. He then moved his family to Rydal Mount, partly to get away from sad memories of their deaths. There, Wordsworth spent the rest of his life.

As Wordsworth grew older, he grew less radical. His growing conservatism, caused by disillusionment over the failure of the French Revolution and Napoleon's ascent to power, was also reflected in a growing literary conservatism. Modern critics generally agree that Wordsworth's later work is but a shadow of his earlier poetry. *The Excursion* (1814), a sequel to *The Prelude; Peter Bell* (1819); and *Memorials of a Tour on the Continent* (1822) are among his more unimaginative works. He rarely wrote poetry after 1835. Wordsworth died at the age of 80 and was buried at Grasmere.

Wordsworth's poetry hardly seems radical today; in our time anyone, regardless of class, can be a "fit subject" for popular poetry. But in those days when the news of revolution—the American Revolution as well as the French Revolution—had only just hit England's shores, there was an implicit threat in the idea that a middle-class gentleman would align himself with the common people. Perhaps Wordsworth's greatest accomplishment, apart from the beauty of his verse, is that he recognized a common humanity among all people as well as the bond between humankind and the natural world.

Selected Bibliography

Bloom, Harold, ed. "Introduction." *William Wordsworth's The Prelude: Modern Critical Interpretations.* New York: Chelsea House, 1986.

Davies, Hunter. *William Wordsworth.* London: Atheneum, 1980.

To Toussaint L'ouverture

[Composed probably August, 1802.—Published February 2, 1803 (Morning Post); 1807.]

William Wordsworth

Toussaint, the most unhappy man of men!
Whether the whistling Rustic tend his plough
Within thy hearing, or thy head be now
Pillowed in some deep dungeon's earless den;—
O miserable Chieftain! where and when   5
Wilt thou find patience! Yet die not; do thou
Wear rather in thy bonds a cheerful brow:
Though fallen thyself, never to rise again,
Live, and take comfort. Thou hast left behind
Powers that will work for thee; air, earth, and skies;   10
There's not a breathing of the common wind
That will forget thee; thou hast great allies;
Thy friends are exultations, agonies,
And love, and man's unconquerable mind.

I Wandered Lonely as a Cloud

William Wordsworth

I wandered lonely as a cloud
That floats on high o'er vales and hills,
When all at once I saw a crowd,
A host, of golden daffodils;
Beside the lake, beneath the trees,   5
Fluttering and dancing in the breeze.

Continuous as the stars that shine
And twinkle on the milky way,
They stretched in never-ending line
Along the margin of a bay: 10
Ten thousand saw I at a glance,
Tossing their heads in sprightly dance.

The waves beside them danced; but they
Out-did the sparkling waves in glee:
A poet could not but be gay,
In such a jocund company: 15
I gazed—and gazed—but little thought
What wealth the show to me had brought:

For oft, when on my couch I lie
In vacant or in pensive mood,
They flash upon that inward eye   20
Which is the bliss of solitude;
And then my heart with pleasure fills,
And dances with the daffodils.

John Keats (1795–1821)

John Keats was the youngest of the second generation of English Romantic poets which included Lord Byron and Percy Bysshe Shelley. Keats died of consumption before he reached his 26th birthday, yet during his short career he composed some of the greatest poems ever written in the English language. He is also known for his literary theory, which codified some of the major ideas of the Romantic movement. Although he never published a formal theoretical essay, the ideas expressed in his letters, most notably the concept of "negative capability," or the complete loss of self during the ascent to the world of imagination, suggest that he was a brilliant and original thinker.

Keats was born in London on Halloween, 1795, to a hostler and his wife. He was orphaned by the age of 15 but was lucky enough to be apprenticed to a surgeon, Thomas Hammond. Keats' interest in medicine grew, and he eventually enrolled in medical school. However, in 1816, a few months before he was to graduate with an apothecary's certificate, his first published poem "O Solitude!" appeared in Leigh Hunt's *Examiner*. Six months later, as the newest member of Hunt's literary circle, Keats had decided that he did not want to be an apothecary but a poet.

Keats' earliest work was ordinary at best, but within a year he had composed the remarkable sonnet, "On First Looking into Chapman's Homer." His first volume, *Poems* (1817), found an enthusiastic audience among his friends, although it failed to interest a wider audience. A year later, he published an earnest and daring allegory, "Endymion." An article in Blackwood's *Edinburgh Magazine* attacked Keats' poem, however, and sales of the volume plummeted. This was the first of many vitriolic attacks on Keats' writing; they became so frequent that Shelley blamed the most vocal critics for Keats' premature death.

Two events of 1818 were to affect Keats for the rest of his life. Over the summer, he met the love of his life, Fanny Brawne; he would spend the remainder of his life in a tumultuous relationship with her. In December, his brother, Tom, died of tuberculosis. He had nursed Tom, on and off, for many months, and had watched him waste away; this loss would lead to what some consider to be Keats' obsession with death.

Keats' most productive year was 1819. He composed the major odes, as well as "La Belle Dame sans Merci," *The Eve of St. Agnes*, and *Lamia,* and revised his epic *Hyperion*. His productivity was all the more remarkable because he was distracted by his love for Fanny Brawne. His passion was clearly that of a possessive young man consumed by jealousy, yet ambivalent about the effect a lasting commitment would have on his creativity. But his work suggested a maturity of reason and of self-reflection uncommon in one so young.

In early 1820, Keats himself began to show the symptoms of tuberculosis; in October, seeking a more hospitable climate than that of the raw English winter, he went to Rome. Emotionally exhausted and in failing health, he no longer wrote poetry; instead, he wrote letters of passionate regret to his friends and family, grieving for his imminent separation from his beloved Fanny and for his self-perceived failure as a writer. His epitaph best describes Keats' own perception of the mark he had made upon the world: "Here lies one whose name is writ in water."

Keats is best known for his poems about the supernatural and for his two most powerful odes, "Ode on a Grecian Urn" and "Ode to a Nightingale." Both express the constant tension between the real world and the world of the imagination: between the mutable, decaying realities of the human body and the natural world, and the ideal of art, which is inherently immortal; they also express the longing the poet has for a complete and lasting retreat into the world of the imagination.

Selected Bibliography

Barnard, John. *John Keats*. New York: Cambridge University Press, 1987.
Bloom, Harold, ed. *The Odes of Keats: Modern Critical Interpretations*. New York: Chelsea House, 1987.
Hirst, Wolf Z. *John Keats*. New York: Twayne, 1981.
Vendler, Helen. *The Odes of Keats*. Cambridge: Harvard University Press, 1985.

Ode to a Nightingale

John Keats

1

My heart aches, and a drowsy numbness pains
   My sense, as though of hemlock I had drunk,
Or emptied some dull opiate to the drains
   One minute past, and Lethe-wards had sunk:
'Tis not through envy of thy happy lot,
   But being too happy in thine happiness,—
     That thou, light-wingéd Dryad of the trees,
       In some melodious plot
   Of beechen green, and shadows numberless,
     Singest of summer in full-throated ease.

2

O, for a draught of vintage! that hath been
   Cool'd a long age in the deep-delvéd earth,
Tasting of Flora and the country green,
   Dance, and Provençal song, and sunburnt mirth!
O for a beaker full of the warm South,
   Full of the true, the blushful Hippocrene,
     With beaded bubbles winking at the brim,
       And purple-stainéd mouth;
   That I might drink, and leave the world unseen,
     And with thee fade away into the forest dim:

3

Fade far away, dissolve, and quite forget
   What thou among the leaves hast never known,
The weariness, the fever, and the fret
   Here, where men sit and hear each other groan;
Where palsy shakes a few, sad, last gray hairs,   5
    Where youth grows pale, and specter-thin, and dies;
      Where but to think is to be full of sorrow
        And leaden-eyed despairs,
    Where Beauty cannot keep her lustrous eyes,
      Or new Love pine at them beyond to-morrow.   10

4

Away! away! for I will fly to thee,
   Not charioted by Bacchus and his pards,
But on the viewless wings of Poesy,
   Though the dull brain perplexes and retards:
Already with thee! tender is the night,   5
    And haply the Queen-Moon is on her throne,
      Cluster'd around by all her starry Fays;
        But here there is no light,
    Save what from heaven is with the breezes blown
      Through verdurous glooms and winding mossy ways.   10

5

I cannot see what flowers are at my feet,
   Nor what soft incense hangs upon the boughs,
But, in embalmèd darkness, guess each sweet
   Wherewith the seasonable month endows
The grass, the thicket, and the fruit-tree wild;   5
    White hawthorn, and the pastoral eglantine;
      Fast fading violets cover'd up in leaves;
        And mid-May's eldest child,
    The coming musk-rose, full of dewy wine,
      The murmurous haunt of flies on summer eves.   10

6

Darkling I listen; and, for many a time
   I have been half in love with easeful Death,
Call'd him soft names in many a muséd rhyme,
   To take into the air my quiet breath;
Now more than ever seems it rich to die,
   To cease upon the midnight with no pain,
     While thou art pouring forth thy soul abroad
       In such an ecstasy!
Still wouldst thou sing, and I have ears in vain—
   To thy high requiem become a sod.

7

Thou wast not born for death, immortal Bird!
   No hungry generations tread thee down;
The voice I hear this passing night was heard
   In ancient days by emperor and clown:
Perhaps the self-same song that found a path
   Through the sad heart of Ruth, when, sick for home,
     She stood in tears amid the alien corn;
       The same that oft-times hath
Charm'd magic casements, opening on the foam
   Of perilous seas, in faery lands forlorn.

8

Forlorn! the very word is like a bell
   To toll me back from thee to my sole self!
Adieu! the fancy cannot cheat so well
   As she is fam'd to do, deceiving elf.
Adieu! adieu! thy plaintive anthem fades
   Past the near meadows, over the still stream,
     Up the hill-side; and now 'tis buried deep
       In the next valley-glades:
Was it a vision, or a waking dream?
   Fled is that music:—Do I wake or sleep?

Ode on a Grecian Urn

John Keats

1

Thou still unravish'd bride of quietness,
   Thou foster-child of silence and slow time,
Sylvan historian, who canst thus express
   A flowery tale more sweetly than our rhyme:
What leaf-fring'd legend haunts about thy shape   5
   Of deities or mortals, or of both,
      In Tempe or the dales of Arcady?
   What men or gods are these? What maidens loth?
What mad pursuit? What struggle to escape?
   What pipes and timbrels? What wild ecstasy?   10

2

Heard melodies are sweet, but those unheard
   Are sweeter; therefore, ye soft pipes, play on;
Not to the sensual ear, but, more endear'd,
   Pipe to the spirit ditties of no tone:
Fair youth, beneath the trees, thou canst not leave   5
   Thy song, nor ever can those trees be bare;
      Bold Lover, never, never canst thou kiss,
Though winning near the goal—yet, do not grieve;
      She cannot fade, though thou hast not thy bliss,
   For ever wilt thou love, and she be fair!   10

3

Ah, happy, happy boughs! that cannot shed
    Your leaves, nor ever bid the Spring adieu;
And, happy melodist, unwearied,
    For ever piping songs for ever new;
More happy love! more happy, happy love!
    For ever warm and still to be enjoy'd,
        For ever panting, and for ever young;
All breathing human passion far above,
    That leaves a heart high-sorrowful and cloy'd,
        A burning forehead, and a parching tongue.

4

Who are these coming to the sacrifice?
    To what green altar, O mysterious priest,
Lead'st thou that heifer lowing at the skies,
    And all her silken flanks with garlands drest?
What little town by river or sea shore,
    Or mountain-built with peaceful citadel,
        Is emptied of this folk, this pious morn?
And, little town, thy streets for evermore
    Will silent be; and not a soul to tell
        Why thou art desolate, can e'er return.

5

O Attic shape! Fair attitude! with brede
    Of marble men and maidens overwrought,
With forest branches and the trodden weed;
    Thou, silent form, dost tease us out of thought
As doth eternity: Cold Pastoral!
    When old age shall this generation waste,
        Thou shalt remain, in midst of other woe
Than ours, a friend to man, to whom thou say'st,
    Beauty is truth, truth beauty,—that is all
        Ye know on earth, and all ye need to know.

Dylan Thomas (1914–1953)

Dylan Marlais Thomas was born in Swansea, Wales, on October 27, 1914, and was formally educated at Swansea Grammar School, where his father taught English. At an early age, Thomas began to write lyrical poetry which later reflected his Welsh heritage in concept, image, mood, and rhythm. He published his first poems in the Grammar School's magazine. Though he had an enormous knowledge of English poetry, he was, at best, a mediocre student. At 16, Thomas left school to work as a reporter on the *South Wales Evening Post,* and when he reached 21, he had written the majority of his poetry.

Thomas published his first book, *Eighteen Poems,* in 1934, and after he relocated to London, published, in 1936, another collection of both original and experimental poems titled *Twenty-Five Poems.* Though he received much praise and recognition for this volume, he received little monetary reward.

In 1937 Thomas married Caitlin MacNamara and had with her two sons and one daughter. With mounting bills and unable to make enough money at the British Broadcasting Company (BBC), where he was employed, he began to write radio scripts and to travel to America to supplement his income. Since Thomas had little business acumen, he was nearly always short of funds. His play "Under Mill Wood" represents a period early in his career when his comedic powers, deep insights, dramatic characterization, and comedic invention were all richly imaginative. However, the humorous and realistic scenes in his *Portrait of the Artist as a Young Dog,* presented in New York in 1953, showed a developing maturity in the poet and made Thomas a success at home and abroad.

As Thomas began drinking heavily and womanizing, his despair increased, and he began to borrow from rich friends. As his marital state worsened, he began to have premonitions of his early death, and his poetry, filled with wit and fraught with puns, began to address themes of sex and death, sin and redemption. Thomas believed that life and death are both part of a process shared by all living things. His collection, *Death and Entrances,* firmly established him as a religious poet. Finally, on November 9, 1953, on a poetry-reading tour, he drank so much that he overdosed and died. After his death, Thomas' poetry was thought by some to be overrated. With the passage of time, his beautiful, powerful, and original works are now recognized and enjoyed throughout the world.

Selected Bibliography

Ferris, Paul. *Dylan Thomas: A Biography.* New York: Dial, 1977.

Do Not Go Gentle into That Good Night

Dylan Thomas

Do not go gentle into that good night,
Old age should burn and rave at close of day;
Rage, rage against the dying of the light.

Though wise men at their end know dark is right,
Because their words had forked no lightning they   5
Do not go gentle into that good night.

Good men, the last wave by, crying how bright
Their frail deeds might have danced in a green bay,
Rage, rage against the dying of the light.

Wild men who caught and sang the sun in flight,   10
And learn, too late, they grieved it on its way,
Do not go gentle into that good night.

Grave men, near death, who see with blinding sight
Blind eyes could blaze like meteors and be gay,
Rage, rage against the dying of the light.   15

And you, my father, there on the sad height,
Curse, bless, me now with your fierce tears, I pray.
Do not go gentle into that good night.
Rage, rage against the dying of the light.

European Narrative

Every period in the history of imaginative literature in Europe has been dominated by a prevailing genre or literary form. This does not mean that there were no minor genres in each of these periods, but there was always one form of literature in which the most important works of the time were written. In ancient Greece it was the epic poem, followed by the tragic drama. In the Elizabethan era in England it was again the drama. At other times and in other places the most important genre was, among others, the short lyric poem or even the sermon. From the 18th century to today, however, the majority of the most important works of imaginative literature have been written in novelistic form. Something should be said here about later novelists who build on the developments of earlier ones.

Two important characteristics set the novel apart from other literary forms that were popular before the 18th century: 1) the novel is a prose narrative, not poetry or drama, and 2) its main characters are "ordinary" men and women, at least compared to the kings and queens of Shakespeare's and Sophocles' plays or to the warriors of Homer's and Virgil's epics. *Robinson Crusoe* (1720) by Daniel Defoe (1660–1731), for instance, one of the earliest European novels, features as its main character an Englishman of middle-class origins, who, after being shipwrecked on an island, reports his adventures in matter-of-fact language, focused not on grand poetic metaphors but on the problems and solutions related to surviving on the island.

The popularity of this focus can be understood when the novel's emergence is linked to the rise of capitalism in Europe. Unlike epic poetry, the novel was not royal entertainment that was generally recited at court, and the novelist was not supported by the king, as was seen in the banquet at Phaeacia in book eight of Homer's *Odyssey*. Like the novel, Shakespeare's plays were not reserved for the privileged few: the Globe Theatre had space provided for the groundlings or common people. Thus, *Midsummer Night's Dream* and *King Lear* were communal experiences, with representatives of all the different levels of Elizabethan society present. In contrast, a novel is a privately experienced commodity, reproduced in large quantities thanks to improvements in the technology of printing. As is true with other commodities within capitalism, the consumer purchases it on the open market and takes it home to read in private.

In other words, a new class of readers had been created by commerce: people who had fashioned comfortable lives for themselves by their own practical-minded ingenuity. They liked the fact that novels were written in prose and not verse, or poetry, for they recognized in these narratives the language they used in everyday life, in business transactions, and in private speech. The fact-oriented language of a character like Crusoe also appealed to these readers because this language seemed scientific, and the successes of science and engineering since the Renaissance were evident everywhere. Furthermore, these readers could understand and identify with the middle-class characters in the novel. At the same time, reading about the struggles of a Crusoe or a Pamela Andrews (in *Pamela*, 1739, by Samuel Richardson, 1689–1761) from the safety and comfort of one's own home was one of the rewards of capitalism: if financially secure readers could retreat to the privacy of their rooms and experience the hustle-and-bustle of the world "out there," vicariously through reading, rather than have to live it themselves. Thus, novels reflected, to some extent, and continue to reflect, the values of society, though they can also contain powerful critiques of those values.

In this regard, it is worth noting that some of Western society's worst attitudes and values permeated the earliest novels. In *Robinson Crusoe*, for instance, racism motivates the main character to exploit a black man on the island where the protagonist has been shipwrecked. In Richardson's novels, *Pamela* and *Clarissa* (1748), sexism is evident in that these stories contain scenes of threatened and actual rape. For some readers, these aspects will contaminate such works through and through. For other readers, these morally mixed fictions contain both objectionable parts and more admirable values. The issue of the extent to which values, both good and bad, count in judging works of literature that reflect those values is one that is hotly debated and that has relevance to how individuals feel about works of Western literature, dating back to its earliest surviving texts.

In any case, in the 18th century, when the novel was getting its start, narratives were generally episodic (that is, containing a series of separate and loosely related incidents) and satirical (poking fun at human vice or folly). These two features linked the novel to such forerunners as *The Golden Ass,* by the Roman Apuleius, in the 2nd century A.D.; *Gargantua and Pantagruel,* published in the 16th century by the French writer Rabelais; and especially *Don Quixote,* produced in 1605 and 1615 by the Spanish writer Cervantes. These early proto-novels and the 18th century novels that resembled them (like Henry Fielding's 1742 English narrative *Joseph Andrews*) generally introduced their often naive, foolish, or fantastically exaggerated main characters and then followed them through a series of adventures which were self-contained and did not refer to earlier or later adventures. One could rearrange the order of the episodes without seriously disturbing the sense of the novel as a whole. The plots of these episodes were largely driven by parody or satire, that is, they often made fun of the poetic literature of the past or of philosophical ideas that shared the past's idealistic notions (as Voltaire satirized the idea that ours is "the best of all possible worlds" in the French narrative *Candide*, 1759). However, before moving on to new ways of thinking, feeling, and seeing, writers had to loosen the grip of the old ways on people's minds. These novels accomplished this task by exaggerating the language and plots of the old stories of knights and of romantic lovers, making them seem silly and clearing the way for a new, more realistic way of approaching life.

Idealistic notions and language did resurge briefly at the end of the 18th and the beginning of the 19th centuries, with the advent of Romanticism. Though Romanticism is generally associated with poetry, there were some Romantic novels, such as Goethe's *The Sorrows of Young Werther* (the 1774 German work) and the English stories *Frankenstein* (1818) by Mary Shelley and *Wuthering Heights* (1847) by Emily Bronte. These works, written like novel-length prose poems, took seriously what the satiric novels of the 18th century had satirized: the supernatural, extreme passion, and fascination with death.

Gradually, however, the inflated language of the satiric and the Romantic novel gave way to realistic observations about the lives of bourgeois or middle-class people, while at the same time the episodic novel was replaced by novels that were carefully and tightly structured. Such novels had reappearing images and symbols to tie them together as a whole, just as recurring motifs in music serve to unify a symphony. This change in the novel culminated in the work of Gustave Flaubert (1821–1880), whose *Madame Bovary* (1856) recorded, in an almost documentary fashion, the appetites, behaviors, and shortcomings of the French middle-class. Flaubert's fellow French novelist Emile Zola (1840–1902) applied the methods of realist fiction to the poorer, working-class levels of society, creating the naturalistic novel, as in *Germinal* (1885), which documents the brutal lives of the French miners. Novelists in other European countries who wrote using the techniques of Realism and Naturalism include Charles Dickens (1812–1870), George Eliot (Mary Ann Evans, 1819–1880), and Thomas Hardy (1840–1928) in England, and Nicolai Gogol (1809–1852) and Leo Tolstoy (1828–1910) in Russia.

Toward the end of the 19th century and the beginning of the 20th century, novelists started to turn their attention away from the "typical" lives of doctors' wives (as in *Madame Bovary*) or even of miners (*Germinal*) and to focus more on "abnormal" characters, outsiders, or people suffering from psychological breakdowns. We can see this trend at work in the Russian *Notes from the Underground* (1864) by Dostoevsky and in the German *The Metamorphosis* (1915) by Franz Kafka. To some extent, the trend was a continuation of the documentary impulse of realistic fiction. Such works can be read as an almost scientific investigation into the minds of characters at the frayed edges of society. At the same time, psychological fiction such as Dostoevsky's and Kafka's presupposes that characters who suffer breakdowns are capable of perceptions and insights into the true nature of life and sensitive to aspects of reality that society tends to deny or block out.

Thus, Dostoevsky's Underground Man is both a little "cracked" and very astute about certain needs of the human soul that the social planners fail to take into account. There is much raving in his diatribes, but the skewed nature of his talk should not blind readers to the valid points he makes, while his story illustrates a level of emotional risk between people that society's conventions and politeness usually keep individuals from realizing. His story shows people breaking past the safety of such conventions to a mode of confrontation in which love and hate are hard to tell apart. Kafka's Gregor, on the other hand, is so dulled and alienated that he has few insights into his own situation, let alone into life in general or into society. But his transformation into a gigantic insect is less remote and fantastic than it seems at first. How many people, like Gregor, work long hours at jobs they hate, only to come home to an emotionally dysfunctional family? Long before his transformation, Gregor had developed a hard exterior, like an insect's exoskeleton, to get him through the daily drudgery and humiliations of his life. At the same time, his emotional inside had gone soft, again like an insect's, through lack of any affectionate relationships with other human beings. Gregor's metamorphosis into an insect, as handled by Kafka, becomes a powerful symbol of the alienation, the lives of "quiet desperation" (to use Thoreau's phrase) lived by so many people in the 20th century.

The modernist fiction that followed Dostoevsky's and Kafka's continued the exploration of people's inner lives by developing new stylistic methods to record characters' conscious and unconscious thoughts. Irish novelist James Joyce, for instance, used the stream-of-consciousness style throughout *Ulysses* (1922), perhaps the most important novel of the 20th century. Joyce recounts less the external events of his characters' lives than the continuous, often irrational flow of their inner thoughts, the "stream-of-consciousness" in their heads. Other important modernist novelists include Marcel Proust (1871–1922) of France and D.H. Lawrence (1885–1930) and Virginia Woolf (1882–1941) of England. Later novelists invented what can be called "metafictions," that is, stories and novels that are less concerned with events and characters than with the act of reading itself. These works by writers like Alain Robbe-Grillet (1922–), Italo Calvino (1923–1985), Umberto Eco (1929–), and Milan Kundera (1929–) are as much philosophical meditations on the nature of storytelling as they are stories about external or internal events. A good example is Kundera's *Unbearable Lightness of Being* (1984), which has strong political and sexual components but ultimately is most concerned with philosophical notions of "heaviness" and "lightness" as they relate to the act of reading.

Today, many European writers have returned to the basically realistic mode of storytelling developed in the 19th century. A good example of this kind of writer is English novelist Iris Murdoch (1919–), who has written more than 20 novels since the mid-1950s and who continues to write. Her work, and that of other novelists, seems to presuppose that life in homes and in society continues to change and to present new problems and that realism is still a valid mode for exploring these new social experiences. Yet she also employs the psychological fictional methods of Dostoevsky, the technique of creating modern fables developed by Kafka, the stylistic innovations of Joyce, and the meditations on aesthetics of metafiction writers as having provided tools that can be used here and there within an otherwise realistic novel. Thus, she and others synthesize, to some extent, the fiction of the last two centuries.

As for the future, fiction in the form of written novels may well be in the process of being replaced by film and other forms of multi-dimensional media developed for use through computers. If that does happen, there can be no doubt that the ways of narrating stories and of imagining human experience developed by writers like Dostoevsky, Kafka, and the others at the forefront of European narrative history will continue to exist, exerting their influence on the new media.

The best critical studies of the novel are Mikhail Bakhtin's *The Dialogic Imagination* (1981) and Gerard Genette's *Narrative Discourse* (1986).

Feodor Mikhailovich Dostoevsky (1821–1881)

Feodor Mikhailovich Dostoevsky was born in Moscow, Russia, on October 30, 1821, and died on January 29, 1881. Unlike some authors, in his life he experienced many of the extreme events that he wrote about in his novels. His family included his father and mother and five siblings—one older brother, two younger brothers, and two younger sisters. The Dostoevskys were middle-class but claimed to be descended from nobility. Dostoevsky attended a military engineering school in Saint Petersburg from 1837 to 1843, then served a year of military service, at which point he began his literary career. His first novel was *Poor Folk* (1846), a critical and commercial success at the time but not at the level of his later masterpieces.

Frequently, there were parallels between Dostoevsky's novels and events in his life. Dostoevsky's father was an alcoholic and a violent disciplinarian. In 1839 he was murdered by peasants, possibly for good reasons, on a small estate he had bought south of Moscow. Dostoevsky drew on this event in his final novel, *The Brothers Karamazov* (1880), in which the drunken, lecherous father is also murdered. All his life, Dostoevsky suffered from epilepsy, so it is not unusual that Prince Myshkin, the main character of *The Idiot* (1868), has epileptic fits. The writer describes the moments just before the fits as instances of supreme awareness, followed by near idiocy. In 1847 Dostoevsky began attending secret meetings to discuss social problems with other utopian socialists. On April 22, 1849, he was arrested with the others and sentenced, in the name of Czar Nicolas I, to execution by firing squad. He was taken out to be shot on December 22, but the Czar granted a last-minute reprieve, and he was sent to a prison labor camp in Siberia for four years. Dostoevsky worked the theme of the last-minute reprieve from execution into *The Idiot*, and he depicted his years in the prison labor camp in *The House of the Dead* (1860–62). In 1859, after an additional five years of exile, he returned to Russia and married a widow who already had children. She grew sick and died, leaving him with dependents and debts. That same terrible year (1864), he published his penetrating psychological study of an alienated man, *Notes from the Underground*.

A long, tortuous love affair with Apollinaria Suslova endured while they lived in Russia, Italy, Switzerland, France, and Germany and became the source for many of the relationships described in his novels. *Crime and Punishment* (like *Notes*, a study of a psychologically disturbed individual) appeared in 1866. In debt from the affair and from a severe gambling addiction, Dostoevsky married his stenographer, Anna Grigorievna Snitkina in 1867. She bore him four children, and with her help he largely straightened out his life and settled down to write his last three novels. *The Idiot* (1868) was followed by *The Possessed* in 1872 and in 1880 by the novel that most critics consider to be his greatest masterpiece, *The Brothers Karamazov,* which includes the famous chapter, "The Grand Inquisitor," a sort of 19th century version of the *Book of Job*. Dostoevsky's death in 1881 came from a hemorrhage in his throat caused by emphysema. He remains one the great psychological novelists.

The authoritative biography in English would have to be Joseph Frank's on-going, multi-volume work, *Dostoevsky*. The best critical study of Dostoevsky is still Russian critic Mikhail Bakhtin's *Problems of Dostoevsky's Poetics*.

Notes from the Underground

Feodor Dostoevsky

Part I

Underground

I am a sick man. . . . I am a spiteful man. I am an unattractive man. I believe my liver is diseased. However, I know nothing at all about my disease, and do not know for certain what ails me. I don't consult a doctor for it, and never have, though I have a respect for medicine and doctors. Besides, I am extremely superstitious, sufficiently so to respect medicine, anyway (I am well-educated enough not to be superstitious, but I am superstitious). No, I refuse to consult a doctor from spite. That you probably will not understand. Well, I understand it, though. Of course, I can't explain who it is precisely that I am mortifying in this case by my spite: I am perfectly well aware that I cannot "pay out" the doctors by not consulting them; I know better than anyone that by all this I am only injuring myself and no one else. But still, if I don't consult a doctor it is from spite. My liver is bad, well—let it get worse!

I have been going on like that for a long time—twenty years. Now I am forty. I used to be in the government service, but am no longer. I was a spiteful official. I was rude and took pleasure in being so. I did not take bribes, you see, so I was bound to find a recompense in that, at least. (A poor jest, but I will not scratch it out. I wrote it thinking it would sound very witty; but now that I have seen myself that I only wanted to show off in a despicable way, I will not scratch it out on purpose!)

When petitioners used to come for information to the table at which I sat, I used to grind my teeth at them, and felt intense enjoyment when I succeeded in making anybody unhappy. I almost did succeed. For the most part they were all timid people—of course, they were petitioners. But of the uppish ones there was one officer in particular I could not endure. He simply would not be humble, and clanked his sword in a disgusting way. I carried on a feud with him for eighteen months over that sword. At last I got the better of him. He left off clanking it. That happened in my youth, though.

But do you know, gentlemen, what was the chief point about my spite? Why, the whole point, the real sting of it lay in the fact that continually, even in the moment of the acutest spleen, I was inwardly conscious with shame that I was not only not a spiteful but not even an embittered man, that I was simply scaring sparrows at random and amusing myself by it. I might foam at the mouth, but bring me a doll to play with, give me a cup of tea with sugar in it, and maybe I should be appeased. I might even be genuinely touched, though probably I should grind my teeth at myself afterwards and lie awake at night with shame for months after. That was my way.

I was lying when I said just now that I was a spiteful official. I was lying from spite. I was simply amusing myself with the petitioners and with the officer, and in reality I never could become spiteful. I was conscious every moment in myself of many, very many elements absolutely opposite to that. I felt them positively swarming in me, these opposite elements. I knew that they had been swarming in me all my life and craving some outlet from me, but I would not let them, would not let them, purposely would not let them come out. They tormented me till I was ashamed: they drove me to convulsions and—sickened me, at last, how they sickened me! Now, are not you fancying, gentlemen, that I am expressing remorse for something now, that I am asking your forgiveness for something? I am sure you are fancying that . . . However, I assure you I do not care if you are. . . .

It was not only that I could not become spiteful, I did not know how to become anything; neither spiteful nor kind, neither a rascal nor an honest man, neither a hero nor an insect. Now, I am living out my life in my corner, taunting myself with the spiteful and useless consolation that an intelligent man cannot become anything seriously, and it is only the fool who becomes anything. Yes, a man in the nineteenth century must and morally ought to be pre-eminently a characterless creature; a man of character, an active man is pre-eminently a limited creature. That is my conviction of forty years. I am forty years old now, and you know forty years is a whole lifetime; you know it is extreme old age. To live longer than forty years is bad manners, is vulgar, immoral. Who does live beyond forty? Answer that, sincerely and honestly I will tell you who do: fools and worthless fellows. I tell all old men that to their face, all these venerable old men, all these silver-haired and reverend seniors! I tell the whole world that to its face! I have a right to say so, for I shall go on living to sixty myself. To seventy! To eighty! . . . Stay, let me take breath . . .

You imagine no doubt, gentlemen, that I want to amuse you. You are mistaken in that, too. I am by no means such a mirthful person as you imagine, or as you may imagine; however, irritated by all this babble (and I feel that you are irritated) you think fit to ask me who I am—then my answer is, I am a collegiate assessor. I was in the service that I might have something to eat (and solely for that reason), and when last year a distant relation left me six thousand roubles in his will I immediately retired from the service and settled down in my corner. I used to live in this corner before, but now I have settled down in it. My room is a wretched, horrid one in the outskirts of the town. My servant is an old country-woman, ill-natured from stupidity, and, moreover, there is always a nasty smell about her. I am told that the Petersburg climate is bad for me, and that with my small means it is very expensive to live in Petersburg. I know all that better than all these sage and experienced counsellors and monitors. . . . But I am remaining in Petersburg; I am not going away from Petersburg! I am not going away because . . . ech! Why, it is absolutely no matter whether I am going away or not going away.

But what can a decent man speak of with most pleasure?

Answer: Of himself.

Well, so I will talk about myself.

II

I want now to tell you, gentlemen, whether you care to hear it or not, why I could not even become an insect. I tell you solemnly, that I have many times tried to become an insect. But I was not equal even to that. I swear, gentlemen, that to be too conscious is an illness—a real thorough-going illness. For man's everyday needs, it would have been quite enough to have the ordinary human consciousness, that is, half or a quarter of the amount which falls to the lot of a cultivated man of our unhappy nineteenth century, especially one who has the fatal ill-luck to inhabit Petersburg, the most theoretical and intentional town on the whole terrestrial globe. (There are intentional and unintentional towns.) It would have been quite enough, for instance, to have the consciousness by which all so-called direct persons and men of action live. I bet you think I am writing all this from affectation, to be witty at the expense of men of action; and what is more, that from ill-bred affectation, I am clanking a sword like my officer. But, gentlemen, whoever can pride himself on his diseases and even swagger over them?

Though, after all, everyone does do that; people do pride themselves on their diseases, and I do, may be, more than anyone. We will not dispute it; my contention was absurd. But yet I am firmly persuaded that a great deal of consciousness, every sort of consciousness, in fact, is a disease. I stick to that. Let us leave that, too, for a minute. Tell me this: why does it happen that at the very, yes, at the very moments when I am most capable of feeling every refinement of all that is "sublime and beautiful," as they used to say at one time, it would, as though of design, happen to me not only to feel but to do such ugly things, such that . . . Well, in short, actions that all, perhaps, commit; but which, as though purposely, occurred to me at the very time when I was most conscious that they ought not to be committed. The more conscious I was of goodness and of all that was "sublime and beautiful," the more deeply I sank into my mire and the more ready I was to sink in it altogether. But the chief point was that all this was, as it were, not accidental in me, but as though it were bound to be so. It was as though it were my most normal condition, and not in the least disease or depravity, so that at last all desire in me to struggle against this depravity passed. It ended by my almost believing (perhaps actually believing) that this was perhaps my normal condition. But at first, in the beginning, what agonies I endured in that struggle! I did not believe it was the same with other people, and all my life I hid this fact about myself as a secret. I was ashamed (even now, perhaps, I am ashamed): I got to the point of feeling a sort of secret abnormal, despicable enjoyment in returning home to my corner on some disgusting Petersburg night, acutely conscious that that day I had committed a loathsome action again, that what was done could never be undone, and secretly, inwardly gnawing, gnawing at myself for it, tearing and consuming myself till at last the bitterness turned into a sort of shameful accursed sweetness, and at last—into positive real enjoyment! Yes, into enjoyment, into enjoyment! I insist upon that. I have spoken of this because I keep wanting to know for a fact whether other people feel such enjoyment? I will explain; the enjoyment was just from the too intense consciousness of one's own degradation; it was from feeling oneself that one had reached the last barrier, that it was horrible, but that it could not be otherwise; that there was no escape for you; that you never could become a different man; that even if time and faith were still left you to change into something different you would most likely not wish to change; or if you did wish to, even then you would do nothing; because perhaps in reality there was nothing for you to change into.

And the worst of it was, and the root of it all, that it was all in accord with the normal fundamental laws of over-acute consciousness, and with the inertia that was the direct result of those laws, and that consequently one was not only unable to change but could do absolutely nothing. Thus it would follow, as the result of acute consciousness, that one is not to blame in being a scoundrel; as though that were any consolation to the scoundrel once he has come to realise that he actually is a scoundrel. But enough. . . . Ech, I have talked a lot of nonsense, but what have I explained? How is enjoyment in this to be explained? But I will explain it. I will get to the bottom of it! That is why I have taken up my pen. . . .

I, for instance, have a great deal of *amour propre*. I am as suspicious and prone to take offence as a humpback or a dwarf. But upon my word I sometimes have had moments when if I had happened to be slapped in the face I should, perhaps, have been positively glad of it. I say, in earnest, that I should probably have been able to discover even in that a peculiar sort of enjoyment—the enjoyment, of course, of despair; but in despair there are the most intense enjoyments, especially when one is very acutely conscious of the hopelessness of one's position. And when one is slapped in the face—why then the consciousness of being rubbed into a pulp would positively overwhelm one. The worst of it is, look at it which way one will, it still turns out that I was always the most to blame in everything. And what is most humiliating of all, to blame for no fault of my own but, so to say, through the laws of nature. In the first place, to blame because I am cleverer than any of the people surrounding me. (I have always considered myself cleverer than any of the people surrounding me, and sometimes, would you believe it, have been positively ashamed of it. At any rate, I have all my life, as it were, turned my eyes away and never could look people straight in the face.) To blame, finally, because even if I had had magnanimity, I should only have had more suffering from the sense of its uselessness. I should certainly have never been able to do anything from being magnanimous—neither to forgive, for my assailant would perhaps have slapped me from the laws of nature, and one cannot forgive the laws of nature; nor to forget, for even if it were owing to the laws of nature, it is insulting all the same. Finally, even if I had wanted to be anything but magnanimous, had desired on the contrary to revenge myself on my assailant, I could not have revenged myself on any one for anything because I should certainly never have made up my mind to do anything, even if I had been able to. Why should I not have made up my mind? About that in particular I want to say a few words.

III

With people who know how to revenge themselves and to stand up for themselves in general, how is it done? Why, when they are possessed, let us suppose, by the feeling of revenge, then for the time there is nothing else but that feeling left in their whole being. Such a gentleman simply dashes straight for his object like an infuriated bull with its horns down, and nothing but a wall will stop him. (By the way: facing the wall, such gentlemen—that is, the "direct" persons and men of action—are genuinely nonplussed. For them a wall is not an evasion, as for us people who think and consequently do nothing; it is not an excuse for turning aside, an excuse for which we are always very glad, though we scarcely believe in it ourselves, as a rule. No, they are nonplussed in all sincerity. The wall has for them something tranquillising, morally soothing, final—maybe even something mysterious . . . but of the wall later.)

Well, such a direct person I regard as the real normal man, as his tender mother nature wished to see him when she graciously brought him into being on the earth. I envy such a man till I am green in the face. He is stupid. I am not disputing that, but perhaps the normal man should be stupid, how do you know? Perhaps it is very beautiful, in fact. And I am the more persuaded of that suspicion, if one can call it so, by the fact that if you take, for instance, the antithesis of the normal man, that is, the man of acute consciousness, who has come, of course, not out of the lap of nature but out of a retort (this is almost mysticism, gentlemen, but I suspect this, too), this retort-made man is sometimes so nonplussed in the presence of his antithesis that with all his exaggerated consciousness he genuinely thinks of himself as a mouse and not a man. It may be an acutely conscious mouse, yet it is a mouse, while the other is a man, and therefore, et cetera, et cetera. And the worst of it is, he himself, his very own self, looks on himself as a mouse; no one asks him to do so; and that is an important point. Now let us look at this mouse in action. Let us suppose, for instance, that it feels insulted, too (and it almost always does feel insulted), and wants to revenge itself, too. There may even be a greater accumulation of spite in it than in *l'homme de la nature et de la vérité*. The base and nasty desire to vent that spite on its assailant rankles perhaps even more nastily in it than in *l'homme de la nature et de la vérité*. For through his innate stupidity the latter looks upon his revenge as justice pure and simple; while in consequence of his acute consciousness the mouse does not believe in the justice of it. To come at last to the deed itself, to the very act of revenge. Apart from the one fundamental nastiness the luckless mouse succeeds in creating around it so many other nastinesses in the form of doubts and questions, adds to the one question so many unsettled questions that there inevitably works up around it a sort of fatal brew, a stinking mess, made up of its doubts, emotions, and of the contempt spat upon it by the direct men of action who stand solemnly about it as judges and arbitrators, laughing at it till their healthy sides ache. Of course the only thing left for it is to dismiss all that with a wave of its paw, and, with a smile of assumed contempt in which it does not even itself believe, creep ignominiously into its mouse-hole. There in its nasty, stinking, underground home our insulted, crushed and ridiculed mouse promptly becomes absorbed in cold, malignant and, above all, everlasting spite. For forty years together it will remember its injury down to the smallest, most ignominious details, and every time will add, of itself, details still more ignominious, spitefully teasing and tormenting itself with its own imagination. It will itself be ashamed of its imaginings, but yet it will recall it all, it will go over and over every detail, it will invent unheard of things against itself, pretending that those things might happen, and will forgive nothing. Maybe it will begin to revenge itself, too, but, as it were, piecemeal, in trivial ways, from behind the stove, incognito, without believing either in its own right to vengeance, or in the success of its revenge, knowing that from all its efforts at revenge it will suffer a hundred times more than he on whom it revenges itself, while he, I daresay, will not even scratch himself. On its deathbed it will recall it all over again, with interest accumulated over all the years and . . .

But it is just in that cold, abominable half despair, half belief, in that conscious burying oneself alive for grief in the underworld for forty years, in that acutely recognised and yet partly doubtful hopelessness of one's position, in that hell of unsatisfied desires turned inward, in that fever of oscillations, of resolutions determined for ever and repented of again a minute later—that the savour of that strange enjoyment of which I have spoken lies. It is so subtle, so difficult of analysis, that persons who are a little limited, or even simply persons of strong nerves, will not understand a single atom of it. "Possibly," you will add on your own account with a grin, "people will not understand it either who have never received a slap in the face," and in that way you will politely hint to me that I, too, perhaps, have had the experience of a slap in the face in my life, and so I speak as one who knows. I bet that you are thinking that. But set your minds at rest, gentlemen, I have not received a slap in the face, though it is absolutely a matter of indifference to me what you may think about it. Possibly, I even regret, myself, that I have given so few slaps in the face during my life. But enough . . . not another word on that subject of such extreme interest to you.

I will continue calmly concerning persons with strong nerves who do not understand a certain refinement of enjoyment. Though in certain circumstances these gentlemen bellow their loudest like bulls, though this, let us suppose, does them the greatest credit, yet, as I have said already, confronted with the impossible they subside at once. The impossible means the stone wall! What stone wall? Why, of course, the laws of nature, the deductions of natural science, mathematics. As soon as they prove to you, for instance, that you are descended from a monkey, then it is no use scowling, accept it for a fact. When they prove to you that in reality one drop of your own fat must be dearer to you than a hundred thousand of your fellow-creatures, and that this conclusion is the final solution of all so-called virtues and duties and all such prejudices and fancies, then you have just to accept it, there is no help for it, for twice two is a law of mathematics. Just try refuting it.

"Upon my word, they will shout at you, it is no use protesting: it is a case of twice two makes four! Nature does not ask your permission, she has nothing to do with your wishes, and whether you like her laws or dislike them, you are bound to accept her as she is, and consequently all her conclusions. A wall, you see, is a wall . . . and so on, and so on."

Merciful Heavens! but what do I care for the laws of nature and arithmetic, when, for some reason I dislike those laws and the fact that twice two makes four? Of course I cannot break through the wall by battering my head against it if I really have not the strength to knock it down, but I am not going to be reconciled to it simply because it is a stone wall and I have not the strength.

As though such a stone wall really were a consolation, and really did contain some word of conciliation, simply because it is as true as twice two makes four. Oh, absurdity of absurdities! How much better it is to understand it all, to recognise it all, all the impossibilities and the stone wall; not to be reconciled to one of those impossibilities and stone walls if it disgusts you to be reconciled to it; by the way of the most inevitable, logical combinations to reach the most revolting conclusions on the everlasting theme, that even for the stone wall you are yourself somehow to blame, though again it is as clear as day you are not to blame in the least, and therefore grinding your teeth in silent impotence to sink into luxurious inertia, brooding on the fact that there is no one even for you to feel vindictive against, that you have not, and perhaps never will have, an object for your spite, that it is a sleight of hand, a bit of juggling, a card-sharper's trick, that it is simply a mess, no knowing what and no knowing who, but in spite of all these uncertainties and jugglings, still there is an ache in you, and the more you do not know, the worse the ache.

IV

"Ha, ha, ha! You will be finding enjoyment in toothache next," you cry, with a laugh.

"Well, even in toothache there is enjoyment," I answer. I had toothache for a whole month and I know there is. In that case, of course, people are not spiteful in silence, but moan; but they are not candid moans, they are malignant moans, and the malignancy is the whole point. The enjoyment of the sufferer finds expression in those moans; if he did not feel enjoyment in them he would not moan. It is a good example, gentlemen, and I will develop it. Those moans express in the first place all the aimlessness of your pain, which is so humiliating to your consciousness; the whole legal system of nature on which you spit disdainfully, of course, but from which you suffer all the same while she does not. They express the consciousness that you have no enemy to punish, but that you have pain; the consciousness that in spite of all possible Wagenheims you are in complete slavery to your teeth; that if someone wishes it, your teeth will leave off aching, and if he does not, they will go on aching another three months; and that finally if you are still contumacious and still protest, all that is left you for your own gratification is to thrash yourself or beat your wall with your fist as hard as you can, and absolutely nothing more. Well, these mortal insults, these jeers on the part of someone unknown, end at last in an enjoyment which sometimes reaches the highest degree of voluptuousness. I ask you, gentlemen, listen sometimes to the moans of an educated man of the nineteenth century suffering from toothache, on the second or third day of the attack, when he is beginning to moan, not as he moaned on the first day, that is, not simply because he has toothache, not just as any coarse peasant, but as a man affected by progress and European civilisation, a man who is "divorced from the soil and the national elements," as they express it now-a-days. His moans become nasty, disgustingly malignant, and go on for whole days and nights. And of course he knows himself that he is doing himself no sort of good with his moans; he knows better than anyone that he is only lacerating and harassing himself and others for nothing; he knows that even the audience before whom he is making his efforts, and his whole family, listen to him with loathing, do not put a ha'porth of faith in him, and inwardly understand that he might moan differently, more simply, without trills and flourishes, and that he is only amusing himself like that from ill-humour, from malignancy. Well, in all these recognitions and disgraces it is that there lies a voluptuous pleasure. As though he would say: "I am worrying you, I am lacerating your hearts, I am keeping everyone in the house awake. Well, stay awake then, you, too, feel every minute that I have toothache. I am not a hero to you now, as I tried to seem before, but simply a nasty person, an impostor. Well, so be it, then! I am very glad that you see through me. It is nasty for you to hear my despicable moans: well, let it be nasty; here I will let you have a nastier flourish in a minute. . . ." You do not understand even now, gentlemen? No, it seems our development and our consciousness must go further to understand all the intricacies of this pleasure. You laugh? Delighted. My jests, gentlemen, are of course in bad taste, jerky, involved, lacking self-confidence. But of course that is because I do not respect myself. Can a man of perception respect himself at all?

V

Come, can a man who attempts to find enjoyment in the very feeling of his own degradation possibly have a spark of respect for himself? I am not saying this now from any mawkish kind of remorse. And, indeed, I could never endure saying, "Forgive me, Papa, I won't do it again," not because I am incapable of saying that—on the contrary, perhaps just because I have been too capable of it, and in what a way, too. As though of design I used to get into trouble in cases when I was not to blame in any way. That was the nastiest part of it. At the same time I was genuinely touched and penitent, I used to shed tears and, of course, deceived myself, though I was not acting in the least and there was a sick feeling in my heart at the time. . . . For that one could not blame even the laws of nature, though the laws of nature have continually all my life offended me more than anything. It is loathsome to remember it all, but it was loathsome even then. Of course, a minute or so later I would realise wrathfully that it was all a lie, a revolting lie, an affected lie, that is, all this penitence, this emotion, these vows of reform. You will ask why did I worry myself with such antics: answer, because it was very dull to sit with one's hands folded, and so one began cutting capers. That is really it. Observe yourselves more carefully, gentlemen, then you will understand that it is so. I invented adventures for myself and made up a life, so as at least to live in some way. How many times it has happened to me—well, for instance, to take offence simply on purpose, for nothing; and one knows oneself, of course, that one is offended at nothing; that one is putting it on, but yet one brings oneself at last to the point of being really offended. All my life I have had an impulse to play such pranks, so that in the end I could not control it in myself. Another time, twice, in fact, I tried hard to be in love. I suffered, too, gentlemen, I assure you. In the depth of my heart there was no faith in my suffering, only a faint stir of mockery, but yet I did suffer, and in the real, orthodox way; I was jealous, beside myself . . . and it was all from *ennui*, gentlemen, all from *ennui*; inertia overcame me. You know the direct, legitimate fruit of consciousness is inertia, that is, conscious sitting-with-the-hands-folded. I have referred to this already. I repeat, I repeat with emphasis: all "direct" persons and men of action are active just because they are stupid and limited. How explain that? I will tell you: in consequence of their limitation they take immediate and secondary causes for primary ones, and in that way persuade themselves more quickly and easily than other people do that they have found an infallible foundation for their activity, and their minds are at ease and you know that is the chief thing. To begin to act, you know, you must first have your mind completely at ease and no trace of doubt left in it. Why, how am I, for example, to set my mind at rest? Where are the primary causes on which I am to build? Where are my foundations? Where am I to get them from? I exercise myself in reflection, and consequently with me every primary cause at once draws after itself another still more primary, and so on to infinity. That is just the essence of every sort of consciousness and reflection. It must be a case of the laws of nature again. What is the result of it in the end? Why, just the same. Remember I spoke just now of vengeance. (I am sure you did not take it in.) I said that a man revenges himself because he sees justice in it. Therefore he has found a primary cause, that is, justice. And so he is at rest on all sides, and consequently he carries out his revenge calmly and successfully, being persuaded that he is doing a just and honest thing. But I see no justice in it, I find no sort of virtue in it either, and consequently if I attempt to revenge myself, it is only out of spite. Spite, of course, might overcome everything, all my doubts, and so might serve quite successfully in place of a primary cause, precisely because it is not a cause. But what is to be done if I have not even spite (I began with that just now, you know). In consequence again of those accursed laws of consciousness, anger in me is subject to chemical disintegration. You look into it, the object flies off into air, your reasons evaporate, the criminal is not to be found, the wrong becomes not a wrong but a phantom, something like the toothache, for which no one is to blame, and consequently there is only the same outlet left again—that is, to beat the wall as hard as you can. So you give it up with a wave of the hand because you have not found a fundamental cause. And try letting yourself be carried away by your feelings, blindly, without reflection, without a primary cause, repelling consciousness at least for a time; hate or love, if only not to sit with your hands folded. The day after tomorrow, at the latest, you will begin despising yourself for having knowingly deceived yourself. Result: a soap-bubble and inertia. Oh, gentlemen, do you know, perhaps I consider myself an intelligent man, only because all my life I have been able neither to begin nor to finish anything. Granted I am a babbler, a harmless vexatious babbler, like all of us. But what is to be done if the direct and sole vocation of every intelligent man is babble, that is, the intentional pouring of water through a sieve?

VI

Oh, if I had done nothing simply from laziness! Heavens, how I should have respected myself, then. I should have respected myself because I should at least have been capable of being lazy; there would at least have been one quality, as it were, positive in me, in which I could have believed myself. Question: What is he? Answer: A sluggard; how very pleasant it would have been to hear that of oneself! It would mean that I was positively defined, it would mean that there was something to say about me. "Sluggard"—why, it is a calling and vocation, it is a career. Do not jest, it is so. I should then be a member of the best club by right, and should find my occupation in continually respecting myself. I knew a gentleman who prided himself all his life on being a connoisseur of Lafitte. He considered this as his positive virtue, and never doubted himself. He died, not simply with a tranquil, but with a triumphant conscience, and he was quite right, too. Then I should have chosen a career for myself, I should have been a sluggard and a glutton, not a simple one, but, for instance, one with sympathies for everything sublime and beautiful. How do you like that? I have long had visions of it. That "sublime and beautiful" weighs heavily on my mind at forty But that is at forty; then—oh, then it would have been different! I should have found for myself a form of activity in keeping with it, to be precise, drinking to the health of everything "sublime and beautiful." I should have snatched at every opportunity to drop a tear into my glass and then to drain it to all that is "sublime and beautiful." I should then have turned everything into the sublime and the beautiful; in the nastiest, unquestionable trash, I should have sought out the sublime and the beautiful. I should have exuded tears like a wet sponge. An artist, for instance, paints a picture worthy of Gay. At once I drink to the health of the artist who painted the picture worthy of Gay, because I love all that is "sublime and beautiful." An author has written *as you will*: at once I drink to the health of "anyone you will" because I love all that is "sublime and beautiful."

I should claim respect for doing so. I should persecute anyone who would not show me respect. I should live at ease, I should die with dignity, why, it is charming, perfectly charming! And what a good round belly I should have grown, what a treble chin I should have established, what a ruby nose I should have coloured for myself, so that everyone would have said, looking at me: "Here is an asset! Here is something real and solid!" And, say what you like, it is very agreeable to hear such remarks about oneself in this negative age.

VII

But these are all golden dreams. Oh, tell me, who was it first announced, who was it first proclaimed, that man only does nasty things because he does not know his own interests; and that if he were enlightened, if his eyes were opened to his real normal interests, man would at once cease to do nasty things, would at once become good and noble because, being enlightened and understanding his real advantage, he would see his own advantage in the good and nothing else, and we all know that not one man can, consciously, act against his own interests, consequently, so to say, through necessity, he would begin doing good? Oh, the babe! Oh, the pure, innocent child! Why, in the first place, when in all these thousands of years has there been a time when man has acted only from his own interest? What is to be done with the millions of facts that bear witness that men, *consciously*, that is fully understanding their real interests, have left them in the background and have rushed headlong on another path, to meet peril and danger, compelled to this course by nobody and by nothing, but, as it were, simply disliking the beaten track, and have obstinately, wilfully, struck out another difficult, absurd way, seeking it almost in the darkness. So, I suppose, this obstinacy and perversity were pleasanter to them than any advantage. . . . Advantage! What is advantage? And will you take it upon yourself to define with perfect accuracy in what the advantage of man consists? And what if it so happens that a man's advantage, *sometimes*, not only may, but even must, consist in his desiring in certain cases what is harmful to himself and not advantageous. And if so, if there can be such a case, the whole principle falls into dust. What do you think—are there such cases? You laugh; laugh away, gentlemen, but only answer me: have man's advantages been reckoned up with perfect certainty? Are there not some which not only have not been included but cannot possibly be included under any classification? You see, you gentlemen have, to the best of my knowledge, taken your whole register of human advantages from the averages of statistical figures and politico-economical formulas. Your advantages are prosperity, wealth, freedom, peace—and so on, and so on. So that the man who should, for instance, go openly and knowingly in opposition to all that list would to your thinking, and indeed mine, too, of course, be an obscurantist or an absolute madman: would not he? But, you know, this is what is surprising: why does it so happen that all these statisticians, sages and lovers of humanity, when they reckon up human advantages invariably leave out one? They don't even take it into their reckoning in the form in which it should be taken, and the whole reckoning depends upon that. It would be no greater matter, they would simply have to take it, this advantage, and add it to the list. But the trouble is, that this strange advantage does not fall under any classification and is not in place in any list. I have a friend for instance . . . Ech! gentlemen, but of course he is your friend, too; and indeed there is no one, no one to whom he is not a friend! When he prepares for any undertaking this gentleman immediately explains to you, elegantly and clearly, exactly how he must act in accordance with the laws of reason and truth. What is more, he will talk to you with excitement and passion of the true normal interests of man; with irony he will upbraid the short-sighted fools who do not understand their own interests, nor the true significance of virtue; and, within a quarter of an hour, without any sudden outside provocation, but simply through something inside him which is stronger than all his interests, he will go off on quite a different tack—that is, act in direct opposition to what he has just been saying about himself, in opposition to the laws of reason, in opposition to his own advantage, in fact in opposition to everything . . . I warn you that my friend is a compound personality and therefore it is difficult to blame him as an individual. The fact is, gentlemen, it seems there must really exist something that is dearer to almost every man than his greatest advantages, or (not to be illogical) there is a most advantageous advantage (the very one omitted of which we spoke just now) which is more important and more advantageous than all other advantages, for the sake of which a man if necessary is ready to act in opposition to all laws; that is, in opposition to reason, honour, peace, prosperity—in fact, in opposition to all those excellent and useful things if only he can attain that fundamental, most advantageous advantage which is dearer to him than all. "Yes, but it's advantage all the same," you will retort. But excuse me, I'll make the point clear, and it is not a case of playing upon words. What matters is, that this advantage is remarkable from the very fact that it breaks down all our classifications, and continually shatters every system constructed by lovers of mankind for the benefit of mankind. In fact, it upsets everything. But before I mention this advantage to you, I want to compromise myself personally, and therefore I boldly declare that all these fine systems, all these theories for explaining to mankind their real normal interests, in order that inevitably striving to pursue these interests they may at once become good and noble—are, in my opinion, so far, mere logical exercises! Yes, logical exercises. Why, to maintain this theory of the regeneration of mankind by means of the pursuit of his own advantage is to my mind almost the same thing . . . as to affirm, for instance, following Buckle, that through civilisation mankind becomes softer, and consequently less bloodthirsty and less fitted for warfare. Logically it does seem to follow from his arguments. But man has such a predilection for systems and abstract deductions that he is ready to distort the truth intentionally, he is ready to deny the evidence of his senses only to justify his logic. I take this example because it is the most glaring instance of it. Only look about you: blood is being spilt in streams, and in the merriest way, as though it were champagne. Take the whole of the nineteenth century in which Buckle lived. Take Napoleon—the Great and also the present one. Take North America—the eternal union. Take the farce of Schleswig-Holstein. . . . And what is it that civilisation softens in us? The only gain of civilisation for mankind is the greater capacity for variety of sensations—and absolutely nothing more. And through the development of this many-sidedness man may come to finding enjoyment in bloodshed. In fact, this has already happened to him. Have you noticed that it is the most civilised gentlemen who have been the subtlest slaughterers, to whom the Attilas and Stenka Razins could not hold a candle, and if they are not so conspicuous as the Attilas and Stenka Razins it is simply because they are so often met with, are so ordinary and have become so familiar to us. In any case civilisation has made mankind if not more bloodthirsty, at least more vilely, more loathsomely bloodthirsty. In old days he saw justice in bloodshed and with his conscience at peace exterminated those he thought proper. Now we do think bloodshed abominable and yet we engage in this abomination, and with more energy than ever. Which is worse? Decide that for yourselves. They say that Cleopatra (excuse an instance from Roman history) was fond of sticking gold pins into her slave-girls' breasts and derived gratification from their screams and writhings. You will say that that was in the comparatively barbarous times; that these are barbarous times too, because also, comparatively speaking, pins are stuck in even now; that though man has now learned to see more clearly than in barbarous ages, he is still far from having learnt to act as reason and science would dictate. But yet you are fully convinced that he will be sure to learn when he gets rid of certain old bad habits, and when common sense and science have completely re-educated human nature and turned it in a normal direction. You are confident that then man will cease from *intentional* error and will, so to say, be compelled not to want to set his will against his normal interests. That is not all; then, you say, science itself will teach man (though to my mind it's a superfluous luxury) that he never has really had any caprice or will of his own, and that he himself is something of the nature of a piano-key or the stop of an organ, and that there are, besides, things called the laws of nature; so that everything he does is not done by his willing it, but is done of itself, by the laws of nature. Consequently we have only to discover these laws of nature, and man will no longer have to answer for his actions and life will become exceedingly easy for him. All human actions will then, of course, be tabulated according to these laws, mathematically, like tables of logarithms up to 108,000, and entered in an index; or, better still, there would be published certain edifying works of the nature of encyclopaedic lexicons, in which everything will be so clearly calculated and explained that there will be no more incidents or adventures in the world.

Then—this is all what you say—new economic relations will be established, all ready-made and worked out with mathematical exactitude, so that every possible question will vanish in the twinkling of an eye, simply because every possible answer to it will be provided. Then the "Palace of Crystal" will be built. Then. . . . In fact, those will be halcyon days. Of course there is no guaranteeing (this is my comment) that it will not be, for instance, frightfully dull then (for what will one have to do when everything will be calculated and tabulated), but on the other hand everything will be extraordinarily rational. Of course boredom may lead you to anything. It is boredom sets one sticking golden pins into people, but all that would not matter. What is bad (this is my comment again) is that I dare say people will be thankful for the gold pins then. Man is stupid, you know, phenomenally stupid; or rather he is not at all stupid, but he is so ungrateful that you could not find another like him in all creation. I, for instance, would not be in the least surprised if all of a sudden, *à propos* of nothing, in the midst of general prosperity a gentleman with an ignoble, or rather with a reactionary and ironical, countenance were to arise and, putting his arms akimbo, say to us all: "I say, gentleman, hadn't we better kick over the whole show and scatter rationalism to the winds, simply to send these logarithms to the devil, and to enable us to live once more at our own sweet foolish will!" That again would not matter, but what is annoying is that he would be sure to find followers—such is the nature of man. And all that for the most foolish reason, which, one would think, was hardly worth mentioning: that is, that man everywhere and at all times, whoever he may be, has preferred to act as he chose and not in the least as his reason and advantage dictated. And one may choose what is contrary to one's own interests, and sometimes one *positively ought* (that is my idea). One's own free unfettered choice, one's own caprice, however wild it may be, one's own fancy worked up at times to frenzy—is that very "most advantageous advantage" which we have overlooked, which comes under no classification and against which all systems and theories are continually being shattered to atoms. And how do these wiseacres know that man wants a normal, a virtuous choice? What has made them conceive that man must want a rationally advantageous choice? What man wants is simply *independent* choice, whatever that independence may cost and wherever it may lead. And choice, of course, the devil only knows what choice.

VIII

"Ha! ha! ha! But you know there is no such thing as choice in reality, say what you like," you will interpose with a chuckle. "Science has succeeded in so far analysing man that we know already that choice and what is called freedom of will is nothing else than—"

Stay, gentlemen, I meant to begin with that myself I confess, I was rather frightened. I was just going to say that the devil only knows what choice depends on, and that perhaps that was a very good thing, but I remembered the teaching of science . . . and pulled myself up. And here you have begun upon it. Indeed, if there really is some day discovered a formula for all our desires and caprices—that is, an explanation of what they depend upon, by what laws they arise, how they develop, what they are aiming at in one case and in another and so on, that is a real mathematical formula—then, most likely, man will at once cease to feel desire, indeed, he will be certain to. For who would want to choose by rule? Besides, he will at once be transformed from a human being into an organ-stop or something of the sort; for what is a man without desires, without free will and without choice, if not a stop in an organ? What do you think? Let us reckon the chances—can such a thing happen or not?

"H'm!" you decide. "Our choice is usually mistaken from a false view of our advantage. We sometimes choose absolute nonsense because in our foolishness we see in that nonsense the easiest means for attaining a supposed advantage. But when all that is explained and worked out on paper (which is perfectly possible, for it is contemptible and senseless to suppose that some laws of nature man will never understand), then certainly so-called desires will no longer exist. For if a desire should come into conflict with reason we shall then reason and not desire, because it will be impossible retaining our reason to be *senseless* in our desires, and in that way knowingly act against reason and desire to injure ourselves. And as all choice and reasoning can be really calculated—because there will some day be discovered the laws of our so-called free will—so, joking apart, there may one day be something like a table constructed of them, so that we really shall choose in accordance with it. If, for instance, some day they calculate and prove to me that I made a long nose at someone because I could not help making a long nose at him and that I had to do it in that particular way, what *freedom* is left me, especially if I am a learned man and have taken my degree somewhere? Then I should be able to calculate my whole life for thirty years beforehand. In short, if this could be arranged there would be nothing left for us to do; anyway, we should have to understand that. And, in fact, we ought unweariyingly to repeat to ourselves that at such and such a time and in such and such circumstances nature does not ask our leave; that we have got to take her as she is and not fashion her to suit our fancy, and if we really aspire to formulas and tables of rules, and well, even . . . to the chemical retort, there's no help for it, we must accept the retort too, or else it will be accepted without our consent. . . ."

Yes, but here I come to a stop! Gentlemen, you must excuse me for being over-philosophical; it's the result of forty years underground! Allow me to indulge my fancy. You see, gentlemen, reason is an excellent thing, there's no disputing that, but reason is nothing but reason and satisfies only the rational side of man's nature, while will is a manifestation of the whole life, that is, of the whole human life including reason and all the impulses. And although our life, in this manifestation of it, is often worthless, yet it is life and not simply extracting square roots. Here I, for instance, quite naturally want to live, in order to satisfy all my capacities for life, and not simply my capacity for reasoning, that is, not simply one twentieth of my capacity for life. What does reason know? Reason only knows what it has succeeded in learning (some things, perhaps, it will never learn; this is a poor comfort, but why not say so frankly?) and human nature acts as a whole, with everything that is in it, consciously or unconsciously, and, even if it goes wrong, it lives. I suspect, gentlemen, that you are looking at me with compassion; you tell me again that an enlightened and developed man, such, in short, as the future man will be, cannot consciously desire anything disadvantageous to himself, that that can be proved mathematically. I thoroughly agree, it can—by mathematics. But I repeat for the hundredth time, there is one case, one only, when man may consciously, purposely, desire what is injurious to himself, what is stupid, very stupid—simply in order to have the right to desire for himself even what is very stupid and not to be bound by an obligation to desire only what is sensible. Of course, this very stupid thing, this caprice of ours, may be in reality, gentlemen, more advantageous for us than anything else on earth, especially in certain cases. And in particular it may be more advantageous than any advantage even when it does us obvious harm, and contradicts the soundest conclusions of our reason concerning our advantage—for in any circumstances it preserves for us what is most precious and most important—that is, our personality, our individuality. Some, you see, maintain that this really is the most precious thing for mankind; choice can, of course, if it chooses, be in agreement with reason; and especially if this be not abused but kept within bounds. It is profitable and sometimes even praiseworthy. But very often, and even most often, choice is utterly and stubbornly opposed to reason . . . and . . . and . . . do you know that that, too, is profitable, sometimes even praiseworthy? Gentlemen, let us suppose that man is not stupid. (Indeed one cannot refuse to suppose that, if only from the one consideration, that, if man is stupid, then who is wise?) But if he is not stupid, he is monstrously ungrateful! Phenomenally ungrateful. In fact, I believe that the best definition of man is the ungrateful biped. But that is not all, that is not his worst defect; his worst defect is his perpetual moral obliquity, perpetual—from the days of the Flood to the Schleswig-Holstein period. Moral obliquity and consequently lack of good sense; for it has long been accepted that lack of good sense is due to no other cause than moral obliquity. Put it to the test and cast your eyes upon the history of mankind. What will you see? Is it a grand spectacle? Grand, if you like. Take the Colossus of Rhodes, for instance, that's worth something. With good reason Mr. Anaevsky testifies of it that some say that it is the work of man's hands, while others maintain that it has been created by nature herself. Is it many-coloured? May be it is many-coloured, too: if one takes the dress uniforms, military and civilian, of all peoples in all ages—that alone is worth something, and if you take the undress uniforms you will never get to the end of it; no historian would be equal to the job. Is it monotonous? May be it's monotonous too: it's fighting and fighting; they are fighting now, they fought first and they fought last—you will admit, that it is almost too monotonous. In short, one may say anything about the history of the world—anything that might enter the most disordered imagination. The only thing one can't say is that it's rational. The very word sticks in one's throat. And, indeed, this is the odd thing that is continually happening: there are continually turning up in life moral and rational persons, sages and lovers of humanity who make it their object to live all their lives as morally and rationally as possible, to be, so to speak, a light to their neighbours simply in order to show them that it is possible to live morally and rationally in this world. And yet we all know that those very people sooner or later have been false to themselves, playing some queer trick, often a most unseemly one. Now I ask you: what can be expected of man since he is a being endowed with strange qualities? Shower upon him every earthly blessing, drown him in a sea of happiness, so that nothing but bubbles of bliss can be seen on the surface; give him economic prosperity, such that he should have nothing else to do but sleep, eat cakes and busy himself with the continuation of his species, and even then out of sheer ingratitude, sheer spite, man would play you some nasty trick. He would even risk his cakes and would deliberately desire the most fatal rubbish, the most uneconomical absurdity, simply to introduce into all this positive good sense his fatal fantastic element. It is just his fantastic dreams, his vulgar folly that he will desire to retain, simply in order to prove to himself—as though that were so necessary—that men still are men and not the keys of a piano, which the laws of nature threaten to control so completely that soon one will be able to desire nothing but by the calendar. And that is not all: even if man really were nothing but a piano-key, even if this were proved to him by natural science and mathematics, even then he would not become reasonable, but would purposely do something perverse out of simple ingratitude, simply to gain his point. And if he does not find means he will contrive destruction and chaos, will contrive sufferings of all sorts, only to gain his point! He will launch a curse upon the world, and as only man can curse (it is his privilege, the primary distinction between him and other animals), may be by his curse alone he will attain his object—that is, convince himself that he is a man and not a piano-key! If you say that all this, too, can be calculated and tabulated—chaos and darkness and curses, so that the mere possibility of calculating it all beforehand would stop it all, and reason would reassert itself, then man would purposely go mad in order to be rid of reason and gain his point! I believe in it, I answer for it, for the whole work of man really seems to consist in nothing but proving to himself every minute that he is a man and not a piano-key! It may be at the cost of his skin, it may be by cannibalism! And this being so, can one help being tempted to rejoice that it has not yet come off, and that desire still depends on something we don't know?

You will scream at me (that is, if you condescend to do so) that no one is touching my free will, that all they are concerned with is that my will should of itself, of its own free will, coincide with my own normal interests, with the laws of nature and arithmetic.

Good heavens, gentlemen, what sort of free will is left when we come to tabulation and arithmetic, when it will all be a case of twice two make four? Twice two makes four without my will. As if free will meant that!

IX

Gentlemen, I am joking, and I know myself that my jokes are not brilliant, but you know one can take everything as a joke. I am, perhaps, jesting against the grain. Gentlemen, I am tormented by questions; answer them for me. You, for instance, want to cure men of their old habits and reform their will in accordance with science and good sense. But how do you know, not only that it is possible, but also that it is *desirable* to reform man in that way? And what leads you to the conclusion that man's inclinations *need* reforming? In short, how do you know that such a reformation will be a benefit to man? And to go to the root of the matter, why are you so positively convinced that not to act against his real normal interests guaranteed by the conclusions of reason and arithmetic is certainly always advantageous for man and must always be a law for mankind? So far, you know, this is only your supposition. It may be the law of logic, but not the law of humanity. You think, gentlemen, perhaps that I am mad? Allow me to defend myself. I agree that man is pre-eminently a creative animal, predestined to strive consciously for an object and to engage in engineering—that is, incessantly and eternally to make new roads, *wherever they may lead*. But the reason why he wants sometimes to go off at a tangent may just be that he is *predestined* to make the road, and perhaps, too, that however stupid the "direct" practical man may be, the thought sometimes will occur to him that the road almost always does lead *somewhere*, and that the destination it leads to is less important than the process of making it, and that the chief thing is to save the well-conducted child from despising engineering, and so giving way to the fatal idleness, which, as we all know, is the mother of all the vices. Man likes to make roads and to create, that is a fact beyond dispute. But why has he such a passionate love for destruction and chaos also? Tell me that! But on that point I want to say a couple of words myself. May it not be that he loves chaos and destruction (there can be no disputing that he does sometimes love it) because he is instinctively afraid of attaining his object and completing the edifice he is constructing? Who knows, perhaps he only loves that edifice from a distance, and is by no means in love with it at close quarters; perhaps he only loves building it and does not want to live in it, but will leave it, when completed, for the use of *les animaux domestiques*—such as the ants, the sheep, and so on. Now the ants have quite a different taste. They have a marvellous edifice of that pattern which endures for ever—the ant-heap.

With the ant-heap the respectable race of ants began and with the ant-heap they will probably end, which does the greatest credit to their perseverance and good sense. But man is a frivolous and incongruous creature, and perhaps, like a chess player, loves the process of the game, not the end of it. And who knows (there is no saying with certainty), perhaps the only goal on earth to which mankind is striving lies in this incessant process of attaining, in other words, in life itself, and not in the thing to be attained, which must always be expressed as a formula, as positive as twice two makes four, and such positiveness is not life, gentlemen, but is the beginning of death. Anyway, man has always been afraid of this mathematical certainty, and I am afraid of it now. Granted that man does nothing but seek that mathematical certainty, he traverses oceans, sacrifices his life in the quest, but to succeed, really to find it, dreads, I assure you. He feels that when he has found it there will be nothing for him to look for. When workmen have finished their work they do at least receive their pay, they go to the tavern, then they are taken to the police-station—and there is occupation for a week. But where can man go? Anyway, one can observe a certain awkwardness about him when he has attained such objects. He loves the process of attaining, but does not quite like to have attained, and that, of course, is very absurd. In fact, man is a comical creature; there seems to be a kind of jest in it all. But yet mathematical certainty is after all, something insufferable. Twice two makes four seems to me simply a piece of insolence. Twice two makes four is a pert coxcomb who stands with arms akimbo barring your path and spitting. I admit that twice two makes four is an excellent thing, but if we are to give everything its due, twice two makes five is sometimes a very charming thing too.

And why are you so firmly, so triumphantly, convinced that only the normal and the positive—in other words, only what is conducive to welfare—is for the advantage of man? Is not reason in error as regards advantage? Does not man, perhaps, love something besides well-being? Perhaps he is just as fond of suffering? Perhaps suffering is just as great a benefit to him as well-being? Man is sometimes extraordinarily, passionately, in love with suffering, and that is a fact. There is no need to appeal to universal history to prove that; only ask yourself, if you are a man and have lived at all. As far as my personal opinion is concerned, to care only for well-being seems to me positively ill-bred. Whether it's good or bad, it is sometimes very pleasant, too, to smash things. I hold no brief for suffering nor for well-being either. I am standing for . . . my caprice, and for its being guaranteed to me when necessary. Suffering would be out of place in vaudevilles, for instance; I know that. In the "Palace of Crystal" it is unthinkable; suffering means doubt, negation, and what would be the good of a "palace of crystal" if there could be any doubt about it? And yet I think man will never renounce real suffering, that is, destruction and chaos. Why, suffering is the sole origin of consciousness. Though I did lay it down at the beginning that consciousness is the greatest misfortune for man, yet I know man prizes it and would not give it up for any satisfaction. Consciousness, for instance, is infinitely superior to twice two makes four. Once you have mathematical certainty there is nothing left to do or to understand. There will be nothing left but to bottle up your five senses and plunge into contemplation. While if you stick to consciousness, even though the same result is attained, you can at least flog yourself at times, and that will, at any rate, liven you up. Reactionary as it is, corporal punishment is better than nothing.

X

You believe in a palace of crystal that can never be destroyed—a palace at which one will not be able to put out one's tongue or make a long nose on the sly. And perhaps that is just why I am afraid of this edifice, that it is of crystal and can never be destroyed and that one cannot put one's tongue out at it even on the sly.

You see, if it were not a palace, but a hen-house, I might creep into it to avoid getting wet, and yet I would not call the hen-house a palace out of gratitude to it for keeping me dry. You laugh and say that in such circumstances a hen-house is as good as a mansion. Yes, I answer, if one had to live simply to keep out of the rain.

But what is to be done if I have taken it into my head that that is not the only object in life, and that if one must live one had better live in a mansion? That is my choice, my desire. You will only eradicate it when you have changed my preference. Well, do change it, allure me with something else, give me another ideal. But meanwhile I will not take a hen-house for a mansion. The palace of crystal may be an idle dream, it may be that it is inconsistent with the laws of nature and that I have invented it only through my own stupidity, through the old-fashioned irrational habits of my generation. But what does it matter to me that it is inconsistent? That makes no difference since it exists in my desires, or rather exists as long as my desires exist. Perhaps you are laughing again? Laugh away; I will put up with any mockery rather than pretend that I am satisfied when I am hungry. I know, anyway, that I will not be put off with a compromise, with a recurring zero, simply because it is consistent with the laws of nature and actually exists. I will not accept as the crown of my desires a block of buildings with tenements for the poor on a lease of a thousand years, and perhaps with a sign-board of a dentist hanging out. Destroy my desires, eradicate my ideals, show me something better, and I will follow you. You will say, perhaps, that it is not worth your trouble; but in that case I can give you the same answer. We are discussing things seriously; but if you won't deign to give me your attention, I will drop your acquaintance. I can retreat into my underground hole.

But while I am alive and have desires I would rather my hand were withered off than bring one brick to such a building! Don't remind me that I have just rejected the palace of crystal for the sole reason that one cannot put out one's tongue at it. I did not say because I am so fond of putting my tongue out. Perhaps the thing I resented was, that of all your edifices there has not been one at which one could not put out one's tongue. On the contrary, I would let my tongue be cut off out of gratitude if things could be so arranged that I should lose all desire to put it out. It is not my fault that things cannot be so arranged, and that one must be satisfied with model flats. Then why am I made with such desires? Can I have been constructed simply in order to come to the conclusion that all my construction is a cheat? Can this be my whole purpose? I do not believe it.

But do you know what: I am convinced that we underground folk ought to be kept on a curb. Though we may sit forty years underground without speaking, when we do come out into the light of day and break out we talk and talk and talk. . . .

XI

The long and the short of it is, gentlemen, that it is better to do nothing! Better conscious inertia! And so hurrah for underground! Though I have said that I envy the normal man to the last drop of my bile, yet I should not care to be in his place such as he is now (though I shall not cease envying him). No, no; anyway the underground life is more advantageous. There, at any rate, one can . . . Oh, but even now I am lying! I am lying because I know myself that it is not underground that is better, but something different, quite different, for which I am thirsting, but which I cannot find! Damn underground!

I will tell you another thing that would be better, and that is, if I myself believed in anything of what I have just written. I swear to you, gentlemen, there is not one thing, not one word of what I have written that I really believe. That is, I believe it, perhaps, but at the same time I feel and suspect that I am lying like a cobbler.

"Then why have you written all this?" you will say to me. "I ought to put you underground for forty years without anything to do and then come to you in your cellar, to find out what stage you have reached! How can a man be left with nothing to do for forty years?"

"Isn't that shameful, isn't that humiliating?" you will say, perhaps, wagging your heads contemptuously. "You thirst for life and try to settle the problems of life by a logical tangle. And how persistent, how insolent are your sallies, and at the same time what a scare you are in! You talk nonsense and are pleased with it; you say impudent things and are in continual alarm and apologising for them. You declare that you are afraid of nothing and at the same time try to ingratiate yourself in our good opinion. You declare that you are gnashing your teeth and at the same time you try to be witty so as to amuse us. You know that your witticisms are not witty, but you are evidently well satisfied with their literary value. You may, perhaps, have really suffered, but you have no respect for your own suffering. You may have sincerity, but you have no modesty; out of the pettiest vanity you expose your sincerity to publicity and ignominy. You doubtlessly mean to say something, but hide your last word through fear, because you have not the resolution to utter it, and only have a cowardly impudence. You boast of consciousness, but you are not sure of your ground, for though your mind works, yet your heart is darkened and corrupt, and you cannot have a full, genuine consciousness without a pure heart. And how intrusive you are, how you insist and grimace! Lies, lies, lies!"

Of course I have myself made up all the things you say. That, too, is from underground. I have been for forty years listening to you through a crack under the floor. I have invented them myself, there was nothing else I could invent. It is no wonder that I have learned it by heart and it has taken a literary form. . . .

But can you really be so credulous as to think that I will print all this and give it to you to read too? And another problem: why do I call you "gentlemen," why do I address you as though you really were my readers? Such confessions as I intend to make are never printed nor given to other people to read. Anyway, I am not strong-minded enough for that, and I don't see why I should be. But you see a fancy has occurred to me and I want to realise it at all costs. Let me explain.

Every man has reminiscences which he would not tell to everyone, but only to his friends. He has other matters in his mind which he would not reveal even to his friends, but only to himself, and that in secret. But there are other things which a man is afraid to tell even to himself, and every decent man has a number of such things stored away in his mind. The more decent he is, the greater the number of such things in his mind. Anyway, I have only lately determined to remember some of my early adventures. Till now I have always avoided them, even with a certain uneasiness. Now, when I am not only recalling them, but have actually decided to write an account of them, I want to try the experiment whether one can, even with oneself, be perfectly open and not take fright at the whole truth. I will observe, in parenthesis, that Heine says that a true autobiography is almost an impossibility, and that man is bound to lie about himself. He considers that Rousseau certainly told lies about himself in his confessions, and even intentionally lied, out of vanity. I am convinced that Heine is right; I quite understand how sometimes one may, out of sheer vanity, attribute regular crimes to oneself, and indeed I can very well conceive that kind of vanity. But Heine judged of people who made their confessions to the public. I write only for myself, and I wish to declare once and for all that if I write as though I were addressing readers, that is simply because it is easier for me to write in that form. It is a form, an empty form—I shall never have readers. I have made this plain already. . . .

I don't wish to be hampered by any restrictions in the compilation of my notes. I shall not attempt any system or method. I will jot things down as I remember them.

But here, perhaps, someone will catch at the word and ask me: if you really don't reckon on readers, why do you make such compacts with yourself—and on paper too—that is, that you won't attempt any system or method, that you jot things down as you remember them, and so on, and so on? Why are you explaining? Why do you apologise?

Well, there it is, I answer.

There is a whole psychology in all this, though. Perhaps it is simply that I am a coward. And perhaps that I purposely imagine an audience before me in order that I may be more dignified while I write. There are perhaps thousands of reasons. Again, what is my object precisely in writing? If it is not for the benefit of the public why should I not simply recall these incidents in my own mind without putting them on paper?

Quite so; but yet it is more imposing on paper. There is something more impressive in it; I shall be better able to criticise myself and improve my style. Besides, I shall perhaps obtain actual relief from writing. Today, for instance, I am particularly oppressed by one memory of a distant past. It came back vividly to my mind a few days ago, and has remained haunting me like an annoying tune that one cannot get rid of. And yet I must get rid of it somehow. I have hundreds of such reminiscences; but at times some one stands out from the hundred and oppresses me. For some reason I believe that if I write it down I should get rid of it. Why not try?

Besides, I am bored, and I never have anything to do. Writing will be a sort of work. They say work makes man kind-hearted and honest. Well, here is a chance for me, anyway.

Snow is falling today, yellow and dingy. It fell yesterday, too, and a few days ago. I fancy it is the wet snow that has reminded me of that incident which I cannot shake off now. And so let it be a story *à propos* of the falling snow.

PART II

A Propos of the Wet Snow

> When from dark error's subjugation
> My words of passionate exhortation
>   Had wrenched thy fainting spirit free;
> And writhing prone in thine affliction
> Thou didst recall with malediction
>   The vice that had encompassed thee:
> And when thy slumbering conscience, fretting
>   By recollection's torturing flame,
> Thou didst reveal the hideous setting
>   Of thy life's current ere I came:
> When suddenly I saw thee sicken,
>   And weeping, hide thine anguished face,
> Revolted, maddened, horror-stricken,
>   At memories of foul disgrace.
>   NEKRASSOV
>   (translated by Juliet Soskice).

I

At that time I was only twenty-four. My life was even then gloomy, ill-regulated, and as solitary as that of a savage. I made friends with no one and positively avoided talking, and buried myself more and more in my hole. At work in the office I never looked at anyone, and was perfectly well aware that my companions looked upon me, not only as a queer fellow, but even looked upon me—I always fancied this—with a sort of loathing. I sometimes wondered why it was that nobody except me fancied that he was looked upon with aversion? One of the clerks had a most repulsive, pock-marked face, which looked positively villainous. I believe I should not have dared to look at anyone with such an unsightly countenance. Another had such a very dirty old uniform that there was an unpleasant odour in his proximity. Yet not one of these gentlemen showed the slightest self-consciousness—either about their clothes or their countenance or their character in any way. Neither of them ever imagined that they were looked at with repulsion; if they had imagined it they would not have minded—so long as their superiors did not look at them in that way. It is clear to me now that, owing to my unbounded vanity and to the high standard I set for myself, I often looked at myself with furious discontent, which verged on loathing, and so I inwardly attributed the same feeling to everyone. I hated my face, for instance: I thought it disgusting, and even suspected that there was something base in my expression, and so every day when I turned up at the office I tried to behave as independently as possible, and to assume a lofty expression, so that I might not be suspected of being abject. "My face may be ugly," I thought, "but let it be lofty, expressive, and, above all, *extremely* intelligent." But I was positively and painfully certain that it was impossible for my countenance ever to express those qualities. And what was worst of all, I thought it actually stupid looking, and I would have been quite satisfied if I could have looked intelligent. In fact, I would even have put up with looking base if, at the same time, my face could have been thought strikingly intelligent.

Of course, I hated my fellow clerks one and all, and I despised them all, yet at the same time I was, as it were, afraid of them. In fact, it happened at times that I thought more highly of them than of myself. It somehow happened quite suddenly that I alternated between despising them and thinking them superior to myself. A cultivated and decent man cannot be vain without setting a fearfully high standard for himself, and without despising and almost hating himself at certain moments. But whether I despised them or thought them superior I dropped my eyes almost every time I met anyone. I even made experiments whether I could face so and so's looking at me, and I was always the first to drop my eyes. This worried me to distraction. I had a sickly dread, too, of being ridiculous, and so had a slavish passion for the conventional in everything external. I loved to fall into the common rut, and had a whole-hearted terror of any kind of eccentricity in myself. But how could I live up to it? I was morbidly sensitive as a man of our age should be. They were all stupid, and as like one another as so many sheep. Perhaps I was the only one in the office who fancied that I was a coward and a slave, and I fancied it just because I was more highly developed. But it was not only that I fancied it, it really was so. I was a coward and a slave. I say this without the slightest embarrassment. Every decent man of our age must be a coward and a slave. That is his normal condition. Of that I am firmly persuaded. He is made and constructed to that very end. And not only at the present time owing to some casual circumstances, but always, at all times, a decent man is bound to be a coward and a slave. It is the law of nature for all decent people all over the earth. If anyone of them happens to be valiant about something, he need not be comforted nor carried away by that; he would show the white feather just the same before something else. That is how it invariably and inevitably ends. Only donkeys and mules are valiant, and they only till they are pushed up to the wall. It is not worth while to pay attention to them for they really are of no consequence.

Another circumstance, too, worried me in those days: that there was no one like me and I was unlike anyone else. "I am alone and they are *everyone*," I thought—and pondered.

From that it is evident that I was still a youngster.

The very opposite sometimes happened. It was loathsome sometimes to go to the office; things reached such a point that I often came home ill. But all at once, *à propos* of nothing, there would come a phase of scepticism and indifference (everything happened in phases to me), and I would laugh myself at my intolerance and fastidiousness, I would reproach myself with being *romantic*. At one time I was unwilling to speak to anyone, while at other times I would not only talk, but go to the length of contemplating making friends with them. All my fastidiousness would suddenly, for no rhyme or reason, vanish. Who knows, perhaps I never had really had it, and it had simply been affected, and got out of books. I have not decided that question even now. Once I quite made friends with them, visited their homes, played preference, drank vodka, talked of promotions. . . . But here let me make a digression.

We Russians, speaking generally, have never had those foolish transcendental "romantics"— German, and still more French—on whom nothing produces any effect; if there were an earthquake, if all France perished at the barricades, they would still be the same, they would not even have the decency to affect a change, but would still go on singing their transcendental songs to the hour of their death, because they are fools. We, in Russia, have no fools; that is well known. That is what distinguishes us from foreign lands. Consequently these transcendental natures are not found amongst us in their pure form. The idea that they are is due to our "realistic" journalists and critics of that day, always on the look out for Kostanzhoglos and Uncle Pyotr Ivanitchs and foolishly accepting them as our ideal; they have slandered our romantics, taking them for the same transcendental sort as in Germany or France. On the contrary, the characteristics of our "romantics" are absolutely and directly opposed to the transcendental European type, and no European standard can be applied to them. (Allow me to make use of this word "romantic"—an old-fashioned and much respected word which has done good service and is familiar to all.) The characteristics of our romantic are to understand everything, *to see everything and to see it often incomparably more clearly than our most realistic minds see it*; to refuse to accept anyone or anything, but at the same time not to despise anything; to give way, to yield, from policy; never to lose sight of a useful practical object (such as rent-free quarters at the government expense, pensions, decorations), to keep their eye on that object through all the enthusiasms and volumes of lyrical poems, and at the same time to preserve "the sublime and the beautiful" inviolate within them to the hour of their death, and to preserve themselves also, incidentally, like some precious jewel wrapped in cotton wool if only for the benefit of "the sublime and the beautiful." Our "romantic" is a man of great breadth and the greatest rogue of all our rogues, I assure you. . . . I can assure you from experience, indeed. Of course, that is, if he is intelligent. But what am I saying! The romantic is always intelligent, and I only meant to observe that although we have had foolish romantics they don't count, and they were only so because in the flower of their youth they degenerated into Germans, and to preserve their precious jewel more comfortably, settled somewhere out there—by preference in Weimar or the Black Forest.

I, for instance, genuinely despised my official work and did not openly abuse it simply because I was in it myself and got a salary for it. Anyway, take note, I did not openly abuse it. Our romantic would rather go out of his mind—a thing, however, which very rarely happens— than take to open abuse, unless he had some other career in view; and he is never kicked out. At most, they would take him to the lunatic asylum as "the King of Spain" if he should go very mad. But it is only the thin, fair people who go out of their minds in Russia. Innumerable "romantics" attain later in life to considerable rank in the service. Their many-sidedness is remarkable! And what a faculty they have for the most contradictory sensations! I was comforted by this thought even in those days, and I am of the same opinion now. That is why there are so many "broad natures" among us who never lose their ideal even in the depths of degradation; and though they never stir a finger for their ideal, though they are arrant thieves and knaves, yet they tearfully cherish their first ideal and are extraordinarily honest at heart. Yes, it is only among us that the most incorrigible rogue can be absolutely and loftily honest at heart without in the least ceasing to be a rogue. I repeat, our romantics, frequently, become such accomplished rascals (I use the term "rascals" affectionately), suddenly display such a sense of reality and practical knowledge that their bewildered superiors and the public generally can only ejaculate in amazement.

Their many-sidedness is really amazing, and goodness knows what it may develop into later on, and what the future has in store for us. It is not a poor material! I do not say this from any foolish or boastful patriotism. But I feel sure that you are again imagining that I am joking. Or perhaps it's just the contrary and you are convinced that I really think so. Anyway, gentlemen, I shall welcome both views as an honour and a special favour. And do forgive my digression.

I did not, of course, maintain friendly relations with my comrades and soon was at loggerheads with them, and in my youth and inexperience I even gave up bowing to them, as though I had cut off all relations. That, however, only happened to me once. As a rule, I was always alone.

In the first place I spent most of my time at home, reading. I tried to stifle all that was continually seething within me by means of external impressions. And the only external means I had was reading. Reading, of course, was a great help—exciting me, giving me pleasure and pain. But at times it bored me fearfully. One longed for movement in spite of everything, and I plunged all at once into dark, underground, loathsome vice of the pettiest kind. My wretched passions were acute, smarting, from my continual, sickly irritability. I had hysterical impulses, with tears and convulsions. I had no resource except reading, that is, there was nothing in my surroundings which I could respect and which attracted me. I was overwhelmed with depression, too; I had an hysterical craving for incongruity and for contrast, and so I took to vice. I have not said all this to justify myself. . . . But, no! I am lying. I did want to justify myself. I make that little observation for my own benefit, gentlemen. I don't want to lie. I vowed to myself I would not.

And so, furtively, timidly, in solitude, at night, I indulged in filthy vice, with a feeling of shame which never deserted me, even at the most loathsome moments, and which at such moments nearly made me curse. Already even then I had my underground world in my soul. I was fearfully afraid of being seen, of being met, of being recognised. I visited various obscure haunts.

One night as I was passing a tavern I saw through a lighted window some gentlemen fighting with billiard cues, and saw one of them thrown out of the window. At other times I should have felt very much disgusted, but I was in such a mood at the time, that I actually envied the gentleman thrown out of the window—and I envied him so much that I even went into the tavern and into the billiard-room. "Perhaps," I thought, "I'll have a fight, too, and they'll throw me out of the window."

I was not drunk—but what is one to do—depression will drive a man to such a pitch of hysteria? But nothing happened. It seemed that I was not even equal to being thrown out of the window and I went away without having my fight.

An officer put me in my place from the first moment.

I was standing by the billiard-table and in my ignorance blocking up the way, and he wanted to pass; he took me by the shoulders and without a word—without a warning or explanation—moved me from where I was standing to another spot and passed by as though he had not noticed me. I could have forgiven blows, but I could not forgive his having moved me without noticing me.

Devil knows what I would have given for a real regular quarrel—a more decent, a more *literary* one, so to speak. I had been treated like a fly. This officer was over six foot, while I was a spindly little fellow. But the quarrel was in my hands. I had only to protest and I certainly would have been thrown out of the window. But I changed my mind and preferred to beat a resentful retreat.

I went out of the tavern straight home, confused and troubled, and the next night I went out again with the same lewd intentions, still more furtively, abjectly and miserably than before, as it were, with tears in my eyes—but still I did go out again. Don't imagine, though, it was cowardice made me slink away from the officer; I never have been a coward at heart, though I have always been a coward in action. Don't be in a hurry to laugh—I assure you I can explain it all.

Oh, if only that officer had been one of the sort who would consent to fight a duel! But no, he was one of those gentlemen (alas, long extinct!) who preferred fighting with cues or, like Gogol's Lieutenant Pirogov, appealing to the police. They did not fight duels and would have thought a duel with a civilian like me an utterly unseemly procedure in any case—and they looked upon the duel altogether as something impossible, something free-thinking and French. But they were quite ready to bully, especially when they were over six foot.

I did not slink away through cowardice, but through an unbounded vanity. I was afraid not of his six foot, not of getting a sound thrashing and being thrown out of the window; I should have had physical courage enough, I assure you; but I had not the moral courage. What I was afraid of was that everyone present, from the insolent marker down to the lowest little stinking, pimply clerk in a greasy collar, would jeer at me and fail to understand when I began to protest and to address them in literary language. For of the point of honour—not of honour, but of the point of honour (*point d'honneur*)—one cannot speak among us except in literary language. You can't allude to the "point of honour" in ordinary language. I was fully convinced (the sense of reality, in spite of all my romanticism!) that they would all simply split their sides with laughter, and that the officer would not simply beat me, that is, without insulting me, but would certainly prod me in the back with his knee, kick me round the billiard-table, and only then perhaps have pity and drop me out of the window.

Of course, this trivial incident could not with me end in that. I often met that officer afterwards in the street and noticed him very carefully. I am not quite sure whether he recognised me, I imagine not; I judge from certain signs. But I—I stared at him with spite and hatred and so it went on . . . for several years! My resentment grew even deeper with years. At first I began making stealthy inquiries about this officer. It was difficult for me to do so, for I knew no one. But one day I heard someone shout his surname in the street as I was following him at a distance, as though I were tied to him—and so I learnt his surname. Another time I followed him to his flat, and for ten kopecks learned from the porter where he lived, on which storey, whether he lived alone or with others, and so on—in fact, everything one could learn from a porter. One morning, though I had never tried my hand with the pen, it suddenly occurred to me to write a satire on this officer in the form of a novel which would unmask his villainy. I wrote the novel with relish. I did unmask his villainy, I even exaggerated it; at first I so altered his surname that it could easily be recognised, but on second thoughts I changed it, and sent the story to the *Otetchestvenniya zapiski*. But at that time such attacks were not the fashion and my story was not printed. That was a great vexation to me.

Sometimes I was positively choked with resentment. At last I determined to challenge my enemy to a duel. I composed a splendid, charming letter to him, imploring him to apologise to me, and hinting rather plainly at a duel in case of refusal. The letter was so composed that if the officer had had the least understanding of the sublime and the beautiful he would certainly have flung himself on my neck and have offered me his friendship. And how fine that would have been! How we should have got on together! "He could have shielded me with his higher rank, while I could have improved his mind with my culture, and, well . . . my ideas, and all sorts of things might have happened." Only fancy, this was two years after his insult to me, and my challenge would have been a ridiculous anachronism, in spite of all the ingenuity of my letter in disguising and explaining away the anachronism. But, thank God (to this day I thank the Almighty with tears in my eyes) I did not send the letter to him. Cold shivers run down my back when I think of what might have happened if I had sent it.

And all at once I revenged myself in the simplest way, by a stroke of genius! A brilliant thought suddenly dawned upon me. Sometimes on holidays I used to stroll along the sunny side of the Nevsky about four o'clock in the afternoon. Though it was hardly a stroll so much as a series of innumerable miseries, humiliations and resentments; but no doubt that was just what I wanted. I used to wriggle along in a most unseemly fashion, like an eel, continually moving aside to make way for generals, for officers of the guards and the hussars, or for ladies. At such minutes there used to be a convulsive twinge at my heart, and I used to feel hot all down my back at the mere thought of the wretchedness of my attire, of the wretchedness and abjectness of my little scurrying figure. This was a regular martyrdom, a continual, intolerable humiliation at the thought, which passed into an incessant and direct sensation, that I was a mere fly in the eyes of all this world, a nasty, disgusting fly—more intelligent, more highly developed, more refined in feeling than any of them, of course—but a fly that was continually making way for everyone, insulted and injured by everyone. Why I inflicted this torture upon myself, why I went to the Nevsky, I don't know. I felt simply drawn there at every possible opportunity.

Already then I began to experience a rush of the enjoyment of which I spoke in the first chapter. After my affair with the officer I felt even more drawn there than before: it was on the Nevsky that I met him most frequently, there I could admire him. He, too, went there chiefly on holidays. He, too, turned out of his path for generals and persons of high rank, and he, too, wriggled between them like an eel; but people, like me, or even better dressed than me, he simply walked over; he made straight for them as though there was nothing but empty space before him, and never, under any circumstances, turned aside. I gloated over my resentment watching him and . . . always resentfully made way for him. It exasperated me that even in the street I could not be on an even footing with him.

"Why must you invariably be the first to move aside?" I kept asking myself in hysterical rage, waking up sometimes at three o'clock in the morning. "Why is it you and not he? There's no regulation about it; there's no written law. Let the making way be equal as it usually is when refined people meet; he moves half-way and you move half-way; you pass with mutual respect."

But that never happened, and I always moved aside, while he did not even notice my making way for him. And lo and behold a bright idea dawned upon me! "What," I thought, "if I meet him and don't move on one side? What if I don't move aside on purpose, even if I knock up against him? How would that be?" This audacious idea took such a hold on me that it gave me no peace. I was dreaming of it continually, horribly, and I purposely went more frequently to the Nevsky in order to picture more vividly how I should do it when I did do it. I was delighted. This intention seemed to me more and more practical and possible.

"Of course I shall not really push him," I thought, already more good-natured in my joy. "I will simply not turn aside, will run up against him, not very violently, but just shouldering each other—just as much as decency permits. I will push against him just as much as he pushes against me." At last I made up my mind completely. But my preparations took a great deal of time. To begin with, when I carried out my plan I should need to be looking rather more decent, and so I had to think of my get-up. "In case of emergency, if, for instance, there were any sort of public scandal (and the public there is of the *most recherché*: the Countess walks there; Prince D. walks there; all the literary world is there), I must be well dressed; that inspires respect and of itself puts us on an equal footing in the eyes of the society."

With this object I asked for some of my salary in advance, and bought at Tchurkin's a pair of black gloves and a decent hat. Black gloves seemed to me both more dignified and *bon ton* than the lemon-coloured ones which I had contemplated at first. "The colour is too gaudy, it looks as though one were trying to be conspicuous," and I did not take the lemon-coloured ones. I had got ready long beforehand a good shirt, with white bone studs; my overcoat was the only thing that held me back. The coat in itself was a very good one, it kept me warm; but it was wadded and it had a raccoon collar which was the height of vulgarity. I had to change the collar at any sacrifice, and to have a beaver one like an officer's. For this purpose I began visiting the Gostiny Dvor and after several attempts I pitched upon a piece of cheap German beaver. Though these German beavers soon grow shabby and look wretched, yet at first they look exceedingly well, and I only needed it for the occasion. I asked the price; even so, it was too expensive. After thinking it over thoroughly I decided to sell my raccoon collar. The rest of the money—a considerable sum for me, I decided to borrow from Anton Antonitch Syetotchkin, my immediate superior, an unassuming person, though grave and judicious. He never lent money to anyone, but I had, on entering the service, been specially recommended to him by an important personage who had got me my berth. I was horribly worried. To borrow from Anton Antonitch seemed to me monstrous and shameful. I did not sleep for two or three nights. Indeed, I did not sleep well at that time, I was in a fever; I had a vague sinking at my heart or else a sudden throbbing, throbbing, throbbing! Anton Antonitch was surprised at first, then he frowned, then he reflected, and did after all lend me the money, receiving from me a written authorisation to take from my salary a fortnight later the sum that he had lent me.

In this way everything was at last ready. The handsome beaver replaced the mean-looking raccoon, and I began by degrees to get to work. It would never have done to act offhand, at random; the plan had to be carried out skilfully, by degrees. But I must confess that after many efforts I began to despair: we simply could not run into each other. I made every preparation, I was quite determined—it seemed as though we should run into one another directly—and before I knew what I was doing I had stepped aside for him again and he had passed without noticing me. I even prayed as I approached him that God would grant me determination. One time I had made up my mind thoroughly, but it ended in my stumbling and falling at his feet because at the very last instant when I was six inches from him my courage failed me. He very calmly stepped over me, while I flew on one side like a ball. That night I was ill again, feverish and delirious.

And suddenly it ended most happily. The night before I had made up my mind not to carry out my fatal plan and to abandon it all, and with that object I went to the Nevsky for the last time, just to see how I would abandon it all. Suddenly, three paces from my enemy, I unexpectedly made up my mind—I closed my eyes, and we ran full tilt, shoulder to shoulder, against one another! I did not budge an inch and passed him on a perfectly equal footing! He did not even look round and pretended not to notice it; but he was only pretending, I am convinced of that. I am convinced of that to this day! Of course, I got the worst of it—he was stronger, but that was not the point. The point was that I had attained my object, I had kept up my dignity, I had not yielded a step, and had put myself publicly on an equal social footing with him. I returned home feeling that I was fully avenged for everything. I was delighted. I was triumphant and sang Italian arias. Of course, I will not describe to you what happened to me three days later; if you have read my first chapter you can guess for yourself. The officer was afterwards transferred; I have not seen him now for fourteen years. What is the dear fellow doing now? Whom is he walking over?

II

But the period of my dissipation would end and I always felt very sick afterwards. It was followed by remorse—I tried to drive it away; I felt too sick. By degrees, however, I grew used to that too. I grew used to everything, or rather I voluntarily resigned myself to enduring it. But I had a means of escape that reconciled everything—that was to find refuge in "the sublime and the beautiful," in dreams, of course. I was a terrible dreamer, I would dream for three months on end, tucked away in my corner, and you may believe me that at those moments I had no resemblance to the gentleman who, in the perturbation of his chicken heart, put a collar of German beaver on his great-coat. I suddenly became a hero. I would not have admitted my six-foot lieutenant even if he had called on me. I could not even picture him before me then. What were my dreams and how I could satisfy myself with them—it is hard to say now, but at the time I was satisfied with them. Though, indeed, even now, I am to some extent satisfied with them. Dreams were particularly sweet and vivid after a spell of dissipation; they came with remorse and with tears, with curses and transports. There were moments of such positive intoxication, of such happiness, that there was not the faintest trace of irony within me, on my honour. I had faith, hope, love. I believed blindly at such times that by some miracle, by some external circumstance, all this would suddenly open out, expand; that suddenly a vista of suitable activity—beneficent, good, and, above all, *ready made* (what sort of activity I had no idea, but the great thing was that it should be all ready for me)—would rise up before me—and I should come out into the light of day, almost riding a white horse and crowned with laurel. Anything but the foremost place I could not conceive for myself, and for that very reason I quite contentedly occupied the lowest in reality. Either to be a hero or to grovel in the mud—there was nothing between. That was my ruin, for when I was in the mud I comforted myself with the thought that at other times I was a hero, and the hero was a cloak for the mud: for an ordinary man it was shameful to defile himself, but a hero was too lofty to be utterly defiled, and so he might defile himself. It is worth noting that these attacks of the "sublime and the beautiful" visited me even during the period of dissipation and just at the times when I was touching the bottom. They came in separate spurts, as though reminding me of themselves, but did not banish the dissipation by their appearance. On the contrary, they seemed to add a zest to it by contrast, and were only sufficiently present to serve as an appetising sauce. That sauce was made up of contradictions and sufferings, of agonising inward analysis, and all these pangs and pin-pricks gave a certain piquancy, even a significance to my dissipation—in fact, completely answered the purpose of an appetising sauce. There was a certain depth of meaning in it. And I could hardly have resigned myself to the simple, vulgar, direct debauchery of a clerk and have endured all the filthiness of it. What could have allured me about it then and have drawn me at night into the street? No, I had a lofty way of getting out of it all.

And what loving-kindness, oh Lord, what loving-kindness I felt at times in those dreams of mine! in those "flights into the sublime and the beautiful"; though it was fantastic love, though it was never applied to anything human in reality, yet there was so much of this love that one did not feel afterwards even the impulse to apply it in reality; that would have been superfluous. Everything, however, passed satisfactorily by a lazy and fascinating transition into the sphere of art, that is, into the beautiful forms of life, lying ready, largely stolen from the poets and novelists and adapted to all sorts of needs and uses. I, for instance, was triumphant over everyone; everyone, of course, was in dust and ashes, and was forced spontaneously to recognise my superiority, and I forgave them all. I was a poet and a grand gentleman, I fell in love; I came in for countless millions and immediately devoted them to humanity, and at the same time I confessed before all the people my shameful deeds, which, of course, were not merely shameful, but had in them much that was "sublime and beautiful" something in the Manfred style. Everyone would kiss me and weep (what idiots they would be if they did not), while I should go barefoot and hungry preaching new ideas and fighting a victorious Austerlitz against the obscurantists. Then the band would play a march, an amnesty would be declared, the Pope would agree to retire from Rome to Brazil; then there would be a ball for the whole of Italy at the Villa Borghese on the shores of Lake Como, Lake Como being for that purpose transferred to the neighbourhood of Rome; then would come a scene in the bushes, and so on, and so on—as though you did not know all about it? You will say that it is vulgar and contemptible to drag all this into public after all the tears and transports which I have myself confessed. But why is it contemptible? Can you imagine that I am ashamed of it all, and that it was stupider than anything in your life, gentlemen? And I can assure you that some of these fancies were by no means badly composed. . . . It did not all happen on the shores of Lake Como. And yet you are right—it really is vulgar and contemptible. And most contemptible of all it is that now I am attempting to justify myself to you. And even more contemptible than that is my making this remark now. But that's enough, or there will be no end to it; each step will be more contemptible than the last. . . .

I could never stand more than three months of dreaming at a time without feeling an irresistible desire to plunge into society. To plunge into society meant to visit my superior at the office, Anton Antonitch Syetotchkin. He was the only permanent acquaintance I have had in my life, and I wonder at the fact myself now. But I only went to see him when that phase came over me, and when my dreams had reached such a point of bliss that it became essential at once to embrace my fellows and all mankind; and for that purpose I needed, at least, one human being, actually existing. I had to call on Anton Antonitch, however, on Tuesday—his at-home day; so I had always to time my passionate desire to embrace humanity so that it might fall on a Tuesday.

This Anton Antonitch lived on the fourth storey in a house in Five Corners, in four low-pitched rooms, one smaller than the other, of a particularly frugal and sallow appearance. He had two daughters and their aunt, who used to pour out the tea. Of the daughters one was thirteen and another fourteen, they both had snub noses, and I was awfully shy of them because they were always whispering and giggling together. The master of the house usually sat in his study on a leather couch in front of the table with some grey-headed gentleman, usually a colleague from our office or some other department. I never saw more than two or three visitors there, always the same. They talked about the excise duty; about business in the senate, about salaries, about promotions, about His Excellency, and the best means of pleasing him, and so on. I had the patience to sit like a fool beside these people for four hours at a stretch, listening to them without knowing what to say to them or venturing to say a word. I became stupefied, several times I felt myself perspiring, I was overcome by a sort of paralysis; but this was pleasant and good for me. On returning home I deferred for a time my desire to embrace all mankind.

I had however one other acquaintance of a sort, Simonov, who was an old schoolfellow. I had a number of schoolfellows, indeed, in Petersburg, but I did not associate with them and had even given up nodding to them in the street. I believe I had transferred into the department I was in simply to avoid their company and to cut off all connection with my hateful childhood. Curses on that school and all those terrible years of penal servitude! In short, I parted from my schoolfellows as soon as I got out into the world. There were two or three left to whom I nodded in the street. One of them was Simonov, who had in no way been distinguished at school, was of a quiet and equable disposition; but I discovered in him a certain independence of character and even honesty. I don't even suppose that he was particularly stupid. I had at one time spent some rather soulful moments with him, but these had not lasted long and had somehow been suddenly clouded over. He was evidently uncomfortable at these reminiscences, and was, I fancy, always afraid that I might take up the same tone again. I suspected that he had an aversion for me, but still I went on going to see him, not being quite certain of it.

And so on one occasion, unable to endure my solitude and knowing that as it was Thursday Anton Antonitch's door would be closed, I thought of Simonov. Climbing up to his fourth storey I was thinking that the man disliked me and that it was a mistake to go and see him. But as it always happened that such reflections impelled me, as though purposely, to put myself into a false position, I went in. It was almost a year since I had last seen Simonov.

III

I found two of my old schoolfellows with him. They seemed to be discussing an important matter. All of them took scarcely any notice of my entrance, which was strange, for I had not met them for years. Evidently they looked upon me as something on the level of a common fly. I had not been treated like that even at school, though they all hated me. I knew, of course, that they must despise me now for my lack of success in the service, and for my having let myself sink so low, going about badly dressed and so on—which seemed to them a sign of my incapacity and insignificance. But I had not expected such contempt. Simonov was positively surprised at my turning up. Even in old days he had always seemed surprised at my coming. All this disconcerted me: I sat down, feeling rather miserable, and began listening to what they were saying.

They were engaged in warm and earnest conversation about a farewell dinner which they wanted to arrange for the next day to a comrade of theirs called Zverkov, an officer in the army, who was going away to a distant province. This Zverkov had been all the time at school with me too. I had begun to hate him particularly in the upper forms. In the lower forms he had simply been a pretty, playful boy whom everybody liked. I had hated him, however, even in the lower forms, just because he was a pretty and playful boy. He was always bad at his lessons and got worse and worse as he went on; however, he left with a good certificate, as he had powerful interests. During his last year at school he came in for an estate of two hundred serfs, and as almost all of us were poor he took up a swaggering tone among us. He was vulgar in the extreme, but at the same time he was a good-natured fellow, even in his swaggering. In spite of superficial, fantastic and sham notions of honour and dignity, all but very few of us positively grovelled before Zverkov, and the more so the more he swaggered. And it was not from any interested motive that they grovelled, but simply because he had been favoured by the gifts of nature. Moreover, it was, as it were, an accepted idea among us that Zverkov was a specialist in regard to tact and the social graces. This last fact particularly infuriated me. I hated the abrupt self-confident tone of his voice, his admiration of his own witticisms, which were often frightfully stupid, though he was bold in his language; I hated his handsome, but stupid face (for which I would, however, have gladly exchanged my intelligent one), and the free-and-easy military manners in fashion in the " 'forties." I hated the way in which he used to talk of his future conquests of women (he did not venture to begin his attack upon women until he had the epaulettes of an officer, and was looking forward to them with impatience), and boasted of the duels he would constantly be fighting. I remember how I, invariably so taciturn, suddenly fastened upon Zverkov, when one day talking at a leisure moment with his schoolfellows of his future relations with the fair sex, and growing as sportive as a puppy in the sun, he all at once declared that he would not leave a single village girl on his estate unnoticed, that that was his *droit de seigneur*, and that if the peasants dared to protest he would have them all flogged and double the tax on them, the bearded rascals. Our servile rabble applauded, but I attacked him, not from compassion for the girls and their fathers, but simply because they were applauding such an insect. I got the better of him on that occasion, but though Zverkov was stupid he was lively and impudent, and so laughed it off, and in such a way that my victory was not really complete; the laugh was on his side. He got the better of me on several occasions afterwards, but without malice, jestingly, casually. I remained angrily and contemptuously silent and would not answer him. When we left school he made advances to me; I did not rebuff them, for I was flattered, but we soon parted and quite naturally. Afterwards I heard of his barrack-room success as a lieutenant, and of the fast life he was leading. Then there came other rumours—of his successes in the service. By then he had taken to cutting me in the street, and I suspected that he was afraid of compromising himself by greeting a personage as insignificant as me. I saw him once in the theatre, in the third tier of boxes. By then he was wearing shoulder-straps. He was twisting and twirling about, ingratiating himself with the daughters of an ancient General. In three years he had gone off considerably, though he was still rather handsome and adroit. One could see that by the time he was thirty he would be corpulent. So it was to this Zverkov that my schoolfellows were going to give a dinner on his departure. They had kept up with him for those three years, though privately they did not consider themselves on an equal footing with him, I am convinced of that.

Of Simonov's two visitors, one was Ferfitchkin, a Russianised German—a little fellow with the face of a monkey, a blockhead who was always deriding everyone, a very bitter enemy of mine from our days in the lower forms—a vulgar, impudent, swaggering fellow, who affected a most sensitive feeling of personal honour, though, of course, he was a wretched little coward at heart. He was one of those worshippers of Zverkov who made up to the latter from interested motives, and often borrowed money from him. Simonov's other visitor, Trudolyubov, was a person in no way remarkable—a tall young fellow, in the army, with a cold face, fairly honest, though he worshipped success of every sort, and was only capable of thinking of promotion. He was some sort of distant relation of Zverkov's, and this, foolish as it seems, gave him a certain importance among us. He always thought me of no consequence whatever; his behaviour to me, though not quite courteous, was tolerable.

"Well, with seven roubles each," said Trudolyubov, "twenty-one roubles between the three of us, we ought to be able to get a good dinner. Zverkov, of course, won't pay."

"Of course not, since we are inviting him," Simonov decided.

"Can you imagine," Ferfitchkin interrupted hotly and conceitedly, like some insolent flunkey boasting of his master the General's decorations, "can you imagine that Zverkov will let us pay alone? He will accept from delicacy, but he will order half a dozen bottles of champagne."

"Do we want half a dozen for the four of us?" observed Trudolyubov, taking notice only of the half dozen.

"So the three of us, with Zverkov for the fourth, twenty-one roubles, at the Hotel de Paris at five o'clock tomorrow," Simonov, who had been asked to make the arrangements, concluded finally.

"How twenty-one roubles?" I asked in some agitation, with a show of being offended; "if you count me it will not be twenty-one, but twenty-eight roubles."

It seemed to me that to invite myself so suddenly and unexpectedly would be positively graceful, and that they would all be conquered at once and would look at me with respect.

"Do you want to join, too?" Simonov observed, with no appearance of pleasure, seeming to avoid looking at me. He knew me through and through.

It infuriated me that he knew me so thoroughly.

"Why not? I am an old schoolfellow of his, too, I believe, and I must own I feel hurt that you have left me out," I said, boiling over again.

"And where were we to find you?" Ferfitchkin put in roughly.

"You never were on good terms with Zverkov," Trudolyubov added, frowning.

But I had already clutched at the idea and would not give it up.

"It seems to me that no one has a right to form an opinion upon that," I retorted in a shaking voice, as though something tremendous had happened. "Perhaps that is just my reason for wishing it now, that I have not always been on good terms with him."

"Oh, there's no making you out . . . with these refinements," Trudolyubov jeered.

"We'll put your name down," Simonov decided, addressing me. "Tomorrow at five-o'clock at the Hôtel de Paris."

"What about the money?" Ferfitchkin began in an undertone, indicating me to Simonov, but he broke off, for even Simonov was embarrassed.

"That will do," said Trudolyubov, getting up. "If he wants to come so much, let him."

"But it's a private thing, between us friends," Ferfitchkin said crossly, as he, too, picked up his hat. "It's not an official gathering."

"We do not want at all, perhaps . . ."

They went away. Ferfitchkin did not greet me in any way as he went out, Trudolyubov barely nodded. Simonov, with whom I was left *tete-a-tete*, was in a state of vexation and perplexity, and looked at me queerly. He did not sit down and did not ask me to.

"H'm . . . yes . . . tomorrow, then. Will you pay your subscription now? I just ask so as to know," he muttered in embarrassment.

I flushed crimson, as I did so I remembered that I had owed Simonov fifteen roubles for ages—which I had, indeed, never forgotten, though I had not paid it.

"You will understand, Simonov, that I could have no idea when I came here . . . I am very much vexed that I have forgotten. . . ."

"All right, all right, that doesn't matter. You can pay tomorrow after the dinner. I simply wanted to know. . . . Please don't . . ."

He broke off and began pacing the room still more vexed. As he walked he began to stamp with his heels.

"Am I keeping you?" I asked, after two minutes of silence.

"Oh!" he said, starting, "that is—to be truthful—yes. I have to go and see someone . . . not far from here," he added in an apologetic voice, somewhat abashed.

"My goodness, why didn't you say so?" I cried, seizing my cap, with an astonishingly free-and-easy air, which was the last thing I should have expected of myself.

"It's close by . . . not two paces away," Simonov repeated, accompanying me to the front door with a fussy air which did not suit him at all. "So five o'clock, punctually, tomorrow," he called down the stairs after me. He was very glad to get rid of me. I was in a fury.

"What possessed me, what possessed me to force myself upon them?" I wondered, grinding my teeth as I strode along the street, "for a scoundrel, a pig like that Zverkov! Of course I had better not go; of course, I must just snap my fingers at them. I am not bound in any way. I'll send Simonov a note by tomorrow's post. . . ."

But what made me furious was that I knew for certain that I should go, that I should make a point of going; and the more tactless, the more unseemly my going would be, the more certainly I would go.

And there was a positive obstacle to my going: I had no money. All I had was nine roubles, I had to give seven of that to my servant, Apollon, for his monthly wages. That was all I paid him—he had to keep himself.

Not to pay him was impossible, considering his character. But I will talk about that fellow, about that plague of mine, another time.

However, I knew I should go and should not pay him his wages.

That night I had the most hideous dreams. No wonder; all the evening I had been oppressed by memories of my miserable days at school, and I could not shake them off. I was sent to the school by distant relations, upon whom I was dependent and of whom I have heard nothing since—they sent me there a forlorn, silent boy, already crushed by their reproaches, already troubled by doubt, and looking with savage distrust at everyone. My schoolfellows met me with spiteful and merciless jibes because I was not like any of them. But I could not endure their taunts; I could not give in to them with the ignoble readiness with which they gave in to one another. I hated them from the first, and shut myself away from everyone in timid, wounded and disproportionate pride. Their coarseness revolted me. They laughed cynically at my face, at my clumsy figure; and yet what stupid faces they had themselves. In our school the boys' faces seemed in a special way to degenerate and grow stupider. How many fine-looking boys came to us! In a few years they became repulsive. Even at sixteen I wondered at them morosely; even then I was struck by the pettiness of their thoughts, the stupidity of their pursuits, their games, their conversations. They had no understanding of such essential things, they took no interest in such striking, impressive subjects, that I could not help considering them inferior to myself. It was not wounded vanity that drove me to it, and for God's sake do not thrust upon me your hackneyed remarks, repeated to nausea, that "I was only a dreamer," while they even then had an understanding of life. They understood nothing, they had no idea of real life, and I swear that that was what made me most indignant with them. On the contrary, the most obvious, striking reality they accepted with fantastic stupidity and even at that time were accustomed to respect success. Everything that was just, but oppressed and looked down upon, they laughed at heartlessly and shamefully. They took rank for intelligence; even at sixteen they were already talking about a snug berth. Of course, a great deal of it was due to their stupidity, to the bad examples with which they had always been surrounded in their childhood and boyhood. They were monstrously depraved. Of course a great deal of that, too, was superficial and an assumption of cynicism; of course there were glimpses of youth and freshness even in their depravity; but even that freshness was not attractive, and showed itself in a certain rakishness. I hated them horribly, though perhaps I was worse than any of them. They repaid me in the same way, and did not conceal their aversion for me. But by then I did not desire their affection: on the contrary, I continually longed for their humiliation. To escape from their derision I purposely began to make all the progress I could with my studies and forced my way to the very top. This impressed them. Moreover, they all began by degrees to grasp that I had already read books none of them could read, and understood things (not forming part of our school curriculum) of which they had not even heard. They took a savage and sarcastic view of it, but were morally impressed, especially as the teachers began to notice me on those grounds. The mockery ceased, but the hostility remained, and cold and strained relations became permanent between us. In the end I could not put up with it: with years a craving for society, for friends, developed in me. I attempted to get on friendly terms with some of my schoolfellows; but somehow or other my intimacy with them was always strained and soon ended of itself. Once, indeed, I did have a friend. But I was already a tyrant at heart; I wanted to exercise unbounded sway over him; I tried to instil into him a contempt for his surroundings; I required of him a disdainful and complete break with those surroundings. I frightened him with my passionate affection; I reduced him to tears, to hysterics. He was a simple and devoted soul; but when he devoted himself to me entirely I began to hate him immediately and repulsed him—as though all I needed him for was to win a victory over him, to subjugate him and nothing else. But I could not subjugate all of them; my friend was not at all like them either, he was, in fact, a rare exception. The first thing I did on leaving school was to give up the special job for which I had been destined so as to break all ties, to curse my past and shake the dust from off my feet.... And goodness knows why, after all that, I should go trudging off to Simonov's!

Early next morning I roused myself and jumped out of bed with excitement, as though it were all about to happen at once. But I believed that some radical change in my life was coming, and would inevitably come that day. Owing to its rarity, perhaps, any external event, however trivial, always made me feel as though some radical change in my life were at hand. I went to the office, however, as usual, but sneaked away home two hours earlier to get ready. The great thing, I thought, is not to be the first to arrive, or they will think I am overjoyed at coming. But there were thousands of such great points to consider, and they all agitated and overwhelmed me. I polished my boots a second time with my own hands; nothing in the world would have induced Apollon to clean them twice a day, as he considered that it was more than his duties required of him. I stole the brushes to clean them from the passage, being careful he should not detect it, for fear of his contempt. Then I minutely examined my clothes and thought that everything looked old, worn and threadbare. I had let myself get too slovenly. My uniform, perhaps, was tidy, but I could not go out to dinner in my uniform. The worst of it was that on the knee of my trousers was a big yellow stain. I had a foreboding that that stain would deprive me of nine-tenths of my personal dignity. I knew, too, that it was very poor to think so. "But this is no time for thinking: now I am in for the real thing," I thought, and my heart sank. I knew, too, perfectly well even then, that I was monstrously exaggerating the facts. But how could I help it? I could not control myself and was already shaking with fever. With despair I pictured to myself how coldly and disdainfully that "scoundrel" Zverkov would meet me; with what dull-witted, invincible contempt the blockhead Trudolyubov would look at me; with what impudent rudeness the insect Ferfitchkin would snigger at me in order to curry favour with Zverkov; how completely Simonov would take it all in, and how he would despise me for the abjectness of my vanity and lack of spirit—and, worst of all, how paltry, *unliterary*, commonplace it would all be. Of course, the best thing would be not to go at all. But that was most impossible of all: if I feel impelled to do anything, I seem to be pitchforked into it. I should have jeered at myself ever afterwards: "So you funked it, you funked it, you funked the *real thing*!" On the contrary, I passionately longed to show all that "rabble" that I was by no means such a spiritless creature as I seemed to myself. What is more, even in the acutest paroxysm of this cowardly fever, I dreamed of getting the upper hand, of dominating them, carrying them away, making them like me—if only for my "elevation of thought and unmistakable wit." They would abandon Zverkov, he would sit on one side, silent and ashamed, while I should crush him. Then, perhaps, we would be reconciled and drink to our everlasting friendship; but what was most bitter and humiliating for me was that I knew even then, knew fully and for certain, that I needed nothing of all this really, that I did not really want to crush, to subdue, to attract them, and that I did not care a straw really for the result, even if I did achieve it. Oh, how I prayed for the day to pass quickly! In unutterable anguish I went to the window, opened the movable pane and looked out into the troubled darkness of the thickly falling wet snow. At last my wretched little clock hissed out five. I seized my hat and, trying not to look at Apollon, who had been all day expecting his month's wages, but in his foolishness was unwilling to be the first to speak about it, I slipped between him and the door and, jumping into a high-class sledge, on which I spent my last half rouble, I drove up in grand style to the Hôtel de Paris.

IV

I had been certain the day before that I should be the first to arrive. But it was not a question of being the first to arrive. Not only were they not there, but I had difficulty in finding our room. The table was not laid even. What did it mean? After a good many questions I elicited from the waiters that the dinner had been ordered not for five, but for six o'clock. This was confirmed at the buffet too. I felt really ashamed to go on questioning them. It was only twenty-five minutes past five. If they changed the dinner hour they ought at least to have let me know—that is what the post is for, and not to have put me in an absurd position in my own eyes and . . . and even before the waiters. I sat down; the servant began laying the table; I felt even more humiliated when he was present. Towards six o'clock they brought in candles, though there were lamps burning in the room. It had not occurred to the waiter, however, to bring them in at once when I arrived. In the next room two gloomy, angry-looking persons were eating their dinners in silence at two different tables. There was a great deal of noise, even shouting, in a room further away; one could hear the laughter of a crowd of people, and nasty little shrieks in French: there were ladies at the dinner. It was sickening, in fact. I rarely passed more unpleasant moments, so much so that when they did arrive all together punctually at six I was overjoyed to see them, as though they were my deliverers, and even forgot that it was incumbent upon me to show resentment.

Zverkov walked in at the head of them; evidently he was the leading spirit. He and all of them were laughing; but, seeing me, Zverkov drew himself up a little, walked up to me deliberately with a slight, rather jaunty bend from the waist. He shook hands with me in a friendly, but not over-friendly, fashion, with a sort of circumspect courtesy like that of a General, as though in giving me his hand he were warding off something. I had imagined, on the contrary, that on coming in he would at once break into his habitual thin, shrill laugh and fall to making his insipid jokes and witticisms. I had been preparing for them ever since the previous day, but I had not expected such condescension, such high-official courtesy. So, then, he felt himself ineffably superior to me in every respect! If he only meant to insult me by that high-official tone, it would not matter, I thought—I could pay him back for it one way or another. But what if, in reality, without the least desire to be offensive, that sheepshead had a notion in earnest that he was superior to me and could only look at me in a patronising way? The very supposition made me gasp.

"I was surprised to hear of your desire to join us," he began, lisping and drawling, which was something new. "You and I seem to have seen nothing of one another. You fight shy of us. You shouldn't. We are not such terrible people as you think. Well, anyway, I am glad to renew our acquaintance."

And he turned carelessly to put down his hat on the window.

"Have you been waiting long?" Trudolyubov inquired.

"I arrived at five o'clock as you told me yesterday," I answered aloud, with an irritability that threatened an explosion.

"Didn't you let him know that we had changed the hour?" said Trudolyubov to Simonov.

"No, I didn't. I forgot," the latter replied, with no sign of regret, and without even apologising to me he went off to order the *hors d'oeuvre*.

"So you've been here a whole hour? Oh, poor fellow!" Zverkov cried ironically, for to his notions this was bound to be extremely funny. That rascal Ferfitchkin followed with his nasty little snigger like a puppy yapping. My position struck him, too, as exquisitely ludicrous and embarrassing.

"It isn't funny at all!" I cried to Ferfitchkin, more and more irritated. "It wasn't my fault, but other people's. They neglected to let me know. It was . . . it was . . . it was simply absurd."

"It's not only absurd, but something else as well," muttered Trudolyubov, naïvely taking my part. You are not hard enough upon it. It was simply rudeness—unintentional, of course. And how could Simonov . . . h'm!"

"If a trick like that had been played on me," observed Ferfitchkin, "I should . . ."

"But you should have ordered something for yourself," Zverkov interrupted, "or simply asked for dinner without waiting for us."

"You will allow that I might have done that without your permission," I rapped out. "If I waited, it was . . ."

"Let us sit down, gentlemen," cried Simonov, coming in. "Everything is ready; I can answer for the champagne; it is capitally frozen . . . You see, I did not know your address, where was I to look for you?" he suddenly turned to me, but again he seemed to avoid looking at me. Evidently he had something against me. It must have been what happened yesterday.

All sat down; I did the same. It was a round table. Trudolyubov was on my left, Simonov on my right, Zverkov was sitting opposite, Ferfitchkin next to him, between him and Trudolyubov.

"Tell me, are you . . . in a government office?" Zverkov went on attending to me. Seeing that I was embarrassed he seriously thought that he ought to be friendly to me, and, so to speak, cheer me up.

"Does he want me to throw a bottle at his head?" I thought, in a fury. In my novel surroundings I was unnaturally ready to be irritated.

"In the N— office," I answered jerkily, with my eyes on my plate.

"And ha-ave you a go-od berth? I say, what ma-a-de you leave your original job?"

"What ma-a-de me was that I wanted to leave my original job," I drawled more than he, hardly able to control myself. Ferfitchkin went off into a guffaw. Simonov looked at me ironically. Trudolyubov left off eating and began looking at me with curiosity.

Zverkov winced, but he tried not to notice it.

"And the remuneration?"

"What remuneration?"

"I mean, your sa-a-lary?"

"Why are you cross-examining me?" However, I told him at once what my salary was. I turned horribly red.

"It is not very handsome," Zverkov observed majestically.

"Yes, you can't afford to dine at cafes on that," Ferfitchkin added insolently.

"To my thinking it's very poor," Trudolyubov observed gravely.

"And how thin you have grown! How you have changed!" added Zverkov, with a shade of venom in his voice, scanning me and my attire with a sort of insolent compassion.

"Oh, spare his blushes," cried Ferfitchkin, sniggering.

"My dear sir, allow me to tell you I am not blushing," I broke out at last; "do you hear? I am dining here, at this cafe, at my own expense, not at other people's—note that, Mr. Ferfitchkin."

"Wha-at? Isn't every one here dining at his own expense? You would seem to be . . ." Ferfitchkin flew out at me, turning as red as a lobster, and looking me in the face with fury.

"Tha-at," I answered, feeling I had gone too far, "and I imagine it would be better to talk of something more intelligent."

"You intend to show off your intelligence, I suppose?"

"Don't disturb yourself, that would be quite out of place here."

"Why are you clacking away like that, my good sir, eh? Have you gone out of your wits in your office?"

"Enough, gentlemen, enough!" Zverkov cried, authoritatively.

"How stupid it is!" muttered Simonov.

"It really is stupid. We have met here, a company of friends, for a farewell dinner to a comrade and you carry on an altercation," said Trudolyubov, rudely addressing himself to me alone. "You invited yourself to join us, so don't disturb the general harmony."

"Enough, enough!" cried Zverkov. "Give over, gentlemen, it's out of place. Better let me tell you how I nearly got married the day before yesterday. . . ."

And then followed a burlesque narrative of how this gentleman had almost been married two days before. There was not a word about the marriage, however, but the story was adorned with generals, colonels and kammer-junkers, while Zverkov almost took the lead among them. It was greeted with approving laughter; Ferfitchkin positively squealed.

No one paid any attention to me, and I sat crushed and humiliated.

"Good Heavens, these are not the people for me!" I thought. "And what a fool I have made of myself before them! I let Ferfitchkin go too far, though. The brutes imagine they are doing me an honour in letting me sit down with them. They don't understand that it's an honour to them and not to me! I've grown thinner! My clothes! Oh, damn my trousers! Zverkov noticed the yellow stain on the knee as soon as he came in. . . . But what's the use! I must get up at once, this very minute, take my hat and simply go without a word . . . with contempt! And tomorrow I can send a challenge. The scoundrels! As though I cared about the seven roubles. They may think. . . . Damn it! I don't care about the seven roubles. I'll go this minute!"

Of course I remained. I drank sherry and Lafitte by the glassful in my discomfiture. Being unaccustomed to it, I was quickly affected. My annoyance increased as the wine went to my head. I longed all at once to insult them all in a most flagrant manner and then go away. To seize the moment and show what I could do, so that they would say, "He's clever, though he is absurd," and . . . and . . . in fact, damn them all!

I scanned them all insolently with my drowsy eyes. But they seemed to have forgotten me altogether. They were noisy, vociferous, cheerful. Zverkov was talking all the time. I began listening. Zverkov was talking of some exuberant lady whom he had at last led on to declaring her love (of course, he was lying like a horse), and how he had been helped in this affair by an intimate friend of his, a Prince Kolya, an officer in the hussars, who had three thousand serfs.

"And yet this Kolya, who has three thousand serfs, has not put in an appearance here tonight to see you off," I cut in suddenly.

For one minute every one was silent. "You are drunk already." Trudolyubov deigned to notice me at last, glancing contemptuously in my direction. Zverkov, without a word, examined me as though I were an insect. I dropped my eyes. Simonov made haste to fill up the glasses with champagne.

Trudolyubov raised his glass, as did everyone else but me.

"Your health and good luck on the journey!" he cried to Zverkov. "To old times, to our future, hurrah!"

They all tossed off their glasses, and crowded round Zverkov to kiss him. I did not move; my full glass stood untouched before me.

"Why, aren't you going to drink it?" roared Trudolyubov, losing patience and turning menacingly to me.

"I want to make a speech separately, on my own account . . . and then I'll drink it, Mr. Trudolyubov."

"Spiteful brute!" muttered Simonov. I drew myself up in my chair and feverishly seized my glass, prepared for something extraordinary, though I did not know myself precisely what I was going to say.

"*Silence*!" cried Ferfitchkin. "Now for a display of wit!"

Zverkov waited very gravely, knowing what was coming.

"Mr. Lieutenant Zverkov," I began, "let me tell you that I hate phrases, phrasemongers and men in corsets . . . that's the first point, and there is a second one to follow it."

There was a general stir.

"The second point is: I hate ribaldry and ribald talkers. Especially ribald talkers! The third point: I love justice, truth and honesty." I went on almost mechanically, for I was beginning to shiver with horror myself and had no idea how I came to be talking like this. "I love thought, Monsieur Zverkov; I love true comradeship, on an equal footing and not . . . H'm . . . I love . . . But, however, why not? I will drink your health, too, Mr. Zverkov. Seduce the Circassian girls, shoot the enemies of the fatherland and . . . and . . . to your health, Monsieur Zverkov!"

Zverkov got up from his seat, bowed to me and said:

"I am very much obliged to you." He was frightfully offended and turned pale.

"Damn the fellow!" roared Trudolyubov, bringing his fist down on the table.

"Well, he wants a punch in the face for that," squealed Ferfitchkin.

"We ought to turn him out," muttered Simonov.

"Not a word, gentlemen, not a movement!" cried Zverkov solemnly, checking the general indignation. "I thank you all, but I can show him for myself how much value I attach to his words."

"Mr. Ferfitchkin, you will give me satisfaction tomorrow for your words just now!" I said aloud, turning with dignity to Ferfitchkin.

"A duel, you mean? Certainly," he answered. But probably I was so ridiculous as I challenged him and it was so out of keeping with my appearance that everyone including Ferfitchkin was prostrate with laughter.

"Yes, let him alone, of course! He is quite drunk," Trudolyubov said with disgust.

"I shall never forgive myself for letting him join us," Simonov muttered again.

"Now is the time to throw a bottle at their heads," I thought to myself. I picked up the bottle . . . and filled my glass . . . "No, I'd better sit on to the end," I went on thinking; "you would be pleased, my friends, if I went away. Nothing will induce me to go. I'll go on sitting here and drinking to the end, on purpose, as a sign that I don't think you of the slightest consequence. I will go on sitting and drinking, because this is a public-house and I paid my entrance money. I'll sit here and drink, for I look upon you as so many pawns, as inanimate pawns. I'll sit here and drink . . . and sing if I want to, yes, sing, for I have the right to . . . to sing . . . H'm!"

But I did not sing. I simply tried not to look at any of them. I assumed most unconcerned attitudes and waited with impatience for them to speak *first*. But alas, they did not address me! And oh, how I wished, how I wished at that moment to be reconciled to them! It struck eight, at last nine. They moved from the table to the sofa. Zverkov stretched himself on a lounge and put one foot on a round table. Wine was brought there. He did, as a fact, order three bottles on his own account. I, of course, was not invited to join them. They all sat round him on the sofa. They listened to him, almost with reverence. It was evident that they were fond of him. "What for? What for?" I wondered. From time to time they were moved to drunken enthusiasm and kissed each other. They talked of the Caucasus, of the nature of true passion, of snug berths in the service, of the income of an hussar called Podharzhevsky, whom none of them knew personally, and rejoiced in the largeness of it, of the extraordinary grace and beauty of a Princess D., whom none of them had ever seen; then it came to Shakespeare's being immortal.

I smiled contemptuously and walked up and down the other side of the room, opposite the sofa, from the table to the stove and back again. I tried my very utmost to show them that I could do without them, and yet I purposely made a noise with my boots, thumping with my heels. But it was all in vain. They paid no attention. I had the patience to walk up and down in front of them from eight o'clock till eleven, in the same place, from the table to the stove and back again. "I walk up and down to please myself and no one can prevent me." The waiter who came into the room stopped, from time to time, to look at me. I was somewhat giddy from turning round so often; at moments it seemed to me that I was in delirium. During those three hours I was three times soaked with sweat and dry again. At times, with an intense, acute pang I was stabbed to the heart by the thought that ten years, twenty years, forty years would pass, and that even in forty years I would remember with loathing and humiliation those filthiest, most ludicrous, and most awful moments of my life. No one could have gone out of his way to degrade himself more shamelessly, and I fully realised it, fully, and yet I went on pacing up and down from the table to the stove. "Oh, if you only knew what thoughts and feelings I am capable of, how cultured I am!" I thought at moments, mentally addressing the sofa on which my enemies were sitting. But my enemies behaved as though I were not in the room. Once—only once—they turned towards me, just when Zverkov was talking about Shakespeare, and I suddenly gave a contemptuous laugh. I laughed in such an affected and disgusting way that they all at once broke off their conversation, and silently and gravely for two minutes watched me walking up and down from the table to the stove, *taking no notice of them.* But nothing came of it: they said nothing, and two minutes later they ceased to notice me again. It struck eleven.

"Friends," cried Zverkov getting up from the sofa, "let us all be off now, *there!*"

"Of course, of course," the others assented. I turned sharply to Zverkov. I was so harassed, so exhausted, that I would have cut my throat to put an end to it. I was in a fever; my hair, soaked with perspiration, stuck to my forehead and temples.

"Zverkov, I beg your pardon," I said abruptly and resolutely. "Ferfitchkin, yours too, and everyone's, everyone's: I have insulted you all!"

"Aha! A duel is not in your line, old man," Ferfitchkin hissed venomously.

It sent a sharp pang to my heart.

"No, it's not the duel I am afraid of, Ferfitchkin! I am ready to fight you tomorrow, after we are reconciled. I insist upon it, in fact, and you cannot refuse. I want to show you that I am not afraid of a duel. You shall fire first and I shall fire into the air."

"He is comforting himself," said Simonov.

"He's simply raving," said Trudolyubov.

"But let us pass. Why are you barring our way? What do you want?" Zverkov answered disdainfully.

They were all flushed, their eyes were bright: they had been drinking heavily.

"I ask for your friendship, Zverkov; I insulted you, but . . ."

"Insulted? *You* insulted *me*? Understand, sir, that you never, under any circumstances, could possibly insult *me*."

"And that's enough for you. Out of the way!" concluded Trudolyubov.

"Olympia is mine, friends, that's agreed!" cried Zverkov.

"We won't dispute your right, we won't dispute your right," the others answered, laughing.

I stood as though spat upon. The party went noisily out of the room. Trudolyubov struck up some stupid song. Simonov remained behind for a moment to tip the waiters. I suddenly went up to him.

"Simonov! give me six roubles!" I said, with desperate resolution.

He looked at me in extreme amazement, with vacant eyes. He, too, was drunk.

"You don't mean you are coming with us?"

"Yes."

"I've no money," he snapped out, and with a scornful laugh he went out of the room.

I clutched at his overcoat. It was a nightmare.

"Simonov, I saw you had money. Why do you refuse me? Am I a scoundrel? Beware of refusing me: if you knew, if you knew why I am asking! My whole future, my whole plans depend upon it!"

Simonov pulled out the money and almost flung it at me.

"Take it, if you have no sense of shame!" he pronounced pitilessly, and ran to overtake them.

I was left for a moment alone. Disorder, the remains of dinner, a broken wine-glass on the floor, spilt wine, cigarette ends, fumes of drink and delirium in my brain, an agonising misery in my heart and finally the waiter, who had seen and heard all and was looking inquisitively into my face.

"I am going there!" I cried. "Either they shall all go down on their knees to beg for my friendship, or I will give Zverkov a slap in the face!"

V

"So this is it, this is it at last—contact with real life," I muttered as I ran headlong downstairs. "This is very different from the Pope's leaving Rome and going to Brazil, very different from the ball on Lake Como!"

"You are a scoundrel," a thought flashed through my mind, "if you laugh at this now."

"No matter!" I cried, answering myself. "Now everything is lost!"

There was no trace to be seen of them, but that made no difference—I knew where they had gone.

At the steps was standing a solitary night sledge-driver in a rough peasant coat, powdered over with the still falling, wet, and as it were warm, snow. It was hot and steamy. The little shaggy piebald horse was also covered with snow and coughing, I remember that very well. I made a rush for the roughly made sledge; but as soon as I raised my foot to get into it, the recollection of how Simonov had just given me six roubles seemed to double me up and I tumbled into the sledge like a sack.

"No, I must do a great deal to make up for all that," I cried. "But I will make up for it or perish on the spot this very night. Start!"

We set off. There was a perfect whirl in my head.

"They won't go down on their knees to beg for my friendship. That is a mirage, cheap mirage, revolting, romantic and fantastical—that's another ball on Lake Como. And so I am bound to slap Zverkov's face! It is my duty to. And so it is settled; I am flying to give him a slap in the face. Hurry up!"

The driver tugged at the reins.

"As soon as I go in I'll give it him. Ought I before giving him the slap to say a few words by way of preface? No. I'll simply go in and give it him. They will all be sitting in the drawing-room, and he with Olympia on the sofa. That damned Olympia! She laughed at my looks on one occasion and refused me. I'll pull Olympia's hair, pull Zverkov's ears! No, better one ear, and pull him by it round the room. Maybe they will all begin beating me and will kick me out. That's most likely, indeed. No matter! Anyway, I shall first slap him; the initiative will be mine; and by the laws of honour that is everything: he will be branded and cannot wipe off the slap by any blows, by nothing but a duel. He will be forced to fight. And let them beat me now. Let them, the ungrateful wretches! Trudolyubov will beat me hardest, he is so strong; Ferfitchkin will be sure to catch hold sideways and tug at my hair. But no matter, no matter! That's what I am going for. The blockheads will be forced at last to see the tragedy of it all! When they drag me to the door I shall call out to them that in reality they are not worth my little finger. Get on, driver, get on!" I cried to the driver. He started and flicked his whip, I shouted so savagely.

"We shall fight at daybreak, that's a settled thing. I've done with the office. Ferfitchkin made a joke about it just now. But where can I get pistols? Nonsense! I'll get my salary in advance and buy them. And powder, and bullets? That's the second's business. And how can it all be done by daybreak? and where am I to get a second? I have no friends. Nonsense!" I cried, lashing myself up more and more. "It's of no consequence! The first person I meet in the street is bound to be my second, just as he would be bound to pull a drowning man out of water. The most eccentric things may happen. Even if I were to ask the director himself to be my second tomorrow, he would be bound to consent, if only from a feeling of chivalry, and to keep the secret! Anton Antonitch. . . ."

The fact is, that at that very minute the disgusting absurdity of my plan and the other side of the question was clearer and more vivid to my imagination than it could be to anyone on earth. But. . . .

"Get on, driver, get on, you rascal, get on!"

"Ugh, sir!" said the son of toil.

Cold shivers suddenly ran down me. Wouldn't it be better . . . to go straight home? My God, my God! Why did I invite myself to this dinner yesterday? But no, it's impossible. And my walking up and down for three hours from the table to the stove? No, they, they and no one else must pay for my walking up and down! They must wipe out this dishonour! Drive on!

And what if they give me into custody? They won't dare! They'll be afraid of the scandal. And what if Zverkov is so contemptuous that he refuses to fight a duel? He is sure to; but in that case I'll show them . . . I will turn up at the posting station when he's setting off tomorrow, I'll catch him by the leg, I'll pull off his coat when he gets into the carriage. I'll get my teeth into his hand, I'll bite him. "See what lengths you can drive a desperate man to!" He may hit me on the head and they may belabour me from behind. I will shout to the assembled multitude: "Look at this young puppy who is driving off to captivate the Circassian girls after letting me spit in his face!"

Of course, after that everything will be over! The office will have vanished off the face of the earth. I shall be arrested, I shall be tried, I shall be dismissed from the service, thrown in prison, sent to Siberia. Never mind! In fifteen years when they let me out of prison I will trudge off to him, a beggar, in rags. I shall find him in some provincial town. He will be married and happy. He will have a grown-up daughter. . . . I shall say to him: "Look, monster, at my hollow cheeks and my rags! I've lost everything—my career, my happiness, art, science, *the woman I loved*, and all through you. Here are pistols. I have come to discharge my pistol and . . . and I . . . forgive you. Then I shall fire into the air and he will hear nothing more of me. . . ."

I was actually on the point of tears, though I knew perfectly well at that moment that all this was out of Pushkin's *Silvio* and Lermontov's *Masquerade*. And all at once I felt horribly ashamed, so ashamed that I stopped the horse, got out of the sledge, and stood still in the snow in the middle of the street. The driver gazed at me, sighing and astonished.

What was I to do? I could not go on there—it was evidently stupid, and I could not leave things as they were, because that would seem as though . . . Heavens, how could I leave things! And after such insults! "No!" I cried, throwing myself into the sledge again. "It is ordained! It is fate! Drive on, drive on!"

And in my impatience I punched the sledge-driver on the back of the neck.

"What are you up to? What are you hitting me for?" the peasant shouted, but he whipped up his nag so that it began kicking.

The wet snow was falling in big flakes; I unbuttoned myself, regardless of it. I forgot everything else, for I had finally decided on the slap, and felt with horror that it was going to *happen now, at once*, and that *no force could stop it*. The deserted street lamps gleamed sullenly in the snowy darkness like torches at a funeral. The snow drifted under my great-coat, under my coat, under my cravat, and melted there. I did not wrap myself up—all was lost, anyway.

At last we arrived. I jumped out, almost unconscious, ran up the steps and began knocking and kicking at the door. I felt fearfully weak, particularly in my legs and knees. The door was opened quickly as though they knew I was coming. As a fact, Simonov had warned them that perhaps another gentleman would arrive, and this was a place in which one had to give notice and to observe certain precautions. It was one of those "millinery establishments" which were abolished by the police a good time ago. By day it really was a shop; but at night, if one had an introduction, one might visit it for other purposes.

I walked rapidly through the dark shop into the familiar drawing-room, where there was only one candle burning, and stood still in amazement: there was no one there. "Where are they?" I asked somebody. But by now, of course, they had separated. Before me was standing a person with a stupid smile, the "madam" herself, who had seen me before. A minute later a door opened and another person came in.

Taking no notice of anything I strode about the room, and, I believe, I talked to myself. I felt as though I had been saved from death and was conscious of this, joyfully, all over: I should have given that slap, I should certainly, certainly have given it! But now they were not here and . . . everything had vanished and changed! I looked round. I could not realise my condition yet. I looked mechanically at the girl who had come in: and had a glimpse of a fresh, young, rather pale face, with straight, dark eyebrows, and with grave, as it were wondering, eyes that attracted me at once; I should have hated her if she had been smiling. I began looking at her more intently and, as it were, with effort. I had not fully collected my thoughts. There was something simple and good-natured in her face, but something strangely grave. I am sure that this stood in her way here, and no one of those fools had noticed her. She could not, however, have been called a beauty, though she was tall, strong-looking, and well built. She was very simply dressed. Something loathsome stirred within me. I went straight up to her.

I chanced to look into the glass. My harassed face struck me as revolting in the extreme, pale, angry, abject, with dishevelled hair. "No matter, I am glad of it," I thought; "I am glad that I shall seem repulsive to her; I like that."

VI

. . . Somewhere behind a screen a clock began wheezing, as though oppressed by something, as though someone were strangling it. After an unnaturally prolonged wheezing there followed a shrill, nasty, and as it were unexpectedly rapid, chime—as though someone were suddenly jumping forward. It struck two. I woke up, though I had indeed not been asleep but lying half-conscious.

It was almost completely dark in the narrow, cramped, low-pitched room, cumbered up with an enormous wardrobe and piles of cardboard boxes and all sorts of frippery and litter. The candle end that had been burning on the table was going out and gave a faint flicker from time to time. In a few minutes there would be complete darkness.

I was not long in coming to myself; everything came back to my mind at once, without an effort, as though it had been in ambush to pounce upon me again. And, indeed, even while I was unconscious a point seemed continually to remain in my memory unforgotten, and round it my dreams moved drearily. But strange to say, everything that had happened to me in that day seemed to me now, on waking, to be in the far, far away past, as though I had long, long ago lived all that down.

My head was full of fumes. Something seemed to be hovering over me, rousing me, exciting me, and making me restless. Misery and spite seemed surging up in me again and seeking an outlet. Suddenly I saw beside me two wide open eyes scrutinising me curiously and persistently. The look in those eyes was coldly detached, sullen, as it were utterly remote; it weighed upon me.

A grim idea came into my brain and passed all over my body, as a horrible sensation, such as one feels when one goes into a damp and mouldy cellar. There was something unnatural in those two eyes, beginning to look at me only now. I recalled, too, that during those two hours I had not said a single word to this creature, and had, in fact, considered it utterly superfluous; in fact, the silence had for some reason gratified me. Now I suddenly realised vividly the hideous idea—revolting as a spider—of vice, which, without love, grossly and shamelessly begins with that in which true love finds its consummation. For a long time we gazed at each other like that, but she did not drop her eyes before mine and her expression did not change, so that at last I felt uncomfortable.

"What is your name?" I asked abruptly, to put an end to it.

"Liza," she answered almost in a whisper, but somehow far from graciously, and she turned her eyes away.

I was silent.

"What weather! The snow . . . it's disgusting!" I said, almost to myself, putting my arm under my head despondently, and gazing at the ceiling.

She made no answer. This was horrible.

"Have you always lived in Petersburg?" I asked a minute later, almost angrily, turning my head slightly towards her.

"No."

"Where do you come from?"

"From Riga," she answered reluctantly.

"Are you a German?"

"No, Russian."

"Have you been here long?"

"Where?"

"In this house?"

"A fortnight."

She spoke more and more jerkily. The candle went out; I could no longer distinguish her face.

"Have you a father and mother?"

"Yes . . . no . . . I have."

"Where are they?"

"There . . . in Riga."

"What are they?"

"Oh, nothing."

"Nothing? Why, what class are they?"

"Tradespeople."

"Have you always lived with them?"

"Yes."

"How old are you?"

"Twenty."

"Why did you leave them?"

"Oh, for no reason."

That answer meant "Let me alone; I feel sick, sad."

We were silent.

God know why I did not go away. I felt myself more and more sick and dreary. The images of the previous day began of themselves, apart from my will, flitting through my memory in confusion. I suddenly recalled something I had seen that morning when, full of anxious thoughts, I was hurrying to the office.

"I saw them carrying a coffin out yesterday and they nearly dropped it," I suddenly said aloud, not that I desired to open the conversation, but as it were by accident.

"A coffin?"

"Yes, in the Haymarket; they were bringing it up out of a cellar."

"From a cellar?"

"Not from a cellar, but a basement. Oh, you know . . . down below . . . from a house of ill-fame. It was filthy all round . . . Egg-shells, litter . . . a stench. It was loathsome."

Silence.

"A nasty day to be buried," I began, simply to avoid being silent.

"Nasty, in what way?"

"The snow, the wet." (I yawned.)

"It makes no difference," she said suddenly, after a brief silence.

"No, it's horrid." (I yawned again). "The gravediggers must have sworn at getting drenched by the snow. And there must have been water in the grave."

"Why water in the grave?" she asked, with a sort of curiosity, but speaking even more harshly and abruptly than before.

I suddenly began to feel provoked.

"Why, there must have been water at the bottom a foot deep. You can't dig a dry grave in Volkovo Cemetery."

"Why?"

"Why? Why, the place is waterlogged. It's a regular marsh. So they bury them in water. I've seen it myself . . . many times."

(I had never seen it once, indeed I had never been in Volkovo, and had only heard stories of it.)

"Do you mean to say, you don't mind how you die?"

"But why should I die?" she answered, as though defending herself.

"Why, some day you will die, and you will die just the same as that dead woman. She was . . . a girl like you. She died of consumption."

"A wench would have died in hospital . . ." (She knows all about it already: she said "wench," not "girl.")

"She was in debt to her madam," I retorted, more and more provoked by the discussion; "and went on earning money for her up to the end, though she was in consumption. Some sledge-drivers standing by were talking about her to some soldiers and telling them so. No doubt they knew her. They were laughing. They were going to meet in a pot-house to drink to her memory."

A great deal of this was my invention. Silence followed, profound silence. She did not stir.

"And is it better to die in a hospital?"

"Isn't it just the same? Besides, why should I die?" she added irritably.

"If not now, a little later."

"Why a little later?"

"Why, indeed? Now you are young, pretty, fresh, you fetch a high price. But after another year of this life you will be very different—you will go off."

"In a year?"

"Anyway, in a year you will be worth less," I continued malignantly. "You will go from here to something lower, another house; a year later—to a third, lower and lower, and in seven years you will come to a basement in the Haymarket. That will be if you were lucky. But it would be much worse if you got some disease, consumption, say . . . and caught a chill, or something or other. It's not easy to get over an illness in your way of life. If you catch anything you may not get rid of it. And so you would die."

"Oh, well, then I shall die," she answered, quite vindictively, and she made a quick movement.

"But one is sorry."

"Sorry for whom?"

"Sorry for life."

Silence.

"Have you been engaged to be married? Eh?"

"What's that to you?"

"Oh, I am not cross-examining you. It's nothing to me. Why are you so cross? Of course you may have had your own troubles. What is it to me? It's simply that I felt sorry."

"Sorry for whom?"

"Sorry for you."

"No need," she whispered hardly audibly, and again made a faint movement.

That incensed me at once. What! I was so gentle with her, and she . . .

"Why, do you think that you are on the right path?"

"I don't think anything."

"That's what's wrong, that you don't think. Realise it while there is still time. There still is time. You are still young, good-looking; you might love, be married, be happy. . . ."

"Not all married women are happy," she snapped out in the rude abrupt tone she had used at first.

"Not all, of course, but anyway it is much better than the life here. Infinitely better. Besides, with love one can live even without happiness. Even in sorrow life is sweet; life is sweet, however one lives. But here what is there but . . . foulness? Phew!"

I turned away with disgust; I was no longer reasoning coldly. I began to feel myself what I was saying and warmed to the subject. I was already longing to expound the cherished ideas I had brooded over in my corner. Something suddenly flared up in me. An object had appeared before me.

"Never mind my being here, I am not an example for you. I am, perhaps, worse than you are. I was drunk when I came here, though," I hastened, however, to say in self-defence. "Besides, a man is no example for a woman. It's a different thing. I may degrade and defile myself, but I am not anyone's slave. I come and go, and that's an end of it. I shake it off, and I am a different man. But you are a slave from the start. Yes, a slave! You give up everything, your whole freedom. If you want to break your chains afterwards, you won't be able to; you will be more and more fast in the snares. It is an accursed bondage. I know it. I won't speak of anything else, maybe you won't understand, but tell me: no doubt you are in debt to your madam? There, you see," I added, though she made no answer, but only listened in silence, entirely absorbed, "that's a bondage for you! You will never buy your freedom. They will see to that. It's like selling your soul to the devil. . . . And besides . . . perhaps, I too, am just as unlucky—how do you know—and wallow in the mud on purpose, out of misery? You know, men take to drink from grief; well, maybe I am here from grief. Come, tell me, what is there good here? Here you and I . . . came together . . . just now and did not say one word to one another all the time, and it was only afterwards you began staring at me like a wild creature, and I at you. Is that loving? Is that how one human being should meet another? It's hideous, that's what it is!"

"Yes!" she assented sharply and hurriedly.

I was positively astounded by the promptitude of this "Yes." So the same thought may have been straying through her mind when she was staring at me just before. So she, too, was capable of certain thoughts? "Damn it all, this was interesting, this was a point of likeness!" I thought, almost rubbing my hands. And indeed it's easy to turn a young soul like that!

It was the exercise of my power that attracted me most.

She turned her head nearer to me, and it seemed to me in the darkness that she propped herself on her arm. Perhaps she was scrutinising me. How I regretted that I could not see her eyes. I heard her deep breathing.

"Why have you come here?" I asked her, with a note of authority already in my voice.

"Oh, I don't know."

"But how nice it would be to be living in your father's house! It's warm and free; you have a home of your own."

"But what if it's worse than this?"

"I must take the right tone," flashed through my mind. "I may not get far with sentimentality." But it was only a momentary thought. I swear she really did interest me. Besides, I was exhausted and moody. And cunning so easily goes hand-in-hand with feeling.

"Who denies it!" I hastened to answer. "Anything may happen. I am convinced that someone has wronged you, and that you are more sinned against than sinning. Of course, I know nothing of your story, but it's not likely a girl like you has come here of her own inclination. . . ."

"A girl like me?" she whispered, hardly audibly; but I heard it.

Damn it all, I was flattering her. That was horrid. But perhaps it was a good thing. . . . She was silent.

"See, Liza, I will tell you about myself. If I had had a home from childhood, I shouldn't be what I am now. I often think that. However bad it may be at home, anyway they are your father and mother, and not enemies, strangers. Once a year at least, they'll show their love of you. Anyway, you know you are at home. I grew up without a home; and perhaps that's why I've turned so . . . unfeeling."

I waited again. "Perhaps she doesn't understand," I thought, "and, indeed, it is absurd—it's moralising."

"If I were a father and had a daughter, I believe I should love my daughter more than my sons, really," I began indirectly, as though talking of something else, to distract her attention. I must confess I blushed.

"Why so?" she asked.

Ah! so she was listening!

"I don't know, Liza. I knew a father who was a stern, austere man, but used to go down on his knees to his daughter, used to kiss her hands, her feet, he couldn't make enough of her, really. When she danced at parties he used to stand for five hours at a stretch, gazing at her. He was mad over her: I understand that! She would fall asleep tired at night, and he would wake to kiss her in her sleep and make the sign of the cross over her. He would go about in a dirty old coat, he was stingy to everyone else, but would spend his last penny for her, giving her expensive presents, and it was his greatest delight when she was pleased with what he gave her. Fathers always love their daughters more than the mothers do. Some girls live happily at home! And I believe I should never let my daughters marry."

"What next?" she said, with a faint smile.

"I should be jealous, I really should. To think that she should kiss anyone else! That she should love a stranger more than her father! It's painful to imagine it. Of course, that's all nonsense, of course every father would be reasonable at last. But I believe before I should let her marry, I should worry myself to death; I should find fault with all her suitors. But I should end by letting her marry whom she herself loved. The one whom the daughter loves always seems the worst to the father, you know. That is always so. So many family troubles come from that."

"Some are glad to sell their daughters, rather than marrying them honourably."

Ah, so that was it!

"Such a thing, Liza, happens in those accursed families in which there is neither love nor God," I retorted warmly, "and where there is no love, there is no sense either. There are such families, it's true, but I am not speaking of them. You must have seen wickedness in your own family, if you talk like that. Truly, you must have been unlucky. H'm! . . . that sort of thing mostly comes about through poverty."

"And is it any better with the gentry? Even among the poor, honest people who live happily?"

"H'm . . . yes. Perhaps. Another thing, Liza, man is fond of reckoning up his troubles, but does not count his joys. If he counted them up as he ought, he would see that every lot has enough happiness provided for it. And what if all goes well with the family, if the blessing of God is upon it, if the husband is a good one, loves you, cherishes you, never leaves you! There is happiness in such a family! Even sometimes there is happiness in the midst of sorrow; and indeed sorrow is everywhere. If you marry *you will find out for yourself*. But think of the first years of married life with one you love: what happiness, what happiness there sometimes is in it! And indeed it's the ordinary thing. In those early days even quarrels with one's husband end happily. Some women get up quarrels with their husbands just because they love them. Indeed, I knew a woman like that: she seemed to say that because she loved him, she would torment him and make him feel it. You know that you may torment a man on purpose through love. Women are particularly given to that, thinking to themselves 'I will love him so, I will make so much of him afterwards, that it's no sin to torment him a little now.' And all in the house rejoice in the sight of you, and you are happy and gay and peaceful and honourable. . . . Then there are some women who are jealous. If he went off anywhere—I knew one such woman, she couldn't restrain herself, but would jump up at night and run off on the sly to find out where he was, whether he was with some other woman. That's a pity. And the woman knows herself it's wrong, and her heart fails her and she suffers, but she loves—it's all through love. And how sweet it is to make up after quarrels, to own herself in the wrong or to forgive him! And they both are so happy all at once—as though they had met anew, been married over again; as though their love had begun afresh. And no one, no one should know what passes between husband and wife if they love one another. And whatever quarrels there may be between them they ought not to call in their own mother to judge between them and tell tales of one another. They are their own judges. Love is a holy mystery and ought to be hidden from all other eyes, whatever happens. That makes it holier and better. They respect one another more, and much is built on respect. And if once there has been love, if they have been married for love, why should love pass away? Surely one can keep it! It is rare that one cannot keep it. And if the husband is kind and straightforward, why should not love last? The first phase of married love will pass, it is true, but then there will come a love that is better still. Then there will be the union of souls, they will have everything in common, there will be no secrets between them. And once they have children, the most difficult times will seem to them happy, so long as there is love and courage. Even toil will be a joy, you may deny yourself bread for your children and even that will be a joy, They will love you for it afterwards; so you are laying by for your future. As the children grow up you feel that you are an example, a support for them; that even after you die your children will always keep your thoughts and feelings, because they have received them from you, they will take on your semblance and likeness. So you see this is a great duty. How can it fail to draw the father and mother nearer? People say it's a trial to have children. Who says that? It is heavenly happiness! Are you fond of little children, Liza? I am awfully fond of them. You know—a little rosy baby boy at your bosom, and what husband's heart is not touched, seeing his wife nursing his child! A plump little rosy baby, sprawling and snuggling, chubby little hands and feet, clean tiny little nails, so tiny that it makes one laugh to look at them; eyes that look as if they understand everything. And while it sucks it clutches at your bosom with its little hand, plays. When its father comes up, the child tears itself away from the bosom, flings itself back, looks at its father, laughs, as though it were fearfully funny, and falls to sucking again. Or it will bite its mother's breast when its little teeth are coming, while it looks sideways at her with its little eyes as though to say, 'Look, I am biting!' Is not all that happiness when they are the three together, husband, wife and child? One can forgive a great deal for the sake of such moments. Yes, Liza, one must first learn to live oneself before one blames others!"

"It's by pictures, pictures like that one must get at you," I thought to myself, though I did speak with real feeling, and all at once I flushed crimson. "What if she were suddenly to burst out laughing, what should I do then?" That idea drove me to fury. Towards the end of my speech I really was excited, and now my vanity was somehow wounded. The silence continued. I almost nudged her.

"Why are you—" she began and stopped. But I understood: there was a quiver of something different in her voice, not abrupt, harsh and unyielding as before, but something soft and shamefaced, so shamefaced that I suddenly felt ashamed and guilty.

"What?" I asked, with tender curiosity.

"Why, you . . ."

"What?"

"Why, you . . . speak somehow like a book," she said, and again there was a note of irony in her voice.

That remark sent a pang to my heart. It was not what I was expecting.

I did not understand that she was hiding her feelings under irony, that this is usually the last refuge of modest and chaste-souled people when the privacy of their soul is coarsely and intrusively invaded, and that their pride makes them refuse to surrender till the last moment and shrink from giving expression to their feelings before you. I ought to have guessed the truth from the timidity with which she had repeatedly approached her sarcasm, only bringing herself to utter it at last with an effort. But I did not guess, and an evil feeling took possession of me.

"Wait a bit!" I thought.

VII

"Oh, hush, Liza! How can you talk about being like a book, when it makes even me, an outsider, feel sick? Though I don't look at it as an outsider, for, indeed, it touches me to the heart . . . Is it possible, is it possible that you do not feel sick at being here yourself? Evidently habit does wonders! God knows what habit can do with anyone. Can you seriously think that you will never grow old, that you will always be good-looking, and that they will keep you here for ever and ever? I say nothing of the loathsomeness of the life here. . . . Though let me tell you this about it—about your present life, I mean; here though you are young now, attractive, nice, with soul and feeling, yet you know as soon as I came to myself just now I felt at once sick at being here with you! One can only come here when one is drunk. But if you were anywhere else, living as good people live, I should perhaps be more than attracted by you, should fall in love with you, should be glad of a look from you, let alone a word; I should hang about your door, should go down on my knees to you, should look upon you as my betrothed and think it an honour to be allowed to. I should not dare to have an impure thought about you. But here, you see, I know that I have only to whistle and you have to come with me whether you like it or not. I don't consult your wishes, but you mine. The lowest labourer hires himself as a workman, but he doesn't make a slave of himself altogether; besides, he knows that he will be free again presently. But when are you free? Only think what you are giving up here? What is it you are making a slave of? It is your soul, together with your body; you are selling your soul which you have no right to dispose of! You give your love to be outraged by every drunkard! Love! But that's everything, you know, it's a priceless diamond, it's a maiden's treasure, love—why, a man would be ready to give his soul, to face death to gain that love. But how much is your love worth now? You are sold, all of you, body and soul, and there is no need to strive for love when you can have everything without love. And you know there is no greater insult to a girl than that, do you understand? To be sure, I have heard that they comfort you, poor fools, they let you have lovers of your own here. But you know that's simply a farce, that's simply a sham, it's just laughing at you, and you are taken in by it! Why, do you suppose he really loves you, that lover of yours? I don't believe it. How can he love you when he knows you may be called away from him any minute? He would be a low fellow if he did! Will he have a grain of respect for you? What have you in common with him? He laughs at you and robs you—that is all his love amounts to! You are lucky if he does not beat you. Very likely he does beat you, too. Ask him, if you have got one, whether he will marry you. He will laugh in your face, if he doesn't spit in it or give you a blow—though maybe he is not worth a bad halfpenny himself. And for what have you ruined your life, if you come to think of it? For the coffee they give you to drink and the plentiful meals? But with what object are they feeding you up? An honest girl couldn't swallow the food, for she would know what she was being fed for. You are in debt here, and, of course, you will always be in debt, and you will go on in debt to the end, till the visitors here begin to scorn you. And that will soon happen, don't rely upon your youth—all that flies by express train here, you know. You will be kicked out. And not simply kicked out; long before that she'll begin nagging at you, scolding you, abusing you, as though you had not sacrificed your health for her, had not thrown away your youth and your soul for her benefit, but as though you had ruined her, beggared her, robbed her. And don't expect anyone to take your part: the others, your companions, will attack you, too, win her favour, for all are in slavery here, and have lost all conscience and pity here long ago. They have become utterly vile, and nothing on earth is viler, more loathsome, and more insulting than their abuse. And you are laying down everything here, unconditionally, youth and health and beauty and hope, and at twenty-two you will look like a woman of five-and-thirty, and you will be lucky if you are not diseased, pray to God for that! No doubt you are thinking now that you have a gay time and no work to do! Yet there is no work harder or more dreadful in the world or ever has been. One would think that the heart alone would be worn out with tears. And you won't dare to say a word, not half a word when they drive you away from here; you will go away as though you were to blame. You will change to another house, then to a third, then somewhere else, till you come down at last to the Haymarket. There you will be beaten at every turn; that is good manners there, the visitors don't know how to be friendly without beating you. You don't believe that it is so hateful there? Go and look for yourself some time, you can see with your own eyes. Once, one New Year's Day, I saw a woman at a door. They had turned her out as a joke, to give her a taste of the frost because she had been crying so much, and they shut the door behind her. At nine o'clock in the morning she was already quite drunk, dishevelled, half-naked, covered with bruises, her face was powdered, but she had a black-eye, blood was trickling from her nose and her teeth; some cabman had just given her a drubbing. She was sitting on the stone steps, a salt fish of some sort was in her hand; she was crying, wailing something about her luck and beating with the fish on the steps, and cabmen and drunken soldiers were crowding in the doorway taunting her. You don't believe that you will ever be like that? I should be sorry to believe it, too, but how do you know; maybe ten years, eight years ago that very woman with the salt fish came here fresh as a cherub, innocent, pure, knowing no evil, blushing at every word. Perhaps she was like you, proud, ready to take offence, not like the others; perhaps she looked like a queen, and knew what happiness was in store for the man who should love her and whom she should love. Do you see how it ended? And what if at that very minute when she was beating on the filthy steps with that fish, drunken and dishevelled—what if at that very minute she recalled the pure early days in her father's house, when she used to go to school and the neighbour's son watched for her on the way, declaring that he would love her as long as he lived, that he would devote his life to her, and when they vowed to love one another for ever and be married as soon as they were grown up! No, Liza, it would be happy for you if you were to die soon of consumption in some corner, in some cellar like that woman just now. In the hospital, do you say? You will be lucky if they take you, but what if you are still of use to the madam here? Consumption is a queer disease, it is not like fever. The patient goes on hoping till the last minute and says he is all right. He deludes himself And that just suits your madam. Don't doubt it, that's how it is; you have sold your soul, and what is more you owe money, so you daren't say a word. But when you are dying, all will abandon you, all will turn away from you, for then there will be nothing to get from you. What's more, they will reproach you for cumbering the place, for being so long over dying. However you beg you won't get a drink of water without abuse: 'Whenever are you going off, you nasty hussy, you won't let us sleep with your moaning, you make the gentlemen sick.' That's true, I have heard such things said myself. They will thrust you dying into the filthiest corner in the cellar—in the damp and darkness; what will your thoughts be, lying there alone? When you die, strange hands will lay you out, with grumbling and impatience; no one will bless you, no one will sigh for you, they only want to get rid of you as soon as may be; they will buy a coffin, take you to the grave as they did that poor woman today, and celebrate your memory at the tavern. In the grave, sleet, filth, wet snow—no need to put themselves out for you—'Let her down, Vanuha; it's just like her luck—even here, she is head-foremost, the hussy. Shorten the cord, you rascal.' 'It's all right as it is.' 'All right, is it? Why, she's on her side! She was a fellow-creature, after all! But, never mind, throw the earth on her.' And they won't care to waste much time quarrelling over you. They will scatter the wet blue clay as quick as they can and go off to the tavern . . . and there your memory on earth will end; other women have children to go to their graves, fathers, husbands. While for you neither tear, nor sigh, nor remembrance; no one in the whole world will ever come to you, your name will vanish from the face of the earth—as though you had never existed, never been born at all! Nothing but filth and mud, however you knock at your coffin lid at night, when the dead arise, however you cry: 'Let me out, kind people, to live in the light of day! My life was no life at all; my life has been thrown away like a dish-clout; it was drunk away in the tavern at the Haymarket; let me out, kind people, to live in the world again.'"

And I worked myself up to such a pitch that I began to have a lump in my throat myself, and . . . and all at once I stopped, sat up in dismay and, bending over apprehensively, began to listen with a beating heart. I had reason to be troubled.

I had felt for some time that I was turning her soul upside down and rending her heart, and—and the more I was convinced of it, the more eagerly I desired to gain my object as quickly and as effectually as possible. It was the exercise of my skill that carried me away; yet it was not merely sport. . . .

I knew I was speaking stiffly, artificially, even bookishly, in fact, I could not speak except "like a book." But that did not trouble me: I knew, I felt that I should be understood and that this very bookishness might be an assistance. But now, having attained my effect, I was suddenly panic-stricken. Never before had I witnessed such despair! She was lying on her face, thrusting her face into the pillow and clutching it in both hands. Her heart was being torn. Her youthful body was shuddering all over as though in convulsions. Suppressed sobs rent her bosom and suddenly burst out in weeping and wailing, then she pressed closer into the pillow: she did not want anyone here, not a living soul, to know of her anguish and her tears. She bit the pillow, bit her hand till it bled (I saw that afterwards), or, thrusting her fingers into her dishevelled hair, seemed rigid with the effort of restraint, holding her breath and clenching her teeth. I began saying something, begging her to calm herself, but felt that I did not dare; and all at once, in a sort of cold shiver, almost in terror, began fumbling in the dark, trying hurriedly to get dressed to go. It was dark; though I tried my best I could not finish dressing quickly. Suddenly I felt a box of matches and a candlestick with a whole candle in it. As soon as the room was lighted up, Liza sprang up, sat up in bed, and with a contorted face, with a half insane smile, looked at me almost senselessly. I sat down beside her and took her hands; she came to herself, made an impulsive movement towards me, would have caught hold of me, but did not dare, and slowly bowed her head before me.

"Liza, my dear, I was wrong . . . forgive me, my dear," I began, but she squeezed my hand in her fingers so tightly that I felt I was saying the wrong thing and stopped.

"This is my address, Liza, come to me."

"I will come," she answered resolutely, her head still bowed.

"But now I am going, good-bye . . . till we meet again."

I got up; she, too, stood up and suddenly flushed all over, gave a shudder, snatched up a shawl that was lying on a chair and muffled herself in it to her chin. As she did this she gave another sickly smile, blushed and looked at me strangely. I felt wretched; I was in haste to get away—to disappear.

"Wait a minute," she said suddenly, in the passage just at the doorway, stopping me with her hand on my overcoat. She put down the candle in hot haste and ran off; evidently she had thought of something or wanted to show me something. As she ran away she flushed, her eyes shone, and there was a smile on her lips—what was the meaning of it? Against my will I waited: she came back a minute later with an expression that seemed to ask forgiveness for something. In fact, it was not the same face, not the same look as the evening before: sullen, mistrustful and obstinate. Her eyes now were imploring, soft, and at the same time trustful, caressing, timid. The expression with which children look at people they are very fond of, of whom they are asking a favour. Her eyes were a light hazel, they were lovely eyes, full of life, and capable of expressing love as well as sullen hatred.

Making no explanation, as though I, as a sort of higher being, must understand everything without explanations, she held out a piece of paper to me. Her whole face was positively beaming at that instant with naive, almost childish, triumph. I unfolded it. It was a letter to her from a medical student or someone of that sort—a very high-flown and flowery, but extremely respectful, love-letter. I don't recall the words now, but I remember well that through the high-flown phrases there was apparent a genuine feeling, which cannot be feigned. When I had finished reading it I met her glowing, questioning, and childishly impatient eyes fixed upon me. She fastened her eyes upon my face and waited impatiently for what I should say. In a few words, hurriedly, but with a sort of joy and pride, she explained to me that she had been to a dance somewhere in a private house, a family of "very nice people, *who knew nothing*, absolutely nothing, for she had only come here so lately and it had all happened . . . and she hadn't made up her mind to stay and was certainly going away as soon as she had paid her debt . . . and at that party there had been the student who had danced with her all the evening. He had talked to her, and it turned out that he had known her in old days at Riga when he was a child, they had played together, but a very long time ago—and he knew her parents, but *about this* he knew nothing, nothing whatever, and had no suspicion! And the day after the dance (three days ago) he had sent her that letter through the friend with whom she had gone to the party . . . and . . . well, that was all."

She dropped her shining eyes with a sort of bashfulness as she finished.

The poor girl was keeping that student's letter as a precious treasure, and had run to fetch it, her only treasure, because she did not want me to go away without knowing that she, too, was honestly and genuinely loved; that she, too, was addressed respectfully. No doubt that letter was destined to lie in her box and lead to nothing. But none the less, I am certain that she would keep it all her life as a precious treasure, as her pride and justification, and now at such a minute she had thought of that letter and brought it with naive pride to raise herself in my eyes that I might see, that I, too, might think well of her. I said nothing, pressed her hand and went out. I so longed to get away. . . . I walked all the way home, in spite of the fact that the melting snow was still falling in heavy flakes. I was exhausted, shattered, in bewilderment. But behind the bewilderment the truth was already gleaming. The loathsome truth.

VIII

It was some time, however, before I consented to recognise that truth. Waking up in the morning after some hours of heavy, leaden sleep, and immediately realising all that had happened on the previous day, I was positively amazed at my last night's *sentimentality* with Liza, at all those "outcries of horror and pity." "To think of having such an attack of womanish hysteria, pah!" I concluded. And what did I thrust my address upon her for? What if she comes? Let her come, though; it doesn't matter. . . . But *obviously*, that was not now the chief and the most important matter: I had to make haste and at all costs save my reputation in the eyes of Zverkov and Simonov as quickly as possible; that was the chief business. And I was so taken up that morning that I actually forgot all about Liza.

First of all I had at once to repay what I had borrowed the day before from Simonov. I resolved on a desperate measure: to borrow fifteen roubles straight off from Anton Antonitch. As luck would have it he was in the best of humours that morning, and gave it to me at once, on the first asking. I was so delighted at this that, as I signed the IOU with a swaggering air, I told him casually that the night before "I had been keeping it up with some friends at the Hotel de Paris; we were giving a farewell party to a comrade, in fact, I might say a friend of my childhood, and you know—a desperate rake, fearfully spoilt—of course, he belongs to a good family, and has considerable means, a brilliant career; he is witty, charming, a regular Lovelace, you understand; we drank an extra 'half-dozen' and . . ."

And it went off all right; all this was uttered very easily, unconstrainedly and complacently.

On reaching home I promptly wrote to Simonov.

To this hour I am lost in admiration when I recall the truly gentlemanly, good-humoured, candid tone of my letter. With tact and good-breeding, and, above all, entirely without superfluous words, I blamed myself for all that had happened. I defended myself, "if I really may be allowed to defend myself," by alleging that being utterly unaccustomed to wine, I had been intoxicated with the first glass, which I said, I had drunk before they arrived, while I was waiting for them at the Hotel de Paris between five and six o'clock. I begged Simonov's pardon especially; I asked him to convey my explanations to all the others, especially to Zverkov, whom "I seemed to remember as though in a dream" I had insulted. I added that I would have called upon all of them myself, but my head ached, and besides I had not the face to. I was particularly pleased with a certain lightness, almost carelessness (strictly within the bounds of politeness, however), which was apparent in my style, and better than any possible arguments, gave them at once to understand that I took rather an independent view of "all that unpleasantness last night"; that I was by no means so utterly crushed as you, my friends, probably imagine; but on the contrary, looked upon it as a gentleman serenely respecting himself should look upon it. "On a young hero's past no censure is cast!"

"There is actually an aristocratic playfulness about it!" I thought admiringly, as I read over the letter. "And it's all because I am an intellectual and cultivated man! Another man in my place would not have known how to extricate himself, but here I have got out of it and am as jolly as ever again, and all because I am 'a cultivated and educated man of our day.' And, indeed, perhaps, everything was due to the wine yesterday. H'm!" . . . No, it was not the wine. I did not drink anything at all between five and six when I was waiting for them. I had lied to Simonov; I had lied shamelessly; and indeed I wasn't ashamed now. . . . Hang it all though, the great thing was that I was rid of it.

I put six roubles in the letter, sealed it up, and asked Apollon to take it to Simonov. When he learned that there was money in the letter, Apollon became more respectful and agreed to take it. Towards evening I went out for a walk. My head was still aching and giddy after yesterday. But as evening came on and the twilight grew denser, my impressions and, following them, my thoughts, grew more and more different and confused. Something was not dead within me, in the depths of my heart and conscience it would not die, and it showed itself in acute depression. For the most part I jostled my way through the most crowded business streets, along Myeshtchansky Street, along Sadovy Street and in Yusupov Garden. I always liked particularly sauntering along these streets in the dusk, just when there were crowds of working people of all sorts going home from their daily work, with faces looking cross with anxiety. What I liked was just that cheap bustle, that bare prose. On this occasion the jostling of the streets irritated me more than ever, I could not make out what was wrong with me, I could not find the clue, something seemed rising up continually in my soul, painfully, and refusing to be appeased. I returned home completely upset, it was just as though some crime were lying on my conscience.

The thought that Liza was coming worried me continually. It seemed queer to me that of all my recollections of yesterday this tormented me, as it were, especially, as it were, quite separately. Everything else I had quite succeeded in forgetting by the evening; I dismissed it all and was still perfectly satisfied with my letter to Simonov. But on this point I was not satisfied at all. It was as though I were worried only by Liza. "What if she comes," I thought incessantly, "well, it doesn't matter, let her come! H'm! it's horrid that she should see, for instance, how I live. Yesterday I seemed such a hero to her, while now, h'm! It's horrid, though, that I have let myself go so, the room looks like a beggar's. And I brought myself to go out to dinner in such a suit! And my American leather sofa with the stuffing sticking out. And my dressing-gown, which will not cover me, such tatters, and she will see all this and she will see Apollon. That beast is certain to insult her. He will fasten upon her in order to be rude to me. And I, of course, shall be panic-stricken as usual, I shall begin bowing and scraping before her and pulling my dressing-gown round me, I shall begin smiling, telling lies. Oh, the beastliness! And it isn't the beastliness of it that matters most! There is something more important, more loathsome, viler! Yes, viler! And to put on that dishonest lying mask again! . . ."

When I reached that thought I fired up all at once.

"Why dishonest? How dishonest? I was speaking sincerely last night. I remember there was real feeling in me, too. What I wanted was to excite an honourable feeling in her. . . . Her crying was a good thing, it will have a good effect."

Yet I could not feel at ease. All that evening, even when I had come back home, even after nine o'clock, when I calculated that Liza could not possibly come, still she haunted me, and what was worse, she came back to my mind always in the same position. One moment out of all that had happened last night stood vividly before my imagination; the moment when I struck a match and saw her pale, distorted face, with its look of torture. And what a pitiful, what an unnatural, what a distorted smile she had at that moment! But I did not know then, that fifteen years later I should still in my imagination see Liza, always with the pitiful, distorted, inappropriate smile which was on her face at that minute.

Next day I was ready again to look upon it all as nonsense, due to over-excited nerves, and, above all, as *exaggerated*. I was always conscious of that weak point of mine, and sometimes very much afraid of it. "I exaggerate everything, that is where I go wrong," I repeated to myself every hour. But, however, "Liza will very likely come all the same," was the refrain with which all my reflections ended. I was so uneasy that I sometimes flew into a fury: "She'll come, she is certain to come!" I cried, running about the room, "if not today, she will come tomorrow; she'll find me out! The damnable romanticism of these pure hearts! Oh, the vileness—oh, the silliness—oh, the stupidity of these 'wretched sentimental souls!' Why, how fail to understand? How could one fail to understand? . . ."

But at this point I stopped short, and in great confusion, indeed.

And how few, how few words, I thought, in passing, were needed; how little of the idyllic (and affectedly, bookishly, artificially idyllic too) had sufficed to turn a whole human life at once according to my will. That's virginity, to be sure! Freshness of soil!

At times a thought occurred to me, to go to her, "to tell her all," and beg her not to come to me. But this thought stirred such wrath in me that I believed I should have crushed that "damned" Liza if she had chanced to be near me at the time. I should have insulted her, have spat at her, have turned her out, have struck her!

One day passed, however, another and another; she did not come and I began to grow calmer. I felt particularly bold and cheerful after nine o'clock, I even sometimes began dreaming, and rather sweetly: I, for instance, became the salvation of Liza, simply through her coming to me and my talking to her. . . . I develop her, educate her. Finally, I notice that she loves me, loves me passionately. I pretend not to understand (I don't know, however, why I pretend, just for effect, perhaps). At last all confusion, transfigured, trembling and sobbing, she flings herself at my feet and says that I am her saviour, and that she loves me better than anything in the world. I am amazed, but. . . . "Liza," I say, "can you imagine that I have not noticed your love? I saw it all, I divined it, but I did not dare to approach you first, because I had an influence over you and was afraid that you would force yourself, from gratitude, to respond to my love, would try to rouse in your heart a feeling which was perhaps absent, and I did not wish that . . . because it would be tyranny . . . it would be indelicate (in short, I launch off at that point into European, inexplicably lofty subtleties à la George Sand), but now, now you are mine, you are my creation, you are pure, you are good, you are my noble wife.

'Into my house come bold and free,
Its rightful mistress there to be.'"

Then we begin living together, go abroad and so on, and so on. In fact, in the end it seemed vulgar to me myself, and I began putting out my tongue at myself.

Besides, they won't let her out, "the hussy!" I thought. They don't let them go out very readily, especially in the evening (for some reason I fancied she would come in the evening, and at seven o'clock precisely). Though she did say she was not altogether a slave there yet, and had certain rights; so, h'm! Damn it all, she will come, she is sure to come!

It was a good thing, in fact, that Apollon distracted my attention at that time by his rudeness. He drove me beyond all patience! He was the bane of my life, the curse laid upon me by Providence. We had been squabbling continually for years, and I hated him. My God, how I hated him! I believe I had never hated anyone in my life as I hated him, especially at some moments. He was an elderly, dignified man, who worked part of his time as a tailor. But for some unknown reason he despised me beyond all measure, and looked down upon me insufferably. Though, indeed, he looked down upon everyone. Simply to glance at that flaxen, smoothly brushed head, at the tuft of hair he combed up on his forehead and oiled with sunflower oil, at that dignified mouth, compressed into the shape of the letter V, made one feel one was confronting a man who never doubted of himself. He was a pedant, to the most extreme point, the greatest pedant I had met on earth, and with that had a vanity only befitting Alexander of Macedon. He was in love with every button on his coat, every nail on his fingers—absolutely in love with them, and he looked it! In his behaviour to me he was a perfect tyrant, he spoke very little to me, and if he chanced to glance at me he gave me a firm, majestically self-confident and invariably ironical look that drove me sometimes to fury. He did his work with the air of doing me the greatest favour, though he did scarcely anything for me, and did not, indeed, consider himself bound to do anything. There could be no doubt that he looked upon me as the greatest fool on earth, and that "he did not get rid of me" was simply that he could get wages from me every month. He consented to do nothing for me for seven roubles a month. Many sins should be forgiven me for what I suffered from him. My hatred reached such a point that sometimes his very step almost threw me into convulsions. What I loathed particularly was his lisp. His tongue must have been a little too long or something of that sort, for he continually lisped, and seemed to be very proud of it, imagining that it greatly added to his dignity. He spoke in a slow, measured tone, with his hands behind his back and his eyes fixed on the ground. He maddened me particularly when he read aloud the psalms to himself behind his partition. Many a battle I waged over that reading! But he was awfully fond of reading aloud in the evenings, in a slow, even, sing-song voice, as though over the dead. It is interesting that that is how he has ended: he hires himself out to read the psalms over the dead, and at the same time he kills rats and makes blacking. But at that time I could not get rid of him, it was as though he were chemically combined with my existence. Besides, nothing would have induced him to consent to leave me. I could not live in furnished lodgings: my lodging was my private solitude, my shell, my cave, in which I concealed myself from all mankind, and Apollon seemed to me, for some reason, an integral part of that flat, and for seven years I could not turn him away.

To be two or three days behind with his wages, for instance, was impossible. He would have made such a fuss, I should not have known where to hide my head. But I was so exasperated with everyone during those days, that I made up my mind for some reason and with some object to *punish* Apollon and not to pay him for a fortnight the wages that were owing him. I had for a long time—for the last two years—been intending to do this, simply in order to teach him not to give himself airs with me, and to show him that if I liked I could withhold his wages. I purposed to say nothing to him about it, and was purposely silent indeed, in order to score off his pride and force him to be the first to speak of his wages. Then I would take the seven roubles out of a drawer, show him I have the money put aside on purpose, but that I won't, I won't, I simply won't pay him his wages, I won't just because that is "what I wish," because "I am master, and it is for me to decide," because he has been disrespectful, because he has been rude; but if he were to ask respectfully I might be softened and give it to him, otherwise he might wait another fortnight, another three weeks, a whole month. . . .

But angry as I was, yet he got the better of me. I could not hold out for four days. He began as he always did begin in such cases, for there had been such cases already, there had been attempts (and it may be observed I knew all this beforehand, I knew his nasty tactics by heart). He would begin by fixing upon me an exceedingly severe stare, keeping it up for several minutes at a time, particularly on meeting me or seeing me out of the house. If I held out and pretended not to notice these stares, he would, still in silence, proceed to further tortures. All at once, *à propos* of nothing, he would walk softly and smoothly into my room, when I was pacing up and down or reading, stand at the door, one hand behind his back and one foot behind the other, and fix upon me a stare more than severe, utterly contemptuous. If I suddenly asked him what he wanted, he would make me no answer, but continue staring at me persistently for some seconds, then, with a peculiar compression of his lips and a most significant air, deliberately turn round and deliberately go back to his room. Two hours later he would come out again and again present himself before me in the same way. It had happened that in my fury I did not even ask him what he wanted, but simply raised my head sharply and imperiously and began staring back at him. So we stared at one another for two minutes; at last he turned with deliberation and dignity and went back again for two hours.

If I were still not brought to reason by all this, but persisted in my revolt, he would suddenly begin sighing while he looked at me, long, deep sighs as though measuring by them the depths of my moral degradation, and, of course, it ended at last by his triumphing completely: I raged and shouted, but still was forced to do what he wanted.

This time the usual staring manoeuvres had scarcely begun when I lost my temper and flew at him in a fury. I was irritated beyond endurance apart from him.

"Stay," I cried, in a frenzy, as he was slowly and silently turning, with one hand behind his back, to go to his room. "Stay! Come back, come back, I tell you!" and I must have bawled so unnaturally, that he turned round and even looked at me with some wonder. However, he persisted in saying nothing, and that infuriated me

"How dare you come and look at me like that without being sent for? Answer!"

After looking at me calmly for half a minute, he began turning round again.

"Stay!" I roared, running up to him, "don't stir! There. Answer, now: what did you come in to look at?"

"If you have any order to give me it's my duty to carry it out," he answered, after another silent pause, with a slow, measured lisp, raising his eyebrows and calmly twisting his head from one side to another, all this with exasperating composure.

"That's not what I am asking you about, you torturer!" I shouted, turning crimson with anger. "I'll tell you why you came here myself: you see, I don't give you your wages, you are so proud you don't want to bow down and ask for it, and so you come to punish me with your stupid stares, to worry me and you have no sus . . . pic . . . ion how stupid it is—stupid, stupid, stupid, stupid! . . ."

He would have turned round again without a word, but I seized him.

"Listen," I shouted to him. "Here's the money, do you see, here it is," (I took it out of the table drawer); "here's the seven roubles complete, but you are not going to have it, you . . . are . . . not . . . going . . . to . . . have it until you come respectfully with bowed head to beg my pardon. Do you hear?"

"That cannot be," he answered, with the most unnatural self-confidence.

"It shall be so," I said, "I give you my word of honour, it shall be!"

"And there's nothing for me to beg your pardon for," he went on, as though he had not noticed my exclamations at all. "Why, besides, you called me a 'torturer,' for which I can summon you at the police-station at any time for insulting behaviour."

"Go, summon me," I roared, "go at once, this very minute, this very second! You are a torturer all the same! a torturer!"

But he merely looked at me, then turned, and regardless of my loud calls to him, he walked to his room with an even step and without looking round.

"If it had not been for Liza nothing of this would have happened," I decided inwardly. Then, after waiting a minute, I went myself behind his screen with a dignified and solemn air, though my heart was beating slowly and violently.

"Apollon," I said quietly and emphatically, though I was breathless, "go at once without a minute's delay and fetch the police-officer."

He had meanwhile settled himself at his table, put on his spectacles and taken up some sewing. But, hearing my order, he burst into a guffaw.

"At once, go this minute! Go on, or else you can't imagine what will happen."

"You are certainly out of your mind," he observed, without even raising his head, lisping as deliberately as ever and threading his needle. "Whoever heard of a man sending for the police against himself? And as for being frightened—you are upsetting yourself about nothing, for nothing will come of it."

"Go!" I shrieked, clutching him by the shoulder. I felt I should strike him in a minute.

But I did not notice the door from the passage softly and slowly open at that instant and a figure come in, stop short, and begin staring at us in perplexity. I glanced, nearly swooned with shame, and rushed back to my room. There, clutching at my hair with both hands, I leaned my head against the wall and stood motionless in that position.

Two minutes later I heard Apollon's deliberate footsteps. "There is some woman asking for you," he said, looking at me with peculiar severity. Then he stood aside and let in Liza. He would not go away, but stared at us sarcastically.

"Go away, go away," I commanded in desperation. At that moment my clock began whirring and wheezing and struck seven.

IX

*"Into my house come bold and free,
Its rightful mistress there to be."*

I stood before her crushed, crestfallen, revoltingly confused, and I believe I smiled as I did my utmost to wrap myself in the skirts of my ragged wadded dressing-gown—exactly as I had imagined the scene not long before in a fit of depression. After standing over us for a couple of minutes Apollon went away, but that did not make me more at ease. What made it worse was that she, too, was overwhelmed with confusion, more so, in fact, than I should have expected. At the sight of me, of course.

"Sit down," I said mechanically, moving a chair up to the table, and I sat down on the sofa. She obediently sat down at once and gazed at me open-eyed, evidently expecting something from me at once. This naivete of expectation drove me to fury, but I restrained myself.

She ought to have tried not to notice, as though everything had been as usual, while instead of that, she . . . and I dimly felt that I should make her pay dearly for *all this*.

"You have found me in a strange position, Liza," I began, stammering and knowing that this was the wrong way to begin. "No, no, don't imagine anything," I cried, seeing that she had suddenly flushed. "I am not ashamed of my poverty. . . . On the contrary, I look with pride on my poverty. I am poor but honourable. . . . One can be poor and honourable," I muttered. "However . . . would you like tea? . . ."

"No," she was beginning.

"Wait a minute."

I leapt up and ran to Apollon. I had to get out of the room somehow.

"Apollon," I whispered in feverish haste, flinging down before him the seven roubles which had remained all the time in my clenched fist, "here are your wages, you see I give them to you; but for that you must come to my rescue: bring me tea and a dozen rusks from the restaurant. If you won't go, you'll make me a miserable man! You don't know what this woman is. . . . This is—everything! You may be imagining something. . . . But you don't know what that woman is! . . ."

Apollon, who had already sat down to his work and put on his spectacles again, at first glanced askance at the money without speaking or putting down his needle; then, without paying the slightest attention to me or making any answer, he went on busying himself with his needle, which he had not yet threaded. I waited before him for three minutes with my arms crossed *à la Napoléon*. My temples were moist with sweat. I was pale, I felt it. But, thank God, he must have been moved to pity, looking at me. Having threaded his needle he deliberately got up from his seat, deliberately moved back his chair, deliberately took off his spectacles, deliberately counted the money, and finally asking me over his shoulder: "Shall I get a whole portion?" deliberately walked out of the room. As I was going back to Liza, the thought occurred to me on the way: shouldn't I run away just as I was in my dressing-gown, no matter where, and then let happen what would?

I sat down again. She looked at me uneasily. For some minutes we were silent.

"I will kill him," I shouted suddenly, striking the table with my fist so that the ink spurted out of the inkstand.

"What are you saying!" she cried, starting.

"I will kill him! kill him!" I shrieked, suddenly striking the table in absolute frenzy, and at the same time fully understanding how stupid it was to be in such a frenzy. "You don't know,

Liza, what that torturer is to me. He is my torturer. . . . He has gone now to fetch some rusks; he . . ."

And suddenly I burst into tears. It was an hysterical attack. How ashamed I felt in the midst of my sobs; but still I could not restrain them.

She was frightened.

"What is the matter? What is wrong?" she cried, fussing about me.

"Water, give me water, over there!" I muttered in a faint voice, though I was inwardly conscious that I could have got on very well without water and without muttering in a faint voice. But I was, what is called, *putting it on*, to save appearances, though the attack was a genuine one.

She gave me water, looking at me in bewilderment. At that moment Apollon brought in the tea. It suddenly seemed to me that this commonplace, prosaic tea was horribly undignified and paltry after all that had happened, and I blushed crimson. Liza looked at Apollon with positive alarm. He went out without a glance at either of us.

"Liza, do you despise me?" I asked, looking at her fixedly, trembling with impatience to know what she was thinking.

She was confused, and did not know what to answer.

"Drink your tea," I said to her angrily. I was angry with myself, but, of course, it was she who would have to pay for it. A horrible spite against her suddenly surged up in my heart; I believe I could have killed her. To revenge myself on her I swore inwardly not to say a word to her all the time. "She is the cause of it all," I thought.

Our silence lasted for five minutes. The tea stood on the table; we did not touch it. I had got to the point of purposely refraining from beginning in order to embarrass her further; it was awkward for her to begin alone. Several times she glanced at me with mournful perplexity. I was obstinately silent. I was, of course, myself the chief sufferer, because I was fully conscious of the disgusting meanness of my spiteful stupidity, and yet at the same time I could not restrain myself.

"I want to . . . get away . . . from there altogether," she began, to break the silence in some way, but, poor girl, that was just what she ought not to have spoken about at such a stupid moment to a man so stupid as I was. My heart positively ached with pity for her tactless and unnecessary straightforwardness. But something hideous at once stifled all compassion in me; it even provoked me to greater venom. I did not care what happened. Another five minutes passed.

"Perhaps I am in your way," she began timidly, hardly audibly, and was getting up.

But as soon as I saw this first impulse of wounded dignity I positively trembled with spite, and at once burst out.

"Why have you come to me, tell me that, please?" I began, gasping for breath and regardless of logical connection in my words. I longed to have it all out at once, at one burst; I did not even trouble how to begin. "Why have you come? Answer, answer," I cried, hardly knowing what I was doing. "I'll tell you, my good girl, why you have come. You've come because I talked sentimental stuff to you then. So now you are soft as butter and longing for fine sentiments again. So you may as well know that I was laughing at you then. And I am laughing at you now. Why are you shuddering? Yes, I was laughing at you! I had been insulted just before, at dinner, by the fellows who came that evening before me. I came to you, meaning to thrash one of them, an officer; but I didn't succeed, I didn't find him; I had to avenge the insult on someone to get back my own again; you turned up, I vented my spleen on you and laughed at you. I had been humiliated, so I wanted to humiliate; I had been treated like a rag, so I wanted to show my power. . . . That's what it was, and you imagined I had come there on purpose to save you. Yes? You imagined that? You imagined that?"

I knew that she would perhaps be muddled and not take it all in exactly, but I knew, too, that she would grasp the gist of it, very well indeed. And so, indeed, she did. She turned white as a handkerchief, tried to say something, and her lips worked painfully; but she sank on a chair as though she had been felled by an axe. And all the time afterwards she listened to me with her lips parted and her eyes wide open, shuddering with awful terror. The cynicism, the cynicism of my words overwhelmed her. . . .

"Save you!" I went on, jumping up from my chair and running up and down the room before her. "Save you from what? But perhaps I am worse than you myself. Why didn't you throw it in my teeth when I was giving you that sermon: 'But what did you come here yourself for? was it to read us a sermon?' Power, power was what I wanted then, sport was what I wanted, I wanted to wring out your tears, your humiliation, your hysteria—that was what I wanted then! Of course, I couldn't keep it up then, because I am a wretched creature, I was frightened, and, the devil knows why, gave you my address in my folly. Afterwards, before I got home, I was cursing and swearing at you because of that address, I hated you already because of the lies I had told you. Because I only like playing with words, only dreaming, but, do you know, what I really want is that you should all go to hell. That is what I want. I want peace; yes, I'd sell the whole world for a farthing, straight off, so long as I was left in peace. Is the world to go to pot, or am I to go without my tea? I say that the world may go to pot for me so long as I always get my tea. Did you know that, or not? Well, anyway, I know that I am a blackguard, a scoundrel, an egoist, a sluggard. Here I have been shuddering for the last three days at the thought of your coming. And do you know what has worried me particularly for these three days? That I posed as such a hero to you, and now you would see me in a wretched torn dressing-gown, beggarly, loathsome. I told you just now that I was not ashamed of my poverty; so you may as well know that I am ashamed of it; I am more ashamed of it than of anything, more afraid of it than of being found out if I were a thief, because I am as vain as though I had been skinned and the very air blowing on me hurt. Surely by now you must realise that I shall never forgive you for having found me in this wretched dressing-gown, just as I was flying at Apollon like a spiteful cur. The saviour, the former hero, was flying like a mangy, unkempt sheep-dog at his lackey, and the lackey was jeering at him! And I shall never forgive you for the tears I could not help shedding before you just now, like some silly woman put to shame! And for what I am confessing to you now, I shall never forgive you either! Yes—you must answer for it all because you turned up like this, because I am a blackguard, because I am the nastiest, stupidest, absurdest and most envious of all the worms on earth, who are not a bit better than I am, but, the devil knows why, are never put to confusion; while I shall always be insulted by every louse, that is my doom! And what is it to me that you don't understand a word of this! And what do I care, what do I care about you, and whether you go to ruin there or not? Do you understand? How I shall hate you now after saying this, for having been here and listening. Why, it's not once in a lifetime a man speaks out like this, and then it is in hysterics! . . . What more do you want? Why do you still stand confronting me, after all this? Why are you worrying me? Why don't you go?"

But at this point a strange thing happened. I was so accustomed to think and imagine everything from books, and to picture everything in the world to myself just as I had made it up in my dreams beforehand, that I could not all at once take in this strange circumstance. What happened was this: Liza, insulted and crushed by me, understood a great deal more than I imagined. She understood from all this what a woman understands first of all, if she feels genuine love, that is, that I was myself unhappy.

The frightened and wounded expression on her face was followed first by a look of sorrowful perplexity. When I began calling myself a scoundrel and a blackguard and my tears flowed (the tirade was accompanied throughout by tears) her whole face worked convulsively. She was on the point of getting up and stopping me; when I finished she took no notice of my shouting: "Why are you here, why don't you go away?" but realised only that it must have been very bitter to me to say all this. Besides, she was so crushed, poor girl; she considered herself infinitely beneath me; how could she feel anger or resentment? She suddenly leapt up from her chair with an irresistible impulse and held out her hands, yearning towards me, though still timid and not daring to stir. . . . At this point there was a revulsion in my heart too. Then she suddenly rushed to me, threw her arms round me and burst into tears. I, too, could not restrain myself, and sobbed as I never had before.

"They won't let me . . . I can't be good!" I managed to articulate; then I went to the sofa, fell on it face downwards, and sobbed on it for a quarter of an hour in genuine hysterics. She came close to me, put her arms round me and stayed motionless in that position. But the trouble was that the hysterics could not go on for ever, and (I am writing the loathsome truth) lying face downwards on the sofa with my face thrust into my nasty leather pillow, I began by degrees to be aware of a far-away, involuntary but irresistible feeling that it would be awkward now for me to raise my head and look Liza straight in the face. Why was I ashamed? I don't know, but I was ashamed. The thought, too, came into my overwrought brain that our parts now were completely changed, that she was now the heroine, while I was just a crushed and humiliated creature as she had been before me that night—four days before.... And all this came into my mind during the minutes I was lying on my face on the sofa.

My God! surely I was not envious of her then.

I don't know, to this day I cannot decide, and at the time, of course, I was still less able to understand what I was feeling than now. I cannot get on without domineering and tyrannising over someone, but... there is no explaining anything by reasoning and so it is useless to reason.

I conquered myself, however, and raised my head; I had to do so sooner or later... and I am convinced to this day that it was just because I was ashamed to look at her that another feeling was suddenly kindled and flamed up in my heart... a feeling of mastery and possession. My eyes gleamed with passion, and I gripped her hands tightly. How I hated her and how I was drawn to her at that minute! The one feeling intensified the other. It was almost like an act of vengeance. At first there was a look of amazement, even of terror on her face, but only for one instant. She warmly and rapturously embraced me.

X

A quarter of an hour later I was rushing up and down the room in frenzied impatience, from minute to minute I went up to the screen and peeped through the crack at Liza. She was sitting on the ground with her head leaning against the bed, and must have been crying. But she did not go away, and that irritated me. This time she understood it all. I had insulted her finally, but... there's no need to describe it. She realised that my outburst of passion had been simply revenge, a fresh humiliation, and that to my earlier, almost causeless hatred was added now a *personal hatred*, born of envy.... Though I do not maintain positively that she understood all this distinctly; but she certainly did fully understand that I was a despicable man, and what was worse, incapable of loving her.

I know I shall be told that this is incredible—but it is incredible to be as spiteful and stupid as I was; it may be added that it was strange I should not love her, or at any rate, appreciate her love. Why is it strange? In the first place, by then I was incapable of love, for I repeat, with me loving meant tyrannising and showing my moral superiority. I have never in my life been able to imagine any other sort of love, and have nowadays come to the point of sometimes thinking that love really consists in the right—freely given by the beloved object—to tyrannise over her.

Even in my underground dreams I did not imagine love except as a struggle. I began it always with hatred and ended it with moral subjugation, and afterwards I never knew what to do with the subjugated object. And what is there to wonder at in that, since I had succeeded in so corrupting myself, since I was so out of touch with "real life," as to have actually thought of reproaching her, and putting her to shame for having come to me to hear "fine sentiments"; and did not even guess that she had come not to hear fine sentiments, but to love me, because to a woman all reformation, all salvation from any sort of ruin, and all moral renewal is included in love and can only show itself in that form.

I did not hate her so much, however, when I was running about the room and peeping through the crack in the screen. I was only insufferably oppressed by her being here. I wanted her to disappear. I wanted "peace," to be left alone in my underground world. Real life oppressed me with its novelty so much that I could hardly breathe.

But several minutes passed and she still remained, without stirring, as though she were unconscious. I had the shamelessness to tap softly at the screen as though to remind her.... She started, sprang up, and flew to seek her kerchief, her hat, her coat, as though making her escape from me. . . . Two minutes later she came from behind the screen and looked with heavy eyes at me. I gave a spiteful grin, which was forced, however, to *keep up appearances*, and I turned away from her eyes.

"Good-bye," she said, going towards the door.

I ran up to her, seized her hand, opened it, thrust something in it and closed it again. Then I turned at once and dashed away in haste to the other corner of the room to avoid seeing, anyway. . . .

I did mean a moment since to tell a lie—to write that I did this accidentally, not knowing what I was doing through foolishness, through losing my head. But I don't want to lie, and so I will say straight out that I opened her hand and put the money in it . . . from spite. It came into my head to do this while I was running up and down the room and she was sitting behind the screen. But this I can say for certain: though I did that cruel thing purposely, it was not an impulse from the heart, but came from my evil brain. This cruelty was so affected, so purposely made up, so completely a product of the brain, of books, that I could not even keep it up a minute—first I dashed away to avoid seeing her, and then in shame and despair rushed after Liza. I opened the door in the passage and began listening.

"Liza! Liza!" I cried on the stairs, but in a low voice, not boldly.

There was no answer, but I fancied I heard her footsteps, lower down on the stairs.

"Liza!" I cried, more loudly.

No answer. But at that minute I heard the stiff outer glass door open heavily with a creak and slam violently; the sound echoed up the stairs.

She had gone. I went back to my room in hesitation. I felt horribly oppressed.

I stood still at the table, beside the chair on which she had sat and looked aimlessly before me. A minute passed, suddenly I started; straight before me on the table I saw. . . . In short, I saw a crumpled blue five-rouble note, the one I had thrust into her hand a minute before. It was the same note; it could be no other, there was no other in the flat. So she had managed to fling it from her hand on the table at the moment when I had dashed into the further corner.

Well! I might have expected that she would do that. Might I have expected it? No, I was such an egoist, I was so lacking in respect for my fellow-creatures that I could not even imagine she would do so. I could not endure it. A minute later I flew like a madman to dress, flinging on what I could at random and ran headlong after her. She could not have got two hundred paces away when I ran out into the street.

It was a still night and the snow was coming down in masses and falling almost perpendicularly, covering the pavement and the empty street as though with a pillow. There was no one in the street, no sound was to be heard. The street lamps gave a disconsolate and useless glimmer. I ran two hundred paces to the cross-roads and stopped short.

Where had she gone? And why was I running after her?

Why? To fall down before her, to sob with remorse, to kiss her feet, to entreat her forgiveness! I longed for that, my whole breast was being rent to pieces, and never, never shall I recall that minute with indifference. But—what for? I thought. Should I not begin to hate her, perhaps, even tomorrow, just because I had kissed her feet today? Should I give her happiness? Had I not recognised that day, for the hundredth time, what I was worth? Should I not torture her?

I stood in the snow, gazing into the troubled darkness and pondered this.

"And will it not be better?" I mused fantastically, afterwards at home, stifling the living pang of my heart with fantastic dreams. "Will it not be better that she should keep the resentment of the insult for ever? Resentment—why, it is purification; it is a most stinging and painful consciousness! Tomorrow I should have defiled her soul and have exhausted her heart, while now the feeling of insult will never die in her heart, and however loathsome the filth awaiting her—the feeling of insult will elevate and purify her . . . by hatred . . . h'm! . . . perhaps, too, by forgiveness. . . . Will all that make things easier for her though? . . ."

And, indeed, I will ask on my own account here, an idle question: which is better—cheap happiness or exalted sufferings? Well, which is better?

So I dreamed as I sat at home that evening, almost dead with the pain in my soul. Never had I endured such suffering and remorse, yet could there have been the faintest doubt when I ran out from my lodging that I should turn back half-way? I never met Liza again and I have heard nothing of her. I will add, too, that I remained for a long time afterwards pleased with the phrase about the benefit from resentment and hatred in spite of the fact that I almost fell ill from misery.

* * * * *

Even now, so many years later, all this is somehow a very evil memory. I have many evil memories now, but . . . hadn't I better end my "Notes" here? I believe I made a mistake in beginning to write them, anyway I have felt ashamed all the time I've been writing this story; so it's hardly literature so much as a corrective punishment. Why, to tell long stories, showing how I have spoiled my life through morally rotting in my corner, through lack of fitting environment, through divorce from real life, and rankling spite in my underground world, would certainly not be interesting; a novel needs a hero, and all the traits for an anti-hero are *expressly* gathered together here, and what matters most, it all produces an unpleasant impression, for we are all divorced from life, we are all cripples, every one of us, more or less. We are so divorced from it that we feel at once a sort of loathing for real life, and so cannot bear to be reminded of it. Why, we have come almost to looking upon real life as an effort, almost as hard work, and we are all privately agreed that it is better in books. And why do we fuss and fume sometimes? Why are we perverse and ask for something else? We don't know what ourselves. It would be the worse for us if our petulant prayers were answered. Come, try, give any one of us, for instance, a little more independence, untie our hands, widen the spheres of our activity, relax the control and we . . . yes, I assure you . . . we should be begging to be under control again at once. I know that you will very likely be angry with me for that, and will begin shouting and stamping. Speak for yourself, you will say, and for your miseries in your underground holes, and don't dare to say all of us—excuse me, gentlemen, I am not justifying myself with that "all of us." As for what concerns me in particular I have only in my life carried to an extreme what you have not dared to carry halfway, and what's more, you have taken your cowardice for good sense, and have found comfort in deceiving yourselves. So that perhaps, after all, there is more life in me than in you. Look into it more carefully! Why, we don't even know what living means now, what it is, and what it is called? Leave us alone without books and we shall be lost and in confusion at once. We shall not know what to join on to, what to cling to, what to love and what to hate, what to respect and what to despise. We are oppressed at being men—men with a real individual body and blood, we are ashamed of it, we think it a disgrace and try to contrive to be some sort of impossible generalised man. We are stillborn, and for generations past have been begotten, not by living fathers, and that suits us better and better. We are developing a taste for it. Soon we shall contrive to be born somehow from an idea. But enough; I don't want to write more from "Underground."

[*The notes of this paradoxalist do not end here, however. He could not refrain from going on with them, but it seems to us that we may stop here.*]

Franz Kafka (1883–1924)

It seems difficult to believe, but Franz Kafka's inner life, his thoughts and feelings were as strange and disturbing as those of Gregor in *The Metamorphosis*, who, in the first lines of the story, turns into a gigantic insect. One finds Kafka, for instance, telling his friend Milena Jesenka Polakova in a 1920 letter that he is dominated by a vague yet powerful sense of dread which runs like an undercurrent through all the surface events of his life (*Letters to Milena*, 1953). Even worse, he believes that if this dread were to cease, his life would end, as well. This dread, though it makes his life nightmarish, is the only alternative to death. At the same time, Kafka's outer life was as dreary, tedious, and uneventful as Gregor's life prior to his transformation. Gregor was a traveling fabric salesman; Kafka, too, spent much of his working life toiling at paperwork in the offices of an insurance company or making short trips to verify workers' compensation claims. He did not move out of his parents' home until the age of 31, never married, and died at the young age of 40 from tuberculosis. In a sense, his real life went into his writings, yet in his lifetime he published just a half-dozen pamphlet-size books, no more than a couple of hundred pages in total. Had his friend Max Brod obeyed his wishes and destroyed all of his remaining manuscripts, these few haunting, enigmatic stories are all one would know of Franz Kafka.

Kafka was born July 3, 1883, in Prague, which, once a part of the Austro-Hungarian empire, is now in the Czech Republic. His family's first language was Czech, but they also spoke German, and Kafka went to German schools after the age of six. The family was of Jewish heritage but was not actively involved in religion. By the time Kafka was bar mitzvahed, he was an atheist. Judaism did become important to him later in life, though only in a cultural and philosophical sense (he never really became a believer). Kafka grew up intimidated by his large, domineering father; in 1919 he wrote a letter of over 100 pages to his father, coolly analyzing the damaging effect of this upbringing (*Letter to His Father*, 1966).

After graduating from law school in 1907, Kafka worked for the next 14 years for insurance companies, until he was forced to retire in 1922 because of his tuberculosis. With women he had a few awkward sexual affairs, one of which produced a child he never knew, who died at the age of six. Kafka was three times engaged to be married (twice to the same person, Felice Bauer) but always broke it off because his father disapproved, and Kafka did not want marriage to interfere with his writing, which he compared to burrowing (his second-to-last story is called "The Burrow") or *Fear* (with a capital *F*), which he associated with existence itself (*Letters to Melena*).

As a writer, Kafka's true talent was the creation of modern parables or fables evoking the terror and alienation of much 20th century life. These works range in length from less than a page (he wrote many such brief meditations throughout his career) to the novel-length masterpieces, *The Trial* (written in 1914 and published in 1925) and *The Castle* (written in 1922 and published in 1926), both of which Max Brod rescued from oblivion by not following Kafka's instructions to burn them. Other notable works include, of course, *The Metamorphosis* (1915), in which a man is transformed into an insect; and its counterpart, "Report to an Academy" (1919), in which an ape teaches itself to think, act, and talk like a human being. The stories "In the Penal Colony" (1919) and "The Great Wall of China," and the related parables, "Before the Law," "An Imperial Message," and "An Old Manuscript," share with *The Trial* and *The Castle* the theme of the nightmarishly mysterious workings of modern, bureaucratic law and authority. "The

Hunger Artist" (1922) and the trilogy of animal fables from Kafka's last year (1923–24), "Investigations of a Dog," "The Burrow," and "Josephine the Singer, or the Mouse Folk," develop Kafka's portrait of the modern artist.

Kafka leaves behind as many diaries and letters as he does fiction, and these personal writings are nearly as compelling (and chilling) as the stories. The most important of these are the two-volume *Diaries* (1948–49), totaling more than 600 pages of text; the *Letters to Felice* (1967), more than 500 pages; the *Letter to His Father,* more than 100; and the *Letters to Milena,* which totals approximately 200 pages.

Kafka died in an Austrian sanatorium on June 3, 1924, from tuberculosis of the larynx. The best biography in English is Ernest Pawel's *The Nightmare of Reason: A Life of Franz Kafka* (1984). The most original critical study is by the French philosophers, Gilles Deleuze and Felix Guattari: *Kafka: Toward a Minor Literature* (1975).

Metamorphosis

(Die Verwandlung)

Franz Kafka

1

As Gregor Samsa awoke one morning from uneasy dreams he found himself transformed in his bed into a gigantic insect. He was lying on his hand, as it were armor-plated, back and when he lifted his head a little he could see his dome-like brown belly divided into stiff arched segments on top of which the bed quilt could hardly keep in position and was about to slide off completely. His numerous legs, which were pitifully thin compared to the rest of his bulk, waved helplessly before his eyes.

What has happened to me? he thought. It was no dream. His room, a regular human bedroom, only rather too small, lay quiet between the four familiar walls. Above the table on which a collection of cloth samples was unpacked and spread out—Samsa was a commercial traveler—hung the picture which he had recently cut out of an illustrated magazine and put into a pretty gilt frame. It showed a lady, with a fur cap on and a fur stole, sitting upright and holding out to the spectator a huge fur muff into which the whole of her forearm had vanished!

Gregor's eyes turned next to the window, and the overcast sky—one could hear rain drops beating on the window gutter—made him quite melancholy. What about sleeping a little longer and forgetting all this nonsense, he thought, but it could not be done, for he was accustomed to sleep on his right side and in his present condition he could not turn himself over. However violently he forced himself towards his right side he always rolled on to his back again. He tried it at least a hundred times, shutting his eyes to keep from seeing his struggling legs, and only desisted when he began to feel in his side a faint dull ache he had never experienced before.

Oh God, he thought, what an exhausting job I've picked on! Traveling about day in, day out. It's much more irritating work than doing the actual business in the office, and on top of that there's the trouble of constant traveling, of worrying about train connections, the bed and irregular meals, casual acquaintances that are always new and never become intimate friends. The devil take it all! He felt a slight itching up on his belly; slowly pushed himself on his back nearer to the top of the bed so that he could lift his head more easily; identified the itching place which was surrounded by many small white spots the nature of which he could not understand and made to touch it with a leg, but drew the leg back immediately, for the contact made a cold shiver run through him.

He slid down again into his former position. This getting up early, he thought, makes one quite stupid. A man needs his sleep. Other commercials live like harem women. For instance, when I come back to the hotel of a morning to write up the orders I've got, these others are only sitting down to breakfast. Let me just try that with my chief; I'd be sacked on the spot. Anyhow, that might be quite a good thing for me, who can tell? If I didn't have to hold my hand because of my parents I'd have given notice long ago, I'd have gone to the chief and told him exactly what I think of him. That would knock him endways from his desk! It's a queer way of doing, too, this sitting on high at a desk and talking down to employees, especially when they have to come quite near because the chief is hard of hearing. Well, there's still hope; once I've saved enough money to pay back my parents' debts to him—that should take another five or six years—I'll do it without fail. I'll cut myself completely loose then. For the moment, though, I'd better get up, since my train goes at five.

He looked at the alarm clock ticking on the chest. Heavenly Father! he thought. It was half-past six o'clock and the hands were quietly moving on, it was even past the half-hour, it was going on toward a quarter to seven. Had the alarm clock not gone off? From the bed one could see that it had been properly set for four o'clock; of course it must have gone off. Yes, but was it possible to sleep quietly through that ear-splitting noise? Well, he had not slept quietly, yet apparently all the more soundly for that. But what was he to do now? The next train went at seven o'clock; to catch that he would need to hurry like mad and his samples weren't even packed up, and he himself wasn't feeling particularly fresh and active. And even if he did catch the train he wouldn't avoid a row with the chief, since the firm's porter would have been waiting for the five o'clock train and would have long since reported his failure to turn up. The porter was a creature of the chief's, spineless and stupid. Well, supposing he were to say he was sick? But that would be most unpleasant and would look suspicious, since during his five years' employment he had not been ill once. The chief himself would be sure to come with the sick-insurance doctor, would reproach his parents with their son's laziness and would cut all excuses short by referring to the insurance doctor, who of course regarded all mankind as perfectly healthy malingerers. And would he be so far wrong on this occasion? Gregor really felt quite well, apart from a drowsiness that was utterly superfluous after such a long sleep, and he was even unusually hungry.

As all this was running through his mind at top speed without his being able to decide to leave his bed—the alarm clock had just struck a quaver to seven—there came a cautious tap at the door behind the head of his bed. "Gregor," said a voice—it was his mother's—"it's a quarter to seven. Hadn't you a train to catch?" That gentle voice! Gregor had a shock as he heard his own voice answering hers, unmistakably his own voice, it was true, but with a persistent horrible twittering squeak behind it like an undertone, that left the words in their dear shape only for the first moment and then rose up reverberating round them to destroy their sense, so that one could not be sure one had heard them rightly. Gregor wanted to answer at length and explain everything, but in the circumstances he confined himself to saying: "Yes, yes, thank you, Mother, I'm getting up now." The wooden door between them must have kept the change in his voice from being noticeable outside, for his mother contented herself with this statement and shuffled away. Yet this brief exchange of words had made the other members of the family aware that Gregor was still in the house, as they had not expected, and at one of the side doors his father was already knocking, gently, yet with his fist. "Gregor, Gregor," he called, "what's the matter with you?" And after a little while he called again in a deeper voice: "Gregor! Gregor!" At the other side door his sister was saying in a low, plaintive tone: "Gregor? Aren't you well? Are you needing anything?" He answered them both at once: "I'm just ready," and did his best to make his voice sound as normal as possible by enunciating the words very clearly and leaving long pauses between them. So his father went back to his breakfast, but his sister whispered: "Gregor, open the door, do." However, he was not thinking of opening the door, and felt thankful for the prudent habit he had acquired in traveling of locking all doors during the night, even at home.

His immediate intention was to get up quietly without being disturbed, to put on his clothes and above all eat his breakfast, and only then to consider what else was to be done, since in bed, he was well aware, his meditations would come to no sensible conclusion. He remembered that often enough in bed he had felt small aches and pains, probably caused by awkward postures, which had proved purely imaginary once he got up, and he looked forward eagerly to seeing this morning's delusions gradually fall away. That the change in his voice was nothing but the precursor of a severe chill, a standing ailment of commercial travelers, he had not the least possible doubt.

To get rid of the quilt was quite easy; he had only to inflate himself a little and it fell off by itself. But the next move was difficult, especially because he was so uncommonly broad. He would have needed arms and hands to hoist himself up; instead he had only the numerous little legs which never stopped waving in all directions and which he could not control in the least. When he tried to bend one of them it was the first to stretch itself straight; and did he succeed at last in making it do what he wanted, all the other legs meanwhile waved the more wildly in a high degree of unpleasant agitation. "But what's the use of lying idle in bed," said Gregor to himself.

He thought that he might get out of bed with the lower part of his body first, but this lower part, which he had not yet seen and of which he could form no clear conception, proved too difficult to move: it shifted so slowly; and when finally, almost wild with annoyance, he gathered his forces together and thrust out recklessly, he had miscalculated the direction and bumped heavily against the lower end of the bed, and the stinging pain he felt informed him that precisely this lower part of his body was at the moment probably the most sensitive.

So he tried to get the top part of himself out first, and cautiously moved his head towards the edge of the bed. That proved easy enough, and despite its breadth and mass the bulk of his body at last slowly followed the movement of his head. Still, when he finally got his head free over the edge of the bed he felt too scared to go on advancing, for after all if he let himself fall in this way it would take a miracle to keep his head from being injured. And at all costs he must not lose consciousness now, precisely now; he would rather stay in bed.

But when after a repetition of the same efforts he lay in his former position again, sighing, and watched his little legs struggling against each other more wildly than ever, if that were possible, and saw no way of bringing any order into this arbitrary confusion, he told himself again that it was impossible to stay in bed and that the most sensible course was to risk everything for the smallest hope of getting away from it. At the same time he did not forget meanwhile to remind himself that cool reflection, the coolest possible, was much better than desperate resolves. In such moments he focused his eyes as sharply as possible on the window, but, unfortunately, the prospect of the morning fog, which muffled even the other side of the narrow street, brought him little encouragement and comfort. "Seven o'clock already," he said to himself when the alarm clock chimed again, "seven o'clock already and still such a thick fog." And for a little while he lay quiet, breathing lightly, as if perhaps expecting such complete repose to restore all things to their real and normal condition.

But then he said to himself. "Before it strikes a quarter past seven I must be quite out of this bed, without fail. Anyhow, by that time someone will have come from the office to ask for me, since it opens before seven." And he set himself to rocking his whole body at once in a regular rhythm, with the idea of swinging it out of the bed. If he tipped himself out in that way he could keep his head from injury by lifting it at an acute angle when he fell. His back seemed to be hard and was not likely to suffer from a fall on the carpet. His biggest worry was the loud crash he would not be able to help making, which would probably cause anxiety, if not terror, behind all the doors. Still, he must take the risk.

When he was already half out of the bed—the new method was more a game than an effort, for he needed only to hitch himself across by rocking to and fro—it struck him how simple it would be if he could get help. Two strong people—he thought of his father and the servant girl—would be amply sufficient; they would only have to thrust their arms under his convex back, lever him out of the bed, bend down with their burden and then be patient enough to let him turn himself right over on the floor, where it was to be hoped his legs would then find their proper function. Well, ignoring the fact that the doors were all locked, ought he really to call for help? In spite of his misery he could not suppress a smile at the very idea of it.

He had got so far that he could barely keep his equilibrium when he rocked himself strongly, and he would have to nerve himself very soon for the final decision since in five minutes' time it would be a quarter past seven—when the front door bell rang. "That's someone from the office," he said to himself, and grew almost rigid, while his little legs only jigged about all the faster. For a moment everything stayed quiet. "They're not going to open the door," said Gregor to himself, catching at some kind of irrational hope. But then of course the servant girl went as usual to the door with her heavy tread and opened it. Gregor needed only to hear the first good morning of the visitor to know immediately who it was—the chief clerk himself. What a fate, to be condemned to work for a firm where the smallest omission at once gave rise to the gravest suspicion! Were all employees in a body nothing but scoundrels, was there not among them one single loyal devoted man who, had he wasted only an hour or so of the firm's time in a morning, was so tormented by conscience as to be driven out of his mind and actually incapable of leaving his bed? Wouldn't it really have been sufficient to send an apprentice to inquire—if any inquiry were necessary at all—did the chief clerk himself have to come and thus indicate to the entire family, an innocent family, that this suspicious circumstance could be investigated by no one less versed in affairs than himself? And more through the agitation caused by these reflections than through any act of will Gregor swung himself out of bed with all his strength. There was a loud thump, but it was not really a crash. His fall was broken to some extent by the carpet, his back, too, was less stiff than he thought, and so there was merely a dull thud, not so very startling. Only he had not lifted his head carefully enough and had hit it; he turned it and rubbed it on the carpet in pain and irritation.

"That was something falling down in there," said the chief clerk in the next room to the left. Gregor tried to suppose to himself that something like what had happened to him today might some day happen to the chief clerk; one really could not deny that it was possible. But as if in brusque reply to this supposition the chief clerk took a couple of firm steps in the next-door room and his patent leather boots creaked. From the right-hand room his sister was whispering to inform him of the situation: "Gregor, the chief clerk's here." "I know," muttered Gregor to himself; but he didn't dare to make his voice loud enough for his sister to hear it.

"Gregor," said his father now from the left-hand room, "the chief clerk has come and wants to know why you didn't catch the early train. We don't know what to say to him. Besides, he wants to talk to you in person. So open the door, please. He will be good enough to excuse the untidiness of your room." "Good morning, Mr. Samsa," the chief clerk was calling amiably meanwhile. "He's not well," said his mother to the visitor, while his father was still speaking through the door, "he's not well, sir, believe me. What else would make him miss a train! The boy thinks about nothing but his work. It makes me almost cross the way he never goes out in the evenings; he's been here the last eight days and has stayed at home every single evening. He just sits there quietly at the table reading a newspaper or looking through railway timetables. The only amusement he gets is doing fretwork. For instance, he spent two or three evenings cutting out a little picture frame; you would be surprised to see how pretty it is; it's hanging in his room; you'll see it in a minute when Gregor opens the door. I must say I'm glad you've come, sir; we should never have got him to unlock the door by ourselves; he's so obstinate; and I'm sure he's unwell, though he wouldn't have it to be so this morning." "I'm just coming," said Gregor slowly and carefully, not moving an inch for fear of losing one word of the conversation. "I can't think of any other explanation, madam," said the chief clerk, "I hope it's nothing serious. Although on the other hand I must say that we men of business—fortunately or unfortunately—very often simply have to ignore any slight indisposition, since business must be attended to." "Well, can the chief clerk come in now?" asked Gregor's father impatiently, again knocking on the door. "No," said Gregor. In the left-hand room a painful silence followed this refusal, in the right-hand room his sister began to sob.

Why didn't his sister join the others? She was probably newly out of bed and hadn't even begun to put on her clothes yet. Well, why was she crying? Because he wouldn't get up and let the chief clerk in, because he was in danger of losing his job, and because the chief would begin dunning his parents again for the old debts? Surely these were things one didn't need to worry about for the present. Gregor was still at home and not in the least thinking of deserting the family. At the moment, true, he was lying on the carpet and no one who knew the condition he was in could seriously expect him to admit the chief clerk. But for such a small discourtesy, which could plausibly be explained away somehow later on, Gregor could hardly be dismissed on the spot. And it seemed to Gregor that it would be much more sensible to leave him in peace for the present than to trouble him with tears and entreaties. Still, of course, their uncertainty bewildered them all and excused their behavior.

"Mr. Samsa," the chief clerk called now in a louder voice, "what's the matter with you? Here you are, barricading yourself in your room, giving only 'yes' and 'no' for answers, causing your parents a lot of unnecessary trouble and neglecting—I mention this only in passing—neglecting your business duties in an incredible fashion. I am speaking here in the name of your parents and of your chief, and I beg you quite seriously to give me an immediate and precise explanation. You amaze me, you amaze me. I thought you were a quiet, dependable person, and now all at once you seem bent on making a disgraceful exhibition of yourself. The chief did hint to me early this morning a possible explanation for your disappearance—with reference to the cash payments that were entrusted to you recently—but I almost pledged my solemn word of honor that this could not be so. But now that I see how incredibly obstinate you are, I no longer have the slightest desire to take your part at all. And your position in the firm is not so unassailable. I came with the intention of telling you all this in private, but since you are wasting my time so needlessly I don't see why your parents shouldn't hear it too. For some time past your work has been most unsatisfactory; this is not the season of the year for a business boom, of course, we admit that, but a season of the year for doing no business at all, that does not exist, Mr. Samsa, must not exist."

"But, sir," cried Gregor, beside himself and in his agitation forgetting everything else, "I'm just going to open the door this very minute. A slight illness, an attack of giddiness, has kept me from getting up. I'm still lying in bed. But I feel all right again. I'm getting out of bed now. Just give me a moment or two longer! I'm not quite so well as I thought. But I'm all right, really. How a thing like that can suddenly strike one down! Only last night I was quite well, my parents can tell you, or rather I did have a slight presentiment. I must have showed some sign of it. Why didn't I report it at the office! But one always thinks that an indisposition can be got over without staying in the house. Oh sir, do spare my parents! All that you're reproaching me with now has no foundation; no one has ever said a word to me about it. Perhaps you haven't looked at the last orders I sent in. Anyhow, I can still catch the eight o'clock train, I'm much the better for my few hours' rest. Don't let me detain you here, sir; I'll be attending to business very soon, and do be good enough to tell the chief so and to make my excuses to him!"

And while all this was tumbling out pell-mell and Gregor hardly knew what he was saying, he had reached the chest quite easily, perhaps because of the practice he had had in bed, and was now trying to lever himself upright by means of it. He meant actually to open the door, actually to show himself and speak to the chief clerk; he was eager to find out what the others, after all their insistence, would say at the sight of him. If they were horrified then the responsibility was no longer his and he could stay quiet. But if they took it calmly, then he had no reason either to be upset; and could really get to the station for the eight o'clock train if he hurried. At first he slipped down a few times from the polished surface of the chest, but at length with a last heave he stood upright; he paid no more attention to the pains in the lower part of his body, how ever they smarted. Then he let himself fall against the back of a near-by chair, and clung with his little legs to the edges of it. That brought him into control of himself again and he stopped speaking, for now he could listen to what the chief clerk was saying.

"Did you understand a word of it?" the chief clerk was asking; "surely he can't be trying to make fools of us?" "Oh dear," cried his mother, in tears, "perhaps he's terribly ill and we're tormenting him. Grete! Grete!" she called out then. "Yes Mother?" called his sister from the other side. They were calling to each other across Gregor's room. "You must go this minute for the doctor. Gregor is ill. Go for the doctor, quick. Did you hear how he was speaking?" "That was no human voice," said the chief clerk in a voice noticeably low beside the shrillness of the mother's. "Anna! Anna!" his father was calling through the hall to the kitchen, clapping his hands, "get a locksmith at once!" And the two girls were already running through the hall with a swish of skirts—how could his sister have got dressed so quickly?—and were tearing the front door open. There was no sound of its closing again; they had evidently left it open, as one does in houses where some great misfortune has happened.

But Gregor was now much calmer. The words he uttered were no longer understandable, apparently, although they seemed clear enough to him, even clearer than before, perhaps because his ear had grown accustomed to the sound of them. Yet at any rate people now believed that something was wrong with him, and were ready to help him. The positive certainty with which these first measures had been taken comforted him. He felt himself drawn once more into the human circle and hoped for great and remarkable results from both the doctor and the locksmith, without really distinguishing precisely between them. To make his voice as clear as possible for the decisive conversation that was now imminent he coughed a little, as quietly as he could, of course, since this noise too might not sound like a human cough for all he was able to judge. In the next room meanwhile there was complete silence. Perhaps his parents were sitting at the table with the chief clerk, whispering, perhaps they were all leaning against the door and listening.

Slowly Gregor pushed the chair towards the door, then let go of it, caught hold of the door for support—the soles at the end of his little legs were somewhat sticky—and rested against it for a moment after his efforts. Then he set himself to turning the key in the lock with his mouth. It seemed, unhappily, that he hadn't really any teeth—what could he grip the key with?—but on the other hand his jaws were certainly very strong; with their help he did manage to set the key in motion, heedless of the fact that he was undoubtedly damaging them somewhere, since a brown fluid issued from his mouth, flowed over the key and dripped on the floor. "Just listen to that," said the chief clerk next door; "he's turning the key." That was a great encouragement to Gregor; but they should all have shouted encouragement to him, his father and mother too: "Go on, Gregor," they should have called out, "keep going, hold on to that key!" And in the belief that they were all following his efforts intently, he clenched his jaws recklessly on the key with all the force at his command. As the turning of the key progressed he circled round the lock, holding on now only with his mouth, pushing on the key, as required, or pulling it down again with all the weight of his body. The louder click of the finally yielding lock literally quickened Gregor. With a deep breath of relief he said to himself. "So I didn't need the locksmith," and laid his head on the handle to open the door wide.

Since he had to pull the door towards him, he was still invisible when it was really wide open. He had to edge himself slowly round the near half of the double door, and to do it very carefully if he was not to fall plump upon his back just on the threshold. He was still carrying out this difficult manoeuvre, with no time to observe anything else, when he heard the chief clerk utter a loud "Oh!"—it sounded like a gust of wind—and now he could see the man, standing as he was nearest to the door, clapping one hand before his open mouth and slowly backing away as if driven by some invisible steady pressure. His mother—in spite of the chief clerk's being there her hair was still undone and sticking up in all directions—first clasped her hands and looked at his father, then took two steps towards Gregor and fell on the floor among her outspread skirts, her face quite hidden on her breast. His father knotted his fist with a fierce expression on his face as if he meant to knock Gregor back into his room, then looked uncertainly round the living room, covered his eyes with his hands and wept till his great chest heaved.

Gregor did not go now into the living room, but leaned against the inside of the firmly shut wing of the door, so that only half his body was visible and his head above it bending sideways to look at the others. The light had meanwhile strengthened; on the other side of the street one could see clearly a section of the endlessly long, dark gray building opposite—it was a hospital—abruptly punctuated by its row of regular windows; the rain was still falling, but only in large singly discernible and literally singly splashing drops. The breakfast dishes were set out on the table lavishly, for breakfast was the most important meal of the day to Gregor's father, who lingered it out for hours over various newspapers. Right opposite Gregor on the wall hung a photograph of himself on military service, as a lieutenant, hand on sword, a carefree smile on his face, inviting one to respect his uniform and military bearing. The door leading to the hall was open, and one could see that the front door stood open too, showing the landing beyond and the beginning of the stairs going down.

"Well," said Gregor, knowing perfectly that he was the only one who had retained any composure, "I'll put my clothes on at once, pack up my samples and start off. Will you only let me go? You see, sir, I'm not obstinate, and I'm willing to work; traveling is a hard life, but I couldn't live without it. Where are you going sir? To the office? Yes? Will you give a true account of all this? One can be temporarily incapacitated, but that's just the moment for remembering former services and bearing in mind that later on, when the incapacity has been got over, one will certainly work with all the more industry and concentration. I'm loyally bound to serve the chief, you know that very well. Besides, I have to provide for my parents and my sister. I'm in great difficulties, but I'll get out of them again. Don't make things any worse for me than they are. Stand up for me in the firm. Travelers are not popular there, I know. People think they earn sacks of money and just have a good time. A prejudice there's no particular reason for revising. But you, sir, have a more comprehensive view of affairs than the rest of the staff, yes, let me tell you in confidence, a more comprehensive view than the chief himself, who, being the owner, lets his judgment easily be swayed against one of his employees. And you know very well that the traveler, who is never seen in the office almost the whole year round, can so easily fall a victim to gossip and ill luck and unfounded complaints, which he mostly knows nothing about, except when he comes back exhausted from his rounds, and only then suffers in person from their evil consequences, which he can no longer trace back to the original causes. Sir, sir, don't go away without a word to me to show that you think me in the right at least to some extent!"

But at Gregor's very first words the chief clerk had already backed away and only stared at him with parted lips over one twitching shoulder. And while Gregor was speaking he did not stand still one moment but stole away towards the door, without taking his eyes off Gregor, yet only an inch at a time, as if obeying some secret injunction to leave the room. He was already at the hall, and the suddenness with which he took his last step out of the living room would have made one believe he had burned the sole of his foot. Once in the hall he stretched his right arm before him towards the staircase, as if some supernatural power were waiting there to deliver him.

Gregor perceived that the chief clerk must on no account be allowed to go away in this frame of mind if his position in the firm were not to be endangered to the utmost. His parents did not understand this so well; they had convinced themselves in the course of years that Gregor was settled for life in this firm, and besides they were so preoccupied with their immediate troubles that all foresight had forsaken them. Yet Gregor had this foresight. The chief clerk must be detained, soothed, persuaded and finally won over; the whole future of Gregor and his family depended on it! If only his sister had been there! She was intelligent; she had begun to cry while Gregor was still lying quietly on his back. And no doubt the chief clerk, so partial to ladies, would have been guided by her; she would have shut the door of the flat and in the hall talked him out of his horror. But she was not there, and Gregor would have to handle the situation himself. And without remembering that he was still unaware what powers of movement he possessed, without even remembering that his words in all possibility, indeed in all likelihood, would again be unintelligible, he let go the wing of the door, pushed himself through the opening, started to walk towards the chief clerk, who was already ridiculously clinging with both hands to the railing on the landing; but immediately, as he was feeling for a support, he fell down with a little cry upon all his numerous legs. Hardly was he down when he experienced for the first time this morning a sense of physical comfort, his legs had firm ground under them; they were completely obedient, as he noted with joy; they even strove to carry him forward in whatever direction he chose; and he was inclined to believe that a final relief from all his sufferings was at hand. But in the same moment as he found himself on the floor, rocking with suppressed eagerness to move, not far from his mother, indeed just in front of her, she, who had seemed so completely crushed, sprang all at once to her feet, her arms and fingers outspread, cried: "Help, for God's sake, help!" bent her head down as if to see Gregor better, yet on the contrary kept backing senselessly away; had quite forgotten that the laden table stood behind her; sat upon it hastily, as if in absence of mind, when she bumped into it; and seemed altogether unaware that the big coffee pot beside her was upset and pouring coffee in a flood over the carpet.

"Mother, Mother," said Gregor in a low voice, and looked up at her. The chief clerk, for the moment, had quite slipped from his mind; instead, he could not resist snapping his jaws together at the sight of the streaming coffee. That made his mother scream again, she fled from the table and fell into the arms of his father, who hastened to catch her. But Gregor had now no time to spare for his parents; the chief clerk was already on the stairs; with his chin on the banisters he was taking one last backward look. Gregor made a spring, to be as sure as possible of overtaking him; the chief clerk must have divined his intention, for he leaped down several steps and vanished; he was still yelling "Ugh!" and it echoed through the whole staircase.

Unfortunately, the flight of the chief clerk seemed completely to upset Gregor's father, who had remained relatively calm until now, for instead of running after the man himself, or at least not hindering Gregor in his pursuit, he seized in his right hand the walking stick which the chief clerk had left behind on a chair, together with a hat and greatcoat, snatched in his left hand a large newspaper from the table and began stamping his feet and flourishing the stick and the newspaper to drive Gregor back into his room. No entreaty of Gregor's availed, indeed no entreaty was even understood, however humbly he bent his head his father only stamped on the floor the more loudly. Behind his father his mother had torn open a window, despite the cold weather, and was leaning far out of it with her face in her hands. A strong draught set in from the street to the staircase, the window curtains blew in, the newspapers on the table fluttered, stray pages whisked over the floor. Pitilessly Gregor's father drove him back, hissing and crying "Shoo!" like a savage. But Gregor was quite unpracticed in walking backwards, it really was a slow business. If he only had a chance to turn round he could get back to his room at once, but he was afraid of exasperating his father by the slowness of such a rotation and at any moment the stick in his father's hand might hit him a fatal blow on the back or on the head. In the end, however, nothing else was left for him to do since to his horror he observed that in moving backwards he could not even control the direction he took; and so, keeping an anxious eye on his father all the time over his shoulder, he began to turn round as quickly as he could, which was in reality very slowly. Perhaps his father noted his good intentions, for he did not interfere except every now and then to help him in the manoeuvre from a distance with the point of the stick. If only he would have stopped making that unbearable hissing noise! It made Gregor quite lose his head. He had turned almost completely round when the hissing noise so distracted him that he even turned a little the wrong way again. But when at last his head was fortunately right in front of the doorway it appeared that his body was too broad simply to get through the opening. His father, of course, in his present mood was far from thinking of such a thing as opening the other half of the door, to let Gregor have enough space. He had merely the fixed idea of driving Gregor back into his room as quickly as possible. He would never have suffered Gregor to make the circumstantial preparations for standing up on end and perhaps slipping his way through the door. Maybe he was now making more noise than ever to urge Gregor forward, as if no obstacle impeded him; to Gregor, anyhow, the noise in his rear sounded no longer like the voice of one single father; this was really no joke, and Gregor thrust himself—come what might—into the doorway. One side of his body rose up he was tilted at an angle in the doorway, his flank was quite bruised, horrid blotches stained the white door, soon he was stuck fast and, left to himself, could not have moved at all, his legs on one side fluttered trembling in the air, those on the other were crushed painfully to the floor—when from behind his father gave him a strong push which was literally a deliverance and he flew far into the room, bleeding freely. The door was slammed behind him with the stick, and then at last there was silence.

II

Not until it was twilight did Gregor awake out of a deep sleep, more like a swoon than a sleep. He would certainly have waked up of his own accord not much later, for he felt himself sufficiently rested and well-slept, but it seemed to him as if a fleeting step and a cautious shutting of the door leading into the hall had aroused him. The electric lights in the street cast a pale sheen here and there on the ceiling and the upper surfaces of the furniture, but down below, where he lay, it was dark. Slowly, awkwardly trying out his feelers, which he now first learned to appreciate, he pushed his way to the door to see what had been happening there. His left side felt like one single long, unpleasantly tense scar, and he had actually to limp on his two rows of legs. One little leg, moreover, had been severely damaged in the course of that morning's events—it was almost a miracle that only one had been damaged—and trailed uselessly behind him.

He had reached the door before he discovered what had really drawn him to it: the smell of food. For there stood a basin filled with fresh milk in which floated little sops of white bread. He could almost have laughed with joy, since he was now still hungrier than in the morning, and he dipped his head almost over the eyes straight into the milk. But soon in disappointment he withdrew it again; not only did he find it difficult to feed because of his tender left side—and he could only feed with the palpitating collaboration of his whole body—he did not like the milk either, although milk had been his favorite drink and that was certainly why his sister had set it there for him, indeed it was almost with repulsion that he turned away from the basin and crawled back to the middle of the room.

He could see through the crack of the door that the gas was turned on in the living room, but while usually at this time his father made a habit of reading the afternoon newspaper in a loud voice to his mother and occasionally to his sister as well, not a sound was now to be heard. Well, perhaps his father had recently given up this habit of reading aloud, which his sister had mentioned so often in conversation and in her letters. But there was the same silence all around, although the flat was certainly not empty of occupants. "What a quiet life our family has been leading!" said Gregor to himself, and as he sat there motionless staring into the darkness he felt great pride in the fact that he had been able to provide such a life for his parents and sister in such a fine flat. But what if all the quiet, the comfort, the contentment were now to end in horror? To keep himself from being lost in such thoughts Gregor took refuge in movement and crawled up and down the room.

Once during the long evening one of the side doors was opened a little and quickly shut again, later the other side door too; someone had apparently wanted to come in and then thought better of it. Gregor now stationed himself immediately before the living room door, determined to persuade any hesitating visitor to come in or at least to discover who it might be; but the door was not opened again and he waited in vain. In the early morning, when the doors were locked, they had all wanted to come in, now that he had opened one door and the other had apparently been opened during the day, no one came in and even the keys were on the other side of the doors.

It was late at night before the gas went out in the living room, and Gregor could easily tell that his parents and his sister had all stayed awake until then, for he could clearly hear the three of them stealing away on tiptoe. No one was likely to visit him, not until the morning, that was certain; so he had plenty of time to meditate at his leisure on how he was to arrange his life afresh. But the lofty, empty room in which he had to lie flat on the floor filled him with an apprehension he could not account for, since it had been his very own room for the past five years—and with a half-unconscious action, not without a slight feeling of shame, he scuttled under the sofa, where he felt comfortable at once, although his back was a little cramped and he could not lift his head up, and his only regret was that his body was too broad to get the whole of it under the sofa.

He stayed there all night, spending the time partly in a light slumber, from which his hunger kept waking him up with a start, and partly in worrying and sketching vague hopes, which all led to the same conclusion, that he must lie low for the present and, by exercising patience and the utmost consideration, help the family to bear the inconvenience he was bound to cause them in his present condition.

Very early in the morning, it was still almost night, Gregor had the chance to test the strength of his new resolutions, for his sister, nearly fully dressed, opened the door from the hall and peered in. She did not see him at once, yet when she caught sight of him under the sofa—well, he had to be somewhere, he couldn't have flown away, could he?—she was so startled that without being able to help it she slammed the door shut again. But as if regretting her behavior she opened the door again immediately and came in on tiptoe, as if she were visiting an invalid or even a stranger. Gregor had pushed his head forward to the very edge of the sofa and watched her. Would she notice that he had left the milk standing, and not for lack of hunger, and would she bring in some other kind of food more to his taste? If she did not do it of her own accord, he would rather starve than draw her attention to the fact, although he felt a wild impulse to dart out from under the sofa, throw himself at her feet and beg her for something to eat. But his sister at once noticed, with surprise, that the basin was still full, except for a little milk that had been spilt all around it, she lifted it immediately, not with her bare hands, true, but with a cloth and carried it away. Gregor was wildly curious to know what she would bring instead, and made various speculations about it. Yet what she actually did next, in the goodness of her heart, he could never have guessed at. To find out what he liked she brought him a whole selection of food, all set out on an old newspaper. There were old, half-decayed vegetables, bones from last night's supper covered with a white sauce that had thickened; some raisins and almonds; a piece of cheese that Gregor would have called uneatable two days ago; a dry roll of bread, a buttered roll, and a roll both buttered and salted. Besides all that, she set down again the same basin, into which she had poured some water, and which was apparently to be reserved for his exclusive use. And with fine tact, knowing that Gregor would not eat in her presence, she withdrew quickly and even turned the key, to let him understand that he could take his ease as much as he liked. Gregor's legs all whizzed towards the food. His wounds must have healed completely, moreover, for he felt no disability, which amazed him and made him reflect how more than a month ago he had cut one finger a little with a knife and had still suffered pain from the wound only the day before yesterday. Am I less sensitive now? he thought, and sucked greedily at the cheese, which above all the other edibles attracted him at once and strongly. One after another and with tears of satisfaction in his eyes to quickly devoured the cheese, the vegetables and the sauce; the fresh food, on the other hand, had no charms for him, he could not even stand the smell of it and actually dragged away to some little distance the things he could eat. He had long finished his meal and was only lying lazily on the same spot when his sister turned the key slowly as a sign for him to retreat. That roused him at once, although he was nearly asleep, and he hurried under the sofa again. But it took considerable self-control for him to stay under the sofa, even for the short time his sister was in the room, since the large meal had swollen his body somewhat and he was so cramped he could hardly breathe. Slight attacks of breathlessness afflicted him and his eyes were starting a little out of his head as he watched his unsuspecting sister sweeping together with a broom not only the remains of what he had eaten but even the things he had not touched, as if these were now of no use to anyone, and hastily shoveling it all into a bucket, which she covered with a wooden lid and carried away. Hardly had she turned her back when Gregor came from under the sofa and stretched and puffed himself out.

In this manner Gregor was fed, once in the early morning while his parents and the servant girl were still asleep, and a second time after they had all had their midday dinner, for then his parents took a short nap and the servant girl could be sent out on some errand or other by his sister. Not that they would have wanted him to starve, of course, but perhaps they could not have borne to know more about his feeding than from hearsay, perhaps too his sister wanted to spare them such little anxieties wherever possible, since they had quite enough to bear as it was.

Under what pretext the doctor and the locksmith had been got rid of on that first morning Gregor could not discover, for since what he said was not understood by the others it never struck any of them, not even his sister, that he could understand what they said, and so whenever his sister came into his room he had to content himself with hearing her utter only a sigh now and then and an occasional appeal to the saints. Later on, when she had got a little used to the situation—of course she could never get completely used to it—she sometimes threw out a remark which was kindly meant or could be so interpreted. "Well, he liked his dinner today," she would say when Gregor had made a good clearance of his food; and when he had not eaten, which gradually happened more and more often, she would say almost sadly: "Everything's been left standing again."

But although Gregor could get no news directly, he overheard a lot from the neighboring rooms, and as soon as voices were audible, he would run to the door of the room concerned and press his whole body against it. In the first few days especially there was no conversation that did not refer to him somehow, even if only indirectly. For two whole days there were family consultations at every mealtime about what should be done; but also between meals the same subject was discussed, for there were always at least two members of the family at home, since no one wanted to be alone in the flat and to leave it quite empty was unthinkable. And on the very first of these days the household cook—it was not quite clear what and how much she knew of the situation—went down on her knees to his mother and begged leave to go, and when she departed, a quarter of an hour later, gave thanks for her dismissal with tears in her eyes as if for the greatest benefit that could have been conferred on her, and without any prompting swore a solemn oath that she would never say a single word to anyone about what had happened.

Now Gregor's sister had to cook too, helping her mother; true, the cooking did not amount to much, for they ate scarcely anything. Gregor was always hearing one of the family vainly urging another to eat and getting no answer but: "Thanks, I've had all I want," or something similar. Perhaps they drank nothing either. Time and again his sister kept asking his father if he wouldn't like some beer and offered kindly to go and fetch it herself and when he made no answer suggested that she could ask the concierge to fetch it so that he need feel no sense of obligation, but then a round "No" came from his father and no more was said about it.

In the course of that very first day Gregor's father explained the family's financial position and prospects to both his mother and his sister. Now and then he rose from the table to get some voucher or memorandum out of the small safe he had rescued from the collapse of his business five years earlier. One could hear him opening the complicated lock and rustling papers out and shutting it again. This statement made by his father was the first cheerful information Gregor had heard since his imprisonment. He had been of the opinion that nothing at all was left over from his father's business, at least his father had never said anything to the contrary, and of course he had not asked him directly. At that time Gregor's sole desire was to do his utmost to help the family to forget as soon as possible the catastrophe which had overwhelmed the business and thrown them all into a state of complete despair. And so he had set to work with unusual ardor and almost overnight had become a commercial traveler instead of a little clerk, with of course much greater chances of earning money, and his success was immediately translated into good round coin which he could lay on the table for his amazed and happy family. These had been fine times, and they had never recurred, at least not with the same sense of glory, although later on Gregor had earned so much money that he was able to meet the expenses of the whole household and did so. They had simply got used to it, both the family and Gregor; the money was gratefully accepted and gladly given, but there was no special uprush of warm feeling. With his sister alone had he remained intimate, and it was a secret plan of his that she, who loved music, unlike himself, and could play movingly on the violin, should be sent next year to study at the Conservatorium, despite the great expense that would entail, which must be made up in some other way. During his brief visits home the Conservatorium was often mentioned in the talks he had with his sister but always merely as a beautiful dream which could never come true, and his parents discouraged even these innocent references to it; yet Gregor had made up his mind firmly about it and meant to announce the fact with due solemnity on Christmas Day.

Such were the thoughts, completely futile in his present condition, that went through his head as he stood clinging upright to the door and listening. Sometimes out of sheer weariness he had to give up listening and let his head fall negligently against the door, but he always had to pull himself together again at once, for even the slight sound his head made was audible next door and brought all conversation to a stop. "What can he be doing now?" his father would say after a while, obviously turning towards the door, and only then would the interrupted conversation gradually be set going again.

Gregor was now informed as amply as he could wish—for his father tended to repeat himself in his explanations, partly because it was a long time since he had handled such matters and partly because his mother could not always grasp things at once—that a certain amount of investments, a very small amount it was true, had survived the wreck of their fortunes and had even increased a little because the dividends had not been touched meanwhile. And besides that, the money Gregor brought home every month—he had kept only a few dollars for himself—had never been quite used up and now amounted to a small capital sum. Behind the door Gregor nodded his head eagerly, rejoiced at this evidence of unexpected thrift and foresight. True, he could really have paid off some more of his father's debts to the chief with this extra money, and so brought much nearer the day on which he could quit his job, but doubtless it was better the way his father had arranged it.

Yet this capital was by no means sufficient to let the family live on the interest of it; for one year, perhaps, or at the most two, they could live on the principal, that was all. It was simply a sum that ought not to be touched and should be kept for a rainy day; money for living expenses would have to be earned. Now his father was still hale enough but an old man, and he had done no work for the past five years and could not be expected to do much; during these five years, the first years of leisure in his laborious though unsuccessful life, he had grown rather fat and become sluggish. And Gregor's old mother, how was she to earn a living with her asthma, which troubled her even when she walked through the flat and kept her lying on a sofa every other day panting for breath beside an open window? And was his sister to earn her bread, she who was sill a child of seventeen and whose life hitherto had been so pleasant, consisting as it did in dressing herself nicely, sleeping long, helping in the housekeeping, going out to a few modest entertainments and above all playing the violin? At first whenever the need for earning money was mentioned Gregor let go his hold on the door and threw himself down on the cool leather sofa beside it, he felt so hot with shame and grief.

Often he just lay there the long nights through without sleeping at all, scrabbling for hours on the leather. Or he nerved himself to the great effort of pushing an armchair to the window, then crawled up over the window sill and, braced against the chair, leaned against the window panes, obviously in some recollection of the sense of freedom that looking out of a window always used to give him. For in reality day by day things that were even a little way off were growing dimmer to his sight; the hospital across the street, which he used to execrate for being all too often before his eyes, was now quite beyond his range of vision, and if he had not known that he lived in Charlotte Street, a quiet street but still a city street, he might have believed that his window gave on a desert waste where gray sky and gray land blended indistinguishably into each other. His quick-witted sister only needed to observe twice that the armchair stood by the window; after that whenever she had tidied the room she always pushed the chair back to the same place at the window and even left the inner casements open.

If he could have spoken to her and thanked her for all she had to do for him, he could have borne her ministrations better; as it was, they oppressed him. She certainly tried to make as light as possible of whatever was disagreeable in her task, and as time went on she succeeded, of course, more and more, but time brought more enlightenment to Gregor too. The very way she came in distressed him. Hardly was she in the room when she rushed to the window, without even taking time to shut the door, careful as she was usually to shield the sight of Gregor's room from the others, and as if she were almost suffocating tore the casements open with hasty fingers, standing then in the open draught for a while even in the bitterest cold and drawing deep breaths. This noisy scurry of hers upset Gregor twice a day; he would crouch trembling under the sofa all the time, knowing quite well that she would certainly have spared him such a disturbance had she found it at all possible to stay in his presence without opening the window.

On one occasion, about a month after Gregor's metamorphosis, when there was surely no reason for her to be still startled at his appearance, she came a little earlier than usual and found him gazing out of the window, quite motionless, and thus well placed to look like a bogey. Gregor would not have been surprised had she not come in at all, for she could not immediately open the window while he was there, but not only did she retreat, she jumped back as if in alarm and banged the door shut; a stranger might well have thought that he had been lying in wait for her there meaning to bite her. Of course he hid himself under the sofa at once, but he had to wait until midday before she came again, and she seemed more ill at ease than usual. This made him realize how repulsive the sight of him still was to her, and that it was bound to go on being repulsive, and what an effort it must cost her not to run away even from the sight of the small portion of his body that stuck out from under the sofa. In order to spare her that, therefore, one day he carried a sheet on his back to the sofa—it cost him four hours' labor—and arranged it there in such a way as to hide him completely, so that even if she were to bend down she could not see him. Had she considered the sheet unnecessary, she would certainly have stripped it off the sofa again, for it was clear enough that this curtaining and confining of himself was not likely to conduce to Gregor's comfort, but she left it where it was, and Gregor even fancied that he caught a thankful glance from her eye when he lifted the sheet carefully a very little with his head to see how she was taking the new arrangement.

For the first fortnight his parents could not bring themselves to the point of entering his room, and he often heard them expressing their appreciation of his sister's activities, whereas formerly they had frequently scolded her for being as they thought a somewhat useless daughter. But now, both of them often waited outside the door, his father and his mother, while his sister tidied his room, and as soon as she came out she had to tell them exactly how things were in the room, what Gregor had eaten, how he had conducted himself this time and whether there was not perhaps some slight improvement in his condition. His mother, moreover, began relatively soon to want to visit him, but his father and sister dissuaded her at first with arguments which Gregor listened to very attentively and altogether approved. Later, however, she had to be held back by main force, and when she cried out; "Do let me in to Gregor, he is my unfortunate son! Can't you understand that I must go to him?" Gregor thought that it might be well to have her come in, not every day, of course, but perhaps once a week; she understood things, after all, much better than his sister, who was only a child despite the efforts she was making and had perhaps taken on so difficult a task merely out of childish thoughtlessness.

Gegor's desire to see his mother was soon fulfilled. During the daytime he did not want to show himself at the window, out of consideration for his parents, but he could not crawl very far around the few square yards of floor space he had, nor could he bear lying quietly at rest all during the night, while he was fast losing any interest he had ever taken in food, so that for mere recreation he had formed the habit of crawling crisscross over the walls and ceiling. He especially enjoyed hanging suspended from the ceiling; it was much better than lying on the floor; one could breathe more freely; one's body swung and rocked lightly; and in the almost blissful absorption induced by this suspension it could happen to his own surprise that he let go and fell plump on the floor. Yet he now had his body much better under control than formerly, and even such a big fall did him no harm. His sister at once remarked the new distraction Gregor had found for himself—he left traces behind him of the sticky stuff on his soles wherever he crawled—and she got the idea in her head of giving him as wide a field as possible to crawl in and of removing the pieces of furniture that hindered him, above all the chest of drawers and the writing desk. But that was more than she could manage all by herself; she did not dare ask her father to help her; and as for the servant girl, a young creature of sixteen who had had the courage to stay on after the cook's departure, she could not be asked to help, for she had begged as an especial favor that she might keep the kitchen door locked and open it only on a definite summons; so there was nothing left but to apply to her mother at an hour when her father was out. And the old lady did come, with exclamations of joyful eagerness, which, however, died away at the door of Gregor's room. Gregor's sister, of course, went in first, to see that everything was in order before letting his mother enter. In great haste Gregor pulled the sheet lower and rucked it more in folds so that it really looked as if it had been thrown accidentally over the sofa. And this time he did not peer out from under it; he renounced the pleasure of seeing his mother on this occasion and was only glad that she had come at all. "Come in, he's out of sight," said his sister, obviously leading her mother in by the hand. Gregor could now hear the two women struggling to shift the heavy old chest from its place, and his sister claiming the greater part of the labor for herself, without listening to the admonitions of her mother who feared she might overstrain herself. It took a long time. After at least a quarter of an hour's tugging his mother objected that the chest had better be left where it was, for in the first place it was too heavy and could never be got out before his father came home, and standing in the middle of the room like that it would only hamper Gregor's movements, while in the second place it was not at all certain that removing the furniture would be doing a service to Gregor. She was inclined to think to the contrary; the sight of the naked walls made her own heart heavy, and why shouldn't Gregor have the same feeling, considering that he had been used to his furniture for so long and might feel forlorn without it. "And doesn't it look," she concluded in a low voice—in fact she had been almost whispering all the time as if to avoid letting Gregor, whose exact whereabouts she did not know, hear even the tones of her voice, for she was convinced that he could not understand her words—"doesn't it look as if we were showing him, by taking away his furniture, that we have given up hope of his ever getting better and are just leaving him coldly to himself? I think it would be best to keep his room exactly as it has always been, so that when he comes back to us he will find everything unchanged and be able all the more easily to forget what has happened in between."

On hearing these words from his mother Gregor realized that the lack of all direct human speech for the past two months together with the monotony of family life must have confused his mind, otherwise he could not account for the fact that he had quite earnestly looked forward to having his room emptied of furnishing. Did he really want his warm room, so comfortably fitted with old family furniture, to be turned into a naked den in which he would certainly be able to crawl unhampered in all directions but at the price of shedding simultaneously all recollection of his human background? He had indeed been so near the brink of forgetfulness that only the voice of his mother, which he had not heard for so long, had drawn him back from it. Nothing should be taken out of his room; everything must stay as it was; he could not dispense with the good influence of the furniture on his state of mind; and even if the furniture did hamper him in his senseless crawling round and round, that was no drawback but a great advantage.

Unfortunately his sister was of the contrary opinion; she had grown accustomed, and not without reason, to consider herself an expert in Gregor's affairs as against her parents, and so her mother's advice was now enough to make her determined on the removal not only of the chest and the writing desk, which had been her first intention, but of all the furniture except the indispensable sofa. This determination was not, of course, merely the outcome of childish recalcitrance and of the self-confidence she had recently developed so unexpectedly and at such cost; she had in fact perceived that Gregor needed a lot of space to crawl about in—while on the other hand he never used the furniture at all, so far as could be seen. Another factor might have been also the enthusiastic temperament of an adolescent girl, which seeks to indulge itself on every opportunity and which now tempted Grete to exaggerate the horror of her brother's circumstances in order that she might do all the more for him. In a room where Gregor lorded it all alone over empty walls no one save herself was likely ever to set foot.

And so she was not to be moved from her resolve by her mother, who seemed moreover to be ill at ease in Gregor's room and therefore unsure of herself, was soon reduced to silence and helped her daughter as best she could to push the chest outside. Now, Gregor could do without the chest, if need be, but the writing desk he must retain. As soon as the two woman had got the chest out of his room, groaning as they pushed it, Gregor stuck his head out from under the sofa to see how he might intervene as kindly and cautiously as possible. But as bad luck would have it, his mother was the first to return, leaving Grete clasping the chest in the room next door where she was trying to shift it all by herself, without of course moving it from the spot. His mother however was not accustomed to the sight of him, it might sicken her and so in alarm Gregor backed quickly to the other end of the sofa, yet could not prevent the sheet from swaying a little in front. That was enough to put her on the alert. She paused, stood still for a moment and then went back to Grete.

Although Gregor kept reassuring himself that nothing out of the way was happening, but only a few bits of furniture were being changed round, he soon had to admit that all this trotting to and fro of the two women, their little ejaculations and the scraping of furniture along the floor affected him like a vast disturbance coming from all sides at once, and however much he tucked in his head and legs and cowered to the very floor he was bound to confess that he would not be able to stand it for long. They were clearing his room out; taking away everything he loved; the chest in which he kept his fret saw and other tools was already dragged off; they were now loosening the writing desk which had almost sunk into the floor, the desk at which he had done all his homework when he was at the commercial academy, at the grammar school before that and, yes, even at the primary school—he had no more time to waste in weighing the good intentions of the two women, whose existence he had by now almost forgotten, for they were so exhausted that they were laboring in silence and nothing could be heard but the heavy scuffling of their feet.

And so he rushed out—the women were just leaning against the writing desk in the next room to give themselves a breather—and four times changed his direction, since he really did not know what to rescue first, then on the wall opposite, which was already otherwise cleared, he was struck by the picture of the lady muffled in so much fur and quickly crawled up to it and pressed himself to the glass, which was a good surface to hold on to and comforted his hot belly. This picture at least, which was entirely hidden beneath him, was going to be removed by nobody. He turned his head towards the door of the living room so as to observe the women when they came back.

They had not allowed themselves much of a rest and were already coming; Grete had twined her arm round her mother and was almost supporting her. "Well, what shall we take now?" said Grete, looking round. Her eyes met Gregor's from the wall. She kept her composure, presumably because of her mother, bent her head down to her mother, to keep her from looking up, and said, although in a fluttering, unpremeditated voice; "Come, hadn't we better go back to the living room for a moment?" Her intentions were clear enough to Gregor, she wanted to bestow her mother in safety and then chase him down from the wall. Well, just let her try it! He clung to his picture and would not give it up. He would rather fly in Grete's face.

But Grete's words had succeeded in disquieting her mother, who took a step to one side, caught sight of the huge brown mass on the flowered wallpaper, and before she was really conscious that what she saw was Gregor screamed in a loud, hoarse voice: "Oh God, oh God!" fell with outspread arms over the sofa as if giving up and did not move. "Gregor!" cried his sister, shaking her fist and glaring at him. This was the first time she had directly addressed him since his metamorphosis. She ran into the next room for some aromatic essence with which to rouse her mother from her fainting fit. Gregor wanted to help too—there was still time to rescue the picture—but he was stuck fast to the glass and had to tear himself loose; he then ran after his sister into the next room as if he could advise her, as he used to do; but then had to stand helplessly behind her; she meanwhile searched among various small bottles and when she turned round started in alarm at the sight of him; one bottle fell on the floor and broke; a splinter of glass cut Gregor's face and some kind of corrosive medicine splashed him; without pausing a moment longer Grete gathered up all the bottles she could carry and ran to her mother with them; she banged the door shut with her foot. Gregor was now cut off from his mother, who was perhaps nearly dying because of him; he dared not open the door for fear of frightening away his sister, who had to stay with her mother; there was nothing he could do but wait; and harassed by self-reproach and worry he began now to crawl to and fro, over everything, walls, furniture and ceiling, and finally in his despair, when the whole room seemed to be reeling round him, fell down on to the middle of the big table.

A little while elapsed, Gregor was still lying there feebly and all around us quiet, perhaps that was a good omen. Then the doorbell rang. The servant girl was of course locked in her kitchen, and Grete would have to open the door. It was his father. "What's been happening?"

were his first words; Grete's face must have told him everything. Grete answered in a muffled voice, apparently hiding her head on his breast. "Mother has been fainting, but she's better now. Gregor's broken loose." "Just what I expected," said his father, "just what I've been telling you, but you women would never listen." It was clear to Gregor that his father had taken the worst interpretation of Grete's all too brief statement and was assuming that Gregor had been guilty of some violent act. Therefore Gregor must now try to propitiate his father, since he had neither time nor means for an explanation. And so he fled to the door of his own room and crouched against it, to let his father see as soon as he came in from the hall that his son had the good intention of getting back into his room immediately and that it was not necessary to drive him there, but that if only the door were opened he would disappear at once.

Yet his father was not in the mood to perceive such fine distinctions. "Ah!" he cried as soon as he appeared, in a tone which sounded at once angry and exultant. Gregor drew his head back from the door and lifted it to look at his father. Truly, this was not the father he had imagined to himself; admittedly he had been too absorbed of late in his new recreation of crawling over the ceiling to take the same interest as before in what was happening elsewhere in the flat, and he ought really to be prepared for some changes. And yet, and yet, could that be his father? The man who used to lie wearily sunk in bed whenever Gregor set out on a business journey; who welcomed him back of an evening lying in a long chair in a dressing gown; who could not really rise to his feet but only lifted his arms in greeting, and on the rare occasions when he did go out with his family, on one or two Sundays a year and on high holidays, walked between Gregor and his mother, who were slow walkers anyhow, even more slowly than they did, muffled in his old greatcoat, shuffling laboriously forward with the help of his crook-handled stick which he set down most cautiously at every step and, whenever he wanted to say anything, nearly always came to a full stop and gathered his escort around him? Now he was standing there in fine shape; dressed in a smart blue uniform with gold buttons, such as bank messengers wear; his strong double chin bulged over the stiff high collar of his jacket; from under his bushy eyebrows his black eyes darted fresh and penetrating glances; his onetime tangled white hair had been combed flat on either side of a shining and carefully exact parting. He pitched his cap, which bore a gold monogram, probably the badge of some bank, in a wide sweep across the whole room on to a sofa and with the tail-ends of his jacket thrown back, his hands in his trouser pockets, advanced with a grim visage towards Gregor. Likely enough he did not himself know what he meant to do, at any rate he lifted his feet uncommonly high, and Gregor was dumbfounded at the enormous size of his shoe soles. But Gregor could not risk standing up to him, aware as he had been from the very first day of his new life that his father believed only the severest measures suitable for dealing with him. And so he ran before his father, stopping when he stopped and scuttling forward again when his father made any kind of move. In this way they circled the room several times without anything decisive happening, indeed the whole operation did not even look like a pursuit because it was carried out so slowly. And so Gregor did not leave the floor, for he feared that his father might take as a piece of peculiar wickedness any excursion of his over the walls or the ceiling. All the same, he could not stay this course much longer, for while his father took one step he had to carry out a whole series of movements. He was already beginning to feel breathless, just as in his former life his lungs had not been very dependable. As he was staggering along, trying to concentrate his energy on running, hardly keeping his eyes open; in his dazed state never even thinking of any other escape than simply going forward; and having almost forgotten that the walls were free to him, which in this room were well provided with finely carved pieces of furniture full of knobs and crevices—suddenly something lightly flung landed close behind him and rolled before him. It was an apple; a second apple followed immediately; Gregor came to a stop in alarm; there was no point in running on, for his father was determined to bombard him. He had filled his pockets with fruit from the dish on the sideboard and was now shying apple after apple, without taking particularly good aim for the moment. The small red apples rolled about the floor as if magnetized and cannoned into each other. An apple thrown without much force grazed Gregor's back and glanced off harmlessly. But another following immediately landed right on his back and sank in; Gregor wanted to drag himself forward, as if this startling, incredible pain could be left behind him; but he felt as if nailed to the spot and flattened himself out in a complete derangement of all his senses. With his last conscious look he saw the door of his room being torn open and his mother rushing out ahead of his screaming sister, in her underbodice, for her daughter had loosened her clothing to let her breathe more freely and recover from her swoon, he saw his mother rushing towards his father, leaving one after another behind her on the floor her loosened petticoats, stumbling over her petticoats straight to his father and embracing him, in complete union with him—but here Gregor's sight began to fail—with her hands clasped round his father's neck as she begged for her son's life.

III

The serious injury done to Gregor, which disabled him for more than a month—the apple went on sticking in his body as a visible reminder, since no one ventured to remove it—seemed to have made even his father recollect that Gregor was a member of the family, despite his present unfortunate and repulsive shape, and ought not to be treated as an enemy, that, on the contrary, family duty required the suppression of disgust and the exercise of patience, nothing but patience.

And although his injury had impaired, probably for ever, his powers of movement, and for the time being it took him long, long minutes to creep across his room like an old invalid—there was no question now of crawling up the wall—yet in his own opinion he was sufficiently compensated for this worsening of his condition by the fact that towards evening the living-room door, which he used to watch intently for an hour or two beforehand, was always thrown open, so that lying in the darkness of his room, invisible to the family, he could see them all at the lamp-lit table and listen to their talk, by general consent as it were, very different from his earlier eavesdropping.

True, their intercourse lacked the lively character of former times, which he had always called to mind with a certain wistfulness in the small hotel bedrooms where he had been wont to throw himself down, tired out, on damp bedding. They were now mostly very silent. Soon after supper his father would fall asleep in his armchair; his mother and sister would admonish each other to be silent; his mother, bending low over the lamp, stitched at fine sewing for an underwear firm; his sister, who had taken a job as a salesgirl, was learning shorthand and French in the evenings on the chance of bettering herself. Sometimes his father woke up, and as if quite unaware that he had been sleeping said to his mother: "What a lot of sewing you're doing today!" and at once fell asleep again, while the two women exchanged a tired smile.

With a kind of mulishness his father persisted in keeping his uniform on even in the house, his dressing gown hung uselessly on its peg and he slept fully dressed where he sat, as if he were ready for service at any moment and even here only at the beck and call of his superior. As a result, his uniform, which was not brand-new to start with, began to look dirty, despite all the loving care of the mother and sister to keep it clean, and Gregor often spent whole evenings gazing at the many greasy spots on the garment, gleaming with gold buttons always in a high state of polish, in which the old man sat sleeping in extreme discomfort and yet quite peacefully.

As soon as the clock struck ten his mother tried to rouse his father with gentle words and to persuade him after that to get into bed, for sitting there he could not have a proper sleep and that was what he needed most, since he had to go on duty at six. But with the mulishness that had obsessed him since he became a bank messenger he always insisted on staying longer at the table, although he regularly fell asleep again and in the end only with the greatest trouble could be got out of his armchair and into his bed. However insistently Gregor's mother and sister kept urging him with gentle reminders, he would go on slowly shaking his head for a quarter of an hour, keeping his eyes shut, and refuse to get to his feet. The mother plucked at his sleeve, whispering endearments in his ear, the sister left her lessons to come to her mother's help, but Gregor's father was not to be caught. He would only sink down deeper in his chair. Not until the two women hoisted him up by the armpits did he open his eyes and look at them both, one after the other, usually with the remark: "This is a life. This is the peace and quiet of my old age." And leaning on the two of them he would heave himself up, with difficulty, as if he were a great burden to himself, suffer them to lead him as far as the door and then wave them off and go on alone, while the mother abandoned her needlework and the sister her pen in order to run after him and help him farther.

Who could find time, in this overworked and tired-out family, to bother about Gregor more than was absolutely needful? The household was reduced more and more; the servant girl was turned off; a gigantic bony charwoman with white hair flying round her head came in morning and evening to do the rough work; everything else was done by Gregor's mother, as well as great piles of sewing. Even various family ornaments, which his mother and sister used to wear with pride at parties and celebration had to be sold, as Gregor discovered of an evening from hearing them all discuss the prices obtained. But what they lamented most was the fact that they could not leave the flat which was much too big for their present circumstances, because they could not think of any way to shift Gregor. Yet Gregor saw well enough that consideration for him was not the main difficulty preventing the removal, for they could have easily shifted him in some suitable box with a few air holes in it; what really kept them from moving into another flat was rather their own complete hopelessness and the belief that they had been singled out for a misfortune such as had never happened to any of their relations or acquaintances. They fulfilled to the uttermost all that the world demands of poor people, the father fetched breakfast for the small clerks in the bank, the mother devoted her energy to making underwear for strangers, the sister trotted to and fro behind the counter at the behest of customers, but more than this they had not the strength to do. And the wound in Gregor's back began to nag at him afresh when his mother and sister, after getting his father into bed, came back again, left their work lying, drew close to each other and sat cheek to cheek; when his mother, pointing towards his room, said: "Shut that door now, Grete," and he was left again in darkness, while next door the women mingled their tears or perhaps sat dry-eyed staring at the table.

Gregor hardly slept at all by night or by day. He was often haunted by the idea that next time the door opened he would take the family's affairs in hand again just as he used to do; once more, after this long interval, there appeared in his thoughts the figures of the chief and the chief clerk, the commercial travelers and the apprentices, the porter who was so dull-witted, two or three friends in other firms, a chambermaid in one of the rural hotels, a sweet and fleeting memory, a cashier in a milliner's shop, whom he had wooed earnestly but too slowly—they all appeared, together with strangers or people he had quite forgotten, but instead of helping him and his family they were one and all unapproachable and he was glad when they vanished. At other times he would not be in the mood to bother about his family, he was only filled with rage at the way they were neglecting him, and although he had no clear idea of what he might care to eat he would make plans for going into the larder to take the food that was after all his due, even if he were not hungry. His sister no longer took thought to bring him what might especially please him, but in the morning and at noon before she went to business hurriedly pushed into his room with her foot any food that was available, and in the evening cleared it out again with one sweep of the broom, heedless of whether it had been merely tasted, or—as most frequently happened—left untouched. The cleaning of his room, which she now did always in the evenings, could not have been more hastily done. Streaks of dirt stretched along the walls, here an there lay balls of dust and filth. At first Gregor used to station himself in some particularly filthy corner when his sister arrived, in order to reproach her with it, so to speak. But he could have sat there for weeks without getting her to make any improvement; she could see the dirt as well as he did, but she had simply made up her mind to leave it alone. And yet, with a touchiness that was new to her, which seemed anyhow to have infected the whole family, she jealously guarded her claim to be the sole caretaker of Gregor's room. His mother once subjected his room to a thorough cleaning, which was achieved only by means of several buckets of water—all this dampness of course upset Gregor too and he lay widespread, sulky and motionless on the sofa—but she was well punished for it. Hardly had his sister noticed the changed aspect of his room that evening than she rushed in high dudgeon into the living room and, despite the imploringly raised hands of her mother, burst into a storm of weeping, while her parents—her father had of course been startled out of his chair—looked on at first in helpless amazement; then they too began to go into action; the father reproached the mother on his right for not having left the cleaning of Gregor's room to his sister; shrieked at the sister on his left that never again was she to be allowed to clean Gregor's room; while the mother tried to pull the father into his bedroom, since he was beyond himself with agitation; the sister, shaken with sobs, then beat upon the table with her small fists; and Gregor hissed loudly with rage because not one of them thought of shutting the door to spare him such a spectacle and so much noise.

Still, even if the sister, exhausted by her daily work, had grown tired of looking after Gregor as she did formerly, there was no need for his mother's intervention or for Gregor's being neglected at all. The charwoman was there. This old widow, whose strong bony frame had enabled her to survive the worst a long life could offer, by no means recoiled from Gregor. Without being in the least curious she had once by chance opened the door of his room and at the sight of Gregor, who, taken by surprise, began to rush to and fro although no one was chasing him, merely stood there with her arms folded. From that time she never failed to open his door a little for a moment, morning and evening, to have a look at him. At first she even used to call him to her, with words which apparently she took to be friendly, such as: "Come along, then, you old dung beetle!" or "Look at the old dung beetle, then!" To such allocutions Gregor made no answer, but stayed motionless where he was, as if the door had never been opened. Instead of being allowed to disturb him so senselessly whenever the whim took her, she should rather have been ordered to clean out his room daily, that charwoman! Once, early in the morning—heavy rain was lashing on the windowpanes, perhaps a sign that spring was on the way—Gregor was so exasperated when she began addressing him again that he ran at her, as if to attack her although slowly and feebly enough. But the charwoman instead of showing fright merely lifted high a chair that happened to be beside the door, and as she stood there with her mouth wide open it was clear that she meant to shut it only when she brought the chair down on Gregor's back. "So you're not coming any nearer?" she asked, as Gregor turned away again, and quietly put the chair back into the corner.

Gregor was now eating hardly anything. Only when he happened to pass the food laid out for him did he take a bit of something in his mouth as a pastime, kept it there for an hour at a time and usually spat it out again. At first he thought it was chagrin over the state of his room that prevented him from eating, yet he soon got used to the various changes in his room. It had become a habit in the family to push into his room things there was no room for elsewhere, and there were plenty of these now, since one of the rooms had been let to three lodgers. These serious gentlemen—all three of them with full beards, as Gregor once observed through a crack in the door—had a passion for order, not only in their own room but, since they were now members of the household, in all its arrangements, especially in the kitchen. Superfluous, not to say dirty, objects they could not bear. Besides, they had brought with them most of the furnishings they needed. For this reason many things could be dispensed with that it was no use trying to sell but that should not be thrown away either. All of them found their way into Gregor's room. The ash can likewise and the kitchen garbage can. Anything that was not needed for the moment was simply flung into Gregor's room by the charwoman, who did everything in a hurry; fortunately Gregor usually saw only the object, whatever it was, and the hand that held it. Perhaps she intended to take the things away again as time and opportunity offered, or to collect them until she could throw them all out in a heap, but in fact they just lay wherever she happened to throw them, except when Gregor pushed his way through the junk heap and shifted it somewhat, at first out of necessity, because he had not room enough to crawl, but later with increasing enjoyment, although after such excursions, being sad and weary to death, he would lie motionless for hours. And since the lodgers often ate their supper at home in the common living room, the living-room door stayed shut many an evening, yet Gregor reconciled himself quite easily to the shutting of the door, for often enough on evenings when it was opened he had disregarded it entirely and lain in the darkest corner of his room, quite unnoticed by the family. But on one occasion the charwoman left the door open a little and it stayed ajar even when the lodgers came in for supper and the lamp was lit. They set themselves at the top end of the table where formerly Gregor and his father and mother had eaten their meals, unfolded their napkins and took knife and fork in hand. At once his mother appeared in the other doorway with a dish of meat and close behind her his sister with a dish of potatoes piled high. The food steamed with a thick vapor. The lodgers bent over the food set before them as if to scrutinize it before eating, in fact the man in the middle, who seemed to pass for an authority with the other two, cut a piece of meat as it lay on the dish, obviously to discover if it were tender or should be sent back to the kitchen. He showed satisfaction, and Gregor's mother and sister, who had been watching anxiously, breathed freely and began to smile.

The family itself took its meal in the kitchen. None the less, Gregor's father came into the living room before going into the kitchen and with one prolonged bow, cap in hand, made a round of the table. The lodgers all stood up and murmured something in their beards. When they were alone again they ate their food in almost complete silence. It seemed remarkable to Gregor that among the various noises coming from the table he could always distinguish the sound of their masticating teeth, as if this were a sign to Gregor that one needed teeth in order to eat, and that with toothless jaws even of the finest make one could do nothing. "I'm hungry enough," said Gregor sadly to himself, "but not for that kind of food. How these lodgers are stuffing themselves, and here am I dying of starvation!"

On that very evening—during the whole of his time there Gregor could not remember ever having heard the violin—the sound of violin-playing came from the kitchen. The lodgers had already finished their supper, the one in the middle had brought out a newspaper and given the other two a page apiece, and now they were leaning back at ease reading and smoking. When the violin began to play they pricked up their ears, got to their feet, and went on tiptoe to the hall door where they stood huddled together. Their movements must have been heard in the kitchen, for Gregor's father called out: "Is the violin-playing disturbing you, gentlemen? It can be stopped at once." "On the contrary," said the middle lodger, "could not Fräulein Samsa come and play in this room, beside us, where it is much more convenient and comfortable?" "Oh certainly," cried Gregor's father, as if he were the violin-player. The lodgers came back into the living room and waited. Presently Gregor's father arrived with the music stand, his mother carrying the music and his sister with the violin. His sister quietly made everything ready to start playing; his parents, who had never let rooms before and so had an exaggerated idea of the courtesy due to lodgers did not venture to sit down on their own chairs, his father leaned against the door, the right hand thrust between two buttons of his livery coat, which was formally buttoned up; but his mother was offered a chair by one of the lodgers and, since she left the chair just where he had happened to put it, sat down in a corner to one side.

Gregor's sister began to play; the father and mother, from either side, intently watched the movements of her hands. Gregor, attracted by the playing, ventured to move forward a little until his head was actually inside the living room. He felt hardly any surprise at his growing lack of consideration for the others; there had been a time when he prided himself on being considerate. And yet just on this occasion he had more reason than ever to hide himself, since owing to the amount of dust which lay thick in his room and rose into the air at the slightest movement, he too was covered with dust; fluff and hair and remnants of food trailed with him, caught on his back and along his sides; his indifference to everything was much too great for him to turn on his back and scrape himself clean on the carpet, as once he had done several times a day. And in spite of his condition, no shame deterred him from advancing a little over the spotless floor of the living room.

To be sure, no one was aware of him. The family was entirely absorbed in the violin-playing; the lodgers, however, who first of all had stationed themselves, hands in pockets, much too close behind the music stand so that they could all have read the music, which must have bothered his sister, had soon retreated to the window, half-whispering with downbent heads, and stayed there while his father turned an anxious eye on them. Indeed, they were making it more than obvious that they had been disappointed in their expectation of hearing good or enjoyable violin-playing, that they had had more than enough of the performance and only out of courtesy suffered a continued disturbance of their peace. From the way they all kept blowing the smoke of their cigars high in the air through nose and mouth one could divine their irritation. And yet Gregor's sister was playing so beautifully. Her face leaned sideways, intently and sadly her eyes followed the notes of music. Gregor crawled a little farther forward and lowered his head to the ground so that it might be possible for his eyes to meet hers. Was he an animal, that music had such an effect upon him? He felt as if the way were opening before him to the unknown nourishment he craved. He was determined to push forward till he reached his sister, to pull at her skirt and so let her know that she was to come into his room with her violin, for no one here appreciated her playing as he would appreciate it. He would never let her out of his room, at least, not so long as he lived; his frightful appearance would become, for the first time useful to him; he would watch all the doors of his room at once and spit at intruders, but his sister should need no constraint, she should stay with him of her own free will; she should sit beside him on the sofa, bend down her ear to him and hear him confide that he had had the firm intention of sending her to the Conservatorium, and that, but for his mishap, last Christmas—surely Christmas was long past?—he would have announced it to everybody without allowing a single objection. After this confession his sister would be so touched that she would burst into tears, and Gregor would then raise himself to her shoulder and kiss her on the neck, which, now that she went to business, she kept free of any ribbon or collar.

"Mr. Samsa!" cried the middle lodger, to Gregor's father, and pointed, without wasting any more words, at Gregor, now working himself slowly forwards. The violin fell silent, the middle lodger first smiled to his friends with a shake of the head and then looked at Gregor again. Instead of driving Gregor out, his father seemed to think it more needful to begin by soothing down the lodgers, although they were not at all agitated and apparently found Gregor more entertaining than the violin-playing. He hurried towards them and spreading out his arms, tried to urge them back into their own room and at the same time to block the view of Gregor. They now began to be really a little angry, one could not tell whether because of the old man's behavior or because it had just dawned on them that all unwittingly they had such a neighbor as Gregor next door. They demanded explanations of his father, they waved their arms like him, tugged uneasily at their beards, and only with reluctance backed towards their room. Meanwhile Gregor's sister, who stood there as if lost when her playing was so abruptly broken off, came to life again, pulled herself together all at once after standing for a while holding violin and bow in nervelessly hanging hands and staring at her music, pushed her violin into the lap of her mother, who was still sitting in her chair fighting asthmatically for breath, and ran into the lodgers' room to which they were now being shepherded by her father rather more quickly than before. One could see the pillows and blankets on the beds flying under her accustomed fingers and being laid in order. Before the lodgers had actually reached their room she had finished making the beds and slipped out.

The old man seemed once more to be so possessed by his mulish self-assertiveness that he was forgetting all the respect he should show to his lodgers. He kept driving them on and driving them on until in the very door of the bedroom the middle lodger stamped his foot loudly on the floor and so brought him to a halt. "I beg to announce," said the lodger lifting one hand and looking also at Gregor's mother and sister, "that because of the disgusting conditions prevailing in this household and family"—here he spat on the floor with emphatic brevity—"I give you notice on the spot. Naturally I won't pay you a penny for the days I have lived here, on the contrary I shall consider bringing an action for damages against you, based on claims—believe me—that will be easily susceptible of proof." He ceased and stared straight in front of him, as if he expected something. In fact his two friends at once rushed into the breach with these words: "And we too give notice on the spot." On that he seized the door-handle and shut the door with a slam.

Gregor's father, groping with his hands, staggered forward and fell into his chair; it looked as if he were stretching himself there for his ordinary evening nap, but the marked jerkings of his head, which was as if uncontrollable, showed that he was far from asleep. Gregor had simply stayed quietly all the time on the spot where the lodgers had espied him. Disappointment at the failure of his plan, perhaps also the weakness arising from extreme hunger, made it impossible for him to move. He feared, with a fair degree of certainty, that at any moment the general tension would discharge itself in a combined attack upon him, and he lay waiting. He did not react even to the noise made by the violin as it fell off his mother's lap from under her trembling fingers and gave out a resonant note.

"My dear parents," said his sister, slapping her hand on the table by way of introduction, "things can't go on like this. Perhaps you don't realize that, but I do. I won't utter my brother's name in the presence of this creature, and so all I say is: we must try to get rid of it. We've tried to look after it and to put up with it as far as is humanly possible, and I don't think anyone could reproach us in the slightest."

"She is more than right," said Gregor's father to himself. His mother, who was still choking for lack of breath, began to cough hollowly into her hand with a wild look in her eyes.

His sister rushed over to her and held her forehead. His father's thoughts seemed to have lost their vagueness at Grete's words, he sat more upright, fingering his service cap that lay among the plans still lying on the able from the lodgers' supper, and from time to time looked at the still form of Gregor.

"We must try to get rid of it," his sister now said explicitly to her father, since her mother was coughing too much to hear a word, "it will be the death of both of you, I can see that coming. When one has to work as hard as we do, all of us, one can't stand this continual torment at home on top of it. At least I can't stand it any longer." And she burst into such a passion of sobbing that her tears dropped on her mother's face, where she wiped them off mechanically.

"My dear," said the old man sympathetically, and with evident understanding, "but what can we do?"

Gregor's sister merely shrugged her shoulders to indicate the feeling of helplessness that had now overmastered her during her weeping fit, in contrast to her former confidence.

"If he could understand us," said her father, half questioningly; Grete, still sobbing, vehemently waved a hand to show how unthinkable that was.

"If he could understand us," repeated the old man, shutting his eyes to consider his daughter's conviction that understanding was impossible, "then perhaps we might come to some agreement with him. But as it is—"

"He must go," cried Gregor's sister, "that's the only solution, Father. You must just try to get rid of the idea that this is Gregor. The fact that we've believed it for so long is the root of all our trouble. But how can it be Gregor? If this were Gregor, he would have realized long ago that human beings can't live with such a creature, and he'd have gone away on his own accord. Then we wouldn't have any brother, but we'd be able to go on living and keep his memory in honor. As it is, this creature persecutes us, drives away our lodgers, obviously wants the whole apartment to himself and would have us all sleep in the gutter. Just look, Father," she shrieked all at once, "he's at it again!" And in an access of panic that was quite incomprehensible to Gregor she even quitted her mother, literally thrusting the chair from her as if she would rather sacrifice her mother than stay so near to Gregor, and rushed behind her father, who also rose up, being simply upset by her agitation, and half-spread his arms out as if to protect her.

Yet Gregor had not the slightest intention of frightening anyone, far less his sister. He had only begun to turn round in order to crawl back to his room, but it was certainly a startling operation to watch, since because of his disabled condition he could not execute the difficult turning movements except by lifting his head and then bracing it against the floor over and over again. He paused and looked round. His good intentions seemed to have been recognized; the alarm had only been momentary. Now they were all watching him in melancholy silence. His mother lay in her chair, her legs stiffly outstretched and pressed together, her eyes almost closing for sheer weariness; his father and his sister were sitting beside each other, his sister's arm around the old man's neck.

Perhaps I can go on turning round now, thought Gregor, and began his labors again. He could not stop himself from panting with the effort, and had to pause now and then to take breath. Nor did anyone harass him, he was left entirely to himself. When he had completed the turn-round he began at once to crawl straight back. He was amazed at the distance separating him from his room and could not understand how in his weak state he had managed to accomplish the same journey so recently, almost without remarking it. Intent on crawling as fast as possible, be barely noticed that not a single word, not an ejaculation from his family, interfered with his progress. Only when he was already in the doorway did he turn his head round, not completely, for his neck muscles were getting stiff, but enough to see that nothing had changed behind him except that his sister had risen to her feet. His last glance fell on his mother, who was not quite overcome by sleep.

Hardly was he well inside his room when the door was hastily pushed shut, bolted and locked. The sudden noise in his rear startled him so much that his little legs gave beneath him. It was his sister who had shown such haste. She had been standing ready waiting and had made a light spring forward, Gregor had not even heard her coming, and she cried "At last!" to her parents as she turned the key in the lock.

"And what now?" said Gregor to himself, looking round in the darkness. Soon he made the discovery that he was now unable to stir a limb. This did not surprise him, rather it seemed unnatural that he should ever actually have been able to move on these feeble little legs. Otherwise he felt relatively comfortable. True, his whole body was aching, but it seemed that the pain was gradually growing less and would finally pass away. The rotting apple in his back and the inflamed area around it, all covered with soft dust already hardly troubled him. He thought of his family with tenderness and love. The decision that he must disappear was one that he held to even more strongly than his sister, if that were possible. In this state of vacant and peaceful meditation he remained until the tower clock struck three in the morning. The first broadening of light in the world outside the window entered his consciousness once more. Then his head sank to the floor of its own accord and from his nostrils came the last faint flicker of his breath.

When the charwoman arrived early in the morning—what between her strength and her impatience she slammed all the doors so loudly, never mind how often she had been begged not to do so, that no one in the whole apartment could enjoy any quiet sleep after her arrival—she noticed nothing unusual as she took her customary peep into Gregor's room. She thought he was lying motionless on purpose, pretending to be in the sulks; she credited him with every kind of intelligence. Since she happened to have the long handled broom in her hand she tried to tickle him up with it from the doorway. When that too produced no reaction she felt provoked and poked at him a little harder, and only when she had pushed him along the floor without meeting any resistance was her attention aroused. It did not take her long to establish the truth of the matter, and her eyes widened, she let out a whistle, yet did not waste much time over it but tore open the door of the Samsas' bedroom and yelled into the darkness at the top of her voice: "Just look at this, it's dead; it's lying here dead and done for!"

Mr. and Mrs. Samsa started up in their double bed and before they realized the nature of the charwoman's announcement had some difficulty in overcoming the shock of it. But then they got out of bed quickly, one on either side, Mr. Samsa throwing a blanket over his shoulders, Mrs. Samsa in nothing but her nightgown; in this array they entered Gregor's room. Meanwhile the door of the living room opened, too, where Grete had been sleeping since the advent of the lodgers; she was completely dressed as if she had not been to bed, which seemed to be confirmed also by the paleness of her face. "Dead?" said Mrs. Samsa, looking questioningly at the charwoman, although she could have investigated for herself, and the fact was obvious enough without investigation. "I should say so," said the charwoman, proving her words by pushing Gregor's corpse a long way to one side with her broomstick. Mrs. Samsa made a movement as if to stop her, but checked it. "Well," said Mr. Samsa, "now thanks be to God." He crossed himself, and the three women followed his example. Grete, whose eyes never left the corpse, said. "Just see how thin he was. It's such a long time since he's eaten anything. The food came out again just as it went in." Indeed, Gregor's body was completely flat and dry, as could only now be seen when it was no longer supported by the legs and nothing prevented one from looking closely at it.

"Come in beside us, Grete, for a little while," said Mrs. Samsa with a tremulous smile, and Grete, not without looking back at the corpse, followed her parents into their bedroom. The charwoman shut the door and opened the window wide. Although it was so early in the morning a certain softness was perceptible in the fresh air. After all, it was already the end of March.

The three lodgers emerged from their room and were surprised to see no breakfast; they had been forgotten. "Where's our breakfast?" said the middle lodger peevishly to the charwoman. But she put her finger to her lips and hastily, without a word, indicated by gestures that they should go into Gregor's room. They did so and stood, their hands in the pockets of their somewhat shabby coats, around Gregor's corpse in the room where it was now fully light.

At that the door of the Samsas' bedroom opened and Mr. Samsa appeared in his uniform, his wife on one arm, his daughter on the other. They all looked a little as if they had been crying; from time to time Grete hid her face on her father's arm.

"Leave my house at once!" said Mr. Samsa, and pointed to the door without disengaging himself from the women. "What do you mean by that?" said the middle lodger, taken somewhat aback, with a feeble smile. The two others put their hands behind them and kept rubbing them together, as if in gleeful expectation of a fine set-to in which they were bound to come off the winners. "I mean just what I say," answered Mr. Samsa, and advanced in a straight line with his two companions towards the lodger. He stood his ground at first quietly, looking at the floor as if his thoughts were taking a new pattern in his head. "Then let us go, by all means," he said, and looked up at Mr. Samsa as if in a sudden access of humility he were expecting some renewed sanction for this decision. Mr. Samsa merely nodded briefly once or twice with meaning eyes. Upon that the lodger really did go with long strides into the hall, his two friends had been listening and had quite stopped rubbing their hands for some moments and now went scuttling after him as if afraid that Mr. Samsa might get into the hall before them and cut them off from their leader. In the hall they all three took their hats from the rack, their sticks from the umbrella stand, bowed in silence and quitted the apartment. With a suspiciousness which proved quite unfounded Mr. Samsa and the two women followed them out to the landing; leaning over the banister they watched the three figures slowly but surely going down the long stairs, vanishing from sight at a certain turn of the staircase on every floor and coming into view again after a moment or so; the more they dwindled, the more the Samsa family's interest in them dwindled, and when a butcher's boy met them and passed them on the stairs coming up proudly with a tray on his head, Mr. Samsa and the two women soon left the landing and as if a burden had been lifted from them went back into their apartment.

They decided to spend this day in resting and going for a stroll; they had not only deserved such a respite from work, but absolutely needed it. And so they sat down at the table and wrote three notes of excuse, Mr. Samsa to his board of management, Mrs. Samsa to her employer and Grete to the head of her firm. While they were writing, the charwoman came in to say that she was going now, since her morning's work was finished. At first they only nodded without looking up, but as she kept hovering there they eyed her irritably. "Well?" said Mr. Samsa. The charwoman stood grinning in the doorway as if she had good news to impart to the family but meant not to say a word unless properly questioned. The small ostrich feather standing upright on her hat, which had annoyed Mr. Samsa ever since she was engaged, was waving gaily in all directions. "Well, what is it then?" asked Mrs. Samsa, who obtained more respect from the charwoman than the others. "Oh," said the charwoman, giggling so amiably that she could not at once continue, "just this, you don't need to bother about how to get rid of the thing next door. It's been seen to already." Mrs. Samsa and Grete bent over their letters again, as if preoccupied; Mr. Samsa, who perceived that she was eager to begin describing it all in detail, stopped her with a decisive hand. But since she was not allowed to tell her story, she remembered the great hurry she was in, being obviously deeply huffed: "Bye, everybody," she said, whirling off violently, and departed with a frightful slamming of doors.

"She'll be given notice tonight," said Mr. Samsa, but neither from his wife nor his daughter did he get any answer, for the charwoman seemed to have shattered again the composure they had barely achieved. They rose, went to the window and stayed there, clasping each other tight.

Mr. Samsa turned in his chair to look at them and quietly observed them for a little. Then he called out; "Come along, now, do. Let bygones be bygones. And you might have some consideration for me." The two of them complied at once, hastened to him, caressed him and quickly finished their letters.

Then they all three left the apartment together, which was more than they had done for months, and went by tram into the open country outside the town. The tram, in which they were the only passengers, was filled with warm sunshine. Leaning comfortably back in their seats they canvassed their prospects for the future, and it appeared on closer inspection that these were not at all bad, for the jobs they had got, which so far they had never really discussed with each other were all three admirable and likely to lead to better things later on. The greatest immediate improvements in their condition would of course arise from moving to another house; they wanted to take a smaller and cheaper but also better situated and more easily run apartment than the one they had, which Gregor had selected. While they were thus conversing, it struck both Mr. and Mrs. Samsa, almost at the same moment, as they became aware of their daughter's increasing vivacity, that in spite of all the sorrow of recent times, which had made her cheeks pale, she had bloomed into a pretty girl with a good figure. They grew quieter and half unconsciously exchanged glances of complete agreement, having come to the conclusion that it would soon be time to find a good husband for her. And it was like a confirmation of her new dreams and excellent intention that at the end of their journey their daughter sprang to her feet first and stretched her young body.

Part III: The African Perspective

African Background

Africa is the second largest continent on the Earth (Asia, the largest). It covers an area of approximately 11¾ million square miles, almost three times the size of the United States. In fact, if the United States, Western Europe, India, and China were put into Africa, they would just about fit. From north to south, the continent is divided almost equally by the equator, but because of the bulge formed by western Africa, the greater part of Africa's territory lies northward. The continent is bordered on the north by the Mediterranean Sea, on the west by the Atlantic Ocean, and on the east by the Indian Ocean, which meets the Atlantic at the Cape of Good Hope. There are a number of islands associated with Africa; the largest of these, lying to the southeast, is Madagascar. In 1990 the population for the entire continent was estimated to be 647,518,000, about one-eighth of the world's total (*The New Encyclopedia Britannica*, 1995 edition).

Until recently, few African Americans knew very much about Africa even though their ancestors came from the African continent. For some time, teachers have taught the histories of many countries—England, Germany, France, Italy, and others—whose native sons became the ancestors of so many Americans. But the contributions of various African cultures to the American "melting pot" have been somewhat ignored. Most Americans know that Africa is the home of the African American. And the images that readily come to mind at the mention of Africa may include big game animals, dense jungles, naked savages, or witch doctors. However, today they do not provide a balanced or accurate picture of Africa.

In the last few years, dynamic changes have taken place on the African continent. So many new countries have been formed that it is difficult for map makers to keep maps up-to-date. Some years ago there were only a few independent states; today there are many more. Exciting and dramatic news is being made every day in Africa. Newspapers, radio, and television bring events into our homes almost as soon as they happen. Names of people and places, unfamiliar and difficult to pronounce, appear in the headlines. New leaders suddenly appear and often suddenly disappear. African geography has played a major role in shaping Africa's past and creating its present problems. Its topography and climate still affect its economic and social development.

Language seems to be the most dynamic of all cultural traits. The people inhabiting Africa probably speak more languages than those of any other continent. The homogeneous region, in terms of languages, is North Africa, where Arabic is predominant from Egypt to Mauritania and the Sudan. With the Maghreb, along the Mediterranean coast, reside the Berberi-speaking people, concentrated in Morocco and Algeria, but Arabic is also widely used. The languages spoken by the sub-Saharan people are more numerous. With the exception of the Khoisan language family of southwestern Africa, the largest area of sub-Sahara is inhabited by people speaking a number of languages known collectively as Bantu, the major language of the Benue-Congo group of the Niger-Congo family. Between the Arabic-dominated northern region and the Bantu-speaking central and southern Africa, reside groups speaking other languages of the Niger-Congo family. Close proximity to the Arabic culture of the Sahara has influenced West Africans, and in a number of countries Islam is the predominant religion.

In essence, it is partly through language diversity that we can say that one group of people is different from another group. This is especially true in Africa. There is no single African people or way of life. When one speaks about the English, French, or Italians, one has in mind certain features that distinguish these people from other groups. Each has a national language, national heroes, national holidays, and anthems. But this is not altogether true of the African people, African tribes, or states.

Religion plays a significant role in the development of African society. Religious beliefs, not necessarily the kind with which we are familiar, are strong among most Africans. Many Europeans equate Africa's religious beliefs with superstitions and witchcraft. But this is not at all true. There are more than 100 million Africans who practice particular tribal religions (Graff 24). Some believe that everything in the world possesses a spirit. Others believe that many objects have magical powers to do good or evil. These beliefs are passed from generation to generation by the medicine man, witch doctor, or elders. The tribal religions have certain basic elements in common: (1) the belief that the world was created by a single god and (2) the worship of spirits. Spirit worship includes both the ancestral spirits and such objects as statues, rocks, or stacks of wood (Graff 24).

God, as a concept, is as old and universal as the word "human"; the idea of God is inseparable from the idea of humankind. Whether God made man in his own image or whether it is the other way around, the African has always believed that there is God, the being to whom he attributes all creation. In Africa, human life is very much conditioned by a person's relation to God. According to Mbonu Ojike, when one uses the word "heathen" in describing Africans, one makes a great philosophical blunder (180). One unifying belief-system in African culture is Animism. However, this religious philosophy does not make any one human being the center of religious worship. Rather, African religion respects virtues, ancestors, and the souls of the dead.

The Islamic faith, founded in the 7th century A.D. by the prophet Mohammed, is the major religion of all the countries north of the Sahara Desert in Africa. Its followers moved south during the next few centuries and made many converts in West Africa, especially in the Sudan; in Central Africa, north of the Congo River; and in the countries along the Indian Ocean, from Somalia to Tanzania. The Moslem religion spread faster than the Christian religion because Islam was not associated in the native mind with the White man's imperialism. In the late 18th century, Protestant and Roman Catholic missionaries from England, Germany, Scotland, and elsewhere went to Africa. They took with them Western concepts of education, hygiene, and cultural relationships. Today, not only are millions of Africans Christians, but one million or more Asians, most of whom are of the Hindu faith, live in eastern and southern Africa (Graff 25). These Hindus make up both the commercial and working class in Uganda, Kenya, Tanzania, and other African countries.

Africa contains hundreds of groups of people who speak different languages and feel that they are different from other groups. These groups are parts of the extended families called "tribes." The tribe is more essential to an African than the nation in which he lives. For example, Africans regard themselves as members of a tribe before they think of themselves as Kenyan or Ghanaian.

Some of the larger tribes are spread over several African countries. The Bakongo, for instance, live in Angola and the Republic of Congo. This tribal dispersion resulted when the conquering Europeans imposed artificial divisions among them. Tribes are different from each other in many ways. Whether large or small, strong or weak, each tribe is ruled by a chief who has a great deal of authority. Africans are fiercely loyal to their chief. In some parts of Africa, closely related tribes elect a "supreme chief" as their leader or ruler.

Family and tribal relations are essential to the African. The basic unit of society in sub-Saharan Africa is the family. However, it is a much larger unit than the European or American family. It is made up of all the descendants of a grandparent or great-grandparent and their wives or husbands and children. The head of such an extended family is often the oldest male member of the group, who controls other members and who is responsible for their well-being. The elder takes care of the every-day needs of his family, is the spokesman of the household on the village council, and is also the family priest. All these units of families within families cooperate in almost all their affairs.

In post-colonial, self-governing Africa, tribal life began to change. As a result of improved education and transportation, which connected both areas and people, the influences of tribal chiefs over their subjects slowly decreased, and governments replaced tribal loyalty with national loyalty. Modern medical care is being increased, thus reducing the hold of the tribal priest or medicine man. New ideas about government, politics, science, and religion are helping to change the Africans' relations to their tribe. However, in spite of all these pressures, customs and traditions still continue to bind many Africans to their age-old ways.

In most African societies, marriage is often a matter of custom and convenience. Marriage can assume any one of the three basic forms. Monogamy unites one man with one woman only, but a society cannot be characterized as monogamous unless plural marriages are either frowned upon or forbidden. Polyandry unites one woman with two or more husbands. However, polyandry is virtually nonexistent in Africa, and monogamy, except in cases of European influence, is confined almost exclusively to the Berbers of North Africa, who are the monophysitic Christians of Ethiopia and the remnant of hunting peoples. Polygamy (polygyny) unites one man with two or more wives. Polygamy is still the preferred form of marriage in African societies. Many African women like this arrangement, for it means sharing among several women such work as baby-sitting, pounding corn, and washing clothes. In addition to farming, the chief duties of African women are to cook and raise children.

This conflict between the old and the new likewise expresses itself in literature. The term African literature, as defined by the Nigerian writer Cyprian Ekwensi, is that self-expression in which the psychology behind African thought manifests and in which the philosophy and pattern of culture are easily understood to be of African origin (703). T. R. M. Creighton, a Canadian critic, states that African literature is any work in which an African setting is authentically handled and in which the experiences which originate in Africa are integral (84). Thus African writing is literature recording experiences as seen through the eyes of the African. It may be safe to conclude that African writing is that piece of self-expression in which the psychology behind African thought is manifest and in which African philosophy and patterns of culture can be understood (703).

It may be safe to conclude that African writing is based on the living heritage of African people. It reflects African history as a background of today's events and tomorrow's crises as well as a critique of present-day society. African writing identifies itself, not only with African history and culture but also with the African's aspirations, failures, hopes, frustrations, and soul. African literature is important as a reinstatement of dignity and pride which Blacks lost through slavery and colonialism. As more and more countries in Africa gain their political independence, there will be a greater desire to re-establish African culture in the modern world.

African literature is understood by most to refer to the written literatures of sub-Saharan Africa. The central irony surrounding African literatures today is that the primary languages of expression are European, not African. This fact has been a consistent source of debate. Modern African literatures are divided into three broad phases, according to Guy Ossito Midiohouan's *L'idéologie dans la littérature négro-Africaine* (1986). The first phase, from 1920 to the mid-1940s, can be characterized as a period of cultural awakening. The second phase extends from 1945 to the early 1960s and covers the independence period for most of sub-Saharan Africa. This was a period of protest and reindictment of the colonial social order. The third phase, from 1960 to the 1980s, turned inward with the emergence of national literatures and literatures written in indigenous African languages.

As African literature moved from its first phase into its second, isolated reactions to the colonial structure by writers, such as Rene Maran or Aimé Césaire were joined by Mongo Beti, Wole Soyinka, Chinua Achebe, and others as literary production in European languages began to take root. The primary factors contributing to the acceptance of European languages were the scholastic system, the publishing infrastructure, and the cross-cultural milieu. African writers did not enter the international literary arena devoid of influences from their own culture. They carried with them an array of indigenous, oral aesthetic patterns that they applied to their creative work, as well as models for the production and dissemination of written literature. The applications resulted in an outlook which downplayed individuality and embraced the social responsibility of authors. This outlook also accounts for a high level of non-literary involvement by successful writers. For instance, renowned poet Léopold Sédar Senghor became president of Senegal; prolific Nigerian writer Chinua Achebe not only became an outspoken social critic, but also he has worked to develop the broadcast media in Nigeria; Nobel Prize-winner Wole Soyinka is noted for his cultural analyses. Other writers such as Ngugi Wa Thiong'o and N. Y. Mudimbe have bridged the gaps between creative writing, social criticism, and philosophy.

In the third phase, covering the emergence of national literatures, many writers relate through their "Africannes"; they articulate a national literature shaped by their country's political and social history. For example, Ngugi Wa Thiong'o from Kenya is one of the best-known early proponents of both the use of African languages in literature and the shift toward national literatures. Many writers from three of the most productive nations, Nigeria, Ghana, and Senegal, include: Chinua Achebe, Cyprian Ekwensi, Flora Nwapa, Wole Soyinka, Efu Sutherland, Mariama Ba, Sembene Ousmane, and Léopold Sédar Senghor.

During the colonial period, female participation was not favored in the educational system. As a result, there is a lack of involvement by women as published writers until the third phase in the development of African literatures. Flora Nwapa is the earliest widely-published woman writer. Her first novel, *Efuru*, appeared in 1966. Other women writers soon followed, including Mariama Ba, Rebeka Njau, Bessie Head, and Ellen Kuzwayo of South Africa. One contemporary African woman writer of this third phase is Simi Bedford, who published *Yoruba Girl Dancing* (1992). African women writers face the same issues that other women face in their struggle to write and publish within male-dominated territories.

The social involvement of African writers, previously mentioned, has been well documented over the years. This involvement in the form of a critique is reflected in the language issue that continues to be important for African writers seeking to balance the need to speak in their authentic voices and the need to reach publishing outlets that are largely outside of Africa. There is a strong link between language and literature that has both cultural and ideological implications. As Abiola Irele states in *The African Experience in Literature and Ideology* (1981), the African writer cannot have full possession of African literature as long as it is elaborated in a language that does not belong to the original or authentic voice.

Nations throughout sub-Saharan Africa are recognized for the epics, legends, stories, fables, riddles, and proverbs so much a part of their oral tradition. Written African literature remains grounded in many of these traditional expressive forms of culture, and this fact creates an on-going challenge for those seeking to categorize and evaluate these literatures.

African art includes the visuals arts, performing arts, and literary arts of native Africa, particularly of the sub-Saharan or black Africa. All familiar media—sculpture, painting, architecture, textiles and other fabrics, costume, jewelry, music, dance, drama, and poetry—are found. What gives art in Africa its special character is the immediate interrelationship between art and other social forms and the variety of art styles; each form is developed in its own particular ecological, historical, and social circumstances. Contemporary African artists, living and working in a modern urban environment, have all the richness of these cultural traditions upon which to draw. However, they may employ different techniques and enjoy a different kind of patronage than did their traditional counterparts.

Usually, when one thinks of African art, one thinks of sculpture. However, the earliest evidence of art is provided by 5,000 year-old engravings and paintings on rock surfaces in the Sahara. In the areas in which Islam and Oriental Christianity linked Africa to the rest of the world in pre-colonial times, architecture predominates among the visual arts. Included here are parts of western and eastern Africa, taking in the magnificent mosques built in Mali; the rock-hewn churches of Ethiopia; and the Islamic monuments of coastal eastern Africa. In areas where pastoral culture predominates, emphasis is placed upon personal and aesthetic values. Among the agricultural peoples of western and central Africa, who share the great river system of the Niger and Congo, sculpture dominates the visual arts.

The performing arts—dance, drama, and music—are as pervasive in African culture as the visual arts. Perhaps the most distinctive features of African music are the complexity of rhythmic patterning achieved by a variety of drums and the relationship between melodic form and language tone structure. Without this relationship, the text of a song is rendered meaningless, but even in purely instrumental music, melodic pattern is likely to follow speech tone.

The literary arts are probably the most universal and the most highly regarded of arts in Africa. They include myths, folktales, chants, proverbs, and, above all, poetry. These are the arts most inaccessible to outsiders, which probably explains why comparatively little attention has been given to them. Most of these forms are oral, but written literatures have existed for several centuries in Hausa, Swahili, and Amharic. In the present century written literatures in other African languages, as well as English, French, and Portuguese, have developed.

Selected Bibliography

"Africa." *The New Encyclopedia Britannica.* 1995.

Andrews, William L., Frances Smith Foster, and Trudier Harris, eds. *The Oxford Companion to African American Literature.* New York: Oxford University Press, 1997.

Creighton, T. R. M. "Attempt To Define African Literature." *African Literature and the Universities.* Ed. Gerald Moore. Ibadan: Ibadan UP, 1965. 84–88.

Ekwensi, Cyprian. "The Dilemma of the African Writers." *West African Review* 27 (1956): 701–704, 708.

Graff, Edward, ed. *Africa: History, Culture, People.* New York: Cambridge Book Company, 1971.

Ojike, Mbonu. *My Africa.* New York: John Day, 1946.

African Poetry

East Africa! West Africa! Central Africa! North Africa! South Africa!

Yoruba hunting songs (*ijala*), Pembe verse, Tishi proverbs, Lango folktales, Bantu praise poems, Bantu poetry, Tiv songs, Nsukka dirges, Chopi poetry, Swahili verse, Ewe dirges, Zulu lyrics, Akkan dirges, Ambo songs, Luo *nyatiti*, Akamba stories, Thonga tales, Somali poetry, *tenzi*—within various cultures is a variety of genres: praise poetry, military, political, hunting, religious, wedding songs, love poems, liturgical verse.

The sweeping vastness of Africa—the second largest continent on earth—embraces diverse cultures and various types of poetry. As the breadth and scope of African poetry range the continent, so does the poetry range over time—historically, culturally, and socially, reaching back to the tradition of oral literature which is the progenitor of modern African poetry. Oral literature is that single characteristic which links the diversity of modern poetry.

Some of the specific characteristics of oral literature are that (1) the poem is for performance; (2) events are often narrated in the third person; (3) there is frequent use of interjections, exclamations, epithets; (4) ideas are presented with references to human life; and (5) problems and incidents are presented in terms of conflict or competition. These characteristics give the oral literature of Africa its commonality with oral literature of other cultures and societies. Where the difference lies is in the multitude of languages, words and phrases, stylistic devices, a variety of structures, interpretations, and improvisations.

As all critics and creative writers concur that poetry is oral-aural, modern poetry is no different. Therefore, using these characteristics of oral literature enables the modern poet to bridge the gap between traditional and modern. The continuity of this bridge is that poetry in all cultures continues to be for a public audience. Thus the reason poetry is so popular is that it is a physical, intellectual, emotional, and often spiritual sharing between poet and reader/listener. Also, poetry serves important functions in daily life; consequently, these functions prompt a variety of themes. The diversity of themes is also prompted by the diversity of cultures.

Just as the themes of oral literature embrace the daily aspects of life (hunting, war, marriage, politics, ethnic customs), so does written modern poetry embrace the vicissitudes of modern life. Let it be noted that the emergence of written modern poetry in English, which is the major focus of this discussion, began approximately 50 to 60 years ago. Some of the major themes of modern African poetry are family life, education, money problems, human relationships, moral values, politics, modern versus traditional, war, famine, civil strife, exile, imprisonment, dictators, and inhumanity. Like versifiers of all cultures and of all times, African poets feel the need to protest their social conditions. Yet amidst the "bad and ugly" themes of anger, there are themes which express the good of life, such as love, aspirations, recovery, renewal, hope, pride in self and ethnicity, and country.

As intimated in the preceding paragraph, the literary motifs are influenced by cultural, political, and socio-economic climates, and because of the shifting of these climates, poets are forced to pen their thoughts and feelings about the conflicts. The foremost of these conflicts is the fight for independence. Just as Africans are wresting freedom from the colonialists in the West, the poets are wrestling with other problems, debating the age-old questions for writers everywhere. Should literature be art for art's sake or should literature be propagandistic/political or written in a second language? Even when the poets write in a second language, they draw upon the images, symbols, customs, folk heroes, and folk myths of Africa. In spite of these internal conflicts, most poets think it is an utmost necessity to poeticize their opinions on colonialism and/or the cultural conflicts, traditional versus modern. While the themes of African poetry deal with indigenous subjects, style and structure are directly and indirectly influenced by English and American poets; Christopher Ogkibo is said to be influenced by T. S. Eliot, John P. Clark imitates Gerard Manley Hopkins. Robert Frost, Ezra Pound, William Yeats, W.H. Auden, and Dylan Thomas are just a few of the non-Black poets who are studied by African poets. Of course, Claude McKay, Countee Cullen, and Langston Hughes are major influences. Hughes has inspired and promoted many poets by publishing his two anthologies: *An African Treasury* and *Poems from Black Africa*.

In addition to the influence of colonialism and/or cultural conflicts on the poetry of Africa, another major thematic influence is the Negritude Movement. Aimé Césaire (Martinique), Leon Damas (French Guyana), and Léopold Sédar Senghor (Senegal), expatriates living and studying in Paris, developed the concept of Negritude, which, in essence, is a call to all Black Africans, those at home and those living on other continents, to eschew all Western values and to assert their Africanness. Emmanuel Obeichina declares Negritude as the right for the African intellectual to protest the colonialist's assimilationist policy and to prove to the colonialist that African culture is not inferior to Western culture but is basically superior. While some call Senghor the chief theoretician of the movement, Césaire is called the chief poet. Cesaire, who coined the term Negritude, succinctly and clearly outlines the concept of the movement in three statements: (1) Black identity is affirmed and accepted; (2) Africa is acknowledged as the source of African peoples' historical, spiritual, and cultural origins; and (3) Africans are united with each other and the rest of the world. Césaire's magnus opus "Cahier d'un Retour au Pays Natal" sets the tone for the movement as it reiterates these three concepts.

It must be mentioned that while the Francophone writers of Africa, the Caribbean, and Western Europe espoused Negritude, there were similar movements in Haiti, Cuba (Negrismo), and the United States (Harlem Renaissance). All of these movements had a profound influence and laid the groundwork for the Black Aesthetic Movement in the United States during the 1960s.

Despite the multitude of factors which affect the study and understanding of modern African poetry, it is important to remember that understanding African poetry, as with all poetry, is to understand African culture and African history, therefore reading with an openness and not with attitudes of ignorance and stereotypical misinformation. Therefore, one should know the history and culture, which will help in understanding the images and symbols. Knowing that the literature reflects the peoples' customs and behavior is also important.

Selected Bibliography

Boyce Davis, Carole and Anne Adam Graves. *Ngambika: Studies of Women in African Literature.* Trenton, NJ: Africa World Press, 1986.

Cook, David. *African Literature: A Critical View.* London: Longman, 1977.

Goodwin, Ken. *Understanding African Poetry: A Study of Ten Poets.* London: Heinemann, 1982.

Gunner, Elizabeth. *A Handbook for Teaching African Literature.* Nairobi: Heinemann, 1984. Rpt. 1989.

James, Adeola. *In Their Own Voices: African Women Writers Talk.* Portsmouth, NH: Heinemann, 1990.

Maja-Pearce, Adewale. *The Heinemann Book of African Poetry in English.* Portsmouth, NH: Heinemann, 1990.

Moore, Gerald, and Ulli Beier. *The Penguin Book of African Poetry.* 3rd ed. New York: Viking/Penguin, 1984.

Obiechina, Emmanuel. *Language and Theme: Essays on African Literature.* Washington, DC: Howard University Press, 1990.

Olney, James. *Tell Me Africa: An Approach to African Literature.* Princeton, NJ: Princeton University Press, 1973.

Wanjala, Chris. *Standpoints on African Literature: A Critical Anthology.* Nairobi: East African Literature Bureau, 1973.

Tsegaye Gabre-Medhen (1935–)

Tsegaye Gabre-Medhen, born in 1935, is a native of Ethiopia. He has served as the Director of Ethiopia's Haile Selassie Theater and is best known for his play *The Oda-Oak Oracle: a Legend of Black Peoples, Told of Gods and God, of Hope and Love, and of Fear and Sacrifices.* Gabre-Medhen's poem "Home-Coming Son" also expresses a theme of hope and love for the exile who is cautioned to walk with pride while listening to the welcoming call of the ancestral spirits.

Selected Bibliography

Miller, James E., Jr., Robert O'Neal, and Helene McDonnell. *Black African Voices.* Glenview, IL: Scott, Foresman, 1970.

Home-Coming Son

Tsegaye Gabre-Medhen

Look where you walk, unholy stranger—
this is the land of the eighth harmony
in the rainbow: Black.
It is the dark side of the moon
brought to light; 5
this is the canvas of God's master stroke.

Out, out of your foreign outfit, unholy stranger—
feel part of the great work of art.
Walk in peace, walk alone, walk tall,
walk free, walk naked. 10
Let the feelers of your motherland
caress your bare feet,
let Her breath kiss your naked body.
But watch, watch where you walk, forgotten stranger—
this is the very depth of your roots: Black. 15

Where the tom-toms of your fathers vibrated
in the fearful silence of the valleys,
shook in the colossus bodies of the mountains,
hummed in the deep chests of the jungles.
Walk proud. 20
Watch, listen to the calls of the ancestral spirits, prodigal son—
to the call of the long-awaiting soil.
They welcome you home, home. In the song of birds
you hear your suspended family name,
the winds whisper the golden names of your tribal warriors, 25
the fresh breeze blown into your nostrils
floats their bones turned to dust.
Walk tall. The spirits welcome
their lost-son-returned.
Watch, and out of your foreign outfit, brother, 30
feel part of the work of art.
Walk in laughter, walk in rhythm, walk tall,
walk free, walk naked.
Let the roots of your motherland caress your body,
let the naked skin absorb the home-sun and shine ebony. 35

Message To Mputu Antoinette, Girl Of The Bush, Friend Of My Childhood

Tshakatumba

African sister black sister
you who do not know Damas or Mackay
you who must learn Césaire and Senghor
you who are ignorant of the boundaries of your continent
and in the half-light go to draw water 5
like an ancient goddess
wearing an Edenic smile
at the only spring in the neighborhood
it is for you above all that I labor
it is for you that the cold benumbs me 10
sister of the sapodilla tree loving sister
Africa will be the fruit of our accord.

Tireless gazelle
who wanders at the close of day
through the hushed thickets of dead wood you gather 15
O black woman! guileless sister
your beanty touches me your beauty enchants me
like the blue wave simmering
in your unfathomable depths
To see moored beneath the intertwined lianas 20
a continent moored in a trance
where the tom-toms beat out the rhythm of life
O loving friend in the giant encrusted lokumé:
Africa will be what together we make it.

Lenrie Peters (1932–)

Lenrie Peters was born in Bathurst (now Banjul) in Gambia. After his elementary schooling there, he moved to his parents' native home in Sierra Leone, where he obtained a Higher School Certificate from Freetown's Prince of Wales School. Entering Trinity College at Cambridge in 1952 where he studied medicine, Peters passed his qualifying examinations in 1959. He then specialized in surgery at a hospital in Guildford, England, for ten years. In 1969 he returned to Banjul, Gambia, to practice as a surgeon, but he is also well known as a singer and broadcaster. He has participated in BBC Programmes, in "Calling West Africa," and was chairman of its "Africa Forum."

Recognized as an urbanized poet, Peters has published a novel set in Freetown, *The Second Round* (1965), and several volumes of poetry: *Poems* (1964), *Satellite* (1967), and *Katchikali* (1971). While Peters' poems reveal his estrangement, the poems also express his feelings of dignity. Wilfred Cartey explains that Peters' "Homecoming" and "We Have Come Home" are not jubilant songs celebrating homecoming, but ones in which, through the contrast of exile and return, of deception and promise, the poet evokes the pathos of homecoming, the resilience of the spirit that comes back to the beauty of the African continent. It is quite evident from "Homecoming" as well as Peters' other poems that, though he writes in English within the European tradition, he uses African themes and images in his poetry.

Selected Bibliography

Goodwin, Ken. *Understanding African Poetry: A Study of Ten Poets.* Exeter, N.H.: Heinemann Educational Books, 1982.

Maja-Pearce, Adewale, ed. *Heineman Book of African Poetry in English.* Portsmouth, N.H.: Heinemann, 1990.

Moore, Gerald and Ulli Beier, eds. *Penguin Book of Modern African Poetry.* 3rd ed. New York: Viking/Penguin, 1984.

Homecoming

Lenrie Peters (*Gambia*)

The present reigned supreme
   Like the shallow floods over the gutters
Over the raw paths where we had been,
   The house with the shutters.

Too strange the sudden change   5
   Of the times we buried when we left
The times before we had properly arranged
   The memoirs that we kept.

Our sapless roots have fed
   The wind-swept seedlings of another age.   10
Luxuriant weeds have grown where we led
   The Virgins to the water's edge.

There at the edge of the town
   Just by the burial ground
Stands the house without a shadow   15
   Lived in by new skeletons.
That is all that is left
   To greet us on the home coming
After we have paced the world
   And longed for returning.   20

Francis Ernest Kobina Parkes (1932–)

The third name of Francis Ernest Kobina Parkes—*Kobina*—is derived from the fact that he was born on a Tuesday to an Akan mother. This name is assigned to all Akan males born on Tuesday. Mr. Parkes was born in Accra, Ghana, in 1932. He has had a variety of work experiences: television script writer, publicity man, newspaper editor, press attaché to the Ministry of Information, radio producer with Radio Ghana, and president of the Ghana Society of Writers. However, Mr. Parkes is most lauded for his volume of poetry, *Songs from the Wilderness* (1965), which focuses significantly on the future of the new Africa upon its independence from colonial rule. His poem "Africa Heaven" is a perceptive embracing of Negritude—the movement of Black African assertion which permeated Western Europe and Africa during the mid-twentieth century.

Selected Bibliography

Hughes, Langston, ed. *Poems from Black Africa.* Bloomington, IN: Indiana University Press, 1969.

African Heaven

Francis E. K. Parkes (*Ghana*)

    Give me black souls,
    Let them be black
    Or chocolate brown
    Or make them the
    Color of dust— 5
    Dustlike,
    Browner than sand,
    But if you can
    Please keep them black,
    Black. 10
    Give me some drums;
    Let them be three
    Or maybe four
    And make them black—
    Dirty and black: 15
    Of wood,
    And dried sheepskin,
    But if you will
    Just make them peal,
    Peal. 20

    Peal loud,
    Mutter.
    Loud,
    Louder yet;
    Then soft, 25
    Softer still
    Let the drums peal.
    Let the calabash
    Entwined with beads
    With blue Aggrey beads 30
    Resound, wildly
    Discordant,
    Calmly
    Melodious.
    Let the calabash resound 35

In tune with the drums.
Mingle with these sounds
The clang
Of wood on tin:
Kententsekenken 40
Ken-tse ken ken ken:
Do give me voices
Ordinary
Ghost voices
Voices of women 45
And the bass
Of men.

Let there be dancers,
Broad-shouldered Negroes
Stamping the ground 50
With naked feet
And half-covered
Women
Swaying, to and fro,
In perfect 55
Rhythm
To *"Tom shikishiki"*
And *"ken,"*
And voices of ghosts
Singing, 60
Singing!
Let there be
A setting sun above,
Green palms
Around, 65
A slaughtered fowl
And plenty of
Yams.

And dear Lord,
If the place be 70
Not too full,
Please
Admit spectators.
They may be
White or 75
Black.

Admit spectators
That they may
See:
The bleeding fowl, 80
And yams,
And palms
And dancing ghosts.
Odomankoma,
Do admit spectators 85

That they may
Hear:
Our native songs,
The clang of wood on tin
The tune of beads 90
And the pealing drums.

Twerampon, please, please
Admit
Spectators!
That they may 95
Bask
In the balmy rays
Of the
Evening Sun,
In our lovely 100
African heaven!

Rebekah Njau (1932–)

Rebekah Njau was born at Kanyiriri in Kenya's Kiambu District and has spent most of her life teaching or being taught. She was educated at Alliance Girl's High School and Makerere University. She taught at A.G.H.S. and Makerere College School before becoming founding Headmistress of Nairobi Girls Secondary School. Her husband, Elimo Njau of Tanzania, is a leading artist and cultural innovator in East Africa. Njau herself is artistic in that she enjoys textile designing and picture-making. Although as a child she was determined to be an actress, Njau is better known for her prize-winning play *The Scar* (1965), another play *In the Round Chain*, and a novel *Ripples in the Pool* (1975). She has edited with Gideon Mulaki a collection of essays, folktales, and fables, *Kenyan Women Heroes and Their Mystical Powers* (1984).

In an interview from Adeola James' *In Their Own Voices,* Njau claims that African literature must be functional, not art for art's sake. This literature must speak directly about social and economic ills, keeping in mind that their primary audience will be young students. Njau's poem "Prayer for a Modern Woman," which appears at the beginning of *Kenyan Women Heroes,* reflects a theme similar to the one in *Ripples in the Pool*. The theme in both the poem and the novel emphasizes an African woman's liberation from her traditional roles and the problems resulting from cultural conflicts. The women portrayed in "The Village," a poem Njau wrote under the pen name of Marina Gashe, are a stark contrast to the women in "Prayers for a Modern Woman" because the village women live in a village of grueling drudgery. They, too, have prayers but not the kind that their modern sisters have.

Selected Bibliography

Hughes, Langston, ed. *Poems from Black Africa.* Bloomington, IN: Indiana University Press, 1969.

James, A'deola. *In Their Own Voices: African Women Writers Talk.* Portsmouth, NH: James Currey, 1990.

Killam, G. D. *The Writing of East and Central Africa.* London: Heinemann, 1984.

Njau, Rebekah. *Ripples in the Pool.* London: Heinemann, 1975.

The Village

Marina Gashe (Rebekah Njau)

Kanyariri, Village of Toil,
Village of unending work.
Like a never drying spring,
Old women dark and bent
Trudge along with their hoes   5
To plots of weedy maize.
Young wives like donkeys
From cock crow to setting of the sun
Go about their timeless duties,
Their scraggy figures like bows set in a row,   10
Plod up and down the rolling village farms
With loads on their backs
And babies tied to their bellies.
In the fields all day they toil
Stirring up the soil with hands and knives   15
Like chickens looking for worms.
Nothing here seems to sit still.
Even the village church is like a favourite well
Where the "Revivalists" with their loudspeakers
Never cease calling people   20
To confess their sins and drink the Water of Life.
At dawn men ride away leaving the womenfolk
To fend for the bony goats and the crying children.

Prayer Of A Modern Woman

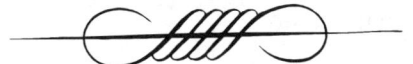

Rebekah Njau

Dear God,
help me to understand myself
help me to come to terms with what I am
for I'm getting more and more confused.
People say I'm blessed to have so much material wealth;   5
I have a beautiful home
and a beautiful large garden;
I also own two cars—a brand new Range-rover
and an almost new Peugeot;
I'm one of the best dressed women in the city   10
I have everything I need to make life comfortable
My four children are in good schools
and I have a well paid job
but I've no joy in life.

I float here and there   15
looking for something big to occupy me;
I thirst for this and that;
I move from club to club
looking for a firm base to place my feet;
Today I join the golf club,   20
Tomorrow I move to a tennis club
And when I feel too depressed
I fly to Mombasa for a swim in the ocean;
but the more I search for peace
the more I get frustrated.   25

My husband is a big boss in a company
He is a respectable gentleman at work
but he has become a big headache to me;
He is never in the house when I need him;
If he is not travelling abroad   30
He is in the bars every evening
to listen, as he says, to the latest political gossip;
He tells me a man of his position
must know what is going on around him

but I doubt this is the reason he frequents the bars
Last week I decided to find out what he is up to
I started following him to the bars
which makes me feel like a fool;
It humiliates me
I feel like a rotten mushroom
all shrivelled up;
I'm in a dilemma
I don't know what to do.

A few months ago
I attended a women's club
which is trying to help women in the rural areas
to uplift their standard of living;
We visited some of these women at their small farms
and when I saw how strong in spirit they were,
When I saw how unconcerned they were
With the kind of things that rule my life
When I saw
they weren't bothered with things like
What dress was in fashion
What hairstyle to adopt
What class of people to be seen with
What kind of car to drive;
When I saw how real
They were to themselves;
I felt shrunken
because I knew, poor as they were in material wealth,
I needed their help more than they needed mine.
I needed to understand what it was that
gave them spiritual strength;
I needed to know what made them look confident
and so unafraid of reality;
I realised their physical poverty
was nothing compared with my mental and spiritual hunger;
I realised I was like a creature
with no identity of its own
I was in chains
I was a prisoner of my own making.

So, Lord, help me
to go back to my roots and find out who I am
Help me to discard the props I've made for myself
So that in understanding who I am
I might help my children to understand who they are
and where they come from.

Francesca Yetunde Pereira (1933–)

Francesca Yetunde Pereira, the daughter of Brazilian repatriates, was born in Lagos, Nigeria in 1933. After graduating with honors from University College in London, England, in 1959, she returned to Lagos to work as an administrative officer with the Federal Service. Pereira is a short story writer as well as a poet, having won first prize for a short story which she entered in the Nigerian Broadcasting contest. She participated as a folk singer at the American Society of African Culture Festival of the Arts in 1961 in Lagos. None other than Wole Soyinka, Nigerian dramatist, accompanied her on the guitar at this festival.

Selected Bibliography

Hughes, Langston, ed. *Poems from Black Africa.* Bloomington, IN: Indiana University Press, 1969.

Mother Dark

Francesca Yetunde Pereira

Mother Land
Long lain asleep
Her people loved
They lived
And killed to live   5
By Nature's law.

Souls to save
The strangers sought,
Riches, some knowledge,
They named her "Dark"   10
Yes, dark was she
In every sense was dark.
They brought "The Light"
And with the light
She saw her children   15
Led in chains
Their wearied steps
Quickened by
The lash of Cain.

The light-bearers   20
Hooded with repentance
Philanthropy
With glib tongue
Took the land
Claimed rulers   25
With gifts of tinsel
Paltry gifts
With crumbs they fed
The children of dark.
The bearers of the light   30
Ate succulent steak.

Mother Dark
She was dark, very dark
Cried out
And her voice shook all the world,   35
Free my people
Set my sons and daughters
Free!

The bearers of light
Made bold retreat   40
Silent dignified farewell
Pomp and splendour, saving grace
The spoilt child
Amidst a thousand shells
Withdrew.   45

Mother Dark
Her rulers chose
All branded with her mark.
Alas! They learned too well the "light"
Then brought home the yoke.   50
Mother Dark
Her wounded heart
Wailed loud in pain,
Is there no hope?
My children perish!   55
But her voice is not heard
For her children now
Oppress her children.

The Paradox

Francesca Yetunde Pereira

     The cross, the icon
     The disciples fought
     They are still fighting
     The whiteman claims
     His god supreme   5
     And blackman muses
White god, in reason can I hope for grace bestowed,
The disciples fought. They are still fighting, maybe
Somewhere in white clouds, somewhere in blackest
Abyss, the white god and the black god dumb,   10
     Look silently on.
     The disciples fought
     They all of them join
     Battle, fierce raging,
     Each god is mighty.   15
They must be. It must be. The world is constant in its chaos.
The world is crumbling and all gods are silent. Evil begets
Good begets evil. Watching. Wenching Eves, empty headed apes
Demanding, exacting. Their folly drowning in spirits flowing.
     And the Infant, crying   20
     For the dried-up stream
     The lapped-up stream
     Caked stream of life
     Is milked in a manger
     Sawdust and straw.   25
     Cool breeze fleeting
     Past suspense, hope,
     And prophecy. Empty.
The age old tree without, magnificent, proudly stands
Its yellowing leaves waft to and fro against the deep   30
Blue sky. The mind persists in calmness, and frenzy
Beats a wild resounding drum within the tortured heart.
     Learn patience
     O frenzied drumbeat
     Be still and rein   35
     Thyself. Advent of

　　　　Destiny. Wildly yours.
　　　　Then canst thou beat
　　　　Wild wild refrain
　　　　And drum and dance　　　　　　　　　　　40
　　　　For joy. Or rend
　　　　Dumb heavens with
　　　　Thy woes. The age
　　　　Old tree, the cheery
　　　　Room, the bright blue　　　　　　　　　　45
　　　　Sky above. The drum
　　　　Still blind, beats on.
The fevered drum still blind beats wildly fiercely on.
No crumbs fall from the orgies of the rich. Eves and apes
With licentious smell trampling the earth.　　　　　　　50
Under their feet the bones of infants. Disciples still
Fighting. Each god is mighty. The world is crumbling. And gods
　　are silent.

Léopold Sédar Senghor (1906–)

Léopold Sédar Senghor, considered by most critics as the most illustrious of African poets, is certainly the best known because of his success as poet, linguist, teacher, and diplomat. Before Senegal gained independence from France, Senghor was a deputy for Senegal in the French National Assembly in Paris, a minister in the French Government, a member of the Council of Europe, and president of the Mali Federal Assembly. Upon the independence of Senegal in 1960, Senghor was installed as the first president of the Republic of Senegal, a position he held until his retirement in 1981.

In addition to his political successes, Senghor is well known because his name is synonymous with Negritude, a movement of Black cultural assertion. While studying in Paris, he met Aimé Césaire from Martinique and Leon Gontran Damas from French Guyana, and the three formulated the concept of the affirmation of Black African identity or, to use Senghor's word, the "revalorization" of African culture.

Born in 1906 into a Roman Catholic family in Joal, Senegal (which is a predominantly Muslim country), Senghor was afforded a superior education by his father, who was a groundnut merchant. He did exceptionally well at the lycee in Dakar and then attended the Lycee Louis le Grand in Paris. He was the first West African to win a degree at the Sorbonne.

The themes of Negritude are prevalent in the poetry of Senghor: (1) the pervasive presence of the dead and their protective guiding influence upon the living ("Night of Sine"), (2) the devastation of ancient Africa and its culture by White Europe ("Paris in the Snow"), (3) the harsh rigidity of the modern West and its desperate need for the complementing qualities of Africa ("New York"), and (4) the warm triumphant beauty of African woman ("You Held the Black Face"). Senghor's poetry also exemplifies his appreciation and understanding of Western achievements and his need to be "a cultural mulatto," a Senegalese and a European Frenchman (Moore and Beier, 19). Despite his very busy political career, Senghor published four volumes of poetry—*Chants d'ombres* (1945), *Ethiopiques* (1956), *Hosties noires* (1958), and *Nocturnes* (1961); he edited an anthology of African poetry and wrote many articles. His works have been published by Editions du Seuil in Paris.

Selected Bibliography

Wanjala, Chris L. *Standpoints on African Literature: A Critical Anthology*. Nairobi: East African Literature Bureau, 1973.

Zell, Hans M. and Helene Silver. *A Reader's Guide to African Literature*. New York: Africana, 1971.

Night Of Sine

Léopold Sédar Senghor

Woman, rest on my brow your soothing hands, your hands
  softer than fur.
Up above the swaying palm trees scarcely rustle in the
  high night breeze.
Not even a lullaby.
Let the rhythmic silence cradle us.
Let us listen to its song, let us listen to the beat of
  our dark blood, let us listen
To the deep pulse of Africa beating in the midst of
forgotten villages.

Now the weary moon sinks toward her bed in the quiet sea
Now the bursts of laughter grow sleepy, the
  story-tellers themselves
Are nodding their heads like babies on the backs of their mothers
Now the feet of the dancers grow heavy, and heavy the
  voices of the alternating choruses.

This is the hour of stars and of the night who dreams
And reclines on the hill of clouds, wrapped in her long
  millky cloth.
The roofs of the huts gleam tenderly. What do they
  say, so confidentially, to the stars?
Inside, the fire dies out among intimate smells bitter and sweet.
Woman, light the lamp of clear oil, that the Ancestors may
  gather about and talk like parents when children are sleeping.
Let us listen to the voices of the Ancients of
  Elissa. Like us, exiled,
They did not want to die and let the torrent of their
  seed be lost in the desert sands.
Let me listen in the smoky hut where welcome spirits visit,
My head on your breast which is warm like a *dang*
  just taken steaming from the fire,
Let me breathe the smell of our Dead, let me recall and
  repeat their living voice, let me learn to
Live before descending, deeper than a diver, into the
  lofty depths of sleep.

The Totem

Léopold Sédar Senghor

I must hide him deep in my veins
The Ancestor with the skin of a tempest streaked by
   lightning and thunder
My Guardian-Animal, I must hide him
Lest I burst the dam of scandals.   5
He is my faithful blood who requires fidelity
Protecting my naked pride against
Myself and the insolence of happy races.

David Diop (1927–1960)

As David Diop and his wife were returning from a vacation in France, they were killed in an airplane crash off the coast of Senegal in 1960, and his manuscripts were destroyed. Therefore, only a volume of poetry *Coups de pillon* (1956), published by Presence Africaine, and some poems included in Léopold Senghor's *Anthologie de la nouvelle poesie negre et malgache* are left. Nevertheless, it is clear from these extant pieces that Diop's poetry expresses simultaneously an intense opposition to European influence on African society and equally intense love of Africa and its people.

Although he was only 33 years old at the time of his death, Diop was recognized as one of the most promising and talented of West Africa's younger French poets. Usually labeled a West African poet, Diop was actually born in 1927 in Bordeaux, France, to Christian parents—a Cameroonian woman and a Senegalese doctor. Diop received his early education in Senegal but continued his training in France, earning two baccalaureates and a *licence-es-lettres*. He returned to Dakar and taught for a year and then went to Kindia, Guinea, where he served as principal of a secondary school.

Albeit a semi-invalid and frequently hospitalized, Diop did not allow any physical weaknesses to intrude into his poetry. Diop's active mind kept him politically aware of the many movements for independence in the various parts of Africa. He felt the anguish of World War II as he saw many of his fellow countrymen and colleagues suffer in a European war. The effects of this war, his exile from Senegal, as well as the work of Aimé Césaire, are considered the main influences of his writings.

James E. Miller exclaims that Diop's poetry, while fierce in its protest, nonetheless retains a beauty usually associated with art for art's sake. In his poem "Africa," Diop accepts the message of these beginnings and hears the singing of the rebirth of his continent. The poem "The Vultures" shows the poet's disdain for the colonialist who did not succeed in killing hope.

Selected Bibliography

Gunner, Elizabeth. *A Handbook for Teaching African Literature*. London: Heinemann, 1984.
Zell, Hans M. and Helene Silver. *A Reader's Guide to African Literature*. New York: Africana, 1971.

The Vultures

David Diop

In those days
When civilization kicked us in the face
When holy water slapped our tamed foreheads
The vultures built in the shadow of their talons
The blood stained monument of tutelage.   5
In those days
There was painful laughter on the metallic hell of the roads
And the monotonous rhythm of the paternoster
Drowned the howling on the plantations.
O the bitter memories of extorted kisses   10
Of promises broken at the point of a gun
Of foreigners who did not seem human,
Who knew all the books but did not know love.
But we whose hands fertilize the womb of the earth
In spite of your songs of pride   15
In spite of the desolate villages of torn Africa
Hope was preserved in us, as in a fortress,
And from the mines of Swaziland to the factories of Europe
Spring will be reborn under our bright steps.

Africa

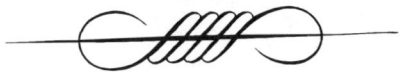

David Diop

Africa, my Africa,
Africa of proud warriors
In ancestral savannas,
Africa of whom my grandmother sings,
On the banks of the distant river 5
I have never known you
But your blood flows in my veins
Your beautiful black blood
That irrigates the fields
The blood of your sweat 10
The work of your slavery
The slavery of your children.
Africa, tell me, Africa,
Is this you, this back that is bent,
This back that breaks 15
Under the weight of humiliation
This back trembling with red scars
Saying *yes* to the whip under the midday sun?
A grave voice answers me:
Impetuous son, this tree, young and strong, 20
This tree there in splendid islolation
Amidst white and faded flowers,
That is Africa, your Africa,
That grows again, patiently, obstinately
As its fruit gradually acquires 25
The bitter taste of liberty.

African Narrative

During the 20th century, the intellectual movements in Africa have been associated, in one way or another, with nationalism. In other words, nationalism and modern African literature have followed closely parallel courses, both being a part of an awakening and a search for a new place in the world for the African. Written literature was already appearing on the continent as early as the beginning of the century. Although the roots of this literature can be traced back to African-American writing of the 18th and 19th centuries, this tradition with its distinctive characteristics did not emerge until the early 1950s.

Culture and language dominate all aspects of reality in the African narrative, both as formal and contextual concerns. That is, the narrative process focuses on the conflicts that inform society as they are represented in language. The language becomes more than the outer shell of meaning; it is the primary subject of the novel in the sense that all the key issues that concern society—the status of women, power politics, clan struggle, culture, and domination—are reflected in and promoted through language.

The African novel is a creative interpretation of history, beginning at the time of the colonial occupation of the continent. The most convenient classification of the novel, therefore, seems to be according to which aspects of this history particular novels depict. These novels portray the process of colonial domination and recreate the struggle for independence and evoke the post-independence social and political climate. But recent novels tend to portray the social and political conflicts of the post-independence era. The African narrative is writing based on the living heritage of the African people. It reflects African history as a background to today's events and tomorrow's crises. It is also a critique of present-day society and a projection into the future.

The colonial situation strongly influenced the upbringing, education, and fictional subject matter of most African novels. This is certainly true of Chinua Achebe. He has written five novels: *Things Fall Apart* (1958), *No Longer at Ease* (1960), *Arrow of God* (1964), *A Man of the People* (1966), and *Anthills of the Savannah* (1987). They each deal primarily with Nigerian citizens from pre-colonial days to the present.

Things Fall Apart first received attention because of the social purposes Achebe assigned to it and to himself as writer. The novel was published two years before Nigeria's independence was gained in 1960. The timing was perfect. While Africans (Nigerians in this case) looked forward with excitement and optimism to the political freedom they would attain after more than a half century of colonial rule, Achebe understood the necessity of showing his countrymen the strength of their own culture to assist in the task of nation building, a strength greatly diminished by the imposition of an alien culture. The fundamental theme was that African people did not hear of culture for the first time from Europeans; that their societies, rather than being mindless as Europeans claimed, exhibited a philosophy of great depth and value; and that their lives were not only poetic but endowed with dignity. It is this dignity that African people all but lost during the colonial period, and it is this quality that they must regain. Achebe's purpose then is to write about and for his own people.

Achebe states that *Things Fall Apart,* a classic, is a tribute to his past and a recognition that Africa's story is at last being told by an African (Carroll 13). The novel primarily recounts the rich heritage of the villagers of Umuofia, prior to its disintegration at the hands of colonial powers. The protagonist, Okonkwo, determined not to be like his father, embodies the qualities most valued by his people: hard work, energy, purpose, communal cooperation, and individuality.

The novel is divided into three parts. The first thirteen chapters, after presenting lifestyles and traditions, introduce readers to Ikemefuna and define Okonkwo's crisis. The second part, the next six chapters, occurs in Mbanta. The third part, the final six chapters, marks Okonkwo's return to Umuofia and depicts the changes that have occurred during his absence. In essence, *Things Fall Apart* dramatizes traditional Ibo life in its first encounter with both colonialism and Christianity at the turn of the century. *Things Fall Apart,* as the title suggests, reflects the dislocation of African society caused by its collision with another way of life.

Selected Bibliography

Carroll, David. *Chinua Achebe.* New York: St. Martin's Press, 1980.

Gakwandi, Shatlo Arthur. *The Novel and Contemporary Experience in Africa.* New York: Africana, 1977.

Gikandi, Simon. *Reading the African Novel.* Portsmouth, NH: Heinemann, 1987.

Innes, C. L., and Bernth Lindfors, eds. *Critical Perspectives on Chinua Achebe.* Washington, D.C.: Three Continents Press, 1978.

Lindfors, Bernth, and Reinhard Sanders, eds. *Dictionary of Literary Biography: Twentieth Century Caribbean and Black African Writers.* Vol. 117. Detroit: Gale Research, 1992.

Ngara, Emmanuel. *Stylistic Criticism and the African Novel.* London: Heinemann, 1982.

Part IV: The Asian Perspective

Asian Background

In his 1956 "Introduction" to *A Treasury of Asian Literature,* John D. Yohannan spoke eloquently of the need to disseminate and to study in the West both secular and religious Asian literature. He lamented the fact that reciprocity between Asia and the West had seldom extended beyond the Asian's study of Western political and natural sciences and, in the case of the Westerner, only Asian language, economics, and geopolitics. Yohannan concluded that literature was the most ignored of all Asian studies, despite the fact that Asian scholars in the West (e.g., Reynold A. Nicholson, A. J. Arberry, Arthur Ryder, and Arthur Waley) had translated into their own tongues a huge number of Asian classics. In nearly the same breath, however, Yohannen conceded that he has omitted from his anthology the entire modern era of Asian literature, for the reason that the impact of Western civilization on this phase of Asian letters all but requires a separate book. Yohannan's observation is not without merit; for the impact of the West on modern Japan, China, and India is indeed formidable—even though, in significant ways, these cultures have reciprocated by influencing the literatures of the West.

In some respects, the least affected by modern Western influence was Japan, which, despite profound changes to its civilization, has managed to retain, substantially unchanged, many of its traditional literary forms. Not a few of the earliest Japanese poems were epic-length myths and semi-myths, as well as folk and erotic songs. With the advent of Chinese-character writing in the fifth-century, Japanese poetry assumed the short, intense, pithy form by which it was to be known for over 1,000 years. By the middle of the eighth century, however, this simpler fifth-century poetic style gave way to sophisticated, extremely well-crafted court poems—poems nonetheless restricted as to subject matter. Then, the lyrical depictions of graphic nature scenes and the poet's emphasis upon such images as leaves, snow, plum or cherry blossoms, the moon, crickets, secretive lovers, ceremonies at court, a monk's tranquil hermitage, and the deaths of important persons were commonplace (Rexroth, xi–xii). Without doubt, this concentration substantially shaped the aesthetic practices of such intense lyrics as *tanka* (a poem of 31 syllables in 5–7–5–7–7 pattern) and *haiku* (a three-lined poem of 17 syllables consisting of lines following the 5-7-5 syllabic pattern).

Yet in the approximately 80 years preceding World War II, the fundamentally lyrical tendency of Japanese poetry, as well as Japanese literature as a whole, eroded. Historians often divide the pre- and post-war periods of Japanese literature according to the reigns of three emperors: Meiji (1868–1912), Taisho (1912–1926), and Hirohito or Showa (1926–1989). During the reign of Emperor Meiji, it seems that Japanese literature reached a nadir in that it appeared formless and prone to triviality or gossip, including impolite, even ugly, anecdotes about well-known courtesans and jabs at the perceived peculiarities of the West. But after the turn of the century, Japanese poetry shifted to a more obscure, symbolist style; and the novel became a more complex psychological medium. In a real way, this movement from an apparently depleted to a more contemporary style went hand-in-hand with modernization and a degree of foreign (especially Western) influence. Even so, the traditional *tanka* and *haiku* are still popular in Japan, and writers still enthusiastically produce them.

Chinese art underwent change to a much greater extent than in Japan. This art had always been diverse: funereal, court, temple, elite, and commercial. Despite this diversity, traditional poetry revealed four functions or roles—*didactic,* involving moral or social instruction; *indi-*

vidualist, offering insight into the heart or the emotions; *technical,* providing a *tour de force* or series of exercises to enhance the verbal agility of the writer; and *intuitionalist,* serving as a means of reflecting upon spirit, life, or nature (Liu, 63–87).

However, following the Communist Revolution in China in 1949, there developed a movement towards a seemingly opposite, functional art, didactic in spirit and socialist in ideology. This new art tended to shun so-called inappropriate subjects and old (seemingly reactionary) styles. The Soviet Union previously had been a testing ground of this new approach, and by the Soviet example, private art schools were closed and the practice of private patronage of art was all but abandoned. With the view of erecting a new national art, Mao Zedong (1893–1976), architect of the Chinese revolution, presented "Talks at the Yan'an Forum on Art and Literature" in which he advocated a state art that realistically critiqued any of the prevailing class and economic conditions. During the People's Congress, held between July 2 and July 19, 1949, the Communist Party went so far as to declare "correct" only Mao's principles of art and literature, particularly his insistence upon social realism. This policy no longer tolerated a "decadent" art for art's sake or the idea that the artist must be a free spirit unfettered by externally-imposed rules or expectations, or the ancient concept that art reveals the inner human being and ennobles human life. On the wings of doctrinal fervor, already distinguished artists such as Xu Beihong, Huang Binhong, and Qi Baishi, were encouraged to depict only revolutionary, military heroes or heroically dedicated workers. To promote such views, the People's Republic employed state-sanctioned painters, sculptors, and graphic artists. These and others then produced a popular folk art which appealed to (and indeed had originated from) the common people. Some new artists, like Jiang Feng, accordingly eliminated from their works ancient religious subjects and figures in favor of more explicit revolutionary content. Though traditional artists continued in post-revolutionary China, they nonetheless were forced to eke out a living either by selling their work in small exhibitions or by fashioning cheap fans, lanterns, and trinkets for export to other countries. Architecturally speaking, there was public support for the decoration of government buildings, and sculptors and painters were put to work completing such tasks. One of these buildings was the Great Hall of the People, which came to be adorned by a now famous party painting, *This Land So Rich in Beauty,* created by Fu Baoshi and Guan Sanyue (Clunas, 209–213). Ironically, immediately after Mao's death in 1976, a reaction set in against a purely doctrinal or party-line approach to art and literature, indicating that the age of the icon (that is, the era of mainly party-approved visual and literary portraits of revolutionary personages and events) was waning; and China once again witnessed interest in traditional art forms (Wang, 243).

As was true in Japan and China, modern India has undergone a struggle, beginning several centuries ago, between native or indigenous styles of art and those imported from Europe—largely through colonial contact (Goetz, 250). Today, because of the diversity in Indian states and territories, in which some 27 Indo-Aryan languages are now spoken by well over 800 million people, the literature of India is unavoidably diverse—falling, in fact, into the three main language categories of Hindi, Bengali, and Marathi, with at least five secondary groupings (Oriya, Panjabi, Gujrati, Assamese, and the unique Hindi variant called Urdu). The literatures which have grown from most, if not all, of these languages were greatly influenced by Sanskrit or classical Hindi, from which modern Indian literature has inherited subjects, vocabulary, and the tendency towards a highly poetic or lyrical expression—a tendency which was modified towards a more prosaic style of expression when India fell under British colonial rule.

Of these language groups, Hindi and Bengali literature hold a special interest. Hindi literature began as early as the eighth century, although the earliest significant secular work, the epic of Chand Bardai of Lahore, appeared in the 12th century (Renou, 100). Though India is well known in the West for ancient Hindu texts, like the *Vedas,* the *Brahmanas,* and the *Upanishads,* one will still find numerous semi-secular manuscripts, often in the form of verse and prose chronicles. The lyric poem comes upon the stage as a dynamic form in the 16th century under the enlightened monarch Akbar (1556–1605), and this strong lyric strain continued through the 1700s. By then, under the skilled pens of Lallu Lal, Dayanand Sarasvali, Harishchandra of Benares, and more recently Premchand (who wrote in Urdu), Hindi literature had reached a new plateau of subtlety and virtuosity (Renou, 105–106).

Also pertinent to a discussion of modern Indian literature is Bengali writing. Bengal had been particulary influenced by British and French literature from as early as the 18th century, through the experiments of author Rammohan Ray (1772–1833). When Ray wrote, there was a blending of Islamic and Hindu art traditions, a synthesis soon disturbed by art influences derived from the interaction between India and early modern Europe. The Portuguese, for instance, had introduced late Renaissance and Baroque styles into India, in such places as Goa, Bassein, Daman, and Diu (Goetz, 243). However, by the last quarter of the 19th century, there had arisen a reaction to this European influence and a corresponding revival of native art (Goetz, 246). Abanindranath Tagore, cousin of Rabindranath Tagore the poet, then cultivated a national style of painting based upon water color, Indian subjects, and traditional techniques; and this style eventually developed into the Bengal School. But in counter-reaction to the seemingly sentimental attitudes of this school, there emerged a style, the Modern School, promoted by a group of young revolutionaries interested in socio-political change, technological advancement, and the uplifting of the masses. These artists were attracted more by international, "modernist" approaches than by the adoration of a national past. This "modernist" style was evident in the planning of Chandigarh (capital of East Punjab) and in administrative buildings and villas. Impressionistic and expressionistic painting formulas were likewise found, with influences from the French painter Paul Gauguin (1848–1903), the Italian artist Amedeo Modigliani (1884–1920), and such Japanese masters as Korin and Koetsu. Prominent among such modernist visual artists was the young woman Amerita Sher-Gil, who died prematurely in 1942 (Goetz, 248–50).

As one considers obvious Western influences on Tagore and others in modern India, one must not lose sight of the fact that Indian literature has likewise influenced that of the West. In fact, the impact of Indian literature has been more pronounced upon the West than that of the West upon India. For example, the Neoplatonist Plotinus was indebted to the *Upanishads,* which Iranian and Asian intermediaries had undoubtedly brought to his attention. Moreover, much of the tradition of Medieval European storytelling seen in fabliaux and other short narrative forms originates, however indirectly, from such Indian prototypes as the *Jatakas* and the *Panchatantra.* This Indian narrative influence culminated in the 19th century German tales of the brothers Grimm, Jacob (1785–1863) and Wilhelm (1786–1859). What is more, the German Romantic writer Johann Wolfgang von Goethe (1749–1832) applauded Sir William Jones' 1789 translation of *Shakuntala;* and German philosophers such as Immanuel Kant (1724–1804) and Georg Wilhelm Friedrich Hegel (1770–1831) have benefited, as well, from the wisdom of India—as did the German[*] thinker Arthur Schopenhauer (1788–1860). Also indebted to Indian literature were the French writers Victor Hugo (1802–1885) and Theophile Gautier (1811–1872); the British authors William Wordsworth (1770–1850), Samuel Taylor Coleridge (1772–1834), Percy Bysshe Shelley (1792–1822), Robert Browning (1812–1889), and Thomas Carlyle (1795–1881); and the American thinkers Ralph Waldo Emerson (1803–1882), Henry David Thoreau (1817–1862), Margaret Fuller (1810–1850), Walt Whitman (1819–1892), and Martin Luther King, Jr. (1929–1968) (Renou, 131).

Thus, influence upon the literatures of Japan, China, and India has been substantial, but not absolute, with the least direct influence being seen in Japan, which has also proved the most successful in retaining its traditional literary heritage. Though China's self-imposed isolation from the rest of the world has retarded Western influence where literature specifically is concerned, that influence nonetheless has worked powerfully through China's general espousal of Karl Marx (1818–1883), although Mao himself must be credited with participating in the development of socialist philosophy, as a whole. Given the fact that the influence of Western upon modern Indian art has been even more profound than in the case of Japan and China, one can see why John Johannan's decision in 1956 to exclude the non-traditional, modern Asian

---

[*] Born in Poland, but studied and taught in Germany.

literature from his *Treasury* made sense. But the question remains as to whether the separation of these literatures from their native roots is in any way permanent. Hermann Goetz at least believes that through the process of fusing the old with the new, Indian literature will give birth to completely new, wholly unforeseen literary attitudes and styles (Goetz, 250). Similar occurrences in Japan and China would not be out of the question.

Selected Bibliography

Clunas, Craig. *Oxford History of Art: Art in China.* New York: Oxford University Press, 1997.
Denton, Kirk A., ed. *Modern Chinese Literary Thought: Writings on Literature, 1893–1945.* Stanford: Stanford University Press, 1996.
Goetz, Hermann. *The Art of India: Five Thousand Years of Indian Art.* 2nd ed. New York: Crown, 1964. 2nd ed., 1964.
Frazer, R.W. *A Literary History of India.* New York: Haskell House, 1970.
Liu, James J. Y. *The Art of Chinese Poetry.* Chicago: U Of Chicago P, 1962.
Renou, Louis. *Indian Literature.* Patrick Evans, trans. New York: Walker Press, 1964.
Wang, Yuein. "Anxiety of Portraiture: . . . Questioning Ancestral Icons in Post-Mao China," *Politics, Ideology, and Literary Discourse in Modern China: Theoretical Interventions and Cultural Critique.* Liu Kang and Xiaobing Tang, eds. Durham, NC: Duke University Press, 1993.
Yasuda, Kenneth. "'Approach to Haiku' and 'Basic Principles,'" *Japanese Aesthetics and Culture.* Nancy G. Hume, ed. Albany, NY: State University of New York Press, 1995.
Yohannan, John D. Introduction, *A Treasury of Asian Literature.* New York: Mentor, 1956.

Chinese Poetry

Seeking a Mooring

Wang Wei (17th Century)

A leaf floats in endless space.
A cold wind tears the clouds.
The water flows westward.
The tide pushes upstream.
Beyond the moonlit reeds,   5
In village after village, I hear
The sound of fullers' mallets
Beating the wet clothing
In preparation for winter.
Everywhere crickets cry   10
In the autumn frost.
A traveller's thoughts in the night
Wander in a thousand miles of dreams.
The sound of a bell cannot disperse
The sorrows that come   15
In the fifth hour of night.
What place will I remember
From all this journey?
Only still bands of desolate mist
And a single fishing boat.   20

Mao Zedong (1893–1976)

One of the philosophical creators of modern Communism, along with Karl Marx (1818–1883) and Vladimir Ilich Lenin (1870–1924), Mao Zedong (or Mao Tse-Tung) helped to found the Chinese Communist Party in Shanghai in 1921 and the People's Republic of China in 1949. Mao was born in Hunan Province in 1893 to a prosperous peasant family. As a young student, he studied the Confucian classics. He served briefly in the republican army and as a library assistant at Peking University, although, because of finances, he did not attend the university himself. Eventually, he became acquainted with radical intellectuals and immersed himself in radical politics, even while he was principal of a Hunan primary school.

He married in 1920 Yang K'ai-hui (later executed by the Chinese Nationalists), in 1930 Ho Tzu-chen (whom he eventually divorced), and in 1939 Chiang Ch'ing. Forced in 1927 to flee to the countryside of south China because of Chiang Kai-Shek's purges of Communists from the Nationalist government, he emerged by the 1937 Japanese invasion of China as a national leader committed to the defense of the Chinese homeland.

Following World War II, from 1946 to 1949, a civil war erupted between the Communists (led by Mao's forces) and the Nationalists (directed by Chiang Kai-Shek). Eventually yielding, the Nationalists fled to Taiwan, leaving the Communists in firm control of mainland China. Rebuffed by the United States in the late 1940s, Mao's government established an alliance with the U.S.S.R.

Disappointment over slow socio-economic development in China and the tendency of many Communist Party members to demand special privileges beyond those enjoyed by average citizens led to reforms which then created reverse hostilities. By the late 1950s, not only had Mao's influence waned, but there developed tensions between China and the U.S.S.R. However, the Great Proletarian Cultural Revolution of the late 1960s, promoted by Chiang Ch'ing, Mao's wife, and supported by loyal students called "Red Guards," propelled Mao back to power. In the early 1970s, Mao implemented a plan to isolate the U.S.S.R. by improving his country's relationship with the United States, culminating in the visit of President Richard Nixon to Beijing in 1972. After Mao's death, late in 1976, there was a reaction to the perceived excesses of the Cultural Revolution and a reduction of Mao's reputation. Nonetheless, Mao is regarded as one of the greatest unifiers of the Chinese people in history.

Selected Bibliography

Chou, Eric. *Mao Tse-Tung, The Man and the Myth.* London: Cassell, 1982.
Schram, Stuart R. *The Thought of Mao Tse-Tung.* New York: Cambridge University Press, 1989.
Uhalley, Stephen. *Mao Tse-Tung, a Critical Biography.* New York: New Viewpoints, 1975.

Tune: "Spring in [Princess] Ch'in's Garden"

Mao Zedong

    Northern landscape,
Thousand miles around covered by ice,
Ten thousand miles under snowdrifts.
    On both sides of the Great Wall,
    I see vast wastes;   5
    Up and down the Great River
    Suddenly the torrents are still;
Mountains wind around like silver serpents,
High headlands ramble about like waxen elephants,
On the verge of challenging heaven.   10
    A sunny day is best
    For watching the red against the white:
    Extraordinary enchantment.

The rivers and mountains have this special charm
That inspires countless heroes to great deeds.   15
Pity the First Sovereign and the Martial Emperor
    Had small talent for literature,
And the founding fathers of T'ang and Sung
    Lacked both grace and charm.
In his own generation—favored by heaven—   20
    Genghis Khan
Knew only how to bend the bow, bringing down the great vulture.
    All these are gone now,
To single out the men of high character,
We must look to now; the present.   25

Declaration

Bei Dau (1949–1970)

Perhaps the last moment is here
I haven't left a will
Only a pen . . . to my mother
I'm not a hero
In an era without heroes
I just wanted to be a man

The quiet horizon
Separated the ranks of the living from the dead
I had to choose the sky
And would never kneel on the ground
To let executioners look gigantic
So they could block the wind of freedom

Out of starlike bullet holes
A bloody dawn is flowing

Japanese Poetry

Fall

Bashō (1644–1694)

The piercing voice
of the autumn wind through
a half-open door

Winter

Bashō (1644–1694)

Withered by winter
the sound of the wind—
one-color world

Spring

Buson (d. 1714)

Spring passes—
the last reluctant
cherry blossoms

Summer

Buson (d. 1714)

Leaves unfold
waters whiten
barley becomes gold

I Stand As Though

Yaichi Aizu (1881–1956)

I stand as though
only I am existing
in heaven and earth—
at this solitariness,
Kannon, you are smiling.   5

Coming stealthily,
who is it hitting the temple bell?
It is late at night
and time for even the Buddha
to go into dreaming.   10
In the Lord Buddha's
drowsy eyes
the ancient
country fields of Yamato
Have their hazy existence.   15

Lemon Elegy

Takamura Kotaro (1883–1956)

So intensely you had been waiting for the lemon
in the sad white light deathbed
you took that one lemon from my hand
and bit it sharply with your bright teeth.
A fragrance arose in topaz   5
and those heavenly drops of juice
flashed you back to sanity.
Your eyes smiled, blue and transparent.
You grasped my hand, how vigorous you were—
There had been a storm in your throat   10
but just before life was gone
you found again yourself,
all life's love into one moment fallen.
As once you did in the depth of mountains
you did then—let out a great sigh   15
and with it your organs stopped.

Today too I shall put a cool fresh piece of lemon
by the cherry blossoms in front of your photograph.

The Girl Cutting Reeds

Suju Takano (1893–?)

The girl cutting reeds
turns her face toward the sky
and combs out her hair.

A temple room's
big heavy eaves—out comes
a spring butterfly.

Now someone else
is beginning to cut down
the distant reeds.

A spider's web—
one strand of it goes across
the front of a lily.

Chinese Narrative

from "The Dream of the Red Chamber"

Ts'ao Hsüeh-Ch'in (1715?–1763?)

(Chen Shih-yin meets the Stone of Spiritual Understanding)

When the Goddess Nügua undertook to repair the Dome of Heaven, she fashioned at the Great Mythical Mountain under the Nonesuch Bluff 36,501 pieces of stone, each 120 feet high and 240 feet around. Of these she used only 36,500 and left the remaining piece in the shadow of the Green Meadows Peak. However, the divine hands of Nügua had touched off a spark of life in the Stone and endowed it with supernatural powers. It was able to come and go as it pleased and change its size and form at will. But it was not happy because it alone had been rejected by the Goddess, and it was given to sighing over its ill fortune.

As it was thus bemoaning its fate one day, it saw coming toward it a Buddhist monk and a Taoist priest, both of uncommon appearance. They were talking and laughing and, when they reached the shadow of the Peak, they sat down by the side of the Stone and continued their conversation. At first they talked about cloud-wrapped mountains and mist-covered seas and the mysteries of immortal life, but presently they changed the topic of their conversation and spoke of the wealth and luxury and the good things of life in the Red Dust. This stirred the earthly strain in the Stone and aroused in it a desire to experience for itself the pleasures of mortal life. Therefore, it addressed the monk and the priest thus:

"Venerable sirs, forgive me for intruding. I could not help overhearing your conversation and I should like very much to have a taste of the pleasures of the Red Dust of which you spoke. Though I am crude in substance, I am not without some degree of understanding or a sense of gratitude. If you, venerable sirs, would be kind enough to take me for a turn in the Red Dust and let me enjoy for a few years its pleasures and luxuries, I shall be grateful to you for eons to come."

"It is true that the Red Dust has its joys," the two immortals answered with an indulgent smile, "but they are evanescent and illusory. Moreover, there every happiness is spoiled by a certain lack, and all good things are poisoned by the envy and covetousness of other men, so that in the end you will find the pleasure outweighed by sorrow and sadness. We do not advise such a venture."

But the fire of earthly desires, once kindled, could not easily be extinguished. The Stone ignored the warning of the immortals and continued to importune them, until the Buddhist monk said to his companion with a sigh, "We have here another instance of Quiescence giving way to Activity and Non-Existence yielding to Existence." Then turning to the Stone, he said, "We shall take you for a turn in the Red Dust if you insist, but don't blame us if you do not find it to your liking."

"Of course not, of course not," the Stone assured them eagerly.

Then the monk said, "Though you are endowed with some degree of understanding, your substance needs improvement. If we take you into the world the way you are, you will be kicked about and cursed like any ordinary stumbling block. How would you like to be transformed into a substance of quality for your sojourn in the Red Dust and then be restored to your original self afterward?"

The Stone agreed, and thereupon the monk exercised the infinite power of the Law and transformed the Stone into a piece of pure translucent jade, oval in shape and about the size of a pendant. The monk held it on his palm and smiled as he said, "You will be treasured now as a precious object, but you still lack real distinguishing marks. A few characters must be engraved upon you so that everyone who sees you will recognize you as something unique. Only then shall we take you down to some prosperous land, where you will enjoy the advantages of a noble and cultured family and all the pleasures that wealth and position can bring."

The Stone was overjoyed on hearing this and asked what characters were to be engraved upon it and where it was to be taken, but the monk only smiled and said, "Don't ask what and where now; you will know when the time comes." So saying, he tucked the Stone in his sleeve and disappeared with the priest to we know not where.

Nor do we know how many generations or epochs it was afterward that the Taoist of the Great Void passed by the Great Mythical Mountain, the Nonesuch Bluff, and the Green Meadows Peak and came upon the Stone, now restored to its original form and substance. Engraved on it was a long, long story. The Taoist read it from beginning to end and found that it was the self-same Stone that was first carried into the Red Dust and then guided to the Other Shore by the Buddhist of Infinite Space and the Taoist of Boundless Time. The story was that of the Stone itself. The land of its descent, the place of its incarnation, the rise and fall of fortunes, the joys and sorrows of reunion and separation—all these were recorded in detail, together with the trivial affairs of the family, the delicate sentiments of the maidens' chambers, and a number of poems and conundrums which one usually finds in such stories. At the end there was this quatrain:

> Without merits that would entitle me to a place in the blue sky,
> In vain have I lived in the Red Dust for so many years.
> These are the events before my birth and after my death—
> Who will transcribe them and give the world my story?

As the material appeared eminently suited for the beguilement of idle moments and the relief of boredom, the Taoist copied it down from beginning to end and gave it the title of *Transcribed by a Priest*. Later, Wu Yü-feng gave it the title of *Dream of the Red Chamber*, while K'ung Mei-ch'i called it *Precious Mirror of Breeze and Moonlight*. Still later, Ts'ao Hsüeh-ch'in studied it for ten years and revised it five times. He divided it into chapters and then composed an analytical couplet for each. He gave it yet another title, *The Twelve Maidens of Chinling*. He also composed a poem on the novel.

> Pages full of unlikely words,
> Handfuls of hot, bitter tears.
> They call the author a silly fool,
> For they know not what he means.

Finally, when "Chih Yen Chai" made still another copy together with a new set of comments in the year *chia-hsu* (1754), he gave it the more appropriate title, *The Story of the Stone*.

Now that the origin of our story has been explained, the reader may turn to what was actually written on the Stone.

In the southeast there was a city named Soochow. The region around Chang-men, one of the city's principal gates, represented one of the foremost centers of wealth and luxury in the Red Dust. Outside Chang-men there was an ancient temple, nicknamed, because of its shape, the Temple of the Gourd. By the side of this temple there lived a member of the gentry by the name of Chen Shih-yin with his wife, Feng-shih. Although not rich, they were one of the well-to-do and respected families of the district.

Shih-yin was a man who cared nothing for fame or fortune. He devoted his time to planting bamboo and watering flowers, sipping wine and writing verses, much after the fashion of the Taoist sages. But unfortunately he lacked one thing to complete his happiness: he was over fifty years of age and had no son. To comfort his old age he had only a three-year-old daughter named Lotus.

One hot summer day, Shih-yin was reading idly in his study. The book dropped from his languid hand and he fell asleep over his desk. He seemed to have traveled far, to some place that he did not recognize. Suddenly he saw a Buddhist monk and a Taoist priest coming in his direction. The Taoist was speaking.

"I am afraid you shouldn't have taken it upon yourself to interfere with the destiny of the Stone. What are you going to do with it?"

"Rest your anxieties," the monk said. "The Stone is, as a matter of fact, involved in a romance that must be enacted on earth. Far from interfering with fate, I am acting as its instrument."

"So another group of spirits have brought upon themselves the curse of incarnation! Where did this drama originate and where is it to be enacted?"

"It is a very amusing story," the monk answered. "As you know, the Stone has been given to wandering about the universe since it acquired supernatural powers. One day it came to the Palace of Vermilion Clouds of the Goddess of Disillusionment. And the Goddess, aware of its unique background and destiny, retained it in her service, conferring upon it the title of the Divine Stone Page. Then one day while roaming along the banks of the Ethereal, it came upon a Crimson Flower growing by the side of the Rock of Three Incarnations. The Stone was struck with the great beauty of the fairy plant and assumed the task of caring for it and feeding it daily with sweet dew. Under this tender care, the Crimson Flower thrived and continued to absorb year after year the cosmic essences of Heaven and Earth until it, too, acquired supernatural qualities and transformed itself into a beautiful fairy goddess. The Goddess manifested, however, a solitary nature and perverse spirit. It was her wont to explore the Realm of Parting Sorrow, to feed upon the Fruit of Unfulfilled Love, and drink from the Fountain of Ineffable Sadness. She was grateful for the care lavished upon her by the Stone and was unhappy because she did not know how to repay it. She used to say to herself, 'I can't pay him back in kind since he has no need of sweet dew. Perhaps I can repay him with my tears, should both of us be sent down to the Red Dust.'

"It was an odd thought but it coincided with the earthly desire of the Stone. The result is that both are to be incarnated, together with a number of other spirits who are in one way or another involved, and all will play their parts in a little drama of the Red Dust."

"It is an odd story indeed," the Taoist said, "I never heard of such a thing as repaying a debt with tears. I imagine the stories of these creatures will be different from the usual 'breeze and moonlight' school."

"Undoubtedly so," the Buddhist answered. "In stories of famous personalities we are usually accorded only the briefest outline of their careers, together with conventional poems by and about them. We are never given any details of their everyday life, what they eat and drink, what they think and say to one another. As to the stories of breeze and moonlight, they all deal with such obvious things as secret meetings and elopements; none venture to describe the real feelings and sentiments that motivate their heroes and heroines. But I have reason to believe that the stories of these creatures will be different, be they good or bad, of subtle sensibilities or gross intemperance."

"I propose," the Taoist said, "that we go down to the mortal world ourselves when the time comes and save a few that are especially worth saving."

"That is what I am thinking myself," the Buddhist answered. "But we must first take the Stone to the Goddess of Disillusionment and have it registered. We must wait until all the spirits involved have descended before we go ourselves. Only half of them have done so now."

Shih-yin heard every word of the conversation and could not resist the urge to break in at this point. "Greetings, immortal masters. I have heard you speak of things I never heard before and which I only half comprehend. Could you elaborate a bit for the benefit of my obtuse mind and thus point the way to salvation?"

"We cannot, unfortunately, divulge the secrets of Heaven," the two immortals replied. "However, if you remember us when the hour comes, you will be able to escape the fiery pits of Hell."

"If you cannot betray the secrets of Heaven," Shih-yin continued, "perhaps you can show me the Stone of which you spoke?"

"That happens to be within your destiny," the monk replied, as he took the Stone from his sleeve and passed it to Shih-yin. It was the same Stone in the shape of a pendant, clear and translucent, but four characters had been engraved upon it: T'ung ling pao yü (Precious Jade of Spiritual Understanding). Before Shih-yin could look at the other side, the monk took it from him, saying, "We have reached the Land of Illusion." Then Shih-yin saw before him a great stone arch, across the top of which were engraved four characters: "Great Void Illusion Land." There was a couplet on the two pillars of the central arch, which read:

> When the unreal is taken for the real, then the real becomes unreal:
> Where non-existence is taken for existence, then existence becomes
> non-existence.

The two immortals passed through the archway, but when Shih-yin tried to follow them, he suddenly heard a crash as if the mountains had collapsed and the earth parted asunder. He woke with a start and saw nothing but the bright sun heating down on the courtyard and the broad leaves of the plantain tree casting a cool shade. He had forgotten most of his dream.

Just then, the nurse came up with his daughter Lotus in her arms, and Shih-yin was filled with joy and pride as he observed how pretty and lovable she had grown to be. He took the child from the nurse and played with her a while and then took her to the gate to watch a procession pass by. As he was about to enter the house, he saw a Buddhist monk and a Taoist priest coming toward him. The monk was barefooted and his head mangy; the priest was lame and his hair disheveled. When they came near and saw Shih-yin with his daughter in his arms, the Buddhist suddenly burst out crying and said, "Kind donor, what are you carrying that ill-fated creature for? She will only bring misfortune upon her parents." Shih-yin ignored him, taking him for a beggar trying to attract attention. The monk continued, "Give her to me as a sacrifice to Buddha. Give her to me!" Shih-yin was annoyed and was about to retreat into the house when the monk as suddenly burst out laughing and, pointing at Shih-yin, recited the following lines:

> Love and tender care will be of no avail;
> The water caltrop will be blighted by snow.
> Rejoice not even though it be the Feast of Lanterns,
> For you may sorrow at what follows in its wake.

As Shih-yin wondered at the significance of the poem and what manner of men the monk and his companion were, he heard the priest say, "We need not go on together from here. Let each go his own way. When the time comes I shall wait for you at Mount Pei Mang and go with you to the Land of Illusion and do what must be done."

"Excellent," the monk replied. And before Shih-yin could speak to them, both had vanished.

Shih-yin realized then that these were not common beggars and regretted that he had not been more attentive to them. His thoughts were interrupted by the appearance of Chia Yu-tsun, a graduate in poor circumstances who lived next door to him in the Temple of the Gourd. A native of Huchow and of a good but impoverished family, he was on his way to the Capital for the Examinations when he found himself stranded in Soochow. He made a precarious living by selling calligraphic scrolls and inscriptions.

"What has brought you to the gate?" Yu-tsun said by way of greeting.

"Nothing," Shih-yin answered. "I was just trying to quiet this crying daughter of mine. You have come at an opportune time. Please come in and help me while away the long summer day." The nurse relieved Shih-yin of Lotus. Tea was served in the study, but presently Shih-yin had to excuse himself because of the arrival of another guest. Yu-tsun amused himself by browsing through the books on the shelves. Suddenly he heard a voice outside the window. It was a maid picking flowers in the courtyard. She was not particularly pretty, but there was something about her features and the way she carried herself that set her apart from the common run of bondmaids, and Yu-tsun found himself staring at her. As she finished her task and was about to leave, she happened to look up and their eyes met.

"This must be Chia Yu-tsun whom the master has often spoken of," the maid thought to herself. "He is evidently in poor circumstances, but he does not look like one who would remain poor for very long. The master is right in prophesying a bright future for him." So thinking, she could not help turning her head to steal another glance at Yu-tsun as she walked toward the inner court. On his part, Yu-tsun was pleased with the impression he seemed to have made. "She is not an ordinary maidservant," he said to himself. "She seems to appreciate me when few in the world do."

On the night of the Festival of the Harvest Moon, Yu-tsun found himself alone in his quarters in the Temple of the Gourd. He had not forgotten the maid, and on this festive occasion his thoughts again turned to her. The bright moon stimulated his fancies, and he composed a poem on their meeting. Then he sighed as he thought how far he was from realizing his ambitions and he recited aloud the couplet in which the poet compared himself to a piece of jade waiting to be discovered by someone who recognized its real worth. He was overheard by Shih-yin, who had come in just at the moment.

"I see that you are a man of ambition, Brother Yu-tsun," Shih-yin said.

"Oh, no," Yu-tsun replied with an embarrassed smile. "I was only reciting the lines of a former poet. What has brought you here, Brother Shih-yin?"

"Tonight is the Harvest Moon, the Festival of Reunion," Shih-yin said. "It occurred to me that on this occasion you might feel like honoring me with your company. I have prepared a small measure of wine in my study and should be delighted if you would share it with me."

Yu-tsun readily accepted the invitation and went with Shih-yin to his house. At first, host and guest poured the wine in small cups and sipped it slowly, but as their spirits rose and good cheer mounted, they called for larger cups and drank more freely. The sound of flutes and strings came from every house, and overhead the moon shone in full splendor. Yu-tsun, emboldened by the wine, improvised a poem to the moon, the wonder and admiration of all during its phase of fulfillment.

Shih-yin applauded heartily: "I have always said you are not one to remain in obscurity. Your poem is a portent of better things to come. Let me congratulate you!" He filled another cup for Yu-tsun, and the latter drained it in one draught.

"If you will forgive me for the lack of modesty," Yu-tsun said, "I would like to say that I am not without a degree of competence in the sort of compositions that the Examinations require. I think I have a fair chance of success. But my purse is empty and the Capital far away. I shall never be able to save enough for the journey through the sort of drudgery I have been doing."

"Why have you not spoken of this before?" asked Shih-yin. "I have often thought of this matter but have not presumed to speak of it. The Metropolitan Examinations are coming up next year, and you must go to the Capital to exercise your talents. I shall consider it a great honor if you will allow me to take care of your traveling expenses." He told his servant to go in and get fifty ounces of silver and two suits of winter clothes. "The nineteenth is a propitious day," he said. "You can hire a boat and start your westward journey. Next winter, I am sure I shall have the pleasure of congratulating you on your return."

Yu-tsun accepted the silver and clothes without any pretense at refusing. When Shih-yin sent two letters of introduction to him the next day, the servant brought back the report that Yu-tsun had started on his journey before dawn, leaving word with the temple attendant to thank Shih-yin for his kindness and to tell him that he did not believe in fortunetellers and that he had therefore left without waiting for the nineteenth.

Truly, time passes quickly when the days are uneventful. In a twinkling, the New Year had come and gone, and soon it was the fifteenth of the First Moon, the Feast of Lanterns. As Shih-yin had no inclination for the diversions of the season, he asked his servant Huo Ch'i to take his daughter to see the fireworks and lantern processions. Having to attend to a trivial but necessary call, the hapless servant left Lotus alone for a moment under the shelter of a gate. When he returned, his charge had disappeared. The servant spent most of the night looking for her and when he realized she must have fallen into the hands of a kidnaper, he too disappeared, not having the courage to face his master and mistress. Shih-yin and his wife were deeply stricken by the loss of their only daughter. Crushed by the burden of their grief, first Shih-yin fell sick and then his wife, so that for a time their days were occupied in consulting physicians and fortunetellers.

Blessing seldom comes in two's, and misfortune rarely comes singly. Two months later, on the fifteenth of the third month, a fire broke out in the Temple of the Gourd. Since wood and bamboo were extensively used for hedges and partitions in that region, the fire was soon out of control and spread to the entire street. Shih-yin's house, being next to the temple, was burned to the ground. He talked things over with his wife and decided they should go to live on their farm. But in the years immediately preceding, flood and drought had followed one another, and gangs of bandits sprang up on every hand. Then came the troops, and between their exactions and the depredations of the bandits, life became all but impossible. Under these circumstances, Shih-yin was glad to take his wife's suggestion to sell their farm and go live with her family.

Now Feng Su, Shih-yin's father-in-law, was a small landowner who had done well. He was not of a generous nature and was none too pleased when his daughter and son-in-law came to him as refugees. Fortunately for Shih-yin, he had some money from the sale of his farm and was able to contribute to the household expenses. But he knew little of financial matters, much less how to drive a bargain. So when he asked Feng Su to invest in some property for him, the latter took advantage of his ignorance and pocketed a good part of the funds. In a year or two, his money was gone, and his father-in-law began to complain about his improvidence, his laziness, and extravagant ways. Shih-yin realized too late that he had thrown himself on the mercy of the wrong man. The long period of illness and misfortune aged Shih-yin rapidly. He took on the appearance of a man approaching the end of his days. He was walking one day on the street, leaning on a cane, when he saw a lame Taoist in hemp sandals and tattered rags coming toward him, chanting this song:

> We all envy the immortals because they are free,
> But fame and fortune we cannot forget.
> Where are the ministers and generals of the past and the present?
> Under neglected graves overgrown with weeds.
>
> We all envy the immortals because they are free,
> But gold and silver we cannot forget.
> All our lives we save and hoard and wish for more,
> When suddenly our eyes are forever closed.
>
> We all envy the immortals because they are free,
> But our precious wives we cannot forget.
> They speak of love and constancy while we live,

But marry again soon enough after we are dead.
We all envy the immortals because they are free.
But our sons and grandsons we cannot forget.
Many there are, of doting parents, from ancient times—
But how few of the sons are filial and obedient!

After hearing this, Shih-yin went up to the Taoist and asked him, "What are you trying to say? All I can get is 'free' and 'forget.'"

"That's all you need to get," the Taoist answered, laughing. "For if you are free, you'll forget, and if you forget, you'll be free. In other words, to forget is to be free and to be free is to forget. That's why I call my song 'Forget and be free.'"

Now Shih-yin had always been a man of great intuitive understanding. He immediately grasped the purport of the Taoist's enigmatic words. "Would you let me elaborate on your theme?" he asked.

"Please do," the Taoist encouraged, and thereupon Shih-yin recited the following lines:

Dingy rooms and desert halls
  Were once filled with insignia of rank.
Fields choked with weeds and blighted trees
  Were once scenes of dancing and song.
While here spiders weave their webs between carved beams
  There they replace window mats with silken gauze.
Boast not that you wear your powder and rouge well,
  But grieve that your temples will soon be covered with frost.
Tonight a pair of cooing doves under red bridal curtains,
  Tomorrow a heap of bleached bones like those of yesteryear.
Chests filled with gold, chests filled with silver—
  In a twinkling, beggars despised by all.
One moment we grieve over a short-lived friend,
  The next we are ourselves overtaken by death.
Careful as we may be with our sons,
  We cannot be certain they will not turn bandits and thieves.
We would all bring up our daughters to be ladies
  But who can say that they will not end up in courtesans' quarters?
Discontent with one's position
  May bring chains upon one's feet.
Yesterday, 'twas the coat because it was not warm enough;
  Today, 'tis the dragon robe because it is too long.
What bustle and confusion, as one set of actors exits and another enters,
  Each taking the illusory for the real.
What stupidity; for in the end, in the end
  One only wears out one's fingers for someone else's trousseau.

"Wonderful! Wonderful!" the Taoist exclaimed, clapping his hands, and Shih-yin relieving the Taoist of the sack he was carrying, said, "Let us be on our way!" And so saying, he went off with the priest.

Shih-yin's wife spared no effort in trying to locate her husband, but how can one find a man who wants to be lost? Fortunately she still had the two maids that she had brought with her from Soochow. With their help she was able to contribute to her own support by sewing and embroidering.

Indian Narrative

Sir Rabindranath Tagore (1861–1941)

The best-known writer, not only in Bengal, but in India as a whole, is Rabindranath Thakur, a name later Anglicized to Tagore. Educated in England, he was quickly acknowledged as a great poet, and his fame increased when he received the Nobel Prize for literature in 1913. In his thinking Tagore often was able to harmonize Asian and Western humanistic values, being particularly committed to negating the pronouncement of the British writer Rudyard Kipling that the cultures of East and West are so greatly different that the two world views can never be reconciled (Renou, 121). Primarily known as a lyrical poet, he likewise has produced diverse dramas, stories, essays, and novels. It is said of Tagore that whatever he may have borrowed from the West he thoroughly re-thought and re-shaped so as to fit this material into an Indian cultural and spiritual context (Renou, 123).

Selected Bibliography

Chatterjee, Bhabatosh. Rabindranath Tagore and Modern Sensibility. Delhi: Oxford University Press, 1996.
Goetz, Hermann. The Art of India: Five Thousand Years of Indian Art. 2nd ed. New York: Crown, 1964.
Renou, Louis. *Indian Literature*. Patrick Evans, trans. New York: Walker Press, 1964.

The Editor

Rabindranath Tagore

As long as my wife was alive, I did not pay much attention to Probha. As a matter of fact, I thought a great deal more about Probha's mother than I did of the child herself.

At that time my dealing with her was superficial, limited to a little petting, listening to her lisping chatter, and occasionally watching her laugh and play. As long as it was agreeable to me I used to fondle her, but as soon as it threatened to become tiresome I would surrender her to her mother with the greatest readiness.

At last, on the untimely death of my wife, the child dropped from her mother's arms into mine, and I took her to my heart.

But it is difficult to say whether it was I who considered it my duty to bring up the motherless child with twofold care, or my daughter who thought it her duty to take care of her wifeless father with a superfluity of attention. At any rate, it is a fact that from the age of six she began to assume the role of housekeeper. It was quite clear that this little girl constituted herself the sole guardian of her father.

I smiled inwardly but surrendered myself completely to her hands. I soon saw that the more inefficient and helpless I was the better pleased she became. I found that even if I took down my own clothes from the peg, or went to get my own umbrella, she put on such an air of offended dignity that it was clear that she thought I had usurped her right. Never before had she possessed such a perfect doll as she now had in her father, and so she took the keenest pleasure in feeding him, dressing him, and even putting him to bed. Only when I was teaching her the elements of arithmetic or the First Reader had I the opportunity of summoning up my parental authority.

Every now and then the thought troubled me as to where I should be able to get enough money to provide her with a dowry for a suitable bride-groom. I was giving her a good education, but what would happen if she fell into the hands of an ignorant fool?

I made up my mind to earn money. I was too old to get employment in a Government office, and I had not the influence to get work in a private one. After a good deal of thought I decided that I would write books.

If you make holes in a bamboo tube, it will no longer hold either oil or water, in fact its power of receptivity is lost; but if you blow through it, then, without any expenditure it may produce music. I felt quite sure that the man who is not useful can be ornamental, and he who is not productive in other fields can at least produce literature. Encouraged by this thought, I wrote a farce. People said it was good, and it was even acted on the stage.

Once having tasted of fame, I found myself unable to stop pursuing it farther. Days and days together I went on writing farces with an agony of determination.

Probha would come with her smile, and remind me gently: "Father, it is time for you to take your bath."

And I would growl out at her: "Go away, go away; can't you see that I am busy now? Don't vex me."

The poor child would leave me, unnoticed, with a face dark like a lamp whose light has been suddenly blown out.

I drove the maid-servants away, and beat the men-servants, and when beggars came and sang at my door I would get up and run after them with a stick. My room being by the side of the street, passers-by would stop and ask me to tell them the way, but I would request them to go to Jericho. Alas, no one took it into serious consideration that I was engaged in writing a screaming farce.

Yet I never got money in the measure that I got fun and fame. But that did not trouble me, although in the meantime all the potential bride-grooms were growing up for other brides whose parents did not write farces.

But just then an excellent opportunity came my way. The landlord of a certain village, Jahirgram, started a newspaper, and sent a request that I would become its editor. I agreed to take the post.

For the first few days I wrote with such fire and zest that people used to point at me when I went out into the street, and I began to feel a brilliant halo about my forehead.

Next to Jahirgram was the village of Ahirgram. Between the landlords of these two villages there was a constant rivalry and feud. There had been a time when they came to blows not infrequently. But now, since the magistrate had bound them both over to keep the peace, I took the place of the hired ruffians who used to act for one of the rivals. Every one said that I lived up to the dignity of my position.

My writings were so strong and fiery that Ahirgram could no longer hold up its head. I blackened with my ink the whole of their ancient clan and family.

All this time I had the comfortable feeling of being pleased with myself. I even became fat. My face beamed with the exhilaration of a successful man of genius. I admired my own delightful ingenuity of insinuation, when at some excruciating satire of mine, directed against the ancestry of Ahirgram, the whole of Jahirgram would burst its sides with laughter like an over-ripe melon. I enjoyed myself thoroughly.

But at last Ahirgram started a newspaper. What it published was starkly naked, without a shred of literary urbanity. The language it used was of such undiluted colloquialism that every letter seemed to scream in one's face. The consequence was that the inhabitants of both villages clearly understood its meaning.

But as I was hampered in my style by my sense of decency, my subtlety of sarcasm very often made but a feeble impression upon the power of understanding of both my friends and my enemies.

The result was that even when I won decidedly in this war of infamy my readers were not aware of my victory. At last in desperation I wrote a sermon on the necessity of good taste in literature, but found that I had made a fatal mistake. For things that are solemn offer more surface for ridicule than things that are truly ridiculous. And therefore my effort at the moral betterment of my fellow-beings had the opposite effect to that which I had intended.

My employer ceased to show me such attention as he had done. The honour to which I had grown accustomed dwindled in its quantity, and its quality became poor. When I walked in the street people did not go out of their way to carry off the memory of a word with me. They even went so far as to be frivolously familiar in their behavior towards me—such as slapping my shoulders with a laugh and giving me nicknames.

In the meantime my admirers had quite forgotten the farces which had made me famous. I felt as if I was a burnt-out match, charted to its very end.

My mind became so depressed that, no matter how I racked my brains, I was unable to write one line. I seemed to have lost all zest for life.

Probha had now grown afraid of me. She would not venture to approach me unless summoned. She had come to understand that a commonplace doll is a far better companion than a genius of a father who writes comic pieces.

One day I saw that the Ahirgram newspaper, leaving my employer alone for once, had directed its attack on me. Some very ugly imputations had been made against myself. One by one all my friends and acquaintances came and read to me the spiciest bits, laughing heartily. Some of them said that however one might disagree with the subject-matter, it could not be denied that it was cleverly written. In the course of the day at least twenty people came and said the same thing, with slight variations to break its monotony.

In front of my house there is a small garden. I was walking there in the evening with a mind distracted with pain. When the birds had returned to their nests, and surrendered themselves to the peace of the evening, I understood quite clearly that amongst the birds at any rate there were no writers of journalism, nor did they hold discussions on good taste.

I was thinking only of one thing, namely, what answer I could make. The disadvantage of politeness is that it is not intelligible to all classes of people. So I had decided that my answer must be given in the same strain as the attack. I was not going to allow myself to acknowledge defeat.

Just as I had come to this conclusion, a well-known voice came softly through the darkness of the evening, and immediately afterwards I felt a soft warm touch in the palm of my hand. I was so distracted and absent-minded that even though that voice and touch were familiar to me, I did not realise that I knew them.

But the next moment, when they had left me, the voice sounded in my ear, and the memory of the touch became living. My child had slowly come near to me once more, and had whispered in my ear, "Father," but not getting any answer she had lifted my right hand, and with it had gently stroked her forehead, and then silently gone back into the house.

For a long time Probha had not called me like that, nor caressed me with such freedom. Therefore it was that to-day at the touch of her love my heart suddenly began to yearn for her.

Going back to the house a little later, I saw that Probha was lying on her bed. Her eyes were half closed, and she seemed to be in pain. She lay like a flower which has dropped on the dust at the end of the day.

Putting my hand on her forehead, I found that she was feverish. Her breath was hot, and her pulse was throbbing.

I realised that the poor child, feeling the first symptoms of fever, had come with her thirsty heart to get her father's love and caresses, while he was trying to think of some stinging reply to send to the newspaper.

I sat beside her. The child, without speaking a word, took my hand between her two fever-heated palms, and laid it upon her forehead, lying quite still.

All the numbers of the Jahirgram and Ahirgrarn papers which I had in the house I burnt to ashes. I wrote no answer to the attack. Never had I felt such joy as I did, when I thus acknowledged defeat.

I had taken the child to my arms when her mother had died, and now, having cremated this rival of her mother, again I took her to my heart.

Appendices

Appendix A: African-American Narrative

African-American Narrative

Equiano

1789: *The Interesting Narrative of the Life of Olaudah Equiano*

Douglass

1845: *Narrative of the Life of Frederick Douglass, An American Slave*
1855: *My Bondage and My Freedom*
1881: *The Life and Times of Frederick Douglass*

Brown

1847: *Narrative of William Wells Brown, A Fugitive Slave*
1880: *My Southern Homes*

Jacobs

1861: *Incidents in the Life of a Slave Girl*

1800s

Novels

1853: William Wells Brown's *Clotel, or the President's Daughter*
1857: Frank Webb's *The Garies and Their Friends*
1859: Harriet Wilson's *Our Nig*
1892: Frances E. W. Harper's *Iola Leroy or Shadows Uplifted*

Autobiographies

Additional slave narratives

Short Stories

1898: Paul Laurence Dunbar's *Folks from Dixie*
1899: Charles Chesnutt's *The Conjure Woman* and *The Wife of His Youth*

1900–09

Novels

1900: Charles Chestnutt's *The House Behind the Cedars*; Pauline Hopkins' *Contending Forces*
1901: Charles Chestnutt's *The Marrow of Tradition*
1905: Charles Chestnutt's *The Colonel's Dream*

Autobiographies

1901: Booker T. Washington's *Up From Slavery*

Short Stories

1910–19

Novels

1912: James Weldon Johnson's *The Autobiography of an Ex-Coloured Man*

Autobiographies

Short Stories

1920–29

Novels

1923: Jean Toomer's *Cane*
1924: Jessie Fauset's *There is Confusion*; Walter White's *Fire in the Flint*
1926: W. Adolphe Roberts' *The Haunting Hand*
1928: W. E. B. DuBois' *Dark Princess*; Nella Larsen's *Quicksand*; Claude McKay's *Home to Harlem*
1929: Jessie Fauset's *Plum Bun*; Nella Larsen's *Passing*; Wallace Thurman's *The Blacker the Berry*

Autobiographies

1923: William Pickens' *Bursting Bonds*

Short Stories

1925: Marita Bonner's "The Hands: A Story"; Zora Neale Hurston's "Spunk"
1926: Zora Neale Hurston's "Sweat"; Eric Walrond's *Tropic Death*

1930–39

Novels

1930: Langston Hughes' *Not Without Laughter*
1931: Jessie Fauset's *The Chinaberry Tree*; George Schuyler's *Black No More*
1932: Rudolph Fisher's *The Conjure Man Dies*; Wallace Thurman's *Infants of the Spring*
1933: Jessie Fauset's *Comedy American Style*; Claude McKay's *Banana Bottom*
1934: Zora Neale Hurston's *Jonah's Gourd Vine*
1935: Arna Bontemps' *Black Thunder*
1937: Zora Neale Hurston's *Their Eyes Were Watching God*

Autobiographies

1933: James Weldon Johnson's *Along This Way*
1937: Claude McKay's *A Long Way from Home*

Short Stories

1933: Arna Bontemps' "A Summer Tragedy"; Rudolph Fisher's "Miss Cynthie"
1934: Langston Hughes' *The Way of White Folks*
1938: Richard Wright's *Uncle Tom's Children*

1940–49

Novels

1940: Richard Wright's *Native Son*
1945: Chester Himes' *If He Hollers Let Him Go*
1946: Ann Petry's *The Street*; Dorothy West's *The Living is Easy*
1947: Chester Himes' *Lonely Crusade* and *The Third Generation*; Ann Petry's *Country Place*

Autobiographies

1940: W. E. B. DuBois' *Dusk of Dawn*; Langston Hughes' *The Big Sea*
1942: Zora Neale Hurston's *Dust Tracks on a Road*
1945: Richard Wright's *Black Boy*

Short Stories

1944: Ralph Ellison's "Flying Home"; Richard Wright's "The Man Who Lived Underground"
1947: Ann Petry's "In Darkness and Confusion"

1950–59

Novels

1952: Ralph Ellison's *Invisible Man*; Chester Himes' *Cast the First Stone*
1953: James Baldwin's *Go Tell It on the Mountain*; Ann Petry's *The Narrows*; Richard Wright's *The Outsider*
1954: John Killens' *Youngblood*
1955: Chester Himes' *The Primitive*
1956: James Baldwin's *Giovanni's Room*
1958: Richard Wright's *The Long Dream*
1959: Paule Marshall's *Brown Girl, Brownstone*

Autobiographies

1956: Langston Hughes' *I Wonder as I Wander*

Short Stories

1950: Langston Hughes' *Simple Speaks His Mind*

1960–69

Novels

1962: James Baldwin's *Another Country*
1964: Kristin Hunter's *God Bless the Child*
1965: Chester Himes' *Cotton Comes to Harlem*
1966: Ronald Fair's *Hog Butcher*; Rosa Guy's *Bird at My Window*; Margaret Walker's *Jubilee*
1967: John A. Williams' *The Man Who Cried I Am*
1968: James Baldwin's *Tell Me How Long the Train's Been Gone*
1969: Chester Himes' *Blind Man with a Pistol*; Ishmael Reed's *Yellow Black Radio Broke Down*

Autobiographies

1965: Alex Haley's *The Autobiography of Malcolm X*
1968: *The Autobiography of W. E. B. DuBois*

Short Stories

1967: Langston Hughes' *The Best Short Stories by Negro Writers*
1969: James A. McPherson's *Hue and Cry*

1970–79

Novels

1970: Toni Morrison's *The Bluest Eye*; Alice Walker's *The Third Life of Grange Copeland*
1971: Ernest Gaines' *The Autobiography of Miss Jane Pittman*; John Killens' *The Cotillion*; Frank Yerby's *The Dahomean*
1972: John A. Williams' *Captain Blackman*
1973: Alice Childress' *A Hero Ain't Nothing but a Sandwich*; Toni Morrison's *Sula*
1974: James Baldwin's *If Beale Street Could Talk*
1976: Ishmael Reed's *Flight to Canada*; Alice Walker's *Meridian*
1977: Toni Morrison's *Song of Solomon*
1979: Octavia Butler's *Kindred*; Barbara Chase-Riboud's *Sally Hemings*

Autobiographies

1970: Maya Angelou's *I Know Why the Caged Bird Sings*; Ida B. Wells-Barnett's *Crusade for Justice*
1971: Nikki Giovanni's *Gemini*
1972: Chester Himes' *The Quality of Hurt*
1974: Maya Angelou's *Gather Together in My Name*
1976: Maya Angelou's *Singin' and Swingin' and Gettin' Merry Like Christmas*; Chester Himes' *My Life of Absurdity*
1977: Richard Wright's *American Hunger*

Short Stories

1973: Arna Bontemps' *The Old South*
1977: James A. McPherson's *Elbow Room*

1980–89

Novels

1981: David Bradley's *The Chaneysville Incident*
1982: Gloria Naylor's *The Women of Brewster Place*; Alice Walker's *The Color Purple*
1983: Ernest Gaines' *A Gathering of Old Men*; Rosa Guy's *A Measure of Time*
1984: Samuel Delany's *Stars in My Pocket Like Grains of Sand*; Andrea Lee's *Sarah Phillips*
1985: Gloria Naylor's *Linden Hills*
1987: Toni Morrison's *Beloved*
1988: Gloria Naylor's *Mama Day*
1989: Steven Corbin's *No Easy Place to Be*

Autobiographies

1981: Maya Angelou's *The Heart of a Woman*
1983: Marita Golden's *Migrations of the Heart*
1984: John Edgar Wideman's *Brothers and Keepers*
1986: Maya Angelou's *All God's Children Need Travelin' Shoes*; Marsha Hunt's *Real Life*

Short Stories

1983: Paule Marshall's *Reena and Other Stories*
1984: J. California Cooper's *A Piece of Mine*
1986: J. California Cooper's *Homemade Love*
1987: J. California Cooper's *Some Soul to Keep*
1989: John Edgar Wideman's *Fever*

1990–

Novels

1990: Charles Johnson's *Middle Passage*; Walter Mosley's *Devil in a Blue Dress*
1991: Tina McElroy Ansa's *Baby of the Family*
1992: Caryl Phillips' *Cambridge*; Darryl Pinckney's *High Cotton*; Brent Wade's *Company Man*
1993: Trey Ellis' *Home Repairs*; Albert French's *Billy*
1994: Walter Mosley's *Black Betty*; Gwendolyn Parker's *These Same Long Bones*; and Edwidge Danticat's *Breath, Eyes, Memory*
1995: Dorothy West's *The Wedding*
1996: Diane McKinney-Whetstone's *Tumbling*; Dawn Turner Trice's *Only Twice I've Wished for Heaven*
1997: Tananarive Due's *My Soul to Keep*; Brian Keith Jackson's *The View from Here*
1998: Toni Morrison's *Paradise*
1999: Colson Whitehead's *The Intuitionist*; and *Juneteeth* by Ralph Ellison, as edited by John F. Callahan

Autobiographies

1990: Arthur Ashe's *Days of Grace*
1991: Lorene Cary's *Black Ice*
1992: Charlayne Hunter-Gault's *In My Place*
1993: Sarah and A. Elizabeth Delany's *Having Our Say: The Delany Sisters' First 100 Years*
1994: Henry Louis Gates, Jr.'s *Colored People*; Nathan McCall's *Makes Me Wanna Holler*
1995: Marcus Mabry's *White Bucks and Black-Eyed Peas*
1996: Veronica Chambers' *Mama's Girl*

Short Stories

1991: J. California Cooper's *The Matter is Life*
1994: Richard Wright's *Rite of Passage*
1995: J. California Cooper's *Some Love, Some Pain, Sometime*; Dorothy West's *The Richer, the Poorer*

Appendix B: Supplementary Biographies

William Wells Brown (1814–1884)

William Wells Brown was one of seven children born to Elizabeth, a slave who was rumored to be the daughter of Daniel Boone, in Lexington, Kentucky in 1814. William's father was George Higgins, a relative of Elizabeth's master. During William's boyhood, the slave owner moved his family and slaves to Missouri where William held a variety of jobs including house servant, field hand, tavern-keeper's assistant, printer's helper, medical office assistant, handyman, and seaman. William, who was determined to be a free man, persuaded his mother to escape with him, but they were discovered in Illinois and returned to their master. William's mother was sent to a plantation in New Orleans, and he was sold to a new master, from whom William successfully escaped on January 1, 1834. Wells Brown, a Quaker, helped the 19-year-old William to flee slavery, and as a result, he adopted the man's nomenclatures as his middle name and surname.

Brown, while basking in his own freedom, never forgot about those still in bondage. While residing in Buffalo, New York, he worked on Lake Erie steamboats where, for nine years, he ferried many slaves to freedom. In one instance, from May to December of 1842, Brown, a solitary but valuable link in the Underground Railroad, carried 69 fugitive slaves to Canada. In 1843, he began lecturing as a representative of western New York's Anti-Slavery Society, and by the time Brown joined Massachusetts' Anti-Slavery Society in 1847, he was recognized as a leading anti-slavery lecturer. In addition to denouncing slavery, Brown orated on behalf of the temperance movement, prison reform, and women's suffrage.

In 1849 Victor Hugo invited Brown to the Paris Peace Conference, and after the Fugitive Slave Law was enacted in 1850, Brown lived in England and delivered many anti-slavery lectures until his friends' purchase of Brown's freedom in 1854 facilitated his return to the United States.

In addition to his work with the Underground Railroad and his anti-slavery orations, Brown, the abolitionist, had an even more potent weapon: writing. He was a prolific author who, regardless of genre, denounced slavery and publicized African-American accomplishments. Among Brown's publications are his first autobiography, *Narrative of William W. Brown, A Fugitive Slave, Written By Himself* (1847); a volume of song-poems, *The Anti-Slavery Harp* (1848); the first travel book by an African American, *Three Years in Europe, or Places I Have Seen and People I Have Met* (1852); the first novel by an African American, *Clotel, or the President's Daughter: A Narrative of Slave Life in the United States* (1853); the first drama published by an African American, *The Escape, or A Leap for Freedom* (1858); one of the first volumes of African-American history, *The Black Man: His Antecedents, His Genius, and His Achievements* (1863); the first military history of African Americans, *The Negro in the American Rebellion* (1867); his most comprehensive history, *The Rising Son; or, The Antecedents and Advancement of the Colored Race* (1874); and his second autobiography, *My Southern Home* (1880). Brown's creative publications have distinguished him as African America's first writer of belles lettres, while his historical publications place him among the earliest African-American historians. Brown died at his Chelsea, Massachusetts home on November 6, 1884.

Selected Bibliography

Andrews, William L., Frances Smith Foster, and Trudier Harris, eds. *The Oxford Companion to African-American Literature*. New York: Oxford UP, 1997.

Nelson, Emmanuel S., Ed. *African American Authors, 1745–1945: A Bio-Bibliographical Critical Sourcebook*. Westport, CT: Greenwood, 2000.

James Weldon Johnson
(1871–1938)

Born of middle-class, African-American and West Indian parentage in Jacksonville, Florida, in 1871, James Weldon Johnson cultivated a love of letters and music at an early age. He attended the Atlanta University Preparatory School and College, graduating in 1894. Afterwards, he became principal of the Black public school in Jacksonville, founded and published a paper, *The Daily American*, in 1895, and studied law. In 1897, he was the first African American to pass the Florida Bar Examination. In the summers from 1899–1901, Johnson went to New York to collaborate with his brother, Rosamond, in the writing of light opera and musical comedy, producing such songs as "Under the Bamboo Tree," "Congo Love Song," "O Didn't He Ramble," and "Lift Every Voice and Sing," commonly known as the Black National Anthem, which Rosamond set to music.

Johnson's interest in politics and knowledge of Spanish won him the position of the United States consul at Puerto Cabello, Venezuela, from 1906 to 1907 and at Corinta, Nicaragua, from 1909 to 1912. During his diplomatic career, Johnson wrote *The Autobiography of an Ex-Colored Man* (1912). This novel marked the beginning of a literary career that, combined with his work as an official of the NAACP, brought Johnson great contemporary distinction. He published three volumes of poetry: *Fifty Years and Other Poems* (1917), *God's Trombones* (1927), *and St. Peter Relates an Incident of the Resurrection Day* (1935). These volumes revealed Johnson's remarkable growth as a poet. In 1933 Johnson published his autobiography, *Along This Way*.

Johnson's poetic works are a good index to changes in themes, techniques, and tone which the Harlem Renaissance introduced. The first volume, *Fifty Years and Other Poems,* evidences most of the faults found in Black writing of the pre-Renaissance era. The title poem, written to commemorate the 50th anniversary of the Emancipation Proclamation, is virtually a catalogue of cliched themes found in Negro poetry since the Civil War. The second volume, *God's Trombones,* appearing only ten years after the first, shows far more than ten years of Johnson's poetic growth and understanding. In *God's Trombones,* using the old-time Black folk sermon as his vehicle, Johnson put his theories into practice. He has shown great skill in transforming folk material into sophisticated art. The third volume, *St. Peter Relates an Incident of the Resurrection Day,* consists of 38 poems, most of them having appeared in *Fifty Years and Other Poems*.

Educator, song writer, man of letters, diplomat, secretary of the NAACP, and successful journalist, James Weldon Johnson was a many-sided and talented figure. A rare combination of creative artist and man of affairs, Johnson had the ambition, the competency, the pragmatic outlook of the successful middle-class American, as well as the sensitivity of the artist.

Selected Bibliography

Davis, Arthur P. *From the Dark Tower: Afro-American Writers (1900 to 1960)*. Washington, D.C.: Howard University Press, 1974.
Henderson, Stephen. *Understanding the New Black Poetry: Black Speech & Black Music as Poetic References*. New York: William Morrow, 1972.

Ralph Waldo Ellison (1914–1994)

Ralph Ellison is best known for *Invisible Man* (1952), a novel that won him a National Book Award and the Russwurm Award. In a 1965 literary poll, the book was deemed the most esteemed work published in the United States since 1945.

Ellison was born on March 1, 1914, in Oklahoma City, the son of Lewis Alfred Ellison, a construction worker, and Ida Ellison. He later observed that growing up in Oklahoma stimulated him to explore the Black experience in a new and complex way, since the state had no tradition of slavery and therefore had better relations between races than could be found in the Old South.

From 1933 to 1936, Ellison attended Tuskegee Institute in Alabama. Although he enrolled as a music major, he soon became interested in writing. At Tuskegee, Ellison took a sociology course that was to change his life. He observed that the course presented such a humiliating portrait of Black Americans that he felt a new sense of urgency to discover the truth about Black culture for himself. When Ellison did not have funds for college, he went to New York to study sculpture. While Ellison was in New York, from 1938 to 1942, he worked with the Federal Writers Project, a federally funded program designed to combat unemployment while supporting the arts. Ellison published short stories and essays in left-wing journals. His two best-known stories from this period are "Flying Home" and "King of the Bingo Game."

Ellison's New York years helped to shape him as a writer. He met the major Black poet Langston Hughes, who suggested that he read the White Marxist writer André Malraux. Ellison later met Black novelist Richard Wright, who urged him to read other key White writers. Although Ellison and Wright became friends, Ellison rejected Wright's portrait of Bigger Thomas in *Native Son*, believing that Wright has portrayed Black people as helpless victims, rather than as people with intelligence and imagination.

In 1942 Ellison briefly edited the magazine, *Negro Quarterly*. From 1955 to 1957, Ellison was a fellow of the American Academy in Rome. He was a visiting professor of writing at Yale University, an instructor in Russian and American literature at Bard College, and visiting professor at Rutgers University. In 1961 Ellison served as an Alexander White visiting professor at the University of Chicago. He was appointed to the American Academy of Arts and Letters in 1964. From 1970 to 1980, he was Albert Schweitzer Professor of Humanities at New York University. He was a charter member of the National Council on the Arts and Humanities, a member of the Carnegie Commission on public television, and a trustee of the John F. Kennedy Center for the Performing Arts.

During World War II, Ellison served in the United States Merchant Marine. After the war, he received a Rosenwald grant that afforded him the time to continue writing. He began *Invisible Man*, which took him seven years to complete. *Invisible Man* is the story of a young Black man, who, on a journey in search of his identity, moves from innocence to knowledge. Ellison makes use of jazz imagery, historical and cultural myths, and the philosophical interests and stylistic innovations of modern European and American writers.

Invisible Man is a distinguished book. It won many awards and much acclaim. It led to lecture tours in Europe and many posts teaching literature and writing at American colleges and universities. The book raises many questions of deep concern, not only to every Black man and woman but also to all Americans.

Selected Bibliography

Harris, Trudier, ed. *Dictionary of Literary Biography: Afro-American Writers 1940–1955.* Vol. 76. Detroit: Gale Research, 1988.
Kranz, Rachel C. *The Biographical Dictionary of Black Americans.* New York: Oxford University Press, 1991.

Adrienne Rich (1929–)

A native of Baltimore, Adrienne Rich was born in 1929 and graduated from Radcliffe College in 1951. *A Change of World,* Rich's first volume of poetry, also was published in 1951 in the Yale series of Younger Poets, a prize awarded by the then judge, W. H. Auden. She has published more than 15 volumes of poetry since 1951, including her most recent work, *Dark Fields of the Republic: Poems 1991–1995* (1995).

Rich's work addresses her role as a female poet and the dichotomies in the lives and experiences of women. After her marriage to the economist Alfred Conrad in 1953 and the birth and nurturing of three sons, Rich published her second volume of poetry, *The Diamond Cutters.* But eight years followed before the publication of her third and fourth books, *Snapshots of a Daughter* (1963) and the *Necessities of Life* (1966). In 1966 after moving to New York City, Rich became involved in radical politics in opposition to the Vietnam War, which would become another concern within her poems, *Leaflets* (1969) and *The Will to Change* (1971). Increasingly she also dedicated herself to feminism, for which she has provided an important context in numerous collections of prose, which include *Of Woman Born , On Lies, Secrets, and Silence: Selected Prose 1966–1978* and *Blood, Bread, and Poetry: Selected Prose 1979–1985*. Some critics have dismissed Rich's work, charging that she has sacrificed her art in the expression of her political views.

Selected Bibliography

Cooper, Jane Roberta. *Reading Adrienne Rich*. Ann Arbor: University of Michigan Press, 1984.
Keyes, Claire. *The Aesthetics of Power: The Poetry of Adrienne Rich*. Athens: University of Georgia Press, 1986.
Rich, Adrienne Cecile. *The Fact of a Doorframe: Poems Selected and New 1950–1984*. New York: W.W. Norton, 1984.

Chinua Achebe (1930–)

Born in Ogidi, the eastern part of Nigeria, in 1930, Chinua Achebe was originally christened Albert Chinua-lumogu. His father, Isaiah Okafor Achebe, was an evangelist and church teacher, although many of his relatives and neighbors adhered to Ibo religion and customs.

Achebe's primary education was in the society's school in Ogidi. He was eight when he began to learn English and fourteen when he was one of the few boys selected to attend the Government College at Umuahia, one of the best schools in West Africa. In 1948 he enrolled at University College, Ibadan, as a member of the first class to attend this new school, which was a constituent college of the University of London. His intention was to study medicine, but he soon switched to English literary studies and followed a syllabus that almost exactly resembled the University of London honors degree program. As a student, Achebe contributed stories, essays, and sketches to the *University Herald*. The stories were reprinted in 1972 in *Girls at War and Other Stories*. After graduating in 1953, he decided to become a writer.

Achebe is probably the most widely read of contemporary African authors, both on the African continent and abroad. He is also the most discussed African writer of his generation. His first novel, *Things Fall Apart* (1958), has become a classic. It has been discussed by readers worldwide and translated into some 40 languages. His other novels include *No Longer at Ease* (1960), *Arrow of God* (1964), *A Man of the People* (1966), and *Anthills of the Savannah* (1987). These highly respected books have been the objects of a substantial body of scholarship and criticism.

Achebe's reputation was quickly established with *Things Fall Apart,* which won him the Margaret Wrong Memorial Prize as well as scholarships and grants. After the publication of *No Longer at Ease,* he was awarded the Nigerian National Trophy for Literature, and for the third novel, *Arrow of God,* he received the New Statesman Jock Campbell Award. *A Man of the People* aroused immediate interest because of its seemingly prophetic insight into subsequent political events in Nigeria. In 1972 he was awarded the Commonwealth Poetry prize for his volume titled *Beware, Soul Brother and Other Poems* (revised and republished as *Christmas in Biafra and Other Poems* in 1973). Achebe has been awarded honorary doctorates by universities in North America and Britain, has been elected an honorary fellow of the Modern Language Association, and has been nominated for the Nobel Prize in literature.

Achebe's lectures and essays have provoked much debate about the criteria for assessing African writers, and his influence on younger novelists has been considerable. He, of course, continues to be the subject of numerous critical essays published in journals throughout the world. Achebe himself has not only been an outspoken social critic, but also he has worked to develop the broadcast media in Nigeria.

Selected Bibliography

Carroll, David. *Chinua Achebe*. 2nd ed. New York: St. Martin's Press, 1980.
Innes, C. L., and Bernth Lindfors, eds. *Critical Perspectives on Chinua Achebe*. Washington, D.C.: Three Continents Press, 1978.

Lindfors, Bernth, and Reinhard Sander, eds. *Dictionary of Literary Biography: Twentieth Century Caribbean and Black African Writers.* Detroit: Gale Research, 1992.

Wren, Robert M. *Achebe's World: The Historical and Cultural Context of the Novels.* Washington, D.C.: Three Continents Press, 1980.

Lorraine Hansberry (1930–1965)

Lorraine Vivian Hansberry, born in Chicago to well-to-do parents, was the youngest of four children. Her mother, Nannie Perry Hansberry, was a teacher who played a major role in the social and cultural life of Black Chicago. Her father, Carl Augustus Hansberry, was a businessman, civic leader, real estate broker, and investor who converted low-priced buildings into kitchenette units for African-American tenants.

Hansberry left Chicago after her 1947 graduation from high school to attend the University of Wisconsin-Madison. In 1950 she moved to Harlem, where she wrote and edited stories for *Freedom*, a newspaper founded by actor/singer Paul Robeson. In 1952 she met Robert Nemiroff, a student from New York University. They married a year later, at which time Hansberry resigned from her position at *Freedom* to devote herself to her writing. She was not financially secure, though, until Nemiroff and a friend made big money selling a song they wrote called "Cindy, Oh Cindy."

Hansberry, who had begun to identify herself as a playwright, went back to her past, to the kitchenette units in Chicago, in imaging forth *A Raisin in the Sun,* a play that many critics now view as the most powerful drama ever written about the American family. After initial resistance from Broadway producers, Hansberry and her supporters took the play on tour in Philadelphia, Chicago, and a handful of other cities. Finally, in March of 1959, *A Raisin in the Sun* opened on Broadway to immediate acclaim. That year Hansberry became the youngest writer and first African American to receive the coveted New York Drama Critics Circle Award.

Following several years of speaking engagements and writing for television and film, she completed a second play, *The Sign in Sidney Brustein's Window,* in 1964. Many theater-goers were disappointed that the play had abandoned the theme of African Americans in struggle. *Sidney Brustein,* with its mainly White cast, examines intellectual choice and social commitment among people living in Greenwich Village. While these issues are important, critics tended to think that *Sidney Brustein* lacked the dramatic intensity of *A Raisin in the Sun,* with its powerful treatment of race and gender.

In 1964 Hansberry was working on a variety of other plays or adaptations. Among them were *Les Blancs,* a play about a revolution in an African country that was edited and produced by Nemiroff five years after Hansberry's death; and *Achnaton,* an unfinished drama about the Egyptian ruler who founded a religion based on the concept of one god, Aton, the sun god.

But 1964 was a disastrous year for Hansberry. She and Nemiroff divorced after a long separation. The cancer that had been discovered a year earlier was progressing, with little hope of remission. She was still well enough, though, to give occasional lectures and to participate in the emerging Civil Rights Movement and in the new feminism.

Lorraine Hansberry died in January of 1965, at the age of 34. She had chosen Robert Nemiroff to be her literary executor. In this capacity, Nemiroff in 1969 put together a theatrical piece, *To Be Young, Gifted, and Black,* a collection of autobiographical sketches and other writings. Both *A Raisin in the Sun* and *To Be Young, Gifted, and Black* have been frequently revitalized for stage, print, screen, and television. Despite the brevity of her life, Lorraine Hansberry continues to make an enduring contribution to American theater.

Selected Bibliography

Baldwin, James. "Lorraine Hansberry at the Summit." *Freedomways* 19 (1979): 269–272. Special Issue.
Carter, Steven R. *Hansberry's Drama: Commitment Amid Complexity.* Urbana: University of Illinois Press, 1991.
Cheney, Anne. *Lorraine Hansberry.* Twayne Series. New York: Macmillan, 1984.
"Hansberry, Lorraine Vivian." *Notable Women in the American Theater: A Biographical Dictionary.* A. M. Robinson, V. Roberts, and M. S. Barranger, eds. *Notable Black Women.* New York: Greenwood Press, 1989, 524–529.
Mayfield, Julian. "Lorraine Hansberry: A Woman for All Seasons." *Freedomways* 19 (1979): 263–268. Special Issue.
Seaton, Sandra. "*A Raisin in the Sun:* A Study in Afro-American Culture." *Midwestern Miscellany* 20 (1992): 40–49.
Shinn, Thelma. "Living the Answer: The Emergence of African American Feminist Drama." *Studies in the Humanities* 17 (1990): 149–59.
Washington, J. Charles. "*A Raisin in the Sun* Revisited." *Black American Literature Forum* 22 (1988): 109–24.

August Wilson (1945–)

August Wilson was born on April 27, 1945, in Pittsburgh, Pennsylvania. During Wilson's teenaged years, his family moved to a predominantly White suburban neighborhood, and Wilson transferred to Gladstone High School, where he was subjected to the racial taunts of his classmates and the prejudice of his teacher, who accused him of plagiarizing his term paper. Fifteen-year-old Wilson dropped out of school, yet he spent the remainder of his teen years in disciplined self-study at a local library before enlisting in the United States Army.

After being discharged from the Army, Wilson moved to a boarding house in Pittsburgh in 1965. He was determined to become a writer, and he supported himself with various low-paying jobs. Hearing a recording by the blues singer Bessie Smith motivated him to document the Black American experience in his writings. Wilson's initial efforts were poetic, and during the late 1960s and early 1970s, his poems were published in several periodicals such as *Negro Digest*, as well as *Black Lines* and in at least one anthology, *The Poetry of Black Americans: Anthology of the Twentieth Century*.

Wilson co-founded two organizations that promoted Black American writing: the Center Avenue Poets Theatre Workshop and Black Horizons. His earliest plays, including *Recycle, The Homecoming,* and *The Coldest Day of the Year* (1977), were written for Black Horizons. In 1975 Wilson became a scriptwriter for the Science Museum of Minnesota, where he authored several brief scripts including "An Evening with Margaret Mead," "How Coyote Got His Special Power and Used It to Help the People," and "Eskimo Song Duel: The Case of the Borrowed Wife." Wilson continued to create plays in his spare time. *Black Bart and the Sacred Hills, Jitney!* and *Fullerton Street* were written prior to Wilson's decision to quit his job as a scriptwriter in order to devote more time to his own plays.

Wilson's dedication to his craft has led to the creation of seven dramas that have generated national attention and critical success. *Ma Rainey's Black Bottom, Fences, Joe Turner's Come and Gone, The Piano Lesson, Two Trains Running,* and *Seven Guitars* have been performed at regional theaters across the United States as well as on Broadway and have received various theatrical awards. Wilson is one of seven American playwrights to win two Pulitzer Prizes for Drama (*Fences* and *The Piano Lesson*) and the first Black American to have two plays (*Fences* and *Joe Turner's Come and Gone*) running simultaneously on Broadway. Wilson's seven plays are elements of an announced ten-drama cycle designed to document 20th century Black American life decade by decade. Thus, he provides a panoramic view of Black identity, culture, and history as he chronicles the Black experience.

Selected Bibliography

Andrews, William L., Frances Smith Foster, and Trudier Harris, eds. *The Oxford Companion to African American Literature.* New York: Oxford University Press, 1997.
Bigelow, Barbara C., ed. *Contemporary Black Biography.* Detroit: Gale Research, 1994. Vol. 7.
Moritz, Charles, ed. *1987 Current Biography Yearbook.* New York: Wilson, 1987.
Nadel, Alan, ed. *May All Your Fences Have Gates: Essays on the Drama of August Wilson.* Iowa City: University of Iowa Press, 1994.

Shannon, Sandra G. *The Dramatic Vision of August Wilson.* Washington, D.C.: Howard University Press, 1995.

DEPARTMENT OF *ENGLISH*

and LANGUAGE ARTS

COURSE SYLLABUS

HUMANITIES 202

Morgan State University

THE FRESHMAN ENGLISH—HUMANITIES—WRITING PROFICIENCY EXAMINATION PROGRAM

Facts That You Should Know:

1. The Freshman English—Humanities—Writing Proficiency Examination Program is a five stage corps of General Education Requirements which every student must satisfy in order to be eligible for graduation. A student must pursue the five stages of the Program in the following order:

    STAGE 1: English 101
    STAGE 2: English 102
    STAGE 3: Humanities 201
    STAGE 4: Humanities 202
    STAGE 5: Writing Proficiency Examination

2. Students may not advance to any stage of the Program until they have satisfied all of the preceding stages. Students found in violation of the proper sequence will be removed from a given stage (course or examination) until they have satisfied all of the prerequisites of that stage.

   Through placement testing, the University will determine the level at which students are to enter the Program. Students must enter the Program at the prescribed level and move forward in proper sequence. They are exempted from all courses that precede the level to which they are assigned.

   Students may meet the course and examination requirements of the Program in the following ways:

   A. **Advanced Placement Exemption:** As a result of placement testing by the University, students may be exempted from any of the stages of the program. If these students are to be exempted from any of the stages of the Program by placement testing, they will be notified of such exemption or advanced placement at the time of their matriculation at Morgan. Students exempted from any one or more of these stages (except ENGL. 100) will receive credit, but no grade, for the course.

   B. **Transfer Credit:** The transcript of students bringing transfer credit from other institutions will be evaluated to determine if those credits meet any of the requirements of the Program. If students are to be exempted from any of the five stages of the Program, they will be notified of such exemption at the time of matriculation at Morgan. No transfer credit is accepted for the Writing Proficiency Examination, and students transferring to Morgan with the A.A. degree should arrange to take the Examination during their first semester at Morgan.

   C. **Regular Course Enrollment:** Students may satisfy any of these stages by enrolling and receiving a passing grade in the relevant course.

   D. **Proficiency Testing:** Students may satisfy the requirement for English 101 and 102 and Humanities 201 and 202 through proficiency tests. Students desiring to pursue credit through proficiency testing should apply in the English Office (Holmes Hall 202) by the end of the third week of classes of the semester in which they seek to be tested.

5. Passing grades in English 101 and 102 are "A," "B," and "C." Any performance below the level of "C" is unsatisfactory and will cause a student to receive an "F."

6. Students may satisfy the Writing Proficiency requirement by enrolling and receiving a passing grade in English 350 (Junior Writing Practicum). Students who fail the Writing Proficiency Examination should also enroll in this course.

7. Student should take the Writing Proficiency Examination in their junior year (after passing Humanities 202) and should register for that Examination in the Office of the English Department well before the date on which the Examination is scheduled. By no means should students wait until their senior year to take the Examination.

CLASS ATTENDANCE POLICY

Students are expected to attend every class. In the event of unavoidable absence, the student will submit written, official verification of the reason for the absence. Students should submit the written, official verification upon their return; the instructor will make the final determination as to the validity of the excuse. The student is responsible for all work, whether or not he/she is present. If a student accumulates more unexcused absences than the number of hours in which the class meets weekly, the student will receive an "F" for the course.

EXIT EXAMINATION

Beginning in the fall semester of 1995, each student in a Freshman English or Humanities course will need to pass a Departmental exit examination in order to pass the course. To be eligible to take the exit examination, the student needs to be passing the course at the time of the examination.

PROCEDURES AND REQUIREMENTS

1. Classes meet three hours a week.

2. Students should note that the indicated readings, including related introductory and auxiliary materials, are to be completed before the class periods in which they are to be discussed.

3. Written reports *will be assigned* on outside reading and on *field experiences* in art, film, dance, music, and drama.

4. In addition to completing a number of requirements (as outlined by the instructor, in writing, at the beginning of the course), students will complete a minimum of one documented essay, which essay will constitute 10–20 percent of the final grade (the percentage to be specified by the instructor at the beginning of the semester). In addition, all of the major examinations will have an essay component.

MAIN TEXTS

Achebe, *Things Fall Apart*
Humanities in the Modern World: an Africana Emphasis

ADDITIONAL TEXTS

Students should check with their instructors *before* purchasing any additional texts.

MATERIALS

Where appropriate, students may be required to purchase supplemental materials, supplies, or tools.

Morgan State University

HUMANITIES 202

OBJECTIVES:

The general objectives of this course are to make students articulate members of the intellectual community, interested in the ideas and literary forms reflective of modern cultures; to make students aware of the personal, social, artistic, and literary values of these cultures; and to make students constantly alert and receptive to opportunities to improve and enlarge their experiences in the humanities.

Specifically, students

1. will become articulate concerning the humanities, observing the communication standards required of Morgan students:

    a. students will become more proficient in research skills and write clearer, more effective documented essays.

    b. students will write clearly structured essay-type examinations that are focused and effectively supported.

2. will recognize (especially in literature) the forms, themes, and movements of the humanities.

3. will develop a keen understanding of the relationship between cultural movements and historical facts.

4. will acquire literary skills, being able

    a. to recognize distinctions among literary forms.

    b. to differentiate specifically among the genres or modes, such as drama, lyric, and narrative.

    c. to discern various modes of presentation within each of the above categories.

5. will acquire increasing sensitivity to women's issues and attitudes and to the roles of women in modern cultures.

HUMANITIES 202

Modern

Introduction 2 weeks
Drama 2 weeks
*Douglas Turner Ward's *Day of Absence* or Lorraine Hansberry's *A Raisin in the Sun* or August Wilson's *Fences*
*Shakespeare's *Lear* or *Othello*
Lyrics 3 weeks
*As a core requirement, each class will study:
   A. A minimum of ten(10) *African-American* poems by such writers as Wheatley, Dunbar, Hughes, Toomer, Cullen, McKay, and Brooks.
   B. At least two poems from each of the following cultures, focussing on authors like those indicated below.
      1. *African:* Senghor, Diop, Peters, Njau
      2. *Asian:* Wang Wei, Mao Tse-Tung, Takamura Kotaro, Yaichi Aizu
      3. *European-American:* Dickinson, Frost, Roethke, Rich
      4. *European:* Petrarch, François Villon, Shakespeare, Keats, Dylan Thomas
      5. *Native American:* James Welch, Ray Young Bear
Narrative 5 weeks
*Chinua Achebe's *Things Fall Apart*
Two Asian Short Narratives Such as Ts'an Hsueh's "[Chen Shih-Yin Meets the Stone of Spiritual Understanding]" and Rabindranath Tagore's "Editor"
*ced*Black Elk Speaks* (Chapter 3)
*Kate Chopin's *The Awakening*
*Frederick Douglass' *Narrative of the Life of Frederick Douglass*
Ralph Ellison's *Invisible Man* (or other complete African-American narrative selected by the Instructor)
*Franz Kafka's "Metamorphosis" or Dostoevsky's *Notes from the Underground*
One or Two Latin American Short Narratives such as Estaban Montejo and Miguel Barnet's "Ma Lucia, the Great Story Teller" or Jorge Luis-Borges' "Labyrinths"
Ann Petry's "In Darkness and Confusion"
Edgar Allan Poe's "The Cask of Amontillado"
*Richard Wright's "The Ethics of Living Jim Crow" and *The Man Who Lived Underground*

Supportive Visual Arts and Music

In addition to studying the above literary texts, the class will have multicultural experiences in the visual arts and music.

---

* The asterisked selections are core or required items.

European-American Painting, Sculpture, and Architecture

Robert Mills (1848–1884)
Washington Monument. Baltimore, Maryland.
Reproduced by permission of Ewing Galloway.

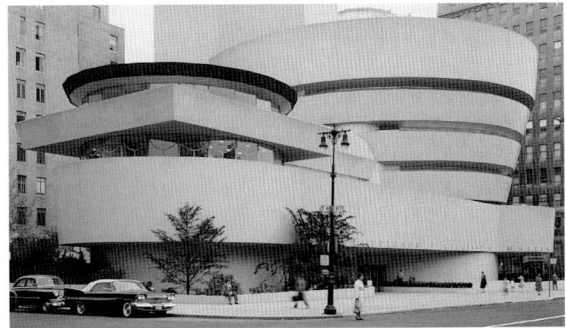

Frank Lloyd Wright (1867–1959) *Interior and Exterior, Solomon R. Guggenheim Museum.*
Photo by Robert Mates. © Solomon R. Guggenheim Foundation, New York.

Andy Warhol (1925–1987) *One Hundred Cans.*
The Andy Warhol Foundation, Inc./Art Resource, New York, © 1998 Andy Warhol Foundation for the Visual Arts./Artists Rights Society, New York.

African-American Painting and Sculpture

Edmonia Lewis (1849–1890?)
Forever Free.
Howard University Art Gallery, Washington, D.C.

A-4 African-American Painting and Sculpture

Horace Pippin (1888–1946) *The End of the War: Starting Home.*
Philadelphia Museum of Art. Gift of Robert Carlen.

Jacob Lawrence (1917–) *During the World War There Was A Great Migration North by Southern Negroes [1940–41].*
Phillips Collection, Washington, D.C.

Faith Ringgold (1934–) *The Flag is Bleeding*.
96˝ x 72˝, Oil on Canvas, 1967. Reproduced by permission of Faith Ringgold.

European Painting, Sculpture, and Architecture

Donato Bramante (c. 1444–1514) Damascus Court. Vatican Palace, Rome. Courtesy Alinari/Art Resource, New York.

A–6

European Painting, Sculpture, and Architecture   A–7

Auguste Rodin (1840–1917)
Le Penseur (The Thinker)
Courtesy Museè Rodin, Paris/Art Resource, New York.

African Art, Sculpture, and Architecture

Mask, Wood, Baule Tribe, Ivory Coast, West Africa.
Courtesy Museè de L'Homme, Paris.

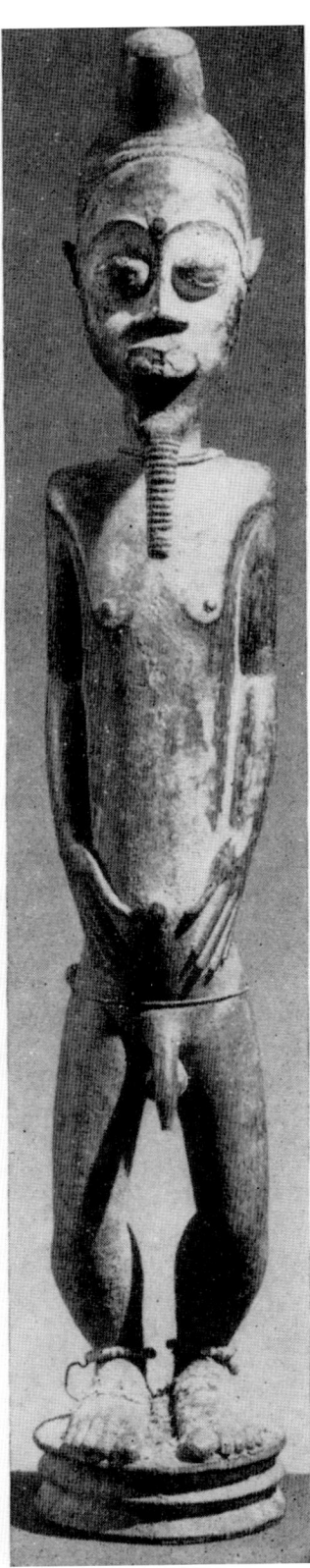
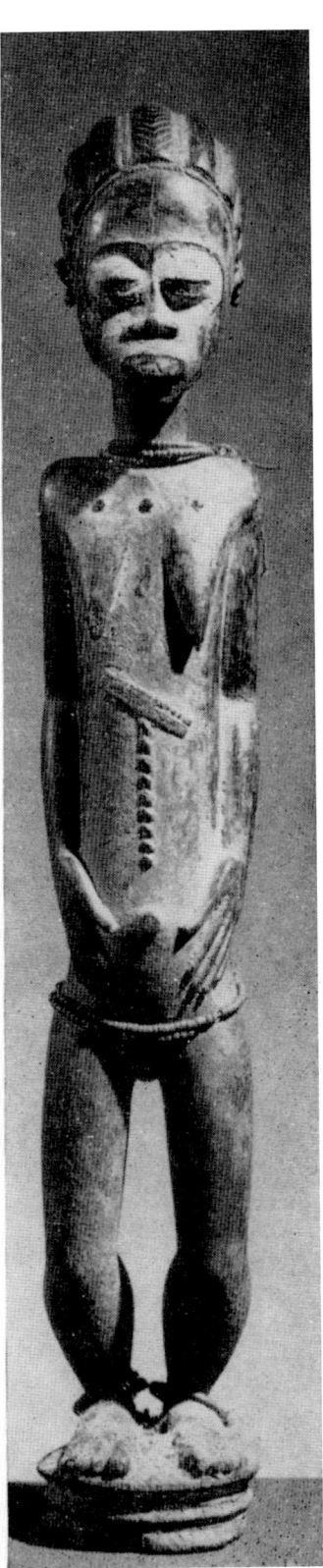

Standing Male and Female Figures. Wood, Baule Tribe, Ivory Coast, West Africa.
Courtesy Museum of Primitive Art, New York.

Head of Oba (King). Edo Peoples, Benin, Court Style, Nigeria.
Photograph by Jeffrey Polonskona. Gift of Joseph H. Hirshhorn. Copyright © 1987 Smithsonian Institution, National Museum of African Art.

African Art, Sculpture, and Architecture   A–11

Head of a Queen-Mother. Brass, Benin Court, Nigeria.
Courtesy British Museum, London.

A–12　African Art, Sculpture, and Architecture

Male Head of Early Period and Male Head of Late Period. Bronzes.
Courtesy Aldo Tutino/Art Resource, New York; Lauros-Giraudon/Art Resource, New York.

African Art, Sculpture, and Architecture   A–13

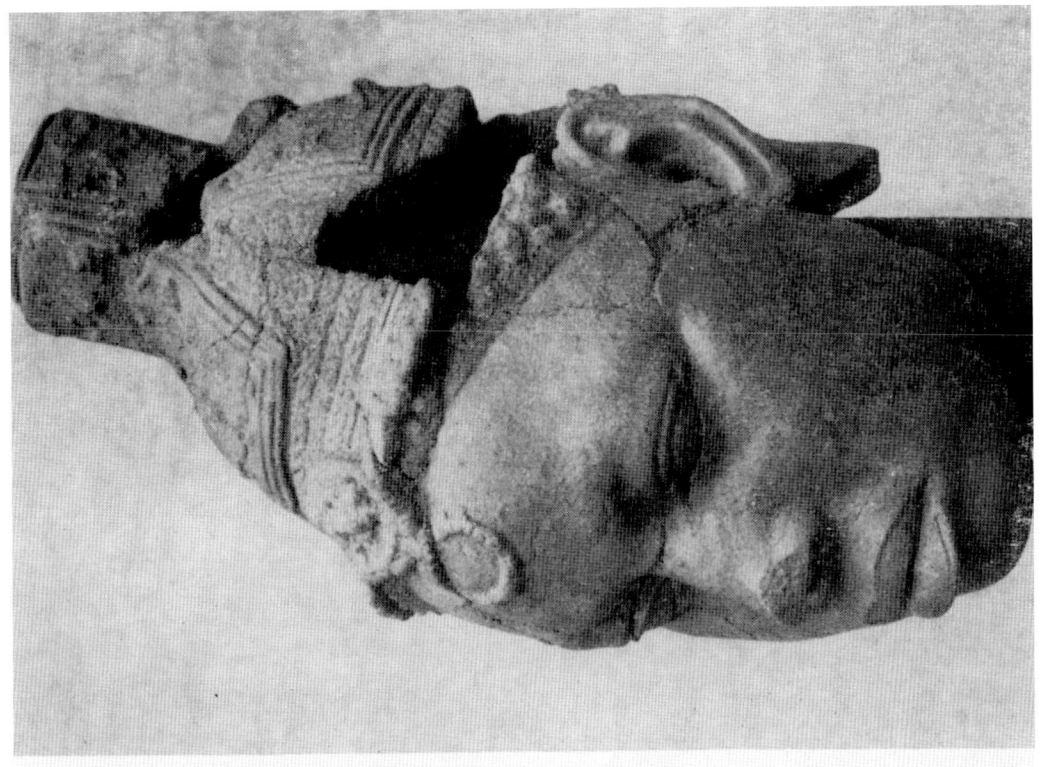

Heads from Ita Yemoo. Terracotta, Ife Culture, Nigeria, West Africa. Courtesy British Museum, London.

A-14 African Art, Sculpture, and Architecture

Mask from Wunmonije and Head from Wunmonije. Bronzes. Ife Culture, Nigeria, West Africa. Courtesy British Museum, London.

African Art, Sculpture, and Architecture   A–15

Palace Door. Wood. Yoruba Tribe, Nigeria, West Africa.
Carved by Arowogun of Osi.
Courtesy British Museum, London.

Asian Painting and Architecture

Ming Dynasty (1368-1644): The Great Wall with Watchtower, Hopei Province.
Photograph © by Erich Lessing/Art Resource, New York.

Kitagawa Sosetsu, "Summer Flowers," Hanging scroll, ink and colors on paper.
Photograph Courtesy John Bigelow Taylor, Newark Museum, Newark, NJ/Art Resource, New York.

A–18 Asian Painting and Architecture

Safawid: The Royal Square, Mosque, and Palace, Isfahan. SEF/Art Resource, New York.

Mughal: The Taj Mahal, Agra.
Scala/Art Resource, New York.

European-American Painting

Jackson Pollock (1912–1956) *Autumn Rhythm.*
© 1998 Pollock-Krasner Foundation/Artists Rights Society, New York. © 1980 by the Metropolitan Museum of Art. Reproduced Courtesy of the George A. Hearn Fund, 1957.

African-American Painting and Sculpture

Robert S. Duncanson (1821–1871) Blue Hole, Flood Waters, Little Miami River.
Cincinnati Art Museum. Gift of Norbert Heerman and Arthur Helbig.

A-22 African-American Painting and Sculpture

Edward Mitchell Bannister (1828–1901) Approaching Storm. [1886]
National Museum of American Art, Smithsonian Institution. Art Resource, New York.

Henry Ossawa Tanner (1859–1937) [1893]
The Banjo Lesson.
Hampton University Museum, Hampton, Virginia.

African-American Painting and Sculpture   A–23

Aaron Douglass (1898–1979)
Building More Stately Mansions.
Oil on Canvas, 1944. Collection of Fisk University, Nashville, Tennessee.

Lois Mailou Jones (1905–1998) Jardin du Luxembourg.
National Museum of American Art, Washington, D.C./Art Resource, New York. Oil on Canvas 23¾″ x 28¾″. Gift of Gladys P. Payne in honor of Alice P. Moore.

Elizabeth Catlett (1919–) *Sharecropper.*
1970, 17$^{13}/_{16}$ x 16$^{15}/_{16}$ in. Linoleum Cut on Paper. © Elizabeth Catlett/Licensed by VAGA, New York, NY. National Museum of American Art, Smithsonian Institution.

James Hampton *The Throne of the Third Heaven of the Nations Millennium General Assembly.*
National Museum of Art, Smithsonian Institution. Gift of anonymous donors.

European Painting

Leonardo Da Vinci (1452–1519).
Mona Lisa. Louvre, Paris.
Courtesy Scala/Art Resource, New York.

A–26   European Painting

The Last Supper.
Refectory, Santa Maria Delle Grazie, Milan.
Courtesy Scala/Art Resource, New York.

Michelangelo (1475–1564)
The Creation of Man. Sistine Chapel, Vatican, Rome.
Courtesy Scala/Art Resource, New York.

A–28 European Painting

Paul Gaugin (1848–1903).
Ta Matete (The Market). Kunstmuseum, Basel.
Courtesy Giraudon/Art Resource, New York.

Henri Matisse (1869–1954).
Poppies.
© 1998 Succession H. Matisse, Paris/Artists Rights Society, New York. Photograph © The Detroit Institute of Arts.
Bequest of Robert H. Tannahill.

A–30　European Painting

Pablo Picasso (1881–1973)
Les Demoiselles D'Avignon.
© 1998 Estate of Pablo Picasso, Paris/Artists Rights Society, New York/Photograph © 1997 The Museum of Modern Art, New York, through the Lillie P. Bliss Bequest.

African Sculpture

A Baule Mask. Wood, Ivory Coast, West Africa.
Courtesy Entwistle Gallery, London/Werner Forman Archive/ Art Resource, New York.